THE
Crucial Decade
—AND AFTER

AMERICA, 1945-1960

E-70
F.C.

BY

ERIC F. GOLDMAN

Vintage Books
A DIVISION OF *Random House*

NEW YORK

Preface
to the Vintage Edition

THIS BOOK was first published in a hardback edition under the title *The Crucial Decade: America, 1945-1955*. In that form it told the history of the United States from the end of World War II in the summer of 1945 to the Geneva Summit Conference in the summer of 1955. This new, Vintage edition includes two fresh chapters and an epilogue which continue the history from 1955 to 1960.

The decade covered by the original volume, 1945-55, was certainly a crazy-quilt era. That taut Thursday when Franklin Roosevelt died, the first sickening fall of an atomic bomb, the heartfelt roar when Jackie Robinson trotted out in a Dodgers uniform, the meat you couldn't buy and the apartment you couldn't rent, high prices and boom times and higher prices and still more boom, a brilliant young man named Alger Hiss, President Harry Truman now fumbling, now making the bold decision to go into Korea, Arnold Toynbee and Mickey Spillane, Ezio Pinza singing "Some Enchanted Evening" and the bloody wastes of the Changjin Reservoir, "We like IKE," "We LIKE IKE," "WE LIKE IKE," pyramid games, the poodle bob, chlorophyll toothpaste, chlorophyll chewing gum, chlorophyll dog food, Senator Joseph McCarthy intoning "Point of order, point of order, Mr. Chairman," President Dwight Eisenhower worrying millions and reassuring still more millions by his folksy middle-roadism—these and a thousand other memories flood back from the frightening, heartening, whirligig years after the end of World War II.

Despite all the swirl of events, it seemed to me while working on *The Crucial Decade*, the years from 1945 to 1955 did have their own genuine unity and their own definable meaning. Beneath everything, two critically important questions were pressing to be answered. One of the questions concerned affairs inside the United States: would America continue, through extensions of the welfare state and of welfare capitalism and through a variety of other techniques, the economic and social revolution which had marked the previous decades? The other question concerned foreign affairs: would the United States keep moving along the path marked out in the early Truman years, a path suggested by the words "containment" and "co-existence" and one which represented a sharp departure from deep-seated American traditions? What seemed to me crucial about the Crucial Decade was that during the years 1945-55 the people of the United States faced these questions, worried and wrangled over the answers, almost spoke a double no, then finally answered both with a decisive affirmative.

In preparing this new Vintage edition of the book, I mulled over, from the perspective of the passage of additional years, whether I still believed 1945 to 1955 was a definable epoch in American history and whether the decade was, more than any other recent one, a "crucial" decade. My conclusion on both points was a clear-cut yes. As a matter of fact, it seemed to me that events since 1955 have made even more plain that during the previous decade the American people, in their haphazard way, arrived at fundamental decisions and that our history now and for the foreseeable future amounts to the working out of those decisions. Consequently, in this extended form of *The Crucial Decade*, the contents and the interpretation of the original book remain the same and the history of the years after 1955 simply builds on the preceding chapters.

The Crucial Decade—And After is, quite consciously, interpretative history, but it is decidedly not the kind of interpretative history which attempts to serve as a tract for the times. The volume is based on no special theories about man or about history; it contains no ringing plea to save America. As a matter of fact, implicit throughout is the assumption that America will be saved—whatever precisely that may mean —not by men with banners but by those who are able to escape the banners long enough to think. *The Crucial Decade—And After* is history in the most direct sense of the word. It is a narrative, written with a careful regard for facts, an attempt to escape partisanship or other bias, an effort to place events in the long perspective, and the assumption that the history of man is the story of men. Insofar as I was able, I have had people take over these pages, the leaders who changed the nation by winning votes and the movers who worked their revolutions oblivious of politics, the bitter and the wise, the indignant and the smug, the faceless millions who proceeded to show a thousand faces ranging from utter inanity to utter good sense.

Naturally, in writing of events so recent and so controversial, I have been especially concerned about the danger of factual inaccuracy. Beyond the usual scholarly checks, I tried to ward off error through a direct appeal to the participants in the story. Wherever it seemed to me feasible or sensible, I sent a copy of the appropriate manuscript pages to the man or woman I had written about and asked for a check on my facts, and I did this without regard to whether the person was a waiter or a world statesman and without regard to whether I had written about him favorably or unfavorably. The comments and corrections that came back were not always the kind that would pass muster in a university seminar. Memories have a way of slipping; they also have a way of being convenient. Yet many genuine errors were caught and I would like to thank very warmly the people who gave time and energy to help keep this history straight. They

and others to whom I am indebted are listed in the
"Note on the Sources and Acknowledgments" which
appears at the end of the book.

E F G

Princeton, N. J.
July 16, 1960

Contents

THE
Crucial Decade
—AND AFTER

AMERICA, 1945-1960

Mood Maybe

A U.S. radio monitor in a little frame house in Oregon caught the first hint. The Japanese were interested in peace, the Domei broadcast said, provided that the prerogatives of the Emperor would not be "prejudiced." Then came two days of diplomacy, a few hours of false armistice, more waiting through an interminable weekend. Finally, on Tuesday, August 14, 1945, reporters were summoned to the Oval Room of the White House. President Truman glanced at the clock to make sure he was holding to the agreement of simultaneous announcement in Washington, London, and Moscow. At exactly 7 p.m. he began reading: Late that afternoon a message had been received from the Japanese Government which "I deem . . . full acceptance of . . . unconditional surrender."

Across America the traditional signs of victory flared and shrieked. In Los Angeles, yelling paraders commandeered trolley cars, played leapfrog in the middle of Hollywood Boulevard, hung Hirohito from scores of lampposts. Salt Lake City thousands snake-danced in a pouring rain and a St. Louis crowd, suddenly hushing its whistles and tossing aside the confetti, persuaded a minister to hold services at 2 a.m. New York City, hardly unaccustomed to furor, amazed itself. With the first flash of V-J, up went the windows and down came the torn telephone books, the hats, bottles, bolts of silk, books, wastebaskets, and shoes, more than five thousand tons of jubilant litter. Whole families made their way to Times Square until two million people were milling about, breaking into snatches of the conga, hugging and kissing anybody in sight, greeting each twinkle of V-J news on the *Times* electric sign with a cheer that roared from the East River to the Hudson. The hoopla swirled on into the dawn, died down, broke out again the next afternoon, finally subsided only with another midnight.

Americans had quite a celebration and yet, in a way, the celebration never really rang true. People were so gay, so determinedly gay. The nation was a carnival but the festivities, as a reporter wrote from Chicago, "didn't seem like so much. It was such a peculiar peace. . . . And everybody talked of 'the end of the war,' not of 'victory.'" The President himself spoke with a mixed tone. When the crowds around the White House chanted "We want Harry," he appeared beaming with Bess on his arm and proclaimed this "a great day." His face quickly sobered as he added warnings of an "emergency" ahead—a crisis "as great . . . as Dec. 7, 1941." At V-J, 1945, the United States was entering the newest of its eras in a curious, unprecedented jumble of moods.

Peace had not come to the nation with the soothing coo of a dove. Instead it came in swift hammer blows of news, smashing old sure stand-bys. Four months before the Japanese surrender, cerebral hemorrhage struck down Franklin Roosevelt, a second father to millions of Americans during their worst depression and their worst war. Another three months and the British were sweeping out of office Winston Churchill, doughty symbol of steadiness to much of Western Civilization. Eleven days later, just before V-J, President Truman announced: "An American airplane [has] dropped one bomb on Hiroshima. . . . It is an atomic bomb. It is a harnessing of the basic power of the universe."

Over all the victory celebrations, the fact of the atomic bomb hung like some eerie haze from another world. Americans tried to make jokes. The Japanese were suffering from atomic ache, people giggled to each other. Or when God made Atom, he sure created a handful for Eve. Americans were sententious. The bomb meant the end of civilization and atomic energy was certain to usher in a golden age of peace and plenty. Americans argued furiously. John Foster Dulles intimated that atomic bombs and "Christian statesmanship" were hardly compatible and scores of leaders answered hotly that a truly Christian nation ended wars as quickly as possible. Somehow neither the arguments nor the jokes nor the sententiousness meant much. People fumbled along, trying to comprehend the incomprehensible, to fit a sense of terrifying newness into their accustomed ways of thinking. And in almost every American mind, there was one corner that could respond to the words reported from a European prison cell. "A mighty accomplishment," the captured Nazi leader Hermann Göring said. "I don't want anything to do with it."

The sense of a scarifying future was accompanied by memories of the last postwar, jabbing, mocking memories. In the America of V-J, the story went around how Franklin Roosevelt had kept a picture of Woodrow Wilson hanging in the meeting room of the War Cabinet, frequently glancing toward it when he discussed the coming years, and everybody got the point of the tale. Woodrow Wilson also had led the United States to victory in a world war. Then came the hard times of 1920-1, less than a decade of prosperity, the brutal depression of the 1930's, and the furies of World War II.

For one large section of the American people, memories were particularly disturbing. Cotton-pickers, professors, and secretaries, auto workers, writers, and the man who collected the garbage, they had given their minds and their hearts to the credo represented by Franklin Roosevelt. The cotton-pickers and the secretaries might speak of the "New Deal"; the professors and the writers were inclined to talk of "liberalism." Whatever the term, the groups joined in a zest for legislation in favor of lower-income groups, for questioning and nose-thumbing, for chopping away at the crust of social castes. Now that World War II was over, the liberals also shared an apprehension provoked by history. The least educated among them were acutely aware that the previous generation's "New Deal," the reformism of Theodore Roosevelt and Woodrow Wilson, had passed through World War I and come out Warren G. Harding.

Worriedly, yearningly, the liberal leaders were talking of sixty million jobs, the figure that Franklin Roosevelt had used in his vista of the postwar. Sixty million jobs, the argument ran, were a symbol of the full employment and social advances which could be; they were also a measuring-rod that would warn of oncoming disaster. And this time, a thousand New Deal commentators added, failure to solve America's domestic problems would mean something worse than hard times. As the end of World War II neared, *Harper's Magazine*, certainly a restrained liberal journal, was running an article which argued that "the veterans are not going to accept unemployment with the bewildered docility which was characteristic of most of the jobless in the last depression. . . . What action will result from that attitude . . . ? Nobody knows, of course. But we have some hints, and they are hints which should make any American start worrying. One of them is the report of a historian who watched fascism rise in Italy and Germany after the last war."

In the eyes of many educated New Dealers, the national scene already included dangerously large areas of rightism. During the month of V-J, Bernard De Voto, a favorite of liberal readers, pointed to the dismissal of Homer Rainey from the presidency of the University of Texas. The situation was complex, De Voto wrote. But basically Rainey was dismissed because of his New Dealish opinions and his insistence on academic freedom for subordinates. The case resulted from a rapidly spreading doctrine of "ruthless industry and finance," which equated both free inquiry and New Dealism with Communism.

This kind of argument, De Voto went on, "is a powerful sentiment, and one easily polarized by a rabble-rouser or an honest deluded man. The communists [so the argument runs] were responsible for the New Deal and they intend to inflict a labor dictatorship on us. . . . They want to destroy initiative and profit, business and freedom, the individual and the United States. . . . Get rid of the communist professors—who are all homosexuals and New Dealers anyway—and everything will be all right once more. We will be back in the days before . . . the New Deal conspiracy was hatched, before labor unions had to be dealt with, . . . before socialists and bureaucrats in Washington could tell us . . . what we had to do and whom we had to hire and how much we had to pay him, before the foundations of our society were undermined by atheism and bolshevism."

De Voto was ready for a grim prediction. Free universities are "the central mechanism of democracy." Yet "as the waves of reaction gather strength in the years immediately ahead of the United States, this same attack will be made repeatedly, in many colleges, always by the same kind of men representing the same interests and forces, employing the same or equivalent means."

The anti-New Dealers, the people who more and more were coming to be called "conservatives," had their portentous reading too. Late in the war, the University of Chicago Press published *The Road to Serfdom*, by an Austrian-born economist, Friedrich A. von Hayek. The Press knew well the usual fate of

scholarly treatises; it printed only two thousand copies. But Hayek had set his scholarship within a general
proposition that caught perfectly the mood of much
of American conservatism. Nazism, he contended,
had not grown up in opposition to New Deal-type
liberalism; such liberalism and Nazism came from
the same roots. All Western Civilization had been relying increasingly on ideas of national economic planning, and the ideas, whether called liberalism, Nazism,
socialism, or Communism, led inevitably to totalitarian
serfdom. Hayek's volume was scarcely in the bookstores before the University of Chicago Press discovered that it had published not only a scholarly mon-
ograph but a manifesto for American conservatism.
Hailed by anti-New Deal publications, purchased in
quantity by a number of American corporations, *The
Road to Serfdom* promptly made its way to the best-
seller list and stayed on month after month into the
V-J period. The severely intellectual Hayek, dumfounded at the sales of the volume and half-protesting
that he did not want to be a spokesman for any political group, found himself lecturing up and down the
country to rapt anti-New Deal audiences.

The defeat of Winston Churchill by the British
Labour Party shortly before V-J stoked the fears of
American conservatives. Here was repudiation of a
beloved national hero for a bluntly socialist regime;
here was precisely the swing toward economic controls against which Hayek was warning. People in
conservative commuter communities read the election
headline with "shock," to use the term of the *New
Canaan* (Conn.) *Advertiser*. The Labour victory,
Business Week added, brought worried reconsidera-
tion of the general strength of "New Deal" forces in
and outside Britain. The most optimistic conservative
survey could not fail to note one great fact. At V-J,
the long-time trend toward controls over economic
life had gone so far that no government in Western
Civilization except Washington gave even lip service

to free enterprise—and in the White House sat Franklin Roosevelt's chosen heir.

Some American conservatives were avid for an all-out effort to get rid of the New Deal and turn America back toward unregulated capitalism. Others acquiesced in what the New Deal had done but insisted upon drawing a stern line, beyond this not one step further. Both conservative groups often talked a formula that was decades old but now had a fresh significance and a new name, "welfare capitalism." Industry itself, the formula ran, should protect the welfare of its employees to such an extent that social legislation, and perhaps unions, would lose their appeal. Whatever the emphasis, conservatives joined with liberals in considering the postwar a battleground on which domestic issues of far-ranging significance would be fought out, with results that could mean heaven or hell.

At V-J, the field of foreign policy brought its own sense of great possibilities for good or evil. Throughout the war, most liberals had been little bothered by the alliance with the Soviet Union. After all, they argued, the Soviet stood for anti-fascism, for collective security against aggression, and for the betterment of the underprivileged. With patience, Russia could be brought more and more to the ways of democratic nations; besides, if the United States did not co-operate with the Soviet, how could it win the war? Many liberals went beyond these sidewise justifications to the argument that the Soviet alliance was a positive good. It meant a peace that would endure because it would be built on unity between the powers that counted, the United States and Russia; it foreshadowed a postwar in which, through the pressure of both New Dealism and Communism, social reform would become a prime concern of world leadership.

During World War II, only a minority among the conservatives sharply differed with the liberal attitude

toward the Soviet alliance. Stalin's public statements
and actions seemed devoid of double-dealing; the
Russians were obviously saving American lives by
smashing Nazi divisions; the fierce Soviet holding
operation at Stalingrad and then the hammer blows
back across Russia had a heroic quality about them
which won general American admiration. Public-
opinion polls indicated that most business executives
were thoroughly optimistic about Russia's postwar
intentions. The powerful anti-New Deal Luce publications were explaining away the Russian secret police
as "a national police similar to the FBI," with the job
of "tracking down traitors," while the high-Republi-
can Main Line filled the hall with cheers when the
Philadelphia Orchestra introduced the new Russian
anthem, "Hymn to the Soviet Union." The Yalta
Conference of February, 1945, seemed a triumph of
Allied unity for purposes on which all groups in the
United States could agree, and the Yalta communiqué
was greeted by almost unanimous praise in the United
States.

Yet beneath the conservative acceptance of the Soviet alliance ran irritations and misgivings. The man
who had long considered the New Deal dangerous
radicalism hardly took real pleasure in joining hands
with out-and-out Bolsheviks. He was the more edgy
because the camaraderie was being promoted by
Franklin Roosevelt. He could not help but feel that a
peace built on a Communist–New Deal understanding would move everything away from the kind of
pattern he considered sensible and decent. This underlying disturbance of the conservatives over the Soviet
relationship was especially marked in the Midwestern
Republican faction led by Senator Robert A. Taft.
"It's all very well to win a war with socialist New
Dealers and Bolsheviks having a love feast," Senator
Kenneth Wherry of Nebraska expressed the attitude,
"but what follows then?"

As the war drew to a close and the day approached

when Russian divisions would no longer be needed,
the conservative restiveness mounted. It was further
increased by headlines which began breaking soon
after the Yalta communiqué of February, 1945. The
news was revealed of a secret Yalta agreement, easily
deemed favorable to the Soviet. The Russians made
moves in flagrant violation of the Yalta provisions for
free elections in the liberated countries of eastern Europe. Stalin seemed to speak contempt for the whole
idea of world peace by announcing that he would send
merely an underling of his Foreign Office to the San
Francisco conference for setting up the United Nations
—a decision that was reversed, it was widely assumed,
only by strong pressure from President Truman.

At the time of the Japanese surrender, most liberals
were still optimistic about American-Russian relations; if they doubted, it was largely because Franklin
Roosevelt had been removed from the negotiating table. But many an anti-New Dealer was beginning to
wonder aloud if the whole Roosevelt policy had not
been a tragic blunder. Some conservatives, particularly the Taftian Republicans, were projecting into
the V-J air doubts whether peace itself could long endure between the United States and the Bolsheviks.

Russians or no Russians, Hayek *vs.* the New Dealers,
atom bomb or not, World War II was over, and all
America joined in a sense of coming home. At V-J,
the first groups of veterans were already fidgeting in
trains and buses, straining for some half-remembered
clump of billboards, a bed of petunias, a funny-shaped
building that meant they were almost there. Defense
workers were pulling out of the Quonsets in Los Angeles and Detroit and Hartford, heading back to Alabama, Oklahoma, and the hills of Maryland. Men and
women who had taken the same commuter train, prepared dinner in the same kitchen, punched the same
time clock for twenty years, were coming home too.
At last they could fill their gasoline tanks, use a second

chunk of butter, watch the long lazy curl of a fishing line flicker in the sunlight, or get royally tight, without feeling that they were cheating some GI in the flak over Berlin or on the bloody ash of Iwo Jima.

It was good to be home; for millions, it was better still to be in what home had become. The America of V-J was prosperous, more prosperous than the country had been in all its three centuries of zest for good living. The boom rolled out in great fat waves, into every corner of the nation and up and down the social ladder. Factory hands, brushing the V-J confetti out of their hair, laid plans for a suburban cottage. Farmers' children were driving to college classes in glossy convertibles. California border police, checking the baggage of Okies returning east, came across wads of hundred-dollar bills.

For many an American, the new era brought an added exhilaration. It offered not only increased income but a break-through in status, a chance at schooling and occupations and ways of living that previously had been barricaded from them. All through the New Deal period and the war years, the powerful thrusts of minorities had been ramming more and more holes in the walls of discrimination. By V-J, Jews seeking admission to professional schools had a ten-to-fifteen-per-cent better chance than the applicant of 1929. First-generation Catholics of eastern or southern European backgrounds reported far less difficulty in purchasing homes in upper-middle-class neighborhoods. During the four swift years of the war, Negroes for the first time knew the white-collar kudos of working as salesgirls in the swank department stores of the North, and Negro representatives on labor grievance committees were becoming accustomed to speaking up as freely as their white colleagues.

If the upsweep was plainest among the minority groups, it touched the whole bottom of American society with a tonic sense of new possibilities. The GI

Bill of Rights became law in 1944 and with the first
release of veterans during the war, the legislation began working its revolution. Men who had entered the
army as employees returned to borrow money from
the government and set up their own businesses. Hundreds of thousands who had thought of the university
as a preserve of the rich found themselves headed toward an A.B.—in many cases, toward the highest of
professional degrees.

In or outside veteran ranks, lower-status groups had
lifted their sights. "Times have changed," Maurice
O'Connell, of the CIO, notified a Los Angeles Chamber of Commerce meeting shortly after the Japanese
surrender. "People have become accustomed to new
conditions, new wage scales, new ways of being
treated." Even the fabled Rosie the Riveter was a different woman. "Rosie the Riveter," O'Connell announced, "isn't going back to emptying slop jars."

Nobody, it seemed, was going back to emptying the
slop jars. Ads for unskilled labor on farms or in factories produced a resounding lack of response; maids
came only at Tiffany prices and then, as likely as not,
with a Tiffany manner. "People were probably never
choosier . . . ," an Indianapolis reporter described
the nation-wide trend. "Job dreams are golden,
bright golden."

The sense of wonderful possibilities ahead kept
breaking into every part of living. In the year when
man mastered the atom, a good many people did not
smile at the feature-page stories which predicted that
the average American would soon work twenty-five
hours a week, return to a dinner cooked by the flick
of a single button, educate his children through the
finest authorities televised into a sun-heated living-
room, and take his vacation a continent away. In a
period when medical research had just produced the
yellow magic of penicillin only to have it promptly
topped by streptomycin, it did not seem utopian to

talk of conquering tuberculosis, infantile paralysis, even cancer. As for the bread-and-butter of living, the U.S. Director of War Mobilization and Reconversion, Fred Vinson, was saying: "The American people are in the pleasant predicament of having to learn to live 50 percent better than they have ever lived before." From somewhere deep in the national psychology came the surest affirmation of tomorrow. Throughout the depression days of the 1930's, well into the war period, millions of couples had made the decision against children or ventured only as far as a single son or daughter. Now a rampant birthrate was turning community life into one vast gurgle.

In St. Louis, an Inquiring Reporter stopped a young mother and asked about her personal expectations for the postwar. "Oh, things are going along just wonderfully," she bubbled. "Harry has a grand job, there's the new baby—"

Then she frowned. "Do you think it's really all going to last?"

A zest in today, wondrous hopes for tomorrow—but always, in the America of V-J, there were shadows. A nation accustomed to the categorical yes and no, to war or peace and prosperity or depression, found itself in the nagging realm of maybe. The liberals worried over the conservatives and the conservatives watched the liberals with an uneasiness akin to dread. Conservatives, liberals, and the half of the nation which was not really either asked: Would events follow the same pattern as during the last postwar? Was unprecedented boom to bring unprecedented delights only to turn into unprecedented bust? Was peace just a prelude to another war?

The questions broke into conversations as persistently, as much up and down the social scale, as the relish in victory and prosperity and a limitless future. Behind these questions was a further one, often too deeply felt to be expressed. If the pattern held, if history repeated itself, wouldn't another war suck everything into doomsday under those billowing atomic mushrooms?

Strikes, Russians, and Harry Truman

THE DAY after V-J, the new President started his morning with a bit of office shifting. He replaced a model gun on his desk with a shiny model plow and he delighted in pointing out the change to visitors. "It's the simple feelings that count," he would say. "I like the feeling of having the new little fellow there."

Life had prepared Harry Truman for the simple. Life was Jackson County, Missouri, where you grew up near-sighted and the other boys snickered, you went courting Bess Wallace in the big house and her parents tried to get rid of you, you came back from the war to start the haberdashery with Eddie Jacobson and the store went broke. But you stuck at it. You kept in mind the simple things that any sensible man in Jackson County knew were the really important ones—a hard day's work, loyalty to your family and your friends, holding your eye on the cheerful side of life, remembering that "nobody is as big as he thinks he is or so small as his enemies are sure." And things had happened in Jackson County, good things, just as you were sure in your bones that they would happen anywhere if a man would only hold to the simple rules.

Despite the uppity parents, you married Bess and

got started in politics under the wing of Tom Pendergast. The "damned New York liberals" might keep attacking Pendergast as a corrupt Boss. Did your friend Tom ever ask you to do anything dishonest? And it was quite a life, this being a County Judge, then United States Senator, riding off to the Capital and coming back to Independence with people gathering around and asking, "Harry, what are they up to in Washington?"

"They're up to getting whatever they can get," you would say. Everybody would laugh and there was a night of bourbon and poker with the boys and a long visit with Mother, who would always send you off with "Now, Harry, hew to the good line." You hewed to the good line. You never went near a tainted dime. You were a loyal Democrat, almost always voting for the New Deal laws proposed by the Democratic President. You liked reading Civil War history and you remembered World War I; this time no smart-aleck businessmen were going to make off with huge war profits. So you stood up from your back bench in the Senate and called for a committee to keep a suspicious eye on the whole hurry and grab. Naturally you were chairman and naturally you worked nights watching over every dollar spent and soon all kinds of people had a good word for Harry Truman's Special Committee Investigating the National Defense Program.

You kept holding to the simple rules and good things went right on happening. 1944 and Democratic party leaders were telling Franklin Roosevelt that Henry Wallace simply would not do. Why not someone who had voted New Deal yet was not too much stamped as a New Dealer, a friendly man who had stirred up few enmities but nevertheless had some national standing, a Senator from the Border States which could easily decide the election? When they first told you at the convention that you were to get the Vice-Presidential nomination, you were so upset an attack of nausea came and you urged that the place should go to Jimmy Byrnes. But you got used to the idea and before many hours you felt like the boyhood day when you came home holding a twelve-inch trout behind your back. "Who's getting the Vice-Presidential nod?" delegates asked. You grinned and said: "Me."

The Vice-Presidency was wonderful. Bess no longer had to work as your secretary and she would have friends in all the way from Independence for bridge. More and more organizations were asking Margaret to sing. And everybody was glad to meet Harry Truman now, even the movie stars like Lauren Bacall, who came and sat on the top of the piano while you played the "Missouri Waltz."

The afternoon it happened you were having a drink in Sam Rayburn's office. You turned ashen and your voice stuck in your throat. The next day you said to the reporters: "Boys, if you ever pray, pray for me now. I don't know whether you fellows ever had a load of hay fall on you, but when they told me yesterday what had happened, I felt like the moon, the stars, and all the planets had fallen on me."

The first weeks in the White House were awful. You had never really wanted this. Sure, you were a good man, good as the next one, and there was no reason why you shouldn't be Vice-President. But that didn't mean you should be President of the United States, especially not after Franklin Roosevelt and in times like these. His shadow was always over your shoulder. You had been let in so little on really important affairs that you had to keep summoning Roosevelt intimates, Harry Hopkins, Admiral Leahy, or Jimmy Byrnes, merely to get the basic facts. And every day there was some tremendous decision to make in that lonely room where Abraham Lincoln and Woodrow Wilson and Franklin Roosevelt had sat. You said it privately and you said it publicly: If only I could be back in the Senate.

But the Senate days were gone; you even had to stop slipping over to the Senate cafeteria for lunch because it made such a fuss. Well, you weren't going to flinch and you weren't going to forget the important things. You kept hard at work, up at 5:30 a.m. and tackling a stack of papers after dinner. You didn't high-hat your friends. You drew them around you, old buddies you knew you could trust, like solid John Snyder, who talked horse sense to all the crackpot theorists buzzing around the White House, and your other sidekick from World War I days, Harry Vaughan, always such a comfort with his funny stories and his booming "I'm still with ya, Chief," and Ed Pauley, who had pitched in and raised hundreds of thousands when the Democratic Party needed money so badly. Above all, you were determined to keep smiling—the newspapers noticed that you referred to reasons for hopefulness seven times in one speech. And there you were behind the big desk with the shiny model plow on it, your suit neatly pressed and your bow tie dapper, good father, good Democrat, good fellow, and the man who also happened to have the most awesome job in the world.

In the final months of 1945, all through 1946, one situation clamored for the attention of the White House more insistently than anything else—the problem that everybody was calling "reconversion." Governmental and business plans for shifting the nation's economy back from war to peace had generally assumed the necessity of a lengthy invasion of Japan. Now that atomic bombs had abruptly ended the hostilities, the economic blueprints were dangerously fuzzy and incomplete.

The arguments concerning reconversion centered on the scores of wartime federal controls, particularly the controls over prices and wages. Everybody wanted to get back to "normal" conditions. Everybody was ready with his prediction of dire depression if reconversion should be mishandled. But the nation's most powerful economic blocs violently disagreed over what was normal and how you arrived there.

The slogans of liberal New Dealism and conservative anti-New Dealism filled the air, and each group varied doctrine in a way to suit its own interest. Organized labor, for years a bulwark of New Dealism, was all for reconversion under stern governmental supervision—which it was inclined to define as price controls but no wage controls. Industry, for so long the chief center of anti-New Dealism, wanted to hurry toward free enterprise—which usually ended up in meaning wage controls but no price controls. Agriculture, deeply divided in its attitudes since the late 1930's, spoke in a dozen voices but always with an insistence that the purchasing power of the farmer was to be kept high.

No one questioned that the war had brought inflation and that the postwar was continuing it. Equally plain was the fact that most industrial labor had worked forty-eight hours during the war—eight at overtime—and now the normal work week was back to forty. Could industrial wages be increased to compensate for these developments without raising prices and thus bringing still more inflation? Businessmen's organizations, with an imposing battery of statistics, proved that it was impossible for industry to go on making a reasonable profit if wages were increased without hiking prices. The labor unions, with an equally impressive array of figures, proved that business was making so much that it could amply afford to absorb large wage increases.

In the White House, Harry Truman sat listening to the endless arguments and forebodings and he wished people would "stop singing the blues." Once in a while he fell into the language of the day and talked of crisis. For the most part he would speak to the public as he did when he dedicated a dam at Gilbertsville, Kentucky, two months after V-J: "We are having our little troubles now—a few of them. They are not serious. Just a blowup after a let-down from war."

When the President acted, he moved along a wavering line. In his mind, being a loyal Democrat meant carrying on at least the New Deal's general tendency to use governmental powers in ways favored by the lower-income groups. On the other hand, he was anxious to get along with a Congress that was controlled by a coalition of anti-New Dealers. His most trusted advisers, particularly John Snyder, were decidedly favorable to the attitudes of business, and he could not entirely down his own feeling that there was something un-American about price controls in peacetime. ("Police state methods," he was soon to call them in a press conference.) During late 1945 and 1946, the President was less either a New Dealer or an anti-New Dealer than a man reacting to the strongest pressures of the moment.

The V-J celebrations were hardly over when he began tossing out by the armloads rationing regulations and other controls affecting prices. At the same time he was supporting the proposal for a Council of Economic Advisers with considerable powers over industry, and in the ensuing tug-of-war Congress did pass a watered-down version of the bill. The President told the livestock men that he would "never, never" lift price controls on meat as long as there was a shortage; twenty-one days later, at the height of the shortage, he scrapped all ceilings on meat. He carried on a sporadic battle with Congress to preserve an OPA with real powers over general prices, sometimes applying full White House pressure, sometimes doing more talking than acting and permitting his subordinates to aid the anti-OPA forces. Because of, in spite of, and in a very real sense regardless of Harry Truman, during most of 1946 price controls were more sieve than ceiling.

All the while labor was up in arms against wage controls. Three months after the Japanese surrender, the United Automobile Workers read out the declaration of war. Inflation or no inflation, forty-eight or forty hours' work, the UAW demanded that its members should take home at the end of the week at least as much purchasing power as they received before V-J. Specifically the union called on General Motors to raise wages thirty per cent.

Soon the country's biggest union and its richest corporation were locked in a bitter strike, and walkouts were spreading across the country. Usually the major struggles ended up on the President's desk. Usually the White House arranged a settlement by proposing an 18 to 22 cent-per-hour wage boost with fringe benefits. And usually one strike was ended only to be followed by two more.

On April 1, 1946 John L. Lewis, refusing a White House compromise, led his four hundred thousand soft-coal miners out, and the nation's economy slowed, faltered, wobbled toward a dead stop. Within a month, freight loadings dropped seventy-five per cent and steel plants were beginning to bank their fires. A fury of anti-labor feeling swept the country, bursting into denunciations on the floors of Congress. Virginia's conservative Senator, Harry Byrd, cried: "[Lewis is] drunk with power." Senator Scott Lucas of Illinois, usually a supporter of the unions, added: "If this Government has not the power to outlaw strikes of this character, then this Government has no power of self-preservation."

After forty days of the crippling coal strike, a truce was arranged only to be followed by the threat of a still more paralyzing walkout. The United States had never gone through a total railroad stoppage but in May, 1946, Alvanley Johnston, Grand Chief of the Brotherhood of Locomotive Engineers, and Alexander F. Whitney, President of the Brotherhood of Railway Trainmen, were ready to pull the switch. Just twenty-six minutes before the deadline, Johnston and Whitney accepted a telephone plea from the White

House to delay the strike for five days while the negotiations continued.

The five days rushed by and still the two union leaders refused to accept compromise terms. Beginning at 4 p.m. on May 23, the United States had a preview of a national rail strike. Within forty-eight hours, air and bus terminals were pandemonium, runs were starting on gas stations and food stores, unemployment in fringe industries was mounting, and news stories were pouring in of fortunes in lettuce rotting away at Salinas, in citrus fruit at Redlands, in vegetables on the Rio Grande. From federal officials came the bluntest possible warning that hundreds of thousands in Europe would starve if shipments of grain and meat to eastern ports were delayed as much as two weeks.

Now Harry Truman was anything but smiling. Years later the White House physician, Dr. Wallace Graham, remembered how disturbed the President was. Johnston and Whitney, Truman was clear in his mind, were taking an impossible position. "What decent American would pull a rail strike at a time like this?"

The President summoned the two union chiefs for a final conference. He had never had much use for Johnston, a grumpy bureaucratic type and "a damned Republican," but he and the sprightly Whitney had been friends for years.

Neither union leader would budge. Whitney said: "I've got to go through with it."

The President hunched forward in his chair. "Well then, I'm going to give you the gun."

That night Harry Truman went on the radio with the toughest public language he had used since entering the White House. A new figure, the St. Louis attorney Clark Clifford, was appearing in the White House inner circle, and Clifford, following the President's mood, drafted sentences that rasped through the loudspeakers like angry blows. "The crisis of Pearl

Harbor was the result of action by a foreign enemy," the President told the nation. "The crisis tonight is caused by . . . men within our own country who place their private interests above the welfare of the nation."

Throughout the night Clifford and other Presidential aides worked feverishly in the White House on the special message Truman was to deliver to Congress the next afternoon. In the Hotel Statler another aide, John Steelman, worked just as feverishly to negotiate a settlement of the strike. Shortly before the President left for the Capitol, word came from the Statler that agreement seemed near, but Truman began his speech with no settlement signed.

The President's face was gray and tight as he read his tartly worded message. He was a warm friend of labor, Truman emphasized; he did not want sweeping anti-strike legislation. But the railroads had been taken over by the government in order to keep them running and he would not tolerate a strike against the government of the United States. He felt compelled to ask for the power which would permit him, as Commander-in-Chief, "to draft into the Armed Forces of the United States all workers who are on strike against their government."

While Truman spoke, Clark Clifford sat in the office of Speaker of the House Sam Rayburn, hoping for word from the Hotel Statler. Finally, after what seemed like an interminable wait, John Steelman telephoned. Clifford scribbled off a note and hurried it to Leslie Biffle, Secretary of the Senate. As the President spoke his final emphatic word, Biffle handed him the slip of paper. Truman read the note out loud: "Mr. President, agreement signed, strike settled." A great roar of applause, from Republicans and Democrats alike, swept across Congress.

So the railroad strike was over and the Congressmen cheered, but an unprecedented paralysis had been prevented only by the threat of an unprecedented curtailment of liberties. Pro-labor liberals were not the only Americans who winced at the Presidential demand for the right to draft strikers. Senator Robert A. Taft stood up in the Senate and declared that the Truman proposal "offends not only the Constitution, but every basic principle for which the American Republic was established. Strikes cannot be prohibited without interfering with the basic freedom essential to our form of Government." With the danger of a railroad stoppage over, the Presidential recommendation was quickly pigeonholed. But the whole episode was a peculiarly disturbing moment for thoughtful Americans of a wide variety of views.

For most Americans, thoughtful or not, the strikes were spectacular evidence that economic affairs were badly askew. Ugly splotches of unemployment began to appear with the first cancellations of war contracts. While the battle over price controls went on, prices kept inching up until by the end of 1946 living costs were an estimated thirty-three per cent above the level of Pearl Harbor Day. All the while, the 1946 strikes were piling up a record loss of 107,475,000 man-days of work, hobbling production and pushing prices toward still higher levels.

The inflation jabbed people wherever they turned. Trolleys and subways went up two cents, then a nickel. The ten-cent Sunday newspaper was disappearing in America. For years the insurance company, Bankers Life, had run a magazine ad which began: "You can become financially independent. Mary and I did . . . we're living on a life income of $150 a month." In June, 1946 the ad changed. Now Mary and I were "happy as kids on a life income of $200 a month."

Still more irritating were the things that were hard to buy at any price. A public with billions of dollars stored up in war bonds and savings accounts, avid to replace the worn-out and push on to a higher standard of living, found itself queuing up in long nerve-jangling lines. Women had trouble getting furniture, nylons, a new electric iron; men found clothing, even a razor blade that would shave clean, in short supply; families were forced on to hopeless-appearing waiting lists for a new car.

Everywhere the housing shortage was the subject of irritated conversation. The potent real-estate lobby fought federal subsidies for low-cost housing; the equally powerful unions were leery of assembly-line construction; the swing toward prefabs ran into the difficulty of using enormous quantities of scarce sheet steel. Housing units kept going up, hundreds of thousands of them, but rarely according to schedule and never enough. Many new dwellings promptly started falling apart. They had been thrown together with green lumber, ersatz plumbing, slapdash carpentry, and a general air of who-cares. Everybody knew a story like the one from Mineola, Long Island: the house had cost $9,950 and now its cellar was flooded with sewage.

Food shortages came grinding in on top of the housing debacle. This city lacked sufficient sugar; another was short of coffee. New Englanders grimaced at a scarcity of beans, and Southerners were forced into cooking like damyankees and boiling vegetables without fatback.

In Detroit, a woman walked into a butcher shop. The butcher eyed the stranger, turned to the boss. "Who is she?"

The boss said: "I don't know. Starve the bitch."

As the summer of 1946 closed, the food shortages were reaching their climax in meat famine. First came a meteoric rise in prices.

PRICES SOAR, BUYERS SORE
STEERS JUMP OVER THE MOON

ran the *New York Daily News* headline. Then the steers disappeared behind the moon. While the White House and the livestock men argued over the wisdom of price ceilings on meat, the producers staged their own strike and refused to send the cattle to market. In some communities, meat of any kind was only a savory memory. In many cities, housewives who did not reach the counters early were lucky to pick up a half-pound of bologna or three frankfurters. Even hospitals were frantically telephoning Washington, asking emergency provisions of red meat for their patients' trays.

But there were ways and ways of getting things. Housewives kept an eye on the front street, alerting each other that a supply truck was on its way to the chain store. Tipping became more and more correct—perhaps a half-dollar to the butcher for the back-breaking labor of handing the chops over the counter. The tie-in sale was commonplace; you could get Scotch if you were also ready to load up on wine and rum. Here and there barter came back. A car would get you an apartment; football tickets, good liquor, soap, auto batteries, and sugar were all part of the day's currency.

And there were the under-the-table deals, on a scale far beyond the wartime activity. The black market was most extensive in the new-car field (an estimated seventy-five per cent), and the techniques took on rococo variety. Customers would drop four or five hundred-dollar bills on the desk and quickly look the other way. You could get a new automobile by trading in your old car for a reasonable price—say ten dollars. In other salesrooms, the customer would look toward a wall a hundred feet away and say: "Bet you five hundred dollars I can hit that wall with my hat." In Oklahoma City, a dealer sold you the car and, for four hundred dollars more, a hound dog. The dog, decidedly a postwar model, would then shuffle back to its master.

"Round and round we go," the *Seattle Post-Intelligencer* editorialized in verse rocky enough to be worthy of the occasion. "And where we stop, nobody, not Harry, not the Chamber of Commerce, not the CIO, not even the *Post-Intelligencer* doth know." To millions of Americans, the country did seem caught in a never-ending circle of vexation. The unhealthy economic situation, especially inflation, produced strikes; the strikes cut down production and thus pressed prices upward; they were settled by wage hikes that were quickly made up by further price increases; and so on.

And so on—to where? As 1946 drew to an end, the answers were many and loud and hardly convincing.

The more Americans fretted over home affairs, the more plain a fact of fundamental importance became. For the first time during an American era of peace, it was next to impossible to discuss domestic problems coherently without having the points become entangled in foreign affairs.

To millions this was an intensely irritating fact. They felt, as generations of Americans had felt before them, that concern over international matters was to be confined to unfortunate periods of war. Foreign policy was something you had, like measles, and got over with as quickly as possible. This attitude was especially common among the Midwestern conservatives led by Senator Robert A. Taft. A number of years later, when circumstances had forced the Ohio Senator into the field of world policy, he remarked with shrewd insight into himself and his following: "I am charged with moving in on foreign policy; the truth is that foreign policy has moved in on me."

The Taftites were strengthened by people from all sections of the country who were simply acting from primordial instincts. American troops around the world were organizing "I Wanna Go Home" demonstrations, and their wives, girl friends, sisters, mothers, and the lady next door were mailing Senators a pair of baby boots with a note that read: "I miss my Daddy." Many businessmen, their fortunes and their careers staked on existing economic relationships, were decidedly suspicious of proposals for world-wide monetary agreements or for an increase in the number of reciprocal tariff agreements. Efforts to determine where the new United Nations organization should be located in the United States produced tortured rationalizations from people who worried about what would happen to property and social values if their suburb was invaded by Greeks and Peruvians, not to speak of Russians. Greenwich, Connecticut, which had as high a percentage of UN enthusiasts as any community in the country, staged an anguished referendum on the subject. Five out of every seven people who voted thought it would be better if the splendid organization would do its magnificent work somewhere else.

Yet all of this was not the main stream. As World War II neared an end, the United States Senate witnessed the most meaningful conversion in modern American history. For two decades Arthur H. Vandenberg of Michigan, top-ranking Republican on the powerful Senate Foreign Relations Committee, had been an all-out isolationist. While the Nazi threat mounted, he voted against repeal of the Neutrality Acts and against the Draft Act, the Draft Act Extension, and Lend-Lease. Four weeks after the Germans invaded Poland, he said: "This so-called war is nothing but about 25 people and propaganda." Then, under the pressures of World War II, Vandenberg began to swing. The final turn in his thinking came when he stood in London in 1944 and listened to German robot bombs snarl overhead. "How can there be immunity or isolation," he mused to a friend, "when man can devise weapons like that?" By early 1945, Vandenberg was ready to renounce formally his lifelong belief.

Before a hushed Senate, his strong voice punching home his points, Vandenberg declared: "I hasten to make my own personal viewpoint clear. I have always been frankly one of those who has believed in our own self-reliance. I still believe that we can never again—regardless of collaborations—allow our national defense to deteriorate to anything like a point of impotence. But I do not believe that any nation hereafter can immunize itself by its own exclusive action. . . . I want maximum American cooperation. . . . I want a new dignity and a new authority for international law. I think American self-interest requires it."

As Vandenberg finished his brief address, both sides of the Senate floor broke into an applause more heartfelt than Washington had heard for years. "A speech of unquestioned greatness," "the most important to come from the Senate Chamber in the last 80 years," "a shot heard round the world," rang the praise from journals of many points of view. Senator Taft, who had little desire to advertise splits in the Republican Party, managed to confine his comment to faint derision. But no degree of derision could gainsay the fact that one thirty-nine-minute address had transformed Vandenberg from just another powerful Midwestern Republican into a leader whose stature was commanding in and outside the Midwest and in and outside the Republican Party.

Consciously or unconsciously, Vandenberg had taken the immemorial path of effective leadership in a democracy: he led where people were going anyhow. In the final stages of the war, most Americans were also making their way toward a great decision. They announced it to no cheering galleries. As a matter of fact, they arrived at the judgment so unobtrusively that experienced politicians and journalists were caught off guard—including men like the *New Republic*'s highly knowledgeable "T.R.B.," who wanted very much to believe that the decision was being made.

"Let me begin by candidly admitting a mistake . . . ," T.R.B. wrote. "Every now and then a wind starts blowing in Washington and suddenly all the little weathervanes point one way. It is blowing now, off the grass roots, and it is saying that Hank Jones, American, is sick of isolationism. . . . Six months ago it seemed impossible that the House would pass the Bretton Woods plan [for international monetary agreements]. Yet it did. . . . Six months ago chances seemed dubious for the reciprocal-trade-agreements bill. . . . But the wind started and the bill passed the House, 239 to 153. It blew some more, and the Senate passed it last week, 54 to 21. Sometimes you can almost see public opinion working on Congress. It is doing so now."

When the ratification of the United Nations Charter came up in the Senate, reporters packed the press gallery, expecting a repetition of the dramatic battle over the League of Nations. The debate had its moments—Burton Wheeler's revealing spleen against a world that was "forcing" him to vote for the Charter, William Fulbright's lone, bold questioning of national sovereignty, the touching appeal for peace by Walter George, whose son had been killed in the Navy Air Corps. But on the whole, the debate produced less clash than many a scuffle over an appropriations bill. At the end only two Senators voted no, and they were men long stamped as lame ducks from another political era.

Most of the country viewed the beginnings of the United Nations with a determined beneficence. So the delegates had hardly assembled before they were at each other's throats. So what? A nation snapping and snarling over nylons and rents, which took pride in the Bronx cheer and the quick punch in the nose, was ready to understand. Television was just coming into use as the UN held its early meetings, and large parts of America went along with the argument that the very difficulties of the new organization, so intimately revealed, showed that diplomacy was being rescued from back-room deals. And there *was* something enormously comforting about having the delegates in full exposure, posturing, sneezing, arguing their cases in your living-room.

The trouble was that the more Americans ventured into the world, the more disconcerting were the facts that confronted them. War-crimes trials were going on and the picture of other civilizations that emerged was hardly encouraging. In France, Pierre Laval, three times Premier of the country, had no defense whatsoever against charges of total collaboration with a bestial and often senseless brutality. He could only stand smirking while the Judge, the Prosecutor, and all twenty-four jurors disgraced the courtroom by trying to shout down anything he said. In the Japanese trials, men who had led millions only months ago turned all American efforts at seriousness into a grisly *opéra bouffe*. Ex-Premier Hideki Tojo sat picking his nose and trying to flirt with an American secretary. Ex-propagandist Shumei Okawa would open his shirt and rub his scrawny chest, dart from his chair to smack Tojo's gleaming pate, shout in weirdly clever English: "I hate the U.S.; it is democrazy."

From the German trials came evidence that sounded like an echo of the primitive forests. There was Major General of Police Otto Ohlendorf matter-of-factly telling how his Task Force D killed ninety thousand men, women, or children. (Other task forces were said to have killed more, the Major General added, but he suspected they were just boasting.) Or the testimony of Dr. Franz Blaha, a Czech surgeon who had managed to live through Dachau: "It was dangerous to have a soft, fine skin. . . . Soft human skin was prized for leather and bindings." Or the reports from the trials of women workers at the Belsen and Oswiecim concentration camps: of gentle-voiced Juana Borman, whose wolfhound enjoyed tearing prisoners to pieces; of wispy Anna Hampel, who took a liking to a French internee and, being rebuffed, beat him daily with a hose; of Irma Grese, she of the delicate features and the warm smile, who calmly fixed her hair while the prosecution showed movies of a bulldozer pushing a huge pile of rotted corpses into a pit. And what thoughtful American could fail to ponder the fact that many an ordinary German was expressing utter bewilderment that the Allies, having won the war, should conduct rigorously fair trials for enemy prisoners?

Whatever the state of people's minds, there was the equally terrifying condition of their bodies. In Europe and Asia, hunger rode the wake of war like some leering devil of man's stupidity. To war's devastation, nature added floods in China and Indochina, a tidal wave in Madras, drought in Australia, South Africa, Greece, and Mexico. After a survey of twenty-four countries, Herbert Hoover broadcast his report on food conditions and the stark facts gave eloquence even to the well-remembered monotony of his voice. Most heartrending of all were the photographs of children that kept appearing in American newspapers, always the same, always the sagging shoulders, the spidery legs, the Adam's apples sticking out, the dull stare of young faces that had never laughed.

Working as friends with a world in such a condition was a formidable enough task but the relationship, the United States was learning, was not going to overflow with camaraderie. Modern Americans, probably more than any other large nation in history, have yearned to be liked by other peoples, and most Americans, rightly or wrongly, had assumed that at least western Europe and Asia looked to them with affection. Now a new and ominous word—"anti-Americanism"—was emphasized in reports from every continent. Even in England, the most friendly of America's former allies or enemies, people were delighting in an acrid jingle about the Statue of Liberty:

I wonder is freedom still holding the light—
Or is she just calling the waiter?

The most widely quoted report came from the

Rev. Renwick C. Kennedy, certainly no alarmist newspaperman but an army chaplain out of small-town Alabama who was home after twenty months in western Europe. "From England to Germany," the Rev. Mr. Kennedy wrote, "they have had enough of us. . . . [The American soldier in Europe has proved] more than a little pathetic. . . . He is not very clear in his own mind about why he fought, nor about what his victory means. As a matter of fact, he is not much interested in such matters. . . . His interests are chiefly three: 1) to find a woman and sleep with her; 2) to buy or steal a bottle of cognac and get stinking drunk; 3) to go home. . . . There he stands in his bulging clothes, fat, overfed, lonely, a bit wistful, seeing little, understanding less—the Conqueror, with a chocolate bar in one pocket and a package of cigarets in the other. . . . The chocolate bar and the cigarets are about all that he, the Conqueror, has to give the conquered."

Americans, naturally enough, bridled at such talk. Yet the reports kept coming and they helped to insinuate into the national mind deeply worrisome questions: Could the United States pull off the new world role it was assuming? Wasn't it especially likely to fail in view of the way the Soviet was acting?

Yes, the Soviet—always the Russians pushed their way into the discussion. Everything about the Soviet Union that bothered the Taftite Republicans at V-J Day was now, in greatly magnified form, troubling a much wider circle. Even for many liberals, Yalta was becoming a goading symbol of American failure in dealing with the Russians. "Oh God, Yalta this and Yalta that!" old Tom Connally, the Democratic foreign-policy leader in the Senate, cried out in weariness at the endless criticism of the Crimean agreements. Soviet threats to eastern Europe were no longer mere threats; the only question left was whether any of the area would remain free. In the UN, the Russian representatives were incessantly vetoing, staging stormy walkouts, presenting their arguments in a shrieking billingsgate. On the most critical issue of all, international control of atomic energy, the Russians conducted themselves in a way which seemed to most Americans categorical proof that the Soviet wanted no genuine international control.

The activities of the American Communist Party itself were taking on a different and sinister meaning. To most Americans the struggles between political parties in the United States had always seemed a kind of family row, bitter perhaps and certainly hard-fought but never raising any question that all groups were loyal to the one flag. In the months after V-J, American Communist leaders began deserting the Party with a jarring set of declarations. The most publicized deserter, Louis Budenz, ex-editor of the *Daily Worker,* quit with a flat statement that Communist parties anywhere were not political parties at all but conspiracies which gave their loyalty first and last to the Soviet Union.

Yet the news from around the world was of continuing gains by Communist parties. In France, Italy, and Czechoslovakia, the Red groups emerged from the war the strongest single political units and their growth was rushing ahead. Aid from the Soviet was helping Red Armies bring one region of China after another under the control of Communists. Even from the Latin countries to the south, which Americans had long considered a region of amenable rumba-dancers, the news was portentous. Communist parties, reliable estimates ran at the end of 1946, would poll a million to a million-and-a-half votes if free elections were held, and their support was mounting with the steadiness of a Cugat beat.

In the middle of it all, a Doukhobor farm girl began testifying in a Canadian court. While working as a cipher clerk in the External Affairs Department, Emma Woikin told her story, she had met Major Sokolov, of the Soviet Embassy. The Major, a "handsome man," and Mrs. Sokolov had been most friendly; repeatedly they invited her to come to their home, where she had "interesting" talks. She "had a feeling of love for Russia," the pathetic young widow said in a tense whisper. "I wanted to help the Soviet but not to hurt Canada." After Emma Woikin came the testimony of thirteen other Canadians who had enjoyed interesting talks with members of the Soviet Embassy, especially about atomic and other defense secrets.

Americans looked homeward; was it going on here too? A Gallup Poll indicated wide support for the proposal to bar all Communists from federal offices in the United States. The House Un-American Activities Committee went to work with increased zeal and members of the Senate Foreign Relations and Appropriations committees sounded alarms. In and outside Washington, another new phrase was rapidly gaining in usage. The Soviet Union, with its brutal imperialism, its sabotaging of the UN, its world-wide spying, was hurrying the nations toward an "East-West" clash.

The phrase caught a special aspect of the situation as it appeared to the American mind. Communism, centered in Russia and spreading most rapidly in eastern Europe and in the Orient, seemed peculiarly eastern. But many of the troubles of the world appeared eastern in a sense not entirely connected with Red armies or parties. Out across the Pacific, along North Africa and the Middle East, colonial peoples were in revolt, sometimes led by Communists and sometimes not but always keeping the eastern regions in a dangerous churning.

What should American policy be? In international affairs as in domestic matters, President Truman kept issuing sunny statements and he kept wavering. After calling for Universal Military Training, he quickly gave in to the popular clamor for demobilization; a military establishment which had included eleven million men on V-J Day was soon down to about one million. The Administration backed large loans for a number of countries in Europe or Asia but permitted food shipments to lag enough so that many a World War II ally was enraged and despairing. It sharpened its notes of protest to the Soviet but built no political, economic, or military arrangements which would give substance to the pieces of paper. Month after month of 1946 the Administration wobbled along and little was clear concerning its foreign policy except that it sincerely backed the UN, hoped for a Soviet-American understanding but was not relying on one, and assumed some responsibility for restoring the war-wrecked economies of Europe and Asia.

As international tensions sharpened in the spring of 1946, Franc L. McCluer, president of tiny Westminster College in Fulton, Missouri, had an idea. It was quite an idea; the awed townsfolk had long since taken to calling their college president "Bullet" McCluer. Westminster had a fund for inviting a speaker of "international importance" each year and Winston Churchill, a man with qualifications, was expected to visit the White House. The Bullet confided his idea to Harry Vaughan, the star football center at Westminster when McCluer was the star debater. Vaughan arranged an appointment with Truman, who endorsed McCluer's letter of invitation with a penned note at the bottom of the paper. Churchill replied that he had some things on his mind he would very much like to say at Fulton.

With the President of the United States sitting on the platform, Churchill reminded his listeners that he had seen World War II coming and "cried aloud to my own fellow-countrymen and to the world. . . . There never was a war in history easier to prevent by timely action. . . . But no one would listen." Now, once again, tyranny was spreading. "From Stettin in the Baltic to Trieste in the Adriatic an iron curtain has descended across the Continent. . . . I do not believe that Soviet Russia desires war. What they desire is the fruits of war and the indefinite expansion of their

power and doctrines. . . . From what I have seen of
our Russian friends and allies during the war, I am
convinced that there is nothing they admire so much
as strength, and there is nothing for which they have
less respect than for weakness, especially military
weakness." Churchill outlined his formula for strength
—an ironclad American-British alliance, possibly
gathering in the other Western powers in time. The
speech sent an unmistakable chill of belligerence into
the balmy Fulton air. To the Soviet it said, with the
authentic Churchillian cock of the head: Desist or
fight.

Churchill, the gallant warrior, was as popular as
ever. The crowd jammed into the little college gymnasium roared its applause for the man, but his doctrine brought few cheers in Fulton or anywhere else
in the United States. President Truman, who later
said that he had sponsored the speech as a trial balloon,
was given an unmistakable view of public opinion.
The typical Congressman or newspaper added the
phrase "iron curtain" to the swiftly growing postwar
vocabulary and wondered out loud if Churchill's proposals would not wreck the UN and provoke the Soviet into war.

The old master, who could read national political
reactions as other men read a billboard, knew he had
not won his real audience. Rumbling off to Richmond
to address the Virginia Assembly, Churchill was decidedly testy. "You have not asked to see beforehand
what I am going to say," he snapped. "I might easily
blurt out a lot of things people know in their hearts
are true."

Six months after Bullet McCluer scored his Fulton
coup, another American had an idea. Henry Wallace,
the Roosevelt intimate and ex-Vice-President who
was now a politically potent member of the Truman Cabinet, considered himself the heir of true New
Dealism, and to Wallace, true New Dealism meant
insistence that the Soviet Union was a peaceful power.

STRIKES, RUSSIANS, HARRY TRUMAN

The stiffening attitude of the Truman Administration toward the Russians, Wallace believed, was warmongering. He was scheduled to address the National Committee of the Arts, Sciences, and Professions in New York City and he determined to use the occasion to rally the forces of "peace"—and perhaps to rally them around Henry Wallace as the Democratic Presidential candidate in 1948.

Wallace wrote out a speech which included passages that amounted to an attack on American policy toward the Soviet. The United States, he charged, had not been trying to meet Russia halfway. If it did, it would find co-operation toward peace. In 1955 Harry Truman stated categorically that he read no part of the speech before it was delivered. In 1956 Henry Wallace stated categorically that he and the President had gone over the manuscript page by page, each with a copy in his hand.

On the afternoon before the speech was to be delivered, the subject came up in a White House press conference. William Mylander, of the Cowles newspapers, had an advance copy in his hand and he quoted from Wallace: " 'When President Truman read these words he said that they represented the policy of his administration.' "

That is correct, the President replied.

"Does that apply just to that paragraph or to the whole speech?" Mylander pressed.

It applies to the whole speech, Truman said.

Later in the press conference Raymond Brandt of the *St. Louis Post-Dispatch* returned to the subject. Did not the Wallace address, Brandt asked, represent a departure from the policy of Secretary of State James Byrnes?

No, the President insisted, the two were right in line.

That evening, Wallace found himself before a crowd that was, at least in part, vociferously pro-Soviet. He adjusted his speech. Once he looked up

from his text and remarked extemporaneously: "I realize that the danger of war is much less from Communism than it is from imperialism." He left out two
points. The first was a reference to "native Communists faithfully following every twist and turn in the
Moscow party line." The second was the sentence:
"The Russians should stop teaching that their form
of Communism must . . . ultimately triumph over
democratic capitalism."

Reaction to the episode was volcanic. Secretary of
State Byrnes, then negotiating with the Russians in
Paris, sent a teletype message to the White House
which stated: "If it is not completely clear in your own
mind that Mr. Wallace should be asked to refrain from
criticizing the foreign policy of the United States
while he is a member of your Cabinet, I must ask you
to accept my resignation immediately." Senator Vandenberg, now the chief symbol of bipartisan foreign
policy, told reporters: "We can only cooperate with
one Secretary of State at a time." The President summoned a special press conference and performed the
inevitable. This time he permitted no questions. He
read off a statement that he had meant only to approve
Wallace's right to express his opinions, not the actual
points that had been made. The next week Wallace
was fired from the Cabinet.

And where did that leave things? Churchill, talking
blunt belligerence toward the Soviet, walked into a
national leeriness; Wallace, calling for faith in the Russians, found himself hustled out of Washington. As
1946 ended, the sagacious *Christian Science Monitor*
ventured a reading of the state of American opinion on
foreign affairs. "Nobody," the paper editorialized,
"seems to be sure what is going to happen. And few
are sure what should be done, no matter what happens."

In New York City, other observers offered their
comment on postwar America. Parfums Weil Paris

Company put out a new perfume called "GriGri." It was designed, the ads explained, "to replace the atom bomb with a dash of the inconsequential."

Americans of late 1945 and 1946, their zest for luxuries pent up by four long years of war, their victory turned into an endless nagging of problems, were hardly averse to the inconsequential. The big football weekend roared back; television sets sold like red meat; women snapped up lamé skirts, sequin-trimmed aprons cartwheel hats with pastel blooms waving in billowing nets. Any night was likely to burst into New Year's Eve. People jammed swish restaurants, lavished millions on dog races that did not even pretend to be honest, wheedled, bribed, and pushed their way to pay $8 to $125 a couple for an evening drinking watered Scotch and having their eardrums clouted by indifferent jazzmen.

"The Year of the Bullbat," "The Year of Frenzy," "The Year of Frustration," journalists were calling 1946, and through all the spreeing there did run an unmistakable sense of displacement, a feverish running away, a bitterness that reveled in the harsh, the mocking, the blatant. The great movie box-office success was Jane Russell in *The Outlaw*, which was announced with the unabashed placard: "The Music Hall gets the big ones. What are the two great reasons for Jane Russell's rise to stardom?" Wider and wider audiences were won by novels of the raw and the amoebic, of men whose calling card was a battered body or women who delivered themselves from temptation by never knowing that you had to be tempted. The new radio sensation was Henry Morgan, master of the melancholy onslaught and "a nice enough fellow," as he would explain, "but all screwed up, like you are."

Hundreds of thousands bought *The Snake Pit*, Mary Jane Ward's novel of a woman's struggle with schizophrenia in a mental hospital. At the sanatorium, the patient went through shock therapy, hydrotherapy, psychoanalytical questionings, paraldehyde dosings, and old-fashioned madhouse discipline.

"I just don't know where it's all going to end," an ex-nurse, now a patient, says.

The head nurse of the ward answers: "I'll tell you. . . . When there's more sick ones than well ones, by golly the sick ones will lock the well ones up."

In every section of the United States, on all levels of society, the ill-tempered, the mean, the vicious in human beings pushed to the fore. These were the months when Justices of the Supreme Court of the United States insulted each other in newspaper head-lines and New England poultry farmers whined to their Congressmen about grain being sent overseas to the starving. They were the months, too, when the North disgraced itself by two major race riots, and the South, by six lynchings; West Coast ruffians threw bricks at the windows of Japanese-American veterans; and Dartmouth's President, Ernest Hopkins, blandly explained that of course his college admitted only a quota of Jews. In Atlanta, violence against Negroes and Negro houses was mounting, Jews were being threatened, and observers pointed to a newly chartered organization which, they warned, might prove the base for another nation-wide Ku-Klux Klan. "All the advances which minorities made during the New Deal and the war seem to be in question," the *Cleveland Plain Dealer* added. "And what is the longtime trend? Who knows?"

Who knew—who could be sure of anything in such an atmosphere? All approaches that offered confi-dence, or at least solace, found ready clienteles. The couches of psychiatrists were kept endlessly warm. Russell Janney, a gagman turned philosopher, scored unprecedented first-novel sales with *The Miracle of the Bells*, which somehow jumbled press agents, a Po-lish stripteaser, and St. Michael "taking on Kid Lucifer and putting him down for the count" into a demon-stration that America would be saved by an "emotion

deeper than love—the emotion of Palship." From the
Federal Council of Churches of Christ came a declaration of incontestable accuracy, which suggested a
major shift in thinking. "For at least half a century
Americans have been drifting away from religion," the
Council pointed out. "But at the present time all
signs—the cheap and the reverent, the serious and the
trivial—lead to only one conclusion. Americans are
going back to God."

Eugene O'Neill was in New York City for the
opening of his new play, *The Iceman Cometh*, and
reporters put the matter to him. "Back to religion?"
O'Neill mused. "Perhaps. Perhaps that will be the
answer for some. At any rate, I realize that I have been
putting my faith in values that are gone. . . . There
is a feeling around, or I'm mistaken, of fate. Kismet,
the negative fate. . . . It's struck me as time goes on,
how something funny, even farcical, can suddenly
without any apparent reason, break up into something
gloomy and tragic. . . . A sort of unfair *non sequitur*,
as though events, as though life were being manipulated just to confuse us."

For almost half a century, intellectual America,
along with its great playwright, had taken its main
sustenance from the exuberantly hopeful liberal tradition. Few were now ready to break with it; fewer still
were yet sure why they were so disturbed. Yet the
sense of that unfair *non sequitur*, of a soiled and be-
fuddled imperative, went on spreading.

In New York, San Francisco, or Greenville, South
Carolina, Americans concerned with words and ideas
waited for the postwar outburst of literary talent that
would mean excitingly fresh emphases. Hadn't 1919
brought Sherwood Anderson's *Winesburg, Ohio*,
Irving Babbitt's *Rousseau and Romanticism*, Joseph
Hergesheimer's *Java Head*, Eugene O'Neill's *The
Moon of the Caribbees*, not to speak of John Maynard
Keynes's *The Economic Consequences of the Peace*
which was about to appear? 1945 gave way to 1946,

1946 careened ahead and the outburst did not come. Restively, irritably, American intellectuals turned toward a hangdog self-criticism.

At least there was one outlet for everyone, whether the troubled writer or the housewife waspish over the disappearance of chops. The President of the United States is many things. He is the symbol of the nation, the head of the dominant political party, the man who makes the crucial decisions. He is also the final focus of the national mood, a subject for adulation when things go well and the butt of anger in a period of turmoil and troubles. As 1946 ended, Harry Truman sat in the President's chair a perfect target. Not since another simple man, Andrew Johnson, tried to fill the place of another strong President in another postwar had such a fury of unpopularity lashed the White House.

Truman's determined optimism, his addiction to his Missouri buddies, to platitudes, and to Mother? "Every day is Mother's Day in the White House," people said with a bitter snicker. His handling of John L. Lewis, symbol of the strikes? "The President lets the public freeze while his guts quiver," roared Robert R. Wason, president of the National Association of Manufacturers. His back-and-forth on price controls? "Poor Mr. Truman," the liberal columnist Samuel Grafton sneered, "an object for pity." His fumbling of the Wallace speech? Even the secretaries were saying: "You just sort of forget about Harry until he makes another mistake." People of a dozen points of view passed around a wisecrack. Why had the President been late to today's press conference? He got up this morning a little stiff in the joints and had trouble putting his foot in his mouth.

For fourteen long years, Republicans had been trying to capture the national mood. They cried: "Roosevelt and Ruin," "Dictatorship," "Bankruptcy," "Warmongering," "Bureaucracy," and "Communism." Nothing had worked. Then, as the Congressional elections of November, 1946, came on, the Harry M. Frost Advertising Company of Boston hit upon two words with magic for the day.

"Had enough?" the Republicans asked the country. A nation which had quite enough of inflation and the Russians, of strikes, shortages, and the atom bomb, of everlasting maybe's about peace and prosperity, rose up in a hiss of exasperation and elected the first Republican Congress since the far-distant days of Herbert Hoover.

The Postwar Takes Shape

GRADUALLY THE store shelves began to fill. Within months after the election of 1946, steaks and roasts were no longer drawing crowds. Canned beer was back and so were white sheets, alarm clocks, nylons, and golf balls. The black-marketeers were slithering away. Here and there startled householders opened the door and actually heard a salesman ask them to buy an automobile.

Shortly after the election John L. Lewis marched his coal miners out on strike and this time a government injunction marched them right back again. Labor leaders, no aspirants for defeat, saw to it that strikes quickly dwindled. Raw materials were becoming plentiful; the reconversion of machinery was nearing completion. "Let 'er rip" was the mood of the front offices and production, already approaching prewar levels, spurted ahead.

Prices kept on climbing. Even the kids of the Cape Cod resort towns, who for years had dived to retrieve pennies thrown in the water by vacationers, now refused to budge except for nickels. But the public was learning to roll with the inflation and the free-spending spree of 1946 was quieting into budget-wary living. Expensive Scotch and bonded bourbon piled up in liquor stores. Despite the most honeyed words of *Vogue* and *Mademoiselle*, women did not rush to buy Paris's new padded hips and the long skirt; instead buttons for home sewing were selling briskly. The great vacation migrations slowed and night-club business was off sharply from Manhattan's Latin Quarter to the Hollywood Mocambo. "The geese are out there," the headwaiter of the Latin Quarter sighed, "but they ain't comin' in here and layin' them golden eggs."

Across the river in Brooklyn, telephones in newspaper offices jangled crazily. Was the terrible rumor true, was Manager Leo Durocher really shifting over to the Giants? "Jeez," one choked-up caller took the news, "it's Poil Hobba for the Dodgers." The nation could smile indulgently at the dither, could find the mood for all the old stand-bys of sports and sentiment. Things were less hectic, less feverish. The divorce rate tumbled; the South staged fewer lynching bees; Supreme Court Justices stopped caterwauling at each other in public. And the pro-feminist novelist, Fannie Hurst, who had managed to find a bright dawn for women over many years, could only complain to her audiences: "A sleeping sickness is spreading among the women of the land. . . . They are retrogressing into . . . that thing known as The Home."

As the nation returned to more workaday acting and thinking, a spectacular fact emerged: the America that was settling was not so much settling down as it was settling upward. The high hopes of V-J were, at least in one important respect, beng realized. Whatever the ravages of inflation, the masses of ordinary Americans were living at a higher material standard than their groups had ever known and with a much greater sense of status in the community.

The postwar period was proving to be the beneficiary of at least fifty years of bloodless but drastic change in the United States. During this Half-Century of Revolution, mass-production techniques in industry and the mechanization of agriculture raced ahead.

Powerful political forces pushed toward a welfare state while businessmen countered with welfare capitalism. Two world wars affected the domestic society like giant leveling bulldozers. The results of all these developments, intertwined in a dozen ways, came to a temporary climax in the amazing America of the late 1940's.

Trim workers' suburbs were rising in testimony to the fact that almost half of organized labor was in or quite near the middle-income brackets of the country. All but the unluckiest or least provident of farmers were living decently, often amid so many machines that a nine-to-five workday was possible for both husband and wife; among the eight million farm families of the top-income group, a year's gross return of ten thousand dollars was average. The rampant inflation itself was in part a result of the fact that the country as a whole was living better. The American Meat Institute issued the most revealing figures. Before the war housewives had turned to macaroni, egg-and-cheese mixtures, or some other inexpensive dish for about half the family meals; in 1947 the average American ate meat five out of seven nights a week.

Economics was only part—and perhaps the least important part—of the developing scene. The sense of heightened status which farmers and workingmen were beginning to feel at the end of the war was now coming in large, deeply satisfying draughts. As a young man Leslie Heiser, a farmer of upstate Illinois, had been so mortified by the clothes he had to wear to town that he cursed the fate which gave him his occupation. In 1947 Heiser was talking the changed attitude of much of agricultural America. His annual income well over six thousand dollars, the whole family trim in Chicago-style clothing, each year bringing the sense of upward movement which came with new farm machinery or more electrical appliances for the home, Heiser deferred to no man. "There isn't a job in New York City that's good enough for me," he would say.

Labor too was lifting its head high. As a new era of union-management relations came in, a team of girls locked in a room on the eleventh floor of the General Motors Building in Detroit finished a secret typing job. Six floors below, a little group of men, haggard from seventeen consecutive hours of collective bargaining, called in reporters and handed out the sensational news: the world's largest automobile manufacturer had agreed to what the union liked so much—a formula for hitching wages to living costs. The GM agreement was many things, including a way of keeping the labor front quieted in an inflationary period while protecting corporations from a sudden deflation. But perhaps most importantly, the pact was another and especially striking indication of the role that unions were coming to play in American life. These organizations may have grown primarily as economic weapons but they had become something far beyond that. Regularly taking on the biggest corporations, winning an increasingly large part in management discussions, raising and distributing vast welfare funds, wielding political power that could mean a key role in picking the President of the United States, the unions were bringing to industrial workers a sense of being men who counted.

In the cities or out across the countryside, the GI Bill of Rights, now in full operation, went on its revolutionary way. In 1947 more than four million young men and women were benefiting from the legislation. Thousands did not need the aid; others used it to take rumba lessons at Arthur Murray's, to learn archery, or, in the case of one veteran from Des Moines, to equip himself with a fine set of burglary tools. But for millions the GI Bill of Rights was opportunity written in large, alluring letters. Turning to it for more education, to set up a business of their own or an independent farm, perhaps to purchase a home, they knew the zest of the upsweep in status. "I've talked to hundreds and hundreds of these kids," James Gardner, a Veterans' Administration official in San Francisco, remarked, "and you get the same story over and over again. They like the idea of making more money but they like even more the idea—as they keep putting it—of 'getting to be somebody.' "

Amid it all, a powerful, lithe Negro was turning the base paths of Ebbets Field into a holy war. For Jack Roosevelt Robinson living had always been fierce competition. Growing up in a Pasadena slum, he made his first money by sneaking onto golf courses, retrieving lost balls, and outrunning the cops. Given athletic scholarships to Pasadena Junior College and U.C.L.A., Jackie Robinson drove himself to stardom in so many different sports that West Coast writers were rhapsodizing about the new Jim Thorpe. After World War II, as Robinson was slugging and darting his way up in the Negro baseball leagues, the Brooklyn Dodger general manager Branch Rickey heightened the competition. Half Barnum and half Billy Sunday, Rickey had decided to defy baseball's ancient color line and sign Robinson to a Brooklyn contract. Now the sensitive, quick-tempered young Negro faced the most brutal kind of contest; this time he had to battle by not battling at all.

Rickey drove at the matter hard the first time Robinson came to his office. At the height of the emotional talk, the Brooklyn owner moved behind his big desk. He posed as a clerk in a Southern hotel, insultingly refusing Robinson a room; as a prejudiced sports writer, twisting a story to make the Negro look bad; as a foul-tongued fan jostling him in a hotel lobby or railroad station. Rickey took off his coat and charged out in front of the desk. "Now I'm playing against you in the World Series. . . . I go into you, spikes first. But you don't give ground. You stand there and you jab the ball into my ribs and the umpire yells, 'Out!' I flare—all I see is your face—that black face right on top of me. So I haul off and I punch you right in the cheek."

A white fist barely missed Robinson's sweating face. The head did not budge.

"What do you do?" Rickey roared. "What do you do?"

The heavy lips trembled for an instant and then opened. "Mr. Rickey," Jackie Robinson said in a taut whisper, "I've got two cheeks."

People who should have known were openly skeptical. "Players on the road live close together," one baseball veteran expressed the feeling. "It just won't work." Rickey was saying very little. Instead he was organizing in each city of the National League a how-to-handle-Robinson committee, composed of leading Negro citizens. Jackie Robinson, it was agreed, would stay away from night spots, endorse no products, leave the ball parks by a secret exit to avoid displays of Negro adulation as well as pop bottles, and, at least for a period, turn down social invitations from blacks or whites.

Robinson took his position at first base and more than occasionally players came smashing against him, at times with spikes out; the Negro ground his teeth and said nothing. Hotels in St. Louis and Philadelphia registered the rest of the Dodgers and refused Robinson a room. He turned away without a word and slept at a friend's home. Some members of his own team walked past without saying hello; some members of other teams poured verbal filth from the dugout or yelled insults as he rounded the bases. "I'd get mad," Jackie Robinson said. "But I'd never let them know it."

The 1947 season rushed ahead. The first baseman's dazzling hitting and running were heading him for sure Rookie-of-the-Year honors, teammates began inviting him for a poker session. Baseball Commissioner Albert Chandler cracked down on the rowdies, national popularity polls showed Jackie Robinson running a close second to Bing Crosby. Down the home stretch in September, with the Dodgers and the Cardinals first and second in the National League, the Cardinals' catcher hurtled into the Negro at first base. Next time at bat Jackie Robinson suddenly was Jackie Robinson. He turned to the catcher and let fly with all the furious language of a rhubarb and the Cardinal, in the routine tradition, rhubarbed back. The stands hushed, then broke into a vast murmur of approval. A newspaperman said to a friend: "By God, there's a black boy squawking just like everybody else and nothing happening. I don't mean to be silly but somehow I think this is one for the history books."

The history books will have to record that Jackie Robinson's triumph, so widely publicized and admired, enormously furthered acceptance for the Negro in many fields of American life. They will also have to record a still more important fact. This revolutionist in a baseball suit was the flashing symbol of an era in the national life when, for all minority groups, for all lower-status Americans, the social and economic walls were coming tumbling down.

In Washington, Congressmen would pause for an occasional pat on the back to Jackie Robinson, an apostrophe to the American Way of Life. Then the chambers hurried back to the main business at hand. The Congress elected in the Republican sweep of 1946, the Eightieth Congress, was led by men with a mission. They had come roaring into the Capital filled with spleen and plannings.

Behind them was a nation-wide rancor. It spurted out from all regions of the country and from a dozen different groups, each with its own special resentment. Democratic Georgia Crackers hated "what the Niggers are getting away with"; Republican businessmen in any community had their furies at the labor unions; New Dealish secretaries, plumbers, and hairdressers in New York, Toledo, or Seattle sputtered every time they saw the size of the withholding tax on their pay checks. But the most powerful thrust of discontent came from one readily identifiable group, the men and women who had come to be called conservatives and who now emphatically did not want to conserve the existing America.

These malcontents were as much a product of the Half-Century of Revolution as the situations which annoyed them so much. All during the years since the 1890's, the emerging society had been making enemies. Many of these foes were members of the high-income strata, who saw the period as one long aggravating process of redistributing their wealth. Foreign and domestic affairs alike seemed to mean increasingly the same thing—spending great sums of money which came disproportionately from their pockets.

Yet the grievance was not wholly economic; men from middle and low economic groups joined wealthy Americans in an impatience with things that had little to do with finances. The Half-Century of Revolution, particularly the jolting changes since 1933, had been a trial to all those whose temperaments yearned for stability. One change was proving particularly upsetting. Once upon a time, white, Protestant, relatively old-stock Americans had been the arbiters of the national life. Small-town storekeepers or big-city bankers, they were "nice people," the "Best People," expecting and receiving a certain deference. Now the established classes were having to make room for groups from the bottom and they were feeling uncomfortable, jostled, almost displaced in an America which they had assumed belonged peculiarly to them. "What kind of a country is it," John Hurst, an old-family small businessman of Champaign, Illinois, cried out the feeling at a druggists' convention, "I ask you, what kind of a country is it that fusses over anybody who makes a big noise and ignores Robert A. Taft?"

Robert A. Taft—here, to an extraordinary extent, was the symbol and the spokesman, the glory and the hope of the malcontents. The Taft family had stood for reputability, for solid, ultra-respectable achievement, ever since grandfather Alphonso doggedly walked from a Vermont farm to New Haven, became the first of twenty-one Tafts to graduate from Yale, quit working in a New York law office because he found his colleagues too grasping ("money is the all in all"), and settled into Cincinnati's most esteemed legal and political circles. Alphonso's son gave the family tradition a firm nudge forward. William Howard Taft was quite a man of achievement; he was also a President of the United States who stood, with all the strength his amiable and decorous self would permit, against the whole social-reform movement of his day. Almost as a matter of course, the President's son, Robert Taft, was number one in his class at Yale University and Harvard Law School, an extraordinarily able attorney giving most of his time to trust funds and impeccable real estate, a United States Senator who took over the leadership of the battle which established America was waging in the 1930's against the New Deal.

The most striking personal qualities of Senator Taft were precisely the ones which this traditional America liked to believe belonged especially to its way of life. His habits were as unpretentious as his baggy serge suits; Taft's idea of a good time was a family picnic where everybody sat around munching drugstore candy bars and playing hearts. He permitted his brilliant mind no heretical adventures, keeping it tightly reined by the logic of the ledger-book. Despite his mounting yearnings to follow his father into the White House, he remained honest, outspoken, almost unbelievably ready to make plain exactly what Robert Taft thought on any public issue. "I look at that man," Mrs. Edith Busbey, an Idaho Taftite phrased what the Senator could mean to his supporters, "and I see everything which my father taught me to hold good."

Taft's greatest political liability before the general public only increased his hold on his special following. The man was a study in discomfiture, a deep-seated, persistent lack of rapport with his America. Taft would go campaigning at fairs or city rallies, where the local titans, crowding and backslapping him, made sure that everybody knew they were as good as any Taft, by God, and the Senator's smile would come out as radiant as a very small and very lopsided persimmon. Republican politicians might shudder. The Senator's devotees, squirming with him amid the incessant leveling of the new era, cherished him the more for the things he could not tolerate.

Taft's doctrine had its compromises; the yearnings for the White House did not leave his policies entirely unaffected. Yet basically Taftism amounted to a call for counter-revolution against the Half-Century of Revolution. The Senator reacted to almost any foreign-affairs situation by trying to limit American commitments; the issue was at home and it was urgent. For too long, as Taft saw things, the emphasis had been on economic and social opportunities. The stress should be returned to the "traditional American heart of things, liberty"—the greatest practicable freedom of the individual in both his economic and his governmental relationships.

The usually flat voice would take on a high-pitched urgency as Taft said: "We have got to break with the corrupting idea that we can legislate prosperity, legislate equality, legislate opportunity. All of these good things came in the past from free Americans freely working out their destiny. . . . That is the only way they can continue to come in any genuine sense." Once the credo was expressed more simply. At the height of the furor over meat prices, reporters asked the Senator for his solution and he replied: "Eat less." It was the purest Taftiana—in its magnificent tactlessness and its bedrock assumption that a real American solved his own problems.

Taft was unquestionably the powerhouse of the new Eightieth Congress and he and most of the other leaders took the Republican victory as a mandate to remake

America along anti-New Deal lines. Committee after committee went under the chairmanship of veterans of the struggle against Rooseveltism. In a kind of caricature of the trend, the chairmanship of the powerful House Appropriations Committee passed to cantankerous John Taber, who in the long-past days of 1940 had roared so loud fighting a New Deal bill that he restored the hearing in the deaf ear of Congressman Leonard Schuetz ("I had spent thousands of dollars on that ear," Schuetz said in grateful wonderment). Now, John Taber stormed, he was going to apply a "meat-axe to government frills."

When the actual record of the Congress began to emerge in 1947, it proved an assault on the legislation and the tendencies of the Half-Century of Revolution. The practical political basis of the session was a deal between Southern Democrats and right-wing Republicans, which meant the end of any hopes for civil-rights legislation. The two most important laws passed were the Taft-Hartley Act, which weakened the power of unions, and a new income tax formula that reduced the disproportion of taxes on high incomes. (The bill cut the levies three per cent for families with incomes of $2,400 or less; eight per cent for those in the $10,000 bracket; fifteen per cent for the $20,000 a year class; and forty-eight to sixty-five per cent for the group over $100,000.) The structure of government aid to farmers was attacked by cuts in funds for soil conservation and for crop storage. The Congress refused demands for federal help in the form of more public housing, strong price controls, extended social security, or aid-to-education. Both what was done and what was not done in the field of immigration legislation reflected distaste for immigrants of southern and eastern European origins. Over the whole session hung the air of wrathful counter-revolution. "T.R.B.," the New Deal columnist of the *New Republic*, was as accurate as he was melancholy when he wrote: "This Congress brought back an atmosphere you had forgot-

ten or never thought possible. . . . Victories fought
and won years ago were suddenly in doubt. Everything
was debatable again."

"It would be ironical," Taft remarked early in the
session, "if this Congress which really has its heart set
on straightening out domestic affairs would end up in
being besieged by foreign problems." The world of
1947 had a way of being ironical. The Eightieth Congress had hardly assembled when news from abroad
was hammering at the door of every Congressman.

Since the end of World War II, the anti-Communist
government of Greece had been under attack from
Red guerillas and had survived only because the British gave it sizable economic and military support. In
February, 1947 the British, hard-pressed financially
and embroiled in troubles throughout the Empire,
notified the American government that they would no
longer be able to serve as the prop in Greece. With
this support removed, Greece almost certainly would
gravitate into the Soviet orbit, the independence of
Turkey would be undermined, and the whole eastern
Mediterranean might slide behind the Iron Curtain.
Secretary of State George Marshall, reaching into his
military past, found the phrase that expressed the
Washington reaction. This was "like the Battle of the
Bulge," the Secretary declared, a sudden thrust of danger that carried within it potential disaster for the
whole defense of the democracies.

Shortly after the bad news from London, Secretary
Marshall flew to a Big Four conference in Moscow
which was supposed to arrange peace treaties for Germany and Austria. For forty-four sessions the meetings ground on, all utterly sterile except in giving the
West an unmistakable indication of what the Soviet
meant by diplomacy. One especially poignant moment was caught on the front pages of the American
newspapers. George Marshall, trying desperately to
break through the Russian twistings of language, read

off a little lecture on what Americans meant by democracy, in central Europe or anywhere else.

"We believe," the Secretary said, "that human beings have certain inalienable rights—that is, rights which may not be given or taken away. They include the right of every individual to develop his mind and his soul in the ways of his own choice. . . . To us a society is not democratic if men who respect the rights of their fellow-men are not free to express their own beliefs and convictions without fear that they may be snatched away from their home or family. . . . [A democratic society must] assure such rights to every individual and effectively prevent any government or group, however powerful or however numerous, from taking such rights away from or imposing any such fears on any individuals, however weak or however few."

Foreign Minister Molotov stirred impatiently. "A number of valuable remarks," he said and then hurried into another tirade against "war-mongering capitalist piracy."

In rapid succession the Soviet Union threw loud-clanging *nyets* into the machinery of the United Nations. One day the Soviet was rejecting more plans for the international control of atomic energy. Another two weeks and it was using its tenth veto—this time to shield Communist Albania from an investigation of the charge that she planted mines which damaged British destroyers. A few days more and the Soviet boycotted the opening session of the UN Trusteeship Council with cries of "barbarous American imperialism." Nothing, not even a sense of the ridiculous, restrained the malevolent self-righteousness of the Russians. Do you know, the Soviet delegate to the UN Commission on Human Rights asked indignantly, that Alabama has a law which permits a man to beat his wife provided that the stick is not more than two inches in circumference?

The White House was in a fury of activity. Legislation was being rushed to cope with the Greek-Turkish crisis and Congressional leaders were soon summoned to smooth the way for quick passage of the bill. Secretary Marshall took the lead in explaining the situation. With his mind on the poverty that was so powerful an ally of the Communists in Greece, the Secretary emphasized the need for economic relief. The Republican leaders stirred irritably. Did this Administration really expect the Congress of Robert Taft to play WPA to the Greeks?

Undersecretary of State Dean Acheson, sensing the trouble, turned to President Truman and asked if he might add some remarks. Acheson said little about economic distress. Instead he moved over to the big wall map with pointer in hand and described in detail just what strategic consequences would follow the fall of Greece to Red armies. The Republican leaders began relaxing and one of the most important of them, Senator Arthur Vandenberg, went away with a co-operative word of advice. As Vandenberg left, he remarked to Truman: "Mr. President, if that's what you want, there's only one way to get it. That is to make a personal appearance before Congress and scare hell out of the country."

On March 12, 1947, Truman went before Congress with a message which would have scared hell out of any nation. He had a good deal to say about the American desire for peace. But basically the speech was a blunt warning that Communist actions were directly and gravely threatening American security. Specifically, the President proposed that Congress should bolster the hard-pressed Greek and Turkish governments by appropriating $400,000,000 in military and economic help and by authorizing the sending of American military and civilian personnel to supervise the use of the aid. He was fully aware, Truman said, of the broad implications involved in such actions. But the time had come when America had to take a stand. "I believe that it must be the policy of the United

States," the President declared in words that immediately became known as the Truman Doctrine, "to support free peoples who are resisting attempted subjugation by armed minorities or by outside pressures."

The Congressional and public debate of the Presidential proposals, wordy as it was, soon made plain that the country was quite ready to authorize the funds and the personnel which Truman had recommended. As the national determination to take action against Soviet imperialism became clear, Bernard Baruch began preparations for a speech he was to make in South Carolina and Baruch turned for assistance to an old friend, the veteran newspaperman Herbert Bayard Swope. About a year before, Swope, working on another address for Baruch, had used the phrase "Cold War" to describe American-Soviet relations but a number of mutual friends thought the term too strong and Baruch removed it. Now Swope wrote into his draft of the South Carolina speech the sentence: "Let us not be deceived—today we are in the midst of a cold war." This time the phrase did not seem too strong and Baruch spoke it in Columbia, South Carolina on April 16, 1947. Walter Lippmann spread it through his widely syndicated column and the public, recognizing "Cold War" as an accurate expression of the situation that had developed, immediately made the term a commonplace of the American language.

Just before Baruch's speech, American bookstores received their first shipment of an abridgment of the massive *Study of History* by the London University professor, Arnold Toynbee. Even in shortened form the work was hardly the usual popular reading; the 589 pages, part history, part philosophy, and part poetry, wound a labyrinthine way through the rise and fall of twenty-six civilizations. Yet the book quickly made its way to best-seller lists and stayed on week after week. Soon the slim, pale professor, with the long grave face and the uncompromising language, was the rage of the American lecture circuit, and Toynbee-ism in some vague and simplified form was reaching amazingly far into the semi-literate public. No matter what Toynbee had meant to say, his brooding discussion of the rise and fall of civilizations bore directly upon a feeling that had been growing in the United States ever since the first postwar difficulties with Communism and was now hardening into a conviction. By the spring of 1947, a good many Americans, whether talking the language of the universities or the corner taverns, were ready to state that the United States faced not simply the threat of war with another country but some kind of vast and fundamental conflict between ways of acting and thinking, the kind of clash, as Professor Toynbee said, which time and again had sent whole civilizations crashing down.

So it was to be war, at least Cold War, certainly a portentous struggle. So it was not to be depression, at least not tomorrow, but social and economic upsurge and inflation and the headaches that inflation brought and the Taftite assault on many of the laws and attitudes associated with the upsurge. The postwar America emerging in the spring of 1947, so zestfully careering, so replete with evidence that the careering would take you fast and far, so formidably threatened, was like nothing so much as some great gaily colored balloon bounding along just above craggy wastes. The people of the United States, more and more aware of their situation, were to react in quite different ways. Their first major national response was to be so rational, so hard-headed, that they utterly dumfounded themselves.

IV

Containment, Foreign and Domestic

THE REPORTERS who covered the White House during the spring of 1947 almost all agreed on one thing. Bert Andrews of the *New York Herald Tribune* put it succinctly: "Harry Truman is becoming President of the United States."

The man in the White House was getting used to the big lonely room where Lincoln and Wilson and Franklin Roosevelt had sat. The year and a half in office had given Truman a chance to catch up on the background of affairs, easing his feeling that he was overwhelmed. ("I don't know how I ever got out of that mudhole," he said as he recalled how he had been forced to rely on Roosevelt holdovers for the most basic facts on this or that situation.) In its own way, the Republican victory in the Congressional elections of 1946 helped to put Truman on his feet. During the first period after Roosevelt's death, he had not been able to down the feeling that he was something of an executor for the deceased President's Administrations. The elections of 1946, however Republican the returns, started things afresh. Now Truman felt freer to be himself, to act on his own in his own ways.

A new air was permeating the White House. The President's incessant cheerfulness of the early days was becoming mixed with a sober recognition of the difficulties facing the United States. The lines of authority tightened. "The boys are learning," Presidential Secretary Charles Ross observed, "that Harry Truman is no pushover." John Snyder still talked blowzy platitudes to the President and Harry Vaughan's brassy laugh was as audible as ever around the White House, but Truman was also recognizing the need for a different type of adviser. Particularly noticeable was the growing role of Clark Clifford, who had first come to public attention because of his part in drafting the Presidential message which marked the end of the 1946 railroad strike.

When Clark Clifford was growing up in St. Louis, all the nice ladies would say: "My, what a beautiful youngster." Half the coeds at Washington University had their eyes on this six feet two inches of graceful muscularity, topped by waves of taffy-colored hair and a smile that dimmed the toothpaste ads. Like many handsome men, Clifford could be annoyed by the fuss over his appearance but he was never so annoyed that he failed to realize how his striking good looks, coupled with a friendly manner and a clear, agile mind, gave him a head start toward success. From college days, Clifford was driving hard. At Washington University he was the biggest of the Big Men on Campus. Entering the Missouri bar, he commanded an income of thirty thousand dollars a year as a trial lawyer before he was out of his thirties. Volunteering for the Navy during World War II, Clifford rose, or rather rocketed, from a lieutenant j.g. to a captain in twenty-one months.

By now success was a habit. When a friendship with a Truman crony, Jake Vardaman, led to Clifford's appointment as a White House naval aide, the bright young man wore his new importance as easily as he wore his faultless clothing. Truman liked the confidence of his young associate. He was no less pleased by Clifford's Missouri colloquialisms, his hardheaded

thinking and his way with words, above all by his habit
of talking to the boss with no intimation that Harry
Truman was a smudged carbon copy of Franklin
Roosevelt. By the spring of 1947 Clark Clifford, just
turned forty, was Special Counsel to the President of
the United States, serving as a combination speech-
writer, political strategist, and general co-ordinator of
White House affairs and doing it all with the bland
assurance that the Truman Administration, like Clark
Clifford, would be quite a success.

Two or three times a week the President and Clifford ate together in the basement lunchroom of the
White House. Six or eight times a day Clifford walked
the twenty paces which were all that separated his
office from Truman's door. Always the counselor
pushed vigorously for positive, broad-gauged policies
in domestic and foreign affairs. 1947 had already
brought action aplenty. That formidable government
injunction had been thrown at John L. Lewis; the
Greek-Turkish proposals were being rushed through
Congress. But none of these moves bespoke a genuine
policy. None offered a comprehensive, practicable
guide for future steps on either the domestic or the
foreign front.

Clifford's own special interest was in domestic affairs, and here his urgings were especially confident.
A nephew and admirer of Clark McAdams, the crusading liberal editor of the St. Louis Post-Dispatch, Clifford had grown up with a marked tendency toward
the kind of policies represented by the New Deal. A
close student of political affairs, he was convinced
that the long lines of development indicated victories
for the party which identified itself with the hopes
and the worries of ordinary men and women. As Clifford looked out at the America of the late 1940's, with
its vast social upsweep, he was more sure than ever that
success for the Truman Administration and continuation of the Half-Century of Revolution were inextricably entwined.

Clifford wanted no emotional New Dealism, no sweeping new programs; such things were foreign to this unideological moderate, as he believed they were foreign to the mood of the country. Clifford sought, as it were, to codify the New Deal. He wanted to protect what it had done by fending off the Eightieth Congress, to improve on its accomplishments by tying together loose ends here and there, to bring it up to date by applying its general approach to certain key problems which had arisen since the war.

Such doctrine sat well with Harry Truman. The President, whatever his allergy to intellectualish New Dealers, had long leaned in the direction of wanting to use the government to help the lower economic groups. An unreconstructable Democrat, he was inclined to believe that anything a Republican Congress did was pernicious. A politician to the bone, he had an instinctive sense of the millions of votes that lay down in the rows of little white houses where men worried about keeping up the payments on the car or getting the daughter a formal.

On through 1947, then during 1948, President Truman, prodded and aided by Clifford, was working out his own variety of liberalism in domestic affairs. Under the circumstances of the Eightieth Congress, it was expressed most conspicuously in negatives. Sixty-two times Truman wielded the Presidential veto and for his most important attempt at blockage, the rejection of Taft-Hartley, he accepted language written by Clifford which was more vigorous than the country had heard since the bellicose vetoing days of Grover Cleveland.

Meanwhile the President spelled out the proposals which represented his program for positive adjustments and updatings of the New Deal: for farmers, a series of minor changes in existing legislation which were intended to make more beneficial the federal aid to agriculture; for labor, a raise in the minimum wage from forty to seventy-five cents; for the foreign-born, an amendment to immigration policy which would remove any stigma from citizens of southern and eastern European birth; for the general public of medium or low incomes, favorable modifications in the social security program, the re-enactment of strict price controls, and a tax bill that would have helped the rich the least by cutting everyone's income tax the same forty dollars. Of all the lower-status groups, the Negroes had received the fewest New Deal laws specifically designed to help them and they were now pressuring the hardest for federal aid. Down to Congress went a strong Truman message urging the heart of the Negro legislative demands—an anti-lynching bill, the elimination of the poll tax, and a permanent Fair Employment Practices Commission.

In foreign affairs, the sheer force of events was helping to push the Administration toward a genuine policy. Even before President Truman received the formal Congressional authorization of aid for Greece and Turkey, the first ships were being loaded with food and bullets for the Mediterranean. Greece and Turkey held. But the foreign crisis only went on mounting. In Asia, almost nothing was improving from the American point of view. In western Europe, conditions were deteriorating so rapidly that an unending stream of Congressmen and government officials were crossing the Atlantic and coming back crying disaster.

The spring of 1947 found Britain and most of the Continent teetering near economic collapse. From Paris to Naples and on up to Oslo, tens of thousands of the undernourished were speaking with a racking cough. Tuberculosis, on the rise in western Europe for the first time in a century, was turning into the region's number-one killer. "What is Europe now?" Winston Churchill declared on May 14, 1947. "It is a rubble-heap, a charnal house, a breeding-ground of pestilence and hate." Bitterness, hunger, and disease could only mean more Communist strength and it was clear that France and Italy were gravely threatened.

The Truman Doctrine itself added to the difficulty of the American position. Edward Barrett, the overseas information specialist, has described how "the Truman Doctrine, well-meant but drafted without enough awareness of foreign reactions, backfired in many parts of the world. Since the then Greek Government had a reputation for corruption and oppression, America seemed to many to be underwriting the forces of reaction. Since . . . the President had said American officials would supervise the use of U.S. dollars in Greece, he seemed to underscore the theme that America was hell-bent on economic imperialism. More important still, it indicated to some that America had embarked on a program of using troubled small nations as pawns in a gigantic contest with the U.S.S.R."

In the State Department lights burned late seven nights a week. President Truman, who more than once publicly called Secretary of State George Marshall "the greatest living American," was leaning heavily on the gnarled, fatherly Marshall for guidance in foreign affairs. The Secretary, no novice at brainpicking, was reaching out for information and ideas. William L. Clayton, who for years had headed the largest firm of cotton brokers in the world and who now was Undersecretary of State for Economic Affairs, was providing a seasoned assessment of the economic state of Europe. The luminous mind of Undersecretary of State Dean Acheson was putting Administration thinking together into a general approach. Speaking in Cleveland, Mississippi, on May 7, Acheson expressed the developing pattern. "Since world demand exceeds our ability to supply, we are going to have to concentrate our emergency assistance in areas where it will be most effective in building world political and economic stability, in promoting human freedom and democratic institutions, in fostering liberal trading policies, and in strengthening the authority of the United Nations. This is merely common sense and sound practice."

Meanwhile Secretary Marshall was turning for additional aid to a board which he himself had set up. The War Department had long contained a Strategy and Policy Section, concerned not with day-by-day affairs but with long-range planning. As Secretary of State, Marshall ordered the establishment of a State Department "Policy Planning Staff," to be composed of specialists whose function would be to formulate foreign policy projected from ten to twenty-five years into the future. The meeting place of the PPS, a spacious room next to the Secretary's office, was deliberately given an atmosphere of unhurried academe. No telephone was to bring a sense of the insistent present; the room contained only a conference table quietly flanked by floor-to-ceiling bookshelves. But whatever the original plan, in the spring of 1947 the present was bursting into the thinking of the policy planners like a fire bell. The group had not even formally met for the first time when, on April 29, Secretary Marshall sent the PPS chief, George Kennan, a written instruction to draw up a specific recommendation of moves to be made by the United States.

The next day Marshall talked with Kennan. The European situation was so bad, the Secretary said, that Congressmen would soon be coming up with all kinds of unworkable schemes. The Secretary wanted a sound program and he wanted it within ten days or two weeks. As the conference closed Kennan asked the Secretary if he had any further instructions. Marshall replied: "Avoid trivia."

George Kennan took his place at the head of the policy planners' table a slender, casually dressed figure with a preoccupied smile and quick-darting words, who somehow suggested both the skeptical man of affairs and the dedicated scholar. The early years of Kennan had been routine enough—a comfortable Milwaukee lawyer's home, a strict Midwestern military academy, a reading of Fitzgerald's *This Side of Paradise* which sent him applying to Princeton in 1921. At college one part of the unusual combination in the man began to develop. Shy, oversensitive, sure that he was crude in manner, he was probably the most obscure and lonely student on the Princeton campus. This very lack of social success threw him together with a rebellious minority who were defying campus conventions, reading with avid excitement the products of the American literary flowering that accompanied their years in college, and arguing philosophy, religion, and politics from dusk to dawn in one of the battered ground-floor rooms of Witherspoon Hall. Twenty-one years in the Foreign Service, years that were concentrated especially on Russian affairs, only developed further the intellectualism of Kennan. Of equal importance, the years added a toughmindedness and the two qualities—the worldliness and the bookishness—blended into a pattern of thinking.

George Kennan proved the scholar-diplomat, if the United States has ever had one. To him being a Foreign Service man came to mean studying thoroughly the nation to which he was accredited, not simply its politics and its economics but its history, its music, its mores, everything which would permit him to lay hold of its inner nature. At the same time Kennan grew impatient with any diplomacy based primarily on academic theorizing or moral and legalistic considerations; the crusadings and the One Worldism of the Roosevelt era particularly bothered him. Kennan sought, as he said later, the diplomacy of "reality"—a diplomacy which demanded a hardheaded handling of a rigorously appraised situation. The job of the Foreign Service man was to be a diplomat "in the most old-fashioned sense of the word." He was not to make the world wonderful but to save it from the worst consequences of its follies. For civilization was in "a constant state of change and flux" and the major function of the diplomat was "to ease its transitions, to temper the asperities to which . . . [the constant change] often leads, . . . to see that these conflicts do not assume forms too unsettling for international life in general."

When World War II ended, Kennan was the number-two man in the American Embassy at Moscow and growing more and more disturbed by the American policy toward the Soviet Union. In February, 1946, just as Churchill was to make his "Iron Curtain" speech, Kennan took the occasion of some queries from the State Department to speak his mind in an eight-thousand-word cable. The American people, he declared, did not remotely understand the Soviet Union and the policy of the government itself was marked by "wishful thinking." Reaching into his profound knowledge of Russian history, he saw the Soviet as dominated by a "neurotic view," a "traditional and instinctive sense of insecurity" stemming from the days when the Russians were an agricultural people living on a defenseless plain amid fierce nomadic tribes. As Russia grew and came into contact with the West centuries ago, its rulers acquired another fear, a disquietude about the societies they were encountering. They "sensed that their rule was relatively archaic in form, fragile and artificial in its psychological foundation, unable to stand comparison or contact with political systems of Western countries. For this reason they have always feared foreign penetration. . . . And they have learned to seek security only in patient but deadly struggle for the total destruction of rival power, never in compacts and compromises with it."

After Communism took power, that dogma became a perfect vehicle for the sense of insecurity of the new Russian rulers. It pictured them as defending idealism against menacing forces within and without, and thus justified the "dictatorship without which they did not know how to rule . . . [and] the cruelties they did not dare not to inflict." In addition, Bolshevism attached to traditional Russian expansionism the whole apparatus of an international revolutionary force. Soviet Communism, in short, was another expression of the centuries-old "uneasy" Russian nationalism and imperialism but in a much more powerful and insidious form.

From such an analysis, one could only deduce that it was useless to try to establish normal relationships with the Soviet Union by compromises, another meeting of the Big Four, or some other reasonable form of give-and-take. The Kennan cable was harsh and disillusioning doctrine, much too disillusioning for early 1946 when the United States was not even ready for Churchill's Iron Curtain speech. Only during succeeding months, as the Soviet acted ever more plainly the dark role which Kennan had assigned it, did his words begin to count. His cable was studied and re-studied in Washington until it was accepted as something of a classic among American diplomatic analyses. Kennan was summoned home, assigned to lecture to two hundred military and civilian leaders at the newly reactivated National War College, then given the vital chairmanship of the Policy Planning Staff.

In working out their recommendations for Secretary Marshall, the policy planners drew upon a number of analytical studies previously made for the State Department, particularly an over-all report written by Clayton after a trip to Europe, and on the judgment of many experts, especially Charles Bohlen, a Counselor of the State Department whose experience in Russian matters was as great as that of Kennan. Using these materials within the framework of Kennan's analysis of Soviet policy, they agreed that the United States had only three alternatives in dealing with the problem presented by Communism: to fight the Soviet in the hope of destroying the center of revolu-

tionary activity; to permit an indefinite expansion of
Bolshevism; or to regulate American foreign policy so
as to halt Red gains. To Kennan and his group, this
third approach was the correct one both because it
avoided war or indefinite Communist expansion and
because it held out the hope of the disappearance of
the Bolshevik disturbance. In ten or fifteen years, the
Policy Planning Staff believed, Stalin would die and
the leaders of the Soviet dictatorship would be fighting among themselves or their rule would be mellow-
ing into a more tractable form.

But meanwhile what kind of a foreign policy would
halt Communist expansion? The policy planners did
not see the problem as primarily a military one. They
were sure that American saber-rattling would only
strengthen the Soviet argument that capitalism was
spoiling to deprive the masses around the world of
their just social advances. Mere anti-Communism in
any form was not the wise approach; the world-wide
disturbances basically came not from Red activities
but from economic maladjustments and "a profound
exhaustion of spiritual vigor" which would be exploited by some other variety of totalitarianism even
if no Communists existed. The sensible program for
the United States was a positive effort to create
healthy societies, primarily through economic aid.
The thinking of the policy planners emphasized heavily that American economic aid alone would not stop
any country from going Communist. It could only
serve as a spark to recovery, and only for those nations which had the will to remain non-Communist
and an economic situation capable of improvement
without fundamental surgery.

Kennan and his group gave considerable attention
to the Chinese civil war. They concluded that China,
under the corrupt and inefficient rule of Chiang Kai-
shek, lacked the kind of economic system which could
be saved by American aid and that further help from
the United States would simply find its way to the

Red armies. They were particularly concerned about western Europe because of the key importance of its military-industrial potential. They thought that China, in view of its poverty in coal, iron, oil, and developed sources of water power, could not become an industrial power, and hence a major menace, in the foreseeable future. (Later, when the Communists had taken over China, Kennan remarked: "I am sure that the Russians would gladly exchange our control of Japan for their control of China. China is a drain on them and is likely to remain one for a long, long time. Europe is different. Germany's potential, added to that of Russia, could tip the scales of world power within a decade.") To the Policy Planning Staff, the vital areas to keep free of Communist control were Japan and western Europe, two great industrial centers which also formed a pincers around the Soviet. And in the circumstances of the spring of 1947, with Japan firmly under American rule while much of western Europe neared chaos, their eyes were fixed steadily westward.

On May 23, Kennan submitted the recommendation of the Policy Planning Staff to Secretary Marshall. The proposal was clean-cut: a massive offer of American resources, directed toward all of Europe with no ideological overtones, in a positive effort to restore the economy of the continent. There were two important provisos. The Europeans had to take the initiative in working out all details, and the program the Europeans submitted had to give promise of doing the "whole job. . . . [of being] the last such program we shall be asked to support in the foreseeable future."

Secretary Marshall sent this memorandum to a number of his top-level assistants, then summoned a series of conferences. On every major point, the memorandum of the policy planners stood. For all hesitancies, all questionings, Kennan was ready with his relentless pragmatism. Was there doubt whether the United States or the European nations should draw up the recovery plans for the various countries and make the initial estimate of the amount of aid to be given each? By all means the European nations, Kennan argued successfully. This would weaken charges of American domination; avoid a long parade of petitioners before Congress, exacerbating feelings that America was pouring out too much money; and create a situation in which the European nations, arguing among themselves, would become irritated at each other rather than the United States.

At another stage in the discussions, Secretary Marshall raised the most tortuous question: "Are we safe in directing such a proposal to all of Europe? What will be the effect if the Soviets decide to come in?"

Again Kennan carried his point. What better way to emphasize that the program is not mere anti-Sovietism? he maintained. And why not make the American proposition one which said to Russia: "You, like ourselves, produce raw materials which western Europe needs, and we shall be glad to examine together what contributions you as well as we could make. This would mean that Russia would either have to decline or else agree to make a real contribution, herself, to the revival of the western European economy."

One point Kennan did not argue too directly; he had not been a diplomat for twenty-one years for nothing. The policy planners' memorandum spoke of "misconceptions" that had arisen concerning the Truman Doctrine, which the proposed program would correct. Actually Kennan had been deeply disturbed by the whole approach of the Truman Doctrine and the memorandum represented a sharp and conscious break with it. Specifically, he sought to get away from the President's earlier hurried message by discarding the implication that American offers of aid were a defensive reaction to Communism; by withdrawing the blanket support which Truman had offered to all nations resisting the Reds, regardless of the quality of their own governments; and by removing from American policy any air of truculence toward the Soviet Union or world Communism.

Pressure, harsh pressure, always the pressure of the onrushing chaos in Europe. A little more than a week after the policy planners' memorandum first reached Secretary Marshall, Bohlen and others were hurriedly preparing a speech which Secretary Marshall would deliver. The Secretary was scheduled to deliver the address at the Amherst commencement exercises on June 16 but the European situation was deteriorating so rapidly that Marshall asked Harvard to revive a former invitation to give him an honorary degree so that he could take advantage of their earlier commencement date. On June 4 the Secretary left for Cambridge. Deeply convinced of the significance of the words he was to speak the next day, Marshall sat in the plane making penciled changes until the last moment.

"Our policy," he declared in the authentic tone of the new program, is "directed not against any country or doctrine, but against hunger, poverty, desperation, and chaos. Its purpose should be the revival of a working economy . . . so as to permit the emergence of political and social conditions in which free institutions can exist. . . . Any government that is willing to assist in the task of recovery will find full cooperation, I am sure, on the part of the United States Government."

No one in the State Department anticipated immediate important results from the speech. The haste was to get the idea in circulation, to begin what was expected to be a slow process of having it sift through the minds of European leaders. But the State Department had not reckoned with British Foreign Minister Ernest Bevin. The Foreign Minister first heard of the speech when already in bed and leaped out, elephantine frame and all, to put his office to work with the words: "This is the turning point." French Foreign

Minister Georges Bidault reacted with almost as much decision. Just twenty-two days after the Marshall speech, a meeting was assembling in Paris to discuss the American idea.

At the conference the Soviet Union soon made plain that it wanted no part of the program, but in a way that leaves a haunting question. American observers had long noted that Foreign Minister Molotov had a bump on his head which swelled when he was under emotional strain. Molotov was discussing the plan, raising only minor objections, when he was handed a telegram from Moscow. The bump swelled high; his manner suddenly became harsh and intractable. Did Molotov believe that his masters in the Kremlin were being stupid? Did he think that the Soviet, as Marshall had uneasily wondered that it might do, should have gone along with the program and sabotaged from within?

As a practical matter, the proposal which went to the American Congress asked for an appropriation of seventeen billion dollars, to be spent in approximately four years beginning in 1948, for the purpose of bolstering the economies of all the European countries outside the Iron Curtain and of Turkey. Officially, the legislation established a "European Recovery Program" to be handled by an "Economic Cooperation Administration" but soon most Americans and Europeans were escaping the jumble of ERP and ECA to refer simply to the "Marshall Plan."

By early 1948 the Secretary of State had his own idea about what the program should be called. He told reporters he wished they would drop the term "Marshall Plan" or at least change it to "Marshall-Vandenberg Plan" and his attitude did not come solely from modesty. As soon as the Eightieth Congress began serious debate of ERP in January, 1948 the program ran into heavy weather. Some of the trouble came from the pressure on Congress of liberal or pro-

Communist groups who were following Henry Wallace in denouncing the whole idea as a war-breeding, anti-Soviet "Martial Plan." Far more serious difficulties were caused by Taft and a group of like-minded Senators. Usually without directly opposing the bill, they complained that it represented some more "global New Dealism" on the part of the State Department, called for a sum which threatened bankruptcy for the United States, and foolishly ignored Asia. The stronger the winds of criticism blew, the more Senator Arthur Vandenberg proved the dexterous skipper of ERP.

Using his full powers as chairman of the Senate Foreign Relations Committee, calling on all the sidewise techniques of a legislative artist, Vandenberg nudged the legislation ahead. So my distinguished colleague is disturbed by this or that aspect of the bill? Of course, of course. Vandenberg was ready for endless compromise—for any amendment that did not affect the substance of the legislation. No doubt seventeen billion dollars was a staggering sum of money; why not merely appropriate five billions for the first year, with an assurance to Europe that further sums would be forthcoming? The State Department certainly could do queer things; let the Marshall Plan be administered by an independent agency, headed by a man who would have to be confirmed by the Senate. And Asia—Vandenberg himself agreed that China was being neglected. The Policy Planning Staff stoutly maintained that any money for Chiang Kai-shek was just so many dollars thrown away, a sop to domestic political prejudices. The Senator was highly interested in domestic political prejudices. He induced President Truman to recommend, outside of ERP, 338 millions in economic help and 125 millions in military aid for Chiang Kai-shek.

Before long Vandenberg acquired a persuasive ally, the impatient men in the Kremlin. In February, 1948 a Communist coup sucked Czechoslovakia under the

Iron Curtain, recalling to the least-informed Americans memories of Munich, 1938. Russian moves to the north made it look as if Finland were next. The Italian elections were coming on April 18 and newspapers in the United States agreed that the Communists were at least a fifty-fifty bet to win.

President Truman appeared before his press conferences making little pretense of chipperness. His faith in ultimate world peace, the President admitted, was being shaken. Reports went out that Secretary of Defense James Forrestal was meeting in Key West with heads of the Army, Navy, and Air Force to iron out their roles in the event of fighting. Two Republican members of the House, Charles Kersten of Wisconsin and Richard Nixon of California, expressed an attitude rapidly spreading in Congress. They presented a resolution giving "solemn warning to the conspiracy in the Politburo that any further step of aggression, internal or external, will be actively resisted by every means at our disposal."

Throughout the country war fears ran rampant. In New England, "wait until the Russians hit" and "when we fight Stalin" were becoming clichés. In Atlanta, friends were greeting each other with: "Well, boy, break out that old uniform." A Seattle newspaper summarized: "Generally, people here have come to feel that war is very definitely on the way."

A Chicago reporter caught the national mood in its fuller nuances. "Cold fear is gripping people hereabouts. They don't talk much about it. But it's just as real and chilling as the current 11-degree weather. Fear of what? Most people don't know exactly. It's not fear of Russia alone. For most think we could rub Joe's nose in the dirt. It's not fear of Communism in this country. Few think there are enough Commies here to put it over. It's not fear of the atom bomb. For most think we still possess a monopoly. But it does seem to be a reluctant conviction that these three relentless forces are prowling the earth and that somehow they are bound to mean trouble for us. Not many months ago, these forces were something to be thought about only in off moments—like when you turned in some commentator by mistake. . . . But all winter, confidence in peace has been oozing away. With the Czech coup, it practically vanished."

On March 1 Vandenberg rose from his second-row desk in the Senate. Observers noted a special poignance: the desk where Vandenberg stood once belonged to Senator William E. Borah, the foreign-affairs powerhouse in a day when Americans could, with a contemptuous toss of Borah's mane, tell the world to go to hell any way it chose. This time the speech contained no histrionics, only the dogged practicality that had marked the preliminary discussions of the Marshall Plan. The legislation, Vandenberg said, "seeks peace and stability for free men in a free world. It seeks them by economic rather than by military means. . . . It recognizes the grim truth—whether we like it or not—that American self-interest, national economy, and national security are inseparably linked with these objectives." And every word Vandenberg spoke only underlined the unspoken argument. Indefinite Communist expansion would mean atomic war; what sounder way to halt the expansion than by revivifying the economic life of that crucial area, western Europe?

As Vandenberg finished, dozens of Senators lined up to shake his hand. His compromises and the mounting Communist threat had undercut any serious blockage to the Marshall Plan. The remaining critics had no broad-based support, no powerful leaders; Senator Taft was now definitely saying that he would vote yes. Working against the deadline set by the Italian elections, the Senate met in night sessions and passed the bill by the resounding majority of sixty-nine to seventeen. The House, with a brief scuffle occasioned by an attempt to include fascist Spain in ERP, quickly followed suit. On April 2, 1948, the Marshall Plan was law with no vital change from the form in which it was first presented to Congress.

So the Administration's basic foreign-policy proposal was turning into fact. Its domestic recommendations were being almost totally ignored. In defeat and in victory, the Administration of Harry Truman, after all the confusion of the early period, was taking on a coherent shape. The post-1946 policies for home or abroad were certainly not conservatism in any sense which Americans had been giving to the word. They carried no tone of Taftism and, at least in their domestic phases, were sharply antagonistic to most business thinking. The Truman programs scarcely resembled liberalism of the 1930's; the dawn-world plannings of Harry Hopkins would have been jarringly out of place amid the restrained vistas of Clark Clifford or George Kennan's wary pursuit of reality. The man named to administer the Marshall Plan, Paul Hoffman, may have been a Republican but he was a faithful replica of the Administration he was serving in at least one respect. Asked for his political philosophy, Hoffman looked puzzled, then expressed the bankruptcy of the old terms: "I would describe myself as a Republican responsible—that means, on some things I'd be liberal and on other things, well—something else."

Shortly after the Marshall Plan was first publicly announced, in July, 1947, the semi-scholarly journal *Foreign Affairs* ran an article entitled "The Sources of Soviet Conduct" by "X." The newspapers quickly identified X as George Kennan and spread across the country the key phrase of the article, "the containment" of Communism. Containment—here, better than any other term, was the expression of the emerging Truman policies in foreign and domestic affairs. Abroad, Communist expansion was to be halted and prevented from affecting American life any further. At home, the basic outline of the America created by the Half-Century of Revolution was to be accepted, to be consolidated, to be carried forward only where some situation was out of line with the larger pattern. "We aim," Truman put it, "to keep America secured inside and out"—to contain a general situation which, the President was sure, could much more easily get worse than better.

It rained frogs, little green frogs in New Bedford, Massachusetts; citizens were sure they saw them. In Spokane, a butcher shop put up a sign: "Choice Meats —The Management Will Accept Cash, First Mortgages, Bonds, and Good Jewelry." The Midwest was telling the story about the farmer who went to the bank to pay off an eight thousand dollar mortgage, discovered that he had handed in ten thousand dollars, and said: "Oh, I must have brought the wrong bucket." The war scare of spring, 1948 was giving way to a relieved, flopdoodle summer.

Whether anybody cared or not—and the nation showed no signs of being transfixed—July brought the Presidential nominating conventions. The Republicans played it safe. Passing by Robert Taft, they named Thomas Dewey, an early friend of the Marshall Plan, an inbetweener on domestic affairs, a carefully disciplined political figure who, if he did not make friends easily, was without the Ohio Senator's formidable talent for making enemies. ("You have to know Dewey well to really dislike him," the faithless chose to put it.) The problem of the Democrats was not so easily solved. They already had their man in the White House and he emphatically wanted to stay there. The trouble was that in all the United States there was scarcely a politician, a pundit, or plain citizen who believed that Harry Truman could, by the remotest chance, under any foreseeable circumstances, win the election of 1948.

Powerful segments of opinion in the South, that usual bedrock of Democratic strength, were furious at the Administration for its civil-rights drive and by convention time were moving toward a third, "Dixiecrat Party." In the North, devotees of Henry Wallace were launching a "Progressive Party" and were talk-ing—not without evidence—of taking at least six mil-lion votes from the Democratic column in crucial states. North or South, among Democrats or Republi-cans, the mention of Truman for another four years was likely to produce a sad shaking of the head if not a snort of protest.

A large part of the country had unquestionably de-veloped a certain affection for the perky, obviously well-intentioned man in the White House. Yet there was a widespread feeling that, however much the President had pulled his Administration together, he was right when he remarked at the beginning of his term that he simply was not a big enough man for the job. The usually Democratic *St. Louis Post-Dispatch* spoke the attitude in explaining why it would support Dewey against a ticket headed by Truman. The news-paper, its editorial ran, liked Truman personally and did not particularly like either Dewey or the policies he would probably push. The *St. Louis Post-Dispatch* simply believed that the President had proved he lacked "the stature, the vision, the social and eco-nomic grasp, or the sense of history required to lead this nation in a world crisis."

As the Democratic convention came on, with Harry Truman announcing that it would be Harry Truman on the first ballot, leaders from all wings of the party frantically sought to escape him. Eisenhower, "Ike" Eisenhower, the war hero with a glowing smile, ad-mired by multitudes who were sure he was an instinc-tive liberal and by other millions just as positive of his bedrock conservatism—Democratic politicians clus-tered around the honey like so many busy, contriving bees. The previous January, the General had spoken a firm, polite no. The week before the convention he repeated the no, more firmly and less politely. Still a crazy-quilt coalition of big-city bosses, New Dealish politicos, and Southern machine leaders labored away.

Claude Pepper, the ultra-New Deal Senator from Florida, sent off a telegram designed to permit Eisenhower to remove his noes without saying yes. Pepper wired the General his "opinion" that the convention should draft Eisenhower as a totally "national" candidate, permitting him to write his own platform, freeing him of all partisan obligations, and instructing the Democratic Party to confine its own activities to Congressional and local contests. At the end of the telegram was the master gimmick: "I neither expect nor desire either an acknowledgement or a reply." Back from Eisenhower came quite a reply: "No matter under what terms, conditions, or premises a proposal might be couched, I would refuse to accept the nomination."

Boss Frank Hague read the Eisenhower telegram and crunched out his cigar. "Truman, Harry Truman. Oh my God."

The Dewey "Victory Special" rolled across the country. The GOP campaign was efficient, trimly, calmly efficient. It was, even more so, magisterial, the movements of a President-elect who somehow had to go through this unseemly business of a campaign. The Victory Special engaged in no grubby vote-chasing; many stops which could easily have been fitted into the schedule were omitted. When the speeches came, they were in cathedral tones, conspicuously above any quarreling over issues. Never, from the Hudson to the Sacramento, did Dewey attack Truman by name. Rarely did he stoop to anger. "We know the kind of government we have now," Dewey would say more in sorrow than in umbrage. "It's tired. It's confused. It's coming apart at the seams. . . . It cannot give this nation what it needs most—what is the real issue of this election—unity."

At the height of the campaign, the Republican candidate hit at a few brass tacks. He spoke of his "pride" in the Republican-controlled Eightieth Congress. He talked a bit about foreign affairs, saying that during his first campaign for the Presidency in 1944 he had founded the bipartisan support which made the Marshall Plan possible. With something akin to indignation, Dewey described "the Administration which happens to be in power at the moment" as "weak" and "fumbling." But soon everything was back to the higher level. In the closing days of the campaign, the Dewey staff talked less of the final swing than of their "real concern"—what Harry Truman might do between now and Inauguration Day to hurt the country. The burdens of power already weighed on them so heavily that one newsman was moved to inquire: "How long is Dewey going to tolerate Truman's interference in the government?"

Clark Clifford was watching it all with a craftsman's eye and he was sure that there was only one strategy for Truman—attack, incessant, razzle-dazzle attack which would shake the political apathy of the country and direct attention to the Republican record on specific issues. "We were on our own 20-yard line," Clifford later recalled his analysis. "We had to be bold. If we kept plugging away in moderate terms, the best we could have done would have been to reach midfield when the gun went off. So we had to throw long passes—anything to stir up labor and the other mass votes." Once again the Presidential adviser was talking congenial doctrine to his boss. Naturally combative, smarting under the general assumption that he could never be elected President in his own right, Harry Truman was ready to throw the stadium at Dewey to win this contest.

Dewey campaigned six weeks; Truman, eight. Dewey covered sixteen thousand miles; Truman, twenty-two thousand. Dewey made 170 speeches; Truman, 271. Up and down the country the President went, clambering out of the confusion of his campaign train to talk to any crowd that gathered at 7 a.m. or 11 p.m. "Give 'em Hell, Harry," somebody would yell. And Harry Truman, the Missouri twang shrill, both hands pumping up and down, would pour it on in the roughest English spoken by a Presidential campaigner since frontier days. So Dewey was proud of the Republican Party? "Those fellows are just a bunch of old mossbacks . . . gluttons of privilege . . . all set to do a hatchet job on the New Deal." So Dewey was above mentioning Truman's name? "That's all a lot of hooey. And if that rhymes with anything, it's not my fault." So the real issue in the campaign was unity? Dewey "is talking mealy-mouthed political speeches. . . . I warn you . . . if you let the Republicans get control of the government, you will be making America an economic colony of Wall Street."

As the campaign went on, Truman concentrated heavily on one subject—"that notorious Republican Eightieth Congress." The Truman-Clifford strategy naturally climaxed in a hammering on the Republican Congressional record of 1947-8 as a consistent assault on the interests of ordinary Americans. More and more the President singled out groups and pointed to what "that bunch has done to hurt you."

To the industrial workers of the country, he said: "The Republicans . . . voted themselves a cut in taxes and voted you a cut in freedom. The 80th Republican Congress failed to crack down on prices. But it cracked down on labor all right." In the agricultural areas, Truman cried out how "they have already stuck a pitchfork in the backs of the farmers by cutting down on funds for crop storage. . . . I warn you, that's their real attitude. First the little cuts, then all price supports would be thrown out." Campaigning among the first- and second-generation voters of the urban centers, he flailed at the "insulting" refusal of the Eightieth Congress to admit DP's and the "anti-Semitic, anti-Catholic" immigration bill it passed. With respect to the Negro issue, Truman's campaign talk was relatively vague; there were those angry Southern states. But he underlined his civil-rights program in unspoken ways—most notably, by being the first

major-party candidate for the Presidency who really
stumped Harlem.

The night after the Harlem rally Truman appeared
at Madison Square Garden in New York City. Dewey
was on his final leisurely swing, touching a number of
places where the President had already campaigned.
The Madison Square Garden speech, the traditional
written-out address winding up the Democratic campaign, was a little stodgy, a little weary. Near its end,
Truman deviated from the prepared text. He had
made this point before, day after day, publicly and
privately, from his deepest personal conviction. Now
he had another way of saying it.

The President's tone was grave. "I have had a consultation with the White House physician," he began
and the crowd stirred uneasily.

"I told him," Truman speeded up his delivery, "that
I kept having this feeling that wherever I go there's
somebody following behind me. The White House
physician told me not to worry. He said: 'You keep
right on your way. There's one place where that fellow's not going to follow you and that's into the White
House.'"

"Mighty game little scrapper," people said. "Too
bad he doesn't have a chance." Elmo Roper had long
since stopped taking public-opinion polls; two months
before election day science declared the election over.
Leading Democratic politicians, students of another
science, were publicly offering their Washington
homes for sale. Bookies quoted odds they would have
refused on Joe Louis at his prime—fifteen-, twenty-,
even thirty-to-one. Families planned an early election
evening, until nine or so when President-elect Dewey
would make his victory statement, and then off to a
good night's rest.

Until nine or so Truman was leading in the popular
and in the electoral votes. This was as expected, the
radio commentators explained; wait until the rural
returns came in. By ten o'clock a good many of the

farm areas were reporting. The figures were not particularly Republican, while Truman went on rolling up majorities in the cities. The voices of the commentators were as authoritative as ever; wait until there were enough rural returns to show the inevitable pattern. The *Chicago Tribune*, no journal for shilly-shallying, was out on the streets with its extra:

DEWEY DEFEATS TRUMAN

Some people stayed up. Ten-thirty, eleven, eleven-thirty—chairs hunched closer to the radio, conversation was shushed, somebody would dart off to telephone and wake up a friend. The Dixiecrats were carrying only three or four states in the South and Henry Wallace was showing no real strength except in California and New York. The Truman majorities in the cities remained substantial and the farm areas were reporting slim Dewey victories or Democratic sweeps. H. V. Kaltenborn of NBC, the voice that had reported Munich, 1938 to America, the voice that had been news incarnate to a large part of a generation, kept saying, crackling and definitive, wait until the full rural returns come in. But the litany was breaking. On the ABC network George Gallup was a shattered man. He could only sigh and tell his audience: "I just don't know what happened."

Later and later the lights burned in living-rooms. It was clear that Truman was holding most of the South and a sizeable bloc of Midwestern and Western states. Would this weird night end without a majority of electoral votes for either the Republican or the Democrat, in the use of a long-forgotten Constitutional provision which gives the selection of the President to the House of Representatives under such circumstances? Would it end—and here the commentators broke into shrill incredulity—in the election of Harry Truman? By dawn the issue was California, New York, or Ohio; the electoral votes of any one of these states would push the Democrat over. New York, with Wallace taking a half-million votes from Truman, went Republican. California and Ohio swung crazily back and forth, with majorities of fifteen hundred this way, twenty-five hundred the other, in states that had well over two million voters apiece.

At breakfast time the Ohio result became definite. After a long twenty minutes, Harry Truman came out of his Kansas City hotel suite. The strut of the bantam cock was gone; the eyes were misty. The President and President-elect of the United States walked slowly into the lobby, arm-in-arm with his brother Vivian, and reporters overheard him whisper tremulously: "I just hope—I hope so much I am worthy of the honor."

Up from the country came a long loud guffaw. Even many Dewey voters went about grinning at strangers, gathering in scoffing clusters with friends. The people of the United States had made fools of all the experts. They had knocked down the smooth and the smug and lifted up the shaggy, spunky underdog. They had brought off the most spectacular upset in American political history. But in those first half-real hours after Ohio came in, nobody had the slightest idea how in the world the Truman victory had happened.

Only gradually, as the experts finished their mouthfuls of crow and studied the situation, did the pattern become clear. The turnout of voters was much heavier than the political apathy at the time of the conventions would have indicated; Truman's shock tactics did not fail. So far as those who voted were concerned, the public-opinion polls had been right up to a point. Until very late in the campaign—when the pollsters had stopped taking soundings—the country was overwhelmingly ready to remove Truman. But then a vast swing had set in—a swing which came so late thousands said they had walked into the polling places intending to vote Republican and ended up casting a Democratic ballot.

To a small extent the swing was involved with foreign policy. Here Truman plainly represented the Marshall Plan and full-measured steps to check Communism. Whatever Dewey's personal position on ERP had been, the public mind inevitably associated him to some degree with the Republican Taftite reluctance to act vigorously abroad. To a much greater extent, the swing came from domestic concerns. The Truman-Clifford strategy had projected the President into everyone's view as the enthusiastic exponent of the Half-Century of Revolution. Dewey, rarely discussing specific issues and expressing general approval of the Eightieth Congress, easily appeared a Taft without the Senator's willingness to say what he meant. The very personalities of the candidates and the nature of their campaigns underlined the public impression of their attitudes toward the workaday hopes and worries of ordinary people. "I kept reading about that Dewey fellow," said Charles Crenshaw of New Lebanon, Ohio, "and the more I read the more he reminded me of one of those slick ads trying to get money out of my pocket. Now Harry Truman, running around and yipping and falling all over his feet—I had the feeling he could understand the kind of fixes I get into."

Millions of farmers were like the citizens of Guthrie County, Iowa, which had turned in regular Republican majorities even during the 1930's and proceeded to go Democratic in 1948. "I talked about voting for Dewey all summer," one Guthrie farmer put it, "but when voting time came, I just couldn't do it. I remembered . . . all the good things that have come to me under the Democrats." Scores of urban communities resembled Arlington, a suburb of Boston, which startled itself by giving Truman a majority. "I own a nice house," an Arlington resident remembered his thinking as he made up his mind how to vote, "I have a new car and am much better off than my parents were. Why change?" A breakdown of the national figures showed that basically Truman won because he received overwhelming backing from labor, Negroes, and most white minority groups, and at least fifty-fifty support from the farmers and all of the newer middle classes—precisely the segments of the population which had benefited most from the Half-Century of Revolution.

Senator Taft sat shaking his head incredulously. "I don't care how the thing is explained. It defies all common sense for the country to send that roughneck ward politician back to the White House." The election did defy sense in Robert Taft's world, where men worried over established patterns of American life and measured the manner of politicians by the yardstick of the big houses on the hill. But this was an America of Jackie Robinson's aspiring cleats and Communist lunges around the world and farmers proudly watching their sons off to college. A nation in economic and social upsurge could have its own defensiveness—against Communism abroad and against Taftism at home. The millions eager to preserve their new-found comforts and opportunities had felt their way, through all their political apathy, through all their misgivings about Harry Truman, to pull the lever for the surest available leader of containment foreign and domestic.

Year of Shocks

INAUGURAL DAY was just right. The weather experts predicted clouds and the skies were brilliantly clear. Harry Truman had an old-home breakfast with his buddies of Battery D ("I don't give a damn what you do after the Inaugural speech but I want you to stay sober until then") and went off to the huge, folksy celebration. For seven and a half miles, almost three hours of marching time, the parade stretched out. Up front was the honor guard from Battery D, at the tail end was a calliope tooting "I'm Just Wild about Harry," and in between were Montana cowboys and a trick dog from California and Missouri mules and a Virginia band that played "Dixie" over and over again, switched to a few bars of "Hail to the Chief" at the reviewing stand, then hurried back to "Dixie." The President grinned; he was almost always grinning and raising his paper coffee cup in acknowledgment of a salute. And the crowds, well over a million men, women, and children, yelled "Hi, Harry," "'Ray Harry," as if they were welcoming the local boy who had hit the big one out of the park.

When the car of the Dixiecrat candidate, Governor Strom Thurmond, approached the reviewing stand, Truman suddenly discovered that he had something very important to say which required turning to the man beside him. A Presidential guest, Tallulah Bankhead, hardly a woman for indirection, let out a foghorn of boos. It was all quite appropriate. On orders from the White House, for the first time in American history Negroes were invited to the top social events of the Inaugural. Even some of the attempts at unofficial Jim Crow were defeated. When the New York delegation arrived at its hotel, rooms were assigned to the whites but refused the Negroes. New York City's Deputy Commissioner of Housing, J. Raymond Jones, insisted that all or none of the delegates would stay at the hotel. The Negroes were registered and immediately telephone trouble developed in their rooms. Deputy Commissioner Jones had an idea. Noting that the owners of the Washington hotel also controlled New York establishments, he mentioned that a reinspection of Manhattan hotels was then in progress. Suddenly all the telephone difficulties disappeared. The attacks on racial segregation, Walter White, head of the NAACP, enthused, "seemed part and parcel of an Inauguration which had about it a special tone of recognizing the new place of all ordinary Americans."

President Truman had a fresh name for his domestic policy now, one he himself had invented in the exhilaration of the election victory. The "Fair Deal" he called his program in a State of the Union message delivered shortly before Inauguration Day, and Truman was soon explaining that the Fair Deal was "an extension of the New Deal; fundamentally, both mean greater economic opportunity for the mass of the people. There are differences, not of principle but of pace and personnel; the New Deal in the beginning, because of the times and its very newness, was marked by a tempo at times almost frenetic. Now there is a steady pace, without the gyrations of certain early New Dealers"—the certain New Dealers whom Truman continued to dismiss as "professional liberals."

The President's foreign policy introduced not only a new phrase but an additional idea. A number of friends had been saying to Truman that some State Department men were taking too much credit for the

Marshall Plan and that the Inaugural Address should direct the foreign policy spotlight back on the White House. Apart from any such consideration, the feeling was growing in the United States that the country should embark on a striking, world-wide offensive against Communism. A former reporter for the *Atlanta Journal*, Benjamin Hardy, now in the Public Affairs division of the State Department, agreed emphatically with this opinion, and he had a quite specific idea what the offensive should be. For a number of years the United States government had been giving technical assistance to Latin American countries and had been encouraging private investment which would speed industrialization. Why not expand this program to all non-Communist under-developed areas of the world?

Two weeks after the election of 1948, Hardy put his idea in a memorandum to his immediate superior in the State Department. Nothing happened. In mid-December Hardy wrote an expanded form of the memo, took it to a White House aide, George Elsey, and a great deal happened. When Clark Clifford prepared the next draft of the Inaugural Address, the speech revolved around four points in foreign policy and number four was Benjamin Hardy's proposal. Two State Department powers, Undersecretary Robert Lovett and the Counselor of the Department, Charles Bohlen, vigorously urged deleting the passage on the grounds that the idea was vague and premature. But Truman was enthusiastic and insisted that it remain in his address.

On Inaugural Day, the President's voice took on a special clipped emphasis as he read his fourth point. The United States was embarking on "a bold new program for making the benefits of our scientific advances and industrial progress available for the improvement and growth of under-developed areas." Much of the money, Truman plainly implied, would have to come from the United States government.

But so far as possible, the enterprise, financially and otherwise, would be co-operative and would be carried out through the United Nations. Private investment would be encouraged. "Our aim," the President summarized, "should be to help the free peoples of the world, through their own efforts, to produce more food, more clothing, more materials for housing, and more mechanical power to lighten their burdens. . . . Only by helping the least fortunate of its members to help themselves can the human family achieve the decent, satisfying life that is the right of all people."

"Point Four," the American newspapers immediately dubbed the proposal. In time peoples around the world would talk of *Punto Cuatro* or *Astle Charom* and American offices in Jordan received an enthusiastic letter addressed to "The Master of the Fourth Spot." Benjamin Hardy would be killed in a plane crash over Iran while serving as chief of the information division of an intensely active Point Four program. More than two thousand Americans from Seattle, Sioux City, and Birmingham were to be explaining sewage disposal or more efficient ways to teach reading in Tegucigalpa, Shiraz, and Djokjakarta, starting rivulets of change down unpredictable centuries. Before many years Jonathan Bingham, an enthusiastic administrator of the program, would write: "What makes Point 4 different from the ordinary concept of economic aid and makes it so infinitely appealing is that it emphasizes the distribution of knowledge rather than of money. Obviously there is not money enough in the world to relieve the suffering of the peoples of the underdeveloped areas, but . . . there is, for the first time in history, enough knowledge to do the job. This is indeed an exciting, even a revolutionary idea." All of this was to happen, but during the period immediately after the Truman Inaugural, Point Four was only a proposal slowly and laboriously turning into reality—so slowly that Congress did not pass its first Point Four legislation until May, 1950.

Meanwhile there was today, the today of jobs and Communists and grocery lists. Less than a month after the Inaugural ceremonies, Americans knew a strange sensation. Prices were going down. The nickel beer returned to Manhattan, the $1.99 shirt to Kansas City, and a Des Moines newspaper discovered that a basket of groceries which cost $4.19 in 1948 could be bought now for $3.29. Here and there people rubbed their eyes at old-fashioned price wars. In Los Angeles police were called to handle the crowds when steak dinners went down to sixty-five cents, women's panties to a quarter, and pie à la mode to one cent. With the deflation came the postwar's first real unemployment—some four million by the summer of 1949.

The more emphatic because of the threatened depression, President Truman urged the enactment of a long list of domestic measures modeled after his demands on the Eightieth Congress. During 1949 the Eighty-first Congress passed a comprehensive public-housing program, revised upward Social Security benefits and extended the coverage, increased the minimum wage, tightened price supports for farmers, and expanded programs for soil conservation, flood control, rural electrification, and public power. But the Congress huffed and puffed and did nothing about the most dramatized issues of the day—civil rights, Taft-Hartley, aid to education, and health insurance. The "ho-hum session," the more eager Fair Dealers were calling the Eighty-first Congress as 1949 ended.

The most important aspect of the Eighty-first Congress lay precisely in what it did not do; it made no significant attacks on the Half-Century of Revolution. The most important aspect of Fair Dealism in general was not what it did but what it threatened. It hung over business, speeding up still more the tendency of industrialists to try to outbid the welfare state by welfare capitalism; over the Republicans, causing even Senator Taft to view more kindly social measures; over the South, bringing a rash of voluntary moves to open educational and economic opportunities to Negroes lest civil-rights legislation should force them open still more widely.

The recession of 1949 halted well short of a depression. Supports on farm prices and the battery of social legislation prevented the deflation and unemployment from setting off a chain reaction; increased military expenditures helped; the Administration resorted to some hasty deficit spending. By the fall of 1949 the economic decline ended. The country was headed back to mounting prices and mounting incomes, high employment, and wide opportunities for climbing the ladder of status—back to more successful operation of the postwar pattern of containment domestic.

Just as surely the containment of Communism in Europe was working. The Marshall Plan did its job; Italy and France skidded past Communism and the economies of all the western European nations swung upward. In the spirit of the Marshall Plan, a series of moves brought the countries of western Europe into closer economic, political, and military relationships. Most importantly, in March, 1949 ten nations of northwestern Europe, Canada, and the United States signed the pact creating the North Atlantic Treaty Organization, under which the signatory countries began coordination of their military organizations and agreed to joint action in the event that any one of the nations was attacked by Russia. By the end of 1949 western Europe showed signs of once again becoming a region able to support itself and able and willing to resist Red blandishments if not Red armies.

It was all fine—and it was all terrible. During 1949 containment foreign might be working effectively in Europe and plans might be forming to project it around the world through Point Four programs; containment domestic might be continuing the miracle of America's social revolution. But for most Americans, Communism as a world force, far from being contained, seemed a much greater, a much more insidious menace than ever before.

Year after year the Chinese Communist armies had been advancing from their northern bases. Year after year the American newspapers had been telling of the shouts going up for Mao Tse-tung, he of the peasant's squatness and guile, incessantly smoking or chewing on melon seeds, unceremoniously stripping himself to the waist in hot weather, for

> *Chairman Mao who can be compared to the*
>   *sun in the east,*
> *Which shines over the world so brightly, so*
>   *brightly.*
> *Heigh-ai-yo, heigh-heigh-heigh-yo.*
> *Without Chairman Mao, how can there be*
>   *peace?*
> *Heigh-ai-yo.*

Late 1948 had brought more ominous reports. Mao's armies, having overrun Manchuria, were pushing southward. January, 1949 and Chiang Kai-shek's Nationalist government fled to Formosa. May, 1949 and the Reds had swept all the way to Shanghai.

A number of Americans were exercised. In particular a group of Republican politicians kept up a loud outcry to do something. But China was far, very far away. American newspapers had been carrying news of wars and civil wars in China for eighteen monotonous years, ever since the Japanese invaded in 1931. Much more clear-cut and dramatic events were happening inside the United States and across the Atlantic. Suddenly, on August 5, 1949, every newspaper, radio station, and television outlet in the nation directed garish floodlights on the Far East. A "White Paper" of the Department of State was officially announcing that China, vast China, had fallen to the Communist armies.

The preface to the White Paper was a strong defense of American policy by Dean Acheson, who had taken over as Secretary of State from the ailing George Marshall. The Truman Administrations, Acheson emphasized, had given large-scale aid to Chiang Kai-shek since V-J—more than two billion dollars in grants and credits, not counting more than a billion dollars in surplus American war stock which had been left with the Nationalists for $232,000,000. "It has been urged that relatively small amounts of additional aid—military and economic—to the National Government would have enabled it to destroy communism in China. The most trustworthy military, economic, and political information available to our Government does not bear out this view. . . . The only alternative open to the United States was full-scale intervention in behalf of a Government which had lost the confidence of its own troops and its own people."

Acheson put the blame for the fall of China squarely on the Chiang Kai-shek government, which he described as corrupt, inefficient, and utterly purblind to the just aspirations of the masses of Chinese people. "The unfortunate but inescapable fact is that the ominous result of the civil war in China was beyond the control of the government of the United States. Nothing that this country did or could have done within the reasonable limits of its capabilities could have changed that result. . . . It was the product of internal Chinese forces, forces which this country tried to influence but could not."

The Acheson explanation was blunt; it was, at least in some important respects, persuasive. Yet no explanation could explain away the fact that China was gone, that with her fall the closely linked Communist leaders of Russia and China ruled almost a quarter of the earth's surface and more than a quarter of its people, and that, as the White Paper itself pointed out, grave danger now existed that Mao's regime would "lend itself to the aims of Soviet Russian imperialism." From one end of the United States to the other the shocked question was asked: Had Communism been checked in Europe only to spread rapidly in Asia?

Just forty-nine days after the White Paper, in the late morning of September 23, reporters were summoned to the big walnut desk of Presidential Press Secretary Charles Ross. "Close the doors," Ross said. "Nobody is leaving here until everybody has this statement." Then he passed out mimeographed sheets of paper. Merriman Smith of the United Press was the first to read enough to catch the gist. Whistling in astonishment, he edged for the door. In a moment all the reporters were tearing through the lobby, smashing the nose of a stuffed deer on their dash to pressroom telephones. The President of the United States had announced: "We have evidence that within recent weeks an atomic explosion occurred in the U.S.S.R."

Having filed their stories, the newsmen hurried to the front of the White House, hoping to question Cabinet members who had just been meeting with the President. Secretary of Defense Louis Johnson was the only one who had not disappeared and the reporters clutched at him with questions as he made his way to the waiting automobile.

Had any change been ordered in the disposition of American armed forces since this fact was learned? No, Johnson said serenely.

Was there more to the situation than had been revealed? No, Johnson replied smilingly.

The Secretary of Defense was smiling and serene throughout and as he got into his car he said: "Now, let's keep calm about this. Don't overplay the story."

The whole Truman Administration labored hard to keep the report from setting off hysteria and most news media followed suit. In his original announcement, President Truman sought to soften the news by stressing that "the eventual development of this new force by other nations was to be expected." Most commentators and editorialists underlined the point; they also emphasized that it was one thing to have a bomb or two and quite another to be able to produce them in large quantities or to deliver them where they would hurt. Yet playing down the Soviet bomb was even more difficult than cushioning the impact of the fall of China. Since Hiroshima almost all American scientists had predicted that the Russians would not be able to perfect the weapon until 1952, and some had not expected the Soviet to succeed before 1955. Here was the fact at least three years ahead of schedule, stripping the American people of whatever security they had felt behind their atomic stockpile, jangling nerves still more because the timetable of the trusted scientists had been wrong.

In Chicago Harold C. Urey, the Nobel Prize leader in atomic research, managed to phrase what so many Americans were feeling. He was "flattened" by the announcement, Urey told reporters. "There is only one thing worse than one nation having the atomic bomb—that's two nations having it."

Weekly, daily, the furor over Communism mounted. The trial of the top Communist Party leaders in the United States went ahead while Judith Coplon was trying to persuade another jury that she had trysts with Valentin Gubitchev for love, not to hand over Justice Department secrets. Congressional investigators, FBI investigators, State Department investigators, Bureau of Entomology and Plant Quarantine investigators thrashed through Washington. At an Omaha businessmen's luncheon, a speaker told a story about an Irishman who insisted on being buried in a Church of England cemetery because "that's the last place the Divil would look for an Irishman." Officials of the Catholic War Veterans who were present got an idea, opined that the last place anybody would look for

Communists would be within the Roman Catholic fold, and started looking. Harold Taylor, president of Sarah Lawrence College, noting the way that charges of Communism were being used to beat down any independence in thinking, got off a definition of a patriotic American as "one who tells all his secrets without being asked, believes we should go to war with Russia, holds no political view without prior consultation with his employer, does not ask for increases in salary or wages, and is in favor of peace, universal military training, brotherhood, and baseball." And month after month during 1949, goadingly, explosively, there was the case of Alger Hiss.

The case had been news as early as August, 1948 when the ex-Communist, Whittaker Chambers, standing in the glare of the House Un-American Activities Committee, first publicly accused Hiss of being a member of the Communist Party at least from 1934 to 1938. The succeeding months brought sensational developments but the affair as yet had little of the momentous about it. Chambers had produced nothing to back his charge except his own thoroughly tainted word. The $75,000 libel suit which Hiss lodged against Chambers seemed the natural act of an innocent man. The President of the United States was dismissing the whole series of Congressional investigations as a political red herring—designed, Truman told his press conference two days after Chambers's first public accusation of Hiss, to distract public attention from the failure of the Republican-controlled Eightieth Congress to cope with inflation. (The President also made a formal statement at the press conference which explained in a different way why he believed the committees could be brushed aside—he said that they were not uncovering anything which was not known to the New York grand jury investigating Communism or to the FBI. But it was the phrase of utter dismissal, red herring, which was left in the public mind.)

After the Democratic victory in November, 1948,

many newspapers carried reports that the House Un-American Activities Committee would probably let the Hiss case lapse, indeed that the Committee itself might disappear. After all, the Democrats now controlled the House, two of the seven members of the Committee had been defeated, and Representative J. Parnell Thomas, the chairman at the time of the Chambers charges, was under indictment for having padded his Congressional payroll.

As 1948 ended, the affair suddenly took a far more serious turn. Whittaker Chambers broadened his charge: Alger Hiss had not only been a member of the Communist Party but had been part of an espionage ring in the 1930's, taking home confidential documents to be copied so that Chambers could pass them on for Soviet eyes. Chambers also produced evidence to back both his old and his new accusations. He turned over copies of classified State Department papers; some of them, he said, were in Hiss's handwriting and some were typed on a machine that had belonged to Hiss. Then Chambers took two House Committee investigators to his Maryland farm. He led the way to a pumpkin patch, reached into a pumpkin that had been scooped out and carefully restored, and pulled forth a wad of microfilm of more classified State Department documents.

After the news of the pumpkin microfilm, a reporter asked at the White House press conference: "Mr. President, do you still feel, as you did in August, that the investigation has aspects of being a red herring?"

Truman shot back: That's what the people thought [by re-electing him].

But, the reporter pressed, did the President still think so now that it had been revealed that the documents were stolen?

He certainly did, Truman replied. The committee was prosecuting nobody and was just seeking headlines.

Four days later, on December 15, 1948, a New York grand jury indicted Hiss for perjury on two counts—his statement that he had not passed "numerous secret, confidential and restricted documents" to Chambers and his statement that he had not seen Chambers after January 1, 1937. The most casual newspaper reader knew what these indictments really meant. The statute of limitations made it impossible to bring in an indictment for espionage. But morally and in common sense, Alger Hiss was being indicted for spying against the United States in behalf of the Soviet Union.

The first trial began in May, 1949 and ended in a hung jury; the second, taking up in November, wound on into January, 1950. No case in American history has offered more in sheer human interest. The lawyers were a fascinating study in contrasts. The testimony wound through a rococo variety. Witnesses discussed light serifs on typewriters, a rickety Model-A Ford, and prothonotary warblers. A tired swarthy man named Touloukian talked of Oriental rugs. Felix Frankfurter, Associate Justice of the Supreme Court, sat like an alert bird in the middle of the big witness chair, and handyman Raymond Sylvester Catlett, very black and very loyal to Hiss, shook his finger at the prosecutor and told him that when he was young he was "taught a lot of things, like God and about fellows like you." Always there were Whittaker Chambers and Alger Hiss, the brilliant editor of *Times vs.* the high-level New Dealer and head of the august Carnegie Endowment for International Peace, the accuser fat and heavy-lidded and brooding, the accused trim, handsome, and so urbane he seemed almost another spectator of the proceedings. One of these extraordinarily gifted men was lying—not the workaday lies of all men's lives but some gigantic contrivance built out of the shambles which Communism had brought to so many able minds in Western Civilization.

It was all fascinating and the Hiss case crowded American dinner-table conversations. But as 1949 went on the color and drama of the trials gave way to a different type of impact. Whittaker Chambers receded into the background; the specific testimony was less and less discussed. Even the figure of Alger Hiss the individual blurred. Everything was turning into Alger Hiss the symbol.

Looking back on the period, Chambers has written: "No feature of the Hiss Case is more obvious, or more troubling as history, than the jagged fissure, which it did not so much open as reveal, between the plain men and women of the nation, and those who affected to act, think and speak for them. It was not invariably, but in general, the 'best people' who were for Alger Hiss and who were prepared to go to almost any length to protect and defend him." That was the way it looked to the man who had left *Time* Magazine's world of glamour and power to fight out some lonely convulsion within himself, who, as Communist or anti-Communist, seemed desperately to need a sense that he was the chosen instrument to save the common man. Yet Chambers's picture, however overdrawn, points to a salient feature of the emerging Hiss symbolism.

Every casual fold of Hiss's Ivy League clothing, every modulation of his perfectly controlled voice spoke the fact that he was a product of genteel Baltimore, Harvard '29, a onetime member of a law firm with the name Choate in it, a New Dealer who was simultaneously in the Washington *Social Register*. He was being assailed by a man who, in appearance, in manner, and in fact, had risen through the demimonde of flophouse days in New Orleans, radical litterateuring, and self-confessed Communist spying. Established America did not entirely desert its beleaguered representative. A striking number of socialites and corporation executives who hated the New Deal, not to speak of Communism, doggedly defended the image of Alger Hiss the respectable success against the image of Whittaker Chambers the grubby upstart.

At the same time the Hiss symbolism was taking a quite different and far more important form. If part of established America rallied to the defense, the larger segment did not. Many upper-status Americans were joining with the general Taft Republican movement in finding a Devil. Irritated at the Half-Century of Revolution in domestic affairs, seeing the world crisis as the result of years of Democratic softness toward Communism, they turned Hiss into a representation of the whole period of New Deal—Fair Deal rule and identified the era with muddle-headedness and suscep- tibility to treason. On the other side of the political fence, Americans were finding a martyr, if not a hero. Many Democrats, particularly those of a New Dealish persuasion, proud of the Half-Century of Revolu- tion, sure that Democratic foreign policy had been basically correct, associating New Dealism with the brilliance and social-mindedness Hiss had shown, also turned him into a representation of the Roosevelt- Truman years and pictured the achievements of that era as now under assault from dark reactionary forces. For both these groups, the Hiss symbolism provoked fierce, blinding emotions.

Distinguished university professors of the pro-Hiss school, ignoring the damaging evidence against Hiss, stated flatly that it was impossible for him to be guilty. Leading attorneys and businessmen of the anti-Hiss faction, disregarding Chambers's general record of un- reliability, baldly stated that the case for conviction was incontrovertible. Members of both the pro- and anti-Hiss groups, anxious to bolster their prepossess- sions, took up rumors for which there was no visible evidence.

Alger Hiss was shouldering the blame for his wife, the pro-Hiss group would say. Or homosexuality ex- plained any enigmas of the case. Or Hiss was a counter- Communist agent reporting directly to Franklin

Roosevelt; as a counter-agent, he was sworn never to reveal his role and with Roosevelt's death the only man who could reveal it for him was gone.

The anti-Hiss faction had its own rumors, equally satisfying and equally unsubstantiated. The Truman Administration had moved heaven and earth to block Hiss's indictment; if the accused ever testified fully, other important ex-New Dealers would be involved in espionage. The expenses of the Hiss defense, the talk went on, were being met by a huge fund raised by pro-Communists. The rumor most widespread in anti-Hiss circles was that the judge at the first trial, Justice Samuel H. Kaufman, was pro-Hiss. Shortly after the trial ended in a hung jury, Representative Richard Nixon declared that Kaufman's "prejudice for the defense and against the prosecution was so obvious . . . that the jury's 8-4 vote for conviction came frankly as a surprise to me."

Near the end of the second trial, the symbolism took, or was made to take, a heightened form. During most of Chambers's testimony in the first trial, a well-known psychiatrist, Dr. Carl Binger, had sat in the audience intently following the proceedings. The Hiss attorneys tried hard to put the doctor on the stand but Judge Kaufman, citing the fact that there was no precedent for psychiatic testimony in federal cases, refused the requests. The judge at the second trial, Henry W. Goddard, was ready to set a precedent. Any evidence bearing upon the credibility of Chambers, he ruled, belonged before the jury. The Hiss defense attorneys took on the air of men who were about to play their ace card.

Dr. Binger, tall and deep-voiced and very professional, started his testimony in a calmly authoritative way. He discussed "a condition known as psychopathic personality, which is a disorder of character, of which the outstanding features are behavior of what we call an amoral or an asocial and delinquent nature." The symptoms of this condition "include chronic, persistent, and repetitive lying; they include stealing; they include acts of deception and misrepresentation; they include alcoholism and drug addiction; abnormal sexuality, vagabondage; panhandling; inability to form stable attachments, and a tendency to make false accusations. May I say that in addition . . . there is a peculiar kind of lying known as pathological lying, and a peculiar kind of tendency to make false accusations known as pathological accusations, which are frequently found in the psychopathic personality." For most of a morning the physician testified in a way that connected a number of these symptoms with Whittaker Chambers. The purport of the psychiatrist's words was inescapable: All of Chambers's accusations against Hiss were pathological lies.

The man who rose to do the cross-questioning for the prosecution was six feet, four inches tall, with a longshoreman's shoulders, a full, florid face, and a king-size mustache straight out of the beer halls of the Gay Nineties. It was not hard to believe that Thomas Murphy was the grandson of a New York cop, the son of a clerk in the Water Supply, Gas, and Electricity Department, a brother of the "Fireman" Johnny Murphy who had been cherished by Yankee fans as their stoppingest relief pitcher. "He's terribly normal," Mrs. Murphy used to say of her "Murph," and Assistant United States Attorney Murphy began his cross-questioning of Dr. Binger every inch the simple, puzzled layman.

To try to get at something an ordinary man could understand, what about the witness's qualifications? Plain Mr. Murphy brought out that Dr. Binger had been a physician for thirty-five years but a "certified" psychiatrist for only three. To anyone who knew much about the field of psychiatry—to, for example, Mr. Murphy who had been giving long hours to studying the profession—it was hardly unusual to find psychiatrists who had practiced for years and were highly esteemed without such certification. The court-room Mr. Murphy let the apparent point sink in.

And what about psychoanalysis? Had Dr. Binger himself ever been psychoanalyzed?

The physician, trying to fend off the implications, replied: "Certainly. Nobody can do psychoanalysis without having been psychoanalyzed."

Plain Mr. Murphy was bothered. "Would you try, doctor, just to say 'yes' or 'no' and we will go much faster?"

Plain Mr. Murphy was particularly bothered by the fact that he had difficulty in getting the physician to give a simple yes or no answer to questions about whether any individual characteristic of Chambers was, in itself, evidence of a psychopathic personality. "I have to consider the totality of the picture," the doctor kept saying, his calm ruffled. "I can't isolate my judgment according to specific parcels of information." But plain Mr. Murphy kept wanting to know about those characteristics. Lying, for example. Surely there was some particular kind of lie that would serve as a symptom of an abnormal personality. What if a man told a lie to his wife to avoid an argument? Pretty normal, Dr. Binger thought. Telling children that there is a Santa Claus? No symptom, the doctor said, just a part of folk mythology. Well, would Dr. Binger say "that telling the children for many, many years that the stork brings the baby—would that indicate that the parent perhaps was manifesting a symptom of psychopathic personality?"

This was the doctor's moment. "If the parents believed the story," Dr. Binger said with a twinkle, "I would think it might," and everybody, including Judge Goddard, had a good laugh. But plain Mr. Murphy was still seeking a plain definition of abnormality. If the parent believed the stork story, he wanted to know, would that be a symptom *merely* of a psychopathic personality?

"Oh no; it would be a symptom of much else."

"You said it," remarked Mr. Murphy, taking back the day.

But to get on with the statements of this puzzling doctor—Dr. Binger had made a point of the way that Chambers on the stand seemed to establish little contact with his questioner and frequently looked up at the ceiling. Mr. Murphy allowed that he had kept a check on Dr. Binger and found that the physician looked toward the ceiling fifty-nine times in fifty minutes. "And I was wondering, doctor, whether that had any symptoms of a psychopathic personality?"

"Not alone," Binger said once again, his calm strained still more.

And those lies of Chambers's—the psychiatrist had counted up what he considered the real ones and arrived at a total of twenty lies over a period of thirty-six years. Doctor, Mr. Murphy wanted to know, what's par for a normal person? The physician expressed the thought that Mr. Murphy had more experience than himself as a basis for answering that question and Mr. Murphy was hurt, very conspicuously hurt, at this slur by a highbrow doctor on a simple American trying to do his duty. Plain Mr. Murphy went right on being conspicuously hurt until Judge Goddard explained, what was not too difficult to see, that the doctor was referring to Mr. Murphy's experience as a prosecutor.

Finally recovered, Mr. Murphy ranged through other symptoms Dr. Binger had found in Chambers. Take this business of bizarre behavior—this bringing up the fact that Chamber had hid the documents in a pumpkin. Was that so queer? Didn't the colonial Founding Fathers put the Connecticut charter in the Hartford oak—were the Founding Fathers bizarre, doctor? Dr. Binger made it testily plain that he did not believe the Founding Fathers were bizarre. Well, Mr. Murphy went on, you say normal people put things in banks for safekeeping; didn't the mother of Moses hide him in the bulrushes?

Then, too, what about personal sloppiness as a symptom? Had the doctor ever seen Albert Einstein walking around in his sweat shirt? Or Will Rogers, Heywood Broun, and Thomas Edison? Was sloppiness really evidence of a psychopathic personality, doctor?

No, not alone, he never said it was, Dr. Binger snapped, his calm completely shattered.

Plain Mr. Murphy was more and more bewildered. He would try to make sense out of all this a different way. The psychiatrist had stressed the fact that Chambers rarely answered questions directly and often prefaced his statement with expressions like "it must have been" or "it could have been." Well, Mr. Murphy was no brilliant doctor but by golly he could count. And during the weekend he and his assistants had gone through 717 pages of official transcript and found that Chambers had used phrases like these a total of ten times. Would the doctor like to know how often Alger Hiss used similar expressions? The doctor showed no overwhelming desire to know. But Mr. Murphy told him anyhow: 158 times in 590 pages of testimony.

Plain Mr. Murphy was at his wit's end. He would presume to ask the learned doctor only a few more questions. Dr. Binger didn't know Chambers, did he? And the psychiatrist said he had analyzed the witness partly from his writings—especially Franz Werfel's *Class Reunion*, which Chambers had translated and which the physician intimated had provided Chambers with a morbid model for his attack on Hiss. Mr. Murphy shook his head in utter befuddlement. Did Dr. Binger find a model in *Bambi*, which Chambers had also translated?

"Who's the Psycho Now?" the headlines asked. Plain Mr. Murphy, who had never lost a case or an appeal in seven years as a government lawyer, had shown why with his tour de force; however unfair to psychiatry he may have been, he had plodded his way brilliantly to trump the defense's ace card. The Murphy handling of Binger had the larger effect of

sharpening the Hiss symbolism to a far more provoca-
tive point. Now the images of Hiss and anti-Hiss were
not only New Dealism *vs*. Taftism in domestic affairs,
a difference in foreign policies, a clash between two
general ways of looking at public problems. More than
ever, the conflict took on an aura of the highbrow and
the heretical *vs*. God-fearing, none-of-your-highfalu-
tin-nonsense, all-American common sense.

And the Hiss symbolism was heightening as most
Americans reached a decision on Alger Hiss the man.
By the close of 1949—nearly the end of the second
trial—it was clear that Chambers was hardly a saint
and that Hiss had led a distinguished career. Neither
fact was half as compelling as the battered old Woodstock typewriter sitting in the courtroom—a typewriter which both sides agreed had once belonged
to Hiss and which the FBI categorically stated had
typed many of the classified State Department documents handed over to Chambers. Fervid devotees of
the pro- or anti-Hiss images might go on insisting that
Hiss was a total martyr or a total scoundrel. For most
Americans the reaction was different—a growing belief that Hiss had carried on espionage activities with
Chambers and with this belief a mounting sense of
questioning. If a man of Hiss's background, achievements, and reputation for character had spied for Communism, who could be trusted? If the New Deal had
promoted Hiss, if President Truman had continued
to call committee activities which were exposing him
a red herring and a good many New Dealish people
went on backing him even after the unfavorable evidence was coming in, if the whole defense of Hiss led
down murky paths, how comfortable could an ordinary citizen feel in the middle of it all?

How comfortable indeed—1949 was proving the
most nerve-racking of all the disquieting periods the
United States had known since V-J. Some years in a
nation's history blur into a long-continuing story.
Some mark a fateful turn. There was, for example, a

period somewhere before 1776 when a strategic number of Americans passed over from thinking like colonists to thinking like rebels. There was a period too when the North and the South decided to draw the sword. The year 1949 was such a turning point. August, the concession of China to the Communists; September, the announcement of the Soviet atom bomb; August and September and the months before and after, the explosive questions raised by the Hiss case—1949 was a year of shocks, shocks with enormous catalytic force.

The shocks were hurtling a good deal of the nation into a new mood. The emotions forming the mood were the more powerful because they tied back into feelings deep in the postwar, deep in the whole modern history of the United States.

V I

The Great Conspiracy

THE SHOCKS of 1949 loosed within American life a vast impatience, a turbulent bitterness, a rancor akin to revolt. It was a strange rebelliousness, quite without parallel in the history of the United States. It came not from any groups that could be called the left, not particularly from the poor or the disadvantaged. It brought into rococo coalition bankers and charwomen, urban priests and the Protestant farmlands of the Midwest, longtime New Deal voters and Senator Robert A. Taft.

Most directly the restiveness resulted from the foreign policy of the Truman Administration. As the Democratic leadership moved after 1946 to meet the Soviet menace, it broke in a jarring way with deep-seated American attitudes. During all the previous decades, the United States had known its internationalist and its isolationist phases but it had never really departed from certain bedrock assumptions. The business of America was America. It was to get on with this business without dependence on other nations and without interference from them. At times, of course, there would be an interruption when some foreign nation, acting in a way that foreigners persist in doing, went berserk. Then the matter was to be settled by diplomacy or war but whatever the technique, quickly and finally.

We are a people whose history has made us the land

of the swift, total solution, brought about by ourselves alone. We faced a wilderness; we hacked it down. We were vexed by slavery; we cut it out of our system. We fought Britishers, Mexicans, Spaniards, Germans, Germans plus Japanese, and licked them all with short shrift. No wonder our movies have a happy ending, and in ninety minutes. No wonder we are the only country in the world which has produced a popular saying like: "The difficult we do immediately, the impossible takes a little time."

Americans were the more inclined to believe in the quick, total solution of any world problem because they were sure that the world was no great problem anyhow. Republicans and Democrats, New Dealers and anti-New Dealers, they tended to assume a general international trend, a trend so certain that it took on the cast of a law of history. Human beings everywhere and at all times, the law ran, seek peace and democracy, want to get ahead to a farm of their own or a house on the right side of the tracks, prefer to do it all gradually and with a decent regard for the amenities. The history of man is consequently a long slow swing toward a world consisting entirely of middle-class democracies. Once in a while, the trouble comes when some country falls under an evil leader, who forces it along a road forbidden by the law of history. Then it is only necessary to remove the leader and let things flow back along their proper path. (Quite characteristically, the United States fought its wars not in the name of fighting a whole people but against a wicked leader or group of leaders—the tyrannical King George III, the militaristic Kaiser, the brutal fascist dictators.) If the natural swing of the world was toward peaceful, democratic middle-class ways, how could foreign policy be a problem requiring anything except the occasional surgical removal of an unnatural growth?

The containment policy which the Truman Administration adopted in 1947 represented the first fundamental break with these attitudes. Dean Acheson, George Kennan, and the other chief foreign-policy advisers of the President assumed no comforting law of history. Instead they were reconciled to a situation in which history, with a mocking toss of her head, seemed off on a roar with shaggy and disreputable suitors. The East-West clash, as they saw it, came fundamentally from a long-running, world-wide social revolution. They doubted whether the resulting problems could ever be totally solved; they were positive that they could not be solved quickly. They were not even sure that the United States should try to solve them by simply smashing Communism because they were plagued by the feeling that the Red surge represented, in a viciously distorted way, the legitimate aspirations of millions for independence, social reform, and self-respect.

Containment was to be no swift, clean-cut process; it was to move along its complicated path for at least a decade, probably over many decades. The containers relied principally on the long-range effects of economic aid to non-Communist countries, not on the more direct method of arming the free world and certainly not on any hope of destroying Communism by war. They promoted co-existence, with its implication that Communism would be powerful for an indefinite period. They showed no faith that America could solve the problem alone, and sought to bolster the American position by strong support of the United Nations and by general coalition diplomacy.

As soon as the containment policy emerged in 1947, the signs of restlessness with it were plain. Did the container insist that millions of men and women, far from moving gradually toward middle-class democracy, were hurtling off in an entirely different direction? Did scores of commentators point out that history was racing along the wrong path? Then the United States was to yank it back and have done with the business. Many Americans, continuing to think along traditional lines, assumed that all the ordinary people of the world wanted peace and democracy and hence the Soviet-American clash could be solved quickly, finally, and with no great dependence on other nations. They spurned co-existence, and put much more emphasis on direct military moves than on the complex processes of economic aid. Though few actually advocated preventive war, thousands showed a marked receptivity to the argument that the disturbance could be ended once and for all by smashing its center, the men in the Kremlin. A considerable part of the population evidenced little enthusiasm for the United Nations, coalition diplomacy, coalition war, or anything else which placed the United States in a position of relying on others.

Nowhere did this way of thinking take more characteristic form than in its attitude toward Asia. For many decades a feeling had been growing in America that the Asiatics were the special mission of the United States under the law of history. It was our duty to help feed them, educate them, convert them, nudge them along toward the middle-class life. The sentiment was plain in President William McKinley as he expressed his conviction that "there was nothing for us to do but to . . . educate the Filipinos, and uplift and civilize and Christianize them." Over the years the attitude was spoken from a thousand pulpits by missionaries returning from China with fervid reports of how many more Chinese had chopped off their pigtails, learned to wear pants, or marched to the baptismal font. The emotion made its way into endless speeches by politicians of the modern era, not to speak of the dictum of Senator Kenneth Wherry, who told a wildly cheering crowd in 1940, "With God's help, we will lift Shanghai up and up, ever up, until it is just like Kansas City."

As a result of this attitude, the swing of Asia toward Communism proved a particularly sore point with many Americans. The Chinese not only proceeded to violate the law of history by going to the extreme left; they brought the added irritation of thumbing their noses at American patronage. Hundreds of thousands of Americans were irreconcilable, above all, to the Chinese revolutionists or to any other Red movements in Asia. In their thinking about American foreign policy, they believed in Asia First; some came close to believing in Asia Only. As a group they had a view of the world deeply colored by the feeling that Communism in Asia was peculiarly intolerable.

For these Americans, the shocks of 1949 were the last straw. The containment policy was upsetting enough; it was downright infuriating when it failed to contain. Western Europe may have been saved but what of the facts that vast China was now in Communist hands, that the Soviet Union could dangle an atomic bomb over American heads, that the Hiss case easily raised the question whether Communist infiltration into the American government was ended?

Some actions and attitudes of the Democratic leaders had not created a situation conducive to quieting the uproar. Ardent followers of Roosevelt and Truman might point out that sweeping world forces had been at work, far longer-running and more powerful than the rule of any one party in Washington. They could emphasize the incontestable fact that Roosevelt in his wartime negotiations with the Soviet had given the Russians little which they could not have taken themselves. With entire accuracy they were able to stress that Chiang Kai-shek's government had been a miserable remnant of feudalism; that the pumpkin microfilm which convicted Alger Hiss was dated not 1949 but 1937-8; and that the Truman Administrations had a long, consistent anti-Communist record, including the brilliantly successful Marshall Plan and a program for removing security risks from the government so sweeping and at times so overzealous that Dean Acheson later apologized for it. Yet there were other, quite different aspects of the situation.

Only the most partisan Democrat could really believe that Roosevelt would have carried on relations with the Russians as he did had he not been proceeding on the misplaced hope that the Soviet would be a cooperative power in the postwar. President Truman hardly strengthened public confidence by his use of the phrase "red herring" in connection with the Congressional investigating committees, particularly after Chambers's charges against Hiss were backed by the pumpkin microfilm. Although Communist sympathizers certainly did not fill any sensitive government post as late as 1949, some Democratic leaders brushed the whole problem of Red infiltration aside with a conspicuous casualness. Under the circumstances, it was inevitable that part of the public would get the impression that these men would not be too disturbed if they did discover a Soviet sympathizer in, say, the State Department. Most important, the Administration's policy in China was a plain failure. Perhaps, as Secretary of State Acheson contended, there had been no way to succeed but if that was the case, the Department of State had done little to prepare public opinion for the inevitable fall of China.

Whatever the merits and deficiencies of the Roosevelt-Truman handling of the Communist problem, the Democratic leadership was a perfect devil to be flayed. What party had been in power while Communism made progress inside and outside the United States? Franklin Roosevelt, New Dealers, Harry Truman, Fair Dealers—the words came out in a hiss of exasperation and fright. The New Deal, Fair Deal Democrats, who had received so much support because of the widening economic and social opportunities, were learning the force of the political maxim of old Senator George Moses of New Hampshire: The party that receives credit when the sun shines also gets the blame for the rain.

In itself the fury over the Communist advances would have created a powerful discontent but Communism was not the whole story. The man who was middle-aged in 1949 had lived through transformations of life within the United States more swift and sweeping than any previous generation of Americans had known. He grew up in a land where free economic enterprise was the normal way; white, Protestant, old-stock families dominated the community; and the whole of everyday activities moved within a basically fixed pattern. In 1949 this American made his living in a crazy-quilt system of free enterprise, the welfare state, welfare capitalism, and the patches of socialism represented by public power. Negroes, Catholics, Jews, and the sons of recent immigrants jostled the one-time elite for jobs and status. Wherever the American turned, whether to the details of the home or the mores of the Presidency, nothing seemed unchanging except change.

"All the standards are harum-scarum," the chronicler of a more stable America, Mark Sullivan, sighed in 1950. "Children running the homes or the President of the United States barnstorming up and down the country—it's all the same dissolution of traditional, dependable ways." The more the sense of quicksand came, the more the disturbed citizen could find evidence of it on all sides. By the heavens, at least there was still such a thing as moral good and bad. But then, come to think of it, was there still such a thing? Hadn't the corrosives of all the old sure standards seeped even into this rock? When the American criticized the man next door for cocktailing with other women, his own wife was likely to quote Dr. Kinsey and ask: "Don't you know that moral codes are relative to social class?" His denunciation of juvenile delinquents was inevitably followed by a news item in which an expert insisted that the fault should be assigned not to the delinquent but to a vague complexity called maladjustments in the home. Well, at least he was sure how to raise his own children. But then, matter of fact, was he really sure what closing hour to impose on his daughter's dates? And when he raised his hand to thwack Junior's bottom, the blows were unsteadied by a crisscross of child-raising theories in his own mind.

Even the type of national leadership had been shifting. As a people, Americans traditionally have put their faith in the man of action, particularly in the man of action who has done the democratic thing of being born poor. An overwhelming percentage of Presidents have been practical politicians, lawyers, generals, or businessmen who made their own ways up in the world, and Presidential advisers generally came from the same groups. But the complexities of the welfare state had begun bringing into prominence a quite different type—the highly educated man, decidedly intellectualish in manner, with a marked, often wise-cracking, impatience for the certitudes of the man of action. To top off their ability to arouse suspicion, many of these Brain Trusters were the sons of wealth and the products of Eastern universities which had long been associated in the popular mind with snobbery.

The Half-Century of Revolution in domestic affairs had reached a climacteric—in social changes and in the dissolution of old ways and old ideas which accompanied the changes. "New Dealism" people called it all and the term was appropriate despite the fact that Franklin Roosevelt was long dead and the New Deal as a specific program had ended years ago. In its simplest form, New Dealism may have been a set of domestic policies but it was also, in just as important a sense, an emphasis, a climate of opinion, a collection of attitudes. It was the assumption that the new was better than the old; that intellectuals ought to be leaders; that morals and religion as well as economics and politics were constantly to be re-examined; that progressive education and Freudianism and planned parenthood were to be furthered; that the cocked eye was man's most proper expression. The Truman Administration broke with many of these attitudes but it never really disassociated itself from them in the public mind. The New Deal and the figure of Franklin Roosevelt loomed over anything a Democrat might do.

No nation can go through such rapid changes in its domestic life without backing up an enormous amount of puzzlement, resentment, and outright opposition. Revolutions provoke counter-revolutions; drastic change, a weariness of change. In this case the reaction was the greater because of the prosperity and enormous social and economic opportunities which had come to exist by 1949. In social movement, nothing quite fails like too much success. New Dealism, having labored mightily to lift low-income Americans, found that it had created a nation of the middle class, shocked at New Dealism's iconoclasm and especially annoyed at its insistence on placing the values of change above those of standard middle-class thinking. Nobody believes more in self-made men than the man who has been made by distant social legislation. No group is more annoyed by reform than those who have benefited from it and no longer need it.

Any irritation with domestic New Dealism was stoked by the Communist threat. The joining of New Dealism and Communism in a troubled American mind was easy, almost axiomatic. Was it not the New Dealers, like the Communists, who talked of uplifting the masses, fighting the businessman, establishing economic controls over society, questioning the traditional in every part of living? Was it not the reformers at home who had called during the war for linking hands with the Bolsheviks abroad? Was not Alger Hiss just the type of which the New Dealers had been so proud? As the postwar went on, Franklin Roosevelt, labor unions, Harry Truman, progressive education, the Marshall Plan, Alger Hiss and a thousand other aspects of New Dealism were becoming jumbled into a bitter thinking which amounted to a theory of conspiracy.

In 1933, so the theory ran, Franklin Roosevelt put into control of the nation a group of men whose ultimate aim was a Communist world. They did not say they were Communists. Instead they called themselves by the sweet-smelling words, "New Dealers," "progressives," "humanitarians," and worked deviously toward their goal. They hurried the destruction of free economic institutions in the United States by manipulating the tax structure and by strangling free enterprise in bureaucracy and controls. When World War II came, they maneuvered American foreign policy to strengthen the forces of world Communism. Roosevelt and his aides propagandized America into a picture of the Soviet Union as a peace-loving democracy, hurried over quantities of lend-lease far beyond military needs, then sold out eastern Europe and China at Yalta. Under Truman, the Communizers went on undermining the American economic system while bringing about the confirmation of Soviet control of eastern Europe at Potsdam and making sure of the final delivery of China to the Reds.

And the conspirators were not only operating in American economic affairs and on the world scene. Their wily hand reached into every aspect of life in the United States, inculcating attitudes destructive of the truly American way of living and thinking. The shocks of 1949 loosed not only a sweeping anti-Communism but a tendency to denounce anything associated with the different or disturbing as part of a Communist conspiracy. With the end of 1949, many an American was attacking Sigmund Freud in the same breath with his denunciation of Alger Hiss. Ladies' committees that stalked the bookstores for pro-Communist writings also wanted to burn John Steinbeck's *Grapes of Wrath*. Textbook boards, setting out to protect the schools from Communism, shielded the young from any praise of minimum-wage laws along the way.

People were beginning to use the word "intellectual" as if it meant some compound of evil, stupidity, and treason.

The heart of the emotional drive behind this whole conspiracy theory lay precisely in the fact that it *was* a theory of conspiracy. The hated developments could all have been prevented; they were all the work of a few wicked men, operating behind a cloak of hypocrisy. The American who was so annoyed at the fact that a Negro sat down beside him in a bus rarely saw the social upsurge in the United States as an ineluctable part of the democratic process. The Negro was there because New Dealers had plotted to put him there. The rise of Communism around the world did not result from long-running historical forces; the Red advances came from the Alger Hisses, who had contrived to bring them about. The sense that any unwanted development could have been prevented was strongest and most bitter with respect to the Communist menace. The danger had been and was within the United States, not from the outer world. It was not really the Russian and Chinese Communists but Reds in the United States who had brought the crisis and who now direly threatened America.

As the sense of conspiracy mounted, its hottest emotions centered on the State Department. In a way this was natural. After all, the State Department played a major part, or was assumed to have played a major part, in the negotiations with the Soviet and the handling of the Chinese problem which were being so much criticized. Yet the excoriation of the State Department involved much more than this. Back in 1889 the *New York Sun* declared: "The diplomatic service . . . is a costly humbug and sham. It is a nurse of snobs. It spoils a few Americans every year, and does no good to anybody. Intead of making ambassadors, Congress should wipe out the whole service." Throughout American history, the State Department has been the subject of intense suspicion in times of international stress. Manned for the most part by products of upper-status families, it aroused charges of aristocracy. Calling more and more upon specialists, it rubbed wrong the faith in the man of action. Above all, its very function—the carrying on of continuous relations with other powers—easily annoyed a nation which believed in its heart of hearts that somewhere, somehow there must be a foreign policy which had the supreme virtue of making foreign policy unnecessary.

As long ago as 1906, that sensitive analyst of American society, Henry Adams, remarked: "The Secretary of State has always stood as much alone as the historian. Required to look far ahead and around him, he measures forces unknown to party managers, and has found Congress more or less hostile ever since Congress first sat. The Secretary of State exists only to recognize the existence of a world which Congress would rather ignore. . . . Since the first day the Senate existed, it has always intrigued against the Secretary of State whenever the Secretary has been obliged to extend his functions beyond the appointment of Consuls. . . ." And to crown the vulnerability of the State Department in 1949, its chief was Dean Acheson.

One afternoon a staid Washington affair reached the point where the Secretary of State was to make a few remarks. Dean Acheson tweaked his perfectly groomed mustache and began in the most cultivated of voices: "All that I know I learned at my mother's knee and other low joints. . . ." There it was—a man in the so easily suspected post of Secretary of State who was the New Dealish type down to the last item of irrepressible kidding. To capsule Acheson is to summarize the things which provoked the devotees of the theory of conspiracy. He was born to the Social Register and he was Groton, Yale, and Harvard Law School. He had been a New Dealer in domestic affairs despite some differences with Franklin Roosevelt, operated as a let's-be-friends-with-Russia man during

the war, and when he shifted in his attitude toward the
Soviet after V-J, did it with a conviction that the
world revolution called for a basic change in traditional American ideas. Acheson and Alger Hiss were
longtime associates; Alger's brother, Donald, was a
member of the law firm of which the Secretary had
been a senior partner. Acheson was not only the Secretary of State who had to announce the fall of China
but he had been a high officer in the State Department
during most of the period when Communism made
its chief advances. And always there was Dean Good-
erham Acheson the man, a goadingly adventurous
mind in irritatingly handsome tweeds.

"Our name for problems is significant," Acheson
declared as early as 1946. "We call them headaches.
You take a powder and they are gone. These pains
. . . [brought by the world situation] are not like that.
They . . . will stay with us until death. We have got
to understand that all our lives the danger, the uncertainty, the need for alertness, for effort, for discipline
will be upon us. This is new for us. It will be hard for
us."

It was hard, infuriatingly hard, for a good many of
Acheson's fellow Americans. "I look at that fellow,"
Senator Hugh Butler of Nebraska exploded for them,
"I watch his smart-aleck manner and his British clothes
and that New Dealism, everlasting New Dealism in
everything he says and does, and I want to shout, Get
out, Get out. You stand for everything that has been
wrong with the United States for years."

To some extent the mounting restiveness simply
represented an intensification of feeling on the part of
a long-running opposition. After all, since 1933 millions of people in the United States had been listening
sympathetically to speakers who charged that New
Dealers were socializing the economy, leading the
nation to ruin in foreign affairs, and leaving the whole
of American life prey to radical intellectuals. Men

who felt this way were usually Taft Republicans and
such Republicanism easily slid over into a theory of
conspiracy under the pressure of the events of 1949.

Most Taftites were either upper-income Americans
or middle- or lower-middle-class people who were
relatively old stock. To wealthy Taftites, the economic
leveling of New Dealism was infuriating. To rich and
poor Taftites, the social leveling and the disruption of
old ideas associated with New Dealism were just as
exasperating. They were ready to believe the worst
of the long years of Democratic rule and when the advances of Communism offered a chance to believe
that New Dealers had plotted its successes, a good
many Taftites eagerly seized the opportunity.

Taft Republicanism moved in this direction the
more easily because of the nature of its own central
doctrine. Long before the crisis of 1949, Senator Taft
had emphasized repeatedly his conviction that the
United States was far less menaced by any foreign foe
than by conditions at home. New Dealism—particularly its great expenditures of money, its economic
controls, and its approval of strong executive actions—
was bankrupting the United States, crushing free enterprise, and generally stifling the atmosphere of sober,
solvent liberty which was the source of America's
power and its surest protection against foreign threats.
Taft argued this way in refusing to support the large
appropriations and the executive moves called for by
New Dealers in the face of rising Nazi power. He repeated the arguments—particularly his opposition to
huge expenditures—in explaining his reluctance to go
along with the Marshall Plan. "Keep America solvent
and sensible," the Senator put it in 1947, "and she has
nothing to fear from any foreign country." From this
way of thinking to a belief that America's worries
came not from Red armies without but from New
Dealish conspirators within was not a long step—certainly not too long a step to be taken in the heated atmosphere of 1949.

Yet to see the emerging bitterness as simply an accentuation of Taft Republicanism is to misunderstand seriously what was happening in American life. Angry suspicion of New Dealism was building in groups which had been largely Democratic since the 1930's and had generally supported the domestic and foreign policies of both Roosevelt and Truman. It was not only that prosperity was releasing groups from their longtime emotional loyalty to Democratic reformism; the shocks of 1949 were so severe that all old alignments were being shattered. These ex-New Deal dissidents, unlike most Taftites, did not assail social legislation which was already enacted. But they joined in the sense of evil pro-Communist plotting and they were likely to snap and snarl at the whole mood of New Dealism. Of the one-time New Deal supporters, three groups were particularly susceptible to some variety of the conspiracy theory because of special historical circumstances—Midwesterners, relatively recent immigrants, and Catholics.

The history of the western part of the United States, particularly of the Midwest, is a confusing one. The Midwest was a great center of Populist social reformism in the 1890's and it gave powerful support to progressivism in the various forms which it took before and after World War I. Yet this Midwestern liberalism contained elements which could easily turn it into anti-New Dealism. It was anti-Eastern America and anti-"aristocracy." To some extent, it was against new immigrants and against any movement with an air of freewheeling cosmopolitanism. In foreign affairs, it was filled with a particularly strong aversion to Europe, a fear and hatred of Britain, and a deeply emotional concern over Asia. There is a direct line from the Midwestern Populist leader, Ignatius Donnelly, denouncing "the oppression of farmers by a devilish conspiracy of bloated Easterners and Britishers" to the *Chicago Tribune* of 1949 with its assault on Dean Acheson as "another striped-pants snob" who "ignores the people of Asia and betrays true Americanism to serve as a lackey of Wall St. bankers, British lords, and Communistic radicals from New York."

Another important part of support for New Dealism had come from recent immigrants living in the great urban centers across the country, most of whom were in the working class during the 1930's. These people had a special sensitivity, to which they could afford to pay little attention during depression times. As the 1940's and 50's moved many of them into the middle classes in income or in actual jobs, the sensitivity became a vital part of their reaction to public affairs. Americans, just because they are so mixed in background, are one of the few peoples in modern history who have shown a great concern with aspiring to full nationality—with being "100% Americans." By 1949, the nature of the population had changed so much that only a minority could feel genuinely old stock; the typical American, if such a person could really be found, was a third-generation immigrant. Rising to the middle class left the Italian-American worker, the Slovak-American accountant, the Russian-American teacher only the more anxious to achieve the further respectability of unhyphenated Americanism. Under the circumstances, he was the more likely to want no part of the New Dealism and the Democratic foreign policy which were being assailed as an un-American conspiracy and he was the more ready to accept that view himself.

A large number of the first- and second-generation immigrants were Roman Catholics, and most of the Catholics were city dwellers and working class or just moving into the middle class. American Catholicism is a vast and complex subject; almost any generalization about it is likely to contain at least some inaccuracies. Yet it can be said with reasonable factuality that millions of these Catholics were subject to all the aspirations for unchallengeable Americanism which were influencing other recent immigrant groups, and they were also under influences that were peculiarly their own. The Catholics may have been prime supporters of the New Deal in the 1930's but the support had an undertone. Basic in the philosophy of the Church is the tenet that Catholicism has its own unique attitude toward all problems, and a part of the American Church, while rarely breaking with Roosevelt, was often standoffish about the government's increasing invasion of the life of the individual.

The phase of New Dealism that was not directly concerned with legislation—its whole pragmatic, iconoclastic approach—provoked still more resistance. In 1864, Pope Pius IX had expressed the Church's flat opposition to such tendencies, and his encyclical blended easily with the natural tendency of many of the priests and diocesan newspapers in the United States. American intellectualism as it was commonly practiced provoked much the same reaction. In 1955 the unabashedly intellectual Bishop John J. Wright, of the diocese of Worcester, looked back over the post-World War II period and summarized: "There have been grave reasons in recent years to fear that in our [Catholic] newspapers and our forums, not to say even on our campuses, we have frequently revealed a nervous spirit of impatient and sullen anti-intellectualism."

After World War II, some parts of the Church led in identifying non-Communist liberal agitations with Communism. Many diocesan papers gave fervid support to the House Committee on Un-American Activities, which was denouncing scores of liberals as Reds. Priests in various parts of the country carried on their own un-American investigations. Typical of many of these efforts was a Cleveland episode of 1948. The priest who was director of the diocesan Holy Name Society attacked a candidate for the Ohio state senate on the ground that he had knowledge that the candidate was "of the left-wing variety," " 'pink,' at least." Specifically, the knowledge was that the candidate had "sought to have the movie censorship lifted, one of the Communist activities."

Toward Communism itself, many American Catholics had long had an attitude of fear and intransigence much deeper than that of the general population. The position of the Church had been made militantly clear in 1937. The encyclical of Pius XI, *Atheistic Communism*, ruled out all co-operation, conferences, or compromises between Communists and non-Communists. "See to it, Venerable Brethren," Pope Pius XI declared, "that the Faithful do not allow themselves to be deceived. Communism is intrinsically wrong, and no one who would save Christian civilization may collaborate with it in any undertaking whatsoever." During World War II, while much of the United States was thinking of the Soviet as a friendly ally, a good part of the American hierarchy was sharply anti-Soviet. When the East-West clash developed after V-J, Francis Cardinal Spellman, the most publicized spokesman of the American Church, delivered address after address which had the tone of war and which directly charged the existence of a powerful Communist conspiracy in American life.

As early as 1946 the Cardinal was talking of the grave need of combating the "aggression of enemies within" the United States. "The fear weighs upon me that we may fail or refuse to realize that Communists, who have put to death thousands of innocent people across the seas, are today digging deep inroads into our own nation. . . ." During 1947-48 the tone heightened. Cardinal Spellman spoke of "this hour of dreadful, desperate need. . . . Once again while Rome burns, literally and symbolically, the world continues to fiddle. The strings on the fiddle are committees, conferences, conversations, appeasements—to the tune of no action today." By 1949 the Catholic prelate was declaring in the bluntest possible language that America would not be safe "until every Communist cell is removed from within our own government, our own institutions, not until every democratic country is returned to democratic leadership. . . ."

In February, 1949 the Cardinal appeared in the pulpit of St. Patrick's Cathedral to speak one of the most passionate sermons ever delivered from an American pulpit. America was in imminent danger of "Communist conquest and annihilation. . . . Are we, the American people, the tools and the fools for which the Communists take us?" The situation called for an immediate end of all "ostrich-like actions and pretenses," particularly in halting the "Communist floodings of our own land."

Throughout the later postwar period, Catholic anti-Communism sometimes took on an emotional tone close to the hysterical. The year before the crises of 1949, the Catechetical Guild of St. Paul distributed a comic-strip pamphlet called *Is This Tomorrow?*, in which Communist mobs were depicted as attacking St. Patrick's Cathedral with torches and nailing the Cardinal to the door. When a widely read Catholic magazine carried the publication as a supplement, the Detroit police banned the issue on the ground that it might provoke violence. The editor of the journal told the police commissioner: "Then you'll be arresting twenty or thirty pastors who will be selling it next week." The Detroit police backed down; other police departments chose not to move. A single New York priest sold more than seven thousand copies of the booklet from the pamphlet rack of his church.

Some leading Catholics deplored this publication, and throughout the postwar era prominent Catholics publicly criticized the extreme positions taken by particular Church figures. The American Church did not respond with one voice to the problems raised by 1949, just as there has rarely been a monolithic Catholic opinion on any issue in the United States. So too, millions of Midwesterners and Taft Republicans did not fit into sweeping generalizations about their attitudes. Yet as the shocks of 1949 took their full effect, it was clear that the mounting restiveness was disproportionately centered in these groups.

In January, 1950 Clark Clifford resigned his White House post; with three growing daughters, Clifford explained, it was time for him to return to the high income of private law practice. Shortly before, George Kennan left the chairmanship of the Policy Planning Staff and soon headed for a post at the Institute for Advanced Study in Princeton. Kennan, friends said, was disappointed with the Administration's foreign policy, not too well, and anxious for time to think and study. The resignations were scarcely noticed in the press. At the close of 1949, attention was hardly centered on Clifford's containment domestic or the containment of Communism in Europe associated with Kennan.

New faces were prominent. Everybody was now familiar with intense, scowling young Congressman Richard Nixon; when the House Un-American Activities Committee was about to give up on Alger Hiss, had Nixon not kept on pursuing him? Old figures of prominence were talking differently. Arthur Vandenberg, for so long a rock of bipartisanship in foreign affairs, was wondering out loud if "bipartisanship means more Chinas and more Hisses and more messes with Russian bombs hanging over us." Robert Taft's face no longer took on a pained look when the discussion turned to international affairs. He had a fresh major theme—"the great problem of Asia" and the "wreckage that is our Far Eastern policy."

President Truman was troubled, testy. He rode over to Arlington to attend a dinner honoring Harry Vaughan, lost his temper completely, told the startled guests that he didn't care about "any s.o.b." who criticized Vaughan. He stood before his press conference talking grimly of the "great wave of hysteria" that was building. It would subside, Truman added stanchly. We had gone through this sort of thing before and "the country did not go to hell, and it isn't going to now."

Presidential Press Secretary Charles Ross went away from the session rubbing his chin reflectively. "Well," he said to a friend, "it all depends on the way Harry defines that word 'hell.'"

Dinner at the Colony

1949 GAVE way to 1950 and nothing changed except the calendar. For the frightened and embittered, there was only more incitement to fright and bitterness.

Early in the afternoon of January 21, 1950, a plump Bronx widow, Mrs. Ada Condell, gave the news in a nervous, almost inaudible voice. "Guilty on the first count and guilty on the second," she said. Alger Hiss could only stand before Judge Goddard and explain lamely: "In the future all the facts will be brought out to show how Whittaker Chambers was able to commit forgery by typewriter." When the onetime New Deal luminary was led to the station wagon handcuffed to a common thief, it was the thief who hid his face from the photographers.

Four days after the conviction, Secretary of State Acheson held his weekly press conference and Homer Bigart of the *New York Herald Tribune* asked: "Have you any comment on the Alger Hiss case?"

Acheson refused to discuss the legal aspects of the trials. Then he edged forward in his chair and with considerable feeling added: "I take it the purpose of your question was to bring something other than that out of me. I should like to make it clear to you that, whatever the outcome of any appeal which Mr. Hiss or his lawyer may take in this case, I do not intend to turn my back on Alger Hiss." The Secretary's face flushed as he continued. "I think every person who has known Alger Hiss . . . had upon his conscience the very serious task of deciding what his attitude is and what his conduct should be." His own conduct would be determined by the twenty-fifth chapter of Matthew, beginning at verse thirty-four, the lines in which Christ called upon His followers to recognize that the man who turned his back on anyone in trouble also turned his back on Him.

Of course the Secretary of State did not mean that he was questioning the verdict of the court or that he intended to remain in friendly association with a man convicted of perjury and, by implication, of espionage. He was simply saying, as Acheson explained later, that he was following "Christ's words setting forth compassion as the highest of Christian duties." In its way, the Secretary's statement spoke as courageous and as genuinely Christian an attitude as American politics has ever produced and it will no doubt earn him a special garland when the furies of recent years have completely died away. The sentence about not turning his back on Hiss was also a remark which, like Truman's red-herring comments, was easily misunderstood or deliberately misconstrued. In the atmosphere of 1950, it was a tremendous and totally unnecessary gift to those who were insisting that the foreign policy of the Truman Administration was being shaped by men who were soft toward Communism. The tone of the outcry was expressed by Congressman Richard Nixon who, in the course of a speech treating the Acheson-Hiss relationship, declared: "Traitors in the high councils of our own government have made sure that the deck is stacked on the Soviet side of the diplomatic tables."

Ten days after the Hiss conviction, on January 31, Presidential Press Secretary Charles Ross handed reporters a statement from President Truman: "It is part of my responsibility as Commander in Chief of the armed forces to see to it that our country is able

to defend itself against any aggressor. Accordingly I
have directed the Atomic Energy Commission to continue its work on all forms of atomic weapons, including the so-called hydrogen or super-bomb." Once
again a terrifying announcement had been made with
all the studied toning down of a mimeographed sheet
—this time the President even saw to it that he was
casually lunching at Blair House when Ross met the
reporters. Once again nothing could really cushion
the news. Not only would a hydrogen bomb have one
hundred to one thousand times the power of the largest atomic weapon. Twelve distinguished scientists immediately issued a joint statement which pointed out
that "in the case of the fission bomb the Russians required four years to parallel our development. In the
case of the hydrogen bomb they will probably need a
shorter time."

Some Americans talked tough. Secretary of Defense
Louis Johnson told an alumni gathering at the University of Virginia: "I want Joe Stalin to know that if
he starts something at four o'clock in the morning, the
fighting power and strength of America will be on the
job at five o'clock in the morning." Other Americans
raised harsh, portentous questions. Senator Brien
McMahon, chairman of the Joint Congressional Committee on Atomic Energy, brought solemn handshakes
from both sides of the chamber by a speech in which
he asked: "How is it possible for free institutions to
flourish or even to maintain themselves in a situation
where defenses, civil and military, must be ceaselessly
poised to meet an attack that might incinerate fifty
million Americans—not in the space of an evening,
but in the space of moments?" The most authoritative
voice of all talked doom. Albert Einstein went on television, the simple sweater jacket, the scraggly gray
hair, the childlike face with the brilliant eyes all adding
to the aura of an otherworldly wisdom beyond the
power of ordinary mortals. With the order of President Truman to produce an H-bomb, Einstein said,

"radioactive poisoning of the atmosphere and hence annihilation of any life on earth has been brought within the range of technical possibilities. . . . General annihilation beckons."

Another four days and another jolting headline. On February 3 the British government announced the confession of Dr. Klaus Fuchs, a high-level atomic scientist. The descriptions of Fuchs sitting behind the cast-iron grill of the prisoner's dock in Bow Street police court, plainly dressed, bespectacled, quiet-mannered, gave him every inch the appearance of the dedicated scientist—"the last man in the world you would expect to be a spy," as one English reporter commented. Yet Fuchs's confession stated that from 1943 through 1947, while engaged in government atomic research in the United States and Britain, he had systematically passed over to Soviet agents the inmost scientific secrets of the Western powers. "I had complete confidence in Russian policy," he told the police, "and I had no hesitation in giving all the information I had." The knowledge Fuchs handed over, his superior, Michael Perren, stated, had been "of the highest value to a potential enemy," and no doubt speeded up the Russian production of an atom bomb "at least a year."

Senator Homer Capehart of Indiana stood up in the Senate and stormed: "How much more are we going to have to take? Fuchs and Acheson and Hiss and hydrogen bombs threatening outside and New Dealism eating away the vitals of the nation. In the name of Heaven, is this the best America can do?" The applause was loud and long, from the floor and from the galleries.

That afternoon the regular plane from Washington to Wheeling, West Virginia, began loading. The stewardess did her duty, noted a United States Senator on the passenger list, and greeted him with a smiling, "Good afternoon, Senator McCarthy." The reply was a bit plaintive. "Why, good afternoon—I'm glad somebody recognizes me."

Getting recognized was no new concern of Joseph McCarthy. The Irish settlement in northern Wisconsin where he grew up respected money and looks; the McCarthys were a struggling brood of nine and Joe was the ugly duckling, barrel-chested and short-armed with thick eyebrows and heavy lips. Mother Bridget McCarthy threw a special protective wing around the shy, sulky boy and when the rough teasing came, he sought out her big warm apron. "Don't you mind," she would console. "You be somebody. You get ahead."

Joe took heed. He would get back; he would show everybody. The shy sulkiness turned into a no-holds-barred ambition curiously mixed with a gawky, grinning likability. The boy worked so furiously on the family farm that neighbors joked he must have spent his babyhood wearing overalls instead of diapers. Starting his education late, he talked, wheedled, and shoved his way through Marquette University with so much corner-cutting that Wisconsin educators still gasp at the record.

Associates noted the fierce, blinding drive in everything McCarthy did. When he boxed and his awkwardness was getting him cut to pieces, he would keep coming in, slashed and bleeding but flailing away in the hope of striking a knockout blow. When he played poker, he played all-or-nothing. He had the "guts of a burglar," one friend remembers. "He was brutal. He'd take all the fun out of the game, because he took it so seriously." When he ran for office in college, he dropped his homework, cut school for weeks at a time, devoted night and day to buying coffees and cokes and making lavish promises. He and his opponent agreed that each would vote for the other until the election was decided. The first ballot was a tie. On the next McCarthy won by two votes.

"Joe," the defeated candidate said, "did you vote for yourself?"

McCarthy grinned his big, disarming, tail-between-the-legs grin. "Sure. You wanted me to vote for the best man, didn't you?"

Once out of Marquette, he bashed his way to a Wisconsin Circuit Judgeship and soon converted it into a political stump, knocking off divorces in five minutes or less, racing around to please people by trying as many cases as possible. After Pearl Harbor he entered the Marine Corps, turning the whole Pacific Theater of War into a headquarters of McCarthy for United States Senator, blithely giving himself the name of "Tail-gunner Joe" although most of the time he was actually serving as an intelligence officer and doing the paper work for a squadron of pilots. Elected to the Senate in 1946, he thrashed about for ways to secure his political hold. McCarthy served the interests of the Pepsi-Cola Company so faithfully he became known to fellow Senators as the "Pepsi-Cola Kid." He delighted the real-estate interests in Wisconsin by battling public housing and he pleased some of his large German-American constituency by defending the Nazis on trial for the murders of Malmédy.

It was a great life, this being a United States Senator. "Pretty good going for a Mick from the backwoods, eh?" McCarthy would grin at the cocktail parties and the ladies thought he was awfully cute—"such an engaging primitive," as one debutante put it. But there was a problem and the engaging primitive was no more patient with a problem than he had ever been.

On January 7, 1950 McCarthy sat having a troubled dinner at the Colony Restaurant in Washington. The get-together had been arranged by Charles H. Kraus, a professor of political science at Georgetown University, and William A. Roberts, a well-known Washington attorney. Kraus in particular had been seeing a good deal of the Senator and had been suggesting books for him to read—especially the potent anti-Communist volume *Total Power* by Father Edmund A. Walsh, vice-president of Georgetown and regent of its School of Foreign Service. (McCarthy was hardly a booklover but he did like to skim hurriedly and he had spoken of his desire "to read some meaty books.") The prime purpose of the dinner was to permit the Senator to meet Father Walsh, whom both Kraus and Roberts profoundly admired.

McCarthy soon brought the conversation around to what was uppermost in his mind. His situation was bad, the Senator said. Here it was already the beginning of 1950, with his term running out in two years, and he had neither the national publicity which would attract Wisconsin voters nor any specific issue likely to stir them.

Within months Kraus, Roberts, and Walsh were all to repudiate McCarthy but at this time they were well disposed toward the youthful Senator. Kraus and Roberts were also Marine veterans of World War II; everyone at the table was a Catholic; the Senator's shaggy affability could attract men as well as women. Eager to help McCarthy, the group threw out suggestions.

"How about pushing harder for the St. Lawrence seaway?" Roberts proposed.

McCarthy shook his head. "That hasn't enough appeal. No one gets excited about it."

The Senator then thought aloud about a Townsend-type pension plan for all elderly Americans. Why not start a campaign to pay one hundred dollars a month to everybody over sixty-five years of age? But the three other men agreed that the idea was economically unsound.

After dinner the group went to Roberts's office in the adjoining DeSales Building and continued the discussion. McCarthy and Roberts, both voluble men, did most of the talking but at one point Father Walsh spoke at length. He emphasized the world power of

Communism and the danger that it would infiltrate any democratic government. He was sure, Walsh declared, that vigilance against Communism was of such importance that it would be an issue two years hence.

The Senator's face brightened. Communist infiltration—wasn't this what everybody was talking about? And wasn't this, after all, a *real* issue? The priest's remarks touched chords that reached far back into McCarthy's life. In the 1930's, the Irish settlement of northern Wisconsin voted for Franklin Roosevelt; the farms were in too desperate a condition for anything else. But the New Dealism had its own Midwestern, new-immigrant, Irish-Catholic coloration. It was filled with suspicion of Easterners, "radicals," "aristocrats," the British, and the "striped-pants fellows" of the State Department. McCarthy had started in politics a New Deal Democrat but as soon as the prosperity came he shifted to a more congenial Taft Republicanism. Whether a Democrat or a Republican, he had always more or less consciously assumed that the big trouble with America, as his boyhood neighbor Jim Heegan used to put it, was "those Leftists."

McCarthy cut in on Father Walsh. "The Government is full of Communists. The thing to do is to hammer at them."

Roberts, a longtime liberal attorney, spoke a sharp warning. Such a campaign would have to be based on facts; the public was weary of "Wolf! Wolf!" cries about "Reds." The Senator said offhandedly he would get the facts.

Lincoln's Birthday, the traditional time for Republican oratory, was approaching, and McCarthy—probably at his own request—was assigned by the Senate Republican Campaign Committee to speak on the topic, "Communism in the State Department." The Senator's office put together some materials drawn mostly from hearings and staff investigations of a House Appropriations subcommittee. Three weeks after Hiss was convicted, ten days after President Truman ordered work on the H-bomb, six days after the British announced the Fuchs confession, on February 9, 1950, McCarthy took the plane to deliver his speech before the Women's Republican Club in Wheeling, West Virginia. He would give it a try. He would see if he could not get someone besides polite airline stewardesses to recognize the name Joseph McCarthy.

"The reason why we find ourselves in a position of impotency [in international affairs]," the Senator told the club, "is not because our only powerful potential enemy has sent men to invade our shores, but rather because of the traitorous actions of those who have been treated so well by this Nation. . . ." Where was the situation most serious? "Glaringly" so in the State Department. And what kind of men were the offenders? "The bright young men who are born with silver spoons in their mouths are the ones who have been worst. . . . In my opinion the State Department, which is one of the most important government departments, is thoroughly infested with Communists." Most dangerous of all was Dean Acheson, that "pompous diplomat in striped pants, with a phony British accent."

McCarthy had always believed that a speaker had to get specific in order to make his points stick. Near the end of his speech he talked about a list "I hold here in my hand." Exactly what he said about the list will probably never be known with certainty. James E. Whitaker and Paul A. Myers, news editor and program director respectively of the Wheeling radio station that broadcast the speech, WWVA, later swore in an affidavit that McCarthy's words were: "I have here in my hand a list of 205—a list of names that were known to the Secretary of State as being members of the Communist Party and who nevertheless are still working and shaping the policy in the State Department." The Senator's friends later insisted that his point was something like: "I have here in my hand 57 cases of individuals who would appear to be either card-carrying members or certainly loyal to the Communist Party, but who nevertheless are still helping to shape our foreign policy." One man who would never be sure what he had said was Joseph McCarthy. Frederick Woltman, the responsible reporter for the Scripps-Howard newspapers, has described how "on a number of occasions—mostly in my apartment at the Congressional—I heard McCarthy and his advisors wrack their brains for some lead as to what he said in that Wheeling speech. He had no copy; he had spoken from rough notes and he could not find the notes. . . . The Senator's staff could find no one who could recall what he'd said precisely. He finally hit on the idea of appealing to ham radio operators in the area who might have made a recording of the speech. He could find none."

For the moment there was no such interesting problem. There was only another plane to catch, another polite stewardess to greet Senator McCarthy. The speech seemed to disappear; it was not even reported except in the Wheeling newspapers and in the *Chicago Tribune*. The Senator kept flailing away. On February 10, in Salt Lake City, he made a speech similar to his Wheeling talk and charged that there were "57 card-carrying members of the Communist Party" in the State Department. The next day he repeated substantially the same talk in Reno and wired President Truman demanding that the White House do something.

Things began to happen. Newspapers in many parts of the country headlined the Salt Lake City and Reno charges. President Truman and Secretary of State Acheson issued angry statements of denial. The Senate stirred, authorizing a subcommittee of the Foreign Relations Committee to investigate the Senator's statements.

But what was happening did not seem to bode well for Joseph McCarthy. The materials that he had used for his speeches were largely old and none too sturdy charges. The Senate subcommittee, chairmanned by the militantly Democratic Millard Tydings of Maryland, kept McCarthy pinned in the worst possible light. Veteran Republican Senate leaders were plainly hesitant about backing this rambunctious upstart.

Then, gradually, support came. By an instinct born of the whole climate of ideas in which he had grown up, McCarthy was attacking precisely in the way most likely to capture the groups in America who were most disturbed about foreign policy—the whole conspiracy theory of international affairs down to the last suspicion of Dean Acheson's striped pants. By the same instinct, he kept broadening the sense of conspiracy, catching more strands of the rebelliousness abroad in the country. Within a month after his Wheeling speech he was assailing as Communists the "whole group of twisted-thinking New Dealers [who] have led America near to ruin at home and abroad." Many others had been saying these things. No one had kept naming names, dozens of specific, headline-making names. And no one had attacked with such abandon—McCarthy politicking as he had done everything else, ignoring the rules, always walking in, taking his beatings, endlessly throwing wild, spectacular punches. Shortly after the Tydings subcommittee did its most telling job on the charge of fifty-seven card-carrying Communists in the State Department, the Senator closed his eyes completely and swung so hard he shook the country.

He would "stand or fall on this one," McCarthy let it be known. He was naming "the top Russian espionage agent" in the United States and a man who had long been "one of the top advisers on Far Eastern policy"—Owen Lattimore. In the ensuing uproar only the most informed Americans could make out the fact that Lattimore was a non-Communist liberal who had been called into consultation infrequently by the State

Department and whose suggestions had been almost totally ignored.

By late March private contributions were pouring into the Senator's office. The awards began. The Marine Corps League of Passaic, New Jersey, announced that it had selected Joseph McCarthy to receive its 1950 citation for Americanism. Leading Taft Republicans, including Senator Taft himself, the two powerhouses, Senators Kenneth Wherry and Styles Bridges, and the chairman of the Republican National Committee, Guy Gabrielson, were giving a respectful and cooperative attention to the rambunctious upstart. Various groups which had their own special uses for McCarthy's kind of anti-Communism came to his support—including the potent manipulators who were soon known as the "China Lobby."

Now the grin was as broad as Mother Bridget's apron. The Senator was affable, endlessly affable. In the course of a discussion in McCarthy's apartment, Mrs. Frederick Woltman asked testily: "Tell me, Senator, just how long ago did you discover Communism?"

The Senator grinned. "Why, about two and a half months ago."

In the office of Herbert Block, the strongly New Dealish cartoonist of the *Washington Post*, there was no grinning. Herblock angrily sketched a harassed Republican elephant, being pushed and pulled by Taft, Wherry, Bridges, and Gabrielson toward a stack of buckets of tar with an extra big barrel of tar on top. The cartoonist hesitated for a moment, thinking over possible one-word labels. Then he was satisfied. On the large barrel of tar he printed the letters, McCARTHYISM.

Immediately, and so naturally that people promptly forgot where the term had first been used, the word McCarthyism passed into the language. The revolt set off by the shocks of 1949 had its name and the expression of its most violent, most reckless mood.

Suspended Moment

THE SUMMER of 1950 came over the eastern seaboard hot and drowsy. Saturday, June 24 found most of America's top foreign-policy men weekending away from thoughts of Joseph Stalin or Joseph McCarthy. President Truman was enjoying a family reunion in Independence. Secretary of State Dean Acheson was at his lovely old farm, "Harewood," in Sandy Spring, Maryland. The U.S. Representative to the United Nations, Warren Austin, walked through his apple orchard near Burlington, Vermont, pruning a bit here, stopping to admire a particularly fine specimen there. Austin's deputy, Ernest Gross, was overwhelmed with a different kind of specimen. In an expansive mood his teen-age daughter had invited twenty of her girl friends to come out and party in the cool of their Manhasset, Long Island, home.

That Saturday evening W. Bradley Connors, the Officer in Charge of Public Affairs for the State Department's Far Eastern Bureau, was relaxing with his wife and children in their Washington apartment. Shortly after 8 p.m. Connors received a telephone call from Donald Gonzales, of the United Press Washington office. Gonzales said that Jack James, the UP man in Korea, was cabling that fragmentary reports indicated a large-scale North Korean attack on South Korea (the Republic of Korea). Could the State Department confirm this bulletin? Connors tried to place a telephone call to the American Embassy in Seoul, the capital of South Korea, but it was early Sunday morning on the other side of the Pacific and the overseas circuits to Korea were closed. He hurried to the State Department and by 9.26 p.m. Connors no longer needed a connection to Seoul. From John J. Muccio, American Ambassador to the Republic of Korea, came an official cable: "North Korean forces invaded Republic of Korea territory at several places this morning. . . . It would appear from the nature of the attack and the manner in which it was launched that it constitutes an all-out offensive against the Republic of Korea." An astonished Bradley Connors reached for his phone to alert an astonished officialdom.

The American government had long known that Korea was a trouble spot. The 38th parallel separating North and South Korea made no sense geographically or economically; it was simply an arbitrary line hastily drawn to define the areas in which Japanese military commanders would surrender to American or Soviet forces. By June, 1949 the occupation armies of both the United States and Russia had withdrawn but efforts of the UN to conduct free elections for a united Korean government had foundered on the refusal of the Communist leaders of North Korea to cooperate. The UN did sponsor elections in South Korea, which resulted in the "Republic of Korea" headed by the fire-eating old nationalist Syngman Rhee. Rhee's government, recognized by the General Assembly of the UN as the only legitimate one in Korea and bolstered by American funds, was nevertheless beset by economic and political troubles and it showed a constant restlessness to bring North Korea under its control. Because of the danger that Rhee might try to use force to bring all Korea under the jurisdiction of his government, the United States, though it kept a military advisory group in South Korea, sent only light defensive arms. North of the 38th parallel the tight Communist dictatorship went on ruling and it persistently proclaimed its intention to "liberate" the south. Periodically North Korea would stage raids across the border, sometimes using as many as fifteen hundred men. In the spring of 1950, the American Central Intelligence Agency was reporting that the North Koreans were continuing to build up their military machine with Soviet assistance and might launch a full-scale offensive.

Yet whatever the tensions in Korea, Washington's attention was not concentrated on that area. If Central Intelligence indicated the possibility of an aggression in Korea, it also indicated an equal possibility at a number of other points in the world. As a matter of fact, when Connors's telephone call reached his superior, Assistant Secretary of State Dean Rusk, the Assistant Secretary was at the house of the columnist Joseph Alsop, where the conversation centered on the threat to Yugoslavia resulting from the build-up of the Rumanian and Bulgarian armies.

Dean Rusk hurried to his office. Lights were going on all over the State and Defense Departments. Rusk conferred with the Secretary of State in Sandy Spring by phone, and Acheson put in a call to the Truman home in Independence. The phone rang just as the President and his family were entering the library after a leisurely dinner.

Truman's impulse was to fly back to Washington immediately but Acheson dissuaded him. It was still not certain whether the North Korean attack was a big raid or the real thing; besides, a dramatic return by the President could precipitate the world into a war scare. Truman and the Secretary of State discussed bringing the invasion formally before the United Nations and agreed that, for the moment, they would merely alert UN headquarters at Lake Success, Long Island.

John Hickerson, Assistant Secretary of State in charge of relations with the UN, put in the call to the Long Island home of UN Secretary-General Trygve Lie. The Secretary-General, who was just about to

tune in a news broadcast, had heard nothing of the
North Korean move and the news Hickerson spoke
profoundly shocked him. "My God, Jack," Lie ejacu-
lated, "this is war against the United Nations."

All Saturday night cables kept coming into Washington from Ambassador Muccio and from General
Douglas MacArthur's headquarters in Tokyo, each one
more ominous. The attack looked less and less like a
mere raid; still more disturbing, evidence mounted
that the invaders were fighting with Russian-made
tanks and guns. At 2 a.m. Acheson put in another call
to the President. They quickly agreed that the United
States should formally bring the invasion before the
Security Council and in the strongest possible manner.
The United States would not present a resolution
which merely called the attack a "dispute." It would
urge the Security Council to categorize it under the
"last resort" clause of the UN Charter—"threats to the
peace, breaches of the peace, and acts of aggression."
Under this heading the Security Council was empowered to take a further step and use economic sanctions,
a blockade, or all-out military action against the
aggressor.

Again, it was John Hickerson's turn for action.
Vermont was too far away in terms of an emergency
Security Council meeting at Lake Success and Hickerson did not contact the senior American representative
to the UN, Warren Austin. Instead the call went to
Long Island, where Deputy Representative Ernest
Gross picked his way through a living-room full of
sleeping teen-agers to get to the phone. Shortly before
3 a.m. Gross roused Secretary-General Lie from a
none too restful sleep to tell him that the United States
was requesting a Security Council meeting at the earliest possible time. Calls went out all over the area
surrounding UN headquarters, summoning Security
Council delegates from their weekend retreats.

When the Council assembled at 2.20 on Sunday afternoon, one of the big green chairs was glaringly va-

cant. For five months the Soviet representative had been boycotting the Council because of its refusal to replace the Nationalist Chinese delegate with a representative of Red China, and the Russian did not appear now. An added figure sat at the glistening horseshoe table, there by request of the United States. He was bespectacled little John Chang, the Republic of Korea's UN Observer.

Secretary-General Lie, shifting his huge body restlessly as he talked, opened the session with a firm statement: "The present situation is a serious one and is a threat to international peace. . . . I consider it the clear duty of the Security Council to take the steps necessary to reestablish peace in that area." Ernest Gross, his gray pin-stripe suit falling trimly over his solid build, heavy brows capping large, clear eyes, looked and talked like a highly successful attorney who was particularly sure of his case this time. The attack on South Korea, Gross declared, was of "grave concern to the governments of all peace-loving and freedom-loving nations" and "openly defies the interest and authority of the United Nations." The resolution which Gross asked the Council to adopt accused North Korea of "armed invasion," demanded that she cease fire immediately and order her troops back across the 38th parallel, and called upon all UN members "to render every assistance to the United Nations in the execution of this resolution."

In quick succession John Chang of South Korea and the representatives of Britain, Nationalist China, France, Ecuador, and Egypt supported the American resolution. But the French delegate and, more emphatically, the Egyptian representative indicated that they wanted time to suggest revisions and at 4.15 the Council recessed. Moves were made to change "armed invasion" to "armed attack" and to direct the cease-fire order not simply at North Korea but at both sides. These and other minor alterations were accepted by the United States without serious argument and the Council convened again at 5.25.

Throughout the session the nervous figure of Djura Nincic had been darting in and out of the chamber. Nincic's lot was hardly a happy one. His superior had not been able to get back to Lake Success in time and Nincic had little authority to act without telephone instructions. Nincic's country, Yugoslavia, was in a scarcely better position. It had broken with Stalin and was moving toward alignment with the West, but it was also looking into Soviet guns. After the recess, the Yugoslav made his move—the presentation of a compromise resolution which merely called for a cease-fire and invited North Korea to state its case before the UN. The only hand that went up for Nincic's proposal was his own (although Egypt, India, and Norway abstained). By 6 p.m. Sunday the American resolution had been adopted with the support of all the representatives except Nincic. Once again he compromised and abstained.

In Independence, Harry Truman had been trying hard to keep the appearance of calm. His original plan had called for having Sunday lunch at the farm which he and his brother Vivian owned in Grandview, near Kansas City. Sunday morning he drove over to Grandview and duly fiddled with a new milking machine, but that morning his interest in milking machines was minimal. By 11.30 he was back in Independence, awaiting further word from Washington.

At 12.35 Secretary Acheson telephoned. The North Korean attack, the Secretary of State informed the President, was undoubtedly an all-out offensive. American advisers in South Korea were asking for emergency supplies of ammunition and General MacArthur was sending arms from Tokyo. The UN, Acheson predicted correctly, would probably vote a cease-fire and the North Koreans, the Secretary went on just as accurately, would no doubt ignore the UN.

Harry Truman had heard enough. He told Acheson that he would order his plane, the *Independence*, readied immediately and asked the Secretary of State to get together with the military chiefs and prepare recommendations. The departure of the *Independence* was so abrupt that aides with clotheshangers over their shoulders were still running for the plane as the motors were tuned up. The President took care to say to newsmen at the airport: "Don't make it alarmist. It could be a dangerous situation, but I hope it isn't. I can't answer any questions until I get all the facts." The reporters noticed other things. Bess Truman waved good-by to her husband with a look very much like the one she had on that eerie evening when Vice-President Truman suddenly became President Truman. Margaret stood a bit apart from the airport crowd, staring at the plane with her hands clasped under her chin as if in silent prayer.

While the *Independence* sped toward Washington on the sunny Sunday afternoon, Truman had the plane's radio operator send a message to Acheson asking him to summon an emergency supper conference at Blair House that evening. For most of the three hours of the flight, the President kept to himself, mulling over the crisis.

During the hectic late 1940's, the Administration had been feeling its way toward a policy for the Far East and in the months immediately preceding the North Korean invasion, Truman and Acheson spelled out their program in a series of public statements. Basically the policy was containment, but with special twists intended to meet the circumstances of the Orient. The fundamental sources of unrest in the Far East, Truman and Acheson declared, were poverty and the hatred of being treated as colonial peoples. Military intervention in Asia by the United States would provoke bitter resentments which the Communists could exploit. America should be particularly careful not to associate itself too closely, militarily or otherwise, with the Nationalist government of Chiang Kaishek, who was identified in the minds of millions of Asiatics with the old, hateful ways of poverty and Western domination and who was now holed up in the only territory he had been able to keep from the Communists, the island of Formosa.

So far as the mainland of China was concerned, Acheson said for the Administration, the American attitude would be to keep hands off and to encourage the Chinese leaders to realize that their real enemy was the Soviet Union. In the case of Formosa, the United States would from now on provide only limited economic assistance and would not send further arms or military experts. With respect to the rest of non-Communist Asia, the policy would be to seek to win the goodwill of the masses through economic aid while bolstering their ability to resist Communism by the shipment of arms.

Five months before the North Korean invasion, as part of a speech before the National Press Club of Washington on January 12, Acheson approached the Far Eastern problem in terms of military strategy. The Secretary spoke of the "defensive perimeter" of the United States in the Pacific and described it as running from the Aleutian Islands off Alaska, to Japan, to Okinawa south of Japan, and on to the Philippines. If any of these points or any areas east of them were attacked, Acheson made plain, the United States would fight. Korea and Formosa lay west of this perimeter and of this outer area the Secretary said: "So far as the military security of other areas in the Pacific is concerned, it must be clear that no person can guarantee these areas against military attack. But it must also be clear that such a guarantee is hardly sensible or necessary within the realm of practical relationship. Should an attack occur—one hesitates to say where such an armed attack could come from—the initial reliance must be on the people attacked to resist it and then upon the commitments of the entire civilized world under the Charter of the United Nations which so far has not proved a weak reed to lean on by any people who are determined to protect their independence against outside aggression."

Did these sentences say that the United States would permit Formosa, South Korea, or similar areas in the Far East to fall to the Communists? The Acheson speech obviously did not state that the United States would go to their defense. On the other hand, it did not state that the United States would refuse to defend them—provided that the United Nations sponsored the action. So far as the whole American attitude toward the Orient was concerned, the Secretary of State stressed in a number of statements, it could be radically changed by war in the region.

Well before the invasion of Korea, this Far Eastern policy of the Truman Administration had been the subject of a mounting attack. The Pacific was the area where Communism had made its most frightening postwar advance—China. It was also the area which aroused all the emotional furies of Asia Firstism. Devotees of the theory of conspiracy saw in the Truman-Acheson Far Eastern policy shocking proof that pro-Communists were guiding American affairs. Angrily they had been demanding that the United States throw its unqualified support behind Chiang Kai-shek, guarantee that Formosa would not be taken by the Chinese Reds, and encourage the Nationalists to attack the mainland. They were inclined to call for unreserved support of all anti-Communists in the Orient, whatever else the anti-Communists represented, and to place the United States on record as ready to fight rather than acquiesce in any further territorial advance of Communism. They found their hero in General MacArthur who, they said, stood for their whole position. These attitudes, so strongly felt by men who held to the theory of conspiracy, marked the thinking of many Republican leaders to a greater or lesser degree. Most notably, Senator Robert Taft had been moving closer and closer to such a position in the months before the North Korean invasion.

There was all this past debate over policy to move through the President's mind as the *Independence* flew east. There were also stark considerations of the present. In or outside any defense perimeter, the Republic of Korea had been set up by the United Nations. If the North Korean invasion overwhelmed the little country, the prestige of the UN would be undermined if not destroyed. And what of the effects on world opinion? Wouldn't millions of Asiatics say that the march of Communism was inevitable? Wouldn't many European leaders, already highly skeptical of the extent to which the United States would go in defending collective security, believe that America was ready to go no further than talk? Above all, the North Korean attack bore a haunting similarity to the fascist aggressions of the 1930's. In his thinking on the flight to Washington, the President had very much in mind the opinions of many experts who believed that World War II could have been prevented if the early aggressions of the 1930's had been stopped.

The *Independence* landed in Washington at 7.15 p.m. Sunday and Truman hurried off to Blair House, where Acheson had assembled the chief State Department aides, the Secretary of Defense, the Secretaries of the three branches of the military, and the Joint Chiefs of Staff. The White House maître d'hôtel Alonzo Fields, was rather proud of the dinner he and his staff managed to get together by calling on the frying-chickens in the freezer, but minds were scarcely on the food. The meal was doubly quick because the President asked that no real discussion of the situation should begin until the servants were out of the room.

After dinner the long mahogany table was cleared and served as a conference board. The President, as was his usual practice, listened to the views of his advisers before expressing his own but it was soon obvious that Truman's thinking on the plane had taken him far. He was the clear-cut leader of the group, grim and decisive. This was no time, Truman made his attitude plain, for worrying over what Administration policy might have been up to now. The worldwide Communist threat was getting out of hand. In the Far East, particularly, the situation was deteriorating to the point where the national security of the United States, the future effectiveness of the UN, and the ability to avoid World War III were gravely endangered. The hour was at hand, the President's whole manner emphasized, for boldness.

Truman asked Acheson to present the joint recommendations of the State and Defense Departments and the Secretary listed a number, of which three were most immediate. MacArthur should be ordered to continue what he was already doing—rushing ammunition to South Korea. The General should be told to furnish ships and planes to protect the evacuation of Americans. American policy toward Formosa should be altered by having the Seventh Fleet sail from the Philippines and protect the island from invasion by the Chinese Reds. At the same time the fleet should see to it that Chiang launched no attack on the mainland.

The Formosa proposal provoked considerable discussion—just how much and how heated the available evidence does not make certain. The conferees also made varying estimates as to how far the United States might have to go in order to check the aggression in Korea. At least two of the military men present brought up the possibility that American ground forces would have to be used. On one point there was absolutely no disagreement. The President has recalled "the complete, almost unspoken acceptance on the part of everyone that whatever had to be done to meet this aggression had to be done. There was no suggestion from anyone that either the United Nations or the United States could back away from it."

Before the meeting broke up, Harry Truman made his decisions. He ordered the ammunition sped to Korea and the evacuation of Americans protected; the latter order followed the general tenor of the discussion and permitted MacArthur wide discretion in defining how much action by American air and naval units was needed to "protect" the evacuation. The President issued no instructions about Formosa but he did order the Seventh Fleet to leave the Philippines and proceed toward the island.

On Monday, June 26, the news from the battlefront steadily darkened. Far from obeying the UN cease-fire, the North Koreans were sweeping ahead in a six-pronged blitz. By late afternoon the reports were so bad another emergency council was summoned at Blair House, this time for 9 p.m. Once again Secretary of State Acheson presented the joint recommendations of the State and Defense Departments. The key proposal was that the United States Navy and Air Force should be ordered to provide cover and support for the South Korean armies although they were not to operate north of the 38th parallel. The Secretary also repeated the recommendation that the Seventh Fleet should neutralize the island of Formosa. He added that the UN Security Council would meet the next day, Tuesday, and urged that the United States press for a resolution calling on members of the UN to give armed assistance to South Korea. In the ensuing discussion, no one raised any important objection to the recommendations. Harry Truman made his affirmative decisions on the spot. Forty minutes after the conference began it was over.

All during Sunday and Monday, opinion in the capitals of the free world had been growing increasingly restive. No real news leaked from the Blair House conferences. A Presidential statement of Monday, which consisted merely of generalities, left most observers with the feeling that another Munich was in the making. Friends of collective security in Washington and the other Western capitals were downcast. They were inclined to agree with the European diplomat who cabled his government from Washington: "The time has come when Uncle Sam must put up or shut up, and my guess is he will do neither." At UN headquarters, delegates smiled wryly at the signs on the bulletin boards which announced: "Monday, June 26 is the fifth anniversary of the signing of the United Nations Charter." June 26 so easily could be the wake of the United Nations.

Early on the morning of Tuesday, June 27, word began to get around Washington that the President would announce he had pledged American arms to the defense of South Korea. Most reporters were astonished. At 12.30 the official statement was released. Washington gulped, then reacted with a massive closing of ranks. The *Christian Science Monitor*'s Washington bureau chief, Joseph C. Harsch, a resident of the capital for twenty years, reported: "Never before in that time have I felt such a sense of relief and unity pass through the city." James Reston of the *New York Times* added: "The decision to meet the Communist challenge in Korea has produced a transformation in the spirit of the United States Government. . . . . There have been some differences in the last seventy-two hours over how to react to the Communist invasion, but . . . these differences have apparently been swept away by the general conviction that the dangers of inaction were greater than the dangers of the bold action taken by the President."

When the Truman statement was read in the House of Representatives, the whole chamber rose cheering except Vito Marcantonio of New York, long a fellow traveler of the Communist Party. In the Senate, a few Republicans asked irritably—to use the words of James Kem of Missouri—whether the orders to the Navy and Air Force meant that Truman "arrogates to himself the power to declare war." A scattering of other questioning remarks were made. While the Democratic leader, Scott Lucas of Illinois, was answering the criticisms, Senator William Knowland of California, a rising figure in the Taft group, interrupted to say: "I believe that in the very important steps the President of the United States has taken to uphold the hands of the United Nations and the free peoples of the world, he should have the overwhelming support of all Americans regardless of their party affiliation." Both sides of the Senate broke into loud, sustained applause.

Throughout the United States opinion rallied to the support of Harry Truman. Telegrams and letters, some of a highly personal nature, flooded the White House, running ten-to-one in favor of the Presidential action. Truman was especially pleased by a wire from his 1948 opponent, Thomas Dewey, which read: "I wholeheartedly agree with and support the difficult decision you have made." The *Chicago Tribune* was unhappy, but most Republican opinion across the country went at least as far as the head of a Warren County, Iowa, organization, who said to reporters: "We don't know who told him [Truman] to do it, but for once he made the right decision." The nation's most respected Republican newspaper, the *New York Herald Tribune*, gave center front page to an editorial that declared: "The President has acted—and spoken—with a magnificent courage and terse decision. . . . It was time to draw a line—somewhere, somehow. . . . The jubilation in the Soviet satellite press over the first successes of the Korean invasion, the dispirited reaction from all peoples who have looked to United States support in their battle for freedom, is sufficient indication of what would have been bound to follow if the United States had supinely accepted this as one more victory for Communist armed infiltration. The President has refused so to accept it; his is an act of statesmanship and this newspaper believes that it is a basic contribution toward genuine peace in our disturbed and distracted world."

As Truman's words went out on Tuesday, an air of intense excitement gathered around UN headquarters. The President's statement declared that he had ordered the use of the American Navy and Air Force in support of the UN resolution of Sunday. The resolution could be interpreted to sanction armed intervention but it certainly did not explicitly call on America or any other member nation to enter the shooting war. Now the Administration, anxious to have clear-cut UN endorsement for its move and to bring other nations to the military support of South Korea, was pressing for a resolution that unequivocally summoned the member nations of the UN to "furnish such assistance to the Republic of Korea as may be necessary to repel the armed attack and to restore international peace and security in the area." Passage of this resolution would mark an epochal step. For the first time in the five thousand years of man's recorded history a world organization would be voting armed force to stop armed force.

Since early Tuesday morning the United States had been pressing hard for a quick assembling of the Security Council. From the point of view of American and overseas opinion every hour counted, but the President of the Security Council, the veteran Indian diplomat Sir Benegal Rau, was not to be rushed. The new American policy presented problems for the countries of Asia and the Middle East, which were becoming more and more neutralist in their attitude toward the East-West struggle. Sir Benegal and the representative of Egypt both wanted fresh instructions from their home governments before they took a position and they were having trouble getting the instructions. Apparently the home governments were none too sure what they wanted to do in the ticklish situation. Besides, the overseas telephone lines on this particular day were filled with squawks and fadeouts.

The minutes and the hours went by and still the Security Council was not called to order.

Lunch hour brought a curious scene in the Stockholm Restaurant on Long Island. The UN Secretary-General, Trygve Lie, had a long-standing date to eat with a group including Ernest Gross and the Soviet delegate, Jacob Malik. Gross and Malik sat on either side of Lie and the three men talked at length about the Korean situation. The Russian insisted that the first, June 25, resolution was "illegal" because no Soviet delegate was present at the meeting and because the Security Council had not seated a representative of Red China. He also charged "intervention by the United States" in Korea. About the time the meal was reaching coffee and dessert, the Secretary-General performed his duty as an international officer and urged the Russian to end his boycott of the Security Council and attend the meeting that afternoon. "Won't you join us?" Lie urged. "The interests of your country would seem to me to call for your presence."

Malik shook his head vigorously. "No, I will not go there."

Lie and Ernest Gross left the luncheon together and got into the Secretary-General's car. Gross's relief was unconcealed. "Think," he said to Lie, "what would have happened if he had accepted your invitation."

It was a moment that recalled the day in Paris when the bump on Molotov's head swelled and he made plain that the Soviet would have no part of the Marshall Plan. What, indeed, would have happened if Malik had attended the Security Council, vetoed the resolution, and left the American Navy and Air Force fighting without explicit UN sanction until the cumbersome machinery of the UN General Assembly could have been brought into action?

By mid-afternoon the Egyptian and Indian representatives were still without instructions and at 3.16

p.m. Sir Benegal gaveled the Council to order. Each country had its first team in now. The senior American delegate, ex-United States Senator Warren Austin, was back from his apple orchard, looking very pink-cheeked and very fatherly and very agitated. The number-one Yugoslav, slim and swarthy Ales Bebler, sat in ramrod alertness. Spectators filled every seat in the Security Council chamber and overflowed into the usually sacrosanct delegates' lounge, where a television set was tuned to the proceedings (more than 5,000 people were being turned away). The summer prints of the women were gay and the men's seersuckers casual, but a tense, hushed atmosphere surrounded the crowd.

Action came in a rapid fire. With a brief speech, Austin presented the American resolution. Bebler immediately countered with a proposal that would have left the United States far out on a limb—a resolution calling merely for a repetition of the cease-fire order and the institution of mediation proceedings.

The crowd strained irritably as it heard the translation of Bebler's words, then returned to complete quiet. John Chang of South Korea was talking now. He had not been to bed since the first news of the invasion and his short speech dragged with weariness. "Moral judgment," Chang said, was not enough. It had to be backed with force sufficient "to expel the invader from our territory and act directly in the establishment of international peace and security." Chang's drawn face seemed to relax as, in quick succession, the representatives of France, Britain, Nationalist China, Cuba, Norway, and Ecuador rose to support the American resolution. When Egypt's turn came shortly after five o'clock, Mahmoud Fawzi could only say that he expected "shortly to receive . . . instructions on this matter of extreme urgency and importance." Sir Benegal, who was in no better position, proposed an adjournment to 6.15.

As Austin walked from the Council chamber to the

delegates' lounge, reporters surrounded him. One
newsman asked if he thought there was any chance
Jacob Malik might show up for the later session.

Austin chewed hard on his cigar. "Oh, Lord, don't
ask me such questions."

Another reporter wanted to know whether the next
step after passing the American resolution would be
the establishment of a permanent United Nations military force. "Now, boys," Austin said, "don't take me
too far. Remember that a big country has to be careful. It's so easy for a big country to give offense."

The spectators were jamming the bar, watching
two children's puppets named Foodini and Pinhead
on the television set, drifting out into the corridors.
At 6.25 it was announced that the Council would stay
adjourned until 9 and a large part of the crowd gave
up and went home for supper. At 9.22 the session was
postponed again, and at 10.20 the delegates finally
filed into the chamber. The seat of Jacob Malik was
still glaringly vacant; Egypt and India were still without instructions from home. The balloting, first on the
American and then on the Yugoslav resolution, followed its preordained course. Egypt and India abstained. Every other country except Yugoslavia voted
for the U.S. resolution. Yugoslavia alone voted for the
Yugoslav proposal.

As the balloting ended, there was a stir at the delegates' table. Sir Benegal turned over the Presidency
to his alternate, Gopala Menon, and the Indian and
Egyptian delegates hurried from the room. "New
Delhi and Alexandria are on the phone," Menon told
the Council. Five minutes went by and it was just past
11 p.m. A messenger whispered to Menon and the
Acting President said: "I understand it has not been
possible to get the phone calls through. The meeting
of the Security Council is adjourned."

The UN was backing Harry Truman; the U.S. was
cheering him. There was still that special principality,
armed and formidable, which went by the name of

Senator Robert A. Taft. He had sat through the Senate discussion on Tuesday, head resting in his hand, wrapped in quiet inscrutability. Not until Wednesday afternoon did Taft take the Senate floor.

In many ways the speech spoke the strongest feelings of the devotees of the theory of conspiracy. The fall of China and the succeeding troubles in the Far East were all the fault of the Administration, "of the sympathetic acceptance of communism." The Democrats had "invited" the North Korean attack. The acceptance of the 38th parallel meant "giving the Russians the northern half of the country, with most of the power and a good deal of the industry, and leaving a southern half which could not support itself, except on an agricultural basis." The "Chinese policy of the administration gave basic encouragement to the North Korean aggression. If the United States was not prepared to use its troops and give military assistance to Nationalist China [Formosa] against Chinese Communists, why should it use its troops to defend Nationalist Korea against Korean Communists?" Taft declared that Acheson's speech of 1950 in which he described the Pacific "defensive perimeter" of the United States as running on the American side of Korea and Formosa offered an especially obvious green light to the Communists. "With such a reaffirmation of our Far Eastern policy, is it any wonder that the Korean Communists took us at the word given by the Secretary of State?"

In the manner of the whole revolt against the Administration foreign policy, the Senator singled out Acheson for his heaviest blows. "The President's statement of policy [on Tuesday] represents a complete change in the programs and policies heretofore proclaimed by the Administration." It meant a "reversal" of Acheson, and "any Secretary of State who has been so reversed by his superiors and whose policies have precipitated the danger of [world] war, had better resign and let someone else administer the program to which he was, and perhaps still is, so violently opposed." In the scattering of applause which followed this statement, the enthusiasm of Senators Joseph McCarthy and the emerging McCarthyite leader, William Jenner of Indiana, was particularly conspicuous.

Taft then went on to question Truman's right to order armed intervention without consulting Congress, whether the intervention was in support of the UN or not. The Senator had not "thoroughly investigated" the matter. But after all, the Constitution gave Congress the exclusive right to declare war and "his action unquestionably has brought about a de facto war. . . . So far as I can see, and so far as I have studied the matter, I would say there is no authority to use armed forces in support of the United Nations in the absence of some previous action by Congress dealing with the subject. . . ."

Yet the questioning and the attack were only one phase of the Taft speech. Throughout he made plain that "I approve of the changes now made in our foreign policy. I approve of the general policies outlined in the President's statement." Had the question of armed intervention in Korea been brought before Congress, the Senator emphasized, he would have voted affirmatively. The seasoned newspaperman William S. White, who was covering Washington politics at the time, has commented: "While Taft was sharp . . . [his] speech was welcomed by the internationalists; they felt that, for him, it was remarkably soft toward the President and toward the whole enterprise."

Truman's press secretary, Charles Ross, put it another way. Told of the Senator's speech, he shook his head incredulously and said: "My God! Bob Taft has joined the UN and the U.S."

At 7 a.m. on Thursday, June 29, the news from Korea took another sharp turn for the worse. General

MacArthur's headquarters, communicating by telecon with the Pentagon, reported that the South Korean casualties were nearing a staggering fifty per
cent. The capital city of Seoul had fallen and the Republic of Korea troops (ROK's) were trying to form
a line at the Han River, south of Seoul, but it was
questionable whether they could. Other disturbing
information followed. By late morning Secretary of
Defense Louis Johnson was on the phone to the White
House, suggesting another top-level conference and
the hour was set for 5 p.m.

At 4 p.m. the President held his first press conference since the North Korean attack. Quickly one of the
reporters got to the inevitable: "Mr. President, everybody is asking in this country, are we or are we not
at war?"

"We are not at war," Truman replied and he
granted the newsmen the unusual privilege of directly
quoting a President's words at a press conference.
Truman also permitted direct quotation of his phrase
that the United States was trying to suppress "a bandit raid" on the Republic of Korea.

Another reporter asked: "Would it be correct to
call this a police action under the United Nations?"

Yes, the President replied, that was exactly what it
amounted to. (Thus, indirectly, Truman became associated with the phrase that was to be so bitter a
part of later foreign-policy debate.)

Reporters did not push the President on the definition. They, like the nation, were not pushing him on
anything these days. Later in the conference a newsman asked about Taft's demand for Acheson's resignation and Truman brushed it aside with a disdainful
remark about political statements in the middle of an
emergency like this. The reporter subsided.

From the press conference the President turned to
the five o'clock meeting of his advisers, which assembled this time at the White House. The council consisted of all the men present at the Sunday and Mon-

day meetings and some additions, including John Foster Dulles, Republican adviser to the State Department who had been in Korea as recently as June 21, and W. Averell Harriman, chief of American economic activities in Europe, who had been summoned from Paris the day before. Defense Secretary Johnson opened the conference with a gloomy review of the military situation. Circumstances were such, he pointed out, that even American naval and air aid were not proving of great help.

Johnson then read a proposed directive to General MacArthur, which had been prepared by the Defense Department and concurred in by the State Department during the day. The order authorized the use of American service troops (primarily signal-corps and transport units) throughout South Korea, and the use of American combat troops for the limited purpose of protecting the port and airfield at Pusan on the southeastern tip of the peninsula. American ships and planes, previously forbidden to strike at Communist supplies and reinforcements until they came south of the 38th parallel, were permitted to attack military targets in North Korea. The directive did not permit MacArthur to send American combat troops into the combat area, which was still nearly two hundred miles north of Pusan.

The President hesitated. He was particularly disturbed by the thought of committing ground troops anywhere in Korea. During the ensuing discussion Secretary of State Acheson contributed the news of the Soviet reply to an American note which had asked Russia to use its influence with the North Koreans to get them to cease fire. The important aspect of the Soviet note, Acheson said, was not the fact that Russia refused. It was rather that the Soviet reply seemed to indicate that the Russians did not plan direct military intervention in the war. This estimate removed some of the President's reluctance to commit American ground troops; the unanimous urging of his military advisers removed the rest. By 5.40 the conference was over and the new orders were being hurried to Tokyo.

That evening Acheson returned to the White House with a communication from Chiang Kai-shek. The Nationalist leader was offering ground forces up to thirty-three thousand men, although he would need American air and naval units to transport and supply his troops. The President's inclination was to accept the offer. Wasn't this what the UN had asked its member countries to do? he said. Moreover, Truman could hardly have failed to be thinking that the more troops fighting with the ROK's, the less likelihood of need for American units in the actual battles. The Secretary of State opposed acceptance of the offer. Chiang Kai-shek's troops would need a great deal of re-equipping before they could go into combat, he argued. Besides, Nationalist China was a special case among the UN members. Formosa was being defended by the American Seventh Fleet and did it make sense for the United States to protect the island while its natural defenders went off elsewhere? The President, still unconvinced, asked Acheson to bring the matter up at a Friday-morning conference.

Before the morning came, at 3 a.m. on Friday, the Pentagon received a lengthy cable from General MacArthur. He had just returned from a personal reconnaissance at the battlefront and his words were blunt. "The South Korean forces," the General declared, "are in confusion, have not seriously fought, and lack leadership. Organized and equipped as a light force for maintenance of interior order, they were unprepared for attack by armor and air. Conversely they are incapable of gaining the initiative over such a force as that embodied in the North Korean army. . . . It is essential that the enemy advance be held or its impetus will threaten the over-running of all Korea." Then MacArthur made his recommendation: "The only assurance for holding the present line and the ability to regain later the lost ground is through the introduction of United States ground combat forces into the Korean battle area. . . . If authorized it is my intention to immediately move a United States regimental combat team to the reinforcement of the vital area discussed and to provide for a possible build-up to a two division strength from the troops in Japan for an early counteroffensive."

General J. Lawton Collins, Chief of Staff of the Army, had a hurried telecon connection put through to Tokyo. The President, Collins told MacArthur, had made it plain that he was reluctant to commit troops to combat, and before giving such an order Truman would probably want to consult advisers. Wouldn't the directive of Thursday—using service troops and moving combat units to Pusan—be enough until the President could hold such a conference?

Time was of the essence, MacArthur answered emphatically. Immediate authorization to use American troops in the fighting was of the highest importance if all South Korea were not to fall.

Collins replied that he would get the President's answer with the greatest possible speed. It was Secretary of the Army Frank C. Pace, Jr. who telephoned Blair House. Harry Truman, always an early riser, was up even earlier these days. Shortly before 5 a.m., already shaved, he took Pace's call at the phone on his bedside table. With only a flicker of hesitation the President authorized the sending of one regimental combat team to the combat zone. On the question of a build-up to two divisions, he promised an answer in a few hours. Top military and State Department officials were tumbled out of bed. There would be a White House meeting at 8.30 a.m., the Presidential message ran, and the conferees were to be prepared to discuss MacArthur's urgent recommendation and the Chiang Kaishek offer of troops.

At the meeting Truman raised the question whether it would not be wise to accept the Nationalist offer.

The number of trained American troops, he stressed, was quite limited and there was no telling where else trouble might break out. What, for instance, was Mao Tse-tung planning? And what might the Russians do in the Balkans, Germany, or Iran?

Acheson continued his opposition. To his arguments of the previous night he added the consideration that the use of Nationalist troops might provoke the Chinese Reds to enter the fighting. The Secretary was backed by all the military chiefs on military grounds. They maintained that Chiang's ill-equipped men would be helpless against the North Koreans. Furthermore, the transportation required would be more profitably used by being assigned to carry American soldiers and supplies from Japan.

Disagreements might arise about particular ways to throw back the North Korean aggression; Harry Truman was not wavering in the slightest in his determination to achieve that purpose. "I was still concerned," he has recalled the close of the conference, "about our ability to stand off the enemy with the small forces available to us, but after some further discussion I accepted the position taken by practically everyone else at this meeting; namely, that the Chinese offer ought to be politely declined. I then decided that General MacArthur should be given full authority to use the ground forces under his command"—not only the build-up to two divisions but all the combat troops he could spare from Japan. At the suggestion of Admiral Forrest Sherman, Chief of Naval Operations, a second order was added, a naval blockade of the Korean coast. At 1.22 p.m. on Friday, June 30, just short of six days after the first shots were fired by the North Koreans, the orders left Washington which put the United States irrevocably in the war—planes, ships, tanks, and infantrymen.

Late Friday afternoon the President left Washington. He had been canceling engagements all week, but now he was going to keep a date to address an international boy scout jamboree at Valley Forge. Then he would meet his daughter Margaret, who was singing at a concert in Philadelphia, and they would board the Presidential yacht *Williamsburg* for a leisurely trip back to Washington. As Truman approached the train in Washington, reporters noted that the lines in his face were receding and his step was regaining its sprightliness. The decision to fight was made and he was confident it was the right one. He was not going to let the United States and its President be pushed around, Truman remarked several times on Friday, and he was not going to let the United Nations be pushed around.

The nation was in no mood to disagree. The order to send combat troops into Korea produced even less dissent than had come with the Tuesday decision to use only the Navy and Air Force. The fact of war, of course, hushed criticism but this was hardly the complete story. A whole concatenation of emotions pulled Americans together in support of the President —a feeling of relief that the United States had at last taken an armed stand against Communism, the hope that Korea would stave off World War III and the dread that it would not, a sense of pride that American deeds were now matching American words, the natural human response to the forthright courage of Harry Truman.

The very nature of the Presidential decisions disarmed critics of the Truman-Acheson foreign policy. Devotees of the theory of conspiracy and many less extreme dissenters had insisted that Asia was being neglected; Asia was now the focus of the national effort. They had demanded American arms to protect Formosa from the Chinese Reds; the Seventh Fleet shielded the island. They had cried out for a line to be drawn against Communism, beyond this not one step further; the line was as plain as guns and bombs could make it. They had put their faith, above all, in General

Douglas MacArthur. It was at the General's recommendation—and this fact was generally known—that
full intervention had been decided upon, and Douglas
MacArthur was in command in Korea.

American acceptance of the Truman moves was
bolstered by the reaction around the free world. Western representatives at the United Nations were jubilant. Delegate after delegate was telling reporters that
the Truman leadership had saved the UN from going
the tragic way of the League of Nations. Newspapers
were filled with descriptions of the stiffened sense of
resolution in western Europe and Asia. From all over
the free world came comments like that of the high
French official who said: "A few days ago I was filled
with despair. I saw as in a nightmare all the horrors repeated that followed the first surrender to Hitler in
1936. Now there is a burst of sun." Even if the intervention failed, the Frenchman went on, that was not
the essential point. "It is the proof of your willingness
to act that makes all the difference. A continent that is
emerging slowly from defeat and demoralization needs
moral assurance as much as material help or proofs of
military preparedness."

Most striking of all was the news from India, huge
and critically important India. For weeks Prime Minister Jawaharlal Nehru had been making increasingly
neutralist statements and Indian newspapers freely predicted that their country would not support the Tuesday resolution of the UN Security Council. On Friday afternoon Sir Benegal Rau finally received his
instructions from New Delhi and he reported that India "accepted" the resolution. The Nehru government
was "opposed to any attempt to settle international
disputes by resort to aggression."

East, west, north, and south, American newspapers
reported overwhelming support of the President in
their areas. "The White House gang is today enormously popular, incredibly popular," even the *Chicago Tribune* found itself saying. In Congress criti-

cism was only a growl here and there on the side aisles. Senator Robert Taft made no speech; instead he observed in the lobby that America should go "all out." Senator Joseph McCarthy found no one to applaud. As a matter of fact, the Democratic leadership had proceeded to suspend the investigation of McCarthy's charges against the State Department without a single Republican protest. The loudest cheers in either the House or the Senate followed a speech of Representative Charles Eaton of New Jersey, ranking Republican on the House Foreign Affairs Committee. Eaton was an ordained Baptist minister and he managed to convey just how much he supported Democrat Harry Truman. "We've got a rattlesnake by the tail," said the Reverend Representative, "and the sooner we pound its damn head in the better."

For one moment, suspended weirdly in the bitter debates of the postwar, the reckless plunge of the North Korean Communists and the bold response of Harry Truman had united America, united it as it had not been since that distant confetti evening of V-J.

The Hills of Korea

THE NEWS was terrible. Day after day, week after week the newspapers read the same—retreat, bloody, humiliating, scarifying retreat.

The UN forces under General MacArthur's command—largely American and South Korean—were pitifully unprepared to stop the powerful North Korean blitz. They were outnumbered three to one, eight to one, even twenty to one in some areas. The light defensive arms of the ROK's bounced helplessly off the huge Soviet-made tanks advancing against them. The Americans who came rushing in from Japan were little better prepared. They had no tanks of their own and the thirty-five-ton Soviet machines laughed at their old World War II bazookas. Only ten to twenty per cent of the Americans were seasoned by combat. All of them were occupation soldiers who, as their field commander Major General William Dean remarked later, were used to being "fat and happy in occupation billets, complete with Japanese girl friends, plenty of beer, and servants to shine their boots."

The desperately needed arms and reinforcements could be sent from the United States only with agonizing slowness. The situation was the product of years of economizing in the military budget, pushed by Republican and Democratic Congresses, tolerated by President Truman, and sanctified by the Secretary of Defense, Louis Johnson, who had done that pontificating about if "Joe Stalin . . . starts something at four o'clock in the morning," the "fighting power" of America would be taking care of things by five. It was way past five o'clock now and the United States was fighting back with a feather.

From the battlefronts came the reports, stark and heart-rending. The retreat of the UN forces was so pellmell that three weeks after the war began headlines told of the capture of General Dean himself. He was last seen, the accounts said, in the front lines of the confused fighting, desperately trying to rally his men against the tanks. Generals or privates, the debacle was the same. The story of tens of thousands of GI's was told by Sergeant Raymond Remp, of Pittsburgh, who fled Taegu after fourteen and a half hours of constant fire.

"Someone fired a green flare, and they saw us," the Sergeant choked out his account to reporters. "All around us in the hills, bugles started in blowing. . . . They were right on top of us in the hills, firing down on us. . . .

"Some colonel—don't know who—said, 'Get out the best way you can.' He stayed behind to hold them. As we went up a draw, they opened fire. I got my rifle belt and canteen shot off. Two men following me got hit. They were so tired they just couldn't move.

"We headed south. An officer and me split up our ammo and rations into a couple of cans. I drank water from the rice paddies. Got cramps—sick as a dog—and my dysentery is awful. . . .

"Tanks fired at us from our own motor pool. We met some more guys cut off. We climbed a big mountain. The guys had machine guns strapped on their backs. One ran with his gun and stooped over. His partner fired. I don't know where they got the strength.

"They ran like goats. We took off and got on top of another mountain. We ran across six of them mountain tops and killed four guys. We were out of ammo. . . .

"For 10 miles outside Taegu, we were fired at. All day and night we ran like antelopes. We didn't know our officers. They didn't know us. We lost everything we had.

"These new shoes were put on me a couple of days ago. The soles were almost ripped off from running. My feet are cut to pieces. I saw lots of guys running barefooted.

"I can't stand it—seeing friends get it and not being able to help them drives you crazy. I thought the Huertgen Forest was bad and Normandy, but they were nothing like this. This was awful.

"How much can you take?

"I guess I'm lucky. I'm not hit. But what it did to me. . . . Oh my God, what it did to me."

It was not only frantic retreat. It was frantic retreat amid savagery. The fighting was not two weeks old when the authenticated stories came of American soldiers lying in ditches, their hands tied behind their backs and bullet holes in the rear of their heads. With or without butchery, almost any aspect of this war was proving peculiarly disturbing to the American reader. MacArthur's command was supposed to be a United Nations force and a scattering of other nations were soon contributing some military aid. But why, influential publications in the United States demanded to know, should America be expected to bear so heavy a share of the fighting?

For the first time ordinary citizens in Portland, Omaha, and Tuscaloosa were discovering just how complicated it was to fight Communists. Foreign correspondents kept pointing out that North Korean propaganda pamphlets emphasized things like: "Today, under the orders of a Southern U.S. President, U.S. planes are bombing and strafing COLORED PEOPLE in Korea." Almost everyone who wrote from Korea stressed that this conflict was not only a war against North Koreans but a highly complex struggle for the feelings of all Asiatics, feelings that had become ex-

traordinarily sensitive under the proddings of nationalism and of Communism.

Americans were reading daily the evidence that
even the GI was no longer his cocky, wisecracking
self. Ever-retreating, outmanned, outtanked, outsup-
plied, outflanked, and outyelled, fighting over saw-
tooth ridges, wreck-littered roads, and paddies ferti-
lized by human excrement, most of the American
soldiers were glum, bitter, confused. The average GI
had not the slightest idea why he was battling on these
far-off hills. "I'll fight for my country," Corporal
Stephen Zeg of Chicago put it, "but I'll be damned if
I see why I'm fighting to save this hell hole." After a
few flourishes at the beginning of the war, troops leaving the United States usually wanted no parades. Once
in Korea, they went in conspicuously little for jokes
and horseplay. No Kilroy announced his sovereign
presence. There was no bouncing "Mademoiselle from
Armentières," which the doughboys had marched to
in World War I, no love song like "Lili Marlene" of
World War II. The most popular GI expression was a
fatalistic, "Well, that's the way the ball bounces." The
Korean GI, if he sang at all, was likely to rasp out lines
like:

> *The Dhow, the Gizee, and Rhee*
> *What do they want from me?*

Finally, on August 6, 1950 the retreat ended. Large
numbers of reinforcements, the stiffening lines of the
ROK's, new tank-killing American arms, and the mur-
derous operations of the U.S. air forces had all told. A
defense perimeter was now stabilized around the port
of Pusan at the southeastern tip of Korea.

On September 15 the UN forces took the offensive.
In a brilliant amphibious operation conceived by General MacArthur, the troops landed at Inchon near the
western end of the 38th parallel and fought their way
east. Other UN armies struck north from Pusan. The
North Koreans, in danger of total entrapment, surrendered by the thousands or ran for the 38th parallel.

The UN forces swept north in hot pursuit, up to the parallel and—authorized by a hasty and vague UN resolution—into North Korea. Soon advance units of the UN armies were on the banks of the Yalu River, which separated North Korea from Chinese Manchuria. On November 24 General MacArthur launched a "final" offensive, designed to crush all remaining resistance in North Korea and leave North and South Korea united under UN supervision. "The war," MacArthur told reporters, "very definitely is coming to an end shortly."

As the UN troops had advanced toward the 38th parallel, the Premier and Foreign Minister of Red China, Chou En-lai, bitterly denounced the "frenzied and violent acts of imperialist aggression" of the United States and stated that the Chinese people would not "supinely tolerate seeing their [North Korean] neighbors being savagely invaded by imperialists." During late October and November, MacArthur's troops encountered considerable units of Chinese "volunteers" as much as fifty miles south of the Yalu.

President Truman had put the danger of Chinese intervention to General MacArthur in a conference at Wake Island on October 15. Just what was said at Wake Island and in subsequent communications between Washington and Tokyo is the subject of furious controversy (Truman and MacArthur have devoted large sections of books to the subject, the President in his *Memoirs*, the General in the authorized volume, *MacArthur: His Rendezvous with History*). What emerges as incontestable fact is that MacArthur told Truman at Wake Island that there was little if any chance of Chinese intervention and that, if the Chinese did come in, their armies would be slaughtered; that the Truman Administration approved the movement north of the 38th parallel and the "final" offensive only on the basis of this assurance; that as the evidence of Chinese fighting increased, the General appealed to Washington for permission to blow up the bridges

across the Yalu and the Administration refused, partly
because it was trying to stay out of war with the Chinese and partly because the river would soon freeze
and be as passable as any bridge; and that McArthur
launched his Yalu offensive with little thought
in his own mind and no indication to Washington that
it might provoke a major Chinese counter-offensive.

Late in November President Truman appeared at
the door of his White House office to summon his
staff for the daily conference. He put his hands on
his hips in the mock impatience he loved to show and
he grinned. But the little ritual had no exuberance.
The President went around the group in his usual
way, taking up the problems each man had on his
mind. Then he moved to the middle of his desk,
shifted papers back and forth, and finally spoke in a
quiet, solemn way. "General Bradley called me at
6.15 this morning," Truman said. "He told me that a
terrible message had come from General MacArthur.
. . . The Chinese have come in with both feet."

The Chinese had come in with both feet and a
roundhouse swing. On November 26 thirty-three divisions hit the UN lines. Night after night the pattern
of attack was the same. Under cover of darkness, specially trained and specially armed units of five to nine
Chinese crawled forward to determine just how the
UN front troops were arranged, to destroy artillery
positions, and to cut supply lines. Then flares lit up,
bugles or cymbals sounded, whistles went off, and the
mass of infantrymen charged, thousands of them, falling unexcited and apparently unafraid only to make
room for more thousands. Quickly the Chinese
smashed down the center of the UN forces. To the
west American and other UN units were able to retreat in orderly fashion, though with heavy casualties.
To the east the situation was desperate. The overwhelming Communist offensive cut off and surrounded masses of UN troops, including the First Marine Division and two battalions of the Seventh Infan-

try Division of the United States. The position of the
First Marine Division was especially critical. It was surrounded on the frigid wastes beside the Chongjin Reservoir, forty miles from the nearest evacuation point
on the east coast.

Major General Oliver P. Smith, a Marine for thirty-
three years and now the proud commander of the
First Division, sent out the defiant word: "Retreat,
hell! We're only attacking in another direction." The
Marines did fight with guts and wits that sent a thrill
through the home country but the newspapers also
had to describe the worst ordeal since Tarawa. Much
of the escape route was a corkscrew trail of icy dirt,
just wide enough for a two-and-a-half-ton truck and
winding by rocky ridges and forested bluffs that
were filled with Chinese. Sub-zero cold, violent snow-
storms, and sudden wild gorges two thousand feet
deep were as much of a menace as the Communists. A
large part of the fighting was during the night and at
close quarters, with pistols, grenades, and subma-
chine guns. 2,651 wounded were flown out in only
four days; once 117 bodies were buried in a single
grave and a bulldozer used to push a covering over
them—there was no time for anything else when a
grave had to be blasted from ground frozen to eighteen inches.

Long-distance telephone lines to Washington were
flooded. "What is the real situation?" "Is it true that
the First Marine Division has been wiped out and the
news is going to be let out slowly?" "Why doesn't
somebody *do* something?" After thirteen days the sur-
vivors began to reach safety. The Marines came in so
many remnants of holocaust, the uninjured with
sunken, staring eyes, the wounded often grimacing
from frostbite as well as their injuries, some of the
dead lying grotesquely across trailers with blood frozen to their skin.

In Washington grim faces grew grimmer. President
Truman confided to a memorandum pad: "We had

conference after conference on the jittery situation facing the country. Attlee, Formosa, Communist China, Chiang Kai-shek, Japan, Germany, France, India, etc. I have worked for peace for five years and six months and it looks like World War III is near." Hastily the Administration, with a scared Congress going along for the most part, moved to bolster the military strength of the non-Communist world. Hurried steps were taken to enlarge the American armed forces, to improve the defenses of Formosa and of the nations in Southeast Asia, to speed the building and co-ordination of armies in the NATO countries, even —what would have seemed so wildly improbable only a few years before—to push the rearmament of West Germany.

The Chinese, stopping and starting, pushed through North Korea and a few miles into South Korea. There the UN forces, regrouped, were able to hold. Day after day, by foot, ox-cart, packhorse, and two-humped Bactrian camel, more of what MacArthur called the "bottomless well of Chinese manpower" crossed the Yalu into North Korea. No one could question that the Chinese armies, now firmly linked with the North Koreans, were getting ready for their own end-the-war offensive and would try to drive the UN troops off the peninsula. On New Year's Eve, in the dark of another night and more zero weather, the onslaught came.

The UN lines bent, Seoul fell again, but the Communists could not break through. As 1951 went on, the UN forces began a slow, punishing advance back toward the 38th parallel.

Corporal William Jensen was shot in the thigh in the first Chinese breakthrough and he was flown home to Hastings, Nebraska. The day after he arrived, he hobbled down along the stores of Second Street and delivered himself of a judgment. "Man," he said, "I never saw anything like it. This town is just one big boom."

During the Korean War the whole United States was one big boom, the boomingest America in all the prosperous years since V-J. Virtually all of the soft spots that were still left in the economy were removed by the Korean War. The most telltale sign, employment, told a tale of historic proportions. Two months after the Korean War began, employment crossed the sixty-two million mark—two million beyond the fondest dreams of New Dealers at V-J. As a matter of fact, by August, 1950 New York State had so few unemployment claims that it fired five hundred people in its compensation division.

It was prosperity, too, within the framework of continuing the Half-Century of Revolution in domestic affairs. Once the Korean War started, Congress passed little domestic legislation but the laws that did go through often inched ahead government aid to lower-income groups. Most notably, the Social Security Act underwent its first comprehensive change since enactment of the bill in 1935 and an estimated ten million Americans, largely farmworkers, domestic servants, and small businessmen, were added to the coverage. Outside the political arena, the steady leveling on the American social scene was still more evident. Once buying stocks may have been a matter for the Fifth Avenues of the nation but now the long-established brokerage firm, Ira Haupt & Co., set up a tent exhibit at the Mineola, Long Island, County Fair. Ernest E. Ruppe, the Haupt man assigned to Mineola, stood on the sodden grass and, amid a great crowing of roosters and cackling of hens, bespoke the era. "Money has changed hands in the last twenty years. The people who used to have it don't. The workingman does. . . . One of my best customers is a potato farmer in Hicksville; I've sold him nineteen thousand dollars' worth of mutual funds."

The walls of discrimination against Negroes, Jews,

and other minorities kept on lowering. The decades-old trend was at work; moreover, the argument that America could not win the Asiatic mind while discriminating against colored men at home was having its effect. In the middle of the Korean War an incident brought a flash of the attitude that was becoming more and more common. The body of a casualty, Sergeant John Rice, was brought to Sioux City for burial and just as the casket was to be lowered in the grave, officials of the Sioux City Memorial Park stopped the ceremony. Sergeant Rice, it seemed, was a Winnebago Indian; he was "not a member of the Caucasian race." The officials made an offer to Mrs. Evelyn Rice. Would she care to sign a statement stating that her husband had "all white blood"? Mrs. Rice emphatically did not care to sign the statement and the body was taken back to the funeral home. The next morning President Truman read of the incident at breakfast. Within minutes Mrs. Rice was invited to bury her husband in Arlington National Cemetery and was informed that the United States Government would be happy to dispatch an Air Force plane to bring the body and the family to Washington. Harry Truman had rarely done anything more popular. A wide variety of opinion across the country agreed that, to use the words of the *Cleveland Plain Dealer*, "it is high time we stopped this business. We can't do it as decent human beings and we can't do it as a nation trying to sell democracy to a world full of non-white peoples."

The Negro scored his most meaningful advance since the issuance of the FEPC order during World War II. Shortly before the election of 1948 President Truman had issued an Executive Order, declaring it to be "the policy of the President that there shall be equality of treatment and opportunity for all persons in the armed services. . . . This policy shall be put into effect as rapidly as possible, having due regard to the time required to effectuate any necessary changes without impairing efficiency or morale." In January,

1950 Secretary of the Army Gordon Gray issued a supplementary policy statement, reiterating the President's general position and going on specifically to direct that soldiers with special skills were to be assigned without regard to race or color. The directives were none too sweeping and they were not rigorously pushed. When the Korean War began, the Air Force was largely integrated; segregation was the general pattern in the Army, Navy, and Marine Corps. But the new currents of thinking were running strong and the practical circumstances gave an opening to the military men who wanted to end Jim Crow or had no particular feelings about it one way or another.

Brigadier General Frank McConnell was a veteran army officer simply interested in doing an efficient job at the post he was assigned when the Korean War began—commandant of the infantry training base at Fort Jackson, South Carolina. The General put into effect the customary pattern of segregation and then, during the North Korean blitz, the draftees came pouring in at the rate of a thousand a day. Treating the whites and Negroes separately in beginning the training of the men was enormously slowing the whole process. McConnell summoned his staff and proposed ignoring the color line.

An aide spoke up. Wasn't there danger that the General would be "going off the deep end"?

McConnell pulled out from his desk the directive of Secretary Gray concerning segregation. "It was all the authority I needed," he recalled later. "I said that if we didn't ask permission, they couldn't stop us." The General issued a verbal order that the next fifty-five draftees who arrived were to be put in a platoon in the order that they arrived and that was the end of segregation at Fort Jackson.

No race incidents followed. "I would see recruits, Negro and white, walking down the street off-duty, all grouped together," McConnell remembered. "The attitude of the Southern soldiers was that this was the army way; they accepted it the same way they accepted getting up at 5:30 in the morning." Word of the new way of doing things at Fort Jackson got around rapidly and some high-ranking military officials, including General Mark Clark, chief of the Army Field Forces, were anything but happy. But soon the color line was disappearing at all Army training bases.

Meanwhile the Army Chief of Staff, General J. Lawton Collins, wrote his overseas commanders a confidential letter calling for integration according to a deliberate, unspectacular program. Again the reasoning was pragmatic. As Collins's assistant, General Anthony McAuliffe, remarked later: "We didn't do it to improve the social situation. It was merely a matter of getting the best out of the military personnel that was available to us."

On the battlefields of Korea, emergency circumstances swept ahead the change. Colonel John G. Hill, another matter-of-fact military man, commanded the 9th U.S. Infantry Regiment, one of the first American units to land in Korea. Hill had ten per cent overstrength in his all-Negro 3rd Battalion but his two white battalions were short of men and battle losses quickly thinned them still further. "Force of circumstances" dictated the next move, Hill told the story later. "We had no replacements. . . . We would have been doing ourselves a disservice to permit [Negro] soldiers to lie around in rear areas at the expense of the still further weakening of our [white] rifle companies." When he ordered the integration of the Negroes, Hill continued, the whites took the situation in stride. As for the Negroes, a remarkable change occurred. The same men who had been unreliable in combat now were entirely dependable under fire. What's more, Negroes suddenly began volunteering for dangerous assignments.

After Hill's move succeeded, other Korean commanders tried integration. They found that the pattern held. Negro units were none too steady in com-

bat. Once integrated, the Negroes fought as well as
the whites and the whites accepted the change with
few incidents. The discovery of this basic practical
fact spurred ahead integration and by early 1951 the
color line was scarcely visible among the U.S. troops
fighting in Korea.

The effects of what the Army was doing spilled over
into many parts of American life. It had shown that
racial barriers could be removed without causing disruption and with a marked increase in the efficient use
of human beings. The Army moves speeded integration in the Navy and the Marine Corps. Outside the
military, they undermined segregation in scores of
ways, tangible and intangible. Tens of thousands of
white men left the service with an experience which
otherwise they never would have had. Some acquired
an increased dislike of Negroes but from the available
evidence most soldiers took home a slant on race markedly different from the previous assumption of segregation. In areas of the United States near Army camps,
military integration inevitably affected nonmilitary
situations. North or South, here and there churches,
USO clubs, cafés, and taxicabs began voluntarily to admit Negroes on an equal or near-equal basis. Just as inevitably, there were instances of military pressure to
change local racial practices—like the Provost Marshal
on a northern post who ended Jim Crow in a near-by
bar by telling the owner that his place would be declared off limits unless all soldiers were served. Old
ways were crumbling; new habits were being formed.

Perhaps most important of all, military desegregation
furthered general desegragation by capturing the emotions of many people. In the atmosphere of the 1950's
few crusades seemed bright and shining; here was an
appealing human cause to which human beings could
respond. Brigadier General Lloyd Hopwood, Deputy
Chief for Air Force Personnel Planning, touched the
note when he stopped one day to talk with Lee Nichols, a journalist who was examining letters from Air

Force commanders attesting the success of their integration program. "I like to go through them myself once in a while," the General said. "It kind of restores my faith in human nature."

More social revolution, more boom, and withal a vast restlessness. The prosperity itself was involved with the irritations of a sharply accelerated inflation. A month after hostilities began the government had to announce a new low in the purchasing power of the dollar; it was now worth just 59.3 cents as compared with 1939 and the value was going right on sinking. The inflation was most severe where it was most annoying—in the price of food. The sale of horse meat tripled in Portland (it tends to be sweet, the *Oregon Journal* advised, so cook it with more onions and fewer carrots). The New Jersey Bell Telephone Company put pot roast of whale on its cafeteria menu. In Toledo the Utopia Auto Laundry added a frozen-meat department with an opening-day special of filet mignon at $1.75 a pound—twenty-five cents more than a car wash. Like all wartime inflations, the Korean price spiral spurred itself upward. Throughout the country many a citizen (considering himself just as patriotic as the next fellow of course) was hoarding everything from automobile tires to metal hair curlers. "Buy Nothing From Fear" Macy's pleaded in full-page ads—and then reported sales twenty-five per cent above normal.

All the while the public was being jabbed by news of scandals of a dozen varieties. In the months before the Korean War, a subcommittee of the Senate Committee on Executive Expenditures began spreading in the headlines the story of the "five percenters" who sold actual or pretended influence with government officials. Before long the subcommittee was proving that these five percenters were no small operators—that, in fact, some of them were working with leading officers in the procurement sections of the armed forces. The investigation climaxed when testimony was given that shortly after the end of World War II a perfume company, which was eager to speed some European oils through the remaining wartime regulations, had presented a $520 deep-freeze unit to Harry Vaughan, a man with a pad of White House stationery which could expedite such matters.

The dust had not settled over these proceedings when Senator J. William Fulbright's subcommittee of the Senate Banking and Currency Committee ran into a cesspool in the Reconstruction Finance Corporation. The American Lithofold Company, thrice turned down for an RFC loan of $565,000, had suddenly received the money after it retained as its lawyer William Boyle, Jr., chairman of the Democratic National Committee. Republicans cried shame. Then the subcommittee discovered that Guy Gabrielson, chairman of the Republican National Committee, had intervened with the RFC in an attempt to get the terms extended on a large-scale loan to the Carthage Hydrocol Company, of which he was president.

Along the line, the investigators came upon a mink coat which immediately took a place alongside Harry Vaughan's deep freeze in the national symbolism. Mrs. E. Merl Young, wife of a former examiner of loans for the RFC, had a $9,540 mink, acquired with the financial help of an attorney whose firm, it so happened, had represented a company in its application for a loan of $150,000 from the RFC. After that Mrs. Blair Moody, wife of the United States Senator from Michigan, went around wearing on her fur coat a sales receipt showing that the fur was mink-dyed muskrat and that the price, including the taxes, was $381.25. The general furor was so great the mink farmers wailed it was threatening their $100,000,000-a-year industry. An "unjust stigma" had been placed on the woman with a mink, said Harold W. Reed of the Mink Ranchers' Association. He wanted everybody to know that most wearers of mink were "highly respectable people of discriminating taste."

Outside of Washington other scandals were breaking, forms of corruption that reached deep into areas of special national pride. Millions had followed the brilliant basketball team of the City College of New York as it whirled its way to consecutive national championships. Now three out of the five members of the first team admitted taking bribes up to fifteen hundred dollars to rig scores. Soon similar cases were revealed at Long Island University, New York University, Bradley University, the University of Kentucky, and Toledo University. New York General Sessions Court Judge Saul S. Streit, before whom many of the cases were tried, took the occasion to study the national sports situation and he could only report that "commercialism" in college sports was "rampant throughout the country . . . .[It] contaminates everything it touches. It has fostered bookmaking and nationwide gambling; it produces illegal scouting, recruiting, proselytizing and subsidization of athletes; it corrupts the athlete, the coach, the college official and the alumnus; it breeds bribery, fraud and forgery; it impairs the standards of integrity of the college."

What a mess, people said; something is decidedly wrong. Then the country was really rocked. West Point, proud West Point, a school that placed character-building above everything else and trained the men who were to lead everybody's son in battle, had to make an announcement. West Point announced that it was dismissing for cheating in examinations ninety cadets, including Robert Blaik, son of the football coach and an All-American quarterback, eight other students on the Army first team, and members of the varsity squads in most other sports.

The nation gulped doubly hard when the dismissed students began talking. Many of them were not contrite and they were bewildered. Everybody had been cheating, they said in puzzlement; as a matter of fact, it was the "honest" students who stated what they had been doing and the "liars" who were still cadets. Earl

H. Blaik, the colonel who had coached football at the Point for ten years, hurried down to an emotion-charged press conference at Leone's Restaurant in New York and insisted that there was "no moral reason" why the dismissed athletes, these "men of character," should not leave the Point with their reputations totally unimpaired. "Stop knocking football," Blaik said in a choked voice. "God help this country if we didn't play football. . . . Gen. Eisenhower came to West Point with his greatest desire to play football."

The national concern over the sports scandals linked closely to the jolting realization of just how serious a problem juvenile delinquency had become. From V-J on through 1948 the rate declined. But then it began to rise and after the outbreak of the Korean War it mounted so swiftly that about a million children a year were getting into trouble with the police. Just as disquieting were the incidents that did not involve actual brushes with the law. Out of small towns and cities, particularly in the Midwest and South, came story after story like those of the teen-age clubs in Borger, Texas, and Mattoon, Illinois. The Borger club staged "house-parties" at which numbers were drawn by the high-school boys and girls and the matched pairs then went off to a shack or an auto for intercourse. In Mattoon each girl was "initiated" by having intercourse with one male in the presence of another male and she pledged herself to have intercourse at least four times a month if she was to remain "in good standing."

Whatever the form of the teen-age problem, the whole situation was showing peculiarly disturbing trends. The age of the children who went astray was rapidly dropping. Housebreaking, for example, had formerly been committed largely by boys sixteen years or older; now the offender was often thirteen to fifteen or even, in a shocking number of cases, ten to twelve. The offenses were growing more serious, with burglary, drug addiction, sex attacks, and murder increasingly frequent. It was no longer possible to dismiss the child in trouble as something which did not happen to nice people. More and more it was the son or daughter of the manufacturer or the professional man who ended up in a jumble.

Nahant, Massachusetts, provided one of the endless newspaper stories. Fifteen-year-old Roberta McCauley, seventeen-year-old Eileen Jeffreys, and sixteen-year-old Marilyn Curry were pert, cutely dressed, apparently happy daughters of middle-class America. One fine summer's night the three girls found themselves together in the course of a baby-sitting job at the home of Dr. Albert Covner. Things were pretty dull, the girls agreed. So they stole eighteen thousand dollars from a box in the bedroom closet and took off on a New York tour of buying $235 Christian Dior suits, handing ten dollar tips to cab drivers, turning Roberta into a blonde and Marilyn into a redhead, and picking up prize-fighter Wayne Eckhart who chose Roberta and registered with her at the Dixie Hotel as Mr. and Mrs. John Daly of Cedar Rapids, Iowa.

The next day Eileen ended the episode with just the words to comfort the parents of the United States. "Don't say I've been smoking," she asked the reporters. "My father would kill me if he knew I had been."

Meanwhile, starting in May, 1950, a Senate committee had been crisscrossing the United States, holding and reholding hearings in a number of large cities. The Special Committee to Investigate Organized Crime in Interstate Commerce was the official name; the Kefauver Committee, people called it after its chairman, Senator Estes Kefauver of Tennessee. In three of the cities visited, the proceedings were televised with a degree of local interest and when the Committee came to the Foley Square Courthouse in New York for public hearings, arrangements were made to set up the cameras. The independent station WPIX was to do the televising and it prepared for a routine public-service assignment. Charles A. Voso, who was in charge of the production crew, later remarked: "We didn't expect much of a public response. Neither did the Committee."

On March 12 Senator Kefauver rapped his gavel and started the proceedings in his mild, schoolmasterish way. The Committee counsel, youthful Rudolph Halley, went along with his questions, mostly in a singsong manner. Things slowly picked up. The convicted gambler, burly Frank Erickson, was asked his occupation and answered, with entire accuracy, "I'm in jail." Then he made his contribution to the English language; he announced he would refuse to answer a question because "it might intend to criminate me." Joe Adonis came to the stand looking cool and dapper and left it just another overdressed hood, mumbling the Fifth Amendment. And always Rudolph Halley's questions were becoming more sharply spoken, more insinuating, more concerned with the activities of one Frank Costello.

When Costello walked to the witness chair, his two hundred dollar suit was trim, his heavily lined face composed, his eyes hard and arrogant. His lawyer, George Wolf, soon insisted that the TV cameras be taken off his client. The Committee agreed to the demand and one of the cameramen had an idea. Why not turn the cameras only on Costello's hands?

While the cameras recorded hands fiddling with papers or pouring water from a glass, Halley drove hard to establish evidence that Costello was what the Committee was perfectly sure he was—head of one of two gigantic crime syndicates operating across many states. Bigger crowds were trying to get into the Foley Square Courthouse now. Thousands more New York sets were tuned to WPIX. TV stations across the country were being fed by WPIX.

Halley asked Costello about the testimony of George M. Levy, who was connected with the Roosevelt Raceway. Levy had said that in 1946 the chairman of the

New York State Harness Racing Commission threatened to revoke the track's license if he did not get rid of the bookmakers operating there. Levy thought of his golfing friend, Costello, paid him fifteen thousand dollars a year for four years, and the bookmakers disappeared. Didn't this suggest, Halley wanted to know, that Costello had at least some control over the bookies?

Costello's answer was unruffled. Of course he controlled no bookies. Levy had talked to him about the matter and "I says, 'What way can I help you?' . . . I says, 'Well, what I can do George, I can spread the propaganda around that they're hurting you there and you're a nice fellow. . . . I don't know how much good it's going to do you, but I'll talk about it.' He says, 'I wish you would,' and I did."

HALLEY: Where did you talk about it?

COSTELLO: Oh, in Moore's Restaurant, Gallagher's Restaurant, a hotel, a saloon, as you would call it, any place, or a night club, whenever I had the chance, just in general. . . .

HALLEY: What did you do in 1946 to earn $15,000?

COSTELLO: Practically nothing. . . .

HALLEY: And what did you do in the second year that made your services more valuable?

COSTELLO: Nothing. I did the same thing I did the first year, and I don't think I did a damn thing.

The Committee and Halley pursued Costello doggedly. How much money did he have in all? Well, he had a sort of "little strong box" at home where he kept "a little cash" but he couldn't remember how much. Couldn't he remember roughly how much? Couldn't he make a guess?

Senator Charles Tobey erupted. The elderly Committee member from New Hampshire had been listening to the evasion and lying with the air of a deacon confronted by saturnalia. Now he cut in: One way to find out how much is in the strong box is for us to send somebody up to look.

Costello's memory suddenly improved. Yes, he thought he had about fifty thousand dollars or so in the box, another ninety thousand dollars to one hundred thousand dollars in his bank account.

The aplomb of the witness was fast disappearing. On the TV screens his hands tore up pieces of paper or jiggled the water glass. Halley shifted the subject, casually asked Costello if he ever paid anyone to check his telephone for wire tapping. "Absolutely not," the witness said. A heavy-set, graying man named James F. McLaughlin took the stand. He testified that in 1945 he checked Costello's phone two or three times a week for about three months, and Costello would hand him fifty dollars or one hundred dollars or one hundred and fifty dollars when he saw him outside the Waldorf-Astoria barbershop. Senator Kefauver's soft voice spoke the harsh words: "Somebody has committed perjury."

When Costello returned to the witness stand, his face was dark and scowling. His client felt awful, George Wolf said. His throat was inflamed, the television lights and the photographers bothered him, and he was just in no condition to testify further. In a very mild and a very firm voice, Kefauver insisted that the witness should try to answer questions.

Costello managed to sound a half-step from the hospital. "I want to testify truthfully, and my mind don't function. . . . With all due respect to the Senators . . . , I have an awful lot of respect for them, I am not going to answer another question. . . . I am going to walk out."

An estimated 30,000,000 Americans watched Frank Costello leave the courtroom—by far the biggest TV audience assembled up to that time. The routine public-service program of WPIX was turning into the nation's first TV spectacular. All the major networks were now carrying the full hearings. New York City was seized as if by some sudden hypnosis. Videodex reported that 69.7% of the city's sets were tuned to the Foley Square Courthouse—a percentage twice as high as the one for the World Series games of the previous fall. Merchants complained to the Committee that their businesses were paralyzed. Movie houses became ghost halls during the hours of the proceedings (some gave up, installed TV, and invited the public to come in free). Housewives did their ironing and fed the baby in front of the set. In many big cities business and home life were noticeably affected. One Chicago department-store manager took a look at the number of customers in his aisles and ran an ad: "Ten Percent Off During Kefauver Hours."

Other witnesses were taking the stand including, as Senator Kefauver said with quiet emphasis, *Mrs.* Virginia Hauser. She was *soignée* in a five thousand dollar silver-blue mink stole, gray suede gloves, black dress, and large-brimmed black hat. She was also annoyed. She pointed to the photographers and screamed: "Make those goddam fools stop. I'll throw something at them in a minute." The Committee had good reason to believe that this witness was the bank courier for some of the key figures in the underworld; they were anxious for her to talk. Senator Kefauver waved the photographers away and soothed her in his best Southern manner. Wouldn't she just tell the Committee something of her life?

Why, she said with drawling innocence, she was just another Alabama girl who came to Chicago, worked for a while, and met some fellows. There was Joe Adonis and Charlie Fischetti and Ben Siegel—

But what about all her money? Where did that come from?

Mrs. Virginia Hauser lolled in the witness chair. "For years I have been going to Mexico. I went with fellows down there. And like a lot of girls that they got. Giving me things and bought me everything I want. . . . Whatever I have ever had was, outside of betting horses, was given to me."

Since she knew these men well, didn't she hear things about their business operations?

Her air of innocence could no longer conceal the smirk. Know anything about their affairs? Why, when any of the fellows talked business she left the room. At Siegel's Flamingo Club in Las Vegas, "on a lot of times, people didn't even know I was there. I was upstairs in my room; I didn't even go out. . . . I was allergic to the cactus."

And with a few more drawls Mrs. Virginia Hauser shrugged her mink stole higher on her shoulders, ran a gauntlet of photographers, and left the courthouse yelling at the cameramen: "You bastards, I hope a goddamn atom bomb falls on every goddam one of you." The Kefauver Committee had not exactly proved her role as the bank courier for gangsters. But it had provided quite an education for those thirty million people at TV sets who had known the Virginia Hausers only as a product of Hollywood's imagination.

Over the weekend Frank Costello decided to come back on the stand and was maneuvered into statements that risked further perjury charges. All the while Halley kept probing the role of money in New York politics and the connections between crime and politics. Along the way the stand was taken by William O'Dwyer, the ex-Mayor of New York and at this time the United States Ambassador to Mexico.

O'Dwyer was amiable, reasonable, practical. He was an honest man, the ex-Mayor's manner said, but no bluenose and he knew the facts of life. Casually fingering a paper clip, he rambled over an account of his career ("I took 190,000 people out of slums"), soliloquized at length that organized crime was bred by Prohibition, slot machines, and too many tattered nerves in family living. O'Dwyer readily admitted that he knew Costello.

Senator Tobey interrupted in his best Biblical manner. "It almost seems to me as though you should say, 'Unclean, unclean' . . . and that you would leave him alone. . . ."

O'DWYER: You have bookmaking all over the country. They say there is a lot of it in New Hampshire, too —thirty million a year. . . .

TOBEY: Well, we haven't a Costello in New Hampshire.

O'DWYER: I wonder. . . . And I wonder who the bookmakers in Bretton Woods support for public office in New Hampshire?

O'Dwyer conceded that large-scale gambling had probably gone on in New York while he was Mayor and that it could not have existed on such a scale without police protection. But with respect to things like that, he explained, all a man who was trying to run a city of eight million could do was to try to appoint good men and then depend on them. The testimony brought out a series of interlockings between New York City politics and the underworld, including the fact that O'Dwyer had named a protégé of Frank Costello to a judgeship and that one of his Fire Commissioners, Frank Quayle, was a friend of Joe Adonis. "There are things that you have to do politically if you want to get co-operation," O'Dwyer said. They had nothing to do with his honesty or the fact that his political powers as Mayor had not been for sale.

Matter-of-factly, Halley asked O'Dwyer whether he knew John P. Crane, president of the Uniformed Firemen's Association. Yes, O'Dwyer knew Crane. Did Crane ever make any campaign contribution through you? No, he did not. Matter-of-factly, Halley went on to other matters.

The next day John Crane took the stand. Did he know O'Dwyer? Yes, Crane had kept wanting the Mayor's support for increasing firemen's salaries and once shortly before a mayoralty election he had gone to see O'Dwyer.

HALLEY: Will you tell the committee what transpired?

CRANE: I told the mayor at that time that I had pro-

mised him the support of the firemen, and I offered
him some evidence of that support on the occasion,
in the form of $10,000. . . .
HALLEY: Was that in cash?
CRANE: That was in cash. . . .
HALLEY: You gave it to the mayor . . . ?
CRANE: Yes.

Late that afternoon, the eighth day of the proceedings, the cameras were taken from the Foley Square
Courthouse. It had been quite an eight days. The New
York hearings of the Kefauver Committee made television (now TV became almost an essential of the ordinary home). They made Estes Kefauver, who the
next year was to go to the Democratic National Convention with 340 delegates pledged to him for the
Presidential nomination. But above all the televised proceedings, with their stark portrayal of the practical
Mayor who might not have been merely practical, of
the sinister arrogance of the Costellos and the Virginia
Hausers, of the endless shadowy fingers that obviously
controlled so much, catalyzed the whole vague feeling
that corruption was moving through all American
life like a swarm of maggots.

Across a full page of the New York newspapers the
advertising firm, Young and Rubicam, expressed the
national reaction:

"With staggering impact, the telecasts of the Kefauver investigation have brought a shocked awakening
to millions of Americans.

"Across their television tubes have paraded the
honest and dishonest, the frank and the furtive, the
public servant and the public thief. Out of many pictures has come a broader picture of the sordid intermingling of crime and politics, of dishonor in public
life.

"And suddenly millions of Americans are asking:
What's happened to our ideals of right and wrong?

What's happened to our principles of honesty in government?

What's happened to public and private standards of morality?

"Then they ask the most important question of all: How can we stop what's going on? *Is there anything we can do about it?*"

Was there anything Americans could do about standards of morality? Was there anything they could do about anything?

The spring of 1951 came to an America caught in a snarl of frustration. On a rain-swept Easter Sunday the UN forces in Korea fought their way north across the 38th parallel. They had crossed the line twice before— once going and once coming—and did the crossing mean any more now? General MacArthur, no man for pessimistic statements, made it unmistakably clear that he expected stalemate. The reports of the war were taking on a peculiarly meaningless quality, the killing of a hundred Communists here when there were thousands a bit further north, the taking of some hill without a name only to lose it, still unnamed, a few days later. The news on the attitude of the soldiers in Korea was that, to use the dispatch of E.J. Kahn, Jr., "the idea of this war as an endless one is almost universally accepted here"—endless war, and endless war in as cheerless a situation as American troops had ever encountered. Even money was worthless, Kahn continued, "since there is absolutely nothing to spend it on. A couple of days ago, I saw two rifle companies playing a softball game on a diamond laid out in a paddy field, for a purse of a thousand dollars."

The descriptions of Korean deadlock came back to a country filled with a sense of stalemate wherever it turned. Why couldn't America make the world realize that it wanted only peace and decency? One of the earliest books on the Korean crisis was by Mrs. Doro-

thy Vieman, the wife of an Army officer stationed in
Korea before the invasion, and Mrs. Vieman wrote: "I
believe other nationalities think we are crazy." Surely
there was some way of getting people to sit down at a
table and straighten out the mess? The Big Four under-
secretaries of foreign affairs were sitting down at a
table in Paris; they were only trying to arrange an
agenda for the secretaries and at that they were getting
nowhere. There was always Assistant Commissar for
Foreign Affairs Andrei Gromyko, sonorous, belligerent, and endlessly obstructive.

Home-front problems kept taking on the same quality of deadlock. Inflation, for example—the jukebox
men announced an anti-inflation song *Once Upon A
Nickel* as they proceeded to retool the jukeboxes to
take only dimes. The hoodlums? In Los Angeles District Court Judge Ben Harrison sentenced gangster
Mickey Cohen with the statement: "His parents came
from abroad . . . and the environment here produced
Mr. Cohen. When he started violating the laws by becoming a gambling commissioner, it could only have
been with the acquiescence of the law enforcement
agencies." The government scandals? Senator Fulbright told the country that the problem was not really
illegal conduct but unethical conduct—a lack of ethics
that ran through the whole community. "How do we
deal with those who, under the guise of friendship, accept favors which offend the spirit of the law but do
not violate its letter? What of the men outside government who suborn those inside it?" The teen-age sex
clubs? When they appeared in Indiana a reporter
thought of asking Dr. Kinsey. He noted that according
to his studies an unmarried male beyond the age of
puberty had premarital experiences at the rate of about
once a week, multiplied this by Indiana's 450,000 unmarried males, and got 450,000 male premarital experiences per week in Indiana. "And that," said Dr.
Kinsey, "is why I don't get excited when the news-

papers report three or four teen-agers having such experiences."

Irritation rasped through American life. The unity of the week when the country cheered intervention in Korea lay in shreds. Harry Truman was being flayed as he had not been since the "Had Enough?" days of 1946. Senator Joseph McCarthy was in the headlines again shrill and confident. Delegations trooped into Washington with block-long petitions demanding the ouster of Dean Acheson.

Irritation, anger, worry, bitterness—and through it all the sense of frustration mounted. The veteran journalist George Creel found the words for the America of spring, 1951. Entertaining a group in San Francisco, Creel tapped the table impatiently and said: "I have never seen anything like it in all my seventy-four years. On any problem it's like those damned hills of Korea. You march up them but there's always the sinking feeling you are going to have to march right back down again."

X

Yearnings and the Fulfillment

ON WEDNESDAY April 11, 1951 the United States forgot all about Estes Kefauver, Chinese infantrymen, or mink coats. The news was released at one a.m. (to coincide with the delivery of a message on the other side of the world) and most Americans did their gasping at the breakfast table. Harry Truman, Captain Harry of Battery D, had upped and fired General of the Army Douglas MacArthur, Commanding General of the U.S. Army Forces, Far East, U.S. Commander-in-Chief, Far East Command, Supreme Commander for the Allied Powers in Japan, and Commander-in-Chief, United Nations Command.

From MacArthur came magisterial silence. Aides of the General talked to reporters in a sepulchral hush. "I have just left him," Major General Courtney Whitney said. "He received the word of the President's dismissal from command magnificently. He never turned a hair. His soldierly qualities were never more pronounced. This has been his finest hour."

From the United States came a roar of outrage. By ten a.m. on April 11, Senator Taft and other major Republican figures were caucusing in the office of the House GOP leader, Joseph Martin, agreeing that MacArthur should be invited to address a joint meeting of Congress and that the whole foreign and military policy of the Administration should be subjected to a Congressional investigation. "In addition," Martin told the press, "the question of impeachments was discussed" and he emphasized the *s* on the word impeachment in a way that left no doubt he meant Secretary of State Acheson as well as President Truman. Senator McCarthy immediately staged his own impeachment of the President. "The sonofabitch," McCarthy said; the decision to fire the General must have come from a night "of bourbon and benedictine." Seventy-eight thousand telegrams or letters, running twenty-to-one against the dismissal, were assaulting the White House. The Gallup Poll sent out its interviewers and they came back with a thumping sixty-nine per cent for MacArthur and only twenty-nine per cent backing the Presidential action.

From San Gabriel, California to Worcester, Massachusetts, Harry Truman was burned in effigy. In Los Angeles the City Council adjourned "in sorrowful contemplation of the political assassination" of the General. In Charlestown, Maryland, a woman tried to send a wire calling the President a moron, was told she couldn't, persisted in epithets until the clerk let her tell Harry Truman he was a "witling." In Eastham, Massachusetts, Little Rock, Houston, and Oakland, flags went down to half-mast. People savored scores of new anti-Truman stories. "This wouldn't have happened if Truman were alive," the wisecracks went. Or "I'm going to have a Truman beer—you know, just like any ordinary beer except it hasn't got a head."

Within five days MacArthur's big Constellation, the *Bataan*, was coming in over the San Francisco Airport. The General paused at the head of the gangway, the trench coat and the frayed battle cap silhouetted in the floodlights, and the crowd roared and surged. When the police and the MP's managed to get the General's party into automobiles, almost two hours were needed to crawl through the fourteen miles to the St. Francis Hotel and only a flying wedge of policemen got the MacArthur family into their suite. Next day the General went to a reception in front of San Francisco's City Hall and said: "The only politics I have is contained in a single phrase known well to all of you—God Bless America!" A hundred thousand people cheered in a way San Francisco had not heard since the visits of Franklin Roosevelt.

On to the national capital and, for a moment, something less than tumult. At the Washington airport MacArthur was greeted by the Joint Chiefs of Staff, who had unanimously recommended his dismissal. Everyone was very polite. Up stepped the personal representative of the Commander-in-Chief, Major General Harry Vaughan. The General and the Major General engaged in hasty greetings and Vaughan scurried away. He was heard muttering "Well, that was simple."

Then the crowds took over and everything was San Francisco redoubled. Wherever MacArthur appeared —at a meeting of the American Society of Newspaper Editors, riding down Pennsylvania Avenue through 300,000 people, before another quarter of a million gathered in front of the Washington Monument— everywhere the reception was thunderous. The DAR was beside itself. The six thousand ladies assembled in their Sixtieth Continental Congress at Constitution Hall went to the ultimate; they took off their hats en masse so that everybody could see a full Douglas MacArthur. "I have long sought personally to pay you the tribute that is in my heart . . . ," the General said in his three-minute talk to the DAR. "In this hour of crisis, all patriots look to you." The next day Recording Secretary General Mrs. Warren Shattuck Currier read from her minutes that MacArthur's speech was "probably the most important event" in the history of Constitution Hall. Mrs. Thomas B. Throckmorton was immediately on her feet. She moved, and the convention promptly agreed, to strike out the word "probably."

At 12.30 on April 19 the Doorkeeper of the House of Representatives intoned: "Mr. Speaker, General of the Army Douglas MacArthur." He walked down the aisle in a short army jacket, his chest bare of ribbons, the back rigid and the face stony. The packed galleries, the Senators and Representatives, the Republicans and Democrats, were on their feet applauding wildly. The General stood calmly at the rostrum and waited for complete silence. "I address you," he declared, "with neither rancor nor bitterness in the fading twilight of life, with but one purpose in mind: To serve my country." Emotion seized the chamber again; thirty times in a thirty-four-minute speech the hall broke into fervid clapping. The words went on, at times sharp with anger, at times sinking to an emotional whisper, but always controlled in a way that Congress had not witnessed since the World War II visits of Winston Churchill. MacArthur presented his differences with the Truman Administration in the most rousing possible manner. "Why, my soldiers asked of me, surrender military advantages to an enemy in the field?" He paused a long few seconds, then said: "I could not answer."

As the General neared the end of the speech, the voice dropped and the words were misty. "I am closing my fifty-two years of military service. When I joined the Army, even before the turn of the century, it was the fulfillment of all of my boyish hopes and dreams. . . . The hopes and dreams have long since vanished, but I still remember the refrain of one of the most popular barracks ballads of that day, which proclaimed most proudly that old soldiers never die; they just fade away. And like the old soldier of that ballad, I now close my military career and just fade away, an old soldier who tried to do his duty as God gave him the light to see that duty. Good-by."

MacArthur handed his manuscript to the clerk, waved to his wife in the gallery, and strode toward the exit. The din swept up, crashed against the musty ceiling of the House chamber, went on and on. More than a few Congressmen had tears in their eyes. Across the country millions snapped off their television sets in a state of high emotion, some raging against corniness, a good many more furious at a President of the United States who would fire such a man.

On to New York City and more cheers and emotion—a reception that exceeded Lindbergh Day or Eisenhower Day or the excitement of V-J. Seven million people turned out for the parade. The torn paper cascaded down until some streets were ankle-deep and TV screens blurred for long periods. Amid all the uproar a quite different kind of feeling kept expressing itself. As MacArthur's limousine went by, men and women would cross themselves. The handkerchiefs came out. And sometimes there were patches of quiet, a strange, troubled, churning quiet.

The limousine took the General to the Waldorf-Astoria for a few days' rest and the furor in New York and in the nation went right on. MP's and police turned away droves of reporters from the hotel. Special switchboard arrangements diverted three thousand telephone calls a day. Hasty recordings of "Old Soldiers Never Die" leaped up on the hit parade (the song, tracing back to a British barrack-room version of an American gospel hymn, "Kind Words Can Never Die," was out in a half-dozen versions). Any store with MacArthur buttons, pennants, or corncob pipes left over from the 1948 MacArthur-for-President flurry was hitting it rich. The flower marts of the country blossomed with a Douglas MacArthur orchid, geranium, cactus, gladiolus, day lily, bearded iris, herbaceous peony, and a hybrid tea rose (the advertisements described the tea rose as rose gold in color and "needing no coddling or favor"). "The country," said

Senator James Duff of Pennsylvania with no one to gainsay him, "is on a great emotional binge."

As MacArthur stayed holed up in the Waldorf-Astoria, reporters became increasingly inquisitive. What were his intentions? Despite his disavowals of political ambition, did he seek the Republican Presidential nomination? The General returned to a lofty silence and his aides were hardly explicit. When asked how MacArthur might react to a Presidential draft, Major General Courtney Whitney replied: "The General told me that if any such question was raised he would advise the questioner to go home and read the Bible. Especially the chapter on St. Thomas, the part pertaining to doubting Thomas." Resorting to their Gospel of John, the reporters read how doubting Thomas had questioned the resurrection of Jesus. Except for the suggestion that MacArthur might be confusing himself with Jesus, an idea that was not exactly news to many of the reporters, they had learned nothing.

After a week MacArthur emerged from the Waldorf-Astoria. A "crusade" he called his next move; a "vendetta" was the name in Democratic circles. Whatever the interpretation, the General engaged in the most substantial and noisiest fading away in history. He went to Chicago and Milwaukee to make speeches at welcome-home celebrations and attacked the Truman Administration. He returned to Washington to testify before a joint Senate Committee which was investigating his dismissal and denounced the Administration some more. Then he went off on a speaking tour that took him Truman-thwacking to the West Coast, into Texas and the South, through Wisconsin, Michigan, Ohio, Pennsylvania, and Massachusetts.

Everywhere the General spoke for an older, more conservative America frightened and irritated by the whirligig of changes which was climaxing during the post-World War II period. In his speeches on domestic affairs MacArthur was Robert Taft in a general's cap. His attacks on the foreign and military policies of the Administration amounted to a repudiation of the whole breakaway from traditional ideas which had begun with the policy of containment and been swept ahead by the Korean War.

The Truman Administration called its policy in Korea "limited warfare" and the name was correct. The American military effort was decidedly constrained by worry that both China and the Soviet might come full scale into the fighting; by concern whether the allies of the United States would support a direct attack on China; by a constant consideration of the way other countries in Asia were likely to react to American moves; and by a hesitancy to commit too large a part of American resources in the Far East lest Communism should move in Europe or in the Middle East. To MacArthur such limited warfare was simply the "appeasement of Communism." The result was "prolonged indecision" and "in war there is no substitute for victory." The quick total solution, brushing aside what other countries might think and emphasizing Asia first—here was the heart of the MacArthur demands and here was an expression of deeply grooved American attitudes which had been causing so much restlessness with the Truman foreign policies since the shocks of 1949.

Apart from specific arguments about international or domestic affairs, MacArthur stood for an older America in a score of less tangible ways. His full-blown oratory recalled ten thousand Chautauqua nights. "Though without authority or responsibility, I am the possessor of the proudest of titles. I am an American," the General would say with a grandiose patriotism straight out of the days of William McKinley. In city after city MacArthur appeared with one arm around Mrs. MacArthur, another around his son Arthur, the unabashed symbol of Home and Motherhood and what he delighted in calling "the simple, eternal truths of the American way."

Like many Americans who were so disturbed by the dominant trends in the national life, the General moved closer and closer to the theory of conspiracy in explaining the developments. An aura of dark conniving surrounded MacArthur's denunciations of "the insidious forces working from within," of those who would "lead directly to the path of Communist slavery." "We must not underestimate the peril," he cried out. "It must not be brushed off lightly. It must not be scoffed at, as our present leadership has been prone to do by hurling childish epithets such as 'red herring,' 'character assassin,' 'scandal monger,' 'witch hunt,' 'political assassination,' and like terms designed to confuse or conceal. . . ."

Harry Truman played it cagily. He expected, the President told friendly reporters, an immediate stormy reaction in favor of the General, then about six weeks of rough sledding, then a swing against MacArthur. Meanwhile Harry Truman knew the uses of a storm cellar.

Gradually the Administration took the offensive. Speaking largely through the authoritative Joint Chiefs of Staff, it used the widely publicized Senate hearings on MacArthur's dismissal to make its case. The Joint Chiefs of Staff hammered on the point that the General had repeatedly and publicly challenged the Korean policies of the Administration and had thus flagrantly violated a basic principle of the American Constitution—that military men must remain subordinate to their civilian superiors. The moves MacArthur was advocating, the Administration spokesmen went on, were tragically wrong. He called for ending the Korean stalemate by permitting Chiang Kai-shek to invade the mainland, using Nationalist Chinese troops in Korea, blockading the whole Chinese coast, and bombing Chinese bases beyond the Yalu. But this, the Truman group insisted, would mean full-scale war with China. It would bring a split with America's allies who, ever since the Chinese intervention in Korea, had been making it increasingly plain that they wanted no expansion of the fighting in the Far East. It would suck American manpower and material into the vastness of China while the real enemy, Russia, stood unassailed. In the course of the hearings the mild-mannered chairman of the Joint Chiefs of Staff, General Omar Bradley, the last man anyone would pick for a spellbinder, got off the really telling phrase summarizing the Administration's case. MacArthur's program, Bradley said, "would involve us in the wrong war, at the wrong place, at the wrong time and with the wrong enemy."

By late May, 1951, the hearings were having a decided effect on public opinion. Douglas MacArthur was having decided effects too. For millions of Americans delighting in their new standard of living the General's speeches on domestic affairs sounded ominously like Herbert Hoover. For a generation including so many who were proud of their blaséness, too much talk of Motherhood and God-bless-America and too much trench coat and battered cap could pall. The polls were showing a tremendous shift away from MacArthur. The talk of MacArthur-for-President was dying down among responsible Republican leaders. The General's public appearances were losing their overpowering quality.

When MacArthur returned to New York and went to the Polo Grounds for a Giant-Phillies game, he and the management did their best. A recording of a seventeen-gun general's salute was played. MacArthur stood up in a box decorated with the Stars and Stripes and a five-star flag and told the crowd how happy he was "to witness the great American game of baseball that has done so much to build the American character." The MacArthur party left before the other spectators, walking across the whole diamond to the

center-field exit while "Old Soldiers Never Die" was
played. But things were different now. As the General neared the exit, the stands roared with laughter
when a voice of purest Bronx vintage yelled: "Hey,
Mac, how's Harry Truman?"

But if Douglas MacArthur the man was at last genuinely fading away, the impact of his dismissal was not
lost. Here was an unquestionably skillful general, intimately associated with the victory in World War II,
now cashiered because he insisted, regulations or no
regulations, on advocating the old-fashioned American remedy of quick total victory. The MacArthur
dismissal was one more event—and a tremendously jarring one—in the whole series of developments which
was leaving so many Americans feeling confused, irritated, utterly frustrated.

All the situations on the home front which contributed to the feeling—the evidences of political corruption, the inflation, the signs of slackening personal
standards—went on worsening. Korea was Korea and
more so. Two days before the MacArthur hearings
ended, on June 23, 1951, the Soviet representative to
the UN, Jacob Malik, intimated in a radio speech that
the Russians were ready for a cease-fire in Korea.
Hopes soared in the United States only to bring the
added bitterness of disappointment. Month after
month the negotiators talked peace in the tent at Panmunjom and month after month the killing went on.

Christmas, 1951 was grisly. On December 18 the
truce talks reached the point where the enemy handed
MacArthur's successor, General Matthew Ridgway, a
compilation of UN prisoners allegedly held in North
Korean prison camps. The list staggered the United
States. It contained the pitifully small total of 11,559
names and of these a mere 3,198 were Americans although Washington recorded 11,224 men as missing in action. Had the Communists murdered seven to
eight thousand American prisoners? To add to the
consternation, there was the possibility that the whole

compilation was a cruel hoax. Were the Americans on the list really alive? President Truman had to issue a heart-rending statement: "This country has no way of verifying whether the list is accurate or inaccurate, true or false, complete or incomplete. For the sake of the families whose sons are missing in action, everyone should treat this list with skepticism." As newspaper pictures of anguished faces studying the names appeared during the Christmas season, no one could disagree with the statement of the *Louisville Courier-Journal:* "This list is mocking everything Christmas is supposed to represent."

The inevitable came and with tremendous force. The shocks of 1949 had given Senator Joseph McCarthy his start. The frustrations of 1950 and 1951 blasted wide his road to power. With America tangled in deadlocks at home and abroad, the man with the simple answer, the furious, flailing answer, had his day. In early 1951 Mickey Spillane's *One Lonely Night* started on its way to selling more than three million copies. The hero, Mike Hammer, gloated: "I killed more people tonight than I have fingers on my hands. I shot them in cold blood and enjoyed every minute of it. . . . They were Commies, Lee. They were red sons-of-bitches who should have died long ago. . . . They never thought that there were people like me in this country. They figured us all to be soft as horse manure and just as stupid." Hammer's tough-guy certainty that he was solving the world's problems by bludgeoning Communists hardly hurt the sales of *One Lonely Night.* It was a day for Mike Hammerism, in books or in politics.

Week after week Senator McCarthy became bolder and more reckless. For years General of the Army George Marshall, the over-all architect of victory in World War II, had been one of the most generally esteemed figures in the United States. But Marshall was associated with the Truman policy in the Far East and on June 14, 1951 McCarthy stood up in the Senate and delivered a sixty-thousand-word speech which charged that Marshall was part of "a conspiracy so immense, an infamy so black, as to dwarf any in the history of man. . . . [a conspiracy directed] to the end that we shall be contained, frustrated and finally fall victim to Soviet intrigue from within and Russian military might from without." The more reckless McCarthy became, the more his influence mounted. Fewer and fewer Senators rose to gainsay him. Pollsters found that steadily increasing percentages of Americans were ready to answer yes to questions like, Do you in general approve of Senator McCarthy's activities?

Outside of politics, the flood of McCarthyism mounted—the people who were chasing alleged Communists, the men and the institutions who were abetting McCarthyism by acquiescing in its attitudes. Some of the furor was simply ridiculous. Monogram Pictures canceled a movie about Henry Wadsworth Longfellow. Hiawatha, the studio explained, had tried to stop wars between the Indian tribes and people might construe the picture as propaganda for the Communist "peace offensive." Wheeling, West Virginia, staged the kind of comic-opera terror that was going on in scores of cities. In Wheeling the hubbub began when a policeman announced his discovery that penny-candy machines were selling children's bonbons with little geography lessons attached to the candies. The very tininess of the messages, half the size of a postage stamp, was suspicious; most rousing of all was the revelation that some of the geography lessons bore the hammer-and-sickle Soviet flag and the message: "U.S.S.R. Population 211,000,000. Capital Moscow. Largest country in the world." City Manager Robert L. Plummer thundered: "This is a terrible thing to expose our children to." Stern measures were taken to protect the candy-store set from the knowledge that the Soviet Union existed and that it was the biggest country in the world.

Much of the furor, far from being ridiculous, was

sinister. The United States Government was tainting
the names of innocent men and costing itself the
services of invaluable specialists. Senator McCarthy decided that Philip Jessup, a distinguished professor of
international law at Columbia and a skilled diplomat,
was a man with "an unusual affinity for Communist
causes"; supinely a subcommittee of the Senate Foreign Relations Committee turned down Jessup's nomination as a delegate to the UN General Assembly.
Trying to fight off McCarthyism, the Truman Administration adopted loyalty procedures that were increasingly dubious. In or out of government, utterly innocent people were losing their jobs. Irene Wicker,
the "Singing Lady" of television, who was soon to
have an audience with the Pope and be given a special
blessing for her work with children, found her TV
contract canceled. The McCarthy-type magazine
Counterattack, which was connected with the pressure to dismiss her, made everything clear. The *Daily
Worker* had listed Miss Wicker as a sponsor of a Red
councilmanic candidate in New York and "the *Daily
Worker* is very accurate; they never make a mistake."

Everywhere in the United States, the fury against
Communism was taking on—even more than it had
before the Korean War—elements of a vendetta against
the Half-Century of Revolution in domestic affairs,
against all departures from tradition in foreign policy, against the new, the adventurous, the questing in
any field. Self-confident Yale University felt it necessary to appoint a committee of distinguished alumni to
protect itself against a recent undergraduate, William F. Buckley, who talked, in the same burst of
indignation at the Yale faculty, about the menace of
Communism and the threat of "atheists" and of men
who criticized "limited government" or economic
"self-reliance." For most of 1951 the best-seller lists of
the country included *Washington Confidential* by two
newspapermen, Jack Lait and Lee Mortimer. The book
was a jumble of breathless revelations about "Commu-

nism" in Washington, quotations like the one from an unnamed Negro dope peddler who told an unnamed federal agent "You can't arrest me. I am a friend of Mrs. Roosevelt," and such observations as "Where you find an intellectual in the District you will probably find a Red." In a number of cities, educators reported, anything "controversial" was being stripped from the schools—and more than a few times the "controversial" writing turned out to be factual information about UNESCO or New Deal legislation. A battle over a textbook in Council Bluffs, Iowa, produced the kind of statement that was commonplace. Ex-Congressman Charles Swanson opened the meeting with a roaring denunciation of "all these books. . . . They should be thrown on a bonfire—or sent to Russia. Why according to this book, Jefferson, Jackson, Wilson and Franklin Roosevelt were outstanding Presidents— what about William Howard Taft?"

In Washington, William Howard Taft's son Robert was in a new phase of his career. "The sad, worst period," his sympathetic biographer, William S. White, has called it. Certainly Senator Robert Taft was moving closer to McCarthyism. Even before the Korean War, in March, 1950, several responsible reporters asserted that Taft had remarked: "McCarthy should keep talking and if one case doesn't work out he should proceed with another." The Senator protested that this quotation misrepresented him but there can be no question about the meaning of statements he made after the Korean intervention. Taft complained that Truman had the bad habit to "*assume the innocence* of all the persons mentioned in the State Department." He also declared: "Whether Senator McCarthy has *legal evidence*, whether he has over-stated or understated his case, is of lesser importance. The question is whether the Communist influence in the State Department *still exists*." (Italics added.) "This sort of thing," William White could only sadly comment, "was not the Taft one had known."

In domestic affairs the Senator's attacks became sharper and edged closer to the argument that Fair Dealism was a conspiracy of socialists. In foreign affairs, all the matters that were "open to question" in Taft's speech at the time the United States entered the Korean War were now settled and settled against the Administration. The American intervention was "an unnecessary war," an "utterly useless war," a war "begun by President Truman without the slightest authority from Congress or the people." And in explaining the international policy of the Administration the Senator was more and more using phrases that suggested a plot on the part of—to use a 1951 statement of Taft—"men who did not and do not turn their backs on the Alger Hisses."

If the Senator was going far, a large part of the GOP was moving in the same direction. In part this trend represented out-and-out McCarthyism. More of it came from the feeling—to use the phrase current then—that "I don't like some of McCarthy's methods but his goal is good." To the largest extent the development resulted from a fundamental disquietude with foreign and domestic affairs that showed itself in a violent anti-Trumanism, particularly on the issue of Far Eastern policy. The feeling was so extreme that it was willing to hit out almost blindly. Senator H. Alexander Smith, certainly no McCarthyite and not always a Taftite, spoke the attitude in explaining the decisive committee vote he cast against the confirmation of Philip Jessup. Smith said he did not agree with McCarthy's portrayal of Jessup as a pro-Communist. But the real issue was "approval or disapproval of our over-all Far Eastern policy. Dr. Jessup has been identified with those forces . . . responsible for the Far Eastern policy which has led to the present crisis. . . . He participated in the unfortunate events which led to the summary dismissal of General MacArthur. He is the symbol of a group attitude toward Asia. . . ."

At the conclusion of the MacArthur hearings, eight

out of the nine Republicans on the Senate Committee signed a policy statement. The men belonged to no one segment of the party—they included at least one representative from every principal faction—but they united in declaring that the reasons given for MacArthur's dismissal were "utterly inadequate"; in talking darkly about a "pro-Communist State Department group," concerning which "the . . . truth has not yet been revealed"; and in denouncing the management of affairs in the Far East "as the most desolate failure in the history of our foreign policy." As for the Administration's Korean policy of limited warfare in close association with the UN and with allies, the Senators spoke bitterly of a program which worried over the attitude of "certain of our associates" and was based on "no positive plan for achieving a decisive victory."

General Republicans, Taftite Republicans, McCarthyite Republicans, McCarthyite Democrats, and the millions of Americans who fitted none of these categories—in late 1951 and 1952 much of the nation was restlessly, irritably seeking to break through the sense of frustration. People flailed Harry Truman as a caged animal lashes at its bars. The President's Gallup rating sank to a minuscule twenty-six per cent and the personal attacks were so extreme the pro-Truman *New York Post* found itself pleading: "After all, the President of the United States is a member of the human race." Men and women were looking for some bright shining light, some road without endless roadblocks. Captain Henrik Carlsen became a national hero by following a simple forthright code and staying for twelve days on his foundering ship, the *Flying Enterprise*. The mounting religious interest was now reaching the scope of a national phenomenon; even Mickey Spillane turned to the church in early 1952—in his case to the appropriately frenetic doctrine of Jehovah's Witnesses. Before 1952 was done that recipe for swift certainties, *The Power of Positive Thinking*, began a sales career which was to break every best-seller record in modern American history. "The patron saint of Americans today is St. Vitus," said the book's author Dr. Norman Vincent Peale, pastor of the Marble Collegiate Church in New York. "The American people are so keyed up it is impossible to put them to sleep even with a sermon."

In Cleveland Louis B. Seltzer, editor of the *Cleveland Press*, sat down at his typewriter and wrote an editorial:

"What is wrong with us? . . .

"It is in the air we breathe. The things we do. The things we say. Our books. Our papers. Our theater. Our movies. Our radio and television. The way we behave. The interests we have. The values we fix.

"We have everything. We abound with all of the things that make us comfortable. We are, on the average, rich beyond the dreams of the kings of old. . . . Yet . . . something is not there that should be—something we once had. . . .

"Are we our own worst enemies? Should we fear what is happening among us more than what is happening elsewhere? . . .

"No one seems to know what to do to meet it. But everybody worries. . . ."

For days afterward Louis Seltzer's life was a madhouse. Phone calls and letters flooded his office. Strangers stopped him on the street to wring his hand and tell him he sure had hit it right. Forty-one publications throughout the United States reprinted the editorial. Louis Seltzer was not alone in yearning for something that was not there, for something that he was sure had once been there, for an older, simpler America without juvenile delinquents and genteel young men turning into Alger Hisses and five percenters and bewildering doctrines of limited warfare.

Shortly after noon on July 11, 1952, the TV cameras caught the banner of Minnesota waving frantically in Chicago's International Amphitheater. Senator Edward Thye was shouting hoarsely into the microphone: "Mr. Chairman, Mr. Chairman, Minnesota wishes to change—" Great roars went up in the hall, the organ broke into "The Minnesota Rouser," snake-dancers started down the aisles. "Minnesota," Thye finally got his words out, "wishes to change its vote to Eisenhower." It was done. After all the efforts of Robert Taft to get the nomination, after all the protestations of Dwight Eisenhower against running for political office, the first ballot had made the General the Republican candidate for the Presidency.

Eisenhower hurried off for a fisherman's vacation near Denver and the country settled back to ponder just what kind of a man had become the GOP standard-bearer. Rarely in American history had so little been known about the views of a major candidate for the Presidency. It was generally agreed that the General was no ecstatic admirer of New Dealism. In fact, while President of Columbia he had gotten off a number of decidedly rightish remarks like "If all that Americans want is security, they can go to prison." On the other hand, it was equally widely assumed that he was much more friendly than Taft to the Half-Century of Revolution in domestic affairs. After all, hadn't liberals pushed Eisenhower for the Democratic nomination in 1948, and was there not a persistent story that he had been offered the 1952 Democratic nomination by no less a Fair Dealer than Harry Truman? As for foreign policy, the General had occasionally made statements such as "If we had been less soft and weak, there might not have been a Korean War." Yet it was unchallengeable fact that all of the most important parts of his career—his leadership during World War II, his period as Army Chief of Staff after V-J, and the NATO command which he resigned to run for the Presidency—had been carried on in intimate association with the Roosevelt-Truman foreign policies.

Eisenhower returned from his fishing trip and was soon talking policy. "The great problem of America today," he said, "is to take that straight road down the middle. . . ." He was for the UN, the General declared. Concerning Korea: "I believe we can point out what appear to all of us, at least from our position, to be the really terrible blunders that led up to the Korean war. But I do not see how these conditions, having occurred and having been created, how you could stay out of the thing, I don't know." In domestic matters he was certain that Americans of all parties approved "social gains" and that the Republicans would administer social legislation more efficiently and honestly than the Democrats had done.

Reporters kept asking about McCarthyism and the attacks on the loyalty of Eisenhower's old superior, General Marshall, by McCarthy and by McCarthy's ally, Senator William Jenner of Indiana. Eisenhower said several times that he would back "all duly nominated Republicans." But he also made a number of statements like "I am not going to support anything that smacks to me of un-Americanism . . . and that includes any kind of thing that looks to me like unjust damaging of reputation." On another occasion the candidate added: "I have no patience with anyone who can find in his [Marshall's] record of service to this country anything to criticize. . . . Maybe he made some mistakes. I do not know about that."

Six weeks after the General was nominated, the nineteen newspapers of the ardently pro-Eisenhower Scripps-Howard chain ran a front-page editorial. "Ike," the editorial declared, "is running like a dry creek." The General's speeches were stamping him "just another me-too candidate" and that would ruin him. Eisenhower was not "coming out swinging"— for example, his comment that he did not know whether Marshall had made mistakes. "If Ike doesn't know, he had better find out. For that's one of the big issues of this campaign. Ask any mother, father or wife of a soldier now in Korea. . . . We still cling to the hope that . . . he will hit hard. If he doesn't, he might as well concede defeat."

Many leading Republican politicians were downcast. Big crowds were turning out for Eisenhower but they seemed more interested in the war hero than the candidate and the General's hazy, fumbling words sent them away unaroused. ("Now he's crossing the 38th platitude again," reporters would sigh.) Senator McCarthy and McCarthyite GOP Senators were taking indirect slaps at Eisenhower. In a number of states Taft men were sulking in their tents. "Until Bob Taft blows the bugle," Indiana's Republican Chairman Cale J. Holder declared, "a lot of us aren't going to fight in the army."

If the General was running like a dry creek, his opponent Adlai Stevenson was rippling along like a spring brook in sparkling sunlight. The country had known little about this one-term Illinois Governor and a good many people were having quite an experience. He would sit on a platform, a smallish man advancing in the hips and retreating at the hairline, so pained by overstatement that when a speaker described him as the "gra-a-a-yate Guv-er-nur" he fussed with his tie and gulped. Then he stood up, cocked his head thoughtfully, started to speak, and electricity came into the hall. "Let's talk sense to the American people," he would say in his taut, clear voice and suddenly people had the feeling that here was a man who had fought out the question within himself and was ready to state his conclusion with no muzziness whatsoever.

Eisenhower went before the American Legion, stumbled through the conventional statements, received ten interruptions of hand-clapping and affectionate cheers when he finished. Adlai Stevenson walked right into the Legionnaires—he kidded them about how he was sure they had been enjoying the many cultural opportunities of New York City. Then the voice took on its special charge. He told the Legion that McCarthy's kind of patriotism was a disgrace and that he was shocked at the attacks on George Marshall. He defined a veteran as a man who owed America something even more than he was owed anything by the nation. The American Legion, citadel of special privilege, hotbed of McCarthyism, loudly cheered Stevenson twenty-five times—especially loudly when he said that the healthy veteran had no claim to favoritism.

And then there was Stevenson on television. "To both the Republican and the Democrat," the well-known TV critic John Crosby wrote in September, "it's now fairly obvious that Gov. Adlai E. Stevenson is a television personality the like of which has not been seen ever before. The man is setting a pace that will not only be almost impossible for succeeding candidates to follow but one that will be pretty hard for Stevenson himself to maintain." The voice would ring like a perfectly cast bell as Stevenson declared: "When an American says he loves his country, he means not only that he loves the New England hills, the prairies glistening in the sun or the wide rising plains, the mountains and the seas. He means that he loves an inner air, an inner light in which freedom lives and in which a man can draw the breath of self-respect." The slightest smile would come and the wit crackled out—a wit that was part Will Rogers, part cocktail lounge. The Republican Party had "been devoid of new ideas for almost 70 years. . . . As to their platform, well, nobody can stand on a bushel of eels." The fact that Eisenhower was accepting so much of the New Deal-Fair Deal record? "I've been tempted to say that I was proud to stand on that record if only . . . the General would move over and make room for me." And the wit that was not merely wit, the cold, stinging indignation: "You can tell the size of a man by the size of the thing that makes him mad, and I hope that regardless of my own political advantage, the matter [of the accusations against Marshall] is not finally resolved by the counsel of those who favor what has been described as the middle-of-the-gutter approach."

Stevenson's platform wizardry was worrying and irritating Republicans. In mid-September the columnist, Stewart Alsop, arrived in Hartford, Connecticut, aboard the Stevenson train. He telephoned his younger brother John, an insurance executive who was head of the Republican Speaker's Bureau in the state, and asked how the campaign was going. When John replied that the situation looked good for the GOP, Stewart brought up the fact that many intelligent and highly educated people who had supported Eisenhower against Taft for the Republican nomination were now switching to Stevenson.

John Alsop bridled. He was a good Republican partisan and he was especially irritated because he knew that what his brother was saying was true. He was also sure, as he recalled later, that "while Stevenson was appealing and appealing strongly to people's minds, Eisenhower, as a man and as a figure, was appealing far more strongly to far more people's emotions." An irascible image of the kind of person who was switching to Stevenson popped into John Alsop's mind—"a large oval head, smooth, faceless, unemotional, but a little bit haughty and condescending."

"Sure," John Alsop remarked on the telephone, "all the eggheads are for Stevenson, but how many eggheads are there?"

To John Alsop, a Yale graduate and anything but an anti-intellectual, the word "egghead" implied no sweeping opprobrium. With the same attitude Stewart Alsop quoted his brother in his syndicated column. Unintentionally the Alsops were adding a new sneer to the American language. Within days the word "egghead" was rapidly spreading, was being applied to Stevenson and the whole group of intellectuals who so ardently supported him, and was taking on bitter connotations. Before long the novelist Louis Bromfield would write that "there has come a wonderful new expression to define a certain shady element of our population. Who conceived the expression, I do not know. . . . It seems to have arisen spontaneously from the people themselves. . . . [It means] a person of intellectual pretensions, often a professor or the protégé of a professor . . . superficial in approach to any problem . . . feminine . . . supercilious . . . surfeited with conceit . . . a doctrinaire supporter of middle-European socialism . . . a self-conscious prig . . . a bleeding heart." If Stevenson won the election, Bromfield concluded, "the eggheads will come back into power and off again we will go on the scenic railway of muddled economics, Socialism, Communism, crookedness and psychopathic instability."

General Eisenhower sat on an Indianapolis platform with the increasingly rabid McCarthyite Senator William Jenner, colored and physically winced as Jenner delivered his diatribe but spoke the words of endorsement for the Senator's reelection. McCarthyite trumpets began to sound for Dwight Eisenhower. Soon the General and Senator Taft had a conference in New York City. The Senator issued a statement saying that any differences between them on matters of foreign or domestic policy were mere "differences of degree," and the Taft men started to go to work.

From the beginning of the campaign the top Republican strategists had more or less agreed that there were three key issues. One day at a conference Senator Karl Mundt, co-chairman of the Speaker's Bureau, lightheartedly referred to the trio of points by the formula K_1C_2 and the phrase was becoming more and more common in GOP strategy letters and conversations. The campaign addresses that were being written for Eisenhower were also increasingly focusing on K_1C_2—the Korean War and charges of corruption and of Communism in the government.

Sharpening up the speeches entirely fitted the General's conception of how the campaign should be fought. At the early strategy conferences Eisenhower had expressed few positive opinions. He pointed out that he was an amateur in this business of politics, that he preferred for a while to listen and ask questions, but he did emphasize one consideration. He wanted to hold his fire at the beginning, to increase it as he went along, and to finish blazing away. Although Eisenhower made no reference to previous Republican campaigns, it was assumed by a number of the men present that he had in mind both the general nature of successful warfare, military or political, and the specific fact that Thomas Dewey's campaigns had closed weakly in 1944 and 1948.

The General's speeches were not only acquiring a more vigorous tone and clearer lines; they were being written with a greater adaptation to the man who was delivering them. Beginning a Midwestern swing, Eisenhower answered Stevenson's wit by K_1C_2 interwoven with a let's-not-be-funny theme. "It would be very, very fine," the General said, "if one could command new and amusing language, witticisms to bring you a chuckle. Frankly, I have no intention of trying to do so. The subjects of which we are speaking these days, my friends, are not those that seem to me to be amusing. . . . Is it amusing that we have stumbled into a war in Korea; that we have already lost in casualties 117,000 of our Americans killed and wounded; is it amusing that that war seems to be no closer to a real solution than ever; that we have no real plan for stopping it? . . . Is it funny when evidence was discovered that there are Communists in government and we get the cold comfort of the reply, 'red herring'?" And what was so uproarious about "the experts in shady and shoddy government operations . . . coming from their shadowy haunts" to corrupt the "very operations of democratic government?"

Things were picking up decidedly. The candidate, gathering ease from his successes, fumbled less and less and the famous smile glowed with confidence as well as friendliness. At the whistle stops in Minnesota, Iowa, Nebraska, and Missouri, there was a striking rapport between Eisenhower and the huge crowds that turned out for him. Correspondents who had followed the General in the early days of the campaign could hardly believe they were watching the same man.

Just as the Republican campaign was rolling, on September 18, 1952, the pro-Stevenson newspaper, the *New York Post*, came out with a full-page headline: SECRET NIXON FUND. A "millionaire's club" in California, the *Post* declared, had collected an eighteen-thousand-dollar "slush fund" for the "financial comfort" of the GOP Vice-Presidential candidate, Senator Richard Nixon. The story did not spread widely until the next day but then bedlam broke.

Democratic National Chairman Stephen Mitchell flatly demanded Nixon's resignation. Nixon cried out: "This is another typical smear by the same left wing elements which have fought me ever since I took part in the investigation which led to the conviction of Alger Hiss." The trustee of the fund, the Pasadena lawyer Dana Smith, was explaining away. The arrangement was set up when Nixon was elected to the Senate in 1950, Smith told reporters, and ended when he was nominated for the Vice-Presidency. Seventy-six contributors had put in an average of two hundred and fifty dollars and the largest contribution was a thousand dollars. Smith did all the disbursing of the money and it went exclusively for expenses connected with the Senator's "campaign against Communism and corruption in government. . . . The whole idea of the Nixon fund program was to enable Dick to do a selling job to the American people in behalf of private enterprise and integrity in government."

Everybody was commenting now and the hubbub was hardly pro-Nixon. The powerful Republican newspaper, the *New York Herald Tribune*, said the Senator should offer to withdraw. The independent but pro-Eisenhower *New York Times* editorialized that the contributors "showed poor judgment in making such a gift, and Senator Nixon had shown poor judgment in accepting it." A survey of almost one hundred representative papers, the majority of which were supporting the Republican ticket, showed disapproval of the Vice-Presidential candidate by a ratio of nearly two-to-one. The CIO was hammering hard on Nixon's voting record in the Senate, arguing that he had voted on taxes, housing, and rent control in a way that brought direct financial profit to a number of men among the donors.

Conflicting advice racked the Eisenhower campaign train and the General delayed taking any decisive action. As the days went by, the newspapermen on the train let it be known that they had voted forty-to-two against Nixon and that they believed preparations were under way for a "whitewash." Infuriated, Eisenhower called an off-the-record press conference. Pounding his fist into his palm, he told the newsmen: "I don't care if you fellows are forty-to-two against me, but I'm taking my time on this. Nothing's decided, contrary to your idea that this is all a setup for a whitewash of Nixon. Nixon has got to be as clean as a hound's tooth."

Then, more calmly, the General went on to explain his attitude. He had been enthusiastically for Nixon, he said, because of his age and because he considered him the earnest, upright young man of the type that America needed. He still had faith in his integrity. However, he felt that in a crusade of the kind that he was conducting—a crusade against unethical as well as illegal practices in government—he had to criticize his dearest friend as quickly as his enemy if the friend fell short of the most exacting standards. The whole matter of the fund would be subjected to the most careful scrutiny, Eisenhower concluded.

Nixon, campaigning on the West Coast, was near explosion. He was sure he had done nothing wrong. He was miffed at Eisenhower's failure to give him all-out support and he was staggered by blows like that of the *New York Herald Tribune*. By the time his train pulled into Portland, he was tight-lipped and snappish. Finally, after frantic telephone calls between Eisenhower's train, Nixon's train, and leading GOP figures all over the country, a decision was made. On the evening of September 23 Nixon would go on coast-to-coast radio and television to answer the charges. An offer of commercial sponsorship was considered but quickly dismissed; the Republican National Committee paid the seventy-five-thousand-dollar bill. Most of the day before the telecast Nixon spent alone, filling legal-sized sheets with notes. Later, speaking before an advertising men's luncheon in New York, he recalled September 23 and remarked that "no TV performance takes such careful preparation as an off-the-cuff talk."

An estimated fifty-five million Americans watched or listened to the candidate fighting for his political life. Some of the speech was an argument that none of the eighteen thousand dollars benefited Nixon personally, that it was all used for "this one message, of exposing this Administration, the Communism in it, the corruption in it." Other parts of the talk were straight political argument. But most of the thirty minutes was a story of a family, told in a tone of utter earnestness by an ordinary-looking young man in a none-too-fashionable suit. He grew up in the "modest circumstances" provided by his father's grocery store in East Whittier, California, Nixon said. Then came "the best thing that ever happened to me. I married Pat, who is sitting over here." The war years were not "particularly unusual. . . . I went to the South Pacific. I guess

I'm entitled to a couple of stars . . . but I was just there when the bombs were falling."

"Like most young couples," the Nixons accumulated their possessions and their debts—the 1950 Oldsmobile car, the mortgage on the house, the $4,000 in life insurance plus his GI policy. Like most doting parents, Nixon kept coming back to his two girls, Patricia and Julia, and he told about a gift which a supporter had sent to "our two youngsters. . . . Do you know what it was? It was a little cocker spaniel dog in a crate that he'd sent all the way from Texas, black and white, spotted, and our little girl, Trisha, the six-year-old, named it Checkers. And you know the kids, like all kids, love the dog, and I just want to say this right now that regardless of what they say about it, we're going to keep it." It all wasn't very much, the possessions of the Nixons, the Senator summarized, "but Pat and I have the satisfaction that every dime that we've got is honestly ours. I should say this—that Pat doesn't have a mink coat, but she does have a respectable Republican cloth coat, and I always tell her that she'd look good in anything.

"And now, finally, I know that you wonder whether or not I am going to stay on the Republican ticket or resign. Let me say this—I don't believe that I ought to quit, because I'm not a quitter. And incidentally, Pat's not a quitter. After all, her name was Patricia Ryan and she was born on St. Patrick's Day, and you know the Irish never quit.

"But the decision, my friends, is not mine. . . . Wire and write the Republican National Committee whether you think I should stay on or whether I should get off, and whatever their decision is, I will abide by it.

"But just let me say this last word—regardless of what happens, I'm going to continue this fight. I'm going to campaign up and down America until we drive the crooks and the Communists and those that defend them out of Washington. And remember, folks, Eisenhower is a great man. Believe me. He's a great man. And a vote for Eisenhower is a vote for what's good for America."

Dwight and Mamie Eisenhower watched the tele-cast sitting in the manager's office at the Cleveland Public Auditorium, where the General was scheduled to speak that night. At the conclusion Mrs. Eisenhower was weeping and the General was obviously trying to control his emotions. Outside in the auditorium Representative George Bender of Ohio was leading wild demonstrations in favor of Nixon.

Eisenhower's press secretary James Hagerty turned to his boss. "General," he said, "you'll have to throw your speech away. Those people out there want to hear about Nixon."

Eisenhower scribbled notes for a new speech and thirty minutes later he was before the crowd. "I have been a warrior and I like courage," the General began. "I have seen many brave men in tough situations. I have never seen any come through in better fashion than Senator Nixon did tonight." But then he added that he needed more than "a single presentation" and that he was asking Nixon to meet him in Wheeling, West Virginia.

Nixon was irritated again. "What more can I explain?" he snapped but he took off for Wheeling. Meanwhile the switchboards of radio and television stations were hopelessly jammed. Where do I send a wire supporting Nixon? the endless voices wanted to know. (Later Nixon said that he had remembered to get into his speech everything he wanted to say except the address of the Republican National Committee.) Wires and letters were addressed to scores of places—to Eisenhower's and Nixon's campaign trains, to Dana Smith, to local Republican committees, to "Richard Nixon" and "Dwight Eisenhower, U.S.A." Western Union officials said that they had never handled as many wires as they did that night. It was a month before the Republican National Committee, using a hundred volunteers, could get the mail opened and sorted. The sentiment was about three hundred and fifty to one in Nixon's favor and enough contributions poured in—mostly in amounts of one dollar or less—to pay sixty thousand dollars of the seventy-five-thousand-dollar cost of the telecast.

As Eisenhower's train moved toward Wheeling, every mention of the Vice-Presidential candidate had the crowds whooping with approval. So many stacks of pro-Nixon telegrams kept being brought aboard that the General pleaded for people to stop wiring. The further the train traveled, the more relaxed Eisenhower became, the more he talked in a folksy vernacular, the more he discussed "Dick Nixon."

The General drove nine miles to the hilltop field at Wheeling and boarded the plane before the Senator could descend. "Boy, am I glad to see you," Eisenhower greeted Nixon.

The Senator had expected to have to seek out Eisenhower in town and he was startled. "You didn't need to come out here," he said.

"Why, you're my boy," Eisenhower replied, putting his arm warmly around Nixon.

The two men talked for six minutes in the plane and then went off to the waiting crowd at Wheeling Stadium. With his first words Eisenhower ended the debate whether Nixon was to continue as the GOP Vice-Presidential candidate. "He is not only completely vindicated as a man of honor but as far as I am concerned he stands higher than ever before."

Democrats cried outrage. Was six minutes of conversation on a plane the careful scrutiny Eisenhower was going to insist upon? Was Nixon's TV speech to settle the matter despite the fact that he had not explained where he got the money for a twenty-thousand-dollar down payment on a home in Washington and another considerable down payment on a house in East Whittier, California? Was this "incredible corn," to use the phrase of the pro-Stevenson *St. Louis Post-Dispatch*, to be accepted as serious political discussion? Even assuming that Nixon had spent none of the money on himself, what about the ethics of taking funds which could easily influence the way a Senator voted? The Stevenson forces cried out and their voices were lost. The whole issue was confused because shortly before Nixon's TV address, the fact was revealed that Stevenson had used money left over from his gubernatorial campaign to augment the salaries of some state employees—a quite different kind of fund, the Democrats insisted, but one which easily sounded the same in the furor. In larger measure the anti-Nixon indignation was swept aside because the Senator had touched a vital nerve.

For two decades Democratic politicians had been benefiting by an emotional identification with the common man as he appeared in the 1930's—the common man worrying over enough food to eat or a decent suit to wear. Nixon, consciously or unconsciously, was identifying himself with the most common American of the 1950's—the man with quite enough food and an entirely respectable suit but worrying over the next step up, a step like Nixon's purchase of an expensive home with a large mortgage hanging over him. And Nixon spoke of this different problem with the same little-man psychology that had been so moving when the little man was worried not about thousands owed to the bank but the week's grocery bill.

Robert Ruark, the Scripps-Howard columnist, caught a good deal of the power of the Nixon performance when he wrote: "Dick Nixon stripped himself naked for all the world to see, and he brought the missus and the kids and the dog and his war record into the act. . . . The sophisticates . . . sneer . . [but] this came closer to humanizing the Republican party than anything that has happened in my memory. Mr. Thomas Dewey never seemed to share much of the problems of the ordinary Joe. Even the immensely

popular Gen. Eisenhower has not been as you and I.
. . . Bob Taft had a President for a father, and
money of his own. Gen. MacArthur is nearly a deity.
. . . Tuesday night the nation saw a little man,
squirming his way out of a dilemma, and laying bare
his most-private hopes, fears and liabilities. This time
the common man was a Republican, for a change. . . .
Dick Nixon . . . has suddenly placed the burden of
old-style Republican aloofness on the Democrats."

Eisenhower and Nixon—it was now genuinely Eisenhower and Nixon for the Vice-Presidential candidate was drawing big crowds—swung back on their
campaign tours. The pattern of their campaign took
final shape. The gains to ordinary men from the Half-
Century of Revolution in domestic affairs would be
preserved and "extended where wise." But these matters and everything else were to be handled in the
"American style"—without Communism, corruption,
or Korea. Further ways were found of stressing Korea
and Communism. More and more directly Eisenhower accused the Administration of softness toward
Communists in the government. ("We have seen this
sort of thing go on and on until my running mate,
Dick Nixon, grabbed a police whistle and stopped
it.") The General swung into Wisconsin, conferred
with McCarthy, and cut from his speech sentences
praising General Marshall. McCarthy and Nixon went
on TV to associate the danger of Communism with
Stevenson. McCarthy said "Alger—" then stopped and
smirked—"I mean Adlai"—was "an out-and-out pro-
Communist." Nixon declared that the Democratic
candidate had "failed to recognize the threat."

In the Hotel Commodore in New York City, Emmet John Hughes, a *Time-Life* editor, was working
away on speeches for Eisenhower. Hughes had an
idea: The General should promise to go to Korea
when elected. Hughes wrote the idea into a draft of a
speech and Eisenhower liked it. Speaking in Detroit,
the candidate denounced the "false answer . . . that

nothing can be done to speed a secure peace. . . . I shall go to Korea." The crowd liked the idea too. It stood up and cheered in a way few American political meetings have ever done. Democratic strategists did not pretend that this speech, with its implication of a quick end to the war, had not hurt and hurt badly.

Specific developments, spectacular developments— but above and beyond these an undefined and almost indefinable image of the Republican ticket was emerging. Richard Nixon, saying "Gee, this is a great country" and going on talking about "my darling wife Pat . . . my little girls," was helping to create the impression, but fundamentally it was emerging from the figure of the sixty-one-year-old General making his first foray into politics. Dwight Eisenhower was the simple American. He used the phrase *status quo* and quickly apologized: " 'Course, I'm not supposed to be the educated candidate." He was the rugged American. The Democrats were firing "red hot salvos" but he was not disturbed because "I've been shot at by real artillerists." He was the God-fearing American. "The issue always and at bottom is spiritual." He was the American free of bewildering ideology who only wanted it said of his Presidency: " 'He has been fair. He has been my friend.' " Somehow everything he said and did created more and more the image of Dwight Eisenhower of Abilene, Kansas, honest and decent and uncomplicated in a way that America had been before the complexities of social revolution at home and of Communist revolutions abroad.

By eleven p.m. on Election Night it was all over. Eisenhower was on his way to a landslide and to the most genuinely national victory since another candidate, the Franklin Roosevelt of 1936, spoke the mood of another generation. Thirty-nine states were moving into the Republican column, only nine into the Democratic line; more than six million popular votes were separating the two candidates. Eisenhower was th

first Republican candidate since 1928 to break the
Solid South. He captured large segments of groups
that had been Democratic for years—Catholics, organized workers, and young voters. He ran rampant in the
areas which most surely characterized the America of
1952, the little white houses of suburbia.

At 11.32 p.m. Adlai Stevenson left the Governor's
mansion in Springfield to read his concession statement
at Democratic headquarters in the Leland Hotel. He
was trying hard to appear jaunty and chipper. His
smile was steady; when he arrived at the hotel, he saw
a newspaperman he knew and gave him an owlish
wink. Stevenson read his concession statement, a generous one, with perfect control and took pains to remind
his followers: "It is traditionally American to fight
hard before an election. It is equally traditional to close
ranks as soon as the people have spoken." Then, suddenly, all the jauntiness was gone. "Someone asked
me, as I came in, down on the street, how I felt, and I
was reminded of a story that a fellow-townsman of
ours used to tell—Abraham Lincoln. They asked him
how he felt once after an unsuccessful election. He said
he felt like a little boy who had stubbed his toe in the
dark. He said that he was too old to cry, but it hurt too
much to laugh." In university towns, among writers,
wherever men and women had been captivated by the
lilt of Adlai Stevenson, people stared at each other
blankly and some wept unabashedly. "It's not just that
a great man has been defeated," Val Jamison, a professor at the University of Utah, expressed the feeling.
"It's that a whole era is ended, is totally repudiated, a
whole era of brains and literacy and exciting thinking."

At Republican headquarters in the Hotel Commodore of New York City, the modish gowns and the
well-tailored suits swirled around as thousands joined
Fred Waring in singing the "Battle Hymn of the Republic," "God Bless America," and "Where Oh Where
but in America Can You Sing True Freedom's

Song?" Throughout the country many a member of upper-income America celebrated the end of twenty hateful years.

The jubilant better neighborhoods and the depressed intellectual groups were not alone in their sense of a new era. The day after the election a Harrisburg reporter set out to discover how ordinary Americans were reacting to the election. The first person he talked to was Mrs. Edith Wilson, wife of a mechanic at a Texaco garage. When the reporter put his question to Mrs. Wilson, she paused and shifted her bundles uneasily. Then she said slowly: "I don't want to be silly or anything. But you know it's so big and wonderful— it's like, well, it's like America has come home."

XI

No Fear of Conservatism

SHORTLY AFTER the election Dwight Eisenhower landed in Korea, took an intense, worried look at the situation, flew back with his advisers to Guam. There they shifted to the U.S.S. *Helena* and at Wake Island the cruiser paused to take on more aides who had flown from the United States. The *Helena* laid a course for Pearl Harbor, three days away, and the men spent the respite on the Pacific getting acquainted with each other and talking plans.

Eisenhower began one session with a statement of some of his own general ideas. He said that he thought of the office of the Presidency not as Roosevelt and Truman had done but according to an older conception—the Executive as one of three equal branches of the government, who was not to try to do too much leading. It was his profound conviction, he went on, that the 156 million citizens of the United States could best live their lives and improve their lot without controls from above. The government's role in domestic affairs was to assure fair play, not to attempt to direct the national economic life. In only one area did the government have a prime responsibility. By means of its handling of the budget and its credit policies, it should insure a sound and stable dollar. The President-elect repeatedly emphasized his fear of inflation, citing his European experiences to back up his point.

Like Taft, Eisenhower closely connected his economic thinking and his ideas about national defense. American power, he said, rested on two pillars—actual fighting strength and a flourishing industry and agriculture. The United States had to have powerful armed forces, but a prodigal outlay of money on military equipment or tremendous expenditures for other purposes would generate more inflation and thus disastrously weaken the country.

When the talk turned to foreign affairs, the incoming Secretary of State, John Foster Dulles, usually took the lead. Dulles especially stressed one point. All the great wars of modern history, he was sure, were started by national leaders who miscalculated and thought they could get away with something that other nations actually were not willing to tolerate. The North Korean invasion in particular had been undertaken as a result of Acheson's speech concerning America's defense perimeter in Asia. Dulles's implications for the present were unmistakable. The Communist nations should be told the consequences if they did certain things—and the consequences should be serious.

The President-elect, accustomed to the crispness of military briefings, sometimes showed impatience at Dulles's long pauses and somewhat oracular manner. But for the most part Eisenhower listened approvingly. Beneath everything Dulles was saying ran a theme quite congenial to the President-elect. The United States, as Dulles would soon express the attitude in a speech, should operate on the three principles which were "in accord with what used to be the great American traditional foreign policy . . . openness, simplicity, and righteousness." A quest for the traditional, for what they were sure was the sounder, the more American way of doing things—here was the point of view that united Eisenhower and his chief aides.

The President-elect became the President, the attitudes of the Administration began to be spoken out, and millions rejoiced. The Rev. Mr. James Miller of Los Angeles offered up a prayer which began: "Now that virtue has been restored to high places. . . ." The DAR and assorted citizens, having worried for years whether the gold at Fort Knox was safe under the free-spending Democrats, soon managed to get it counted. (When the count of the nation's assets was over and it was found that the United States did have the $30,442,415,581.70 it was supposed to have except for ten dollars which the ex-Treasurer of the United States, Mrs. Georgia Clark, said—some thought Mrs. Clark was being sarcastic—she would send a check to cover.) Of serious import, a large part of the country's businessmen and those with business attitudes, who for twenty long years had felt themselves pushed aside, believed that they and their ideas would now return to their rightful place.

They looked at the new Cabinet and they winced at the Secretary of Labor, who was none other than Martin Durkin, the pro-Stevenson, anti-Taft-Hartley president of the United Association of Journeymen Plumbers and Steamfitters. But for the most part the business world could not have been more pleased. "Eight millionaires and a plumber," "T.R.B." wise-cracked in the *New Republic* and the remark, whatever its inaccuracies, did catch the board-of-directors' tone of the group of Presidential advisers. Even before the administration formally began, Charles Wilson, the president of General Motors who was slated to be Secretary of Defense, got off a cardinal point of the businessman's traditional credo before the Senate Armed Forces Committee. For years, Wilson said, he had assumed that "what was good for our country was good for General Motors, and vice versa." The phrase immediately made its way across the United States, usually in the simplified and somewhat distorted form of "what's good for General Motors is good for the country." Democrats cried I-told-you-so. (In his first major speech after the election Stevenson smiled mischievously and remarked: "While the New Dealers have all left Washington to make way for the car dealers, I hasten to say that I, for one, do not believe the story that the general welfare has become a subsidiary of General Motors.") As for Wilson, he was puzzled at the uproar. After all, was he not speaking precisely the feeling of generations of Americans who had labored to build grocery stores or corporations in the firm belief that what was good for their businesses was good for America, the land of business?

Things not only sounded different; they were quite different in fact. From the beginning of Eisenhower's term until Robert Taft's death in July 1953, the Senator from Ohio was an important part of the Administration, advising the President and working closely with him. Before and after Taft's death, the influence of a Taft Republican, George Humphrey, was steadily mounting in the Presidential circle.

Shortly after Humphrey entered the Cabinet as Secretary of the Treasury, a reporter asked whether he had read Ernest Hemingway's *The Old Man and the Sea*. The Secretary replied: "Why would anybody be interested in some old man who was a failure and never amounted to anything anyway?" Humphrey's father, a prosperous lawyer of Saginaw, Michigan, had permitted no one in his home to forget the importance of material success. The mother, when she found it absolutely necessary to use the word, had an unbreakable rule to spell Franklin Roosevelt's name with a small *r*. From boyhood, it was the material, the pecuniary drive, the practical that appealed to George Humphrey. Starting out as a lawyer in Saginaw, he soon realized, as he remarked later, that "in the law business you put your heart and soul into a client. When you finished with his trouble, then you went through it again with the next client. All you could build in the law business was a personal reputation. I was much more interested in building something you could see or touch." In 1918 he turned to the highly touchable and seeable; he went to Cleveland as general counsel for M. A. Hanna and Co., the ore house in which Mark Hanna had been a leading partner. Year after year Humphrey proved his business prowess—pulling the Hanna firm out of a two million dollar deficit, rising to its presidency, expanding it to a giant holding company with subsidiaries in everything from steel-making to plastics and banking. And year after year George Humphrey personally became more the businessman's businessman—a pleasant, vigorous figure, working hard and playing hard, with a mind of impressive clarity, a passion for facts, and an assumption that New Dealism was spending the country into bankruptcy and planning it into chaos.

Secretary of the Treasury Humphrey told President Eisenhower he had only one request. "When anyone talks to you about money, will you ask him if he has seen George?" People saw George and the new Administration hurried toward the Taftite essentials in domestic affairs. The hiring of government exployees was drastically curbed; the number of federal construction projects was cut down. The wage and price controls imposed in the course of the Korean War were abolished. Moves were made toward putting into effect tax, budget, public-resources, and power policies long sought by corporate America. One of the first pieces of legislation urged by the Administration concerned a matter which had become something of a symbol of the clash between New Dealish and pro-business thinking. The Administration called for and Congress passed a bill turning over to state jurisdiction a large part of the tidelands oil.

In March the new order of things was expressed in a form so extreme that it amounted to a caricature. The Secretary of Commerce, the industrialist Sinclair Weeks, had come to Washington anxious, as he expressed it, "to create a 'business climate' in the nation's economy." On March 31 the Department announced the resignation "by request" of Dr. Allen Astin, head of the National Bureau of Standards. When Secretary Weeks testified before the Senate Small Business Committee it became clear that Astin's dismissal was involved with a Bureau of Standards report. The laboratory tests of the Bureau showed results unsatisfactory to Jess Ritchie, the manufacturer of a battery additive.

Secretary Weeks was profoundly dissatisfied with the Bureau, he told the Senate Committee, because of its lack of awareness of "the business point of view." He intended to "get the best brains I can find to examine into the functions and objectives of the Bureau of Standards and re-evaluate them in relation to the American business community." One question the Secretary would raise was whether any product should be subjected to government approval before going on the market. "As a practical man I do not see why a product should be denied an opportunity in the market place." In the ensuing furor Weeks backed down and Astin was re-employed. But a point of view had been pictured, with strokes that a Herblock would not care to improve upon.

In the Department of Agriculture the new Secretary, Ezra Taft Benson, his plain face and plain clothes contrasting incongruously with his huge, glossy office, was working away on a farm program. Benson is a distant blood relative of Robert Taft and ideologically he is a brother. One of the Twelve Apostles, the ruling group of the Mormon Church, he has all of the Mormon's zeal for self-reliance and a commensurate skepticism of federally subsidized agriculture. The President not only agreed with Benson's general attitude; he felt peculiarly close to his Secretary of Agriculture because the two men shared a strong religious bent and a tendency to equate the "spiritual" side of democracy with an individualistic economy. Benson set out to put farm products back in the free market as quickly as possible. In late 1953 his program was emerging—the legislation which was passed by Congress in August 1954. The bill took a decided step toward a free market by replacing rigid price supports with flexible supports. Benson fought hard to provide a price flexibility on all products of between 75 and 90 per cent of parity. Congress decreed that the range should be only 82½ to 90 per cent on the basic commodities—cotton, corn, wheat, rice, peanuts, and tobacco. But in the case of other products, the level of support was at the Secretary's discretion.

Six months after he took office Eisenhower discussed the direction and achievements of his Administration in several South Dakota speeches. The Republicans, he declared, had "instituted what amounts almost to a revolution in the Federal Government as we have known it in our time, trying to make it smaller rather than bigger and finding things it can stop doing instead of seeking new things for it to do." This, he emphasized, was a matter of no small import because "in the last twenty years creeping socialism has been striking in the United States." The fault was not exclusively that of "a few long-haired academic men in Washington." In part it came because some Americans had "not been quick enough to resent socialism if we thought it would benefit us." The next week Eisenhower was pressed at his press conference to give an example of "creeping socialism" and he named TVA. Clarence Manion, chairman of Eisenhower's Commission on Inter-Governmental Relations, promptly advocated the sale of TVA to private utility companies. Did he agree? the President was asked by reporters. Eisenhower replied that his views were well known—he believed in the maximum of free enterprise. But he did not know whether TVA could be sold without bringing about circumstances that would wreck it.

Just as the Administration was getting fully under way headlines reported the physicians' bulletins.

March 4, 1953: STALIN GRAVELY ILL AFTER STROKE. March 5: STALIN SINKING: LEECHES APPLIED. March 6: STALIN DEAD. Within days the new premier, Georgi Malenkov, was making speeches about solving all "troublesome and unresolved questions . . . by peaceful negotiations." With a rush of hope the American public asked: Did the end of the tough old dictator mean the end of the Korean War?

During his postelection trip to Korea, Eisenhower had become convinced that continuation of the stalemate was intolerable. The one major remaining issue between the UN and the Communist negotiators was whether the more than 22,000 North Korean and Chinese prisoners of the UN who said they did not want to go home would be forced to return. Nothing had seemed to be able to break this deadlock, including a proposal made to the UN by India in November, 1952. Prisoners unwilling to be repatriated, New Delhi urged, should be supervised by a commission made up of Poland and Czechoslovakia, both Communist, and Sweden and Switzerland, both neutral, and a fifth nation to be named. The mildest comment any Communist leader made about the plan at the time was Andrei Vishinsky's "unacceptable, unsuitable, unbelievable." Eisenhower agreed with Dulles that the Communists should be told that the new American policy was: Peace or else. The Administration would continue to negotiate sincerely. But if the stalemate went on, the United States would fight to win, and this meant air attacks beyond the Yalu and the tactical use of atomic arms. The Secretary of State undertook to see to it that the Chinese thoroughly understood the American position. He explained it personally to Prime Minister Nehru of India—a man with decidedly good communication lines to Peiping.

In 1956 Dulles expressed his belief that the American threats broke the deadlock in the truce negotiations. Other experts have argued that the prime difference was the willingness of the new Soviet regime to permit an armistice. Indian spokesmen have pointed to their proposal, maintaining that it provided a sensible solution which the Communists ultimately recognized as sensible. Whatever the reason or reasons, things happened in early 1953.

On February 22 the UN commander, General Mark Clark, had written the Communists another in a long series of letters urging that something be done about exchanging sick and wounded prisoners. He did not receive a reply until March 28 but he was startled at its contents. The Communists were not only ready to arrange such an exchange; they wanted to discuss "the smooth settlement of the entire question of prisoners of war." Truce negotiations which had been given up since the fall were resumed, the sick and the wounded were exchanged, and the conferences moved toward peace. By June 17 a settlement seemed close.

But the postwar remained the postwar, endlessly productive of jarring news. That June 17 the Associated Press carried eighteen special bulletins in the day period, sixteen in the night report, and for one twenty minute period news came in so fast that nothing was put on the trunk wire except flashes. East Berlin, restive after Stalin's death, broke into open revolt. Supreme Court Justice William Douglas stayed the execution of the convicted atom spies, the Rosenbergs. Near Tokyo a C-124 crashed in the worst air tragedy up to that time, killing 129 soldiers and airmen. And 78-year-old Syngman Rhee, determined that there should be no truce except one which united Korea under him, capped all the bulletins with an act of utter defiance.

At 2 a.m., June 18, Dulles was awakened by the ringing of a telephone in the bedroom of his Washington home. An officer at the State Department was calling to say that Rhee's soldiers were cutting through the wire compounds and freeing thousands of North Korean and Chinese prisoners. Dulles listened quietly, grunting an occasional "yow" and trying to shake off the sleep. As he reached over to switch on the light, he broke through the heaviness and realized that the United States was close to major fighting, perhaps on the verge of a nuclear World War III. Wouldn't the Communists now walk out of the peace conference, bringing into effect the drastic measures which he and Eisenhower had agreed upon? "This is as critical as June, 1950," the Secretary believed.

Dulles picked up his direct phone to the White House and had the President awakened. Both men were ready to go ahead. The bombing targets beyond the Yalu had already been carefully picked so as to limit them to areas of indisputable military importance.

But the Communists really wanted a truce. Their representatives stormed and they sulked but they went right on negotiating. Soon the final papers were ready. The military demarcation line was fixed near the 38th parallel. (South Korea gained 2,350 square miles of North Korean territory and North Korea added 850 square miles south of the 38th parallel.) The forced repatriation issue was settled approximately along the lines of the Indian proposal. During the months of bitter negotiations each side had made important concessions. The UN had not gained acceptance of an inspection system trustworthy enough to make sure that preparations for another attack did not go ahead in North Korea. The Communists, although they won face-saving amendments to the original Indian proposal, were denied forced repatriation.

Promptly at 10 a.m. on Monday, July 28 (it was 9 p.m. Sunday, July 27 in Washington) the two senior negotiators entered the little truce building at Panmunjom—the mild-mannered General William K. Harrison, tieless and without decorations, and the bristling North Korean, General Nam Il, sweltering in a heavy tunic sagging with gold medals. Aides carried back and forth nine copies of the main documents (three each in English, Chinese, and Korean) and the two men sat at separate tables, silently writing their signatures. By orders of Syngman Rhee, no South Korean signed. When Harrison and Nam Il had finished, they rose and departed without a handshake or a word.

After thirty-seven months and two days the war that was never officially a war, which had cost America alone 25,000 dead, 115,000 other casualties, and twenty-two billion dollars, was over. The UN and the U.S. had stopped aggression; they had neither won nor lost the war. They had managed to arrange a truce; the truce was as flimsy as the bitterness of Syngman Rhee or the plans of the Communists might make it. They had established emphatically before the world that Communist advances could be resisted. They had not necessarily contributed to anti-Communist feeling in pivotal Asia.

Along the front lines UN soldiers heard the news broadcast in nine languages, smiled and yelled a bit but mostly stood around talking quietly. Once in a while somebody would grin and say something like: "Don't forget where you put your gun. You'll need it next week." General Mark Clark told reporters: "I cannot find it in me to exult at this hour." Foreign correspondent Dwight Martin cabled back that many top U.S. military men in Korea were perfectly aware of the arguments that freedom had been defended and aggression repelled but took little joy in the truce. "They all seem concerned," he added, "that some day they will be called on to explain why they signed the present armistice. Several I've talked to specifically think in terms of investigating committees demanding to know whether it is a fact that they sold out Korea. They frankly admit that complex justifications and explanations, currently acceptable, may look pretty lame in a year or so."

The evening of the armistice President Eisenhower appeared on television solemn-faced. He spoke of his relief that the killing had been stopped but he quickly added that what had been gained was "an armistice on a single battleground, not peace in the world. We may not now relax our guard nor cease our quest." Here and there in the United States celebrations started up and quickly petered out. In Philadelphia a soldier who had already managed quite an evening tried to keep things going. He went up to a man standing on the corner. "Wonerful, ishn't it? Jus' plain dern wonerful."

The man hailed his cab and paused for a moment. "I don't know whether it's wonderful, son. But anyhow it's over."

The removal of the specific pressures of the Korean War permitted the Administration to develop more rapidly its general defense and foreign policies. In part they sprang from a strategic calculation—that there was no longer any one year in which the danger of war was greatest but that policies must be laid down to take care of a number of years, any one of which might be critical. But more basically the change came from an impatience at the Democrats' dependence on the policy of containment, with its huge year-after-year expenditures for armament and for economic aid to other countries, its tremendous concern for the opinion of allies, and its assumption of the necessity for adjustment to a world-wide social revolution that would probably go on for decades. The Republican policies were heavily influenced by the Taftite insistence on economy and the Taftite skepticism that talk of adjusting to a world social revolution was just so much more global New Dealism.

The basic decisions were made in late 1953 and summarized in a speech which Secretary of State Dulles delivered before the Council on Foreign Relations on January 12, 1954. The Administration, the Secretary said, was aiming for "a maximum deterrent" of aggression at "a bearable cost." To achieve this, it was going to de-emphasize "local defense" and rely more on "the deterrent of massive retaliatory power . . . a great capacity to retaliate, instantly, by means and at times of our own choosing." Instant retaliation by means and at times of America's own choosing—the United States was not going to be too concerned about the attitude of allies. Less dependence on local defense —the United States was going to cut down expensive ground forces and rely more on air power and atomic weapons.

In line with the policy of massive retaliation the Administration took what Admiral Arthur Radford, chairman of the Joint Chiefs of Staff, called a "New Look" at the defense budget. It trimmed $2,300,000,-000 in expenditures and $5,247,000,000 in defense-spending authority from the Truman proposals for the fiscal year 1954. At the same time the Administration was taking a new and skeptical look at the whole policy of economic aid abroad. A raft of statements came from officials which gave credence to the report that Eisenhower would propose cutting off all economic aid by June 30, 1956.

The new defense and foreign policies, particularly the massive retaliation speech, provoked strong and sustained opposition. Adlai Stevenson, dropping his banter, solemnly charged that the Administration was putting dollars before defense and threatening the unity of the Western world. Within the Administration itself General Matthew Ridgway, a member of the Joint Chiefs of Staff, fought the whole trend so hard that he brought about some amendments to the plans for cutting the ground forces. But for the most part the Administration stood its ground and with a way of arguing that emphasized the heart of its policies.

At the heart was restlessness, the restlessness of generations of Americans at having to deal with a strange and unruly world, a restlessness enormously magnified by the exasperations and fears of the post-World War II period. The massive retaliation speech was essentially another declaration of peace-or-else; it probably marked, as the strongly pro-Eisenhower historian

Merlo Pusey has commented, "the zenith of the cold war." A dozen speeches implied that the United States was not willing to settle for containing Communism. We were going to be "positive," the President said. He had not given up his policy of "liberation," Dulles added. Cantankerous allies as well as Communists were not to be dallied with indefinitely. The French, the Secretary of State made plain, could bring about "an agonizing reappraisal of basic United States policy" if they did not do as America wanted and join the European Defense Community. And always there was the traditional American assumption that only a few evil leaders stood in the way of a world-wide acceptance of American values and hence of peace.

"What we need to do," Dulles declared, "is to recapture the kind of crusading spirit of the early days of the Republic when we were certain that we had something better than anyone else and we knew the rest of the world needed it and wanted it and that we were going to carry it around the world."

On Capitol Hill Senator Joseph McCarthy was asked his judgment of the new Administration and he smiled loftily. The Administration's record on anti-Communism, he said, was "fair."

Circumstances were hardly such as to curb the arrogance of Joseph McCarthy. The Republican capture of the Senate in 1952 had made him for the first time the chairman of his own committee—the powerful Committee on Government Operations—and he also headed its formidable subcommittee, the Permanent Subcommittee on Investigations. With a handful of exceptions the whole Senate treated him with respect or at least with care. He seemed to have proved what a politician respects most—an awesome ability to affect votes. He himself had been re-elected in 1952 by a majority of more than 140,000. No less than eight of the men in the Senate—six who had been elected in 1952—were thought to owe their seats largely to his campaigning. Around the country his name had an increasing potency. A belligerent if small pro-McCarthy faction was making itself heard even among the group which had shown the most solid bloc resistance to him, the intellectuals of the United States.

Probably most important of all, the man in the White House had a conception of his role which very specifically ruled out openly battling McCarthy. Eisenhower not only wanted to respect the Constitutional division between the Executive and legislative divisions. He was keenly aware that he was the head of a divided party and anxious to unite it along the lines of his own thinking. Whatever the President's own tendencies toward the right, his views were quite different from those of the right-wingers, who for the most part were bitter anti-New Dealers, all-out isolationists with respect to Europe, all-out interventionists with respect to Asia, and enthusiasts for the kind of anti-Communism represented by McCarthy. These men followed the President reluctantly when they followed him at all and Eisenhower wanted to do nothing to increase the friction. It was the President's "passion," his aide C. D. Jackson remarked, "not to offend anyone in Congress" and this attitude soon permeated most of his subordinates.

Month after month McCarthy went to further extremes and month after month the Administration sidestepped, looked the other way, or actually followed his bidding. At the beginning of the Administration McCarthy declared that he believed there were still Communists in the State Department and that Dulles could go a long way toward rooting them out by naming a good security officer. The Secretary named a good security officer—Scott McLeod, widely assumed to be a McCarthy disciple. March 1953 and the Senator announced that he had negotiated with Greek shipowners to stop trading at Soviet and satellite ports. Director of Mutual Security Harold Stassen angrily pointed out that this was a flagrant Senatorial inter-

ference with the functions of the Executive Branch
and that by negotiating with a small group "you are
in effect undermining and are harmful to our objective" of stopping the general trade with the Communists. Immediately a mollifying statement came from
Frank Nash, Assistant Secretary of Defense for international affairs, and Secretary of State Dulles and Mc-
Carthy got together for a congenial lunch. At his press
conference, the President did the final smoothing over
by suggesting that both McCarthy and Stassen had
gone a bit far. The Senator had probably made a "mistake" and the Director of Mutual Security probably
meant "infringement" rather than "undermining."

All the while McCarthy was stepping up his campaign against the State Department's overseas information program. The country began to hear about the
two 27-year-olds, Roy Cohn, the Subcommittee's chief
counsel, and G. David Schine, an unpaid Subcommittee consultant. They left on an eighteen-day whirl
through western Europe to ferret out "subversion" in
the overseas program. Seventeen hours in Bonn,
twenty hours in Berlin, nineteen hours in Frankfurt
—these and a sprinkling of other stops and McCarthy
was proclaiming "appalling infiltration." The State
Department reacted dutifully. It asked for resignations
—including those of men like Theodore Kaghan who
had probably dabbled with radicalism in the late 1930's
and who now was known through central Europe as
one of the most effective organizers of anti-Communist propaganda. (When the Subcommittee made its
charges Leopold Figl, the ultraconservative former
Chancellor of Austria, wrote Kaghan: "What goes on?
After all, April Fool's day has long passed by. . . .")
The State Department also issued a new directive banning from American information activities all "books,
music, paintings, and the like . . . of any Communists, fellow travelers, *et cetera*" and ordering that
"librarians should at once remove all books and other
material by Communists, fellow travelers, *et cetera*,

from their shelves and withdraw any that may be in circulation."

Many librarians, taking no chance on having a work by an *et cetera* on their shelves, removed the books of authors like Bert Andrews, chief of the Washington bureau of the Republican *New York Herald Tribune;* Walter White, head of the anti-Communist National Association for the Advancement of Colored People; Richard Lauterbach, former European correspondent of *Time;* Clarence Streit, chief figure in the strongly democratic movement for a federal union of the North Atlantic democracies; and Foster Rhea Dulles, a decidedly anti-Communist professor at Ohio State and cousin of the Secretary of State. Some librarians stored the books they removed; others burned them.

At the height of the book purge, on June 14, President Eisenhower went to Dartmouth to receive an honorary degree. Among those sharing honors with him were his friend John J. McCloy, Judge Joseph M. Proskauer of New York, and Lester B. Pearson, Canadian Secretary of State for External Affairs. The President overheard these three discussing with horror the book burnings and joined in the conversation. When he rose to make his extemporaneous remarks, Eisenhower said: "Don't join the book burners. Don't think you are going to conceal faults by concealing evidence that they ever existed. Don't be afraid to go in your library and read every book as long as any document does not offend our own ideas of decency. That should be the only censorship.

"How will we defeat communism unless we know what it is? What it teaches—why does it have such an appeal for men? . . . We have got to fight it with something better. Not try to conceal the thinking of our own people. They are part of America and even if they think ideas that are contrary to ours they have a right to have them, a right to record them and a right to have them in places where they are accessible to others. It is unquestioned or it is not America."

Anti-McCarthy opinion in the United States was jubilant. At last the President was taking a stand; now the Senator would have the whole prestige and power of the Administration thrown against him. Many papers were like the *Baltimore Sun* in calling the Dartmouth remarks an "important turning point."

The day after the speech Secretary Dulles met his regular press conference and reporters quickly got around to the book purge. Yes, books had been burned, Dulles said, but after all they were only a small number of titles among the more than two million volumes in the libraries.

But didn't the President's speech indicate a new policy? the newsmen asked.

No, just the use of more sense in applying the directive, the Secretary of State replied. As the reporters pressed on, Dulles abruptly changed the subject.

On June 17 Eisenhower met the press for the first time since his Dartmouth speech. He was asked if he intended the remarks to be "critical of a school of thought represented by Senator McCarthy." The President replied that he must refuse to talk personalities. The speech was not a stand in favor of using government money to propagate Communist beliefs. He was against book burning, which to him meant a suppression of ideas.

No, he had not ordered any directives canceled, although he had asked Dulles to see him about the problem. He really didn't know much about the whole matter.

A newsman asked about the "controversial" but non-Communist books. The President replied that if they were on the shelves of libraries in this country, it was all right to have them in our libraries abroad, generally speaking. Then Eisenhower added that if the State Department was burning a book which was an open appeal to everybody in a foreign country to be a Communist, then he would say that the book falls outside the limits in which he was speaking. The State

Department could do as it pleased to get rid of such books.

For two weeks reporters harried Eisenhower for clarification. At one press conference Raymond Brandt, chief Washington correspondent for the *St. Louis Post-Dispatch*, questioned the President sharply and at length. Eisenhower was having trouble keeping his temper as he answered.

Brandt: "Do you and Secretary Dulles hope to get a clear directive [about overseas library policy] eventually?"

The President: Well, certainly.

Brandt: "Is that possible?"

The President: Certainly, he hoped that it was.

Brandt: "Is it possible?"

The President: It should be; yes, it should be. There was no question as to where he stood. Now, he thought we could make it clear so that any reasonable person could understand exactly what was meant.

Brandt: "I think there was some confusion between your Dartmouth speech and your press conference speech in which you said it was perfectly all right for the State Department to burn books or do as they pleased with them."

By now the President was glowering. He snapped back that he didn't believe he said that. He said that the Government would be foolish to promulgate and help to support the distribution of a book that openly advocated its own destruction by force.

Brandt: "One of the writers was Dashiell Hammett, who writes detective stories. So far as I know—and I have read several of them—I don't see anything Communistic about them, but they were thrown out by the libraries. . . ."

Eisenhower smiled and his composure returned. He thought someone got frightened, he said. He didn't know why they should—he wouldn't. He would tell them that—he wouldn't. And there the discussion ended.

McCarthy rampaged on. With the opening of 1954 he and his staff concentrated increasingly on the Department of the Army and a number of top Army officials tried hard to work with them. In January the Senator began to hammer on the case of Major Irving Peress, a New York dental officer. Peress had been permitted to receive his regularly due promotion and granted an honorable discharge after he had refused to sign an Army loyalty certificate and after he had refused, on the grounds of possible self-incrimination, to answer a number of questions at a Subcommittee hearing. In a letter to McCarthy, Secretary of the Army Robert Stevens acknowledged that the Peress case had been mishandled and stated that if he found the promotion had been anything but routine he would discipline the officers involved. He also ordered that in the future Reserve officers who refused to sign a loyalty certificate were to be given an other than honorable discharge.

Unappeased, the Senator summoned Peress and a group of Army officials, including Brigadier General Ralph Zwicker, to a Subcommittee hearing. At one point, when the hearing was in executive session, McCarthy demanded that Zwicker answer questions concerning the processing of the Peress case and Zwicker replied that such information was inviolate under a Presidential order. The Senator was furious. According to Zwicker, McCarthy shouted at the General: "You are a disgrace to the uniform. You're shielding Communist conspirators. You are going to be put on public display next Tuesday. You're not fit to be an officer. You're ignorant."

Zwicker was a highly esteemed officer who was obviously simply following orders. The Army seethed with resentment. Secretary Stevens heatedly accused McCarthy of humiliating Zwicker and of undermining Army morale, and ordered two officers not to appear before the Senator's Subcommittee. McCarthy promptly replied that Stevens was an "awful dupe" and

summoned the Secretary himself to testify. Stevens
decided to go and prepared a strong statement which
he intended to read at the hearing. But the statement
was never read. Instead Stevens met with McCarthy
and other members of the Subcommittee and accepted
a "Memorandum of Agreement." When the memorandum was released few commentators, pro- or anti-Mc-
Carthy, interpreted it as anything but complete and
abject surrender on the part of the Secretary of the
Army.

That afternoon the White House was filled with
glum discussions of ways to do something about the
Stevens debacle. In the Capitol a reporter passed by
the hearings room of the Subcommittee, noticed the
door open, and looked in. He saw McCarthy and Roy
Cohn sitting at the end of the table and "laughing so
hard," the newsman remembered, "that the room
seemed to shake."

During the Administration efforts to counteract
the Memorandum of Agreement, photographers
snapped the President out on the White House lawn
practicing his putting. He was taking the respite, as
was his habit, to calm his boiling temper. But to many
serious observers the symbolism was perfect for the
trend of American affairs in the winter of 1953-4.

An amiable, well-intentioned President was taking
his model from leadership of pre-F. D. R. days. Government was "teamwork." You got together a team,
primarily of executives from corporations, and put
them to work on their specialties. You struck up cordial relations with Congress. Then the President presided over the ensuing co-operation much like a constitutional monarch and the nation moved gently,
sensibly toward sound, economical, thoroughly Amer-
can ways.

All the while men and women with programs of
rancor worked away. In both houses of Congress
and throughout the country the right wing of the

Republican Party was making a bold bid for power. Word kept coming from the Senate that the Bricker Amendment, the isolationist's dream, might well pass. Movements were building to strip away the substance of New Deal domestic legislation that had long been considered inviolate. Informed pro-Eisenhower observers wondered aloud whether the smiling General had not lost control of his party and of the nation. In December 1953, Walter Lippmann proclaimed a "crisis," brought about by the "abdication of the powers of the Executive and the usurpation of Congress."

McCarthyism was permeating every state and every occupation, sometimes ridiculous, sometimes frightening, sometimes bordering on the incredible. Five distinguished ex-diplomats warned that the assaults on the State Department were having "sinister results. . . . A premium has been put upon reporting and upon recommendations which are ambiguously stated or so cautiously set forth as to be deceiving. . . . The ultimate result is a threat to national security." The major drama publisher, Samuel French, announced a playwriting contest in which one of the conditions was that the sponsor "reserves the right at any time to declare ineligible any author who is, or becomes publicly involved, in a scholastic, literary, political, or moral controversy." The crackdown on scientists and teachers had reached the point where Albert Einstein was advising his correspondents to resort to the "way of non-cooperation in the sense of Gandhi's"—a refusal to testify before any Congressional committee about personal beliefs and a willingness to go to jail as a result.

In Indiana Mrs. Thomas J. White, a member of the State Textbook Commission, charged that "there is a Communist directive in education now to stress the story of Robin Hood. They want to stress it because he robbed the rich and gave it to the poor. That's the Communist line. It's just a smearing of law and order." Governor George Craig declined comment and State

Superintendent of Education Wilbur Young announced that he would reread *Robin Hood* to consider the merits of Mrs. White's charge. The 1953 Sheriff of Nottingham, England, William Cox, was more definite. "Why, Robin Hood was no Communist," he said.

Paul Hoffman, chairman of the board of the Studebaker-Packard Corporation, was taken aback when he finished a speech on freedom at a large southwestern university. A student came up to him and asked: "Do you think there ought to be any study of communism in a school such as this?"

"Yes," Hoffman said, "I think we ought to teach what communism *is*, so that the new and most important generation of Americans can know exactly why it is such a menace to our way of life."

"I think so, too," the student said, "but it's dangerous to say that around here now."

In Washington Martin Merson, an ex-Dixie Cup executive who gave up his plans for a business of his own in the flush of his pro-Eisenhower enthusiasm, tried to function as an official of the United States Information Administration. When the McCarthyite thrusts undermined the whole organization, Merson assumed that there must be something he could do to save the agency. He helped arrange a dinner meeting with Senator McCarthy, Cohn, Schine, and George Sokolsky, a pro-McCarthy columnist, and later they were joined by others. McCarthy was relaxed, jovial, and a bit puzzled why Merson was so exercised.

Finally something brought a real reaction from McCarthy and his group. Cohn mentioned the composer Aaron Copland, whose music was used in the overseas information programs. Sokolsky argued that the music should not be blacklisted and Cohn felt strongly that it should be banned. "As I sat quietly listening to the Copland colloquy," Merson remembered later, "I was suddenly struck by the ludicrousness of the whole evening's performance. Cohn, Schine, Mc-

Carthy, Sokolsky, and for that matter the rest of us, meeting to discuss the manners and morals of our times. By whose appointment? By what right?" The question was asked by many people. The answer was lost somewhere in the miasma of the winter of 1953-4.

On February 6, 1954, the President and 7,500 Republican leaders gathered at a Lincoln Day box supper in Uline Arena in the Capital. Herbert Hoover made a surprise appearance and was given a tremendous ovation. Everybody munched his box of fried chicken and joined in singing "God Bless America" and Eisenhower made a little speech in which he included the term "conservative." He paused, then added firmly: "And don't be afraid to use the word." The crowd cheered loudly.

In the winter of 1953-4, for the first time in twenty years, the term "conservative" was being used in the United States widely and without embarrassment. With the exultant thrust of the right-wing Republicans and with the way the Eisenhower Administration reacted, some Americans worried that the word would be not simply conservative but reactionary.

XII

The Eisenhower Equilibrium

AT FIRST the war scares kept right on coming. The Korean truce was hardly signed when the civil war in Indochina, which had been dragging on since 1946, erupted into a major Communist assault on Dien Bien Phu. A number of high Administration figures, including Vice-President Nixon and Secretary of State Dulles, let it be known that the United States might well send troops. Dien Bien Phu fell, an armistice was signed (giving the Communists 60,000 square miles containing a population of 14,000,000), and Indochina quieted. Six months more and the Chinese Communists seized Yikiang, north of Formosa, and talked loudly of invading Quemoy, Matsu, and Formosa itself. President Eisenhower asked Congress for broad authority to use American armed forces in the area and, with the country expecting a Chinese thrust any day, the Senate passed the resolution by the sweeping majority of 85 to 3.

Over everything, more than ever, hung the knowledge that another major war could be a war of oblivion. On March 1, 1954 American scientists set off the first explosion of an H-bomb and the scientists themselves were surprised at the range of its ability to injure.

Radioactive ash fell on a Japanese fishing boat eighty miles away and twenty-three fishermen were hospitalized for burns. A chill went through the United States. Scores of cities reported that automobile windshields were suddenly pock-marked as if by some exhalation from the H-bomb. The scientific explanation was normal erosion—plus mass jitters.

Yet during all the fears of 1954 and 1955 a quite different feeling was growing in the United States. Cautiously, incredulously, Americans were asking: Was not the danger of World War III definitely receding? For one thing, whatever the threats to peace, armies were no longer fighting each other. With the signing of the Indochinese truce on July 20, 1954, no shooting war existed anywhere on the globe for the first time since the Japanese invaded Manchuria twenty-three years before. The failure of the Chinese Communists to carry out their threats continued the fact of actual peace. For another thing, strange and hopeful events were happening in the Soviet Union. The post-Stalin Russian leaders were not only continuing their conciliatory language. On occasion they were acting in a way which strongly suggested that the bear could change his habits.

Early in 1955 Premier Georgi Malenkov resigned with the explanation of "insufficient experience . . . I see clearly my guilt" and went right on staying alive while the premiership was taken over by Nikolai Bulganin and Nikita Khrushchev emerged as the power in the Communist Party organization. On the international scene, the Soviet government did things which had the authentic ring of a desire to soften the East-West clash. In June 1955 Americans really rubbed their eyes. Russian fliers shot down a United States plane over the Bering Strait and the Soviet government quickly expressed its regrets and offered to pay half the cost of the plane.

Probably most important of all, the feeling was growing in America that science had made large-scale

war so terrifying that no nation would start one.
1954-5 was the period when it became clear that both
the United States and the Soviet Union had an effective H-bomb and that both were far along in the development of intercontinental missiles. President Eisenhower expressed the spreading American attitude
when he said: "We have arrived at the point. . .
[where] there is just no real alternative to peace."

In the new climate of expectations of peace the
United States naturally relaxed and sought to go back
to its customary ways. But just what was normal for
1954-5? To what extent could one apply the pre-
F.D.R. conception of America as a nation determining
by itself its role in the world, zestfully individualistic,
cherishing Home and Mother, delighting in a free economy and all the values that went with it?

Certainly the tug toward the traditional was powerful in American thinking. Every area of living showed
the trend. Most of the college girls were telling the
pollsters they wanted babies, not careers. The vogue
among men was to stay home at night and do-it-
yourself (insurance statisticians said more than 600,000
men a year were cutting their fingers with saws, setting themselves afire with spray paints, or shocking
themselves with electrical tools). The intellectuals
were showing greater and greater interest in a "new
conservatism." And Dwight Eisenhower, who more
than any President since William McKinley liked to
deliver little homilies on Home and Mother, held on to
his enormous popularity—in part, observers agreed,
because of his emphasis on traditional values.

Yet if the trend was unmistakable, it was no plainer
than certain counter facts. One of the assumptions of
old-style America had been the acceptance of a society in which great differences in economic and social
standing existed. The United States of 1954-5 was not
only a product of the Half-Century of Revolution in
domestic affairs; the revolution was not only continu-

ing; the pressures for still more economic and social
gains were strong and sustained. By 1955 the inflation
had definitely slackened. The Republicans said their
policies had brought about the change; the Democrats
declared it came from long-term programs and the end
of the Korean War. Whatever the cause, the result was
a girding of all lower- and middle-income groups to
see to it that the altered situation brought no wage
cuts or other obstacles in the way of a continually rising standard of living.

Citizens of lower social status kept pressing hard for
opportunities to improve their standing in the community. Those of less esteemed nationality and religious backgrounds had never been so persistent. Negro
leaders battled untiringly. On May 17, 1954 they won
the critically important Supreme Court decision declaring that no child could be barred from a public
school simply because of his color. Without a pause,
the National Association for the Advancement of Colored People threw tremendous energies into efforts to
get the decision speedily enforced and to remove Jim
Crow from further parts of American life.

Partly because of the techniques that had been used
to bring the social upsweep, partly for a dozen other
reasons, millions of Americans now found themselves
in a position where the genuine attitudes of individualism were not so much wrong as irrelevant. The average industrial worker belonged to a union and the
average farmer was deeply involved in at least one occupational organization. The typical clerical worker
was employed by a corporation or a business with
more than two hundred employees, and the typical
executive was not the owner but an employed manager
of the business. A web of relationships bound most
Americans in with state and federal governments. The
very manner of living was having its effects. The unquestionable trend was toward a home in a suburb—
the mushrooming miles of middle-class and worker's
suburbs—where the prime virtue was adjustment to

what the neighbors thought and did. Under the circumstances the urge was not so much for individualism as it was for getting oneself into the most profitable and comfortable relationship with some larger group or organization.

Particular developments in the United States were making large numbers fearsome of facing society by themselves and deeply concerned with keeping and extending special governmental and nongovernmental protections. In the existing state of the American economy and of the world market, farming was simply not profitable without a subsidy. The decades-old urbanization of the nation had brought a huge segment of the population to the complexities and the anonymity of city living. The relative number of women had been steadily mounting and many of them were in a vulnerable economic position; in 1954 a female headed about one in ten households. The population was growing older, bringing all the fears and uncertainties of age. In 1900, one person in seven was forty-five to sixty-four; by the early 1950's the ratio had changed to one in five and one in every twelve persons was sixty-five or over. The white, Protestant, "Anglo-Saxon" had long felt especially secure in the United States. But now year after year a smaller percentage of Americans were white, Protestant, and born of parentage which traced back to "Anglo-Saxon" lands.

Whether in a special category or not, the American of 1954-5 was likely to be a man who could not forget the crash of 1929. No matter the rampant boom, no matter the fact that during all the years since the beginning of World War II most families had been prospering; the edginess about a possible depression continued. Any dip in the economy, any flutter of the stock market brought wide concern. The very quieting of the international scene had many Americans asking: Wouldn't a peaceful situation and the cutting down of defense expenditures bring the crash? "Depression psychosis," the economist John Galbraith called it. Whether it was psychosis or good sense, the apprehensions about depression brought an added element into the national response to any governmental talk or action that smacked of the 1920's.

As for Home and Mother, attitudes were inevitably adjusting somewhat to the facts. In a thousand ways, little and big, the general reactions of the American had been growing less sentimental. Family living itself had been undergoing important changes. There was not only the possibility that mother was the head of the household; there was the decidedly better chance that she was out working (women were making up about 21,000,000 out of a total working force of roughly 64,000,000). Scores of other developments in the home, decidedly unsettling of the old ways in themselves, were dwarfed by the television revolution. By 1954-5 it had gone so far that for many Americans home was close to meaning the place where the TV set was located.

In 1954 the Water Commissioner of Toledo, puzzled why water consumption rose so startlingly during certain three-minute periods, checked and rechecked his charts, theorized and retheorized, finally hit on the answer: Toledo was flushing the toilets during the commercials. That same year the "TV dinner" was born—the turkey, sweet potatoes, and peas pre-cooked in a compartmented tray—and the family did not have to talk to each other even during supper. The offerings of TV were hardly dominated by lavender and lace. The plunging necklines had plunged to a point where only an abyss could provoke comment. More people were murdered on TV in 1954, one dour commentator estimated, than the United States lost in Korea. And Lucille Ball of *I Love Lucy*, redefining the decorous, proceeded to give a week-by-week viewing of most of her pregnancy period, including Desi Arnaz's sympathetic morning sickness.

If the American scene itself was sharply untradi-

tional, the feelings of world peace which were settling
over the nation were still more unconventional. They
lacked the fundamental of the usual American conception because they did not permit the country to forget
about the world. The Soviet leaders might be cooing,
but Communism in and outside Russia was obviously
as much of a reality as ever and constantly threatening to increase in strength. In fact, the apparent Soviet
swing away from attempts to advance Bolshevism by
wars was merely being replaced by an intensified
drive to extend Communism by internal subversion
and by political, diplomatic, and economic techniques.
If this was peace, it was plainly no 1865 or 1919 or
even 1945 but a peace that constantly had to be
worked at.

A strong urge toward the traditional amid situations
that were inescapably new—here was the general
pattern of the America that was relaxing in 1954-5.
Such a nation could find its normality only along
some wavering, in-between path.

Ever since the beginning of the 1952 campaign,
Dwight Eisenhower had frequently used the term
"middle-of-the-road" in describing his approach to
public affairs. His Administration up to the winter
of 1953-4, with its restrained Executive leadership, its
toleration of extreme right-wing Republicans, its tendency toward the past in domestic and foreign policies, had certainly moved down the right side of the
middle. But even in the most conservative days of
1953-4, other elements were present in Eisenhower's
thinking.

All the while that he was emphasizing that the Executive should respect Congress and pointing to Roosevelt and Truman as men who had tried to lead too
much, the President liked to repeat some remarks
made by his old friend, General George Patton. One
day Patton was discussing leadership and his eye fell
on a plate of spaghetti. Leadership was like trying to

get a piece of spaghetti across a table, Patton said. Push it and you would only break it. But get a bit in front of the piece of spaghetti, pull it gently, and you would get it across the table intact. Dwight Eisenhower, however much he was a leader who wanted to keep the Republican Party intact, nevertheless was quite conscious of the importance of getting out ahead a bit and pulling gently.

The President's attitude toward specific domestic and foreign problems also had its varying aspects. He was, as he frequently remarked, "basically conservative." But it was just as true to say that he was—and more so than any President in recent American history—generally non-ideological. Eisenhower tended to look for an *ad hoc* solution to a given situation and was willing to listen sympathetically to quite contrasting points of view. If he was inclined to believe that a successful businessman had thereby proved his sagacity, he deeply admired his younger brother Milton ("Milt inherited all the brains in the family"), whose mind had been shaped by years of high New Deal and Fair Deal positions.

Any policy in any field had to stand the test of the President's persistent tendency to react less along the lines of doctrine than according to the human aspects of the problem. The journalist Stewart Alsop has recalled an incident of the 1952 campaign. At first Eisenhower was strongly inclined to make a major issue of what seemed to him the excessively pro-labor attitude of Truman in dealing with a serious steel strike. Before committing himself, he asked to be briefed on the facts and some of his labor advisers explained the demands of the union in terms of what the benefits meant to the men's families in a period of rising prices. Eisenhower's reaction was, "Why maybe they ought to have had more than that," and the steel strike never became an important campaign issue.

Around the President were a group of men who were also "basically conservative," most of them more so than Eisenhower, but they had their own flexibility. All of the principal aides had spent their mature careers learning to operate within a New Deal-Fair Deal society. A number of them had served in specific functions for a Democratic Administration. This was particularly true of Eisenhower's chief adviser on foreign affairs, Secretary of State Dulles, who had worked with the State Department during most of the post-World War II period and who played a part in bringing about the highly untraditional decision to intervene in Korea. The two most influential advisers in domestic and defense matters, Secretary of the Treasury George Humphrey and Secretary of Defense Charles Wilson, were decidedly not businessmen of the 1920's type. They were part of the new, more adaptable managerial class.

In 1948 Wilson, wearied by the struggles between General Motors and the United Automobile Workers, had invented the famous "escalator clause" (tying wages to the cost of living) which labor liked so much and which was important in preserving industrial peace in the following years. In 1947 Humphrey demonstrated a similar flexibility. Facing a coal strike, he and Benjamin Fairless of United States Steel met with John L. Lewis for private talks and brought about a settlement largely on Lewis's terms. Many industrialists and a large section of Congress were indignant but Humphrey defended the move on pragmatic grounds, including the statement that Lewis's demands were largely reasonable. Discussing these episodes, the astute journalist Robert Coughlan has commented that "Wilson and Humphrey . . . have about as much resemblance to the Republican Big Businessman of the Coolidge-Hoover era as the Indian elephant has to the hairy mammoth—the general outline is the same, but there are vital differences in detail. . . . These two performances were neither 'conservative' nor 'liberal.' They were, however, practical."

Practical men, headed by an essentially non-

ideological President, trying to govern a nation with
conflicting urges—after the winter of 1953-4 the Administration moved increasingly from the severe conservatism of its early phase. The shift was evident in
many ways, but it was clearest of all in the fact that
Eisenhower was departing somewhat from his pre-
F.D.R. conception of the Presidency.

He talked less and less about offending no one in
Congress, left fewer major decisions to subordinates,
spoke out more frequently on public issues. He was
giving the appearance at press conferences that he no
longer merely tolerated them but intended to use them
to press forward his purposes. Only occasionally did
he still remark that he just didn't know about the matter under discussion. No one quite said it but a dozen
newsmen now came close to applying to this President
Bert Andrews's remark about Harry Truman after the
election of 1946: Dwight Eisenhower is becoming
President of the United States.

The most immediate problem facing an Executive
who was genuinely trying to lead was the rampant
right-wing of the Republican Party, particularly one
Joseph McCarthy. A relaxing America was stirring
against the extremities of the Senator from Wisconsin.
As Secretary of the Army Stevens apparently yielded
to McCarthy on February 24, 1954, feelings were at
white heat throughout the country. Within the next
ten days Adlai Stevenson bluntly called the Republican Party "half McCarthy and half Eisenhower." The
Republican Senator from Vermont, Ralph Flanders,
took the floor of the Senate with anger and scorn.
"He dons his warpaint," the elderly Vermonter said.
"He goes into his war dance. He emits his warwhoops.
He goes forth to battle and proudly returns with the
scalp of a pink Army dentist. We may assume that this
represents the depth and seriousness of Communist
penetration at this time." That night Edward R. Mur-
row used his CBS documentary TV show, "See It
Now," for a film-clip program which was potently

anti-McCarthy. CBS stations reported a flood of applauding calls (15-1 against the Senator in San Francisco and New York, 2-1 against him in Chicago).

From the day of the Memorandum of Agreement the Administration moved against McCarthy, sometimes indirectly but steadily. Secretary Stevens countered the Memorandum with a strong statement and the President made plain that he backed his Secretary "one hundred percent." On March 11, 1954 the Army attacked with the charge that Senator McCarthy, Roy Cohn, and Francis Carr, the Subcommittee staff director, had sought, separately and collectively, by improper means, to obtain preferential treatment in the Army for G. David Schine, the Subcommittee consultant who was now a private in the Army. McCarthy and "associates" promptly replied with forty-six charges against the Army, of which the key one was that Secretary Stevens and John Adams, the department counselor, had tried to stop the Subcommittee's exposure of alleged Communists at Fort Monmouth and that they used Private Schine as a "hostage" to this end. Four more days and the Subcommittee voted to investigate the Army-McCarthy clash, with TV cameras in the room and with McCarthy temporarily replaced by the next ranking Republican, Senator Karl Mundt of South Dakota. Once again a TV spectacle would transfix the country and once again television would have a major part in shaping opinion on a critical national issue.

Shortly after 10 a.m. on April 22, 1954 the red lights in the cameras went on amid the florid Corinthian columns and the brocaded curtains of the large Senate Caucus Room. Senator Mundt tapped his big pipe, leaned forward, and delivered a little speech about how everything was going to be done with "dignity, fairness, and thoroughness." The ranking Democrat, John McClellan, said a few words to the same effect.

"Thank you very much, Senator McClellan," Chairman Mundt declared. "Our counsel, Mr. Jenkins, will now call the first witness." Ray Jenkins opened his mouth but the words came from down along the table. "A point of order, Mr. Chairman," McCarthy was saying. "May I raise a point of order?"

For thirty-six days and more than 2,000,000 words of testimony the hearings went on. A thousand impressions were driven into the public mind—Senator Mundt, roly-poly and pliable and so torn between his McCarthyite sympathies and the fact that he was supposed to be an impartial chairman that someone thought to call him the "tormented mushroom"; the Subcommittee's special counsel, Ray Jenkins, the homicide lawyer from Tellico Plains, Tennessee, chin stuck forward, intoning away with his questions; Senator John McClellan of Arkansas, the real terror of the Subcommittee, cadaverous and saturnine and pursuing everyone with a rasping logic; Robert Stevens, earnest and decent but having to pour out his, the Secretary of War's, pathetic attempts to mollify the friends of buck private G. David Schine; Roy Cohn, leaning over to make a point to McCarthy with a mouth that seemed perpetually pouting, obviously tremendously attached to Schine, obviously tremendously attached to Roy Cohn; Cohn and Schine, endlessly Cohn and Schine. But with each passing day one impression was having an increasingly potent effect on the millions at their TV sets. It was Joseph McCarthy, full-life, acting precisely like Joseph McCarthy.

"Point of order, point of order, Mr. Chairman," the Senator would interrupt in his scowling, sneering way until the children of the United States were imitating him on the streets. He repaid loyalty, like that of bumbling Senator Henry Dworshak of Idaho, by riding contemptuously over what the supporter was trying to say. He seized the floor from opponents by physical force, repeating in his strong, singsong voice until the opponent wearily gave way. McCarthy flung smears and constantly accused others of smearing; his aides tried to use a cropped photograph and he cried deceit at the Army; he sidetracked, blatantly sidetracked, and demanded the end of "diversionary tactics." Day after day he was still Joe McCarthy of the boyhood fights, ceaselessly, recklessly swinging for the knockout.

The more reckless McCarthy became, the more strongly the Administration opposed him. In mid-May the President threw the Constitution of the United States at him. McCarthy became involved in demands that were flagrant violations of the rights of the Executive and from the White House came a blunt statement of those rights, which "cannot be usurped by any individual who may seek to set himself above the laws of our land." No one, not even the President of the United States, not even a President of his own party, was immune to the Senator's standard weapon, the charge of softness toward Communism. McCarthy's answer to Eisenhower was to talk once again of "the evidence of treason that has been growing over the past twenty—" Then he paused and added darkly: "twenty-one years."

The hearings ground on. The changing national mood, the Presidential opposition, and the appearance McCarthy was making on TV were costing the Senator heavily in public support. But he was still not a ruined man. The evidence was certainly not giving either side a clear-cut victory in the issues immediately at stake. Had the McCarthy group sought preferential treatment for Schine? Clearly they had. Had the Army tried to stop McCarthy's investigation at Fort Monmouth? Equally clearly it had—though it was emphasizing that it was anxious to get "that type" of hearing ended because it demoralized the Army. Other charges and countercharges were tangled in a maze of conflicting testimony. Throughout the country a good many pro-McCarthy or anti-anti-McCarthy people were wavering but they were only wavering. The Senator could have emerged from the hearings partially intact if he had now made some moves to present himself as a reasonable, responsible person. But Joseph McCarthy was not interested in being partially intact. He went on looking for the hay-maker and the right man was present to see to it that when the Senator swung his wildest, he swung himself flat on his face.

The chief Army counsel, Joseph Welch, was a senior partner of the eminent Boston law firm of Hale and Dorr and he had a well-deserved reputation as an infinitely shrewd trial lawyer. But friends emphasized more Welch's innate sense of human decency and his gift of ironic laughter. They associated him with his spacious colonial home in Walpole, where he puttered around studying his thermometers (there were twelve in the house), spending a day fishing or an evening in a game of carom or cribbage, delighting more than anything else in kindly, bantering talk about the cosmos. Mrs. Welch had a favorite story about the whimsicality of the man. She liked to tell how she had urged him to take up gardening, which he loathed, and he countered that he would garden if she would drink beer, which she detested. So on weekends the two would alternately garden in the broiling sun and stop for a beer in the shade, both grinning through their periods of suffering.

At the hearings Welch sat questioning away, his long, drooping face quizzical, his questions softly spoken and deftly insidious, dropping a damaging little jest and looking utterly surprised when people laughed. The sessions were only eight days old when the Army counsel drew blood. Welch was driving hard at a photograph which the McCarthy forces had produced, cropped to show only Stevens and Schine together although the original photograph contained two other men. The Army counsel brought out that the original had hung on Schine's wall and he questioned James Juliana, a Subcommittee employee who had arranged the cropping, as to why he had not brought the whole picture.

JULIANA: "I wasn't asked for it. . . ."

WELCH: ". . . You were asked for something different from the thing that hung on Schine's wall?"

JULIANA: "I never knew what hung on Schine's wall. . . ."

WELCH: "Did you think this came from a pixie? Where did you think this picture that I hold in my hand came from?"

JULIANA: "I had no idea."

There was a stir of voices and McCarthy interrupted. "Will counsel for my benefit define—I think he might be an expert on that—what a pixie is?"

Welch's face was beatific. "Yes. I should say, Mr. Senator, that a pixie is a close relative of a fairy. Shall I proceed, sir? Have I enlightened you?"

The spectators roared. Roy Cohn's pouting lips hardened into angry lines. The Senator glowered.

In the world of Joseph McCarthy nothing was more alien than the deft, and the Senator's feelings about Welch steadily mounted. He denied the Army counsel, or was wary of giving him, what he considered the ordinary camaraderie. McCarthy would walk up to friends and opponents alike, hand extended and the other hand grasping an arm, but he moved a wide circle around Joseph Welch. He first-named almost everybody—Secretary Stevens was "Bob" and the obviously hostile Senator Stuart Symington was "Stu." Welch was "Mr. Welch" or "the counsel."

Eight days before the hearings ended, on June 9, the Army counsel led Roy Cohn through a mocking, destructive cross-examination and McCarthy sat fuming. Now Welch was pressing Cohn as to why, if subversion was so serious at Fort Monmouth, he had not come crying alarm to Secretary Stevens. When Welch went ahead along this line, McCarthy began to grin broadly.

The Army counsel got in another dig at Cohn: "May I add my small voice, sir, and say whenever you know about a subversive or a Communist or a spy, please hurry. Will you remember these words?"

McCarthy broke in, bashed his way to attention. "In view of Mr. Welch's request that the information be given once we know of anyone who might be performing any work for the Communist Party, I think we should tell him that he has in his law firm a young man named Fisher whom he recommended, incidentally, to do work on this committee, who has been for a number of years a member of an organization which was named, oh, years and years ago, as the legal bulwark of the Communist Party. . . ."

The Senator was grinning ever more broadly, pausing now and then to lick his lips and savor his words. Roy Cohn sat in the witness chair, his legs dangling apart, the blood drained from his face, and once his lips seemed to be forming the words "Stop, stop." McCarthy went on: "Knowing that, Mr. Welch, I just felt that I had a duty to respond to your urgent request. . . . I have hesitated bringing that up, but I have been rather bored with your phony requests to Mr. Cohn here that he personally get every Communist out of government before sundown. . . .

"I am not asking you at this time to explain why you tried to foist him on this committee. Whether you knew he was a member of that Communist organization or not, I don't know. I assume you did not, Mr. Welch, because I get the impression that, while you are quite an actor, you play for a laugh, I don't think you have any conception of the danger of the Communist Party. I don't think you yourself would ever knowingly aid the Communist cause. I think you are unknowingly aiding it when you try to burlesque this hearing in which we are trying to bring out the facts, however."

Welch was staring at McCarthy with the look of a man who was watching the unbelievable. The puck was gone; his face was white with anger. "Senator McCarthy," Welch began, "I did not know—"

McCarthy turned away contemptuously and talked to Juliana. Twice the Army counsel demanded his attention and the Senator talked to Juliana in a still louder voice, telling him to get a newspaper clipping about Fisher so that it could be put in the record.

Welch plunged ahead. "You won't need anything in the record when I have finished telling you this.

"Until this moment, Senator, I think I never really gauged your cruelty or your recklessness. Fred Fisher is a young man who went to the Harvard Law School and came into my firm and is starting what looks to be a brilliant career with us.

"When I decided to work for this committee I asked Jim St. Clair . . . to be my first assistant. I said to Jim, 'Pick somebody in the firm who works under you that you would like.' He chose Fred Fisher and they came down on an afternoon plane. That night, when we had taken a little stab at trying to see what the case was about, Fred Fisher and Jim St. Clair and I went to dinner together. I then said to these two young men, 'Boys, I don't know anything about you except that I have always liked you, but if there is anything funny in the life of either one of you that would hurt anybody in this case you speak up quick.'

"Fred Fisher said, 'Mr. Welch, when I was in law school and for a period of months after, I belonged to the Lawyers Guild.' . . . I said, 'Fred, I just don't think I am going to ask you to work on the case. If I do, one of these days that will come out and go over national television and it will just hurt like the dickens.'

"So Senator, I asked him to go back to Boston.

"Little did I dream you could be so reckless and so cruel as to do an injury to that lad. It is true that he is still with Hale & Dorr. It is true that he will continue to be with Hale & Dorr. It is, I regret to say, equally true that I fear he shall always bear a scar needlessly inflicted by you. If it were in my power to forgive you for your reckless cruelty, I would do so. I like to think I am a gentle man, but your forgiveness will have to come from someone other than me."

The Senate Caucus Room was hushed. McCarthy fumbled with some papers, began saying that Welch had no right to speak of cruelty because he had "been baiting Mr. Cohn here for hours."

Welch cut off McCarthy. "Senator, may we not drop this? We know he belonged to the Lawyers Guild, and Mr. Cohn nods his head at me." Cohn was quite plainly nodding.

WELCH: "I did you, I think, no personal injury, Mr. Cohn."

COHN: "No, sir."

WELCH: "I meant to do you no personal injury, and if I did, I beg your pardon."

Cohn nodded again. The Army counsel turned back to McCarthy and his emotion was so great that on the TV screens his eyes seemed to be filling with tears. "Let us not assassinate this lad further, Senator. You have done enough. Have you no sense of decency, sir, at long last? Have you left no sense of decency?"

McCarthy tried to ask the Army counsel a question about Fisher. Welch cut him off again. He had recovered his composure now and his voice was cold with scorn. "Mr. McCarthy, I will not discuss this with you further. You have sat within 6 feet of me, and could have asked me about Fred Fisher. You have brought it out. If there is a God in heaven, it will do neither you nor your cause any good. I will not discuss it further. I will not ask Mr. Cohn any more questions. You, Mr. Chairman, may, if you will, call the next witness."

For a long few seconds the hush in the room continued. One of the few rules Chairman Mundt had tried hard to enforce was the one against demonstrations and six policemen were present to assist him. But suddenly the room shook with applause. For the first time in the memory of Washington observers, press photographers laid aside their cameras to join in the ovation for Welch. Chairman Mundt made no effort to interfere and instead soon called for a five-minute recess.

Joseph McCarthy sat slouched in his chair, breathing heavily. Spectators and reporters avoided him. Finally he found someone to talk to. He spread out his hands in a gesture of puzzlement and asked: "What did I do wrong?"

Joseph McCarthy would never know. And that June day, 1954, millions at their TV sets learned once and for all that Joseph McCarthy would never know.

The children stopped saying "Point of order, point of order." The housewives went back to *I Love Lucy*. A different subject was filling conversations. Agricultural prices were dropping, the textile and auto industries were laying off workers, general unemployment was mounting (by mid-1954 the government figures put it over 2,000,000). Everywhere in the United States there was talk of depression.

November 1954 was not far away and GOP political leaders shuddered at the thought of a Republican Administration having to face the polls during a decline in the economy. They were keenly aware that the success in 1952 had been much more an Eisenhower than a Republican victory and they did not ignore the association in so many people's minds between Republicanism and the depression of 1929. The elections of 1954 came, the Democrats did take both houses of Congress, and the point went on having its effects in high GOP circles. It was a continuing prod to an Administration which was not indisposed for other reasons to move from the conservatism of its early period.

The domestic policies that emerged in 1954 and 1955 represented no sharp break. The Administration kept its businessman tone. Just before the elections of 1954, Secretary of Defense Wilson was at it again with his observation, in discussing unemployment, that "I've always liked bird dogs better than kennel-fed dogs myself—you know one who'll get out and hunt for food rather than sit on his fanny and yell." As late as May 1956 another high Administration official, a deputy assistant to the President, Howard Pyle, was apologizing for his "off-hand comment" that the "right to suffer [by unemployment] is one of the joys of a free economy." Particularly in its policies toward government finance, power, and public resources the Administration continued the lines of its first period to such an extent that the New Dealish had tart words. Which was the more serious corruption? they demanded to know. Mink coats and deep-freezers or disposals of the national forests and utility contracts which could mean millions for a few corporations? And Administration figures were still capable of providing caricatures of the conservative leeriness of welfare expenditures by the federal government. When the Salk polio vaccine was announced on April 12, 1955, the problem arose as to how poor families were to get the protection without having to go through the humiliation of declaring that they could not pay for it. A bill was presented in Congress to have the federal government provide free vaccine for all children. Mrs. Oveta Culp Hobby, Secretary of Health, Education and Welfare, was horrified. The bill was "socialized medicine"—by "the back door."

Yet the shift, however restrained, was on. In late 1954 a White House adviser remarked: "The President's changed, George Humphrey's changed—we've all changed since we came here." Eisenhower was seeing more and more of Dr. Arthur Burns, a Columbia economist and now chairman of the Council of Economic Advisers, who believed that "it is no longer a matter of serious controversy whether the Government should play a positive role in helping to maintain a high level of economic activity. What we debate nowadays is not the need for controlling business cycles, but rather the nature of governmental action, its timing and its extent." Humphrey, who had taken Taftite steps to raise interest rates, was encouraging measures that would bring them down. "The first moves," he explained in his pragmatic way, "were to stop price rises and inventory inflation. Then, finding we had credit a little tight, we turned around and loosened it."

In April 1954 Secretary of Agriculture Benson cut the price support of butter from 90 to 75 per cent of parity. The dairy industry was furious but Benson, probably the most dogged free-enterprise man in the Cabinet, indicated he would stand firm. The Secretary of Agriculture was soon summoned to the White House. "Ezra," the President said, "I think maybe we went a mite too far this time." Eisenhower pulled a pad of paper toward him and drew a base and a summit line. He pointed to the bottom line. "This is where we are." Then he tapped the upper line. "And this is where we eventually want to arrive. But we'll have to go more slowly with our changes—like this." The pencil zig-zagged up the length of the sheet. "This is the way we'll have to go—first this way, then that. But we'll always be headed here"—*here* meaning an agriculture more responsive to the play of market forces.

The threatened depression did not come but the Administration shift continued. The trend is summarized by a comparison of the President's 1953, 1954, and 1955 State-of-the-Union messages. The 1953 document had an unmistakable Taftite tone. By 1955 the nature of the address had changed to one which the *New York Times* correctly characterized as a call "for limited extension of measures along the lines of the New Deal." The new direction was plain in the highway, school, slum-clearance, medical insurance, and widened social security bills sent to Congress. They were decidedly un-New Dealish in the amounts of money called for, some of the methods proposed, and the extent to which the Administration pressed for their passage. But they were also decidedly non-Taftian in their assumption that the federal government had to assume responsibility for broad social needs. So far as amount of expenditure was concerned, the programs would raise federal spending in these categories to an annual level four billion dollars higher than it had been under Truman.

Throughout the shift of his Administration, Eisenhower was feeling his way toward some general statement of the domestic aims of his Presidency. He no longer emphasized "conservatism" alone. He tried "dynamic conservatism," "progressive, dynamic conservatism," "progressive moderation," "moderate progressivism," "positive and progressive." But more and more he adopted a formula along the lines of the one he expressed in December 1954. The Administration, Eisenhower remarked then, "must be liberal when it was talking about the relationship between the Government and the individual, conservative when talking about the national economy and the individual's pocketbook."

Adlai Stevenson met a Chicago press conference and said: "I have never been sure what progressive moderation means, or was it conservative progressivism? [Laughter] I have forgotten, and I am not sure what dynamic moderation or moderate dynamism means. I am not even sure what it means when one says that he is a conservative in fiscal affairs and a liberal in human affairs. I assume what it means is that you will strongly recommend the building of a great many schools to accommodate the needs of our children, but not provide the money. [Laughter]" Unquestionably there was something ludicrously muddled about the Administration's efforts to describe itself in its new direction, but the very confusion bespoke the essence of where it was going. Conservative in economic matters and liberal in human affairs—the social gains of the New Deal and the Fair Deal were to be preserved, some extensions would be advocated but for the most part not vigorously pressed, and the whole was to be set within a severe budget consciousness.

The most striking fact about the Eisenhower domestic policies, in their earlier or later phase, was the same characteristic that had marked the programs of the Truman years—action on the home front was usually much less significant than action abroad.

In the all-important foreign field, the Administration was paralleling its domestic shift. It held to the main lines of the New Look defense policy. But it went along with an increasing number of amendments to it. It was noticeable, too, that the Administration was defending the policy less and less in terms of budget-balancing and more by that totally non-ideological argument—the world situation and the development of new weapons dictated a shift in the American defense. As time went on, the question arose just how new the New Look was. How much was it a reversion to Taftism and how much simply another instance of the immemorial American habit—practiced after every war and decidedly practiced by the Truman Administration—of slashing defense expenditures when the guns were quiet?

Still more change from the early Eisenhower days was evident in the attitude toward economic aid and technical assistance. The talk within the Administration of ending all such expenditures died down. The smallness of the appropriations asked for by the President continued to distress deeply men of a Point Four persuasion. Chester Bowles, Ambassador to India during the Truman Administration, cried out: "Let it not be said by future historians that in the second decade after World War II freedom throughout the world died of a balanced budget." But a degree of

economic aid continued, with the Administration
fighting off right-wing attempts to cut severely the
amount or add hamstringing restrictions. Meanwhile
Eisenhower was putting into effect something of an
atomic age Point Four—his plan for the United States
to join in spreading the peaceful uses of atomic energy by giving knowledge and by selling atomic reactors at half price.

The change in the Administration's policy toward
the world was most marked in the most important aspect, the matter of general attitude. The basic question
was the same as it had been throughout the post—
World War II period: To what extent was the United
States going to break with its deeply felt tradition of
the quick, final solution, brought about largely by the
United States alone? The specific debate was now less
over the word "containment" than the word "coexistence," with all its implications of a long, slow process
of adjustment during which the continued power of
Communism would be assumed and the world would
stay thoroughly entangled.

Any favorable mention of coexistence brought from
McCarthy-type sentiment cries of treason. To many
Americans of less extreme views, the idea was dangerous nonsense. In particular Senator William Knowland,
the Republican leader in the Senate, was arguing forcibly that coexistence was a "Trojan horse" that would
lull America into a sense of false security, to be followed by disaster. The United States, Knowland solemnly warned, must take "every possible step"—often
the Senator sounded as if this included war—to throw
back Communism or in time it would find itself overwhelmed. "The civilizations that flourished and died
in the past had opportunities for a limited period of
time to change the course of history. Sooner or later,
however, they passed 'the point of no return,' and the
decisions were no longer theirs to make."

1954-5 saw Secretary Dulles move appreciably toward the coexistence position. His speeches became a

good deal less impatient and bellicose. He dropped any emphasis on liberation and instead gave most of his enormous energies to building the Southeast Asia Treaty Organization—a NATO-type defense organization which certainly assumed a long, hard pull. Of still greater importance, President Eisenhower, who had never entirely shared his Secretary's belligerence, was more and more determining the general outlines and the tone of the country's foreign policy.

With each passing month the President increased his emphasis on the importance of the slow processes of conciliation and adjustment in world affairs. In July 1954 UN headquarters were filled with talk that Red China was about to be admitted. Senator Knowland, speaking for a considerable body of opinion in the United States, was bitter. America, he declared, should make plain that it would leave the UN the day Red China entered. As for himself, if the UN made the move he would resign his Republican leadership in the Senate to lead an agitation to take the United States out of the world organization. What did President Eisenhower think? reporters wanted to know. He did not believe that Red China would be admitted, Eisenhower replied. But if the UN should make this mistake, the attitude of the American government would have to be decided on the basis of how it could best advance the cause of peace. But what about Knowland's insistence on American withdrawal? the newsmen pressed. The President said he had not yet reached any such decision. No, he hadn't.

In November 1954 Red China announced that it had sentenced as spies thirteen Americans, eleven of them fliers who had fought in the Korean War. It was not only obvious that the charges against the fliers were fraudulent; Red China had clearly violated the Korean armistice agreement by not repatriating the airmen. A good many Americans besides William Knowland were furious, and the Senator demanded that the Chinese should be handed an ultimatum: Release the fliers or the United States would impose a naval blockade.

Eisenhower made plain to his press conference that he believed a blockade meant war and he was against imposing one. The President went further. He delivered a little fifteen-minute speech which he permitted the reporters to quote directly. A President, Eisenhower said, "experiences exactly the same resentment, the same anger, the same kind of sense of frustration almost, when things like this occur, as other Americans, and his impulse is to lash out. . . . In many ways the easy course for a President, for the Administration, is to adopt a truculent, publicly bold, almost insulting attitude." But the easy course had one terrible flaw—it led toward war. The sensible path was the hard way and "the hard way is to have the courage to be patient, tirelessly to seek out every single avenue open to us in the hope finally of leading the other side to a little better understanding of the honesty of our intentions. . . ."

The courage to be patient, the slow, hard way, using every possible avenue—a climax of coexistence was near and Eisenhower did not stand in its way. During all the bitternesses over foreign affairs in the postwar, one image in particular had inflamed the critics of the Roosevelt-Truman policies. It was their picture of the President of the United States sitting in Big Four conferences, joking and tossing off Martinis with the Soviet leaders, signing secret agreements that sold more millions down the river to Communism. As the summer of 1955 came on, the pressure for a Big Four conference steadily mounted. The Russians were calling for one; a good deal of world opinion agreed; in the Democratic-controlled Congress, Senator Walter George of Georgia, chairman of the powerful Senate Foreign Relations Committee, was pressing hard. President Eisenhower moved warily. He attempted to make certain that the time and the conditions were propitious for American purposes and he announced firmly that there would be no secret agreements—probably no agreements at all but merely exploratory talks. Then, on July 18, 1955, he joined the leaders of Britain, France, and the Soviet Union at a Big Four conference in Geneva.

The Russians tried hard to tell the world that they were men of peace. Party chief Nikita Khrushchev grinned endlessly for the photographers and said: "Things are different now." Premier Nikolai Bulganin went around in an open car beaming at everybody and waving his gray fedora. Foreign Minister Vyacheslav Molotov, he of the eternal *nyets* in the UN, got to talking of the photograph of him on a recent American visit wearing a ten-gallon hat. He'd like people to think of him, the Foreign Minister said to reporters, "as something more than a man who says no." The hat didn't fit, Molotov added, "but it's more important to have good publicity than to have a hat that fits."

If the Russians were friendly, Dwight Eisenhower was coexistence incarnate. He opened the conference with a moving appeal for "a new spirit. . . . No doubt there are among our nations philosophical convictions which are in many respects irreconcilable. Nothing that we can say or do here will change that fact. However, it is not always necessary that people should think alike and believe alike before they can work together." The President overlooked no amenity. Eisenhower, Bulganin later recalled delightedly, "opened the Martini road." When the President learned that the daughter of his World War II colleague, Soviet Marshal Georgi Zhukov, was about to be married, he promptly sent to Moscow gifts of a desk pen inscribed "From the President of the United States" and a portable American radio. And then as the conference neared its end, with many observers declaring that it was really getting nowhere, the President rose from his seat, began reading his formal paper prepared by the State Department, put it aside. He took off his glasses, laid them on the table, continued extemporaneously.

"Gentlemen," he said, "I have been searching my heart and mind for something that I could say here that could convince everyone of the great sincerity of the United States in approaching this problem of disarmament." Eisenhower turned and directly faced the Russians. "I should address myself for a moment principally to the delegates from the Soviet Union, because our two great countries admittedly possess new and terrible weapons in quantities which do give rise in other parts of the world, or reciprocally, to the fears and dangers of surprise attack."

The translations of the President's words were not yet coming through but his face alone, cocked to the side in earnestness and gravity, told that he was speaking important words. The usual bustle of the conference room quieted. "I propose, therefore," Eisenhower went on, "that we take a practical step, that we begin an arrangement very quickly, as between ourselves—immediately. These steps would include: to give each other a complete blueprint of our military establishment. . . . Next, to provide within our countries facilities for aerial photography to the other country." Firmly Eisenhower added: "What I propose, I assure you, would be but a beginning."

The Russians were sitting bolt upright. In the United States experts broke into puzzled discussion. How practical was the plan? Why should the Soviet exchange something it had, knowledge of the American military establishment, for something the United States might well not have and very much wanted—information about the Russian facilities? What was the essence of the Eisenhower foreign policy anyhow, with its wariness toward the world on the one hand and on the other hand its invitation to fly Soviet planes over America? The President found no phrase to express his program in international affairs, at least nothing as simple as his conservative-liberal description of his domestic policies. Perhaps it was because the emerging program for abroad, with its restraints on defense money, its hesitancies about large-scale economic aid, and its acceptance of coexistence, was—even more confusingly than the domestic policy—a blend of conservatism and of New Dealism. Perhaps it was because the Eisenhower foreign policy, in a very real sense, was Robert Taft in many of its tactics and Dean Acheson in its larger strategy.

When the President's plane, the *Columbine III*, neared the Washington airport, a summer shower was spattering the Capital. Vice-President Richard Nixon issued an instruction to the officials going out to the airport. No umbrellas, the Vice-President said, because people might be reminded of Prime Minister Neville Chamberlain coming back with his umbrella from the Munich appeasement of Hitler. Nixon need hardly have been concerned. By the summer of 1955 Eisenhower's in-between concept of the President's role, his conservative-liberal domestic policies, his mixed attitudes in foreign affairs, his warm but unaggressive personality, were sweeping him to a political potency unapproached since the heyday of Franklin Roosevelt.

The right wing of the Republican Party lay at his feet, powerless if not shattered. Senator Knowland was issuing no more calls for ultimatums and he was making it very plain that he was for Eisenhower first and last. To the farthest right there were only occasional yawps breaking the still of the cemetery. Senator McCarthy was now duly censured by the Senate of the United States and by a vote of 67 to 22. Flailing away at the descending oblivion, he summoned a press conference and "apologized" for having supported Eisenhower in 1952. The President smiled and the nation yawned.

Harry Truman was stirring restlessly. Where were

the give-'em-hell assaults? Why were there so few calls
for "real" liberalism? The head of the Democratic
Party, Adlai Stevenson, would soon answer: "We must
take care lest we confuse moderation with mediocrity,
lest we settle for half answers to hard problems. . . .
[But] I agree that it is time for catching our breath; I
agree that moderation is the spirit of the times."

Moderation, middle-of-the-road—the phrases were
filling the country until Charles Comiskey, vice-
president of the Chicago White Sox, could say with a
straight face: "Henceforth, we'll do our trading in
moderation, we'll be middle-of-the-roaders." In every
part of America, in every part of American living,
people were working out the clashes created by a decade of turbulent change with a thousand conscious
and unconscious compromises. If women were saying
they wanted babies, not careers, they were also making sure that the phone number of a baby sitter was
at hand. If the intellectuals were discussing a "new conservatism," the new conservatism, for the most part,
was heavily streaked with the old liberalism. The trend
was emphasized by the reports from the oncoming
generation. The pollsters polled, the magazines questioned away, and in Los Angeles a UCLA coed summarized the findings in a few words. What, in general,
did she want out of living? "Why, a good sensible life."
The coed added quickly: "But, you know, of course
not too darned sensible."

Somehow, amid all the bitter disagreements of the
post–World War II period, the United States had felt
its way to a genuinely national mood. It was not the
kind of arrival that could be announced in ringing
tones. It contained, in fact, a determination not to be
too sure where you were or where you ought to go.
It was nothing more or less than the decision on the
part of a people who were so in-between in so many of
their attitudes to go on cautiously, hopefully maintaining equilibrium. In the murky way of history, another
era in the life of the United States was closing. The

ten years from the end of World War II in the summer of 1945 to the Geneva Summit Conference in the summer of 1955 were over—and over not only in a chronological sense.

Some astute observers have found little good in the decade, only a muddled descent of American civilization. The "Dismal Decade," the "Years of Neuroses," the "Age of the Vacuum Tube," they have called the period. They see in it the culmination of deeply disturbing trends in the national life, and picture the end-product as a country dominated by a banal mass culture, a worship of the material, the gaudy, the violent, and the mediocre.

Certainly such portrayals cannot be airily waved aside. After all, the America of 1955 was a country where Altman's in New York City had quite a run on mink-handled openers for beer cans and a women's shop in Beverly Hills, California sent out charge plates made of fourteen-carat gold; where the disc jockeys took off "O, Happy Day" only to put on "If a Hottentot taught a tot to talk ere the tot could totter"; where the stock-market craze reached the point that millions of shares of blatantly wildcat uranium ventures were snapped up; where a major crime was committed every fifteen seconds; where approximately one hundred million dollars a year—or just about four times the expenditures on public libraries —were paid out for comic books; where the most popular of all its citizens, Dwight Eisenhower, defined an intellectual as "a man who takes more words than is necessary to say more than he knows."

Yet there is another way of viewing the decade, a way with a quite different emphasis. The ten years from 1945 to 1955 were a decade of high importance in American history, a Crucial Decade. When World War II ended, the Half-Century of Revolution in domestic affairs had reached a critical state. It had gone far enough to influence profoundly American living and to pile up a strong and bitter opposition. During the years immediately after V-J Day, the problem of international affairs reached a similar critical juncture. The emergence of the world-wide Communist threat brought changes in American foreign policy fully as revolutionary as the trends which had been developing on the domestic scene, and these jolting breaks with tradition also provoked potent resistance. Intermingling with the mounting storm, taking strength from it and giving strength to it, was the surge of McCarthyism which, in essence, amounted to an exasperated urge to club everything back into a simpler, more comfortable pattern. At the height of the drive for the traditional, during the tensions of the goadingly untraditional Korean War, two fateful questions were emerging. Would the United States continue, through extensions of the welfare state and of welfare capitalism and a variety of other techniques, the Half-Century of Revolution in domestic affairs? Would it continue moving along the new international path marked by the attitudes clustering around the concepts of containment and coexistence? What is crucial about the Crucial Decade is that during the years from 1945 to 1955 the American people faced these questions and they answered them.

Whatever the swings from Democrats to Republicans, McCarthyism to moderation, intellectualish New Dealers to practical-minded businessmen, there was a basic continuity in the era. Gradually, with many a contrary movement and sidewise venture, a greater and greater percentage of the population decided that the Half-Century of Revolution in domestic affairs was here to stay and that it should be forwarded. Still more gradually, and with much more bridling, an increasing percentage came to the conclusion that the traditional idea of a quick, total solution to international problems, executed largely by the United States alone, simply would not do. The coming of a general attitude of equilibrium in the summer of 1955 was accompanied by the arrival of a broad consensus in

the thinking of Americans about the basic public issues of the day. Most of them had come to agree on
continuing social change at home, if not so much, so
swiftly, and on a shift in their attitude toward the
world, if not so sharply, so expensively.

The continuity of the period also expressed itself in
political terms. In a very real sense, the Truman and
the early Eisenhower years blended into one development. It was the Truman Administration that began
codifying New Dealism in domestic affairs—slowing
down its pace, pushing its attitude only in areas of outstanding need. (It is easy to overlook the fact that as
early as 1949 Truman was describing his domestic
policy as the "middle-course" and defining the phrase
in a way that Eisenhower would not have found too
hard to accept.) Meanwhile the Truman years were
also bringing the departures in foreign policy. The
Eisenhower Administration, whatever its modifications, continued the codification in domestic affairs
and accepted and extended the breakaways in the foreign field. Moreover, it was bringing the Republican
Party, a large part of which had been talking for
twenty years as if it would do everything drastically
differently, into line with the long-running policies
and thus changing them from partisan to national programs. The consensus on fundamental public issues that
was reached in the summer of 1955 was so genuine a
consensus because it developed slowly and survived
the test of savage political warfare.

From the perspective of future years the arrival at
this consensus may well be considered one of the most
important facts in all the American story. Over the
centuries more than one powerful nation has, out of
meanness and shortsightedness, tried to walk against
a great tide of human aspirations and been swallowed
ignominiously. The two problems Americans faced
during the years 1945-55 were actually parts of one
such tide—a world-wide struggle of poor people or
men of lower status to achieve more income and more

of a sense of human dignity. Inside the United States the surge took the form of the demands for the Half-Century of Revolution. Around the world it appeared as the stirrings of underdeveloped colonial lands under Communist, partially Communist, or non-Communist impetus. On occasion during the exasperating, frightening years after World War II, the American people came close to saying that they had enough of aspirations, foreign or domestic. But they never quite said it and in time they managed to say something quite different.

As the Crucial Decade closed in the summer of 1955, the American people could face the onrushing years and the onrushing crises with one solid fact to buttress them. Whatever their addiction to chrome, comic books, and comic-book politics, whatever their yearning for the prepackaged, one-minute solution to everything, they had not, however sorely tempted, committed the supreme foolishness of trying to defy history.

XIII

More of the Same

THREE WEEKS after the Geneva Summit Conference, on August 14, 1955, President Eisenhower left Washington for a long vacation at the Denver home of his mother-in-law, Mrs. John S. Doud. In the mornings the President would do a quick run-through of official tasks; most afternoons he was off to the golf course or to the sparkling Rocky Mountain trout streams. On the afternoon of Friday, September 23, he played twenty-seven holes of golf and then spent a quiet evening with Mrs. Eisenhower and Mrs. Doud. In the middle of the night he was awakened by a pain in his chest and his physician, Major General Howard Snyder, hurried to his bedside. Shortly after 2 p.m. on Saturday, Acting Press Secretary Murray Snyder made the announcement: Dwight Eisenhower had suffered a heart attack and had just been taken to Fitzsimons Army Hospital.

The nation gasped, then fidgeted uneasily. Suddenly fervid Republicans realized to what extent their hopes for victory in 1956 rested on this one sixty-four-year-old human being. Suddenly ardent Democrats, who had developed a hatred for Richard Nixon such as had never before been visited on a mere Vice-President, recognized how close they might be to having Nixon in the White House. And suddenly too millions of Americans, who were neither particularly Democratic nor Republican, became aware just how much their troubled transition from old ways of thinking in public affairs had been eased by its association with this amiable national hero who made all the innovations seem so common sense, so American.

The President pulled through the first critical days in the oxygen tent. A few more weeks and he appeared out of any immediate danger. Five months after the attack, Eisenhower's physician, the distinguished heart specialist Dr. Paul Dudley White, assured the nation: "The President has made a good recovery. . . . Medically the chances are that the President should be able to carry on an active life satisfactorily for another five to ten years." People settled back again, as they wanted so much to do. The Crucial Decade was over, its decisions made; now let the details be worked out with as little fuss as possible.

The Presidential election of 1956 seemed hardly a contest. Adlai Stevenson, the lilt gone from his voice, ran with all the zest and decisiveness of a man taking the final steps to the gas chamber. The landslide reelection of Eisenhower was accompanied by a victory of the Democrats in the Congressional race. They held their majority in the Senate and increased it in the House—for the first time since 1848 a Presidential candidate had won without giving control of at least one branch of Congress to his party. Even this situation scarcely ruffled the scene. Since World War II, different parties had controlled the White House and at least one branch of Congress for almost one-third of the time; Americans were growing accustomed to split authority in Washington. What's more, the atmosphere of consensus had so affected the parties that one had to find the distinctions between them largely in matters of degree, of emphasis, of nuance. People were smiling understandingly at the story about the political writer who was hard pressed at a dinner party to answer the question, What *really* is the difference between a Republican and a Democrat nowadays? He tried, tried again, and was embarrassed by his own pronouncements. Finally he said: "A Republican, why a Republican when he makes a highball takes a jigger and measures out the whisky. A Democrat, a Democrat just pours."

Before and after the election, from 1955 on through 1957, the decisions of the Crucial Decade were executed in both domestic and foreign affairs. The Half-Century of Revolution at home inched ahead. For the most part the Eisenhower Administration, always budget-wary, held back on large-scale federal expenditures; for the most part, the Democratic majorities in Congress were less reluctant. Everything was compromise, adjustment, but some bills became law. Many Democrats in the House and Senate wanted a considerably liberalized social-security system; Eisenhower, fewer extensions. They agreed on legislation adding somewhat to the categories of people eligible. After a similar hassle, 70,000 more low-rent public-housing units were authorized. A thirty-three-billion-dollar proposal for highway building pleased the President and conservative Congressmen because of defense and general considerations, and delighted New Dealish Representatives and Senators because it would serve as economic pump-priming in the event of a recession. The debate was over where the money was to come from and finally all sides settled for a user's tax. Eisenhower successfully vetoed a Democratic bill to return to high, rigid price supports for agricultural products but accepted a billion-dollar "soil bank" plan, which smacked of Henry Wallace's Triple A by paying farmers to take land out of production.

In the most sensitive area of economic and social legislation, rights for Negroes, the disagreeing went on across party lines in Congress as well as between Congress and the Administration. The unreconstructable Dixiecrat Presidential candidate of 1948, now Democratic Senator Strom Thurmond of South Carolina, set a new filibuster record of twenty-four hours, and eighteen minutes trying to talk away any civil-rights legislation. But a bill reached the statute books, the first such legislation in eighty-two years, and it established a Federal Civil Rights Commission with the kind of functions which in time could undermine the power of the Thurmonds in Southern life.

Outside the field of legislation, the social upsweep continued. In 1956, almost without notice, the United States hurried by a milestone comparable in significance to the disappearance of the American frontier in the 1890's. The government issued figures indicating that the number employed in the worker's job of producing things was now less than the number making their livings from largely middle-class occupations. More than half the population had reached or was just about to reach the cherished status of the white collar. Other signs of the social upsurge were less statistical, more satisfying. Ivy League colleges were scouting the secondary schools to enroll able students regardless of family background. More miles of suburbia were stretching out, inhabited not only by the $25,000-a-year old-stock American but by the automobile worker, the man who ran the pharmacy in the city, the children of immigrants. Month after month, in one area of life after another, Negroes scored more "firsts." 1957 brought a later-day Jackie Robinson story. For centuries tennis had been a decidedly upper-class sport. On July 6, 1957, Althea Gibson, daughter of the Harlem streets, curtsied before the Queen of England, murmured "at last, at last," and received the Wimbledon trophy.

Of most basic importance in the Negro's advance, the 1954 Supreme Court decision ordering the desegregation of schools was chipping away at the ancient crust of custom. When the fall term opened in September 1957, desegregation troubles were plentiful. Alabama, Georgia, Mississippi, and South Carolina refused to budge; Virginia was talking "massive resistance." The Border State of Arkansas so brazenly de-

fied the Supreme Court that President Eisenhower
ordered federal troops into Little Rock. Yet most seasoned observers agreed with Harry S. Ashmore, the
moderate editor of the Arkansas *Gazette*, whose edi-
torials said in a dozen different ways: Here in Little
Rock, and throughout the United States, it's only a
matter of time.

From abroad the scare headlines kept coming. The
Chinese Communist leaders would make threatening
noises, subside, start up again. The Hungarians, long
restless under their Russian rulers, erupted into street
fighting and the Soviet, sending huge tanks clanking
over the bodies of men armed only with rifles or
sticks, reminded the United States that Communists,
coexisting or not, could be utterly ruthless. All the
while the turbulent Middle East was made more turbulent by the rabid nationalism of Egypt's new leader,
Gamal Abdel Nasser.

In 1956 Nasser was busy making deals with the
Soviet Union for guns, bombers, and tanks. Many of
the guns went into the hands of Egyptian comman-
does for hit-and-run raids on Israeli territory, and it
was hardly a secret that Nasser yearned to find the
right opportunity to launch a full-scale attack against
the Jewish state. The United States, trying to turn
Egyptian nationalism to the amelioration of Egyptian poverty, offered to help finance a gigantic dam
at Aswan on the Nile, which would irrigate some
2,000,000 acres of land and increase the arable territory of the country by more than thirty per cent.
Nasser liked the idea of American dollars for an Aswan
Dam; he also cuddled closer and closer to the Soviet
Union. In July 1956, Secretary of State John Foster
Dulles abruptly canceled the American offer of financial aid. Nasser exploded. In the course of a three-hour
tirade, he announced that he was "nationalizing" the
largely British and French-owned Suez Canal and that
the Aswan Dam would be built from the profits of
the Canal. The Canal, he stormed, "belongs to Egypt

. . . and it will be run by Egyptians! Egyptians! Egyptians!" What's more, Egypt was mobilizing. "We will defend our freedom to the last drop of our blood."

In Israel, political leaders had their own theory about the reason for the Egyptian mobilization. Our only choice now, one of them remarked, is whether "to wait and be wiped off the map and then be eulogized and mourned by our friends, or to attack, to survive, and then explain to our friends." On October 29, 1956, Israeli troops attacked and slashed across the Sinai Peninsula in triumph. (Later 6,000 Egyptian prisoners were exchanged for four Israelis.) The British and French, equally anxious to get rid of Nasser, joined the assault with air and naval units. From the Kremlin came a rapid-fire of statements. The Soviet Union would not let Egypt stand alone against "imperialist aggression"; Russian "volunteers" were eager to intervene. Inferentially, the Soviet threatened to bombard Britain and France with nuclear missiles if the invasion were not halted. In Washington, responsible men talked nervously about the coming of World War III.

Alarms, missile-rattling, intimations of nuclear doomsday—but somehow it all settled down. The United States, working with the UN, threw its full weight behind restoring peace in the Middle East. Under this pressure and the pressure of the Soviet threats, Israel, Britain, and France backed down. The Middle Eastern crisis even produced a promising new UN technique. To keep Egypt and Israel from each other's throats, the international organization set up a "United Nations Emergency Force" consisting of 2,600 troops from Colombia, Denmark, India, Norway, and Sweden. Shortly after 9 p.m. on March 7, 1957, advance battalions of Danes and Norwegians, riding in jeeps and trucks flying the blue-and-white flag of the UN, went splashing through the ancient mud of Gaza—history's first international task force to keep the peace.

Even the most pessimistic Americans were heartened by the Soviet political shake-up that came in July 1957.

Out went the tough old Bolshevik, First Deputy Premier Vyacheslav Molotov, and the Stalin protégé, Deputy Premier Georgi Malenkov—Molotov all the way out to Outer Mongolia, where he was to serve as "Ambassador," and Malenkov to remote Kazakhstan, where he would manage a hydroelectric plant. Bulganin was still Premier, Khrushchev still First Secretary of the Communist Party. But in describing state occasions, *Pravda* now started listing Khrushchev first —roly-poly, wisecracking, gladhanding Nikita Khrushchev, whom most observers said was a strong advocate of seeking an understanding with the West.

As 1957 drew to a close and the first period after the Crucial Decade ended, the United States ambled down its middle road, worried now and then, even having its frenetic moments, but usually happily absorbed in private affairs. The decisions made during the Crucial Decade seemed to be doing their job and they seemed enough. The great waves of prosperity kept rolling in, overwhelming any concerns about the world. In 1957 the government could issue figures establishing that, despite the slowly continuing inflation, most Americans were enjoying more real income than ever before. The signs were everywhere, in the way people lived, played, risked their money. In 1954 the New York Stock Exchange had ordered a public-opinion poll, which found that only twenty-three per cent of the population knew what a stock was and only ten per cent were even considering putting a penny in the market. Now, one in nine adults owned stock—in some cities, Berkeley, Hartford, Pasadena, St. Petersburg, and Wilmington, for example—one in every five people, babies included, were receiving dividends. Vacation time brought migrations bigger than the original march across the continent. In the summer of 1957 well over half the population, some 90,000,000, was going somewhere and spending about two and a half billion dollars to do it.

Middle-class Americans found money for whisky-flavored toothpaste; glass poles that were guaranteed to frustrate suburban woodpeckers; and radar-type fishing rods that sent out an electric wave to locate the fish and report back where it was. Everyone who served the rampant middle classes was lifting his sights. The new Montgomery Ward catalogue had two pages of "live listings"; you could get a Great Dane pup for $120 or a Shetland pony for $300. At drive-in restaurants in the Southwest, the girl in the cute uniform rushed out, placed a portable air conditioner around you as you ordered your hot-dog.

People who couldn't purchase things rented them—the booming rental business now included a secretary from the Kelly Girl Service, garden tools, silverware, cocktail glasses, and zircons. People who couldn't buy things or rent them got them by credit. Men who understood the America of 1957 were building the Diner's Club into a multi-million-dollar operation and launching a new national habit that reached a temporary climax when a Duluth businessman proudly exhibited to photographers his fifty-eight credit cards, each readied for instant use in a special accordion-type wallet. Department stores were not lagging behind. They were advertising their programs whereby a housewife could remain indefinitely in debt up to a certain sum, say $500. And if it was all too much bother, firms were springing up that called themselves "debt counselors." For a fee, they took your check each month, gave you a living allowance, parceled out the remainder to your creditors.

The form of prosperity most enjoyable to Americans, prosperity which permitted exhibiting each new step up the social ladder, kept offering its fresh delights. Was a new dress no longer enough to impress the neighbors? Millions of American women (an estimated one in three) had the money to go to a beauty shop and have their hair tinted practically any color it was not—Golden Apricot, Sparkling Sherry, Fire Silver, or Champagne Beige. Could anyone go off to a vacation of lying on the beach? The magazines said "the influentials" were turning to skin-diving and the sales of web feet were up by more than a quarter of a million. Did the crummiest homes in town have TV these days? Hi-fi sets were roaring in and, to make sure the neighbors knew you had one, they were being played so loud that a professor of psychology announced a new neurosis, "audiophilia," turning up the sound until it "reaches the level of physical pain."

The automobile, traditional yardstick of status in America, was swept into rococo phases. Yearly the American cars grew longer, wider, cushier, more gadgety, and with bigger, shinier fins. If you wanted to be sniffish about chrome, the pint-sized foreign cars were coming in—only 56,000 imported in 1955, more than 200,000 in 1957. General Motors stirred to take care of those who couldn't find a sufficiently expensive car. It announced for $13,074 the Cadillac Eldorado Brougham, which offered on its dashboard a tissue box, vanity case, lipstick, and four gold-finished drinking cups. Those who wanted to assert status above all status-seeking could turn to the ultimate in inverted snobbery: the plain black Ford station wagon.

For the most part, intellectuals were glum, warning. They kept insisting that the decisions made in the Crucial Decade were not enough in either foreign or domestic affairs. They added that the very roads Americans had chosen brought their own great dangers. A nation dedicated to lifting endlessly the standard of living and to a long-time coexistence with a powerful enemy could easily turn into a militarized, overfat, numb civilization, increasingly oblivious to the value that had stoked American progress—individualism. Among such critics, the phrase of the immediate post-Crucial Decade years undoubtedly was "organization man," taken from the title of the 1956 volume by William H. Whyte, Jr., a part-descriptive, part-satirical, and all hortatory analysis of the civilization that was emerging in the United States. The dissidents went on reading and writing their books; encouraging the few rebels of the oncoming generation such as youthful Jules Feiffer, whose sad, fragile humor reflected his feeling that the new America made real satire impossible—"satire doesn't stand a chance against reality any more"; huddling together with the talismans of their unhappiness, like the mimeographed sheets that were passed around with waspish glee in intellectual circles.

On the sheets were the anonymous words of some newspaperman in Washington. Fed up with President Eisenhower's middle-of-the-roadism and his muddled way of expressing it, the reporter rewrote the "Gettysburg Address" as Eisenhower would have delivered it: "I haven't checked these figures, but 87 years ago, I think it was, a number of individuals organized a governmental setup here in this country, I believe it covered certain eastern areas, with this idea they were following up, based on a sort of national independence arrangement. . . .

"Well, now of course we are dealing with this big difference of opinion, civil disturbance you might say, although I don't like to appear to take sides or name any individuals. . . . Here we are, you might put it that way, all together at the scene. . . . We want to pay our tribute to those loved ones, those departed individuals who made the supreme sacrifice here on the basis of their opinions about how this setup ought to be handled. It is absolutely in order and 100 per cent OK to do this.

"But if you look at the overall picture of this, we can't pay any tribute—we can't sanctify this area—we can't hallow, according to whatever individual creeds or faiths or sort of religious outlooks are involved, like I said about this particular area. It was those individuals themselves, including the enlisted men—very brave individuals—who have given this religious character to the area. The way I see it, the rest of the world will not remember any statements issued here, but it will never forget how these men put their shoulders to the wheel and carried this idea down the fairway. . . .

"We have to make up our minds right here and now, as I see it, they didn't put out all that blood, perspiration and—well, that they didn't just make a dry run here, that all of us, under God, that is, the God of our choice, shall beef up this idea about freedom and liberty and those kind of arrangements, and that government of all individuals, by all individuals and for the individuals shall not pass out of the world picture."

The intellectuals satirized and gloomed and warned, and the general public did not listen. The general public, if it was harking to anything except the incessant wheels of upper mobility, was responding to the voice of religion. The increased interest noticeable soon after World War II now burst into a full-scale revival. Some of the new attention to religion was undoubtedly a sincere turning to the rigors and consolations of faith; knowledgeable and hardheaded religious leaders could point to incontrovertible facts. But a good deal of it was certainly a false religiosity, compounded of social aspirations and a fervid desire to avoid thinking. In 1956 the Reverend Dr. John Sutherland Bonnell, minister of the Fifth Avenue Presbyterian Church in New York City, began running a highly successful ad. "FOR A SPIRITUAL LIFT IN A BUSY DAY," the ad said, "DIAL-A-PRAYER. CIrcle 6-4200. One minute of inspiration in prayer." The bookstores were offering *Go with God* or *The Power of Prayer on Plants* or *Pray Your Weight Away*, while the juke boxes joined in with "I've Got Religion," "Big Fellow in the Sky," and "The Fellow Upstairs." *Modern Screen* magazine ran a series called "How the Stars Found Faith," in which Jane Russell announced: "I love God. And when you get to know Him, you find He's a Livin' Doll."

Week after week Billy Graham, a sincere Fundamentalist evangelist who was now organized into a tremendous operation with the efficiency and impersonality of a Dewey campaign, went around saving more cities, not to speak of the Los Angeles hoodlum Mickey Cohen. Shortly after Cohen declared his conversion, it seems, he got together with W. C. Jones, a member of the governing board of the Billy Graham Crusade. Brother Cohen and Brother Jones prayed together over breakfast, then Cohen addressed a meeting of the Los Angeles Union Rescue Mission at which five men made decisions for Christ. "After that," Jones recalled, "I was convinced that Michael—I always called him Michael in those days—was converted," and after that Michael, who said he needed "a little stake" for his new life as a Christian, borrowed about $5,000 from the Graham organization which he never repaid. "I don't begrudge him the money," Jones added sadly. "But I've now come to the conclusion he wasn't sincere when he said he was following Billy Graham." The Crusade rolled on, on to its climactic New York meeting in 1957, where a $1,300,000 budget had taken care of everything, including special climate studies to predict when to schedule outdoor meetings and special surveys of the habits of strap-hangers to learn the most effective placement for subway ads.

In Minnesota, a wholesale groceryman listened to a re-broadcast of Billy Graham's opening sermon at Madison Square Garden, drove off with a friend for some fishing. In ten minutes his new radar-type rod had produced an eight-pound trout. He put the fish in his ice container, opened a beer, and settled back for a bit of heavy thinking. "You know," he said to his friend, "those Russians talk and talk and bluster. But with God and with good old American know-how"—he tapped his glistening rod—"with those on our side, I just can't get bothered."

XIV

The Middle Road
Grows Bumpy

THE UNITED STATES read the headlines on Saturday morning, October 5, 1957. The Soviet news agency, Tass, announced: "The first artificial earth satellite in the world has now been created. This first satellite was successfully launched in the U.S.S.R. . . . Artificial earth satellites will pave the way for space travel and it seems that the present generation will witness how the freed and conscious labor of the people of the new socialist society turns even the most daring of man's dreams into reality."

Americans took another astonished gulp of coffee, read on eagerly. The Tass dispatch was not reticent. The satellite was twenty-two inches in diameter, weighed 184.3 pounds, was whirling about the earth at a maximum height of 560 miles and at a speed of 18,000 miles an hour, circling the globe once every hour and thirty-five minutes. Inside were two radio transmitters that continually beeped scientific information to earth. The Russians called the satellite a "sputnik," meaning an object that was traveling with a traveler—that is, an object that was traveling with the earth which in turn was traveling through space. By nightfall of this strange Saturday, the most eerie day since Harry Truman announced the atomic bomb in far-off 1945, the word "sputnik" had a firm place in the American language.

The reactions came in a caterwaul of disagreement. Here and there Americans pooh-poohed, including Rear Admiral Rawson Bennett, Chief of the Office of Naval Research, who wanted to know why all the fuss over a "hunk of iron almost anybody could launch." Leading Democrats cried shame. "If this now known Soviet superiority," Senator Stuart Symington, of the Armed Services Committee, said for them, "develops into supremacy, the position of the free world will be critical." Yet "for fiscal reasons this Government . . . continues to cut back and slow down its own missile program." Symington demanded an investigation by the Senate Armed Services Committee. "Only in this way can the American people learn the truth. Putting it mildly, they have not been getting the truth." "The launching," added Senator Henry M. Jackson, chairman of the military applications panel of the Joint Congressional Committee on Atomic Energy, was "a devastating blow to the prestige of the United States as the leader in the scientific and technical world." It corroborated, Jackson said, the Soviet claim of the previous August that it had launched an intercontinental ballistic missile and had developed an effective missile-propulsion system.

Republicans varied in their emphases but most took the line which President Eisenhower expressed through his press secretary. The satellite, said James Hagerty calmly, was "of great scientific interest."

But what about its defense and security aspects? reporters pressed.

He was staying with its "scientific interest," Hagerty replied. His manner became still more nonchalant. The sputnik "did not come as a surprise." Besides, "we never thought of our program as one which was in a race with the Soviet's." Other Administration statements had the same unruffled tone. The United States had decided to separate its military-missile and its space-missile programs and to emphasize the former. Hence the Soviet success in getting a satellite up first.

It soon became clear that many scientists engaged in government research had opposed this separation. A number now spoke out, not only arguing against continuation of the separation, but maintaining that their progress on both programs had been slowed by interservice rivalries and by the Administration's insistence on holding down costs. Almost all scientists agreed that the launching of the sputnik proved that the Russians were well ahead of the United States in building and controlling rockets. After all, they pointed out, the United States in its most optimistic planning had expected to launch a satellite of only 21.5 pounds—seven times lighter than the sputnik. Dr. Joseph Kaplan, chairman of the American program for the International Geophysical Year, spoke the general scientific estimate of the Russian achievement. It was nothing less than "tremendous." Dr. Kaplan added: "If they can launch one that heavy, they can put up much heavier ones."

Just twenty-nine days later, on November 3, the Soviet put up a whale of a lot heavier one—Sputnik II, weighing 1,120.29 pounds and orbiting as much as 1,056 miles away. About half its weight was a labyrinth of scientific instruments reporting back to earth. Sputnik II also contained the sure harbinger of a coming Russian attempt to put a man into space. In a hermetically sealed, air-conditioned compartment was a live dog of the laika breed, with instruments strapped to the animal's chest which broadcasted its reactions to space conditions.

In Washington, people had a new story. It was about the reporter who called up the U.S. Space Agency and asked how the American program was going. The girl in the office replied: "Sir, are you calling *for* information or *with* information?" Throughout the United States a sense of alarm, exasperation, humilia-

tion, and confusion mounted. Sputniks I and II dramatized as nothing else could have done that the chief
thing on which Americans had depended for their
national security and for victory in a competitive
coexistence with Communism—the supremacy of
American technical know-how—had been bluntly
challenged.

At the White House James Hagerty was no longer
issuing casual statements. The President moved up a
speech scheduled to be delivered on November 13.
Four days after Sputnik II, on November 7, he
made the address and it included an announcement
of the appointment of James R. Killian, Jr., president
of the Massachusetts Institute of Technology, as Special Assistant to the President for Science and Technology "to have the active responsibility for helping
me to follow through on the scientific improvement
of our defense." The next day Secretary of Defense
Neil H. McElroy revised a long-standing Administration policy. Heretofore the American satellite program
had been under the charge of the Navy, with all
other branches concentrating on long-range ballistic
missiles. Now McElroy ordered the Army, which had
a well-tested Jupiter-C rocket, to take over on satellites and to get an artificial moon into orbit.

The Defense Department was soon issuing press
releases: on December 4 the United States would put
a satellite into orbit at Cape Canaveral, Florida. Tens
of thousands of spectators and hundreds of reporters
gathered. The countdown started at 5:30 a.m. and was
stopped; a fuel valve was not working. Another countdown, another halt because of mechanical failure. In
early afternoon the announcement came that the
launching would be delayed forty-eight hours, until
December 6. The foreign press broke into loud hee-
haws. "Flopnik," "Stay-putnick," "Kaputnik," British
papers labeled the American satellite. The Ameri-
canized Japanese press wrote about "Sputternick."
The Communist East German papers took the Ger-

man word for "late," *spaet*, and sneered "Spaetnik."
In Washington, people passed around another wry
wisecrack: "The American satellite ought to be called
Civil Servant. It won't work and you can't fire it."

At Cape Canaveral, December 6 came in a startlingly
beautiful day. The thousands gathered again, buzzed
expectantly as the reports said all was going well. Precisely on schedule, at 11:45 a.m. the satellite blasted
off, its orange blaze seething against the blue of the
sky. Seconds later the orange turned into a dingy
brown-black smoke. The satellite had started up, exploded, crashed back burning on its pad. This time a
comment came from the First Secretary of the Communist Party of the Soviet Union. Nikita Khrushchev
was playful, condescending. The Soviet sputniks were
"lonely." They were "waiting for American satellites
to join them in space." Then the cold, crunching truth:
"Who wants to overtake whom in science? The United
States would like to overtake the Soviet Union."

More frantic weeks, in Washington and at Cape Canaveral. On January 31, 1958, President Eisenhower
was vacationing in Augusta. At about 5:30 p.m. Hagerty began going back and forth between the press
room and the President's cottage, giving Eisenhower
the latest word from Cape Canaveral. After dinner, he
brought the President firm news. The satellite would
definitely be fired that night; the blast-off would come
at 10:48 p.m. A direct telephone line was connected
from Eisenhower's cottage to Dr. J. Wallace Joyce at
the National Science Foundation in Washington. Dr.
Joyce received word that the satellite had been
launched faultlessly. He waited seven minutes, giving
it time to reach a height permitting it to go into orbit.
He waited another 114 minutes while his instruments
told him that it was making a first swing around the
earth. Then Dr. Joyce put the call through to Atlanta.
"It's in orbit," the scientist said. The Eisenhower smile
had never been more radiant. "That's wonderful, simply wonderful," the President replied.

The whole United States heaved a sigh of relief. But for a considerable part of the population the old, post-Crucial Decade days of assurance were gone. The American satellite, the Explorer, weighed only 30.8 pounds; whirling proudly in space, it nevertheless was a conspicuous symbol that the United States was second best in a field that could prove decisive. Under the circumstances the unending crises abroad took on a greatly heightened power to worry and to frighten.

About three months after the Explorer went into orbit, on March 27, 1958, Khrushchev became clear-cut boss of the Soviet Union, and four days later his government issued an ambiguous but decidedly trouble-brewing statement that it intended to suspend nuclear tests while reserving the right to resume them if the United States and Britain did not follow suit. By the summer of 1958, the Middle East was again in such turmoil that American Marines were ordered into Lebanon. Fall brought more threats from the Chinese Reds about the islands lying off Formosa, Quemoy and Matsu. On November 27, 1958, Khrushchev delivered what sounded like an ultimatum on the delicate subject of Berlin. Within six months, he said, West Berlin must be "free," which was standard Communist language for putting West Berlin in a situation where it would end up Communist-controlled. Spring 1959, and the most remote region of the world rang an alarm bell. Chinese Communists were cracking down on the Tibetans, sending the Dalai Lama fleeing to India.

"When are we going to land on the moon?" a Muscovite asked Khrushchev. The Soviet leader slapped his thigh and laughed. "Why should we go there? We're doing all right here on earth." Scores of respected American commentators were pointing out that the Soviet was doing fine in impressing, cajoling, and pressuring nations here on earth. In a number of "neutral" countries both pro-Communism and anti-Americanism, whether pro-Communist or not, seemed to be increasing. Americans had to watch the process going on just

ninety miles south of Florida. On January 1, 1959,
Fidel Castro's bearded revolutionaries took over Cuba.
Within months some Communist infiltration of the
government was plain. A few more months and
most of Cuba's institutions were marked by a bitter
and systematized anti-Americanism. The press of the
United States was filled with dispatches like the description of the new educational process in the Havana
schools:

The teacher of the third-grade class asks: "What did
José Marti do?"

The eight-year-old boy answers: "José Marti freed
Cuba from the Spaniards."

"And what did Fidel Castro do?"

"Fidel freed Cuba from the United States, which
seized all our land."

"Correct," the teacher says. She turns to a girl student: "What happened on February 15, 1898?"

"The United States blew up the *Maine* so they could
intervene in Cuba."

The Portland *Oregonian* spoke a national mood
when it commented in connection with the Castro
movement: "All this sort of thing was bad enough
when we were first learning about the Communist
menace. It is downright terrifying with those sputniks
staring down at us."

The new apprehension in the United States ranged
beyond events in foreign countries, particularly to the
area most sensitized by the Soviet sputnik success—
the American attitude toward learning in general and
toward science in particular. The Soviet schools,
Americans were being told, were tough, purposeful,
heavily emphasizing science in every year from the
fourth grade up, ruthlessly ready to separate the mediocre from the outstanding students and to push the
latter. And the schools of the United States? "I will
tell you about the American schools," a Nobel Prize
physicist said to a New York City group. "This is the
way they decide how to teach. People who know

what they are talking about say, 'We should teach that the world is round, not square.' The superintendent, one eye on the mommas of the Parent-Teachers-Association, the other eye on the Chamber of Commerce, the labor unions, the Croatian-American Society, and what-have-you, says, 'I will find out how many voters in this town think that the world is round and how many think that it is square.' "

Five months after Sputnik I, *Life* began a series of articles which summarized and prodded the growing national concern. "Crisis in Education," the series was called. For years, *Life* said, "most critics of U.S. education have suffered the curse of Cassandra—always to tell the truth, seldom to be listened to." Now the sputniks had brought "a recognized crisis" and its "salient points" were:

"The schools have been overcrowded for years. . . .

"Most teachers are grossly underpaid (some are not worth what they get). A great many . . . have to work without help, understanding or proper tools.

"In their eagerness to be all things to all children, schools have gone wild with elective courses. They build up the bodies with in-school lunches and let the minds shift for themselves.

"Where there are young minds of great promise, there are rarely the means to advance them. The nation's stupid children get far better care than the bright. The geniuses of the next decade are even now being allowed to slip back into mediocrity.

"There is no general agreement on what the schools should teach. A quarter century has been wasted with the squabbling over whether to make a child well adjusted or teach him something.

"Most appalling, the standards of education are shockingly low."

Shockingly low—in the post-sputnik era, Americans were reading harsh words about their schools and, beyond their schools, about their whole way of life. Intellectuals said it, now more vigorously than ever.

Democrats and dissident Republicans said it, worriedly, angrily. Quite different people were also speaking up. Mrs. Clare Boothe Luce, high Republican and so often a spokesman of American self-satisfaction, now declared: The beep of the Russian sputniks is an "outer-space raspberry to a decade of American pretensions that the American way of life is a gilt-edge guarantee of our national superiority."

In the week that Sputnik I went up, a band blared "When the Saints Go Marching In" and 1,753 delegates of the International Brotherhood of Teamsters marched into the Miami Beach Auditorium. Fat President David Beck bellowed for an hour a sentiment no one could deny—"God never created me in the crucible of infallibility"—and was retired to a $50,000-a-year pension and indictments for wholesale fleecing. Up went the roars for Jimmy Hoffa, the abundantly exposed prime target of Senator John McClellan's Labor Rackets Committee. A Chicago Teamster, Thomas Haggerty, tried to run against Hoffa on moral grounds and the delegates had a wonderful time. "We got a new slogan," they said with roars of rib-poking laughter. "Haggerty for integrity, Hoffa for President." When Hoffa was duly named President of the nation's largest union, some Teamsters could not contain their pride. "Jimmy," they chanted over and over again, "is the greatest little bastard who ever put on shoes." Many another American wondered what was happening to the simplest, the most basic conceptions of morality in the United States.

They were getting none too comforting answers. The McClellan Committee went on revealing sleazy union practices, often condoned by the rank-and-file members and often connived in by management. The House Subcommittee on Legislative Oversight, headed by Representative Oren Harris of Arkansas, reported that Bernard Goldfine, a businessman with decided needs for connections in Washington, had paid

the cost of a vicuna coat and of hotel stays for none
other than the chief assistant to the President of the
United States, Sherman Adams. Still protesting that
he had "done no wrong," Adams had to be forced off
the national scene by Republican politicians worried
about the coming Congressional election. American
politics, Republican or Democratic, continued to produce peculiarly disconcerting incidents. In 1958 a federal grand jury indicted for income-tax evasion the
Reverend Mr. Adam Clayton Powell, Jr., minister of
the Abyssinian Baptist Church, a Democratic Congressman rhapsodically popular in Harlem, and one of
the most vigorous spokesmen of the upcoming Negro
minority (the jury disagreed and returned no verdict).
At the same time the mass media were picking up a
book by Professor Philip E. Jacob of the University of
Pennsylvania, who had surveyed the American colleges
and concluded that cheating "is so widespread as to
challenge the well-nigh universal claim of students
that they value honesty as a moral virtue. Frequent
cheating is admitted by 40% or more at a large number
of colleges, often with no apology or sense of wrongdoing." And all the while, the clouds were gathering
around the one folk hero who had emerged in post-
Crucial Decade America.

Week after week during late 1956 and 1957 Charles
Van Doren had been seen on the NBC program
Twenty-One. On the TV screen he appeared lanky,
pleasant, smooth in dress and manner but never
slick, confident but with an engaging way of under-
stating himself. The long, hard questions would come
at him and his eyes would roll up, squeeze shut, his
forehead furrow and perspire, his teeth gnaw at his
lower lip. Breathing heavily, he seemed to coax information out of some corner of his mind by talking to
himself in a kind of stream-of-consciousness. Like a
good American, he fought hard, taking advantage of
every rule. ("Let's skip that part, please, and come
back to it.") Like a good American, he won with no

crowing. And, like a good American, he kept on winning, downing corporation lawyers or ex-college
presidents with equal ease on questions ranging from
naming the four islands of the Balearic Islands to
explaining the process of photosynthesis to naming the
three baseball players who each amassed more than
3,500 hits. Charles Van Doren was "the new All-
American boy," the magazines declared, and to millions he was that indeed—a crew-cut, gray-flannel
image to an America yearning for the crew-cut, gray-
flannel life.

After Van Doren finally lost and NBC made him a
$50,000-a-year commentator on Dave Garroway's
Today show, the arrival of the sputniks soon gave him
an even more solid place as a folk hero. Was he not
the son of America's most famous intellectual family?
Had he not won his celebrity on an egghead program
and continued to teach the youth at Columbia for
$4,400 a year despite his large NBC salary? Of the
letters that continued to pour in to Van Doren, one in
four was written by a parent or teacher telling him that
he was an idol for the young who counteracted Elvis
Presley, that he had taken the curse off studying, that
he had proved an egghead could be as glamorous as
Gary Cooper or Mickey Mantle. "I am damned happy
about these letters," said Charles Van Doren.

From the beginning of the big-money TV quizzes,
some people had been unhappy. They argued that
the programs were giving the public the dangerously
distorted idea that learning consisted of knowing petty,
disconnected facts for a fat fee. Others were skeptical
about the reality of the contests; they insisted that at
least some of the shows must be fixed. Evidence
emerged that some of the minor shows were in fact
fixed; the New York County Grand Jury became interested. Most unhappy of all was a chunky, bristle-
haired, abundantly articulate young man, Herbert M.
Stempel, a C.C.N.Y. student who had won $49,500 on
Twenty-One before losing to Van Doren.

Stempel had problems. His big winnings had been tossed away. His psychiatrist bills were mounting. Worst of all of Stempel's problems was his ego. He kept saying to friends that the producers of *Twenty-One*, Daniel Enright and Albert Freedman, had made him muff questions to which he knew the answers ("I was forced to say that Gothic architecture originated in Germany when I know damn well it was France"). Enright had instructed him in unnatural grimaces and gestures, insisting that he "think violently" in the isolation booth ("I call it the Dan Enright school of acting"). Then, because "we've reached a plateau, we need a new face," Enright ordered him to "take a dive" to Charles Van Doren, "a guy that had a fancy name, Ivy League education, parents all his life, and I had the opposite. . . . All of this [fame and money of Van Doren] should have been coming to me." The more Stempel thought about what had happened, the more his psyche bothered him. He was especially upset one night "when I took my wife to the theater . . . and I overheard somebody saying, 'That's the guy who was beaten by Van Doren.' It hurt me egotistically." In April 1958 Stempel massaged his bruised ego by talking to District Attorney Frank Hogan and to the New York *World-Telegram and Sun*. His story amounted to the charge that *Twenty-One*, including Van Doren's participation, was rigged.

Reporters hurried to Van Doren's smartly redecorated Greenwich Village home. The All-American boy was "sad" and "shocked" at such talk. Of course he had played "honestly. . . . At no time was I coached or tutored."

The Grand Jury finished its investigation and Judge Mitchell Schweitzer impounded the record on the ground that it contained allegations that could seriously hurt people who had not had an opportunity to reply. Stories leaked from the Grand Jury; more ex-contestants were talking. The reporters went back to Van Doren again. This time the All-American boy showed a proper American indignation. "It is an insult," he said, "to keep asking me these questions."

"Well," a reporter pressed, "is it absolutely true that you have never been coached in any way?"

"Hell, no!"

The leaks, the rumors went on. A new Grand Jury convened. District Attorney Hogan was calling people in, including Van Doren. Under oath he flatly denied any part in rigging. On October 6, 1959, Representative Oren Harris's Special Subcommittee on Legislative Oversight (in this case oversight over the Federal Communications Commission) began closed hearings on the quiz shows. Van Doren telegraphed to the Committee a categorical statement that he had not been "assisted in any form." He was "available" to the Committee any time it might like to question him.

A few more days of testimony and the Committee decided it would very much like to question him. It sent Van Doren a telegram inviting him to appear voluntarily; the telegram was not answered. The Committee issued a formal subpoena for his appearance. The process-server could not find him.

Six days went by. On October 14 Van Doren appeared at the Hotel Roosevelt in New York City, was handed the subpoena, and walked into a jammed press conference. Smiling but showing strain, he read a prepared statement. He had not been evading the subpoena. He had been "distressed" by the rush of events, asked for a week's leave of absence from Columbia, and went with his wife to New England "to gather my thoughts . . . in the October beauty of the region." He did not know he was being sought until yesterday.

Reporters closed in with questions. How could he have failed to know about the subpoena when it was the big news in the newspapers and on radio and TV? When was he going to tell the real story? Van Doren paled, clutched the rostrum until his knuckles showed white. He would say no more. He respected the

United States Congress too much to answer questions until he reached the "appropriate forum," the Harris Committee.

On November 2 Van Doren made his way into the House Caucus Room, a pale, tense young man in an Oxford-gray suit and a dark-figured tie. The huge, high-ceilinged chamber was jammed and standees flowed into the corridor; 120 reporters and seventeen photographers scrambled for vantage points. Van Doren eased himself uncomfortably into the witness chair, asked for some water. A hush fell over the room as he began to read a prepared statement in a low, taut voice: "I would give almost anything I have to reverse the course of my life in the last three years. . . . I have learned a lot in those three years, especially in the last three weeks. . . . I've learned a lot about good and evil. They are not always what they appear to be. I was involved, deeply involved, in a deception."

Van Doren's voice steadied as he became accustomed to the still of the room. He was reading calmly now, with none of the gestures that millions had associated with him. He had not been gradually lured into the deception; the faking started "with my first actual appearance on 'Twenty-One.' I was asked by Freedman to come to his apartment. He took me into his bedroom where we could talk alone. He told me that Herbert Stempel . . . was unpopular, and was defeating opponents right and left to the detriment of the program. He asked me if, as a favor to him, I would agree to make an arrangement. . . . Freedman guaranteed me $1,000 if I would appear for one night. I will not bore this committee by describing the intense moral struggle that went on inside me. . . . The fact is that I unfortunately agreed, after some time, to his proposal."

Van Doren had not faked occasionally; everything was rigged. "I met him [Freedman] next at his office, where he explained how the program would be controlled. He told me the questions I was to be asked, and then asked if I could answer them. Many of them I could. But he was dissatisfied with my answers. They were not 'entertaining' enough. He instructed me how to answer the questions: to pause before certain of the answers, to skip certain parts and return to them, to hesitate and build up suspense, and so forth. On this first occasion and on several subsequent ones he gave me a script to memorize, and before the program he took back the script and rehearsed me in my part. This was the general method which he used through my fourteen weeks on *Twenty-One*."

Van Doren was fully aware of the dishonesty of what he was doing. He was "deeply troubled" but "the show ballooned beyond my wildest expectations. . . . I became a celebrity. I received thousands of letters and dozens of requests to make speeches, appear in movies, and so forth. . . . I was winning more money than I had ever had or even dreamed of having. I was able to convince myself that I could make up for it after it was over."

As the weeks went by, he grew "terribly uncomfortable. . . . Frankly, I was very much afraid." He told Freedman of his fears and asked "several times" to be released from the program. Freedman explained that Van Doren would have to leave by being defeated in "a dramatic manner." Van Doren went on performing on *Twenty-One*. An attractive blonde attorney, Mrs. Vivienne Nearing, appeared on the program as an opponent of Van Doren; Freedman apparently liked her performance. She played a series of dramatic tie games and then Freedman "told me that . . . I would be defeated by her. I thanked him."

When the revelations began to close in on Van Doren, he was "horror-struck. . . . I simply ran away. . . . Most of all, I was running from myself." After he was served the subpoena, he "spent the rest of the week trying hopelessly to seek a way out. . . . There was one way out which I had, of course, often considered, and that was simply to tell the truth." But "emotionally" he did not find this a "possible" solution.

Van Doren's voice was tensing up again. He looked up from his manuscript, glanced nervously at the crowd. In the end, he said, "it was a small thing that tipped the scales. A letter came to me . . . from a woman, a complete stranger, who had seen me on the Garroway show and who said she admired my work there. She told me that the only way I could ever live with myself, and make up for what I had done—of course, she, too, did not know exactly what that was —was to admit it, clearly, openly, truly. Suddenly I knew she was right. . . ."

His voice calmed again. "In the morning I telephoned my attorney and told him my decision. He had been very worried about my health and, perhaps, my sanity, and he was happy that I had found courage at last. He said 'God bless you.'" Charles Van Doren laid aside his manuscript, turned to his lawyer, and smiled.

Rarely, in the long history of public confessions, had anyone revealed an episode of more thoroughgoing fraudulence. Van Doren had knowingly entered into a total deception and received huge returns for it, in money and in non-pecuniary returns. Then, when the charges came, he had lied to his family, his lawyer, the Grand Jury, the reporters, and a Congressional Committee. In his appearance before the Committee, he had lied, or at least not told the whole truth, even in the course of confessing that he had lied. The woman who liked Van Doren on the Garroway show may have influenced him finally to tell the truth; he could hardly have been uninfluenced by the fact that his appearance at the Congressional hearing was the last possible moment when he could avoid a perjury charge. He stated that he had asked producer Albert Freedman to let him off the show but that Freedman refused. He did not explain why he did not simply leave the program or, if he preferred to be extra polite, just miss a question he was not supposed to miss.

As Van Doren finished his statement, the room was in dead silence. Chairman Oren Harris spoke first. He wanted to "compliment" Van Doren on his statement. Other Congressmen or Committee officials hastened to "commend" him for his "soul-searching" statements, his "fortitude," his "forthrightness." Congressman Peter F. Mack, Jr., Democrat of Illinois, expressed the hope that NBC would not fire Van Doren; Representative William E. Springer, Republican of Illinois, that Columbia University would not act "prematurely." The crowd applauded at each remark.

Representative Steven B. Derounian, Republican of Nassau County, New York, was a little restless at all this. "I don't think," he said coldly, "an adult of your intelligence ought to be commended for telling the truth." There was no applause.

Chairman Harris ended the brief proceedings. He had some further thoughts that anybody who "tells the whole truth in a matter that is so important to the American people and the public interest is to be highly complimented. . . ." He turned to Van Doren, smiled benignly. "I think you have a great future ahead of you. . . . I think I could end this session by saying what your attorney did say to you the other day; that is, 'God bless you.'"

Five hours after the Committee adjourned, Columbia University announced it was accepting Van Doren's "resignation"; the next morning NBC fired him without circumlocution. Newspaper editors competed with the pulpits in their sermons on the state of American morality. The networks fell over each other trying to show that each was fumigating the fastest until the actor Walter Slezak moaned: "Everybody in TV is so suspicious that if you say 'Oh, my God' on television, they think you're being paid off by the Holy Father." CBS, the wags added, was about to move *Church of the Air* to prime evening time.

But the general public showed no such reaction; its tone was like that of Chairman Harris and most of his Committee. Letters flooded into NBC; they were 5 to 1 against the firing of Van Doren. At Columbia a large group of students held a rally to protest his dismissal. Several colleges hinted they would like to employ him, including his alma mater, St. John's, which prided itself on a special emphasis on the values of Western Civilization. In Hollywood, the well-known producer Mervyn LeRoy said he was offering Van Doren an acting position—as a prosecutor in a movie. The "punishment" had gone too far; besides, "it's time someone gave him a job that would pay a living wage." Newspapers and magazines, checking the general reaction, found a majority of Americans fully supporting Van Doren. One responsible journal declared that three out of four were saying that "most people" would have done what Van Doren did for the money and the fame.

At the end of 1959, *Look* magazine sent out a team of twelve experienced reporters to question all kinds of Americans about their general moral attitudes. Editor William Attwood, summarizing the findings, said that they were capsuled by the remark of a young woman in Pennsylvania: "Who am I to say what's right and wrong?" For most Americans, "moral relativism" had replaced moral certitudes and brought in its wake moral lassitude and confusion. Out of the confusion, Attwood continued, "a new American code of ethics seems to be evolving. Its terms are seldom stated in so many words, but it adds up to this: Whatever you do is all right if it's legal or if you disapprove of the law. It's all right if it doesn't hurt anybody. And it's all right if it's part of accepted business practice."

The essential fact behind the new code was the group, "that is, you no longer refrain from doing something because you couldn't live with yourself— you refrain from doing something because you couldn't live with your neighbors." In most group codes, some cheating was tolerated—even approved and demanded. A *Look* reporter had found an extreme and ironic case of group morality in Colorado, where a man who did *not* chisel on his income tax boasted that he did in order to be well regarded by his friends. "So it would seem that your changing code of ethics is creating a fifth American freedom—the freedom to chisel."

In or outside group morality, Attwood was sure, "moral indignation is out of fashion. It isn't smart to get mad. Nor are people concerned with making moral judgments unless they are discussing clearly criminal behavior. The thing to be these days is cool, sophisticated—and tolerant of wrongdoing. . . ."

A cool abstention from indignation, a "group" morality that put relatively few restraints on the individual, scandal after scandal culminating in the Van Doren episode and even more in the public reaction to it—ever since the Kefauver Hearings of 1950 thoughtful Americans had been increasingly concerned about the trend of American attitudes toward right and wrong. Now John Steinbeck wrote a passionate letter to his friend, Adlai Stevenson. "If I wanted to destroy a nation," the novelist declared, "I would give it too much and I would have it on its knees, miserable, greedy, and sick. . . . [In rich America] a creeping, all pervading, nerve-gas of immorality starts in the nursery and does not stop before it reaches the highest offices, both corporate and governmental. . . . On all levels American society is rigged. . . . I am troubled by the cynical immorality of my country. It cannot survive on this basis."

The Steinbeck letter was printed, reprinted, re-reprinted, endlessly discussed. And as people discussed it, they read that eight Chicago policemen were under arrest for serving as lookouts while their burglar friends looted businesses and that you could pay New York agencies to take your college exam or to write your Ph.D. dissertation.

Three days after the Van Doren testimony, reporters brought up the quiz scandals at the White House press conference. President Eisenhower said he was "astounded and almost dismayed," stated that he did not believe that such things meant "America has forgotten her own moral standards," and dropped the matter.

During 1959 and 1960, the President was pushing little on the home scene. He had never really been inclined to strong action in the domestic area. Now he was an old man, moving in the shadow of his heart attack, hankering for the surcease of the golf course. As he said of himself, he was holding to the middle road but growing "more conservative," and in modern America, conservatism in home affairs has meant largely inactivity, particularly inactivity in using Presidential prestige, federal powers, or public money to bring about social and economic change. The Congressional elections of 1958 confirmed Eisenhower's natural tendency. The returns, as the gagsters said, made even Alf Landon look good. The Democrats swept everything, electing more Congressmen and getting control of more State Houses than at any time since the F.D.R. landslide of 1936. President Eisenhower was bewildered, hurt—and wary. He saw the incoming Congress as a band of Treasury marauders and braced for a crusade of inactivity in the realm of spending.

Endlessly the President talked economy, balanced budget, cutting down the national debt. (If he were to tell his grandson a bedtime story, Eisenhower remarked without a smile, even it would make the point: "I am not supporting you—you are supporting me.") The President's economy-mindedness was successful enough in arousing public opinion so that the Democratic Rayburn-Johnson team in Congress, which had its own reservations about spending, led a House and a Senate which did not push very hard. A labor-reform bill, including a "bill of rights" for rank-and-file members, became law; so, too, did another civil-rights measure, providing for federal-court-appointed "referees" who were to help give Negroes the vote in the South. The admission of Hawaii rounded out the fifty states of the Union. Beyond that, the internal life of the United States was left untouched by important new legislation.

The President was the less inclined to push domestic action because, with each passing day, his heart and his mind were concentrated more on foreign affairs. During his Administrations, Eisenhower's conception of his role in history gradually changed. He had prided himself on ending the Korean War and of having taken some of the acrimony out of the American political atmosphere; restoring and maintaining fiscal "prudence" were always on his mind. But increasingly he saw for himself one overarching historic mission, to further a "just and lasting peace." He had run for re-election in 1956, he told friends, because "I want to advance our chances for world peace, if only by a little, maybe only a few feet." In 1958 he stated to a press conference: "There is no place on this earth to which I would not travel, there is no chore I would not undertake, if I had any faintest hope that, by so doing, I would promote the general cause of world peace." Eisenhower's sense of mission in world affairs became still more compelling after the death of the strong-minded Secretary of State John Foster Dulles in May 1959, when the President tended to concentrate foreign policy in his own hands.

The situation looked propitious. Despite the continuing crises in American-Soviet relations, Khrushchev appeared genuinely to wish an end to the Cold War, or at least an armistice. The prevailing theory in Washington was that the Soviet leader personally was a man of peace and that his people were pressing for consumer's goods, thus making him the more willing to reach a *détente* which would permit him to shift the Soviet economy from its overwhelming emphasis on armaments.

Genuine improvement in the relations between the Soviet and the United States would be especially furthered by some settlement of the recurrent Berlin crisis and by steps toward disarmament, particularly steps toward an international agreement for the ending of nuclear tests and for the control of existing nuclear weapons. Khrushchev had a standard proposition to settle these or almost any difficulties: Call a summit meeting. President Eisenhower was leery. He had been none too happy with the Geneva Conference of 1955, which offered a magnificent occasion for Soviet propaganda and produced no solid results. But pressures were building for another meeting of the Big Four. In the United States a large number of thoughtful and influential people were saying that such a conference could produce a real breakthrough in the world deadlock. Some of America's allies, especially the Macmillan government of Britain, agreed. Khrushchev was constantly stepping up his own pressure for a summit meeting. He went barnstorming around the world presenting the Soviet as the true friend of peace because it was ready and eager for such a conference. Ever more openly he used the Berlin situation. Something had to be done soon to "free" West Berlin or the Soviet would move, he declared in increasingly blunt ways, and the only way to get something done was a summit meeting.

Meanwhile a number of things, little and big, made it seem that this time a summit conference could produce real results. A flurry of exchanges between Soviet and American scientists, students, athletes, and politicians went off well. In July 1959 Vice-President Richard Nixon flew into Moscow, was greeted pleasantly along the streets, spent a cordial night at Khrushchev's cream-colored *dacha* twenty miles from Moscow. The two men visited the United States National Exhibition set up in Moscow and wandered into the kitchen of a model house. There, amid the glistening gadgets, the Vice-President of the United States and the Premier of the Soviet Union got themselves into a curiously heartening donnybrook.

Khrushchev: "You Americans think that the Russian people will be astonished to see these things. The fact is that all our new houses have this kind of equipment."

Nixon: "We do not claim to astonish the Russian people. We hope to show our diversity and our right to choose. We do not want to have decisions made at the top by one government official that all houses should be built the same way."

The Premier made some vagrant remarks about washing machines, but the Vice-President pushed the argument. "Is it not far better to be talking about washing machines than machines of war, like rockets? Isn't this the kind of competition you want?"

Khrushchev's voice rose angrily. "Yes, this is the kind of competition we want. But your generals say they are so powerful they can destroy us. We can also show you something so that you will know the Russian spirit."

Nixon's face tightened. "You are strong and we are strong. In some ways you are stronger, but in other ways we might be stronger. We are both so strong, not only in weapons but also in will and spirit, that neither should ever put the other in a position where he faces in effect an ultimatum."

The scores of officials, reporters, and security guards in the kitchen crowded closer, tense and wide-eyed, as Nixon went on with his obvious reference to Khrushchev's threats about Berlin. "I hope the Prime Minister has understood all the implications of what I said. What I mean is that the moment we place either one of these powerful nations, through an ultimatum, in a position where it has no choice but to accept dictation or fight, then you are playing with the most destructive force in the world."

The muscles in Khrushchev's face tightened. He wagged a stubby finger near Nixon's face. "We too are giants. If you want to threaten, we will answer threat with threat."

Nixon bent close to the Premier and tapped his lapel. "We never engage in threats."

Khrushchev: "You wanted indirectly to threaten me. But we have means at our disposal that can have very bad consequences."

Nixon: "We have too."

Khrushchev's tone became friendlier. "We want peace with all other nations, especially America."

Nixon relaxed too. "We also want peace," he said. He mentioned Russian Foreign Minister Andrei Gromyko, "who looks like me but is better looking." "Only outwardly," Khrushchev replied with a grin. Soon the Vice-President of the United States and the Premier of the Soviet Union wandered out of the kitchen, talking with pleasant casualness.

The Gallup Poll rating for Nixon shot up—and so did the percentage in the United States favoring a summit meeting. The kitchen hassle, projected into millions of American living rooms by TV, seemed heated, but it also presented Nikita Khrushchev, wagging a high-spirited finger, giving and taking blows, joshing his own foreign minister, as a very human human being, one you could do business with. The next step came soon. On August 3, 1959, President Eisenhower and Premier Khrushchev announced reciprocal visits, to be opened by the Premier's arrival in America on September 15.

Nineteen hours before Khrushchev's arrival, Soviet scientists hit the moon with a 858.4-pound missile complete with metal pennants bearing the Communist sickle and hammer—hit it just eighty-four seconds later than they predicted and just about where they had anticipated (near, of all places, the "Sea of Tranquillity"). The Premier swept into Washington in his big white jet and presented a model of the lunik to

President Eisenhower, who took it with cool politeness. The whole receptions in Washington and New
York were cool and polite and the atmosphere was
not improved by some of Khrushchev's heavy-handed
remarks. To an especially unsmiling Allen Dulles, director of the American Central Intelligence Agency,
the Premier said: "I believe we get the same reports
—and probably from the same people."

Khrushchev took off for California and the goodwill
trip almost ended. "Disneyland" was removed from
his itinerary because the police were worried about
his safety in the labyrinth of gewgaws. Khrushchev
glowered, snarled at the reporters. "Just imagine, I, a
Premier, a Soviet representative . . . told that I could
not go. . . . Why not? . . . Do you have rocket-
launching pads there? . . . Or have gangsters taken
hold of the place?" Hollywood, forgetting that atheistic Bolsheviks can also have a puritanical streak,
proudly showed the Premier the shooting of a dance
scene for *Can-Can*. The Premier let it be loudly
known that he thought the dance was "immoral," fit
only for the "insatiable." Besides, "a person's face is
more beautiful than his backside."

That night, at a dinner in the Ambassador Hotel in
Los Angeles, Mayor Norris Poulson tried a bit of
grandstanding for the home folks. Recalling the celebrated remark by Khrushchev that "we shall bury
you," the Mayor struck his best Patrick Henry stance
and declaimed: "You shall not bury us. . . . If challenged, we shall fight to the death." The Premier,
dark-faced, hurried through his prepared text, then
turned coldly to Poulson. He had already made clear
to the United States, Khrushchev said, what he meant
by the remark—he meant that the inevitabilities of history would bring about a Communist world. "I trust
that even mayors read the newspapers." More tongue-
lashing of Poulson and then Khrushchev pounded the
rostrum and his voice rose to a yell. "It is a question of
war or peace between our countries, a question of the

life or death of the people. . . . If you think the cold war is profitable to you, then go ahead." As for himself, "I can go, and I don't know when, if ever, another Russian Soviet Premier Minister will visit your country."

San Francisco was San Francisco. The city had on its fall charm, the crowds were friendly. Khrushchev relaxed, rolled unannounced into a union meeting, swapping his felt hat for a worker's white cap, toured an IBM plant and jovially lined up for lunch in the company cafeteria. From then on the Premier was all smiles, pleasant quips, and good fellowship. In Des Moines he exuberantly downed his first hot-dog. In the corn fields near Coon Rapids, Iowa, he roared with laughter as a farmer shied fodder at newsmen who were crowding and shoving. In Pittsburgh he fingered a machine tool admiringly and startled reporters by saying: "We can learn much from you." The American crowds, responding to Khrushchev's new mood, gave him warmer and warmer receptions.

The height of the cordiality came at the climax of the visit, the leisurely period which President Eisenhower and Premier Khrushchev spent at Camp David. For three days the two leaders ate their meals together, ambled along the winding gravel paths, talked freely and fully. As Khrushchev was taken to the airport for the flight home, he was beaming. The President and he, the Premier said, had agreed that all disputes "should be settled not by force but by peaceful means —by negotiation." Khrushchev added firmly: "Let us have more and more use for the short American word *O.K.*" At his next press conference, Eisenhower appeared equally pleased by the results of the visit and mentioned a specific consequence of great importance. The conversations at Camp David had "removed many of the objections that I have heretofore held to a Big Four meeting." Reporters knew what the President meant. By now the news was out that at Camp David Eisenhower had refused to go to the summit under Khrushchev's ultimatum about Berlin, and the Premier had agreed to remove it.

With a Big Four meeting so obviously approaching, Eisenhower decided to play what so many Administration men considered the American ace card—his own world prestige and world popularity—to bring as much neutral opinion as possible behind the West and to iron out differences among the Western allies. On December 3 he began a 22,000-mile, eleven-nation swing that took him along the southern tier of Europe and Asia, then back to a meeting of the Western allies in Paris. Through one ancient capital after another the President went, Rome and Ankara and Teheran and Athens, armed with his smile, a slogan ("peace and friendship—in freedom"), and a promise delivered in scores of different forms: "We want to help other peoples to raise their standards of living." By car and bicycle, on foot, by camelback, and in bullock carts, millions crowded into the cities along his route and gave him a reception of enormous warmth.

The welcome in India staggered the President and had him shaking his head in incredulity. Twilight was falling as Eisenhower and Prime Minister Nehru began the drive from the airport to New Delhi. Thousands of bonfires and thousands of lanterns swung high by hollow-eyed Hindu functionaries lit the way. An estimated million and a half Indians of every class— disease-scaled peasants, trim little civil servants, fierce-looking Sikhs, bare-bottomed children, old men smoking their hookahs, lovely women clad in rich saris —a million and a half human beings jammed the road, cheering, stomping, shrieking. Some of the enthusiasm had an eerie undertone. People had walked with their children ten or twelve miles to see the figure they were sure was the reincarnation of Vishnu, the "protector" in the Hindu trinity. "Did he not send us wheat when we needed it and build us dams?" explained seventy-year-old Kanthi from a village eleven miles south of New Delhi. "Could he not destroy the world by a mere wish but never uses his power except as a shield against evil?"

The police were helpless to clear a path for the President's big black Cadillac. Worried, Prime Minister Nehru got out of the car, entered an escorting jeep, and rode along shouting for the people to make way. His voice was lost in the din. Nehru climbed back in the car and, chin in hand, gazed stoically ahead while the Cadillac inched along. Once the caravan reached New Delhi, the enthusiasm was even wilder. WELCOME PRINCE OF PEACE, the endless signs screamed. Flowers by the pound flew at Eisenhower until he was standing foot deep in them and the Secret Service men were panting from batting down the clumps of blossoms. In the closing hour of Eisenhower's visit, Prime Minister Nehru told the President: "As you go, you take a piece of our heart." Newsmen with decades of experience agreed that at no time, anywhere, had they seen so rhapsodic a reception of a public figure.

On to more capitals, more cheers, and then to Paris for the meeting with the leaders of England, France, and West Germany. Here the President ran into problems that were anything but flower-laden. In particular, President Charles de Gaulle of France wanted to get some things straight about NATO and Algeria before he mounted any summit. Eisenhower and Macmillan wheedled and smoothed, agreed to disagree on this or that until more staff work was done, and the four men were ready: the invitation was to go out to Khrushchev for a summit meeting in May 1960.

Never, in all the ups and downs of opinion since the beginning of the East-West clash, had the world shared such optimism. From the Kremlin, from Western capitals, from the centers of neutralism came agreement with British Prime Minister Macmillan's statement: "At this wondrous moment we seem on the threshold of genuine, practical steps toward peace." In the United States, the *Bulletin of Atomic Scientists*, which had been talking nuclear doom since 1945, reset the ominous clock that regularly appeared on its cover. The hands of the clock had stood at two minutes to twelve. Now they were moved back to seven minutes to twelve.

Just eleven days before the summit meeting, on May 5, 1960, Prime Minister Khrushchev came near the end of his three-and-a-half-hour address to the Supreme Soviet. He paused, glowered, then went on: "I am duty bound to report to you on the aggressive acts . . . by the United States of America." On May 1 the Soviet Union had shot down over Russian territory a plane on a mission of "aggressive provocation aimed at wrecking the Summit Conference." Eisenhower, the Premier declared, seemed to want peace but was surrounded by "imperialists" and "militarists."

The rest came in trip-hammer blows of news:

May 5. The U.S. National Aeronautics and Space Administration states that a high-flying U-2, the plane used by Americans for weather observation, is missing on a flight in Turkey after the pilot reported oxygen trouble. It suggests that the plane strayed over Soviet territory.

May 6. Lincoln White, State Department press officer, agreeing that the plane in question is a weather one, adds: "There was absolutely no—N—O—no deliberate attempt to violate the Soviet air space, and there has never been." When asked by newsmen to identify the missing pilot, White begs off, saying that the pilot's mother is suffering a serious heart condition and should not be shocked.

The efforts of the State Department and the NASA are not co-ordinated. NASA releases the name of the "weather pilot," Francis G. Powers, and thus gives Khrushchev the final detail he needs to catch the United States in a bald lie.

May 7. Khrushchev springs his trap. He announces

that the Soviet had captured Powers "alive and kicking," that he had been shot down near the industrial
city of Sverdlovsk, some 1,300 miles inside Russia,
and that the pilot had confessed to being on a spy
flight which began in Pakistan and was to end in
Norway. Triumphantly the Premier displays the
equipment allegedly found in the plane, including a
poison needle with which the spy was to commit
suicide if caught and pictures of Soviet airfields developed from Powers's camera.

The State Department admits that the flight was
one of "surveillance." It states that such flights had
gone on for four years, ever since the Soviet rejected
the American "open skies" proposal made at the
Geneva Summit Conference of 1955. In all of his
statements, Khrushchev seemed to be exonerating
Eisenhower of any blame. The State Department
goes along with this by saying that "the authorities"
had not authorized "any such flights as described
by Mr. Khrushchev."

May 8. Dismay throughout the Western world over
the timing of the flight, the trapping of the United
States in a lie, and the statement which implied that
the President of the United States did not know that
something so important as spying on the Soviet Union eleven days before a summit meeting was being
carried on by his own subordinates.

May 9. The Eisenhower Administration reverses itself.
Secretary of State Christian Herter declares that the
President had authorized the general program of
spying though not specific missions. Herter adds a
sentence which unmistakably implies that the
United States intends to continue the intelligence
flights over the Soviet: "The United States has not
and does not shirk this responsibility."

May 10-14. The Eisenhower Administration continues
to leave the impression that it will continue the spy
missions. President Eisenhower speaks of them in
the present tense—as a "distasteful but vital neces-

sity." White House Press Secretary James Hagerty categorically knocks down a story by James Reston of the *New York Times* that the President has ordered a suspension of the flights.

May 15. The Big Four arrive in Paris. De Gaulle, Macmillan, and Khrushchev confer and the Russian lays down his terms for participating in the summit conference: (1) a cessation of the flights; (2) an American apology for "past acts of aggression"; and (3) punishment of "those responsible." Informed of these terms, Eisenhower states that the flights have already been stopped but the other terms will never be accepted by the United States.

May 16. The summit meeting opens, without a single exchange of pleasantries or a single handshake. At the first opportunity, Khrushchev takes the floor, curt, rude, and defiant. He repeats his three-point demands, accuses President Eisenhower of "treachery" and a "bandit" policy. He startles his listeners by the statement that the U-2 incident "deeply involves" the "internal politics" of the Soviet and by the suggestion that the summit be postponed for six to eight months in the hope that "another United States government will understand the futility of pursuing aggressive policies." Khrushchev has one more insult for the President of the United States. "Conditions have now arisen which make us unable to welcome the President with the proper warmth which the Soviet people display toward fond guests." The invitation for the reciprocal Eisenhower visit to Russia is therefore canceled.

President Eisenhower sits tight-lipped and grim. In carefully controlled words, he repeats that the overflights are ended but that the Khrushchev "ultimatum" is utterly unacceptable to the United States. The President returns to the American Embassy and explodes. "He was not just angry," an aide recalls. "He was absolutely furious."

May 16 and 17. De Gaulle and Macmillan make last-

ditch efforts to save the conference. At 3 p.m. on
May 17, the Big Three assemble for the first business session. Khrushchev is not present; he is off visiting the French countryside, chopping wood and
joking with the peasants. An aide telephones to ask
whether Eisenhower is ready to apologize for the
flights and to punish those responsible. At 5 p.m. on
May 17 the summit meeting that never started ends.
May 18. Khrushchev summons a press conference in
the Palais de Chaillot and for two and a half hours
delivers himself of a public spleen unprecedented
even in the annals of Cold War diplomacy. Pounding the table, sneering, shouting, he calls the actions
of the United States "thief-like," "piratical," and
"cowardly," and denounces Eisenhower as a "fishy"
friend. American "aggressors," he storms, should
be treated the way that he as a boy handled cats that
stole cream or broke into pigeon lofts. "We would
catch such a cat by the tail and bang its head against
the wall, and that was the only way it could be
taught some sense." He threatens "devastating"
rocket blows at any nation used as a base for
American espionage flights and announces that the
Soviet will take action about Berlin by signing a
treaty with Communist East Germany—just *when*
is "our business."

What did it all mean—the sudden transition of the
exuberant apostle of coexistence to a snarling, rocket-
rattling exponent of Cold War? Responsible observers
in the Western capitals agreed that the U-2 incident
was not the primary cause of the Premier's shift; it was
more of a pretext. They believed that in the weeks
immediately preceding the summit gathering, firm
statements by American State Department officials
had made it clear that the Soviet was not going to get
from the summit what it most wanted—concessions
concerning Berlin. At the same time Khrushchev was
under increasingly heavy pressure from the Chinese
Communist leaders and from a faction in the Kremlin.

both of which groups were Stalinist in tendency, had never agreed with Khrushchev's coexistence policies, and had been asking more and more sharply: What are you gaining by the friendship line? Expecting to win nothing important from the meeting, having positive reasons not to participate in it, the Premier had snatched at the U-2 episode as an excuse to blow up the conference—and to get in some tirading that would sound good in Moscow and Peiping.

Most commentators added that the American handling of the U-2 incident had been unwise. Permitting a flight so close to the time of the Paris meeting gave hostages to Khrushchev. The confusion in Washington at receipt of the news bewildered and frightened friendly and neutral nations. The American admission that the U-2 flight was a spy mission, and that such missions had been going on for four years, made a mockery of Khrushchev's repeated assurances to his people that the Soviet was invulnerable and made it essential, if he was to maintain his stature at home, to talk tough. The action of President Eisenhower in taking personal responsibility for the flight hardly made it politically expedient for Khrushchev to sit down in friendly conference with him.

Khrushchev arrived at the Paris airport and got in a warning to Foreign Minister Gromyko, who was about to fly to a UN meeting in New York: "Be careful of those imperialists. Be careful to cover your back. Don't expose your back to them." Then he climbed in his own plane, headed for East Germany, and abruptly changed his tone. There would be no swift move about West Berlin, he told a disappointed Communist crowd. The existing situation would be preserved "until the heads of government meeting which, it is hoped, will take place in six or eight months." A few weeks later the Premier took the occasion of a Bucharest Communist assemblage to rap "left-wing opportunists" among the Red leaders, to declare that the only sensible course was coexistence and negotiation, and to describe the "present deterioration" in East-West relations as a "passing phase." On the other hand, Moscow radio was back to its old ways, competing with Peiping in hurling slurs at the United States. And, ever more truculently, the Soviet pushed its campaign to get rid of the American bases which ringed it.

What did it all mean in the long run? Was the world back to the furies and the dangers of full-scale Cold War or, as Khrushchev said, only passing through an unfortunate phase? The answer was hardly clear, but one fact was eminently plain. Any assumption of an easy coexistence, of steady progress toward peace through hot-dog munching guests and flower-strewn visits and genial get-togethers at the summit, of an American-Soviet relationship which would permit the United States the luxury of complacency and bungling —any such assumption simply would not hold.

Epilogue

SHORTLY AFTER the Administration bungling in handling the U-2 incident, the Gallup Poll asked Americans its periodic question about whether they approved of the way the President was carrying out his job. The answer was a thumping 68 percent approval—a near all-time high in the phenomenal record of Eisenhower popularity. But at the same time, one segment of American opinion was disturbed as it had not been since the first emergence of the seriousness of the East-West clash in 1947.

This division in American attitudes, present throughout the Crucial Decade and the immediate post-Crucial Decade years, had widened and deepened with each jarring event after Sputnik I went up in 1957. In part the split was partisan. Naturally the opposition Democrats did the most worrying, and this tendency was increased by the fact that so large a part of the long-dissident intellectual class was Democratic. But partisanship was not the whole story, and probably not the most important part of it. Some leading Republican commentators, like Walter Lippmann, were among the most forceful spokesmen of the criticism. The generally pro-Eisenhower publications, *Life* and the *New York Times*, were joining in. Two weeks after the summit debacle, one of the country's most prominent Republican political figures, Governor Nelson Rockefeller of New York, spoke out his disquietude with basic trends in American political leadership and in American society. It was noticeable too that Rockefeller's statement was drafted by Emmet John Hughes, a long-time aide of the President who had now broken not only with Eisenhower but with Eisenhowerism as a way of thinking.

Except for a few shrill voices on the far right, none of the critics were quarreling with the two great decisions of the Crucial Decade. They assumed that the New Deal and the Fair Deal were here to stay and that social changes within the pattern of the Half-Century of Revolution would and should go ahead. They also assumed that the only sensible foreign policy was coexistence with world Communism and patient efforts to work out specific agreements. The criticisms concerned developments that had accompanied the decisions of the Crucial Decade and they carried an insistence that the decisions of the past years, sound as they were, had to be extended by fresh and bold policies.

In the language of the dissidents, one phrase was becoming especially persistent: "national purpose." It was projected into the discussion as early as Khrushchev's visit to America, when Walter Lippmann wrote in his potent prose: "The critical weakness of our society is that for the time being our people do not have great purposes which they are united in wanting to achieve. The public mood of the country is defensive, to hold on to and to conserve, not to push forward and to create. We talk about ourselves these days as if we were a completed society, one which has achieved its purposes, and has no further business to transact." Discussion of the point received even greater impetus a few weeks later when the widely respected George Kennan went before the Women's National Democratic Club in Washington, asked a disturbing question, and gave a still more disturbing answer: "If you ask me . . . whether a country in the state this country is in today: with no highly developed sense of national purpose, with the overwhelming accent of life on personal comfort and amusement, with a dearth of public services and a surfeit of privately sold gadgetry, with a chaotic transportation system, with its great urban areas being gradually disintegrated by the headlong switch to motor transportation, with an educational system where quality has been extensively sacrificed to quantity, and with insufficient social discipline even to keep its major industries functioning without grievous interruptions—if you ask me whether such a country has, over the long run, good chances of competing with a purposeful, serious, and disciplined society such as that of the Soviet Union, I must say that the answer is 'no.' " The jolting events of mid-1960, during which the basic direction of the United States seemed anything but clear, stimulated talk about the national purpose still further. Soon *Life* and the *New York Times* were joining in running a series of articles on the subject by men ranging from Adlai Stevenson through Professor Clinton Rossiter on to David Sarnoff, chairman of the board of RCA.

Most of the talk about national purpose was more notable for its insistence that we ought to have a clear-cut purpose than for its statement of what the purpose should be. Yet the usual critic did make a connection between the national purpose and the national leadership. As Eisenhower's Administrations closed in 1960, the dissidents were coming to something of an agreement concerning his place in history. Some, usually of a strongly Democratic bent, considered his whole tenure in office a mistake, if not a disaster. A far greater percentage assigned to his first Administration, whatever its demerits, a highly constructive role in bridging deep political divisions within the country and in leading an almost united nation to acceptance of continuing social change at home and coexistence abroad. In this process, the President's vague generalities, his assumption that good will would solve almost anything, even his ability to render the English language nearly incomprehensible, could be deemed assets.

"The first term, yes, I can see its merits," remarked the strongly Democratic Professor Walter Johnson of the University of Chicago, "but the second term— there I draw the line." Most critics felt that the President, his healing mission performed, became a symbol of drift to a nation already far too ready for drift, an exponent of materialism in a country overwhelmed by chrome, a spokesman of the easy solution to an America that had been getting itself into trouble by yearning for easy solutions ever since World War II. Critics were especially sharp in pointing to the Eisenhower of the second term as the glaring example of a new school of leadership in which personality was assumed to be the prime need, public relations the sure method, and the end product was a grinning nothingness—"the bland leading the bland," in the angry phrase of the day.

What positive goals did the critics want, what kind of leadership toward what ends? They were sure that the rampant drive of the individual American for more money and more status was self-defeating. In individual terms, it meant an ever more frantic quest of an ever more evanescent prize. In national terms, it was totally inadequate as a way of life which would attract the uncommitted peoples of the world and give the United States a chance in the decades-long competition with Communism that lay ahead. The situation should be drastically changed by strong leadership, the critics were sure, building on the decisions of the Crucial Decade, sweeping beyond them to a new atmosphere and new decisions.

In foreign policy, the critics insisted that mere acceptance of coexistence was not enough. The United States had to make very clear what it stood for in the world—and in doing this the repetition of snappy phrases about freedom would not be sufficient. It had to give up budget-pinching in appropriating funds for matters connected with foreign policy. Millions more had to be appropriated to make sure that the United States was keeping up with—and getting ahead of—the Soviet Union in the race for scientific knowledge. Millions more had to be appropriated for economic aid abroad.

In domestic policy, the critics went on, the United States must rid itself of the emphasis on the endless increase in consumer goods. What was needed was not the better-equipped American but the American who was a better human being, his life enriched by an altered community atmosphere and by greatly improved facilities for education, medical care, and recreation. Just as the sputniks were going up, the Harvard professor of economics, John Kenneth Galbraith, gave the critical mood tartly effective expression in his widely acclaimed book, *The Affluent Society*. The ideas of a good society on which the United States was operating, Galbraith wrote, were carry-overs from a period when the country had to worry about widespread poverty. They did not fit a society of widespread affluence. Obsolescent thinking was committing us to a senseless pursuit of goods while the human beings floundered. What Galbraith called the "social balance" was wobbling, to a degree where it could take a dangerous plunge.

As the bipartisan hammering went on and the bipartisan counterblasts came, it was clear that the United States was heading into a basic issue. Should the nation continue, in gradually altered form, the mood, the kind of leadership, the basic domestic and foreign policies that it had agreed upon in the Crucial Decade of 1945-55? Or did it need breakaways, genuine breakaways? Was it to be consolidation or innovation—more circumspect consolidation of the decisions of the Crucial Decade or venturesome innovation to a new kind of leadership, basically different ideas, a rethinking if not a redefinition of the whole national purpose?

The answer to the question lay somewhere in the realm of murky imponderables. For those who were certain that the United States would choose and hold to the path of genuine innovation, there was always history's yawning reminder. Fat and satisfied nations like the America of 1960 have rarely been innovating societies. For those who were positive that the answer would be more consolidation, there were circumstances which even 5,000 years of history had never previously produced. The fat and satisfied America of 1960 faced annihilation if its foreign policy did not adequately meet swiftly changing circumstances. Having geared its life to endless upper mobility, it was endlessly subjected to the demands of millions for the better life in a constantly expanding definition of that phrase.

Americans of the Crucial Decade, catching the earlier intimations of these extraordinary situations, had moved—uncertainly, irritably, but with notable speed—to meet the fiat of facts. A nation that had adjusted that fast and that far in ten years could surprise the world, not to speak of itself, by the way it responded to more decades that were certain to have their own crucial qualities.

Note on the Sources and Acknowledgments

THIS BOOK rests in large part on the mass of printed materials which concern the years 1945-60. In a few instances, where manuscript collections were available and seemed of importance, I turned to them. The sources were also supplemented by interviews and by correspondence with men and women who made the history. Most of the interviews and some of the correspondence were undertaken to gather material for a particular episode and occurred before the writing. In addition, as is indicated in the Preface, I used extensive correspondence (and in a few cases interviews) after the manuscript was prepared, asking people who were participants in the history to check my factual accuracy.

About eighty-five per cent of the men and women to whom I wrote responded and their letters contain a good deal of contemporary history, not all of which is incorporated in this book and some of which is completely confidential. It is my hope that in time these materials may be deposited in the Princeton University Library, where they could be consulted by people with a serious research purpose.

Some of the participants in the history of the period have requested that I make no public acknowledgment of their aid. The others who helped me by letters or interviews are (all titles are omitted): Dean Acheson, John Alsop, Stewart Alsop, Warren R. Austin, Lauren Bacall, Bernard M. Baruch, Ales Bebler, Leslie L. Biffle, Herbert Block, Vannevar Bush, James F. Byrnes, John M. Chang, Winston Churchill, Mark W. Clark,

Clark M. Clifford, J. Lawton Collins, W. Bradley Connors, Claude B. Cross, Willard Edwards, George M. Elsey, Morris L. Ernst, Alonzo Fields, Thomas K. Finletter, Cody Fowler, Karl M. Frost, J. W. Fulbright, Walter F. George, Donald J. Gonzales, Wallace H. Graham, Gordon Gray, Ernest A. Gross, Leslie R. Groves, Rudolph Halley, Friedrich A. von Hayek, John D. Hickerson, John G. Hill, Paul G. Hoffman, Cale J. Holder, Lloyd P. Hopwood, Emmet John Hughes, J. Raymond Jones, H. V. Kaltenborn, Samuel H. Kaufman, George F. Kennan, Renwick C. Kennedy, Alfred C. Kinsey, Charles H. Kraus, Trygve Lie, A. C. McAuliffe, F. L. McCluer, Frank C. McConnell, Joseph W. Martin, Jr., Stephen A. Mitchell, Mrs. Blair Moody, John J. Muccio, Karl E. Mundt, Thomas F. Murphy, Paul A. Myers, W. H. Mylander, Djura Nincic, Frank Pace, Jr., Norman Vincent Peale, Mrs. John R. Rice, Branch Rickey, William A. Roberts, Dean Rusk, Mrs. Dorothy Schiff, Louis B. Seltzer, Merriman Smith, Oliver P. Smith, John R. Steelman, Adlai E. Stevenson, Herbert Bayard Swope, Strom Thurmond, Edward J. Thye, Harold C. Urey, Charles A. Voso, Henry A. Wallace, Mary Jane Ward, and Frederick Woltman.

In some instances, a relative or associate took care of my inquiries. These included Louis J. Gallagher, Murray Glaubach, Victor J. Hammer, Arthur Mann, and Richard Wallace.

Friends and strangers, who were not mentioned as part of the history but who have a special knowledge about some phase of the story, criticized parts of the manuscript or aided in other ways. In this connection, I would particularly like to thank Jack Anderson, Robert J. Butow, Harold W. Chase, Marquis Childs, Kenneth W. Condit, W. Frank Craven, Benjamin J. Custer, Frederick S. Dunn, Robert F. Futrell, E. Harris Harbison, James A. Kritzeck, J. Norman Lodge, Mrs. Helen Taft Manning, John Miller, Jr., Walter Millis, Newton N. Minow, Louis Morton, James Rorty,

Roger W. Shugg, Harold Stein, Gordon B. Turner, and John J. Wright.

I am very genuinely indebted to the above men and women and, in thanking them, I would like to repeat with special emphasis the customary statement that any factual errors or inadequacies of interpretation are exclusively my responsibility. Some of the people who were kind enough to aid me disagreed with my interpretation of a particular event or personality or even of the whole decade. Others disagreed not only with respect to interpretation but in the area of factual statements. Their recollection was different, in more or less important degree, from the form which I decided to report after consideration of the total evidence that I was able to discover.

Writing a book inevitably piles up other types of debts, and in the case of this particular volume they are so numerous that I will not try to describe most of them. I can only hope that I was able to express something of my appreciation along the way toward completion of the book. I do want to mention here that in the preparation of the original *Crucial Decade*, Mr. Bennett Hill gave me able assistance for many months, and that at a critical juncture in the work Mr. Fredrick Aandahl's generous readiness to call on his bibliographical skill removed a considerable worry. I would also like to state, with my appreciation, that the Princeton University Research Fund provided financial assistance which expedited the research and that a number of members of the firm of Alfred A. Knopf, Inc., gave unstinted co-operation and encouragement.

Index

ERIC FREDERICK GOLDMAN was born in Washington, D. C., in 1915. He was educated at the Johns Hopkins University, where he received his Ph.D. in history in 1938. He has taught at Hopkins and, since 1940, at Princeton University, where he is now Professor of History and one of the most popular lecturers. He has been a Guggenheim Fellow; a Library of Congress Fellow; and, since 1957, a member of the Board of Councillors of the Society of American Historians. Mr. Goldman has written articles for the leading scholarly journals as well as for *Harper's Magazine*, *Holiday*, the *Reporter*, and the *Saturday Review*, and is a regular reviewer for the *New York Times* and the *New York Herald Tribune* Sunday book sections. He is the author of a number of books of which the most famous is *Rendezvous with Destiny* (1952), winner of the Bancroft Prize for distinguished American history (also available in the Vintage series).

THE TEXT of this book was set on the Linotype in *Janson*, an excellent example of the influential and sturdy Dutch types that prevailed in England prior to the development by William Caslon of his own incomparable designs. Composed, printed, and bound by The Colonial Press Inc., Clinton, Mass. Cover design by BEN SHAHN.

A free catalogue of VINTAGE BOOKS will be sent at your request. Write to Vintage Books, 457 Madison Avenue, New York 22, New York.

VINTAGE POLITICAL SCIENCE
AND SOCIAL CRITICISM

V-726	Marcuse, Herbert	SOVIET MARXISM
V-102	Meyers, Marvin	THE JACKSONIAN PERSUASION
V-19	Milosz, Czeslaw	THE CAPTIVE MIND
V-101	Moos, Malcolm (ed.)	H. L. MENCKEN ON POLITICS
V-192	Morgenstern, O.	QUESTION OF NATIONAL DEFENSE
V-251	Morgenthau, Hans J.	PURPOSE OF AMERICAN POLITICS
V-703	Mosely, Philip E.	THE KREMLIN AND WORLD POLITICS: *Studies in Soviet Policy and Action* (*Vintage Original*)
V-46	Philipson, M. (ed.)	AUTOMATION: *Implications for the Future* (*Vintage Original*)
V-128	Plato	THE REPUBLIC
V-719	Reed, John	TEN DAYS THAT SHOOK THE WORLD
V-212	Rossiter, Clinton	CONSERVATISM IN AMERICA
V-220	Shonfield, Andrew	ATTACK ON WORLD POVERTY
V-253	Stampp, Kenneth	THE PECULIAR INSTITUTION
V-179	Stebbins, Richard P.	U. S. IN WORLD AFFAIRS, 1959
V-204	Stebbins, Richard P.	U. S. IN WORLD AFFAIRS, 1960
V-222	Stebbins, Richard P.	U. S. IN WORLD AFFAIRS, 1961
V-244	Stebbins, Richard P.	U. S. IN WORLD AFFAIRS, 1962
V-53	Synge, J. M.	THE ARAN ISLANDS *and Other Writings*
V-231	Tannenbaum, Frank	SLAVE & CITIZEN: *The Negro in the Americas*
V-206	Wallerstein, Immanuel	AFRICA: THE POLITICS OF INDEPENDENCE (*Vintage Original*)
V-145	Warren, Robert Penn	SEGREGATION
V-729	Weidlé, W.	RUSSIA: ABSENT & PRESENT
V-249	Wiedner, Donald L.	A HISTORY OF AFRICA: *South of the Sahara*
V-208	Woodward, C. Vann	BURDEN OF SOUTHERN HISTORY

VINTAGE HISTORY AND CRITICISM OF LITERATURE, MUSIC, AND ART

V-22	Barzun, Jacques	THE ENERGIES OF ART
V-93	Bennett, Joan	FOUR METAPHYSICAL POETS
V-57	Bodkin, Maud	ARCHETYPAL PATTERNS IN POETRY
V-51	Burke, Kenneth	THE PHILOSOPHY OF LITERARY FORM
V-75	Camus, Albert	THE MYTH OF SISYPHUS
V-171	Cruttwell, Patrick	THE SHAKESPEAREAN MOMENT
V-4	Einstein, Alfred	A SHORT HISTORY OF MUSIC
V-177	Fuller, Edmund	MAN IN MODERN FICTION
V-13	Gilbert, Stuart	JAMES JOYCE'S "ULYSSES"
V-56	Graves, Robert	THE WHITE GODDESS
V-175	Haggin, Bernard	MUSIC FOR THE MAN WHO ENJOYS "HAMLET"

The
Cyclist's
Anthology

Compiled by
NICKY SLADE

TRAILBLAZER PUBLICATIONS

The Cyclist's Anthology
First edition: 2015

Publisher
Trailblazer Publications
The Old Manse, Tower Rd, Hindhead, Surrey, GU26 6SU, UK
www.trailblazer-guides.com

British Library Cataloguing in Publication Data
A catalogue record for this book is available from the British Library

ISBN 978-1-905864-69-0

Editors: Nicky Slade & Jane Thomas
Layout: Bryn Thomas
Proofreading: Jane Thomas
Cover image: Cycles Griffon Poster by Georges Faivre
© Swim Ink 2, LLC/CORBIS

NICKY SLADE has worked in publishing since graduating from the University of Nottingham with a degree in English and Linguistics. She has always had a passion for being outdoors, and recently rediscovered her love of cycling after a few years' break. She particularly enjoys cycling with her husband and sons in the beautiful South Downs National Park around her home in West Sussex.

Printed in China; print production by D'Print (☎ +65-6581 3832), Singapore

CONTENTS

3: CYCLE TOURING

4: THE SPORT OF CYCLING

5: WORKING BIKES

6: CITY CYCLING

7: EXTREME CYCLING

To my boys – Andy, Ben, Matthew and Oliver –
with thanks for all your love and support.

INTRODUCTION

While the basic design of a human-powered vehicle comprising a wooden frame on two in-line wheels had already been in existence for some time, in 1817 Baron Karl von Drais added a rudimentary steering mechanism. This simple development drastically improved balance as well as the more obvious directional control and, with that, the ancestor of the modern bicycle was born.

Most of us learn to ride a bike as a child and barely remember our first foray on two wheels, any more than we remember our first steps, but imagine how the fear of falling would haunt the attempts of the average adult learning to ride a bicycle for the first time. Then imagine if that adult rider was seated over a metre off the ground on a penny-farthing bicycle with the pedals on that tall front wheel! So the introduction of a chain-drive system in the 1880s, enabling the pedals to turn the rear wheel rather than the front one, was a significant advance in making it more user-friendly.

This was undoubtedly the first step towards cycling for the masses, and brought a truly universal mode of transport into the world, available to young and old, rich and poor, city-dweller and countryman, commuter and cycle-tourer alike. Upon mastering the mystery of balance, something that cannot truly be 'taught', only imperfectly explained and acquired through practice, almost anyone from young children to the elderly can propel themselves to school, work or out into the wide world.

Further refinements have since been made with gears and revolutionary materials that reduce the weight of the machine, but the fact remains that the basic design is very little changed in well over 100 years.

Although in Britain in the early and mid 20th century the bicycle was often the most practical choice of transport for work purposes (postmen, policemen, district nurses, delivery boys), fast forward to the 21st century and the car has taken on the majority of those roles. While it might still be used for city commuting or by cycle couriers, the bicycle now features far more in the leisure and sport arenas for most. In less developed countries, such as China and India, the bicycle continues to rule supreme. China still has nearly half of the world's population (estimated at over a billion) of bicycles but even there the car is beginning to win out over pedal power.

Similarly in literature, while the humble bicycle has often been there in the background, it has rarely taken centre stage.

So this anthology brings it into the spotlight, showing how, as well as being a tool for those with a job to do, from serving the community to solving crimes, it has been a means of immersing ourselves fully in other cultures and natural environments, a self-sufficient method of carrying our own little world wherever we wish to explore, to bond with companions or meet new friends. For a child it may have been a status symbol like the Raleigh Chopper in the 1970s (ideally in purple, like my brother's) or a BMX bike in the 1980s. For an adult it may be a means of facing a personal challenge, overcoming a mental crisis or turning a dream into reality.

But whatever your own personal experience of bikes and cycling, the key theme that emerges from much of the writing in this anthology is one of the bicycle as liberator: for women, from the confines of uncomfortable restrictive clothing and the need for a chaperone; for the poor, who previously could only rely on their own two feet for transport; for the thrill-seeker on any downhill run; for the child with a sense of adventure; for the traveller, who could carry enough to be self-reliant yet still interact with the people and landscape through which he or she travelled.

I'll finish with the words of 19th century author Mark Twain who, on concluding his account of his own efforts to learn to ride the terrifyingly-challenging penny-farthing as an adult (see p11), offers the following incisive and succinct imperative:

Get a bicycle. You will not regret it – if you live.

Nicky Slade, West Sussex, 2015

LEARNING TO RIDE

The Nothing of the Day, 1819
JOHN KEATS

Summarily dismissed in a few words written in a letter to relatives George and Georgiana Keats in America, the poet was clearly not impressed with the forerunner to the bicycle.

The nothing of the day is a machine called the Velocepede – It is a wheel carriage to ride cock-horse upon, sitting astride & pushing it along with the toes, a rudder wheel in hand. They will go seven miles an hour. A handsome gelding will come to eight guineas, however they will soon be cheaper, unless the army takes to them. I look upon the last month, & find nothing to write about, indeed I do not recollect one thing particular in it – It's all alike, we keep on breathing.

(From a letter by John Keats to George & Georgiana Keats, 17 Mar 1819)

A Curious Invention, 1819
ACKERMAN'S REPOSITORY OF ARTS AND SCIENCES

Interestingly, although contemporary with Keats' 'nothing of the day' letter, the writer of this piece seems more open to the possibilities presented by this new 'curious invention'. Clearly it is so new that the component parts, such as handlebars, have not yet even been named.

The principle of this invention is taken from the art of skating, and consists in the simple idea of a seat upon two wheels propelled by the feet acting upon the ground. The riding seat or saddle, is fixed on a perch upon two double shod wheels running after each other, so that they can go upon the footways. To preserve the balance, a small board, covered and stuffed, is placed before, on which the arms are laid, and in front of which is a little guiding pole, which is held in the hand to direct the route.

The swiftness with which a person well practised can travel is almost beyond belief – eight, nine and even ten miles may, it is asserted, be passed over within an hour on good level ground. The machine, it is conjectured, will answer well for messengers, and even for long journeys; it does not weigh more than fifty pounds, and may be made with travelling pockets. The price, we are informed, varies from eight to ten guineas.

(From *Ackerman's Repository of Arts and Sciences*, 1819)

Iconic bicycle designs – the Laufmaschine (c1817)

Necessity is the mother of invention, as the saying goes – and that is as true of the bicycle as any other invention. In the early 19th century, German civil servant Baron Karl von Drais (1785-1851) needed an alternative to the horse for travelling along the narrow tracks of the forestry estate where he worked. His invention, the *Laufmaschine* – which literally translates as 'running machine' – was made mainly of wood and used in-line wheels. Other similar machines already existed, but what set the Laufmaschine apart was the addition of rudimentary steering. Although steering obviously allows the rider to control the direction of their travel, it has an even more fundamental bearing on balance. The ability to make small adjustments to the front wheel allowed riders to rebalance their weight and stay seated on the Laufmaschine without having to touch the ground, thereby potentially reaching speeds far in excess of running alone.

It was not long before similar designs, known variously as dandy horses and hobbyhorses among other names, were being manufactured by enthusiasts and coach builders the world over.

So bicycle design moved on and the *Laufmaschine* was consigned to history – or was it? In fact, if you go to a family play park today you'll see children as young as two years old confidently propelling themselves by 'running' on wooden 'balance bikes' that are a remarkable echo of the earliest days of bicycle design.

Falling forwards from a bicycle is by no means a difficult

On Learning to Dismount, 1893
MARK TWAIN

When reading Mark Twain's *account of getting to grips with riding a bicycle the reader is left with the overwhelming impression that it is a miracle anyone is ever actually successful.*

I thought the matter over, and concluded I could do it. So I went down and bought a barrel of Pond's Extract and a bicycle. The Expert came home with me to instruct me. We chose the back yard, for the sake of privacy, and went to work.

Mine was not a full-grown bicycle, but only a colt – a fifty-inch, with the pedals shortened up to forty-eight – and skittish, like any other colt. The Expert explained the thing's points briefly, then he got on its back and rode around a little, to show me how easy it was to do. He said that the dismounting was perhaps the hardest thing to learn, and so we would leave that to the last. But he was in error there. He found, to his surprise and joy, that all that he needed to do was to get me on to the machine and stand out of the way; I could get off, myself. Although I was wholly inexperienced, I dismounted in the best time on record. He was on that side, shoving up the machine; we all came down with a crash, he at the bottom, I next, and the machine on top.

We examined the machine, but it was not in the least injured. This was hardly believable. Yet the Expert assured me that it was true; in fact, the examination proved it. I was partly to realize, then, how admirably these things are constructed. We applied some Pond's Extract, and resumed. The Expert got on the OTHER side to shove up this time, but I dismounted on that side; so the result was as before.

The machine was not hurt. We oiled ourselves up again, and resumed. This time the Expert took up a sheltered position behind, but somehow or other we landed on him again.

He was full of surprised admiration; said it was abnormal. She was all right, not a scratch on her, not a timber started anywhere. I said it was wonderful, while we were greasing up, but

exploit, indeed the difficulty is to avoid performing it.
VISCOUNT BURY, 1887

he said that when I came to know these steel spider-webs I would realize that nothing but dynamite could cripple them. Then he limped out to position, and we resumed once more. This time the Expert took up the position of short-stop, and got a man to shove up behind. We got up a handsome speed, and presently traversed a brick, and I went out over the top of the tiller and landed, head down, on the instructor's back, and saw the machine fluttering in the air between me and the sun. It was well it came down on us, for that broke the fall, and it was not injured.

Five days later I got out and was carried down to the hospital, and found the Expert doing pretty fairly. In a few more days I was quite sound. I attribute this to my prudence in always dismounting on something soft. Some recommend a feather bed, but I think an Expert is better.

The Expert got out at last, brought four assistants with him. It was a good idea. These four held the graceful cobweb upright while I climbed into the saddle; then they formed in column and marched on either side of me while the Expert pushed behind; all hands assisted at the dismount.

The bicycle had what is called the 'wabbles,' and had them very badly. In order to keep my position, a good many things were required of me, and in every instance the thing required was against nature. Against nature, but not against the laws of

---

Iconic bicycle designs – the Velocipede (c1860s)
Moving on from the *Laufmaschine*, the next step towards the bicycle we know today was the introduction of pedals. This enabled the rider to attain faster speeds, but steering and balance was not quite so instinctive as on the 'running machine' because the rider had to be seated further forward with legs stretching to reach the pedals which were attached to the centre of the front wheel. Known as the velocipede ('fast foot'), these pedal cycles were also dubbed 'boneshakers', as increased speeds highlighted the poor ride quality of solid wooden or metal wheels.

Life is like riding a bicycle – in order to keep

nature. That is to say, that whatever the needed thing might be, my nature, habit, and breeding moved me to attempt it in one way, while some immutable and unsuspected law of physics required that it be done in just the other way. I perceived by this how radically and grotesquely wrong had been the life-long education of my body and members. They were steeped in ignorance; they knew nothing – nothing which it could profit them to know. For instance, if I found myself falling to the right, I put the tiller hard down the other way, by a quite natural impulse, and so violated a law, and kept on going down. The law required the opposite thing – the big wheel must be turned in the direction in which you are falling. It is hard to believe this, when you are told it. And not merely hard to believe it, but impossible; it is opposed to all your notions. And it is just as hard to do it, after you do come to believe it. Believing it, and knowing by the most convincing proof that it is true, does not help it: you can't any more DO it than you could before; you can neither force nor persuade yourself to do it at first. The intellect has to come to the front, now. It has to teach the limbs to discard their old education and adopt the new.

The steps of one's progress are distinctly marked. At the end of each lesson he knows he has acquired something, and he also knows what that something is, and likewise that it will stay with him. It is not like studying German, where you mull along, in a groping, uncertain way, for thirty years; and at last, just as you think you've got it, they spring the subjunctive on you, and there you are. No – and I see now, plainly enough, that the great pity about the German language is, that you can't fall off it and hurt yourself. There is nothing like that feature to make you attend strictly to business. But I also see, by what I have learned of bicycling, that the right and only sure way to learn German is by the bicycling method. That is to say, take a grip on one villainy of it at a time, and learn it – not ease up and shirk to the next, leaving that one half learned.

When you have reached the point in bicycling where you can balance the machine tolerably fairly and propel it and steer it,

your balance you must keep moving. ALBERT EINSTEIN

Iconic bicycle designs – Penny-farthing (c1870s)
Most people know that a penny-farthing, more properly
known as a High-Wheeler or Ordinary, was so called because its
two unequalled sized wheels were reminiscent of the difference
in size between those two Victorian coins. English inventor
James Starley recognised that enlarging the front wheel of the
velocipede would increase the distance travelled with one revolution of the wheel. Ride quality was also improved by replacing the solid wooden or metal wheels with solid rubber tyres on
metal rims. However, actually riding the penny-farthing was
not for the faint-hearted as mounting and dismounting was
notoriously difficult with the saddle possibly over a metre off
the ground, and many a rider would 'take a header'. Back to the
drawing board...

then comes your next task – how to mount it. You do it in this
way: you hop along behind it on your right foot, resting the other
on the mounting-peg, and grasping the tiller with your hands. At
the word, you rise on the peg, stiffen your left leg, hang your
other one around in the air in a general and indefinite way, lean
your stomach against the rear of the saddle, and then fall off,
maybe on one side, maybe on the other; but you fall off. You get
up and do it again; and once more; and then several times.

By this time you have learned to keep your balance; and also
to steer without wrenching the tiller out by the roots (I say tiller
because it IS a tiller; 'handle-bar' is a lamely descriptive phrase).
So you steer along, straight ahead, a little while, then you rise forward, with a steady strain, bringing your right leg, and then your
body, into the saddle, catch your breath, fetch a violent hitch this
way and then that, and down you go again.

But you have ceased to mind the going down by this time;
you are getting to light on one foot or the other with considerable
certainty. Six more attempts and six more falls make you perfect.
You land in the saddle comfortably, next time, and stay there –
that is, if you can be content to let your legs dangle, and leave the

One thing that cycling has taught me is that if you can

pedals alone a while; but if you grab at once for the pedals, you are gone again. You soon learn to wait a little and perfect your balance before reaching for the pedals; then the mounting-art is acquired, is complete, and a little practice will make it simple and easy to you, though spectators ought to keep off a rod or two to one side, along at first, if you have nothing against them.

And now you come to the voluntary dismount; you learned the other kind first of all. It is quite easy to tell one how to do the voluntary dismount; the words are few, the requirement simple, and apparently undifficult; let your left pedal go down till your left leg is nearly straight, turn your wheel to the left, and get off as you would from a horse. It certainly does sound exceedingly easy; but it isn't. I don't know why it isn't but it isn't. Try as you may, you don't get down as you would from a horse, you get down as you would from a house afire. You make a spectacle of yourself every time.

(From *What Is Man? And Other Stories: Taming the Bicycle*, 1893)

A Wobbling Will vs A Wobbling Wheel, 1895
FRANCES WILLARD

After being told by an English naval officer 'You women have no idea of the new realm of happiness which the bicycle has opened to us men', American temperance reformer and women's suffragist Frances Willard *decided she must learn to master bicycle riding herself, despite being 53 years old and forced to wear an 'unnatural style of dress'.*

Gradually, item by item, I learned the location of every screw and spring, spoke and tire, and every beam and bearing that went to make up Gladys. This was not the lesson of a day, but of many days and weeks, and it had to be learned before we could get on well together. …I found a whole philosophy of life in the wooing and the winning of my bicycle.

Just as a strong and skilful swimmer takes the waves, so the bicycler must learn to take such waves of mental impression as the passing of a gigantic hay-wagon, the sudden obtrusion of black cattle with wide-branching horns, the rattling pace of high-

achieve something without a struggle it's not going to be satisfying. GREG LEMOND

stepping steeds, or even the swift transit of a railway-train. At first she will be upset by the apparition of the smallest poodle, and not until she has attained a wide experience will she hold herself steady in presence of the critical eyes of a coach-and-four. But all this is a part of that equilibration of thought and action by which we conquer the universe in conquering ourselves.

I finally concluded that all failure was from a wobbling will rather than a wobbling wheel. I felt that indeed the will is the wheel of the mind – its perpetual motion having been learned when the morning stars sang together. When the wheel of the mind went well then the rubber wheel hummed merrily; but specters of the mind there are as well as of the wheel. In the aggregate of perception concerning which we have reflected and from which we have deduced our generalizations upon the world without, within, above, there are so many ghastly and fantastical images that they must obtrude themselves at certain intervals, like filmy bits of glass at the turn of the kaleidoscope. Probably every accident of which I had heard or read in my half-century tinged the uncertainty that by the correlation of forces passed over into the tremor that I felt when we began to round the terminus bend of the broad Priory walk. And who shall say by what original energy the mind forced itself at once from the contemplation of disaster and thrust into the very movement of the foot on the pedal a concept of vigor, safety, and success? I began to feel that myself plus the bicycle equalled myself plus the world, upon whose spinning-wheel we must all learn to ride, or fall into the sluiceways of oblivion and despair. That which made me succeed with the bicycle was precisely what had gained me a measure of success in life – it was the hardihood of spirit that led me to begin, the persistence of will that held me to my task, and the patience that was willing to begin again when the last stroke had failed. And so I found high moral uses in the bicycle and can commend it as a teacher without pulpit or creed. He who succeeds, or, to be more exact in handing over my experience, she who succeeds in gaining the mastery of such an animal as

Those who wish to control their own lives, and move

Gladys, will gain the mastery of life, and by exactly the same methods and characteristics.

☆ ☆ ☆

As nearly as I can make out, reducing the problem to actual figures, it took me about three months, with an average of fifteen minutes' practice daily, to learn, first, to pedal; second, to turn; third, to dismount; and fourth, to mount independently this most mysterious animal. January 20th will always be a red-letter bicycle day, because although I had already mounted several times with no hand on the rudder, some good friend had always stood by to lend moral support; but summoning all my force, and, most forcible of all, what Sir Benjamin Ward Richardson declares to be the two essential elements – decision and precision – I mounted and started off alone. From that hour the spell was broken; Gladys was no more a mystery: I had learned all her kinks, had put a bridle in her teeth, and touched her smartly with the whip of victory. Consider, ye who are of a considerably chronology: in about thirteen hundred minutes, or, to put it most mildly of all, in less than a single day as the almanac reckons time – but practically in two days of actual practice – amid the delightful surroundings of the great outdoors, and inspired by the bird-songs, the color and fragrance of an English posy-garden, in the company of devoted and pleasant comrades, I had made myself master of the most remarkable, ingenious, and inspiring motor ever yet devised upon this planet.

Moral: *Go thou and do likewise!*

(From *A wheel within a wheel: How I learned to ride a bicycle: with some reflections by the way*, Fleming H. Revell Company, 1895)

beyond existence as mere clients and consumers – those people ride a bike. WOLFGANG SACHS

Education of the Nerves, 1896

MUNSEY'S MAGAZINE

This article from an American magazine suggests that learning control of 'the wheel' is mostly a question of mind over matter...

Probably if every woman in the beginning had realized the difficulties of learning to ride, she would never have essayed her first lesson. But the feat looks so easy, that probably there was not one woman in ten who did not believe that she could gracefully mount and forthwith ride away in triumph. The schools hold traditions of women who have actually done this thing, but they are the glorious exceptions that prove the rule of preliminary falls; and they prove something else as well. These favoured ones are generally women who have been noted for excellence in some other sport. They are good skaters, who have been in the habit of balancing themselves on the steel blades over the glaring ice; or fine shots, whose trained eyes and steady arms have shown the bullet the path to the bull's eye; or billiardists whose balls knew their way through the mysteries of 'draws', 'drives', and 'follows'.

Steady nerves have everything to do with bicycling, and the chief value of the sport is its education of the nerves, and through them of the character. Most of the women who took up the wheel had already learned the theories of Delsarte. They knew that a dignified carriage was the result of a well organized and a well controlled temperament; that an acquired dignity would react upon the mind, and cultivate the qualities that go to make the attitude real. They speedily discovered that no enemy had ever found out their weaknesses so readily as the bicycle. The woman who would ride must be patient, watchful, self-reliant. The least lapse in purpose, the thousandth part of a second's indulgence in indecision, was recorded, usually by a bruise on some portion of her anatomy which had come in contact with the floor.

Physicians say that science has discovered no new remedy of incipient brain disease equal to the bicycle. It gives sufficient

A woman without a man is like

enjoyment to make it fascinating to the patient, and it provides for a constant concentration of the mind. The play it gives the muscles is extraordinary. The first long spin brings the rider home with a realization that every fiber of the body has been brought into active use. There is no comparison between horseback riding and bicycling in this respect. While the horse is a companion to the true horsewoman which she is loath to give up, her wheel becomes something much better. It is soon identified with its owner as a horse never can be.

☆ ☆ ☆

The beginner should take her lessons and learn her pace from a competent instructor. It may be that in the beginning, if she tries it alone or with the assistance of someone as ignorant as herself, all the benefit may be destroyed. The machine must be adjusted to the nature, habits, and physique of the woman who is to ride it. It may be that too light a wheel is given to the very nervous woman. She will come home a bundle of nerves, shaken into bewilderment and pain by the vibration which would only be an added delight to her stronger sister. Her saddle should be set well over her pedals, and so low that her heel can touch the pedal when it is at the lowest point.

A woman should never go upon the road until she can mount and dismount with confidence, and thoroughly understands her machine. A fright or any accident in the beginning may 'break the nerve' of a raw rider until confidence can never be fully regained. The wheel means too much to woman, when it is fully appreciated and enjoyed, to be considered lightly, or trifled with. It is the best gift that the nineteenth century has brought her.

(From *Munsey's Magazine: The World Awheel*, 1896)

Mulga Bill's Bicycle, 1896
A.B. 'BANJO' PATERSON

After Waltzing Matilda *this ballad, first published in* The Sydney Mail, *is probably the next most famous of this Australian bush poet's works. There is now a Mulga Bill's Bicycle Trail in Bendigo which takes riders round the Eaglehawk mining site.*

'Twas Mulga Bill, from Eaglehawk, that caught the cycling craze;
He turned away the good old horse that served him many days;
He dressed himself in cycling clothes, resplendent to be seen;
He hurried off to town and bought a shining new machine;
And as he wheeled it through the door, with air of lordly pride,
The grinning shop assistant said, 'Excuse me, can you ride?'

'See here, young man,' said Mulga Bill, 'from Walgett to the sea,
From Conroy's Gap to Castlereagh, there's none can ride like me.
I'm good all round at everything as everybody knows,
Although I'm not the one to talk – I hate a man that blows.
But riding is my special gift, my chiefest, sole delight;
Just ask a wild duck can it swim, a wildcat can it fight.
There's nothing clothed in hair or hide, or built of flesh or steel,
There's nothing walks or jumps, or runs, on axle, hoof, or wheel,
But what I'll sit, while hide will hold and girths and straps are tight:
I'll ride this here two-wheeled concern right straight away at sight.'

'Twas Mulga Bill, from Eaglehawk, that sought his own abode,
That perched above Dead Man's Creek, beside the mountain road.
He turned the cycle down the hill and mounted for the fray,
But 'ere he'd gone a dozen yards it bolted clean away.
It left the track, and through the trees, just like a silver streak,
It whistled down the awful slope towards the Dead Man's Creek.

It shaved a stump by half an inch, it dodged a big white-box:
The very wallaroos in fright went scrambling up the rocks,
The wombats hiding in their caves dug deeper underground,
As Mulga Bill, as white as chalk, sat tight to every bound.

He blended with his bicycle like a musician with his

It struck a stone and gave a spring that cleared a fallen tree,
It raced beside a precipice as close as close could be;
And then as Mulga Bill let out one last despairing shriek
It made a leap of twenty feet into the Dead Man's Creek.
'Twas Mulga Bill, from Eaglehawk, that slowly swam ashore:
He said, 'I've had some narrer shaves and lively rides before;
I've rode a wild bull round a yard to win a five-pound bet,
But this was the most awful ride that I've encountered yet.
I'll give that two-wheeled outlaw best; it's shaken all my nerve
To feel it whistle through the air and plunge and buck and
    swerve.
It's safe at rest in Dead Man's Creek, we'll leave it lying still;
A horse's back is good enough henceforth for Mulga Bill.'

(From *Mulga Bill's Bicycle*, 1896)

Iconic bicycle designs – Dursley Pedersen (1894)

Danish designer and inventor Mikael Pedersen was a keen cyclist and became convinced that the comfort and strength of the Safety bicycle could be improved. He set about reconfiguring the entire set up, starting with the saddle. He devised a seat that was made from a woven sling hung like a hammock from a frame consisting of fourteen thin steel rods. However, this seat design required a complete rethink of the bicycle frame itself. It was made up of a series of triangles to obtain the maximum amount of rigidity and was significantly lighter than the diamond frame of the Rover Safety.

The bicycle was manufactured from 1896 in Dursley, hence the name, and was claimed by the manufacturers, R.A. Lister, to be 'the only perfect bicycle in existence'. Unfortunately, although he was clearly an innovative designer, it seems Pedersen was not such a good businessman and the Dursley Pedersen became more of a collector's item than a commercial success.

---

instrument. Jacques Goddet (on Tour de France winner Anquetil)

The Bruises Tell the Story, 1896
H. G. WELLS

Draper's assistant Mr Hoopdriver is determined to spend his annual holiday on a cycling tour of the south coast of England, but his efforts in acquiring the necessary skill to do so are evidently not without consequence…

Now if you had noticed anything about him, it would have been chiefly to notice how little he was noticeable. He wore the black morning coat, the black tie, and the speckled grey nether parts (descending into shadow and mystery below the counter) of his craft. He was of a pallid complexion, hair of a kind of dirty fairness, greyish eyes, and a skimpy, immature moustache under his peaked indeterminate nose. His features were all small, but none ill-shaped. A rosette of pins decorated the lappel (sic) of his coat. His remarks, you would observe, were entirely what people used to call cliché, formulae not organic to the occasion, but stereotyped ages ago and learnt years since by heart. 'This, madam,' he would say, 'is selling very well.' 'We are doing a very good article at four three a yard.' 'We could show you something better, of course.' 'No trouble, madam, I assure you.' Such were the simple counters of his intercourse. So, I say, he would have presented himself to your superficial observation.

But real literature, as distinguished from anecdote, does not concern itself with superficial appearances alone. Literature is revelation. Modern literature is indecorous revelation. It is the duty of the earnest author to tell you what you would not have seen – even at the cost of some blushes. And the thing that you would not have seen about this young man, and the thing of the greatest moment to this story, the thing that must be told if the book is to be written, was – let us face it bravely – the Remarkable Condition of this Young Man's Legs.

Let us approach the business with dispassionate explicitness. Let us assume something of the scientific spirit, the hard, almost professorial tone of the conscientious realist. Let us treat this

To ride a bicycle properly is very like a love affair—chiefly it

young man's legs as a mere diagram, and indicate the points of interest with the unemotional precision of a lecturer's pointer. And so to our revelation. On the internal aspect of the right ankle of this young man you would have observed, ladies and gentlemen, a contusion and an abrasion; on the internal aspect of the left ankle a contusion also; on its external aspect a large yellowish bruise. On his left shin there were two bruises, one a leaden yellow graduating here and there into purple, and another, obviously of more recent date, of a blotchy red – tumid and threatening. Proceeding up the left leg in a spiral manner, an unnatural hardness and redness would have been discovered on the upper aspect of the calf, and above the knee and on the inner side, an extraordinary expanse of bruised surface, a kind of closely stippled shading of contused points. The right leg would be found to be bruised in a marvellous manner all about and under the knee, and particularly on the interior aspect of the knee. So far we may proceed with our details. Fired by these discoveries, an investigator might perhaps have pursued his inquiries further – to bruises on the shoulders, elbows, and even the finger joints, of the central figure of our story. He had indeed been bumped and battered at an extraordinary number of points. But enough of realistic description is as good as a feast, and we have exhibited enough for our purpose. Even in literature one must know where to draw the line.

Now the reader may be inclined to wonder how a respectable young shopman should have got his legs, and indeed himself generally, into such a dreadful condition. One might fancy that he had been sitting with his nether extremities in some complicated machinery, a threshing-machine, say, or one of those haymaking furies. But Sherlock Holmes (now happily dead) would have fancied nothing of the kind. He would have recognised at once that the bruises on the internal aspect of the left leg, considered in the light of the distribution of the other abrasions and contusions, pointed unmistakably to the violent impact of the Mounting Beginner upon the bicycling saddle, and that the ruinous state of the right knee was equally eloquent of the con-

is a matter of faith. Believe you do it, and the thing is done; doubt, and, for the life of you, you cannot. HG WELLS

cussions attendant on that person's hasty, frequently causeless, and invariably ill-conceived descents. One large bruise on the shin is even more characteristic of the 'prentice cyclist, for upon every one of them waits the jest of the unexpected treadle. You try at least to walk your machine in an easy manner, and whack! – you are rubbing your shin. So out of innocence we ripen. Two bruises on that place mark a certain want of aptitude in learning, such as one might expect in a person unused to muscular exercise. Blisters on the hands are eloquent of the nervous clutch of the wavering rider. And so forth, until Sherlock is presently explaining, by the help of the minor injuries, that the machine ridden is an old-fashioned affair with a fork instead of the diamond frame, a cushioned tire, well worn on the hind wheel, and a gross weight all on of perhaps three-and-forty pounds.

The revelation is made. Behind the decorous figure of the attentive shopman that I had the honour of showing you at first, rises a vision of a nightly struggle, of two dark figures and a machine in a dark road – the road, to be explicit, from Roehampton to Putney Hill – and with this vision is the sound of a heel spurning the gravel, a gasping and grunting, a shouting of 'Steer, man, steer!' a wavering unsteady flight, a spasmodic turning of the missile edifice of man and machine, and a collapse. Then you descry dimly through the dusk the central figure of this story sitting by the roadside and rubbing his leg at some new place, and his friend, sympathetic (but by no means depressed), repairing the displacement of the handle-bar.

Thus even in a shop assistant does the warmth of manhood assert itself, and drive him against all the conditions of his calling, against the counsels of prudence and the restrictions of his means, to seek the wholesome delights of exertion and danger and pain. And our first examination of the draper reveals beneath his draperies – the man! To which initial fact (among others) we shall come again in the end.

(From *The Wheels of Chance: A Bicycling Idyll*, 1896)

Perhaps people, and kids especially, are spoiled today,

Boy Scouts on Bicycles, 1918

D.G. DOLLERY

Baden-Powell's Boy Scouts were still a relatively new organisation in 1918 and this article was at pains to explain how Scouting helped to channel boys' energy in a positive manner.

Frequenters of the open road are naturally apt to associate the word Scout with the figure – once, at any rate, familiar – of the AA man. The object of this article, however, is to show how great a bond should exist between cyclists and the young followers of 'B.P.'

Possibly many wheelmen do not realise to what a great extent cycling and its allied pursuits are being encouraged by the Boy Scout movement. It is significant that one of the very first sketches in 'Scouting for Boys' depicts Lord Edward Cecil and some cyclist Boy Scouts in Mafeking. The next illustration, too, is a reproduction of a special postage stamp used during the siege. This particular stamp bore the figure of a cadet bicycle orderly, and Sir Robert Baden-Powell refers to the splendid work of boy cyclists in maintaining a postal system between the various forts, even amidst danger.

The Value of Cycling

Scouting naturally stands for healthy open-air activity, and it is therefore a *sine qua non* that cycling is recognised to be of great value. A handbook for cyclist Scouts has been published, and frequent references to the great pastime occur in the periodicals of the movement. Rallies of cyclist Scouts have been held from time to time in various centres, and the cycle has proved of the utmost utility for despatch riding and travelling to camp, whilst thousands of scouts have rendered the country service of real importance by means of their cycles during war.

Among the varied proficiency badges which may be gained by Boy Scouts there is to be found the Cyclist Badge, the emblem of which is the bicycle wheel. To obtain this, the boy is required

because all the kids today have cars, it seems. When I was young you were lucky to have a bike. JAMES CAGNEY to sign a certificate that he owns a bicycle in good working order, which he is willing to use in the King's service if called upon at any time, in case of emergency. He must be able to ride the machine satisfactorily and repair punctures, etc. He must also be able to read a road map and repeat correctly a verbal message. Many troops include a cyclist patrol of boys who hold this badge.

(From *Boy Scouts on Bicycles: How Scouting encourages the use of Bicycles,*
published in *Cycling* magazine, 1918)

Learn to Ankle Your BSA Bicycle, 1945
BSA BICYCLES LTD

So what do you put in a child's bicycle advertisement if wartime restrictions mean you don't actually have any bicycles to sell? Well, you could always give children tips on how to ride their bicycle efficiently when they do eventually get one...

When you're riding your BSA do you ever think about what your feet and ankles are doing? No? Well, here's what they should be doing if you want to get the best out of your BSA.

The ball of the foot – that is the forepart – should be on the pedals, because the proper movement is to swing the pedal round instead of just pushing it down. You can get this swing movement by using your ankles. When the pedal is down, use your toes to drive it under the centre of the bottom bracket. When it's up, push it over the top centre by raising your toes. This is known as 'ankling', and it makes all the difference to easy riding. Try it and see.

If you haven't a BSA yet but want one, ask your parents to put your name on the nearest BSA dealer's waiting list. He'll do his best for you – but you'll have to be patient.

BSA – the bicycle you can't beat.

(From *The Meccano Magazine,* 1945)

Directly he gets on wheels he is as cocky as if he owned the universe, his manner to boys who have only their feet to take

Goodnight, Mister Tom, 1945

MICHELLE MAGORIAN

In a fragile state after everything he has gone through, WWII evacuee Will is further devastated by the death of his friend Zach, but is determined to learn to ride Zach's bike in an effort to feel close to him again.

Will carried on until he was well out of sight of the cottages and when he had found a reasonably smooth stretch of road he swung his leg over the saddle and sat still for a moment. He placed the toe of his foot on one of the pedals. Gritting his teeth and taking a deep breath, he pushed it down and wobbled forward. The bicycle curved and swooped into a near-by hedge. He picked himself up and climbed back onto the seat. Again the bicycle skidded over to one side so that he grazed his knees on the rough road. Undaunted, he clambered back on again and each time he swerved and fell, he only grew more determined.

In spite of the hoar frost that covered the hedgerows and surrounding fields, learning to ride was hot work and soon his overcoat was left dangling from the branch of a near-by tree.

At times he managed to keep the bicycle balanced for a few yards only to swerve into another clump of brambles or icy nettles. He could hear his Dad's words over and over again inside his head. 'Takes yer time, everythin' 'as its own time.' But whether it was because it was Zach's bicycle or because the colours were so intense, he felt frustrated and impatient. He wanted to learn now. When, at last, he managed to ride it for a reasonable distance he rewarded himself with Aunt Nance's blackcurrant jelly sandwiches and the ginger beer. Perspiration trickled down his face and into his shirt and jersey. Soon the crisp January air was freezing it into a cold clammy sweat. He hung the bag on a branch and pushed the bicycle forward. The break had been a good idea for when he set off again it seemed easier, far less of a struggle.

Soon he began to grow confident. He put his coat back on, leaving it undone and slung the bag over his head and shoulder.

them along is always patronising and occasionally insolent.
WINDSOR MAGAZINE, 1906

He understood now why Zach loved riding so much. There was a marvellous feeling of freedom once you'd got the hang of it.

As he rode, his coat flapping behind him, the crisp wind cooling his face, he suddenly felt that Zach was no longer beside him, he was inside him and very much alive. The numbness in his body had dissolved into exhilaration.

(From *Goodnight, Mister Tom*, Puffin, 2010. Copyright © Michelle Magorian, 1981)

Starting young

For a child, learning to ride a bike is only the first hurdle. Learning to deal with traffic on our increasingly busy roads in the 21st century is an altogether more serious challenge, and to that end RoSPA, the Royal Society for the Prevention of Accidents, introduced the Cycling Proficiency Test to serve as a minimum recommended standard for cycling on British roads.

The first Cycling Proficiency Test was held for seven children on 7 October 1947. The National Cycling Proficiency Scheme was introduced by the Government in 1958, with statutory responsibility for road safety being given to local authorities in 1974, including the provision of child cyclist training.

The first child to get 100% for this test was Stephen Borrill of Scunthorpe in 1962 and he was featured on the front page of *The News of the World*. Stephen was given the honour of 'Knight of the Road', presented by the Mayor of Scunthorpe at the council offices in Central Park.

Now branded Bikeability (🖥 bikeability.org.uk), the training is designed to give primary school children the requisite skills and confidence to ride their bikes on today's roads.

'I won! I won! I don't have to go to school anymore.'

Cycling is Grand Fun, 1959

ANDREW CRAWFORD

Although written for the kind of book that a boy of twelve or thirteen in the 1950s might have been given by a well-meaning great-aunt to keep him out of mischief, this is a marvellous evocation of childhood in simpler times, with a direct tone unlikely to be seen in print nowadays.

Cycling is grand fun – at least, it is if you go the right way about it. It is grand fun to explore the countryside near and far or to go to sand-dunes where you can bird-watch, or cycle to a safe spot on the river for a bathe, or take sandwiches and a bottle of pop for a picnic. Of course, you won't think it fun if you don't like adventure; but are there any boys who have tasted adventure that do not want more?

Perhaps you have just received your first bicycle. It is to be hoped that it has been chosen carefully. None of this nonsense about buying a large bicycle so that you will be able to ride it when you have stopped growing. You run the risk of not living that long if you cannot reach the ground with your toes without getting off the saddle.

A 'sports' model, one with flat or slightly upturned bars, is best for a beginner. Make sure that you can sit a few inches behind the pedals, not directly above them, and lean forward slightly so that a little of your weight is on the front wheel. Now, do not bend your arms to do this. If the bicycle is right the handlebar will be low enough and far enough forward for you to lean sufficiently without crouching like a witch over a broom-stick.

If you are learning to ride, keep away from busy roads. Wobbles and swerves, whether accidental or by 'big-heads' trying to show off, are dangerous. Besides, it is not fair to other road users who expect a cyclist to ride almost in a straight line, and to act as he is told to do in the Highway Code.

Cycling is made easier by using the feet correctly, and by a number of other gimmicks, having the tyres inflated board-hard, and if you have a three-speed, by using a fairly low gear, not one that makes you sway like a goose! Don't stick your heels on the pedals and ride flat-footed. The ball of the foot is the part of the foot to use. Work your ankles, raising the toes to push forward and down when the pedal is at the top, and clawing it round at the bottom. Practice will be needed, and your muscles may ache until you have learned to do it smoothly but it is a good exercise.

The whole movement of cycling is exercise. That is one of the great advantages of cycling. It will keep you fit, provided that you avoid standing about in the cold after getting warm, and that you change any damp clothing immediately you finish a ride. Sufficient clothing for warmth and plenty of common-sense are needed on cold days. Carry a spare pullover in your touring-bag, if you have one, and use common-sense when fog blots out the road in front. Ride slowly, or walk – it is safer.

Now that you have been for a ride on your bicycle, lean it against a wall and take a good look at it. Which part do you think has worked the hardest? The chain? Good! That shows you understand something about a machine. Did you notice any bicycles with rusty chains while you were riding? It is awful that people should neglect their bicycles in that way. If a cyclist cannot be bothered to test his brakes and oil his chain regularly he ought to be banned from the road. Yes! Anyone who uses a bicycle that is not in good working order and properly oiled is a danger. Mechanical faults often cause wobbles and swerves.

(From *The Boys' Book of Hobbies: Cycling as a Hobby*, Spring Books, 1959)

Toleration is the greatest gift of the mind; it requires the

Call the Midwife, 1950s

JENNIFER WORTH

Writing about her work in the East End of London in the 1950s, Call the Midwife *author Jennifer Worth had the task of helping her colleague, the blue-blooded Camilla 'Chummy' Fortescue-Cholmeley-Browne, 'six foot two inches tall, with shoulders like a front row forward and size eleven feet' learn to ride a bike for the first time.*

For all the genteel education and ladylike accomplishments, no one had thought it necessary to teach her to ride a bicycle. A horse yes, but a bicycle, no.

'Never mind, I can learn,' she said cheerfully. Sister Julienne said it was hard for an adult to acquire the skill. 'Not to worry, I can practise,' was her equally exuberant response.

Cynthia, Trixie and I went with her to the bicycle shed, and selected the largest – a huge old Raleigh, of about 1910 vintage, made of solid iron with a scooped-out front and high handlebars. The solid tyres were about three inches thick, and there were no gears. The whole contraption weighed about half a ton, and for this reason no one rode it. Trixie oiled the chain and we were ready for the off.

The time was just after lunch. We agreed to push Chummy up and down Leyland Street until she found her balance, after which we would travel in convoy to where the roads were quiet and flat. Most people who have tried to ride a bicycle in adult life for the first time will tell you that it is a terrifying experience. Many will say that it is impossible and give up. But Chummy was made of sterner stuff. The Makers of the Empire were her forebears, and their blood flowed in her veins. Besides which, she was going to be a missionary, for which it was necessary that she should be a midwife. If she had to ride a bicycle to achieve this, so be it – she would ride the thing.

We pushed her, huge and shaking, shouting 'pedal, pedal, up, down, up, down' until we were exhausted. She weighed about twelve stone of solid bone and muscle, and the bike anoth-

same effort of the brain that it takes to balance oneself on a bicycle. HELEN KELLER

er six stone, but we kept on pushing. At four o'clock the local school ended, and children came pouring out. About ten of them took over, giving us girls a well-earned rest as they ran along beside and behind, pushing and shouting encouragement.

Several times Chummy fell heavily to the ground. She hit her head on the kerb, and said, 'Not to worry – no brains to hurt.' She cut her leg, and murmured, 'Just a scratch.' She was indomitable. We began to respect her. Even the Cockney children, who had seen her as a comic turn, changed their tune. A tough-looking cookie of about twelve, who had been openly jeering at first, now looked solemnly at her with admiration.

The time had come to venture further than Leyland Street. Chummy could balance, and she could pedal, so we agreed to half an hour cycling together around the streets. Trixie was in front, Cynthia and I on either side of Chummy, the children running behind, shouting.

We got to the top of Leyland Street and no further. It had not occurred to us to show Chummy how to turn a corner. Trixie turned left, calling 'just follow me', and rode off. Cynthia and I turned left, but Chummy kept going straight ahead. I saw her fixed expression as she came straight for me, and after that all was confusion. Apparently a policeman had been in the act of crossing the street when the two of us hurtled into him. We came to rest on the opposite pavement. Seeing a representative of the law hit full frontal by a couple of midwives was joy for the children. They screamed with delight, and doors opened all down the street, emitting even more children and curious adults.

I was lying on my back in the gutter, not knowing what had happened. From this position I heard a groan, and then the policeman sat up with the words, 'What fool did that?' I saw Chummy sit up. She had lost her glasses, and peered round. Maybe this could account for her next action or maybe she was dazed. She slapped the man heavily on the back with her huge hand and said, 'No whingeing, now. Cheer up, old bean. Stiff upper lip and all that, what?' Clearly she was unaware that he was a policeman.

(From *Call the Midwife* published by Phoenix, an imprint of Orion Books Ltd, London, 2012. Copyright © Jennifer Worth, 2002)

One of the most important days of my life

Riding a Bike, 2009
RONALD CHAPMAN

Whether you take the words of this poem literally or metaphorically, there is good counsel in it.

I'm learning to ride a bike,
And I'm learning to fly on my own,
And I'm learning to sing,
Not to cry, when I fall,
And I'm learning not to give up,
As I ride though life,
And I'm learning to try try try again,
To get back up on that bike,
And I'm learning (although it sometimes really hurts me) ,
Not to run away from pain,
And I'm learning to fly high,
While I speed through the hills of life,
And I'm learning that it's much,
Much easier to look ahead at my future path,
Than looking in my mirror,
To see the past.

(Reprinted by permission of Ronald Chapman, 2009)

Scouts Cyclist Activity Badge, 2015

There are two parts to achieving this badge. Complete all tasks for Part 1. **1**. Use a bicycle that is properly equipped. Keep it in good working order for at least six months. **2**. Show that you can carry out essential maintenance and repairs, including:

- checking and adjusting the brakes
- checking and adjusting the gear change
- adjusting the seat and handlebars to a correct height
- removing a wheel and locating and repairing a puncture
- checking and adjusting your cycle helmet
- maintaining a set of lights.

For Part 2 of this activity badge, choose one of these options then complete all the tasks for that option.

Option 1: road cycling You can automatically complete Option 1 if you gain Bikeability Level 2 or 3. Otherwise, here's what you need to do for this option.

1. Explain what extra precautions you should take when cycling in the dark or in wet weather. Show you understand why motor vehicles take longer to stop in the wet.

2. Learn the basics of first aid and what to do if an accident happens.

3. Develop a working knowledge of map reading. Orientate a map using a compass or conspicuous features. Estimate distances and times taken to travel.

4. Plan and carry out an all-day cycle ride of at least 40km (25 miles).

5. Complete one of these:

- Show you can control a cycle along a slalom course.
- Show you understand the Highway Code, including road signs and helmet use.

Option 2: off-road cycling

1. Show you understand the Mountain Bike Code of Conduct.

2. Show you can control your cycle over different types of terrain.

3. Show you're aware of the damage that may be caused to the environment through careless cycling across the countryside.

4. Learn the basics of first aid, including the treatment of hypothermia and find out what to do in the case of an accident.

5. Gain a working knowledge of map reading. Orientate a map using a compass or conspicuous features. Estimate distances and times taken to travel.

6. Plan and carry out an all-day ride of at least 30 km (20 miles).

(Scout Cyclist Badge requirements, © 2015 The Scout Association; reproduced by permission)

The Costume of Women, 1895
FRANCES WILLARD

It is clear that Frances Willard *was speaking from direct experience when describing the difficulty of cycling in cumbersome, restrictive clothing for the sake of public opinion.*

We saw that the physical development of humanity's mother-half would be wonderfully advanced by that universal introduction of the bicycle sure to come about within the next few years, because it is for the interest of great commercial monopolies that this should be so, since if women patronize the wheel the number of buyers will be twice as large. If women ride they must, when riding, dress more rationally than they have been wont to do. If they do this many prejudices as to what they may be allowed to wear will melt away. Reason will gain upon precedent, and ere long the comfortable, sensible, and artistic wardrobe of the rider will make the conventional style of woman's dress absurd to the eye and unendurable to the understanding. A reform often advances most rapidly by indirection. An ounce of practice is worth a ton of theory; and the graceful and becoming costume of woman on the bicycle will convince the world that has brushed aside the theories, no matter how well constructed, and the arguments, no matter how logical, of dress-reformers.

A woman with bands hanging on her hips and dress snug about the waist and chokingly tight at the throat, with heavily trimmed skirts dragging down the back and numerous folds heating the lower part, and with tight shoes, ought to be in agony. She ought to be as miserable as a stalwart man would be in the same plight.

(From *A wheel within a wheel: How I learned to ride a bicycle: with some reflections by the way*, 1895, Fleming H. Revell Company)

On Cycling in Corsets, 1896

MUNSEY'S MAGAZINE

While recognising the freedom that cycling had brought to women of the late 19th century, the writer of this article seems more concerned about appearance than practicality, cautioning against adopting a style of dress that would attract the undesirable attention of the 'caricaturist'.

A great deal has been said about bicycle costumes. Rationally regarded, it will be seen that women have treated the question of dressing for the bicycle exactly as they have treated every other sport that required a change from the conventional wear of every day. It is nonsense to say that the bicycle had revolutionized women's dress, and has glorified Mrs Bloomer. The most daring costume worn on the wheel cannot approach the ordinary bathing dress as a bold departure from the accepted standards of feminine gowning upon conventional occasions.

When women began to ride, they found themselves hampered by long skirts, and they promptly had them shortened. Many women wore bloomers, and a few appeared in knickerbockers, but they were never those whom the great majority would care to imitate. The well bred rider of the bicycle – and the average American woman is always tactful and adaptable enough to have that appearance – sees to it that her dress is dainty and picturesque, without holding out any temptations to the caricaturist. It must be no more pronounced in cut and style than her walking dress. It must be neat, tailor made, and elegant, without a frill or a ribbon to catch the eye or the wind.

It has been boasted that the wheel has done what the physical culturists have never been able to do – made women set stays aside, and rely upon their own muscles for support. The fact is, that the best physical trainers of girls do not ask them to put aside whalebone entirely. When they mount the wheel, it is only a small minority who discard their corsets. Because she has found a new delight in living, a way to get out of beaten paths, and into the open air of the country, there is no reason why a woman should change every habit of her life in the twinkling of an eye. At any rate

Let me tell you what I think of bicycling. I think it has done more to emancipate women than anything else in the world. It gives women a feeling of freedom and self—reliance.

🚲 The Emancipated Cyclist

Here in the early 21st century, a woman wanting to go for a bike ride need only pull on some suitable clothes, hop on and pedal off, without attracting any negative attention, or indeed any attention at all. Her 'suitable clothes' more than likely comprise comfortable, close-fitting trousers or shorts and a stretchy top for ease of movement. Yet the earliest female cyclists attracted a great deal of criticism, focused not only on their desire to ride a bicycle as a man could, but on their choice of attire whilst doing so.

Of course this was nothing new – women riding horses had been battling since the 17th century against the view that riding astride was 'unseemly'. As late as 1913 the redoubtable Queen Mary tried to issue a royal ban on women riding astride in Hyde Park. The impracticalities of the side-saddle are obvious, from the impossibility of mounting without assistance from at least two people, through the difficulty of controlling a horse when both the rider's legs are on the same side of her mount, to the increased risk of being injured by the horse in a fall rather than being thrown clear. The solution, adopted by a few brave souls, was a divided skirt, yet even this relatively modest garment scandalised some.

In the same way that the side-saddle is a design driven by social niceties rather than practicality, the early involvement of women in the bicycle story gave rise to a variety of impractical inventions. Initially a women on wheels was more likely to be seated on a heavy tricycle for two, known as a 'sociable', alongside her husband or chaperone. In 1884 *Tricycles of the Year* described 220 such machines. Yet once the high-wheeled 'Ordinary' had been superseded by the far more rider-friendly 'Safety', women soon discovered that once the requisite skill had been acquired it was lighter, easier to mount and dismount, capable of negotiating most road surfaces and easier to stop. However, corsets and heavy skirts were a distinct disadvantage and a long divided skirt was not going to be the solution this time, as anyone who has tried cycling in loose trousers will realise.

(cont'd overleaf)

(cont'd overleaf)

CYCLING FOR ALL

I stand and rejoice every time I see a woman ride by on a wheel ... the picture of free, untrammeled womanhood.
SUSAN B. ANTHONY

The Emancipated Cyclist

(cont'd from p37) The recommended costume was known as 'rationals', which substituted the dangerously flapping long skirts with pantaloons combined with a knee length skirt. It was said to be originally inspired by Oriental harem dress and first adopted by the women of a progressive community in America in the 1840s, not for cycling purposes but so that they could more easily manage the physical work of helping the men of their community build a meeting house. Although first sported outside that community by a Mrs Elizabeth Smith Miller, they became known as bloomers after being championed by Mrs Amelia Bloomer in her reform magazine *Lily*, but then fell out of fashion before being rediscovered some years later as the perfect solution to the problem of practical women's cycling attire.

The rest, as they say, is history – but what kind of history? This is not the history of fashion, like the scandal of skirts shortening from floor length to calf length in the 1920s, to knee length in the 1940s, to barely there in the 1960s, but the history of social change. It's the history of women's position in a society that was organised and dominated by men. Women who battled to be able to enjoy the same freedom as men, who could choose to cycle where they pleased in clothing suited to the purpose, were fighting a different battle in the same campaign as the suffragettes who chained themselves to railings to win the vote.

That vote was achieved in some measure by 1918, although it was to be another 10 years before women received the right to vote on the same terms as men. In the meantime the pressure of the war years had exerted its own influence on women's dress, and by the 1930s a BSA advertisement proclaiming 'Get Fit, Keep Fit' depicted a smiling man and woman cycling through the countryside together, both clad in loose shorts.

If I could change one single thing in British cycling then it

she had not done so. If she has ridden her bicycle into new fields, becoming in the process a new creature, it has been gradually and unconsciously. She did not have to be born again in some mysterious fashion, becoming a strange creature, a 'new woman'. She is more like the 'eternal feminine', who has taken on wings, and who is using them with an ever increasing delight in her new power.

(From *Munsey's Magazine: The World Awheel*, 1896)

Sherlock Holmes and the Solitary Cyclist, 1903
ARTHUR CONAN DOYLE

Miss Violet Smith is a governess who teaches music to a young girl in Surrey and cycles from her employer's house to the station to return to her home in London every weekend. When she calls upon Mr Sherlock Holmes to ask for his help in discovering the identity of a lone cyclist who regularly follows her, he is typically intrigued by the puzzle that the case presents.

From the years 1894 to 1901 inclusive Mr. Sherlock Holmes was a very busy man. It is safe to say that there was no public case of any difficulty in which he was not consulted during those eight years, and there were hundreds of private cases, some of them of the most intricate and extraordinary character, in which he played a prominent part. Many startling successes and a few unavoidable failures were the outcome of this long period of continuous work. As I have preserved very full notes of all these cases, and was myself personally engaged in many of them, it may be imagined that it is no easy task to know which I should select to lay before the public. I shall, however, preserve my former rule, and give the preference to those cases which derive their interest not so much from the brutality of the crime as from the ingenuity and dramatic quality of the solution. For this reason I will now lay before the reader the facts connected with Miss Violet Smith, the solitary cyclist of Charlington, and the curious sequel of our investigation, which culminated in unexpected tragedy.

CYCLING FOR ALL

would be to put an elite female in a high-up role within the structure. VICTORIA PENDLETON

With a resigned air and a somewhat weary smile, Holmes begged the beautiful intruder to take a seat and to inform us what it was that was troubling her.

'At least it cannot be your health,' said he, as his keen eyes darted over her; 'so ardent a bicyclist must be full of energy.' She glanced down in surprise at her own feet, and I observed the slight roughening of the side of the sole caused by the friction of the edge of the pedal.

'Yes, I bicycle a good deal, Mr. Holmes, and that has something to do with my visit to you to-day.

'You must know that every Saturday forenoon I ride on my bicycle to Farnham Station in order to get the 12.22 to town. The road from Chiltern Grange is a lonely one, and at one spot it is particularly so, for it lies for over a mile between Charlington Heath upon one side and the woods which lie round Charlington Hall upon the other. You could not find a more lonely tract of road anywhere, and it is quite rare to meet so much as a cart, or a peasant, until you reach the high road near Crooksbury Hill.

'Two weeks ago I was passing this place when I chanced to look back over my shoulder, and about two hundred yards behind me I saw a man, also on a bicycle. He seemed to be a middle-aged man, with a short, dark beard. I looked back before I reached Farnham, but the man was gone, so I thought no more about it. But you can imagine how surprised I was, Mr. Holmes, when on my return on the Monday I saw the same man on the same stretch of road.

'My astonishment was increased when the incident occurred again, exactly as before, on the following Saturday and Monday. He always kept his distance and did not molest me in any way, but still it certainly was very odd. I mentioned it to Mr. Carruthers, who seemed interested in what I said, and told me that he had ordered a horse and trap, so that in future I should not pass over these lonely roads without some companion.

'The horse and trap were to have come this week, but for some reason they were not delivered, and again I had to cycle to the station. That was this morning. You can think that I looked out when I came to Charlington Heath, and there, sure enough,

When the spirits are low, when the day appears dark, when work becomes monotonous, when hope hardly seems worth

was the man, exactly as he had been the two weeks before. He always kept so far from me that I could not clearly see his face, but it was certainly someone whom I did not know. He was dressed in a dark suit with a cloth cap. The only thing about his face that I could clearly see was his dark beard. To-day I was not alarmed, but I was filled with curiosity, and I determined to find out who he was and what he wanted. I slowed down my machine, but he slowed down his. Then I stopped altogether, but he stopped also. Then I laid a trap for him. There is a sharp turning of the road, and I pedalled very quickly round this, and then I stopped and waited. I expected him to shoot round and pass me before he could stop. But he never appeared. Then I went back and looked round the corner. I could see a mile of road, but he was not on it. To make it the more extraordinary, there was no side road at this point down which he could have gone.'

Holmes chuckled and rubbed his hands. 'This case certainly presents some features of its own,' said he.

(From *The Adventure of the Solitary Cyclist*, 1903)

Perfect in Every Part, 1920
B.S.A. BICYCLES LTD

Newspapers in the 1920s featured many adverts such as this, illustrated with drawings of smiling men in suits who had made the 'right' choice of bicycle.

To the business man a rapid, economical, and ever-ready means of transit is a great boon. Such a convenience is the B.S.A. Bicycle.

Easy running, comfortable, convenient, of strong construction and perfect finish, it is the choice the world over, of the cyclist who buys with a thought to the future. And with the recent increases in tram and train fares, the economy of the B.S.A. is more pronounced than ever. B.S.A. Bicycles have a reputation for reliability and excellence extending over half a century, and ensure the maximum of riding comfort with the minimum of attention.

(B.S.A Bicycles Limited, Birmingham, 1920)

having, just mount a bicycle and go out for a spin down the road, without thought on anything but the ride you are taking.
ARTHUR CONAN DOYLE

Keeping Up Appearances, 1930

SOMERSET MAUGHAM

As the nephew of a Kent vicar, fifteen-year-old William Ashenden should know his place in society and behave accordingly, but his earnest desire to learn to ride a bicycle brings him into contact with other riders of a quite different social status.

I do not know how long the safety bicycle had been invented, but I know that it was not common in the remote part of Kent in which I lived, and when you saw someone speeding along on solid tyres you turned round and looked till he was out of sight. It was still a matter for jocularity on the part of middle-aged gentlemen who said Shank's pony was good enough for them, and for trepidation on the part of elderly ladies who made a dash for the side of the road when they saw one coming.

I was determined to ride by myself, and chaps at school had told me that they had learned in half an hour. I tried and tried, and at last came to the conclusion that I was abnormally stupid, but even after my pride was sufficiently humbled for me to allow the gardener to hold me up I seemed at the end of the first morning no nearer to being able to get on by myself than at the beginning. Next day, however, thinking that the carriage drive at the vicarage was too winding to give a fellow a proper chance, I wheeled the bicycle to a road not far away which I knew was perfectly flat and straight, and so solitary that no one would see me making a fool of myself.

I tried several times to mount, but fell off each time. I barked my shins against the pedals, and got very hot and bothered. After I had been doing this for about an hour, though I began to think that God did not intend me to ride a bicycle, but was determined (unable to bear the thought of the sarcasms of my uncle, His representative at Blackstable) to do so all the same, to my disgust I saw two people on bicycles coming along the deserted road. I immediately wheeled my machine to the side and sat down on a stile, looking out to sea in a nonchalant way, as though I had been for a ride and were just sitting there wrapped in contemplation of the vasty ocean. I kept my eyes dreamily averted from the two persons who were advancing toward me, but I felt that they were coming nearer, and through the corner of my eye I saw that they were a man and a woman. As they passed me the woman swerved violently to my side of the road and, crashing against me, fell to the ground.

'Oh, I'm sorry,' she said. 'I knew I should fall off the moment I saw you.'

'I think bicycling's lovely, don't you?' she said, looking at my beautiful new machine which leaned against the stile. 'It must be wonderful to be able to ride well.'

I felt that this inferred an admiration for my proficiency.

'It's only a matter of practice,' I said.

'This is only my third lesson. Mr Driffield says I'm coming along wonderfully, but I feel so stupid I could kick myself. How long did it take you before you could ride?'

I blushed to the roots of my hair. I could hardly utter the shameful words.

'I can't ride,' I said. 'I've only just got this bike, and this is the first time I've tried.'

I equivocated a trifle here, but I made it all right with my conscience by adding the mental reservation: except yesterday at home in the garden.

'I'll give you a lesson if you like,' said Driffield in his good-humoured way. 'Come on.'

'Oh no,' I said. 'I wouldn't dream of it.'

'Why not?' asked his wife, her blue eyes still pleasantly smiling. 'Mr Driffield would like to and it'll give me a chance to rest.'

Driffield took my bicycle and I, reluctant but unable to withstand his friendly violence, clumsily mounted. I swayed from side to side, but he held me with a firm hand.

'Faster,' he said.

I pedalled and he ran by me as I wobbled from side to side. We were both very hot when, notwithstanding his efforts, I at last fell off. It was very hard under such circumstances to preserve

CYCLING FOR ALL

but few understand. JIM BURLANT

the standoffishness befitting the vicar's nephew with the son of Miss Wolfe's bailiff, and when I started back again and for thirty or forty thrilling yards actually rode by myself and Mrs Driffield ran into the middle of the road with her arms akimbo shouting: 'Go it, go it, two to one on the favourite,' I was laughing so much that I positively forgot all about my social status. I got off of my own accord, my face no doubt wearing an air of immodest triumph, and received without embarrassment the Driffields' congratulations on my cleverness in riding a bicycle the very first day I tried.

(From *Cakes and Ale*, William Heinemann, 1930)

Billy Bunter Stops the Cycling Thief, 1933
FRANK RICHARDS

Greyfriars' schoolboy Billy Bunter looms large, in more ways than one, in stories originally published in the boys' weekly publication The Magnet *from 1908 to 1940. Here Bunter's refusal to let an impatient cyclist past him and Harry Wharton on a narrow icy road draws him unwittingly into helping to apprehend a villain in the crime of a stolen diamond tiepin.*

From the Wimford road they turned into the lane that led to the village and the local station. Bunter grunted and groused at every step. It was undoubtedly rather an exertion to get through frozen snow. Bunter had never liked exertion. Elmdale – the village where there was a railway station – was only a half mile from Wharton Lodge, but the fat Owl of the Remove was puffing and blowing before he had done a tenth of that distance. He threw a great deal of weight on Wharton's arm, which the captain of the Remove bore with manly fortitude.

A sound of swishing in the snow behind caused Wharton to glance round. The cyclist he had seen coming from Wimford had turned into the lane and was coming on after them. Now that he was close at hand Harry looked at him rather curiously. Difficult as it was to ride on such a road, he was putting on some speed, evidently exerting himself to the uttermost. And he was not an athletic fellow to look at. He was short and slightly built, with a thin, narrow face and pale red eyebrows and eyelashes. His exertions were telling on him, judging by the beads of perspiration that ran down his sallow cheeks in spite of the bitter cold.

He buzzed his bell impatiently as he drew near the two schoolboys, who were walking in the middle of the narrow lane. Wharton jerked at Billy Bunter's fat arm.

'Stoppit!' hooted Bunter. 'Beast! You nearly made me slip! Wharrer you dragging at a fellow for, you beast?'

'Get aside, old fat bean!'

'Shan't!'

'There's a bike behind!'

'He can go round us, can't he?' snorted Bunter.

'You silly ass, get out of the man's way!' roared Wharton.

'Beast!'

Buzz, buzz, buzz! came angrily on the bell behind. The cyclist was close now and Wharton had already noted that the man was, for some reason of his own, in hot haste.

The lane was narrow, and going round the fellows walking in the middle of it meant going among deep cart-ruts ridged with frozen snow, at the imminent peril of a crash.

'Hi!' yelled the man with the ginger eyebrows. 'Hi! Get out of the way! Hi! Have you bought this road? Hi!'

'Bunter, you ass…'

'Beast!'

Harry Wharton tugged at a fat arm. Bunter was dragged out of the way by main force. With a snort of wrath, the Owl of the Remove wrenched his arm from Wharton's grasp. He staggered as he got it loose, slipped on icy snow, and spun.

'Yarooooh!' roared Bunter, as he went.

He rolled over, fairly in the way of the oncoming bicycle. The rider had just time to twist aside and avoid him, or certainly he and his machine would have been heaped on the sprawling Owl.

But that sudden twist of the bike on a slippery road did the trick. The wheels ceased to grip, the machine shot away in a skid,

CYCLING FOR ALL

between a bicycle accident and the collapse of civilization.
GEORGE BERNARD SHAW

and the next moment it was crashing into a hedge.

'Crash! Smash! Bump!

'Oh, my hat!' gasped Wharton.

'Yaroop!' roared Bunter, struggling in the snow. 'Whoop! Help me gerrup! Oh crikey! Oh lor'! Beast! Help!'

But Wharton did not heed him. He ran across to the over-turned cyclist, who was much more in need of help.

The bicycle was jammed in the hedge, and looked as if it was tied in a sailor's knot. Obviously that jigger was badly damaged. Its rider was damaged too, apparently. He sat up in the snow, clasping an ankle with both hands, and gasping and spluttering. Harry Wharton reached him swiftly.

'Hurt?' he panted.

'Hang you! Yes, I'm hurt!' howled the man with the ginger eyebrows. 'You cheeky young scoundrel, why couldn't you clear the road?'

Harry Wharton stepped back, his eyes glinting. He was wholly blameless in the matter. Bunter was rather to blame, but the fact that the sandy man had been riding fast on a frozen road was the chief cause of the accident.

The man staggered to his feet.

He did not give Wharton another look. He glanced back quickly in the direction of the Wimford road. Then he gave a look at the wrecked bike, muttered something between his teeth, and started to walk. Evidently he was sorely pressed for time, as he had abandoned his machine where it had fallen and was going as fast as he could move, in spite of a damaged leg.

'Have you seen him?'

'Whom, sir?'

'That thief!' roared the stout gentleman. 'A shrimp of a man with a sandy complexion! He was on a bicycle! He snatched my tiepin and jumped on his machine and got away! By Chove, he has got away with a diamond worth a hundred pounds!'

(From *Billy Bunter's Diamond*, The Magnet, 1933)

Myfanwy, 1940
JOHN BETJEMAN

Poet Laureate from 1972 until his death in 1984, Betjeman *was read and loved by large audiences. His trademark nostalgia is evoked here in typically well-chosen lines.*

Kind o'er the kinderbank leans my Myfanwy,
White o'er the playpen the sheen of her dress,
Fresh from the bathroom and soft in the nursery
Soap scented fingers I long to caress.

Were you a prefect and head of your dormit'ry?
Were you a hockey girl, tennis or gym?
Who was your favourite? Who had a crush on you?
Which were the baths where they taught you to swim?

Smooth down the Avenue glitters the bicycle,
Black-stockinged legs under navy blue serge,
Home and Colonial, Star, International,
Balancing bicycle leant on the verge.

Trace me your wheel-tracks, you fortunate bicycle,
Out of the shopping and into the dark,
Back down the avenue, back to the potting shed,
Back to the house on the fringe of the park.

Golden the light on the locks of Myfanwy,
Golden the light on the book on her knee,
Finger marked pages of Rackham's *Hans Anderson*,
Time for the children to come down to tea.

Oh! Fullers angel-cake, Robertson's marmalade,
Liberty lampshade, come shine on us all,
My! What a spread for the friends of Myfanwy,
Some in the alcove and some in the hall.

CYCLING FOR ALL

with bicycling. JAMES E STARRS

Then what sardines in half-lighted passages!
Locking of fingers in long hide-and-seek.
You will protect me, my silken Myfanwy,
Ring leader, tom-boy, and chum to the weak.

(*Myfanwy* from *Collected Poems* by John Betjeman © 1955, 1958, 1962, 1964, 1958,
1970, 1979, 1981, 1982, 2001; reproduced by permission of John Murray Press, an
imprint of Hodder and Stoughton Limited).

Schwinn – For the Ride of a Lifetime, 1941
ARNOLD, SCHWINN AND COMPANY

Bursting with endorsements from the celebrities of the day, bike manu-facturer Schwinn pulled out all the stops in this catalogue copy to encourage American adults to buy modern American-built bikes rather than 'old-time bicycles' from England.

Buck Jones – famous 'Western' hero, declares: 'There's a heap of riding health and pleasure in my Schwinn-Built Lightweight. I'm for anything that gives a human being a healthy body'. When you see Buck on the screen in his next picture, you will agree that Buck demands perfection in both his horses and bicycles.

For the Ride of a Lifetime!
Schwinn-Built Bicycles
Everybody's Favorite...

And what a grand time they are having! In Hollywood and Honolulu. In New York and New Orleans. At Princeton and Vassar. Everybody, everywhere, seems to be discovering that there's a new thrill in cycling... ridin' Schwinn-Built bicycles! We are sending you this to show you why and tell you why – to make you see the picture we see... a picture of bicycles so much finer than old-time bicycles that they actually make cycling seem like a new sport, just invented. The difference is real, not just some-thing we imagine. The heads of this firm, son following father,

CYCLING FOR ALL

have been building nothing but fine bicycles, for half a century and more.

Today Schwinn experts are devoting every ounce of energy – of engineering knowledge, of skilled craftsmanship, of technological progress – to making bicycles that are just as fine in their way as the new automobiles and clipper planes. New steels, new processes, new machines, new tests, new ideal, new safety and luxury and comfort... all go into the making of these superb bicycles that we proudly mark as Schwinn-Built. In one of the most modern factories in America, we are building for you the bicycles that set the pace for the cycle industry. We invite you to read about these bicycles... and to imagine yourself spinning off on one of them. Boy or man, girl or woman – there's no age limit to a thrill like this. It's great to ride... when you ride a Schwinn-Built bicycle – the only bicycle guaranteed for life!

Captivating Constance Bennett – and her son, Peter Plant, have lots of fun together on their Schwinn-Built Bicycles. 'Peter is the family mechanic,' says the slim, lovely star. 'He's completely sold on riding Schwinn ... and I love to go along, because we have loads of fun and exercise together.'

Bing Crosby and his Boys – all riding Schwinn! Master Lindsay's riding the handlebars of Bing's Schwinn-Built Lightweight, with Gary next, and the twins, Dennis and Philip bringing up the right. The famous radio and screen star writes: 'Schwinn got our vote for its written Lifetime Guarantee. When a maker does that it's got to be good.'

Ride Schwinn-Built Bicycles
With Lifetime Guarantee

(Arnold, Schwinn and Company, Chicago, Illinois, 1941)

CYCLING FOR ALL

Soldiers Need Bicycles, 1944
BSA BICYCLES LTD

During World War II, everyone had to make sacrifices for the sake of the war effort, as this newspaper advertisement shows.

Johnny will be six in October...

... but the war has taken away his birthday present – that BSA Junior bicycle his Dad promised him.

We're sorry to disappoint you, Johnny – but we promise not to forget you. We can't make your machine now because soldiers need bicycles – and it's our job to supply the soldiers first.

But we'll tell you something – we've learned a lot about making bicycles in wartime, and by waiting until the war ends, you're going to get a much better one than you've ever imagined.

When you go riding down the street on your post-war BSA Junior bicycle you'll be the envy of all your friends, and they'll be asking you for a ride on your exciting new bicycle. You'll be glad you waited then.

Until that time we can only supply WAR-TIME STANDARD MODELS for grown-ups, with pump and tools (but without tool-bag), from the BSA dealer in your district.

Price £8.19.5 including Purchase Tax, and even these are scarce!

(From *The CTC Gazette*, August 1944)

The Patriotic Duty of All Cyclists, 1944
JOHN BULL RUBBER CO LTD

This tyre manufacturer's wartime newspaper advertisement certainly didn't pull any punches.

In a recent survey it was found that only 14% of tyres examined were correctly inflated and, therefore, capable of giving the full mileage built into them. No fewer than 59% were definitely soft and likely to give only about half their proper mileage, while 27% were so soft that early and complete failure was inevitable.

In truth it wasn't medals that really inspired me to cycle.

Because rubber is now the nation's most vital war material, it is the patriotic duty of all cyclists to make their tyres last as long as possible. To neglect tyres by running them soft is directly to sabotage the war effort.

Look at the accompanying illustrations. To which category do you belong? If to the second (Careless) or third (Sabotage), get an inflator NOW and PUMP YOUR TYRES REALLY HARD.

REMEMBER, when the enemy has been beaten and rubber is again plentiful, the high quality, lively and reliable tyres for which we were well known will again flow from the factory of John Bull.

(From *The CTC Gazette*, 1944)

Iconic bicycle designs: Flying Pigeon PA-02 (c1950)

In 1949 The Flying Pigeon Bicycle Company was officially sanctioned by Chairman Mao as New China's first bicycle manufacturer, and the first Flying Pigeon bicycle was produced the following year. Since then more than 500 million have been made. In tightly regulated Communist China, the bicycle was the approved form of transport – indeed the Chinese word for bicycle, *zi xing che*, literally translates as 'individual means of transportation'.

The Flying Pigeon was a sturdy steel beast of burden, weighing 45lb with a reinforced cross bar to carry pigs. With no gears, and available in any colour as long as it was black, the Flying Pigeon became one of the defining images of Communist China – so much so that 1970s reformist leader Deng Xiaoping defined prosperity as 'a Flying Pigeon in every household'.

But fast forward to 2006 and a news report proclaimed that 'These days Chinese cyclists won't be seen dead on a Flying Pigeon.'

As in many other world cities, the car has become king and cycle lanes are being rebranded highways. Bicycles have been banned in parts of Shanghai to ease congestion, and the brave cyclists who persevere on two wheels are increasingly taking their lives into their hands. Even the chairman of the China Bicycle Association, Wang Fenghe, abandoned his bike after an accident.

It's my love of riding that inspired me to win medals.
SIR CHRIS HOY

3 CYCLE TOURING

A New Enigma, 1787
'OBSERVATOR'

Though some perhaps will me despise
Others my charms will highly prize
Yet, ne'ertheless, think themselves wise.
Sometimes, 'tis true, I am a toy,
Contriv'd to please some active boy;
But I amuse each Jack O'Dandy,
E'en great men sometimes have me handy,
Who, when on me they're got astride
Think that on Pegasus they ride.

(From *County Magazine*, 1787)

A Very Trying Road, 1874
TEXT BOOK FOR RIDERS

As every cyclist knows, the road condition will have a significant impact on your rate of progress, hence this rather specialised guide to the roads of Britain in the late 19th century.

Liverpool to Prescot, 8 miles good road, then within 6 miles of Newcastle-under-Lyme a very bad bit full of holes…after leaving Lichfield there is a very trying road, short lengths being good and bad alternately… From Mansfield to Doncaster stiff clay, very rutty and uneven. Tadcaster to York is quite impassable. From York to Knaresborough it is in some places three inches deep in mud, but improves to Ripley, there to Ripon is perfect…

… From Rivesby to Horncastle nearly all loose flint: after this the road degenerates into two wheel ruts and a horse track.

The road between Birmingham and Wolverhampton is very bad and wearying: in fact it is full of holes and tramway ruts. The bicyclist had better train this bit …

(From *Text Book for Riders*, 1874)

The Right Accessories, 1882
JAMES STURMEY

All cycle tourers need lights on their bikes, and that was just as much the case in 1882 as it is now, although the choices then were rather different according to the Indispensable Bicyclist's Handbook…

LAMPS are extremely useful to those who ride at night, beside which they are, as well as bells, now made compulsory in most districts. They are of numerous shapes and sizes, qualities and prices.

In order to insure a good light, they should be so constructed as not to be blown out by the wind, and also to be proof against sudden jerks caused by the unevenness of the road; they should also give a clear flame, without smoke, and ought to throw the light well forward and over as large as space as possible, besides being neat in appearance and compact in size. To describe all the slight differences in detail between most of them would be useless; the best only, therefore, I will mention, and would here remark that it is useless to spend money on a cheap lamp, as the majority of them give but a poor light or go out on the least provocation, to say nothing of the danger of their falling to pieces, and causing a bad and dangerous fall.

Lucas's King Head Lamp
This is attached to the head [set] in the usual way, and has a stout rubber handle to deaden vibration and sudden shocks as much as possible. It also has a shade to throw the light down on the road and a wind-up burner on the outside to regulate the wick. ... They have their objections in that in case of a fall they are almost sure to get smashed, that the vibration is such that in most patterns the act of riding over rough ground at a high rate of speed will either extinguish them or reduce the flame to a mere speck. They are also sometimes in the way, and besides send forth a not too pleasant odour if the rider leans much over the handles.

(From *Indispensable Bicyclist's Handbook*, 1888)

CYCLE TOURING

Nothing compares to the simple pleasure of a bike ride.
JOHN F. KENNEDY

Daisy Bell (Bicycle Built for Two), 1892
HARRY DACRE

English songwriter Harry Dacre *went to America and took his bicycle, for which he had to pay import duty. His friend William Jerome, another songwriter, remarked lightly: 'It's lucky you didn't bring a bicycle built for two, otherwise you'd have to pay double duty.' And the rest, as they say, is musical history...*

There is a flower
Within my heart,
Daisy, Daisy!
Planted one day
By a glancing dart,
Planted by Daisy Bell!
Whether she loves me
Or loves me not,
Sometimes it's hard to tell;
Yet I am longing to share the lot
Of beautiful Daisy Bell!

Daisy, Daisy,
Give me your answer do!
I'm half crazy,
All for the love of you!
It won't be a stylish marriage,
I can't afford a carriage
But you'll look sweet upon the seat
Of a bicycle made for two.

We will go 'tandem'
As man and wife,
Daisy, Daisy!
'Peddling' away
Down the road of life,
I and my Daisy Bell!

CYCLE TOURING

There's a certain amount of romance to bikes.

When the road's dark
We can both despise
P'licemen and 'lamps' as well;
There are 'bright lights'
In the dazzling eyes
Of beautiful Daisy Bell!

Daisy, Daisy,
Give me your answer do!
I'm half crazy,
All for the love of you!
It won't be a stylish marriage,
I can't afford a carriage
But you'll look sweet upon the seat
Of a bicycle made for two.

I will stand by you
In 'weal' or woe,
Daisy, Daisy!
You'll be the bell(e)
Which I'll ring you know!
Sweet little Daisy Bell!
You'll take the 'lead'
In each 'trip' we take,
Then if I don't do well,
I will permit you to
Use the brake,
My beautiful Daisy Bell!

(From *Daisy Bell*, © Harry Dacre, 1892)

CYCLE TOURING

They're both beautiful and utilitarian. DAVE EGGERS

No Pain, No Gain, 1898

ELIZABETH ROBINS PENNELL

Elizabeth Robins Pennell, probably one of the earliest female cycle-tourers, eloquently describes how the torture of the ascent is amply off-set by the thrill of the descent.

My Fourth Pass: The Simplon

The same afternoon we started for the Simplon. We followed the straight-ruled line, the road we had seen from the Col de la Forclaz. But everybody goes up the Rhone Valley in the train, a few go on bicycles. As is the way with Alpine valleys, it is shut in by high mountains which shut out the view, and it is infested by tourists, and is fearfully hot. The road is bumpy, there is a gradual rise, but only at the upper end are there any hills worth speaking of. We got to Sion, to Visp, to Brieg, and the next morning were ready to start upon our first great pass by eleven, when, for our comfort, we ought to have been at the top.

A blazing, blinding hot sun was shining, and the road beyond Brieg was shadeless and deep in dust. It set out in a business-like way from the very middle of the town to scale the lower green slopes. The heat was so fierce that the perspiration rolled in great drops from my face and the machine was like fire to my touch. I had to stop every few minutes to cool off, and once we both clambered over a fence and lay full length under a tree, watching the diligence come down in a whirlwind of dust and a cycler following at a speed that would have whirled him into eternity, but for the special providence that watches over the fool-hardy wheelman as well as the drunkard.

If it was odious to push up under the scorching sun, it was still more insufferable to sit there getting no further on our journey. I wish I could reconstruct my psychological emotions under these circumstances. When I grumble, people think it is because I am not enjoying myself. But they do not understand. If a coach and six had been placed at my disposal that afternoon, I would not have taken it, though J. alone knows how ill-tempered I was. I had the grace to be ashamed, and I tried to explain my attitude

To be a cyclist is to be a student of pain ...

to him. I hated what I was doing. I hated to walk, to push the machine, to be sweltering in July sunshine, and smothered in dust. But after it was over I knew I should be immensely proud of my achievement, and I was 'game' to the end. He said that was the way you felt when you were climbing the high peaks – it was the true sporting spirit – and so we did what we could to make the best of my temper.

The road left the slope to zigzag through woods that were no protection against the sun. Then it skirted the bare mountain side, and I pushed and I plodded, higher and higher, until I stopped in sheer exhaustion at a solitary house – the Second Refuge provided by Napoleon – and we ate our third substantial meal that day. It is amazing how much you can eat when you are crossing a pass. And then the road kept on winding along the brink of the precipice, with such a gradual ascent that for a while I rode, and could have ridden further, so well did the French engineers do their work, if the Swiss knew how to do theirs and could keep it in order. Then it crossed a bridge and went climbing up more steeply to Berisal, and more steeply still, and interminably beyond. The diligence overtook me, and so did a perambulator with a baby in it, and a French nurse from Berisal. I was furious. I watched the diligence crawling along, disappearing round a turn and reappearing further up, still crawling, but now like a big fly in a crack on the slopes. And I pushed and I plodded, past the Fourth and Fifth Refuges, while away below and behind, Brieg kept falling lower and lower and growing tinier and tinier. And I pushed and I plodded, until my shoulder ached with the perpetual pushing and my feet were like lead, to where a great glacier came flowing over the mountains, and patches of snow whitened the rocks to the right, and the road escaped into covered galleries from the waterfalls that dashed and roared down all around it, and now and then broke even into the tunnels, giving me a good shower bath as I passed; and on to the Sixth Refuge, and out upon a sort of open moorland. We were at the highest point of the pass, 6,595 feet above the sea.

I had climbed, with my own legs, fifteen and a quarter miles from Brieg, and steadily for seven and a half hours to get there,

CYCLE TOURING

If you never confront pain, you're missing the essence of the sport. SCOTT MARTIN, PARALYMPIAN and now I was there I did not care in the least about anything but the Hospice, where we hoped to spend the night, and the Hospice did not as much as show itself until we were almost at the door of the big building that stands back in its semicircle of peaks directly beneath a glacier. If Napoleon put it there to shelter the weary traveller no one had a better right than I to beg a night's lodging. I was never so dead tired in my life.

☆ ☆ ☆

It was bitter cold in the morning, an icy wind blowing over the glacier, snow all around us. We passed the old Hospice, a grim, weather-beaten stone house with a tower, in a much more exposed position, a little further on, showing Napoleon's good sense in choosing the present site. You do not know what a great man he was, even if you have read Professor Sloane, until you have gone over the Alps on a bicycle. Napoleon's cleverness seemed nothing to mine when I put my feet on the rests and coasted down the road he had hung in mid-air. And there was no question of my courage. The occasional memorial cross on the Simplon, put up to mark the spot, perhaps, where the traveller had been lost in the snow or pitched over the precipice, was an eloquent reminder that the danger was not all imaginary. But the pneumatic was pumped up tight, and I held the front brake by means of an ingenious and simple device with a leather strap, that left some power and feeling in my right hand and arm. For kilometres, with only occasional intervals of back-pedalling, I coasted after J. – too far after he said – down the side of the mountain; down the long zig-zags, where the driver of the diligence, with unexpected courtesy, gave me the inner, which was the wrong side of the road, but then he was an Italian; through the Ravine of Gondo, with waterfalls booming above and the stream thundering below, and the road crossing and crossing again over airy bridges, and clinging to the side of the precipice, and diving into dark tunnels, and taking sharp turns round the walls of rocks, just where carriages were creeping up; to the Swiss frontier, where the custom officer forced back our money upon us. We wanted to wait until we left Switzerland for good and for all. But he said, and as a Swiss he must have known, we had better take it when

If I can bicycle, I bicycle.

we could get it. And I coasted down through the pines, down through the chestnuts, into a land of vineyards and tropical heat, when little more than an hour before I had been shivering.

(From *Over the Alps on a Bicycle*, 1898, T. Fisher Unwin, London)

Ingenious Solutions to Unexpected Problems, 1899
GEORGE FOSTER

When cycling through the Pyrenees with a group of friends, George Foster *discovered that the weather and the need to made emergency bicycle repairs can disrupt a carefully planned itinerary.*

Sunday 14th May

After *café au lait* we started off up the street, a somewhat queer looking crowd. Bertie's cycling shoes were approaching collapse, so far as walking was concerned, so he was attired in a borrowed pair of boots 'a la navvy Anglais'. We others of course congratulated him loudly as he strode along to the manner born, so to speak, Alpenstock in hand. After following the road for an hour or so we left the mules with their novel and awkward burdens and followed the guide along a path. About 7am just as we came in sight of the Pic – still of course a good distance away – rain began to fall. We were soon obliged to make for some shepherds huts – now deserted, being used only as summer 'residences' when the sheep stay up in the mountains all night, in the hope that the rain would stop and allow us to proceed.

In about an hour's time we descried the mules away along the road and after a deal of energy had been expended in shouting they were brought over, unloaded and put in one of the cabins. We were now in a curious plight. The rain increased, we could hear the snow falling down the sides of the peaks with a noise like thunder, and here we were tied up in a rough stone hut miles from anywhere. We had brought some wine, bread and sausage with us so we soon lit a fire and made things as comfortable as we could. We burnt up the shepherd's 'bed' – which consisted mostly of heather – and all the wood that was handy, sang songs and talked.

CYCLE TOURING

DAVID ATTENBOROUGH

As the day wore on it became obvious that the ascent of the pic was out of the question. The alternatives were staying up there until the rain stopped, or making a dash through, despite the cold and the wet, for the nearest village over the col. We decided on the latter. The mules were brought out and loaded in the pouring rain. Bertie changed his boots, and once more we started off. We soon gained the road that led to the col, or pass, and sooner still found it blocked up with snow. We could see the road further on and the guide essayed to take the mules through the drift. He laid hold of one which then began to plunge and stumble and threatened to 'demoralise' the machines, whilst the other made down the mountainside – worse still! We got the latter gentleman in the right however and got through the snowbank, which came up to about our knees, safely. We were all pretty well wet through by now, and after negotiating another snow drift soon reached the top of the col, 7,100 feet high. We unloaded the machines and bade farewell to the guide who returned to Bareges.

Mr B. shot his last film, all in the pouring rain, and essayed to travel the downward track. Riding was practically 'off' owing to the snowdrifts. Moreover when one tried to back-pedal against the descent, one's foot simply slipped and squashed in one's shoe. Grippe, the nearest village, lay 12 kilos (*sic*) down the valley. The gradients on the road were at times very heavy and the turns sharp; whilst there several flocks of sheep, apparently without shepherds, scattered about blocking the roadway. Bertie, as of yore, soon got on ahead, Mr B. following closely, whilst William and yours truly brought up the rear. Bertie bethought himself, so it turned out, of tying a young tree to his saddle and with such an efficient brake to 'moderate his transports' rode probably more of the distance than anyone and so reached the hotel first.

In the fullness of time Bill and I reached the place and were welcomed by Bertie and Mr B. who had prepared a good fire, dry clothes and a hot cognac for us. We had a large room all to ourselves and were soon at peace with the world, quite cheerful in fact. We were soon surveying each other, dressed in French shirts, French trousers, French socks and slippers. Bill, however,

Inconvenience yourself: ditch the remote, the garage door

for some reason or other, which was not quite apparent, had lavender trousers served out to him! The 'little girl' who looked after us worked like a Trojan. Nor did she stand on ceremony, but took no more notice of our state or doings than if she had been a hospital nurse! This hotel is celebrated for its trout, and needless to remark we were in a likely position to enjoy them. We found a pack of cards after dinner and so whiled away the Sunday night.

☆ ☆ ☆

Tuesday 16th May

Awoke to find that fine sunshine had returned at last. The machines seemed none the worse for the snow and rain, and about 9.30am we bade goodbye to Grippe and its hospitable hotel. We parted here from Mr B. who had yet another col to mount, as he intended to reach Adorre if possible before he returned. He had shown himself to be a sound fellow and a real acquisition to our party. We promised to look him up at the Pickwick Cycle Club after our return home.

The road was in a fair condition and improved as we got farther on. It was market day at the nearest large village to Grippe so that with the vehicles and cattle the road was at times rather lively. We eventually reached Bagnières de Bigorre (the baths of Bigorre) and stayed for a while to buy some photos and look about generally. We had reckoned on getting here on the wet Sunday we spent near the Col du Tourmalet, so that we had practically lost two days owing to the weather.

We were now 5,000 feet below the summit of the col and thought the host of the Hotel des Voyageurs at Gavarnie put it to us thus picturesquely: 'Col du Tourmalet phsst! (circular forward motion with clenched fists) – Bagnières de Bigorre!' As has been noticed things did not quite work out that way!

We had left Bagnières about 6 kilos (*sic*) behind when, whilst going along I felt the machine shiver a bit and heard spokes twanging. I thought the chain had broken but saw that it had not, and hearing the air hissing from the back tyre, got down. Just then Bill, who was close behind, and who had also dismounted called out 'here it is, it came from that field!' He had in his hand a large flint about the size of half a brick, and it was obvious to

CYCLE TOURING

opener, the leaf-blower; buy a bike, broom, rake and snow shovel. DAN BUETTNER (ENDURANCE CYCLING RECORD HOLDER)

me that it had gone through my back wheel – after narrowly escaping Bill's ribs. It had demolished the valve and broken four spokes.

We went back a little distance and to investigate and saw a man in the field. There was a ditch and hedge between us so we could not 'fall on him' at once. When, however, he heard our shouts and understood what he had done he seemed greatly upset and we could not make out what he was saying. All I could understand was 'parfaitement, parfaitement'. He soon became so frightened however that he gathered up his tools and hurried off down the field, and so we lost him. We looked about for the valve but could not find it. Bagnières was the nearest place where we could get the repairs done so that all we could do was retrace our steps thither.

Bertie kindly undertook to run my machine whilst riding his own, and he and Bill dashed on so as to save a little time if possible, leaving me to walk back. Needless to remark, the circumstances under which I was suffering did not make that four mile walk feel particularly pleasant or exhilarating. I had reached the heart of the town and was wondering which way the others had taken when I saw them coming. The machine was being attended to and was to be ready in about an hour and a half. I interviewed the *mechanicien* who seemed an intelligent fellow (like all his fellows in that line) and then we did the best thing possible – went and enjoyed a good *déjeuner*.

We left Bagnières once more but after doing a few kilos found the back tyre deflated. This was rather a 'damper' and amidst plenty of 'remarks' and growling I searched for punctures which did not exist. The only conclusion to which we could come was that the valve, being made in a different style to the English ones, and having been put in in a too short space of time, was leaky. We plugged it around with canvas and started off again. It was not of much use however and we had stop at the first place we could find where water was available. This was at some roadside cow sheds where there was a well. We had to manoeuvre slightly as the well bucket was not detachable. It was still the

Like dogs, bicycles are social catalysts that

valve that was defective and after partially resetting it we started off once more, being about six hours behind on the day's ride. There was nothing for it but to ride hard. It was a lovely evening and the road was fairly good. About 7.30 we reached Lannemezan and put up for the night.

☆ ☆ ☆

Wednesday 17th May

We were soon on the main road for Auch, which town we reached in time for *déjeuner* although my tyre wanted re-pumping about every three hours and the road was very hard and bumpy. The weather was perfect; the sky being a lovely colour and just enough breeze to counteract the warm sun. The views we obtained of the Pyrenees which lay on our right and left and behind us seemed to me to be an improvement on the one from Pau. Auch, although the capital of the department of Gers, seemed almost dead. It lies on the slopes of an eminence, crowned by the cathedral and has a celebrated large flight of steps leading from the lower to the upper town, from which a good view of the Pyrenees can be obtained. From Auch we made for Montestruc but upon arriving there found no accommodation for stopping the night, and so perforce had to go on to Fleurance, a much larger place where we put up at the Hotel Barriac.

☆ ☆ ☆

Friday 19th May

It being a question now of riding every day for all we were worth in order to reach Bordeaux with a few hours to spare, we were up early. I found both my tyres deflated and speedily came to the conclusion that the use of a fountain basin six or eight feet in diameter in such a case was not to be despised. Here was a means of finding leakages and punctures which I quickly availed myself of, although possibly enough it is not used so often as it might be! Both tubes were soon in a sound and reliable condition and we started off in good time and spirits. We had now one more stoppage before reaching Bordeaux, *viz* Langon. The road lay along the banks of the Garonne, which is also closely followed by the railway. Almost every inch of the soil in these parts is cultivated,

CYCLE TOURING

attract a superior category of people. CHIP BROWN

there being very little waste or woodland – much different from what obtains in the district of the Landes. We made a stop at Mahmand, and in due course reached Langon where the river is crossed by an artistic suspension bridge. Langon is a thriving business like little town and possesses a good hostelry – The Cheval Blanc – recommended by The English C.T.C. The church here is very fine and together with the bridge helps to form an artistic picture from the river bank.

☆ ☆ ☆

Saturday 20th May

Started early hoping to reach Bordeaux by noon, and so have a few hours to spend in the town. When about half way on the road however, Bill found that one of his cranks was cracked where the pedal pin screwed in, and was in a fair way to break. After wasting some time with it, Bertie and I decided to tow Bill and so get him along. This made slow work of it, but worse still a strong headwind had sprung up. After another mile or two the pedal dropped off altogether, and Bill's front tyre which had had to be bound almost every day through the tour with canvas bursted outright, and so put an end to the towing business. After *dejeuner*, we arrived at the Bordeaux custom house well on in the afternoon, to find business almost at a standstill and a large crowd waiting to be attended to. After waiting our turn and going the necessary formalities found the paying out office shut, which necessitated a visit (with more waiting) to the shipping office, in order to give them the authority to deal with the matter. This brought dinner time upon us and after that there was a journey to the other end of the town to procure William's overcoat which had been left at the Medoc Railway Station. As ill luck would have it the station was closed, but after digging up some clerks who were doing overtime (?) in an office there we obtained the overcoat. The shops were now closed and after a visit to one of the large cafés that boasted an orchestra of Viennese ladies we made for the Hirondelle, which we reached about 11pm.

(From *George's Journey*, 1899)

CYCLE TOURING

My father is the Hollywood equivalent of a clean, fillet-brazed frame. My brother is like one of those fat-tubed aluminum

Spinning Along in Splendid Fashion, 1900
R.H. MORTON

Not many nowadays would attempt a trip in the Kashmir region of India on a bicycle with no brakes, but in 1900 R.H. Morton *simply took it in his stride.*

We arrived at our destination [of Rawal Pindi] late at night and found the only hotel full up, so I proceeded to the *dak* bungalow, or public rest-house, where I secured a comfortable room, sleeping soundly after the long journey in the stuffy train.

Next day I interviewed Mr Danjihhoj, a well-known transport and coolie contractor of Rawal Pindi, concerning the best way of reaching remote Kashmir – for as yet there is no railway from Rawal Pindi to Srinagar, the capital. I had an idea of performing the journey on my bicycle, but I didn't quite know how to manage about my servant and my baggage. But the agent settled all that for me. As I was not pressed for time, he said, the best thing I could do was to put the man and traps in an 'ekka', a one-horse native conveyance, which will do thirty or forty miles daily with ease. This would cost me only 22s. for the 200-mile journey to Srinagar. Accordingly I hired an 'ekka', and with the servant and my baggage installed therein, and myself astride my machine, we made a start. The going was excellent, and I soon left the carriage far behind, spinning along the level road in splendid fashion.

Presently, however, the way grew steeper and steeper, and I had to dismount and wheel the machine. I constantly met long strings of camels laden with merchandise from Kashmir, and coolies with baskets, filled with juicy apples, on their way to the markets of the Punjab. Almost every variety of animal transport – except, perhaps, elephants – was represented. The scene was most interesting but I was not sorry when I reached the dak bungalow of Tret. These bungalows, by the way, are the Indian traveller's sheet-anchor. They are to be found on every main road at convenient intervals, and are usually very clean.

CYCLE TOURING

Next morning we were up betimes, but as the road to Murree, the next station, was all uphill, I tried to get an 'ekka' to carry myself and bicycle. The scenery was magnificent. The gradients just here, however, were a little too severe for cycling. Failing in my efforts to obtain a conveyance, I had to walk my machine to a place called Ghora Gully, where I hired an 'ekka' and was driven into Murree. There is a brewery here which turns out very good beer; but the town itself appeared quite deserted. All the hotels and public resorts were closed, this being the 'slack' season of the year. When I arrived it was bitterly cold, and Powell's Hotel, where I put up (and which had not completely closed its doors to travellers), was almost at the highest point of the station; so I felt the cold keenly. I got an excellent breakfast, however, and the views from the hotel windows were grand – snowy, pine clad mountain slopes stretching away as far as the eye could reach.

After breakfast I rode downhill for a couple of miles to Sunnybank, where I met my 'ekka' with the baggage. From here I pushed on to Kohala, a distance of twenty-seven miles, and downhill all the way. Cyclists will know what this means, and will appreciate it more when I tell them that the road was in splendid condition. I had no brake on my machine, but moderate back-pedalling proved quite sufficient to negotiate the gradients. Heavy-laden mules, camels, and donkeys passed me continually; and when near Kohala I saw for the first time the River Jhelum, miles below me in a deep valley.

☆ ☆ ☆

At Rampore I passed a little post-office and, remembering that I wanted some stamps, dismounted to get them. The postmaster was a most hospitable fellow, for he not only gave me a cup of tea to keep out the cold, but insisted on my accepting some apples, which I munched as I rode along.

As soon as the sun had risen somewhat I got off my machine and sat down to have a smoke. Basking there in the warm sunlight, with my head on my saddle and out of the wind, was very pleasant indeed; and such things as cold head-winds and steep and stony gradients seemed very far off.

CYCLE TOURING

I wouldn't recommend people to go up and ride their road

Soon after this I reached Baramoola, which stands at the entrance to the Vale of Kashmir, a vast plain some 150 miles long by eighty wide, surrounded on all sides by snow-clad mountains. From Baramoola to Srinagar the road is almost dead level and the surface is good. On either side there is a row of tall poplars – pretty enough, no doubt, but decidedly monotonous. I got utterly tired of the poplars as I cycled along that interminable road towards the capital of Kashmir, which is thirty-four miles from Baramoola.

I entered Srinagar in fine style, but it was necessary to keep on shouting continually in order to clear away the crowds of interested natives who thronged around me.

(From *A Cycle Tour in Kashmir* published in *The Wide World Magazine*, 1900)

One Candle Power, 1901

MARCUS TINDAL

What could you do in 1901 if you found yourself far from home with night falling and no lamp on your bike? Here's one possible solution, as long as you were able to cycle in the dark with one arm stretched out before you...

Sometimes a cyclist needs protection from the arm of the law, as when he finds himself many miles from home at lighting-up time, and without a lamp. Many and ingenious are the devices which cyclists have been known to adopt on such occasions of pressing need. A Chinese lantern, if obtainable, and a bit of candle will save the situation; though I cannot recommend the idea of the man who collected all the glow-worms he could find on the roadside, and carried them triumphantly before him in a handkerchief in place of a lamp!

But here is a simple and reliable method for overcoming the difficulty. Let the benighted cyclist obtain a bottle – there should be no great difficulty in this in a civilised country – and a piece of candle. An ordinary white glass bottle with a long neck is best for this purpose. Then let him knock a hole in the bottom of the bottle, light the candle, and push it up the bottle's neck.

CYCLE TOURING

bikes in Kenya. Bikes are not meant to be on the roads. But the mountain biking is fantastic. CHRIS FROOME

An excellent light, even though only of one candle power, is thus given, and the cyclist, holding out his bottle before him, may ride on boldly without fear of falling foul of the law.

(From *Pearson's Magazine: Self Protection on a Cycle*, 1901)

Tandem Trouble, 1914

Jerome K. Jerome

The sequel brings back the three companions who figured in Three Men in a Boat, *this time on a bicycle tour through the German Black Forest. They take one bicycle and a tandem.*

There is always unpleasantness about this tandem. It is the theory of the man in front that the man behind does nothing; it is equally the theory of the man behind that he alone is the motive power, the man in front merely doing the puffing. The mystery will never be solved. It is annoying when Prudence is whispering to you on the one side not to overdo your strength and bring on heart disease; while Justice into the other ear is remarking, 'Why should you do it all? This isn't a cab. He's not your passenger:' to hear him grunt out: 'What's the matter—lost your pedals?'

Harris, in his early married days, made much trouble for himself on one occasion, owing to this impossibility of knowing what the person behind is doing. He was riding with his wife through Holland. The roads were stony, and the machine jumped a good deal.

'Sit tight,' said Harris, without turning his head.

What Mrs. Harris thought he said was, 'Jump off.' Why she should have thought he said 'Jump off,' when he said 'Sit tight,' neither of them can explain.

Mrs. Harris puts it in this way, 'If you had said, 'Sit tight,' why should I have jumped off?'

Harris puts it, 'If I had wanted you to jump off, why should I have said 'Sit tight!'?'

The bitterness is past, but they argue about the matter to this day.

Be the explanation what it may, however, nothing alters the

fact that Mrs. Harris did jump off, while Harris pedalled away hard, under the impression she was still behind him. It appears that at first she thought he was riding up the hill merely to show off. They were both young in those days, and he used to do that sort of thing. She expected him to spring to earth on reaching the summit, and lean in a careless and graceful attitude against the machine, waiting for her. When, on the contrary, she saw him pass the summit and proceed rapidly down a long and steep incline, she was seized, first with surprise, secondly with indignation, and lastly with alarm. She ran to the top of the hill and shouted, but he never turned his head. She watched him disappear into a wood a mile and a half distant, and then sat down and cried. They had had a slight difference that morning, and she wondered if he had taken it seriously and intended desertion. She had no money; she knew no Dutch. People passed, and seemed sorry for her; she tried to make them understand what had happened. They gathered that she had lost something, but could not grasp what. They took her to the nearest village, and found a policeman for her. He concluded from her pantomime that some man had stolen her bicycle. They put the telegraph into operation, and discovered in a village four miles off an unfortunate boy riding a lady's machine of an obsolete pattern. They brought him to her in a cart, but as she did not appear to want either him or his bicycle they let him go again, and resigned themselves to bewilderment.

Meanwhile, Harris continued his ride with much enjoyment. It seemed to him that he had suddenly become a stronger, and in every way a more capable cyclist. Said he to what he thought was Mrs. Harris:

'I haven't felt this machine so light for months. It's this air, I think; it's doing me good.'

Then he told her not to be afraid, and he would show her how fast he could go. He bent down over the handles, and put his heart into his work. The bicycle bounded over the road like a thing of life; farmhouses and churches, dogs and chickens came to him and passed. Old folks stood and gazed at him, the children cheered him.

CYCLE TOURING

In this way he sped merrily onward for about five miles. Then, as he explains it, the feeling began to grow upon him that something was wrong. He was not surprised at the silence; the wind was blowing strongly, and the machine was rattling a good deal. It was a sense of void that came upon him. He stretched out his hand behind him, and felt; there was nothing there but space. He jumped, or rather fell off, and looked back up the road; it stretched white and straight through the dark wood, and not a living soul could be seen upon it.

☆ ☆ ☆

The young man... suggested the police station at the next town. Harris made his way there. The police gave him a piece of paper, and told him to write down a full description of his wife, together with details of when and where he had lost her. He did not know where he had lost her; all he could tell them was the name of the village where he had lunched. He knew he had her with him then, and that they had started from there together.

The police looked suspicious; they were doubtful about three matters: Firstly, was she really his wife? Secondly, had he really lost her? Thirdly, why had he lost her? With the aid of a hotel-keeper, however, who spoke a little English, he overcame their scruples. They promised to act, and in the evening they brought her to him in a covered wagon, together with a bill for expenses. The meeting was not a tender one. Mrs. Harris is not a good actress, and always has great difficulty in disguising her feelings. On this occasion, she frankly admits, she made no attempt to disguise them.

(From *Three Men on the Bummel*, 1914)

CYCLE TOURING

It is by riding a bicycle that you learn the contours of a country best, since you have to sweat up the hills and coast down

Europe *en vélo*, 1929

JEAN BELL

In 1929, American graduate Jean Bell *worked his sea passage across 'the Pond' to Europe, bought a bike, had a rack fitted and became a truly independent cycle tourer.*

8 July 1929 – Arrival in Antwerp

We seem to have taken an extremely long time getting here but the seaman's pay which got us to Europe puts us quite a bit ahead of the game financially; the voyage finally ended, the crew paid off.

9 July 1929 – Buying bicycles

After breakfast, we set out in search of a bicycle shop. The call of the open road is strong and we're anxious to be on our way, really to begin our vagabonding abroad.

At first glance, Belgian bicycles look just like our bikes back home. Two wheels, two pedals, one chain, one seat, all that a cyclist needs for around-town riding; our plans for making a long-distance ride, however, require a luggage rack. We also would like to have a coaster brake and a tool kit which will permit us to make emergency roadside repairs. Obviously there is a need to upgrade our vélos for long-distance traveling. The salesman calls in the mechanic and we explain why we need a rack. We will probably be cycling to Paris, we tell them. The mechanic nods, 'Oui. C'est possible.' With a rack mounted over the rear wheel we now have a place to lash our 'carry-on' luggage.

Our next request. 'Can you install coaster brakes?' Here we foul out. What in the world is the French for 'coaster brake?' Eventually we drew a 'Pas possible,' followed by a vigorous shake of the head. We gather from his response that this technology apparently has not yet crossed the Atlantic from west to east. Brakes on these bikes consisted of a lever mounted on the handlebar which, when squeezed, activated a pad on the front wheel which served to slow down progress ... more or less. But the lack of coaster brakes, at that moment at least, did not seem worth

CYCLE TOURING

them. Thus you remember them as they actually are, while in a motor car only a high hill impresses you... ERNEST HEMINGWAY

wrestling for, so we skip to our next request: single [solid] tires.

Well, 'win some, lose some'. We would get the rack but struck out everything else. And, oh yes, the price. Would you believe it, their grand total selling price per bicycle was 1100.25 Belgian francs ... the equivalent of US$25, all of which we recaptured when we sold them in Bulgaria some four months later.

I don't know why the rims on the wheels of my bike are wooden; Amos's rims are metal. Some thousand miles later, the significance of this difference will become clear.

Weight and simplicity are significant factors in long-distance cruising. Our plans for the road are to wear blue jeans, blue work shirts and tennis shoes. Our baggage includes changes of shirt, underwear, socks and pyjamas, also a blue-knit 'UC' sweater. Add maps, camera and film, a water bottle ... the list grows with astonishing speed.

Ah yes, let me not forget to mention the $300 letter of credit Mom had tucked away with my passport and seaman's papers. Incidentally, this map mentioned above, is a Rand McNally pocket map of Europe and the Near East which I had bought in a New York drug store. This funny little map guided us all the way across Bulgaria and, eventually, to Jerusalem.

13 July 1929 – Amsterdam

I have one major goal in Amsterdam: to see the Rijksmuseum and that famous painting by Rembrandt, The Night Watch. All by itself the sight of this memorable canvas pays off the time and effort of getting there.

We decide to make an effort to end each day in a small town ... the smaller the better for a number of reasons: 1. The prices are more subject to bargaining. 2. The prices are usually lower. 3. Probably most important, your host is not so busy with other guests and an evening with him around the fire is a heart-warming experience. Some of our most interesting nights have been spent with the host and his wife. Their questions are exceedingly interesting and, hopefully, ours are too. Perhaps the best advice a traveler gets is 'Avoid stopping in big cities.'

CYCLE TOURING

Well, you go to Holland and everybody's on a bike – nobody

23 July 1929 – Amiens

Noontime found us, like Goldilocks, lost in the woods outside Amiens. We were hungry, very hungry. Eventually we reached a promising peasant dwelling. An old lady in a black apron and white lace cap was feeding the chickens as we drew near. We told her we were hungry and wonder if she could sell us something to eat. What is outstanding in my memory of these strangers whom we approached with requests for favors such as this was their almost universal smiling and obliging acquiescence. Wiping her hands she said lunch had finished but if the messieurs would care to wait? We would! And while she podded peas and peeled potatoes for our three-course lunch we sat in her kitchen, spoke bad French and told her of our travels and of America. What a lunch!

With such experiences are the scrapbooks of vagabonds filled. Nothing stereotyped, nothing pre-arranged by a travel agency, nothing staged for its effect on tourist pocketbooks. Only a desire to please, a warm glow of friendship which steps across barriers of race and language. Such are the true joys of wandering.

16-28 September 1929 – Austria

What a lot of ground for two college boys to have covered in approximately two months!! Belgium, Holland, France, Germany! One thing about Amos and me, we are more than willing to 'dream big'.

7-14 October 1929 – Bulgaria

We expect to reach Svilengrad in three days. The map shows a 'very good road' most of the way. Seven days later we drag into Svilengrad cussing all Bulgarian road maps. We expected to find paved roads. We did! They were paved with a six-inch layer of yellow dust which concealed rocks. Bicycling is evidently not the accepted mode of transport over lonely Bulgarian roads. We nearly cause a runaway or a smash-up each time we meet or pass an animal-drawn vehicle.

By mid-afternoon we have reached the foothills and begin what promises to be a long, steep climb. Suddenly there is a very loud bang and I find myself sprawling over the handlebars into

CYCLE TOURING

would think to have a car. STONE GOSSARD (ROCK MUSICIAN)

the gravel. My wooden rim has shattered when my tire exploded and the inner tube is tangled in the chain. So ... here is our very first accident in all those long miles from Antwerp.

Have you ever tried pushing a loaded bicycle backwards and on one wheel? It seems that I have been pushing forever when we finally reach the small village of Razgrad. We eat our first meal since dining on bread and sausage the night before. That accomplished, we show the waiter our bike. He is all smiles and indicates that we should follow him. About a block up the street we come upon a bicycle shop. To our great surprise we are greeted in very passable English. Here, in the middle of the Balkan Mountains, we have found a bike shop owner who had put in some 15 years as a waiter in Chicago and only recently returned home to retire. Our needs do not faze him. 'Of course I can get you a new wheel'. He will phone in the order and we should be ready to roll in two days. 'Two days?' I am very dubious. I had seen no phone lines; nor had we encountered either a UPS or Fed Ex van on the road.

Believe it or not, my damaged wheel is replaced and as good as new. We bid goodbye to all our friends (by this time it seems that we have become old friends with everybody in the village) and after three hours of steep hill climbing, we reach the pass. Some 3000ft below lies a broad valley through which the Maritza River flows gently, reminiscent of the Los Angeles River in late summer.

My nine-month trip around Europe, Asia and Africa cost a total of $265.67, almost all of which I managed to cover in various jobs along the way. Not as tourists, or statesmen, or students but as *wandervogel* we 'did' the Old World on a minimum of cash and a maximum of exuberance.

(From *A 90 year Journey Through the 20th Century*, 1st Book Library, 2000, © Jean Bell, available from 🖳 www.amazon.com)

CYCLE TOURING

I thought then, as I still do, that if someone enjoys cycling

On Being a Goddam Nut-Case, 1963
DERVLA MURPHY

For her tenth birthday, Dervla Murphy was given a bicycle and a world atlas, and not long afterwards she resolved to cycle all the way to India. Twenty years later she set off with her bicycle, 'Roz', to make this very journey, and her motivation for such a solo trip continued to be as much of a mystery to those she met on her travels as they had been to those she'd left behind in Ireland. Three months into the journey, she is cycling from Tehran to the Afghan Frontier.

Abbas-Abad, 3 April

We covered eighty-three miles today, but that meant breaking my 'not-after-dark' rule and cycling till 9.30pm. However, in such uninhabited country I don't think there's any danger and bright moonlight showed the way; it was indescribably beautiful on the huge sand-dunes, which looked like mountains. I'm at last getting used to the uncanny silence of desert landscape and to the odd experience of seeing things that disappear as you approach them. Also I've discovered that what looks like a village two miles ahead is actually a village twenty miles ahead, and I've got acclimatized to fine dust permeating every crevice of self and kit. In short, I'm broken in!

There was an amusing interlude today when an American engineer going back by jeep to his work in Afghanistan pulled up to investigate me and the following conversation took place:

American: 'What the hell are you doing on this goddam road?'

Me: (having taken an instant dislike to him) 'Cycling.'

American: 'I can see that – but what the hell for?'

Me: 'For fun.'

American: 'Are you a nut-case or what? Gimme that bike and I'll stick it on behind and you get in here and we'll get out of this goddam frying-pan as fast as we can. This track isn't fit for a camel!'

Me: 'When you're on a cycle instead of in a jeep it doesn't feel

CYCLE TOURING

and wishes to go to India, the obvious thing is to cycle there.
DERVLA MURPHY

like a frying-pan. Moreover, if you look around you you'll notice that the landscape compensates for the admittedly deplorable state of the road. In fact I enjoy cycling through this sort of country – but thank you for the kind offer. Goodbye.'

As I rode on he passed me and yelled; 'You are a goddam nut-case!'

I regard this sort of life, with just Roz and me and the sky and earth, as sheer bliss. My one worry at the moment is Roz's complete disintegration. So far the rear-lamp, the rear mud-guard and half the front mud-guard have fallen off; the straps tying saddle-bag to saddle have both broken; the left pannier-bag holder has come apart and the right pedal has loosened. Everything is being held together by a system of rope and wire more complicated than you'd believe possible, but fortunately none of these disabilities is serious. The trouble will start when wheels or frame crack up. It's astonishing that I haven't had a puncture since leaving Teheran – a tribute to the extreme care with which I'm cycling. But obviously my claim that cycling is the best way to see a country just isn't valid in this region. I daren't take my eyes off the road for one second and my 'seeing' is confined to the walking intervals and to the frequent stops I make just to look around me.

This village is the most primitive place I've hit so far, with not even a gendarmerie barracks. It's a collection of the usual mud huts, very roughly constructed, and in the tea-house everything is of mud – the 'counter', the seats all around the walls and the steps leading up to an attic where men are smoking opium.

☆ ☆ ☆

I feel it's just as well I arrived late: the fewer people who know about my presence the better. I'll sleep on one of the long mud seats with Roz tied to me and my knapsack under my head with its straps round my neck – though it's not clear how me being strangled by my own straps will help the situation if someone tries to rob me!

(From *Full Tilt: Ireland to India with a Bicycle*, 2010; © Dervla Murphy 1965; reprinted by permission of Eland Publishing Ltd)

CYCLE TOURING

I simply haven't the nerve to imagine a being, a force, a cause which keeps the planets revolving in their orbits and

The Towpath Less Travelled, 1987

ᴇʀɪᴄ Nᴇᴡʙʏ

For cycle tourers, choosing an interesting off-road route on a map, such as a canal-side path, is one thing, but cycling it on the ground can be quite a different matter, as Eric Newby *and his wife Wanda found out on their tour of Ireland.*

After a few hundred yards it became impossible to ride at all, and we had to push our bikes the rest of the way. This was partly because the Shimano transmissions, in their element hacking down the north face of Fujiyama, rock-hopping along some beach on Shikoku Island or even descending a forest ride in the Quantocks, here got so fouled up with Irish cow parsley that they would barely function; and partly because even if they had, the track was so muddy and full of holes and cow crap that you only had to make one mistake and fall off to the left rather than the right and you would end up in about five feet of water. But the principal obstacles were the cows themselves, out in force enjoying the weather and all refusing to move in any sensible direction.

Twice we came to the boundary of one farmer's land with another's where what in more friendly times had been a stile was now an object so festooned with barbed wire that it look like something in the Hindenberg Line, and here in both cases the animals turned and prepared to make a last stand, ankle-deep in mud. The only thing to do was the drive them down the Canal embankment using the only weapons we had, our bicycle pumps, unload both bikes completely, then lift them five feet in the air and over the fence, trying to avoid puncturing the tyres on the wire, wishing all the time that we had lightweights instead of mountain bikes weighing in at 38 pounds, and when it was done re-loading everything before setting off to deal with another herd, all fresh and ready for an encounter. We were a bit like one of those competing naval teams at the Royal Tournament which take guns to pieces, sling them across a yawning gulf on a wire

CYCLE TOURING

then suddenly stops in order to give me a bicycle with three speeds. Qᴜᴇɴᴛɪɴ Cʀɪsᴘ

rope, and then re-assemble them, except that we had no competition.

However, we did not lack an audience. Apart from the cows, which had been getting a lot of mileage out of us, across the Canal on the real towpath was a meagre line of semi-comatose fisherman, to whom we appeared to be the principal objects of interest. Surrounded by the incredible amount of gear coarse fishermen seemed to need (almost as much as required to cycle across Ireland), including large green umbrellas to protect their complexions from the pernicious effects of the sun, they watched our exertions with all the animation of a band of fork-tongued lizards about to eat a dinner of flies, although occasionally one would raise himself to a sitting position and shout across to us, 'You'se are on the wrong bank!' What we really needed was a Flymo.

Altogether it took an hour to cover the two miles to the Lucan Road Bridge, by which time we were almost as knocked out, physically and emotionally, as if we had covered forty miles on the N18.

'You've had some pretty crazy ideas in your life, Newby,' Wanda said, rather unfairly I thought, while we were pouring water on our nettle stings, getting the herbage out of our transmissions, scraping cow-shit off our trousers, swatting horseflies rendered torpid by over-indulgence in our blood, and generally smartening up, 'but this towpath of yours is the craziest of the lot.'

(From *Round Ireland in Low Gear*, reprinted by permission of
HarperCollins Publishers Ltd, © 1987 Eric Newby)

CYCLE TOURING

If I'm ever feeling tense or stressed ... I'll put on my iPod

'What this bike needs is....', 1987
QUENTIN BLAKE

What begins as an ordinary bike ride for Mrs Armitage becomes an exercise in modifying her bike to suit her needs, much like any other cycle-tourer on the road – but with a notable lack of concern about carrying additional weight! As we join her she's already added three loud horns, a bucket of water, soap and a towel to wash her hands after putting the chain back on, a proper tool kit in a large metal box, a picnic basket, a seat for her dog Breakspear and some umbrellas to keep off the rain.

Riding through the rain, Mrs Armitage began to feel rather down-hearted. 'What this bike needs,' said Mrs Armitage to herself, 'is a bit of cheerful music.'

So she got a transistor radio-cassette player and a lot of cassettes of cheerful music and a mouth-organ so that she could join in; and she fixed them all to the bike, and off they went.

Mrs Armitage was turning the pedals so fast and blowing the mouth-organ so hard that soon she was nearly exhausted.

'What this bike needs,' said Mrs Armitage to herself, 'is a bit of extra oomph.'

And so she got some wood and some ropes and some tarpaulin. She rigged up a mast and a sail and she added a few yards of bunting and an anchor into the bargain.

And off they went with the wind behind them, faster and faster and faster until...

CRASH! CRUNCH! CLANG! CLATTER! THUD! Paheehahurh!

'What this bike needs, Breakspear,' said Mrs Armitage as she picked herself from the wreckage, 'is taking to the dump.'

(From *Mrs Armitage on Wheels* by Quentin Blake, 1987, published by Jonathan Cape, reprinted by permission of the Random House Group Limited)

CYCLE TOURING

and head to the gym or out on a bike ride along Lake Michigan with the girls. MICHELLE OBAMA

Maybe Alone on My Bike, 1975
WILLIAM STAFFORD

I listen, and the mountain lakes
hear snowflakes come on those winter wings
only the owls are awake to see,
their radar gaze and furred ears
alert. In that stillness a meaning shakes;

And I have thought (maybe alone
on my bike, quaintly on a cold
evening pedaling home), Think!—
the splendor of our life, its current unknown
as those mountains, the scene no one sees.

O citizens of our great amnesty:
we might have died. We live. Marvels
coast by, great veers and swoops of air
so bright the lamps waver in tears,
and I hear in the chain a chuckle I like to hear.

(*Maybe Alone On My Bike* from *Smoke's Way*, © 1975 by William Stafford,
Graywolf Press)

Riding Every Inch of the Way, 2010
STEPHEN LORD AND CHRIS SCOTT

*So after years of dreaming and months of planning, you're finally off on
your pedal-powered adventure trip of a lifetime. Is it cheating if you
hitch a lift or hop on a bus now and again? Discuss.*

Many cycle tourers set off with a vow to cycle all the way,
except when absolutely unavoidable – usually ferries to cross
seas or rivers. Indeed first-timers often assume it ought to be
done this way; that they've somehow cheated themselves and
betrayed the greater cause should they take the train or a bus
when a perfectly rideable road exists. On this view the ride is an
act of purification or a political statement; it's just you, your

CYCLE TOURING

The bicycle is the most civilized conveyance known to man.

bike and the world. Recognise this as a not uncommon over-adventurous reflex to the humdrum and predictable life you may be leaving behind; you're up for it and want to get your teeth into a challenge!

In the car-dominated west the environmentally affirmative activity of cycling as full-time transportation (as opposed to widely practised recreation) encourages a certain zeal which might eschew any form of engine-powered assistance. It's something that more experienced riders get over once they realise it's not necessarily about riding, it's about travelling. It doesn't mean you have to hail down a local farmer in a pickup every time a stiff climb or an annoying headwind presents itself; it merely recognises that a bicycle's great advantages includes its natural portability – and that one of the better lessons learned on the road is flexibility.

Riding it all is challenging stuff indeed; the downside of this kind of commitment is clear: a fair amount of discomfort and even danger at times – heading out of towns on busy motorways or through run-down shanty-towns, riding in extremes of heat and cold, unable to catch up with the favourable seasons for travel.

Lashed to a bus roof, in a train or on a ferry or plane, you can cut out a busy or boring stretch or have a chance to meet some locals and so enrich your experience. Refusing to consider these options is to make a rod for your own back. So you slogged your way resolutely across the endless Kazakh steppe. Was it a month well spent? Or would you have rather shot ahead to ride the alpine meadows and heavenly mountains of Kyrgyzstan before the first winter snows? Some hardy blogs conjure up contorted reasoning as to why, under their rules, it was permissible to take transport in one situation but not in others.

If your time is unlimited, you might want to ride every inch of the way. Otherwise, you'll have a lot more fun and get further if you press 'fast-forward' once in a while. This is the key: it's your ride, not someone else's.

(From *Adventure Cycle-Touring Handbook*, 2nd edition, © Stephen Lord 2010, Trailblazer Guides)

Other forms of transport grow daily more nightmarish. Only the bicycle remains pure in heart. IRIS MURDOCH

A Bike Ride Through the Countryside, 2010
Elizabeth Shield

This poem is a subtle evocation of sounds, senses and rambling thoughts while cycling on a summer's evening.

The grass flickers, as the
Wind pushes it down, in
A gentle but determined
Motion, sweeping upwards to
Swirl the blue-grey clouds
Around the radio tower, before
Dissipating into the milky
Sky, which at this moment
Is the lightest shade of
Blue, an open innocent shade
Of blue, like an angelic birthday
Cake, the pinker clouds, whose
Graceful tendrils embrace the
Air, and dancing twirl across the
Peaceful summer skyscape

Down below them, the
Emerald stalks of corn stand,
Silent sentinels, awaiting the
Coming of the dawn, they too
Feel the pushing of the wind, but
Brush it off, over their shoulders,
And continue their silent watching
On the sloping sides of the hill, the
Growling pines, resplendent in their
Glimmering needles, reflect the fading
Light, off the clouds, as the sun sinks,
Beneath the horizon, and I watch them
Silently on my bike, the only thing
I can hear, is the swish of the wind,

CYCLE TOURING

And the hum and whirring of the
Pedals, as my bike and I, we glide up
The hill, and down the hill, and
Around the posts that are meant
To keep the cars from disturbing, this
Peaceful walking path

A while later, we crest a hill, now
Having passed the town, I see the work
Of the persistent wind, the clouds
Now whipped into a curling wave,
Of pink and blue-black, spilling
Over the horizon, behind the red-roofed
Country houses, which are strangely
Reminiscent of those old, red, barns
Which would sit abandoned in
Fields of perpetual wheat, and,
Through the turning of the seasons,
Would rot away into timbers, with
No one left to remember, what
They were, or why they remain

Now we have ridden in a loop, my
Bike clicks as I change gears, to
Crest a hill and coast down, at high
Speed, between the guard rails and
The road, with the wind kicking
Up behind me and whisking an
Upcoming tree in to a fluttery
Flurry of leaves and branches, while
Below a stream cuts a field, and,
Skirting a pen, passes by a pinto
Pony, I think it was, that was just
Standing there, as we rode past,
Onto the cobblestones and around
A bend, the group splits, some going
A different route, but I want to come

CYCLE TOURING

vehicle of novelists and poets. CHRISTOPHER MORLEY

Back the way I came, and I ride
Beside the highway, listening to
The chirp of the crickets and the
Hum of the wheels against the
Cold, pavement, while up the hill
The verdant pines bob their boughs,
Up and down, waving, waving,
The cresting blue-black wave has
Rolled, on past the tower now, it
Is crashing down over the silent
Sentinels, and I watch quietly as
The wind rolls down the hill, and
Whirls some leaves, making the
Grass flicker in the setting sun.

What-Ifs in Myanmar, 2014

STEPHEN FABES

Adventure cycle-touring veteran Stephen Fabes *recounts biking the remote Chin State in Myanmar in the wet season where mud, leeches and landslides were the price worth paying for an adventure through an anachronistic, seldom-reached wilderness where hospitality abounds.*

More villages marched by, draped over ridges instead of cut into mountainsides, perhaps because of a particular peril of the season: landslides. I saw their aftermath every five or ten kilometres, blocking the road and allowing only motorbikes past so I no longer shared the mud with trucks or cars. I knew if there was a mechanical problem with my bike I'd be walking out, and that could take a week or more. This realisation collided with a new click from my right pedal: the bearings were shot. I couldn't make repairs here, and, deciding it was better not to listen, reached for my iPod. With Motown in my ears, a disaster felt unlikely.

I think the thing to do is enjoy the ride

CYCLE TOURING

I was still riding the precipice-edged mountain road an hour later when a flurry of fist-sized rocks cascaded down the mountain and into my path. I looked up, chose my moment, and pedaled madly past the raining earth and slate. I turned to watch the ongoing tumble. It was hypnotic: this mimicry of elements. For an instant land became water. The earth looked to flow and boil, a splash of rock here, a foam of shattering shale there. At once a huge section of soil slipped downwards, and then the entire slope subsided, bringing three trees crashing down the mountain and obliterating the road.

I spent the next hours pondering what-ifs and playing back that day's small events, giving myself reasons to have passed the road moments earlier, when the mountain would have claimed me within it. I came out of the clouds at last and cycled on a road furnished with mud and dozing buffalos, and I had to stop often to haul my bike through the gunk. This was no longer bicycle touring – it had degenerated into an undefined sport which combined the brutish power of Sumo with the grace of care-home Pilates and the pointless cruelty of bear-baiting. By night I rough-camped, waking each morning to find bloody patches on the wall of my tent where leeches had attached themselves and feasted through the darkness.

☆ ☆ ☆

At last – a proper village, a place to feast on rice and curried meat. As I ate a girl shot to my side, armed with a dog-eared and faded pamphlet entitled 'English for Ladies and Gentlemen of Business'.

'Do you have any rubies or gems to trade?' she asked, reading from the book. I shook my head, took it and leafed through to find the appropriate response.

'I'm afraid, Madam, the matter is quite one-sided' I told her. The girl, in her early twenties, struck me as unusually forthright for a Burmese lady. Her intentions soon became clear.

'Are you married?' she said, again reading from the book before landing her eyes on mine.

'No.'

CYCLE TOURING

while you're on it. JOHNNY DEPP

'Do you have fiancée or lover?' she fired back.

'Um, no'.

'I don't believe you! Give me your passport.'

I handed it over.

'Beautiful,' she cooed as she appraised my photo, which was odd. I had always considered my passport photo to smack of a vagrant with several restraining orders.

'I want to travel so much' she continued. 'But I have no sponsor for my passport' Then she looked me dead in the eye, her stare suffused more with determination than desire.

'My name is Maiah, you will remember me. This is where I work. You can come back here any time.'

I hadn't washed for uncountable days. My beard was of vagabond proportions. I smelt of feet and recently, when getting dressed, had inserted my entire leg through a rip in my shorts instead of through the leg hole. I could only look back at her, that poor girl. She must really, really have wanted out of Myanmar.

Cycling through Chin State I wondered if my being here would find its way into stories. My stories, of a country then unmarred by mass tourism, and those of the children of Chin State who may one day recount tales of the old Burma to the next generation. Their memories might include the flagship tourist they glimpsed as a child – a hairy, odorous man on a bicycle, tired enough to wear an air of disaster, but grinning manically too.

Stephen Fabes is a medical doctor, award-winning freelance writer, hiphop DJ and adventure cyclist passionate about the world's back roads and wild places. Stories from his six year, six continent bike ride can be found at 💻 www.cyclingthe6.com.

CYCLE TOURING

Marriage is a wonderful invention: then again, so is a bicycle repair kit. BILLY CONNOLLY

THE SPORT OF CYCLING

An Early Cycling Record, 1871

Designed by James Starley in 1870, the Ariel bicycle was the first penny-farthing style machine and was launched on an unsuspecting public the following year with a grand, record-setting publicity stunt. This is a contemporary account of their challenge.

To demonstrate to the bicycling fraternity the qualities of the new bicycle now being manufactured by Messrs. Starley and Hillman of Coventry, these two gentlemen undertook to ride their machines from London to Coventry within the day. Mr James Starley is well-known as an inventor and is prominent in the sewing-machine industry. Lately he has turned his inventive ability to the improvement of the velocipede. Mr Starley was one of the first to master the art of riding the bicycle, as the modern machines are called, and is often to be seen in the saddle. Mr William Hillman is an enthusiastic bicyclist and has taken part in several races. The bicycles are of the latest design with iron-spoked wheels, and rubber tyres and are fitted with Mr Starley's ingenious improvements.

The two gentlemen took their bicycles by train to Euston Station, spending the night in the Station Hotel. Arranging to be called before daylight, they had a light breakfast and mounted their machines just as the sun was rising. At that hour only the early workers were about to witness the unusual sight of velocipedes speeding through the streets. The cobbled roads caused the bicyclists some discomfiture… Once through London, the country roads were smoother and the two bicyclists made good progress, reaching St Alban's at about 8.30am, where they stopped to have an ample breakfast before starting on the most arduous part of the journey.

Watling Street from St Albans to Dunstable runs over part of the Chiltern Hills, but the road is well graded and smooth, and although on some of the steeper hills, the bicyclists had to walk, compensation came in the long down-hill portions, and there, so Mr Hillman says, Mr Starley's weight gave great velocity to his machine, a speed of at least twelve miles an hour being attained. Disaster might have overtaken the gentlemen who wished to take full advantage of the hills, had it not been for Mr Starley's ingenious brake.

By one o'clock the riders had covered nearly half of the distance and halted at an inn near Bletchley to partake of a dinner and to rest for an hour. When they remounted, Mr Starley complained of strain to his leg muscles. From here the condition of the road deteriorated and great care had to be taken to avoid loose stones. They plodded on through Stony Stratford and Towcester, cheered by the inhabitants of towns and villages, few of whom had seen a bicycle.

Only one mishap befell the adventurous bicyclists – Mr Hillman was thrown from his machine when the rubber tyre of his front wheel came off, but escaped with nothing worse than a grazed hand. He was able to bind the tyre on again and proceed without further trouble.

Both gentlemen admitted that the last few miles from Daventry to Coventry daunted them. By this time they were both tired and when night fell there was the added difficulty of avoiding stones and holes in the road, and Mr Starley, who is no longer a young man, admitted that he was near the limit of his endurance before they saw the lights of Coventry and pedalling bravely they reached Mr Starley's residence just as the clock of St Michael's struck the hour.

This astonishing feat has been acclaimed as a triumph for the bicyclists, who completed the journey of ninety-six miles, and for the bicycles which had no mechanical trouble, except for the tyre mishap. It demonstrates that the bicycle that has been developed by Messrs. Starley and Hillman from the velocipede is a most efficient form of human transport. It may be recorded that the two intrepid gentlemen, though tired and stiff, after their long ride, were no worse for their adventure.

Perhaps the single most important element in mastering the techniques and tactics of racing is experience. But once

Racing With Style, 1890
HEWITT GRIFFIN

In the early day of cycle racing, members of the London Athletic Club frowned upon those forsaking style for speed...

A graceful attitude on a Safety, when racing, is almost an impossibility, and old race goers may well sigh for the style in which such riders as Lt Byng and Jack Keen sat their machines. The first amateur champion, H.P. Whiting, was one of the introducers of the 'grasshopper' style of leaning over, which is almost imperative on the latter-day dwarf bicycles. The very latest fad of Safetyists is to get the saddle back as far as possible, so the position is still more like that on the boneshakers, and riders rely more on the forward push than the downward thrust. Bad habits are easily acquired, and as the rider improves, he should strive to attain style as well as speed, and above all never stoop and wag the head. If, owing to the exertion, the shoulders are dropped, the head must be kept up and held still; it neither adds to the speed, nor does it impress the spectators, for a man to put out his tongue and wag his head like a china mandarin.

(From *All England Series: Cycling*, 1890)

La France Sportive, 1926
ERNEST HEMINGWAY

Deep in 1920s Basque country, Hemingway *glimpsed the world of bicycle road-racing. Although intensely competitive, the participants also seemed to be enjoying themselves whilst off their bikes.*

Later when it began to get dark, I walked around the harbor and out along the promenade, and finally back to the hotel for supper. There was a bicycle-race on, the Tour du Pays Basque, and the riders were stopping that night in San Sebastian. In the dining-room, at one side, there was a long table of bicycle-riders, eating with their trainers and managers. They were all French and Belgians, and paid close attention to their meal, but they were having a good

you have the fundamentals, acquiring the experience is a matter of time. GREG LEMOND

time. At the head of the table were two good-looking French girls, with much Rue du Faubourg Montmartre chic. I could not make out whom they belonged to. They all spoke in slang at the long table and there were many private jokes and some jokes at the far end that were not repeated when the girls asked to hear them. The next morning at five o'clock the race resumed with the last lap, San Sebastian-Bilbao. The bicycle-riders drank much wine, and were burned and browned by the sun. They did not take the race seriously except among themselves. They had raced among themselves so often that it did not make much difference who won. Especially in a foreign country. The money could be arranged.

The man who had a matter of two minutes lead in the race had an attack of boils, which were very painful. He sat on the small of his back. His neck was very red and the blond hairs were sunburned. The other riders joked him (*sic*) about his boils. He tapped on the table with his fork.

'Listen,' he said, 'to-morrow my nose is so tight on the handlebars that the only thing touches those boils is a lovely breeze.'

One of the girls looked at him down the table, and he grinned and turned red. The Spaniards, they said, did not know how to pedal.

I had coffee out on the *terrasse* with the team manager of one of the big bicycle manufacturers. He said it had been a very pleasant race, and would have been worth watching if Bottechia had not abandoned it at Pamplona. The dust had been bad, but in Spain the roads were better than in France. Bicycle road-racing was the only sport in the world, he said. Had I ever followed the *Tour de France*? Only in the papers. The *Tour de France* was the greatest sporting event in the world. Following and organizing the road races had made him know France. Few people know France. All spring and all summer and all fall he spent on the road with bicycle road-racers. Look at the number of motor-cars now that followed the riders from town to town in a road race. It was a rich country and more *sportif* every year. It would be the most sportif country in the world. It was bicycle road-racing did it. That and football. He knew France. *La France Sportive*. He knew road-racing. We had a cognac. After all, though, it wasn't bad to

The ideal Tour would be one in which only one rider survived

get back to Paris. There is only one Paname. In all the world, that is. Paris is the town the most *sportif* in the world. Did I know the *Chope de Negre*? Did I not. I would see him there some time. I certainly would. We would drink another *fine* together. We certainly would. They started at six o'clock less a quarter in the morning. Would I be up for the *depart*? I would certainly try to. Would I like him to call me? It was very interesting. I would leave a call at the desk. He would not mind calling me. I could not let him take the trouble. I would leave a call at the desk. We said goodbye until the next morning.

In the morning when I awoke the bicycle-riders and their following cars had been on the road for three hours.

(From *The Sun Also Rises*, 1926)

Steel Grandpa, 1951
SPORTS ILLUSTRATED

In 1951, 66-year-old Gustaf Hakansson cycled the length of Sweden on a heavy-framed, old bike – and became a cycling legend

The most punishing bicycle race in Swedish history was about to end. At any moment the first cyclist would appear in sight after five days of pedaling 1,000 miles from Haparanda near the Finnish border in the north to Ystad in the south. Thousands of people were lined up along the colorful main street of Ystad on that day in July 1954. Brass bands waited for the signal to play. A welcoming committee of civic officials were ready at the finish line. As the leading cyclist rounded the distant bend in the high street, a great roar went up and the cheering crowd surged forward into the road to greet the winner. A lithe young man in neat shorts and singlet on a sleek racing bicycle? Not a bit of it. The cyclist first over the line was an old man with a fluffy white beard that reached halfway down his chest and almost covered the figure '0' on his vest. Moreover, he was mounted on a lady's heavy-framed bicycle with a large hamper at the front and a flat tire at the rear.

The event had been heralded as the 'killer race,' a test of strength and human endurance that only superfit athletes could

the ordeal. HENRI DESGRANGE (FOUNDER OF THE TOUR DE FRANCE)

hope to survive. Yet here, winning the race, with his nearest rival 23 hours behind, was a retired truck driver turned amateur cyclist, 66 years of age, father of 10 and grandfather of five. As a result, the name Gustaf Hakansson became the most celebrated in all Sweden.

When old Gustaf heard in 1951 that the Stockholm newspaper Tidningen was sponsoring a race from the top of the country to its southernmost point with a $1,000 prize for the winner, he promptly sent in an entry form, as did some 1,500 somewhat younger Swedes. All the entrants were told that they would have to pass a strict medical examination before they could be accepted for such a severe test of strength and stamina. This compulsory test whittled down the number of competitors to a mere 50, and Gustaf

---

Iconic bicycle designs: Breezer mountain bike (1978)
In the early 1970s a group of young cycling enthusiasts began spending their evenings and weekends racing down the Mount Tamalpais trails in northern California. Starting out using pre-war balloon-tyre Schwinn cruisers, the riders soon began to modify their machines with better brakes, tyres and strengthened frames. These heavily adapted bicycles, referred to by the riders as 'klunkers', continued to develop and gears were soon added to help the riders reach new rides farther up the mountain trails. Eventually, the limitations of using modified bicycles became too great and it became necessary to build bespoke machines. In 1978 Joe Breeze built a prototype of the Breezer Series 1 – the first purpose-built mountain bike.

As the popularity of the mountain biking increased, regular races were held. These started to attract riders from further afield and by the mid-1980s the sport of mountain biking was fully established across both the United States and Europe.

Not many people can claim credit for helping to create an entirely new discipline of cycling, but this group of friends and acquaintances had sown the seeds of a bicycling subculture that would have an impact they could hardly have imagined.

Mountain biking's cult status died the day

was not among them – not officially at any rate. A huge crowd was gathered in Haparanda to give them a rousing sendoff. The greatest excitement of the crowd came, however, 20 seconds after the start when a lone, bearded figure in overalls shot over the line and set off in pursuit of the 50 powerful young racers. Hakansson, riding his lady's bicycle, had made his unofficial challenge.

Out on the open road, Gustaf settled down to a steady pace; it was not spectacular, but Gustaf, tortoise like, knew that he could maintain it for days. After the first 50 miles he was a full 10 miles behind the leaders, who were all bunched out in the lead. After 300 miles, however, he was still cruising along at the same rate – but now 20 miles in front.

The old man's remarkable progress was explained by one vital difference in his racing strategy. He cheated. Unlike the other riders, he did not observe the rule by which competitors were required to stop each night at check points and restart in the morning. After an hour's rest on the first night, Gustaf was back in the saddle, plodding on alone through the darkness. Still, since he was not an official entrant, one could hardly complain that he was taking an unfair advantage.

Official or not, the eyes of the whole country became focused on Gustaf's progress, which was both astonishing and appealing. Could the old man maintain such a pace without reasonable sleep? Might he not collapse and even suffer irreparable damage as a result of such a strain on his heart? As the miles were covered, the race itself became of secondary interest. What mattered was Gustaf. Shrewdly, the sponsoring newspaper's competitors splashed Hakansson's story and pictures all over their front pages, and the whole nation came to marvel at the gnomelike figure with the 18 inch beard, crouched over the handlebars of his antique lady's bicycle.

As all Sweden followed the mile-by-mile account of his journey, Gustaf became a national hero. They called him Stl Farfar (Steel Grandpa). At every town, village and hamlet through which Gustaf rode, people lined the streets to cheer him, slap his back, pelt him with flowers and present him with food. After

Madonna started riding. BIKE MAGAZINE

three days he had had only five hours' sleep, but he was leading the field by more than 120 miles... By the end of the fourth day, with only seven hours' sleep since the start, he had extended his lead to more than 150 miles.

Everything was set for a triumphal entry. Then – with only about 800 yards to go – Steel Grandpa suddenly came to a halt. After nearly 1,000 miles, his bike suffered its first flat tire.... Even a man with less sense of the theatrical than Gustaf could sense that this was no time to stop and fix a puncture; with a sprightly movement, the old man remounted and wobbled the last few hundred yards on the flat, crossing the line at exactly 2:15 p.m. on July 7, 1951. He had completed the 1,000-mile course in five days and five hours – almost a full day ahead of the leading official competitor... The greatest pleasure for Gustaf was the satisfaction that he had effectively replied to the young doctors who had suggested that he was more suited to a rocking chair than a marathon cycle race.   (From *Sports Illustrated*, 1970)

Iconic bicycle designs: BMX (1982)

Like the Raleigh Chopper, the inspiration for BMX bikes came from the coolest of American motorbikes – in this case, those used for the sport of cross-country motorbike racing, known as motocross. BMX, or bicycle motocross began in the 1970s when a group of friends began to organise dirt-track bicycle races in California using bikes like the Chopper or Schwinn Stingray. They were soon being purpose-made for the sport. By the early 1980s, children the world over had seen BMX bikes in the hugely popular Steven Spielberg film *E.T. The Extra-Terrestrial*, where the hero Elliott used his BMX bike to escape the authorities and carry the homesick extra-terrestrial back to his rendezvous point with the alien mothership. Many of today's most famous cyclists, including the Olympian Sir Chris Hoy, were inspired by *E.T.* to try BMX.

Today BMX is still highly popular, whether it's BMX Racing or Freestyle BMX, involving tricks and stunts at skate-parks.

**It's one of the most iconic sporting places on the planet.
Even people who don't follow cycling could tell you the**

Bradley Wiggins – A Hunger Within, 2012
BRADLEY WIGGINS

On 22 July 2012 Bradley Wiggins *made history as the first British cyclist ever to win the Tour de France. His description of the final minutes of the race, the culmination of years of intensive physical and mental training, shows the mindset of a true winner.*

The further we go into the race, the more I'm beginning to realise: 'This is it, I've won the Tour, I've done it.' With each kilometre going by, I'm a little more inspired by that thought and that makes me push even more; there is a sort of aggression, a hunger within me, an urge to keep gaining as much time as possible. I want to win this race. There is no sense of, 'Oh, you've done it now, you can back off slightly.' No: I want more, more, more.

So then we come off the big wide main roads on to smaller roads in the last 10km and it's at that point that it's starting to get painful at this pace. The physical effort is beginning to take its toll: the first twenty minutes are almost easy, the next twenty minutes you're having to concentrate more, but the last twenty minutes is where the pain starts kicking in. In that first forty minutes you feel: 'Yeah, I can sustain this power, at any stage I could take it up twenty, thirty watts.' In the last 10km that's gone and you're thinking, 'I'm actually struggling to hold this now.' But in spite of the pain, I'm still able to lift it up. And at about 5km to go we turn left onto this little road and then the gradient starts ramping up, and I'm still pushing and it's really hurting and with every kilometre that's going past, once we're within 5km to go, I'm beginning to think of a lot of other things, and that is inspiring me to push on even harder.

The thoughts come, but not to the detriment of the effort. I'm not wavering and losing concentration or slowing down. I'm going just as hard, and what's going through my head is inspiring me more and more.

Tour de France finishes on the Champs-Elysées.
MARK CAVENDISH

The contest for the yellow jersey

When the first sixty riders set off from the Café au Reveil Matin, Paris, in 1903 the Tour de France was a chaotic scramble around France, conceived as a publicity stunt by founder Henri Desgrange to promote his newspaper *L'Auto*. Now it is the biggest annual cycling event in the world.

Initially a pure endurance test with little scope for teamwork, the Tour gradually took on its modern format, one unique in the sporting world for being a team sport in which only the team leader gets the glory – and the rewards.

The famous and photogenic yellow jersey – the *maillot jaune* – worn by the leader at the end of each stage was introduced by Desgrange in 1919. The colour was chosen to match the paper on which *L'Auto* was printed. In 1953 a green jersey was introduced for the points winner of the day, and in 1975 a polka-dot jersey for the King of the Mountain joined the set, although the King of the Mountain competition had been part of the race since 1933.

While the route changes each year and alternates between clockwise and anticlockwise circuits of France, the format of the race always includes time trials, passes through the mountain chains of the Pyrenees and the Alps, and always culminates in the high-profile finish on the Champs-Elysées in Paris. The modern day Tour de France has 21 day-long stages over a 23-day period and covers around 3,500 kilometres).

Multiple winners of the Tour de France are legendary heroes – Frenchman Louison Bobet became the first man to win three consecutive tours in 1951, 1952 and 1953. Jacques Anquetil (France), Eddy Merckx (Belgium), Bernard Hinault (France) and Miguel Indurain (Spain) have all won it five times. In 2005 American Lance Armstrong appeared to surpass them all by clocking up his seventh win, but he was stripped of his titles in 2012 amid the furore of the infamous doping scandal. Bradley Wiggins became the first ever British winner in 2012 and was knighted in December 2013 for his services to cycling.

The only part of the race I enjoyed was the last weekend. The rest of the time, I didn't enjoy it. I was the favourite, so every day felt like I was walking a tightrope, knowing that at any

☆ ☆ ☆

This is what it's all been about; Cath and the kids, all the sacrifices they've made to get me here…

We're getting into those last kilometres and I'm thinking of those things, thinking of my childhood, when I started dreaming about the Tour, how I started cycling when I was twelve. I'm about to win the Tour de France, and I'm taking my mind back to riding my bike as a kid going to my grandparents', thinking of everything I've gone through to be at this point now.

☆ ☆ ☆

So I am emptying it to the line as if it is a training effort in Tenerife and I have to get out every last bit. And that's where the punch in the air happens as I cross the line. It comes from all that emotion I was going through in that last couple of kilometres, for all that hour, for all that morning, for all the days before that time trial. It all comes out in that punch in the air as I go across the line. That's the defining image of the Tour for me: crossing the line and the punch. It is an incredible, incredible feeling.

(From *Bradley Wiggins: My Time by Bradley Wiggins,* 2013; published by Yellow Jersey Press; reprinted by permission of The Random House Group Limited)

second a little crash or a puncture could ruin everything. So you end up just ticking off the days. BRADLEY WIGGINS 2012

5

WORKING BIKES

British Army Regulations for the Training of Cyclists, 1911
HMSO

Once the British Army had accepted the use of the bicycle, of course regulations were required governing its use in drilling and ceremonial occasions as well as in the field. One suspects that they were written by someone with little personal experience of handling a bicycle…

Regulation 64
A cyclist standing with his cycle, with rifle attached to it, will salute with the right hand, as laid down in Section 19, returning the hand to the point of the saddle on completion of the salute. When at ease, the cyclist, whether mounted or leading his cycle, will salute by coming to attention, and turning his head to his officer as he salutes. A party of cyclists on the march will salute on the command Eyes Right, which will be followed by Eyes Front, from the officer or NCO in charge.

Regulation 65
The position of the cyclist at attention is the same as that of the dismounted soldier, except that he will grasp the left steering handle with his left hand, and place the right hand at the point of the saddle, elbow to the rear.

(HMSO, 1911)

The Cyclists of the Signal Corps, 1915
SIR JOHN FRENCH

This despatch written by Sir John French brings to the attention of Sir Redvers Buller the value of the cyclist in the Great War.

'I am anxious in this despatch to bring to your Lordship's special notice the splendid work which has been done throughout the campaign by the Cyclists of

Military bicycles in the Boer War, 1899-1902

Pressed into service by British troops for the first time in The Boer War, bicycles proved to be a very useful transport option to support the cavalry, and at the height of the campaign there were several hundred bicycle-mounted soldiers in South Africa.

Unfortunately there was little support for the Cycle Corps amongst the regular cavalry and their official role was mainly to carry despatches. However, it soon became apparent that cyclists were particularly effective on scouting and spying missions. They tended to be quieter than horses, and easier to hide.

Cyclists were sometimes given unusual tasks, such as the transport of carrier pigeons, which were said to be upset by being carried on horseback but didn't mind being loaded onto a bicycle. One such task, which later received much media attention, was undertaken by Scout Callister of the Cape Cycle Corps who cycled 120 miles, 'gaining a vantage point, lying *perdu* (hidden) for several days, and then releasing birds whenever he saw Boer activity.'

Brother of the Scouts organisation founder, Major B.F.S. Baden-Powell of the 1st Battalion Scots Guards had a folding bicycle which carried a kite. The kite was used at first for taking photographs of the camp by a remotely controlled camera, and later for raising an aerial for experiments in wireless telegraphy between Modder River Station and Belmont.

In another highly unusual application, a special 'War Cycle' was built for use on railway lines. It was introduced into South Africa by the Royal Australian Cycle Corps and had a detachable rim which was fitted to the pneumatic tyres, so it could be used on rails as well as on normal roads when the rim was removed. These bikes were put to use for reconnaissance, carrying despatches, checking the railway line for demolition charges, and also for removing the wounded from a skirmish taking place near a railway.

By the time of World War I motorised vehicles had come to the fore and bicycles, being of limited use on rough terrain, returned mainly to their original role of carrying despatches.

Source 🖳 bsamuseum.wordpress.com/military-bicycles-in-the-boer-war

WORKING BIKES

the Signal Corps. Carrying despatches and messages at all hours of the day and night in every kind of weather, and often traversing bad roads blocked with transport, they have been conspicuously successful in maintaining an extraordinary degree of efficiency in the service of communications. Many casualties have occurred in their ranks, but no amount of difficulty or danger has ever checked the energy and ardour which has distinguished this corps.'

(From *War Illustrated*, 1915)

WORKING BIKES

Onion Johnnies in the 1920s & 1930s

It was from Roscoff in 1828 that the first French onion salesman to try his luck in England set sail, the trip across the Channel being far shorter and less hazardous than an overland journey to the markets of Paris. Having returned with tales of how quickly he had sold his cargo, he established a tradition that was to continue well into the 20th century.

In the 1920s and 1930s there were as many as 1500 French onion pedlars who regularly travelled from Brittany to England, Wales and even Scotland, selling their merchandise door-to-door.

Sporting berets at a jaunty angle, Gauloises cigarettes drooping from their lips, bicycles laden with plaited strings of onions – each of which weighed between one and two kilos – French onion sellers were once a familiar sight on the streets of Britain, plying their trade from door to door. At its peak in 1929 there were some 1500 so-called Onion Johnnies – all of whom came from one tiny area around the Breton port of Roscoff, giving rise to the familiar cliché of the Frenchman in a beret and stripy jersey. There are still a dozen or so Onion Johnnies in business in Roscoff, and even a museum, the *Maison des Johnnies et de L'Oignon Rose* celebrating Roscoff's famous pink onion, now designated appellation d'origine contrôlée (AOC).

When I was young, I used to expect Parisians to wear little black berets, to bicycle about with strings of onions around

Reconstructing the Crime, 1931

DOROTHY L. SAYERS

Lord Peter Wimsey is determined to work out whether the death of an artist in Scotland is an accident or murder – but with six possible suspects in the frame, how can he identify the culprit? His main suspect, Ferguson, seems to have a watertight alibi – a clipped train ticket to Glasgow – but could he have used a bicycle to leave the train and rejoin it later? There's only one way to find out if it can be done…

'That is all very well, Wimsey, and it sounds very convincing, but unless you can break down Ferguson's alibi, it goes for nothing at all. We know that he – or somebody – went from Gatehouse to Dumfries with the 9.8 and on to Glasgow. The ticket was clipped at three points on the journey, and given up at Glasgow. And besides, Ferguson was seen at Glasgow by those magneto people, and by Miss Selby and Miss Cochran. Are you suggesting that he had an accomplice to impersonate him, or what?'

'No. He hadn't an accomplice. But he was a student of detective literature. Now, I'll tell you what I propose to do, with your permission. Tomorrow is Tuesday again, and we shall find all the trains running as they did on the morning of the alibi. We will go down to the cottage tonight and reconstruct the whole course of events from beginning to end. I will undertake to show you exactly how the thing was worked. If I break down at any point, then my theory breaks down. But if I get through, I will not only prove that the thing is possible but also that it was done that way.'

☆ ☆ ☆

At 11.25 Wimsey rose regretfully.

'Corpse-time,' he said. 'Here, Sir Maxwell, is the moment when you go bumpety-bump into the water.'

'Is it?' said the Chief Constable, 'I draw the line there.'

'It would make you rather a wet-blanket on the party,' said Wimsey. 'Well, we'll suppose it done. Pack up, you languid aristocrats, and return to your Rolls-Royce, while I pant and sweat upon this confounded bicycle. We had better take away the Morris and

WORKING BIKES

their necks, and to brandish long sticks of bread, just like they used to do in school textbooks. CRAIG BROWN

the rest of the doings. There's no point in leaving them.'

He removed Campbell's cloak and changed the black hat for his own cap, then retrieved the bicycle from its hiding place, and strapped the attache-case to the carrier. With a grunt of disgust he put on the tinted spectacles, threw his leg across the saddle and pedalled furiously away. The others packed themselves at leisure into the two cars. The procession wound out upon the Bargrennan Road.

Nine and a half miles of crawling in the wake of the bicycle brought them to Barrhill. Just outside the village, Wimsey signalled a halt.

'Look here', said he. 'Here's where I have to guess. I guess that Ferguson meant to catch the 12.35 here, but something went wrong. It's 12.33 now, and I could do it. The station is just down that side-road there. But he must have started late and missed it. I don't know why. Listen! There she comes!'

As he spoke, the smoke of the train came in view. They heard her draw up into the station. Then, in a few minutes, she panted away again.

'Well on time,' said Wimsey. 'Anyway, we've missed her now. She's a local as far as Girvan. Then she turns into an express, only stopping at Maybole before she gets to Ayr. Then she becomes still more exalted by the addition of a Pullman Restaurant Car, and scorns the earth, running right through to Paisley and Glasgow. Our position is fairly hopeless, you see. We can only carry on through the village and wait for a miracle.'

He remounted and pedalled on, glanced back from time to time over his shoulder. Presently, the sound of an over-taking car made itself heard. An old Daimler limousine, packed with cardboard dress-boxes, purred past at a moderate twenty-two or three miles an hour. Wimsey let it pass him, then, head down and legs violently at work, swung in behind it. In another moment, his hand was on the ledge of the rear window, and he was free-wheeling easily in its wake. The driver did not turn his head.

'A-ah!' said Macpherson, 'It's our friend Clarence Gordon, by Jove! And him tellin' us he'd passed the man on the road. Ay,

I look at being a capitalist businessperson

imph'm, an' he wad be tellin' nae mair nor less than the truth. We'll hope his lordship's no killt.'

'He's safe enough,' said the Chief Constable, 'providing his tyres hold out. That's a very long-headed young man, for all his blether. At this rate, we'll be beating the train all right. How far is it to Girvan?'

'Aboot twelve miles. We ought tae pass her at Pinmore. She's due there at 12.53.'

'Let's hope Clarence Gordon keeps his foot down. Go gently, Macpherson. We don't want to overtake him.'

Clarence Gordon was a careful driver, but acted nobly up to expectation. He positively put on a spurt after passing Pinwherry, and as they attacked the sharp rise to Pinmore, they caught sight of the black hinder-end of the train labouring along the track that ran parallel and close to the road. As they topped the hill, and left the train behind them, Wimsey waved his hat. They span merrily along, bearing to the left and winding down towards the sea. At five minutes past one, the first houses of Girvan rose about them. The pursuer's hearts beat furiously as the train now caught them up again on their right and rushed past them towards Girvan Station. At the end of the tow, Wimsey let go his hold on the car sprinting away for dear life to the right

---

🚲 **Stop me and buy one!**

The first ice cream bicycles in London were used by Walls in London in about 1923. Cecil Rodd of Walls came up with the slogan 'Stop Me and Buy One' after his experiments with doorstep selling in London. In 1924 they expanded the business, setting up new manufacturing facilities and ordering fifty new tricycles. From initial sales in 1924 of £13,719, in just three years they had increased to £444,000.

However, during World War II manufacture of ice cream was severely curtailed, and the tricycles were requisitioned for use at military installations. In October 1947 Walls sold 3,300 tricycles and instead invested in freezers for shops.

---

like riding a bike – if I go too slowly, I'll fall over.
ANDREW MASON (FOUNDER OF GROUPON)

down the station road. At eight minutes past he was on the platform, with three minutes to spare. The police force, like the ranks
of Tuscany, could scarce forbear to cheer.

(From *Five Red Herrings* (*A Lord Peter Wimsey Mystery*), 1931 Victor Gollanz Ltd)

Tradesman's Carry-All Carrier:
Model TCC Code no. 242, 1936
THREE SPIRES

*This advertisement for a trade delivery bike clearly emphasises the
strength of the machine, but given that it uses the word 'heavy' no less
than six times, we can only guess how much the thing weighed even
before it was piled high with goods for the unlucky shop delivery boy to
struggle with every day.*

FRAME: Specially designed 22" with Heavy gauge weldless steel
tubes, extra large lugs and ball races.
FORK: Very strong, fitted with safety liner.
WHEELS: 20" x 1 ¼" front, 26 x 1 ¼" rear, extra heavy hubs, large
cones and heavy SAFETY SPOKES.
TYRES: Front wheel 20" x 2" Dunlop Carrier, rear wheel, 26" x 1
¼" Dunlop Carrier
BRAKES: Two roller lever on raised handlebars, special carrier.
PEDALS: Extra wide and heavy black finish.
GEAR: 63" heavy Carrier cranks and chain wheels
MUDGUARDS: Special heavy section
NAMEPLATE: Detachable
FRONT CARRIER: Very strong, brazed to frame, fitted with lamp
brackets and bottom plate. Size of Carrier 19" x 14" x 9" deep.
Stand operating from front side of carrier.
SADDLE: Middlemore's special Carrier.
FINISH: Bonderised, absolutely rustproof, all parts enamelled
black.
ACCESSORIES: Toolbag, tools, spanners, inflator and reflector.
Price: £6-17-6

(From *Three Spires* catalogue, 1936)

He didn't riot. He got on his bike

An Ode to Bicycles, 1956
PABLO NERUDA

Chilean poet-diplomat and politician Pablo Neruda *won the Nobel Prize for Literature in 1971 'for a poetry that with the action of an elemental force brings alive a continent's destiny and dreams'.*

A few bicycles
passed
me by,
the only
insects
in
that dry
moment of summer,
silent,
swift,
translucent;
they barely stirred
the air.

Workers and girls
were riding to their
factories,
giving
their eyes
to summer,
their heads to the sky,
sitting on the
hard
beetle backs
of the whirling
bicycles
that whirred
as they rode by
bridges, rosebushes, brambles
and midday.

WORKING BIKES

and looked for work. NORMAN TEBBIT

WORKING BIKES

I thought about evening, when
the boys
wash up,
sing, eat, raise
a cup of wine
in honour
of love
and life,
and waiting
at the door,
the bicycle,
stilled,
because
only moving
does it have a soul,
and fallen there
it isn't
a translucent insect
humming
through summer
but a cold
skeleton
that will return to
life
only
when it's needed,
when it's light,
that is,
with
the
resurrection
of each day.

(© Pablo Neruda, 1956)

I'd like to ride my bike all day but I've got this

The Cycle Courier's Instinct, 2015
JON DAY

Life as a London cycle courier gave Jon Day *a totally new perspective on the city he thought he knew…*

As a courier you learn to inhabit the places in between the pick-ups and the drops. You learn the secret smells of the city: summer's burnt metallic tang; the sweetness of petrol; the earthy comfort of freshly laid tarmac. Some parts of London have their own smells, like olfactory postcodes. The shisha bars on Edgware Road fill the area with a sweet smoky haze; the mineral tang of Billingsgate fish market wafts over the Isle of Dogs.

You learn to read the road too, calculating routes, anticipating snarl-ups, dancing round potholes almost unconsciously. With its signs and painted hieroglyphics the road is an encyclopaedia of movement: drive here, walk here, park here, no stopping here. Look down and the tarmac tells you what to do. Traffic lights regulate the entire mechanism like enormous clocks, telling you when to move and when to stop.

☆ ☆ ☆

At 8.30am, Old Street is clogged with other cyclists. Lycra-clad bankers head into the City on their carbon-framed racers, wobbly commuters on Boris bikes hug the gutter. Suited Brompton riders glide through the gaps. Graphic designers and web developers, bound for Soho, drift by on their track bikes, studiously ignoring everyone else. I join the peloton, attacking when I see a space until I've moved to the front of the bunch. I cast a wide loop around a pedestrian on a zebra crossing, grabbing the side of a bus to pull myself through a gap. Cycling in traffic like this is an opportunistic business, part instinct and part analysis. You have to navigate the flow with the detached concentration of a boulderer addressing a climbing problem.

At the lights the exhaust of a bus blasts my feet like the warm nuzzling of some enormous dog. The aerial of my radio sticks out

WORKING BIKES

thing called a job that keeps getting in the way. BILL WALTON

from the strap of my bag at an angle and extends for a few inches beyond my shoulder, functioning like a cat's whiskers, alerting me to the width of gaps as I squeeze through them. My shoulders are no wider than my handlebars, so I know that if I can fit them through then the rest of my body will follow.

Though I'd lived in London all my life, until I began working as a courier I never quite realised how it all fits together. The city is too vast to be seen from any single point; too fragmented to be reduced to a predictable series of sectors or arrondissements. No Haussmann has ever succeeded in standardising its layout. At street level it remains untamed.

(From *Cyclogeography: Journeys of a London Bicycle Courier* by Jon Day, © 2015, Notting Hill Editions)

WORKING BIKES

The life of a rickshaw wallah in Dhaka

In 2002, police in Bangladesh began a campaign to remove unlicensed cycle rickshaws from the capital, Dhaka. The authorities said the long-term aim was to halve the city's estimated 400,000 cycle rickshaws.

Life is hard for the rickshaw wallahs of Dhaka. They ride all day earning tiny amounts in stifling heat and ferocious rain. There are police officers to pay off, suicidal coach drivers to be avoided and some of the world's most crowded and pot-holed roads to be navigated. Not to mention the air pollution from the ceaseless flow of traffic.

But thousands of rickshaws can be seen every day, either carrying up to four passengers or transporting huge loads which are often twice their bodyweight.

In what remains a distinctly hierarchical society, rickshaw wallahs are regarded as the lowest form of life on the roads. There is no enforcement of the highway code in Bangladesh, other than the widely held principle that if you are smaller you should get out of the way. That means that trucks, lorries and coaches move over for no one. Cars are in the second tier, two-stroke three-wheelers – or auto rickshaws – are in category three and the cycle rickshaw is at the bottom of the pile. Their low ranking means that if there is an accident, the riders are inevitably held responsible and frequently beaten up for their troubles.

But despite these hardships, rickshaw wallahs are well known for their resilience and cheerfulness.

CITY CYCLING

The Fittest Use of the Bicycle... 1870
CHARLES SPENCER

Spencer *was an ex-champion gymnast who ran a business selling sports equipment. He imported a velocipede from France in the 1860s but soon realised that the potential of this machine was much more than just as an aid to getting fit. He placed advertisements for this 'Paris model of the new two-wheel velocipede', and demonstrated its durability with a ride from London to Brighton. He wrote a book,* The Bicycle: Its Use and Action, *extolling the virtues of this new machine...*

The fittest use of the bicycle is not to treat it as a toy, to be ridden on a smooth boarded surface, without impediment of any kind, and where all the riders are careful to follow each other in the same direction; but to use it as a vehicle, as an ordinary means of transit from one place to another, over roads rougher or smoother as the case may be. Thus, starting through the crowded streets at evening, as is my wont, and working at moderate speeds through omnibuses, cabs, drays, etc. etc. till gradually the road gets clearer, and extra steam may be put on: until at length the long country roads give full score for the greatest speed consistent with a due regard for the proposed length of journey, taking care, of course, not to be so exhausted at the end as to spoil all the pleasure.

This has been my practice for months on returning from business in the city to my residence at Harrow-on-the-Hill, and I can assure my readers that the 'Hill' occupies a very conspicuous part in the affair, particularly in wet or foggy weather, when it is a very different thing indeed to travel along dark, sloppy and hilly roads, to gliding swiftly round the brilliantly lighted and smooth area of the Agricultural Hall.

(From *The Bicycle: Its Use and Action,* 1870)

Dangerous Wide Spaces, 1897
MRS F. HARCOURT WILLIAMSON

It seems even in the early days of popular cycling, women in London could be just as fearless as men...

History has not recorded which of the fashionable women was first to discover the delight of whirling all over the country on two wheels; but it was certainly Lady Norreys who first excelled in this direction, and I can well remember seeing quite a little crowd collected at her door in Great Cumberland Place to see her start upon her ride, when, regardless of her admiring audience, she jumped lightly onto her machine, and ringing her bell smartly once or twice as warning, wheeled away, with her dogs frisking and barking behind her. She knows nothing whatever of fear; and with quite unruffled countenance will cross that dangerous wide space between Constitution Hill and Piccadilly, and turn up the hill of Hamilton Place, as unconcerned and cool as though she were on one of those beautiful broad level roads in France, where vehicles are so delightfully few and far between. She is always very neatly dressed, generally in dark blue, with white revers on her coat and a natty sailor hat.

Another little lady who led the way where this fashion was concerned was Lady Cairns, who, like Lady Norreys, is very small in stature and slim, while it is well known that slender figures look their best on wheels. She is a very plucky rider too, and one hears of her in the neighbourhood of Windsor flying downhill with two or three companions as daring as herself, all hand-in-hand, and not one of them even attempting to guide their machines, but trusting entirely to balance. The very good riders all pride themselves upon being able to ride without touching their handles; and Miss Muriel Wilson, who is another smart cyclist, has been seen again and again in Hull, which is the nearest town to Tranby Croft, with one hand thrust into her coat pocket and the other engaged in holding up her parasol.

(© Mrs F. Harcourt Williamson, 1897)

The bicycle is just as good company as most husbands and, when it gets old and shabby, a woman can dispose of it and

London Through the Eyes of a Poet, 1914

EDWARD THOMAS

Cycling in 21st century cities is not for the faint-hearted and requires total focus on the road and the traffic, but a hundred years ago there was time and space for a writer beginning a cycle tour from central London to observe and ponder every detail of his surroundings.

This is the record of a journey from London to the Quantock Hills to Nether Stowey, Kilve, Crowcombe, and West Bagborough, to the high point where the Taunton-Bridgwater road tops the hills and shows all Exmoor behind, all the Mendips before, and upon the left the sea, and Wales very far off. It was a journey on or with a bicycle. The season was Easter, a March Easter.

☆ ☆ ☆

Whatever happened, I was to start on Good Friday. I was now deciding that I would go through Salisbury, and over the Plain to West Lavington, and thence either through Devizes or through Trowbridge and Bradford. Salisbury was to be reached by Guildford, Farnham, Alton, Arlesford, but perhaps not Winchester for I could follow down the Itchen to King's Worthy, and then cross those twenty miles of railwayless country by way of Stockbridge, visiting thus Hazlitt's Winterslow. To Guildford there were several possible ways. The ordinary Portsmouth road, smooth enough for roller-skating, and passing through unenclosed piny and ferny commons one after another, did not overmuch attract me. Also, I wanted to see Ewell again, and Epsom, and Leatherhead, and to turn round between hill and water under Leatherhead Church and Mickleham Church to Dorking. Thus my ways out of London were reduced. I could, of course, reach Ewell by way of Kingston, Surbiton, and Tolworth, traversing some of Jefferies' second country, and crossing the home of his ' London trout.' But this was too much of a digression for the first day.

At any rate the Quantocks were to be my goal. I had a wish of a mildly imperative nature that Spring would be arriving among the Quantocks at the same time as myself, that 'the one

CITY CYCLING

red leaf the last of its clan,' that danced on March 7, 1798, would have danced itself into the grave : that since my journey was to be in a month before the month of May, Spring would come fast, not slowly, up that way. Yes, I would see Nether Stowey, the native soil of 'Kubla Khan,' 'Christabel,' and 'The Ancient Mariner,' where Coleridge fed on honeydew and drank the milk of Paradise.

If I was to get beyond the Quantocks, it would only be for the sake of looking at Taunton or Minehead or Exmoor. Those hills were a distinct and sufficient goal, because they form the boundary between the south-west and the west. Beyond them lie Exmoor, Dartmoor, the Bodmin Moor, and Land's End, a rocky and wilder land, though with many a delicate or bounteous interspace.

On this side is the main tract of the south and the south-west, and the Quantocks themselves are the last great strongholds of that sweetness. Thither I planned to go, under the North Downs to Guildford, along the Hog's Back to Farnham, down the Itchen towards Winchester, over the high lands of the Test to Salisbury; across the Plain to Bradford, over the Mendips to Shepton Mallet, and then under the Mendips to Wells and Glastonbury, along the ridge of the Polden Hills to Bridgwater, and so up to the Quantocks and down to the sea.

I was to start on roads leading into the Epsom road. Some regret I felt that I could not contrive to leave by the Brighton road. For I should thus again have enjoyed passing the green dome of Streatham Common, the rookery at Norbury, the goose-pond by the 'Wheatsheaf' and 'Horseshoe,' and threading the unbroken lines of Croydon shops until Haling Park begins on the right hand, opposite the 'Red Deer.' The long, low, green slope of the Park, the rookery elms on it, the chestnuts above the roadside fence, are among the pleasantest things which the besieging streets have made pleasanter. Haling Down, a straight-ridged and treeless long hill parallel to the road, is a continuation of that slope. In the midst it is broken by a huge chalk-pit, bushy and weathered, and its whole length is carved by an old road, always clearly marked either by the bare chalk of its banks or the stout

What Paris has done right is to make it awful to get around by

thorn-bushes attending its course. Blocks of shops between the grass and the road, a street or two running up into it, as at the chalk-pit, and the announcement of building sites, have not spoiled this little Down, which London has virtually imprisoned. Anywhere in the chalk country its distinct individuality, the long, straight ridge and even flank, would gain it honour, but here it is a pure pastoral. It is good enough to create a poem at least equal (in everything but length) to 'Windsor Forest' or 'Cooper's Hill,' if we had a local poet to-day. Beyond it, enclosed by the Eastbourne and Brighton roads, is a perfect small region of low downs, some bare, some wooded, some bushy, having Coulsdon in the centre. . . . But that was not to be my way.

☆ ☆ ☆

I had planned to start on March 21, and rather late than early, to give the road time for drying. The light arrived bravely and inno-cently enough at sunrise; too bravely, for by eight o'clock it was already abashed by a shower. There could be no doubt that either I must wait for a better day, or at the next convenient fine inter-val I must pretend to be deceived and set out prepared for all things. So at ten I started, with maps and sufficient clothes to replace what my waterproof could not protect from rain.

The suburban by-streets already looked rideable; but they were false prophets: the main roads were very different. For example, the surface between the west end of Nightingale Lane and the top of Burntwood Lane was fit only for fancy cycling in and out among a thousand lakes a yard wide and three inches deep. These should either have been stocked with gold-fish and aquatic plants or drained, but some time had been allowed to pass without either course being adopted. It may be that all the draining forces of the neighbourhood had been directed to emp-tying the ornamental pond on Wandsworth Common. Empty it was, and the sodden bed did not improve the look of the com-mon flat by nature, flatter by recent art. The gorse was in bloom amidst a patchwork of turf, gravel, and puddle. Terriers raced about or trifled. A flock of starlings bathed together in a puddle until scared by the dogs. A tall, stern, bald man without a hat strode earnestly in a straight line across the grass and water, as if

CITY CYCLING

car and awfully easy to get around by public transportation or by bike. SERGE SCHMEMANN (*INTERNATIONAL HERALD TRIBUNE*)

pleasure had become a duty. He was alone on the common. In all the other residences, that form walls round the common almost on every side, hot-cross buns had proved more alluring than the rain and the south-west wind. The scene was, in fact, one more likely to be pleasing in a picture than in itself. It was tame: it was at once artificial and artless, and touched with beauty only by the strong wind and by the subdued brightness due to the rain. Its

---

🚲 Cycling in London today – Boris bikes boom

The London bicycle sharing scheme was launched in July 2010 amid fanfare and scepticism in equal measure, but has since proved itself highly popular.

In 2014, a record year for the number of hires from London's cycle hire scheme, more than 10 million journeys were made – up 5% on 2012 (the previous highest year) and 25% on 2013. The mayor of London, Boris Johnson, announced his final intentions for the new east-west and north-south superhighways early in 2015, saying 'These amazing numbers show how cyclists are becoming ubiquitous in London and prove, if further proof were needed, why we need to crack on with catering for them. Cycle hire continues to grow in popularity and there can be no doubt that our trusty bicycles have changed the way people get around our great city.'

There are now more than 10,000 bikes available from over 700 docking stations, up from 6600 bikes and 400 docking stations when the cycle hire scheme was launched. There was much enthusiasm for 'Boris bikes' from the start, with a million rides clocked up in the first ten weeks.

Now sponsored by Santander, the bikes cost just £2 for 24 hour access, with free hire for the first half hour after removal from the self-service docking station, which encourages short journeys and prompt return to docking stations keeping as many bikes as possible available at any one time. You can take as many rides of under 30 minutes as you like within your 24 hour period, all for free, so it represents a fantastically economical way for visitors to see London.

London should be in many ways a perfect city to ride a bike. We have a flat or gently undulating landscape – much less

breadth and variety were sufficient for it to respond something as Exmoor or Household Heath or Cefn Bryn in Gower would have responded to the cloudily shattered light, the threats and the deceptions, and the great sweep of the wind. But there was no one painting those cold expanses of not quite lusty grass, the hard, dull gravel, the shining puddles, the dark gold-flecked gorse, the stiff, scanty trees with black bark and sharp green buds, the comparatively venerable elms of Bolingbroke Grove, the backs and fronts of houses of no value save to their owners, and the tall chimney-stacks northwards.

Perhaps only a solitary artist, or some coldish sort of gnome or angel, could have thoroughly enjoyed this moment. That it was waiting for such a one I am certain; I am almost equally certain that he could create a vogue in scenes like this one, which are only about a thousandth part as unpleasant as a cold bath, and possess, furthermore, elements of divinity lacking both to the cold bath and to the ensuing bun.

It is easier to like the blackbird's shrubbery, the lawn, the big elm, or oak, and the few dozen fruit trees, of the one or two larger and older houses surviving for example, at the top of Burntwood Lane. The almond, the mulberry, the apple trees in these gardens have a menaced or actually caged loveliness, as of a creature detained from some world far from ours, if they are not, as in some cases they are, the lost angels of ruined paradises.

☆ ☆ ☆

As I left the Green I noticed Huntspill Road. Why is it Huntspill Road? I thought at once of Huntspill in Somerset, of Highbridge on the Brue, of Brent Knoll, of Burnham and Hunt's Pond, and the sandhills and the clouded-yellow butterflies that shared the hollows of the sandhills with me in the Summer once. Such is the way of street names, particularly in London suburbs, where free play is given to memory and fancy. I suppose, if I were to look, I should find names as homely as the Florrie Place and Lily Place at lower Farringdon near Alton, or the Susannah's Cottage and Katie's Cottage near Canute's Palace at Southampton. But Beatrice, Ayacanora, or Megalostrate would be as likely. To the

CITY CYCLING

casual, curious man, these street names compose an outdoor museum as rich as any in the world. They are the elements of a puzzle map of England which gradually we fill in, now recognizing from a bus-top the name of a Wiltshire village, and again among the Downs coming upon a place which had formerly been but a name near Clapham Junction.

Not far beyond Huntspill Road, at what is called (I think) New Wimbledon, I noticed a De Burgh Street. Do you remember how Borrow, speaking of the tricks of fortune, says that he has seen a descendant of the De Burghs who wore the falcon mending kettles in a dingle? He counted himself one of the De Burghs. De Burgh Street is a double row of more than dingy better than dingy swarthy, mulatto cottages, ending in a barrier of elm trees. The monotony of the tiny front gardens is broken by a dark pine tree in one, and by an inn called the 'Sultan', not 'Sweet Sultan', which is a flower, but 'Sultan', a dusky king. And out of the 'Sultan' towards me, strode a gaunt, dusky man, with long black ringlets dangling from under his hard hat down over his green and scarlet neckerchief. His tight trousers, his brisk gait, and his hairless jib, were those of a man used to horses and to buyers and sellers of horses. He came rapidly and to beg. Rapid was his begging, exquisitely finished in its mechanical servility. His people were somewhere not far off, said he. That night he had travelled from St. Albans to rejoin them. They were not here: they must be at Wandsworth, with the vans and horses. All questions were answered instantly, briefly, and impersonally. The incident was but a pause in his rapid career from the 'Sultan' to Wandsworth. He took the price of a pint with a slight appearance of gratitude, and departed with long, very quick steps, head down, face almost hidden by his bowler.

But there was much to be seen between Huntspill Road and De Burgh Road. The scene, for instance, from the corner by the 'Plough', the 'Prince Albert' and the 'White Lion' at Summerstown, was curious and typical. These three great houses stand at the edge of the still cultivated and unpopulated portion of the flatland of the Wandel, the allotment gardens, the

CITY CYCLING

On a bike, being just slightly above pedestrian and car eye

watercress beds, the meadows plentifully adorned with advertisements and thinly sprinkled with horse and cow, but not lacking a rustic house and a shed or two, and to-day a show of plum-
blossom. This suburban landscape had not the grace of Haling
Park and Down, but at that moment its best hour was beginning.
The main part visible was twenty acres of damp meadow. On the
left it was bounded by the irregular low buildings of a laundry, a
file and tool factory, and a chamois- leather mill ; on the right by
the dirty backs of Summerstown. On the far side a neat, white,
oldish house was retiring amid blossoming fruit trees under the
guardianship of several elms, and the shadow of those two tall
red chimneys of the Electricity Works. On my side the meadow
had a low black fence between it and the road, with the addition,
in one place, of high advertisement boards, behind which lurked
three gypsy vans. A mixture of the sordid and the delicate in the
whole was unmistakable.

Skirting the meadow, my road led up to the Wandel and a
mean bridge. The river here is broadened for a hundred yards
between the bridge and the chamois-leather mill or Copper Mill.
The buildings extend across and along one side of the water; a
meadow comes to the sedgy side opposite. The mill looks old, has
tarred boards where it might have had corrugated iron, and its
neighbours are elms and the two chimneys. It is approached at
one side by a lane called Copper Mill Lane, where the mud is of
a sort clearly denoting a town edge or a coal district. Above the
bridge the back-yards of new houses have only a narrow waste
between them and the Wandel, and on this was being set up the
coconut-shy that would have been on Garratt Green twenty years
ago.

☆ ☆ ☆

For some distance yet the land was level. The only hill was made
by the necessity of crossing a railway at Morden station. At that
point rows of houses were discontinued; shops and public- houses with a lot of plate-glass had already ceased. The open stretches were wider and wider, of dark earth, of vegetables in squares,
or florists' plantations, divided by hedges low and few, or by

CITY CYCLING

level, one gets a perfect view of the goings-on in one's own
town. DAVID BYRNE (ROCK MUSICIAN – TALKING HEADS)

lines of tall elm trees or Lombardy poplars. Not quite rustic men and women stooped or moved to and fro among the vegetables: carts were waiting under the elms. A new house, a gasometer, an old house and its trees, lay on the farther side of the big field: behind them the Crystal Palace. On my right, in the opposite direction, the trees massed themselves together into one wood.

It is so easy to make this flat land sordid. The roads, hedges, and fences on it have hardly a reason for being anything but straight. More and more the kind of estate disappears that might preserve trees and various wasteful and pretty things: it is replaced by small villas and market gardens. If any waste be left under the new order, it will be used for conspicuously depositing rubbish. Little or no wildness of form or arrangement can survive, and with no wildness a landscape cannot be beautiful. Barbed wire and ugly and cruel fences, used against the large and irresponsible population of townsmen, add to the charmless artificiality. It was a relief to see a boy stealing up one of the hedges, looking for birds' nests. And then close up against this eager agriculture and its barbed wires are the hotels, inns, tea-shops, and cottages with ginger-beer for the townsman who is looking for country of a more easy-going nature. This was inhospitable. On many a fence and gate had been newly written up in chalk by some prophet : 'Eternity,' 'Believe,' 'Come unto Me.'

I welcomed the fences for the sake of what lay behind them. Now it was a shrubbery, now a copse, and perhaps a rookery, or a field running up mysteriously to the curved edge of a wood, and at Morden Hall it was a herd of deer among the trees. The hedges were good in themselves, and for the lush grass, the cuckoo-pint, goose-grass, and celandine upon their banks. Walking up all the slightest hills because of the south-west wind, I could see everything, from the celandines one by one and the crowding new chestnut leaves, to the genial red brick tower of St. Laurence's Church at Morden and the inns one after another, the 'George', the 'Lord Nelson', the 'Organ', the 'Brick Kiln', the 'Victoria'.

(From *In Pursuit of Spring*, 1914)

Portland, Oregon won't build a mile of road without a mile

A Passage to India, 1924

E.M. FORSTER

E.M. Forster's novel, based on his own experiences in India, shines a harsh light on the relationship between the British Raj and the educated Indian in the 1920s. Neatly juxtaposing aspects of both cultures, the novel begins with the young Indian Dr Aziz dining with two Indian friends in the city of Chandrapore when he receives a summons from Major Callendar, his superior at the hospital.

India – a hundred Indias – whispered outside beneath the indifferent moon, but for the time India seemed one and their own, and they regained their departed greatness by hearing its departure lamented, they felt young again because reminded that youth must fly. A servant in scarlet interrupted him; he was the chuprassi of the Civil Surgeon, and he handed Aziz a note.

'Old Callendar wants to see me at his bungalow,' he said, not rising. 'He might have the politeness to say why.'

'Some case, I daresay.'

'I daresay not, I daresay nothing. He has found out our dinner hour, that's all, and chooses to interrupt us every time, in order to show his power.'

'On the one hand he always does this, on the other it may be a serious case, and you cannot know,' said Hamidullah, considerately paving the way towards obedience. 'Had you not better clean your teeth after pan?'

'If my teeth are to be cleaned, I don't go at all. I am an Indian, it is an Indian habit to take pan. The Civil Surgeon must put up with it. Mohammed Latif, my bike, please.

The poor relation got up. Slightly immersed in the realms of the matter, he laid his hand on the bicycle's saddle, while a servant did the actual wheeling. Between them they took it over a tintack. Aziz held his hands under the ewer, dried them, fitted on his green felt hat, and then with unexpected energy whizzed out of Hamidullah's compound.

'Aziz, Aziz, imprudent boy...' But he was far down the bazaar, riding furiously. He had neither light nor bell nor had he

CITY CYCLING

a brake, but what use are such adjuncts in a land where the cyclist's only hope is to coast from face to face, and just before he collides with each it vanishes? And the city was fairly empty at this hour. When his tyre went flat, he leapt off and shouted for a tonga.

He did not at first find one, and he had also to dispose of his bicycle at a friend's house. He dallied furthermore to clean his teeth. But at last he was rattling towards the civil lines, with a vivid sense of speed. As he entered their arid tidiness, depression suddenly seized him. The roads, named after victorious generals and intersecting at right angles, were symbolic of the net Great Britain had thrown over India. He felt caught in their meshes.

(From *A Passage to India*, 1924)

Ciclovía – City Cycleways

Spanish for 'cycleway', *Ciclovía* means that once a week in a few fortunate cities, the cyclist is king.

Ciclovía was first introduced in Bogota, Colombia in December 1974 and has continued to grow in popularity. Each Sunday and public holiday from 7am until 2pm certain main streets of Bogotá, Cali, Medellín, and other municipalities are blocked off to cars for runners, skaters, and bicyclists. At the same time, stages are set up in city parks. Aerobics instructors, yoga teachers and musicians lead people through various performances. Bogotá's weekly ciclovías are used by approximately two million people (about 30% of the population) on over 120 kilometres of car-free streets.

The Ciclovía concept has since spread to several other South American cities, including Rosario, Argentina and Mexico City. Other world cities in USA and Australia have held Ciclovía days but apart from in Ottowa, Canada, these tend to be far less regular, perhaps only one a year.

CITY CYCLING

When I'm in New York, I bike everywhere.

Spring Morning Commute, 2014

RICK BROWN

Wheels spin round and round
Traversing the paved terrain
They roll in cadent unison
Along the paved bike lane

Fresh air breezes past me
As fragrances abound
Spring charms once dulled senses
As my wheels spin round and round

Songbirds serenade me
With their musical delights
A cavalcade of sweet tunes
To start the day off right

One pedal before the next
While shifting gears in time
In constant, subtle harmony
A soothing, recurrent rhyme

Away from the congestion
Through canopies of bliss
My wheels roll ever onward
Cloaked in the morning mist

Freed from harried schedules
As the wheels spin on and on
To enjoy keepsake moments
Amid the day-breaking dawn.

(© Rick Brown, 2014)

CITY CYCLING

It's the only way to go. WOODY HARRELSON

🚲 Cycle Commuting – Smart Move or Suicide?

Cities the world over are choked up with gridlocked, motorized transport, exacerbated by costly and insufficient car parking. Public transport infrastructures are frequently equally congested and are certainly expensive. Frustrated commuters might picture the freedom of the nippy cycle commuter beating the traffic down little-known back streets and alleyways. Or is it actually more about risking the blind side of buses, lorries and the distracted motorist? Is it safe?

Of course it depends on the city. Beijing, for example, has generous, fenced off cycle lanes down most major roads. Clearly an improvement on a strip of tarmac separated from traffic by a painted line. Until you discover that Beijing cycle lanes must still be shared with bus stops and taxis pulling in, as well as pedestrians and even other cyclists going in the wrong direction.

Some cities, such as Amsterdam and Copenhagen, have had little trouble in encouraging their citizens to get on their bikes. Amsterdam first started introducing measures to improve cyclist safety in the 1970s. According to 🖥 iamsterdam.com, an estimated 63% of Amsterdammers now use their bike on a daily basis. The 500km of bike paths offer a great incentive, along with geographical circumstances – the city is flat and compact.

So what would encourage more cycle commuters? Like Beijing, many cities have introduced separate cycle lanes on roads, but better still are dedicated cycling paths, like in Portland, Oregon, USA. Cycle paths there connect the urban areas, allowing riders to bypass roads altogether. With 260 miles of trails and paths, Portland achieves a commuter rate of nearly 9%, remarkable for car-addicted America.

Obviously not all cities have the topography of Amsterdam so the problems of getting around the natural features of a city require creative solutions. In the Norwegian city of Trondheim the disincentive of a stiff up-hill climb that would mean arriving at work hot and sweaty has been surmounted by a trick from the skiing industry – there is a uphill bike tow mechanism.

If you see me in New York, you'll probably see me on my bicycle riding furiously between a city bus and a taxi cab,

Tackling Delhi, 2013
HUGH BERGIN

City cycling inevitably means coping with traffic – lots of traffic. But traffic in Delhi is a bit different to traffic in Dublin, as Hugh Bergin discovered on his fundraising bike ride from Ireland to Myanmar.

I collected my passport with visa from Myanmar embassy and was itching to get back on the road. A few weeks in Delhi had been more than enough urban intensity for this cycle traveller. And so without much mourning I farewelled the guesthouse and pushed the loaded black Cadillac out the narrow alleys of Paherganj. New Delhi is laid out with colonial-era planning. What a task, however, to find my way out of Old Delhi, its main thoroughfares and higgledy-piggledy side streets evolved over millennia. It took hours picking my way through the traffic jams.

That term 'traffic jam' conjures up in the mind slow moving, bumper to bumper vehicles at 5pm of an evening in Dublin, the traffic lights changing and barely any progress. Crawling forward, frustration barely contained. This was of a different class.

First of all cars were in the minority, it was mainly three-wheeled auto and bicycle rickshaws edging into the most impossible spaces, motorbikes and scooters with sometimes three or four aboard darting forward, hand-drawn two-wheeled carts piled high with boxes and ox-drawn four-wheeled ones slowly plodding a step at a time. Some trucks and buses added their belching fumes, revving to keep the engines from giving up before lurching a few feet forward. And when the traffic wedged itself into immobility, I felt helpless. If all these (mostly) nimble vehicles were stuck so most certainly was I. It was a lesson in patience.

© Hugh Bergin 2013. Hugh cycled from Kilkenny to Burma to raise funds for two charities. See 🖳 Bicycletoburma.com/delhi-nepal for more information.

CITY CYCLING

hitting one of them on the side and yelling at them.
DENIS O'HARE

EXTREME CYCLING

On the Wheels of Love, 1881
H. J. Swindley

In this extract from a story serialised in Wheel World *in 1881, our hero, Tom, returns from two years abroad to find that Alice, the love of his life, has been persuaded by her father to marry another man and the wedding takes place that very day. Can Tom reach Alice before the vows are made?*

'You could get there now, Tom, old boy,' suddenly remarked, from a corner, his brother Harry, as all started at the sound of his voice. 'You could get there now,' he continued, 'if you could spin a bit, as you did when you thrashed the beast for the Championship.'

'How, then?' quickly asked Tom.

'Why, ride, of course; your machine is all right, I have only been cleaning it this morning, and it is fit to go for a man's life.'

'God bless you, Harry,' said Tom, 'where is it?'

'Go and slip into your togs,' returned his brother, 'you'll find 'em all in the old place, but they'll be rather tight. I'll have the crock ready. Sprint! You've got an hour and ten minutes to do the 15 miles and start.'

'I'll do it or ride my heart out,' replied Tom, as he vanished up the stairs. In a few moments he reappeared clad in the uniform of the Barmouth Bicycle Club, his face white with the deadly pallor of a determination to risk all for the happiness of Alice and his own, for well he knew that he alone possessed her true affection.

'Get up, Tom,' said his brother, 'you've no time to lose.'

'Now, Harry,' cried Tom, and with a push off which would not have disgraced a Sopper or a Cortis, young Harry Ruston sent forward his brother upon that 15 mile ride, the issue of which was to brighten or begloom his fresh young life forever. Who could – or indeed would –

essay to portray the conflicting emotions of our hero during his swift flight, which ever after marked an era in, and stood out in the past as, the turning point of his life. As he flew along the road what a tide of recollections rolled back on him – recollections once as sweet as honey, now turned to bitterness of gall as he fully realised the purpose of his present errand.

But now, as the tenth milestone whirred by, he began to feel the want of that peculiar training, without which no man can hope to become a bicyclist pure and simple. His muscles felt like bars of iron, and his whole body ached with the violence of his exertions. Should he be in time – in time to avert that baleful union? The hills, those cruel rises, up which in the past he had so often shown the way, now appeared to be insurmountable. 'Oh, for a lead, for a lead!', he gasped, as he gained the summit of Horse Shoe Clump – the most trying on the road, and two miles from that church where he knew she now must be standing at the altar with the man who had, near this very spot, attempted his life in the dead of night, two years ago. Perhaps, by this time, she had become his wife, and lost to him forever. The thought was madness, death; and summoning all his remaining energies, he rushed the last mile down the straight to the church as if he was riding a London Handicap with the desperate energy of a scratch man.

'Alice, Alice,' he moaned as, but two hundred yards from the gate, a sickening giddiness seized him, and he swerved dangerously across the road. With the energy of despair he steadied the machine, and, nearly fainting, fell rather than dismounted, before the church. The machine dropped with a clang on the roadway, and the crowd, awaiting in the churchyard the appearance of the bridal party, gazed with horror at the spectacle presented to them. A cyclist, whose features they knew not, covered with dust, his face a deadly whiteness, and utter exhaustion marking his features, was entering the church. As he gained the porch, so great was the silence that the words of the minister were plainly audible. 'Wilt thou have this man to be thy wedded…'

The door opened with a crash, and all within rose to their feet at the interruption. Up the aisle rushed Tom, with a cry of 'Alice, I am here,' his arms outstretched towards the veiled figure at the altar.

'Tom!', and with a piercing cry the girl swooned in her father's arms…

(From *A Ride for a Wife*, published in *Wheel World*, 1881)

EXTREME CYCLING

The Bicycle as Spirit-Level, 1893
Mark Twain

Many's the cyclist who has been surprised to find that a road they've often walked or driven along and have previously considered flat is actually nothing of the sort.

I have been familiar with that street for years, and had always supposed it was a dead level; but it was not, as the bicycle now informed me, to my surprise. The bicycle, in the hands of a novice, is as alert and acute as a spirit-level in the detecting of delicate and vanishing shades of difference in these matters. It notices a rise where your untrained eye would not observe that one existed; it notices any decline which water will run down. I was toiling up a slight rise, but was not aware of it. It made me tug and pant and perspire; and still, labor as I might, the machine came almost to a standstill every little while. At such times the boy would say: 'That's it! take a rest—there ain't no hurry. They can't hold the funeral without YOU.'

(From *What Is Man? And Other Stories: Taming the Bicycle* by Mark Twain (Samuel Clemens), 1893)

Over the Gobi Desert, 1894
Thomas Gaskell Allen, Jr. & William Lewis Sachtleben

This account of the adventures of two American students cycling across inhospitable Asian landscapes describes how their 'machines' caused surprise and bafflement in everyone they met. Here they are about to attempt to cross the Gobi Desert.

Upon assurance of at least official consent to hazard the journey to Peking, a telegram was sent to the chief of police at Tomsk, to whose care we had directed our letters, photographic material, and bicycle supplies to be sent from London in the expectation of being forced to take the Siberian route. These last could not have been dispensed with much longer, as our cushion-tires, ball-bearings, and axles were badly worn, while the rim of one of the rear

Pain is a big fat creature riding on your back. The farther you pedal, the heavier he feels. The harder you push, the tighter

wheels was broken in eight places for the lack of spokes. These supplies, however, did not reach us till six weeks after the date of our telegram, to which a prepaid reply was received, after a week's delay, asking in advance for the extra postage. This, with that prepaid from London, amounted to just fifty dollars. The warm weather, after the extreme cold of a Siberian winter, had caused the tires to stretch so much beyond their intended size that, on their arrival, they were almost unfit for use. Some of our photographic material also had been spoiled through the useless inspection of postal officials.

Our work of preparation was principally a process of elimination. We now had to prepare for a forced march in case of necessity. Handle-bars and seat-posts were shortened to save weight, and even the leather baggage-carriers, fitting in the frames of the machines, which we ourselves had patented before leaving England, were replaced by a couple of sleeping-bags made for us out of woolen shawls and Chinese oiled-canvas. The cutting off of buttons and extra parts of our clothing, as well as the shaving of our heads and faces, was also included by our friends in the list of curtailments. For the same reason one of our cameras, which we always carried on our backs, and refilled at night under the bedclothes, we sold to a Chinese photographer at Suidun, to make room for an extra provision-bag. The surplus film, with our extra baggage, was shipped by post, via Siberia and Kiakhta, to meet us on our arrival in Peking.

The blowing of the long horns and boom of the mortar cannon at the fort awoke us at daylight on the morning of July 13. Farewells had been said the night before. Only our good-hearted Russian host was up to put an extra morsel in our provision-bag, for, as he said, we could get no food until we reached the Kirghiz aouls on the high plateau of the Talki pass, by which we were to cut across over unbeaten paths to the regular so-called imperial highway, running from Suidun. From the Catholic missionaries at Kuldja we had obtained very accurate information about this route as far as the Gobi desert. The expression Tian Shan Pe-lu, or northern Tian Shan route, in opposition to the Tian Shan Nan-lu, or southern Tian Shan route, shows that the Chinese had fully

he squeezes your chest. The steeper the climb, the deeper he digs his jagged, sharp claws into your muscles. SCOTT MARTIN appreciated the importance of this historic highway, which continues the road running from the extreme western gate of the Great Wall obliquely across Mongolian Kan-su, through Hami and Barkul, to Urumtsi. From here the two natural highways lead, one to the head-waters of the Black Irtish, the other to the passes leading into the Ili valley, and other routes of the Arolo-Caspian depression. The latter route, which is now commanded at intervals by Chinese forts and military settlements, was recently relinquished by Russia only when she had obtained a more permanent footing on the former in the trading-posts of Chuguchak and Kobdo, for she very early recognized the importance of this most natural entry to the only feasible route across the Chinese empire. In a glowing sunset, at the end of a hot day's climb, we looked for the last time over the Ili valley, and at dusk, an hour later, rolled into one of the Kirghiz aouls that are here scattered among the rich pasturage of the plateau.

Even here we found that our reputation had extended from Kuldja. The chief advanced with amans of welcome, and the heavy-matted curtains in the kibitka doorway were raised, as we passed, in token of honor. When the refreshing kumiss was served around the evening camp-fire, the dangers of the journey through China were discussed among our hosts with frequent looks of misgiving. Thus, from first to last, every judgment was against us, and every prediction was of failure, if not of something worse; and now, as we stole out from the tent by the light of the rising moon, even the specter-like mountain-peaks around us, like symbols of coming events, were casting their shadows before. There was something so illusive in the scene as to make it very impressive. In the morning, early, a score of horsemen were ready to escort us on the road. At parting they all dismounted and uttered a prayer to Allah for our safety; and then as we rode away, drew their fingers across their throats in silence, and waved a solemn good-by. Such was the almost superstitious fear of these western nomads for the land which once sent forth a Yengiz Khan along this very highway.

Down the narrow valley of the Kuitun, which flows into the Ebi-nor, startling the mountain deer from the brink of the tree-arched rivulet, we reached a spot which once was the haunt of a band of those border-robbers about whom we had heard so much from our apprehensive friends. At the base of a volcano-shaped mountain lay the ruins of their former dens, from which only a year ago they were wont to sally forth on the passing caravans. When they were exterminated by the government, the head of their chief, with its dangling queue, was mounted on a pole near-by, and preserved in a cage from birds of prey, as a warning to all others who might aspire to the same notoriety. In this lonely spot we were forced to spend the night, as here occurred, through the carelessness of the Kuldja Russian blacksmith, a very serious break in one of our gear wheels. It was too late in the day to walk back the sixteen miles to the Kirghiz encampment, and there obtain horses for the remaining fifty-eight miles to Kuldja, for nowhere else, we concluded, could such a break be mended. Our sleeping-bags were now put to a severe test between the damp ground and the heavy mountain dew. The penetrating cold, and the occasional panther-like cry of some prowling animal, kept us awake the greater part of the night, awaiting with revolvers in hand some expected attack.

Five days later we had repassed this spot and were toiling over the sand and saline-covered depression of the great 'Han-Hai,' or Dried-up Sea. The mountain freshets, dissolving the salt from their sandy channels, carry it down in solution and deposit it with evaporation in massive layers, forming a comparatively hard roadway in the midst of the shifting sand-dunes. Over these latter our progress was extremely slow. One stretch of fifteen miles, which it took us six hours to cover, was as formidable as any part of the Turkoman desert along the Transcaspian railway. At an altitude of only six hundred feet above the sea, according to our aneroid barometer, and beneath the rays of a July sun against which even our felt caps were not much protection, we were half-dragging, half-pushing, our wheels through a foot of sand, and slapping at the mosquitos swarming upon our necks and faces. These pests, which throughout this low country are the largest and most numerous we have ever met, are bred in the intermediate swamps, which exist only through the negligence of

you'd never get on. LANCE ARMSTRONG

the neighboring villagers. At night smoldering fires, which half suffocate the human inmates, are built before the doors and windows to keep out the intruding insects. All travelers wear gloves, and a huge hood covering the head and face up to the eyes, and in their hands carry a horse-tail switch to lash back and forth over their shoulders. Being without such protection we suffered both day and night.

The mountain freshets all along the road to Urumtsi were more frequent and dangerous than any we had yet encountered. Toward evening the melting snows, and the condensing currents from the plain heated during the day, fill and overflow the channels that in the morning are almost dry. One stream, with its ten branches, swept the stones and boulders over a shifting channel one mile in width. It was when wading through such streams as this, where every effort was required to balance ourselves and our luggage, that the mosquitos would make up for lost time with impunity. The river, before reaching Manas, was so swift and deep as to necessitate the use of regular government carts. A team of three horses, on making a misstep, were shifted away from the ford into deep water and carried far down the stream. A caravan of Chinese traveling-vans, loaded with goods from India, were crossing at the time, on their way to the outlying provinces and the Russian border. General Bauman at Vernoye had informed us that in this way English goods were swung clear around the circle and brought into Russia through the unguarded back door.

With constant wading and tramping, our Russian shoes and stockings, one of which was almost torn off by the sly grab of a Chinese spaniel, were no longer fit for use. In their place we were now obliged to purchase the short, white cloth Chinese socks and string sandals, which for mere cycling purposes and wading streams proved an excellent substitute, being light and soft on the feet and very quickly dried. The calves of our legs, however, being left bare, we were obliged, for state occasions at least, to retain and utilize the upper portion of our old stockings. It was owing to this scantiness of wardrobe that we were obliged when taking a bath by the roadside streams to make a quick wash of our linen, and put it on wet to dry, or allow it to flutter from the

Cycling used to be how you got about when you were poor ... now, though, it has evolved into something more. It's gone

handle-bars as we rode along. It was astonishing even to ourselves how little a man required when once beyond the pale of Western conventionalities.

(From *Across Asia On A Bicycle: The Journey Of Two American Students From Constantinople To Peking,* The Century Co., 1894)

EXTREME CYCLING

On Being Hurled Through Space (Euclidian), 1895
GEORGE BERNARD SHAW

A newspaper report from the The Sheffield Independent *in 1895 tells of a bicycle accident between George Bernard Shaw and Bertrand Russell, while on a cycling trip with Sidney Webb to Tintern Abbey. Their minds were apparently taken up with loftier concerns…*

ADVENTURE OF THREE DISTINGUISHED CYCLISTS

Mr George Bernard Shaw tells in a letter a 'piece of catastrophic news' about three distinguished persons – to wit, himself, Mr Sidney Webb, and the Hon. Bertrand Russell, brother of Earl Russell.

'On Thursday afternoon, on the road from Trelleck to Chepstow,' he writes, 'we three rode on our bicycles down a steep hill on our way to Tintern Abbey. Russell is rather absent-minded, as he is preoccupied at present with a work on non-Euclidian space. He suddenly woke up from a fit of mathematical absorption, and jumped off his machine to read a signpost.'

The consequences may be imagined. G.B.S. was just behind him and there was 'a terrific smash', and the great critic and Fabian was hurled 'five yards through space (Euclidian)' and landed impartially on several parts of himself. The Hon Mr Russell was unhurt. Mr Shaw was able to ride home after, as he explains, lying flat on his back on the roadway for a while, and defending himself against all proposals to poison himself with brandy, and he attributes his escape from serious consequences to the splendid quality of bone and muscle produced by vegetarian diet and Jager clothing. He is badly strained, however, and moves about like the rheumatic hero of Waterloo at the Lyceum.

(Published in the *Sheffield Independent*, Friday 20th September 1895)

beyond a way of life and become a political statement. A movement. JEREMY CLARKSON

All Pace and Fizzle, 1896
H. G. WELLS

Sometimes a leisurely cycle through the countryside turns out to be anything but leisurely…

In the fulness of time, Mr. Hoopdriver drew near the Marquis of Granby at Esher, and as he came under the railway arch and saw the inn in front of him, he mounted his machine again and rode bravely up to the doorway. Burton and biscuit and cheese he had, which, indeed, is Burton in its proper company; and as he was eating there came a middle aged man in a drab cycling suit, very red and moist and angry in the face, and asked bitterly for a lemon squash. And he sat down upon the seat in the bar and mopped his face. But scarcely had he sat down before he got up again and stared out of the doorway.

'Damn!' said he. Then, 'Damned Fool!'

'Eigh?' said Mr. Hoopdriver, looking round suddenly with a piece of cheese in his cheek.

The man in drab faced him. 'I called myself a Damned Fool, sir. Have you any objections?'

'Oh! – None. None,' said Mr. Hoopdriver. 'I thought you spoke to me. I didn't hear what you said.'

'To have a contemplative disposition and an energetic temperament, sir, is hell. Hell, I tell you. A contemplative disposition and a phlegmatic temperament, all very well. But energy and philosophy...!'

Mr. Hoopdriver looked as intelligent as he could, but said nothing.

'There's no hurry, sir, none whatever. I came out for exercise, gentle exercise, and to notice the scenery and to botanise. And no sooner do I get on the accursed machine, than off I go hammer and tongs; I never look to right or left, never notice a flower, never see a view, get hot, juicy, red – like a grilled chop. Here I am, sir. Come from Guildford in something under the hour. Why, sir?'

Mr. Hoopdriver shook his head.

'Because I'm a damned fool, sir. Because I've reservoirs and reservoirs of muscular energy, and one or other of them is always leaking. It's a most interesting road, birds and trees, I've no doubt, and wayside flowers, and there's nothing I should enjoy more than watching them. But I can't. Get me on that machine, and I have to go. Get me on anything, and I have to go. And I don't want to go a bit. Why should a man rush about like a rocket, all pace and fizzle? Why? It makes me furious. I can assure you, sir, I go scorching along the road, and cursing aloud at myself for doing it. A quiet, dignified, philosophical man, that's what I am – at bottom; and here I am dancing with rage and swearing like a drunken tinker at a perfect stranger.

'But my day's wasted. I've lost all that country road, and now I'm on the fringe of London. And I might have loitered all the morning! Ugh! Thank Heaven, sir, you have not the irritable temperament, that you are not goaded to madness by your endogenous sneers, by the eternal wrangling of an uncomfortable soul and body. I tell you, I lead a cat and dog life. But what is the use of talking? It's all of a piece!'

He tossed his head with unspeakable self-disgust, pitched the lemon squash into his mouth, paid for it, and without any further remark strode to the door. Mr. Hoopdriver was still wondering what to say when his interlocutor vanished.

There was a noise of a foot spurning the gravel, and when Mr. Hoopdriver reached the doorway, the man in drab was a score of yards Londonward. He had already gathered pace. He pedalled with ill-suppressed anger, and his head was going down. In another moment he flew swiftly out of sight under the railway arch, and Mr. Hoopdriver saw him no more.

(From *The Wheels of Chance: A Bicycling Idyll*, 1896)

EXTREME CYCLING

Taking a Header, 1898

ELIZABETH ROBINS PENNELL

As cycle touring pioneer Elizabeth Robins Pennell *discovered, a moment's lapse of concentration can have unfortunate consequences for rider and bicycle.*

Like Heine's Philistine, I began to sing my little Ti-ri-li of exultation to find myself in Italy again. It seemed to me the sky was more tender, the landscape more luxuriant, the people more graceful. I was thinking out an elegant phrase for my note book, and attempting to pass a cart, when, the first thing I knew, the bicycle had caught in deep sand at the side of the road, and I was over in front and the back wheel of the bicycle was under the cart, and there I was, miles and miles from a repair shop, with the rim bent out of shape, the wheel buckled and the frame twisted. In fact, the machine looked more like the folding bicycle of the French army than the Rover I had been riding a second before, and I thought I should have to carry it to the nearest railway station, which was I did not know how far away. But J. took hold of it, shook it viciously, kicked it, pulled it about, and it recovered itself almost miraculously — all but the rim.

It was ridable, but I went with a limping, dot-carry-one action which was as quaint as unusual. The next party of Americans we met shoving up thought it was some strange foreign invention, and said so in our great universal language. However, I managed to ride to the wonderful curve in the road that gives that first perfect view of the Val D'Ossola; on to Domo D'Ossola for lunch; on across the valley fighting a mad wind; on round the shores of Lago Maggiore; on to Baveno. Across the Lake at Intra was a factory, and a mechanic clever enough to put a new rim on an old wheel.

This, for the sake of sensation I regret to say, was the one big smash of the ride, and it happened, not on a Pass, but on a nearly level stretch of road.

(From *Over the Alps on a Bicycle* by Elizabeth Robins Pennell, T. Fisher Unwin, London, 1898)

Life is like a ten speed bicycle. Most of us have

A Cycle Tour in Kashmir, 1900

R.H. MORTON

There is no doubt that cycling in the Kashmir region of India requires courage and a good head for heights, as traveller R.H. Morton *discovered for himself.*

Next morning I set out for the Banikal Pass, 9000ft above sea-level. A coolie carried my bicycle, and I selected the old road to the summit as being the shortest. The way was rough and difficult, however; the footpaths were covered with frozen snow, on which one's feet slipped continually, and the wind was piercingly cold. We did not reach the summit of the pass until about twelve o'clock, but the descent on the other side was much easier.

From Banikal I made my way to Ramband, some thirty miles farther on. The road itself is good, but somewhat trying to the nerves, being only 5ft or 6ft wide in places, with sheer precipices on the outer side going down thousands of feet to the far-away river. The path was not only narrow, but it twisted and turned and rose and fell in a most appalling fashion. At first I did not even like the idea of walking along it, but by-and-by, when I got in a measure used to it, and could look with something approaching indifference into the depths below, I mounted my machine, and rode warily along at a steady pace. Once, in going round a nasty corner, I had actually to lean against the side of the cliff and dismount as best I could.

Whilst drinking my afternoon tea near this place I was suddenly startled to see a number of large stones come hurtling past my head and plunge into the river beyond. The coolie and I promptly got behind the rocks, from which safe retreat I shouted to the coolie to tell the idiots up aloft to stop hurling boulders about. By way of reply he pointed upwards, and I saw on the crest of the hill above us a troop of monkeys going along in Indian file. It was the passage of these beasts which had dislodged the rocks.

(From *A Cycle Tour in Kashmir* published in *The Wide World Magazine*, 1900)

gears we never use. CHARLES M. SCHULZ

Self Protection on a Cycle, 1901

MARCUS TINDAL

Subtitled 'How you may Best Defend Yourself when Attacked by Modern Highwaymen', *this article gave instructions and illustrations explaining how plucky cyclists could avoid falling prey to 'highway robbers' – assuming they had sufficient presence of mind when put on the spot.*

Self-protection awheel is an art full of possibilities. The cyclist who is a skilful rider, who possesses pluck and dash, who has mastered the elementary rules of defence on a bicycle, and who is armed with a knowledge of how to use a machine to the best advantage as a weapon, may rest content when he is able to defend himself perfectly when attacked under the majority of conditions.

Perhaps the commonest occasion when a little knowledge of the art of self-defence awheel would prove of greatest use is when a rider is menaced by a rough who blocks the road. A lady, say, is riding alone on a country road, when an approaching tramp suddenly assumes a hostile attitude, standing before her with legs apart and arms outstretched, effectively barring the way. Now this is the secret for removing the tramp, and for riding past in safety. Let the lady put on a spurt, and ride, point blank, at her assailant, then swerve at the last moment. Certainly this requires nerve, but it is really simple, and marvellously effective. The tramp cannot overcome the instinct of self-protection which makes him jump to one side, when the cyclist, of course, at once swerves in the other direction.

Nearly every cyclist carries a weapon on his machine which, under many circumstances, he may use with great effect: a strong, long, heavy metal pump offers as convenient a weapon as one could desire. Let the rider who is threatened by a foot-pad flourish his pump in his assailant's face, and he will be surprised how quickly and precipitously the assailant jumps back. A formidable blow could be delivered in a man's face with a heavy pump, especially when riding at speed. If the pump is carried in spring clips attached to the top bar of the machine – or in the case

Caution is the key to safe cycling. I'm aware that cars are

of a lady's machine to the handlebars – it is ready to hand in case of emergency, and may be detached in a moment.

It is well to know how to utilise the momentum of a cycle in disabling an opponent to the best effect. To deliver a blow whilst riding – say, at the head of an objectionable small boy who has been indulging in the dangerous practice of throwing a cap at your wheel, and stands in need of punishment – or at the head of an assailant of larger growth – it is necessary to swerve suddenly as you come alongside, so that you throw the balance of your machine over towards your assailant! Leaning well over you deliver a swinging, slightly upward, and *forward*, blow with your hand or your weapon. If the blow is timed well, the shock of the recoil – which, it must be understood, would otherwise be disastrous – will have no other effect than to throw your machine back into an upright position, and to cause you to regain your balance easily, when you may ride on in triumph.

(From *Pearson's Magazine: Self Protection on a Cycle*, 1901)

Sherlock Holmes Reads the Tyre Tracks, 1904
ARTHUR CONAN DOYLE

When the ten-year-old son of a Lord inexplicably goes missing from his boarding school at the same time as the German master and his bicycle, Sherlock Holmes & Watson must get to the bottom of the mystery without delay. Where Watson sees simply tyre tracks, Holmes, of course, sees a great deal more…

With high hopes we struck across the peaty, russet moor, intersected with a thousand sheep paths, until we came to the broad, light-green belt which marked the morass between us and Holdernesse. Certainly, if the lad had gone homewards, he must have passed this, and he could not pass it without leaving his traces. But no sign of him or the German could be seen. With a darkening face my friend strode along the margin, eagerly observant of every muddy stain upon the mossy surface. Sheep-marks there were in profusion, and at one place, some miles down, cows had left their tracks. Nothing more.

bigger than me, but I feel quite safe. I'm in control, liberated and free, when I'm on my bike. ERIN O'CONNOR (SUPERMODEL)

'Check number one,' said Holmes, looking gloomily over the rolling expanse of the moor.

'There is another morass down yonder and a narrow neck between. Halloa! halloa! halloa! What have we here?'

We had come on a small black ribbon of pathway. In the middle of it, clearly marked on the sodden soil, was the track of a bicycle.

'Hurrah!' I cried. 'We have it.'

But Holmes was shaking his head, and his face was puzzled and expectant rather than joyous.

'A bicycle, certainly, but not the bicycle,' said he.

'I am familiar with forty-two different impressions left by tyres. This, as you perceive, is a Dunlop, with a patch upon the outer cover. Heidegger's tyres were Palmer's, leaving longitudinal stripes. Aveling, the mathematical master, was sure upon the point. Therefore, it is not Heidegger's track.'

'The boy's, then?'

'Possibly, if we could prove a bicycle to have been in his possession. But this we have utterly failed to do. This track, as you perceive, was made by a rider who was going from the direction of the school.'

'Or towards it?'

'No, no, my dear Watson. The more deeply sunk impression is, of course, the hind wheel, upon which the weight rests. You perceive several places where it has passed across and obliterated the more shallow mark of the front one. It was undoubtedly heading away from the school. It may or may not be connected with our inquiry, but we will follow it backwards before we go any farther.'

We did so, and at the end of a few hundred yards lost the tracks as we emerged from the boggy portion of the moor. Following the path backwards, we picked out another spot, where a spring trickled across it. Here, once again, was the mark of the bicycle, though nearly obliterated by the hoofs of cows. After that there was no sign, but the path ran right on into Ragged Shaw, the wood which backed on to the school. From this wood the cycle must have emerged. Holmes sat down on a boulder and rested his chin in his hands. I had smoked two cigarettes before he moved.

The wheel that squeaks the loudest is

'Well, well,' said he, at last. 'It is, of course, possible that a cunning man might change the tyre of his bicycle in order to leave unfamiliar tracks. A criminal who was capable of such a thought is a man whom I should be proud to do business with. We will leave this question undecided and hark back to our morass again, for we have left a good deal unexplored.'

We continued our systematic survey of the edge of the sodden portion of the moor, and soon our perseverance was gloriously rewarded. Right across the lower part of the bog lay a miry path. Holmes gave a cry of delight as he approached it. An impression like a fine bundle of telegraph wires ran down the centre of it. It was the Palmer tyre.

'Here is Herr Heidegger, sure enough!' cried Holmes, exultantly. 'My reasoning seems to have been pretty sound, Watson.'

'I congratulate you.'

'But we have a long way still to go. Kindly walk clear of the path. Now let us follow the trail. I fear that it will not lead very far.'

We found, however, as we advanced that this portion of the moor is intersected with soft patches, and, though we frequently lost sight of the track, we always succeeded in picking it up once more.

'Do you observe,' said Holmes, 'that the rider is now undoubtedly forcing the pace? There can be no doubt of it. Look at this impression, where you get both tyres clear. The one is as deep as the other. That can only mean that the rider is throwing his weight on to the handle-bar, as a man does when he is sprinting. By Jove! he has had a fall.'

There was a broad, irregular smudge covering some yards of the track. Then there were a few footmarks, and the tyre reappeared once more.

'A side-slip,' I suggested.

Holmes held up a crumpled branch of flowering gorse. To my horror I perceived that the yellow blossoms were all dabbled with crimson. On the path, too, and among the heather were dark stains of clotted blood.

(From *The Adventure of the Priory School*, 1904)
Read the whole story at 🖳 sherlock-holmes/stories/pdf/a4/1-sided/prio.pdf

the one that gets the grease. JOSH BILLINGS

EXTREME CYCLING

The Hunt for the Right Saddle, 1914

JEROME K. JEROME

It is a truth universally acknowledged among cyclists that a saddle which seemed perfectly comfortable in the shop could turn out to be an instrument of torture on the road...

'Then there are saddles,' I went on – I wished to get this lesson home to him. 'Can you think of any saddle ever advertised that you have not tried?'

He said: 'It has been an idea of mine that the right saddle is to be found.'

I said: 'You give up that idea; this is an imperfect world of joy and sorrow mingled. There may be a better land where bicycle saddles are made out of rainbow, stuffed with cloud; in this world the simplest thing is to get used to something hard. There was that saddle you bought in Birmingham; it was divided in the middle, and looked like a pair of kidneys.'

He said: 'You mean that one constructed on anatomical principles.'

'Very likely,' I replied. 'The box you bought it in had a picture on the cover, representing a sitting skeleton – or rather that part of a skeleton which does sit.'

He said: 'It was quite correct; it showed you the true position of the—'

I said: 'We will not go into details; the picture always seemed to me indelicate.'

He said: 'Medically speaking, it was right.'

'Possibly,' I said, 'for a man who rode in nothing but his bones. I only know that I tried it myself, and that to a man who wore flesh it was agony. Every time you went over a stone or a rut it nipped you; it was like riding on an irritable lobster. You rode that for a month.'

'I thought it only right to give it a fair trial,' he answered.

I said: 'You gave your family a fair trial also; if you will allow me the use of slang. Your wife told me that never in the whole course of your married life had she known you so bad tempered,

I'm lazy. But it's the lazy people who invented the wheel

so un-Christian like, as you were that month. Then you remember that other saddle, the one with the spring under it.'

He said: 'You mean 'the Spiral.''

I said: 'I mean the one that jerked you up and down like a Jack-in-the-box; sometimes you came down again in the right place, and sometimes you didn't. I am not referring to these matters merely to recall painful memories, but I want to impress you with the folly of trying experiments at your time of life.'

(From *Three Men on the Bummel*, 1914)

William the Determined, 1922

RICHMAL CROMPTON

Schoolboy William Brown, hero of the Just William *stories, manages to get into the most incredible scrapes, apparently quite by accident, and is always in trouble with someone. This time he has upset his brother Robert by monopolising the lovely Miss Cannon's attention with a game of Red Indians when she comes to tea. So a birthday picnic is planned for Robert, to which William is not invited. Surely that should keep him out of harm's way?*

They comforted Robert's wounded feelings as best they could, but it was Ethel who devised the plan that finally cheered him. She suggested a picnic on the following Thursday, which happened to be Robert's birthday and incidentally the last day of Miss Cannon's visit, and the picnic party was to consist of Robert, Ethel, Mrs. Clive and Miss Cannon, and William was not even to be told where it was to be. The invitation was sent that evening and Robert spent the week dreaming of picnic lunches and suggesting impossible dainties of which the cook had never heard. It was not until she threatened to give notice that he reluctantly agreed to leave the arrangements to her. He sent his white flannels (which were perfectly clean) to the laundry with a note attached, hinting darkly at legal proceedings if they were not sent back, spotless, by Thursday morning. He went about with an expression of set and solemn purpose upon his frowning countenance. William he utterly ignored. He bought a book of poems at

and the bicycle because they didn't like walking or carrying things. LECH WALESA

a second-hand bookshop and kept them on the table by his bed.

They saw nothing of Miss Cannon in the interval, but Thursday dawned bright and clear, and Robert's anxious spirits rose. He was presented with a watch and chain by his father and with a bicycle by his mother and a tin of toffee (given not without ulterior motive) by William.

They met Mrs. Clive and Miss Cannon at the station and took tickets to a village a few miles away whence they had decided to walk to a shady spot on the river bank.

William's dignity was slightly offended by his pointed exclusion from the party, but he had resigned himself to it, and spent the first part of the morning in the character of Chief Red Hand among the rhododendron bushes. He had added an ostrich feather found in Ethel's room to his head-dress, and used almost a whole cork on his face. He wore the door-mat pinned to his shoulders.

After melting some treacle toffee in rain-water over his smoking fire, adding orange juice and drinking the resulting liquid, he tired of the game and wandered upstairs to Robert's bedroom to inspect his birthday presents. The tin of toffee was on the table by Robert's bed. William took one or two as a matter of course and began to read the love-poems. He was horrified a few minutes later to see the tin empty, but he fastened the lid with a sigh, wondering if Robert would guess who had eaten them. He was afraid he would. Anyway he'd given him them. And anyway, he hadn't known he was eating them.

He then went to the dressing-table and tried on the watch and chain at various angles and with various postures. He finally resisted the temptation to wear them for the rest of the morning and replaced them on the dressing-table.

Then he wandered downstairs and round to the shed, where Robert's new bicycle stood in all its glory. It was shining and spotless and William gazed at it in awe and admiration. He came to the conclusion that he could do it no possible harm by leading it carefully round the house. Encouraged by the fact that Mrs. Brown was out shopping, he walked it round the house several times. He much enjoyed the feeling of importance and possession that it gave him. He felt loth to part with it. He wondered if it was

At that age, it's one of the worse things in the world to

very hard to ride. He had tried to ride one once when he was staying with an aunt. He stood on a garden bench and with difficulty transferred himself from that to the bicycle seat. To his surprise and delight he rode for a few yards before he fell off. He tried again and fell off again. He tried again and rode straight into a holly bush. He forgot everything in his determination to master the art. He tried again and again. He fell off or rode into the holly bush again and again. The shining black paint of the bicycle was scratched, the handle bars were slightly bent and dulled; William himself was bruised and battered but unbeaten.

At last he managed to avoid the fatal magnet of the holly bush, to steer an unsteady zig-zag course down the drive and out into the road. He had had no particular intention of riding into the road. In fact he was still wearing his befeathered headgear, blacked face, and the mat pinned to his shoulders. It was only when he was actually in the road that he realised that retreat was impossible, that he had no idea how to get off the bicycle.

What followed was to William more like a nightmare than anything else. He saw a motor-lorry coming towards him and in sudden panic turned down a side street and from that into another side street. People came out of their houses to watch him pass. Children booed or cheered him and ran after him in crowds. And William went on and on simply because he could not stop. His iron nerve had failed him. He had not even the presence of mind to fall off. He was quite lost. He had left the town behind him and did not know where he was going. But wherever he went he was the centre of attraction. The strange figure with blackened, streaked face, mat flying behind in the wind and a head-dress of feathers from which every now and then one floated away, brought the population to its doors. Some said he had escaped from an asylum, some that he was an advertisement of something. The children were inclined to think he was part of a circus. William himself had passed beyond despair. His face was white and set. His first panic had changed to a dull certainty that this would go on for ever. He would never know how to stop. He supposed he would go right across England. He wondered if he were near the sea now. He couldn't be far off. He wondered if he

would ever see his mother and father again. And his feet pedalled mechanically along. They did not reach the pedals at their
lowest point; they had to catch them as they came up and send
them down with all their might.

It was very tiring; William wondered if people would be
sorry if he dropped down dead.

I have said that William did not know where he was going.
But Fate knew.

The picnickers walked down the hill from the little station to
the river bank. It was a beautiful morning. Robert, his heart and

Iconic bicycle designs: Raleigh Chopper

If Richmal Crompton had been writing the *Just William*
stories in the 1970s rather than the 1920s, William's bicycle of
choice would certainly have been a Chopper. The Raleigh
Chopper represented a significant departure from earlier bike
designs in that it was specifically targeted at children and
designed more for its image than its practicality. Inspired by
motorbikes like the one in films such as Easy Rider, it featured
'ape-hanger' handlebars, a rear wheel larger than the front, and
a spongy motorcycle-style saddle that incorporated a backrest.

It certainly achieved iconic status among kids growing up in
the 1970s, even though it was less stable than a conventional
bike, slow and heavy with wide tyres that created greater rolling
resistance. Kids didn't care though, because the Mk 2 Chopper
had a frame mounted T-bar-style shifter and came in cool
colours like purple or red.

These days they are collectors' items and an unrestored Mk
2, with all the original features, can change hands for over £600.

Memories of Chopper owners

*'Well, what can you say about the Chopper except it was a triumph of
design over practicality. I had a yellow Chopper when I was 8 or 9 and
I loved it. Why, I'll never know because it really was a bit of a pig to
ride, the central gear lever felt really fragile and it was a pain to
change the back wheel if you got a puncture. It might have something*

Well, I don't ever get excited. I haven't been excited since

hopes high, walked beside his goddess, revelling in his nearness to her though he could think of nothing to say to her. But Ethel and Mrs. Clive chattered gaily.

'We've given William the slip,' said Ethel with a laugh. 'He's no idea where we've gone even!'

'I'm sorry,' said Miss Cannon, 'I'd have loved William to be here.'

'You don't know him,' said Ethel fervently.

'What a beautiful morning it is!' murmured Robert, feeling that some remark was due from him. 'Am I walking too fast for

---

to do with the fact that it really was the coolest bike. You can keep yer Grifters and Mongooses. No bike summed up funk and flash quite like a Chopper.'

'What a great bike this was! I had a blue 5-speed in the mid 70s and no idea of how lucky I was to have this weird bike. It was style, form over function all the way. Speed not so much, but the long handlebars made for good sprint times, as you crank side to side, standing up, from the starting line to the finish line. Take it anywhere far though, and it tired you out. If you were willing to push it though, my Chopper was an off-road champ compared to anything else available at the time. Many great hours riding up and down trails taking jumps few others dared.'

'Who remembers coming to a sudden stop, sliding off the seat and landing squarely on the gear-shift? Those hideous minutes of innocent agony rolling around on the ground? My chopper eventually died when I pulled my last wheelie, only to have the handlebars snap at the stem, with the front in the air! That landing was unpleasant too...'

'The thing I remember most was the little warning on the back of the seat saying 'Not to be used to carry passengers' (or something similar) – well of course, due to the sheer size of the massive seat, that was like a red rag to a bull! We used to give each other 'backies' all the time – one of you got to sit back in luxury, while the 'driver', had to use all his strength just to get the bike actually moving and had no choice but to stand up the entire journey...'

I got a Chopper bicycle when I was about 12. JACK DEE

you – Miss Cannon?'

'Oh, no.'

'May I carry your parasol for you?' he enquired humbly.

'Oh, no, thanks.'

He proposed a boat on the river after lunch, and it appeared that Miss Cannon would love it, but Ethel and Mrs. Clive would rather stay on the bank.

His cup of bliss was full. It would be his opportunity of sealing lifelong friendship with her, of arranging a regular correspondence, and hinting at his ultimate intentions. He must tell her that, of course, while he was at college he was not in a position to offer his heart and hand, but if she could wait... He began to compose speeches in his mind.

They reached the bank and opened the luncheon baskets. Unhampered by Robert the cook had surpassed herself. They spread the white cloth and took up their position around it under the shade of the trees.

Just as Robert was taking up a plate of sandwiches to hand them with a courteous gesture to Miss Cannon, his eyes fell upon the long, white road leading from the village to the riverside and remained fixed there, his face frozen with horror. The hand that held the plate dropped lifelessly back again on to the table-cloth. Their eyes followed his. A curious figure was cycling along the road – a figure with blackened face and a few drooping feathers on its head, and a door-mat flying in the wind. A crowd of small children ran behind cheering. It was a figure vaguely familiar to them all.

'It can't be,' said Robert hoarsely, passing a hand over his brow.

No one spoke.

It came nearer and nearer. There was no mistaking it.

'William!' gasped four voices.

William came to the end of the road. He did not turn aside to either of the roads by the riverside. He did not even recognise or look at them. With set, colourless face he rode on to the river bank, and straight amongst them. They fled from before his charge. He rode over the table-cloth, over the sandwiches, pat-

As a kid I had a dream – I wanted to own my own bicycle. When I got the bike I must have been the happiest boy in

ties, rolls and cakes, down the bank and into the river.

☆ ☆ ☆

They rescued him and the bicycle. Fate was against Robert even there. It was a passing boatman who performed the rescue. William emerged soaked to the skin, utterly exhausted, but feeling vaguely heroic. He was not in the least surprised to see them. He would have been surprised at nothing. And Robert wiped and examined his battered bicycle in impotent fury in the background while Miss Cannon pillowed William's dripping head on her arm, fed him on hot coffee and sandwiches and called him 'My poor darling Red Hand!'

She insisted on going home with him. All through the journey she sustained the character of his faithful squaw. Then, leaving a casual invitation to Robert and Ethel to come over to tea, she departed to pack.

Mrs. Brown descended the stairs from William's room with a tray on which reposed a half-empty bowl of gruel, and met Robert in the hall.

'Robert,' she remonstrated, 'you really needn't look so upset.'

Robert glared at her and laughed a hollow laugh.

'Upset!' he echoed, outraged by the inadequacy of the expression. 'You'd be upset if your life was ruined. You'd be upset. I've a right to be upset.'

He passed his hand desperately through his already ruffled hair.

'You're going there to tea,' she reminded him.

'Yes,' he said bitterly, 'with other people. Who can talk with other people there? No one can. I'd have talked to her on the river. I'd got heaps of things ready in my mind to say. And William comes along and spoils my whole life – and my bicycle. And she's the most beautiful girl I've ever seen in my life. And I've wanted that bicycle for ever so long and it's not fit to ride.'

'But poor William has caught a very bad chill, dear, so you oughtn't to feel bitter to him. And he'll have to pay for your bicycle being mended. He'll have no pocket money till it's paid for.'

'You'd think,' said Robert with a despairing gesture in the direction of the hall table and apparently addressing it, 'you'd

Liverpool, maybe the world. I lived for that bike... the first night I even kept it in my bed. JOHN LENNON

think four grown-up people in a house could keep a boy of William's age in order, wouldn't you? You'd think he wouldn't be allowed to go about spoiling people's lives and – and ruining their bicycles. Well, he jolly well won't do it again,' he ended darkly.

Mrs. Brown, proceeded in the direction of the kitchen.

'Robert,' she said soothingly over her shoulder, 'you surely want to be at peace with your little brother, when he's not well, don't you?'

'Peace?' he said. Robert turned his haggard countenance upon her as though his ears must have deceived him. 'Peace! I'll wait. I'll wait till he's all right and going about; I won't start till then. But – peace! It's not peace, it's an armistice – that's all.'

(From *Just William*, 1922, published by George Newnes)

Numerous Ups and Downs, 1922
WARD LOCK RED GUIDE

Signs specifically for 'motor traffic' were still a relative novelty in the 1920s, as apparently was the concept that they might also be informative for non-motorised road users.

Cycling in Lakeland is enjoyable, if arduous. The triangles and other signs for motor traffic erected by the County Council serve equally well for the cyclist and should be carefully regarded, especially on inclines and long mountain passes. During the past twenty years there has been considerable improvement both on main roads and by-ways. Surfaces throughout are well made, and dangerous corners have been almost eliminated in the central area. Cyclists should note that some of the by-roads are still crossed by gates; a sharp look-out should be kept for them. Cycling in the outlying districts is less severe, but the ups and downs are numerous and often abrupt and less official attention has been paid to improvements.

☆ ☆ ☆

Between Keswick and Seatoller there are numerous ups and downs, some of them quite sharp. The cyclist has always to be

I still feel that variable gears are only for people over forty-

vigilant, for, despite improvements, the lane is still narrow, and hedged by tall stone walls which mask the approach of the modern low motor car. From Seatoller it is almost all push to Honister House (sic). Here the cyclist must on no account mount, but must walk down the rough pass till the comparatively level ground at the foot of Honister Crag is reached. This route is not for motorists.

(From *Guide to the English Lake District*, Ward Lock, 1922)

EXTREME CYCLING

A Reckless Ride, 1936
D.H. LAWRENCE

Paul Morel is simultaneously longing to get closer to Miriam and also afraid to upset his intense mother. After another frustrating evening studying with Miriam, his reckless downhill cycle home without properly working brakes is cathartic.

Well,' he said, 'get that French and we'll do some – some Verlaine.'

'Yes,' she said in a deep tone, almost of resignation. And she rose and got the books. And her rather red, nervous hands looked so pitiful, he was mad to comfort her and kiss her. But then he dared not – or could not. There was something prevented him. His kisses were wrong for her. They continued the reading till ten o'clock, when they went into the kitchen, and Paul was natural and jolly again with the father and mother. His eyes were dark and shining; there was a kind of fascination about him.

When he went into the barn for his bicycle he found the front wheel punctured.

'Fetch me a drop of water in a bowl,' he said to her. 'I shall be late, and then I s'll catch it.'

He lighted the hurricane lamp, took off his coat, turned up the bicycle, and set speedily to work. Miriam came with the bowl of water and stood close to him, watching. She loved to see his hands doing things. He was slim and vigorous, with a kind of easiness even in his most hasty movements. And busy at his work he seemed to forget her. She loved him absorbedly. She

five. Isn't it better to triumph by the strength of your muscles than by the artifice of a derailer? HENRI DESGRANGE

Endurance riding, 1939 vs 2015

In 1939, 27-year-old Tommy Godwin rode 75,065 miles in a single year to set an endurance riding record that some believe will never be beaten. The distance is the equivalent of three times around the world in a single year, or riding from John O'Groats to Land's End and back every week, all achieved on a heavy steel bike with only three gears.

Tracking devices did not exist in 1939, so Godwin's mileage was verified by respected figures such as police officers, and posted daily to *Cycling* – the magazine that originally set up the challenge.

Stoke-on-Trent cycling legend Brian Rourke said: 'In theory, the record should be breakable because new road surfaces and modern bikes offer a huge advantage. They can do 500 miles in a day now. But to do over 200 miles, every day for a year, on a three-speed bike made of steel, is basically impossible. Nobody could ever match his record. Even if it was broken, the conditions just aren't comparable.'

After the feat, Godwin had to learn to walk normally again and uncurl his hands. Yet within weeks, he was serving his country in the RAF.

It has been described as an 'unbreakable' record. Or is it?

In 2015, two cyclists are taking on the year-long challenge to break Tommy Godwin's record. British man Steve Abraham started his attempt on January 1, 2015, while American Kurt Searvogel started his official riding on January 10, 2015. Each will have their mileage tracked over a continuous 365-day period using the Strava GPS application. The UMCA Ultra Marathon Cycling Association is sanctioning the records. Unfortunately Abraham suffered a broken ankle after being involved in a collision with a moped in March 2015, but he is determined to pursue his record attempt. Follow his progress at ⌨ oneyeartimetrial.org.uk.

Pain is temporary.

wanted to run her hands down his sides. She always wanted to embrace him, so long as he did not want her.

'There!' he said, rising suddenly. 'Now, could you have done it quicker?'

'No!' she laughed.

He straightened himself. His back was towards her. She put her two hands on his sides, and ran them quickly down.

'You are so FINE!' she said.

He laughed, hating her voice, but his blood roused to a wave of flame by her hands. She did not seem to realise HIM in all this. He might have been an object. She never realised the male he was.

He lighted his bicycle-lamp, bounced the machine on the barn floor to see that the tyres were sound, and buttoned his coat.

'That's all right!' he said.

She was trying the brakes, that she knew were broken.

'Did you have them mended?' she asked.

'No!'

'But why didn't you?'

'The back one goes on a bit.'

'But it's not safe.'

'I can use my toe.'

'I wish you'd had them mended,' she murmured.

'Don't worry – come to tea tomorrow, with Edgar.'

'Shall we?'

'Do – about four. I'll come to meet you.'

'Very well.'

She was pleased. They went across the dark yard to the gate. Looking across, he saw through the uncurtained window of the kitchen the heads of Mr. and Mrs. Leivers in the warm glow. It looked very cosy. The road, with pine trees, was quite black in front.

'Till tomorrow,' he said, jumping on his bicycle.

'You'll take care, won't you?' she pleaded.

'Yes.'

His voice already came out of the darkness. She stood a moment watching the light from his lamp race into obscurity

EXTREME CYCLING

along the ground. She turned very slowly indoors. Orion was wheeling up over the wood, his dog twinkling after him, half smothered. For the rest the world was full of darkness, and silent, save for the breathing of cattle in their stalls. She prayed earnestly for his safety that night. When he left her, she often lay in anxiety, wondering if he had got home safely.

He dropped down the hills on his bicycle. The roads were

The Hour Record

The Hour Record is one of the most prestigious records in cycling with roots dating back to 1893 when it was set by Henri Desgrange, the creator of the *Tour de France*. Described as 'Man and machine against the clock', to take it on means cycling the greatest distance in 60 minutes.

In the mid 1990s the record was repeatedly broken on increasingly advanced equipment forcing the sports governing body, the UCI, to create a set of regulations that unwittingly stifled record attempts and confused the record books. However, the record was effectively reset in May 2015 when the UCI standardised the equipment regulations, bringing them in line with Olympic track cycling and announcing that the current record of 49.7km would stand as the mark to beat.

This was first cracked by Jens Voigt who successfully set a new record of 51.115km in Switzerland on 18 September 2014. That stood for only six weeks before being bettered by Matthias Brandle's 51.850km on 30 October 2014, then was again overtaken by Australian Rohan Dennis on 8 February 2015 with a new mark of 52.491km.

It was not long before this was exceeded by over 400 metres, by Britain's Alex Dowsett on 2 May 2015, with 52.937km. However, the challenge was then taken up by World and Olympic time trial champion Sir Bradley Wiggins whose successful record attempt on 7 June 2015 increased the distance to an astonishing 54.526km.

At that continuous speed a cycle ride the length of Britain, from Land's End to John o'Groats, would take just under 26 hours.

But to say that the race is the metaphor for the life is to miss

greasy, so he had to let it go. He felt a pleasure as the machine plunged over the second, steeper drop in the hill. 'Here goes!' he said. It was risky, because of the curve in the darkness at the bottom, and because of the brewers' waggons with drunken waggoners asleep. His bicycle seemed to fall beneath him, and he loved it. Recklessness is almost a man's revenge on his woman. He feels he is not valued, so he will risk destroying himself to deprive her altogether.

The stars on the lake seemed to leap like grasshoppers, silver upon the blackness, as he spun past. Then there was the long climb home.

'See, mother!' he said, as he threw her the berries and leaves on to the table.

'H'm!' she said, glancing at them, then away again. She sat reading, alone, as she always did.

(From *Sons & Lovers*, 1936)

Empire of the Sun, 1941
J.G. BALLARD

Born and raised in Shanghai, even up to 1941 eleven-year old Jim's war experience is still the life of the privileged colonial. Then the Japanese attack on Pearl Harbor and sinking of British and American warships in the Yangtze changes everything and, separated from his parents in the confusion, Jim finds himself at home entirely alone.

Leaving the garden, Jim wheeled his bicycle through the verandah door. Then he did something he had always longed to do, mounted his cycle and rode through the formal, empty rooms. Delighted to think how shocked Vera and the servants would have been, he expertly circled his father's study, intrigued by the patterns which the tyres cut in the thick carpet. He collided with the desk, and knocked over a table lamp as he swerved through the door into the drawing-room. Standing on the pedals, he zig-zagged among the armchairs and tables, lost his balance and fell on to a sofa, remounted without touching the floor, crash-landed into the double doors that led into the dining room, pulled them

the point. The race is everything. It obliterates whatever isn't racing. Life is the metaphor for the race. DONALD ANTRIM

back and began a wild circuit of the long polished table. He detoured into the pantry, swishing to and fro through the pool of water below the refrigerator, scattered the saucepans from the kitchen shelves and ended in a blaze of speed towards the mirror in the downstairs cloakroom. As his front tyre trembled against the smudged glass Jim shouted at his excited reflection. The war had brought him at least one small bonus.

(Reprinted by permission of HarperCollins Publishers Ltd.
From Empire of the Sun, © J.G. Ballard, 1984)

A Wounded Passenger, 1944
SHIRLEY HUGHES

With the help of his beloved bicycle, thirteen year old Paolo finds himself playing a vital part in rescuing Joe, a Canadian prisoner-of-war on the run in Nazi-occupied Florence in 1944.

There was a lot of shouting then and confusion. A bullet hit the wall behind Paolo's head. The plaster shattered and fell to the ground, but he was too stunned to be frightened. He reacted blindly, without hesitation.

'This way,' he said, pulling Joe along with one hand and clutching his bicycle with the other. Two more shots followed as they made their way off around the corner. He felt Joe stumble and fall against him, but Joe quickly righted himself and kept running. Other doors were being flung open now and people were coming out into the street: women were screaming; men were gesticulating. The panic that ensued gave them a few seconds' lead. Paolo pulled Joe into a side alleyway which led through to another street. It was then that he remembered the ice-cream shop.

☆　☆　☆

He gave the back door a push. It creaked open. Quickly he shoved his bicycle inside and then, after dragging Joe inside, shut the door behind them. He could hear running footsteps very close at hand – booted feet on cobbles – and orders shouted in

German. Joe and Paolo stood together in the half-dark. Joe was leaning heavily on him, heaving for breath. Paolo gripped his arm and encountered something warm and sticky – blood.

'They got me in the shoulder with that second shot,' Joe whispered hoarsely.

Paolo was too scared to answer. Instead he looked around. It was the ice-cream shop, all right. They seemed to be in the kitchen. It smelt of damp, decay and urine but there were two big fridges looming up out of the dark. Outside the soldiers were kicking open doors all along the alley. Paolo shoved his bicycle into a corner and pulled Joe behind one of the fridges. There was just room for them, if they pressed up against the wall.

A second later the door from the alleyway was flung open and two soldiers burst in. Torches flashed around the room, packing cases were pulled aside and cupboards searched. Both fridge doors were wrenched open. Paolo held his breath. One man was so near to him that he could have reached out and touched Paolo's arm.

Then one of the soldiers spotted the bicycle. There was an exchange and the door that led into the shop was kicked open. The soldiers rushed through, rifles at the ready.

'Come on,' whispered Paolo. He grabbed the bike and he and Joe slipped out silently into the alley. Paolo peered down the street. He could hear excited voices nearby, but in the immediate vicinity there was nobody about and all was quiet. He motioned for Joe to follow him but, looking back, he saw that Joe was not in a good way. He was staggering, and blood had soaked through the left arm of his jacket and was dripping down his hand. Paolo ran back to him. Somehow he managed to support the wounded man as far as the bicycle and lever him onto the seat.

'It's OK. Hang on to me,' he said.

Then, with Joe clinging onto his waist with his good arm, Paolo shoved off. He cycled hard, standing high on the pedals, and within minutes they were away up the darkened street.

The way home was the worst journey Paolo had ever made. He took the back streets out of the city, dreading at every turn they would run into another German patrol. Joe was tall and

something wrong with a society that drives a car to work out in a gym. BILL NYE

broad, and he seemed a dead weight to Paolo, who was finding it almost impossible to support him, even along the flat. As they began their ascent up the road towards home Paolo had to dismount and push his bicycle with Joe slumped upon it.

It was hard-going. They went on in silence, with Paolo heaving for breath. They were both thinking of David and how they had had to abandon him to his fate at the hands of his German captors. They had run out on him – they both knew that all too clearly, though they also knew that any attempt to save him would have been futile and would probably have resulted in all three of them being captured or shot, Paolo tried to concentrate on reaching home. It was the only thing that mattered now.

Ice cycling record, 2013

On the 27th December 2013, Maria Leijerstam became the first person in the world to cycle from the edge of the Antarctic continent to the South Pole. She also set the new World Record for the fastest human-powered coast to pole traverse, completing her 638km journey on her specially designed recumbent PolarCycle in 10 days, 14hrs and 56 minutes.

www.whiteicecycle.com

Cycle tracks will abound in Utopia.
H.G. WELLS

BIBLIOGRAPHY

Allen, Jr, Thomas Gaskell & Sachtleben, William Lewis *Across Asia On A Bicycle: The Journey Of Two American Students From Constantinople To Peking* (The Century Co., 1894)

Ballard, J.G. *Empire of the Sun* (HarperCollins Publishers Ltd, 1984)

Bell, Jean *A 90-Year Journey Through the 20th Century* (1st Book Library, 2000)

Bergin, Hugh *Bicycle to Burma* (2013)

Betjeman, John *Collected Poems* (John Murray Press, Hodder & Stoughton, 2001)

Blake, Quentin *Mrs Armitage on Wheels* (Jonathan Cape, Random House, 1987)

Brown, Rick *Spring Morning Commute* (2014)

Chapman, Ronald *Riding a Bike* (2009)

Conan Doyle, Arthur *The Adventure of the Solitary Cyclist* (1903); *The Adventure of the Priory School* (1904)

Crawford, Andrew *The Boys' Book of Hobbies* (Spring Books, 1959)

Crompton, Richmal *Just William* (George Newnes, 1922)

Dacre, Harry *Daisy Bell* (1892)

Day, Jon *Cyclogeography: Journeys of a London Bicycle Courier* (Notting Hill Editions, 2015)

Dollery, D.G. *Boy Scouts on Bicycles* (Cycling magazine, 1918)

Fabes, Stephen *The Wild Corner of Myanmar* published in *Adventure Cycling Touring Handbook, 3rd edition* (Trailblazer, 2015)

Forster. E.M. *A Passage to India* (1924)

Foster, George *George's Journey* (1899)

French, Sir John *The Cyclists of the Signal Corps* (War Illustrated, 1915)

Griffin, Hewitt *All England Series: Cycling* (1890)

Harcourt Williamson, Mrs F. *Dangerous Wide Spaces* (1897)

Hemingway, Ernest *The Sun Also Rises* (1926)

Hughes, Shirley *Hero on a Bicycle* (Walker Books, 2012)

Jerome K. Jerome *Three Men on the Bummel* (1914)

Keats, John *The Nothing of the Day* (1819)

Lawrence, D.H. *Sons and Lovers* (1936)

Lord, Stephen *Adventure Cycle Touring Handbook*, 2nd edition (Trailblazer, 2012)

Magorian, Michelle *Goodnight, Mister Tom* (Puffin, 2010)

Maugham, Somerset *Cakes and Ale* (William Heinemann, 1930)

Morton, R.H. *A Cycle Tour in Kashmir* (The Wide World Magazine, 1900)

Murphy, Dervla *Full Tilt: Ireland to India with a Bicycle* (Eland, 2010)

Neruda, Pablo *An Ode to Bicycles* (1956)

Newby, Eric *Round Ireland in Low Gear* (HarperPress, Harper Collins, 2011)

Paterson, A.B. 'Banjo' *Mulga Bill's Bicycle* (1896)

Richards, Frank *Billy Bunter's Diamond* (The Magnet, 1933)

Robins Pennell, Elizabeth *Over the Alps on a Bicycle* (T. Fisher Unwin, 1898)

Sayers, Dorothy L *Five Red Herrings* (Victor Gollanz Ltd, 1931)

Shaw, George Bernard Letter to the Sheffield Independent (1895)

Shield, Elizabeth *A Bike Ride Through the Countryside* (2010)

Spencer, Charles *The Bicycle: Its Use and Action* (1870)

Stafford, William *Smoke's Way* (Graywolf Press, 1975)

Sturmey, James Bicyclist's *Indispensable Handbook* (1882)

Swindley, H.J. *A Ride for a Wife* (Wheel World, 1881)

Tindal, Marcus *Self Protection on a Cycle* (Pearson's Magazine, 1901)

Thomas, Edward *In Pursuit of Spring* (1914)

Twain, Mark *What is Man? And Other Stories* (1893)

Wells, H.G. *The Wheels of Chance: A Bicycling Idyll* (1896)

Wiggins, Bradley *My Time* (Yellow Jersey Press, Random House, 2013)

Willard, Frances *A Wheel within a Wheel* (Fleming H. Revell Company, 1895)

Worth, Jennifer *Call the Midwife* (Phoenix, Orion Books Ltd, 2012)

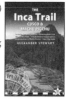

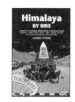

INDEX

The Wars of the Roses

The Wars of the Roses
Military Activity and English Society, 1452–97

Anthony Goodman

Routledge & Kegan Paul
London, Boston and Henley

To the memory of my mother

First published in 1981
by Routledge & Kegan Paul Ltd
39 Store Street, London WC1E 7DD,
9 Park Street, Boston, Mass. 02108, USA, and
Broadway House, Newtown Road,
Henley-on-Thames, Oxon RG9 1EN

Set in 10/11pt Plantin by
Computacomp (UK) Ltd
Fort William, Scotland
and printed in Great Britain by
Billing & Sons Ltd
Guildford, London, Oxford and Worcester

British Library Cataloguing in Publication Data

Goodman, Anthony
The Wars of the Roses
1. Great Britain — History — Wars of the Roses,
1455–1485
I. Title
942.04   DA 250

ISBN 0-7100-0728-0

4-21-85

Contents

Illustrations

Preface

Yet another book about the Wars of the Roses needs to start with an apology. For the battles have often been refought, and in recent years historians have gone far in reweaving the fabric of the political backcloths. Nevertheless, I felt it might be worthwhile to review in particular strategic, technical and logistic aspects of the wars which were important factors in them and in the evolution of English military skills. I have, besides, examined the tangled subject of the effects of the wars on society: I suspect that one important effect was to intensify feelings of regional particularism, facilitating Tudor rule over communities which found it hard to combine against the crown.

I owe especial thanks to Professor Kenneth Fowler for his comments on chapter 8, and to Dr Angus MacKay for introducing me to Mosén Diego de Valera's and Andres Bernaldez's lively reactions to the turbulent and ferocious English. I hope that my incidental remarks about institutions and society adequately reflect the stimulating teaching of my former colleagues Professor Ted Cowan and Professor Alan Harding, with whom I taught a senior course on such aspects of late medieval British society for several years. I am grateful to the officers of county record offices who have helpfully answered my inquiries about urban financial accounts – particularly to Jennifer Hofmann, Senior Assistant Archivist at the Dorset County Record Office, who brought the Bridport Muster Roll to my attention. Anna P. Campbell typed the manuscript with her customary skill.

But, above all, I owe thanks to the encouragement of my wife, Jacqueline, and to the patience of my daughter, Emma. Regrettably, my mother, Ethel Lilly Eels, did not live to see this book, to whose completion she looked forward eagerly.

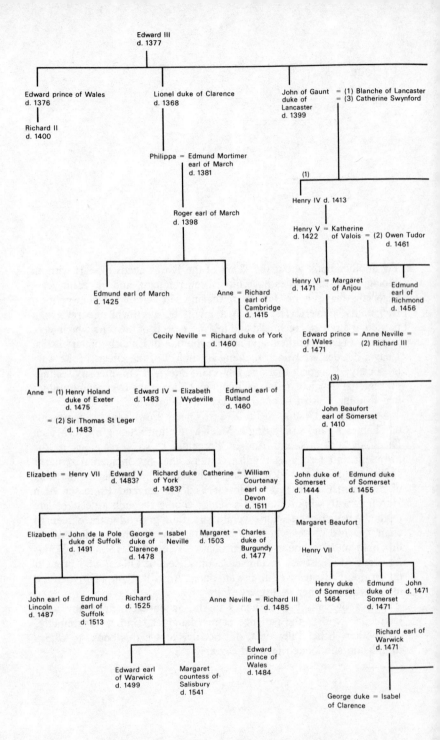

The succession to the English throne in the later fifteenth century

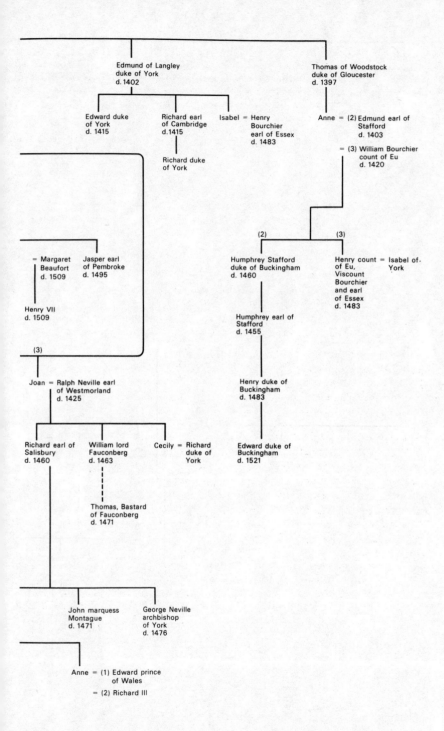

Introduction

'The Wars of the Roses' is the name commonly given by modern historians to campaigns in the second half of the fifteenth century which were fought mainly in England and Wales, but also spilled over on to Irish, French and Scottish soil, and had important international repercussions and involvements. Their starting-point has usually been taken to be the brief revolt in May 1455 headed by the richest secular magnate in the realm, Richard duke of York, a great lord in that part of Wales known as the Marches as well as in northern England. York was protesting against the enmity shown to him by those favoured by Henry VI, notably Edmund Beaufort, duke of Somerset.

Henry's grandfather, Henry of Bolingbroke, duke of Lancaster, had gained the throne in 1399 as Henry IV, by procuring the deposition of Richard II. The claim to the succession of York's uncle Edmund Mortimer, earl of March (whose heir York was), was passed over then. In 1459 and 1460 York again headed rebellions against courtiers and councillors whose hostility towards him was strongly sustained by the forceful queen, Margaret of Anjou. The wars began as a lengthy political, and eventually armed, struggle, predominantly for influence at court and in the localities, between alliances of magnates and gentlefolk. But after the success of the 1460 revolt York gave primacy to the dynastic issue. He laid claim to the throne in right of his Mortimer descent before parliament, which recognized that he should succeed Henry, displacing as heir the latter's son, the young Edward prince of Wales. Soon afterwards, however, York died fighting against the queen's and prince's supporters who opposed the parliamentary compromise.

In March 1461 York's eldest son, the earl of March, was acclaimed in London by his supporters as Edward IV. Though the young king speedily drove Henry and Margaret from the realm, it was not until 1464 that the last serious Lancastrian stir was defeated. Thereafter the queen and her son maintained a threadbare court over the water, a centre for intrigue, and Henry's standard was still on occasion defiantly raised in Wales.

The strenuous military and financial demands which Edward made on his subjects in order to oust the Lancastrians in the early 1460s disillusioned them with his rule, which consequently remained vulnerable. In the late 1460s Richard Neville, earl of Warwick, head of the magnate family which since 1455 had given the most notable support to the Yorkist cause, became alienated from Edward, whose favour to some other leading supporters – such as the kinsmen of his queen, Elizabeth Wydeville – provoked tensions. Warwick, like York in the 1450s, used his formidable prestige, wealth and local influence to instigate rebellions in 1469 and in March 1470, with the aim of establishing his primacy at court, in alliance with Edward's brother George duke of Clarence, who married the earl's daughter Isabel. Like York, but more quickly, the pair were driven to dynastic plotting, since their ostensibly 'reformist' agitation, with its aim of personal domination of the crown, received enthusiastic support widely only from the commons. In October 1470 Clarence and Warwick succeeded in driving Edward into exile and in restoring the passive Henry VI, who had been a prisoner in the Tower since 1465. This 'Readeption' of Henry, inspired by Louis XI of France, turned out disastrously for Warwick and his uncomfortable Lancastrian bedfellows. In 1471 Edward resolutely reconquered the realm, slaying in battle Warwick, his brother Marquess Montague, Henry's son Prince Edward, executing the last male Beaufort, Edmund duke of Somerset, imprisoning Margaret of Anjou and apparently having Henry murdered in the Tower.

For the rest of his life Edward's rule was not seriously challenged, but soon after his twelve-year-old son succeeded him as Edward V in 1483, Edward IV's surviving brother, Richard duke of Gloucester, usurped the throne. Within months Richard III faced and convincingly crushed a major rebellion, whose public aim was to put an obscure exile, Henry Tudor, on the throne. Henry claimed it in right of his mother, Margaret Beaufort, as the surviving male representative of the house of Lancaster. In 1485 he defeated and killed Richard at the battle of Bosworth, assumed the crown, and in January 1486 married Edward IV's eldest child, Elizabeth. Bosworth has often been taken by historians as marking the end of the Wars of the Roses, and the beginnings of a new era of relative Tudor political stability and internal peace.

Implicit in the phrase 'the Wars of the Roses' are the propositions that a number of campaigns occurring in a thirty-year period had a causal link, and that this link was the enmity between the houses of

Lancaster and York, symbolized respectively by red and white roses. In fact the white rose was only one of several badges used by the Yorkist family, and was to become the prime emblem of the distinctive dynastic links of some of their sixteenth-century descendants.[1] There is no definite evidence that Lancastrian princes and their supporters displayed a red rose. A mixed red and white one was invented for Henry VII and Elizabeth of York to symbolize the intention of their marriage to reconcile the two warring families. The mixed rose became a favourite Tudor emblem.[2]

Contemporaries have left few direct analytical comments about the wars as a whole, since a total concept of them was embryonic. A connection between troubles was perceived because of their relevance to disputes over the crown, whose rightful tenure was widely regarded as being of vital importance. Calamities were regarded as the inevitable corollaries of attempts to dethrone lawful kings and of rule by usurping ones. Also literary criticism and satire about the state of the polity – such as that in surviving English verses – shows the strength of contemporary convictions that there were other current disintegrative social trends: persistent royal failures to provide justice, burdensome royal financial demands, and the protection which nobles gave to law-breakers.[3] Some became concerned at the commons' propensity to rebel.[4]

One of the origins of later dynastic interpretations of the wars is to be found in the declaration of Edward IV's title to the throne in parliament (November 1461), where the usurpation of Henry IV was cloudily linked with all the troubles which the realm had experienced since 1399:

> whereof the heavy explanation in the doom of every Christian man soundeth into God's hearing in heaven, not forgotten in the earth, specially in this Realm of England, which therefore hath suffered the charge of intolerable persecution, punition and tribulation, whereof the like hath not been seen or heard in any other Christian Realm, by any memory or record.[5]

But to help justify Henry VII's rule, a non-dynastic explanation was put forward more specifically for the troubles in the thirty or so years before 1485 – an explanation providing the tenacious idea that Tudor rule had then ushered in, as pre-ordained, a new era of lasting domestic peace. Henry, born in 1456, the year after the first battle of St Albans, was of mixed Welsh and English parentage, with a strain of French royal blood from his grandmother Katherine of Valois, which he was to value highly.[6] In the 1460s he was brought up in the household of Edward's leading Welsh supporter, Lord Herbert. Henry's alleged descent from Cadwalader (who according to Geoffrey of Monmouth was the last king of Great Britain, driven out by the Saxons) may have made him especially aware of Welsh beliefs, based on prophecies, that a native prince would arise to crush the Saxons – predictions which some people associated with Edward IV's accession, and some, more briefly, with the Herberts' invasion of England in 1469.[7]

Henry's residence in Brittany (1471–84) and in France (1484–5), as a dependant of their respective courts, may have confirmed a tendency to view English history and politics in an alien interpretative and critical spirit. At the Breton court the legendary British history embodied in Geoffrey of Monmouth's *Historia Regum Britanniae* was cherished as a glorification of ancient Breton independence and greatness. In the definitive history of Brittany written in the late 1490s by Alain Bouchard with the encouragement of Charles VIII's queen, Anne duchess of Brittany, the struggles of the kings of Great Britain against the restless, perfidious Saxons were outlined, with the fall of Cadwalader.[8]

The British history also provided material for the French court's current interpretation of English history, which emphasized the violence and perfidy with which kings were habitually overthrown. This received new publicity in January 1484, when Charles VIII's chancellor, at the estates general of Tours, contrasted his happy accession with Richard III's murder of his nephews.[9] Henry Tudor's princely foreign patrons firmly believed in the ingrained political viciousness of the English, once more exposed in recent dissensions and usurpations. In this context he and they are likely to have been excited by the possible significance of his descent from Cadwalader, a sign that he was intended to restore the more Christian, more glorious polity of Great Britain.

The panegyric biography written for Henry the mature ruler by the French Augustinian friar Bernard André related the downfall of Cadwalader and emphasized Henry's descent from him. André also emphasized that Henry's destiny had been to calm the deep-rooted *saevitia Anglorum*, to block the influence of that *malignus spiritus* which had brought Britons and Saxons into collision, which had shown itself once more in the rage against Henry VI, and which Henry VII's English 'Juno', Edward IV's sister Margaret, dowager duchess of Burgundy, attempted to kindle against him.[10]

Henry's likely conviction that he had been divinely ordained to destroy the ancient vice, whose recurrence since Henry VI's accession had filled the realm with turbulence, is probably reflected in court verses celebrating a new era of peace, such as those written by Pietro Carmeliano and Giovanni de' Giglis, and in the florid address to Henry by Walter Ogilvie, written soon after James IV's marriage in 1502 to Henry's daughter.[11]

Thus the foreign elements in Henry's upbringing provided him with a novel sort of justification for his rule, focusing on the dissidence of the previous thirty years, and treating it as a distinct phenomenon terminated by what was implicitly alleged to be a 'new monarchy' – aptly symbolized by the ancient British name of Arthur given by Henry to his first-born son in 1486, by the imperial coin-image introduced possibly as early as 1487, and by the kneeling effigy of himself receiving the crown from God at Bosworth field which he willed to be placed over the most sacred shrine of English monarchy, St Edward's tomb in Westminster abbey.[12]

The view held at Henry's court that he had inaugurated a peaceful era after one of deeply entrenched division was to be powerfully developed in the early sixteenth century by Polydore Vergil in his *Anglica Historia*, and by Edward Hall's *The Vnion of the two noble and illustre famelies of Lancastre and Yorke*, published in 1548 by Richard Grafton. Vergil established the interpretation that the original cause of division was not *saevitia Anglorum*, but the usurpation of 1399. These views were to be propagated by the oft-printed chronicles of Grafton and Holinshed, and by Shakespeare's history plays, and were to be succinctly summed up by the phrase 'the Wars of the Roses', invented, apparently, by Sir Walter Scott.[13]

Recent historians have tended to play down the Tudor propositions that the wars were caused by the dynastic issue, and that they long engulfed society in chaos and misery. But they have mostly continued to see a value in looking at a scattering of conflicts over three decades as a whole, treating them as symptomatic of social, institutional and political tensions connected particularly with the role of the nobility. David Hume, in his *History of England*, had placed particular emphasis on the allegedly factious practices of the pre-Tudor nobility, and on how Henry VII's firm government induced cultural and social change:

There scarcely passed any session during this [Henry's] reign without some statute against engaging retainers, and giving them badges or liveries – a practice, by which they were in a manner enlisted under some great lord, and were kept in readiness to assist him in all wars, insurrections, riots, violences and even in bearing evidence for him in courts of justice. This disorder, which had prevailed during many reigns, when the law could give little protection to the subject, was then deeply rooted in England; and it required all the vigilance and rigor of Henry to extirpate it. . . . The nobility, instead of vying with each other in the number and boldness of their retainers, acquired by degrees a more civilised species of emulation, and endeavored to excel in the splendor and elegance of their equipage, houses, and tables: the common people, no longer maintained in vicious idleness by their superiors, were obliged to learn some calling or industry, and became useful both to themselves and to others.[14]

Hume's emphasis on the importance of aristocratic turbulence and its institutional forms was to be reinforced and refined by Charles Plummer's well-known critical edition (Oxford 1885) of Sir John Fortescue's brief treatise *The Governance of England*. Fortescue had been chancellor to Henry VI and his son Prince Edward in the 1460s: the *Governance* dates in its present form from soon after 1471, when Fortescue had perforce to accept Edward IV's allegiance. The work distils the mature reflections of a former chief justice of the King's Bench and royal councillor, about current problems of English monarchy which had absorbed his own career for at least a decade. He entitled his ninth chapter: 'Here he showith the perils that may come to the king by over mighty subjects':

> Whereof it hath come that often times, when a subject hath had also great livelihood of his prince, he hath anon aspired to the estate of his prince, which by such a man may soon be got. . . . For the people will go with him that best may sustain and reward them. . . . We have also seen late in our own realm, some of the king's subjects give him battle, by occasion that their livelihood and offices were the greatest of the land, and else they would not have done so.[15]

In his introductory discussion of this passage, Plummer put forward ideas about how changes in the system of military service in the fourteenth century increased the danger to the crown from the influence of 'over-mighty subjects': the reign of Edward III

> saw the beginning of that bastard feudalism, which, in place of the primitive relation of a lord to his tenants, surrounded the great man with a horde of retainers, who wore his livery and fought his battles, and were, in the most literal sense of the words, in the law courts and elsewhere, 'Addicti jurare in verba magistri;' while he in turn maintained their quarrels and shielded their crimes from punishment. This evil, as we shall see, reached its greatest height during the Lancastrian period.[16]

Plummer's casual phrase 'bastard feudalism' was to be given wider currency by the late K. B. McFarlane, who used it in his penetrating – and more sympathetic – explorations of later medieval patronage and clientage, especially in papers published in the 1940s, and in the Ford Lectures for 1953.[17] McFarlane bequeathed a new understanding of the social and political mechanics of later medieval aristocracy – in some ways a parallel achievement to Sir Lewis Namier's exposition of eighteenth-century 'connection'. In a similar vein, McFarlane regarded gentlefolk as generally motivated by self-interest rather than ideological conviction: the Wars of the Roses presented them with no 'cause worth dying for'; 'it is easy to see why opportunism rather than loyalty prevailed among those with most to lose, the heads of the great landed families'. He used the word 'opportunism' in a non-pejorative sense, taking a Whiggish view of noble patronage as social cement rather than (as Plummer) dissolvent. McFarlane denied that civil war was caused by the existence of armed bands of retainers or that it grew out of the local quarrels of magnates: the reason for central government's collapsing authority was the inanity of Henry VI.[18]

More recently, historians have illuminated facets of the politics of the nobility, and of the workings of 'bastard feudalism' in the period, confirming previous historians' insistence on their relevance to an understanding of the wars. Professor R. L. Storey has surveyed the widespread, increasing violence of 'faction' up to 1461, and, in a masterly biography, Professor C. Ross has shown how Edward IV gradually asserted his control over the disordered political scene.[19] Professor Ross has also written a succinct account of the Wars of the Roses.[20] The work of Storey and Dr R. A. Griffiths in particular has taught us much about the origins of the political instability of northern society, which was to help prolong the wars.[21] As yet less is known about political relationships in Henry VII's reign, though his methods of government have been studied exhaustively.

This book is intended to illuminate the Wars of the Roses through a study of the campaigns, military organization and methods, and social consequences. Indeed, the consequences were not as profound as those of the Hundred Years War in France, since commanders were especially concerned to keep campaigns brief and localized, and to minimize disruption of civilian life. But military activity does not have to be prolonged, wide-scale and devastating to produce significant social and political effects. As we are experiencing, late-twentieth-century society is vulnerable to mere threats from minute groups of terrorists. Normally, the main consequence of warfare for fifteenth-century society was the cost of sustaining soldiers, unwonted burdens on a largely subsistence economy. However few, however briefly engaged, the soldiers of the Wars of the Roses had to be armed, fed and billeted. Artillery, munitions, entrenching tools, transports and camp gear had to be assembled. The efforts required – even though no blows might be exchanged – had complex social effects, as did casualties, executions and forfeitures. An examination of such phenomena may help to explain the sixteenth-century conviction – transmuted by Tudor historians and poets into flights of classically inspired hyperbole – that recent ancestors had profoundly experienced the agonies of civil tumult.

Modern historians' concentration on socio-political aspects of the wars has led many to neglect their military context.[22] Indeed, patchy evidence about the armies and campaigns has been a deterrent to study – and has led all too often to surmise in the following pages. Contemporary descriptions of engagements are often so vague that it is impossible to pinpoint details topographically with assurance, or even fix on their sites. Changing land-usage has often altered sites drastically. But one can walk round the centre of St Albans and trace the course of the 1455 *mêlée*. One certain, relatively unchanged battle-site, Bosworth, has recently been adorned with flag-poles and notices purporting to explain the course of the battle.

It has generally been too readily assumed that military methods in the Wars of the Roses were of little intrinsic significance. Supposedly they were insular and conservative – surprising suppositions, considering that before the wars the English had been so heavily involved in Continental warfare, and that during them there were notable Continental developments in the roles of infantry, cavalry and artillery. In the later stages of the wars foreign mercenaries were particularly prominent. Scientific study of warfare was encouraged at the highest levels of English society, and mercenary service by veterans of the wars was valued on the Continent. It is argued in this book that the wars helped to adapt historic English military methods to what was required of expeditionary forces crossing the Channel to the Continent in the new military age of the Italian wars.

In this study, the period of the Wars of the Roses has been taken as running from 1452 to 1497, not from 1455 to 1485. The 1452 campaign – which Professor Storey has described[23] – was the first large-scale one, with more magnates and soldiers involved than in 1455. It ended without the threatened battle, but its military and political lessons had some influence on subsequent campaigns. In a long-term perspective the battle of Bosworth in 1485 marks a decisive turning-point – the inauguration of the Tudor dynasty. But it did not, as Henry VII's propaganda suggested, inaugurate an era of peace. His seizure of the crown prolonged the rebelliousness which had reappeared in 1483. In 1486–7 his rule was dangerously beleaguered. Perkin Warbeck's attempted invasions in 1495, 1496 and 1497 petered out so quickly that they have not been seriously considered as a phase in the wars. But the forces he mustered on each occasion were not negligible – they were just mustered to little purpose. Henry would have faced a more formidable dynastic rebellion in the 1490s but for his success in penetrating his opponents' plans and arresting noble dissidents. 1497, not 1485, is the year in which the last dynastic rebellion occurred.

With one major exception, the literary sources used in this study were all written in the fifteenth century. Persuasive details given by Edward Hall and later Tudor writers have been ignored, because it is impossible to check on the sources of much of their information. There is a large amount of historical writing surviving from the later fifteenth century, much of it anonymous and primitively annalistic in form and content. Historiography was in a transitional phase. The tradition of monastic chronicle-writing was moribund: only two abbeys provide important sources for the wars. Abbot Whethamstede of St Albans (d. 1465) compiled a *Register* concerned mainly with the abbey's affairs, written up in its surviving form after his death. This contains a valuable, independent account of national politics up to 1461, with vivid details about the battles fought, so to speak, on the abbey's doorstep in 1455 and 1461.[24] At Crowland abbey (Lincs.) continuations of older chronicles produced in the house were made in the fifteenth century, which are prime sources for the wars. The 'first continuation', compiled by a former prior, narrated events until Warwick's triumph over Edward IV in 1469. The 'second continuator', who wrote in more polished vein some time after April 1486, started his account of events up to that year in October 1459: weight is added to it by information derived from an anonymous doctor of canon law who had been a councillor of Edward IV.[25]

The writing of Latin chronicles had become rare outside as well as inside monasteries. A particularly valuable non-monastic example, with many unique details, is that ending in 1462 and transcribed into his commonplace book before 1471 by John Benet, vicar of Harlington (Beds.). The single author of this account of events from 1440 onwards was probably a cleric living in London, perhaps Benet himself.[26] Another Latin writer who contributed unique details of early stages of the wars was an annalist writing in 1491, whose account of events from November 1459 to May 1463 contains a number of autobiographical entries. K. B. McFarlane disproved the accepted ascription of the chronicle of which this forms a section to William Worcester, a gentleman-bureaucrat of literary and antiquarian tastes whose Latin notebooks contain information about some episodes in the wars.[27] Humanist Latin historiography was slow to take root in England, and had few major practitioners. The founder of humanist historiography there (as practised in the vernacular as well as Latin) was Polydore Vergil of Urbino. When he arrived in England in 1502, he already had a distinguished scholarly reputation; and with some encouragement from Henry VII, Vergil undertook to write a history of England from Romano-British origins to the present day. He completed a draft up to September 1513, which he subsequently altered and added to: the first edition was published in Basel in 1534. Vergil set new standards of literary elegance and interpretative coherence for English historians. For events of the later fifteenth century he obtained information from those who had held high office in the period. This is reflected in the many unique details which he gives of rebellions and campaigns of the 1480s and '90s.[28]

The most powerful influence on the form of chronicle-writing in the fifteenth century was the spread of vernacular literacy among secular elites of gentlefolk and citizens. Many of their commonplace books have survived, into which they copied or had copied material relating to history and politics, such as royal genealogies, exhortatory and satirical verses, and chronicles of Anglo-British history going back to mythical times, notably the *Brut Chronicle*, so called after Brutus, the legendary Trojan founder of the ancient kingdom of Great Britain. Owners were eager to bring chronicles up to date, copying sets of borrowed annals, sometimes making personal insertions as they copied, or composing their own continuations. The Wars of the Roses in themselves probably helped to stimulate these literary activities. The largest corpus of burgeoning contemporary or near-contemporary annals, overshadowing all others in bulk and influence by the later fifteenth century, were the 'chronicles of London'. Dozens of manuscripts of these survive, some of them continuations of the *Brut* or older city chronicles, all differing in various degrees, but inter-related in complex patterns. They were written in the first instance for or by London citizens and residents: their preoccupations are reflected in the prominence allotted to city as well as national affairs, and to the record of commodity prices and matters of urban gossip.[29]

The London chronicles have drawbacks as sources for national politics. They are mostly anonymous compilations, a patchwork of annals, and their authors characteristically lacked literary skill or good sources of information about court politics and distant events. The annals are consequently often a hotch-potch of bald and inaccurate facts. But their great value is that they reflect contemporary rumour and prejudice – the marked pro-Yorkist bias of London annals dealing with the events of the 1450s and early '60s is a pointer to opinion in the city. An example is *An English Chronicle from 1377 to 1461* (a continuation of the *Brut*), the last eleven years of which, the work of a single author, are fullest, and distinguished by their Yorkist fervour.[30] Strong personal opinions about events in the early stages of the wars (notably about the second battle of St Albans in 1461) are found in the continuations of a city chronicle to 1470, in a commonplace book written in a fifteenth-century hand. There is tantalizing evidence that one of its continuators may have been William Gregory, a skinner who was mayor in 1451–2.[31] These are London chronicles with an exceptional amount of unique information for periods of the wars. More generally in this book recourse has been had to a London chronicle which embraces their whole span, and contains a great deal of information found in other London chronicles – British Museum, Cottonian MS Vitellius A XVI, which C. L. Kingsford edited in *Chronicles of London* (Oxford 1905). The core of this is a version of what he termed the 'Main City Chronicle, 1440–85'.

One of the few vernacular chronicles of the period whose authorship is definitely known is the short but valuable one which John Warkworth, master of Peterhouse, Cambridge, tacked on to a *Brut Chronicle* which he presented to the college in 1483.[32] Warkworth gave an account of national politics from Edward IV's accession in 1461 to the end of the last rebellion against him, the surrender of St Michael's Mount in 1474. Warkworth coolly appraised Edward's fumbling responses to the problems confronting his early rule, and provides one of the few accounts of the struggles of 1469–70. Knowledge of some campaigns in this period is provided by two early manuscript examples of a genre which was to be stimulated by the growth of vernacular literacy and printing – the propaganda pamphlet. The *Chronicle of the Rebellion in Lincolnshire, 1470*[33] is a brief account of Edward IV's campaign in the shire and its aftermath, which makes use of rebel confessions to prove Clarence's and Warwick's complicity. Another, more polished and informative official account is the *Historie of the Arrivall of King Edward IV, A.D. 1471*, written by 'a servant of the King's that presently saw in effect a great part of his exploits, and the residue knew by true relation of them that were present at every time'.[34]

These two works have affinities with documentary genres, now written mainly in the vernacular, numerous examples of which survive – public proclamations and political manifestos, semi-public letters of denunciation and summons addressed to individuals, and private newsletters. All these were heavily utilized by chroniclers. The Castilian Mosén Diego de Valera incorporated the substance of his letter to the Catholic kings about Richard III's fall and Henry VII's early months of rule in his *Crónica de los Reyes Católicos*.[35] Newsletters, and news items in letters, are to be found in the English family collections of vernacular correspondence, which become a substantial source in the second half of the fifteenth century. Our knowledge of politics and domestic conflict in the period would be a great deal poorer but for the survival of its most voluminous correspondence, that of the Norfolk family the Pastons.[36] The fact that their propertied fortunes were especially bound up with magnate politics made them great retailers of political gossip. Shafts of information about politics can also be found in the correspondence of two knightly families, the Yorkshire Plumptons, dependants of the Percies, and the Stonors of Stonor (Oxon).[37]

The frequent international repercussions and involvements of the Wars of the Roses led not only to the writing of informative diplomatic reports about them by foreigners, but to mentions of them in foreign chronicles – particularly in the compendious and sophisticated works produced for the edification of courtiers and councillors by French and Burgundian historians. Thomas Basin, bishop of Lisieux, was interested in recording information particularly about Anglo-French relations in the 1460s;[38] Philippe de Commynes, in his celebrated *Memoirs*, made some characteristically succinct judgments about English politics and warfare.[39] In view of the close English links with the Low Countries, and the marriage of Edward IV's sister Margaret to Charles the Bold, duke of Burgundy, in 1468, it is not surprising that the official historiographers of the ducal house of Burgundy provide considerable information about English affairs. Georges Chastellain (d. 1475) provides some about early stages of the wars; his official successor and the continuator of his chronicle, Jean de Molinet (d. 1507) was interested in the invasions of England from 1485 onwards.[40] Another servant of the ducal house, Jean de Waurin (d. *c.* 1474) produced a collection of sources of English history from the earliest times (for which he depended heavily on the *Brut*) to 1471. The section from 1444 onwards is more original: it contains the fullest account of the wars from 1459 to 1471. He used the official accounts of the rebellion of March 1470 and of Edward's campaigns in 1471 – but the sources of most of his unique details (such as those of the battle of Edgcote) are unknown. Like Froissart when writing about English affairs from abroad, he demonstrably relied on muddled hearsay on occasion, and gave garbled versions of English personal and place-names. Possibly this is why his accounts have sometimes been neglected – an undeserved fate for the commentator with the best appreciation of military matters to write about a broad sweep of the Wars of the Roses.[41]

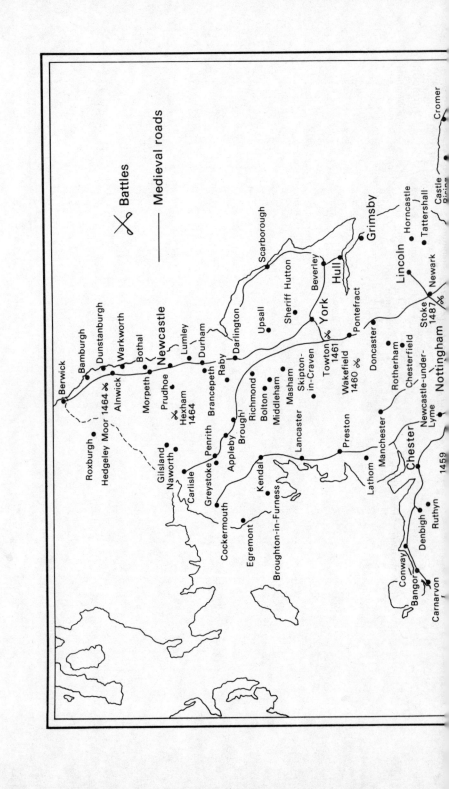

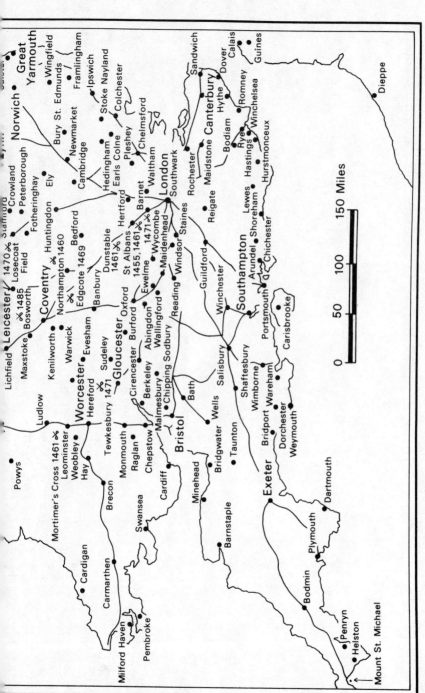

Map 1   *England and Wales during the Wars of the Roses*

Part One

The Campaigns

Chapter 1

Yorkist Rebellions, 1452–60

Richard duke of York's elaborate and widespread propaganda campaign in the winter of 1451–2 gave the court ample warning of rebellion. In September 1451 he wrote to towns and individuals in Norfolk requesting support for his aims. In November, according to later indictments, his chamberlain Sir William Oldhall was inciting uprisings in eastern England.[1] Tense reactions at court are reflected in a letter which the duke wrote to Henry VI from his castle at Ludlow on 9 January 1452. Informed that, as a result of defamations, Henry was displeased with him, he had declared himself a true liegeman to Reginald Boulers, bishop of Hereford, and the earl of Shrewsbury. He had asked them to report to Henry his willingness to swear his loyalty on the Sacrament in the presence of two or three lords, if Henry cared to send them to Ludlow.[2]

The duke is unlikely to have received such deferential treatment. He was visited by the mere clerk of the council, who set out from Westminster on 1 February to summon him to a council at Coventry.[3] The mission proved vain. York was on the verge of rebellion. On 3 February he wrote a letter from Ludlow castle addressed to the bailiffs, burgesses and commons of Shrewsbury, blaming the duke of Somerset for the great losses in France, and for the king's failure to implement the articles which York had put before him in 1450, and accusing Somerset of continually labouring about the king for York's undoing. Consequently the latter had 'fully concluded to proceed in all haste against him [Somerset] with the help of my kinsmen and friends'. He requested the town of Shrewsbury to send him in support as many 'goodly and likely men as ye may'.[4]

The clerk of the council, who returned to Westminster on 12 February, doubtless confirmed rumours of York's warlike intentions. There were reports, too, of stirrings in the West Country, where the earl of Devon was preparing to join the duke in arms: on 14 February the duke of Buckingham and Lord Bonville were appointed chief commissioners to proceed against the rebels there.[5] Two days later the king rode northwards out of London, getting that day as far as Barnet, on his way to meet and consult with lords in arms, and perhaps to confront York, in case he advanced eastwards through the Midlands from Ludlow.[6] A peremptory royal mandate to Lord Cobham dated 17 February, upbraiding him for failure to attend the king like other lords who had been summoned, and enjoining immediate attendance, shows suspicion that he was involved in the rising.[7] The king headed for Northampton, where he stayed on 22–23 February, and 'took his counsel and sent for his lords'. He then turned back towards London, pausing at Dunstable, where he was well attended by magnates – the dukes of Exeter, Buckingham and Norfolk; the earls of Salisbury, Shrewsbury, Worcester and Wiltshire; Viscounts Beaumont and Lisle; Lords Clifford, Egremont, Moleyns, Stourton, Camoys and Beauchamp. By their advice he sent letters to the duke of York. These may have been carried by the envoys whom he dispatched to the duke – William Waynflete, bishop of Winchester, Viscount Bourchier and Lord Stourton. They relayed the royal prohibition of the rising: York tried to justify it and refused to obey. Henry also wrote, on 24 February, to the mayor, aldermen and commons of London, forbidding them to receive the duke.[8]

Henry's advance northwards and speedy concentration of formidable support posed a serious threat to the rising. Between 19 and 23 February there were Yorkist demonstrations in eastern England, but the assembly of the royal army may have deterred the demonstrators from moving westwards to join the duke.[9] York 'went another way' to avoid confrontation with the king, possibly through the southern Midlands, a convenient region in which to meet his southern allies, Devon and Cobham. The king's reversal of direction and message to the Londoners were probably responses to this Yorkist line of advance. The duke may have hoped to make Henry amenable by occupying the city. He and his allies sent a herald requesting the citizens to give them and their army passage. But the governors, obeying the royal command, refused and manned their defences. The Yorkist army abandoned the direct approaches to London, crossing the Thames into Surrey over Kingston bridge.[10]

York remained at Kingston for three days, perhaps waiting for reinforcements to come in, perhaps debating the next move, in view of the strength of royal support. But on 29 February, having traversed Surrey, the Yorkists arrived at Dartford in north-west Kent. The following day they were arrayed nearby at Crayford. Possibly they occupied ground between Crayford and the Darent estuary, with the Thames shore on their right flank, and on their left the river Cray, a tributary of the Darent crossed by Watling Street just south-east of Crayford church. York commanded the 'middleward', with Devon in command of a 'battle' 'by the South side' (bounded by the Cray?) and Cobham of one 'at the water side' (near the Thames shore?). There was a considerable array of ordnance – perhaps aligned in front of these positions in anticipation of a royal advance from the East along Watling Street.[11]

To counter York's move from Kingston to the vicinity of Dartford, the royal army had returned to London. Its 'foreward' had arrived there early in the morning of 27 February and passed over London Bridge, lodging in Southwark. The following morning it set out for Kent. That afternoon Henry VI reached London with the rest of his army, and lodged in Southwark at the bishop of Winchester's hostel by the church of St Mary Overy (now Southwark cathedral). Thence he dispatched bishops to negotiate with York. The latter 'said he would have the Duke of Somerset, or else he would die therefore'. His situation was not hopeless. Some chroniclers stress that he had a large, well-equipped army in a strong defensive encampment. Though the author of *An English Chronicle* said that his army was 'not strong enough for the king's party', the author of Arundel MS 19 said that allegedly he had as many soldiers as the king, and 'great stuff and ordnance'. Seven ships laden with 'stuff' kept open a line of riverine communication for the duke.[12]

On 1 March Henry moved from Southwark with his troops, to Blackheath, and over Shooter's Hill to Welling, where he lodged that day and the one following, about three miles from the Yorkist position. Bishop Waynflete of Winchester and the bishop of Ely, the earls of Salisbury and Warwick, Viscount Bourchier and Lord Sudeley rode to and fro from the king's camp as royal emissaries. Strenuous conciliatory efforts may have undermined the will of nobles on both sides to commence what promised to be bloody slaughter of their peers and kinsmen. The Yorkist lords' will to fight may have been sapped too by the amount and quality of noble support the king had rallied, and by the Kentishmen's failure to bring promised support. Henry, who hated the effusion of Christian blood, consented to receive York's petition. Terms were agreed on the afternoon of 2 March, presumably laying down conditions for York's reception, the disengagement of the armies and the right of Yorkist soldiers to unharmed egress. About noon the next day York, Devon and Cobham rode with forty horsemen into the royal army, which had withdrawn to Blackheath. The Yorkist lords knelt before the king, and the duke presented his articles of accusation against Somerset. To no avail: York was escorted to London, and before being allowed to return to Ludlow he was obliged to make public oath in St Paul's cathedral that he would never again instigate a rising.[13]

York's political humiliation stemmed from strategic failure. He had failed to co-ordinate the widespread stirrings which he had incited into a united movement. Constrained by the need to avoid outrageously rebellious behaviour, he did not move boldly against the king. The duke's unsure progress gave the royal commanders time to assess and respond to the challenge. The king's strategy may have benefited from the presence in his army of the most famous English soldier of the day, the venerable John Talbot, earl of Shrewsbury. The following year Talbot was to be killed at Castillon in Périgord, leading an Anglo-Gascon army as aggressively against the French as Henry's army had gone against York, and attempting an assault on a camp fortified with artillery like York's at Crayford.[14]

In his 1455 rising York avoided the mistakes of 1452. By basing it on the support of magnates coming from the remote north of England, instead of attempting to appeal widely to southern communities, he achieved a degree of surprise. By heading swiftly for the king's person, he kept the initiative. The campaign was one of the shortest in the Wars of the Roses. Henry, whose retinues were under Buckingham's command, was overwhelmed when defending the town of St Albans by York's forces and those of 'the captains of this field' under him, the earl of Salisbury and his eldest son, the earl of Warwick.[15] The king had set off from Westminster the previous day (21 May) on his way to Leicester. There he intended to hold a great council, which the insurgent lords feared might be turned to their disadvantage. About Christmas 1454 or New Year 1455, Henry VI had recovered from the mysterious illness which had incapacitated him mentally. The protectorship of the realm conferred on York to cope with the crisis had been terminated, and his deadly enemy Somerset had been released from prison and reinstated in favour at court. York and his Neville allies felt the situation to be intolerably threatening to their political interests.

When Henry set out from Westminster, he had fewer adult lay peers in his company than at Welling in 1452, and some of these may have come prepared to give counsel rather than military aid. Nevertheless, his tally of thirteen such peers was respectable, and there were well-founded hopes that he would soon be joined in arms by other lords and retinues, belatedly summoned to muster probably for his arrival at St Albans. In response to a royal mandate, the town of Coventry was preparing to send a contingent there, which was disbanded on news of the battle. The earls of Oxford and Shrewsbury, Lord Cromwell and Sir Thomas Stanley all arrived with contingents in the vicinity just too late to participate.[16]

The three Yorkist magnates probably had at most only four adult peers in their company, three of them minor barons.[17] But they had a larger army, perhaps outnumbering the king's, Mr Armstrong conjectures, by two or three thousand men. The date and place of their assembly is not known. A large number of the Yorkist troops were raised in the Marches towards Scotland. Warwick had 'the March men' fighting in his retinue, and the Northumbrian knight Robert Ogle led 600 'men of the Marches'.[18] Salisbury's castle at Middleham in Yorkshire, so often to be used as a rallying-point in the wars, is a likely place of assembly. The council knew of the rising by 18 May. On the 20th the Yorkists were as far south as Royston (Herts.) and on the 21st were at Ware. They may have been hoping to reach London before the king left, or were moving parallel to his intended route to Leicester because they were as yet hesitant about a direct confrontation. Moreover, York was particularly anxious to gain the duke of Norfolk's support, and felt perhaps that an easterly route would facilitate a juncture with his East Anglian contingents. In the event Norfolk brought a retinue into Hertfordshire, but remained militarily neutral.[19]

The king and his army spent the night of 21–22 May at Watford. Alerted about his advance there, the Yorkists had turned westwards from Ware in the direction of St Albans. When the king set out on his way there early on the morning of 22 May, news was brought indicating that the Yorkists were much nearer than expected. In a council of war, the duke of Buckingham argued in favour of pushing on to St Albans ($7\frac{1}{2}$ miles from Watford), confident that York would wait to negotiate.

This course was adopted, and Buckingham's assessment proved correct. The king's army moved unmolested into the town, which they 'strongly barred and arrayed for defence'.[20] The topographical spine of the town – which lacked stone fortifications – was formed by a south-west to north-east succession of streets running from the river Ver about 900 yards to St Peter's church. Holywell street, the road from Watford, climbs up from the river, with the abbey lands to the west of it, into the centre of the town, the market-place, which extends north-east as the broad St Peter's street. On the abbey and river sides, to the south-west, the ground slopes away steeply. But to the north-east the approaches are more level, especially to St Peter's street. Its wide northern end was particularly accessible: here 'at the barrier of the said town . . . which is high near the parish church [St Peter's]' York's emissary Mowbray Herald was challenged on one of his missions.[21] The comparative difficulty of assaulting the town up its western slopes – and the inherent danger of becoming involved in an assault on the abbey – probably determined the Yorkists' lines of attack from the east on the royal position centred on the market-place. The direction of their approach to the town inclined them the same way.

The Yorkist army arrived to the east, probably approaching from Hatfield, soon after the king was installed. They halted the length of a crossbow shot away, in Key Field, and barred exits from the town. The

Yorkist lords failed in their strenuous attempts to secure an undertaking from Buckingham that Somerset (in the royal army) should be imprisoned and tried: they were threatened with the penalties of treason. On the stroke of 10 o'clock, according to the *Dijon Relation*, battle commenced. York's main assault may have been around the barrier near St Peter's church. His attacks were frustrated: Lord Clifford 'kept strongly the barriers'.[22] Warwick attempted to break the deadlock by a diversionary attack to the south, through the back closes of Holywell street. He and his men

> ferociously broke in by the garden sides between the sign of the Key and the sign of the Chequer [inn signs] in Holywell Street; and anon as they were within the town, suddenly they blew up trumpets, and set a cry with a shout and a great voice. 'A Warwick! A Warwick! A Warwick!'[23]

Entering 'the other end of the town' (further south-west than expected?) Warwick's men disconcerted the defenders. When Ogle's Marchmen penetrated to the market-place, 'the alarm bell was rung, and every man went to harness, for at that time every man was out of their array, and they joined the battle anon; and it was done within di [a half] hour'.[24] The alarm bell may have been the early-fifteenth-century bell in the clock tower in the market-place, built between 1403 and 1412.[25]

The king's men had rallied desperately to defend Henry, who took his stand under his banner in St Peter's street. The Yorkists burst into the street in several places. Their opponents, hemmed in and densely packed, were unable to deploy effectively, and presented a good target for archers. They soon disintegrated into a rabble seeking mercy or attempting flight. Shamefully the royal banner was abandoned, propped against a house, and so was the king, his neck bleeding from an arrow wound, in a tanner's.[26] The author of *Benet's Chronicle* estimated that about 100 were killed in the battle.[27] Somerset, Northumberland and Clifford perished. Buckingham was among the prisoners, as was the king himself. He was escorted to the abbey, where the Yorkist lords treated him with due reverence. Next day they took him back to London.

The Yorkist victory was facilitated by royalist tactical miscalculations and failures. The crucial decision was the one pressed by Buckingham – to head for St Albans rather than make a stand on the way. He may have considered that, since the king's forces were probably outnumbered, it would be easier for them to hold out, well victualled and housed, in a town, until the anticipated reinforcements arrived. If this was his reasoning, he probably hoped that negotiations would meanwhile sap the Yorkist lords' determination to attack. Hence his willingness to hear their envoy, Mowbray Herald, and his insidiously tempting suggestion that they might retreat to Barnet or Hatfield for the night.[28]

Yet Buckingham's preference for a defence of St Albans had its disadvantages. When a king and his banner could be clearly viewed in the open field – as at Ludford in 1459 – his troops enjoyed a psychological advantage over rebels.[29] It is unlikely that the Yorkists attacking barriers and breaking down houses and pales at St Albans were daunted by a clear view of majesty. Moreover, an army in the field – particularly a small one, like the king's – could be more tightly controlled and mutually supportive than one strung out to defend a lengthy urban perimeter. The royal soldiers at St Albans had at most a few hours to familiarize themselves with the town and improvise defences. The failure to prevent or plug Warwick's breach in Holywell street, and the unpreparedness of many men to defend the market-place, imply serious defects in Buckingham's co-ordination of defences. Had he been able to prolong negotiations overnight, these might have been remedied. So might a possible fundamental tactical defect dictating the decision not to stand in the open: it is very likely that the royal army was short of archers.[30] But York did not oblige Buckingham by surrendering the initiative, as he had done in 1452. The Yorkist commanders daringly scrambled to the attack within hours of their arrival at St Albans: *their* gamble paid off.

No more fighting centring on the person of Henry VI occurred for four years. The Yorkists who had fought at St Albans were anxious to reaffirm their allegiance to the king and excuse themselves from blame for causing the disgraceful fight. A parliamentary Act of 1455 embodied a justification for their actions at St Albans and a pardon for nearly all the participants. In November York was appointed protector in parliament on conditions similar to those of 1454. But in February 1456 the king personally relieved York of the protectorate in parliament. The duke did not resort to extremes. His reluctance was shared by his opponents, headed at court by the queen, Margaret of Anjou.[31]

The circumstances which sparked off the Yorkist rising of 1459 had some resemblances to those of 1455. Several years of muted political tensions between the court and York and his allies erupted into violence after the king had held a great council at Coventry in the summer of 1459. York and his friends were conspicuous by their absence. At the queen's instigation, indictments were made against them.[32] According to the Act of Attainder passed on the leading rebels in the Coventry parliament the following November, the Yorkist lords planned to come in arms to Kenilworth, taking the king by surprise there.[33] If so, they probably had in mind their success of 1455. But Henry had advantages on this occasion. He was already centrally placed in the Midlands, whereas the Yorkist lords were widely scattered. York was in the Marches of Wales, probably at Ludlow; Salisbury was in Yorkshire at Middleham castle, and his son Warwick was across the Channel in his captaincy of Calais.[34] The king's councillors, with the lessons of 1452 and 1455 in mind, reacted promptly to the threat of a rising. They showed a disconcerting grasp of the strategic situation, giving priority to the need to move and recruit, and to isolate the northern Yorkists who had bruised the royal household so violently at St Albans.

Warwick, having to cross the Channel and traverse southern England to meet his allies, was a man in a hurry, with no time to attempt extensive Kentish recruitment. On 20 or 21 September he was admitted into London with a few hundred well-armed soldiers. He stayed in the city only for one night and next day rode out through Smithfield on his way to Warwick castle. Possibly that was the rendezvous for the Yorkist lords before their confrontation with the king at Kenilworth. In fact royal soldiers were active thereabouts. They were at Warwick before the earl's arrival, and he narrowly missed an encounter with Somerset at Coleshill. Warwick's small numbers, the lack of support from his allies, and the king's northward movement from Coventry determined his exit from the Midlands in another direction, towards the duke of York at Ludlow.[35]

Shortly before the earl of Salisbury set out from Middleham, the king, according to the Act of Attainder on the 1459 Parliament Roll, had taken the field with those lords about him, and advanced 'with great celerity' towards the earl's line of march. From Coventry Henry went to Nottingham, whence he summoned the Lancashire landowner Lord Stanley – and probably other northern lords – to bring military aid. The royal advance, according to the official version, caused Salisbury 'to divert from his first enterprise and purpose [i.e. to go to the king] and to take another way' to assemble with York and Warwick.[36]

Probably in order to block Salisbury, the king shifted his headquarters westwards, from Nottingham into Staffordshire. But Salisbury nearly got through unscathed to the duke of York at Ludlow. The king's main force was not responsible for his interception, but one raised mainly in the young prince of Wales's earldom of Chester, under commission from his father. In the prince's name the queen sent out from Chester urgent summonses for military support, to which there was a ready response from her 'gallants', the local knights and esquires among whom she had recently held open house, and to whom her son had given livery tokens depicting swans (a Lancastrian badge). Margaret and her son moved to Eccleshall castle (Staffs.), the residence of the bishop of Coventry and Lichfield, probably on their way to join the king.[37] But the prince's army apparently intercepted Salisbury without having linked up with the forces which the king was bringing. Moreover, it lacked an important component – the 2,000 Lancashiremen whom Lord Stanley had under arms. In answer to the prince's summons, Stanley sent only fair promises to Chester and Eccleshall, according to the charges brought soon afterwards against him in parliament. On the day on which the prince's forces fought Salisbury at Blore Heath (23 September), this circumstantial dossier alleged, Stanley lay idle with his men within six miles of the heath: in default of his aid, the king's people were 'distressed' there. Moreover, his brother William Stanley had sent reinforcements to the earl of Salisbury before the battle.[38]

There are no detailed accounts of Blore Heath.[39] Under the command of James Tuchet, Lord Audley (a prominent landowner in Staffordshire, Shropshire and Cheshire), the prince's army may have moved out from the neighbourhood of Eccleshall. They intercepted the northerners as they approached Market Drayton along the road from Newcastle-under-Lyme. Salisbury was forewarned of Audley's approach and tried in vain to negotiate an unmolested passage. Chroniclers had the impression that Salisbury was heavily outnumbered, though 'Gregory' was unique in thinking that he had only 500 men as against the prince's 5,000 – 'a great wonder that ever they might stand the great multitude not fearing'. He says that the battle lasted from one to five o'clock 'and the chase lasted unto seven at the bell in the morning. And men were maimed many one in the Queen's party.'[40] Perhaps borderers from the Anglo-Scottish Marches, as at St Albans, displayed their ferocious skills, this time against particularly green troops. The official account on the Parliament Roll does not minimize royal losses: Audley, and many Cheshire knights and esquires, were slain; others, including Lord Dudley, were captured.[41]

Salisbury spent the night a little further along the road to his objective, at Market Drayton. Morale was boosted by a congratulatory letter from Lord Stanley, promising future support, which the earl sent to Sir Thomas Harington. He showed it around, exclaiming, 'Sirs, be merry, for yet we have more friends.' But Harington was soon to be downcast. Next day he and Salisbury's younger sons Sir Thomas and Sir John Neville were captured in Cheshire, at Acton Bridge on the road between Nantwich and Tarporley. They may have been trying to get to Lancashire, seeking a haven for the brothers, who had been wounded in the fray.[42]

Their journey may have jeopardized their father's enterprise. For he lingered dangerously long at Drayton, perhaps in the hope of hearing news of his sons, or of distracting attention from their eccentric and hazardous movements. 'Gregory' believed that the earl narrowly escaped capture on the night after the battle:

But the Earl of Salisbury had been taken, save only a Friar Austin shot guns all that night in a park that was at the back side of the field [battlefield], and by this means the earl came to Duke of York. And in the morrow they found neither man nor child in that park but the friar, and he said that for fear he abode in that park all that night.[43]

Who was meant by 'they' in this passage? It is likely that they were part of the king's main force, belatedly arriving to reinforce the disarrayed Cheshiremen. That morning Salisbury was still at Drayton: a servant of Lord Stanley brought him a message there that his master had been summoned by the king, and that Stanley intended to ride to Henry with his 'fellowship', though he would continue to give the earl secret support. Stanley's abrupt change of conduct may have reflected the proximity of the king, and have snuffed out the embers of Salisbury's expectations of the previous night. The earl decamped from Drayton. It may have been a reflection of his haste that he left behind one of Lord Stanley's cooks, who had been wounded when fighting in William Stanley's company at Blore Heath. The cook was interrogated by gentlemen in the fellowship of one of the king's supporters, the earl of Shrewsbury, when they occupied Drayton.[44]

Salisbury's escape from the trap set for him was a measure of his desperate courage and that of his men. But fundamentally it resulted from failures to concentrate the much larger royal forces in time to stop him. The main army must have been near Salisbury's line of march, for, when the battle was fought, Henry was within ten miles of Blore Heath, and had on the day of the battle dubbed seven knights who fought there.[45] But the sources insist that the Cheshire army – handicapped by Stanley's absence – alone confronted Salisbury. Perhaps lack of co-ordination resulted from the separation of its command, nominally under the prince, from that of the main army. The Cheshiremen may have been eager to go it alone and their patroness, the queen, sympathetic in order to reflect honour on her son. Yet, even when the Cheshiremen had failed disastrously, the main command seems to have lost an opportunity to capture or rout Salisbury, resting with his battered force.

The sluggishness of Henry's command may have been increased by preoccupation with the need to co-ordinate the probably large number of noble retinues which he was soon to lead against the duke of York.[46] The duke of Somerset – possibly bringing a West Country contingent to join the king – was only at Coleshill in Warwickshire soon after 21 September, perhaps on the day of Blore Heath.[47] On 7 October the earl of Northumberland, his brother Thomas Percy, Lord Egremont, and Ralph Neville, earl of Westmorland, probably the leaders of the king's northern contingents, rode through Nottingham.[48]

The first known action of the united forces of Warwick, Salisbury and York was their move, probably from Ludlow, to the neighbourhood of Worcester. Their objective may have been to block a royal advance south from Drayton into the Midlands, which threatened to confine them to the Marches and cut them off from London and their English sympathizers. Probably on the road between Kidderminster and Worcester, the Yorkist army barred the way to the king's. Henry and his lords advanced to the attack with the royal banner displayed. York, not wishing to fight the king, retreated to Worcester.[49] This display of reluctance added credence to the indenture to which the three Yorkist leaders subscribed by oath after receiving the Sacrament in Worcester cathedral. In this they asserted their obedient respect to the royal 'estate and to the pre-eminence and prerogative thereof'. The dispatch of the prior of Worcester and other divines to present the indenture to the king seems to have had no effect on royal strategy. Henry advanced on Worcester: the duke retreated again, south to Tewkesbury.[50]

Henry, though he amply displayed his wonted mercy during and after the campaign, may have been in an uncharacteristically bellicose mood, moved by the slaughter of his faithful lieges, especially those dear to his wife and child, at Blore Heath. Whilst he paused at Worcester to take counsel and refresh his foot soldiers, he studied military problems, probably having in mind particularly those posed to his many hastily raised and ill-equipped levies by Salisbury's patently formidable company, and the professionals whom Warwick had brought from Calais. He considered accounts of past deeds in many annals, and was above all struck by the passage in the classic military textbook, Vegetius' *Epitoma Rei Militaris*, in which he affirmed that a small well-trained force usually defeated a large but inexperienced one, as the example of the ancient Romans' conquests of more numerous peoples showed.[51] The decision to send Richard Beauchamp, bishop of Salisbury, to the Yorkist lords with royal offers of pardons if they submitted was probably made at Worcester. This amnesty was publicly rejected on their behalf by Warwick. The king's army advanced on the Yorkist position at Tewkesbury. The Yorkists crossed the Severn and headed for Ludlow, with Henry in pursuit.[52]

The Yorkist retreat across the Severn was the turning-point of the campaign. York's decision to defend his Marcher lordships against plundering and confiscation involved the abandonment of immediate hopes to gain a wider spectrum of English support.[53] He and his colleagues may have hoped that the relative inaccessibility of Ludlow would shake off pursuit by a large army. But by 10 October the king was at Leominster. On that day the Yorkist leaders addressed a letter to him from Ludlow, protesting their loyalty and their intent to 'the prosperity and augmentation of your common weal of this realm', in accordance with the terms of the Worcester indenture and their subsequent letters to king and lords, and a message conveyed by Garter King of Arms. In effect, they served notice of their intention to defend themselves against royal attack.[54]

South of Ludlow, on the opposite side of the river Teme, near Ludford Bridge, the Yorkists were drawn up on 12 October. According to the official account, they 'fortified their chosen ground, their carts with Guns set before their Battles, made their Skirmishes, laid their Ambushes there, suddenly to have taken the advantage of your Host'. These traps, and the customary skill with which York had chosen his position, slowed royal progress. Because of the 'impediment of the ways and straitness [narrowness] and by let of the waters, it was nigh even' before the king was able to get his men into battle order and his tents pitched. He had it proclaimed within the enemy's earshot that whoever came over to him would be pardoned. The Yorkists fired their guns at his lines.[55]

Despite the strength of the Yorkist lords' encampment, that evening they considered their troops' morale to be critically low. An accumulation of factors contributed to this. It was probably clear that the king had a much larger army.[56] Salisbury and Warwick, dashing to link up with York, had not had time to recruit extensively in their 'countries', but the king's circuitous journey through the Midlands had given him the opportunity for widespread recruitment. The Yorkist lords probably had as scant support from their fellow peers as at St Albans: only two adult ones, both relatively insignificant, participated – Clinton and Grey of Powis. The king is likely to have been supported by an impressive number of peers and their 'fellowships'.[57] The Yorkist army had endured a prolonged retreat in face of the king's advances, involving at least one demoralizing failure to stand up to him in the field. Discontent may have been long simmering among Warwick's Calais soldiers at being brought into the field to oppose their royal master. Dissension in the ranks may have come to a head with the appearance of the 'army royal' in battle order at Ludford and the spread of rumours about the royal offer of pardons.

The Yorkist lords allegedly resorted that day to the desperate expedient of bringing persons before their soldiers who swore that Henry was dead. If so, this carried little conviction. Many deserted, to take advantage of the king's mercy – under cover, probably, of fading light. The key desertion, according to several chronicles, was that of Andrew Trollope, who led over a group of Calais soldiers.[58] The Yorkist leaders certainly left precipitately. According to the official version, about midnight they pretended that they were going to 'refresh' themselves across the river in Ludlow. Leaving their army arrayed with standards and banners flying, they fled from the town with a few companions. Desertion from the field when the banners were flying, as Dr Keen has shown, was regarded as particularly ignoble.[59] York made his way to Ireland, where he had been well liked as royal lieutenant, with his second son Edmund earl of Rutland. His eldest son, Edward earl of March, with Salisbury and Warwick, managed to reach Calais. But on the morning of 13 October, York's shamefully deserted army had to capitulate, and the king's men occupied Ludlow. Many of the leading Yorkists who were to purchase pardons were probably captured then. The king dismissed his arrays, by now weary and undisciplined, and returned to Worcester. The sudden end of the campaign may have come just in time to prevent his army from disintegrating, after the privations in which he had shared, eloquently outlined on the Parliament Roll:

> not sparing for any impediment or difficulty of way, nor of
> intemperance of weather, jeopardy of your most Royal person, and
> continuance of labours thirty days or thereabouts, not to rest any one
> day where Ye were another save only on the Sundays, and sometime
> as the case required lodged in bare field sometime two nights together
> with all your Host in the cold season of the year.[60]

The crown still had the problem of rooting out the fugitives from their havens overseas. Arguably the royal councillors underestimated the rebels' ability to maintain themselves there, and to organize an invasion. Such laxity is not the impression given in the poem *Knyghthode and Bataile*, a vernacular treatise on warfare based mainly on Vegetius' precepts. This was composed probably in the period between the Yorkist lords' flight to Calais and their return to England in June 1460. It was intended by the poet's patron, Viscount Beaumont, for Henry's edification.[61] The anonymous poet was above all concerned with the military and naval problems posed by the Yorkist occupation of overseas posts, drawing out lessons from recent as well as classical campaigns. He probably reflected military thinking current among magnates with influence in the royal council, and their wish to stiffen Henry's martial backbone.

His councillors were confronted with the difficulties of striking at the Yorkist bases in wintertime, probably with financial resources depleted by the costs of the recent campaign. They persisted doggedly with measures of defence and attack.[62] In November measures were being taken to fit out a force of 1,000 at Sandwich (Kent) to recover Calais, commanded by Somerset (the son of the duke killed at St Albans), who had officially superseded the attainted Warwick as its captain. But when the duke appeared before Calais, he was resisted by the garrison and deserted by some of his ships. With Trollope in his company, he was lucky to secure Guines castle.[63] Thence the pair of them harried the

Yorkists in Calais, a thorn in their side, posing a threat to the loyalty of the Calais garrison.[64] Meanwhile efforts had been made in England to reinforce Somerset and check Warwick's privateering navy. On 10 December orders were given for the muster near Sandwich of forces commanded by Lord Rivers and Sir Gervase Clifton. But soon after Christmas, John Dinham and a force sailing from Calais surprised the defenders of Sandwich in a pre-dawn attack, capturing Rivers and 300 of his men (15 January 1460).[65]

The failure of royal plans to recover Calais and the appearance of Yorkist forces on English and Welsh soil in the New Year may have led the council to give priority to naval action, in case of an invasion attempt in the spring. The author of *Knyghthode and Bataile* certainly envisaged the final defeat and submission of the attainted lords as taking place in a vigorously imagined naval battle.[66] On 1 February Sir Baldwin Fulford was empowered to keep the seas, and on 19 March the duke of Exeter, admiral of England, contracted to do so for three years. Their forces were ready by the third week in April. Preparations may have been spurred on by news presaging a Yorkist initiative: Warwick boldly sailed from Calais to Ireland, where by 16 March he was reunited with the duke of York.[67] In his absence Somerset attacked. But his loss of many men near Newnham Bridge altered the balance of forces in the March of Calais decisively in Yorkist favour.[68] However, around 25 May royal forces again took the initiative. Exeter embarked from Sandwich with fourteen ships and 1,500 men. Tension probably mounted along the south coast, especially in the Cinque Ports. It may have been about then that Rye corporation paid 6d. to John Pampulon for his trouble in sailing to Camber to inquire for news of Warwick from mariners coming from the west. Flosie, mariner of Rye, received 8d. for his expenses in going to Lydd to inquire what was the great fleet at sea. The duke of Exeter may have had good intelligence about Warwick: his timing was superb. About 1 June he sighted the earl's ships, returning from Ireland, off the Cornish coast. But the duke, despite superior force, showed no more eagerness to attack than the earl. One chronicler says that Exeter lacked confidence in his men's loyalty: he put in at Dartmouth and discharged them, short of victuals and pay. Perhaps Exeter would have been better advised to send reinforcements to the duke of Somerset during Warwick's absence – which had been causing tension at Calais. His fleet's collapse opened the Channel to Yorkist invasion, for subsequent royal naval activity was negligible, as a result, probably, of lack of funds.[69]

Somerset had not been completely neglected by the crown since the reverse at Newnham Bridge. On 23 May Osbert Mountfort, esquire, and John Baker were appointed to take reinforcements to him. Mountfort collected several hundred men at Sandwich, where they waited for a favourable wind, intending to escort Somerset back from France. He had presumably concluded that his presence in England was militarily more crucial. But Mountfort apparently failed to take adequate precautions against another cross-Channel attack on Sandwich. This is extraordinary, for he was a professional soldier – he had been marshal of Calais in 1452. One might have expected the recent capture of Rivers at Sandwich to have been much in the minds of its defenders. The author of *Knyghthode and Bataile* may have been alluding to it:

> For fault of watch, has worthy
> >   not mischieved
> Now late, and all too soon?
> >   Is this not proved?

Nevertheless, in June Lord Fauconberg (Salisbury's brother), Dinham and Sir John Wenlock sailed across and seized Sandwich (which had stone fortifications), capturing Mountfort. Dinham and Wenlock re-embarked, but Fauconberg garrisoned Sandwich. The Yorkists were once more embattled on English soil. This proved to be the spearhead of their invasion from Calais.[70]

Fauconberg's temerity signalled a striking revival of Yorkist opportunities. The Yorkist lords had taken unseasonable risks which had paid off handsomely. Royal councillors had certainly been tireless in devising counter-measures. But there had been a dismal series of royal failures, partly perhaps because no magnate was prepared to co-ordinate efforts in a recalcitrant region – and because some of those willing to captain wearisome and sometimes unglamorous enterprises showed incompetence. Buckingham, as constable of Dover castle and warden of the Cinque Ports, and a noble of some popular repute, would have been well placed to direct south-eastern efforts.[71]

As a consequence of royal failures and Yorkist improvisation, the Calais lords were able to maintain their outpost gallantly through the winter of 1459–60. But their future, and York's, remained dubious. They were cut off from their main regions of territorial influence, which the crown and its partisans gobbled up. Their fellow magnates remained ranged against them, though the sympathies of some may have been veering their way. No foreign power offered real help, though Warwick set store by the projects of the legate Francesco Coppini, bishop of Terni, who hoped by such partisan schemes to favour Milanese diplomatic interests rather than the reconciliatory papal ones he was supposed to forward.[72]

Yorkist political and military strategy was probably concerted during the Irish conference. It was decided to launch appeals championing popular grievances, more in the style of 1452 than of 1455 or 1459. According to Waurin, a decision was taken at a council of war in Ireland, and confirmed in Calais, to invade England, despite the strong feeling in Calais that Guines should be dealt with. York was to land in the north, the Calais lords in Kent.[73] They were doubtless aware of the grudging response on the south-east coast to measures against them. In Kent the habit of criticizing the court, which had erupted particularly in 1450, may have again intensified in the winter of 1459–60, because of the unseasonable attempts to raise soldiers, sailors and finance against Warwick, popular as a result of his naval attacks on aliens. Royal attempts to cut English communications with rebel Calais may have been particularly annoying in east Kent, for which it was in some respects a commercial and social centre.[74] According to 'Gregory', the Yorkist lords

> sent letters unto many places of England how they were advised to
> reform the hurts and mischiefs and griefs that reigned in this land;
> and that caused them much the more to be loved of the commons of
> Kent and of London; and by this means the commons of Kent sent
> them word to receive them and to go with them in that attempt that
> they would keep true promise and as for the more part of this land
> had pity that they were attaint and proclaimed traitors by the
> Parliament that was held at Coventry.[75]

In a series of articles addressed to the archbishop of Canterbury (Thomas Bourchier) and the 'Commons of England', York, March, Warwick and Salisbury said that they had sued to come into the king's presence, to declare to him a comprehensive list of ills afflicting the realm. But the earls of Shrewsbury and Wiltshire, and Lord Beaumont, 'our mortal and extreme enemies, now and of long time past having the guiding about' Henry, would not allow him to receive them, as he wished. These evil counsellors dreaded that oppressions would be laid to their charge. They had procured the condemnations in the Coventry parliament 'to the intent of our destruction and of our issue, and that they might have our livelihood and goods'. The Yorkist lords declared that they would offer again to come into the royal presence and declare these mischiefs 'in the name of the land', humbly suing remedy. They requested assistance and gave fulsome assurance of their faithful allegiance.[76]

This manifesto probably accompanied, or shortly preceded, their renewal of domestic conflict in June 1460. Near the end of the month March, Salisbury and Warwick, supported by their former prisoner, Audley, joined Fauconberg at Sandwich with their main force, estimated by one contemporary as 2,000 strong.[77] On 26 June, according to the chronicler John Stone, they approached Canterbury.

Next morning those appointed by the king to resist – Robert Horne, John Scot and John Fogge – met them at St Martin's church outside the walls, and negotiated the city's surrender. Despite their local renown, these Kentishmen can have had little hope of standing up to popularly supported lords of the king's blood, especially when two Kentish peers, Cobham and Abergavenny, were about to join the Yorkists, or perhaps had already done so.[78]

The Yorkist lords summoned help from the Cinque Ports. The mayor and bailiff of Rye, receiving a letter from March and Warwick summoning them to Canterbury next day, prudently dispatched Morris Gedard by boat to Winchelsea, to inquire whether the mayor and bailiff there intended to answer a similar summons.[79] The Yorkist lords, having paid their respects at the shrine of St Thomas of Canterbury, moved swiftly via Rochester and Dartford towards London, recruiting by the time they arrived on Blackheath what contemporaries considered to be a large army. Meanwhile the government of London, as in 1452, had taken measures of safeguard. But in the two days before the army reached the banks of the Thames (1 July), Common Council changed its mind and negotiated terms of admission with the lords. Next day the bishops of Ely and Exeter met the lords in Southwark and accompanied them across London Bridge. This was a crucial bloodless victory for the Yorkists. Had the mayor and commonalty accepted the counsel of those who urged them to lay guns at the bridge to keep the Yorkists out, a delay diminishing their chances of victory might have been imposed.[80]

The sudden capitulation of London was a blow to the king's party – and apparently an unexpected one.[81] There were a reasonable number of loyal peers in or near the city, though no leading lay magnate. The lieutenant of the Tower was the energetic veteran Lord Scales, eager to take command of the city and keep the rebels out. He was joined by Jean de Foix, earl of Kendal, and Lords Delaware, Lovell, Hungerford and Vescy.[82] One might have thought that their presence, the relative proximity of the king in the Midlands, and memories of the Kentishmen's conduct in 1450, would have kept the citizens in their resolve not to admit the Yorkist lords. But we know that they were divided in opinion.[83] One reason why the appeasers among them won the day may have been fear of the London commons. The latter 'would not have' Scales as captain of London.[84] Perhaps, as initially in 1450 and 1471, they were sympathetic to the Kentish rebels. Moreover, the city government may have been swayed by more weighty Yorkist sympathizers. Several peers in the vicinity were about to join the Yorkists in arms, or had already done so – the archbishop of Canterbury's brother Viscount Bourchier, Lords Abergavenny, Clinton, Say and Scrope. It was a fortunate conjunction for the Yorkists that the convocation of Canterbury was then meeting at St Paul's.[85] For even bishops opposed to them found it hard to stand out against the exhortations of the papal legate in their company. On 4 July, in full convocation at Paul's Cross, Coppini published the text of a lengthy letter to Henry VI echoing the Yorkist case, which was immediately dispatched to the king.[86] Whilst in London, March, Salisbury and Warwick swore an oath in St Paul's, in the presence of Archbishop Bourchier and two bishops, that they intended nothing contrary to the estate of King Henry.[87]

Henry had been in the Coventry region from the latter part of May, showing concern for defence measures. On 11 June a royal proclamation had been issued denying the Yorkist allegation that he had not freely consented to the attainders of York and his partisans enacted in the Coventry parliament of 1459, and bidding obedience to commissioners of array.[88] Henry may have stayed in the Midlands because his councillors considered, not unreasonably, that the main threat lay in a landing by York in Wales to raise support in his former Marcher lordships in order to strike at the court as he had attempted in 1452 and 1459. His supporters had been active in Wales as recently as the month of March.[89] Till the end of May it may have seemed less likely that the main threat would come through Kent from Calais, since Exeter had his powerful fleet based on Sandwich, and Warwick lingered in Ireland. The deterioration of Somerset's position, the collapse of Exeter's and Mountfort's commands, and the speed with which the Yorkists invaded Kent so soon after Warwick's return from Ireland may have taken the court by surprise.[90]

Probably in response to the invasion, the king shifted his base nearer London, from Coventry to Northampton.[91] But he made no attempt to recover the city or relieve the beleaguered Tower garrison.[92] The royal army covered the southern approaches to Northampton, on the banks of the Nene, across the river from the town, in an encampment positioned rather like York's at Ludford Bridge. The royal commanders may have wished to use the formidable arsenal accumulated at Kenilworth, difficult to transport far, and to wait for more distant regional contingents. In answer to summonses, Shrewsbury dispatched fifty-one men, and Beverley (Yorks) twenty.[93] Soon it was to be rumoured in London that the duke of York was about to invade. In the royal camp there may have been fears that, if the king moved further south, the duke might intercept or deter remoter supporters.[94]

The Calais lords did not waste time waiting for York. Their objective, once they had gained entry to London, was to reach the king before the bulk of his supporters could rally – as they had failed to do the previous year when he was in the Midlands. Their concern about being vulnerably bogged down before an impregnable royal redoubt may be reflected in the report that they feared that Henry and his army intended to withdraw to the Isle of Ely, 'where the king's counsel had proposed as was said to have left the king and for their strength and safeguard thereto have hidden'.[95] As early as 5 July, according to *Benet's Chronicle*, Fauconberg set out from London northwards with an advance-guard of 10,000.[96] Salisbury remained in London with 2,000 of the Yorkist army and the city forces, to safeguard London and besiege the Tower.[97] The main army, under March and Warwick, set out for St Albans, meeting reinforcements on the way, and spending the night there. They went on to pause two days at Dunstable, allowing contingents to assemble.[98] The first Yorkist soldiers arriving near the royal encampment at Northampton may have occupied Hunsbury Hill, to the south-west, whence they could keep it under observation.[99]

The sight may well have been a daunting one. The king, according to a pro-Yorkist London chronicler, had 'ordained a strong and mighty field beside a nunnery, having the river at his back'. His position was entrenched and provided clear fields of fire for his batteries. It was in low fields on the river bank, with Delapré abbey to the west, Sandyford mill to the east, the river Nene to the north, and open fields rising to the village of Hardingstone to the south.[100] Sticking to their manifesto and their oaths, the Yorkist lords attempted, as on previous occasions, to negotiate the peaceful presentation of their petitions to Henry. The fact that they were accompanied or joined by the papal legate, the archbishop of Canterbury and a bevy of mostly sympathetic bishops gave them a powerful mediating hand. But the envoys whom they sent, bishops and heralds, got nowhere. Buckingham in particular was credited by chroniclers with a brusquely dismissive attitude.[101] He was probably supported in this by his sons-in-law Shrewsbury and Beaumont, and by Lord Egremont.[102] They may have feared that the pious king would give in before formidable clerical pressure. On the 1459 campaign he had shown himself eager to pardon the rebels – and in the different circumstances of that campaign his mercifulness had been an effective weapon. Beaumont's concern about Henry's readiness to believe the honest intent of his adversaries is probably reflected in the recent warning to him in *Knyghthode and Bataile* against oaths sworn on the Sacrament 'thy true intent for to beguile'.[103]

Fears of Henry's pliability may have been a principal reason why Buckingham and his fellow magnates rejected the good reasons which they had to temporize. For the royal army was outnumbered: contingents were still on the way.[104] Besides Buckingham, his two kinsmen and Egremont, there was only one other lay peer in the king's company – Edmund Grey, lord of Ruthin. But the Yorkist leaders, for the first time, had a respectable company of lay as well as clerical peers with them – Viscount Bourchier, and Lords Abergavenny, Audley,

Fauconberg, Say, Scrope of Bolton, possibly Clinton, and perhaps even Stanley.[105]

But there were other likely reasons for the royalist readiness to give battle. Buckingham and his colleagues may have misjudged the strength of their encampment and the loyalty of the soldiers. They may have been impressed by the urgent need to relieve the beleaguered garrison in the Tower, and by the opportunity to defeat March and Warwick whilst they were separated from York and Salisbury. Despite the presence of eminent veterans in the Yorkist army, notably Bourchier and Fauconberg, the king's command may not have been over-impressed by its leadership. Warwick's performance at Ludford had been lamentable, and March was young and untried. Buckingham may have misread Warwick's frenetic attempts to put the Yorkist case to the king as a sign of weakness.

The battle was fought on 10 July 1460, less than three weeks after the main Yorkist landing in Kent.[106] According to Whethamstede, the Yorkist lords divided their army into three 'battles' (*turmae*), the first commanded by March, the second by Warwick and the third by Fauconberg. These, he says, did not attack in turn, but simultaneously, along different sections of the entrenchments. In order to overcome a difficult obstacle, the Yorkists took advantage of their superior numbers, making an enveloping assault.[107] The heavy rainfall put the royal artillery out of action, and also probably made the entrenchments sodden and slippery. Progress was made by the attackers when the soldiers of Lord Grey, commanding the 'vaward', helped them up, in accordance with his prior understanding with Warwick. This precipitated the collapse of the royal army. Within half an hour or so of 2 o'clock, when the assault commenced, the battle was over, a cheap victory for 'the true commoners of Kent', to whom it was attributed soon afterwards in some anonymous celebratory verses.[108] 'So few men slain in so great a fight', rejoiced the poet. The Yorkist casualties were negligible, but a number of royal soldiers perished in the pursuit, many of them drowning whilst trying to escape through the swollen river near Sandyford mill.[109] According to one London chronicler, Buckingham, Shrewsbury, Beaumont and Egremont were slain by the Kentishmen beside the king's tent; according to another, Buckingham was slain 'standing still at his [own] tent'.[110] The king was captured by an archer, one Henry Mountfort. Warwick, March and Fauconberg found Henry sitting in his tent. They showed him due obeisance. He was escorted first to Delapré abbey, then to Northampton. Within a few days the lords took him to London, where the Tower garrison soon capitulated.[111]

The battle of Northampton was a day's work in some ways reminiscent of that at St Albans five years before. The fact that Henry

and his faithful nobles were trapped near the tents suggests that they did
not anticipate that they and the main 'battle' needed to be ready to engage. The vanguard, as was to be so often the case in the Wars of the
Roses, was to fight beforehand. The débâcle compounded military and
political miscalculations. If the guns had cut Warwick's men up badly,
Grey might not have given the order to help them. The reason why he
was granted command of the vanguard is puzzling. He was less
distinguished by rank and military experience than other peers present.
Perhaps the honour was conferred on him for his prompt assistance to
the king.[112] Since he had considerable landed power in neighbouring
parts, he may have staked a claim to high command by bringing along
many of his tenants. Even without Grey's treachery, it is likely that the
Yorkists would have won at Northampton, through weight of numbers.
But the battle would have been longer and bloodier: there would have
been less chance for the Yorkists to emerge personally unscathed, with
the king a prisoner and all the opposing nobles dead.

The aim of the lords who rose in arms in the period 1452–60 was
simple and consistent. They wished to go to the king and get him to deal
satisfactorily with grievances which they had against other nobles. They
went in this politically explosive manner because they were convinced
that it was the only way in which to make their influence felt in royal
council and court. Their imperative need was to take the king by
surprise – a difficult task, since they had to organize military
contingents from their several 'countries'. Once the king had had time
to summon the superior forces he could command, and put his
opponents publicly in the posture of rebels, their determination and that
of their men to confront the sovereign and other nobles in battle started
to decline. York, forced on the defensive by royal armies in 1452 and
1459, resorted to an expedient popular in Continental warfare. He
drew up his forces in a fortified camp, defended by entrenchments and
batteries, and on rivers which provided or protected lines of
communication. He doubtless hoped that royal commanders would be
deterred from making potentially bloody assaults with hastily raised
levies, and would therefore become more amenable to political
compromises. In 1452, when he was entrenched at Crayford, the king
was certainly prepared to negotiate a settlement. York may have
believed, mistakenly, that he had won concessions. But at Ludford
Bridge the royal army seems to have been more willing to assault field
fortifications. They were never tested, as a result of the disintegration of
Yorkist morale.

But the defensive encampment was not discredited, at least among
royal councillors. Their concentration of artillery at Kenilworth castle
suggests their belief that the king needed a defensive base, centrally
placed, to guard against threats from different directions, and to which

reinforcements could be summoned from different parts of the realm. The circumstances before the Yorkist invasion in 1460 particularly fitted in with this concept. It was applied at Northampton by Buckingham, Shrewsbury and Beaumont who, taught in the same school of warfare as York, resorted to his expedient of the armed encampment.[113] The utter débâcle which they suffered there, though stemming only in part from inherent military problems, may have finally discredited such defensive strategy in the eyes of younger nobles, such as Somerset, Exeter, Warwick and March, who were to play dominant roles in the next stages of the conflict.[114]

Chapter 2

The War of Succession, 1460–1

The consequences of the battle of Northampton differed greatly from those of the first battle of St Albans. The latter had so shocked contemporaries that it had ushered in a period of political compromise, leading eventually to the new court ascendancy against which York rebelled in 1459. But the compromise after Northampton rested on a novel, even more unstable basis – the recognition of Yorkist dynastic claims. York's acceptance as Henry's heir in parliament in October 1460 immediately provoked a struggle for the crown, a war of succession, producing widespread involvement and lasting bitterness as it developed into what some contemporaries regarded as a war of the north against the south.[1] Once the dynastic issue had been raised, with such dramatic and extreme consequences, it was hard to bottle up again, and, in various guises, it was to be a long-lasting problem in English politics and a principal cause of the recurrence of the wars.

The duke of York returned to England in September 1460. He was determined never again to be treated as a political outcast and branded as a traitor. The only way which he could fix on to prevent this was to put forward his own claim to the throne in parliament, despite adverse reactions, even among some of his closest allies. By the compromise Act of Settlement (10 October), Henry was to keep the throne for life, but York and his heirs were recognized as Henry's heirs. This cut out the claims of Henry's son, Edward prince of Wales. Such disinheritance was totally unacceptable to the boy and his mother, who after Northampton had fled with him from Eccleshall through Cheshire and taken refuge in a Welsh castle.[2] It was also unacceptable to a formidable body of magnates who had not experienced defeat at Northampton or been present in parliament to accept the settlement. The queen consulted Henry's half-brother, Jasper Tudor, earl of Pembroke. She summoned Somerset, Devon and Sir Alexander Hody to meet her speedily with armed companies, informing them that Exeter, with

Lords Roos, Clifford, Greystoke, Neville and Latimer, were to meet her at Hull. Similar summonses were sent to her chief officers. Somerset, who had surrendered Guines to his opponent Warwick, had returned to England about 21 September and taken up residence at Corfe castle (Dorset). He and Devon, with a strong force including many western knights and gentlemen, moved via Bath, Cirencester, Evesham and Coventry to York. The concentration in Yorkshire of an army from different regions (though mainly from the north) out of the campaigning season was a striking achievement, a measure of the fury caused by the Act of Settlement. According to the Londoner 'Gregory', it was achieved in such secrecy that the duke of York and his supporters were taken unawares.[3]

The Yorkist lords could not ignore such a challenge in their own 'country'. Early in December, York secured a loan of 500 marks from the Common Council of London towards the expenses of his intended campaign – though their grant was only half what he had requested, since he would not provide satisfactory securities.[4] The Londoners watched York riding off through Cheapside with a few hundred men, accompanied by Salisbury with at most a hundred. Recruiting on the way, they went northwards, passing through Nottingham, and in three or four days arrived at the duke's town of Wakefield, in or by which their forces encamped. They had already suffered a reverse. According to the *Annales*, their 'aforeriders' (*praeeuntes sui*) were killed by Somerset's men at Worksop (Notts.).[5] York and Salisbury seem to have underestimated Lancastrian determination to force the issue, and the strength the queen's captains had to do so. Lord Neville visited the duke of York, receiving his commission to array under pretence of being an ally, but joined the enemy with his recruits. Somerset also visited the duke and arranged a truce to last till after Epiphany.[6] Nevertheless, on 30 December the Lancastrians launched a full-scale attack at Wakefield. They fielded a respectable array of peers with their retinues – Exeter, Somerset, Devon, Northumberland, Clifford, FitzHugh, Greystoke, Neville and Roos. York and Salisbury had no adult peers in their company.[7] Waurin has a circumstantial but largely uncorroborated account of the ruses which the Lancastrians employed to undermine Yorkist defences. The day before the attack, they had insinuated 400 of their best men into the duke of York's garrison, welcomed by it as a reinforcement from Lancashire. At dawn more Lancastrians, under Trollope's command, appeared before the defences, claiming to be reinforcements for York, and flaunting Warwick's badge of the ragged staff. This lured the unsuspecting duke out to greet them. Somerset's men then attacked, aided by all the pretended reinforcements.[8] Writers in southern England lacked convincing details of the engagement. They were uncertain which side had numerical superiority.[9] The Milanese agent Antonio della Torre, in a letter of 9 January 1461, gave a version which had probably circulated in London. York and Salisbury, he said, were three times stronger than their adversaries, but gave them opportunity to attack through lack of discipline – they allowed a large part of their force to go pillaging and searching for victuals.[10] Whethamstede had heard that the northerners had attacked in bad faith, before the day agreed for battle, when they realized that the southerners were foraging without proper precautions.[11]

To southern writers the battle was a disaster – 'execrabile bellum' in the author of the *Annales'* phrase. Many Yorkists were killed. Among the dead in the field were York, Salisbury's son Sir Thomas Neville, Sir Thomas Harington, Sir Thomas Par, Sir Edward Bourchier, Sir James Pickering and Sir Henry Retford. In the pursuit Lord Clifford killed York's young son Rutland on Wakefield bridge. That night Salisbury was captured by a servant of Trollope and was executed next day at Pontefract.[12]

The Wakefield campaign reveals a new style of military leadership among the Yorkists' opponents – devious, inventive and quick to exploit opportunities. The complacency shown by York and Salisbury over Christmas may have stemmed partly from a failure to grasp that they were dealing with opponents no longer prepared to keep faith with them. But, even during periods of truce, lax discipline within a few miles of the enemy was militarily inexcusable. The Yorkists, unlike their opponents, do not seem to have reconnoitred well. Moreover, their strategy was fundamentally flawed. They lost, as the bishop of Terni wrote, because they made a 'rash advance'.[13] It was imprudent to advance into enemy territory and there remain passive. York might have been better advised to halt at Doncaster, or even at Nottingham, accumulating supplies from the south and tempting the northern army to take the offensive in less favourable circumstances. But he led his army to Wakefield, according to Whethamstede, in order to have better lodging.[14] A middle-aged man who had returned from exile to his greatest political triumph, he may not have relished this irritating, unseasonable campaigning, consoling himself with the prospect of celebrating the New Year peacefully in one of his own castles. His men could expect a better welcome in his lordship. He and Salisbury were doubtless anxious to rescue their Yorkshire tenants from the harassment which they had endured.[15] Such considerations may have inclined the Yorkist leaders to commit a cardinal military sin – the underestimation of their opponents. The Lancastrians had, indeed, recently lost some of their most experienced and forceful captains (Buckingham, Shrewsbury, Beaumont and Egremont); and two of their present commanders, Somerset and Exeter, had recently failed dismally.

The quality of the northern command was again demonstrated after Wakefield in their ability and determination to launch an invasion of the south in midwinter, culminating in a second victory only about seven weeks after the first. The queen, 'Gregory' exaggerated, 'came ever on from the journey of Wakefield till she came to St. Albans'. The northern army, said another London chronicler, 'came down suddenly to the town of Dunstable'.[16] The Yorkist leaders had set in motion widespread defence measures, and heightened tensions, by encouraging the belief that the queen's army of northerners was licensed to plunder the south.[17] On 5 January 1461 Warwick, Bourchier and Lords FitzWarin and Rugemont-Grey came before the London Common Council, and had a gratifying response to their request for a loan for the defence of the realm. Two thousand marks were at once granted by unanimous consent.[18] On 12 January a civic assembly at Norwich considered a royal demand for military aid dated 3 January, and decided to engage and finance a company of 120 men in response.[19] On 17 January the royal council ordered the burgesses of Stamford (Lincs.) to co-ordinate local defences.[20] On 23 January Clement Paston wrote from London: 'I have heard said the further Lords [the queen's supporters] will be here sooner than men wean, I have heard said, ere three weeks to an end.'[21] On 28 January the royal council drafted letters to county arrayers and to the urban officials of Bury St Edmunds and Ipswich (Suffolk), Salisbury (Wilts.) and Colchester (Essex) requesting them to hasten contingents: the council had sure knowledge that the 'misruled and outrageous people in the north parties' were coming.[22] On 5 February the royal council ordered Sir William and Thomas Bourchier and other arrayers to call together the Essex lieges and bring them to the king.[23] On 12 February a civic assembly at Lynn (Norfolk) ordained measures for the defence of the urban constabularies under the captain appointed, and for the keeping of night watches.[24] John Devyn, warden of the town of Henley (Oxon.), paid out of his own pocket the costs of having a watch kept in the guildhall and of having staples and rings made for the bars of the bridge over the Thames.[25]

The effects of the widespread measures stimulated by the king's council may have been to thwart the plans of the queen's sympathizers in the Midlands and south. This deprived the northern army of one vital source of support, just as the earl of March's rout of the army coming to its aid from Wales was to knock away another. Yorkist propaganda's success has concealed the fact that the queen had support in the Midlands and southern England. Amongst those who were attainted for fighting for Henry in March were twenty-four whose residence was given as being in those parts.[26] The council had certainly feared subversion in the regions under its control as well as their invasion. On 12 January the bailiffs and constables of Kingston-upon-Thames

(Surrey) were commissioned to arrest and imprison anyone uttering false news and carrying bills and letters to disturb the peace. On the 20th Richard Hotoft and the sheriff of Leicestershire were ordered to suppress dissentients who made unlawful gatherings or hindered those coming to defend the king. On 3 February Sir John Howard was appointed to head a similar commission in Suffolk.[27] On 28 January and 7 February measures were ordered to prevent the shipment of victuals to the rebels from Norfolk and Cambridgeshire respectively.[28] There may have been a Norfolk conspiracy to aid the northerners. On 7 February the council gave orders for the seizure and garrisoning of Rising castle.[29] The youngest John Paston's remarks in an undated letter probably have a bearing on this order: 'there is at the Castle of Rising, and in other two places, made great gathering of people, and hiring of harness, and it is well understood they be not to the King ward, but rather the contrary, and for to rob.'[30] Rising castle was the residence of one of the best-known partisans of the Lancastrian court in Norfolk, Thomas Daniel, esquire.[31] He had been associated with William de la Pole, duke of Suffolk's, government of Norfolk in 1447–8.[32] In 1449 he was squire for the king's body and in 1450 steward of the duchy of Lancaster beyond Trent.[33] In December 1451 he was closely associated with the duke of Somerset, father of the queen's leading partisan in 1461.[34] In a letter written by Friar Brackley to John Paston senior probably in October 1460 he is denounced as one of her partisans in Norfolk about whom Brackley wanted Paston to warn the earl of Warwick. If the friar was not exaggerating, there was dangerous anti-Yorkist activity in the shire. He names Bishop Lyhert of Norwich and the dowager duchess of Suffolk among the disaffected.[35] Daniel was to be attainted for fighting in the Lancastrian cause at Towton in March 1461, and in 1464 he was said to be in Cheshire, involved in the rising associated with Somerset's pro-Lancastrian treason.[36] It may be that before the queen's army came south Daniel was a leader of a Norfolk conspiracy to support it, whose success would have been a considerable aid.

That there was a sound basis for the fear of the queen's army felt in the south is shown by the pillage carried out at Beverley (Yorks.) by Lord Neville's soldiers on 12 January.[37] Plundering *en route*, the army advanced south via Grantham, Stamford, Peterborough, Huntingdon, Melbourn (Cambs.), and Royston, then turned west to Luton (Beds.) and on 16 February defeated the defenders of Dunstable.[38] On 12 February Henry VI and the duke of Norfolk had led one retinue out of London through Barnet, linking up at St Albans with one which Warwick had led out on the same day through Ware.[39] The earl's preliminary line of advance may have been a precaution in case the northerners failed to swing westwards to St Albans, as he had swung when advancing from Royston in 1455. The difference was that, unlike the king on that occasion, he now easily beat his opponents to St Albans. Nevertheless, as 'Gregory' makes clear, Warwick failed to realize how near the northerners were to St Albans on the 16th.[40] The Yorkist leaders thought that they had time to shift their main position: 'The lords in King Harry's party pitched a field and fortified it full strong, and like unwise men brake their array and took another.'[41] The new position was $1\frac{1}{2}$ miles north-east of St Albans, on Nomansland Common, west of Sandridge.[42] Why was there a radical change of plan? The original Yorkist position may have centred on St Albans, in whose market-place Warwick had signally helped to hem in the king's army in 1455. Warwick now led a much larger army than the king had had then, with levies from Kent and neighbouring shires, London and East Anglia.[43] Since the leading magnates with him – the dukes of Norfolk and Suffolk, and the earl of Arundel – lacked his military experience and repute, they probably deferred to his judgment.[44] Warwick may have become convinced that the army needed to occupy a larger, flatter and more open ground in order to deploy properly. The new choice of field implies the expectation that the northern army would advance on St Albans down either the Luton or the Wheathampstead road, threatening the town from the north-east. Thus the move perhaps indicates indecisiveness and hidebound thinking on Warwick's part.

Opposed to him were Exeter, Somerset, Devon, Northumberland, Shrewsbury and Lords Clifford, FitzHugh, Grey of Codnor, Greystoke, Roos, Welles and Willoughby, most of them recently engaged at Wakefield.[45] The Lancastrian command, showing the flair which Waurin attributes to them at Wakefield, were able to achieve a degree of surprise by moving on the town of St Albans along the Dunstable road, from the north-west, so threatening the main Yorkist position from the rear, on 17 February. The fullest account of the battle is that by Abbot Whethamstede of St Albans, who had known the ground since childhood and was at the abbey during the fighting.[46] He says that the northerners got into St Albans, but were forced back to the western outskirts by the fire of a few Yorkist archers stationed at the Great Cross. The attackers managed to bypass this blockade of the centre of the town by getting up a lane which led to the northern end of St Peter's street, the street leading to the main Yorkist position. Before advancing on that, they had to overcome the stiff resistance of a company of commons who blocked their exit from the town. These delaying actions presumably alerted the Yorkist camp. The vanguard was got into the field to counter this unexpected attack from the south rather than the north. The defence was for a time well maintained, but suddenly collapsed. The Yorkist soldiers did not attempt to stave off their opponents in hopes of relief by reinforcements from their main 'battle'.

Instead they scattered in blind panic in all directions, pursued and slaughtered by northern horsemen, as the appalled bystander Whethamstede graphically recounted. Many were saved, he says, only by the fading light. The main Yorkist 'battle', guarding the king, melted away, leaving him in the company of a few apprehensive nobles. Soon he was to be reunited with his vengeful queen and triumphant little son.[47]

Scraps of information retailed by correspondents and chroniclers reflect contemporaries' awe, and in some cases fear, at the magnitude of the Yorkist disaster. Some attempted to explain it. The Londoner 'Gregory', possibly present among the city levies, railed at the scouts' incompetence, the commanders' untimely decision to shift camp, and the uselessness of the foreign gunners' paraphernalia.[48] Others blamed the defeat on the treachery of the captain of Kentishmen, Lovelace.[49] Two days after the battle an Italian correspondent relayed the generally accurate information which he had gleaned about it.[50] The battle had begun, he said, about one o'clock with a skirmish with the king's vanguard, and lasted until six. Despite the rout of the Yorkists and the loss of the king to their opponents, 'there is less harm done', he remarked mysteriously, because the Kentishmen, said to be commanded by the duke of Norfolk and the earl of Arundel, were not at full strength.[51] Prospero di Camulio wrote from Ghent on 9 March that many of the king's men at St Albans deserted for lack of victuals, and that Somerset attacked after midday with 30,000 horse. The duke wore down his opponents: Warwick decided to quit the field, by breaking through their lines (presumably, in order to get back to London). With 4,000 men he pushed into St Albans, but being heavily outnumbered withdrew to his camp. Hearing shouting thence to the queen's men, he feared treason and fled.[52] Warwick and most of his fellow nobles escaped. Lords Berners and Bonville, and Warwick's brother John Neville, were captured.[53]

According to 'Gregory', most of the northern army had proved useless: 'the substance that got that field were household men and feed men'.[54] The sources give the impression that the bulk of both armies was made up of hastily raised levies whom their commanders were unable to train, discipline or feed adequately. The disintegration of the northern army was well under way by the time it reached St Albans – success in the field, with the attendant orgy of slaughter and plundering, probably accelerated the process. The Yorkist levies, who had not come so far but may have been awed by rumours of their opponents' ferocity, disintegrated in the fight. Some, indeed, may have felt lukewarm about the Yorkist cause. One wonders how wholehearted the duke of Suffolk's retainers were, in the light of Brackley's doubts about the loyalty of the Suffolk political interest, and his opinion that it would be good for the young duke with his knights and esquires to use his spurs and prove in battle where his loyalty lay — though in fact he amply demonstrated himself a Yorkist in 1461.[55]

How did the Lancastrian commanders win with such a volatile army? They boldly exploited Warwick's strategic errors, concentrating their more reliable troops in a disciplined and well-led attacking group. Warwick and his colleagues proved unable to recoup initial mistakes by a similar concentration. Their spirited archers in the market-place at St Albans, the company defending the exit from St Peter's street, the good troops in the vanguard, and the foreign mercenaries, all seem to have fought without cover and reinforcement from their fellows. By getting the vanguard into line the Yorkist commanders reasserted some control, but after that their grip once again fatally slackened. In retrospect, it seems that Warwick was taking unnecessary risks by advancing to St Albans when he did, with the sort of forces he had. He might have won by sitting tight in London with a smaller and more reliable levy, and waiting for March's victorious army to arrive from the west before striking at exhausted and probably retreating northerners.[56] Such a course would have called for single-minded generalship which put strategic considerations before popularity. To some extent the Yorkists were victims of their own propaganda. Their emphasis on evil northern intents had helped to raise a large levy which it would have been difficult to maintain garrisoned in London. The fears there and in the neighbouring regions put pressure on Warwick to go out and repel the invaders long before they approached the city walls, thus enhancing his popular reputation. Ten years later, Warwick was to show that he had learned the wisdom of not always sallying forth to answer the call to battle, but instead braving reproaches passively behind city walls.[57]

'On an Ash Wednesday we lived in mykel dread', wrote a Yorkist versifier, recalling emotions felt the day after the second battle of St Albans.[58] Bishop Beauchamp sonorously recounted his experience of the 'general dread'.[59] The scattering Yorkist leaders were too demoralized to organize the defence of London. Mayor and aldermen kept the city under guard, and hastily opened negotiations for its surrender with the king and queen, who advanced to Barnet. They shared the citizens' anxiety about letting their undisciplined troops near London, and withdrew to Dunstable. Some of their men rode in to Westminster, but the prime royal concern seems not to have been to pluck the natural fruits of victory, by occupying the city. Rather, the Lancastrians were anxious to receive pickings in the shape of urban victuals. Whatever the reason for the Lancastrian command's priorities, their hesitation was fraught with danger when there was another Yorkist army — a victorious one — in the offing. The London commons were emboldened to prevent the dispatch of victuals by the city governors to the king and so hamper negotiations. Less than a fortnight after St Albans, March, accompanied by Warwick, who had met him in the Cotswolds, was welcomed into London at the head of his troops. If the Lancastrians had not already withdrawn northwards from Dunstable, March's arrival necessitated their retreat – a galling decision for mettlesome, victorious young nobles such as Somerset.[60]

Edward earl of March, York's eldest son, had celebrated Christmas at a friary in his father's town of Shrewsbury,[61] and it was probably there that he heard the terrible news of the deaths at Wakefield of his father, his brother Edmund, his cousin Thomas Neville and Neville's father Salisbury. March levied forces from various shires and was preparing to set forth against the northern army when he received news that the earls of Wiltshire and Pembroke had landed in Wales. Their intention, according to what Pembroke was to write on 25 February, had been to go to the king's support. March promptly reversed direction. He mustered his forces outside the town wall at Hereford, and at the beginning of February confronted the two Lancastrian earls at Mortimer's Cross on the river Lugg, about six miles north-west of Leominster. They were utterly defeated. Pembroke and Wiltshire managed to escape, but many of their captains were taken and executed. The engagement is one of the obscurest decisive battles of the Wars of the Roses. What is known about the leadership and composition of the armies suggests a Yorkist advantage.[62] March, though only eighteen, was militarily experienced. He had been present at St Albans in 1455 and Ludford Bridge in 1459, and had been a leader of the advance from Calais to Northampton in 1460. In his company at Mortimer's Cross were many from the Yorkist lordships in the Marches of Wales, probably keen not to see their estates overrun by their opponents and their local interests threatened, as were three leading supporters from the Anglo-Welsh border regions – Lord Audley, Sir Walter Devereux and Sir William Herbert. Other notable knights then with March were Lord Grey of Wilton, Lord FitzWalter and Sir William Hastings. But the Lancastrian force consisted chiefly of Welsh squires. Its leaders were militarily unimpressive. Pembroke had not yet distinguished himself, and Wiltshire's more prominent roles in 1455 and 1460 had provoked insinuations about his lack of martial attributes.[63]

March, as we have seen, speedily capitalized on his victory, averting the ruin staring his father's surviving allies in the face. The queen's cruel invasion, the horror at St Albans and the spiriting of the king northwards help to account for the readiness of many southerners to cast off their tenacious allegiance to the House of Lancaster and acquiesce in the acclamation by his soldiers of the little-known, youthful earl of March as Edward IV in London on 4 March. Despite the time of year, the insecure, fledgling king showed determination to proceed against his rival. There may have been fears of a renewed Lancastrian offensive. Henry's carver Sir Edmund Mountfort, Sir Harry Everingham and the prince of Wales's squire William Elton may have recently visited Coventry in the Lancastrian interest.[64] On the day after his acceptance of the crown, Edward wrote to the governors of Coventry exhorting them to keep the city safely against the rebels, and promising them relief if necessary.[65] On the same day the duke of Norfolk set off hastily into his 'country' to recruit.[66] On 7 March, Warwick left London with a large number of men to secure support in the Midlands; on the 11th the new king's footmen, mainly Welsh and Kentish, set out, and on the 13th Edward himself rode out through Bishopsgate.[67] He passed through St Albans, Barkway (16 March) and Cambridge (17th), where Sir John Howard met him with a contribution of £100 from the abbot and convent of Bury St Edmunds 'by way of love'. Contingents joined him *en route*.[68] He may have had a good deal of urban support. Coventry arrayed and financed a company of 100 men in response to his request of 12 March, and an anonymous poem on the battle of Towton may allude to the presence, besides, of contingents supplied by London, Canterbury, Bristol, Salisbury, Worcester, Gloucester, Leicester, Nottingham and Northampton.[69]

According to Waurin, reports reached Edward that Henry VI was based on Nottingham. Edward arrived there by 22 March, when it was reported that Somerset and Rivers were holding Ferrybridge on the river Aire. One might have expected the Lancastrians to try to hold the line of the Trent at either Nottingham or Newark, but perhaps they decided it was necessary to withdraw nearer York to 'refresh' their troops and link up with northern reinforcements. At a Yorkist council of war, the decision was made to advance to Ferrybridge.[70] Waurin, who gives unique details of the engagement, says that the Yorkist vanguard, commanded by the duke of Suffolk, fought the Lancastrians south of Ferrybridge – this may have been on 28 March.[71] The duke had halted within two miles of the enemy, but was drawn into battle in order to save his reconnoitring force, which had got too near the enemy. The vanguard threw the Lancastrians back to the southern end of the ferry bridge. Edward, informed of the encounter, came up with his main force. He said that the river passage must be gained and ordered an attack. The following month Bishop George Neville recalled what a stiff fight took place. The Lancastrians (presumably after withdrawing to the northern bank) sabotaged the ferry bridge. The Yorkists constructed a narrow raft to get their troops across, but their opponents seized it, and it was recovered only after bloody hand-to-hand fighting.[72] The Yorkist Lord FitzWalter was killed, and many of his men were killed and drowned; Warwick was injured in the leg.[73] The Yorkists got across the river, however, and encamped there amidst snow and hail.[74] A powerful Lancastrian force, with Somerset, Devon, Exeter and Lords Grey of Codnor, Willoughby and Roos present, had been worsted.[75]

The significance of the battle of Ferrybridge needs to be stressed. The Yorkists surmounted a highly defensible natural obstacle on the road to York. Their command demonstrated superior generalship – which Waurin attributed to Edward. The vanguard had been determinedly reinforced in order to gain a crucial advantage. But though the Lancastrian commanders on the spot showed equal determination, it seems that they were not reinforced by many of the nobles whose companies were in the field next day. An opportunity to tip the wavering balance in the fight at the ferry, and inflict a bloody check on Edward, seems to have been lost.

Next day (29 March) Edward's army was drawn up in battle array at Towton, near Sherburn-in-Elmet, about six miles north of Ferrybridge on the road to Tadcaster and York. Dr Richmond has listed eight peers in his company.[76] Opposing him in Henry's army were at least nineteen peers.[77] Contemporary correspondents and English chroniclers had little information about the tactics at Towton: they agreed in thinking that the armies were very large and that the death-toll was quite exceptionally large.[78] The governors of York recalled in 1485 that, whereas they had sent contingents of 400 to support the Lancastrians at the battles of Wakefield and St Albans, more than 1,000 men from the city went to 'the lamentable battle of Towton . . . of which many was slain and put in exile'.[79]

Waurin gives the one detailed account of the battle which, though largely uncorroborated, is followed here.[80] He says that Henry's vanguard, under Somerset, Exeter and Rivers, initiated the fight by attacking and putting to flight Edward's cavalry wing. They continued in hot pursuit, believing that Northumberland, in command of the main Lancastrian 'battle', had also joined the fray. But he was slow to engage. This gave Edward time to retrieve the situation, preparing and putting heart into his remaining troops. A tough struggle ensued, especially in Warwick's part of the line. Eventually the Lancastrians broke and fled. Many died on the road to York. At Tadcaster, according to George Neville, there were heavy drownings in the river Ouse, as the bridge had been broken down to stop the Yorkist advance.[81] The earl of Northumberland and Lords Clifford, Randolph Dacre, Neville and Welles were among the Lancastrian dead.[82]

Correspondents and chroniclers give a few scraps of information about the battle. According to Richard Beauchamp, the outcome remained doubtful all day. The author of *Hearne's Fragment* said that the battle was long, and that it snowed throughout. He believed that Norfolk's reinforcement of Edward during the fight with 'a band of good men' was important.[83] Though we cannot be certain why the Yorkists won, it may be that both sides had a problem in imposing command on exceptionally large forces – and that Edward achieved a unity of aim which eluded the huge number of peers fighting against him.

Next day Edward entered York, where he captured Devon and others, who had taken refuge in the old castle there but were apparently unable to withstand their opponents long enough to make terms. Devon and Wiltshire – a habitual fugitive whose luck had also run out – were executed.[84] Edward resumed the pursuit north of York, but returned there to celebrate Easter (5 April). Henry VI, Margaret of Anjou, the prince of Wales, Somerset and a few others had escaped to Newcastle, George Neville reported on 7 April. Exeter and Roos also got away. Edward raised new levies – a contingent went from Beverley – and after Easter passed through Durham to Newcastle, where he arrived on 1 May. He left next day, entrusting the custody of Newcastle to Fauconberg, and set out for Westminster and the coronation for which he had fought so tenaciously. Edward's striking victories had not brought him full control of the realm, however: he had failed to assert control of the Marches towards Scotland, probably because his troops and resources were exhausted.[85]

Why did the Yorkists win the war of succession in 1461 after the vicissitudes they had experienced? The forces which Edward confronted on the Yorkshire plains in March reflected, in their size and composition, the continuing strength of Lancastrian allegiances. At Towton Edward could muster probably fewer than half the peers that Henry could. Lancastrian commanders had recently inflicted shattering defeats on Edward's father and Neville kinsmen. The new Lancastrian leadership had displayed a more dynamic style of warfare than the static mode favoured by their predecessors at Northampton. Who was principally responsible for their ruses, surprise attacks and the daring winter march on London? Waurin rated highly the military partnership in 1459–61 of Somerset and his councillor, the veteran Trollope.[86] Waurin was not alone in singling out the fighting qualities of duke and esquire. Chastellain described Somerset as 'un des beaux jeusnes chevaliers qui fussent au royaume anglois'.[87] 'Gregory' was impressed by the duke's 'manly' assaults on Calais in 1459–60.[88] The author of the *Annales* remarked on his sterling support of Edward at the siege of Alnwick in January 1462 – and Edward's astonishingly favourable treatment of him showed how highly he valued his support.[89] Another English chronicler described Trollope as 'magno capitaneo et quasi ductore belli' at St Albans, and singled out his capture and wounding for comment.[90] 'Gregory' says that Trollope was wounded in the foot by a caltrop, and was the first of those knighted by the prince of Wales after the battle, to whom he declared, 'My lord, I have not deserved it for I slew but fifteen men, for I stood still in one place and they came unto me, but they bode still with me.'[91]

The dashing exploits of Somerset and Trollope may have masked and, indeed, exacerbated weaknesses and tensions in the Lancastrian command. 'Gregory's' testimony suggests that many of the northern levies had lost any military value by the time they reached St Albans. Waurin names southern lords as leading the attack at Towton, poorly supported by a force commanded by a northern one. Perhaps Somerset or a group of southern lords pressed bold courses on reluctant northerners who were dubious of the prolonged effectiveness of their forces.

The winter invasion of the south is the most striking strategic feature of the war of 1460–1. Persistence with it, after the suppression of southern and Welsh allies, was hazardous. Its failure exposed the queen's relative military weakness and created in the south a political climate for the acceptance of Edward's usurpation. He capitalized on this by mobilizing the superior resources of the richer parts of the realm in his control and striking swiftly at the Yorkshire heart of his opponents' resistance.

Thus the overthrow of the old Lancastrian leadership in 1460 had facilitated the emergence and dazzling successes of Somerset, a kind of Prince Rupert. But his efforts probably exhausted the resources of the Lancastrians' somewhat restricted provincial base of resistance. Moreover, the Lancastrian victories killed off or discredited the Yorkist leaders of 1455–60, facilitating the political and military emergence of Edward IV. His ability to organize armies and lead men to victory appeared conspicuously in 1461, strongly suggesting that he had considerable military talent, or recognized it in his counsellors, as Somerset did in Trollope.

and realm. Leaders of invading foreigners in 1487 and 1496 – Lincoln and Warbeck – showed awareness of the need to reassure subjects and protect them against their troops.

In the 1450s the Yorkist leaders had angled for foreign support, but it was Margaret who effectively 'internationalized' the domestic conflict.[1] The diplomatic precedents set by the Lancastrians in the 1460s after Towton were to be copied by those who wished to prolong dynastic strife for the rest of the century – for instance, there are many parallels between Lancastrian activity then and Yorkist attempts against Henry VII. Foreign rulers saw advantages to be gained in embarrassing English kings by aiding dynastic attempts. Plotters saw the foreign mercenaries and financial aid they could gain abroad as providing a more reliable backbone for domestic rebellion. Conversely, for English kings – for Edward IV in the 1460s and Henry VII in the 1480s and '90s – one key to dynastic peace came to be the establishment of good relations with neighbouring powers.

Frequent commissions of array in the spring and summer of 1461 testify to Edward IV's fears of insurrection and invasion. He had no certainty that Towton had halted the violent reversals of fortune of the last few years. The Lancastrian leaders showed no disposition to allow him peace.[2] His prolonged failure to consolidate his rule in the March of Calais must have seemed ominous, in view of the Calais garrisons' propensity to support rebellion as a means of getting wage arrears, and Charles VII of France's Lancastrian sympathies. In April 1461 a Lancastrian garrison in Hammes castle was besieged by Lord Duras, marshal of Calais, and Richard Whetehill, lieutenant of Guines. They raised the siege when Charles VII appeared with a force nearby. In July Duras, Whetehill and others were empowered to negotiate terms for the castle's surrender. But on 4 October it was reported that Sir Walter Blount, treasurer of Calais, was heavily involved in besieging it with a large force from the Calais garrison. Hammes was handed over by treaty by the end of the month – the defenders having first received £250 in Blount's name.[3]

But it was in the far north of England, in regions where many had allegiances to 'Lancastrian' families, and within reach of Scottish aid, that the first serious threats to Edward's rule developed in the summer of 1461. As early as 18 April Thomas Playter reported the story that the Lancastrians were hanging on to a Yorkshire castle and that its besiegers, Sir Robert Ogle and 'Conyrs' (Sir John Conyers?), had repulsed a relieving force led by Percy squires, inflicting heavy losses. The Percy force had been sent to 'bicker' with them, in order that King Henry 'might have been stolen away at a little postern on the back side. . . . Some say the Queen, Somerset and the Prince [of Wales] should be there.'[4] In fact Henry and 1,000 horsemen had entered

Scotland with safe-conducts by the first week in April. He, his wife, son, and principal lords, such as Somerset and Exeter, were honourably lodged there, and secured an offensive alliance with the regency government of the young James III, headed by his mother Mary of Guelders. In return, they ceded a great English prize to the Scottish crown – Berwick.[5] Probably in June 1461, Margaret, her son, Exeter, Lord Rugemont-Grey, Sir Humphrey Dacre, Sir Edmund Hampden, Sir Robert Whittingham, Sir Henry Bellingham and Sir Richard Tunstall crossed the Border with Scottish support, besieged Carlisle and burnt its suburbs.[6] On 3 June Edward IV wrote to Archbishop Booth of York ordering him to have proclamations made for his clergy to be ready to serve under Fauconberg and Warwick's brother Montague. On 18 June Coventry waged forty soldiers to serve under Warwick for twenty days.[7] Montague soon succeeded in worsting the besiegers of Carlisle and relieving the town.[8]

The Lancastrians promptly tried their luck on the eastern side of the Pennines, where they were probably well entrenched in Northumberland. Some of the Carlisle besiegers linked up with reinforcements, before advancing to threaten Durham, perhaps even hoping to move on York. On 26 June, 'Standards and Guidons' were raised at Ryton, and at Brancepeth, perilously close to Durham, by King Henry, Lords Roos and Rugemont-Grey, Dacre, Sir John Fortescue, Sir William Tailboys, Sir Edmund Mountfort, Thomas Neville, clerk, and Humphrey Neville, esquire, of Brancepeth. The attempt on Durham probably petered out because the bishop, Laurence Booth, held the bishopric's forces to Edward's allegiance – and because the Yorkist Nevilles were not far off.[9] On 28 August Giovanni Pietro Cagnolla reported from Bruges to the duke of Milan that Warwick had frustrated the Yorkshire Lancastrians' intention to rise.[10] Lancastrian strength in Northumberland faded. On 13 September Sir William Bowes assumed the keeping of the Percy castle at Alnwick for Edward IV, and before the end of the month Sir Ralph Percy (younger brother of the earl of Northumberland killed at Towton) had submitted to Edward and was holding the royal coastal castle at Dunstanburgh on his behalf.[11]

By July 1461 the balance in the north had swung in favour of the Yorkists. Both sides were now preoccupied with the fate of King Henry's supporters in Wales, where they held several castles. Edward planned an expedition to supplement the efforts of his local supporters. The Lancastrians essayed a powerful counter-move. An embassy, nominally headed by Hungerford but covertly including Somerset, was dispatched from Scotland to Charles VII. One of its aims was to procure from him 2,000 men to operate in Wales and a loan of 20,000 crowns. But the death of Charles on 22 July, before the embassy's arrival, and the succession of his son Louis, hitherto pro-Yorkist, fatally upset Lancastrian plans. The envoys lacked safe-conducts from the new king. A doleful letter from Hungerford and Whittingham, written at Dieppe on 30 August, and intercepted on its way to Margaret in Scotland, revealed that they were under arrest, and that Somerset was confined nearby at Arques.[12] Two letters written by Italian envoys towards the end of August show that men were breathing more easily at Edward's court, as the likelihood of French intervention dimmed. A recent Yorkist convert, Lord Rivers, crowed to Ludovico Dallugo that Henry's cause was 'lost irremediably'.[13]

Some urgency probably went out of the preparations for the intended royal expedition to Wales. Edward arrived at Hereford on 17 September, nine days after the date set for the muster of his army. He stayed at his castle of Ludlow from the 18th to the 26th, then abandoned the expedition. It must have been concluded that his lieutenants, notably Ferrers and Herbert, could deal with the Welsh Lancastrians. Commissioned to take Pembroke castle, they received it from Sir John Scudamore, who was granted a pardon by Herbert dated at Pembroke on 30 September.[14] On 4 October Henry Wyndesore reported from London that all the castles in North and South Wales were yielded into the king's hands, and that the duke of Exeter and Jasper Tudor, earl of Pembroke, had fled into the mountains.[15] On 16 October or earlier in the year they and Thomas Fitzherry, esquire, of Hereford were in the field at Tuthill near Caernarvon − perhaps in the hope of surprising the town and castle.[16] The Lancastrians hung on to Harlech castle till 1468, but lost Carreg Cennen castle in 1462. Herbert sent his brother Sir Richard to besiege it with Sir Roger Vaughan of Tretower. The garrison submitted, and 500 men were employed to demolish the castle, to prevent it from becoming a refuge for 'rebels and robbers'.[17]

Lancastrian plans in 1462 once again depended on substantial foreign as well as domestic support. They received a blow through the discovery of a conspiracy whose leadership was promisingly rooted in southern England. According to an official Yorkist account written in March 1462 by Antonio della Torre, Edward set out for Northumberland on 24 February to deal with the Scottish threat. Eleven days before his departure, a conspiracy headed by the Essex magnate the earl of Oxford was discovered. The plotters had intended to follow the king with his 1,000 horse northwards, leading retinues of 2,000 or more as if to support him, but in reality to attack. Meanwhile Somerset, then in Bruges, would sail to England, King Henry would cross the Border with the Scots, and Pembroke would come from Brittany.[18] Nevertheless, Somerset's safe voyage with Hungerford from Flanders to Scotland in March appeared to presage an invasion, and defence measures were put in hand.[19] In the north the Yorkists took successful preventive action against Scottish intervention. That month the earl of Douglas, long an exile at the English court, struck a blow at possible Lancastrian allies by raiding the Scottish West March.[20] In April Margaret, despairing of immediate Scottish support, left Kirkcudbright to sail to Brittany, with her husband's commission to treat with Louis XI. In May or June Warwick raided across the Border and captured a castle. At the end of June Mary of Guelders came to Carlisle and made a truce with him, to last till 24 August. There were impressions in England that this would lead to a more comprehensive and lasting settlement. It was rumoured that the Scots had agreed to hand over Henry and his adherents. In return, Warwick had leashed Douglas, who was ordered south, 'a sorrowful and a sore rebuked man'. The Yorkists were able to concentrate on reducing isolated northern strongholds: Dacre yielded his ancestral castle at Naworth to Montague, and on 30 or 31 July Tailboys surrendered Alnwick castle, which had been once more in Lancastrian hands. Sir Ralph Grey, who had commanded the siege with Lord Hastings, was made captain at Alnwick.[21]

The Lancastrian situation was not as hopeless as these diplomatic and military reverses seemed to imply. It was transformed by Margaret's successful diplomacy. In June she had reached agreement with Louis XI: the Lancastrians were to receive a subsidy from him and were authorized to recruit in France. With this aid they attempted to re-establish control in Northumberland in the autumn. Factors in the decision to strike there were probably the expectation of renewed help from the Scots and from Percy adherents, and appreciation that strong castles in the region could be held in defiance of a regime based in the remote south of England. Though the Lancastrians were to fail to extend their power significantly outside Northumberland, their incursions there from October 1462 to June 1464 placed a grave burden on Edward's resources. He had to continue exasperating his subjects by financial demands. Moreover, the Yorkist efforts to reconquer Northumberland led to his continued dependence on the Neville brothers, and their consequent aggrandizement. This contributed to the political strains which resulted in the decline and overthrow of his rule (1469–70) and the brief re-establishment of Henry VI.

The Lancastrian invasion of Northumberland in 1462 thus had a profoundly disquieting effect on Edward's and, indeed, his successors' rule, helping to revive and prolong traditions of dynastic revolt which persisted to the end of the century. Yet, arguably, the decision to strike in Northumberland was a mistake, for Scottish support had previously been wavering and of only limited military value. In 1496 Lord

Bothwell opined that a projected Scottish invasion of Northumberland was a hazardous enterprise, and that the army would agitate to return home after four or five days, being 'so weary for watching and for lack of victuals'.[22] As Perkin Warbeck found on this expedition, Scottish forces, plundering as usual, alienated any local inclination to support a dynastic claimant.[23] Perhaps the Lancastrians would have been better advised to delay their invasion until the spring of 1463, and then concentrate on reviving Welsh support. For the aggrandizement of Edward's lieutenants is likely to have caused as much resentment in Wales as in the north of England,[24] and landing in Wales had the advantage, as Henry Tudor showed in 1485, of providing speedy access to the English heartlands.

The queen embarked at Honfleur in Normandy and landed on the Northumbrian coast near Bamburgh on 25 October 1462. With her was a sizeable French force, at most about 2,000 strong, commanded by the distinguished soldier Pierre de Brézé, *grand sénéchal* of Normandy – according to the chronicler Warkworth 'the best warrior of all that time'. Henry VI, Somerset and some Scottish soldiers had been picked up in Scotland on the way.[25] The invaders speedily took the royal coastal castles at Bamburgh and Dunstanburgh, and the Percy castles at Alnwick and Warkworth, 'which they had victualled and stuffed both with Englishmen, Frenchmen and Scotsmen; by the which castles they had the most part of all Northumberland'.[26]

The Yorkist government reacted quickly: Edward had for some time been alert to the threat of a new Lancastrian invasion.[27] The king 'did make great guns and other great ordnance at London, and did do carry it into the north country'.[28] But the organization and movement of a royal expedition northwards took time. Meanwhile Warwick was commissioned to attack the Lancastrians.[29] Henry VI, his queen and Brézé did not feel strong enough to challenge the Yorkists in the field, and on 13 November they withdrew to seek reinforcements in Scotland, leaving garrisons in the castles which they had captured. The shipwreck of a large company of the queen's Frenchmen on the Northumbrian coast was a blow. The fact that two local gentlemen, the Bastard of Ogle and John Manners, esquire, attacked and overcame them on Holy Island shows that there were limitations to Lancastrian control even in the parts of Northumberland where they were strongest.[30]

Early in November Edward set out from London for the north.[31] He arrayed probably the largest number of peers to serve in a later medieval English army – there were thirty-nine adult ones on service, including recent Lancastrian activists and 'neutrals' who doubtless considered it politic to demonstrate their commitment to the new allegiance.[32] At Durham Edward was incapacitated by measles. He had to leave Warwick to conduct the sieges.[33] On 21 December garrison strengths within Alnwick and Bamburgh castles were said to be 300, in Dunstanburgh 120. Somerset, Pembroke, Roos and a deserter from Edward's allegiance, Sir Ralph Percy, were in Bamburgh, Sir Richard Tunstall and Sir Thomas Finderne in Dunstanburgh. Hungerford and Whittingham were at Alnwick, whose garrison was probably predominantly French.[34] John Paston the youngest, in the duke of Norfolk's military retinue at Newcastle, wrote on 11 December that Warwick was staying not far from Alnwick, at Warkworth castle, 'and he rideth daily to all these castles for to oversee the sieges'. The earl of Kent (Fauconberg) and Rivers's son Lord Scales were at the siege of Alnwick, the earl of Worcester and Sir Ralph Grey at Dunstanburgh, and Lords Montague and Ogle at Bamburgh.[35]

Bamburgh and Dunstanburgh were formally surrendered on 26 and 27 December respectively. Most of the gentlefolk received safe-conducts to withdraw from the realm, but Somerset and Percy paid allegiance to Edward, Percy receiving custody of the two castles.[36] Edward probably had pressing reasons for granting imprudently generous terms. He is likely to have been reluctant, as he was to be in 1464, to cause damage by bombardment to castles useful for the defence of the realm. The continued maintenance of his army was presenting problems. His forces at Alnwick were soon to show that 'they had lie there so long in the field, and were grieved with cold and rain, that they had no courage to fight'.[37] Above all, Edward believed that belated Scottish intervention to save the tottering Lancastrians was imminent. On 31 December, in a mandate under his signet seal dated at Durham and addressed to Archbishop Booth of York, he alleged that the Scots intended to enter the realm on 3 January to rescue 'our enemies of France closed within our castle of Alnwick' and to give him battle. The archbishop was to warn the clergy of the province to be with the king in defensible array on Newcastle moor on 4 January, to assist him in the battle which he anticipated the next day.[38] Edward's appraisal is likely to have been based on reports of the concentration of an army in the Borders by George Douglas, earl of Angus, warden of the Marches.[39] In response to appeals to relieve the hard-pressed and famished garrison in Alnwick, Angus selected his best troops for a foray across the Border. But he was to show no desire to stay for a confrontation with Edward. At about five o'clock on the morning of 6 January he and Brézé reached Alnwick with their forces. Its besiegers withdrew in some confusion, and part of the garrison sallied forth and disappeared with their rescuers. Angus, the Scottish chronicler Major boasted, set the Frenchmen free, and in sight of the mighty English army, carried them with him into Scotland; the English were paralysed by divided counsels as to whether or not they should attack Angus. The English chroniclers Warkworth and the author of the *Annales*, though under no illusions as to their countrymen's poor showing, professed themselves unimpressed by Angus's achievement. They thought that the invaders, fearing a trap, had missed an opportunity to defeat the disarrayed Yorkists. The upshot was in fact to the latter's gain: those remaining in the castle surrendered on terms.[40]

Angus's brief foray and the surrender of Alnwick virtually ended the winter campaign. Edward and his great army withdrew southwards, leaving Warwick to guard the frontier, which he did energetically. One English chronicler commented scornfully on the failure of 'practically the whole knighthood of England' to achieve anything memorable in their long stay, apart from the capture of three castles.[41] His attitude perhaps reflects Englishmen's expectations of brief campaigns and decisive battles in the dynastic conflicts, and their failure to appreciate the handicaps of winter campaigning in the region. Nevertheless, the Yorkist showing was not brilliant. Edward's enforced absence at Durham may have hampered firm directions. Warwick may have found it difficult to impose discipline on a great, motley assembly of fellow nobles, all doubtless as concerned with their precedence and the comforts of their winter quarters as with the business, novel to some, of prosecuting sieges. The Lancastrian leaders, on the other hand, had no cause to celebrate. They had failed to consolidate their hold in Northumberland. Scottish help had been disappointing. Their French force was depleted, and one of their principal supporters had deserted the cause.

Despite disillusion among the French soldiers, in 1463 the chivalrous Brézé displayed his habitual loyalty and tenacity in supporting Lancastrian efforts in Northumberland. There castellans on whom Edward had been constrained to rely, treacherously undermined the recent Yorkist success. In March 1463 Sir Ralph Percy, captain at Bamburgh and Dunstanburgh, delivered the castles to Henry. By May Alnwick castle was once again in Lancastrian hands, betrayed to Hungerford and the French by Sir Ralph Grey. Yorkist counter-measures were entrusted principally to the Nevilles.[42] They were soon faced with a more serious threat: on 11 July Warwick wrote as royal lieutenant from Middleham castle (Yorks.) to Archbishop Booth, saying that he knew for certain that the Scots and 'the king's traitors and rebels' had entered the realm 'with great puissance'. The earl wanted the clergy of the province to be assembled, defensibly arrayed, at Durham on 15 July.[43] Henry and Margaret, Mary of Guelders, the youthful James III, and Brézé laid siege to the bishop of Durham's exposed castle on the frontier at Norham – a move more calculated to suit Scottish than Lancastrian interests. After eighteen days of siege, Warwick and Montague relieved the castle with local forces and put the invaders to flight. Hotly pursued, in great disarray, Margaret fled to the

Northumbrian coast with Brézé and the French. It was the end of Franco-Scottish military co-operation in the Lancastrian interest in the Borders. Waurin, Basin and Chastellain all reflect French bitterness at the failure of the Scots to provide them with the anticipated support in the Border campaigns.[44]

Margaret, with the prince, Exeter, Brézé, Fortescue and other councillors sailed to Flanders. The conclusion of an Anglo-French truce in October 1463 dashed their hopes of aid against Edward. The truce made his threatened invasion of Scotland more dangerous: in December an Anglo-Scottish truce was concluded.[45] The renegade Somerset, Edward's travelling-companion and even, on occasion, bedfellow, may have ruefully reflected that autumn that the Lancastrian cause looked as if it might indeed be irretrievably lost, unless he helped to revive it. Since he was so unpopular with Yorkist partisans, some time after 25 July Edward sent him from court for his own protection to a royal castle, probably in Wales. The king showed his continued trust in Somerset by sending the duke's men to guard Newcastle. But before 20 December the duke, without royal licence, left North Wales for Newcastle, which he had plotted with his men to betray. On the way he was recognized and had to flee from his bed near Durham, in his shirt and barefoot. He reached the Lancastrian garrison at Bamburgh safely, but his supporters in Newcastle had to flee too. The king made the town secure for the winter by sending a force of his household men there and appointing Lord Scrope of Bolton captain of the town.[46]

There were other ramifications of Somerset's plot to be dealt with. On 1 March 1464 John Paston the youngest, in the duke of Norfolk's retinue at Holt castle (Cheshire), wrote about the duke's progress in suppressing and punishing Somerset's adherents in the region. Welsh gentlemen who had assisted his flight had to be dealt with. The commons of Lancashire and Cheshire had risen to the number of 10,000, 'but now they be down again'.[47]

Nevertheless, the Lancastrians were sufficiently well based in Northumberland to conduct offensives without foreign or other substantial help. They captured Langley and Bywell castles, and the town tower at Hexham, establishing a threatening presence in upper Tynedale. They even seized a Yorkshire castle, at Skipton in Craven.[48] On 1 April the irrepressible Humphrey Neville of Brancepeth, breaking the terms of his pardon, joined the Lancastrians at Bamburgh.[49] That month they attempted to disrupt the intended Anglo-Scottish negotiations. Somerset and Sir Ralph Percy placed Neville with eighty spears and bowmen in a wood near Newcastle to ambush Montague on his way to Norham to meet the Scottish envoys and escort them to York. He evaded the trap, but about nine miles from Alnwick, at Hedgeley Moor, was attacked by Somerset, Roos, Hungerford, Sir

Ralph Percy, Sir Richard Tunstall and Sir Thomas Finderne, leading 500 men-at-arms, on 25 April. The attack was repulsed and Percy was killed, a blow to Lancastrian loyalties in Northumberland.[50] Montague carried on to Norham and brought in the Scots, returning to Newcastle. Despite the reverse, the Lancastrian leadership, including Henry, held on in Tynedale. Presumably they hoped to score a success before Edward could bring up overwhelming southern reinforcements. But Montague caught them unprepared: on 15 May, with Lords Greystoke and Willoughby, and, according to the *Annales*, 4,000 men against not more than 500 Lancastrians, he attacked by Hexham. The common soldiers deserted the Lancastrian lords, who were captured thereabouts or hunted down in the next few days. Henry VI made a lucky escape from Bywell castle, leaving behind his helmet with its crown, and his sword. Montague was able to publicize the downfall of the Lancastrian leadership in a series of executions, at Hexham, Newcastle, Middleham and York. Somerset, Roos, Hungerford and Finderne were among the victims.[51]

As a result of Hexham there was a general crumbling of the Lancastrian cause in Northumberland. Commanders of castles abandoned them or negotiated terms.[52] After the battle some fugitives took refuge in Bamburgh castle.[53] Diehard gentlefolk from Northumberland and Westmorland may have congregated there from the end of May.[54] Warwick arrived before Alnwick castle on 23 June and received its surrender, as he did that of Dunstanburgh castle, where he lodged the next day. On 25 June he and his brother Montague (newly created earl of Northumberland) laid siege to Bamburgh castle, whose hard-core garrison was led by Sir Ralph Grey and Neville of Brancepeth. Chester and Warwick Heralds were sent to offer pardons to all the besieged except these two. Grey's reply was defiant, but he was told by a herald, 'My Lords ensurith you, upon their honour, to sustain siege before you these seven years, or else to win you.' Grey had changed his coat too many times. The king, it was intimated, was particularly anxious that the castle should not be damaged by artillery – every shot fired would cost a defender's head. Nevertheless, the besiegers had to bombard: Warwick 'ordained all the King's great guns that were charged at once to shoot'. *Newe-Castel*, the king's great gun, and *London*, 'The second gun of iron', knocked stones off the castle walls into the sea. *Dysyon* (i.e. *Dijon*), a brass gun, often loosed shot through Grey's chamber. He was concussed by a fall of masonry and given up for dead. The bombardment assisted an assault on the castle, but Neville managed to bargain for his life and the lives of the other defenders, except for Grey, who was to pay the penalty for his tergiversations.[55]

From Margaret of Anjou's landing in Northumberland in October

1462 till the surrender of Bamburgh in June 1464, Lancastrian resources were concentrated on controlling this peripheral part of the realm. The attempt was intensely troublesome and repeatedly alarming to Edward IV. Lancastrian threats contributed to his failure to consolidate his rule until after 1471. But at no time were the Lancastrians able to tighten their hold in the Marches sufficiently for the invasion of the realm. They never secured the requisite base — a major town. The attempts to take Carlisle in 1461 and Newcastle in 1464 were failures. The numerous, well-maintained Northumbrian castles provided a means of maintaining their interest there, but local factors made it necessary for them to devote their energies just to hanging on to the castles. Supplies were difficult to come by; local nobles and commons were by no means unanimously pro-Lancastrian, and were liable to flinch from a cause supported by Scottish arms. Apart from Perkin Warbeck in 1496, no claimant to the throne after the 1460s was to make his principal effort in the Marches towards Scotland. The invaders of 1469-71, 1485 and 1487 preferred other entry points, and pushed as fast as they could towards the central parts of the realm, sometimes with foreign support less impressive than that at Margaret's disposal in 1462. Lancastrian strategy took a disastrous turn in the 1460s. The choice of and persistence with the Northumbrian option cost the lives of some of the best of Henry's knights and disillusioned many English and foreign supporters. Nevertheless, it must be remembered that concurrent attempts were made to develop an alternative strategy.

Chapter 4

Local Revolts and Nobles' Struggles to Control the Crown, 1469–71

From 1464 onwards the few remaining prominent Lancastrians were unable to pose a major threat to Edward IV, who was militarily and diplomatically successful. Henry VI was captured, hiding in Lancashire, in 1465 and imprisoned in the Tower. Margaret of Anjou and her son Prince Edward maintained a threadbare court in Lorraine. Their former patron Louis XI had his hands full with the revolts headed by Charles the Bold of Burgundy, and Margaret's doughty champion Brézé died in them, at the battle of Montlhéry in 1465.[1] Somerset's heir, his brother Edmund Beaufort, became absorbed in fighting for Charles, not Henry.[2] Only in Wales did continued Lancastrian activity necessitate royal counter-measures. The bailiffs of Shrewsbury accounted in the year 1466–7 for the financing of soldiers raised on royal command to accompany John Tiptoft, earl of Worcester, to Denbigh and Harlech castles. Men were sent from the town to ascertain the truth of rumours that the Lancastrian Sir Richard Tunstall was at Wrexham with a force, and whether he and other men of Harlech 'intended any evil to this town or not'.[3] In September 1467 the Milanese agent Panicharolla reported from Paris: 'the Welshmen have taken up arms against King Edward and proclaim King Henry, whose next brother [Jasper Tudor], late resident here, is going over there, and the late queen is sending him some of her followers to make their party take the field if possible'. Jasper was provided with enough aid by Louis XI to equip a tiny force of three ships and fifty soldiers. His landing in Wales was reported by Panicharolla on 2 July 1468, and on the next day Lords Herbert and Ferrers were commissioned to array men in the Marches of Wales and adjacent shires for service against him. Jasper Tudor raised enough support to occupy Denbigh, but was defeated by Herbert and his brother Sir Richard. Harlech castle at last capitulated the following month.[4]

The crown was alarmed by the possibility that prominent

Englishmen were involved in this resurgence of Lancastrian activity. Heads of noble families which had lost estates or influence as a result of past rebellion were especially suspect. Among those arrested in the autumn of 1468 were Henry Courtenay, brother and heir of the earl of Devon attainted in 1461, Thomas Hungerford, whose father was also attainted then, and John de Vere, earl of Oxford, whose father and elder brother had been executed in 1462. Oxford was soon released, but in January 1469 Courtenay and Hungerford were convicted of plotting with Margaret of Anjou and executed.[5]

But in 1469–70 it was northern discontent with aspects of Yorkist rule, discontent encouraged by leading Yorkist nobles, which posed dire threats to Edward's rule. The Lancastrian exiles were not to be involved until the summer of 1470 – and then not of their own volition. The first major stirrings were in the spring of 1469. There were popular assemblies centred on Yorkshire, about which the sources are confusing and unenlightening. One aim of the rebels in the East Riding, captained by 'Robin of Holderness', had possible Lancastrian, and certainly anti-Neville, overtones. They wanted the restoration to the earldom of Northumberland of Henry Percy, whose father had forfeited it in 1461. The present earl, Warwick's brother John Neville, took the lead in suppressing these stirs.[6] But about 28 May there started another Yorkshire outbreak, whose leaders had completely different sympathies. Captained by 'Robin of Redesdale', they complained, according to the first Crowland continuator, that they were grievously oppressed by taxes and annual tributes instigated by the favourites of the king and his queen Elizabeth Wydeville. This rising was in fact firmly controlled by Yorkshire gentlefolk acting in the interests of a Neville coterie – Warwick, his brother George archbishop of York, and the king's brother George duke of Clarence, allied to destroy the influence of rivals at court. 'Robin of Redesdale' was probably Sir John Conyers of Hornby (Yorks.), related to the Nevilles by marriage. In his company were the sons of Lords Latimer, FitzHugh and Dudley, also Neville kinsfolk. The royal response to the rising was sluggish. Edward may at first have regarded it as another of the tiresome Yorkshire discontents whose impact had been mainly local. In the first week of June he set out on a tour of East Anglia. The first day on which there is evidence that he was preparing to act against the risers in person is 18 June. On 5 July he addressed a signet letter from Stamford (Lincs.) to the mayor of Coventry, expressing his determination to go into northern parts to suppress the riots, and asking him to send hastily 100 archers in assistance. Five days later he wrote even more urgently from Newark asking for whatever support Coventry could send. When at Newark, he found himself outnumbered by the northern rebels by three to one. He retreated to Nottingham and remained there, presumably unwilling to give the appearance of flight, and hopeful that he would be reinforced in response to the privy seal letters he had sent into the north, Wales and the West Country.[7]

The northerners, remonstrating against royal favourites, were as anxious as Edward's father had been to avoid the appearance of attacking the king. They bypassed Nottingham, moving southwards into the Midlands, doubtless with the intention of linking up with their Neville mentors as soon as possible. Warwick re-enacted his 1460 role as a 'Calais lord'. On 4 July he, his brother-in-law Oxford, and Clarence crossed to his captaincy of Calais. There his daughter Isabel married the duke. On 12 July Clarence, Archbishop Neville and Warwick set their signets and sign manuals to a letter addressed to a 'right trusty and beloved' correspondent. In it they declared that subjects had delivered to them bills containing articles about the 'deceivable rule and guiding of certain seditious persons' – Lord Rivers and his wife the duchess of Bedford (the queen's parents), William Herbert, recently created earl of Pembroke, Humphrey Stafford, recently created earl of Devon, Lord Scales (Anthony Wydeville, the queen's brother), Lord Audley, Sir John Wydeville and his brothers, Sir John Fogge and their supporters. The three said that they intended with other lords to show these articles to the king, and asked for military support to accompany them. They would be at Canterbury on 15 July. In fact they crossed the Channel the day after, to be greeted by a large number of Kentishmen at Canterbury. On 18 July they left the city for London, whose governors allowed them to pass through on their way to join the northerners.[8]

But before the conjunction could be made, the issue was settled in battle. The northerners intercepted a Welsh force commanded by Pembroke, hurrying to reinforce the king, on the 'plain of Edgcote' near Banbury (Oxon.) and decisively defeated it on 26 July. Contemporary accounts of the battle are meagre, apart from Waurin's, whose circumstantial details lack independent confirmation – and who is contradicted by English sources on an important point. Waurin says that the armies converged on a river crossing (presumably on the Cherwell) and encamped at some distance on either side for the night. Next morning both armies advanced to secure the crossing. Pembroke, not realizing how near the enemy was, went on ahead of the infantry with his horsemen, who had to defend themselves against heavy attack. They held the passage, however. The bruised northerners drew off, inclining to wait for Warwick to reinforce them. But two insistent knights got them into line for another assault to secure the crossing. Sir William Par ('Appare') and Sir Geoffrey Gate ('Guat') may have arrived with some reinforcements, part of the vanward of the magnates' army. Waurin says that Pembroke, though now reinforced, was outnumbered, and that the Welshmen were overwhelmed when Devon and his men withdrew from the fight on hearing that Clarence was coming to aid the northerners. However, Warkworth and the author of *Hearne's Fragment* state that Devon and his company had parted company with Pembroke before the battle. The latter author thought that the northerners owed their victory to the 15,000 household men and soldiers from Calais under Clapham whom Warwick sent ahead as a reinforcement from London. Contemporaries regarded the death-toll as high on both sides, but disastrous for the Welsh. Pembroke and his brother Sir Richard Herbert were captured, and executed the following day on Warwick's arbitrary orders. The earl was able to dismiss his Kentish supporters. Too late, on 29 July Edward at last left Nottingham, moving southwards. At Olney (Beds.) he heard about the battle. Deserted by his men, he had to submit to Archbishop Neville. Probably early in August, Earl Rivers and his son Sir John Wydeville were captured and executed.[9]

Warwick's ambitious strategy in 1469, involving the conjunction of forces from the south-east and north, echoed that in which he had been disastrously involved ten years before. But in 1469 he laid the ground well, working up prior support in Yorkshire and Kent, and was sufficiently well informed and organized after reaching London to react speedily to the needs of his northern allies when things did not go according to plan. Edward, however, seems to have been more than usually misled by the fog of war. He failed to exploit interior lines in the Midlands, unlike the royal commanders in 1459. Unlike Henry then, he remained for too long at Nottingham, perhaps hanging on for reinforcements, perhaps uncharacteristically relying on a subordinate commander, Pembroke – who had a good military reputation. Had Edward made a dash to place himself at the head of the Welsh and western men, he would have had a good chance of defeating the northerners at Edgcote, before they were able to link up with Warwick, and consequently might have enforced the latter's submission or flight. For the royal army, though outnumbered at Edgcote, was an excellent one. Its weakness lay in the enmity of its commanders, two parvenu earls. The royal presence would have damped that down, and disheartened the northerners. Basically Edward lost because he failed to achieve a sufficient concentration of forces, whereas his enemies did so.

The civil war of 1469 demonstrated to Lancastrian sympathizers the enmities splitting the Yorkist establishment and the slender hold which Edward and some of his magnates had over local loyalties. Northern Lancastrians attempted to exploit Edward's humiliating tutelage under Warwick's control. Humphrey Neville of Brancepeth had escaped from the rout of Hexham in 1464 and since lived in hiding around Derwentwater. He and his brother Charles now raised revolt in the

Borders. Warwick found that his imprisonment of the king was so unpopular that he could not raise sufficient arrays until Edward was released and appeared at liberty in York. Humphrey Neville was captured by Warwick in Holderness: he and his brother Charles were executed at York on 29 September in the king's presence.[10]

Clarence and Warwick thus soon found that the 1469 rebellion had brought them few political gains. So they planned a repeat performance for 1470, possibly with the more extreme aim of deposing Edward. They covertly encouraged rebellion in the north, planning to join up with the rebels – this time with forces brought from nearer at hand – and trap the unwary king. But Edward had learnt a bitter lesson. Though again operating in a haze of misapprehension, he grappled with the local rebels as quickly as possible. They were unable to withstand the king. Their leaders lacked the calibre of the previous year's, and this time Clarence and Warwick were not in time to give help. Once Edward had won in battle, he began to bring up support, and the frantic efforts of the two lords were unable to stop theirs from petering out.

At the start, besides hoping for support in Yorkshire once again, they tried to exploit tensions among Lincolnshire gentlefolk. Richard Lord Welles and Willoughby, his son Sir Robert Welles, his brother-in-law Sir Thomas de la Launde, and Sir Thomas Dymoke resented the aggrandizement of a knight of the king's body, Thomas Burgh of Gainsborough. He was driven out of the shire and his house was sacked. The Welles interest's fears of royal disfavour for local stirs inclined them to accept the patronage of Clarence and Warwick: some even succumbed to their incitement to rebel.[11] On Sunday 4 March 1470 Sir Robert Welles, 'great captain of the commons of Lincolnshire', had proclamations made in churches, in the name of the king, Clarence, Warwick and himself, ordering the people to meet him armed on Ranby Hawe (seven miles north of Horncastle) in order to resist the king, who was coming, so he said, to destroy the commons of the shire. But fears of royal displeasure had driven other members of the Welles interest to adopt what turned out to be a disastrously contradictory policy. When Sir Robert was having his proclamations made, his father and Dymoke were in London, in answer to royal summonses – and they and, indeed, Sir Robert received pardons for previous disturbances. Sir Robert, according to his confession, relied on Clarence's promises to go to London, excuse Lord Welles to the king, and delay the latter's counter-measures. The duke in fact arrived at court on 4 March, the day of Sir Robert's proclamations, but he does not seem to have effectively delayed Edward's expedition or cleared Lord Welles. The king set out northwards from London on 6 March, the day of the intended assembly at Ranby, and on the following morning, at Waltham (Herts.) received news of the Lincolnshire proclamations. He promptly summoned Welles and Dymoke from London. Clarence's dissimulation left Edward disinclined to believe that his brother and Warwick were mixed up in the business. From Royston (Herts.), where he arrived on 8 March, he dispatched the commissions of array made out to them at Waltham.[12]

Edward reached Huntingdon on 9 March, and his ancestral castle of Fotheringhay (Northants.) on the 11th. There it was reported that the rebels were south of Grantham, less than forty miles away. But they were veering south-west, out of his path, towards Leicester, in response to Warwick's promise to meet them there on Monday 12 March with 20,000 men. According to the Lincolnshire captains' later confessions, the plan was for the rebels at Leicester to allow the king to pass northwards, then cut off his retreat, surrounding him with their northern allies – such as, presumably, the Yorkshire dissidents. This alleged intention seems to have relied heavily on Edward displaying uncharacteristic foolhardiness. In fact he undermined enemy strategy, unknowingly, by a neat piece of psychological warfare. On the 11th Sir Robert received a letter from his father, in the king's army, making plain that Edward would have him executed unless Sir Robert submitted. Sir Robert made a fateful decision. Calculating that the king would get from Fotheringhay as far as Stamford on 12 March and spend the night there, he decided to turn away from Leicester, attack the king's army as it settled into Stamford, and rescue his father.[13]

However favourably this sudden decision displayed Sir Robert's filial and chivalrous instincts, by rushing at Edward single-handed he was providing the king with an opportunity to nip rebellion in the bud. He was negating the strategy agreed with his sluggish magnate allies, whose fair promises had not relieved his father's plight. Early on the morning of 12 March the royal army took the road from Fotheringhay. When it reached Stamford the same day, the rebels were still five miles to the. west of the town, at Empingham. Edward pushed his 'foreward' on towards them. A message to him from Clarence and Warwick saying that they would be at Leicester that night and promising help did not delay him. Edward's generalship is seen at its best in his determination to force the issue that day, after a hard march. His soldiers were probably impressed by the ruthless execution of Lord Welles and Dymoke, in accordance with his nobles' wishes, before engagement. Sir Robert Welles, shocked by what he regarded as royal perfidy, refused an offer of grace. But his rustics, daunted by the sight of Edward's great host, soon broke and scattered in what contemporaries referred to contemptuously as Losecoat Field – so unmemorable, if decisive, a fight that no surviving chronicle records details.[14]

One of the fruits of victory was firm evidence of Clarence's and Warwick's complicity. On the battlefield the corpse of one of

Clarence's servants was found to be carrying in a casket 'many marvellous bills, containing matter of the great sedition'. In the pursuit Sir Thomas de la Launde was captured; Sir Robert Welles and Richard Waryn were among the rebel captains brought to the king when he had moved on to halt at Grantham (14–15 March). These three publicly confessed in the royal presence that Clarence and Warwick had promised them assistance, and they confirmed this at their executions. The magnates' repeatedly asserted purpose, Welles alleged, was to make Clarence king.[15]

After his victory, Clarence and Warwick were disinclined to attack the king. On 13 March Edward dispatched a squire of the body, John Donne, from Stamford with letters to them at Coventry, commanding them to dismiss the bulk of their troops and attend on him with select retinues. But they dissimulated, hoping to stir rebellion anew, north of the Trent. They sent messages charging Yorkshiremen to make proclamations ordering military assistance to them on pain of death. From Coventry they went with their whole fellowship through Burton-on-Trent and Derby, arriving at Chesterfield on 18 March.

Moving on a parallel course, an increasingly recalcitrant Edward set out northwards from Grantham: he had information that there were rebellious moves in Yorkshire, in the honour of Richmond. He arrived at Newark on 16 March; there signet letters were drafted to the two magnates, summoning them to the royal presence to answer the charges against them. *En route* from Newark to Doncaster, Edward received a message from them promising to meet him at Retford. This they failed to do. After his arrival at Doncaster (18 March), their envoys came requesting sureties if they were to come to Edward's presence, which he brusquely refused. The execution of Sir Robert Welles and another Lincolnshire captain there on the 19th showed his confidence and determination. He had beaten his indecisive opponents, who were advancing less directly, in the race for Yorkshire. Appreciating their dilemma, he determined to bring matters to a head. On 20 March 'at nine of the bell, the King took the field, and mustered his people; and it was said that were never seen in England so many goodly men, and so well arrayed in a field'. Abandoning the route north, the royal army turned aside to advance on the lords at Chesterfield. Edward spent the night at Rotherham, since the lords' aforeriders had been there to requisition lodgings. Their appearance may have been a feint, or part of a move to trap the king in conjunction with the Yorkshire rebels, whose leaders were to confess that they were to have 'drawn to' Rotherham, encountered the king there and attacked his host. But at Rotherham Edward had firm news that the lords had given him the slip. They retreated westwards towards Manchester, hoping that Lord Stanley would reinforce them with his Lancashiremen before they joined up with their Yorkshire allies. But it may be that a crisis in the lords' camp necessitated a drastic change of plan. Waurin picked up a story that at some point Warwick was prepared to fight the king, but that the night before, one of his 'great captains', son of the renowned 'Thalbot', deserted with his company of about 3,000 to the king's side so suddenly that Warwick and his army had to make a disorderly flight. 'Thalbot' may have been either John Talbot, earl of Shrewsbury, or his brother Sir Gilbert, grandsons of the great fighting earl who died in 1453.[16]

Acting on the counsel of his lords, Edward broke off the pursuit, deciding to go to York before venturing into Lancashire. Pausing for a night at Pontefract castle, he entered York on 22 March. He wished to 'refresh' his army and secure the submission of Yorkshiremen who remembered well the rout of his army the previous year. Lord Scrope's efforts to raise Richmondshire, in the North Riding of Yorkshire, had been deterred by news of Edward's victory near Stamford and of his commissions of array directed to the Border shires and the earl of Northumberland. At York he received the submissions of Scrope, Sir John Conyers, 'young Hilyard of Holderness' and others who liberally confessed that they had been incited to revolt by Clarence and Warwick. Edward had now decided to treat the pair as incorrigible traitors. In a proclamation dated York, 24 March, he accused them of collusion in the Lincolnshire rising and of subsequent rebellious defiance. He charged them to appear before him on 28 March at the latest, or else be branded as rebels and traitors. They were both denounced as such in commissions of array dated 26 March.[17]

About 27 March Edward set out from York in pursuit. The rebel magnates' plans for resistance in the north collapsed. Finding no support in Lancashire, they retreated south-west all the way to Exeter. Edward, advancing through Nottingham, Coventry and Wells, arrived there on 14 April to find that they had taken ship with their wives and a small fellowship. Heading for Calais, they put in at Southampton, hoping to seize Warwick's great ship the *Trinite*, docked there. But Anthony Wydeville, Earl Rivers, and Lord Howard staved them off. The Calais garrison, despite the sympathy of Warwick's deputy there, Lord Wenlock, made clear that it would oppose the landing. The earl and Clarence had to take refuge in Normandy, putting in at Honfleur about 1 May.[18]

Why were the risings of March 1470 so unsuccessful, despite Edward's dangerous slowness in realizing who the instigators were? Their defeat was due in large measure to Edward's energy and speed of action. He was determined not to be overtaken by events, as he had been in 1469. He matched the ruthlessness his opponents had displayed then by his executions before Losecoat Field, at Grantham and Doncaster, tempered by a politic willingness to grant pardons to the volatile Yorkshiremen. But Clarence and Warwick again relied too readily on raising rebellion by proxy: Welles and his army lacked the ability which their Yorkshire allies of 1469 had exhibited. The sudden, solitary collapse which the Lincolnshiremen brought upon themselves caught the two magnates and their sympathizers in the north on the wrong foot. They were never able to get back into their stride for a challenge to the victorious Edward. Welles's confession strongly suggests that Clarence had a large share of responsibility for inciting the rising prematurely.

The failure of Clarence and Warwick enabled Louis XI of France to give an extraordinary twist to dynastic allegiances by reconciling them to Margaret of Anjou and the prince of Wales. They reverted to the allegiance of Henry VI (still a prisoner in the Tower), and Warwick betrothed his daughter Anne to the prince.[19]

Warwick once more planned an invasion of England – bewilderingly, in the Lancastrian interest with French royal backing. On 2 June commissions of array were appointed for defence against Clarence and Warwick in southern and western shires.[20] On 28 July Sforza de' Bettini, Milanese envoy at the French court, reported from Angers that in two days Warwick would leave for his fleet to undertake the enterprise of England. Just over a week later he reported that the earl had departed for Normandy, and that news of his sailing was expected at any moment.[21] On 5 August Sir John Paston reported from London that 'it is said Courtenays [the Lancastrian family which had held the earldom of Devon] be landed in Devonshire, and there rule' and that Clarence and Warwick 'will essay to land in England every day, as folks fear'.[22] But Warwick was unable to invade. Delays were imposed by organizational problems and a blockade instigated by Charles the Bold of Burgundy, whose alliance with Edward IV was the motive for Louis XI's support of Warwick's extraordinary enterprise.[23]

In anticipation of the earl's arrival, his English adherents rose in arms. In the north, Neville supporters – probably smarting at their recent humiliation and angry at Henry Percy's restoration to the earldom of Northumberland in place of John Neville in March – were dry tinder. In Yorkshire they rose in July under Henry Lord FitzHugh, Warwick's brother-in-law. On 5 August Sir John Paston commented on the inability of Percy to suppress the northern rebels: 'and so the King hath sent for his feedmen to come to him, for he will go to put them down'. On 8 August Coventry dispatched forty soldiers to the king at Nottingham. By mid-August Edward was once again in arms in Yorkshire, advancing from York to Ripon. Deterred by Warwick's failure to appear, and by news of Edward's approach, FitzHugh fled to Scotland.[24]

At last, on 9 September, Clarence and Warwick were able to embark from Normandy, after the Burgundian fleet had been dispersed in bad weather. On 13 September their English and French ships put into West Country ports. In the company were the earl of Oxford, Jasper Tudor, and Warwick's cousin Thomas Neville, Bastard of Fauconberg (the son of Lord Fauconberg). Edward was still at York. His delay there has been considered ill-adjudged; but he may have been concerned about a recurrence of northern rebellion, and he was well placed for a swift advance southwards towards Nottingham and Leicester, to rally retainers and secure London, as he was to do in 1471.[25]

In fact the start of the invasion was inauspicious. It was late in the campaigning season. Due possibly to prevailing winds, Clarence and Warwick had landed in a remote part of the realm, where they had little influence, far away from their Kentish adherents, who were to rampage in Southwark in a manner little calculated to win over London citizens.[26] The invaders advanced into the Midlands, presumably in order to cut Edward off in the north and to recruit in Warwick's shires. By the time they reached Coventry, according to the city's official account, they were 30,000 strong.[27] Edward was moving southwards, perhaps intending, as in 1469 and 1471, to make Nottingham his base for rallying supporters. But, whilst his numbers were still insignificant, he was undone by an outstanding act of treachery. He was roused from his bed by the serjeant of the minstrels, Alexander Carlisle, who came in great haste with the news that his enemies were poised to capture him. Warwick's brother John Neville, Marquess Montague, aggrieved at being recently deprived of the earldom of Northumberland in favour of the Percy, was advancing with 6,000 men arrayed under commission from Edward – against him. The king, with less than 2,000 under arms in his company, could not make a stand. With his young brother Richard duke of Gloucester, Earl Rivers, and Lords Hastings, Howard and Say he fled to Lynn (Norfolk). On 2 October they embarked, seeking refuge in Charles the Bold's county of Holland.[28]

On 5 October Archbishop Neville entered London with a strong force and took over the Tower from the garrison which the perplexed civic authorities had placed in it. Next day Clarence and Warwick appeared in the city. With the archbishop, the earl of Shrewsbury and Lord Stanley, they escorted Henry VI from the Tower to the bishop's palace by St Paul's, and made him take the crown once more.[29]

About five months later, on 11 March 1471, Edward sailed from Flushing to challenge Henry's title, with a force not exceeding 2,000, subsidized by Charles of Burgundy.[30] Next day his ships hove to off Cromer (Norfolk). Sir Robert Chamberlain and Sir Gilbert Debenham landed to reconnoitre. But it was clear that the Lancastrians had a tight grip on East Anglia. One of Oxford's brothers, Thomas de Vere, with the Norfolk levies, appeared too strong.[31] Prevailing winds probably forced Edward to adopt the disagreeable alternative of sailing away from the routes to London and his Midland and southern sympathizers, towards the northern parts whose lukewarm loyalty to his person had undermined his rule since 1469. The weather was so bad that the ships ran for the Humber estuary. Edward landed on the tip of Holderness at Ravenspur on 14 March. Gloucester landed four miles away, and Rivers fourteen away at Paull – he nearly sailed into Hull. By the next day Edward had assembled his force. A council of war was held, and the decision was made to march boldly on York. Local levies to the number of 6,000–7,000 milled menacingly, but luckily for Edward no local noble appeared to give them leadership. He descended to the abject but effective expedient of meeting one of their leaders, to whom he exhibited a letter from Henry Percy, earl of Northumberland, and explained that he had come only to claim his patrimony of the duchy of York. This blatant deception continued to bemuse the more gullible Yorkshiremen. The Holderness levies let Edward pass and, though Hull would not receive him, Beverley did. York, too, where he arrived on 18 March, presented a grudging official face. He was permitted to enter with a few companions. The north was mainly stony ground, however, and Edward moved quickly southwards, reaching Tadcaster the next day, and on 20 March skirted round the hostile but indecisive Montague, whose force was based on Pontefract castle, to pick up some recruits in the Yorkist lordship of Sandal and Wakefield. From Wakefield he moved via Doncaster to Nottingham. There, poised on the borders of southern England, he first issued royally styled proclamations, and received his first significant reinforcements.[32]

Yorkist 'scourers' based on Nottingham reported that a large Lancastrian force – 4,000 strong – had occupied Newark, north-east of Nottingham. This was commanded by the duke of Exeter, Oxford and Lord Bardolf. It comprised levies from East Anglia, Cambridgeshire, Huntingdonshire and Lincolnshire. On 19 March (the day Edward had left York), Oxford had written to his supporters from Bury St Edmunds (Suffolk), asking them to bring contingents to the Norfolk array at Lynn on the 22nd. Thence they would set out for Newark, to combat the invaders in the north – an intention fulfilled with admirable speed.[33]

Edward reacted to their presence at Newark by setting out to attack. Within three miles of the town, he found that they had abandoned it. The Lancastrians had decamped at two o'clock in the morning, precipitating large-scale desertions. Why did their leadership show signs of panic? The author of the *Arrivall* says that they thought the reconnaissance of Edward's aforeriders foreshadowed his arrival, and that they would not be able to withstand him. Warwick, writing on 25 March, emphasized the insignificance of the force with which Edward had landed, and the fewness of his recruits. But the Lancastrian command at Newark may have worried that their levies would be no match for Edward's foreign mercenaries – and perhaps they were rattled by Montague's failure to oppose him or reinforce them. The Yorkist scouts' appearance from higher up the Trent may have intensified their alarm, for it suggested that Edward had outflanked them and might cut their communications with Warwick in the Midlands. Welles's defeat in 1469 was a warning to them – and earlier to Montague – not to face Edward before linking up with Clarence and Warwick. Edward may by then have had a high reputation as a field commander, and this could have been a significant factor in his opponents' calculations. According to Basin, the Lancastrians in the West Country were soon to be reluctant to face him in battle because of his great reputation – this was after his victory at Barnet.[34]

Edward returned to his base at Nottingham. The curious Lancastrian behaviour at Newark may have convinced him of the necessity of getting to grips with Warwick in the Midlands before the latter could concentrate the forces of his hesitant regional allies. He advanced on Leicester. Warwick apparently did not oppose him, but withdrew his substantial forces behind the town walls of Coventry, one of the finest urban defence systems in the realm. On 29 March, only ten days after leaving Tadcaster, and with a greatly increased force – albeit one probably inferior to Warwick's – Edward encamped outside Coventry. For four days he tried to persuade Warwick to come out and fight. But the earl stuck to his policy of waiting for his allies to come up, even when Edward tried to tempt or shame him out by withdrawing to the earl's castle and town of Warwick. Unlike Malory's King Mark, Warwick was not to be shamed into emerging from behind his walls. Up to a point, the earl's policy worked: Edward failed to intercept completely reinforcements which reached him, commanded by Exeter, Montague and Oxford.[35] But as so often in the campaigns of 1469–71, success or failure was swayed by defections. Warwick was probably waiting above all for Clarence before attacking Edward. The duke, who moved south-westwards from Bristol to Wells soon after Edward's landing, recruited over 4,000 men and turned back towards the Midlands, reaching Burford (Oxon.) by 2 April.[36] But Edward suborned him, as he probably suborned other magnates. Probably on 3 April he and Gloucester met their errant brother for a formal reconciliation. They all moved with their men to Warwick. They tried to tempt the earl of Warwick with offers. But even he lacked the nerve to turn traitor again, nor would he and the Lancastrian lords who had joined him come out of Coventry. Despite the blow of Clarence's abysmal defection, he had hopes of reinforcement.[37]

Heartened by Clarence's support, Edward and his council took the bold decision to turn their backs on Coventry and attempt the seizure of London. On 5 April they withdrew south-eastwards, reaching Daventry the next day, and passing through Northampton and Dunstable to arrive at St Albans on the 10th. Warwick set off urgently in pursuit. He wrote to his brother Archbishop Neville in London, urging him to hold the city until his imminent arrival. Neville called together his supporters – not exceeding 7,000 – and paraded Henry VI round the city in an attempt to raise recruits. But the appearance of the saintly king and the worldly ecclesiastic failed to stir military ardour. In fact the Lancastrian lords who could have organized resistance – Somerset, his brother John Beaufort, and Devon – had recently left London for the West Country, to prepare for the arrival from France of Margaret of Anjou and Prince Edward.[38]

The city governors, with their militia in harness, and in receipt of contrary exhortations from Edward and Warwick, were in a fearful dilemma. One king was in their midst, another practically at their gates. Two opposed armies were on the horizon; they risked the penalties of treason and an assault on the city by defying either. In the event they decided not to oppose Edward: it may have been some consolation that his army was well disciplined, and not composed of northerners. On the night of 11 April his supporters opened a way into the city by gaining control of the Tower. Edward entered London next morning. The city governors had got their harnessed men out of the way by telling them to go home to dinner.[39]

Warwick, who had advanced from Coventry via Northampton, may have pinned his hopes on a swift attack on Edward whilst he and his forces were busy celebrating Easter and settling down in London. But Edward, however conventionally pious, was not the man to be distracted by religious observance, unlike King Henry, once more in his hands. He set out with his army from London two days after entering it, on 13 April, the eve of Easter Sunday. In his company, besides his brothers, were Henry Bourchier, earl of Essex, his brother Lord Berners and his son Lord Cromwell, and Lords Hastings and Say – some of whom had swelled Edward's ranks in London. In the afternoon Edward's aforeriders flushed Warwick's from Hornsey Park back towards Barnet, whence the earl's men were driven too. The main body of the Yorkist army came up against the Lancastrians lining a hedge half a mile or so out of Barnet. Despite the fading light, Edward had pushed his men on to camp ready for a dawn attack – in fact, they were closer to the earl than Edward at first realized. Edward's insistence on getting his men into position that night had significant consequences. Warwick failed to realize how close the royal encampment was, and his night bombardment overshot it. But Edward had failed to align his troops precisely opposite Warwick's: on the eastern flank his men overlapped the earl's, and vice versa on the west. When battle commenced early the following morning, the need for swift action may have prevented commanders from altering their alignment, and weather conditions in any case may have prevented them from fully appreciating the situation.[40]

In Warwick's company were Exeter, Montague, Beaumont and Oxford. The sources agree that they outnumbered Edward's army. Zannoto Spinula reported from Bruges on 26 April that Edward had about 7,000 men on entering London, and that Warwick's force was then about 10,000 strong. The author of the *Arrivall* (intent on glorifying Edward) put his forces at Barnet at not more than 9,000 against 30,000. Warkworth says that the day after entering London Edward's strength had risen to 7,000, and that on the eve of Barnet, according to Edward's information, Warwick had about 20,000. The conviction that his opponent had a considerable numerical superiority may have made Edward anxious to take him by surprise at Barnet: he may have recalled how successfully Somerset had hustled the earl at St Albans in 1461, and that the latter had been unable then to assert control over his large army.[41]

On Easter morning (14 April), despite heavy mist, Edward launched his attack between four and five o'clock. The effects of surprise may to some extent have been nullified by those of non-alignment. Though the right (eastern) wing of Edward's 'battle' wheeled in effectively against Warwick's left flank, Edward's left wing was routed by Warwick's overlapping western one, commanded by Oxford. But these reverses did not spread panic down either line because mist concealed what was happening. Fighting was intense in the centre. Edward's right wing, after their preliminary success, joined the fight here. On the western flank, Oxford's victory was so complete that he had difficulty in extricating his men from Barnet to regroup for an attack on Edward. In the mist Warwick's men mistook the livery of Oxford's returning company for Edward's, and attacked them. This brought to the surface the Lancastrian fears that Warwick might do a deal with Edward, which must have simmered since Clarence's desertion. Oxford and his men cried 'Treason! treason!' and, 800 strong, they fled. This apparently was decisive: after at least three hours' fighting, Lancastrian resistance broke. Montague and Warwick were killed; Exeter lay, seriously wounded, abandoned among the dead. Casualties were heavy on both sides. Sir John Paston, writing on 18 April, listed among the slain the king's supporters Cromwell and Say, Berners's son Sir Humphrey Bourchier 'and other people of both parties to the number of more than 1,000'. The author of the *Arrivall* noted that Edward's household had sustained heavy casualties. It was probably a chastened royal army which returned to London that day. Edward's determination to press home a dawn attack in the particular circumstances had created a tricky tactical situation for both sides. But in the fight Warwick does not seem to have maintained as firm control over an army which, despite its fighting qualities, was flawed by suspicions.[42]

The same evening (14 April), Margaret of Anjou and her son landed at Weymouth, with 'knights, squires, and other men of the King of France'. They moved inland to Cerne abbey, where they were met by the duke of Somerset and John Courtenay, earl of Devon. On receiving news of Edward's victory at Barnet, it was decided not to challenge him directly, but pass as quickly as possible through western England, via Bristol, Gloucester and Chester, to recruit skilled Lancashire archers – and link up with Jasper Tudor, earl of Pembroke, who had gone to rally Welsh support. Arrayers were sent to raise contingents in Somerset, Dorset and parts of Wiltshire. Queen, prince and lords first went westwards to Exeter: their appearance helped to attract the 'whole might' of Devon and Cornwall. To disguise their intention to head north-west, the Lancastrian commanders dispatched aforeriders on routes implying an eastward advance.[43]

Edward moved from London to Windsor, the assembly-point for his army, on 19 April.[44] He needed to know as soon as possible which way the Lancastrians would jump, in order to intercept them before they could roll up more support. Intelligence sources soon convinced him that their main force, advancing through Taunton, Glastonbury and Wells, was indeed heading for the Welsh Marches. His objective was to prevent them crossing the Severn, at either Gloucester, Tewkesbury or, further north, at Worcester.[45]

The race was on for the bridges. On 24 April Edward set out from Windsor with his army, arriving at Abingdon on the 27th, Cirencester on the 29th. At Cirencester he had sure information that the Lancastrian army would be at Bath the next morning (as indeed they were) and that on 1 May they would come up against his position. So on the night of 29th–30th, he insisted that his army should lodge, not in the comfort of Cirencester, but three miles away, ready for battle. The next morning, having no news of the Lancastrians' advance, Edward turned southwards towards Bath to seek them out. At Malmesbury he learnt that they had given him the slip, avoiding battle by taking the road from Bath to Bristol, which they triumphantly entered.[46]

From Coventry on 12 May Edward was to write accusing the men of Bristol of having recently broken their allegiance, naming certain persons who had 'largely offended' against him – Nicholas Hervy (the city recorder slain at Tewkesbury), John Schepherd the elder, Robert Straunge, John Cogan, mercer, William Spencer, William Hynde, John

Sutton, goldsmith and John Body, 'staynour'.[47] The Lancastrians, refreshed and reinforced in the city, 'took new courage' to challenge Edward. On 2 May their aforeriders advanced nine miles east of Bristol to Chipping Sodbury, and Sodbury Hill was chosen to make a stand. Edward hastened to meet the challenge: advance elements of both armies skirmished at Sodbury. But when in the afternoon he reached the vicinity of Sodbury Hill, he found no sign of his opponents. He dispatched his scourers, but they could get no certain information. With his army exposed on 'a great and a fair large plain, called a wold', and believing the enemy to be near, he decided to encamp rather than advance without sure intelligence. The king and the main body of the army lodged at Sodbury Hill, the 'vaward' beyond it, in a valley between the hill and the town.[48]

Where was the Lancastrian army? The main force, before reaching Sodbury, had wheeled left, towards the Vale of Berkeley. Most unusually for an army of the period, it kept going all night, heading for Gloucester. Had the thrust towards Sodbury been a feint? The author of the *Arrivall* thought not. The night march bespeaks a desperate change of plan, likely to add to the weariness and demoralization of troops repeatedly marched away from the enemy. Perhaps the Lancastrian commanders' plans to fight at Sodbury were countermanded because the encounter there with Edward's harbingers convinced them that he would forestall their intention to prepare a strong defensive position.[49]

Soon after three o'clock on the morning of 3 May, Edward received news of the Lancastrian line of march. Clearly his opponents might cross the Severn at Gloucester or Tewkesbury. At about ten o'clock they arrived before Gloucester. The captain of the castle, Sir Richard Beauchamp, reassured by Edward's promise of relief, refused demands for entry. The Lancastrians had to go on towards Tewkesbury. They arrived there about four o'clock in the afternoon:

> By which time they had so travailled their host that night and day that
> they were right weary for travelling; for by that time they had
> travelled 36 long miles, in a foul country, all in lanes and stony ways,
> betwixt woods, without any good refreshing.

There, too weary to press on, they determined to spend the night and 'take a field'.

Meanwhile Edward had set out from Sodbury Hill early on 3 May with his army in battle array. The description of his march that day in the *Arrivall* is so vivid that it probably reflects the personal experience of a participant. His army covered over thirty miles 'through the champain country, called Cotswold' to Cheltenham. They shadowed the Lancastrians moving on Tewkesbury – whose pause at Gloucester had probably enabled the king to make up lost ground: 'all that day was evermore the King's host within five or six miles of his enemies; he in the plain country and they amongst woods; having always good espialls upon them'. But the Yorkists suffered from lack of victuals. They were parched in the warm sunlight, and had small refreshment at a brook which 'was so soon troubled with the carriages that had passed it'. At Cheltenham, having sure intelligence that his enemies had just halted five miles away at Tewkesbury, Edward was able to rest and feed his troops, before pushing on to encamp about dusk within three miles of the enemy position.[50]

Next day (Saturday 4 May) the Yorkists advanced to the attack. The Lancastrians held a strong defensive position on a hill not far from Tewkesbury abbey, approaches to which were hindered by dykes, enclosures and woods – 'it was right hard to approach them near' according to the *Arrivall*. But, once bombardment commenced, the defenders did not all remain in position. The foreward, commanded by Somerset, launched an attack which soon ran into difficulties; its retreat produced a swift crumbling of the Lancastrian defences. The prince of Wales, Devon, Wenlock and John Beaufort were killed in the rout. Many leading Lancastrians took refuge in the abbey and fell into Edward's hands. At Tewkesbury he executed many implacable opponents, including Somerset.[51]

Lancastrian tactics at Tewkesbury are hard to account for. Perhaps Somerset was a chivalrous hothead, frustrated by the failures to challenge Edward in recent days, and burning to emulate the deeds of his elder brother and of Charles the Bold, in whose army he had served. Perhaps the Lancastrian command decided that a desperate throw with their best troops was needed, rather like what Oxford may have tried at the start of the battle of Bosworth, and Richard III in its later stages. The Lancastrians had been beaten strategically in a nerve-racking advance through the West Country, and they may have rightly suspected that the bulk of their tired and perhaps demoralized levies had no stomach for a long defence.

The decisive move in the western campaign had been Edward's arrival at Cirencester. This had threatened Lancastrian strategy. But, going on from Bath, then from Bristol, the Lancastrians had shown considerable skill in shaking off Edward's threat. Their command may, indeed, have been divided at Bristol as to whether to go out and confront Edward or to run for the Severn bridges, for there seems to have been a drastic change of plan during the advance on Sodbury. The decision taken then turned out badly, for Edward could not be shaken off and was able to bring his men into battle less weary than their opponents.

Despite the death of the prince of Wales and the capture of Margaret of Anjou, Edward's labours were, he anticipated, not yet over. Rebels were stirring in Wales and the north. The day after the battle, Clarence wrote to Henry Vernon saying that Edward intended to go to the north in haste to establish peaceful government, and requesting Vernon to join him (Clarence) with an arrayed company at Coventry on 12 May. The king's need for fresh troops is reflected in his dispatch of signet letters requesting Vernon's aid on two successive days, from Tewkesbury on 7 May and Worcester on the 8th. In the second, Edward expatiated on the 'murmurs and commotions' being made by the commons in various parts of the realm. Clarence, again summoning Vernon, from Coventry on 10 May, elaborated on the destruction threatening the land. By 14 May, however, it was clear to Edward that there would be no large-scale northern rebellion: those in the field had submitted to the earl of Northumberland.[52]

But Edward received news of a dangerous rising in the south-east which he had been too busy to safeguard against. On 12 May a force commanded by the Bastard of Fauconberg, hoping to rescue Henry VI, appeared before London. Fauconberg, commander of his kinsman Warwick's ships in the Channel, had landed in Kent and raised the commons. Backbone was added to his army by the 300 soldiers under Sir George Broke sent from the Calais garrison by Sir Walter Wrottesley and Sir Geoffrey Gate. Edward, setting out from Coventry, reached London with 30,000 horsemen on 21 May, after the rebels' retreat. Many of them went home, but the Bastard with a nucleus of soldiers went via Rochester to Sandwich, which he garrisoned strongly, according to the *Arrivall*. The Bastard's attempt to rescue Henry seems to have been his death-warrant: on the night Edward entered London, Henry perished in the Tower.[53]

On 22 May Edward's forward set out from London into Kent under Gloucester's command; Edward soon followed with the rest of his army. He arrived at Canterbury on the 26th, making, according to the chronicler Stone, an impressive display of strength. His army was said to be 40,000 strong, and he was well supported by peers – the dukes of Clarence, Gloucester, Norfolk and Suffolk; the earls of Arundel, Wiltshire and Kyme; Lords Scales, Talbot, Grey of Ruthin, Hastings and Mountjoy. The Bastard of Fauconberg had probably not seriously intended to defy such an array at Sandwich, but to negotiate favourable terms of surrender. On 27 May Gloucester received his submission and took possession of his ships at Sandwich, and the Bastard received the promised pardon on 10 June. Edward was now well placed to regain control of Calais, whose soldiers also wished to bargain for its surrender. In July the new lieutenant of Calais, Lord Hastings, and Lord Howard crossed the Channel with a large force. Gate and his fellow captains submitted and gained pardons.[54]

After his arrival at Canterbury Edward was never again to campaign on English soil. Embers of rebellion flickered dimly, despite Louis XI's desultory attempts to breathe life into them. Sforza de' Bettini reported to the duke of Milan on 16 July 1471 that Louis, desirous of encouraging continued disturbance in England, had ordered financial assistance to Jasper Tudor who, with Scottish help, was holding 'a good number of towns' in Wales. On 27 August William Herbert, earl of Pembroke, and Lord Ferrers were commissioned to array in South Wales and adjacent shires and Marches against Jasper, and on 11 September the earl of Shrewsbury was commissioned to array in Shropshire, Staffordshire and the northern Marches to resist the rebels in North Wales and the Marches. Jasper soon had to give up, taking ship for France with his young nephew Henry, the future Henry VII. In 1473 Oxford, who had escaped abroad after Barnet, attempted with assistance from Louis to invade southern England, unsuccessfully. It is difficult to judge in whose dynastic interest Jasper Tudor and Oxford were operating, after the deaths of Henry VI, his son and Beaufort kinsmen. Contemporary sources are not explicit, and later writers were uninterested in these failures. It is hard to avoid the conclusion that Jasper's stir was the first attempt to put Henry Tudor on the throne – since there was no other Lancastrian heir available. The seriousness with which his claim was taken in Yorkist circles in 1483 may have been because it had become familiar to them in 1471.[55]

How good a general was Edward? Commynes certainly thought it was remarkable that he had fought in so many battles and never been on the losing side. The reasons for his failure in June 1469 are mysterious, but clearly he made a feeble and ineffective military showing. The Lincolnshiremen over whom he triumphed in March 1470 may not have been of high calibre, and his other opponents then were badly organized. Nevertheless, Edward's strategy in that campaign was impeccable: his army was well organized, and his speedy movements hampered co-ordinated resistance. The loss of his crown in September was simply due to betrayal – as in the previous March, and probably early in 1469, his military dispositions were influenced by faulty political assessments.

Edward's greatest test as a general was his invasion in 1471: he landed, like so many others in the period, as an adventurer, with a miniature army – though with considerable expectations of gaining support. The fullest source for the invasion is, unfortunately, completely biased in his favour: the *Arrivall* was written as a semi-official account of it. But other sources do not contradict its impression. There seems little doubt that Edward's forces were led in 1471 with speed, tenacity and, on occasion, great boldness in face of numerical superiority. Despite the considerable changes of size and composition in the Yorkist army during a campaign which ranged over most of the length and breadth of England, it remained well organized, efficient. Edward repeatedly took the initiative, against the threats from levies in Yorkshire and at Newark, against Warwick at Coventry and his allies in Leicester, against London, against Warwick advancing on London. Then there was Edward's brilliant disruption of the western Lancastrians' tricky and tenaciously executed strategy, a feat particularly admired by the second continuator of the *Crowland Chronicle*. After all this, Edward immediately prepared to mount expeditions, first against his northern opponents, then against his south-eastern ones. It cannot be proved that Edward was the military genius responsible for these achievements. At the very least the campaign of 1471 demonstrates that he had a flair for picking expert war counsellors, and for recognizing – and putting into execution – exceptionally good advice. Yorkist military efforts in 1471 showed a high degree of concentration. This was successful against the odds because Edward's opponents failed to concentrate their efforts against him. They had good commanders and good troops, but no captain-general with the authority to impose unity. Yet Warwick's passivity at Coventry may have had more justification than his tardiness in supporting allies in the previous two years. He probably appreciated that he would find Edward a tough opponent to take on single-handed, and that he needed time to get his Lancastrian allies to co-operate with him in the field. At Barnet he came near to destroying Edward. But the decision of the Lancastrian lords in the west after Barnet not to challenge Edward directly is less defensible than Warwick's passivity at Coventry. In the days after the battle Edward was vulnerable: his smallish army had been badly mauled and he had not had time to recruit widely. Lancastrian forces were astir at Calais and in the Channel. The Lancastrian cause died, and so did Henry, because the western lords lacked the offensive spirit to march on London to his rescue – as the young Edward had marched to save a faltering cause in 1461.

Chapter 5

The Later Risings, 1483–97

More is known, mainly from Polydore Vergil's account, of the complex plotting leading up to the rising in October 1483 against the new king, Richard III, than about the seemingly desultory fighting.[1] The second continuator of the *Crowland Chronicle* says that there was discontent in southern shires over the imprisonment of Edward IV's sons – and, presumably, over the dramatic deposition of Edward V and Richard's seizing of the crown. Nobles angered by these events fomented and attempted to exploit dissident feeling. According to Vergil, there was devised in London a 'ladies' plot' between Edward IV's widow, Elizabeth Wydeville, whose family had, as in 1469, been violently ejected from influence at court, and Margaret Beaufort, Lord Stanley's wife. Margaret was the daughter of John Beaufort, duke of Somerset (d. 1444), and the widow of Henry VI's half-brother Edmund Tudor, earl of Richmond (d. 1456). The ladies' objective was to displace Richard on the throne by Margaret's son Henry Tudor, who was to swear to marry one of Edward IV's daughters. He had fled abroad as a boy after the Lancastrian débâcle in 1471 and had lived ever since in the duke of Brittany's protective custody.[2]

Margaret Beaufort appointed as her 'chief dealer' in the conspiracy Reginald Bray, who speedily received oaths of adherence from gentlefolk, including Giles Daubeney, Richard Guildford, Thomas Romney and John Cheyney. The dowager queen drew in her kinsfolk and their adherents, notably her son Thomas Grey, marquess of Dorset, who, like his mother, had sought refuge from Richard in sanctuary. Other distinguished plotters were Peter Courtenay, bishop of Exeter, and his cousin Edward Courtenay, heir to the earldom of Devon.[3] Dissidence among Yorkist nobles, as in 1469–70, aroused the expectations of those sympathetic to 'the old cause'.

In its early stages the plot was given a new impetus and focus through the curious treason of the 'kingmaker' who had aided Richard's elevation to the throne – Henry Stafford, duke of Buckingham, who had been lavishly rewarded by his master.[4] Buckingham confided in John Morton, bishop of Ely, a former Yorkist councillor – and, before then, staunch attendant of Henry VI – whose arrest had been ordered by Richard when he was protector of the realm, and who was in the duke's custody at Brecon castle. Morton put the dissident duke in touch with Bray, the agent of Margaret Beaufort – who was Buckingham's aunt. Plans were laid for Buckingham to raise revolt in South Wales, at Brecon. In Brittany, Henry Tudor was visited by a succession of envoys who urged him to stake his claim. His mother's agent Hugh Conway brought money and the advice that he should land in Wales – advice echoed by Guildford's agent Thomas Romney. Buckingham accepted Morton's counsel to send a message to Henry, urging him to hasten over in order to marry Edward IV's daughter Elizabeth, and with her take the throne. Henry conferred with the duke of Brittany, whose strained relations with Richard inclined him to encourage Henry's attempt and offer substantial support.[5]

A revolt in Wales intended to link up with an invasion force from Brittany, and with widely scattered risings in southern England, was crucially dependent on good timing. Buckingham needed to rally his Welsh tenants and cross the Severn speedily in order to link up with his allies in England before the king could concentrate an army. But surprise was lost because the plot proved leaky: royal spies ferreted out information about it, and the king was able to plan his strategy. He entrusted the safeguard of London to the duke of Norfolk, who on 10 October summoned John Paston's aid for its defence against the Kentishmen who he said were 'up [in arms] in the weald'.[6] Richard concentrated his own and his other supporters' energies on the defeat of Buckingham. In the principality and Marches of Wales the king's men were warned to be prepared to occupy the duke's properties as soon as he made his move. His envious neighbours Roger Vaughan of Tretower and the latter's brothers and kinsmen needed little incitement to keep a watch on the duke's lordship of Brecknock. The Worcestershire landowner Humphrey Stafford raised a force to guard the passes and river crossings into England. On 11 October Viscount Lovell, in the king's company at Lincoln, wrote to the Oxfordshire landowner Sir William Stonor, relaying the command to Stonor to bring his company to the royal presence at Leicester on 20 October.[7] Next day Richard wrote confidently in his own hand to the chancellor Bishop Russell about the measures against Buckingham: 'We assure you there was never false traitor better purveyed for as this bearer Gloucester [a herald] shall show you.'[8] A royal signet letter dated Lincoln, 13 October, informed the corporation of Southampton of Buckingham's treasonable intentions and ordered the dispatch of an urban contingent, to report to the king at Coventry on 22 October.[9] Richard 'by word of mouth' issued a general commission of array to Lovell to raise forces against the duke, dated at Leicester on 23 October.[10]

Richard's foreknowledge of the rebels' plans gave him the luxury – unusual for a king defending his crown in this period – of being able to time counter-measures confidently. The plotters may have unwittingly given him time to prepare, and have let the campaigning season go by, because they were anxiously awaiting the arrival on British soil of Henry, an unsullied leader, better able to win men's hearts than the dubious Buckingham.[11] But royal preparations may have at last forced their hands. According to the 1484 Acts of Attainder passed against about 100 participants in the revolt, on 18 October there were risings at Brecon, Maidstone (Kent), Newbury (Berks.), Salisbury (Wilts.) and Exeter (Devon).[12]

Richard moved south-west from Leicester through the Midlands to isolate and confront Buckingham. The duke was unable to put up any opposition. He was effectively hemmed in by neighbouring Ricardians. His sullen Welsh soldiery deserted. At Weobley (Herefs.) he seems to have tried in vain to rally the local gentlefolk. Whilst he was there, the Vaughans sacked his castle at Brecon. From Weobley Buckingham vanished into hiding: betrayed, he was executed at Salisbury, during the king's stay there, on 2 November.[13] Richard soon afterwards reached Bridport (Dorset), and it was probably on this occasion that a prominent burgess of the town, Richard Orchard, provided 'the Kings Wyne' for which he was paid 13s. 4d. by the borough cofferer.[14] Richard's aims were to secure the coast and advance on the rebels in Exeter, who were headed by the marquess of Dorset and the Courtenays. Meanwhile the Kentish and other south-eastern rebels, prominent among whom was Sir Richard Guildford, seem to have been deterred from attacking London by the duke of Norfolk's defence. They may have concentrated at Guildford (Surrey), hopefully awaiting the arrival of Welsh, western or Breton allies.[15]

But the rebel leaders in Exeter were not prepared to trust to its sound defences till Henry arrived. They were intent on escaping from Richard. He occupied the city without difficulty, and there executed the captured Sir Thomas St Leger and Thomas Romney.[16] Henry, whose army of 5,000 Bretons in fifteen ships had been scattered in a storm, hove to off the West Country coast just too late. He prudently refrained from landing and sailed to Normandy.[17] The south-eastern rebels dispersed.

Edward Plumpton's letter of 18 October records how Lancashiremen had been troubled 'marvellously, that they know not what to do', as rumours had spread of Buckingham's strength, and messengers came daily from him and the king. They had particular reason for equivocation. The local magnate, Lord Stanley, an experienced 'trimmer', was Margaret Beaufort's husband. His son Lord Strange was about to set out from their place at Lathom with 10,000 men 'whither men cannot say'.[18] Such equivocations early in the campaign may have been resolved by Richard's success in catching Buckingham and his allies wrong-footed, and in pressing home his advantage. Other nobles besides Norfolk and Lovell had rallied to the king's support. By commission dated Bridport, 5 November, William Herbert, now earl of Huntingdon, was ordered to array in Wales to resist the rebels. Norfolk's son the earl of Surrey and Lord Cobham were commissioned (Exeter, 8 November) to besiege Bodiam castle (Sussex), and Lords Scrope of Bolton and Zouche to array against and punish rebels in western counties (Exeter, 13 November).[19] Among peers rewarded in 1484 for good service against the rebels were Viscount Lisle and Lords Cobham, Grey of Codnor, and Neville.[20] Richard's success against Buckingham seems to have disheartened the remaining rebels – though it might be viewed as a blessing in disguise for Henry's cause. They lacked the temerity displayed by West Country Lancastrians after Barnet in 1471, abandoning the game even though a powerful foreign force was hastening to their support. Had they known Henry's resolute character better, they might have shown more courage.

Despite Richard's brilliant victory, the revolt had ominous implications for his rule. Henry had been seriously promoted as a candidate for the throne: the tensions aroused by Richard's usurpation had revived dynastic conflict, quiescent since 1471. The flight abroad of distinguished dissidents and rebels gave continued credit to Henry's claim. Among his adherents were the queen dowager's brother Sir Edward Wydeville and her son Dorset, and Bishops Morton and Courtenay.[21] For the first time since 1470, a king was menaced by a formidable body of gentlefolk in exile. The large number of attainders enacted in 1484 partly reflect Richard's failure to reconcile opponents, though he did not give up hope of doing so.[22]

Henry's invasion in August 1485 was not unexpected. In a proclamation issued on 7 December 1484 and re-issued on 23 June 1485, Richard had particularized Henry's alleged machinations, and warned subjects to be prepared to resist in case he landed, and to array when commanded.[23] Henry cast off in the Seine estuary on 1 August. According to the newsletter written on 1 March 1486 to the Catholic kings of Spain by their retired councillor Mosén Diego de Valera, Charles VIII of France provided him with 2,000 soldiers paid up for four months, a loan of 50,000 crowns and a fleet for transport. In size, provision of finance, and calibre of leadership Henry's expedition compares favourably with foreign-backed invasions in 1462, 1470 and 1471.[24]

He landed on 7 August in Milford Haven (Pembrokeshire).[25] His sally at a remote part of west Wales rather than the heartlands of southern England was probably influenced by his own and Oxford's failures on the latter's shores, and by Jasper Tudor's successes since the 1460s in gaining support in his former earldom of Pembroke and elsewhere in Wales. Lovell's naval and defence measures centring on Southampton may also have been a determining factor.[26] Thus Henry eschewed the invasion strategy in vogue from 1469 to 1483, and adopted the Welsh option often considered by Lancastrians in the 1460s, and urged on him in 1483.

Henry's Welsh strategy paid off. Officials, gentlefolk and townsmen, when they did not actually welcome him, were slow to oppose his initially vulnerable and nervous force. Henry, his captain-general Oxford, and the captain of his French troops, Philibert de Chandée, were probably agreed on the desirability of getting through Wales quickly, not least in order to draw out Henry's sympathizers in England who had encouraged his enterprise.[27] He wrote to his mother, his stepfather Lord Stanley, the latter's brother Sir William Stanley (chamberlain of North Wales), Lord Talbot and other English lords that he was determined to cross the Severn and march through Shropshire towards London. He requested that they meet him in arms. With impressive speed he acted on his word. Evading potential opponents and exploiting their hesitations, he moved so rapidly up to and along the coast of Cardigan Bay, and inland through what the Crowland continuator described as 'rugged and indirect tracts', that he was before the gates of Shrewsbury on 15 August. *En route* he had attracted some recruits, notably, at Newton, Rhys ap Thomas, whose opposition he had feared, and who was won over, according to Polydore Vergil, by the promise of the 'perpetual lieutenantship of Wales'.[28] But perhaps memories of how their hopes of crushing 'the Saxons' in 1469 had been disappointed, deterred many Welshmen from joining this undoubtedly British prince. Thomas Mytton, one of the bailiffs of well-fortified Shrewsbury, put up what turned out to be only a token resistance.[29] Soon after Henry had left the town, when he was encamped at Newport, the earl of Shrewsbury's uncle Sir Gilbert Talbot joined him with over 500 men. Henry may have been moving north-eastwards towards Stafford because of news that Lord Stanley had advanced from Lancashire to hold the town with nearly 5,000 men. But when he heard of Henry's approach, Stanley abandoned Stafford and went south-eastwards as far as Atherstone (Warwicks.), presumably on the line of Henry's anticipated advance towards London. Sir William Stanley, who appears to have been operating with a retinue independently of his brother (as he had at Blore Heath in 1459), visited Henry at Stafford, but did not join him or send troops. There was a more urgent reason than usual for Stanleyan equivocation. Lord Stanley's son Lord Strange, who had plotted with Sir William to aid Henry, was in the king's hands. Henry thus found himself in the middle of England without the overt support of the nobles on whom he had particularly relied to augment his invasion force.

Richard had been in the north since May. He was at Nottingham when he received news of Henry's landing on 11 August.[30] Vergil says that he was relying particularly on Walter Herbert and Rhys ap Thomas, 'who ruled Wales with equal authority', to dispose of Henry's force. Perhaps he was remembering how Buckingham's rising had been hampered by Welsh opposition, and how Jasper Tudor's numerous attempts to raise revolt in Wales had never had more than local success. Nevertheless, he prudently summoned the military aid of Henry Percy, earl of Northumberland, and other nobles. Sir Robert Brackenbury, lieutenant of the Tower, was ordered to bring up a southern force. But Richard experienced some shocks. Lord Stanley, on the excuse of illness, evaded obedience to his summons. The thwarting of Strange's flight from court induced his confession of treason plotted with his uncle and Sir John Savage. The news of Henry's capture of Shrewsbury reached Richard on 15 August: he was enraged by it and the broken promises which had facilitated it.[31] He determined to go against Henry as quickly as possible. His decisiveness in 1483 showed that he had digested the lesson of the 1469–71 campaigns that chief rebels must be encountered before they could bring up support. Royal 'scurriers' reported Henry's encampment at Lichfield, threatening Richard's southern communications.

On 19 August the king moved from Nottingham southwards to Leicester. Next day the rebel army took a converging course from Lichfield to Tamworth. On the way Henry lost touch with his army. That night, with only twenty soldiers, he 'stayed by the way, uncertain what was best as to deliberate what he might do'. Vergil's elliptical words perhaps hint at contemplated flight – desertion by commanders was not uncommon in the Wars of the Roses. No wonder there was uneasiness in Henry's army. His appearance at Tamworth 'in the grey of morning' may have prevented its disintegration in the nick of time. It speaks volumes for his pertinacity.

On 21 August the large, augmented royal army set out westwards from Leicester, towards the line of Watling Street running south-east of Tamworth through Atherstone. Leading royal supporters were Norfolk and his son Surrey, Northumberland, Lovell and Lords Ferrers and Zouche.[32] On the night of the 21st, royal and rebel armies – and the ambivalent Stanley forces – were encamped at most a few hours' march from each other. Next morning Richard's army manned the eastern crest of Ambien Hill, less than two miles south of Market Bosworth, and the tip of higher ground running near Sutton Cheney.[33] Henry's army probably bivouacked between Atherstone and Ambien Hill (under six miles distant as the crow flies). His men foraged at Atherstone and places about three miles and less from it – at Witherley, Mancetter, Fenny Drayton and Atterton to the south and east.[34]

According to Vergil, Richard's army was more than twice as large as Henry's army of 5,000, well supplied with cavalry as well as infantry, and well equipped with artillery.[35] But Henry had some advantages. Nervousness about treason in the royal camp on the eve of battle is strongly attested: it may have affected Richard's tactical judgment the next day. Well-paid foreign mercenaries, such as Henry deployed, had often fought more tenaciously than native conscripts.[36] Henry had some artillery, though probably of light calibre.[37] He had experienced captains in Jasper Tudor and Oxford, and a galaxy of competent knights, including Edward Wydeville, John Cheyney, John Savage, Robert Willoughby, Richard Edgcombe, Edward Poynings, Giles Daubeney and Richard Guildford.[38] Above all, in conference with the Stanley brothers at Atherstone on 21 August, according to Vergil, Henry gained what he considered a firm commitment of Stanleyan aid in the imminent battle.

Early on the morning of 22 August, Henry's army deployed for battle. To his consternation, Lord Stanley sent an evasive reply to his request to set his soldiers in array, instead approaching the field 'as in the mid way betwixt the two battles' (Vergil). Thus far committed, Henry had to go on. He sent his vanguard forward, captained by Oxford, with archers in the front iine, and himself followed with a meagre main 'battle' – a troop of cavalry and a few footmen. Confronting them was the king's much larger vanguard, comprising horse and foot, with archers to the fore, according to Vergil, 'like a most strong trench and bulwark'. Norfolk and Brackenbury were in command.[39] Richard followed with the main 'battle', a 'choice force of soldiers'. According to Vergil, the rebel army's line of approach took advantage of a marsh between the armies, skirting to the left of it, and getting the rising sun behind them. This is puzzling. The east is not the direction from which one would have expected Henry's army to assault the king's force, and nothing in the sources suggests that it did. If the marsh mentioned by Vergil was the one at the bottom of the long southern slopes of Ambien Hill, it may be that Oxford advanced there, on the enemy's southern flank below the marsh, then turned back to approach the enemy's front from the south-east. This unconventional manoeuvring might have been aimed at disconcerting the royal forces and getting closer to them with the marsh's protection. Scraps of evidence give some support to Vergil's statement, and hint at the reasons for his manoeuvre. According to the poem *The Rose of*

England, the 'blue boar' (Oxford) who commanded Henry's van,

> the right hand of them [the king's troops] he took
> the sun and wind of them to get.[40]

In so doing he would have applied precepts laid down by the classical military writer Vegetius, who stressed the advantages to be gained from overlapping the enemy's flank, and from having the sun and wind behind one.[41] Such may have seemed crucial advantages in neutralizing royal firepower and increasing the effectiveness of Henry's archers. According to Molinet, Richard had his guns fired at the rebels: then Henry's Frenchmen, gauging the king's position by the firing, counselled that, to escape bombardment, the assault should be made on the flank (*costé*) of the king's 'battle', not on its front – and as a result of this course, the royal vanguard was eventually defeated.[42]

Vergil says that as soon as the king saw that the rebels had passed the marsh, he commanded his men to charge them. Oxford's expert direction and the good discipline of his troops enabled them to withstand and confuse the royal vanguard. Whilst the two vans were engaged, Richard received reports that Henry was 'afar off' with a small force, which he confirmed by personal observation. It may be that, in the movements before the battle, a wide gap had opened up between Henry's van and main 'battle'. But the separation may have been deliberate. Perhaps it had been decided that Oxford and some of his best troops should test the uncertain will of the royal army whilst Henry held off, so that, in the event of disaster, Henry could escape the fate of the prince of Wales at Tewkesbury in 1471. He and Oxford were to follow similar tactics at Stoke in 1487, and near Blackheath in 1497 Henry apparently remained stationary with the main 'battle' again, whilst the vanguard under Daubeney engaged the western rebels.[43]

The crisis of the battle resulted from Richard's reaction to the gap between Henry's vanguard and unimpressive main 'battle'. The king may have discerned in this an opportunity to curtail Henry's challenge abruptly – and one which might speedily evaporate, since Oxford's defeat would leave the retreating Henry a chance to fight another day. Vergil says of the king: 'all inflamed with ire, he struck his horse with the spurs, and runneth out of th'one side without the vanwards against him'. In face of the violence of Richard's attack, Henry's retinue faltered and his life was in danger. He was rescued by the intervention of the hitherto neutral Sir William Stanley with 3,000 men. The king's supporters broke under this pressure – and the earl of Northumberland failed to come to his rescue, possibly because he had an understanding with Henry.[44] Richard rejected a captain's expert advice to flee: 'Salaçar, please God that I do not take one step backwards, for I want to die like a king or win victory in this battle.' Donning the royal crown, he encouraged his remaining supporters to fight to the death.[45] Molinet says that, after fighting valiantly, crown on head, Richard, finding himself utterly abandoned, in the end tried to escape. But his horse leapt into marshy ground. Whilst the king floundered, a Welshman killed him with a halberd's blow.[46] According to Henry's proclamation after the battle, Richard was killed at a place called 'Sandeford', which Gairdner plausibly identified as a ford across a brook, nearby where there is now a road between Shenton and Sutton Cheney.[47] This low-lying, damp spot, seen on a wet August day, conjures up a vision of Molinet's marsh.[48]

Once the king's death was known, his remaining soldiers fled or surrendered. Oxford had already independently routed the royal van.[49] According to Vergil, about 1,000 were killed, scarcely 100 of them on Henry's side.[50] Among the slain were Norfolk, Ferrers and Brackenbury. Lovell and Salaçar made good their escape. Surrey was captured on the field, injured.[51]

Richard's defeat can be attributed to treacheries in the field. The day after the battle, the council of the city of York debated reports that Richard III 'through great treason of the Duke of Norfolk [*sic*] and many other that turned against him . . . was piteously slain and murdered'.[52] But were Northumberland's and Lord Stanley's failure to support the king, and Sir William Stanley's intervention against him, inevitable? The earl and the Stanleys played a waiting game – had tactical developments been different, perhaps they would have felt obliged to support Richard. When his impressive vanguard was skilfully pinned down by Oxford, the orthodox move for him would have been to reinforce it with his main 'battle'. But Richard – presumably, with his picked household cavalry – moved boldly out of his lines. His erratic boldness perhaps confirmed the lukewarm in their desire not to hazard themselves, and gave the dissident hopes of picking him off. It is remarkable that two widely separated sources, the Crowland continuator and Vergil, emphasized Richard's disturbed spirits on the morning of the battle. Perhaps the treasons already manifest, and his fears that others might occur, clouded his tactical judgment, so that he angrily cast away his crown and his life, and the fortunes and lives of loyal followers.

Yet the course of the battle might not have gone so badly for Richard but for Oxford's initial success in confronting his vanguard. Though Ambien Hill is a good place for an overnight encampment, it is flawed as a defensive position. The marshy ground to the south provides cover for attackers as well as defenders, and the frontal western slopes can be rushed. Richard had been schooled in his brother's campaigns – and may have learnt his preference for the offensive. Perhaps he never intended to fight at Ambien Hill, but to advance thence on Henry's camp. Henry's captains, some of whom were familiar with the methods of the Yorkist princes, may have decided that their only hope of victory lay in seizing the initiative and forestalling an attack from the much larger royal army, whose size would make it slower to get under way. The Crowland chronicler mentions incidents in Richard's camp which might imply that his troops had to array in haste in face of an unexpected emergency. At daybreak there were no chaplains present to perform divine service for the king, and there was no breakfast prepared for him. Yet it is unthinkable that he should have been in the field without chaplains or cooks. A likely explanation is that they were still asleep, and Richard had to arm and array hastily. Then, says the Crowland continuator, as the rebels advanced, Richard ordered the traitor Strange to be executed instantly. But his servants delayed carrying out the order. Richard's failure to make an example of Strange is in glaring contrast to Edward's execution of Lord Welles before his troops engaged the Lincolnshiremen in 1470, and bespeaks too a Richard thrown off balance by an unexpected attack. He may have underestimated the offensive spirit of his opponents, some of whom had not shown any in 1483.

On the morrow of Bosworth, Henry doubtless realized that his victory, despite its magnitude, gave no prospect of stable rule. Though he had declared his intention of marrying Edward's eldest daughter, Yorkist claimants were likely to be countenanced by some of that majority of subjects who had shown no interest in his claim to the throne. The triumph of the candidate supported by Lancastrian, Wydeville and Buckingham partisans automatically threatened the interests of those favoured by Richard, including leading families such as the de la Poles, Howards and Scropes. Richard's overthrow unbalanced the precarious stability of northern society. He had gained popularity in the north by reconciling and favouring the interests of gentlefolk and townsmen. As Edward's lieutenant, and as lord protector and king, he had used his control of former estates of Warwick the Kingmaker as a means of attaching loyalties and asserting authority. Neville adherents there, and in Warwickshire, Worcestershire and other Midland and southern shires, had no initial expectation of a ladder to royal redress and patronage under the rule of a Tudor with whom they had no 'natural' ties. They were attracted by the claim to the throne of an impeccably Neville and Yorkist candidate, Clarence's fifteen-year-old son, Edward earl of Warwick – heir, since the death of his aunt, Richard's wife Anne Neville, in 1484, to the whole of the Kingmaker's inheritance.[53] Thus Henry's conquest of England had a disruptive effect, producing, like Edward's in 1461, dynastic strife fuelled by the disarray of lords' interests, particularly in the north.

But swift action by Henry after Bosworth was to hobble dynastic opposition. Before he left Leicester for London, he dispatched Sir Robert Willoughby to Sheriff Hutton castle (Yorks.) to secure Warwick's person and bring him south, to be kept in custody in the Tower.[54] But according to the Castilian correspondent, Valera, Henry, after he was installed in London, ordered the arrest of 'lord Tamorlant', who, he had been informed, really intended Clarence's son to be king, and to marry one of his daughters. 'Tamorlant' was released only after Clarence's son had been received into royal custody, and after two 'counts' who were his kinsmen had sworn homage and perpetual fealty to Henry. Valera's informants may have been referring to the earl of Northumberland. It is plausible that he was tempted by the prospect of Warwick as a pliant young son-in-law on the throne, confirming and enhancing a Percy hegemony in the north which Richard had limited, and which there was no certainty that Henry would promote. The earl was certainly imprisoned by Henry: Giovanni de' Giglis reported on 6 December that he had been released 'sub cautione' of the lords and commons in parliament.[55]

One reason for Henry's imprisonment of Northumberland may have been his fear that the earl would be unable or unwilling to control hostile northern reactions to Richard's overthrow. On 15 October Henry wrote to Lords Stanley and Strange and Sir Edward Stanley, sheriff of Lancashire, ordering them to have the county's levies ready to move under their leadership, since the Scots intended to besiege Berwick and plunder the Marches, trusting to the favour of local dissidents.[56] In a letter to Henry Vernon requesting his armed attendance, dated two days later, Henry stated that rebels allied with the Scots were making insurrections in the northern parts – rebels who, in a spirit reminiscent of 1469, took captains with pseudonyms associated with popular protest – 'Robyn of Riddesdale, Jack St[raw], Thomolyn at Lath and Maister Mendall'.[57] But the alarms quickly subsided. In a proclamation of 20 October, Henry allowed the preparations for arrays to be suspended, since the rebels, understanding that he had made 'politic and mighty purveyance for the recounter and subduing of their said malice and rebellion', had dispersed.[58] Nevertheless, it was realized at court that this was unlikely to be the end of the affair. A correspondent, Betanson, wrote from London on 13 December that there were expectations there of rebellion 'and no man can say of whom; but they deem of Northernmen and Welshmen. And much speech is in the King's house and of his householdmen.'[59] It may have been as a bold device to quieten the north that Northumberland had recently been released, and in January 1486 received northern commissions.[60] Moreover, according to Betanson's letter of 15 February, 'the King proposeth northward hastily after the Parliament, and it is said he purposes to do execution quickly there on such as have offended against him' accompanied 'as it is said, with ten hundred men in harness and with him more than five or six score lords and knights'.[61] Betanson was writing to a Yorkshire landowner: if such rumours gained currency in the shire, it is not surprising that (as in Lincolnshire in 1470) men were prepared to resist the king, and dissident nobles quick to exploit their fears. About 11 April, when Henry had progressed as far as Lincoln, it was reported to him that notable fugitives from Bosworth, Viscount Lovell and Humphrey Stafford, had abandoned sanctuary at Colchester.[62] When he arrived in Ricardian York, there was news that Lovell had assembled a large force a little beyond the Neville castle of Middleham, attracting support within its lordship and that of Richmond, and intending to march on York. Stafford, it was reported, had raised revolt in Worcestershire. According to the testimony of some of his indicted sympathizers, he had spread the false news that the king had pardoned his attainder, and that he was a true liegeman. He may have been trying the old trick of arraying under the pretence of supporting the king against rebellion – whereas in fact he intended to go to Lovell's aid. But many of his supporters wanted to promote the earl of Warwick's claim to the throne, including, possibly, some of the townsfolk of Warwick who received general pardons in 1486–7 – Oliver Alwode, clerk; Robert Beverley, chaplain; William Wellys, mercer alias vintner; John Smyth, barber alias vintner; Robert Barlowe and Ralph Betery, yeomen.[63] Henry, at York, and militarily unprepared, was, according to Vergil, 'struck by great fear'. Nevertheless, he scotched these over-hasty risings by wresting the initiative. He dispatched his poorly armed retinue, 3,000 strong, against the northern rebels' encampment. The Yorkshiremen accepted the terms offered to them; Lovell fled. Alarmed by news of this débâcle, and despite his success in gaining entry to Worcester, Stafford also deserted his men, entering sanctuary at Culham (Berks.) on 11 May.[64]

Pardons enrolled in 1486 reflect Henry's anxiety to reconcile dissidents. On 6 August Sir William Tyler and others were empowered to receive into the king's grace and to grant pardons of life and lands to all rebels in Yorkshire, especially in the lordships of Middleham and Richmond.[65] Pardons granted to north-westerners show how Henry's rule stimulated continued discontent among gentlefolk there, upsetting Ricardian loyalties and the relative influence of rival affinities. Writs to the sheriffs of Northumberland, Cumberland and Yorkshire dated 16 July alleged that Sir Thomas Broughton, Sir John Hudleston, William a Thorneburghe, William Ambrose and others 'for their great rebellions and grievous offences lately by them done . . . keep them in huddle and secret places and over that have disobeyed divers and many his [the king's] letters and Privy Seals'. They were charged to appear before the king within forty days or be reputed traitors.[66] This threat elicited some response. General pardons dated 17 August were granted to them and to Richard Middleton, Geoffrey Fraunke and Henry Hudleston, esquires, and George Middleton, gentleman.[67] By commission dated the following day Sir Richard Tunstall, one of Henry's most trusted retainers, and Sir Thomas Wortley were empowered to take oaths of allegiance and sureties from this group, with the addition of Sir James and Sir Robert Harington and Sir Robert Middleton, who had all been attainted in the 1485 parliament.[68] Sir Thomas Broughton was lord of Broughton-in-Furness (Lancs.).[69] Sir John Hudleston of Millom (Cumberland) was a kinsman and long-time associate of Sir James Harington. Another of his old allies was Sir Thomas Pilkington of Pilkington (Lancs.), attainted in 1485 and fully pardoned on 14 August 1486.[70]

The reason for the reluctance of Harington and his friends to swear allegiance to Henry may have been that they feared he would favour north-western landowners whose interests were inimical to theirs. One of these may have been Tunstall – royal councillor and knight of the body in 1487. As Henry VI's chamberlain, he had faithfully helped to hide the fugitive king in Lancashire and Westmorland after the battle of Hexham (1464). Sir James Harington had played a leading part in Henry VI's capture in 1465, and was rewarded by a royal grant of Tunstall's forfeited Lancashire lordship of Thurland.[71] Harington also had a long-standing, bitter dispute with the Stanleys. He was the younger son of Sir Thomas Harington of Hornby castle (Lancs.), who was killed fighting in the Yorkist interest at Wakefield in 1460. His eldest son, John, was mortally wounded there, leaving two infant daughters, Ann and Elizabeth, as co-heirs to the Harington estates. In 1468 they were in the custody of their uncle Sir James and of Sir John Hudleston. In an undated petition to the king the girls complained that Sir James had 'kept them as prisoners contrary to their will, in divers places by long space, intending the utter destruction and disinheritance of the said complainants'. In 1468 Sir James was occupying Hornby castle and other estates of the inheritance, including Brierley (Yorks.) and a group of properties granted him by Archbishop Neville, Hudleston and others of his father's feoffees in 1463.[72]

But a powerful kinsman of the Haringtons, Lord Stanley, emerged as the girls' self-interested protector. His influence may have procured the commissions appointed in 1468 to inquire into the heirs and inheritance of Sir Thomas and John Harington. The verdict of the inquests, that the girls were the co-heirs, and that Sir James had held the manors and lands since their father's death without title or right, was accepted by the chancellor on petition, and he committed the culprit and Hudleston to the Fleet prison. On 6 December the pair appeared in chancery to present a bond guaranteeing the submission of their disputes with Stanley, especially concerning the wardship and marriage of the girls, to arbitrators headed by the earl of Warwick. Ann and Elizabeth were in fact delivered from Sir James's to Stanley's keeping. Stanley married the former to his younger son Edward, and the latter to his nephew John Stanley.[73]

Sir James clung tenaciously to the family estates, however. On 5 March 1471, a few days before Edward IV's invasion, the government of Henry VI and Warwick ordered provision of a carriage to convey the cannon *Mile Ende* from Bristol to Hornby castle, to assist in Stanley's siege of it, doubtless against Harington's supporters.[74] Not surprisingly, Harington was one of the first to bring a company in support of Edward, to Nottingham, according to the *Arrivall*. But Warkworth says that Stanley's brother Sir William joined Edward with a company there – a characteristic piece of Stanleyan reinsurance.[75] In June 1473 a commission headed by Gloucester, and including Hudleston, Sir John Pilkington, and Thomas Pilkington, esquire, was ordered to take all the properties of the late Sir Thomas and John Harington into the king's hands, displacing the possessors, Sir James Harington and his brother Sir Robert. Seemingly Edward was not prepared to back Sir James fully at the Stanleys' expense. But in Edward's later years Sir James was holding on to Farleton and Brierley (Yorks.), and in 1476 his offences against the crown, and debts to it, were pardoned. The 1483 revolt against Richard III, involving Stanley's wife, may have raised the expectation among Sir James and his friends that their interest might be revived at Stanley expense: conversely, they may have considered that Henry Tudor stood for unalterable Stanley hegemony. Sir James, Sir Robert and Pilkington fought for Richard at Bosworth, and afterwards Henry granted Sir James's forfeited estates to Stanley's son Edward.[76]

These complications hampered Henry's attempts to win north-western allegiances. In 1487 Sir Thomas Broughton, Thomas Harington, Broughton's brother John, James Harington, Edward Frank and Richard Middleton joined in an invasion aimed at overthrowing Henry's rule.[77]

This invasion, escalating from an implausible posture originating among relatively humble folk, demonstrated Henry's continued dynastic weakness, despite his marriage to Elizabeth of York and the birth of their hopefully named son Arthur. A 'lowborn' priest studying at Oxford, William or Richard Symonds, trained the 'ignoble' Lambert Simnel, son of an artisan – perhaps an organmaker or a joiner – to impersonate a Yorkist prince. Symonds cannily conveyed his protégé to Ireland, where pro-Yorkist nobles and townsmen readily accepted him as the earl of Warwick and the rightful king. They sought the support of

Edward IV's sister Margaret (widow of Charles the Bold of Burgundy), and of dissidents in England, notably Lovell, who crossed to Flanders to encourage the co-operation of the dowager duchess. The wide network of plotting alerted king and council that a rising was afoot, but royal offers of pardon did not deter Sir Thomas Broughton from crossing to Flanders. More ominously, Suffolk's eldest son, John de la Pole, earl of Lincoln – the Yorkist kings' nephew – took the same route. On 3 April the earl of Northumberland wrote from his house at Leconfield (Yorks.) to the mayor of York that the previous day he had received the king's letters informing him of Lincoln's departure. According to Vergil, the latter aimed at the crown for himself.[78]

At first Henry feared that Lincoln would invade East Anglia, his ancestral 'country'. In the week commencing 12 March the king rode into Essex, and thence to Bury St Edmunds. On Maundy Thursday (12 April) he was at Norwich with Bishop Fox of Exeter, the earls of Oxford and Derby, Lord FitzWalter, Sir Robert Willoughby 'and in Substance all the Nobles of that Parties'. News arrived daily of invasion preparations on the coasts of Zealand and Flanders, but, like all recent kings threatened with invasion, Henry decided that it was more prudent to take up a central position in the realm, where recruits could reach him more easily from all directions, and whence he could reach the vulnerable north as well as the south-east. On 16 April he went to Walsingham, 'where he prayed devoutly before the image of the Blessed Virgin Mary . . . that he might be preserved from the wiles of his enemies'. He moved via Cambridge to Huntingdon, where on 20 April he wrote to the city council of York, warning them to safeguard the city against any rebel assault. Passing through Northampton, he arrived at Coventry on the 22nd. There his servants and subjects rode in to give support, and on 28 and 30 April he wrote letters to the city council of York about the measures concerted for that city's defence. He ordered the constable of Scarborough castle, William Tunstall, to deliver to the citizens twelve serpentines. On 1 May John Vavasour, recorder of York, reported from Coventry that a royal servant had ridden with 'writing and money' to Sir Richard Tunstall and leading Yorkshire knights, for their assistance in the defence of York in case of need. 'The King', Vavasour told his fellow citizens, 'is greatly accompanied and hath yet no certain knowledge when his enemies will take their shipping.'[79]

Three days later, however, Henry wrote to the York council saying he had sure knowledge that the rebels had left Flanders and departed westwards: consequently, he and his council thought that 'ye shall not need to have any strength or company of men of war for this season' under arms. He licensed the 'Nobles of the South Parties', expensively maintaining their retinues at Coventry, to return to their 'Countries' and make preparations for a summons. But some would not leave, sending 'Part of their People into their Countries for their Relief' till required. Henry retired to Kenilworth castle, writing from there to the mayor and aldermen of York on 8 May, commending their provision of victuals and other 'stuff' for the 'men of worship and their retinues' whom he had commanded to defend the city, and reassuring them that these would be ordered to return if danger threatened again; 'also our cousin the Earl of Northumberland intendith hastily to be in the country nigh unto you'. On the 13th, Henry wrote to the earl of Oxford, telling him that the rebels had landed in Ireland eight days previously, and requesting him to come and give advice and counsel on measures to subdue them.[80] A noble – possibly Oxford – wrote to the Norfolk landowner Sir Edmund Bedingfield about this time, saying that he had shown the king Bedingfield's letter about the execution of a commission of array. Henry, grateful for 'the right good minds and disposition of you and of other gentlemen there towards his Grace', would not as yet put them to 'any further labour or charge', as the rebels were in Ireland:

> nevertheless his Grace will that the country be ready at all times to do his Highness service upon reasonable warning; for so much as the King's Grace intendeth to make provision to send an army into Ireland in haste, not knowing as yet whether that ye, and other about you shall be desired to bear any charge thereto or no.[81]

On 24 May, in Dublin, Simnel was crowned as 'Edward VI' before a motley group, notable among whom was the leading Irish magnate Gerald FitzGerald, earl of Kildare. The most formidable rebel support was a force of German and Swiss mercenaries, 1,500 and 2,000 strong, supplied from the Low Countries by Duchess Margaret. They were commanded by the highly reputed Swiss colonel (and former Augsburg shoemaker) Martin Schwarz. The rebels moved on to the offensive with disconcerting speed, and soon shattered any illusions Henry may have had that he could tie them down in Ireland. The English dissidents, foreign mercenaries and a large Irish force commanded by Thomas Geraldine sailed to Lancashire, landing on 4 June at Piel castle on the Isle of Foudray, belonging to Furness abbey. This invasion point, on the tip of the Furness peninsula, was probably recommended by Broughton. Christopher Urswick, whom Henry had dispatched to Lancashire to ascertain which ports were capable of berthing the rebels' ships, brought him news of the invasion. Immediately the king summoned his council to concert military measures. Already he may have had seven secular peers or heirs presumptive to peerages in his company – the earls of Oxford and Shrewsbury, Viscount Lisle, and

Lords Grey of Ruthin, Hastings, Ferrers of Chartley, and Grey of Powis.[82]

There are four especially valuable accounts of the 1487 campaign. An anonymous account probably written by a soldier in Henry's army is graphically informative about its progress up to the battle of Stoke; but the author was largely ignorant of what went on elsewhere. The York civic archives contain an account of the campaign which is uniquely informative about events in the city and its environs. Two historians, Vergil and Molinet, were less well informed about particulars, but put the whole campaign into a general political context. Vergil was concerned to minimize the support which the invaders received in England; Molinet, sympathetic to the Yorkist cause, stressed the augmentation of their numbers in an allegedly favourable north.[83] Indeed, they aimed particularly to stir Yorkist and Neville sentiment there. James Taite alleged on 31 May before the mayor and leading officials of York that on 25 March he had fallen in with travellers who had a white horse which he recognized as the earl of Lincoln's 'hobby', stabled with Taite when the earl had been with the king in York the previous year. These travelling London merchants' servants reportedly had a bold line in subversive conversation, for example:

> John of Lincoln shall give them all a breakfast that oweth him no love
> nor favour . . . thou shall hear tell that right good gentlemen shall
> take my Lords part. Can ye oght me how far I have to Sir Thomas
> Mallevery place for we must have him writing or else send it to him?

When the merchants arrived in York, said the aspiring spy Taite, 'a servant of theirs showed me that they should meet the Prior of Tynmouth at the sign of the boar' – an appropriately named hostelry![84] At least two Yorkshiremen were attainted for their part in the rebellion – Robert Percy of Knaresborough, and William Kay of Halifax, gentleman. A week after the battle of Stoke, the earl of Northumberland wrote from Richmond to Sir Robert Plumpton with some urgency, saying that 'for [his] own discharge and mine' he should arrest 'divers gentlemen and other commoners' within the keepership of Knaresborough who had assisted the rebels in battle or otherwise, especially John Pullen and Richard Knaresborough.[85]

The most distinguished northern adherents were John Lord Scrope of Bolton and his younger kinsman Thomas Lord Scrope of Masham. They had Neville links – Scrope of Bolton had attempted to rally support in Yorkshire for the Kingmaker against Edward IV in March 1470, and Scrope of Masham was married to the Kingmaker's niece.[86] Nevertheless, the support the rebels gained in the north seems disappointing. In Yorkshire there may have been doubts as to who this

'Edward VI' was, as Henry's men had taken the real earl of Warwick from Sheriff Hutton in 1485. Henry's vigorous showing at York and Lovell's poor one at Middleham in 1486, may have been a deterrent to rebellion, as may the outlandishly foreign complexion of much of the present Yorkist army: the city of York no more wanted to admit Lincoln's German mercenaries in 1487 than it had Edward's in 1471.[87]

Taite had pertinently asked the agitator whom he had met in March whether Lincoln stood 'in condition' with the earl of Northumberland, and received the telling answer that 'as therefor we set little by him'. The preparedness of Northumberland and leading Yorkshire landowners stiffened the defensive backbone of the citizens of York and lessened the rebels' chances of capturing the city. Henry had worked strenuously to safeguard it. On 6 June Northumberland wrote from Leconfield to the York council, giving news of the rebels' landing and affirming his intention to resist: he would be in York for the purpose on the 10th. On the 8th he was still at Leconfield, promising the York citizens that he would be at Pocklington the following evening: '[I] shall not rest there but be with you the same night . . . and upon Sunday next coming [10 June] I will not fail to be with you at the farrest, and tofore if ye think it requisite.' But the earl was sluggish compared to the rebels, who speedily made the arduous crossing of the Pennines, descending through Wensleydale. On 8 June 'Edward VI' wrote a signet letter from Masham to the city of York, testing the water by requesting admission. In fact, like Edward IV in 1471, the rebels put a swift southward drive above securing the city's allegiance. The city chamberlains, returning from a meeting with Lincoln and Lovell the following day, reported that they were bypassing the city through Boroughbridge. Later that day, the pro-Tudor Lord Clifford was admitted through Micklegate Bar with 400 foot and horse; the following day (10 June), Northumberland, doubtless galvanized by the enemy's proximity, arrived at noon 'with many knights and lords of this country'.[88]

Clifford was chivalrously determined to take a crack at the disappearing enemy on his own. The prudent citizens laconically recorded the disastrous outcome. On the afternoon of Northumberland's arrival in York, Clifford sallied out, encamping that night at Tadcaster. In fact he had got too close to the rebels lying on Bramham Moor, and that night they attacked and scattered his panicked force. Clifford fled back to York, his baggage abandoned and captured. Two days later he set off again, with Northumberland and the Tudor Yorkshire forces (estimated by the city at 6,000), intent on linking up with the king. Once more Northumberland and Clifford were the victims of poor intelligence – there were other Yorkist forces hovering in the vicinity. The two Lord Scropes rode up to Bootham

Bar, 'there cried King Edward', and assaulted the gates, but the commons acting as watchmen put up a good defence and beat the rebels off. Northumberland, still within six miles of the city, returned with Clifford and garrisoned York for over a week, leaving on 14 June – not to link up with Henry in Nottinghamshire, but to go northwards, presumably to mop up Scrope's following.[89]

Thus Henry's commanders north of the Trent, though hanging on to York, had signally failed to hold the invasion forces there, and were deterred by relatively insignificant forces from adding to the king's main strength. If an uncorroborated episode related by Molinet is true, Tudor ineffectiveness in stopping the rebels was even more striking. Molinet says that Sir Edward Wydeville, with an advance force of 6,000 from the royal army, penetrated into Yorkshire as far as Doncaster, to reconnoitre the rebels' position. But their strength forced Wydeville to retreat for three days through Sherwood Forest to Nottingham, to link up with the king's main force.[90] Perhaps Lincoln and Lovell concluded that poorly co-ordinated enemy forces were reacting similarly to the opponents of Edward's bold advance through south Yorkshire and Nottinghamshire in 1471.

Henry, at Kenilworth when the invasion took place, had his main forces assembled and moving northwards within a week – as fast as might be expected, but too late to halt the rebels north of Trent.[91] According to the anonymous memorialist, he passed through Coventry and Leicester, enforcing strict discipline at Leicester and Loughborough, where he arrived on 11 June.[92] The following day, the army advanced north to encamp for the night 'under a Wood called Bonley [Bouley?] Rice'. This may have been the encampment near Nottingham described by Vergil as 'the wood which is called Banrys in the vernacular'. Possibly Henry's bivouac was at Bunny (Notts.), where 'Boneyris' is recorded in 1330 ('Bonnyrise' in 1572, 'Bonney Reyce' in 1582).[93] On 13 June, in fine weather, the army set out again, but may have lost its way, failing to reach Nottingham, perhaps the day's objective. The foreward and the main 'battle' spent the night in hastily selected quarters, the former below a hill, the latter in a village (where the king lodged in a gentleman's house) and adjacent beanfield. The village may have been Ruddington, three miles south of Nottingham.

Next day (the feast of Corpus Christi), after Henry had heard Mass in the parish church, and trumpets had sounded to horse, he seems to have puzzled some of his soldiers by leaving the army, riding 'backwards'. But this turned out to be (consciously or not) a neat morale-booster, for he returned with Lord Strange, who was accompanied by 'a great Host'. Nevertheless, there was some nervousness in camp that evening; many fled after a disturbance. Next day Henry had sure intelligence about the enemy's movements: they were just north of the Trent, passing away from him through Southwell towards Newark. So as not to be outflanked, on the 15th Henry moved, south of the river, on a parallel course, halting for the night at Ratcliffe. The nervousness in the army showed itself in the same way as the previous night. On the morning of 16 June, Henry, as before Bosworth, got his men on the road very early in the morning: guides from Ratcliffe led Oxford's foreward and the main 'battle' to arrive before nine o'clock at Stoke, not far out of Newark, where, now on Henry's side of the river, the rebels had encamped.

Lincoln responded vigorously to the king's challenge, leading his troops into attack. His force, which was to be officially estimated at 8,000, was heavily outnumbered: the observer in Henry's army thought that the 'great Host' which Lord Strange had brought to Henry's support was 'enough to have beaten all the king's enemies, only of Lord Derby's and his own folk'. The royal council of war at the start of the expedition had set up a powerful foreward under Oxford's command: with him were the earl of Shrewsbury, Viscount Lisle, Lords Grey of Ruthin, Hastings, and Ferrers of Chartley. There were appointed as foreriders, and as the 'right hand' of the foreward, Lord Powis, Sir Edward Wydeville, Sir Charles Somerset, and Sir Richard Haute, 'with many other Gallants of the King's House'; Sir Richard Pole was on the left hand. Some changes in the foreward command may have taken place by the time Stoke was fought: the York civic account mentions the presence there of the latecomer Lord Strange, and Molinet says that the right wing was commanded by Wydeville, the left by Sir John Savage.[94]

Despite the creditable array of magnates to support the king, he may not have been fully confident of noble support, especially in the light of his predecessor's experience at Bosworth. Before the invasion Henry had had the marquess of Dorset arrested by the earl of Oxford, as the marquess was coming to meet him at Bury St Edmunds; he had dispatched the duke of Suffolk, Lincoln's father, honourably to Windsor.[95] Henry's observation of the high morale of Lincoln's men in battle at Stoke convinced him, rightly in Vergil's opinion, that they were relying on secret allies. But the 'naked' Irish were ill equipped for English warfare: the rebels were unable to resist the powerful royal foreward which, alone committed to the fray, at length broke resistance in a vigorous charge. Lincoln, Geraldine, Schwarz and possibly Lovell were killed in the intense fighting. Simnel and his priestly mentor were captured. According to an Irish source, the *Book of Howth*, more than 4,000 Irish were slain. On the day of the battle, Henry wrote from Newark that it had been won 'without death of any noble or gentleman on our part'. Two days later, he dismissed thence all but 3,000 to

4,000 of his soldiers, according to Vergil, going to Lincoln, where several captives were executed, and then south to Kenilworth castle before a progress to York 'in order to reform the territory bordering on Scotland, in which his enemies had shortly before raised an army against him'. Henry arrived at York on 30 July with an army of 10,000 'with his banner displayed' and stayed a week, during which judgments for treason were pronounced and an execution was carried out.[96] Then 'with many lords and nobles' he set out for Durham and Newcastle, returning through Boroughbridge and Pontefract – he was at Pontefract on 25 August.[97]

Henry won a victory for which he had worked hard against a dangerous enemy. Like Richard in 1485, he had had ample warning of the danger of invasion, and gathered, at the same base, an army superior in numbers. But, again like Richard, he was unable to prevent the enemy from penetrating to the Midlands from the fringes of the realm, or to rely fully on the loyalty of his noble supporters. There were many to his rear, in the south, who did not rate his chances high, or who were eager for a Yorkist restoration. According to Molinet, on the day on which Henry's vanguard abandoned Nottingham, lord 'de Veals' (Welles?), who was bringing up a retinue of 10,000 to the king's support, turned in flight and retreated through London. The Yorkists in sanctuary there, thinking that Henry had been defeated, sallied out to rob his servants and well-wishers, and cry for Warwick as king.[98] A London chronicler tells a similar story:

> And yet was that time false Englishmen that were between the field
> and the king's true people that were coming towards him, which
> untrue persons said that the king was fled and the field lost; whereby
> the king was put from much of his aid.[99]

The rumour-laden atmosphere in London, and the danger it presented to Henry, is reflected in the story told by Thomas Howard, earl of Surrey, that the lieutenant of the Tower, where Surrey had been imprisoned since Bosworth, offered to release him.[100] Perhaps, if the real Warwick was also in the Tower, the lieutenant had it in mind that Surrey could have him proclaimed king. Surrey shrewdly stayed put. He may not have relished setting up as a rival kingmaker to his fellow East Anglian, Lincoln, or promoting Lincoln's kingmaking.[101]

How did Henry survive the crisis, amidst widespread lack of confidence in the outcome and treacherous meditations? Perhaps some nobles sympathetic to the Neville–Yorkist cause hesitated to support the invasion because they feared that it boded ill for the genuine Warwick. The frequently ambivalent Stanleys had in 1487 a strong stake in upholding Henry's rule, for it had aggrandized them – and the invasion was in part a protest against their gains. Despite Henry's suspicions of treason, he apparently kept calm at Stoke – unlike Richard at Bosworth – and, as was his wont, tried to remain detached and immune from the fighting. He had good reason for confidence in experienced commanders who had fought together for him in 1485.

The lack of a convincing, free Yorkist candidate for the throne, the formidable repute of Henry's commanders, and the tendency of his principal opponents to die in battle, may after 1487 have acted as deterrents to the continuing impulses to plot dynastic risings. In 1489 and 1491–2 there were popular rebellions in regions which had not been securely in Henry's allegiance since his accession. But they failed notably to develop into more general dynastic stirs. According to Vergil, in 1489 northerners refused to contribute to the subsidy for the Breton war, 'either because they found it too onerous or because they were instigated and urged not to pay it by certain individuals who secretly hated Henry'. When the earl of Northumberland reported to him that it was impossible to make them pay, the king ordered the earl to force those who refused.[102] On 24 April Northumberland wrote to Sir William Plumpton, summoning him on the king's behalf to come with an armed company, together with the earl's nephew Sir William Gascoigne, to attend the earl at Thirsk by the evening of 27 April.[103] The next day Northumberland met the commons at Cocklodge, his house nearby in his lordship of Topcliffe. There the commons slew him. Vergil's succinct explanation of their action was that when they heard the intransigent royal reply about the payment of subsidy, they 'assaulted the earl as though he were the author of their wrongs'. This rings true. Northerners looked to their magnates to represent and protect their interests at a southern court which, except under Richard III, they were inclined to regard as unsympathetic and alien.[104]

Contemporaries regarded the failure of the earl's retinue to protect him as the most shocking aspect of the affair. Dr Hicks has adduced reasons why his followers may have been lukewarm in their loyalty. Former retainers of Gloucester whom he had recruited may have had a cooling effect.[105] Their passivity probably stiffened the resolve of the more intransigent risers to prolong and indeed widen the scope of their protest. Writing from Hedingham (Essex) probably just before 12 May, William Paston relayed reports current in the south that the risers were still around the place where the earl was killed 'and not with no great number, they say not past with 5 or 600'. But they had made proclamations to meet others of their affinity, probably on 7 May. Paston had got hold of a copy of their proclamation: every 'lord, knight, esquire, gentleman and yeoman' in the north parts was to appear in defensible array, either on Allerton Moor (near Pontefract) 'in the east part' or on Gatherley Moor, in Richmondshire, 'in the west part'. No overt treason was suggested: they were 'to gainstand such persons as is aboutward for to destroy our sovereign Lord the King and the Commons of England, for such unlawful points at St. Thomas of Canterbury died for'.[106] But the rebels seem to have attracted insignificant 'gentle' support. Sixty-two out of sixty-six Yorkshiremen indicted for participating were yeomen, husbandmen, artisans and tradesmen. More noteworthy were Eli Casse and Thomas Bullock, two of the four governors of Beverley; Thomas Wrangwish, alderman of York; and Sir John Egremont, a former servant of Richard III who had enjoyed some favour from Henry.[107] According to the earl of Surrey, they captured York, 'won with assault by force' – this was before 17 May, when Egremont summoned the mayor to All Hallows church there, 'showing unto him and his brethren that there might be prepared shortly pretty men with horses to attend and go with certain fellowship of his into Richmondshire'. The mayor complied, for Egremont 'had rule and his people here'.[108]

Soon after Northumberland's death Henry VII had determined to lead a large army into the north. On 6 May the earl of Oxford requested Sir John Paston to meet him with a retinue armed for the king's service at Cambridge on 12 May.[109] Henry set out northwards with his army from Hertford castle. He appointed as 'chief Captain' of the vanguard the earl of Surrey, recently released from the Tower. Among those appointed under Surrey were familiar figures from Henry's campaigns: the earl of Shrewsbury, Lord Hastings (the son of William Hastings), Sir William Stanley, Sir Rhys ap Thomas, Sir Thomas Bourchier, Sir John Savage and Sir John Rysely. Vergil says that on the king's approach to York the rebels dispersed: according to a London chronicle, before Henry arrived, Surrey had 'distressed' the rebels and captured their captain John a Chamber, who with some of his supporters was hanged at York. Egremont showed Yorkist colours by fleeing to the court of Duchess Margaret.[110] Surrey's funeral inscription says that

> for the singular trust, that the King had to the said Earl, and the
> activity that he saw in him, he left him in the North, and made him
> his Lieutenant-general from Trent Northward, and Warden of the
> East and Middle Marches of England against Scotland, and Justice of
> the Forests from Trent Northwards.

At last Henry had found a magnate able and dedicated enough to rule the north in his interest, whose Ricardian background perhaps made him acceptable there. In the second year of his lieutenancy, however, Surrey had to face an insurrection in 'the West part of the Country', but defeated the rebels at Ackworth near Pontefract. He captured and executed their captains, but sued the king for pardons for the rest, a successful intermediacy (unlike Northumberland's in 1489) which 'won . . . the favour of the Country'.[111]

Surrey's ability to rule the north, and the measures which Henry took to strengthen his position in Ireland, deprived Yorkist plotters in the 1490s of promising bases of support.[112] But tensions between Henry and his former patron Charles VIII of France, James IV, who succeeded as king of Scots in 1488, and the rulers of the Low Countries, gave Yorkists continued hopes of foreign help. Perkin Warbeck, claiming to be a Yorkist prince, landed in Ireland at Cork in November 1491. Henry dealt effectively with the threat that Warbeck's claim might be exploited by Irish lords, as Simnel's had been, by dispatching a force the following month under the lieutenant's deputy James Ormond and Captain Thomas Garth. Warbeck found what appeared a more promising field of support in France: in March 1492 he was received as a prince by Charles VIII. A consequence of Henry's invasion of France the following October was to scotch these hopes. For a condition of the Anglo-French peace of Etaples in November was the banishment of Warbeck from France. But he soon received encouragement from Duchess Margaret and the principal rulers of the Low Countries – her son-in-law Archduke Maximilian, king of the Romans, and his son Philip.[113] A letter from Henry to Sir Gilbert Talbot (20 July 1493), requesting that Talbot have a military company in readiness, reflects his fears that the duchess would soon once again launch a mercenary force in favour of a Yorkist impostor.[114] Warbeck's plotting in 1493-4 had some distinguished connections in England, but his hopes of gaining support there were badly dented by the information about it elicited through the activities of Henry's spies in the Low Countries. In January and February 1495 there were treason trials. Among those convicted were the Norfolk landowner Lord FitzWalter, Sir Simon Mountfort of Coleshill (Warwicks.), William Worsley, dean of St Paul's, William Richford, provincial of the Dominicans in England, and Thomas Powys, prior of their house at Langley, Herts. Most spectacularly of all, a man to whom Henry was heavily indebted for his crown – his chamberlain, Sir William Stanley – confessed to having been in contact with Warbeck in 1493. He was executed.[115]

Disappointed by the arrest of plotters in England, Warbeck nevertheless persisted in attempting invasion. In Flanders, with the aid of Duchess Margaret and Maximilian, he collected ships, troops, victuals and artillery, sailing with what Vergil termed the 'human dregs' of neighbouring regions, including English exiles (his denigration is characteristically sweeping). According to Molinet, Warbeck had in his company Roderick de Lalain and other experienced soldiers. Lalain was an ornament of chivalry, who was to excel in Scottish jousts. One of

Warbeck's two Spanish captains, Don Fulano de Guevara, was referred to by de Puebla, the Spanish envoy in England, in a letter to the Catholic kings, in terms which implied their familiarity with his family. One of his English captains, Mountfort, was the son of the recently executed Warwickshire landowner. Warbeck's expedition was comparable in size as well as calibre with other invasion forces during the Wars of the Roses − he probably had at least 1,300 men. He planned to raise the Kentishmen. According to what his captured English captains were to tell Robert Albon of Yarmouth, the intention was to seize 'a town of strength', with Sandwich in mind − Warwick the Kingmaker's and the Bastard of Fauconberg's old base. With over fourteen sails, Warbeck hove to in the Downs off Camber sands near Deal. Calm weather facilitated operations. On 3 July a landing party reconnoitred, to see if Kentishmen would give support. Though tempted, the locals decided to dissimulate with the invaders until levies could assemble to oppose them. Warbeck prudently remained on shipboard with a majority of his troops, but landed reinforcements who fanned out to raise standards over three neighbouring villages. They were attacked − and probably taken badly by surprise − by the mayor of Sandwich and a scratch force of commons. Kentish archery took its toll. The invaders were driven back to their ships. It was a disaster: besides about 150 killed, there were many captives, including a clutch of captains.[116]

Very soon afterwards Warbeck's fleet slipped away from its anchorage. There was speculation as to his intentions. One captured captain, Belt, told Albon 'they will have Yarmouth or they shall die for it'. Another report received by Yarmouth corporation was that 'they be forth out of Camber westwards'. De Puebla reported from London on 19 July that the fleet was believed to have gone to Ireland or Scotland.[117] But Warbeck returned to Flanders, according to Vergil. At Duchess Margaret's court it was planned that he should attempt an invasion of the west of England, first having raised Irish support, or, if this did not work out, that he should sail to Scotland and attempt to exploit the bad relations between James IV and Henry VII.[118] Warbeck appeared in the summer off the earl of Desmond's territory of Munster, the region where he had been welcomed in 1491. From 23 July to 3 August he and Desmond besieged the vigorously defended port of Waterford. It was relieved by Henry's lieutenant, Sir Edward Poynings, with a force from Dublin. As in 1491, Warbeck found the Tudor interest too strong in Ireland to use it as a base for the invasion of England. He moved on to Scotland: in November or December he was received as a prince by James IV.[119]

Henry VII seems to have particularly appreciated the value of spying as a means of disrupting plots − a lesson probably imprinted during his youthful exile. He had penetrated the plotting centring on Warbeck in 1493–4; prior to James IV's invasion of September 1496 in support of Warbeck, he knew what was afoot at the Scottish court. His informant was Lord Bothwell, who emphasized in his letters the unpopularity of James's intention to go to war with England. He recounted his own attempts to temper the king's determination to promote the claim of the 'fenyt boy'. Nervousness among English Border gentlefolk is reflected in his report that on 28 August Warbeck had a visitor from Carlisle. 'I was informit secretely yat yis man sould have commyn fra Randell of Dacre, broder to ye lord Dacre, and fra the Sceltonis for mekyll [Michael?] Scelton yat is her had ye convoyanc[e] of him.'[120] On 8 September Bothwell wrote that five days previously Warbeck had agreed conditions with the king and council for royal intervention in support of his claim. Warbeck was to hand over Berwick, and pay 50,000 marks towards James's military costs. It was planned that the Scottish army and Warbeck's international company, 1,400 strong, should rendezvous at Ellem kirk on 15 September, and cross the Border two days later, despite the opposition of nearly all the barons and people both 'for ye danger that thereof might follow, and for the inconvenience of the season'. Bothwell believed that James was ill prepared for war, and predicted that within four or five days of invading, his men would be 'so weary for watching and for lack of victuals' that they would oblige James to go home. He advised Henry on how to entrap the Scottish army. Besides describing Warbeck's Scottish support unflatteringly, Bothwell insinuated that some of his leading followers were less than devoted to his cause. He represented Warbeck's principal councillor, Sir George Neville, as an unprincipled adventurer. His captain of 1495, Roderick de Lalain, who arrived from Flanders with two little ships and sixty 'Almains' (Germans), emphasized that he had come to serve James, snubbing Warbeck in the royal presence. Perhaps Lalain had been disgusted by Warbeck's failure to attempt the rescue of his captains near Deal.[121]

The invasion got under way not long after Bothwell predicted that it would. On 13 September carters received their wages. The artillery was assembled near the coast east of Edinburgh, at Restalrig: on 14 September the priests of the collegiate church at Restalrig received payment to say Masses for the king before Our Lady and St Triduana, and that day royal forces probably reached Haddington. The army set out to cross the Lammermuirs, probably going up from Garvald by Whiteadder Water, and down from Ellem to Langton. The treasurer made payments on 16 September 'For walking of the guns that night at Johnscleugh' (in Whiteadder valley), and on the 17th for their being 'walked' at Langton. On the 19th, payments were made to 'Henric, gunnar, at Ellem' and to 'the man and the wif of the hous quhar the

King lugyit at Ellem'. Some difficulty was encountered in getting heavy equipment across the Tweed. The treasurer records under 21 September payment to 'The cobill men of Tweid, that helpit the artail3erj oure the watir'; the next payment is 'to the men that brocht the clos cart furth of the watir, quhen scho stude in the watir all nycht'. R. L. Mackie thought that the invaders crossed near Coldstream: that is where Warbeck received a large sum at the king's command on the 21st. The army probably crossed and bivouacked south of the confluence of the Tweed with the Till, so that the cumbersome equipment was protected from the English garrisons at Norham and Berwick by this tributary. James appears to have confined his operations to the Till valley. Presumably Twizel bridge, a key feature, was quickly seized and guarded: peels on the north bank at Twizel, Tillmouth and as far east as Duddo were sacked, probably in part to prevent them from being used as forward English bases. The centrepiece of James's campaign turned out to be a test of his siege equipment, a brief and unsuccessful siege of Heaton castle on the south bank of the Till. This was conducted with some urgency, probably because James feared an attempt at relief. On 24 September, drinksilver was paid to masons 'to mine all night at the house of Hetoune', and on the 25th payment was made to workmen to work in the mine that night.[122] According to a London chronicler, James withdrew into Scotland in some disorder, on receiving news that Lord Neville with 4,000 men and other companies of marchmen were approaching. The Londoner crowed that the Scots had only 'Entered four miles within this land, and burnt houses and cast down two small Towers or peels, making great boast and brag'.[123] Heaton is, indeed, less than four miles from the frontier. Vergil, untainted by London chauvinism, painted a bleaker picture of the effects of invasion. James 'penetrated a considerable distance into the country and ... widely devastated the countryside of Northumberland'; terrified by the Scots' pillage and slaughter, the gentlefolk took refuge in their castles. When his men were sated with booty, and the gentlefolk's resistance stiffened, James retreated. Vergil's account makes plain that Henry's fears that northern nobles would embrace the Yorkist cause proved groundless. The brusque reply which James made to Warbeck's complaint about Scottish ravaging may have stemmed from disillusion with a similar overestimation.[124]

In his limited strategic commitment, as well as his failure to curb pillaging, James had displayed a disinclination to do much to help the Yorkist cause militarily. His achievement in 1496, in terms of his own as well as Yorkist interests, was unremarkable. But he had shown realism. He got away with more than Bothwell thought he would deserve, and rattled the English. The greatest feat was getting the artillery all the way from Edinburgh, across the Lammermuirs and the

Tweed, and back again – an experiment probably not previously tried by a Scottish king on the same scale, which could have easily ended in disaster, and which provided useful operational lessons. To achieve this, there had been hired in Edinburgh 143 carters with 196 horses, to carry guns, covered carts, gunstones, pavilions and other gear, and 76 men with spades, shovels, and pick mattocks to pass with the artillery and draw the guns 'in peththis and myris'.[125]

Why, then, after parting the mountains, did James merely manoeuvre and mine mouselike for a few days in the Till valley? He may have felt that he had insufficient time and resources for deeper penetration, for the reasons outlined by Bothwell. The carters hired on 13 September had received wages from the treasurer for only fourteen days 'fra this day furth'.[126] The hope of Yorkist rebellion provided another reason for sitting down near the frontier. So did a military constraint currently imposed on Scottish royal expeditions by frontier conditions. The prized artillery train, cumbersome to move in an emergency, had to be put at risk across the Tweed – and even on the Scottish bank there was no formidable fortress to protect it from pursuit. Possession of Berwick, taken by the English in 1482, was the best strategic remedy. But Berwick was difficult to besiege, being well fortified, strongly held, and easy to reinforce by land and sea.

The 1496 invasion appears to have been a trial run for James's later forays, in which he again threatened the English higher up the Tweed, hoping, perhaps, to lure and disarray their field forces, then rush the defences of isolated Berwick. In 1497 he besieged Norham castle and attempted to get the earl of Surrey to fight. On his last campaign, in 1513, James again advanced along Whiteadder Water and through Ellem to attack castles in the Till valley, and to meet his death at Flodden.[127]

The 1496 invasion demonstrated what the Lancastrians had discovered in 1462–3: that Scottish intervention in the dynastic quarrel was likely to be of little military value. Moreover, it revealed that the north, in the energetic and tactful care of Surrey, was a barren field for Yorkist rebellion. Warbeck's preoccupation with Scotland and Ireland, and his failure to rebuild a network of supporters in England after the arrests of 1494, led to his inability to exploit fully a dangerous rebellion against Henry in the summer of 1497, a rebellion which was an indirect consequence of his invasion of Northumberland. Rising in protest against taxation for the war with Scotland, the commons of Cornwall were a principal constituent of a West Country army which advanced, recruiting support, through Wells, Salisbury and Winchester and across Surrey, to Henry's mortification encamping intact on Blackheath, the *champ de Mars* of Kentish rebels. They intended to punish the councillors whom they held responsible for taxation, especially

Archbishop Morton of Canterbury and Sir Reginald Bray. But the mayor and aldermen of London took firm defence measures and kept in daily communication with the king and the chancellor, Morton. George Grey, earl of Kent, Lords Abergavenny and Cobham, and Kentish gentlefolk guarded against a rising in their shire. Henry left London with his army to confront the western men. His captains, the earls of Essex and Suffolk, Sir Rhys ap Thomas and Lord Daubeney, surrounded and overcame them with comparative ease at Blackheath on 17 June.[128]

The 1497 rebellion was the first major one since 1460 in which the dynastic issue was not raised. Contemporaries surely expected it to be. It is inexplicable that a peer, Lord Audley, took the captaincy of the rebels at Wells unless he thought he was the first swallow in a Yorkist summer. According to a somewhat suspect allegation made in 1506, Abergavenny, when with soldiers at Ewelme near Wallingford (Berks.) to oppose the rebels' advance, urged the later Yorkist claimant the earl of Suffolk to join them. A letter to the earl when he was a Yorkist pretender (1505?) shows that his circle then affected to believe that Warbeck had indeed been the duke of York. Perhaps in 1497 Suffolk was hesitant about asserting his own claim because he was not sure whether Warbeck was an impostor. On the other hand, if 'York' had appeared at the head of the westerners, Suffolk might have been inclined to join them.[129]

Three days after the battle, on 20 June, the sheriffs of Cornwall, Devon, Somerset, Dorset, Gloucestershire, Wiltshire, Hampshire and Surrey were ordered to have it proclaimed that pardons would be granted on submission to the king's mercy of all offenders in the insurrection subdued at 'the Blackheath beside Greenwich'. But some rebels probably remained recalcitrant, fearful of harsh punishments. On 28 June the earl of Devon was appointed to head a large commission to inquire into all insurrections in those counties and elsewhere, and to punish or pardon the delinquents. On 5 July Sir John Digby and Sir Robert Clifford were appointed to execute respectively the offices of constable and marshal with respect to the rebels who had levied war.[130]

Warbeck was slow to take advantage of the smoulderings of rebellion. Rejected by James IV, he left Scotland on 6 July, and appeared at Cork on the 26th, but was unable to raise support there. On 7 September he landed on the far tip of Cornwall, at Whitesand Bay near Land's End.[131] By 12 September Henry VII, at Woodstock (Oxon.), had heard that Warbeck was on his way from Ireland to Cornwall with two small ships and a Breton pinnace. The king wrote to Sir Gilbert Talbot that he had sent Lord Daubeney westwards to array against Warbeck, and Lord Willoughby of Broke with a fleet to cut off his retreat. He assured Talbot that, if necessary, he would go without delay to subdue Perkin.[132] Reports from Milanese and Venetian agents in London gave particulars of Warbeck's landing, his favourable reception by the Cornishmen, and the impressive royal counter-measures. The agents were confident of Henry's victory. Raimondo de Soncino, writing on 16 September, said that Warbeck had landed with eighty 'savage' Irishmen, and that Henry had dispatched against him the earl of Devon and the lord chamberlain (Daubeney). Next day Andrea Trevisan wrote that Warbeck had raised 6,000–8,000 insurgents and marched sixty miles inland. Among royal measures he mentions the dispatch of the chamberlain and the earl of Kent with 12,000 men.[133]

Warbeck secured St Michael's Mount and, passing through Penryn, displayed remarkable energy by arriving before and assaulting Exeter on 17 September. His attempts to rush the defences on that day and the one following failed against a hastily organized but energetic defence by the earl of Devon, leading gentlefolk of Devon and Cornwall, and the citizens. Why did Warbeck attempt to seize Exeter? Henry VII was to note with satisfaction that, on the 18th, Warbeck had not one gentleman with him. He can hardly have hoped that, once he had occupied the city, the local pro-Lancastrian and pro-Courtenay gentry would flock in. Perhaps both he and the Cornishmen believed that possession of the city would be a counter with which to bargain for pardons and favour from Henry.[134]

On 18 September the earl of Devon wrote to Henry that the rebels had withdrawn from Exeter to Collumpton, and that many had deserted. According to what was reported to the mayor and aldermen of London, Warbeck withdrew to Taunton on hearing of the approach of the king's forces.[135] Like the Lancastrians in the West Country in 1471, Warbeck was anxious to avoid confrontation with a royal army. On 20 September Henry sent news of Perkin's invasion and assaults on Exeter to Oliver King, bishop of Bath and Wells. If, he said, Perkin and his company 'come forward' (eastwards?), they would find 'before' them Daubeney, Willoughby of Broke, Seymour, Sir John Cheyney and the noblemen of South Wales, Gloucestershire, Wiltshire, Hampshire, Somerset and Dorset, and 'at their back' the garrison of Exeter. Henry with his 'host royal' would be not far off for the conclusion. Vergil confirms this strategy of encirclement. Henry dispatched light cavalry, then moved with his main force towards Taunton. He was joined by the duke of Buckingham and an impressive force of western knights. Characteristically, Henry sent on ahead with the main body of his army Daubeney, Broke and Rhys ap Thomas, following himself to trap Warbeck.[136]

At Taunton Warbeck soon concluded that the game was nearly up. He had already shown himself adept at escaping from the Kentishmen and the men of Waterford. With John Heron, Edward Skelion, Nicholas Ostelay and a small company, he rode off from his men at Taunton by night. They were to escape south-eastwards, where, probably, the ways were less infested with Henry's cavalry and the ports less closely guarded than in the West Country. Warbeck nearly reached the Hampshire coast, but had to take refuge in sanctuary at Beaulieu abbey. By 12 October the king was able to inform the mayor and aldermen of London that Warbeck had voluntarily surrendered.[137] According to Vergil, almost all of his deserted followers at Taunton had received pardons on submission. Henry had entered Exeter and sent his cavalry to secure St Michael's Mount.[138]

Thus was extinguished what was arguably the last flare-up of the Wars of the Roses. In the 1490s, the far-flung demonstrations that the persistent and impressively patronized 'duke of York' was an inept plotter and military leader, and his unmasking in 1497 as an impostor, may have discredited Yorkist rebellion as a respectable and legitimate course in noble eyes. Dynastic rebellion had always been hazardous, and the efficiency of Henry's intelligence sources and military system and the competence of his captains worsened the odds. Moreover, gentlefolk may have looked more doubtfully at concepts of rebellion when in 1489 and 1497 they were so boldly appropriated by peasants and artisans – who in the second 1497 revolt had the temerity to take over the dynastic issue and proclaim 'Richard IV'. From the 1450s onwards the rule of kings, their councillors and courtiers was repeatedly and often successfully challenged – by risings of discontented magnates, dynastic plotting and popular demonstrations of discontent. These sorts of movement interacted to give each other more strength and impetus. By 1497 they were manifestly no longer doing so. Such kinds of rebellion all revived in the sixteenth century, with novel features, sometimes in a heady and potent mix. Even the old Yorkist claims were to be canvassed. But this was part of a different drama.[139]

Part Two

Military Organization and Society

Chapter 6

Military Convention and Recruitment

In the fourteenth century, English kings' involvement of subjects' resources and fortunes in the pursuit of royal claims in Scotland and France had led to a renewed emphasis on their personal duty to lead armies, displaying the strength of their resolve to defend subjects against the oft-proclaimed malice of foreigners, and to secure a just peace. Edward I, Edward II and Edward III went abroad at the head of armies. Richard II and Henry IV both led invasions of Scotland, and had their intentions of invading France affirmed on occasion in parliament.

When faced with domestic uprisings, too, kings had powerful incentives to appear armed in the field. Their presence was likely to spur recruitment of levies and infuse them with zeal. According to an official account, the gentlefolk in Henry VI's army in 1459 were stimulated to make great efforts by his exhortation

> made by your own mouth, in so witty, so knightly, so manly, in so comfortable wise, with so Princely apport and assured manner, of which the Lords and the people took such joy and comfort, that all their desire was only to haste to fulfil your courageous Knightly desire.[1]

It may have been with Henry's behaviour then in mind that the author of *Knyghthode and Bataile* wrote

> Therefore our eye is to the king's sign,
>   We hear his voice, as trump and clarion,
> His eyes are obeyed, we incline
>   At once unto him, his legion
> We are . . .[2]

The king's demeanour could have a vital effect on morale. At St Albans in 1461 the Yorkist lords in Henry VI's company despaired and fled from the field when it was clear that he would not attempt to rally his men, since his sympathies lay with their opponents: 'nec spiritum esse, nec animum, immo, nec vultum nec alloquium, ad consolandum sive animandum populum suum'.[3]

Another incentive for the king to ride against rebels was to emphasize the dubiousness of their undertakings. Aquinas had written that the first condition for a just war was 'the authority of a ruler by whose order war is declared, for no private individual may declare war, since he may seek justice at the hands of a superior'.[4] Canonists insisted on the restriction of the right to wage public war to superior authority: 'Every hostile act except immediate self-defence required superior authority.'[5] A state of public war was declared by the unfurling of the prince's banner: subjects who then rode in warlike array in the realm, displaying unauthorized banners, courted the penalties of treason.[6] To do so in the king's presence demanded cool nerve.

York and his noble allies, to counter the unfavourable impressions which they made by raising warlike banners in Henry's vicinity in 1452, 1455, 1459 and 1460, implicitly defended themselves against charges of waging unlawful public war, and flaunting the king's declarations of it. For in their proclamations they asserted that they were in fact petitioning their royal superior, their unconventional manner of proceeding necessitated by scandalous circumstances. They were bearing arms merely in self-defence against the malign intent of the traitors around the king. Rather than risk the accident of an assault on the king's person, at St Albans in 1455 they strenuously tried to negotiate a settlement, protesting that they were loyal subjects whose aim was to procure the condemnation and punishment of traitors. York urged his men to attack only after Henry threatened them with the penalties of treason, refusing to accept the duke's explanation of 'the intent that we be come hither and assembled for and gathered at this time'. York argued that they were cornered men with no alternative to self-defence, for, if they were taken, Henry would 'give us a shameful death losing our livelihood and goods and our heirs shamed for ever'.[7] Immediately after the battle, and in the following months, the Yorkist lords tried to eradicate the treasonable impression which they had made by resorting to arms against a king whose banner was displayed. They escorted him back to London with royal honours, reaffirmed their oaths of fealty at a solemn crown-wearing ceremony, and secured pardons which were ratified in parliament. These pardons put the blame for the battle on the deceased duke of Somerset and two relatively obscure royal bureaucrats, Thomas Thorpe and William Joseph. The pardons cited in some detail the Yorkist lords' attempts to negotiate and the frustration of these efforts by their enemies in the royal entourage.[8]

Chroniclers' accounts of the Ludford Bridge campaign of 1459 and the battle of Northampton reflect the Yorkist lords' attempts to publicize the fact that their primary intention was to negotiate rather than to fight.[9] A conversation between two Nottingham men, probably referring to news of the Yorkist retreat in face of the royal army in October 1459, emphasized the risers' political disadvantage. According to Thomas Bolton:

> Robert Shirwood, baker, said that if the Lords [i.e. Henry's supporters] would have put the King's banner from them, the Earl of Salisbury would have fought with them and proved on them that he had been true lord, as he heard it reported. And I answered again, that it were no wisdom to put ye King's banner away, if they might have it with them.[10]

At Ludlow the Yorkist lords made a virtue of necessity by claiming:

> hereto we have forborne and avoided all things that might serve to the effusion of Christian blood, of the dread that we have of God and of your royal majesty, and have also eschewed to approach . . . [Henry] of the humble obedience and reverence whereon we have and during our life will have the same.[11]

But according to the crown, once Henry had approached them, they did not hesitate to attack him: they 'falsely and traitorously reared war against You [Henry], and then and there shot their said Guns, and shot as well at your most Royal person, as at your lords and people with You then and there being'.[12] The raising of the dynastic issue in 1460 provided a different justification for much of the subsequent campaigning. Resort to public warfare was authorized by rival sovereigns: the waging of battle was an appeal to God's judgment on their royal claims. Pro-Neville, ostensibly non-dynastic rebels in 1469–70 publicly alleged supplicatory or defensive motives for their appearance in arms, but after Wakefield there were no more elaborate attempts by risers to negotiate over grievances before attacking. The sort of negotiations which took place in the later stages of the wars (e.g. in March 1470 and in 1486) were concerned with offers of pardon to rebels and terms of submission.[13]

The dynastic basis of confrontation gave an added incentive to kings and claimants to appear regally in arms, prepared to put themselves to divine judgment. In his proclamation against the Lancastrians who invaded the West Country in 1471, Edward IV emphasized his recent military success. His right to the throne had been made manifest 'by Victory given unto us by our Lord Almighty God in divers Battles against our Great Adversary Harry and his adherents'.[14] To stress his regality, Richard III – like Henry V at Agincourt – appeared crowned at Bosworth. Henry VII's reception of the crown, allegedly found discarded, on the field, and the degradation and exposure of Richard's corpse, were ritual occurrences, unmistakable signs of the divine will.[15] Henry VII was always prepared to ride in person against rebels, including comparatively insignificant ones, like those in Yorkshire in 1489 and in the West Country in 1497. But, perhaps with Richard's fate in mind, he always held back whilst the foreward went on ahead to probe the opposition.[16]

By the mid-fifteenth century, kings of England had for long habitually commissioned lieutenants to exercise royal rights in the waging of war, in the areas of their particular commands. Jurisdiction as lieutenants was conferred on commanders of expeditions abroad, on wardens of the Marches towards Scotland, and on the captain of Calais for its march, within their spheres of operation. The lieutenancies in the north conferred by Edward IV on Lord Fauconberg in 1461 and Warwick in 1462 were probably similar in terms, with powers to raise and discipline soldiers, lead them on expeditions and make local truces.[17] In March 1471, on Edward's invasion, Warwick apparently exercised general military command by virtue of a royal commission: he styled himself 'Lieutenant to the king our sovereign lord Henry VI'.[18] Those who patently lacked such justification for raising war in a land at peace sometimes invoked, besides the right of self-defence, the ideal of championship of those being oppressed: allusions were sometimes made to Robin Hood.[19] In 1471 the Bastard of Fauconberg, anxious perhaps not to be caught out in a deception by the governors of London, or not to give offence to eminent Lancastrians, carefully refrained from claiming to act as Henry VI's lieutenant. He styled himself clumsily 'Captain and leader of our liege lord King Henry's people in Kent'.[20]

Before moving on St Albans in 1455, Henry VI appointed the duke of Buckingham as constable and lieutenant to command the army. The appointment may have been considered especially appropriate because the duke held the office of constable of the realm, by hereditary right.[21] The constable and marshal of the realm were the king's chief customary lieutenants, exercising military justice as well as command.[22] In 1464 some of the Lancastrians captured around Hexham, and Sir Ralph Grey, were convicted of treason in the court of the constable, the earl of Worcester.[23] In 1495 Sir John Digby, the king's marshal, was commissioned to cite before himself and pronounce sentence on the rebels and aliens from Warbeck's invading force captured at Deal, and in 1497 he and Sir Robert Clifford were ordered to execute the office of constable and marshal with respect to the West Country rebels.[24] The constable and marshal of the realm, and the *ad hoc* constables and marshals appointed for particular campaigns, were responsible for

trying offences against the code of discipline issued by the king or his
lieutenant – the ordinances of war.[25] The importance of discipline was
appreciated in English military circles. The author of *Knyghthode and
Bataile* emphasized it,[26] and so did the anonymous author of the
account of the Stoke campaign. At the start of this campaign Henry
'ordained by his proclamations, for good rule of his host'. At Leicester,
by the archbishop of Canterbury's command, the royal proclamations
were put in execution: 'And in especial voiding Common Women, and
Vagabonds, for there were imprisoned great number of both.
Wherefore there was more Rest in the King's Host, and the better
Rule.' At Loughborough 'the Stocks and Prisons were reasonably filled
with Harlots and Vagabonds. And after that were but few in the Host,
unto the Time the field was done.' In 1489 Henry VII wrote to the earl
of Oxford that the English army in Brittany 'blessed be God, hath
among themself kept such love and accord that no manner of fray or
debate hath been between them since the time of their departing out of
this our Realm'.[27] In ordering the proclamation of disciplinary
ordinances in 1487, Henry was probably following a standard practice
in the Wars of the Roses. The key role of the marshal is reflected in his
injunction that every man should endeavour to bring makers of quarrels
and affrays into 'the marshal's ward to be punished according to their
deserts'.[28] The task of disciplining the often hastily assembled, motley
armies of the wars was probably eased by the royal presence – except
perhaps in the case of the notoriously merciful Henry VI. Abbot
Whethamstede recounted how, after the second battle of St Albans, he
prevailed on Henry to issue a proclamation against plundering – which,
the abbot said, was disobeyed. Malory's ideal king had no such
problem.[29]

The roles of kings and magnates in decision-making about strategy
and tactics in the wars are difficult to discern. Chroniclers tended to
attribute initiatives uncritically to leading protagonists. Waurin's
accounts of Somerset's consultations with Trollope, 'ung tres soubtil
homme de guerre', are an unusual acknowledgment of an expert
subordinate's influential counsel.[30] The commander, the author of
Knyghthode and Bataile opined, must rely for counsel on 'olde and
exercised sapience'.[31] Most chroniclers failed to stress the importance
of councils of war – they were ill placed to find out what went on in
these highly confidential and unrecorded sessions. The anonymous
writer about the Stoke campaign knew something about the 'ordering of
his Host' settled by the council which Henry VII summoned for the
purpose. There are mentions of councils held in armies faced with a
tricky set of circumstances – in Henry VI's on the road from Watford
to St Albans in 1455, in Edward IV's after the landing in Holderness in
1471. Later that year the nobles in Margaret of Anjou's army

'deliberated in council how they might contrive most speedily to pass along the west coast'.[32] Waurin is almost the only writer who shows considerable appreciation of the vital significance of councils of war.[33]

I have argued above that, as kings, Edward IV and Richard III took a leading role in strategic and tactical decision-making, whereas Henry VII, lacking comparable field experience on his accession, tended to be a figurehead, relying heavily on the expertise of his skilled commanders.[34] There was one king to whom contemporaries did not usually attribute an active role in command – Henry VI. As we have seen, he delegated it in 1455, and may have done so in 1459 and 1460. Buckingham's refusal to allow Yorkist envoys to have direct dealings with the king at Northampton may have rested on his possession of a lieutenancy again.[35] But Henry's detachment from command, at least in the early campaigns, must not be exaggerated, though his interest may have been characteristically bookish. There is some evidence that he bestirred himself particularly in 1459 and 1460. As we have seen, his strenuous part in the 1459 campaign was officially emphasized, and Whethamstede pictures him on it pondering Vegetian doctrine. The author of *Knyghthode and Bataile* bestowed on Henry the title 'Tryumphatour' afterwards. The author, in order to provide counsel for Henry's war against the fugitive, attainted Yorkists, with Viscount Beaumont's encouragement presented the king with his updated translation of the classical writer Vegetius into English ballad form. Beaumont may have hoped to keep alive Henry's military interest by a work written, congenially, by a cleric professedly ignorant of warfare, and keen on religious symbolism.[36]

The traditional English preference was that noblemen should command armies and their constituent 'battles'.[37] The majority of English lieutenants in France during the Hundred Years War were of royal or noble birth, and captains of English-held coastal fortresses there were usually from either baronial or knightly families.[38] Peers expected to receive commands which they considered commensurate with their rank and honour. Lord Stanley allegedly requested Margaret of Anjou and the prince of Wales in 1459 'forasmuch as he understood, that he was had in jealousy, that he might have the vaward against the earl of Salisbury, and his fellowship'. When the prince, whose council considered that Stanley's force was too small to challenge Salisbury, ordered him to join up with the rest of the army, he disobeyed. In 1487, before Henry's army set forth to fight the rebels, 'the Earl of Oxford desired and besought the King to have the Conduct of the Forward, which the King granted, and accompanied him with many great courageous and lusty knights'.[39]

In a society which inculcated the divine sanction behind hierarchical proprieties, peers, especially those of royal blood and highest rank, were, next to kings, best fitted to secure obedience. The aristocratic Malory would probably have found commoners as well as gentlefolk who agreed that association with noble knights was most desirable and beneficial. His Sir Pryamus declared: 'I had liever have been torn with four wild horses than any yeoman had such a loose won of me, other else any page other pricker should win of me the prize in this field gotten.' Pryamus placed reliance in knights: 'harlots and henchmen will help us but a little, for they will hide them in haste for all their high words'.[40] Nobles were most likely to have funds or credit available to lay out on arms, armour, supplies and wages, and to have the patronage and prestige necessary to recruit large and skilled retinues. The political circumstances of the Wars of the Roses enhanced traditional needs for noble command: authoritative example and persuasion were needed to stir or restrain men in the potentially anarchical conditions of civil war. York in 1455 and Montague in 1470 were probably not alone in having to commit their personal prestige by cajoling their soldiers.[41] In the disturbed situation in London after the surrender of the Tower in 1460, Warwick's intervention was needed to restore order. He 'rode to the Tower, and there he made a proclamation, and all about the city, charging that no manner of person should not slay, nor steal, nor murder, on pain of death'.[42]

But there were precedents from the Hundred Years War for the elevation in command and rank of gentlefolk of lower status (esquires and gentlemen) and of men of non-gentle status. In 1460 John Harowe, mercer of London, was a commander of Yorkist companies (probably ones raised by the city) both there and at Wakefield.[43] The ten Lancastrian captains captured at Mortimer's Cross and executed at Hereford in 1461 were esquires. They included, besides a knight's son and the exalted Owen Tudor, father of the earls of Richmond and Pembroke, an estate steward, an esquire with an income of five marks *per annum*, and a lawyer.[44] Sir Edmund Fish, one of the Lancastrian leaders executed after the battle of Hexham in 1464, was a former tailor (*scissor*) of York.[45] The 'chief captain of the army' of southern rebels in 1483, Edward Peningham, like some of the other rebels, does not seem to have been a knight – perhaps he was selected for his military experience.[46]

Methods of recruitment and the nature of the forces recruited probably encouraged the appointment of captains with professional skills or influence over their non-noble neighbours, but of lesser or no gentility. Urban corporations, concerned that their well-equipped and -financed contingents should honour the town's name, were anxious to appoint captains for competence and trustworthiness, rather than because of their great name. William Tybeaudis, appointed as captain of Coventry's company to support the king, by the mayor and council in May 1455, was not accorded any title of rank in the city's records.[47] William Rokewode, who, the mayor of Norwich declared in January 1461, as a result of 'great labour and supplication' had consented to be captain of the city's company going to the king, was a local esquire.[48] In the early 1460s a Nottingham company intending to join Edward IV at York was captained by the city sheriff, Walter Hilton.[49] However, sophisticated burgesses are likely to have been especially concerned to avoid laughably incompetent captaincy by any of their number. The London author of *Gregory's Chronicle* parades his military expertise and mercilessly denigrates the noble Yorkist commanders at St Albans in 1461, but he also pours contempt on the butcher of Dunstable who had been beaten out of town by the northerners, and as a result of whose 'simple guiding' the contingent of which he was 'chiefest captain' was routed.[50]

The involvement of the commons threw up such rustic captains. According to Warkworth, after Edward landed at Ravenspur in 1471 there was a rising against him of 'all the country of Holderness', captained by a local parson, John Westerdale. The author of the *Arrivall* says that the leaders of the assembly, which was 6,000–7,000 strong, were a vicar and a gentleman called 'Martyn of the See'. Their indecisiveness illustrated the need for the superimposition of noble command on the captains of rural arrays, impressively organized as they often may have been.[51] Prejudice in favour of noble commanders was not just a noble prejudice. Vergil says that the West Country rebels of 1497 were at first captained by 'two men out of the dregs of the population, to wit Thomas Flammock, a lawyer, and Michael Joseph, a blacksmith'. The rebels, though not likely to have put the point with Vergil's elitist waspishness, would have agreed with him, for, when Lord Audley joined them, they acclaimed him as a leader.[52] In default of such leadership, Jack Cade, leading the rebels of 1450, bestowed on himself the aristocratic name of John Mortimer, dressed in the guise of a knight and kept table like one, with a gentleman to carve his meat.[53] Nevertheless, it is likely that noble commanders of armies were often highly dependent on rustic captains of low rank, as well as on captains of mercenaries and urban companies with little or no nobility. The constables of townships played a key role in recruiting and arraying contingents; they may often have been given command roles after contingents had joined up. Rustics were most likely to obey their richer neighbours, men possessed of or aspiring to gentility who knew them and spoke the same dialect. When Audley was in command of the rebels in 1497, he would have remained highly dependent on the mediation of rural captains such as Flammock and Joseph, for most of his men are unlikely to have spoken English, and he is unlikely to have spoken Cornish.

There is a little information about a few men of relatively low status who rose to high military influence through their expertise. One such was the esquire Lovelace. By February 1461 he 'had the reputation of being the most expert in warfare in England': according to Waurin, Warwick had made him captain of Kent and steward of his household, and given him command of the foreward in his campaigns.[54] He took the Yorkist guns and supplies through London northwards in October 1460 and was captured at Wakefield. But by the time the queen's northern army had reached St Albans, he was acting as captain of the Kentishmen in the Yorkist forward. He betrayed the Yorkists there by withdrawing the Kentishmen. A London chronicler had heard that this was because Lovelace had saved his life after Wakefield by taking an oath never to fight against the northerners. Waurin says that he confessed to Edward IV that he had been bought by the queen, who had promised to have him created earl of Kent with a suitable endowment.[55]

Another soldier who rose to high command in the wars was Andrew Trollope, who considered his advancement to knighthood after the second battle of St Albans to be a reward for valour, not a right of birth.[56] Master porter of Calais, he crossed with Warwick from Calais in 1459, and his desertion to the king, and persuasion of Calais soldiers to desert, was an important element in the royal success at Ludford Bridge.[57] According to Waurin, Warwick, having 'greater faith in him than any other', had put Trollope in command of the foreward, but he was suborned by a secret message from the duke of Somerset. Thereafter Waurin represents him as the duke's principal military counsellor, advising him over the defence of Guines and negotiations with Warwick for its surrender, and over his assembly of forces to support the queen, suggesting and helping to execute the plan which brought victory at Wakefield.[58]

For over a century before the outbreak of the Wars of the Roses, the crown's need to mount campaigns and maintain garrisons in the wars with the French, Scots and other foreigners had led to the development of well-tried methods of military recruitment and of the organization of companies. A principal method, the raising of companies by contracted captains, was used mainly in a modified form in the domestic conflicts, and continued to flourish in its normal form as a means of raising forces for service abroad into the sixteenth century. The crown negotiated with its lieutenants and captains to settle their individual terms of service and those of the retinue which they would be responsible for raising, leading, and paying the king's wages. The terms were embodied in indentures interchangeably sealed by the contracting parties. They contained variations on standard, largely traditional conditions – stipulations as to the nature and duration of the captain's and his men's service, as to their rates of pay, and obligations and entitlements regarding war profits and losses. The retinue captain, after his company had been mustered to the satisfaction of the king's or his lieutenant's officials, received a wages advance. He had responsibility for the pay and conduct of his retinue.[59]

In order to recruit the retinue which he had contracted to provide, the retinue captain made a series of indentures with knights and men-at-arms, very similar in form to those which he had made with the crown, stipulating their terms of service and those of the men-at-arms and archers which they often undertook to contribute to the retinue.[60] The captain is likely to have sought to find such subcontractors among kinsmen, servants, tenants and neighbours, and among soldiers with whom he had become acquainted on previous campaigns. Since peers and knights were often eager to contract with the crown as leaders of military retinues, they had an incentive to take permanent contingency measures, so that they would be well placed to respond to a call to arms. This was probably one of the main purposes which led magnates to contract for the service of retainers for life. Indentures were made between the parties stipulating that a knight or esquire was to do service to the lord in peace and war when required: the conditions on which he was to serve in war, such as reception of the king's wages, are often laid down in quite specific detail, reflecting terms usually found in the purely military, and temporary, war contracts. The life retainer, his indenture stated, was to receive a generally substantial annuity, in the form of fee or rent. Such retainers, who were frequently officers in the lord's household or in his estate administration, were presumably expected to provide key segments of his military retinues. Thus a characteristic organizational device of the Hundred Years War stimulated magnates' development of the means of constituting military companies.[61]

In the period of the Wars of the Roses there are numerous examples of customary indentures for paid military service made between the crown and its lieutenants and captains. For instance, there are the indentures contracted by Edward IV with the earl of Northumberland for the keeping of the East and Middle Marches in July 1470, and with Lord Howard as lieutenant and captain of the king's forces for the invasion of Scotland in 1481.[62] But the crown did not normally make this sort of contract with English subjects intending to serve in the wars. An exception is the contract made by Sir Baldwin Fulford in February 1460. He undertook to serve Henry VI at sea with 1,000 men, receiving royal wages for himself and his men for three months. The object of the expedition was to destroy Warwick's naval power based on Calais.[63] The contract reflected conventional aspects of the proposed service, more characteristic of foreign than domestic war. Fulford was undertaking a voluntary command, with a strong profit motive, which would take him to sea and perhaps overseas. He had several weeks in which to prepare and receive finance for his expedition.

In many of the campaigns in the Wars of the Roses, the swift defensive measures required by the crown precluded the negotiation and fulfilment of such elaborate terms of service, which the frequently sudden and unexpected turn of events might render unrealistic. Moreover, when there was rebellion the king was not going into the market-place to negotiate for his nobles' voluntary proffers for a command. He was peremptorily and desperately demanding, on pain of allegiance, whatever support subjects could muster in the time available – an obligation especially pressing on peers, members of the royal household, and other livery-holders of the crown. Even when there was time to commission a commander – in the case of domestic sieges – he was not contracted as for service against foreign enemies, though provision to cover expenses was probably made for him.[64]

Wages were indeed the fuel of warfare: compelled for service or not, men hoped to receive wages from one source or another. The Yorkist leaders of 1459, according to the Act of Attainder passed against them, rebelled at Ludford 'with other Knights and people, such as they had blinded and assembled by wages, promises, and other exquisite means'.[65] The capture of William Tailboys near Newcastle in 1464 with the Lancastrian war-chest of 3,000 marks was a crushing blow to the cause. Henry VI 'had ordained harness and ordnance enough, but the men would not go one foot with him till they had money. And they waited daily and hourly for money that this Tailboys should have sent unto them or brought it.' Instead, the money went to the men of the opposing commander, Montague: it 'was a very wholesome salve' for their wearisome labours.[66] The 1483 revolt may have attracted support because Margaret Beaufort's agent Reginald Bray 'had made up no small sum of money to pay soldiers' wages withall'.[67] But when kings peremptorily summoned nobles to bring retinues for service in the wars, they had no formal obligation to provide the latter with wages for their men, and often no means of doing so. Nevertheless, it was unrealistic to expect individuals to provide expensive service, digging deep into their pockets for their companies' wage bills, without inducement. During the crisis of Edward V's reign, on 11 June 1483, Richard of Gloucester wrote to Lord Neville, asking for his support with a military retinue: 'And, my lord, do me now service, as ye have always before done, and I trust now so to remember you as shall be the making of you and yours.'[68] More tartly than usual, this distilled what is likely to have been an essential spirit in the generation of military support in the wars. Henry VII, thanking Sir Robert Plumpton in 1491 for his part in suppressing Yorkshire commotions, needed only to hint at royal practice: 'we . . . shall not forget the disposition you have been of in that behalf, etc.'.[69] Writing 'in haste' from Knaresborough on 17

September 1497 to his cousin Sir William Calverley, Sir Harry Wentworth relayed news of Warbeck's landing and urged his cousin to prepare a company for the king's service 'for the which I doubt not but his highness shall give you thanks according'.[70]

There are numerous examples of royal cash remunerations for past military service in the wars. Sir John Clay received his costs after serving Edward in the north in the campaign of 1462–3.[71] Edward, after his victories in 1471, ordered payment of '£100 by way of reward' to Lord Grey of Codnor, for the costs which he had incurred in 'attending in his own person upon us in this our great journey as in bringing unto us a great number of men defensibly arrayed at his cost and charge'.[72]

Rewards sometimes took the form of life-grants of offices, annuities and estates, and of perpetual grants of property. The long-term return on some of these rewards represented a potentially large profit on the individual's military investment. A factor determining participation must have been the noble's ability and preparedness to lay out a large sum in the hope of winning a lasting income. The esquire Lovelace dreamt of getting the earldom of Kent – but Lord Fauconberg actually did so.[73] The inducement of large-scale profit was as important in getting men to fight in the Wars of the Roses as in the Hundred Years War, though the mechanics of compensation and reward were markedly dissimilar. Indeed, pressure for compensation and reward, particularly on kings who in the early stages of the wars were short of ready cash, led to the employment of a means of gratification which was a key factor in perpetuating rebellion. The trend was initiated by Henry VI's government after the 1459 forfeitures. Nobles who had given unpaid service against the rebels were rewarded with grants of their lands; lesser men received appurtenant fees and offices.[74] These grants – and the similar ones made by Edward IV after his attainders of 1461 – created a new dimension to the wars: they became recurrent flare-ups between claimants to inheritances as well as to the crown. The earl of Pembroke and Lord Roos, who surrendered at Bamburgh in 1462, did not enter into Edward's allegiance, since they were unable to receive back their lands – presumably because he had granted them to his supporters.[75] Richard III's supporters eagerly occupied Buckingham's lands when he rebelled in 1483, for the king had already promised them ducal wealth.[76] The exiled Henry Tudor's pledge to marry Edward IV's daughter may have been seen as some sort of guarantee that his accession would not lead to an upheaval of the existing landed settlement. Indeed, in his first parliament there was bitter but unavailing opposition to his determination to date the start of the reign from the day before Bosworth, threatening with the penalties of treason any who had taken arms against him. But Henry soon showed his sensitivity to the need to preserve landed stability, in his attempts to reconcile past and potential opponents, and provision of guarantees against forfeiture for all those who supported the crown against rebellion.[77]

We have seen that the nature of the domestic conflicts precluded resort to customary forms of military contract between crown and gentlefolk. The raising of many noble retinues probably stemmed from verbal, sometimes secret, agreements between kings and their noble allies, perhaps sworn on the Sacrament. But agreements for foreign help doubtless continued to be embodied in written contracts. Treaties were made with foreign princes, such as the rulers of France, Scotland and Brittany, which contained promises of aid. The making of written contracts and the provision of wage advances are likely to have been standard practices in gaining the services of reputable foreign mercenary captains and their companies.[78] The text of a distinctly idiosyncratic agreement for foreign noble help survives. On 22 November 1462, at Edinburgh, Henry VI and George Douglas, earl of Angus, sealed an indenture by which Angus was retained to pass with the king into England against the rebels. Within a month of recovering his realm, Henry promised to grant Angus a duchy with lands to the value of 2,000 marks in the north of England. He would be free to hold it in time of war between England and Scotland, and, when fighting in support of the king of Scots, to send up to twenty Scotsmen to govern his lands in England, where they would be treated as if they were Englishmen.[79] The indenture reveals well the kind of ambition which may have animated English as well as foreign nobles' participation. But it is a mad agreement. The implementation of the grant under a restored Henry would have been likely to provoke new domestic conflicts, with greater Scottish involvement.

To resist rebellion, as we have seen, kings perforce relied heavily on the support of influential individuals whom they trusted to bring retinues. Among those whom they turned to were the men whose services in peace they had retained, especially the leading denizens and officers of their households. Under the pressure of domestic conflict, royal military needs became a factor in their retaining policies, and the satisfaction of these needs a more pressing obligation of royal retainers. In 1459 the queen was attempting to rally provincial support; she 'allied unto her all the knights and squires of Cheshire' and had her little son distribute a 'livery of Swans' among them. Some of the recipients were probably among 'the Queen's gallants' who were soon to suffer heavy losses at Blore Heath.[80] At the second battle of St Albans, according to 'Gregory', 'The substance that got that field were household men and feed men.'[81] After Edward's accession, some former members of the Lancastrian household showed tenacious dynastic loyalty, doubtless inspired partly by the conviction that only the reinstatement of King Henry could lead to the recovery of their lost offices and annuities. In 1462 his former steward of the household Sir Thomas Tuddenham, intensely unpopular in some Norfolk circles, was executed for his part in Oxford's conspiracy.[82] A number of former household servants were captured in and after the battle of Hexham in 1464 and executed.[83] A tenacious loyalist was Robert Whittingham, esquire, receiver-general to the prince of Wales in 1456.[84] He was with Somerset at Guines in 1459–60, was knighted by the prince after the second battle of St Albans, in 1461, and later in the year was plotting in France in the Lancastrian interest, for which he died fighting at Tewkesbury in 1471.[85] Richard Tunstall of Thurland (Lancs.) was luckier. In 1452 he was appointed for life as one of Henry's four esquires of the body; in 1457 he was the king's knight and carver, and in 1459–60 his chamberlain.[86] He was with the Lancastrian invaders in Northumberland in November 1462, and took part in the epic defence of Harlech castle.[87] Pardoned by Edward IV in 1468, during Henry's Readeption he was again high in Lancastrian favour: in October 1470, when royal chamberlain, he received a grant made verbally by Henry. The restored Edward immediately pardoned him and made him a king's knight, and he was to serve Richard III and Henry VII as knight of the body.[88]

Edward IV and his immediate successors placed particular reliance on the ability of their retainers to give military as well as political support.[89] In a commission of array by signet letter sent to Coventry corporation (9 February 1470), Edward commanded military service in person or by substitute from all those holding offices of his or the queen's gift with wages of 3*d.* or more a day.[90] On 5 August following, Sir John Paston wrote that the king had 'sent for his feedmen to come to him' to put down the northern rebels.[91] Advancing south from Yorkshire in 1471, Edward rallied his household men. At Barnet many of his 'menial servants' were slain.[92] In 1473 he relied heavily on John Fortescue, esquire of the body, and other household men to oppose the earl of Oxford in the West Country.[93] At Bosworth loyal retainers probably charged with Richard and defended him against odds: Valera says that 'the majority of those who loyally served the king were killed'.[94] Henry VII, according to Vergil, instituted a bodyguard of about 200 retainers, who were among those dispatched from York against rebels in 1486.[95] According to Trevisan's memorialist (1498):

the present King Henry has appointed certain military services, to be performed by some of his own dependants and familiars [*suoi domestici, e famigliari*], who he knows can be trusted on any urgent occasion; and can be kept on a much smaller number of fees [than *milites* can].[96]

In the 1495 parliament it was enacted that all those in receipt of royal 'grants and gifts of offices fees and annuities', having the obligation to give military attendance in person on the king, were to forfeit their grants if they defaulted, unless licenced not to attend, or sick.[97] In 1504 this Act was extended to include all those holding grants of property from the crown, with the proviso that all those in these categories giving attendance 'shall have the King's wages from the time of coming from his House toward the King when they come to the King, and from the King home again at the time of their departing . . . and whilst they be with the King's Grace to have also the King's wages'.[98]

After the battle of Tewkesbury, when Edward was at Coventry preparing for a new campaign (May 1471), he 'forgot not to send from thence his messengers, with writings, all about the countries near adjoining, to such in especial as he trusted best that they would do him service'.[99] Some examples of royal summonses to individuals – not all royal retainers – survive. They seem to reflect a trend towards more insistent, and more elaborately specific requests, and a tendency for kings to make prior agreement with individuals about the nature of the support which they would provide in emergencies. On 13 March 1461, by signet letter dated at York, Henry VI wrote to Sir William Plumpton outlining the 'earl of March's' misdeeds: 'we therefore pray and also straitly charge you that anon upon sight hereof' you come as soon as possible 'with all such people as ye may make defensibly arrayed' to Henry 'as ye love the surety of our person, the weal of yourself, and of all our true and faithful subjects'.[100] Thomas Stonor received a signet letter from Edward IV dated at Coventry, 3 April 1470, informing him of the flight of Clarence and Warwick westwards, and of the royal intent to pursue them and suppress their traitorous purpose: 'Wherefore we will and strictly charge you that immediately after the sight of these our letters ye array you, with such a fellowship on horseback in defensible array as ye goodly can make, to come unto us wheresoever ye shall understand that we then shall be.'[101] Edward's signet letter to William Swan, gentleman, dated at York 7 September following, charged him to array with a fellowship 'upon the faith and liegance that ye bear unto us'. Since the strategic circumstances differed from those of the previous April, Edward did not specify that Swan's company must be horsed, and, in anticipation of a landing in Kent or nearby by Clarence and Warwick, commanded him to be ready to act on several alternatives, in accordance with the information he might receive about rebel movements.[102] In contrast to these summonses, Edward's signet letter to Henry Vernon, esquire (Tewkesbury, 7 May 1471), specified the size of Vernon's company; he was charged 'as our trust is in you' to bring twenty men, defensibly arrayed, to meet the king for his entry into Coventry. But more urgent circumstances made the king less specific and more peremptory. Edward's letter to Vernon from Worcester the following day desired and charged him to bring 'such fellowship defensibly arrayed as ye goodly can make' immediately to meet the king – to resist the rebellious commons – on his allegiance 'and forfeiture of all that ye may forfeit'.[103] Richard III's signet letter dated Beskwood Lodge, 11 August 1485, willing and strictly charging Vernon, squire for his body, to attend the king with a company to resist the malice of Henry Tudor, is also insistent on the penalty of forfeiture. Vernon is to attend 'without failing, all manner excuses set apart'. The king in fact had made prior agreement with Vernon as to the numbers and equipment of the company that he should bring at need: he was to come 'with such number as ye have promised unto us sufficiently horsed and harnessed'. Richard's desire to have his followers' strength prepared is reflected in a list in the duke of Norfolk's papers, dated 26 February 1484, giving some particulars of the 1,000 men 'that my Lord hath granted to the King'. Men were listed under the duke's lordships 'to be ready at all times at my Lord's pleasure': individuals who had promised to come, with or without men, were listed, some with the proviso 'at my Lords cost'.[104]

Though, in a military summons to Vernon, Henry VII did not allude to any prior agreement about the nature of the fellowship that Vernon was willed and desired to bring, his letter to Sir Robert Plumpton dated Sheen, 28 May 1491, shows that he, too, was concerned to have companies organized by trusted gentlemen ready for use in emergencies:

> We therefore, intending to provide for the time to come, desire you that forthwith and by as wise wages as ye can, ye put yourself in a surety of your menial servants and tenants, and to know assuredly how many of them will take your part in serving us according to your and their duties foresaid. When ye have demeaned the matter in this wise, which we would that you did as above with all diligence, then we pray you to certify our cousin, the Earl of Surrey, of the number of such assured men, etc.[105]

In a letter to Sir Gilbert Talbot (July 1493), he willed him to have a company in readiness to resist the malice of Margaret of Burgundy. Henry was highly specific about the composition of Talbot's company. It was to be horsed, eighty strong, 'whereof we desire you to make as many spears, with their custrells [attendants], and demi-lances, well horsed as ye can furnish, and the remainder to be archers and bills, ye be thoroughly appointed and ready to come upon a day's warning for to do us service of war in this case'. The king laid down the rates of pay which Talbot was to receive for different categories of soldier.[106] Thus Richard III and Henry VII appear to have made greater efforts than their predecessors to constitute a select force in readiness to oppose rebellion or invasion, consisting of private companies commanded by trusted gentlefolk, about whose terms of service and composition there was a degree of prior agreement.

In 1497 Henry expected Talbot to bring to his aid promptly a company of 120 men. The need of gentlefolk, especially magnates, to widen potential military as well as political support because of the wars may have encouraged the habit of breaking the 1399 statute enacting that no one 'shall use or give any livery or sign of company'. In 1468 it was enacted that all statutes and ordinances hitherto made against the giving or receiving of liveries and badges should be kept. Great numbers of people were said to be daily breaking them. The grant of liveries or badges was prohibited: no one was to retain another except his menial servant or a lawyer by any writing, oath or promise.[107]

But a body of evidence indicates that one leading participant in the wars, Edward's chamberlain Lord Hastings, retained by indenture for services for life in peace and war, partly as a means of forming companies to participate in the wars. There survive sixty-nine indentures which he entered into in the period 1461–83 with sixty-seven out of the total of two peers and eighty-eight knights, esquires and gentlemen whom he is known to have retained. According to Professor Dunham's analysis of these contracts, the retainer commonly agreed to ride and go with Hastings, to aid and succour him, and to take his part and quarrel against all others, his liege lord the king excepted. The retainer was to come, upon reasonable warning, with as many men defensibly arrayed as he could assemble, or as accorded with his rank. In forty-two contracts, the obligation to attend Hastings was restricted to English soil – a restriction indicating their relevance to the Wars of the Roses. In all but a few cases, Hastings was required to pay the costs and expenses of the retainer and his company for their service.[108]

Other peers and gentlefolk may not have reacted to contemporary domestic political and military stresses with such a widespread making of life-contracts. Some apparently preferred to make relatively few contracts and to grant fees on a less permanent basis.[109] The nature of Hastings's indentures may reflect exceptional features in his political and military career. Something of a parvenu, he came to exercise great influence in some Midland shires, and needed to build up networks of connection: by far the greatest number of his known retainers, thirty-two out of ninety, were from Derbyshire, though his principal family estates were in Leicestershire. Identifying his political fortunes closely with Edward's, he habitually fought for him, and consequently required ready military support, for which he was well placed to guarantee remuneration.[110]

There are some surviving letters from magnates summoning

individuals to bring military support in the wars. Presumably the recipients had made verbal or written promises to provide such support, or it was hoped that they would do so because of their tenure of offices, fees and land grants. The responses to the letters provide some indications as to whether expectations were fulfilled. Henry Vernon, esquire, an officer of the duke of Clarence, received the first of a series of summonses from his master, by signet letter dated Bristol, 15 March 1471. He was to 'see that as well all your tenants and servants as ours in those parts be ready upon an hour's warning to wait upon us in def[ensible] array whensoever we send for you and them'. The following day, from Wells, the duke reiterated this request, emphasizing the importance of the preparations in the light of rumours of Edward IV's imminent invasion, and on 23 March, when sure news of it had arrived, he desired and prayed Vernon to join him immediately with as large a defensibly arrayed company as possible, on the king's service, and that ye fail not hereof as our special trust is in you'.[111] But two days later Warwick dispatched a letter to Vernon with news of Edward's landing, willing him to join him with a company at Coventry 'as my vray singular trust is in you and as I mowe do thing to your weal or worship hereafter'. The earl tellingly added the autograph postscript: 'Henry I pray you fail not now as ever I may do for you.' However, Vernon must have failed either Warwick or Clarence – possibly both of them. Though he sent information to the duke about Edward's movements, Clarence had to send further requests to him for military service in similar urgent terms from Malmesbury on 30 March and Burford on 2 April. Vernon did not take part in the battle of Tewkesbury: Edward IV's signet letters to him (7–8 March) reinforced one from Clarence desiring him to join king and duke with soldiers for the latter's retinue on the northern expedition projected after the battle. Writing on 6 May from Tewkesbury, with Edward's weight behind him, Clarence had adopted a more peremptory tone with Vernon: 'we desire and for your weal advise you, and also in my said lord's [the king's] name charge you, to dispose you to come and attend upon us'. But, summoning him again four days later, Clarence accepted the reasons reported to him for Vernon's failure to attend, and assured him of ducal favour on compliance:

> letting you weet that it hath been reported to us that ye have heretofor
> put you in devoir to have come to us if ye had mought, wherof we
> thank you, the matters and causes of the let and impediment of your
> coming now ceased, blessed be God. . . . [The summons follows.]
> And ye shall find us your good lord, and thereof ye shall not need to
> doubt in any wise.[112]

The group of summonses received by Vernon provide a unique

insight into the pressures for military support on one influential esquire, and the difficulties experienced by lords in mobilizing a retainer or well-wisher in a doubtful politico-military situation. Not all other surviving summonses by magnates were complied with. On 11 October 1483 Viscount Lovell wrote to his 'cousin' Sir William Stonor about the arrangement approved by the king that their companies should go together, Stonor's men in Lovell's livery. Lovell held out in return promise of his future goodwill – but Stonor joined the rebels.[113] The day before Lovell addressed his summons to Stonor, the duke of Norfolk wrote to a well-to-do East Anglian neighbour, his 'welbeloved friend' John Paston, requesting his help to defend London with a company of 'six tall fellows in harness', promising 'ye shall not lose your labour, that knoweth God'.[114] In 1485 he prayed Paston to meet him at Bury, in order to join the king,

> and that ye bring with you such company of tall men as ye may goodly make at my cost and charge . . . and I pray you ordain them jackets of my livery, and I shall content you at your meeting with me. Your lover, J. Norffolk.[115]

Since Paston was appointed sheriff of Norfolk and Suffolk soon after Bosworth, it is unlikely that he complied.[116]

It seems, then, that it was not uncommon for lords (like kings) to be disappointed in domestic emergencies by the gentlefolk they had trusted and favoured. Kings could, indeed, call on a firmer obligation to allegiance – but there is no evidence that they resorted to forfeiture as a penalty for its non-fulfilment. Both kings and nobles punished failure by loss of office, fees, goodwill. Because Sir William Skipwith did not comply with York's summons to join his army in 1455, the duke revoked his offices and annuities. But in 1459, after York's forfeiture, they were restored to Skipwith by the crown.[117] This illustrates limitations on the crown's and nobles' ability to punish the unwilling. They were reliant on gentlefolk to extend their local political influence: if they withheld gracious lordship, there was likely to be someone else eager to step in with it. Clarence in 1471 was being realistic when he accepted Vernon's excuses with a good grace, despite the fact that Vernon was failing him at a crucial stage of his career. For king and lords, the key to gaining the military support of substantial followers was the offer of inducements rather than the threat of disfavour.

There was one other principal means of raising forces in the later Middle Ages, besides the recruitment of companies by individuals. Commissions of array were used more especially to provide for the defence of the realm, as well as for expeditions abroad. This system had its roots in Anglo-Saxon obligations owed by men of shire and borough to give armed support to the king and his officers. In the thirteenth century, able-bodied men between the ages of sixteen and sixty were sworn to allegiance, grouped under the constables of cities and boroughs, hundreds and vills, and were obliged to have adequate arms. They were summoned and mustered to serve under the sheriff or regional constable, and followed his orders to hunt down criminals or rebels, or guard the coasts against invasion. The Statute of Winchester (1285), which laid down the types of arms which possessors of chattels or rents of various worth were to have in readiness for service, remained the basic legislation on military obligation until the sixteenth century.[118]

The systematic use of commissions of array to assemble selected communal recruits for expeditions out of the realm, as well as to supply the backbone of local defences, was developed by Edward I for his Welsh and Scottish wars, and exploited by Edward II and Edward III for their commitments abroad. Under Edward III, arrayers were appointed to raise a company for a French campaign within a single shire or borough. The shire arrayers were usually gentlefolk – particularly knights – with some military experience. The number of men whom they were asked to raise varied according to the size of the county.[119] The sort of instructions which they received were to choose, test and array, ensuring that recruits were suitably clothed, equipped and mounted,[120] and had received pay. Thus communities were expected to supply some finance and, in some circumstances, equipment and weapons.[121] Sheriffs, bailiffs and other officers as well as the faithful men of the communities were bidden by writ to assist the arrayers. Constables of townships probably had some responsibility for securing recruits, ensuring that they were adequately set up, and levying aid from their neighbours. The constables may have also made preliminary groupings of the men into scores and hundreds (*vintaines* and *centaines*) for inspection by the arrayers.

The political weakness of the crown after Edward III's accession in 1327, and his increasing dependence, for waging the French wars which commenced in 1337, on political and financial support from parliament, induced royal concessions in answer to the communities' protests at harsh exploitation by the crown of this system of military obligation. A statute of 1327 conceded that levies were to arm at their own expense only in the manner laid down by the Statute of Winchester, and were not obliged to provide the elaborate and expensive arms which Edward II had on occasion specified. The ancient obligation of men to provide unpaid service was not to be stretched: they were not to have to go out of their counties at their own costs except in the case of the sudden coming of foreign enemies into the realm. From 1343 men could gain exemptions from service by payment of fines. In 1344 it was enacted that those chosen to go on the king's service outside England were to receive his wages from the day on which they left the county in which they were chosen until the day they re-entered it. But for service out of the country in other parts of the realm, the community remained obliged to provide wages. In 1402, at the request of the commons, the statutes of 1327 and 1344 were re-enacted, as was one of 1352 which curbed royal demands on individuals to pay soldiers' costs.

Therefore the kings of the later fifteenth century could turn for defence against rebels to a traditional, well-tried, universally accepted and understood system of raising troops from communities in general. Many commissions to counter internal rebellion and invasion during the Wars of the Roses were of the customary kind, letters patent addressed to a group of influential, reliable military gentlefolk in a shire, or to the ruling elite in a city or borough. Such were the commissions issued in December 1459, intended to prepare forces to resist invasions by the attainted Yorkist lords.[122] But domestic emergencies often led to less conventional, less cumbersome authorization and greater reliance on influential individuals to control arrays. According to William Paston, it was being said that Henry VI, on his way to London in January 1460, 'reareth the people as he come'.[123] In 1471 the Lancastrian forces in the West Country raised men as they moved, presumably by virtue of the prince of Wales's commission of lieutenancy.[124] Kings sent privy seal or signet letters requesting cities and boroughs to dispatch companies, such as those sent by Edward IV to the mayor of Coventry under his signet in July 1469.[125] They turned too to trusted noble friends. In February 1460, to guard against Yorkist invasion, Henry VI's half-brother the earl of Pembroke was empowered to call up all Welsh lieges.[126] In January 1461, when preparations were being made to resist the queen's advance on London, Sir John Wenlock had his commission to suppress her sympathizers strengthened by the power to call together the lieges of Hertfordshire and five other shires north of the city.[127] The following month, the earl of March was empowered to call together, to resist the rebels, the lieges of Bristol, Staffordshire, Shropshire, Herefordshire, Gloucestershire, Worcestershire, Somerset and Dorset.[128] Two letters in the Paston correspondence show magnates acting under a commission of array addressed to them. In March 1471, the earl of Oxford, citing his commission for Norfolk to resist Edward, wrote to five individuals commanding them to come 'with as many men as ye may goodly make'.[129] In October 1485 the duke of Suffolk wrote to John Paston as sheriff of Norfolk and Suffolk, reciting the ducal commission to array received from Henry VII, and ordering Paston to have proclamations made 'in all possible haste' warning 'all manner men able to do the King service, as well knights, esquires, and gentlemen, as townships and hundreds, as well within franchise and liberties as without' to be prepared to attend on king and duke when required. The promptness with which commissions were expected to be fulfilled is reflected in Suffolk's stipulation that the arrayed men were to be ready at all times upon an hour's warning, and his information to Paston that his letter was dispatched 'this same day we received the King's commission at four after noon'.[130]

The need to rely on individual nobles to enforce commissions posed dangers. They might use the arrayed men against instead of in support of the author of the commission. In 1460 Lord Neville raised men under a commission from the duke of York and subsequently joined with them in the attack on him.[131] Even when a lord could not exhibit a commission, there was a danger that he might hoodwink men into believing that he was ordering them to serve at the king's command. Warwick's letter of 28 June 1469 to his 'servants and wellwillers within the city of Coventry' disingenuously asserted that he wished them to array to accompany him in answer to the king's summons for attendance against the northern rebels – when in fact the latter were acting *for* Warwick. Edward was to realize that deceits were being practised against him, for in a signet letter commanding a Coventry array dated 10 July he ordered that

> in no wise ye make any rising or assemblies with any person whatsoever he be, nor suffer any of our subjects within our City of Coventry to do upon the said pain, without that we under our privy seal or signet or sign manual command you to do.[132]

In 1470 Clarence and Warwick perverted the purposes of the commissions which they had received from Edward. According to his proclamation of 24 March,

> his said Highness authorised them by his commission under his great seal to assemble his subjects in certain shires, and them to have brought to his said Highness. . . . [they] under colour thereof, falsely and traitorously provoked and stirred, as well by their writings as otherwise, Sir Robert Welles . . . to continue the said insurrections and rebellions, and to levy war against him, as they, by the same, so did with banners displayed.[133]

Fear of their misuse of the commissions of array which he had issued was probably the spur to his proclamations of 13 March commanding

> that none of his subjects presume, nor take upon him, to rise, nor make any assembly or gathering, by reason of any of the said commissions or writings, nor by moving, stirring, writing, or commandment made, or hereafter to be made, by any person or persons of what estate, degree, or condition soever he be of, lest that

it be by the King's commission, Privy Seal, or writing under his signet, of new to be made after this the 13 day of March.[134]

Nevertheless, later in the year Marquess Montague destroyed Edward's rule by misusing his commission of array.[135]

Such notorious treacheries may have made some men wary. In 1487 Sir Edmund Bedingfield had difficulty in persuading Norfolk gentlemen to assist him in executing a commission of array received by the earl of Oxford, until he could authenticate it:

> it was thought I ought not to obey no copy of the commission, without I had the same under wax, wherein hath been great arguement, which I understood by report a fortnight past, and that caused me to send unto my lord [Oxford] to have the very commission, which he sent me.[136]

Commissions of array indicate the powers granted to arrayers, and provide some information about the recruitment and nature of the forces raised, and their intended spheres of operations. The arrayers in Westmorland in June 1463 were authorized to summon all lieges, who were to array according to their degree. The arrayers were to hold a muster and ensure that the men were continually prepared to serve. On receiving a royal summons, they were to lead the shire levy to the king or others, and were to exercise powers of command over it on the journey. All sheriffs, mayors, bailiffs, constables and other officers within and without liberties (areas of private jurisdiction) were to assist the arrayers in their tasks.[137] In May 1464 sheriffs of sixteen counties were instructed to have proclamations made ordering every man between the ages of sixteen and sixty to prepare to attend Edward IV at a day's notice 'well and defensibly arrayed'.[138] The commission for Cornwall to guard against invasion threats (July 1468) specified that 'hobelars' (light horsemen) and archers were to be arrayed, and that arrayers were to divide them into companies of a thousand, subdivided into hundreds and twenties.[139] Since the direction of threats was often uncertain in the wars, arrayers had on occasion to prepare the levies for a variety of contingencies. A commission for South Wales and its Marches to guard against the return of Edward IV (January 1471) specified that the levy was to repel invasions of particular regions, suppress rebels there or go to the king or his deputies.[140]

Writs to the sheriffs of Kent and Sussex, the mayor of Canterbury, and the constable of Dover and warden of the Cinque Ports, dated August 1492, commanded:

> all and every his subjects inhabited within this his shire of Kent, having harness of his own and being of ability in his person to serve his highness if need be, that they and every one of them prepare

themself to be ready in their said harness, upon an hour warning, to
serve our said sovereign lord at his wages.

Constables of hundreds were to make search for all inhabitants 'of
ability and harnessed to serve' and to certify the king of their names and
apparel without delay.[141] The workings of the array system are more
fully revealed in a writ under Henry VII's sign manual to the
chancellor, dated November 1509, which was intended as a basis for
writs ordering the shires communities to overhaul the system. Those
able in person and goods to serve the king were to prepare 'horse and
harness competent, and weapons convenient' for themselves and, if
their 'degree, power and substance' warranted it, for two or three more.
Those wealthy enough to serve, but unable to do so because of sickness
or old age, were to provide, equipped, one, two or more soldiers.
Sheriffs, bailiffs and constables of cities, towns and boroughs, and
constables of hundreds, were to warn every city, town, borough, village
and hamlet within their offices to prepare one or more able men
harnessed and weaponed. All the prospective soldiers were to remain
during the following months ready to appear and muster before the
commissioners of array whom the king would commission, at the time
and place appointed by them.[142]

Features of this system as it worked in the Wars of the Roses may be
reflected in a hostile account of the Bastard of Fauconberg's levy in
Kent in 1471, raised by authority allegedly received from the earl of
Warwick, Henry VI's lieutenant:

> Other of Kentish people that would right fain have sitten still at
> home, and not to have run into the danger of such rebellion . . . for
> fear of death, and other great menaces, and threatenings, were
> compelled, some to go with the bastard, in their persons; such
> specially, as were able in their persons if they had array, and might
> not wage to such as would go, they were compelled, by like force, to
> lend them their array, and harness; and such as were unharnessed,
> aged, and unable, and of honour, they were compelled to send men
> waged, or to give money wherewith to wage men to go to the said
> bastard's company.[143]

It may be that other arrays during the wars were as unwelcome as
this, involving what was perceived as compulsion and extortion.
Proclamations ordering an array in May 1464 enjoined obedience
'under the Pain that shall fall thereupon'.[144] A hostile writer alleged that
Warwick, as Henry VI's lieutenant in 1471, 'whereas he could not
arraise the people with goodwill, he straitly charged them to come forth
upon pain of death'.[145] The comprehensive powers to array throughout
the realm granted to the prince of Wales in March 1471 threatened the

disobedient with the penalties of treason.[146] Richard III is said by a hostile writer to have dispatched letters in 1485 threatening those who failed to respond to his summonses with forfeiture and death.[147]

The provision of wages for the levy must have been one of the most widespread and resented burdens of the arraying system. The account of the Bastard's recruitment in the *Arrivall* implies that he expected the Kentishmen arrayed to have their wages provided by themselves or their neighbours. Chamberlains' accounts in urban records often state sums provided for the wages of companies raised: urban sources sometimes record in detail the raising of taxes for military wages in the wars and how they were allotted.[148] A letter written by John Paston in 1461 gives information about the 'waging' of Norfolk levies summoned to resist the northerners:

> most people out of this country have taken wages . . . the towns and
> the country that have waged them shall think they be discharged
> . . . . And yet it will be thought right strange of them that have waged
> people to wage any more, for every town hath waged and sent forth,
> and are ready to send forth, as many as they did when the King
> [Henry VI] sent for them before the field at Ludlow [in 1459].[149]

The chronicler Warkworth, discussing the reasons for Edward's loss of the crown in 1470, lists among the common people's discontents the fact that throughout his reign they had 'at yet at every battle to come far out their countries at their own cost'.[150]

Knowledge of the array system is handicapped by a dearth of information about its local organization. There survives a partially defective roll of a muster held at Bridport (Dorset) on 4 September 1457 before the town's two bailiffs and two constables. This may have had some connection with a commission issued on 16 December following, according to which arrayers delivered indentures into the Exchequer, certifying how many archers shires and ten cities were to supply. The respective totals were 10,993 (254 for Dorset) and 1,602.[151] The Bridport Muster Roll lists over 180 individuals with the 'harness' which they presented for inspection, and a note of the additional equipment which some were ordered to produce, often within a fortnight, under pain of fine. No harness is listed after at least sixty names – perhaps because these were absentees or for some reason incapable of complying. Just under two-thirds out of about 100 of those who presented arms had either a bow and sheaf of arrows (or half a sheaf or a specified number of arrows). Seventy or so were equipped with parts or the whole of what seems to have been the standard full complement for an arrayed man-at-arms – a sallet (helmet), jack (reinforced tunic, not unlike a modern flak jacket), sword (the commonest weapon at the muster after bow and arrow), buckler and dagger. Ten had the full equipment; about a dozen lacked buckler and dagger. A few duplicated one or more items: one man had three sallets. With seeming arbitrariness – but presumably in accordance with assessments of property and wealth – some who lacked items of the standard harness were ordered to provide one or more of them, such as a sallet and jack, or a dagger; bucklers, less in evidence, were not *de rigueur*. Some who paraded sallets nevertheless had to provide an additional one.

A sprinkling of other sorts of weapons were produced, often supplementing bows, swords and daggers – there were poleaxes, glaives, spears, axes, custills (two-edged daggers), bills, staves and a hanger (short sword). One man, in addition to a bow, twelve arrows and a sword, had a gun, but despite this unique weapon he had to double his bundle of arrows. There were also odd items of armour, some possibly cannibalized from gentlefolk's superior armours – habergeons (jackets of mail or scale armour), pairs of gauntlets and brigandines (body armour of metal on material), leg harness and a kettle hat. At least two arrayed men brought a pavis – a large shield, probably of a sort fixed on the ground in front of an archer. The bailiffs' and constables' consciousness that more pavises were needed is reflected in their orders to individuals to provide them, in two cases with a lead mallet, presumably intended to hammer pavises into place, or protective stakes set up in front of archers.

The Bridport Muster Roll gives the impression that the leaders of the community were determined that well-equipped archers should be provided. There was a good stock of harness among the inhabitants: some, indeed, were excellently equipped, such as the man who had two sallets, two jacks, three bows and sheaves, two poleaxes, two glaives and two daggers. As a compact, relatively wealthy community uncomfortably close to the Channel coast, Bridport was armed to the teeth.

A few documents concerned with arrays survive from the archives of noble families. A valuable survival is a muster certificate of the later fifteenth century compiled for Sir William Stonor on the information of the constables of the half hundred of Ewelme (Oxon.), 'of men that make harness and be able to do the king service and not able to make harness'. The constables of seventeen vills named more than eighty men, a few of whom were said to be not able for service. All except two of the constables categorized their men as being with or without harness. Over forty had harness. John Pallyng of Ewelme may have inherited his from someone of different build, for he was 'not able to wear it'. Constables often noted whether their men were archers – as many of them were – or whether they fought with what were the other characteristic weapons in this region: bill or staff. Some were noted down as good archers or able with bill or staff. One Brightwell man was armed with an axe. Sir William Stonor thus had precise information about the military strength of the half hundred. The compilation of such certificates was probably unexceptional. Other sorts of array records are to be found copied into a book which contains household accounts of John de Vere, earl of Oxford. There is the commission to the earl to array in Essex, Norfolk, Suffolk, Cambridgeshire and Huntingdonshire for Henry VII's northern expedition after the battle of Stoke, dated Lincoln, 21 June 1487. There follow Oxford's instructions to the arrayers, telling them to inform all knights, esquires, gentlemen and constables of townships about the king's victory, the royal intention to lead 'a mighty power' into the north, and the royal command that individual gentlefolk and townships 'after their degree and substance' should assist the king by personal service or by the provision of men or money. The commissioners were to examine what services had been done in the recent campaign and what would be in the coming one 'and there of make a remembrance, to the intent that the King . . . may give every of his subjects thank after his demerit': those who had aided the Stoke campaign were excused further obligation. The commissioners were also to command constables to ascertain whether men were adequately arrayed, and to certify defaults.[152]

The book also contains notes of the numbers of soldiers that individual gentlemen had undertaken to 'find and purvey' to 'await upon my Lord into the North Country' and of those whom other gentlemen had undertaken to bring at the costs of the king and earl. Also listed were those who 'found men with my Lord in the other voyage' (i.e. the Stoke campaign) at their own cost, and those who paid 'to wage men with' on the same expedition. The latter included Lord Willoughby (£12 for six men) and the towns of Bury St Edmunds, Walden and Ipswich (respectively, £10 for five men, £12 for six, £15 for blank). There follows a list of 'such receipts as I have received of certain hundreds and townships' for the wages of those attending Oxford northwards, waged from 18 July for a month. Some sums were sent to the receiver by a whole hundred, some by an individual township, and in some cases he noted that a constable had given him the money – though a knight, Thomas Grey, did so for three townships.

Some precise information about the organization of arrays is to be found in urban archives. The administrative mechanisms of leading cities were well fitted to raise, equip and provide pay for contingents. In May 1455 the mayor of Coventry received a royal signet letter addressed to him and the sheriffs, summoning them to come armed with a retinue. He convened the council; he and his brethren decided that 100 'of good-men defensibly with bows and arrows, Jakked and saletted, arrayed', should be provided hastily for the king. A captain was appointed, and 38s. 6d. was spent on a new ribanded and tasselled standard for the company, a gaudy multi-coloured garment for its captain, and 'bends' of green and red cloth to be worn by the soldiers. As the company never went to war, these accoutrements were committed to the city wardens' keeping.[153] In a Norwich assembly of 12 January 1461, a royal commission dated 3 January ordering the mayor to summon military aid from the city for Henry VI was read out. It was decided that the aldermen and past and present sheriffs should find forty soldiers and the commonalty eighty: costs were to be assessed by wards and parishes at the mayor's discretion. On 26 January he reported that the captaincy of the company had been filled and that the soldiers were pledged to serve for six weeks at the city's wages. The costs of the captain's outlay were to be borne by the city treasury and sums paid by the cathedral prior and various ecclesiastical bodies.[154] The Nottingham chamberlains' accounts for 1463–4 list expenses of 56s. 3d. for the cost of making jackets for the soldiers riding to the king at York. Payments were made for red cloth for the soldiers' jackets and fine red cloth for their captain's, the sheriff, for white fustian to make letters, and for the cutting out and threading on of the letters.[155]

Unfortunately we lack descriptions or illustrations of the appearance of arrays in the Wars of the Roses. Clearly some of the urban levies were, in their way, as brave a sight as the knights whose deeds and accoutrements were of more interest to courtly chroniclers and illuminators. Perhaps the nearest we can get to a description of levies is Dominic Mancini's one of the soldiers whom he observed in London in 1483, summoned there by the dukes of Gloucester and Buckingham. Among those he saw may have been the northerners (who included a company raised by the city of York) and Welshmen prominent among the dukes' supporters:

There is hardly any without a helmet, and none without bows and arrows: their bows and arrows are thicker and longer than those used by other nations, just as their bodies are stronger than other peoples', for they seem to have hands and arms of iron. The range of their bows is no less than that of our arbalests; there hangs by the side of each a sword no less long than ours, but heavy and thick as well. The sword is always accompanied by an iron shield. . . . They do not wear any metal armour on their breast or any other part of the body, except for the better sort who have breastplates and suits of armour. Indeed the common soldiery have more comfortable tunics that reach down below the loins and are stuffed with tow or some other soft material [i.e. jacks]. They say that the softer the tunics the better do they withstand the blows of arrows and swords, and besides that in summer they are lighter and in winter more serviceable than iron.[156]

Bishop Latimer, in a sermon preached before Edward VI, gave a vivid glimpse of how as a boy he had helped to equip his father, Hugh, setting out to serve Henry VII against the Cornish rebels in 1497:

> My father was a yeoman, and had no lands of his own, only he had a farm of three or four pounds by year at the uttermost, and thereupon he tilled as much as kept half a dozen men. He had walk for a hundred sheep; and my mother milked thirty kine. He was able, and did find the king a harness, with himself and his horse, while he came to the place that he should receive the king's wages. I can remember that I buckled his harness when he went unto Blackheath Field.[157]

His father, a well-to-do tenant at Thurcaston (Leics.), possessing his own harness and mount, was doubtless better equipped than the generality of levies.

How efficiently were commissions of array fulfilled? Many contingents were doubtless tardy, inexperienced, ill equipped, unruly. There were the green Cheshiremen slaughtered at Blore Heath, the inadequately armed ('naked') men in the royal army which advanced to Ludlow, the 'new men of war' routed by the northern army at Dunstable in 1461, and the king's people who, at St Albans the next day, 'would not be guided nor governed by their captains'.[158] Whether the arrays were adequate, and whether they came at all, was highly dependent on the zeal and ability of the arrayers, and on the co-operativeness of local communities. Dire threats in proclamations from kings desperate for support are more likely to have repelled than attracted their services. On occasion arrayers were confronted by a stubborn refusal to budge. At Newark in 1469 Edward IV had to give up his intention of confronting the northern rebels, 'finding that the common people came into him more slowly than he had anticipated'.[159] Later in the year Warwick was unable to get an adequate response to proclamations ordering the lieges to rise against the northern rebels, because the king was his prisoner.[160]

But it is likely that arrays often provided sturdy, reliable companies, especially in the years 1459–64 and 1469–71, when frequent summonses tested arraying organization. The formidable military reputation of northerners may have been based partly on their more habitual arraying, to combat Scottish raids. Cities and boroughs, needing defence against sack, and the goodwill of crown and nobles to maintain their privileges and interests, had incentives to keep their arraying capacity in good order. In February 1460 the mayor of Coventry was concerned because no action had been taken on a royal commission received over a fortnight before ordering a muster in preparation against any invasion attempt by the exiled Yorkists. By the advice of the city council, the mayor waited on the duke of

Buckingham, then lodging in Coventry at 'the Angell', to have the duke's advice 'of his demean in the said commission because his receipt was so late, if any peril or hurt might grow unto the city for the late certificate thereof'.[161] Cities' good repute as paymasters and providers of equipment doubtless enabled them to attract able services.[162] It was probably a point of pride and prestige that civic companies should behave creditably: as we have seen, they were sometimes decked out with a banner and smart new uniforms. Shires and their constituent hundreds, like cities and towns, probably vied to make good array for war, as they did for peace. William Paston reported to his brother in 1489:

> Sir, my lord [the earl of Oxford] hath sent on to the most part of the gentlemen of Essex to wait upon him at Chelmsford, where as he intendeth to meet with the King, and that they be well appointed, that the Lancashire men may see that there be gentlemen of as great substance that they be able to buy all Lancashire. Men think that ye among you will do the same. Your country [Norfolk] is greatly boasted of, and also the inhabitors of the same.[163]

Had Sir William Stonor arrayed a scarecrow levy from the half hundred of Ewelme – like the Essex levy in 1471 and the Cornish levy in 1497 which were sneered at as ragtag and bobtail by London chroniclers – he might have earned ridicule, and certainly no royal thanks.

Edward IV may had some impressive arrayed levies as well as lords' companies when he mustered his army at Grantham in March 1470. According to a correspondent of John Paston, 'it was said that were never seen in England so many goodly men, and so well arrayed in a field. And my Lord [the duke of Norfolk] was worshipfully accompanied, no lord there so well; wherefore the King gave my Lord a great thank.'[164] But even poor contingents had their uses. Their inadequate equipment or inexperience might be compensated for by the quality of nobles' retinues and by a weight of artillery. Massed behind ditches and hedges, relatively 'naked' men, armed with bows, bills, staves, axes, could fill in or extend a defensive position. Their manpower was required to assist carts, particularly those loaded with guns and shot, through foul ways, and to set up artillery positions and encampments. In 1486, when threatened with rebellion in Yorkshire, Henry VII summoned Lincolnshire levies to come unarmed, wishing, says the Crowland continuator, 'to appear rather to pacify than exasperate the people who were opposed to him'.[165] Perhaps he – and other commanders in the wars – had another motive for arraying: to prevent the enemy from recruiting.[166]

A crucial organizational point was the timing of the summons of arrayed men. This is reflected in the emphasis in commissions that arrayers should select their contingents in readiness to array at short notice. John Paston's comments on the Norfolk levy in January 1461 illustrate the importance of timing. He thought that the council's and the commission of array's procrastinations were in danger of causing the disintegration of the levy. Most of the arrayed men believed that their services were needed in London. They had therefore drawn their wages, 'but they have no captain, nor ruler assigned by the commissioners to wait upon, and so they straggle about by themselves, and by likeliness are not like to come at London half of them'. Orders had come from London that people should not come till sent for, but they were unlikely to get more men than the mere 400 or so who had reportedly passed Thetford without the issue of new commissions. Since the communities considered themselves discharged of all expenses, they would think it 'right strange' if they had to pay for new levies.[167]

The exceptional circumstances of January 1461, when the invasion by the northern army was feared, may account for the urgency with which Norfolk constables and bailiffs had organized levies, and the latter's unwonted zeal to commence their service and even depart from the county. But the basic problem on this occasion was a normal one: communities were prepared to 'wage' soldiers for only a few weeks' service. Some of the frequent military débâcles of the Wars of the Roses may have been basically caused by mistimings of summonses. Kings and captains had an incentive to delay them dangerously – the need to husband the short period of waged service available. Paston's letter suggests that Warwick may have been deprived of support at St Albans because arrays had been summoned too early. Henry VI in June 1460, Edward IV in July 1469 and September 1470, Richard III in 1485, and Henry VII in 1486 may have jeopardized their cause by leaving summonses late.

The prolongation of levies' service beyond the period for which they had been paid was also risky, unless the commander could provide wages – and even then, some levies may have murmured against the extension of their term. 'Gregory' thought it worthy of remark that in February 1461, March, when he met Warwick at Burford (Oxon.), was 'sorry that he was so poor, for he had no money, but the substance of his men came at their own cost'.[168] The disintegration of the northern army in the same month may have been because the wages which their communities had provided had run out – they may have been in arms for several months.[169] John Paston wrote to his elder brother John from Newcastle on 11 December 1462

> In case we abide here, I pray you purvey that I may have here more money by Christmas Eve at the farthest, for I may get leave for to send none of my waged men home again; no man can get no leave

for to go home but if they steal away, and if they might be known, they should be sharply punished.

This prolongation of service, and probable delays in receiving extra wages, help to account for the dismal performance of Edward's army at Alnwick the following month.[170] In his reconquest of the realm in 1471 (14 March to 26 April), faced with a sequence of threats, he raised a succession of levies round a stable nucleus of nobles' and royal retainers' companies. After the hard-fought battle of Barnet, he 'sent to all parts to get him fresh men' to meet the Lancastrian threat in the west.[171] These levies, after their victory at Tewkesbury, were presumably dismissed, for to oppose the rebels in the north he promptly 'prepared a new army'.[172] Until the fresh levies arrived, Edward was so low in manpower that he 'by possibility could not by power have resisted the Bastard' (of Fauconberg). But he 'made out commissions to many shires of England; which in a ten days there came to him, where he was, to the number of 30,000'.[173] Edward's need to rotate arrays, and the intermediate periods of vulnerability which he endured, reveal defects in the array system. Yet in 1471 he got speedy and weighty support from arrays arriving from different parts of the realm – as, indeed, did his opponents. The system, put to the test in preceding years, seems to have been working well – though not necessarily to the advantage of the throne's occupant.

Why did rulers continue to rely on methods of recruitment which produced variable levels of support for limited periods, and which might be turned against them? One reason was that these obligations were accepted as customary by communities. Rulers and their opponents struggling to win military and political support in emergencies could not risk alienation by making demands for unfamiliar services. The crown could not afford to maintain large standing forces as an alternative to arrays: it had a struggle to pay the wages of its frontier garrisons. The largest concentration of frontier troops, in the March of Calais, tended to grow mutinous when pay was in arrears – hardly an encouragement to kings to increase standing forces.

Nevertheless, some royal councillors may have toyed with the idea of establishing a standing army, as the French crown had done in the 1440s. In their 1460 manifesto the Yorkist lords alleged:

now begin a new charge of imposition and tallages upon the said people which never afore was seen; that is to say, every township to find men for the king's guard, taking example thereof of our enemies and adversaries of France: which imposition and tallage if it be continued to their heirs and successors, will be the heaviest charge and worst example that ever grew in England.[174]

Sir John Fortescue, in *The Governance of England*, completed in the 1470s, argued that it would not be to the king's advantage if the commons were rendered poor, as some advocated, on the grounds that then, like the French commons, they would not be equipped to rebel. Fortescue's rejection of the idea was based partly on the argument that it would destroy the arraying system:

> Forsooth these folk consider little the good of the realm of England, whereof the might standith most upon archers, which be no rich men. And if they were made more poor than they be, they should not have wherewith to buy them bows, arrows, jacks, or any other armour of defence, whereby they might be able to resist our enemies, when them list to come upon us. . . . Item, if poor men may not lightly rise . . . how then, if a mighty man made a rising should he be repressed, when all the commons be so poor, that after such opinion they may not fight, and by that reason not help the king with fighting? And why maketh the king the commons every year to be mustered; since it were good they had none harness nor were able to fight? O, how unwise is the opinion of these men.[175]

This is powerful testimony, from a leading participant in the Wars of the Roses, to the efficacy of the array system in the period. Indeed, that ancient system was to continue as the bedrock of Tudor and early Stuart military organization.[176] The fact that it had been found politically preferable and reasonably adequate in the Wars of the Roses had important long-term political consequences. Henry VIII and his successors, with their urgent new military requirements, found it simpler to adapt this existing system, revitalized by the wars and in full working order – a system which in the fourteenth century had had constitutional safeguards built into it to restrain its operations from oppressiveness.

As a complement to arrays and the hiring of foreign mercenaries, under Henry VIII the crown continued to rely for service abroad and during domestic disquiets on the recruitment and captaincy by nobles of military companies composed particularly of men customarily in some way in their 'lordship'. The survival of this complementary system owed something to its vigorous use in the Wars of the Roses. To cope with the problems of inducement in civil conflict, 'neo-feudal' ties had been emphasized. Grantors of offices and fees tried to extract support from retainers by promises to pay military wages and give rewards; indentures were drawn up with the object of guaranteeing military support. Random surviving evidence suggests that Richard III, Henry VII and some of their adherents were particularly concerned to secure the promise of service by specified companies beforehand.

The operations of 'neo-feudalism' in the Wars of the Roses have often been viewed as the characteristic expression of noble power threatening royal rule. But arguably 'neo-feudalism' in the long run strengthened rather than weakened the crown. For as a means of raising military support in domestic conflict, retaining had deficiencies which kings were best qualified to overcome. The fact that summonses to arms were on the whole occasional hardened the inclination of office-holders and fee'd men to regard such 'neo-feudal' military obligations as options attached to more basic administrative or political services. The crown was best placed to enforce the association of military demands with patronage, because it could invoke superior obligations of allegiance, and threaten the withdrawal of its exceptional stock of favour. From the 1470s onwards, the increase of royal resources enabled kings to offer more dazzling inducements. Moreover, in the legislation against livery and maintenance, they had a weapon with which to deter potentially hostile magnates from competing with their bounty. The relative infrequency of revolts after 1471 – except during the periods of unusual political tension triggered off by the usurpations of 1483 and 1485 – and the failure of all except one of these revolts, probably stem partly from the crown's successful manipulation of 'neo-feudalism'.

Chapter 7

Supply, Billets and Ordnance

The English, wrote the Milanese Raimondo de Soncino in 1497, 'require every comfort even in the ardour of war'. His words were echoed in the report written for the Venetian envoy Andrea Trevisan in 1498: 'I have it on the best information, that when war is raging most furiously, they will seek for good eating, and all their other comforts, without thinking of what harm might befall them.'[1] One of Malory's knights warned against such temptation: 'They will put forth beasts to bait you out of number.'[2]

There were well-tried methods of providing victuals for English armies and navies in the fifteenth century. The rights of purveyance customarily exercised by royal household officers were extended to licensed victuallers, sheriffs and other local officers, and to the soldiers themselves. These rights, and the limitations on them, were defined by Sir John Fortescue:

> the king, by his purveyors, may take for his own use necessaries for
> his household, at a reasonable price, to be assessed at the discretion
> of the constables of the place, whether the owners will or not: but the
> king is obliged by the laws to make present payment, or at a day to
> be fixed by the great officers of the king's household. The king
> cannot despoil the subject, without making ample satisfaction for the
> same.[3]

An example from the Wars of the Roses of a customary military licence to purvey is the commission granted to two officers in March 1460 to purchase provisions with funds in the duke of Exeter's hands for the fleet under his command, intended to flush out the Yorkists abroad.[4]

The author of *Knyghthode and Bataile* (c. 1460) emphasized the importance that commanders should attach to ensuring that there were sufficient victuals for their men on the march, and in camp or castle. They should show foresight, denying stocks to the enemy:

Have purveyance of forage and victual
For man and horse; for iron smiteth not
So sore as hunger doth if food fail.[5]

Malory appreciated the importance of stockpiling and foraging. One of his armies 'had great plenty of victual by Merlin's provisions'. Arthur declared, 'My folk is waxen feeble for wanting of victual', and dispatched knights to forage in forests where he was convinced his enemies had beasts.[6]

In the Wars of the Roses, prior provision of stocks was peculiarly difficult, for often commanders had not had either the time or the finance to accumulate them and the transports necessary to convey them. Urban and county communities do not seem to have customarily provided much in the way of victuals for the companies which they dispatched. Beverley's contingents for the Lancastrian armies in 1460–1 received wine for a send-off.[7] The forty soldiers which Coventry sent to Edward at Nottingham in August 1470 had been given by the city 16d. 'ad bibendum', a gallon of wine and six pennyworth of ale.[8] Footmen were expected to carry their rations: the author of *Knyghthode and Bataile* advised that they should be regularly sent on practice route marches in full harness, 'Vitaile eke born withal'.[9] Their dependence on daily foraging is suggested by 'Gregory's' remark that 'spearmen they be good to ride before the footmen and eat and drink up their victual'.[10] In 1471 Edward's soldiers were unable to forage in the Cotswolds 'in all the way, horse-meat, nor mans meat'. It was a tribute to his care for the commissariat, especially as his expedition had been hurriedly launched, that at Cheltenham he 'a little comforted himself, and his people, with such meat and drink as he had done to be carried with him, for the victualling of his host'.[11]

The armies' dependence on foraging emphasized the danger that they might oppress the civilian population and alienate support. Henry VII's army foraged in Atherstone and neighbouring villages in 1485 without payment.[12] He had with him many French troops whom he may have found difficulty in restraining from their extortionate customs. Sir John Fortescue, in exile in France in the 1460s, had graphically denounced these to the young, warlike prince of Wales (with whom French troops landed in England in 1471) as oppressive and impoverishing:

the soldiers, though quartered in the same village a month or two, yet
they neither did nor would pay any thing for themselves or horses;
and, what is still worse, the inhabitants of the villages and towns
where they came were forced to provide for them *gratis*, wines, flesh,
and whatever else they had occasion for; and if they did not like what

they found, the inhabitants were obliged to supply them with better from neighbouring villages: upon any non-compliance, the soldiers treated them at such a barbarous rate, that they were quickly necessitated to gratify them. When provisions, fuel and horse meat fell short in one village, they marched away full speed to the next; wasting it in like manner. They usurp and claim the same privilege and custom not to pay a penny for necessaries . . . such as shoes, stockings and other wearing apparel.[13]

Henry VII, despite his Breton sojourn, soon showed an appreciation of contrary English practice, and determination to guarantee more certain payment – and perhaps surer provision of victuals – than he had been able to do in 1485. He compensated property-owners who had suffered losses by his army's encampment before the battle of Bosworth.[14] On 5 June 1487, at the start of his campaign against the Simnel rebels, he had it proclaimed:

and for that his highness nor his said company in no wise should be destitute or wanting of victuals for man or horse: He strictly chargeth and commandeth every victualer, and all other his subjects dwelling in every town or place where his said highness and his said company shall come, to provide and make ready plenty of bread and ale, and of other victuals, as well for horse as for man, at reasonable price in ready money therefor to them: And every of them truly to be contented and paid.[15]

In the ordinances of war which he issued for the campaign at about this time, he insisted that no one 'take nor presume to take any manner of victual, horse meat, or man's meat, without paying therefor the reasonable price thereof assigned by the clerk of the market or other the king's officer therefore ordained, upon pain of death'.[16] His opponents, with foreign mercenaries in their army, feared that they would meet with opposition from those who believed their men would not follow such English conventions. On 8 June 'Edward VI' wrote to the civic governors of York: 'it will like you that we may have Relief and ease of lodging and victuals within our city there and so to depart and truly pay for that We shall take'. The York civic councillors were anxious to respond to Henry's determination to deal fairly: in anticipation of his arrival with an army the following month, they ordained that proclamation was to be made in the city that the common victuallers were to have adequate supplies for the army during his proposed sojourns. The council was concerned to prevent exploitation by the sale of unwholesome or dear food. A price limit of 10*d*. per gallon was fixed for red and white wine, and for claret.[17]

In the often large-scale, prolonged and unseasonable campaigning of the early 1460s it had been particularly important for commanders to ensure availability of stocks. Richard of York's troops at Wakefield in December 1460 were imperilled 'vagantibus per patriam pro victualibus quaerendis'.[18] The poor discipline and plundering habits of the queen's army on its advance southwards in February 1461 may have been intensified by seasonal shortages. The soldiers 'compelled, despoiled, robbed and destroyed all manner of cattle, victuals and riches'. After victory at St Albans their commanders were anxious to obtain 'both bread and victual' from London. But Henry VI, his wife, son and lords had to be content with relief from the city of York 'in victuals and other goods to the uttermost of their powers'.[19]

Possibly the Lancastrian army got into such dire straits because of the disruption of its victualling arrangements in fertile eastern regions before it crossed south of the Trent. On 28 January 1461 a Norfolk squire had been commissioned by the Yorkist government to inquire from what part of the country wheat and victuals were being shipped to the rebels, and to arrest the ships and men involved. Just under a fortnight later a commission was appointed to inquire where in Cambridgeshire wheat, malt and victuals were being shipped for transport to the rebels.[20] The rebels' base at Hull (whose corporation provided fodder for the queen's men) may have been the port to which shipments were being sent. But Yorkist control of Lynn, at the head of an extensive river network, must have hampered any efforts to victual the Lancastrian army from the south.[21]

The Yorkist army which was attacked by the northern men at St Albans may, like theirs, have had an inadequate commissariat. Prospero di Camulio reported that many of the Yorkist soldiers deserted for lack of victuals.[22] Next month Edward, organizing the large army he intended to take north from London, probably made strenuous efforts to overcome the difficult supply situation. Waurin remarks on the great number of waggons with victuals and ordnance parked in the fields outside the city.[23] Towns may have been scoured for contributions: the accounts of the jurats of Lydd record payment 'for vitelle sent to London, to the journey of York, £3. 11s. 9d.'[24]

In the struggle to control Northumberland and neighbouring parts which intensified with Margaret of Anjou's landing in November 1462, shortage of victuals in these relatively barren regions was a key factor: a memory of shortages 'in the extreme pressure of his wars in the parts of the North' was preserved by Henry VI's hagiographer, John Blacman:

> it is told by some who came from that region, that when there was for a time a scarcity of bread among his [Henry's] fellow-soldiers and troops, out of a small quantity of wheat, bread was so multiplied by his merits and prayers that a sufficiency and even a superfluity was

forthcoming for all of his who sought and asked for it, whereas the rest that were opposed to him had to suffer from lack of meat.

The speed with which castles changed hands in the northern Marches was probably due in part to inadequate stocking. The Lancastrians achieved some success because it took time for the Yorkists to organize the provision of supplies from further south on the scale necessary if they were to deploy their numerical superiority. Newcastle was probably the main Yorkist base to which shipments were sent. In a letter of 11 December 1462, John Paston referred to Yorkist victualling arrangements. From his base at Warkworth the earl of Warwick was supervising the sieges of Alnwick, Dunstanburgh and Bamburgh castles, 'and if they want victuals, or any other thing, he is ready to purvey it for them to his power'. Edward, at Durham, had commanded the duke of Norfolk to convey victuals and ordnance from Newcastle to the earl at Warkworth; the duke sent East Anglian knights and esquires to escort the convoy – 'and so we were with my Lord of Warwick with the ordnance and victuals yesterday'.[25] In the years 1461–3 Hull was obliged to provision Edward's forces in the north with corn and beer, without payment.[26]

Thus availability of victuals was crucial in determining the location, duration and outcome of campaigns. In relatively prosperous and accessible eastern parts of England, it was important to keep control of ports and coastal shipping. Domination of these regions depended on possession of towns on or near intersecting north-south and east-west routes, such as Newcastle, York, Pontefract, Doncaster, Newark, Nottingham, Stamford, Leicester, Coventry, Northampton – and, above all, London, the key not only to the Thames valley and estuary, but, with Canterbury and the Cinque Ports, to Kent and the main routes to northern France. In the west of England, the towns of the Severn valley and the cities of Exeter and Bristol were the keys which Welsh and western armies sought to turn, to give them access to the wealth of the Midlands and the eastern plains. Strategic dominance over the realm – including control of its major supply sources – depended on securing the route from London to York. This was demonstrated in the campaign of March–April 1470. Edward's victory near Stamford sealed his control of London, East Anglia and the eastern Midlands. Clarence and Warwick conceded this by withdrawing northwards from Coventry. They hoped to establish an alternative base in Yorkshire. But Edward, operating along the eastern plains, moved north too fast for them, forcing them westwards towards barren Lancashire. He broke off the pursuit,

as it was thought by his highness, his lords, and other noble[men there bei]ng with him that he might not conveniently p[roceed] with

so [great an] host, for that the said duke and earl, with their
fellowship [had consum]ed the [vitaile] afore him, and the country
afore himself wo[s] not able to sustain so great an host as the king's
highness had with him without a new refreshing.[27]

The rebels may have shaken off Edward by denying him supplies, but
they had handed to him their principal northern source. He advanced to
York 'fully determined there to have refreshed and vitailed his said
host', which he did, before forcing the rebels to flee south-west.[28]

Principal towns were important strategic objectives for a number of
reasons: one form of 'refreshment' which they provided was billets. In
May 1471 Edward refreshed his army in Coventry for three days, not
long after his victory at Tewkesbury; Warwick had recently billeted
there for much longer.[29] In 1469 variance over lodging in a town
(possibly Banbury) had, according to Warkworth, led to the split in the
king's army.[30] The author of *Knyghthode and Bataile* described the
task of assigning billets, performed by the harbinger ('herbagere'):

> A Mesurer, that is our Herbagere,
> For paviloun and tent assigneth he
> The ground, and saith 'Be ye there, be ye here!'
> Each hostel eek, in castle and city,
> Assigneth he, each after his degree.[31]

The author of the *Arrivall* mentions the arrival of five or six of
Edward's harbingers in Sodbury in advance of his army in 1471,
intending to 'purvey' his lodgings, and their 'distress' by the enemy's
harbingers.[32] Henry VII's 1487 ordinances of war outlined the powers
of the king's harbinger:

> Also that no manner of person or persons, whatsoever they be, take
> upon them to lodge themself nor take no manner of lodging nor
> harborage but such as shall be assigned unto him or them by the
> King's harbinger, nor dislodge no man, nor change no lodging after
> that to be assigned, without advice and assent of the said harbinger,
> upon pain of imprisonment and to be punished at the will of our said
> sovereign lord.

The anonymous author of the account of Henry's campaign thought
that the 'Marshals and Harbingers of his Host' let him down one day
on the march northwards: they

> did not so well their diligence that Way; for when the King removed,
> there was no proper Ground appointed where the King's Host
> should lodge that Night then following. . . . And the King and his
> Host wandered here and there a great Space of Time, and so came to

a fair long Hill, where the King set his Folks in Array of Battle.[33]

'In England', Fortescue wrote, 'no one takes up his abode in another man's house, without leave of the owner first had: unless it be in public inns.'[34] Malory describes how Sir Marhaute and a damsel

> came into a deep forest, and by fortune they were benighted and rode long in a deep way, and at the last they came unto a curtilage and there they asked harborage ['herborow']. But the man of the curtilage would not lodge them for no treaty that they could treat.

They accepted his refusal.[35] Kings and commanders probably considered it important that their harbingers controlled billeting in order to minimize the abuses of a compulsory enforcement which clearly went against the grain for Englishmen. They also wanted to minimize quarrels such as that which allegedly disrupted the royal army in 1469, and ensure particularly that every man was lodged 'after his degree'. For reasons of prestige as well as comfort kings and peers were anxious to secure the best billets on campaign, soft beds in castles, and religious or town houses. But necessity often forced them to lodge in their tents in fields, as Henry VI frequently did in 1459.[36] Elaborate camping gear was probably carted round for their convenience. But it is unlikely that the common soldier had much shelter, if he was forbidden to enter within town walls, or when the available dwellings in a village were occupied by the entourages of king or peers. Commanders were often keen to station their men in the open, to maintain good battle order as well as to avoid inconvenience to civilians. At Ludlow in 1459 and Northampton in 1460 armies encamped across the river from the town. In 1461 the Yorkist lords moved the bulk of their army to a heath near St Albans, possibly out of the town itself. In 1471, when engagements were thought to be imminent, Edward would not allow his men to billet in townships. Coming to Barnet, and understanding Warwick was encamped nearby, he 'would [not] suffer one man to abide in the same town, but had them all to the field with him, and drew towards his enemies, without the town'. At Cirencester he expected to encounter the Lancastrians the following morning, 'For which cause, and for that he would see and set his people in array, he drove all the people out of the town, and lodged him, and all his host, that night in the field, three miles out of the town.' At Sodbury, when uncertain of the enemy's whereabouts, he pitched camp outside the town.[37] In 1487 Henry VII kept his jittery army out of Nottingham.[38]

In domestic strife royal and noble commanders did not expect to have to provide the bulk of their soldiers with arms, armour, victuals, camping equipment, horses or transport. Officers inspected these commodities, and regulated their use and those of available billets. But there was one highly specialized branch of armaments which commanders were eager to make full provision for – ordnance. John Lord Howard's household accounts for April 1481 show him having serpentines cast – doubtless for use in the Scottish war.[39] The crown's long tradition of maintaining ordnance equipped it especially well to make such provision. By the mid-fifteenth century there was a permanent royal officer for ordnance commissioned primarily to supervise the receipt, upkeep and issue of the firearms and ammunition stocked in the Tower of London.[40]

The shock of York's rebellions in 1452 and 1455, as well as of the débâcles in France in 1449–51 and 1453, may have galvanized the Lancastrian council into improving its ordnance as well as its fortifications.[41] The warrant appointing John Judde, merchant of London, as master of the king's ordnance (21 December 1456) admitted that 'we [Henry VI] be not yet sufficiently furnished of guns, gunpowder and other habilments of war'. Judde contracted to 'do make and ordain' sixty field guns (serpentines) and twenty tons of saltpetre and sulphur for gunpowder.[42] He certainly fulfilled part of this contract, for on 19 May 1457 he was assigned at the Exchequer £133. 8s. 5½d. as payment for twenty-six new serpentines with their apparatus for the field, quantities of sulphur, gunpowder and saltpetre, a culverin and a mortar, and the cost of carriage and two carts to go from London to Kenilworth castle.[43] Judde was energetic in royal service till his death in 1460.[44] In the autumn of 1459, as master of the king's ordnance, he was commissioned to assist in fitting out ships for Somerset's expedition to Calais, to seize armaments which had belonged to York, Warwick and Salisbury, and to ensure that the royal ordnance scattered about in castles and walled towns throughout the realm was ready for use.[45]

The Lancastrian armaments programme of the mid-1450s probably stimulated the use of firearms in the wars, providing a substantial part of the stock of heavier ones deployed. Frequent domestic use of firearms may in turn have helped to stimulate the expansion of the royal ordnance department's activities and personnel. In the later fifteenth century there is more evidence for control of the purchase and manufacture of firearms and ammunition by the master of the ordnance, the king's smith, or a specially commissioned royal squire. They controlled workmen not only in the Tower but in various parts of the realm.[46] The function of the Tower arsenal as a munitions factory as well as a storehouse is seen in Richard III's appointment in 1484 of Patrick de la Motte as 'chief cannoneer' or master founder, surveyor and maker of all the king's cannon there and elsewhere, at a daily wage of 18d. Under his command were the 'gunnoures' Theobald Ferrount, Gland Pyroo and William Nele, who were paid 6d. a day for making cannon in the Tower and elsewhere.[47] The importance of the ordnance office is reflected in Henry VII's appointment of a more socially exalted master than hitherto – Sir Richard Guildford, a substantial landowner and early Tudor supporter experienced in warfare. In September 1485 he was granted for life the offices of master of ordnance and of the king's armour; according to his patent of March 1486, he was to receive wages of 2s. a day, and have a clerk, a yeoman and twelve gunners receiving royal wages from him as master of the ordnance.[48]

Thus the manifold use of artillery in the Wars of the Roses – and, doubtless, the royal invasions of France in 1475 and 1492, as well as other expeditions abroad – probably stimulated the expansion of the royal ordnance department. By the end of the wars, in size, activity and prestige it had attained a level which made it capable of worthily supporting the crown's ventures into sixteenth-century European warfare. Henry VII had good reason for pride in his ordnance, when he took Philip I of Castile to London from Barking abbey, probably up the Thames, in 1506: 'and so the Tower, and gun shot'. The Tower had been celebrated as an arsenal a few years before, by a Scottish poet – possibly William Dunbar: 'by Julyus Cesar thy Tour founded of old may be the hous of Mars victoryall, whose artillary with tonge may not be told'. In the year when Henry was showing off his guns there, Guildford, his old master of the ordnance, *en route* to Jerusalem, inspected with an expert eye the 'wondre and straunge ordynaunce' in the Arsenal at Venice. The English knight abroad on pilgrimage now had another interest besides the traditional pious and chivalrous ones.[49]

Chapter 8

Methods of Warfare

English fighting methods in the mid-fifteenth century, like English military organization, were heavily influenced by the experiences of the Hundred Years War. In the fourteenth century one classic form of attack perfected on expeditions in France and Scotland was *la chevauchée* – the 'ride' through hostile terrain by swiftly moving, unencumbered columns of mounted men-at-arms and archers. Such expeditions varied greatly in size, from armies of several hundreds or thousands down to raiding parties from garrisons of a few score. Besides specific strategic objectives, *chevauchées* had the general ones of undermining the enemy's resources and morale by destroying crops, beasts, buildings and chattels, and of enjoying the pickings of war – victuals, booty, prisoners. Unhampered by the drag of siege equipment or a long tail of non-combatants, the force on *chevauchée* cut a swathe through the fields, less concerned than more elaborately constituted armies about scarcity of victuals or the proximity *en route* of menacing enemy forces and garrisons.[1]

But when, during the Hundred Years War, the conquest of territory by the siege of towns was the principal strategic objective, expeditionary forces were in major respects differently constituted and equipped. Then they included siege engineers, miners, carpenters, smiths, carters and a swarm of servants to maintain an appropriate life-style for lords, who presided in the luxurious tents which are often such a prominent feature in contemporary manuscript illustrations of sieges. There were columns of waggons to bring up siege equipment, prefabricated residences and their furnishings, and to shuttle to victualling bases for supplies of foodstuffs. The army which Henry V led from Harfleur to Calais in 1415 – and with which he won at Agincourt – was fit for a *chevauchée*; that with which he landed in Normandy in 1417 was an army of conquest.

Both sorts of armies were commonly grouped for movement and for engagements into formations known as 'battles', often into the specific triple division of vanguard (also called 'foreward', *avauntguard*), main 'battle', and rearguard.[2] In the field the archers were concentrated in the front or on the wings of the vanguard. The longbowman, protected by the sharp-headed stake he planted before him, loosed off from his bow – six feet of yew, maple or oak – volleys which were highly effective at up to 165 yards' range.[3] The devastating effect of English and Welsh longbowmen's rapid and accurate fire was repeatedly demonstrated during the Hundred Years War – notably against the Scots at Halidon Hill (1333), and against the French at Crécy (1346), Poitiers (1356) and Agincourt (1415). The English military leadership's appreciation of the value of archers is reflected in contracts made by the crown with retinue leaders for military service abroad in the later fourteenth and early fifteenth centuries: these frequently show a ratio of three archers to one man-at-arms.[4] In the fifteenth century the French and Burgundians persistently copied the English use of longbowmen. Philippe de Commynes asserted that 'in my opinion archers are the most necessary thing in the world for an army; but they should be counted in thousands, for in small numbers they are worthless'.[5]

Edward III at Crécy and his son the Black Prince at Poitiers both commanded heavily outnumbered armies. Consequently they dismounted their forces, enabling knights and men-at-arms to seek defensive cover in woods and behind hedges, ditches and archers' stakes. The English commanders' good fortune on these occasions confirmed the advantages of using their usually mounted troops as blocs of infantry, co-operating closely with groups of archers, who enfiladed attacking cavalry and infantry.[6] In 1363 these infantry tactics were successfully introduced to Italian warfare by the White Company, partly English in composition. In Italy dismounted men-at-arms developed offensive tactics, advancing shoulder-to-shoulder, gripping in pairs a heavy cavalry lance.[7] Commynes's accounts of French and Burgundian armies in action in the 1460s and '70s, and his appreciative remarks about the excellence of English infantry, also reflect the deep impression which the English development of infantry tactics made on Continental warfare. In 1465, he says, 'it was . . . the most honourable practice amongst the Burgundians that they should dismount with the archers, and always a great number of gentlemen did so in order that the common soldiers might be reassured and fight better. They had learnt this method from the English.'[8]

The most striking technical innovation in warfare during the Hundred Years War was the development of artillery. Surviving fortifications in England dating from the second half of the fourteenth century onwards are commonly provided with gunports.[9] By the accession of Henry VI the defences of Calais were studded with them, and the artillery its captain had at his disposal included sixty iron guns to shoot stones, forty-nine brass guns, and nineteen iron and four brass guns designed to shoot lead pellets. During the reign additional works were carried out at Calais castle to accommodate the heaviest guns. In 1438–9 an opening was made in the east curtain wall for the insertion of a timber 'loop' through which the 'great bombards' were to shoot. By the mid-1450s two of the earthen bulwarks for artillery, projecting from the enceinte, had in recent years been rebuilt in more permanent materials, one in stone and mortar, the other in brick.[10]

From the 1370s onwards heavy guns had been inflicting significant damage on stone fortifications. Their effectiveness is referred to in the earliest English version of Vegetius, made in 1408 for Lord Berkeley, besieging Aberystwyth castle: 'Also great guns that shoot nowadays stones of so great weight that no wall may withstand them as have been well showed both in the north country and also in the wars of Wales.'[11] The guns of heaviest calibre were known as bombards. At Edinburgh castle can be seen one of the largest bombards ever made – *Mons Meg*, constructed at Mons in 1449 by order of Duke Philip of Burgundy, and sent in 1457 as a gift to James II of Scotland. It weighs about 8½ tons, has a calibre of nine inches, and it cast iron shot of 1125 lb, stone shot of 549 lb. By the 1450s there was such a variety of firearms that the author of *Knyghthode and Bataile* could not be bothered to enumerate them all: 'bombards . . . / And gun and serpentine . . . / Fowler, covey, crappaude and culverin / And other sorts more than eight or nine'.[12]

Heavier pieces were even more difficult to deploy effectively in the field than in sieges. They and their ponderous ammunition presented transport problems, their rate of fire was slow, and they lacked manoeuvrability. The use of more convenient, cheaper portable firearms spread more extensively in the early fifteenth century. By the 1430s there is growing evidence for the presence of companies of hand-gun men in Italian field armies.[13] In the mid-fifteenth century a Norfolk lady was well acquainted with the use of hand-guns: Margaret Paston wrote telling her husband how the company holding Gresham manor-house against him had made five holes for their shot with hand-guns 'scarce knee high' from the floor.[14] By then artillery was becoming more adaptable and efficient. The modern fixed-wheeled gun-carriage appeared, and the development of the trunnion facilitated speedier elevation and depression of the barrel.[15] In the 1440s the brothers Jean and Gaspard Bureau had begun their improvement of French royal artillery. Its deployment was probably a factor in the swift English surrender of towns and fortresses during Charles VII's conquest of Normandy (1449–50). According to the contemporary historian

Thomas Basin, the French besieging force at Castillon in Périgord (1453) had entrenched its artillery round its encampment. They had 'dug a deep ditch and added a wall of earth and even great tree trunks around it, placing on this elevation a very large number of machines of war named serpentines and culverins'. The assault on the camp by the relieving Anglo-Gascon force under the earl of Shrewsbury was broken up by their bombardment.[16] In the Wars of the Roses, by 1462 field artillery was clearly distinguished from siege artillery.[17]

In the phase of the wars up to 1460, most noble commanders had learnt the business of war in the Anglo-French conflict. Their knowledge may have sometimes turned out to be dated, inappropriate or rusty. Richard of York (d. 1460) had been Henry VI's lieutenant in France in 1436–7 and 1440–7, his rival Somerset (d. 1455) in 1447–50. Buckingham (d. 1460) had contracted to take a retinue to France as long before as 1421. He had been appointed constable of France in 1430 and granted the *comté* of Perche in 1431. But Lord Bonville (d. 1461) had probably taken part in Henry V's Norman conquests in 1418.[18] Lord Hungerford (d. 1464) had been captured in France in 1453.[19] Lord Scales (d. 1460) had had a distinguished career of service in France, stretching back to 1421. He was, a London chronicler wrote, 'well approved in the wars of Normandy and France'.[20] Another well-reputed noble veteran was Warwick the Kingmaker's diminutive uncle William Neville, 'little' Lord Fauconberg (d. 1463). He had accompanied York to France in 1436, and was captured there in 1449.[21] The youthful Warwick and March probably relied heavily on Fauconberg's expertise, and his part in the Wars of the Roses must have enhanced his military reputation. He performed a crucial task for Warwick in 1459 by maintaining control of his captaincy of Calais whilst the earl took to arms in England. In June 1460 the Yorkist lords dispatched him from Calais to Sandwich in command of the advance-guard of their invasion. The following month he set out from London towards Northampton with the vanguard of the Yorkist army, and he was to be a commander in the Towton campaign in 1461. After the king's withdrawal from the north he was given responsibilities to safeguard it, and on 1 November he was created earl of Kent. In July 1462 he was appointed admiral of England, and in September he raided Le Conquêt near Brest.[22] No other veteran of the Anglo-French wars won such distinction in the Wars of the Roses. Indeed, the reverses then endured by some veterans suggest difficulties in adjusting to the different conditions of civil war. Younger men, less blinkered by experience of command in other circumstances, proved more adaptable – notably Warwick, Henry duke of Somerset, and March.[23]

The major handicap of the civil-war commander was that many of his troops were likely to be less reliable than those usually recruited for campaigns in the Hundred Years War. A captain who had contracted with the crown to lead a military retinue to France often had weeks in which to select and subcontract with experienced soldiers, to inspect their weapons and general fitness, and to 'shake down' with them as a company on the bivouac at the port of embarkation, on the voyage, and on preliminary manoeuvres in France. In the Wars of the Roses, the captain often had to rely on men who were hastily recruited, inexperienced and inadequately equipped, and whom it was essential to deploy speedily. Nobles were consequently eager to secure the services of veterans, just as Sir John Fastolf (d. 1459) had been, when he recruited 'the old soldiers of Normandy' at Southwark in 1450 to guard his house against Jack Cade's rebels.[24] Fastolf was a distinguished veteran, whose secretary William Worcester collected materials for his biography.[25] Worcester's interest in veterans of the French wars led him to list those who fought at Mortimer's Cross in 1461. On Queen Margaret's side, he says, there were the brothers Sir John and Sir William Scudamore, 'in arms in France'. Six of the earl of March's esquires were either 'of war', 'a man of war' or 'a man of the war of France' – notably Philip Vaughan, 'captain of Hay, a man of the war of France, the most noble esquire of lances among all the rest'.[26] Chroniclers' accounts of the 1459–60 campaigns imply that the professional soldiers and veterans of the Calais garrisons exercised an important influence on their outcome. The desertion of Warwick's Calais contingent in 1459 was a prime blow to the Yorkists.[27] The captain responsible, Andrew Trollope, who was to play a notable military role in the next two years, had distinguished himself as a 'lance' in the Anglo-French conflict.[28]

Inexperience in warfare seems to have been recognized as a characteristic of English captains and men-at-arms in many campaigns in the Wars of the Roses. The author of *Knyghthode and Bataile* (*c.* 1460) wrote for the novice in command an elementary and comprehensive textbook, turning Vegetius' precepts into homely, and distinctly creaking, English verse. He was encouraged to do so by the veteran Beaumont.[29] In the epilogue to his translation of Christine de Pisan's compilation *Le Livre des Faits d'Armes et de Chevalerie*, William Caxton said that Henry VII willed him in Westminster palace on 23 January 1489

> to translate this said book and reduce it in to our English and natural tongue and to put it in enprint to the end that every gentlemen born to arms and all manner men of war captains, soldiers, victuallers and all other should have knowledge how they ought to behave them in the feats of war and of battles.

The veteran earl of Oxford, attending the king, handed Caxton a copy of Christine's book.[30]

The need to season raw levies with veterans strengthened the natural inclination of protagonists to stick to traditional formations and well-tried tactics. But the fact that captains and soldiers often lacked the capability of performing as well as the English were accustomed to do in France, and that opposing veterans had often been trained in the same school, stimulated some tactical diversification. Commanders relied on entrenching, brought up artillery and hand-gunners, and cherished cavalry. Experiment, indeed, had its pitfalls. 'Gregory' scornfully related how Warwick's foreign gunners at St Albans in 1461 failed to make an impression with their outlandish contrivances. All depended on the good old skills of the native infantryman:

> And as the substance of men of worship that will not gloss nor curry favour for no partiality, they could not understand that all this ordnance did any good or harm but if it were among us in our part with King Harry. Therefore it is much left, and men take them to mallets of lead, bows, swords, glaives, and axes.[31]

'Gregory's' scornful contrasts reflect a notable feature of the wars: their particular conditions stimulated attempts to combine innovations with traditional methods.

One tactical feature which outlasted the wars, and is sometimes referred to in accounts of them, is the threefold division of armies for movement or action, a traditional − one might almost say, natural − means of making a host more manageable. Henry VI's army advanced into Kent in 1452 in three divisions, and in 1482 Edward's ally the duke of Albany was said to have invaded Scotland 'in three battles'.[32] Henry VII's army at Calais in 1492, and Henry VIII's there in 1513, were organized in three wards. Henry VII's vanguard, commanded by Oxford, went by a separate route for its advance from base, and his son's three 'wards' all did in 1513. They were self-sufficient fighting forces of all arms, as were probably Henry VII's 'wards' in 1492.[33] In the Wars of the Roses, the need to recruit on the way and to link up with allies coming from different regions had sometimes reinforced logistic and strategic reasons for splitting armies into independent columns. On three occasions in 1460−1 Yorkist armies left London in two or more columns, often on different roads and days, with a rendezvous. On the first occasion, the Northampton campaign of 1460, the army was to go through a series of regroupings.[34] Bishop Neville wrote that Edward IV departed from London in March 1461 'having a week previously dispatched my said brother [Warwick] to muster forces': all the retinues linked up in Yorkshire.[35] However, in 1485, Richard III ordered his whole army into a tight defensive formation for the advance from Nottingham to Leicester, probably to guard against further desertions as well as attack: 'he commanded the army to march forward in square battle [*quadrato agmine*] that way by the which they understood their enemies would come . . . all impediments being gathered into the midst of the army'.[36]

The day before the battle of Tewkesbury in 1471, Edward, anticipating an engagement, 'divided his whole host in three battles'.[37] In 1487 Henry VII, when approaching the earl of Lincoln's camp at Stoke, 'formed his whole force into three columns'.[38] But commanders did not always adhere to the threefold battle order. At Stoke, Lincoln tried to co-ordinate and give greater weight to his ill-matched and outnumbered forces by concentrating them in one 'battle'.[39] Circumstances may have sometimes made the threefold order somewhat academic. The author of *Knyghthode and Bataile* – perhaps with the royal army of 1459 in mind – had warned about how slow and cumbersome 'Too great an host' was: it was preferable to take a smaller one 'of proved and achieved sapience . . . a learned host'.[40] The need for a reliable, speedy striking force led to a frequent division between the main 'battle' and a powerful vanguard, operating independently from it on the march and in the field. According to Waurin, the Yorkist vanguard set off from London to Northampton ahead of the main army in 1460: the following year, the Yorkist vanguard was engaged at St Albans and Ferrybridge before the main army arrived.[41] In 1470 Edward sent his vanguard ahead from Stamford against the Lincolnshire rebels, and in 1471 ahead from London against the Kentishmen.[42] At Bosworth, according to Vergil, Richard arrayed a formidable vanguard, 'stretching it forth of a wonderful length . . . that to the beholders afar off it gave a terror for the multitude'.[43] Both he and Henry committed their vanguards first (the latter's commanded by Oxford) and waited to see how they would fare before joining in with their main 'battles'. The deployment of a powerful advanced striking force moving ahead of the main force and engaging separately in the field became standard practice under Henry VII, perhaps as a result of Oxford's influence in particular. In 1486, when the king was taken unawares by rebellion whilst at York, 'since it was essential to act quickly . . . he dispatched against the enemy his whole retinue, including his bodyguard . . . even although they were ill-equipped'. This force advanced against Lovell at Middleham: Henry meanwhile assembled levies.[44] At Stoke 'the first line of the king's army . . . was alone committed to the fray and sustained the struggle'.[45] In 1489 Henry dispatched his 'foreward' under Surrey's command ahead of himself against the Yorkshire rebels.[46] When confronting the Cornishmen near Blackheath in 1497 he again dispatched the vanguard to envelop them, whilst remaining unengaged with the main 'battle'.[47]

The same year, to suppress Warbeck's revolt in the West Country, he sent the vanguard on ahead under Lord Daubeney's command.[48] Chroniclers had long recognized that a great deal hinged on the conduct of the vanguard in battle, where it was often first in line and heavily engaged. Some of them alleged that the Lancastrian defeat at Northampton and the Yorkist defeats at Ludford Bridge and St Albans stemmed from the treachery of vanguard commanders. The blame for the Lancastrian defeat at Tewkesbury was put on the indifferent command and consequent rout of its vanguard.[49] The Yorkist kings recognized the need to build up and deploy vanguards. The sources give the impression that under Henry VII they were elite bodies of veterans and professionals. The names of some of their commanders recur. Sir John Savage commanded the left wing of Henry's vanguard at Bosworth and, according to Molinet, at Stoke, and he was one of the commanders in the vanguard in 1489.[50] Probably he was a crack cavalryman.

As had become customary in English armies in the Hundred Years War, commanders concentrated archers in the vanguard for a preliminary 'shoot-out'. At Barnet they occupied the centre of Warwick's line, and at Bosworth were in front of Henry's vanguard – their importance in both cases recognized by the captaincy of a magnate.[51] But since England and Wales were nurseries of skilled archers, commanders are likely to have found it more difficult to establish tactical edge with the longbow in the Wars of the Roses than had often been the case abroad, unless they had a special recruiting advantage. There are hints that in a few fights one side enjoyed a telling preponderance of bowmen. At St Albans in 1455 Henry VI had to fight before many local levies could join him: he and his household suffered particularly from arrow wounds.[52] The failure of '7,000 of archers of the west country' to support the Welsh at Edgcote in 1469 was probably an important factor in their defeat.[53] At Tewkesbury Edward's bowmen may have gained an ascendancy over their West Country colleagues, who had not been joined by the Lancashire archers whom their commanders wished to recruit. His vanguard 'so sore oppressed' their opponents 'with shot of arrow, that they gave them right-a-sharp shower'. This barrage, combined with gunshot, the author of the *Arrivall* surmised, may have provoked the Lancastrian vanguard's fatal advance.[54] But at Bosworth, Vergil relates, there was an inconclusive, if fierce, preliminary archery duel between the vanguards.[55] This may have been because the rebels' oblique angle of approach brought them within close range of royal shot for a relatively brief period before battle was joined.[56] One battle in which English archers probably displayed their ancient mastery of the field was Stoke. Lincoln's oddly constituted German-Irish army, unlike French or Burgundian ones of the period, was not well supplied with archers, and was not sufficiently armoured: consequently their 'battle' 'could not withstand the fire of the archers of England'.[57]

Since commanders could not usually assume, as the English had often done abroad, that they would have supremacy in archery, they had an incentive to use, as a supplement in the field, artillery and hand-guns, and, when on the defensive, to reduce the effectiveness of the enemy's firepower by making field fortifications. A weight of noisily impressive guns and protective entrenchments might also reassure and steady raw recruits. These expedients are found in Continental warfare of the period: as we have seen, entrenched artillery contributed to the English defeat at Castillon in 1453.[58] Concerning Italian warfare in the fifteenth century, Dr Mallett has argued that it was the development of field fortifications which hastened the transfer of cannon from ramparts and siege emplacements to the battlefield.[59] Commynes's account of the manoeuvres of Louis XI and his princely opponents on the Seine in 1465 provides graphic illustrations of the combined use of artillery and entrenchments.[60] He also provides examples of the Burgundian use in this campaign of another fifteenth-century development – the *champ de guerre*. This comprised the formation round an army of a defensive enclosure made up of waggons and wooden barriers, which could strengthen slow-moving, encumbered forces and bivouacs against surprise attack.[61] The count of Charolais's army in 1465 had 'such a number of waggons that his alone could enclose the greater part of his host'.[62] After the battle of Montlhéry, the Burgundians used their waggons as a laager, and subsequently, when Charolais's army was encamped between Charenton and Conflans, along the Seine, the count 'enclosed a great stretch of country with his baggage train and artillery, putting all his army inside the enclosure'. When once more expecting battle, this allied army took up a position surrounded by its waggons, except for some cavalry.[63]

The chroniclers of the Wars of the Roses generally lacked Commynes's keen tactical eye. Their evidence of employment of entrenchments, laagers, and firearms is casual and patchy. As early as 1452, the duke of York resorted to characteristic Continental field fortifications. Near Dartford, in expectation of the advance of Henry's army, he 'marvellously fortified his ground with pits, paveys and Guns'.[64] The circumstances at St Albans in 1455 did not allow more than makeshift defensive measures by the royal army: it is not known whether they had guns, though their opponents did.[65] The only evidence for the presence of guns at Blore Heath in 1459 is 'Gregory's' tale of the versatile friar who facilitated Salisbury's escape by shooting guns off all night after the battle.[66] However, soon afterwards, at Ludford Bridge, York once more occupied an impressive field fortification: he 'let make a great deep ditch and fortified it with guns, carts, and stakes', and fired his guns at the royal army.[67] The Lancastrian command in 1460 shared the duke's enthusiasm for entrenchment, and to pander to it the author of *Knyghthode and Bataile* relayed reams of classical technical advice.[68] At Northampton the king held 'a strong and mighty field ... armed and arrayed with guns'. There were 'great ditches which they had dug around the field to the river banks, which enclosed the whole army'. Whethamstede attributed the intransigence of the king's lords partly to confidence in their artillery and entrenchments.[69] But 'the ordnance of the king's guns availed not, for that day was so great rain, that the guns lay deep in the water, and so were quenched and might not be shot'.[70] Apparently the royal high command – like the Yorkist command at St Albans the following year – had not fully grasped the limitations to the reliance which could be placed on artillery in the field. Perhaps the recent death of the master of the king's ordnance, John Judde, had removed an expert whose advice might have been heeded by the lords.[71] In December 1460 the Yorkist lords transported guns northwards from London – they now had possession of the royal arsenal. At Wakefield the duke of York probably once again created a strong defensive position with entrenchments and guns, but, since his soldiers were surprised while out of their lines, these would have been of no avail.[72]

In subsequent campaigns, chroniclers hardly mention field fortifications, and often say little or nothing about the presence of guns. One reason may be that these ceased to be novelties, as domestic conflict became frequent. But possibly recourse to elaborate field fortifications, the panacea of commanders in the fights of 1452–60, declined, since guns became better adapted to field use, and entrenchment was associated with too static a strategic approach. Commanders often placed priority on mobility, with the objectives of seizing towns, spreading recruiting nets, and above all intercepting the enemy chiefs before they could get their campaign rolling. In those circumstances commanders may have been in too much of a hurry to take any except the lightest field pieces and hand-guns. Guns were not a necessity. In November 1462, to counter the Lancastrian invasion, Edward rushed up to Durham with his men, leaving the artillery to follow when it could.[73]

The most detailed account of gunners in action in the Wars of the Roses is one which highlights their limitations – 'Gregory's' incredulously mocking account of the débâcle suffered at St Albans in 1461 by Warwick's foreign company of 'goners and borgeners' [Burgundians?]. This illustrates commanders' interest in bringing in foreign specialists, the cumbersome construction of some early field pieces, and the difficulties of co-ordinating action by specialists with that of the rank and file. This company's guns, unlike the single-barrel pieces more familiar in England, were 'ribaudekins' – multiple-barrels designed to fire simultaneously lead pellets, iron-headed arrows and 'wild fire'. They were aimed through the shutters of pavises, part of the gunners' elaborate defences. At St Albans the gunners were probably attacked before they could erect their booby-traps satisfactorily. Levelling their guns hastily, they injured themselves: 'in time of need they could not shoot not one of these, but the fire turned back upon them that would shoot these three things'.[74]

There is, surprisingly, no record of the presence of artillery at the battle of Towton in 1461, nor in the preliminary engagement at Ferrybridge, though Waurin says that Edward had set out from London with plenty of artillery, and one might have expected it to be useful in helping to force the Aire crossing.[75] But perhaps the foul weather – probably much worse than at Northampton in the summer of 1460 – again dampened the charges. Moreover, the destruction of the ferry may have made it impossible to get heavy artillery across in time for the fight at Towton. Later in the year Edward was having artillery prepared for his projected Welsh expedition, and in 1462 his army in Northumberland was reinforced with it. In September 1461 Philip Herveys, master of the king's ordnance, started out for Hereford with ordnance for the royal expedition.[76] On 11 December 1462 John Paston wrote from Newcastle that the royal commanders in Northumberland had been sent thence enough ordnance 'both for the sieges and for the field, in case that there be any field taken'.[77] In the 1460s artillery was certainly used against Lancastrian fortresses there and in Wales, but it is not evident that guns were used in the relatively small-scale engagements with Lancastrian risers and their foreign supporters – or at Edgcote in 1469.[78] In 1470, at Losecoat Field, Edward 'loosed his guns of his ordnance' on the Lincolnshire rebels.[79] When he invaded the realm in 1471, on landing in Holderness he had in his company 'three hundred of Flemings with hand-guns' – a quarter of his force, according to Warkworth.[80] At Barnet, according to the author of the *Arrivall*, he was outgunned by Warwick – probably because the earl had equipped his army from the royal ordnance. But, as at St Albans ten years before, Warwick does not seem to have benefited from his superior firepower. His night bombardment overshot Edward's army. The king kept most of his guns silent in case their fire enabled the earl's gunners to correct their range. The heavy mist the next morning may have prevented the earl from exploiting his artillery advantage, if he had enough ammunition left to do so.[81] Warwick's guns, undoubtedly among the spoils of Edward's victory, gave him an advantage over the Lancastrian army forming in the West Country. He was certainly concerned to equip his army with ordnance for the new campaign, and the *Arrivall*'s account of the battle of Tewkesbury implies that he outgunned his opponents.[82] Very little is known about the role of artillery in the later campaigns of the wars. It is unlikely that Henry Tudor, speeding through the Midlands in 1485 from a remote part of Wales, transported any but light guns to Bosworth. Richard III, long anticipating his invasion, had had an opportunity to prepare superior ordnance, but the haste with which he moved from Nottingham may have necessitated a reduction of his superiority. Molinet's account of the battle suggests that the royal artillery was superior, nevertheless. Henry's foreign specialists recognized his disadvantage and deployed his troops so as to benefit from defects in the siting of the king's guns.[83]

By then the use of a variety of guns had become a commonplace of warfare in England, no longer a wryly regarded wonder. Viscount Lisle had written to his enemy Lord Berkeley in 1470: 'I marvel ye come not forth with all your Carts of guns, bows, with other ordnance, that ye set forward to come to my manor of Wotton to beat it down upon my head: I let you wit, ye shall not need to come so nie.'[84] In 1475, on his expedition to France, Edward IV had an artillery train which impressed contemporaries, and which was clearly intended to provide for field actions as well as sieges. He had at least thirteen pieces of heavy artillery, including bombards, five 'fowlers' (long-range field guns), a 'curtowe' (short-range field gun) and three 'potguns' (mortars).[85] This splendid train – and the expansion of the royal ordnance department which was responsible for it – bear witness to how the Wars of the Roses had enabled new generations of English captains to keep abreast of military technology, which was developing relatively quickly in the period.[86]

Nevertheless, it is difficult to ascertain how generally and judge how effectively artillery was used in the Wars of the Roses. Chroniclers' references to the presence of guns suggest that they considered them to have been an important factor on occasion. Their presence may have been particularly useful in steadying hastily organized men. The manufacture of artillery and its ammunition was, in fifteenth-century terms, a complex and consequently expensive technology. Kings and nobles would not have paid out for field guns and the costs of transporting them, nor handicapped their progress by taking them sometimes long distances, if they had not considered it worthwhile. But since armies were frequently assembled in haste and on the move to deal with swiftly developing crises, the time factor probably made it difficult to assemble a formidable ordnance train such as Edward accumulated for his French invasion in 1475. In 1460 Henry VI's forces had lost the strategic initiative by tying themselves to their Midlands arsenal: the subsequent technical failure showed that reliance on entrenched artillery was a gamble. But Edward – perhaps inheriting an enthusiasm which his father had gained in the French wars – seems to have been particularly adept in the deployment of field artillery. However, in circumstances when it proved difficult for a force to bring a weight of supporting artillery into the field, commanders in the wars seem to have been prepared to go ahead regardless. Like the tank in twentieth-century warfare, artillery had become a symbol of military virility and prestige. A great bombard was a present fit for a prince to give a king. The 'long fowler' and the 'bumbardelle' which Edward took to France in 1475 were both named the *Edward*.[87] Yet leaders of risings and invasions in the fifteenth century were no more deterred than leaders of 'liberation movements' are today by a dearth of such prestige weapons.

The general vagueness of chroniclers about the use of artillery in the wars is symptomatic of their tendency to neglect tactical detail. Waurin, 'Gregory' and the author of the *Arrivall* are the main ones who write as if they had personal experience of soldiering. Most chroniclers inclined to regard the issue of battle as being settled, if not by treachery, then by flights of arrows followed by 'hand-strokes'. Because infantry fighting was a characteristic skill of the English, the chroniclers are rarely explicit as to whether soldiers had mounts, or whether engagements were entirely fought on foot. The tactical circumstances of some engagements imply that to all intents and purposes they were. At St Albans in 1455, Warwick's men must have been on foot when they penetrated the royal defences, bursting through pales, houses and street barricades.[88] The bulk of the Yorkists at Crayford in 1452 and Ludford Bridge in 1459, and of the royal army at Northampton in 1460, are likely to have been dismounted behind their entrenchments: the assault on them at Northampton must have been on foot. Vergil says that on the king's side there 'many of the horsemen had put their horses from them, and, as their manner [i.e. the English manner] is, fought on foot'.[89] According to *Benet's Chronicle*, in 1461 Edward fought on foot at Ferrybridge, and was unable to pursue the Lancastrians, who commandeered many of the Yorkist horses – presumably being held by pages whilst their owners, like the king, fought dismounted. The next day at Towton, according to Waurin, Edward dismounted at a crucial stage of the battle to encourage his men, saying that he intended to live or die with them that day.[90] Ten years later, at Barnet, Warwick was on foot when he decided to flee: he 'leapt on horse-back'.[91] Commynes, like Vergil, is more explicit about English practice. Edward IV, he says, won nine important battles 'all of which were fought on foot'.[92] Dominic Mancini described the practice of horsed English soldiers in 1483:

Not that they are accustomed to fight from horseback, but because they use horses to carry them to the scene of the engagement, so as to arrive fresher and not tired by the fatigue of the journey: therefore they will ride any sort of horse, even pack-horses. On reaching the field of battle the horses are abandoned, they all fight together under the same conditions so that no one should retain any hope of fleeing.[93]

Most arrayed men were trained only to fight on foot: they did not possess horses suitable for cavalry engagements. Moreover, they were probably anxious to dismount in the field, so as not to risk the loss of their horses, with no certainty of compensation. John Welles, esquire, was fortunate to receive 3s. 4d. as compensation authorized by the governors of Beverley for the loss of his horse at Northampton in 1460. The cryptic entry in their accounts seems to imply that Welles, a soldier in the royal army, had had his horse tethered in a wood during the engagement, but that a fugitive from the rout tried to swim the beast across the Nene, and it drowned in the mill race.[94]

Mancini, describing the troops which Richard III and Buckingham brought to London in 1483, says that 'there were horsemen among them'. There was an important difference between characteristic infantry forces in English armies abroad and those in the Wars of the Roses. Whereas the former had mounts, the bulk of the latter probably did not. When the crown contracted with a captain to bring a retinue of men-at-arms for service on expedition in France or Scotland, it could insist that they should be horsed for mobility. But in the often hasty, desperate conditions of civil war, commanders were anxious to increase manpower above all. The author of *Knyghthode and Bataile* frequently alludes to 'horsemen' and 'footmen', and is concerned about their mutually supportive roles on the march.[95] The distinction is probably not derived simply from his classical source, but based as well on the constituents of the royal army in 1459. Its 'naked men' are unlikely to have been horsed.[96] According to *Bale's Chronicle*, the Yorkist army which reached London in July 1460 had 500 horsemen and 'a host of footmen of commons of Kent, Sussex and Surrey numbered at 60,000'.[97] Advancing on Northampton, its leaders waited for two days at Dunstable for all the contingents to assemble, 'for those on foot could not go as fast as those on horse', especially since bad weather had rendered the ways foul.[98] John Harowe, a London mercer, was described as *dux peditum* ('captain of foot'?) in the Yorkist army at Wakefield.[99] Ruminating on the Lancastrian victory at St Albans in 1461, 'Gregory' expressed the footman's animus against mounted troops: 'As for spearmen they be good to ride before the footmen and eat and drink up their victual, and many more such pretty things they do, hold me excused though I say the best, for in the footmen is all the trust.'[100] Next month, when Edward was preparing to combat the Lancastrians in the north, his 'foot people' set out from London a few days ahead of him.[101] One of those who fought against him at Towton was Sir Thomas Hammys, 'captain of all the footmen'.[102] At Losecoat Field in 1470 Robert Waryn was 'captain of the footmen' in the Lincolnshire army. After the royal victory there, Clarence and Warwick promised to come to Edward from Coventry, leaving their footmen behind. Their excuse for taking a route away from the king was that they were going to contact a force of their footmen.[103] In 1471 Coventry sent twenty 'footmen' and twenty 'horsemen' to Barnet field, presumably to support Warwick.[104] The Lancastrians had to make a stand at Tewkesbury because only their horsemen could go on, in the general state of exhaustion, and 'the greater part of their host were footmen'. Edward achieved a notable feat by forcing on through the Cotswolds, his parched, hungry army, 'whereof were more than 3,000 footmen'.[105] Few of Warbeck's supporters in the West Country in 1497 are likely to have had mounts. Those who were at Bodmin when he was proclaimed Richard IV were 'men of Rascal and most part naked men'. The larger force which he and sixty horsemen abandoned at Taunton were 'poor and naked'.[106]

The fact that armies were partly or in substance composed of marching rather than mounted infantry probably had important tactical consequences. It may have stimulated the formation of specialized mounted vanguards to spearhead attacks. It may have encouraged the carriage of armaments which could not have kept up so easily with mounted troops – artillery, cannon balls and, besides, entrenching tools. But such slower forces were vulnerable to surprise attacks, all the more so as mounted contingents tended to move separately. There was an enhanced need for troops of light horse – 'scourers' (also termed 'aforeriders' or 'prickers') to protect the flanks of footmen and waggons, and maintain contact between columns, as well as watching enemy movements and reconnoitring objectives. Incidentally, aforeriders might cut fine figures: they were able to secure plum billets, and to avoid tramping along muddied lanes, well equipped to make a quick exit from a tight corner, and doubtless expert at scanning the horizon and detecting the whereabouts of a camouflaged pig, chicken or barrel of ale.

The author of *Knyghthode and Bataile* recognized the need for horsemen to provide good intelligence and protection for marching infantry. 'Escouring is to have of every coast', he wrote; the best horsemen, light-harnessed, were to shepherd the footmen.[107] The need for good intelligence was emphasized by some notable failures early in the wars. In May 1455, when Henry VI's retinue was leaving Watford for St Albans, the assembly-point for the royal army, his commanders were startled to discover that York had forestalled them, being near enough to offer battle, or occupy St Albans before them.[108] In 1459 the opponents Warwick and Somerset both passed through Coleshill (Warwicks.) without realizing their proximity.[109] Salisbury's peril at Blore Heath sprang from his failure to realize that superior forces were enveloping him.[110] Yorkist intelligence continued to be abysmal. After their scourers' defeat at Worksop (Notts.) in December 1460, York and Salisbury consistently failed to appreciate their opponents' dispositions in Yorkshire.[111] At St Albans the following February, Warwick's scourers failed him more seriously than at Coleshill. His army was attacked whilst moving to a new position, 'and then', declares the trenchant 'Gregory', 'all thing was to seek and out of order, for their prickers came not home to bring no tiding how nigh that the Queen was, save one, come and said that she was nine miles off'.[112] Waurin's account suggests that in the following months Edward was served better by his *avant coureurs* in the north.[113]

The militarily minded author of the *Arrivall*, in his account of the 1471 campaign, gives the best insights into scouting activities. By then there was probably more light horse available skilled in the techniques of observation and liaison. After his cautious advance from Holderness, Edward 'being at Nottingham, and or he came there, sent the scourers all about the countries adjoining, to aspie and search if any gatherings were in any place against him'. Those who reconnoitred the Lancastrian force at Newark in fact precipitated its withdrawal in the belief that they foreshadowed the imminent arrival of Edward's army.[114] The day before the battle of Barnet, Edward's 'afore-riders' secured an advantage by beating Warwick's out of the village.[115] When the king's army was soon afterwards pursuing the western Lancastrians through the Cotswolds, he always had 'good espialls' on them. The 'certain knowledge' that he had at Cheltenham of their halt at Tewkesbury enabled him to rest his weary army.[116] It seems that Edward appreciated the need for good intelligence, perhaps as a result of his seniors' failures to get it in 1459–61. It was certainly to be crucial to the opponents in the 1485 campaign. In his operations in Wales, Henry Tudor, unsure at each stage of his reception, was highly dependent on his scourers' reports; Richard's were eventually able to pick up his line of march in the Midlands. Henry's aforeriders in 1487, who also apparently formed 'the Wing of the Right Hand of the Forward', were from the pick of his household knights.[117]

Besides detecting and shadowing enemy movements, masking their own forces and securing advance positions, 'scourers' and aforeriders were by 1471 being used for a variety of tasks. In that year, to deceive Edward into believing that they intended to advance on London rather than northwards, the Lancastrians dispatched aforeriders on sweeps from Exeter to Shaftesbury and Salisbury, and from Wells to Yeovil and Bruton. They were to 'call and array the people to make towards them', and to spread false information that the army would advance on Reading, and, through Oxfordshire and Berkshire, on London.[118] In 1487 a weaker side was again resorting to deception measures. Whilst Henry VII confronted the earl of Lincoln's army at Stoke, the latter's scouts may have been spreading hostile rumours on approach routes to the royal army.[119] Vergil hints at another task of scourers, in forces which commanders often with good reason suspected of a lack of enthusiasm for fighting. He claims that many in the royal army would have deserted at the start of the battle of Bosworth 'if for king Richard's scurryers, scouring to and fro, they might so have done'.[120]

There is little evidence of light horse protecting companies of foot and waggon trains on the march, or maintaining contact between them and mounted retinues, but doubtless these were among their principal tasks. Edward, when advancing from Northampton to London in 1471, always left 'behind him in his journey a good band of spears and archers, his behind-riders, to counter, if it had needed, such of the Earl's [Warwick's] party as, peradventure, he should have sent to have troubled him on the back half if he so had done'.[121] As we have seen, on the march from Nottingham to Leicester in 1485, Richard covered the flanks of his army with wings of horsemen.[122] Thus the wars may have stimulated the development of light cavalry in England, and of expertise in its scouting roles.

The question arises whether, despite the heavy weight of assertions that the English habitually fought as infantry in set-piece battles, companies of horse were on occasion remaining mounted in the field. According to the author of *Knyghthode and Bataile*, horsemen were normally set in battle at each 'horn' or 'wing', covering the flanks of archers and other footmen.[123] But he is paraphrasing Vegetius. The frequent deployment, in the wars, of artillery and large numbers of sometimes ill-equipped and unreliable infantry suggests that there were flanking roles for cavalry. There are some tantalizing scraps of information hinting at cavalry actions. At Towton, according to Waurin, Edward concentrated his horsemen on a wing (*sus hesle*): they were put to flight early in the battle and pursued by the Lancastrian vanguard, presumably also mounted.[124] Though Commynes says that the battle of Barnet, ten years later, was fought on foot, Vergil, who had circumstantial, if not wholly accurate, information about it, recounts that Warwick arrayed his 'battles' 'with part of the horsemen in the left wing'. When his men were under heavy pressure, he 'relieved them who fought in the first front with a troop of light horsemen, and caused the enemy somewhat to give ground'.[125] According to the *Arrivall*, at

Tewkesbury Edward feared that the Lancastrians might place horsemen in ambush in a park on their right flank. Therefore he detached 200 spears, setting them in a 'plump' nearly a quarter of a mile from the field to watch the wood. But the Lancastrian command, lacking his tactical insight, failed to exploit the park. The Yorkist plump-commander, realizing this, used his initiative boldly by making a surprise charge against the flank of the Lancastrian vanguard, whilst it was heavily engaged with Edward's 'middleward'.[126] At Bosworth Richard led a charge against Henry Tudor: he 'struck his horse with the spurs, and runneth out of the one side without the vanward against him'.[127] Though the tactical circumstances were different, at both Tewkesbury and Bosworth we find Yorkist cavalry being used in an attempt to sway the balance when opposing infantry were heavily engaged. The Wars of the Roses probably produced a revival of English cavalry fighting, as well as of scouting.

Do contemporary manuscript illuminations and chivalrous romances throw any light on this? Indulgence in artistic and literary licence makes their evidence suspect, but it deserves some consideration, as a reflection of contemporary ideals. A manuscript of the French version of the *Arrivall* has miniatures depicting the battles of Barnet and Tewkesbury.[128] At Barnet the principal engagement is shown as taking place between heavily armoured cavalrymen fighting with swords and couched lances, whilst in the foreground a much smaller number of fully armoured men-at-arms fight on foot with sword and lance. At Tewkesbury the Lancastrians are shown in flight from Edward in a cavalry engagement, whilst in the foreground his more numerous archers gain the ascendancy in a shoot-out with their Lancastrian counterparts. Clearly the artist has taken considerable licence with his text, reversing the preponderance indicated in it of footmen over horsemen at Tewkesbury, depicting the horsemen as uniformly heavily armed, and suggesting that the battles were primarily cavalry engagements.

The series of drawings executed between 1485 and 1490 to illustrate the life of a chivalrous hero, Richard Beauchamp, earl of Warwick (d. 1439), besides being of much higher artistic quality, display a more detailed knowledge of arms and armour than the miniatures in the manuscript of the *Arrivall*. The drawings of the rout of Glyn Dŵr's forces show pursuing English spearmen charging on horseback accompanied by foot archers. Some of the horsemen are fully armoured, but others lack plates on their arms, and have helmets which do not cover the neck or the whole face. Perhaps the latter are wearing the equipment of the light cavalry which played such essential roles in the Wars of the Roses.[129]

The principal English literary work of the period concerned with fighting is Sir Thomas Malory's redaction into the vernacular of Arthurian romances, completed in 1469-70. The battles which Malory recounts, fascinatedly describing individual combats, commence as cavalry engagements, though knights perforce conclude struggles on foot sometimes. Malory echoed the traditional horse-fighting conventions of his sources. Having probably fought in France in the retinue of Richard Beauchamp, earl of Warwick, he was well aware of conventional English infantry methods. His opinion that mounted troops were more useful than foot soldiers was compatible with these as well as with the romance idiom. His King Lot exclaimed, 'ye may see what people we have lost and what good men we lose because we wait always on these footmen; and ever in saving of one of these footmen we lose ten horsemen for him'. Malory's descriptions of campaigns reveal an old soldier's eye. He was nervous about the need for good scouting. Merlin sends forth 'foreriders to skim the country' who encounter the northern army's foreriders and force them to reveal its line of approach. He mentions the scout watch in camp, and an army commander's shame at the destruction of his vaward before he could bring up his main force. Characteristically, Malory valued the military worth of gentlefolk above that of others.[130]

What Malory was particularly interested in applying to his delineation of Arthurian warfare was the methods and conventions of the contemporary tournament. 'A more jolier jousting was never seen on earth' is the comment on one battle. He may have been eager, as Caxton was to be, to promote among gentlefolk admiration for and the desire to emulate the cavalry skills and 'noble' qualities learnt in jousting on horseback.[131] Indeed, the need for cavalry in the Wars of the Roses may have given tournament techniques of controlling a horse in combat renewed practical relevance. There was a revival of interest in tournaments at Edward IV's court, which perhaps can be seen in this context as well as that of courtly splendour. The most famous combats at the Yorkist court were those held before the king at Smithfield on 11-12 June 1467, when his brother-in-law Lord Scales met the challenge of the Bastard of Burgundy. On the first day mounted combats were held – running at large, and tourneying with the sword. On the second day there were foot combats with axes and daggers.[132] It was this chivalrous sporting background which inspired Malory's battle scenes and those illustrated in so many contemporary manuscripts. The decorator of the *Arrivall* was seemingly adding another propaganda slant to the narrative by decking out some of Edward's grim triumphs in 1471 with a Burgundian chivalrous aura. Artistic and literary evidence therefore provide uncertain guides to the realities of the contemporary battlefield. But the impression so often conveyed by contemporary chroniclers, of struggles between dismounted hosts of men-at-arms and archers, also needs to be scrutinized hard and sceptically. In reality, infantry, cavalry and artillery were used in conjunction in the field, probably in increasingly sophisticated combinations which foreshadowed the tactical manoeuvring of early sixteenth-century armies.

The Wars of the Roses have the appearance of wars of movement, in which most commanders sought a speedy decision, if necessary by risking all in battle, rather than attempting to maintain a static defence in fixed fortifications. The traditional view of the relative insignificance of siege warfare in the struggles is implicit in A. Emery's statement: 'apart from the activities of Queen Margaret's troops in the north between 1461 and 1464, and the seizure of the rebel castles in Wales by Herbert, few castles were besieged'.[133] This absence of sieges cannot be attributed entirely to the lack of adequate fortifications. Generally, indeed, England and Wales did not have the density of fortification found in most neighbouring Continental provinces. One reason was that there were comparatively fewer cities than in northern France and the Low Countries. By the early fourteenth century London may have had approaching 50,000 inhabitants; in 1524 not more than fifteen other English towns exceeded 5,000. The typical town, of which there were hundreds, was what we would consider to be a large village, with a range of 500–1,500 inhabitants.[134] But as many as 108 English towns had walls built in the Middle Ages, and others had ditches and embankments, with wooden barriers and palisades.[135] Many of these fortifications are likely to have been in disrepair by the mid-fifteenth century, and were in any case constructed on too small a scale and in too old-fashioned or basic a manner to cater for majority military needs in the wars. The duke of York at Ludlow in 1459 and Henry VI at Northampton in 1460 did not use town walls as part of their defences, but constructed independent ones.

Nevertheless, a number of towns, particularly ports, and those near the sea or potentially hostile Marches, continued to repair and improve their defences. London, the greatest urban prize in Britain, had imposing fortifications, which the commons of Kent were unable to take by assault in 1450. The problems involved in mounting a siege of the city gave its governors power to bargain with the commanders of approaching armies on occasion.[136] Coventry had a particularly fine set of walls, which Warwick manned effectively in 1471. Edward IV and his brothers, unable to provoke the earl to sally forth, decamped, 'not thinking it behoveful to assail, nor to tarry for the assieging thereof; as well for the avoidance of great slaughters that should thereby ensue, and for that it was thought more expedient to them to draw towards London'.[137]

Though in the first half of the fifteenth century foreign threats and domestic discord were not sufficiently serious and prolonged to provide general stimulants to the improvement of English fortifications, the evolution of artillery and the consequently increasing vulnerability of defences provided some added incentive for work on them. The crown spent heavily, if intermittently, on its castles in the Anglo-Scottish Borders, and considerable sums were laid out on repairing castles in the principality of Wales damaged by Glyn Dŵr's rebellion. From 1399 onwards there was continuous building activity at some of the fine castles of the Lancastrian inheritance which Henry IV joined to the crown – at Bolingbroke, Lancaster, Leicester, Pontefract and Tutbury. This activity continued well into the reign of Henry VI at Bolingbroke, Pontefract and Tutbury. But, according to H. H. Colvin, 'with the exception of Nottingham, Windsor and Wallingford, few of the old royal castles in the midlands and south were now maintained in a defensible – or even in a habitable – condition'.[138] Colvin detects a decline in the tempo of work on royal fortifications under Henry VI. Available money was swallowed up by defence works on the perennially disturbed Anglo-Scottish Marches, on works in Normandy, and by the enormous cost of harbour works and repairs to fortifications necessitated by erosion at Calais. The long domestic peace of Henry VI's minority provided little inducement to reverse habitual neglect of ancient royal castles of the interior, though officials of the principality of Wales and the duchies of Cornwall and Lancaster strove conscientiously to maintain castles for which they were responsible.[139]

Nevertheless, there are a few indications that in the 1450s some efforts were made to strengthen royal castles, perhaps with the growing political tensions in mind. Ideas of fortifying them were certainly in the air: in 1450 the duke of Suffolk, constable of Wallingford castle, was accused in parliament of fortifying the castle for his own nefarious ends, and Jack Cade, withdrawing from London later in the year, contemplated barricading himself in Queenborough castle.[140] At Halton castle (Cheshire), in a region where Queen Margaret was soon to display particular diligence in rallying loyalties to its lord, her son, a new gatehouse was built at the main entrance in 1450–7.[141] At Tutbury castle (Staffs.), which she acquired as part of her jointure in 1446, she completed the new South Tower by 1450 and built the North Tower, completed in 1461.[142] At the Lancastrian castle of Bolingbroke (Lincs.), the entrance bridge was rebuilt and walls were repaired in 1457–9, and at Dunstanburgh (Northumberland), another duchy of Lancaster castle, a new tower was built in 1458 and the fortifications were strengthened in 1459.[143] Repairs were done at Newcastle (1458); and Pontefract – occupied by York's opponents in the 1460 campaign – had a lot of attention in Henry's last years.[144] In 1460 the royal council meeting at Coventry decided to make the well-maintained

Lancastrian castle at Kenilworth (Warwicks.) – exceptional in area and in the strength of its water defences – into the king's principal base: 'they determined to fortify . . . [it], and the king rode there and sent for all the guns and armaments in the Tower of London and filled up from these forty carts and transported them to Kenilworth and so armed that castle very strongly'.[145] The king's capture at Northampton after the complete rout of his army prevented the defences of Kenilworth from being put to the test. The laborious effort made to fortify it, to so little effect, suggests some of the reasons why strategy in the Wars of the Roses was not based mainly on the defence of fortifications. The long-term planning and large expenses required to set up and maintain a major base with victuals, batteries and ammunition were deterrents to such a strategy. Kings and nobles were not used to shouldering these burdens for domestic contingencies. Their familiarity with the great costs of maintaining the realm's frontier castles (e.g. at Roxburgh, Berwick, Calais and Guines) was likely to increase their reluctance. Moreover, a strong castle might in an emergency turn out to be strategically irrelevant: in 1460 the king's army moved away from Kenilworth, probably denuding it of artillery. There was a preference for settling domestic issues in short, sharp fights, which were relatively cheap and less annoying to the inhabitants than the tedious presence of soldiers inherent in static warfare. But castles certainly had important strategic roles in these wars of movement. They provided breathing spaces, into which king or magnate might dodge like a *banderillero*, to rally levies in comparative security, wait for allies to come to the rescue, and (not least) negotiate pardons from a position of vantage, or, if they were not forthcoming, a promise of sparing life and limb.

Yet, according to Colvin, by Henry VI's reign there was in some regions a dangerous imbalance between royal and private fortifications: 'The Midlands and the north were studded with private fortresses built and maintained by the over-mighty subjects into whose quarrels the Crown was soon to be drawn. The king still had castles in these areas, but they were no longer the largest, the strongest, or those that were most up-to-date in their defensive contrivances.'[146] There had indeed been some notable private castle-building in the later fourteenth century, particularly in the north to provide defences against Scottish incursions. The Percies' building works at Alnwick and Warkworth are notable examples of this.[147] William Worcester remarks on two magnates who had notably improved castles, though unfortunately he does not usually make clear how far their works were military or domestic. Ralph Neville, earl of Westmorland (d. 1425), he says, built or re-edified (*fundauit, edificauit*) the Yorkshire castles of Guiseley, Sheriff Hutton and Middleham, and the castles of Raby and Brancepeth in the bishopric of Durham.[148] The earl of Warwick (d. 1439) 'rebuilt (*de nouo renouauit*) the south side of Warwick castle, with a splendid new tower and various domestic offices'; he also renovated the castles of Hanley and Elmley (Worcs.), Baginton (Warwicks.) and Hanslope (Bucks.).[149] However, Emery's judgment that there was a marked decline in purely military building in England in the first half of the fifteenth century is surely correct, and should be applied as much to private as to urban and royal fortification.[150] Impressive remains survive of three notable private castles built early in Henry VI's reign. In the early 1430s Sir John Fastolf and Ralph Lord Cromwell, respectively, commenced major projects at Caister (Norfolk) and Tattershall (Lincs.), and in 1440 Roger Fiennes received a licence to crenellate his house at Hurstmonceux (Sussex). None of these castles, though provided with gunports, appear to have been built to withstand bombardment by heavy siege cannon.[151] Caister was in fact besieged from 21 August to 27 September 1469 by a force of 3,000, in a quarrel between the Paston family and the duke of Norfolk, guns being used in defence and assault. The castle was badly damaged by bombardment.[152] Most of the licences to crenellate granted to private individuals in the fifteenth century seem to have been intended for fortifications on a small scale, or of a relatively flimsy nature. They were erected by lords and gentlefolk who wanted to impress their neighbours, and guard against the dispossessions and mayhem endemic in shire society with an imposing tower or elaborately parapeted walls and gatehouse.[153] It is, indeed, difficult to detect any imbalance between royal and noble castles proving dangerous to the crown in the wars.

Control of castles became a major problem for the Lancastrian government after its victory at Ludford Bridge in 1459. There was the fear that the Yorkist lords might invade the realm and seize bases. At the start of December, Judde, master of the king's ordnance, was commissioned to visit all castles, fortified towns and fortalices in the realm, survey their ordnance and have it repaired.[154] Henry VI appointed his half-brother Pembroke constable of York's forfeited Marcher castle of Denbigh; but when the earl tried to take possession, entry was refused. On 16 February 1460 Henry referred to a recent letter from his brother requesting money and ordnance for the siege: the following month the defenders were still defiant.[155] The major siege of 1460 occurred after the Yorkist invasion in June, however. Royal supporters held out in the Tower of London, so as to deny the Yorkists full control of the capital. Lord Scales conducted a vigorous defence, firing his guns at the Yorkist army on its arrival in London.[156] The earl of Salisbury took command of the besieging force, a large part of which probably consisted of civic militia.[157] Scales's gunners continued to show their mettle: they 'cast wild fire into the city, and shot in small guns, and burnt and hurt men and women and children in the streets'.[158] The Yorkist batteries replied effectively: 'they of London laid great bombards on the further side of the Thames against the Tower and crazed the walls thereof in divers places'.[159] Scarcity of victuals, fading hopes of relief, and the distress of ladies sheltering in the Tower were among the factors which soon induced Scales to negotiate surrender,[160] but the intensity of the siege bears witness to the strategic importance of the Tower. Had the Yorkists not won so decisively at Northampton, Scales's continued pressure on the Londoners might have undermined Salisbury's ability to hold them in line.

After their victory, the Yorkist lords feared that their opponents in Wales, reluctant to give up York's forfeited properties, would garrison castles, opposing him on his return from Ireland. On 9 August the keeper of the privy seal was instructed to dispatch letters to the constables of Beaumaris, Conway, Flint, Hawarden, Holt and Ruthin castles. They were to be told to keep the castles securely, not allowing anyone to enter and fortify them. Jasper Tudor, earl of Pembroke, and his deputy at Denbigh castle, Roger Puleston, esquire, were ordered to surrender it to York's deputy.[161] Just over a week later Henry wrote to the Marcher Yorkists Sir William Herbert, Walter Devereux and Roger Vaughan, saying that reportedly certain persons 'usurp and take upon them to victual and fortify divers castles, places and strengths in our country of Wales'. The king enjoined them to take and keep these places securely on his behalf.[162] York's opponents were not able to obstruct his reinstatement, but the need for his presence in parliament in October and in the north in December left him little opportunity to reassert his ascendancy in Wales. The fact that the queen sought refuge in a castle there, that York dispatched his eldest son to the Welsh Marches, and that the latter had to fight a large-scale battle to retain them in February 1461 showed that the council's forebodings the previous August had substance.[163] The defiance of the Yorkists in Wales after Northampton started that prolonged resistance to Edward's rule there, and to the concomitant ascendancy of the Herberts and Vaughans, in which the seizure of some of the fine local baronial and 'Edwardian' castles figured prominently.

No siege played a decisive role in the bitter struggles of 1461 for the crown. But the northern army's advance and Edward's conquests probably led to the most widespread manning of fortifications in the wars. In January, to deal with the queen's threat, the council ordered the aldermen and burgesses of Stamford to have the town's defences manned, and the bailiffs of Shrewsbury to have theirs repaired and manned. Commissioners in Norfolk and adjacent shires were to deal with the disaffected who had fortified castles and fortalices.[164] On 3 February Nicholas Morley and John Bensted, esquires, were commissioned to array the lieges of Hertfordshire, Cambridgeshire and

Huntingdonshire as garrisons for castles and towns.[165] Many landowners, like William Grey, bishop of Ely, probably looked to their own defences: he garrisoned the Isle of Ely and Wisbech castle with men summoned from all his manors in Essex, Norfolk, Suffolk and Cambridgeshire, stiffened by thirty-five Burgundians armed with guns and crossbows.[166] However, the fortifications which turned out to be important in the queen's campaign were those of London, for her army's inability to threaten them negated her victory at St Albans.[167] Edward's victory at Towton, on the other hand, so disrupted the Lancastrian army that York and Newcastle could not be held against him. But the defeated party – as after Ludford Bridge or Northampton – tried hard to retain as toe-holds castles on the periphery of the realm.[168] For a time the Lancastrians may have even maintained a garrison in Northamptonshire. On 31 March William Lee, joiner, was empowered to find carriage, carters, horses and oxen to take three 'great bombards' which Edward IV had ordered to be sent for the siege of Thorpe Waterville castle – where the garrison may have held out since the Lancastrian retreat from St Albans. The siege commander was Sir John Wenlock, who had aided the siege of the Tower in 1460.[169]

Edward's government long remained apprehensive that the Lancastrians would seize castles. At the end of May 1461 Geoffrey Gate was ordered to safeguard Carisbrooke castle and the Isle of Wight.[170] But not until October 1462 were the Lancastrians able to reverse dramatically the defeat of their attempts to keep castles.[171] After the surrender of Bamburgh castle in June 1464, however, there remained only one substantial, menacing pillar of their 'castle-strategy' of the early 1460s. David ap Jevan ap Eynyon, whose levying activities as constable of Harlech castle for King Henry harmed Yorkist loyalists in North Wales in 1461, clung for years to this remote, forbidding fortress, a refuge for Lancastrian adherents. 'Gregory' wrote that 'that castle is so strong that men said that it was impossible to get it'. In the autumn of 1464 Lord Herbert, granted its constableship, commenced a serious siege. He was allowed £2,000 for costs by the crown, and was supplied with 'divers habilments of war' by the master of the king's ordnance. To no avail: David held out. In 1468, when Jasper Tudor was once more stirring in Wales, Herbert made another strenuous attempt against Harlech. This time, in August, he managed to negotiate terms of surrender.[172]

On the outbreak of 'Robin of Redesdale's' rising in 1469, Edward's favourites sought refuge in castles in Norfolk and Wales, but Earl Rivers and his son Sir John Wydeville, ensconced in Herbert's castle at Chepstow, had to surrender.[173] The fall of the Herberts encouraged rebelliousness in South Wales. In December 1469 Gloucester was granted full power to subdue the royal castles of Carmarthen and

Cardigan, which the rebellious gentlemen Morgan and Henry ap Thomas ap Griffith had seized, and from which they were raiding.[174] When Clarence and Warwick invaded England in September 1470, Edward's queen, Elizabeth Wydeville, then in an advanced state of pregnancy, 'well victualled and fortified' the Tower of London, and retired there. Her husband's flight made resistance futile, however. She went into sanctuary at Westminster, and the Tower was eventually surrendered to the mayor and aldermen of London, and to Warwick's man Sir Geoffrey Gate, who thus secured an important prize – King Henry, long a prisoner there.[175]

In 1471 Warwick garrisoned Coventry strongly and effectively, but erred gravely in failing to ensure that London was held on his behalf in sufficient strength.[176] The western Lancastrian army of 1471 was to gain an advantage by its uncontested admittance to Bristol. But a major factor in its defeat was the captain at Gloucester's refusal to surrender the castle and town.[177] Despite the débâcle at Tewkesbury, the irrepressible Jasper Tudor tried to hold South Welsh castles and fortified towns. He retreated with his retinue to Chepstow. After foiling Roger Vaughan's attempt against him there, he withdrew westwards to Pembroke castle. He was besieged by Morgan Thomas, 'and kept in with ditch and trench that he might not escape', but, just over a week later, was rescued by David Thomas. Nevertheless, Jasper had to give up Pembroke, and with his young nephew Henry Tudor he fled from Tenby to France.[178] But there may yet have been a Lancastrian attempt to revive the saga of Harlech: on 11 September 1471 the chief justice of North Wales, the earl of Shrewsbury, was empowered to give grace to any lieges within the castle.[179]

The previous May there had occurred the one major siege in the warfare of 1469–71, the only considerable assault on urban fortifications in the wars. This was the siege of London by the deceased Warwick's former sailors and their allies from Kent and Essex, led by his kinsman the Bastard of Fauconberg. He arrived on the Surrey bank of the Thames on 12 May. Denied entry to the city by the mayor and aldermen, he led his men up-river to cross Kingston bridge, intending to seize, and threatening to plunder, Westminster and the extensive London suburb between it and the walls. Such an attack might have induced the citizens to commit their forces rashly outside their gates, or to negotiate; but the Bastard speedily abandoned this bold strategy, which would have left his forces exposed to a royal advance from the west, with vulnerable lines of communication across the Thames. Warkworth condemned the Bastard's folly for not striking westwards directly at Edward, who 'by possibility could not by power have resisted the Bastard'. The latter's return to Southwark, not far from his ships, committed him to an assault on the city at its strongest points, after a display of indecision likely to hearten the defence. When he had guns brought from the ships and lined in battery to bombard the city from the south bank, the city gunners returned such accurate fire that the batteries could not hold position. The Bastard had to resort to assaults. One force tried in vain to burst across London Bridge after it and the houses on it had been fired. The author of the *Arrivall* considered this a hopeless attempt, because the defenders had such strong ordnance commanding the causeway. More worrying attacks were made by 3,000 troops ferried across to St Katherine's, near the Tower. They divided into two companies to assault Aldgate and Bishopsgate, shooting guns and arrows into the city with some effect and firing the gates. But the defences were well ordered by the earl of Essex, who stiffened the civic levies by mixing them with gentlefolk whom he had under arms. The rebels at the gates had a serious disadvantage: their line of communications was menaced by the Tower garrison, commanded by a spirited soldier, Earl Rivers. In one sally from a postern with 400–500 men, he drove the rebels from their position at Aldgate to the waterside. The assaults on the gates were finally repulsed when the defenders sallied out, routed the besiegers and drove them to their ships. Regrouping on the south bank, the Bastard's men made an orderly retreat to Blackheath, but held on there only from 16 to 18 May before dispersing, fearful of the king's approach.[180]

In the remaining desultory campaigns of the wars there occurred one memorable siege. About Michaelmas 1473 the Lancastrian earl of Oxford, who had fled abroad from the field of Barnet, sailed into Mount's Bay, Cornwall, and seized the fortified monastery on St Michael's Mount there, as a base from which to rally West Country loyalties. He had embarked at Dieppe with twelve ships equipped at Louis XI's expense, and had hovered for some time off English coasts. Warkworth remarked that the Mount was 'a strong place and a mighty, and cannot be got if it be well victualled with a few men to keep it; for twenty men may keep it against all the world'. He says that Oxford had 397 men to hold it, Worcester that he had only 80. Among his companions were his three brothers and two members of families which had suffered by supporting the Lancastrians, William Beaumont and Thomas Clifford. King and council commissioned Henry Bodrugan, 'chief ruler of Cornwall', to lay siege. He did not press the matter, being content to parley, and apparently even allowed the Mount to be victualled – perhaps running with the tide of local opinion. For when the earl and his men had seized the Mount, they reconnoitred the countryside 'and had right good cheer of the commons'. By 7 December news of these jaunts reached the court: they are alluded to in a commission appointing to the command of the siege, besides the slack Bodrugan, John Fortescue, squire of the king's body, and Sir John

Croker. Fortescue had 200 soldiers under his command. John Wode, master of the king's ordnance, organized the transport of cannon from the Tower. Operations may have been hampered by the enmity between Fortescue and Bodrugan, but the siege took a more serious turn, with daily skirmishes punctuated by brief truces.[181] The arrival of the reinforcements authorized by the king in December probably effectively cut Oxford off from any hope of Cornish support. The blockade commenced on 3 February 1474 by the king's ship *le Caricou*, with 260 soldiers and mariners aboard captained by William Fetherston, probably made surrender inevitable.[182] Warkworth was convinced that Oxford was eventually compelled to surrender because king and council had suborned his men with offers of pardons and rewards: 'and so in conclusion the Earl had not passing eight or nine men that would hold with him; the which was the undoing of the Earl'. It was, Warkworth concluded with unaccustomed joviality, a classic case of the proverb that 'a castle that speaketh, and a woman that will hear, they will be gotten both'.[183] For Oxford, the worst effect of the desertions was that they lessened his ability to bargain for good personal terms of surrender. His life was spared, but he was clapped into prison, and there he remained for the rest of Edward's reign.

A few attempts to hold and overcome fortifications in the later campaigns are to be noticed. In the 1483 rebellion Bodiam castle (Sussex) was held against Richard III, possibly by its owner, Sir Thomas Lewknor, who was attainted as a rebel.[184] Perhaps the object of holding it was to provide a base near the coast, in case Henry Tudor, sailing from Brittany, decided to land nearby and rally his Kentish supporters for an attack on London. His ally Buckingham's original base in the rising, Brecon castle, was successfully attacked by Sir Thomas Vaughan and his brothers Roger and Watkin.[185] In 1484 the earl of Oxford, imprisoned at Hammes castle in the March of Calais, suborned its captain, Sir James Blount. The pair fled to Henry Tudor in France, leaving a garrison in the castle. Perhaps they hoped to use Hammes as a base from which to win over the March and launch an attack through Kent. But the garrison at Calais remained loyal: a large part of it besieged Hammes in the winter of 1484–5. Oxford arrived nearby with a relieving force, and stiffened the garrison's resistance by passing to them a reinforcement of thirty men under Thomas Brandon. The royal commander (probably Lord Dinham), menaced by Oxford's proximity, allowed the Hammes garrison to march out, as the earl had hoped. He then withdrew with them from English territory. Considerable amounts of 'stuff' had been brought up during the siege, including stones for serpentines, powder for arquebuses, and scaling-ladders. The seriousness of the threat to Richard's rule posed by this Tudor attempt to gain the March has perhaps been underestimated.[186]

In 1496 James IV of Scotland, in support of the Yorkist claimant Warbeck, sacked peel towers in the Till valley, a characteristic activity in Border warfare.[187] When Warbeck landed in Cornwall in 1497, one of his aims was 'to capture wherever he went fortified places which might usefully serve in his defence', according to Vergil. He took and held St Michael's Mount, as Oxford had done.[188] The earl of Devon's retreat to Exeter may have given him hopes that he could occupy the city, as the Cornishmen had done earlier in the year, despite his lack of siege equipment.[189] We are fortunate in possessing an account of the first day of siege (17 September) written by Henry VII on the 20th, which almost certainly retails information contained in a letter to him from the commander, Devon, sent on the actual day. A letter from Devon to Henry dated 18 September survives, recounting that day's events.[190] According to Henry, the earl was well supported by the gentlefolk of Devon and Cornwall.[191] The rebels arrived at Exeter at about one o'clock on the 17th, 'and there ranged themselves in the manner of a battle, by the space of two hours'. Warbeck's request for the surrender of the city was refused by Devon. His men then assaulted the East Gate and the North Gate – both of which were in good repair.[192] They were driven off with losses of between 300 and 400. On the following day, Devon says, they once again assaulted the gates, concentrating on the North Gate. The defence was maintained strongly there, and the besiegers sustained heavy casualties, especially from gunfire. They requested a truce in order to regroup and withdraw from the city. This was granted, as the garrison, wearied and depleted by casualties, was not strong enough to attack. At about eleven o'clock in the morning the rebels withdrew: 'thanked be God [wrote the earl] there is none of your true subjects about this business slain, but divers be hurt. And doubt not again, one of yours is hurt, there is twenty of theirs hurt and many slain.' Gallantry forbade him from saying that he was one of those hurt: he was wounded by an arrow in the arm.[193] Vergil remarks on the fierceness of the fighting, and the martial conduct of the citizens. When the rebels fired the gates, the defenders, unable to extinguish the blaze, banked it up to drive them back. They dug ditches within the gates to provide new defences and repulsed attempts to scale the walls.[194]

The Wars of the Roses stimulated the strengthening of fortifications. Kings recognized the need to have some strategically placed interior castles in defensible condition. At the Tower of London Edward constructed *c.* 1480 the brick outwork on Tower Hill known as 'the Bulwark', perhaps an artillery emplacement.[195] In 1474 Richard Patyn had been commissioned to arrange the carriage of ordnance to Nottingham castle. Several months later he received a life grant of 4*d.* a day from a nearby mill and meadow: perhaps he was responsible for the custody of artillery there.[196] Between 1476 and 1480 Edward spent over £3,000 on the castle: a new tower was finished, but the works were apparently primarily residential.[197] Richard III planned and partially built impressive new defence works at Warwick castle where, like Henry VII, he probably kept artillery.[198] To strengthen his northern power-base, Richard also embarked in 1484 on a complete reconstruction of York castle: in 1478 Edward had already made clear his intention of repairing it. Events had shown the need for a royal stronghold there to overawe the citizens and the turbulent Yorkshire baronage.[199]

Urban corporations had an incentive to strengthen their defences, and the crown a reason to encourage them. Worcester's walls had apparently not been strong enough to prevent the rebel lords of 1459 from occupying the city. Soon afterwards, in November, the town received a royal grant of stones, including broken ones from the castle walls, for the repair of walls, bridge and gates. This was in response to the citizens' petition that the fortifications were so ruinous that 'a few ill-disposed persons could freely enter and have so done in the days last past'.[200] London was probably the city most frequently in fear of assault in the wars. The most thorough repairs of London Wall were initiated by Ralph Jocelyn (mayor 1476–7): 'and or his year came to an end he had made a good part of that which is new made, beside provision of lime and Brick' for further repairs. Traces of these brick repairs can be seen in surviving fragments.[201]

Since dynastic strife tended to increase the characteristic insecurities of landowners, there were incentives for them to maintain and improve fortifications. Newly rich and powerful gentlefolk built to impress neighbours and provide a refuge from their enemies. The most spectacular surviving example is Raglan castle (Monmouthshire), with its great gatehouse and its hexagonal moated keep, the 'Yellow Tower of Gwent'. The castle reflects the new and much-resented power of Edward IV's 'supremo' in South Wales, William Herbert, earl of Pembroke.[202] Another recently elevated servant of Edward, William Lord Hastings, gave expression to the influence which he had gained in Leicestershire by adding a keep to the old castle at Ashby de la Zouch (1474–83), and commencing in 1480 the building of an impressive castle at Kirby Muxloe.[203]

Though concerned to maintain the defences of the realm, Henry VII does not seem to have shared Edward's and Richard's determination markedly to improve royal strongpoints in the interior of the country. The projected works at York and Warwick castles lapsed, and during Henry's reign many royal castles entered what was to be a lasting phase of neglect and decay.[204] Perhaps youthful experience made him wary of putting his trust in castles. He had seen his guardian, Herbert, fall in

1469, without being able to rely on Raglan's splendid defences. In 1471 Henry had probably had to flee from Chepstow and Pembroke castles.[205] His invasions of the realm in 1483 and 1485 had taught him that men's loyalties were its keys. He may have felt safe in not building up royal fortifications because so many of the best private ones – such as the fine castles of the Nevilles – came to him by escheat or forfeiture. With some exaggeration, the Venetian commentator of 1498 asserted that fortresses, apart from those of the bishopric of Durham, were in royal hands.[206] Since, after 1486–7, dynastic revolt attracted little domestic support, magnates may have been glad of the excuse not to spend money on maintaining fortifications. Lord Hastings's son failed to complete his father's new buildings at Kirby Muxloe. Thus the petering-out of the Wars of the Roses in Henry's reign ended the recent revival of interest in developing fortifications in the interior of the country, and led to a resumption of the neglect generally characteristic of the first half of the fifteenth century. But the Anglo-Scottish Border region remained exceptional. There, frontier tensions intensified, exacerbated by the accession of the anglophobe James IV in 1488. In 1491 Henry VII showed interest in acquiring from the dissident earl of Angus the grim castle of Hermitage in Liddesdale, which would have given him an advanced base from which to control the troublesome local reivers. James's invasion of 1496 is likely to have made northern English landowners look to their defences. In 1497 the king of Scots besieged and bombarded Norham, Bishop Fox of Durham's exposed fortress on the Tweed, necessitating major repairs.[207]

The conditions and aims of warfare in the domestic conflicts certainly did not encourage prime reliance on fortifications. Yet there were some crucial sieges and many brief occupations of castles. Those which figure prominently are mostly the ones in regions where they were generally well maintained – in the far north, Wales, and the March of Calais. Castles and fortified towns were usually occupied briefly, as bases for the rallying of support, or as refuges from which to bar pursuers. However, our knowledge of siege warfare in the wars may be particularly defective. Except when London or a leading town was threatened with assault, or the siege of a castle attained peculiar fame, chroniclers were little interested. They concentrated on the decisive battle, the *iudicium Dei*. There are a number of sieges which we know about only because of casual mention in a record source. If the *Arrivall*, a detailed and expert account of Edward's campaigns in 1471, had not survived, we would not know about the importance of Gloucester castle, however brief, in the western campaign. Our knowledge of the defence of Chepstow and Pembroke in 1471 and Hammes in 1484–5 stems mainly from Polydore Vergil's particular interest in and sources of information about the early life and struggles of his patron Henry VII. In the local bickering which was a concomitant of the grand campaigns of the wars, there may have been considerable fighting around fortifications, even if on a relatively small and brief scale. At times this may have been an influence on the general outcome which is hidden from us. For instance, we may speculate that in February 1461 many men in the East Midlands, East Anglia and the south-east were, like the bishop of Ely, looking to the defence of their properties against the dreaded advent of Queen Margaret's northerners. If so, their static local defences may have been a factor in the odd outcome of the main campaign, in which both sides suffered defeat. Warwick's army may have lacked reliable levies (*pace* the choleric 'Gregory') because many men stayed at home at their masters' behest. The queen's precipitate and lengthy withdrawal, after her failure to secure London, may have been hastened by embattled manor-houses and townships along her line of communications, whose inhabitants were desperate to prevent their beasts from being herded off and their meagre winter food stocks from being seized.

It is difficult to be sure that the Vegetian advice given by the author of *Knyghthode and Bataile* about complex tactical formations and manoeuvres was more than a literary fancy, as far as the Wars of the Roses were concerned.[208] Probably masses of hastily arrayed contingents, often brought into battle within days of assembling, could only be expected to line up for a frontal assault or defence with their traditional weapons, bow and bill. But these very limitations may have stimulated commanders' use of elite bodies of specialist troops, often foreign mercenaries: there are references to the deployment of ordnance and flanking cavalry in the field, in conjunction with bowmen and billmen. The distinctive equipment and roles of light and heavy cavalry may have been well understood, for besides frequent references to the scouting and protecting roles for cavalry, there is Vergil's description of a cavalry charge against a main body of troops at Bosworth. Forewards often operated separately from the mass of troops: perhaps there was a trend to concentrate in them more experienced and manoeuvrable companies. Unfortunately few writers were interested in analysing tactical organization or assessing how responsive to sophisticated commands individual and grouped companies were. Vergil, whose military interests were based on the study of classical authorities, got veterans of Bosworth to explain tactics with unusual precision. He gives a Vegetian account of the formation and deployment of the forewards, which with other tactical details suggests a degree of professional expertise in captains and soldiers hardly hinted at by the customarily more pedestrian accounts of the wars. Vergil's Bosworth is anything but a formless slogging match between old-fashioned forces commanded by bull-headed traditionalists.[209]

Therefore the blending of traditional and innovatory methods in early Tudor armies was probably a development of precedents from the Wars of the Roses, not a completely new one. Why then has there been a tendency to dismiss the skills displayed in the wars as relics of the Hundred Years War? Perhaps it derives in no small measure from the judgments of a penetrating contemporary commentator, Philippe de Commynes. As we have seen, he admired traditional English skills in infantry fighting, particularly in archery, and appreciated their influence on Burgundian practice.[210] The one substantial English army which he personally observed was that with which Edward IV invaded France in 1475: 'never before had an English king brought across such a powerful army at one time . . . nor one so well prepared to fight'. The men-at-arms were 'very well equipped and accompanied'.[211] The army had good camping gear and a large number of scourers.[212] But Commynes also emphasized the English soldiery's deficiencies – significantly, in order to stress the lack of judgment of Edward's ally, Charles of Burgundy: 'these were not the Englishmen of his father's day and the former wars of France. They were inexperienced and raw soldiers, ignorant of French ways.'[213] Commynes watched them from Amiens with his master Louis XI, as they approached to encamp for the conclusion of the Anglo-French truce: 'I tell no lie when I say that Edward's troops seemed to be very inexperienced and new to action in the field as they rode in very poor order.' Soon afterwards he formed a low opinion of their discipline when sent to mop up their drunken disorders in Amiens.[214]

Perhaps Commynes's unfavourable impressions were somewhat harsh, and should not be taken as his considered judgment on English military methods. He was struck by Edward's fortunate experience of war in his domestic conflicts. In 1475 many of Edward's retinue commanders and soldiers were also highly experienced. But such a large army must have included raw arrayed men too. The invasion of France probably presented the English command with unaccustomed logistic problems. Armies of the Wars of the Roses are unlikely to have transported so much ordnance and equipment as the 1475 expedition, or to have been used to coping with victualling problems in a country where town gates were firmly shut against them and the ground had been rigorously scorched. Such conditions may have produced unimpressively sluggish progress, which a wealth of tactical expertise could not improve. Moreover, Commynes may not have realized that English infantry were not so used to having mounts as in earlier French campaigns. Molinet remarked more sagely that Edward's army was 'poorly mounted and little used to going on horseback'.[215] The consequent poor riding and bad order in his 'battles' on the move may have given Commynes a misleading impression of their tactical capabilities which his political stance made him eager to emphasize. Moreover, he observed the English army at a time when the news had probably penetrated to the ranks that there would be no fighting. English troops relaxing abroad, having a party on the local wine, have often given foreigners a misleadingly low impression of their military capabilities. In battle they could be transformed. Thus the chronicler Bernaldez recounted how, at the siege of Loja in Granada in 1486, Sir Edward Wydeville dismounted according to English custom (*a uso de suo tierra*), to fight with his 300 men on foot, devastatingly wielding their battleaxes against the Moors.[216]

Chapter 9

The Wars and Society

Contemporary annalists – mainly London chroniclers – on whom we rely heavily for accounts of the Wars of the Roses, dwell mainly on the wars' immediate political causes and effects. Their more general comments are focused on abuses of kingship and on the dynastic issue, with occasional reflections on the times being out of joint. They largely lacked the hindsight and historiographical concepts which enabled Tudor writers to view the wars as an integral episode or at least as a connected sequence of events, and predisposed them to moralize about the evils they inflicted on society.[1] There were, indeed, some contemporary writers who considered the wars more generally. The first continuator of the Crowland abbey chronicle, a Benedictine monk who chronicled events up to January 1470, wrote that the dissensions which had sprung up between Henry VI and Richard of York 'were only to be atoned for by the deaths of nearly all the nobles of the realm'. He alleged that divisions had spread within a variety of social organizations: 'And not only among princes and people had such a spirit of contention arisen, but even in every society, whether chapter, college, or convent, had this unhappy plague of division effected an entrance.' He summarized the dire results in a passage which has earned him the denigration of modern historians: 'the slaughter of men was immense: for besides the dukes, earls, barons, and distinguished warriors who were cruelly slain, multitudes almost innumerable of the common people died of their wounds. Such was the state of the kingdom for nearly ten years.'[2]

The chronicler Warkworth, ruminating on the reasons why Edward IV lost his crown in 1470, takes a perspective back to the start of his reign, and fixes on the miseries caused by continued warfare as the cause of subjects' alienation from him. He was probably referring principally to the costs of the Northumbrian campaigns (1461–4):

when King Edward IVth reigned, the people looked after all the foresaid prosperities and peace, but it came not; but one battle after another, and much trouble and great loss of goods among the common people; as first, the 15th of all their goods, and then an whole 15th, at yet at every battle to come far out their countries at their own cost.[3]

Warkworth also gives an illuminating description of how a region might suffer through the indiscriminate extortion of fines for pardons after rebellion. He describes how, after the suppression of the Bastard of Fauconberg's rising, royal commissioners sat on

all Kent, Sussex, and Essex, that were at the Blackheath, and upon many others that were not there; for some men paid 200 marks, some a £100, and some more and some less, so that it cost the poorest man 7s. which was not worth so much, but was fain to sell such clotheing as they had, and borrowed the remnant, and laboured for it afterwards; and so the King [Edward IV] had out of Kent much goods and little love. Lo, what mischief grows after insurrection, etc.![4]

This kind of comment on the regional consequences of rebellion is largely lacking in London chronicles, the principal literary source for later accounts. Their authors were unlikely to be concerned about the reduction of provincials to beggary, especially troublesome Kentishmen. Sporadic concern about the latter's designs on the city's wealth is one of the few signs of war nervousness shared by London chroniclers. Their general lack of a sense of civic and personal involvement is a valuable indication of wealthy Londoners' experience of the wars, but cannot be taken as a pattern of Englishmen's experience generally.[5]

To explore the latter, the comments of the Crowland monk and Warkworth respectively about heavy casualties and impoverishment through exactions provide a surer starting-point. It may be significant, however, that they do not picture widespread devastation and general social upheaval as consequences of the wars, unlike French polemicists, notably Alain Chartier and Thomas Basin, lamenting the effects of the Hundred Years War in France. One Englishman certainly argued that domestic strife had generally increased lawlessness in England. He had a partisan aim in doing so, for he was a royal official arguing before the Commons in 1474 to persuade them to grant a subsidy for the proposed royal expedition to France, on the grounds that war against the realm's 'outward' enemies would draw off disorderly elements.[6] What he said is in fact a valuable indication of people's feelings about the effects of the wars, for to be effective his arguments had to ring true for shire knights and burgesses. Dissension and discord, he said, had led to poverty and desolation, and Englishmen had generally suffered ills because of the civil wars: 'every man of this land that is of reasonable age hath known what trouble this realm hath suffered, and it is to suppose that none hath escaped but at one time or other his part hath be therein'. Though general acceptance of Edward's title had stilled dissension

> yet is there many a great sore, many a perilous wound left unhealed, the multitude of riotous people which have at all times kindled the fire of this great division is so spread over all and every coast of this realm, committing extortions, oppressions, robberies, and other great mischiefs.

Accounts of England written by foreigners in the later fifteenth century do not attribute evils to domestic warfare in the manner of the Crowland monk and Warkworth. In 1466 a Bohemian noble, Leo of Rozmital, landed at Sandwich and travelled via Canterbury to London, thence to Windsor and Salisbury, re-embarking at Poole. Two members of his retinue, his standard-bearer Schasek and Gabriel Tetzel of Nuremberg, wrote accounts of his travels.[7] They certainly do not give the impression that London and south-east England were lacking in prosperity. Perhaps Tetzel's account of what he considered the exceptional magnificence of Edward's court and the extraordinary reverence shown to the king and queen by kinsfolk and magnates reflects a style deliberately emphasized to assert the regal dignity of the new dynasty. Schasek remarked how Edward's sailors 'when they saw the King's letters, they all fell to their knees and kissed the letters. For they have the custom that when they hear the King's name or see his letters, they show their respect for them thus.'[8] Such obeisance seems over-elaborate, artificial, but perhaps prudent in a realm the title to which was in dispute.

The Venetian envoy Trevisan had written for him in 1498 by a fellow Italian a brief description of England and English affairs. The writer's personal knowledge of the realm seems to have been confined to London and the south — on this limited observation he was highly impressed with the wealth of the realm, particularly that of the London merchants who had entertained him. But he believed that the nobility had suffered as a result of domestic faction. He says that the peers ('li Signori honorati di Titolo') had patronized many clients, with whose support they had terrorized the crown and their own localities, and on whose account they were at last all executed.[9] This is indeed garbled stuff, but it cannot be entirely dismissed: it is a valuable if tantalizingly distorted echo of some Englishmen's notions that there had been an upheaval in their society. Enigmatic judgments of English government and society in the period are implicit in a famous treatise – *The*

Governance of England, by Sir John Fortescue, former chief justice of the King's Bench and chancellor to the exiled Henry VI. This short work, distilling a lifetime's bureaucratic and political experience near the centres of power, was finalized sometime between Fortescue's transference of his allegiance to Edward after Tewkesbury field in 1471 and his death *c*. 1479. In the *Governance* he defined what he considered to be the historic nature of the English polity, and diagnosed and prescribed for the crown's recent problems, clearly recalling his personal experience, particularly of those in Henry VI's majority. Fortescue distinguished the realm as being free from the arbitrary exercise of the royal will, but subject to 'Jus polliticum et regale', which entitled subjects to participate in law-making and settling grants of subsidy. He attributed the commons' prosperity and military strength to the effects of this 'mixed' rule, and Frenchmen's lack-lustre poverty to the authoritarian government burdening them. He argued that the English crown could recover its strength, and reduce the influence of 'overmighty' subjects clogging its institutions, by a vigorous implementation of what were in fact traditionally prescribed remedies for its better financial endowment, and for the appointment of a more effective council.

Fortescue's diagnosis is hard-hitting, but one wonders whether his conservative prescriptions and praise of English institutions cloak a deep anxiety about the possible political and constitutional consequences of recurrent domestic strife and disorder. He may have been arguing against advocates of harsh exercises of royal will as a remedy for instability: the king's representative in the 1474 parliament whose speech to the Commons survives projected 'outward' war as an alternative to stiff government. Though Fortescue had not lived under Edward's allegiance in the 1460s, he may have believed, like Warkworth, that Edward's heavy demands to suppress risings had alienated his subjects, so that the 'overmighty' could threaten his rule. Rebellion was begetting rebellion. Perhaps Fortescue was expressing a pious hope about Edward's restored rule rather than a considered judgment of it when he wrote:

> He hath done more for us, than ever did king of England, or might
> have done before him. The harms that hath fallen in getting of his
> Realm, be now by him turned into the good and profit of all of us.
> We shall now more enjoy our own goods, and live under justice,
> which we have not done of long time, God knoweth.[10]

On the other hand, this may be a sincere retraction: looking back, he may now have felt that the extinction of domestic strife mattered more than the perpetuation of the Lancastrians, and that the war of 1471 had given Edward an unrivalled opportunity to restore lasting peace and sound rule.

Literary comments do not provide much indication of the extent to which different social groups participated in the wars. The group likely to be involved most heavily was the secular peerage, because of close personal ties with the crown and dependence on court favour. But there were considerable variations in the extent of peers' participation, as individuals and as a group. Edward's Neville kinsmen were habitual participants, but his brother-in-law Suffolk stayed at home as much as possible. Dr Richmond has calculated that there were sixty secular peers in September 1459, joined by ten more between then and March 1461, and that fifty-six out of the seventy participated in the fighting of 1459–61.[11] The high active proportion indicates that this was the period of greatest peerage participation. At St Albans in 1455 eighteen secular peers were present, and at least sixteen were probably active in the campaign of 1459. The number rose to thirty-two in 1460, thirty-three in 1461 and reached thirty-eight, the highest point in the wars, in December 1462, when Edward took an exceptional number of peers northwards.[12] In the peripheral Lancastrian campaigns of 1463–4 and the Neville revolt against Edward in 1469 little more than a handful of peers were engaged. As the crisis of Yorkist rule intensified, more peers were drawn in – twelve in 1470, thirty-one in 1471. But totals as high as those of 1460–2 and 1471 were probably never approached again. In 1483 at least twelve peers were in the field, in 1485 ten, in 1487 thirteen or fourteen, and in 1497 four. Dr Richmond remarks that the low figure for Bosworth demonstrates the growing passivity of the nobility.[13] Other factors too may have lain behind these small numbers. The peerage was depleted by natural wastage – only thirty-eight peers were summoned to the 1484 parliament.[14] Changes in military method may have lessened royal reliance on a levy of peers – against rebels Richard III and Henry VII depended particularly on the military support of a few trusted peers and on that of their own retainers; they were anxious to nip rebellion in the bud rather than wait about for more distant, sluggish or hesitant nobles.[15]

The extent of participation by most other social groups, and the factors determining it, are harder to discern. Among gentlefolk – knights, esquires and gentlemen – it is likely that those closely linked by clientage to kings and participating nobles were most active. Chroniclers sometimes relate how men in receipt of fees were prominent in fighting and, as we have seen, kings and nobles tried to secure their active support.[16] Even kinds of retainers who would not normally be expected to fight were sometimes caught up in battle. Among the Lancastrians captured at Hexham (1464) was John Nayler, *cursarius* of chancery.[17]

Gentlefolk, like peers, were probably particularly active in the years

1459–63 and 1471. In January 1463, when Edward had assembled so many peers in the north, there was present in his army 'almost the whole English knighthood (*milicie*)'.[18] In regions on which risings were based, or on which special reliance was placed to oppose them, a higher percentage of gentlefolk is likely to have been recruited. Cheshire gentlefolk rallying to the young prince of Wales suffered high casualties at Blore Heath in 1459.[19] Where gentlefolk had become especially used to forming networks of clientage and political alliances, in order to support or oppose controversial magnate hegemonies – as in the north and Wales – they were more prone to joining in or indeed generating revolt. William Worcester's lists of recruits to the Tudor and Mortimer armies before Mortimer's Cross in 1461 suggest that Welsh and Herefordshire gentlefolk had flocked *en masse* to the respective standards. In the Edgcote campaign (1469), the Herberts had a large retinue of Welsh gentry.[20] Knights and esquires from the north-western shires figured prominently among the opponents of Henry VII's rule, expressing actively the regret felt by many northern gentlefolk at the destruction of the Neville hegemony cultivated by Richard of Gloucester, and their dislike of the Tudor, Stanley and Percy influence which had replaced it.[21]

It must not be too readily assumed that gentry participation in the last campaigns – for which information about participants is sparse – was negligible. The lists of those attainted for their part in the 1483 rebellion suggest a widespread involvement by south-eastern gentry.[22] Vergil names over sixty gentlemen in the king's army in 1487, and a selection of thirty-nine campaigning for him in the West Country in 1497.[23]

Clergy and burgesses were, by virtue of their avocations, generally regarded as exempt from military summons for personal service. But in the north, clergy as well as laity were customarily obliged to array against the Scots. In the early 1460s, Edward IV and Warwick dispatched mandates to Archbishop Booth of York for the array of the provincial clergy against threatened invasion in support of King Henry.[24] Clerics were also more generally present in armies acting as councillors, secretaries and chaplains. The future cardinal Morton, a steadfast servant of Henry VI, shared the privations of Lancastrian forces in Northumberland in the 1460s, and was captured at Tewkesbury in 1471. Earlier in the year William Dudley (later promoted to the see of Durham) had joined Edward at Doncaster at the head of 160 men.[25] But it is unlikely that such as Morton or Dudley had the inclination or skill to act the combatant as much as the friar who loosed off guns all night after Blore Heath.[26]

As landed magnates, bishops may have been expected to provide military contingents. When the bishop of Winchester took leave of

Henry VII at Coventry before the Stoke campaign, he left the 'substance of his company' to serve under the standard of his kinsman the earl of Devon; the archbishop of Canterbury departed at Loughborough, leaving his folk under his nephew Robert Morton's command, to be put under Oxford's standard in the foreward. The main clerical involvement was political and financial. Dr Knecht has shown how the aristocratic links of Henry VI's bishops generated episcopal partisanship.[27] The Crowland monk wrote with feeling of how the dissensions rippled through corporate bodies of ecclesiastics.[28] Henry VII, despite the papal sanction of 1486 for excommunication of plotters against his rule, suffered from clerical dissentients. Richard Symonds, Simnel's priestly *éminence grise*, presumably hoped that rebellion would lead him to high office. Among those convicted of treason in 1495 were some prominent and well-reputed ecclesiastics.[29] Specifically clerical grievances, exacerbated by the wars, may have contributed to clerical dissent, besides dynastic, familial and patronal ties. The convocation of Canterbury's grant in 1463 of an exceptional subsidy of 13s. 4d. from every priest with a minimum annual income of ten marks is alleged to have caused bitter complaints.[30] The curtailment under Henry VII of the recognition of rights of sanctuary for fugitive traitors at common law may have provoked clerical misgivings.[31] In 1497 Warbeck accused Henry and his adherents of 'great and execrable offences daily committed . . . in breaking the liberties and franchises of our Mother Holy Church, to the high displeasure of Almighty God'.[32]

Citizens and burgesses were obliged to don armour and head the defence in person when their town was threatened by rebel advances. There were numerous occasions in the wars when they prepared to do so, but few actual urban sieges. Town dwellers probably assisted in defending Carlisle against assault in 1461, and York in 1487: the burgesses of Exeter manned their gates and walls with spirit in 1497. The London mercer John Harowe helped to besiege the Tower in June 1460.[33] In 1471 London burgesses helped to repel the Bastard of Fauconberg's attacks: leading citizens were knighted by Edward IV for their steadfastness.[34] But on occasion burgesses and other townsmen ventured to fight outside their walls, enrolling as captains or soldiers in the summoned urban contingents, in order to fulfil obligations of clientage, or in search of adventure, or for pay and reward.[35] Harowe died fighting for Richard of York at Wakefield in December 1460, and the account in *Gregory's Chronicle* of the second battle of St Albans strongly suggests that the writer (a Londoner) was present as a soldier in Warwick's army.[36] 'Master Hervy, the recorder of Bristol' was killed on the Lancastrian side at Tewkesbury.[37] Nicholas Faunt, mayor of Canterbury, was a principal abettor of the Bastard of Fauconberg's rising, and, as Dr Richmond has shown, over 200 men from the city were involved in it.[38]

Evidence of urban participation in particular suggests that many of the campaigns were more than clashes between aristocrats and their rural clients and tenants. This is contrary to the impression often given by chroniclers, who in their accounts of battles tended to concentrate on the actions of the principals, and were hardly concerned to analyse the composition of armies, to indicate the relative strengths of noble retinues, shire levies and town companies. A poem on the battle of Towton uniquely celebrates the participation of urban as well as noble contingents – no other literary source mentions the presence of the former there.[39]

Chroniclers, moreover, concentrated on the forces which fought in major battles. But it is clear that many others were in arms, whose less decisive activities are shadowy. Forces were raised to guard towns and coasts which were never engaged: in 1461, many places in southern England were guarded against the northern men. The speed with which the issue was sometimes settled in battle precluded the involvement of some contingents. In 1455 the numbers engaged at St Albans may indeed have been surpassed by those under arms who did not arrive in time or were deliberately withheld.[40] In all three major campaigns of 1469 and 1470 the armies commanded by Warwick and Clarence remained on the sidelines, since the issue was settled by the actions of supporters commanding subordinate and separate forces. In 1471 sizeable Lancastrian forces were raised in Wales and the north about which nothing is known, since they were disbanded after Edward's victory at Tewkesbury. In 1483 there was clearly a large-scale rebellion in the south-east, but, because it petered out after Buckingham's débâcle, it is ill documented.

London chroniclers, writing for an elite especially sensitive about the city's corporate and individual relations with kings and magnates, emphasized their decisive clashes in the wars. Another sensitive interest was the often threatening behaviour of the amorphous, ambiguously termed 'commons' – hence an emphasis on their resort to arms with minimal encouragement or support from nobles and gentlefolk, categorized as being inspired by righteous indignation at misgovernment or malignant, covetous turbulence. As McFarlane indicated, commoners certainly expressed violent opinions about the matters at issue between lords, and communities were rent by resulting quarrels at a popular as well as at elite levels. The passage of Lancastrian lords through Nottingham in October 1459 provoked divisions in the town, as depositions soon after in the borough court show.[41] Two men deposed that Thomas Bolton had said that there were traitors to the earl of Northumberland and Lord Egremont in the town, 'and owed them no good will, and that he would make good and fight, and waged his glove, because he was born and fostered on their ground'. Bolton himself deposed that he had heard John Whitele say that 'there rode many strong thieves with my Lord of Northumberland and my Lord of Westmorland through the town' and that he had argued against the baker Robert Shirwood's assertions in favour of the earl of Salisbury. Thus the quarrels of lords might widen the cracks underlying laboriously maintained urban unity and peace, besides threatening that a town might give offence to a lord. External demands for financial support in the wars might also have the same effects. Early in Edward's reign, at a Nottingham peace session, John Michell accused Thomas Skrymshire of having spoken treasonably:

> [when] John asked if he would go with the King in his journey northward, Thomas said 'Nay, his money should go, but he would not go himself, and it was nought that they went about, for the King was not king, but that he was made King by the Kentishmen, and the very right King and the Prince were in Scotland'.[42]

Commoners often behaved, in the context of the wars, with a violence which their superiors found difficult to control. In 1460 the Yorkist lords at Calais were anxious that the captured Rivers and his son should not enter the town till the evening, 'pour doubte du commun qui ne les amoit point'.[43] In London, to their chagrin, their sailors lynched Lord Scales after his submission.[44] Allegedly the earl of Salisbury might have been ransomed after his capture at Wakefield, had not the common people of the region violently extricated him from Pontefract castle and beheaded him.[45] In 1461, when the queen's army was threatening London, 'communes civitatis' disrupted the pact between her and the city government, seizing victuals which the aldermen had ordered to be dispatched for her to Barnet, and threatening her knights Baldwin Fulford and Alexander Hody at Westminster.[46] In 1463, when the former Lancastrian duke of Somerset rode through Northampton with Edward IV, the commons thereabouts rose up to kill the duke despite the royal presence.[47] Soon after the battle of Edgcote in 1469 the commons at Bridgwater (Somerset) captured an erstwhile leader of the royal army, Humphrey Stafford, earl of Devon: there he was beheaded.[48] It is no wonder that, as Fortescue says, 'Some men have said that it were good for the king, that the commons of England were made poor, as be the commons of France. For then they would not rebel, as now they do oftentimes.'[49]

The commons' interest in expressing opinions about what was at issue in the wars and in participating – even on occasion initiating risings – was facilitated and stimulated by the continuing failure of magnates to resolve the political rifts which deepened between them from the 1440s onwards, and their desire, when resort was made to arms, to widen the basis of support. In what other period has a leading Yorkshire landowner, in order to gain popular support, assumed the nickname of a heroic mythical lawbreaker? Sir John Conyers's apparent assumption of the pseudonym 'Robin of Redesdale' echoed the recent use of the name Robin by leaders of popular protest in Yorkshire[50] – an allusion to Robin Hood. In 1485 northern rebel leaders allegedly had the names of Robin of Redesdale, Jack Straw (a leader of the Peasants' Revolt in Kent in 1381), and Master Mendall (recalling the Robin Mend-All of 1469).[51] The Yorkshire rebels of 1489 summoned support 'in the name of Master Hobbe Hyrste, Robin Goodfellow's brother he is, as I trow'.[52]

Southern popular revolt lacked a vague, but powerfully emotive, unitary symbol such as that provided in Yorkshire by the ballad images of Robin Hood. But it relied perhaps more on relatively sophisticated rallying-points – political manifestos, and allusions to noble causes. The south-eastern rebels of 1450 drew up elaborate petitions and their leader, Jack Cade, used the politically charged, aristocratic pseudonym of Mortimer. The rioters in the London suburbs in May 1486 displayed homely 'Ploughs Rokkes Clowtes Shoes and Wolsakkes', but also two standards blazoning the ragged staff (badge of the imprisoned earl of Warwick) and the Yorkist badge of the white rose.[53]

Why were the common folk often willing participants in the wars? Many, especially those who had suffered financial and judicial hardships, may have been convinced by propaganda denouncing court favourites, such as was disseminated by the Yorkists and later by Clarence and Warwick. As the Peasants' Revolt and Cade's rebellion had strikingly demonstrated, there was a firm connection in the popular mind between evil counsel given to kings and the financial and judicial oppressions and default of royal redress suffered by the 'poorest he'. Moreover, even the lowliest may have felt concern about the dynastic issue. The usurper was a hideous crack in the chain of nature, *ipso facto* incapable of fulfilling his royal functions as mediator between God and his subjects, consequently visiting them with wrath divine and human. In a period when all ranks of society were concerned with the rightful inheritance of property, and when the economic factors stimulating exceptional tensions between landlords and peasants early in the century had declined, one must not underestimate the force of conviction among commons that they should be ruled by the noble as well as royal families who had customarily done so.[54] Practical as well as numinous benefits flowed from rightful tenure – the true inheritor was trusted to mediate, like his forbears, between the men in his lordship and the royal power. When Sir Robert Welles, supported by other local gentlefolk, told the Lincolnshire commons that they could not mitigate the royal wrath in 1470, he appears to have been unhesitatingly believed and widely followed in rebellion. The previous year, there had been a revolt in Yorkshire in favour of restoring the young Henry Percy to the earldom of Northumberland forfeited by his father in 1461, in place of the 'usurping' John Neville.[55] In 1471, soon after Percy was restored and Neville demoted to Marquess Montague, the latter's influence had shrunk in Yorkshire, and the former was all-powerful, simply because he was the Percy, not as a result of his personality and policy: 'great part of [the] noble men and commons in those parts were towards the Earl of Northumberland, and would not stir with any lord or noble man other than with the said Earl, or at least by his commandment'.[56] Later in the year Westcountrymen reputedly joined the Lancastrian invaders because they considered Edmund Beaufort, duke of Somerset, and John Courtenay, earl of Devon, as 'old inheritors of that country'.[57]

Recurrent forfeitures by magnates and gentlefolk therefore often created conditions in the localities which provoked revolt. 'New men', and sometimes the newly restored, found it hard to assert authority and gain trust. Their efforts to do so might exacerbate hostile feelings; they were easily defamed. Few English fingers were lifted in defence of Edward's newly aggrandized favourites, an easy target for noble incitement, in 1469. According to a Gloucester abbey annalist, the Kentishmen and northerners rose in arms to crush the recently elevated earl of Pembroke, William Herbert, 'since he was a cruel man prepared for any crime, and, it was said, he plotted to subdue the realm of England and totally plunder it'.[58]

Bereft of trusted protectors, commons were easily persuaded to take up arms to restore them, or to defend themselves against royal 'oppressions' or anticipated punishment. Thus in 1486 Yorkshiremen, fearful of the imminent arrival of a probably hostile Henry VII, and lacking confidence in the recently imprisoned earl of Northumberland's ability to moderate royal anger, flocked to Lovell's Yorkist standard. In 1497 Westcountrymen clearly did not rate Edward Courtenay, granted the earldom of Devon by Henry VII, as capable of modifying royal subsidy demands or, subsequently, protecting them against punishment for their revolt. The extraordinary trust which Warwick the Kingmaker had widely and tenaciously inspired as a champion of popular grievances, making him such a formidable threat to Edward, may have been enhanced because many men's ties with their traditional lords had been weakened as a result of the vicissitudes of the wars.

Such were among the local factors determining the commons' willingness to participate. But the imprecision of the sources makes it difficult to be specific about the parts played by commons' grievances over landlords' and urban oligarchies' policies, royal taxation, and about the effects of economic depression and competitiveness. There are hints in London chronicles that economic tensions between the city and its hinterlands helped to provoke rural rebellion. The Kentish supporters of Warwick who in September 1470 'Robbed and despoiled divers Dutchmen and their beer houses' in the London suburbs, were intent on undermining competition to their ale-brewing for the London markets.[59] A Londoner scornfully described how Essex peasants joined the Bastard of Fauconberg's rising:

> The faint husbands cast from them their sharp Scythes and armed them with their wives' smocks cheese cloths and old sheets and weaponed them with heavy and great Clubs and long pitchforks and ashen staves, and so In all haste sped them toward London, making their avaunt as they went that they would be Revenged upon the mayor for setting of so easy pennyworths of their Butter, Cheese, Eggs, pigs and all other victual, and so Joined them unto the Kentishmen.[60]

Kentishmen took a major part in risings in 1460, 1469, 1470, 1471 and 1483. Their rebellious tendencies seem to have been widely recognized – Richard of York in 1452, Warbeck in 1495 and the Cornishmen in 1497 assumed too readily that they would give armed support. These Kentish tendencies may have been fostered by political, military and economic factors hinging on the shire's proximity to London, and its domination of vital commercial and strategic routes from London to Calais. The shire's prosperous gentry and yeomen – uncontrolled by any one great secular lord – looked to the court for patronage and to London markets for agrarian profits. They were consequently sensitive to currents of opinion in court and city – and to those circulating among merchants (many of them Londoners) and soldiers at Calais, the other main external centre for Kentish trade. Kentish gentlefolk and commons were financially vulnerable to the effects of failures to keep the narrow seas safe for commerce, and of crises over pay between the crown and the Calais garrison. They were geographically vulnerable to the implementation of harsh royal fiscal and judicial policies. Kentish commons, in defence of their interests, may have cherished the example set by the saint in their midst, Thomas of Canterbury, of defence of liberties against tyranny, and may have cherished, too, memories of how they and their forbears had occupied London in 1450 and 1381 to save the realm from treason.[61] Some of the Kentish elites may have looked kindly on these sentiments. The fact that many Kentishmen could afford good military equipment, and that they were accustomed to arraying because of their long coastline, contributed to their military weight.

In parts of Yorkshire, too, the commons repeatedly joined in rebellions or instigated them in our period. One origin of these tendencies lay in the struggle for dominance over the shire in the early

1450s between the Percies and the Nevilles, into which gentlefolk, townsmen and commons were drawn. The force with which the Percies ambushed the Nevilles at Heworth (Yorks.) in 1453 included more than a hundred citizens of York, about a third of whom were either merchants or else engaged in the cloth and leather trades.[62] Susceptibility in York – and its hinterland – to noble patronage may have been increased by the city's economic decline.[63] Moreover, the continued instability of noble power in Yorkshire – except during Richard of Gloucester's hegemony – was an incitement for men to take up arms for gain or to air their grievances. The strategic importance of the Yorkshire plain as a launching-pad from which to invade the north-east or the Midlands probably brought upon the region – as upon more prosperous Kent – particularly burdensome financial levies and arrays in the wars. The heavy casualties which Yorkshire Lancastrians suffered in the campaign there in 1461 were bitterly remembered a decade later by gentlemen and others:

> having in their fresh remembrance, how that the King [Edward], at the first entry-winning of his right to the Realm and Crown of England, had and won a great battle in those same parts, where their Master, the Earl's [Northumberland's] father, was slain, many of their fathers, their sons, their brethren, and kinsmen, and other many of their neighbours.[64]

Such weighty testimony to a heavy casualty rate in the wars is exceptional, and gives some support to contemporaries' assertions that the numbers involved in the Towton campaign, and the casualties suffered, were unusually large. Soon afterwards Bishop Beauchamp had written: 'There consequently perished an amount of men nearly . . . hitherto unheard of in our country, and estimated by the heralds at 28,000, besides the wounded and those who were drowned.'[65]

The related questions of the numbers involved and the size of casualties in the wars are vexed and insoluble ones, because of the lack of documentary evidence for the total size of most armies, and the tendency of some chroniclers to repeat uncritically the conflated figures often circulating. One contemporary observer certainly felt acutely embarrassed by these. Prospero di Camulio wrote to Francesco Sforza from Ghent in March 1460 about the St Albans campaign: 'My Lord, I am ashamed to speak of so many thousands, which resemble the figures of bakers, yet everyone affirms that on that day there were 300,000 men under arms, and indeed the whole of England was stirred, so that some even speak of larger numbers.'[66] Nevertheless, chroniclers make it clear that forces engaged in some famous battles were small, or briefly engaged – in these cases casualties were relatively light. Armies were small at St Albans (1455) and at Hedgeley Moor and Hexham (1464).

At Ludford Bridge (1459) only skirmishing took place; Northampton (1460) and Losecoat Field (1470), though bloody, were brief. Before Northampton the Yorkist lords proclaimed that no one was to 'lay hand upon' king or commons, only on lords, knights and esquires. The rule that only the commons should be allowed quarter was a frequent convention in the Wars of the Roses.[67] Nevertheless, there were large-scale routs in which many common soldiers were doubtless put to the sword – Blore Heath (1459), St Albans and Towton (1461), Edgcote (1469), Barnet and Tewkesbury (1471), Bosworth (1485) and Stoke (1487). William Worcester says that about 168 'validioribus gentibus Wallie' were killed at Edgcote.[68] Casualty rates may have tended to be higher than average for English (and Anglo-Welsh) armies because skilled longbowmen were often deployed on both sides.

The convention of executing gentlefolk captured on or near the field became general after Wakefield, but was not always rigorously observed. According to *Gregory's Chronicle*, forty-two Lancastrian knights were executed after Towton.[69] Apart from the leading protagonists, gentlefolk who evaded capture by the opposing army were generally safe: John Paston, on the losing side at Barnet, fled and lay low without mortal anxiety, waiting for a pardon to be sued out.[70] K. B. McFarlane demonstrated that the wars were not responsible for the wholesale destruction of the 'old nobility': the percentages of failures in the male line of peers for the last two quarters of the fifteenth century were in fact below average.[71] Nevertheless, there was a large-scale slaughter of peers in the wars. In the period 1455–87 at least thirty-eight adult peers were killed in battle, or afterwards because of their participation: of these, eighteen were killed in the years 1460–1, and only four after 1471. The deaths in domestic warfare of so many peers, unparalleled in scale in any recent period (and the deaths of some of their kinsfolk and faithful servants besides) is likely to have had profound psychological effects on the nobility. Chroniclers' singling out of the demise in battle of sprigs of nobility hints that this was especially galling.[72] For losers and their families there were many possible vicissitudes. Professor Lander has calculated that between 1453 and 1504, 397 people (excluding members of the houses of Lancaster and York) were condemned for treason. At least 256 of these (about 64 per cent) had their attainders reversed.[73] But years might elapse before a reversal: in the meantime families might be in at least relative poverty, and see their court and local influence decline swiftly – on Hastings's execution in 1483, his servants speedily entered Buckingham's service.[74] Participants risked personal privations: as plotters, fugitives or exiles they sometimes discovered, painfully, the life of a penurious, despised commoner. Sir William Tailboys, hiding from the Yorkists near Newcastle in 1464, experienced life in a coalpit.[75] Commynes saw the exiled duke of Exeter 'begging his livelihood from house to house without revealing his identity'.[76] As a fugitive in 1483 Buckingham lived in a cottage, and may have been discovered because of his inability to adjust his life-style: suspicion was aroused 'in consequence of a greater quantity of provisions than usual being carried thither'.[77] To keep his son and heir, Henry Stafford, safe from search, Dame Elizabeth Delabeare had the boy's head shaved and dressed him in girl's clothes. When searchers were near, she took him in her lap, waded a brook and sat for four hours in a park till they had gone. Later she took him to Hereford, dressed as a gentlewoman, riding pillion behind a faithful servant.[78] There were worse vicissitudes. After Barnet field, Exeter, 'greatly despoiled and wounded', was left for dead.[79] The earl of Oxford's leap from the walls of Hammes castle, where he had been imprisoned for over five years, was widely interpreted as a suicide attempt.[80]

Civil war affected the lives of noble ladies too. In 1461 the aldermen of London sent the duchesses of Bedford and Buckingham to the queen 'pro gratia et pace civitatis habenda'.[81] The sisters of Edward IV and Clarence helped in their reconciliation in 1471.[82] In 1483 Elizabeth Wydeville (who had had some grim political experiences) and Margaret Beaufort were prime movers in the plot to revive their families' fortunes. Many ladies suffered privations as a result of the wars. In October 1459 the duchess of York probably witnessed the pillage of her residence at Ludlow, and was subsequently 'kept full strict and many a great rebuke' in her brother-in-law Buckingham's household.[83] Her sister-in-law the countess of Salisbury had the experience – unusual for a woman – of being attainted.[84] In January 1460 Rivers's wife, the duchess of Bedford, was taken off with him to Calais by Dinham's raiders.[85] Other court ladies, including the duchess of Exeter, endured short commons and hot bombardment in the Tower the following June, and begged the commander to surrender.[86] In 1467 Eleanor Dacre, widow of an attainted Lancastrian, received a royal grant of one of his forfeited manors: 'she has been despoiled of her goods by the Scots and other rebels and has no means of support'.[87] After the collapse of the rebellions instigated by Warwick and Clarence in April 1470, their wives took flight with them. The pregnant duchess of Clarence, whose ship was not allowed to dock at Calais, gave birth at sea to a baby which soon died.[88] In 1488 a royal grant was made for the sustenance of the attainted Lord Zouche's wife and children, in consideration of their 'poverty and wretchedness'.[89]

Bitter mutual feelings about deaths, privations, and insults to ladies are likely to have helped prolong plots and risings after Edward's victories in 1461. The nobility's lack of solidarity facilitated the intrigues of aspiring claimants and kingmakers. But, in the long run, may not there have been a significant noble revulsion against participation in domestic strife? We are handicapped by a dearth of surviving expressions of feeling. Margaret Lady Hungerford, in her will of 1476, referred to heavy debts incurred, 'caused by necessity of fortune, and misadventure that hath happened in this seasons of troubled time last past'.[90] The family fortunes had been blasted by the French ransom of her son Robert Lord Moleyns, and his persistent attachment to the Lancastrian cause, leading to attainder and death. Lady Hungerford's solution was to make her bequests to her grandsons contingent on their continued allegiance to Edward IV and his heirs.

Another noble exasperated by the wars, despite the eminence which he attained as a result of them, was Edward's brother-in-law Anthony Wydeville, Earl Rivers. In the prologue he wrote to his translation *The Dictes or Sayengis of the Philosophres*, published by Caxton in 1477, he says that he had endured perplexity because of worldly adversities and, when released from them by divine grace, had set off on pilgrimage abroad.[91] Rivers had indeed experienced adversities. As a youthful knight he was ignominiously captured with his father in 1460 and was again captured at Towton in 1461.[92] In 1469 he was lucky to escape death, unlike his father and brother. In 1470–1 he shared Edward's hazardous escape abroad, his precarious exile and hard-fought recovery of the crown. With Edward re-established, and despite the king's tart expression of irritation, Rivers determined to escape further politic cares by going on pilgrimage abroad. He wanted to absorb himself in the world of shrines and scholarship, but his nearness in blood to the crown was eventually to shatter his retreat from the violence that had filled his youth.[93]

Some magnates certainly seem to have displayed caution and a reluctance to take up arms when their interests were eclipsed. Henry Percy, whose father and grandfather had died defending King Henry and opposing the Neville challenge to their northern interests, failed to show similar determination – above all, it is likely, he wanted to keep his earldom and avoid the pains of treason. He acquiesced in the limitation of his northern influence by Richard duke of Gloucester in the last decade of Edward's reign. He failed to play the kingmaker when opportunities arose in 1471, 1485, 1486 and 1487.

After the earl of Lincoln's death at Stoke in 1487, his family, the de la Poles, eschewed treason and the promotion of their claim to the throne till 1500, when Lincoln's brother Edmund earl of Suffolk fled abroad after discrediting himself. He and his father, John duke of Suffolk, had acquiesced in the 1480s in the eclipse of their influence in East Anglia by that of Henry VII's favourite, Oxford. When John died in 1491, Edmund peaceably accepted the humiliating royal admonition that he should succeed to an earldom rather than a duchy. It was to be alleged that in 1497 Lord Abergavenny tried to tempt him to put himself at the head of the Cornish rebels. According to the story, Suffolk was shocked by the suggestion and speedily dissociated himself from the rebellion, riding off wearing Abergavenny's shoes, presumably to stop him from following.[94] Another magnate who learnt caution was Thomas Howard, earl of Surrey. His lengthy funeral inscription, formerly at Norwich, is likely to have been based on his own reminiscences of his experiences in the wars.[95] It emphasized his faithfulness to Edward IV in the vicissitudes of 1469–71, his support for him at Edgcote and Losecoat Field, and when the king was 'taken by the Earl of Warwick at Warwick'. After Edward's flight to Flanders, Howard, unable to get abroad, took sanctuary at Colchester, and rejoined the king on his return. At Barnet he was 'sore hurt' and he was wounded and captured at Bosworth. But he prudently passed up an opportunity to escape from his prison in the Tower during the Stoke campaign, and after release from an imprisonment of over three years, worked hard and loyally to maintain Henry VII's interests in the north, despite Oxford's predominant political interest in his native 'country' and Henry's failure to restore to him his father's duchy of Norfolk.

For many lesser participants the experience of the wars was uncomfortable and expensive. Thomas Denyes claimed that, fighting for Warwick at St Albans in 1461, 'there lost I £20 worth horse, harness, and money, and was hurt in divers places'.[96] John Paston, probably in hiding a fortnight after his flight from Barnet, had exhausted his credit, as he wrote to his mother:

> I beseech you, and ye may spare any money, that ye will do your alms on me and send me some in as hasty wise as is possible; for by my troth my leech craft and physic, and rewards to them that have kept me and conducted me to London, hath cost me since Easter Day [the date of the battle] more than £5, and now I have neither meat, drink, clothes, leechcraft, nor money but upon borrowing; and I have assayed my friends so far, that they begin to fail now in my greatest need that ever I was in.

He requested that two of his shirts, three long gowns, two doublets, a jacket of 'plonket chamlett' and a murray bonnet should be sent to him.[97] Such experiences may have increased the reluctance to participate of those with anything to lose. Commentators on some of the later campaigns note this reluctance. According to the official account, though many Kentishmen eagerly joined the Bastard of Fauconberg, others 'would right fain have sat still at home, and not to have run into the danger of such rebellion'.[98] According to Vergil, Warbeck found the Kentishmen reluctant to revolt in 1495: 'they recalled that all their recent revolts had always fallen out badly for themselves and they decided to remain obedient'.[99] He says that the Cornishmen at Blackheath found them in a similar frame of mind, 'remembering only too well that their elders had often paid the penalty for similar rashness'.[100]

How did the wars in general affect non-participants? The fact that Englishmen became so divided, and spilt each other's blood so freely, depressed the reflective, inducing gloomy clerical rhetoric, notably that of Abbot Whethamstede of St Albans, witness to savage killings, and of the first Crowland continuator. The unhappy events led to theorizing even by the unreflective about the unstable temperament of the English. Recounting Sir Mordred's usurpation, which resulted in the destruction of King Arthur's realm, Sir Thomas Malory exclaimed (*c.* 1470):

> Lo, ye all Englishmen, see ye not what a mischief here was? For he that was the most king and noblest knight of the world . . . yet might not these Englishmen hold them content with him. Lo thus was the old custom and usage of this land, and men say that we of this land have not yet lost that custom. Alas! this is a great default of us Englishmen, for there may no thing us please no term.[101]

In 1490, in his prologue to *Eneydos*, Caxton commented on the instability of the English: Vergil's elaborate theory of how their nourishment on faction had been subdued by Edward IV and revived by the example of his brother Richard may have been derived from the discourse of the early Tudor elite.[102] Vergil's views, as we have seen, were to influence heavily those of subsequent sixteenth-century historians. But the long-lasting nervousness about faction and rebellion which was so conspicuous in sixteenth-century politics was nourished by more than literary tradition. It was founded on living folk-memories, as John Smyth's seventeenth-century record of village recollections of the battle at Nibley Green (Gloucs.) in 1470 shows: 'And the blood now spilt was not clearly dried up till the seventh year of King James, as after in many places of these relations appeareth.'[103]

But it is necessary to inquire whether the understandable and long-remembered gloom of contemporaries reflected widespread experience of losses by non-participants – and whether, indeed, the wars had significant material effects on society and the economy in general. Professor Dunham has emphasized the brevity of campaigns:

> Actual fighting probably occupied less than 12 weeks between 1450 and 1485; and the battles, seldom lasting longer than an eight-hour day, were well dispersed among the English counties. So there was really no physical disruption of normal life for over 95 % of the people for about 97 % of the time.[104]

Professor Lander has underlined these points: 'These almost miniature campaigns bear no comparison with the scale of warfare in the rest of Europe.. . . The English suffered hardly at all compared with the damage which they had inflicted on many of the provinces of France during the Hundred Years' War.'[105] In the Appendix an attempt has been made to calculate the total number of days' campaigning (not fighting) in the wars between 1455 and 1485. Sieges and manoeuvres which were of local importance, and desultory land and naval warfare such as that centring on Calais and Sandwich in the winter of 1459–60, have been omitted. The Northumbrian campaign of 1462–3 has been included because, although localized, it involved major efforts by both sides. The length of campaigns has been calculated from the date when the first army in the field set out on the march till the date when the last one was dismissed. As initial and terminal dates are often unknown, on this definition the lengths calculated err on the short side. Some companies clearly had earlier starting or finishing dates. The conclusion is that there were at least sixty-one weeks' campaigning, and that there were major campaigns in ten out of the thirty years. There were, indeed, few actual days of fighting, and the battles seldom lasted more than eight hours, but this was characteristic of medieval warfare. Some of the campaigns were short even by short medieval standards.

Most of the campaigns in the wars are likely to have had far-flung effects, since armies often travelled long distances, sometimes splitting on to different roads, or traversing the same one in different groups. Most parts of the realm experienced the movement of armies, and the people of the Cinque Ports, London, Leicester, Nottingham, York and Newcastle, and those living along the routes between them, at various times became particularly familiar with their movement. The main regions which saw practically no fighting were parts of the north-west, East Anglia and some of the southern shires along the Channel coast.

Commanders in the wars sometimes countenanced the harrying of opponents' estates and servants, as deterrent or punishment. But they were mostly anxious to abate plundering, in order to avoid damage to opponents' estates which they and their followers coveted, but more generally in order to keep and win friends and open town gates. Englishmen's fear and hatred of suffering the ravages which they had often inflicted abroad was the most effective deterrent to plundering in the wars. Until the wars escalated, most English folk were unused to large-scale military operations within the realm. The London writer of *Gregory's Chronicle* remarked in shocked wonder that Cade's encampment at Blackheath in 1450 was fortified 'as it [had] been in the land of war'.[106] It behoved captains to prevent their soldiers from behaving as if they were in such a land. In 1465 (?) Margaret Paston (?) alluded to the force of public opinion about military unruliness in Norfolk: 'for and your soldiers be of such disposition that they will take that they may get it, shall no worship be to you, nor profit in time to come'.[107]

Consequently commanders ordered their soldiers to behave, and promised that they would enforce discipline, while their opponents alleged that they had given licence to plunder. York requested the citizens of Shrewsbury in 1452

> that such strait appointment and ordinance be made, that the people which shall come into your fellowship, or be sent unto me by your agreement, be demeaned in such wise, by the way, that they do no offence, nor robbery, nor oppression upon the people, in lesion of justice.[108]

In 1460 the corporation of London admitted the Yorkist lords on condition that their men did not misbehave and, Warwick in person diligently attempted to enforce this in the difficult conditions created by the siege and surrender of the Tower.[109] A Yorkist partisan alleged that about this time proclamations made in Lancashire and Cheshire in Henry VI's name promised that the king's soldier should be able to 'take what he might and make havoc' in Kent, Essex, Middlesex, Surrey, Sussex, Hampshire and Wiltshire.[110] As the queen concerted resistance that autumn in Yorkshire, Yorkist propaganda played on southern fears that men from poor, remote parts of the realm were being promised that they could plunder southern wealth. The prince of Wales wrote denying this allegation.[111] But denials were in vain. According to Clement Paston, 'the people in the north rob and steal, and [have] been appointed to pillage all this country, and give away men's goods and livelihoods in all the south country, and that will ask a mischief'.[112] The conduct of the queen's army seemed to confirm Yorkist propaganda. Abbot Whethamstede of St Albans prevailed on Henry VI to make proclamation against pillage in the aftermath of the battle there, but, he says, to no avail: 'For they were all at liberty and licenced, as they asserted, by the Queen and Northern lords, to plunder and seize anything they could find anywhere on this side of the Trent, by way of remuneration and recompense for their services.'[113] In a vain attempt to reassure the Londoners, the queen withdrew her army to Dunstable − to protect the goods of the Londoners, according to the author of the *Annales*, who thought this was a calamitous decision for the Lancastrian cause: 'Et hoc fuit destructio regis Henrici et reginae suae.'[114] In September 1470, by proclamation, Warwick forbade his soldiers to loot and rape, and at the start of the 1487 campaign Henry VII issued detailed ordinances designed to protect civilians' rights from outrage by his army. In 1487 Lincoln and Lovell seem to have made a great effort to discipline their foreign troops after their difficult march across the Pennines – 'Edward VI' wrote to the citizens of York promising to pay for victuals, and Vergil noted that Lincoln entered Yorkshire 'offering no harm to the local inhabitants, for he hoped some of the people would rally to his side'.[115] In 1489, playing on memories of the northern invasion of 1461, Henry VII proclaimed that the Yorkshire rebels intended 'to rob, despoil, and destroy all the south parts of this his realm, and to subdue and bring to captivity the people of the same'.[116] When Warbeck invaded Northumberland with James IV, he was upset by the Scots' impolitic plundering: he 'besought the king to harry his [Warbeck's] people no further and to damage his native land with no more flames'.[117]

Whatever the good intentions of commanders, it must have been difficult for them to prevent their men from oppressing non-participants – especially difficult if pay was in arrears or not controlled by them, or if troops were poor and ill equipped. Commanders' difficulties in accumulating victuals made them acquiesce in their men's procuring of crops, beasts, ale. When harvests had been poor, or when, as in 1460–1 and 1462–3, campaigning continued in winter, foraging doubtless caused regional hardships. Moreover, after battles and sieges, it was hard, as it always has been, to control troops whose blood was up, and to prevent the injuries to non-participants which Abbot Whethamstede recounted with horror. Two documents perhaps reflect the anxiety of commanders to protect individuals from their soldiers' depredations. March, Warwick and Salisbury issued a safe-conduct under their signets, dated London, 24 August 1460, to the Bridgwater merchant John Davy to protect his goods from pillage.[118] Possibly during the campaigns of 1469–71, Clarence issued letters of protection forbidding on pain of death the spoliation of Lord Mountjoy's manors of Barton and Elveston (Derbyshire) or of any of his servants, farmers or tenants there or elsewhere.[119]

There are numerous allusions to losses inflicted by land and sea. The Yorkist lords at Ludlow complained to Henry VI in October 1459 that 'our lordships and tenants [have] been of high violence robbed and spoiled'.[120] The town of Warwick may have been one of the places alluded to.[121] After the Yorkist lords' flight, a partisan chronicler alleged that York's town of Ludlow 'was robbed to the bare walls'.[122] Waurin says that the devastation of the Yorkist lords' lands was general.[123] The versifying parson of Calais, unable to reach his benefice because of the Yorkist lords' presence there, alleged that they plundered by land and sea: Warwick certainly seized merchant ships on his voyage thence to Ireland.[124] Late in 1460 the queen's army in Yorkshire plundered the duke of York's and the earl of Salisbury's tenants: York's manor of Sandal suffered losses and no herons nested in the park that year.[125] But Professor Lander's suggestion that 'rumours and tradition seem to have exaggerated' the horrors of her army's advance southwards may well be right.[126] Though the chroniclers who recounted the plundering were mostly Yorkist in sympathy, they reflected the widespread southern belief that her soldiers were exceptionally ill behaved – and beliefs can be as potent in their effects as deeds. Southern reactions may have been decisive for the dynastic conflict. The conviction that the Lancastrian cause was associated with northern threats to south-eastern prosperity, and that Edward and Warwick were sure shields against them, may have persuaded many people in some of the wealthiest parts of the realm reluctantly to reject their traditional allegiance and accept a usurper.

In the years following 1461 it was the extremities of the realm which endured depredations. Property in Carlisle suffered damage as a result of the Lancastrian siege in 1461.[127] In 1463 Edward IV granted £100 to Alnwick abbey, in recompense for its losses in goods at the hands of French and Scots, and of the Yorkist force which had besieged Alnwick castle.[128] An inventory from Durham priory recorded that in 1464 the value of the priory's properties in Norhamshire and Islandshire (now part of Northumberland) was reduced by the depredations of the Lancastrian rebels, particularly by the occupation of Sir Ralph Percy's and Sir Ralph Grey's men.[129] In 1468 the bailiffs and burgesses of Bamburgh were allowed by the crown remissions in their fee farm 'on account of the losses which they have sustained from the king's enemies of France and the rebels, who held the town and castle as a refuge' in 1462–4.[130] The Welsh too suffered in the 1460s. In verses addressed to Lord Herbert, the poet Guto'r Glyn refers to the 'total war and slaughter' which Herbert's expedition against Lancastrian rebels loosed in Gwynedd. In fact the poet pleaded with Herbert to moderate vengeance: 'be not Savage, loosing fire on men'.[131]

The outbreaks of domestic conflict in England in 1469–71 once more posed threats to communities which had been free from them for ten years. In 1470 the Kentishmen committed depredations in Southwark.[132] The next year, under the Bastard's indulgent leadership, they were once more swarming over the London suburbs in search of pickings. Kentishmen and shipmen led away fifty of the hundred oxen which the London butcher William Gould was grazing in a meadow by the Tower – their meat, intended for Elizabeth Wydeville's household, presumably graced the rebels' tables.[133] The recent West Country operations had also involved some depredations. The Lancastrian army sacked the bishop's palace at Wells (Somerset), and Edward's army, after its deprivations and victory, entered town and monastery at Tewkesbury with violence, despoiling many people and stealing monastic goods.[134]

The later risings and invasions of the 1480s and '90s probably caused only desultory damage. In 1483 the Kentish rebels were reported as saying that they intended to rob London.[135] Henry VII, a conscientious man not hardened in warfare, in 1485 authorized the disbursement of £72. 2s. 4d. to townships whose harvests had been seized by him and his army on the way to Bosworth field, and the following month the abbot of Merevale, near Atherstone (Warwicks.), was granted 100 marks for his house's losses resulting from the army's march.[136]

There is, however, a dearth of evidence about the general economic effects of campaigns, which has led to the frequent assumption that the effects were negligible. The assumption is supported by evidence of the continued normal functioning of royal administration – but this may not have always been the case. In April 1470 Thomas Flemmyng, esquire, former escheator of Surrey and Sussex, was pardoned debts owed to the king: 'owing to rebellions and insurrections in divers parts of England' he dared not carry out his office.[137] In 1472 debts were pardoned to Thomas Tempest owed for the shrievalty of Lincoln by his late brother Sir Richard, who 'lost a great part of the profits which should have accrued to him in office and was hindered from exercising it by an insurrection in that county' and was removed from office by the rebels.[138] Robert Throckmarton, appointed sheriff of Warwickshire and Leicestershire soon after the battle of Bosworth, was pardoned arrears of account in February 1486 on his petition that, in the period of about a month in which he had occupied the office, he could not execute it to the king's profit, 'in which time of [his] occupation was within this your realm such rebellion and trouble, and your laws not established'.[139]

Dr Reynolds has written that the wars' effects on trade and urban life 'look fairly limited'; overseas trade may have been especially vulnerable to disruption.[140] The royal embargo on trade with Calais during the winter of 1459–60, and the Readeption government's war with Burgundy, threatened the main arteries of English trade, which were particularly dominated by London merchants.[141] Overseas trade probably suffered also by the impressment of ships into royal service to assist against rebellion and threats of invasion: the support that the Lancastrians received from Bristol in 1471 may have been stimulated partly by exasperation at Edward's shipping demands in the 1460s.[142]

The passage of armies may, in varying circumstances, have stimulated sales, reduced potential profits, or caused food shortages.[143] Rumours about their lines of march may have disrupted trade more than their actual destructiveness. The Shrewsbury bailiff's account for 1458–9 graphically reflects tensions among the townsmen during the 1459 rebellion. They were threatened with possible sack, or loss of privileges and patronage, if they backed the losing side, as they may have done in 1452 in response to York's summons. Men were dispatched in 1459 to negotiate with the king and others at Nottingham, and to reply to a royal letter; as the campaign developed, others were dispatched to ascertain the truth about reports of Salisbury's victory at Blore Heath, about the route he was taking and the situation between the king and the opposing lords at Worcester, and to take a letter to the duke of York and receive his reply. Watches were set at gates and bridges, and a banner was bought for the day watch in the tower of St Mary's church.[144]

It is unlikely that in these circumstances the normal flow of commerce continued through Shrewsbury – circumstances paralleled in many other towns during the wars. Shrewsbury was to feel threatened again. In January 1461 the burgesses were probably apprehensive about the advance of the forces of the earls of Pembroke and Wiltshire from Wales. In 1468 they feared assault by the Welsh Lancastrians. In 1485 the Welsh and their foreign allies at last stood at the gates; the townsmen put up a token resistance of twenty-four hours, probably in the hope of escaping Richard III's wrath and of negotiating guarantees of good conduct by Henry Tudor's dubious army.[145]

For Shrewsbury in 1459 – and for other towns – escape from physical involvement still entailed expense: repairs to defences had to be made, arms had to be bought, guards, spies and messengers paid. A commission was appointed in February 1471, on petition in parliament, by the burgesses and inhabitants of Great Yarmouth for pardon of a great part of their fee farm owed to the crown, because of the port's decline. Among other expenses Yarmouth men listed 'watches for defence against the king's enemies, the repair of the walls of the town and the cleansing of the moats, bombards and powder for the defence of the town'.[146]

Moreover, since ready supplies of money were concentrated in towns and soldiers could be quickly recruited there, townsmen probably contributed disproportionately to the costs of warfare. The surviving evidence suggests that leading towns were obliged to provide large numbers of paid-up companies for the campaigns of 1460–3. Royal demands for such – and for financial and material aid – were frequent in the wars (the Coventry and Norwich archives contain particularly full records of war taxation). But, since the evidence for contributions in urban archives is generally patchy, it remains unclear whether such demands were repeatedly wide, and whether they imposed a significant burden on many towns. K. J. Allison's analysis of war expenses incurred by Hull shows that the conflict 'had seriously depleted Hull's financial resources and the chamberlains in 1460–1 ended their year in office with a huge deficit'. In the years 1461–4 the inhabitants had to make heavy contributions in victuals, shipping, money and soldiers for the king's forces in the north. In 1468–9 they sent twelve soldiers; in

1470 thirty-two, to support the king. Not surprisingly, Hull refused to admit the suppliant Edward in 1471.[147]

When Edward IV was at Durham in the winter of 1462, the prior handed him a bill petitioning for compensation for the 400 marks that Margaret of Anjou had forcibly borrowed from the house, and for the total of £66. 9s. 4d. which the earl of Northumberland and other Lancastrians had borrowed. The prior also wrote to Lady FitzHugh (Warwick's sister), among others, complaining about the money which Margaret 'had of me, utterly against my will, through dread and fear of her and other lords of her counsel, at that time having rule of these North parties'.[148] The Lancastrians had wrung out the wealth of Durham priory, and its experience is unlikely to have been unique. There was a price to be paid for non-participants' relative immunity from sack and disruption in the Wars of the Roses: they had to find much of the war finance. Chroniclers' comments imply that men thought they were having to shoulder a heavy burden of war taxation in the early 1460s.[149] Much has been written in recent years about the relative wealth of Englishmen in the fifteenth century, and the optimism of their elites, with the Wars of the Roses as puffs of cloud on the horizon. But for many non-participants, the strife involved heavy financial burdens: the fact that recurrent demands were for hated internecine strife, not glorious war against foreigners, probably soured feelings further.

Moreover, it would be misleading to see the violence of the wars as more or less satisfactorily contained between the combatants, with a minimal spillage into the lives of non-participants. For the origin of the wars themselves lay in Henry VI's inability in the 1440s to contain the spread of local faction and violence, inherent in the elites' concern for property, office and influence. The outbreak of major revolts from the 1450s onwards and the relative political weakness of novel rulers, both kings and magnates, increased existing social tensions and gave opportunities for the violent pursuit of quarrels and for haphazard mayhem.

Fear of sack in London in 1461, like the passage of soldiers through Nottingham in 1459, provoked individual quarrels.[150] Governors and commons in London sometimes differed sharply in their attitudes to approaching armies.[151] Scores were settled under the cloak of general conflict. John Stafford, who loved Sir William Lucy's wife, had him killed in the confusion at the end of the battle of Northampton.[152] John Paston the youngest described how Norfolk misdoers exploited the dynastic struggles of 1460–1:

there was a certain person forthwith after the journey at Wakefield, gathered fellowship to have murdered John Damme, as is said; and also there is at the Castle of Rising, and in other two places, made great gathering of people, and hiring of harness, and it is well understood they be not to the King ward, but rather the contrary, and for to rob. . . . my brother has ridden to Yarmouth for to let [prevent] bribers that would have robbed a ship under colour of my Lord of Warwick, and belong nothing to him ward [are unconnected with him].[153]

Humphrey Neville of Brancepeth's 'Lancastrian' revolts of the 1460s may have been basically the pursuit of his feud with Durham priory, whose prior wrote in October 1461 to the chancellor George Neville (Warwick's brother) that Humphrey had been 'a cummerouse man to me and my house, and if he come again to our country to have liberty and rule, as he had afore, I dread that I and my brethren shall not rejoice our goods in peace'.[154] Soon after Edward's restoration in 1471, a defendant before the mayor of London's court alleged that a property had been wrongfully occupied in the recent 'troublous season' and that the occupier 'menaced him to flee and also openly noised him that he was a false traitor to Henry late called King of England the sixth'.[155] The wars had emboldened and hardened misdoers, according to one commentator, author of the speech drafted for the 1474 parliament, who alluded to 'the multitude of the misdoers, the readiness of them to mischievous and adventurous deeds by custom had and taken therein during the time of this long trouble and dissension'.[156] The proclamation which Henry VII made immediately after the battle of Bosworth vividly suggests how misdoers were accustomed to exploit uncertain and disordered situations after battles:

upon pain of death, that no manner of man rob or spoil no manner of commons coming from the field; but suffer them to pass home to their countries and dwelling-places, with their horse and harness. And, moreover, that no manner of man take upon him to go to no gentleman's place, neither in the country, nor within cities nor boroughs, nor pick no quarrels for old or for new matters; but keep the king's peace, upon pain of hanging etc.[157]

Gentlefolk were quick to take advantage of the disturbed conditions in the realm by defiantly holding and besieging castles, even by fighting private battles, to gain advantages in their quarrels. In November 1460 two esquires, John and William Knyvet, occupied Buckenham castle (Norfolk), despite its being in the king's hands. When Sir Gilbert Debenham and other royal commissioners entered the outer ward of the castle to remove them, in February 1461, they could get no further than the foot of the raised drawbridge over the moat surrounding the inner ward. This was being held in defensive array by a garrison of about fifty, for whom John Knyvet's wife Alice spoke defiantly from a little tower over the inner foot of the drawbridge: 'if ye begin to break the peace or make any war to get the place of me I shall defend me, for liever I had in such wise to die than to be slain when my husband cometh home, for he charged me to keep it'. The royal commissioners were nonplussed by this.[158]

In August 1469, just after the battle of Edgcote had given Warwick shaky control of the realm, the duke of Norfolk commenced a regular siege of Caister castle (Norfolk), in which he and the defender, John Paston the younger, used cannon. Paston was eventually forced to capitulate.[159] In March 1470, when Edward was defending his crown in the north, Viscount Lisle and Lord Berkeley arranged through their heralds to fight a pitched battle at Nibley Green (Gloucs.); in the bloody little conflict Lisle was killed.[160]

Historians of the Hundred Years War have been particularly concerned to trace gains as well as losses, and to assess their general social effects.[161] Some of the Hundred Years War's characteristic avenues of profit – ravaging, and ransoming noble prisoners – were partly barred in the Wars of the Roses, because of their particular political character. Nevertheless, forfeitures for treason and dynastic changes provided opportunities to gain estates, offices, annuities and chattels. The rise in status of some participants – not always sustained – was due in part or wholly to their military services. Fauconberg's elevation to the earldom of Kent in 1462 is probably a case in point.[162] Warwick's brother John Neville is said to have been granted the earldom of Northumberland as a reward for his victories in 1464, and Herbert the earldom of Pembroke for capturing Harlech castle.[163]

The Hundred Years War, if it did not create the English professional soldier, mightily advanced his sphere of opportunities. The Wars of the Roses helped to maintain the profession, threatened with unemployment by the dramatic loss of most of its French stamping-grounds in the 1440s and '50s.[164] Urgent demands for soldiers in the domestic emergencies tended to drive wage rates up. In November 1459 the crown was arranging to pay Somerset's and Rivers's 1,000 men 6d. a day, the rate granted by Norwich to its company in January 1461.[165] But in 1461–2 Nottingham hired ten men to fight in the north for two months at 8d. a day, and in 1469 Coventry, recruiting to support the king against Robin of Redesdale, 'could get no soldier under xd. a day, and so they were paid'.[166] In April 1470 Coventry made a levy to pay forty soldiers to accompany the king southwards against Clarence and Warwick, waged for a month at 12d. a day.[167] This was the rate which Rivers's horsemen received for their service to the crown in Kent in 1471, and which the city of York contracted to give eighty men for ten days in 1485, to support Richard III.[168]

A glimpse of the hiring of professional soldiers is provided by a letter of 1468 from Sir John Paston to his brother, giving an account of the four he was providing to help safeguard Caister castle against the duke of Norfolk's menaces:

> they be proved men, and cunning in the war, and in feats of arms, and they can well shoot both guns and crossbows and amend and string them, and devise bulwarks, or any things that should be a strength to the place; and they will, as need is, keep watch and ward. They be sad and well advised men, saving one of them, which is bald, and called William Peny, which is as good a man as goeth on the earth, saving a little he will, as I understand, be a little copschotyn [high-crested], but yet he is no brawler, but full of courtesy.[169]

Sir John may have been able to hire good men with comparative ease because there was then little domestic military employment − in such periods English soldiers tended to go abroad into Burgundian service.[170] Those who stayed were probably often seen (as has frequently been the case in England) as a disruptive burden, brawlers and beggars. The author of the 1474 speech in parliament argued that one benefit of war with France would be that 'the men of war, that had none other purveyance' would 'be set in garrisons and live by their wages, which else were like to continue the mischief in this land that they now do'.[171] Unemployed English soldiers, at home and on the Continent, prepared for desperate ventures in the hope of gain, may have formed a pool of support for dynastic pretenders in the 1480s and '90s. The brevity of the English invasions of France in 1475 and 1492 and of Scotland in 1482 must have been sorely disappointing to professionals. One can glimpse some of them on the crusade of Granada in May 1486, distinguishing themselves at the siege of Loja, where Sir Edward Wydeville led a company of 300 Englishmen. In 1488 men flocked to Southampton to join Wydeville's expedition to Brittany. When it was countermanded, 200 of them set off without royal licence in a Breton ship to try their fortunes. Next year Henry VII's occupation of Breton ports in defence of the duchess Anne against the French crown seemed to be reopening a traditional field of English military activity, but the French victory at St Aubin-du-Cormier, where the English were allowed no quarter, dashed such hopes.[172]

Though non-combatants paid heavily towards the costs of the Wars of the Roses, some profited. During most major campaigns, when well-disciplined armies passed through towns, their markets doubtless boomed, sucking in the hinterland's produce. London, Coventry, Nottingham, Newcastle and York were among the principal beneficiaries. When Henry VII visited York it was 'drunk dry'.[173]

Cloth production was stimulated by the demand for uniforms, 'bends', etc.[174] There was need for weapons and armour. In 1472 the crown commissioned two specialists from as far afield as Ecclesfield and Sheffield to take smiths for the manufacture of arrowheads in Yorkshire.[175] Arms and armour were often imported, particularly from Brabant. In 1482 Harry Bryan at Calais wrote to George Cely at Bruges: 'I must within this eight days send you word to pray you to lay out money for six hor[se] harness for my lord of Buckingham.'[176]

English 'merchant venturers' – particularly Londoners – probably profited from entrepreneurial roles in importing war *matériel* or purchasing it from native manufacturers. On 28 September 1459 Henry Waver, citizen and draper of London, appeared in the mayor's court and declared that his enemies had charged him in the king's household and elsewhere with having 'contrary to the king's most dreadful commandment now of late . . . sold furnished and stuffed for the earl of Warwick divers harness and armour'. He deposed that the previous month he had possessed 29 'harneys of milen [Milan] touche', which on 2 September he had sold in London to William Eliot, citizen and mercer, for twenty-nine 'buttes of red rommeney', and denied the sale of any harness or armour for Warwick's use.[177] In 1467 reference was made to the purchase by the master of the king's ordnance, John Wode, of gunpowder to the value of £559. 10s. 8d. from the London grocer John Nicolle.[178]

England has often been depicted as a realm which in the fifteenth and sixteenth centuries was becoming more unified on several levels – in economic development, political organization, and national sentiment. How may the Wars of the Roses have affected such developments? As regards the economy, it seems unlikely that they caused general falls of production and shortages. They may indeed have provided local stimuli, particularly helpful to the commercial dominance of leading towns of the eastern seaboard and Midlands. In politics, they were the major cause of that revival and development of royal authority whose consequences are reflected so strikingly in Edmund Dudley's treatise, *The Tree of Commonwealth*.[179]

It is easy to fall into anachronistic traps when discussing 'national sentiment' in the later Middle Ages. Nevertheless, it does seem that the Hundred Years War and the involvement of natives in economic competition with aliens developed a common sense of national identity, on occasion expressed by 'the commons', as well as by the elites of gentlefolk and merchants among whom it was strongest.[180] But, as the second Crowland continuator and other chroniclers bewailed, the Wars of the Roses were internecine struggles. The terms in which armies are often described make it clear that they might be distinguished as the levies of a particular shire or group of shires. The attack at St Albans in

1455 of the 'marchmen' – from the Marches towards Scotland – was remarked on; at Blore Heath northerners battered a force from Cheshire and Shropshire.[181] The Yorkist lords marched on Northampton in 1460 'with much other people of Kent, Sussex, and Essex'.[182] A poem celebrated the lord's victory there, accompanied by 'the true commoners of Kent'.[183] Chroniclers assert that the queen's army which invaded the south in 1461 was mainly a northern one. She was opposed by a great army drawn from Kent, Essex, Norfolk and Suffolk,[184] and soon afterwards March and Warwick entered London with an army of 'Western men and Welshmen, Kents men and Essex men together'.[185] Predominantly northern armies stood against predominantly southern ones at Ferrybridge and Towton. In 1469 there were distinct northern, western, Kentish (and Welsh) forces in the field; in 1470 a Lincolnshire army operated on its own, and in 1471 so did armies from East Anglia and neighbouring counties, the West Country, and Kent and Essex.

But men often fought against their neighbours, and often forged ties with allied arrays from distant shires. Despite the antagonism of Kentishmen and northerners in 1460–1, in 1469 'communitas de Kente, et communitas ex boriale parte Anglie' rose separately with a common aim.[186] Nevertheless, frequent clashes between levies from unfamiliar shires are likely to have hardened natural antipathies. So was the passage of strangers through communities, not only Welshmen, Cornishmen and others whose native tongue was not English, but Englishmen whose speech seemed thick to the inhabitants. As we have seen, a Nottingham man was moved in 1459 to doubt the honesty of passing northern soldiers. A few years later, another Nottingham man viewed Edward as the Kentishmen's king. One shire's pride in reforming the realm may have sometimes seemed a humiliating imposition to other shires.

On the whole the wars probably increased local patriotism at the expense of an embryonic sense of English nationality. London chroniclers recounting the campaigns of 1460–1 were indignant at what one of them termed 'the malice of the Northermen'.[187] When, in January 1461, the northerners' approach southward was rumoured, Clement Paston described the southern levies' eagerness to attack them: 'My Lords that be here have as much as they may do to keep down all this country more than four or five shires, for they would be up on the men in north, for it is for the weal of all the south.'[188] Abbot Whethamstede of St Albans harped on the warlike, penurious and plundering nature of the northerners, and saw the conflict from Wakefield to Towton as a revolt by them against the south.[189] The endurance of such attitudes is perhaps reflected in Henry VII's proclamation of 1489 asserting that the Yorkshire rebels intended the destruction of the south.[190] But the view of northerners current in East Anglia, the East Midlands and the south-east was not necessarily shared elsewhere. A monk of Crowland abbey in Lincolnshire saw them as deliverers of the English in 1469 from invasion by the Welsh, so puffed up that they thought to gain the mastery of England.[191] A Gloucester monk, more frightened by the Welsh than the northerners, was similarly relieved by the Welsh defeat.[192]

Generally the effects of the wars may have been to stiffen shire communities' resolve to rely on their own military strength and that of their neighbours, and to hesitate over relying on co-operation with strangers, or on moving far from their own 'countries' to combat them. In 1469 the western men apparently deserted their Welsh allies, and the Kentishmen gave minimal aid to their Yorkshire ones. In 1470 the Lincolnshiremen fought on their own in defence of their shire. In 1471 Yorkshire, East Anglian, Midlands, West Country, Welsh, northern and south-eastern opponents of Edward gave him victory against the odds as a result of failures to co-ordinate. In 1483 the southern English rebels seem to have moved timidly: south-eastern and south-western groups failed to link up. The débâcles can be explained in terms of the personal deficiencies of magnate leaders: perhaps the limited horizons of shire communities were more of a constraint on their strategy than has been recognized.

Memories of inter-provincial antagonisms, which had sharpened particularly in the campaigns of 1459–61 and 1469–71, may have increased the difficulty of launching national military efforts. In 1489 Yorkshiremen jibbed at helping to finance a Breton war that was of concern to southern coastal communities; in 1497 Westcountrymen felt similarly about financing a war with Scotland in aid of Marcher security. Provincial movements against Henry VII in 1486, 1487, 1489 and 1497 failed to widen the scope of their appeal. One legacy of the Wars of the Roses which helped to strengthen royal authority against rebellion was a tradition of inter-regional distrust, demonstrated in the resolutely provincial character of Tudor rebellions.

Appendix

Campaigning Periods, 1455–85

The totals given are the minimum numbers of mostly continuous days on which one or more major forces were in arms. The sum total suggests that there was an equivalent in the period of at least sixty-one weeks' domestic campaigning. The majority of campaigns appear to have lasted not much more than three weeks. The most prolonged and intensive were those of 1462–3 and 1471; in 1460, 1461 and 1470 there was prolonged campaigning but more sporadic fighting. The length given for Edward IV's first royal campaign, in 1461, may appear excessive: it includes the time after Towton when he and some of his forces remained on a war footing in the north to consolidate his position there.

	Number of days
1455	
18 May: Yorkist lords in arms (Armstrong, 17).	
22 May: first battle of St Albans.	5
1459	
Henry VI in the field 'thirty days or thereabouts' (*Rot. Parl.*, V, 348).	30
1460	
26 June: Yorkist lords in arms in Kent (Stone, 79).	
10 July: battle of Northampton.	
19 July: surrender of the Tower of London (*Benet's Chron.*, 227n).	24
9 December (or several days earlier): Yorkist lords go north (*ibid.*, 228 and n).	
30 December: battle of Wakefield.	22

Number of days

1461

2 or 3 February: battle of Mortimer's Cross (*ibid.*, 229 and n).

17 February: second battle of St Albans.

26 February: Yorkist lords enter London (*ibid.*, 229 and n).   24

13 March: Edward IV sets out northwards (*ibid.*, 230 and n).

29 March: battle of Towton.

1 May: Edward enters Newcastle (Scofield, I, 175).   50

1462–3

25 October: Lancastrian invasion of Northumberland (Ross, *Edward IV*, 50).

6 January: Scottish raid on Alnwick (*Chronicles of London*, 178).   74

1469

5 July: Edward reaches Stamford in arms (Ross, *Edward IV*, 129).

26 July: battle of Edgcote.   22

1470

6 March: Edward sets out from London – assembly date for Lincolnshire levies (*ibid.*, 140).

14 April: Edward reaches Exeter (*ibid.*, 145).   40

13 September: Warwick's invasion (Scofield, I, 536).

6 October: Warwick enters London (*ibid.*, 541–2).   24

1471

14 March: Edward lands at Ravenspur (*Arrivall*, 2).

27 May: Bastard of Fauconberg submits (Richmond, 'Fauconberg's Kentish rising of May 1471', 682).   75

1483

18 October: various risings (*Rot. Parl.*, VI, 244ff.).

8 November: Richard III at Exeter (Chrimes, 26n).   22

1485

7 August: landing of Henry Tudor (*ibid.*, 40).

22 August: battle of Bosworth.   16

Total number of days   428

Glossary

aforerider	see *forerider*
avant coureur	see *scourer*
battle	main or large body of soldiers
bend	riband, band or strap often worn to display allegiance
bombard	cannon throwing very large shot
brigandine	body armour composed of iron rings or small thin iron plates, sewn on canvas, linen or leather, and covered over with similar materials
caltrop	spiked iron ball used to obstruct cavalry; snare to trap feet and hooves
covey	type of gun
crapaud	type of gun
culverin	type of cannon
forerider	scout; one who rides ahead of an army or as part of its vanguard
foreward	first line or 'battle' of an army; vanguard
fowler	type of light cannon
harbinger	one sent ahead of an army to secure lodgings; advanced company sent out to prepare camping ground
middleward	middle body or 'battle' of an army
mortar	short type of ordnance with large bore and steep trajectory
pavis	shield large enough to cover the whole body
sallet	light globular helmet, either with or without a vizor, but lacking a crest
scourer, scurrier	scout; one sent out to reconnoitre
serpentine	type of cannon
ward	one of the three main divisions of an army – the van, middle and rear wards or 'battles'

Abbreviations

BIHR	*Bulletin of the Institute of Historical Research*
CCR	*Calendar of Close Rolls*
CDS	*Calendar of Documents Relating to Scotland*
CP	*The Complete Peerage*
CPR	*Calendar of Patent Rolls*
CSP	*Calendar of State Papers*
EETS	Early English Text Society
EHR	*English Historical Review*
HMC	*Royal Commission on Historical Manuscripts*
PRO	Public Record Office
Rot. Parl.	*Rotuli Parliamentorum*
TRHS	*Transactions of the Royal Historical Society*
VCH	*Victoria History of the Counties of England*

Notes

Introduction

1 S. Anglo, *Spectacle, Pageantry and Early Tudor Policy* (Oxford 1969), 36n. For popular references to York and March as a rose in 1460–1, C. L. Kingsford, *English History in Contemporary Poetry*, II (London 1913), 40–1; 'Gregory', 215. In 1460 York had displayed his livery of the fetterlock ('Gregory', 208); in 1556–7 Edward Courtenay, earl of Devon, was described in a list of Paduan students as 'Curtinek nob. anglus ex regia Albae Rosae britannorum familia' (A. Goodman, *A History of England from Edward II to James I* (London 1977), 300, 333).

2 Anglo, 36–7, 36n.

3 See some of the political verses in *Historical Poems of the XIVth and XVth Centuries*, ed. R. H. Robbins (New York 1959).

4 See below, pp. 151, 203.

5 *Rot. Parl.*, V, 463–4.

6 For what follows on Henry's career, S. B. Chrimes, *Henry VII* (London 1972); for the interpretation of Henry's view of English history, A. Goodman, 'Henry VII and Christian renewal', *Religion and Humanism. Studies in Church History*, 17, Ecclesiastical History Society (Oxford 1980).

7 Anglo, 44–5; *Historiae Croylandensis Continuatio*, ed. W. Fulman (Oxford 1684), 542–3.

8 Bouchard, *Les croniques Annales des pays dangleterre et Bretaigne* (Paris 1581), especially fols li *seq.*; cf. Goodman, 'Henry VII and Christian renewal'.

9 P. S. Lewis, 'Two pieces of fifteenth-century political iconography', *Journal of the Warburg and Courtauld Institutes*, 27 (1964), 319–20; Dominic Mancini, *The Usurpation of Richard III*, ed. C. A. J. Armstrong (Oxford 1969), 24–5; Goodman, 'Henry VII and Christian renewal'.

10 Bernard André, *De vita atque gestis Henrici septimi ... historia*, in *Memorials of King Henry the Seventh*, ed. J. Gairdner (Rolls ser. 1858), 9–11, 13–14, 68.

11 *Memorials*, lvi ff; Edinburgh, National Library of Scotland, Adv. MS 33. 2. 24 (Ogilvie's address); cf. Goodman, 'Henry VII and Christian renewal'.

12 Goodman, 'Henry VII and Christian renewal'.

13 D. Hay, *Polydore Vergil* (Oxford 1952), 141ff; M. McKisack, *Medieval History in the Tudor Age* (Oxford 1971), 105ff; J. R. Lander, *Crown and Nobility 1450–1509* (London 1976), 57 and n; M. Aston, 'Richard II and the Wars of the Roses', in *The Reign of Richard II*, ed. F. R. H. Du Boulay and C. M. Barron (London 1971), 280ff.

14 D. Hume, *The History of England*, III (London 1834), 307–8; first published in 1762.

15 Sir John Fortescue, *The Governance of England*, ed. Charles Plummer (Oxford 1885), 127–30.

16 *Ibid.*, 14ff.

17 K. B. McFarlane, 'Parliament and "bastard feudalism" ', *TRHS*, 4th ser., 26 (1944); 'Bastard feudalism', *BIHR*, 20 (1947). The Ford Lectures were published in McFarlane, *The Nobility of Later Medieval England* (Oxford 1973).

18 K. B. McFarlane, 'The Wars of the Roses', *Proceedings of the British Academy*, 50 (1964), 95ff. Dr J. A. F. Thomson has suggested that dynastic loyalties may have been a stronger political motive among nobles and gentry than McFarlane allowed ('The Courtenay Family in the Yorkist Period', *BIHR*, 45 (1972), 244–5).

19 R. L. Storey, *The End of the House of Lancaster* (London 1966); C. Ross, *Edward IV* (London 1974); see also Lander, *Crown and Nobility*, and D. A. L. Morgan, 'The King's Affinity in the Polity of Yorkist England', *TRHS*, 5th ser., 23 (1973).

20 C. Ross, *The Wars of the Roses* (London 1976).

21 Storey, *End of the House of Lancaster*; R. A. Griffiths, 'Local rivalries and national politics: the Percies, the Nevilles, and the Duke of Exeter, 1452–1455', *Speculum*, 43 (1968); cf. also M. A. Hicks, 'Dynastic Change and Northern Society: the Career of the Fourth Earl of Northumberland, 1470–89', *Northern History*, 14 (1978).

22 Some of the battles were briskly reconstructed by the late Lt.-Col. A. H. Burne in *The Battlefields of England* (London 1950) and *More Battlefields of England* (London 1952).

23 Storey, *End of the House of Lancaster*, 98ff.

24 Whethamstede in *Registra quorundam Abbatum Monasterii S. Albani*, ed. H. T. Riley, I (Rolls ser. 1872); C. L. Kingsford, *English Historical Literature in the Fifteenth Century* (Oxford 1913), 151–4.

25 *Historiae Croylandensis Continuatio*, ed. Fulman; translated by H. T.

Riley in *Ingulph's Chronicle* (etc.) (London 1854); see A. Hanham, *Richard III and His Early Historians* (Oxford 1975), 74ff.

26 *John Benet's Chronicle for the years 1400 to 1462*, ed. G. L. Harriss and M. A. Harriss, in *Camden Miscellany*, vol. XXIV (London 1972), 151ff.

27 *Annales rerum anglicanum* (henceforth referred to as *Annales*) in *Letters and Papers Illustrative of the Wars of the English in France*, ed. J. Stevenson, II, pt 2 (Rolls ser. 1864); K. B. McFarlane, 'William Worcester, A Preliminary Survey', in *Studies Presented to Sir Hilary Jenkinson*, ed. J. Conway Davies (London 1957), 206–7; William Worcestre, *Itineraries*, ed. and trans. J. H. Harvey (Oxford 1969).

28 *The Anglica Historia of Polydore Vergil A.D. 1485–1537*, trans. D. Hay (Camden ser. 1950); *Three Books of Polydore Vergil's English History . . . from an early translation*, ed. Sir Henry Ellis (Camden Soc. 1844); cf. Hay, *Polydore Vergil*.

29 Kingsford, *English Historical Literature*, 70ff.

30 *An English Chronicle from 1377 to 1461*, ed. J. S. Davies (Camden Soc. 1856); see Kingsford, *English Historical Literature*, 127–9.

31 Printed in *The Historical Collections of a London Citizen in the Fifteenth Century*, ed. J. Gairdner (Camden Soc. 1876) and referred to henceforth as 'Gregory'. Cf. Kingsford, *English Historical Literature*, 96–8, and J. A. F. Thomson, 'The Continuation of "Gregory's Chronicle" – A Possible Author?', *British Museum Quarterly*, 36 (1971–2), 92ff.

32 Warkworth, *A Chronicle of the First Thirteen Years of the Reign of King Edward the Fourth*, ed. J. O. Halliwell (Camden Soc. 1839); Kingsford, *English Historical Literature*, 171–2; Lander, *Crown and Nobility*, 259–61 and 260n.

33 *Chronicle of the Rebellion in Lincolnshire, 1470*, ed. J. G. Nichols (Camden Soc. 1847).

34 *Historie of the Arrivall of King Edward IV, A.D. 1471*, ed. J. Bruce (Camden Soc. 1838); cf. J. A. F. Thomson, ' "The Arrivall of Edward IV" – The Development of the Text', *Speculum*, 46 (1971).

35 A. Goodman and A. MacKay, 'A Castilian report on English affairs, 1486', *EHR*, 88 (1973), 92ff.

36 *The Paston Letters 1422–1509*, 3 vols, ed. J. Gairdner (Edinburgh 1910). Two volumes of Professor N. Davies's definitive edition, *Paston Letters and Papers of the Fifteenth Century* (Oxford 1971–6) have been published. In this book the 1910 edition by Gairdner has been used.

37 *Plumpton Correspondence*, ed. T. Stapleton (Camden Soc. 1839); *The Stonor Letters and Papers 1290–1483*, ed. C. L. Kingsford, 2 vols (Camden ser. 1919); J. Taylor, 'The Plumpton Letters, 1416–1552', *Northern Hist.*, 10 (1975).

38 Basin, *Histoire de Louis XI*, ed. C. Samaran and M.-C. Garand, I–II (Paris 1963–6).

39 Commynes, *Memoirs*, editions by J. Calmette, III (Paris 1925); M. Jones (London 1972); S. Kinser and I. Cazeaux, II (Columbia, S. Carolina 1973).

40 Chastellain, *Chronique*, in *Oeuvres*, IV–V, ed. K. de Lettenhove (Brussels 1864); *Chronique de Jean Molinet*, ed. G. Doutrepont and O. Jodogne, I–II (Brussels 1935).

41 Waurin, *Recuiel des Croniques et Anchiennes Istories de la Grant Bretagne, à present nommé Engleterre*, 5 vols, ed. W. Hardy and E. L. C. P. Hardy (Rolls ser. 1864–91); cf. Kingsford, *English Historical Literature*, 136–7.

Chapter 1: Yorkist Rebellions, 1452–60

1 Storey, *End of the House of Lancaster*, 94.

2 Text in *Paston Letters*, ed. Gairdner, introductory vol., p. cxi.

3 Storey, 98.

4 Text in *Paston Letters*, ed. Gairdner, introductory vol., pp. cxii–cxiii. For York's appeals to other towns, see Storey, 98. Shrewsbury sent a contingent (*HMC, Fifteenth Report, Appendix, part x, The MSS of Shrewsbury Corporation*, 1899, 29; H. Owen and J. B. Blakeway, *A History of Shrewsbury*, I (London 1825), 223n).

5 Storey, 98–9.

6 *Benet's Chron.*, 206; *Chronicles of London*, 163; *Arundel MS 19*, 297; *John Piggot's Memoranda*, 372–3.

7 *Proceedings and Ordinances of the Privy Council*, VI, 116. By then the council was well informed about the ramifications of the rebellion in south-east England (Storey, 98).

8 *Piggot's Memoranda*, 373; *Benet's Chron.*, 206; *English Chron.*, 69–70; *Arundel MS 19*, 297. Bourchier was referred to by the author of *Benet's Chron.*, as occasionally by other chroniclers, as count of Eu, his Norman title.

9 Storey, 99.

10 *English Chron.*, 69–70; *Arundel MS 19*, 297; *Benet's Chron.*, 206. The Yorkist army may have advanced through the Thames valley via Oxford, which was one of the towns to which the duke was alleged to have written inciting rebellion (Storey, 98).

11 *Benet's Chron.*, 206; *A Yorkist Collection*, 367–8.

12 *Piggot's Memoranda*, 373; *Benet's Chron.*, 206–7; *English Chron.*, 70; *Arundel MS 19*, 298; Whethamstede, I, 161ff; *Yorkist Collection*, 367–8. The author of *Benet's Chron.* thought that, at the climax of the campaign, the royal army was larger than the duke's, 24,000 to 20,000.

13 *Benet's Chron.*, 206–7; *Arundel MS 19*, 298; *Yorkist Collection*, 368;

Piggot's Memoranda, 373; *English Chron.*, 70; Whethamstede, I, 161ff; Waurin, V, 265–6. Out of the seven towns to whom (the council learnt on 17 February) York had sent letters allegedly inciting rebellion, three (Canterbury, Maidstone and Sandwich) were in Kent, and one (Winchelsea) was nearby in Sussex (Storey, 98).

14 See below, pp. 164–5.

15 'Gregory', 198. My account is heavily indebted to C. A. J. Armstrong's thorough article, 'Politics and the Battle of St Albans, 1455', *BIHR*, 33 (1960), 1ff.

16 Their lateness may indeed have been deliberate. In view of Stanley's behaviour near the fields of Blore Heath in 1459 and Bosworth in 1485, it is doubtful whether he would have given Henry more than fair words (see below, pp. 27–8, 92ff).

17 Lord Clinton was with them, and so was Richard Grey of Powis, first summoned to parliament just after the battle. Viscount Bourchier and Lord Cobham may have been with them too. (Armstrong, 27; *Benet's Chron.*, 213 and n).

18 *Chronicles of London*, 165; *Paston Letters*, I, no. 240; cf. Whethamstede, I, 171. Ogle had been one of the leaders of a raiding-party which burnt Dunbar in 1448 (*The Auchinleck Chron.*, ed. T. Thomson (1819), 39).

19 Cf. *Benet's Chron.*, 213.

20 *English Chron.*, 72.

21 *Fastolf Relation*, 67.

22 *Ibid.*, 65; *Paston Letters*, I, no. 239; *English Chron.*, 72; *Dijon Relation*, 63–4.

23 *Paston Letters*, I, no. 239.

24 *Ibid.*, no. 240.

25 Royal Commission on Historical Monuments (England), *An Inventory of the Historical Monuments in Hertfordshire* (London 1911), 188.

26 Whethamstede, I, 168; *English Chron.*, 72; *Paston Letters*, I, no. 240; *Dijon Relation*, 64; 'Gregory', 198.

27 *Benet's Chron.*, 214; cf. Armstrong, 49–50.

28 *Fastolf Relation*, 66–7.

29 *Bale's Chron.*, 148; cf. M. H. Keen, *The Laws of War in the Late Middle Ages* (London 1965), 107–8.

30 See below, p. 169.

31 For York's second protectorate, see Lander, *Crown and Nobility*, 74ff; Ross, *Edward IV*, 18–20.

32 *Benet's Chron.*, 223. Among the absentees were Thomas Bourchier, archbishop of Canterbury; Salisbury and Warwick; William Grey, bishop of Ely; Warwick's brother George Neville, bishop of Exeter; the earl of Arundel; and the archbishop's brother Viscount Bourchier.

33 *Rot. Parl.*, V, 348.

34 *English Chron.*, 80.

35 *Benet's Chron.*, 223–4; 'Gregory', 204–5; *Bale's Chron.*, 147–8; Waurin, V, 274. Warwick's presence at Coleshill is difficult to account for: perhaps he was attempting a solitary stroke against the king or his supporters.

36 *Rot. Parl.*, V, 348, 369.

37 *Ibid.*, 369; 'Gregory', 204; *Benet's Chron.*, 224; *English Chron.*, 79–80. Whethamstede (I, 338) says that 'totam quasi militiam' of Shropshire as well as Cheshire was to fight against Salisbury.

38 *Rot. Parl.*, V, 348, 369–70; *English Chron.*, 80; 'Gregory', 204.

39 F. R. Twemlow, using expert topographical knowledge and relying heavily on Waurin's inaccurate accounts of the battle, attempted a detailed but highly speculative reconstruction of it (*The Battle of Bloreheath*, 1912).

40 *Benet's Chron.*, 224; *Chronicles of London*, 169; 'Gregory', 204. Waurin thought that Salisbury had 400 against 6,000–8,000 (V, 269); the author of *Benet's Chron.* that he had 3,000 against 8,000; Whethamstede (I, 338) that he had at most 3,000 against almost 10,000; the author of *Bale's Chron.*, 148, 3,000 against 12,000; the author of *Short English Chron.*, 72, 4,000 against 14,000. The official account put his force at '5,000 persons and more' (*Rot. Parl.*, V, 348).

41 *Rot. Parl.* V, 348; cf. Whethamstede, I, 338; *Benet's Chron.*, 224; *Chronicles of London*, 169; *English Chron.*, 80; *Bale's Chron.*, 148; Waurin, V, 269. According to *Benet's Chron.*, 2,000 of the royal army were killed or captured.

42 *Rot. Parl.*, V, 369; 'Gregory', 204; *Benet's Chron.*, 224; *Chronicles of London*, 169; C. L. Scofield, *The Life and Reign of Edward the Fourth* (London 1923), I, 33n.

43 'Gregory', 204.

44 *Rot. Parl.*, V, 369–70.

45 'Gregory', 204.

46 For the nobles who probably participated in the Ludford campaign, see below, p. 237 n. 57.

47 See above, p. 26.

48 *Records of the Borough of Nottingham*, II, 1399–1485 (London 1883), 368–9.

49 *Benet's Chron.*, 224.

50 *English Chron.*, 80–1; *Benet's Chron.*, 224.

51 '. . . coepit revolvere res gestas varias, annaliaque multa, praecipue tamen, inter alia, illud quod sententiat Vegetius in Libro suo "De Dogmatibus Rei Militaris" ' (etc.) (Whethamstede, I, 338–9). This probably refers to Vegetius, I, i. For the interest of Henry and his supporter Beaumont in Vegetius' *Epitoma Rei Militaris*, see below, p. 124.

52 Whethamstede, I, 338–41; *Benet's Chron.*, 224.

53 For the Yorkist leaders' resentment at being proclaimed traitors and at the

plundering of their estates, see their letter of 10 October to the king (*English Chron.*, 81–3).

54 Scofield, I, 35; *English Chron.*, 81–3.

55 *Rot. Parl.*, V, 348; Whethamstede, I, 341ff.

56 According to Whethamstede, the king had almost 60,000 men before he reached Worcester (I, 338); according to *Short English Chron.*, 72, he had 50,000 at Ludlow; according to *Benet's Chron.*, 224, 40,000 to York's 25,000; according to *Bale's Chron.*, 148, 50,000 to York's 20,000. 'Gregory', 205, said that the king had 30,000 'harnessed' men, besides 'naked' men, and that York was 'over weak'.

57 Salisbury's brother Lord Fauconberg, in the king's retinue at St Albans, safeguarded Calais for Warwick during the 1459 campaign (Waurin, V, 278; Whethamstede, I, 368). Dr Richmond has listed the peers who in the months after the encounter received rewards for service against the rebels, and who may therefore have served at Ludford Bridge. They were the dukes of Buckingham and Exeter, the earls of Arundel, Devon, Northumberland, Shrewsbury and Wiltshire, Viscount Beaumont, and at least ten barons of parliament ('The Nobility and the Wars of the Roses, 1459–61', *Nottingham Mediaeval Studies*, 21 (1977), 74). For glimpses of military movements in the weeks before Ludford Bridge by Somerset, Shrewsbury's fellowship, Westmorland, Northumberland and Egremont, see above, pp. 26, 28.

58 The most circumstantial account is that of Waurin (V, 276–7), who says that Trollope was won over by a secret message from Somerset. If he had indeed been given command of the *avantgard* by Warwick, as Waurin says, his desertion is likely to have made the Yorkists particularly vulnerable. Waurin says that Trollope's men attacked the Yorkist lords as they withdrew.

59 Keen, 108.

60 *Rot. Parl.*, V, 348–9; Whethamstede, I, 342ff, 368; Waurin, V, 276–7; *Chronicles of London*, 169–70. Grey of Powis, Walter Devereux, esquire, and Sir Henry Retford were among those who submitted and were granted their lives at Ludford (*Rot. Parl.*, V, 349).

61 *Knyghthode and Bataile*, ed. R. Dyboski and Z. M. Arend, EETS, 1935; cf. D. Bornstein, 'Military Manuals in Fifteenth-Century England', *Mediaeval Studies*, 37 (1975), 472. I do not think that the editors' discussion of the date of the poem's composition is conclusive.

62 Commissions of array to resist the rebellion of the attainted lords were issued, dated 21 December 1459 (*CPR, 1452–61*, 557ff). For the fixing in February 1460 of Coventry's contingent of forty soldiers to support the king if they landed, *Coventry Leet Book*, 308–10; cf. *Paston Letters*, I, no. 346.

63 *Wars of the English in France*, ed. Stevenson, II, pt 1, 512; *Chronicles of London*, 170; Scofield, I, 50–1. Two of Somerset's leading

supporters, Lord Audley and Humphrey Stafford, esquire, were captured; another, Lord Roos, had returned to England by 28 January 1460 (Whethamstede, I, 369–70; *Benet's Chron.*, 224; Waurin, V, 284; *English Chron.*, 84; *Paston Letters*, I, no. 346; Scofield, I, 62).

64 *Annales*, 772; Waurin, V, 281–2; 'Gregory', 206.

65 *English Chron.*, 84–5; *Annales*, 771–2; Waurin, V, 282–4; Scofield, I, 50ff. Ships under guard at Sandwich belonging to Warwick were also seized and taken to Calais. For a commission of 6 December 1459 to take measures for their safeguard, especially in the spring tides, *CPR, 1452–61*, 525; cf. *ibid.*, 526. For Lydd's contribution of soldiers to Rivers at Sandwich, *HMC, Fifth Report*, I, *MSS of the Corporation of Lydd*, 522.

66 *Knyghthode and Bataile*, 103ff.

67 Scofield, I, 53–4, 59–61.

68 *Annales*, 772.

69 *Benet's Chron.*, 225; *Annales*, 772; *English Chron.*, 85; Waurin, V, 287ff; *Chronicles of London*, 170–1; *HMC, Fifth Report*, I, *MSS of the Corporation of Rye*, 492; Scofield, I, 64–5. For the raising of 4,000 marks in loans by the end of March, to pay for Exeter's and Fulford's naval expedition, *Wars of the English in France*, ed. Stevenson, II, pt 2, 515–16. For Wiltshire's abortive naval measures, Scofield, I, 70.

70 *English Chron.*, 85–6; *Annales*, 772; Whethamstede, I, 370–1; *Paston Letters*, I, no. 181; *Knyghthode and Bataile*, 19; Scofield, I, 63–5.

71 C. Rawcliffe, *The Staffords, Earls of Stafford and Dukes of Buckingham 1394–1521* (Cambridge 1978), 26.

72 Scofield, I, 71ff.

73 Waurin, V, 286–7, 290–1.

74 P. Clark, *English Provincial Society from the Reformation to the Revolution: Religion, Politics and Society in Kent 1500–1640* (Hassocks, Sussex 1977), 11.

75 'Gregory', 206.

76 *English Chron.*, 86–90.

77 *Ibid.*, 94; 'Gregory', 207; *Bale's Chron.*, 149; *Short English Chron.*, 73; *Annales*, 772; Scofield, I, 76. The legate Coppini wrote on 4 July that the lords crossed the Channel on 26 June. He apparently accompanied them to London (*CSP Milan*, I, pp. 23ff, no. 37; *Annales*, 772).

78 John Stone, *Chronicle*, ed. W. G. Searle (Cambridge 1902), 79; *Short English Chron.*, 73; *English Chron.*, 95; Waurin, V, 292–3. Horne, Scot and Fogge had been appointed on a commission of array in Kent in February, in which Abergavenny was second-named after Buckingham, but from which Cobham was prudently excluded (*CPR, 1452–61*, 561). Horne and Fogge had certainly been active in the royal interest, for the men of Lydd sent a deputation to Canterbury to them to intercede for

March's imprisoned men (*HMC, MSS of the Corporation of Lydd*, 523).
But they and Scot joined the Yorkists : royal letters dated 28 January 1461
ordered them (with Cobham, Abergavenny and others) to lead the Kentish
array to the king for service against the northern army (*Proceedings and
Ordinances of the Privy Council*, VI, 307–8).

79 *HMC, MSS of the Corporation of Rye*, 492. The Rye and Winchelsea
officials appear to have gone off to join the Yorkists. A Lydd contingent
may have gone too, and fought at Northampton (*HMC, MSS of the
Corporation of Lydd*, 523).

80 Stone, 79–80; *Short English Chron.*, 73–4; *English Chron.*, 94–5;
Waurin, V, 293–5; *Bale's Chron.*, 149–50; *Annales*, 772; Scofield, I,
77ff. The author of the *Annales* put the size of the Yorkist army when it
arrived at 20,000; the author of a pro-Yorkist London chronicle and
Whethamstede mentioned the figure 40,000 as their nearest
approximation (*Annales*, 772; *English Chron.*, 73; Whethamstede, I,
372).

81 *Bale's Chron.*, 150–1.

82 *Short English Chron.*, 73; *English Chron.*, 95–6; *Annales*, 772.

83 *English Chron.*, 94.

84 *Short English Chron.*, 73.

85 *English Chron.*, 94–5. Bourchier may have fought for York in 1455,
Clinton did then and in 1459 (see above, p. 235 n.17, p. 30).

86 *CSP Milan*, I, pp. 23ff, no. 37.

87 *Annales*, 773.

88 *Benet's Chron.*, 225 and n; *Foedera*, XI, 454–6. Royal letters were
dated at Coventry on 5, 11 and 26 June (*ibid.*, 454–6).

89 *Foedera*, XI, 444–6; commissions to the earl of Pembroke and prince of
Wales. Cf. below, p. 184.

90 As late as 5 June Somerset was empowered to grant pardons to the rebels
at Calais (*ibid.*, 454).

91 *English Chron.*, 95; *Benet's Chron.*, 225–6.

92 For the siege, see below, pp. 184–5.

93 Stone, 80; *HMC, MSS of Shrewsbury Corporation*, 29; G. Poulson,
Beverlac, I (London 1829), 226ff. The Beverley governors' account for
1460–1 raises doubts as to whether the town contingent got to
Northampton in time.

94 *CSP Milan*, I, p. 27, no. 38.

95 *Bale's Chron.*, 150–1.

96 *Benet's Chron.*, 226.

97 See below, pp. 184–5.

98 Waurin, V, 295–6. According to *Bale's Chron.*, 150–1, one part of the
army was routed through St Albans, the other through Ware – the latter
intended to forestall any move by the king to the Isle of Ely. If so, the wait
at Dunstable may have been to allow the Ware force to catch up.

99 Waurin, V, 299–300. Hunsbury Hill, an ancient encampment, may have been the *montagne* which, according to Waurin, Warwick used as an observation post.

100 Stone, 80; *Benet's Chron.*, 226; *Short English Chron.*, 74; Scofield, I, 86 and n.

101 Whethamstede, I, 372–3; Waurin, V, 296ff; *English Chron.*, 95–7; *Short English Chron.*, 74. The chroniclers mention as being with the Yorkists, besides the legate and archbishop, the prior of St John's and the bishops of Exeter, Ely, Salisbury and Rochester. See also *Benet's Chron.*, 226; *CSP Milan*, I, p. 27, no. 38.

102 For Buckingham's family connections with Shrewsbury and Beaumont, see Rawcliffe, 21 and n.

103 *Knyghthode and Bataile*, 43. The author probably had in mind the oaths of the Yorkist leaders at Worcester in 1459. They probably swore on the Sacrament in St Paul's before Northampton (see above, p. 36).

104 'Gregory', 207.

105 *English Chron.*, 95; *Short English Chron.*, 74; Waurin, V, 296; Richmond, 'The Nobility and the Wars of the Roses, 1459–61', 74. Scrope was one of the two captains whom, according to Waurin, V, 299, Warwick had put in charge of the vanguard until the army had completely assembled near Northampton.

106 Sources used for the battle are Whethamstede, I, 373–5; Waurin, V, 299–300; *English Chron.*, 97–8; *Benet's Chron.*, 226; 'Gregory', 207; *Short English Chron.*, 74; Stone, 80. A succinct account is in R. Ian Jack, 'A Quincentenary: the Battle of Northampton, July 10th, 1460', *Northamptonshire Past and Present*, 3 (1960).

107 Whethamstede I, 372, says that the Yorkists had an 'infinite number of commons', in the region of 160,000; *Bale's Chron.*, 151, attribute to them a superiority of 160,000 to 20,000; Waurin, V, 299, of 80,000 to between 40,000 and 50,000; *Benet's Chron.*, 226, 60,000 to 20,000.

108 *Historical Poems of the XIVth and XVth Centuries*, ed. R. H. Robbins (New York 1959), 210ff.

109 Stone, 80. *Benet's Chron.*, 226, says that about 400 royal troops were killed, the *Annales*, 773, that 300 of them were killed and others drowned, *Bale's Chron.*, 151, that 50 of them were killed.

110 *English Chron.*, 97; 'Gregory', 207.

111 See below, pp. 184–5.

112 Grey had gained royal favour in the Coventry parliament, perhaps after allaying suspicions that he was pro-Yorkist. An observer wrote that Warwick's brother Bishop Neville and Grey 'have declared them full worshipfully to the King's great pleasure' (*Paston Letters*, I, no. 342). For Grey's motives for treason, J. S. Roskell, *The Commons in the Parliament of 1422* (Manchester 1954), 176–7.

113 For a recent assessment of Buckingham's role in the conflicts, and

particularly the impact he made on them in 1459–60, see Rawcliffe, 24ff.
114 For entrenched camps, see also below, pp. 170–1.

Chapter 2: The War of Succession, 1460–1

1 This was how it was seen by Whethamstede, who personally experienced its ferocity (I, 386ff); cf. 'The Battle of Towton', Robbins, 215ff.

2 *Annales*, 773.

3 'Gregory', 208–10; Waurin, V, 324–5; *Annales*, 774–5; Scofield, I, 114. Hull may have been chosen as a base because of the opportunities which it provided for victualling by river and sea (cf. below, pp. 156–7, 219–20).

4 R. R. Sharpe, *London and the Kingdom*, I (London 1894), 118. On 2 December, a few days before the loan was granted, common council had received letters from the queen, the prince of Wales and Pembroke: no reply was sent.

5 *Bale's Chron.*, 152; *Chronicles of London*, 172; *Benet's Chron.*, 228; 'Gregory', 210; *English Chron.*, 106; Whethamstede, I, 381; *Annales*, 775. According to *English Chron.*, the Yorkist lords lodged at Sandal castle and Wakefield; according to *Annales*, at Sandal castle, where they kept Christmas, whilst Somerset and Northumberland were at Pontefract castle.

6 *English Chron.*, 106–7; *Brief Notes*, 154. Greystoke had been appointed on the Yorkist commission in Yorkshire in August.

7 Richmond, 'The Nobility and the Wars of the Roses, 1459–61', 75.

8 Waurin, V, 325–6.

9 *C.* 20,000 Lancastrians and 12,000 Yorkists (*Benet's Chron.*, 228); 15,000 Lancastrians and, on the Yorkist side, 'great people' ('Gregory', 210); 800 with Somerset and Devon, 8,000 with Neville and, on the Yorkist side, 'a few persons' (*English Chron.*, 106); 'a great army' on the Lancastrian side and 6,000 Yorkists (*Annales*, 775).

10 *CSP Milan*, I, pp. 42–3, no. 54.

11 Whethamstede, I, 381–2; cf. *Annales*, 775.

12 *Annales*, 775; *English Chron.*, 106–7; Whethamstede, I, 382. Whethamstede (I, 386–7) put the Yorkist death-toll at 700; the author of *Benet's Chron.* at about 1,000; the author of *Annales* at about 2,000; the author of *English Chron.* at 2,200; 'Gregory', who says that the queen's party lost 200, at 2,500.

13 *CSP Milan*, I, p. 39, no. 52.

14 Whethamstede, I, 381.

15 *Annales*, 774.

16 'Gregory', 212; *English Chron.*, 107.

17 See below, p. 215; cf. the bishop of Terni's and Antonio della Torre's

letters of 9 January, *CSP Milan*, I, pp. 37ff, nos 52, 54.

18 Sharpe, I, 128; cf. 119.

19 *The Records of the City of Norwich*, ed. W. H. Hudson and J. C. Tingey, I (Norwich 1906), 405–6.

20 *CPR, 1452–61*, 657.

21 *Paston Letters*, I, no. 367.

22 *Proceedings and Ordinances of the Privy Council*, VI, 307ff.

23 *CPR, 1452–61*, 658.

24 *HMC, MSS of the Corporation of King's Lynn*, 167.

25 *Henley Borough Records. Assembly Books i–iv, 1395–1543*, ed. P. M. Briers, 63.

26 *Rot. Parl.*, V, 477–8. These included five esquires and a grocer from London, an esquire from Southwark, one from Lambeth, and an esquire and yeoman from Westminster. Some others attainted, whose residence was not stated, such as Sir Edmund Mountfort and Sir Edmund Hampden, were from regions in Yorkist control.

27 *CPR, 1452–61*, 657–9.

28 *Ibid.*, 658–9; cf. below, p. 156.

29 *Ibid.*, 658.

30 *Paston Letters*, II, no. 384.

31 *Ibid.*, I, nos 83, 172, 260, 319.

32 *Ibid.*, nos 53, 56.

33 *Ibid.*, nos 68, 96.

34 *Ibid.*, no. 172.

35 *Ibid.*, III, no. 997.

36 *Rot. Parl.*, V, 477–8; *Paston Letters*, II, no. 486.

37 Poulson, I, 234.

38 Whethamstede, I, 388ff; *Brief Notes*, 154–5; 'Gregory', 212; *Annales*, 776. For the fight at Dunstable, see below, p. 126.

39 *Benet's Chron.*, 229 and n; cf. *CSP Milan*, I, p. 48, no. 63, and Waurin, V, 328.

40 See below, p. 177; cf. *English Chron.*, 107. On 14 February an Italian reported from London that the northerners did not seem to have got past Northampton (*CSP Milan*, I, p. 48, no. 63).

41 'Gregory', 212–13.

42 *Brief Notes*, 154–5; *Benet's Chron.*, 229; *English Chron.*, 107; 'The Battle of Towton', Robbins, 216.

43 *CSP Milan*, I, p. 43, no. 63.

44 The more experienced Bourchier, Bonville and Fauconberg were also with Warwick (Richmond, 'The Nobility and the Wars of the Roses, 1459–61', 75).

45 *Annales*, 776; cf. Richmond, 'The Nobility and the Wars of the Roses, 1459–61', 75.

46 Whethamstede, I, 390ff.

47 *Brief Notes*, 155, puts the total killed in the battle at 7,500; *Benet's Chron.*, 229, at about 4,000; 'Gregory', 212, at over 3,500; George Neville at nearly 3,000 (*CSP Venice*, I, p. 99, no. 370); *Annales*, 776, at 2,000; *English Chron.*, 108, at 1,916.

48 'Gregory', 212ff; see below, pp. 177, 171–2.

49 *English Chron.*, 107–8; Waurin, V, 328ff, 334.

50 *CSP Milan*, I, pp. 48–9, no. 64.

51 One explanation for this may be that Lovelace had kept them out of the battle.

52 *CSP Milan*, I, p. 54, no. 71.

53 *English Chron.*, 108; *Annales*, 776; *CSP Venice*, I, p. 99, no. 370. Bonville's switch to the Yorkist side was regarded with particular indignation – he was speedily executed.

54 'Gregory', 212. According to *Annales*, 776, the queen's army was 80,000 strong.

55 *Paston Letters*, III, no. 997.

56 On 12 February, March was commissioned by the Council, as Edward duke of York, to array the lieges of Bristol, Staffordshire, Shropshire, Herefordshire, Gloucestershire, Worcestershire, Somerset and Dorset to go with him against the king's enemies (*CPR, 1452–61*, 659). Two days after the battle of St Albans he was reputed in London to be in the Cotswolds (*CSP Milan*, I, p. 49, no. 64).

57 See below, p. 77.

58 'The Battle of Towton', Robbins, 216.

59 *CSP Venice*, I, p. 101, no. 371.

60 See below, pp. 156, 204, 215.

61 *Annales*, 775.

62 Ibid., 775ff; *Short English Chron.*, 76–7; *Chronicles of London*, 172; 'Gregory', 211; *English Chron.*, 110; *Benet's Chron.*, 229; Worcestre, *Itineraries*, ed. J. Harvey, 202ff; H. T. Evans, *Wales and the Wars of the Roses* (Cambridge 1915), 139. According to *Annales*, March had 50,000 men and Pembroke 8,000; according to *Short English Chron.*, March raised 30,000. *English Chron.* says that his opponents were slain to the number of 4,000.

63 *Paston Letters*, I, no. 239; 'Gregory', 198; *English Chron.*, 90.

64 *Coventry Leet Book*, 313.

65 Ibid., 314.

66 *Chronicles of the White Rose of York*, ed. J. A. Giles (1845), 8, henceforth cited as *White Rose*.

67 Ibid., 8; *Chronicles of London*, 175; *CSP Venice*, I, pp. 99ff, nos 370–1. A commission of array dated 8 March empowered Warwick to raise levies from Northamptonshire, Warwickshire, Leicestershire, Staffordshire, Worcestershire, Gloucestershire, Shropshire, Nottinghamshire, Derbyshire, and Yorkshire (*CPR, 1461–7*, 31).

68 Waurin, V, 335–6; Scofield, I, 162.
69 *Coventry Leet Book*, 314–16; 'The Battle of Towton', Robbins, 215ff.
70 Waurin, V, 336–7; *Benet's Chron.*, 230. The latter says that Edward passed through Newark, as one might expect from his previous route, and does not mention his presence at Nottingham.
71 Waurin, V, 336–7; cf, *White Rose*, 8; *Benet's Chron.*, 230; 'Gregory', 216; *Annales*, 777. The author of *Hearne's Fragment*'s chronology of the battles of Ferrybridge and Towton differs from that of other sources (*White Rose*, 8). The fact that the battles were fought on successive days confused some chroniclers, who failed to distinguish them (*Short English Chron.*, 77; *Chronicles of London*, 175; Stone, 83). Even Warwick's brother George, in his account, fails to make the distinction clear (*CSP Venice*, I, pp. 99–100, no. 370).
72 *CSP Venice*, I, pp. 99–100, no. 370; Waurin, V, 337–8.
73 'Gregory', 216.
74 Waurin, V, 338.
75 *Benet's Chron.*, 230.
76 The duke of Norfolk, the earl of Warwick, Viscount Bourchier, Lords Clinton, Dacre (Richard Fiennes), Fauconberg, Grey of Ruthin, and Scrope of Bolton (Richmond, 'The Nobility and the Wars of the Roses, 1459–61', 75).
77 The dukes of Exeter and Somerset; the earls of Devon, Northumberland, and Shrewsbury; Viscount Beaumont; Lords Clifford, Randolph Dacre, de la Warre, FitzHugh, Grey of Codnor, Lovell, Neville, Rivers, Roos, Rugemont-Grey, Scales, Welles, and Willoughby (*ibid.*).
78 Bishop Beauchamp and the author of *Benet's Chron.* both thought that the army which Edward took north reached around the 200,000 mark (*CSP Venice*, I, p. 102, no. 371; *Benet's Chron.*, 230). According to William Paston and Thomas Playter, immediately after the battle Edward believed there were about 20,000 Lancastrian dead. Beauchamp wrote that the total death-toll on both sides, as estimated by the heralds, came to 28,000; they had not counted drowned or wounded. The heralds' estimate was given by other writers (*Paston Letters*, II, no. 385; *Chronicles of London*, 175). But some went much higher (*White Rose*, 8; *Short English Chron.*, 77). It is not clear whether Ferrybridge casualties were included in the totals. *Annales*, 778, is exceptional in putting the total deaths for all these engagements merely at over 9,000. Bishop O'Flanagan wrote on 8 April that 800 of Edward's troops were killed (*CSP Venice*, I, p. 103, no. 372).
79 *York Civic Records*, I, 135.
80 Waurin, V, 339ff.
81 *CSP Venice*, I, p. 100, no. 370.
82 Richmond, 'The Nobility and the Wars of the Roses, 1459–61', 75.
83 *CSP Venice*, I, p. 102, no. 371; *White Rose*, 8. For an interesting

news-letter about the battle and its aftermath, written from Bruges on 11 April, see J. Calmette and G. Périnelle, *Louis XI et l'Angleterre* (Paris 1930), 273–4.

84 *Chronicles of London*, 175; *Short English Chron.*, 77; 'Gregory', 217.

85 *White Rose*, 8; *Chronicles of London*, 175; *CSP Venice*, I, p. 100, no. 370; *Benet's Chron.*, 230–1; 'Gregory', 217–18; Poulson I, 239ff; Scofield, I, 174ff.

86 See below, p. 123.

87 *Oeuvres de Georges Chastellain*, ed. K. de Lettenhove, IV, 66.

88 'Gregory', 206.

89 *Annales*, 781.

90 *Brief Notes*, 154–5.

91 'Gregory', 214; cf. below, p. 127.

Chapter 3: Lancastrian Risings and Invasions, 1461–4

1 The meeting of Margaret and her son with James II's widow Mary of Guelders at Lincluden in the winter of 1460–1 laid the foundations of subsequent close Lancastrian–Stewart relations (A. I. Dunlop, *The Life and Times of James Kennedy, Bishop of St Andrews* (Edinburgh 1950), 215ff).

2 For Lancastrian disturbances in many parts of England and Yorkist fears of an invasion supported by the French in 1461 and 1462, Ross, *Edward IV*, 42ff.

3 Scofield, I, 205 and n; *Paston Letters*, II, no. 416. Whetehill received the surrender of Guines castle before 25 February 1462 (F. Devon (ed.), *Issues of the Exchequer*, I (London 1837), 486–7).

4 *Paston Letters*, II, no. 386.

5 *Ibid.*, nos 385, 387; John Major, *A History of Greater Britain*, trans. and ed. A. Constable (Scottish Hist. Soc., Edinburgh 1892), 387. Berwick was ceded on 25 April (Dunlop, 221).

6 *Rot. Parl.*, V, 478; Scofield, I, 180.

7 *The Priory of Hexham*, I (Surtees Soc. 1864), p. c; *Coventry Leet Book*, 317–19. The Coventry contingent served till 29 July.

8 *Paston Letters*, II, no. 391; Scofield, I, 180. The initiative of Richard Salkeld, esquire, probably helped to save Carlisle from capitulating before Montague's relief. In 1467 he was said to have seized the city and castle and successfully defended them against Scots and English (*CPR*, 1467–77, 25).

9 *Rot. Parl.*, V, 478; Scofield, I, 186. On 30 June Prior Burnby of Durham wrote from there to the earl of Warwick asking for grace and good lordship for his poor kinsman Richard Billingham who had adhered to and accompanied Humphrey Neville (*Priory of Hexham*, I, p. ci). On

31 July the earl was appointed warden of the East and West Marches (Ross, *Edward IV*, 31).

10 *CSP Venice*, I, pp. 110–11, no. 384.

11 Scofield, I, 204. For Edward's garrisons at Newcastle and Tynemouth, *ibid.*, 204n.

12 *Oeuvres de Georges Chastellain*, ed. K. de Lettenhove, IV, 64ff; *Paston Letters*, II, nos 413, 416; Scofield, I, 187ff; Calmette and Périnelle, 6ff and 6n. For references to preparations for Edward's Welsh expedition in July and August, see, besides Scofield, *Paston Letters*, II, nos 409–10, 413. For the commission of 8 July 1461 to Ferrers, Herbert and James Baskerville to array in Herefordshire, Gloucestershire and Shropshire for defence against enemies in France and Scotland, and Lancastrians, *CPR, 1461–7*, 36.

13 *CSP Venice*, I, pp. 110–12, nos 384–5.

14 H. T. Evans, *Wales and the Wars of the Roses* (Cambridge 1915), 135ff; Scofield, I, 201–2; *Rot. Parl.*, VI, 29–30.

15 *Paston Letters*, II, no. 416. For Jasper's determination to hold Denbigh castle, Evans, 140. Thomas Cornwall, constable of Radnor castle, probably held it for a while for King Henry (Scofield, I, 197).

16 *Rot. Parl.*, V, 478.

17 *King's Works*, II, 602.

18 *CSP Milan*, I, pp. 106ff, no. 125; *Annales*, 779; Scofield, I, 230ff. Other leading conspirators were Oxford's eldest son, Aubrey de Vere, and Henry VI's former keeper of the wardrobe and treasurer of the household, Sir Thomas Tuddenham of Oxborough (Norfolk). According to *Brief Latin Chron.*, 175, the Veres had prepared for a landing in Essex by Somerset. For the release of the duke and his companions from arrest in France, Calmette and Périnelle, 8–9.

19 *Annales*, 779; Scofield, I, 241ff. For diplomatic and shipping movements on the Continent, helping to produce the alarm felt by Edward particularly in March 1462, Calmette and Périnelle, 15–17.

20 *Brief Notes*, 159.

21 *Annales*, 779–80; *Paston Letters*, II, nos 452, 458–9; Scofield, I, 246ff; Calmette and Périnelle, 18ff; Dunlop, 227–9. For the activities of Dacre and Tailboys in 1461, see above, p. 57. Warwick had already met Mary of Guelders at Dumfries in April (Dunlop, 227–8).

22 A. F. Pollard, *The Reign of Henry VII from Contemporary Sources*, I (London 1913), 137ff; cf. below, p. 111.

23 See below, p. 112.

24 For the powers conferred on William Herbert and his brothers in Wales after Towton, Evans, 135ff.

25 'Gregory', 218; Warkworth, 2; *Annales*, 780; Waurin, V, 431; Scofield, I, 261. The chronicler Thomas Basin denounced the meagreness of Louis' aid (*Histoire de Louis XI*, ed. Samaran, I, 80ff). Calmette and

Périnelle, 25ff, discuss the Lancastrian preparations at Honfleur and the reasons for an embarkation late in the year. They date it on 9 October and estimate the size of the expedition as 2,000, the figure given in *Annales* and by Waurin.

26 Warkworth, 2; cf. *Short English Chron.*, 79; *Annales*, 780. Any soldiers they placed in Warkworth castle were probably soon withdrawn to nearby Alnwick, as there is no mention of a Yorkist siege of Warkworth.

27 Warkworth, 2; *Brief Notes*, 157–8; *Paston Letters*, II, no. 460. In August the city of London had agreed to lend the crown £1,000, in response to a request by the earl of Worcester and others of the royal council for a loan of £3,400 to protect Calais from attack, and in October the city lent a further 2,000 marks (Sharpe, I, 308). In October a possible invasion of Scotland by the earl of Douglas was being envisaged (*CDS*, IV, no. 1332).

28 *Short English Chron.*, 79; cf. Scofield, I, 262 and n.

29 Scofield, I, 262.

30 *Chronicles of London*, 177–8; *Annales*, 780; *Brief Latin Chron.*, 175–6; 'Gregory', 218–19; *White Rose*, 13; *Priory of Hexham*, I, pp. cviii–cix; Scofield, I, 262–3. For the connection between the Ogle and Manners of Etal families, R. B. Dobson, *Durham Cathedral Priory 1400–1450* (Cambridge 1973), 197ff.

31 Scofield, I, 263–4. Sir John Clay commenced his attendance on the king for the expedition on 2 November (*CDS*, IV, no. 1342). According to *Annales*, Edward departed on 3 November.

32 *Brief Notes*, 157–8.

33 Scofield, I, 264.

34 *Brief Notes*, 158–9; *Annales*, 780; 'Gregory', 219; Scofield, I, 264ff.

35 *Paston Letters*, II, no. 464. According to *Brief Notes*, 158–9, Warwick, Kent, Grey of Powis, Greystoke and Cromwell besieged Alnwick; Wenlock and Hastings were at Dunstanburgh; and Worcester, Arundel, Ogle and Montague were at Bamburgh.

36 *Brief Latin Chron.*, 176; 'Gregory', 219; *Annales*, 780; Scofield, I, 265.

37 Warkworth, 2; cf. Scofield, I, 265–6.

38 *Priory of Hexham*, I, p. cvii.

39 Major, 388.

40 *Brief Latin Chron.*, 176; Warkworth, 2; 'Gregory', 220; *Annales*, 780–1; Major, 388; Waurin, V, 433. Major says that Angus reached Alnwick castle at noon, implying a less impressive achievement than the night crossing of the Border implicit in his arrival there, according to 'Gregory', at dawn.

41 *Brief Latin Chron.*, 176; *Chronicles of London*, 178; Scofield, I, 266ff.

42 *Annales*, 781–2; *Brief Latin Chron.*, 176; 'Gregory', 220; *Rot. Parl.*, V, 511; Scofield, I, 274, 287–8. Montague received powers as warden

general of the East March on 1 June (*Foedera*, XI, 550ff).

43 *Priory of Hexham*, I, pp. cvii–cviii.

44 'Gregory', 220–1; *Annales*, 781; Waurin, V, 431–3; Thomas Basin, *Histoire de Louis XI*, I, ed. Samaran, 82ff; Chastellain, IV, 278–9; Scofield, I, 293–4, 300; Dunlop, 236–7.

45 'Gregory', 220; Basin, I, 84ff; Chastellain, IV, 279ff; Scofield, I, 301, 306, 308ff; Calmette and Périnelle, 38–9, 38n, 40ff; Dunlop, 238ff.

46 *Rot. Parl.*, V, 511; 'Gregory', 221ff; Scofield, I, 312–13.

47 *Paston Letters*, II, no. 486; Scofield, I, 318–19.

48 *Brief Latin Chron.*, 178–9. According to this, Norham castle was also captured – but the Lancastrians cannot have held it long.

49 *Rot. Parl.*, V, 511.

50 'Gregory', 223–4; *Brief Latin Chron.*, 178; Waurin, V, 440–1; *Priory of Hexham*, I, p. cix and n; Scofield, I, 329–30.

51 *Annales*, 782; 'Gregory', 224–6; *Brief Latin Chron.*, 178–9; *Priory of Hexham*, I, pp. cix–cx; Scofield, I, 333–4. For a discussion of the site of the battle, Charlesworth, 'The Battle of Hexham, 1464', *Archaeologia Aeliana*, 4th ser., 30 (1952), 63ff.

52 *Brief Latin Chron.*, 179.

53 *Annales*, 782.

54 *Rot. Parl.*, V, 511.

55 College of Arms MS, in Warkworth, 37–9; *Annales*, 782–3; Scofield, I, 336ff.

Chapter 4: Local Revolts and Nobles' Struggles to Control the Crown, 1469–71

1 Scofield, I, 380ff, 478.

2 *White Rose*, 18–20; Scofield, I, 384–5.

3 *HMC, MSS of Shrewsbury Corporation*, 30.

4 *CSP Milan*, I, p. 121, nos 154, 162; Ross, *Edward IV*, 114, 120; *CPR, 1467–77*, 103. For the siege of Harlech, see below, p. 186.

5 Scofield, I, 480ff; Ross, *Edward IV*, 122ff. For the accusations against a rich draper, former mayor of London, M. A. Hicks, 'The case of Sir Thomas Cook', *EHR*, 93 (1978).

6 *Brief Latin Chron.*, 183. The risings and the sources for them are thoroughly discussed by Ross, *Edward IV*, 126ff and Appendix IV (439–40).

7 *Hist. Croylandensis Continuatio*, 542–3; Warkworth, 6; Waurin, V, 548; Worcestre, *Itineraries*, 340–1; *White Rose*, 24; *Coventry Leet Book*, 341–3; Scofield, I, 488–9, 491–3; Ross, *Edward IV*, 127ff. According to Warkworth, the northern rebels were 20,000 strong; according to the first Crowland continuator, about 60,000.

8 Warkworth, 6, 46ff; *Hist. Croylandensis Continuatio*, 542–3; Waurin, V, 579; Stone, 110–11; Scofield, I, 493ff; Ross, *Edward IV*, 129ff. Cf. Warwick's disingenuous requests to Coventry for military support (*Coventry Leet Book*, 341–2).

9 Waurin, V, 581–3; Warkworth, 6–7; *White Rose*, 24; *Hist. Croylandensis Continuatio*, 543, 551; *Gloucester Annals*, 356–7; Scofield, I, 496–8; Ross, *Edward IV*, 130ff. Warkworth says that Pembroke had 43,000 men and Devon 7,000; *Hearne's Fragment* (in *White Rose*) that Pembroke had 7,000–8,000 and Devon 4,000–5,000; Waurin, that Devon had 7,000–8,000. The first Crowland continuator says that allegedly 4,000 were killed on both sides, Warkworth that 2,000 Welshmen were slain. Worcester lists 24 Welshmen killed or executed, and says that about 168 others of the wealthier persons of Wales were killed. He puts the northerners' alleged death-toll at 1,500, including the sons of Lords Latimer, FitzHugh and Dudley (*Itineraries*, 338ff).

10 *Priory of Hexham*, I, p. cx; Warkworth, 7; *Hist. Croylandensis Continuatio*, 551–2; Scofield, I, 501ff; Ross, *Edward IV*, 134–5. In 1469 Shrewsbury paid 10s. to a messenger sent to York 'ad scrutandum de rumoribus domini Regis' (*HMC, MSS of Shrewsbury Corporation*, 30).

11 Warkworth, 8; Scofield, I, 509ff; Ross, *Edward IV*, 138ff. For Burgh's career, see R. L. Storey, 'Lincolnshire and the Wars of the Roses', *Nottingham Mediaeval Studies*, 14 (1970), 71ff.

12 *Lincolnshire Rebellion*, 5ff; *Chronicles of London*, 180; Waurin, V, 587ff; *Foedera*, XI, 652–3; Scofield, I, 510ff. On 9 February, by signet letter, Edward commanded Coventry to send him an armed contingent, to meet him at Grantham on 12 March. He asserted that 'we be ascertained that our rebels and outward enemies intend in haste time to arrive in this our Realm', to be joined by domestic adherents (*Coventry Leet Book*, 353–4). Reference to the threat from external enemies in his commission to Clarence and Warwick also suggests that he may have thought the disturbances were Lancastrian-inspired.

13 *Lincolnshire Rebellion*, 6ff; Waurin, V, 589ff.

14 *Lincolnshire Rebellion*, 9ff; Waurin, V, 592–3; *Chronicles of London*, 180–1. Waurin says that the Lincolnshiremen were more than 30,000 strong, and that most of them would have been killed had not Edward taken pains to stop the slaughter.

15 *Lincolnshire Rebellion*, 10–11, 21ff; Waurin, V, 593–4; Warkworth, 53ff. The proclamation forbidding arrays which Edward dispatched from Stamford to Warwickshire and Leicestershire the day after his victory reflects but does not specify his suspicions (Warkworth, 52–3). De la Launde and John Neille, 'a great captain', were executed at Grantham on 15 March, Welles and another great captain were at Doncaster on the 19th (*Paston Letters*, II, no. 638).

16 *Lincolnshire Rebellion*, 10ff; Waurin, V, 593ff, 602–3; Warkworth, 53ff; *Paston Letters*, II, no. 638. Edward was probably joined at Grantham by the Coventry contingent sent in response to his February request (*Coventry Leet Book*, 353–5).

17 Warkworth, 53ff; Waurin, V, 595, 600ff; *Foedera*, XI, 655–6; cf. *ibid.*, 654–5.

18 Scofield, I, 518–20; Ross, *Edward IV*, 145–6. A royal proclamation dated Nottingham, 31 March, declared Clarence and Warwick traitors, since they had not submitted. The confessions made at York were cited as evidence of their further treasons (Warkworth, 56ff). For the levy at Coventry for the soldiers 'that went with the king into the south country', *Coventry Leet Book*, 355–6. Gifts, notably of wine, to the duke of Norfolk and Lords Dinham and Scales, recorded in the Bridport cofferers' account for 1469–70, may reflect their presence in the royal army in the West Country (Dorset County Record Office, B3/M6).

19 Scofield, I, 523ff; Ross, *Edward IV*, 146–7.

20 *CPR, 1467–77*, 220.

21 *CSP Milan*, I, pp. 141–2, nos 192, 194.

22 *Paston Letters*, II, no. 648.

23 Waurin, V, 606–7; T. Basin, *Histoire de Louis XI*, ed. C. Samaran and M.-C. Garand, II, 20ff; *Oeuvres de Georges Chastellain*, ed. K. de Lettenhove, V, *Chronique*, 468.

24 Waurin, V, 606–7; *White Rose*, 28–9; *Paston Letters*, III, no. 648; *Coventry Leet Book*, 356–7; Ross, *Edward IV*, 150ff. Professor Ross discusses pro-Neville assemblies centring on Carlisle. Also this summer Oxford fled to Normandy to join Clarence and Warwick, but a conspiracy by Sir Geoffrey Gate and Clapham to pass over from Southampton was foiled by the earl of Worcester and Lord Howard (*White Rose*, 28–9).

25 Warkworth, 10; *Brief Latin Chron.*, 183; *Chronicles of London*, 181; *CSP Milan*, p. 142, no. 195; Basin, II, 48ff; Chastellain, *Oeuvres*, V, 468–9; *Coventry Leet Book*, 358; Scofield, I, 536; Ross, *Edward IV*, 151–2; Calmette and Périnelle, 118–19.

26 Scofield, I, 538.

27 *Coventry Leet Book*, 358.

28 Warkworth, 10–11; *Hist. Croylandensis Continuatio*, 553–4; *Chronicles of London*, 181; *Coventry Leet Book*, 358–9; Scofield, I, 538–9; Ross, *Edward IV*, 152–4. Chastellain says that Edward had granted command of his *avant-garde* to Montague (*Oeuvres*, V, 499ff).

29 *Coventry Leet Book*, 359; *Chronicles of London*, 182; Sharpe, I, 311–12; Scofield, I, 541–2. Shrewsbury and Stanley had probably joined the rebels with companies in the Midlands. Jasper Tudor had gone to Wales to rally support (Scofield, I, 538).

30 *Arrivall*, 1–2; Warkworth, 13; Scofield, I, 567–8. Warwick wrote on 25 March that Edward had landed with Flemings, 'Esterlinges'

(= Germans?) and Danes, and that his company did not number more than 2,000 (*HMC, Rutland MSS*, I, 3–4). For Warwick's preparations, Ross, *Edward IV*, 160.

31 *Arrivall*, 2; Warkworth, 13; *Paston Letters*, II, no. 663; Scofield, I, 568–9.

32 *Arrivall*, 2ff; Warkworth, 13–14; *York Civic Records*, I, 136; Scofield, I, 569ff. According to one source, Edward reached the Trent on 25 March (J. A. F. Thomson, ' "The Arrivall of Edward IV" – The Development of the Text', *Speculum*, 46 (1971), 91. Sir William Par and Sir James Harington joined him at Nottingham with two well-arrayed 'bands' totalling 600 (*Arrivall*, 7). According to Warkworth, 14, Sir Wiliam Stanley, Sir William Norys and men and tenants of Lord Hastings came in there, bringing Edward's force to over 2,000. The author of the *Arrivall*, 8–9, says that Hastings's supporters joined up at Leicester, to the number of 3,000.

33 *Arrivall*, 7–8; *Paston Letters*, II, no. 664.

34 *Arrivall*, 8; *HMC, Rutland MSS*, I, 3–4; Basin, II, 80–1.

35 *Arrivall*, 8–9, 12; Basin, II, 66–7; Warkworth, 14; Malory, *Works*, II, 621–2; Scofield, I, 571–2. The author of the *Arrivall* says that Warwick had 6,000–7,000 soldiers in Coventry. According to Basin, Edward heard that Oxford, Beaumont and many others were coming to reinforce Warwick, and sent against them, at Leicester, part of his forces, which on 3 April defeated Oxford and his men (Basin, II, 68–9; cf. Thomson, ' "The Arrivall of Edward IV" ', 91).

36 *Arrivall*, 10–11. For Clarence's movements, see his letters to Vernon, *HMC, Rutland MSS*, I, 2–4.

37 *Arrivall*, 9ff; Scofield, I, 573–4. On 27 March a commission had been issued to the prince of Wales (still in France) granting him powers to array and make proclamations throughout the realm (*Foedera*, XI, 706–7).

38 *Arrivall*, 12ff; Warkworth, 15; Scofield, I, 574–5.

39 *Arrivall*, 15–17; Warkworth, 15; *CSP Milan*, I, p. 153, no. 213; Scofield, I, 574ff.

40 *Paston Letters*, III, no. 668; *Arrivall*, 19ff; Warkworth, 16–17; Scofield, I, 578ff.

41 *CSP Milan*, I, p. 153, no. 213; *Arrivall*, 20–1; Warkworth, 15.

42 *Arrivall*, 19ff; Warkworth, 16–17; *Paston Letters*, III, no. 668; Scofield, I, 578ff. Warkworth says that 4,000 were killed on both sides.

43 *Arrivall*, 22ff; Warkworth, 17–18; *Hist. Croylandensis Continuatio*, 555.

44 For Edward's preparations, Ross, *Edward IV*, 169–70. Coventry sent 'new soldiers' to him at London, having just probably contributed a company to Warwick's army which fought at Barnet (*Coventry Leet Book*, 364–6, 369).

45 *Arrivall*, 24–5; Basin, II, 80–1.

46 *Arrivall*, 25. By 28 April Edward received at Abingdon a letter addressed by the prince of Wales to the civic governors of Coventry, dated Chard, 18 April (*Coventry Leet Book*, 366–7). It is difficult to surmise how Edward would have interpreted the prince's presence at Chard. The prudent Coventry citizens probably sent the letter to him promptly because of the support they had given Warwick at Barnet (*ibid.*, 364–6).

47 *The Little Red Book of Bristol*, ed. F. B. Bickley, II, 130–1.

48 *Arrivall*, 25–6.

49 *Ibid.*, 25–6; Basin, II, 80–1.

50 *Arrivall*, 26–8; Basin, II, 82–3.

51 *Arrivall*, 28ff; Warkworth, 18–19; *Paston Letters*, III, no. 671. For a discussion of Somerset's attack, see below, pp. 178–9. According to *MS Tanner 2*, in *Six Town Chronicles*, 168, Wenlock 'proditor pugni a suis in vestigio occisus est'.

52 *HMC, Rutland MSS*, I, 4–6; *Arrivall*, 31–3.

53 *Arrivall*, 33ff; *Hist. Croylandensis Continuatio*, 555–6; Warkworth, 19–20; Basin, II, 84ff; *Yorkist Notes*, 374–5. For the Bastard's siege of London, see below, pp. 187–8.

54 *Arrivall*, 38ff; Stone, 116; Richmond, 'Fauconberg's Kentish Rising of May 1471', 681–3. The earl of Essex and Lord Dinham led a force into Essex to pursue the rebels from that shire who had rebelled with the Bastard.

55 *CSP Venice*, I, p. 129, no. 437; Calmette and Périnelle, 145; *CPR, 1467–77*, 289, 281. For Oxford's 1473 invasion, see below, pp. 188–9.

Chapter 5: The Later Risings, 1483–97

1 This account is based on Polydore Vergil, *English Hist.*, 192ff; *Hist. Croylandensis Continuatio*, 567; *Chronicles of London*, 191–2. For a recent account of the rebellion, A. Hanham, *Richard III and His Early Historians 1483–1535* (Oxford 1975), 14ff.

2 For Henry Tudor's early life, see S. B. Chrimes, *Henry VII* (London 1972).

3 For a discussion of Peter Courtenay's possible motives for joining the rebellion, J. A. F. Thomson, 'The Courtenay Family in the Yorkist Period', *BIHR*, 45 (1972), 241–2.

4 For a recent discussion of Buckingham's motives, and his role in the 1483 rebellion, Rawcliffe, 30ff.

5 *Letters and Papers illustrative of the reigns of Richard III and Henry VII*, I, ed. J. Gairdner (Rolls ser., 1861), 54–5, for reference by the duke of Brittany on 22 November 1483 to 10,000 crowns delivered as a loan to the 'sire de Richemont' (Henry Tudor). For Margaret's raising of

loans to support the rebellion in the city of London and elsewhere, Chrimes, 329.

6 *Paston Letters*, III, no. 876.

7 *Stonor Letters and Papers*, II, no. 333.

8 P. Tudor-Craig, *Richard III* (Ipswich 1977), 78–9.

9 *HMC, MSS of Southampton Corporation*, 31.

10 *CPR, 1476–85*, 370. Commissions of array dated Leicester, 23 October, were issued to various counties and towns (*ibid.*, 371).

11 According to a rebel proclamation, Buckingham had repented of his past conduct (*Hist. Croylandensis Continuatio*, 568). For a hostile reaction to his attempts to raise revolt, see Edward Plumpton's letter of 18 October (*Plumpton Letters*, no. vi). There were suspicions current that the duke really wanted the throne for himself (Vergil, *English Hist.*, 195).

12 Chrimes, 328–9.

13 Cf. Owen and Blakeway, 241; Rawcliffe, 32ff.

14 *CPR, 1476–85*, 370. For the wine payment, Dorset County Record Office, Bridport Borough Records, B3/M6, Cofferer's Account, 1483–4. I owe this reference to the kindness of the Rev. E. B. Short.

15 There were rebels at Rochester on 20 October, Gravesend on 22nd, and Guildford on 25th (Chrimes, 328).

16 For the connections of St Leger's daughter the duchess of Exeter with the marquess of Dorset, Bishop Courtenay and possibly Buckingham, see *Grants, Etc. from the Crown during the Reign of Edward the Fifth*, ed. J. G. Nichols (Camden Soc., 1854), pp. lxv–vi.

17 Chrimes, 26–7 and 26n.

18 *Plumpton Letters*, no. vi.

19 *CPR, 1476–85*, 370–1.

20 *Ibid.*, 427–8, 433, 479.

21 Others were Sir Robert Willoughby, Sir Giles Daubeney, Thomas Arundel, John Cheyney, William Brandon and Richard Edgecombe (Vergil, *English Hist.*, 200; *Paston Letters*, III, no. 883). For a list of Henry's companions in exile, Chrimes, 327.

22 For Richard's subversion of Dorset, Chrimes, 38.

23 *Paston Letters*, III, no. 883; Hanham, 19–20. In June the city of London advanced £2,000 to assist the king against the rebels, daily expected to land, and precautions were taken to safeguard the city (Sharpe, I, 326).

24 A. Goodman and A. MacKay, 'A Castilian report on English affairs, 1486', *EHR*, 88, 92ff; for the text of Valera's letter, Tudor-Craig, 67–8, and Hanham, 54ff. Valera also says that Henry had with him 3,000 Englishmen who had fled from Richard. Vergil says that he had a total of 2,000 men, Molinet that Charles provided him with 1,800 soldiers and 60,000 francs, Commynes that he raised 3,000 men of low fighting quality in Normandy (Vergil, *English Hist.*, 216; Molinet, I,

434; *The Memoirs of Philippe de Commynes*, ed. and trans. Kinser and Cazeaux, II, 414–15; cf. Chrimes, 40 and n). John Major (393) says that Charles gave Henry the aid of 5,000 men, including 1,000 Scots captained by John Haddington.

25 The account of the campaign is based mainly on those of Vergil (*English Hist.*, 216ff) and the second Crowland continuator (*Hist. Croylandensis Continuatio*, 573ff). For a recent account, Chrimes, 40ff.

26 *Hist. Croylandensis Continuatio*, 572–3.

27 For Oxford's command and for Chandée, Bernard André, *De vita atque gestis Henrici septimi* ... *historia*, 25, 27, 29; cf. Goodman and MacKay, 94–5.

28 Cf. Chrimes, 42ff and 42n.

29 Pollard, I, 14–15; Owen and Blakeway, 245ff, 247n; H. L. Turner, *Town Defences in England and Wales* (London 1971), 208. For Richard Crompe's part in the surrender of Shrewsbury, *Materials for a History of the Reign of Henry VII*, I, p. 156.

30 Chrimes, 45.

31 *Ibid.*, 46.

32 Cf. *ibid.*, 63 and n. Norfolk had intended to rally his company at Bury St Edmunds (Suffolk) on 16 August, the day on which he expected the king to set forth (*Paston Letters*, III, no. 884). Richard had been joined by Brackenbury's force, though on the way, at Stony Stratford, Sir Thomas Bourchier and Sir Walter Hungerford deserted it to join the rebels.

33 For the topography of the battlefield, J. Gairdner, 'The Battle of Bosworth', *Archaeologia*, 55 (1896), 159ff; A. H. Burne, *The Battlefields of England* (London 1950), 140–1.

34 *Materials*, I, 188; cf. 201.

35 Gairdner's argument that Richard had no artillery (an exceptional situation for a royal army in the period) is contradicted by Molinet's mention of his 'grande quantité d'engiens volans' and by the roll of Henry's first parliament ('The Battle of Bosworth', 169; Molinet, *Chronique*, I, 434; *Rot. Parl.*, VI, 276).

36 Salaçar, Archduke Maximilian's renowned Spanish captain who fought for Richard, may have had a mercenary company (cf. Goodman and MacKay, 95 and n; Hanham, 54n). For the Salazar family, see Commynes, *Mémoires*, ed. Calmette, III, 148 and n, and P. Contamine, *Guerre, état et société à la fin du moyen âge* (Paris 1972), 446.

37 According to Commynes, Charles VIII furnished Henry with artillery. Cannonballs have been dug up on the brow of Ambien Hill, presumably fired by Henry's men at the royal army there (Gairdner, 'The Battle of Bosworth', 167ff). For finds of cannonballs fired at Bosworth, Burne, *Battlefields of England*, 151; Tudor-Craig, 73.

38 These knights were to distinguish themselves in warfare after 1485. According to Vergil, Savage, Brian Sandford and Simon Digby joined

Henry with a 'choice band' late in the afternoon of 21 August. Sir John Savage the younger described as 'eminent in arms as in character and counsel' was rewarded for his service to Henry at Bosworth 'with a multitude of his brothers, kinsmen, servants and friends' (*CPR, 1485–94*, 101–2).

39 For Brackenbury's command, Molinet, *Chronique* I, 434–5.

40 Pollard, I, 16.

41 Vegetius, *Epitoma Rei Militaris*, III, 20, 14.

42 Molinet, *Chronique*, I, 434.

43 Vergil, *Anglica Historia*, 96–7.

44 Molinet says (*Chronique*, I, 435) that Northumberland and his retinue failed to charge Henry's Frenchmen as they should have done, but did nothing and fled, because the earl had an understanding with Henry. For other reflections on Northumberland's conduct and a discussion of his motives, Goodman and MacKay, 95ff. Valera says that 'my lord Tamorlant', commanding Richard's left wing, circled with a large number of soldiers to fight against the king's vanguard, in front of Henry's men (*ibid.*, 92). For the tentative identification of 'Tamorlant' with Northumberland, see below, p. 96 and n. 55.

45 Goodman and MacKay, 92; cf. Vergil, *English Hist.*, 225–6.

46 Molinet, *Chronique*, I, 435. The story that the crown was found abandoned on a hawthorn bush has been rejected by modern scholarship (Chrimes, 49n). Molinet says that another Welshman took the royal corpse, laid 'like a sheep' on horseback with the hair hanging down. Is it not possible that the killer of an anointed king was frightened by what he had done, and removed and abandoned the crown before having the corpse presented, so that it was not clear that he had known what he was doing?

47 Chrimes, 51; Gairdner, 'The Battle of Bosworth', 177. Richard's putative place of death, north-west of Ambien Hill, may have a bearing on the positions of Henry's main 'battle' and the Stanleys' forces.

48 Richard's standard now evocatively hangs at the place.

49 According to Molinet (*Chronique*, I, 435), the royal van was attacked in flight by Lord Stanley.

50 Molinet says that only 300 were killed on both sides in the battle (*Chronique*, I, 436).

51 According to his funeral inscription, in J. Weever, *Ancient Funerall Monuments* (etc.) (London 1631), 835.

52 Pollard, I, 17; cf. *ibid.*, 17n, for John Payntor's remark in 1491 that the earl of Northumberland had betrayed the king.

53 On the day after Bosworth, York city council recorded that Richard 'was piteously slain and murdered, to the great heaviness of this City' (Pollard, I, 17). For Richard's relations with northern society, R. R. Reid, *The King's Council in the North* (London 1921), 42ff; A. J. Pollard, 'The Tyranny of Richard III', *Journal of Medieval Hist.*, 3 (1977); M. A.

Hicks, 'Dynastic Change and Northern Society: the Career of the Fourth Earl of Northumberland, 1470–89', *Northern Hist.*, 14 (1978).

54 Vergil, *Anglica Historia*, 2–3.

55 Goodman and MacKay, 93, 95ff; Pollard, I, 28–9; Hanham, 55–6; but cf. Tudor-Craig, 69.

56 Pollard, I, 19–20. Henry commissioned John de la Pole, duke of Suffolk, to lead the lieges of Suffolk and Norfolk to attend on the king, and suppress 'certain his rebels associate to his old enemies of Scotland' (Suffolk to the sheriff, John Paston, 20 October, Pollard, I, 21–2).

57 *Ibid.*, 21.

58 *Tudor Royal Proclamations*, I, ed. P. L. Hughes and J. F. Larkin, no. 4, p. 5.

59 Pollard, I, 31–2.

60 Goodman and MacKay, 96 and n; Hicks, 92ff.

61 Pollard, I, 34–5.

62 Vergil, *Anglica Historia*, 10–11. Lovell and Stafford had been among Richard's adherents attainted in the 1485 parliament (Pollard, I, 32). The party which had taken sanctuary at Colchester after Bosworth was a large one, and included Stafford's brother Thomas (Vergil, *English Hist.*, 225).

63 Pollard, I, 45; *CPR, 1485–94*, 89, 156, 94–5, 115. The account of the 1486 rebellion is based mainly on Vergil, *Anglica Historia*, 10–13, and C. H. Williams, 'The Rebellion of Humphrey Stafford in 1486', *EHR*, 43 (1928), 181ff.

64 Stafford was forcibly extracted from sanctuary, condemned and executed; his brother Thomas was pardoned. General pardons were granted in 1487 to John Griffith, late of Worcester, and Simon Mawditt, late constable of Worcester castle (*CPR, 1485–94*, 155–6).

65 *Ibid.*, 112.

66 *Tudor Royal Proclamations*, I, p. 10, no. 8. Broughton was a feedman of the earl of Northumberland in 1483–4 (Cockermouth Castle MSS, Carlisle Record Office, Receiver's Account Roll, 1–2 Richard III, D/Lec/29/8). Sir John Hudleston senior had received a fee from the estates of the Kingmaker's uncle Lord Latimer in 1462 and 1465–6 (Cockermouth Castle MSS, Account Rolls of the receiver of the Latimer estates in Cumberland and Westmorland, D/Lec/28/28–9).

67 *CPR, 1485–94*, 119.

68 *Ibid.*, 133; Pollard, I, 32. Sir Robert Harington and Sir Robert Middleton received general pardons and reversals of attainder dated 17 August (*CPR, 1485–94*, 119).

69 *VCH, Lancs.*, VIII, 402–3.

70 I. Grimble, *The Harington Family* (London 1957), 48, 53–4; *CCR, 1468–76*, no. 136; *CPR, 1467–77*, 426–7; *CPR, 1485–94*, 130; Pollard, I, 32.

71 *CPR, 1485–94*, 169; Waurin, V, 344–5; Scofield, I, 381 and n; Grimble, 53–4; *VCH, Lancs.*, VIII, 232–3.

72 Grimble, 44ff; *CCR, 1468–76*, no. 136; *VCH, Lancs.*, VIII, 191ff.

73 Grimble, 54–5; *CCR, 1468–76*, no. 136.

74 *Foedera*, XI, 699.

75 *Arrivall*, 7; Warkworth, 14.

76 *CPR, 1467–77*, 426–7; Grimble, 55ff.

77 Pollard, I, 52–3.

78 Vergil, *Anglica Historia*, 12ff; André, 49ff; Molinet, I, 562ff; Pollard, I, 51–2 and 3, 246–7, 261–3; *York Civic Records*, II, 6–7. For the reasons for Irish support of the Yorkist cause in Henry's reign, Chrimes, 73ff.

79 Hearne, *Collectanea*, IV, 209; Vergil, *Anglica Historia*, 20–1; *York Civic Records*, II, 10–13.

80 *York Civic Records*, II, 13–14, 16; Hearne, 209–10; Pollard, I, 47.

81 *Paston Letters*, III, no. 895.

82 Vergil, *Anglica Historia*, 20–3; Molinet, I, 562–3; Pollard, III, 262–3, 265–6; *York Civic Records*, II, 20; F. Redlich, *The German Military Enterpriser and his Work Force*, I (Wiesbaden 1964), 107–8; *VCH, Lancs.*, VIII, 287, 309, 402–3; Hearne, 210.

83 Hearne, 209–14; *York Civic Records*, II, 22–3; Vergil, *Anglica Historia*, 22ff; Molinet, I, 563.

84 *York Civic Records*, II, 3ff.

85 Pollard, I, 52–4.

86 *York Civic Records*, II, 22; *CP*, XI, 544–5, 569–70; *Testamenta Vetusta* ed. N. H. Nicholas, 2 vols (London 1826), II, 587; Hicks, 89, 97–8. The York records say that the Scropes made their assault on the city 'constrained as it was said by their folks'; perhaps by an appearance of half-heartedness they secured the gentle treatment which Henry gave them (*CPR, 1485–94*, 190, 199, 238, 264). Scrope of Bolton's half-heartedness in rebellion in 1470 had turned out to his advantage. He was a councillor of Richard III (*CPR, 1476–85*, 501–1).

87 For northern gentlefolk who joined Henry, Vergil, *Anglica Historia*, 23n.

88 *York Civic Records*, II, 4–6, 16, 20–22. Molinet says that the invaders passed over great mountains to 'Scanfort', where many local lords came into the Yorkist obedience (*Chronique*, I, 563). Perhaps he meant Carnforth.

89 *York Civic Records*, II, 22–3. On 23 June Northumberland was at Richmond (Yorks.) (Pollard, I, 54).

90 Molinet, I, 563–4.

91 This account of the movements of Henry's army is based on the anonymous account printed by Hearne.

92 For an impressive list of Henry's supporters, Vergil, *Anglica Historia*, 22n. For agreements by the community of Henley (Oxon.) to finance

soldiers on 25 May and on 8 and 10 June, 'pro domino rege intendente transmeare versus partes boreales', *Henley Borough Records. Assembly Books i–iv*, 94–5.

93 Vergil, *Anglica Historia*, 22–3; *The Place-Names of Nottinghamshire*, ed. J. E. B. Gover, Allen Mawer and F. M. Stenton (Cambridge 1940), 245.

94 Vergil, *Anglica Historia*, 24–7; Pollard, I, 53; Hearne, 213–14; *York Civic Records*, II, 22–3; Molinet, I, 564–5.

95 Vergil, *Anglica Historia*, 20–1; Hearne, 209.

96 Vergil, *Anglica Historia*, 24–7; Pollard, III, 263–4; *York Civic Records*, II, 23ff.

97 *York Civic Records*, II, 28–9. For the expedition under Sir Richard Edgecombe which reasserted Henry's authority at Dublin, Chrimes, 78–9.

98 Molinet, I, 563–4; *Letters and Papers*, I, 94–5.

99 Pollard, I, 51.

100 Weever, 835.

101 Some southerners were attainted for rebellion in 1487 – four of the Mallary family from Northamptonshire and Robert Mannyng of Dunstable, Beds. (Pollard, I, 52–3).

102 Vergil, *Anglica Historia*, 38–9.

103 *Plumpton Correspondence*, letter XXV, p. 61.

104 Vergil, *Anglica Historia*, 38–9; M. E. James, 'The Murder at Cocklodge', *Durham Univ. Jnl*, n.s., 26 (1964–5), 80ff; Hicks, 78ff.

105 Pollard, I, 72ff; Hicks, 79–80, 100.

106 *Paston Letters*, III, no. 916; cf. no. 915.

107 Hicks, 78; Vergil, *Anglica Historia*, 38–9; James, 85.

108 Pollard, I, 80; James, 86n.

109 *Paston Letters*, III, no. 915.

110 Vergil, *Anglica Historia*, 38–9; Pollard, I, 79–81; James, 86–7. Henry was in Yorkshire by 22 May, but departed before the end of the first week in June (*ibid.*, 87n).

111 Pollard, I, 81 and n. For Surrey's return to favour, see M. J. Tucker, *The Life of Thomas Howard Earl of Surrey and Second Duke of Norfolk 1443–1524* (The Hague 1964), 48ff.

112 R. L. Storey, *The Reign of Henry VII* (London 1968), 148–9, 144–5.

113 A. Conway, *Henry VII's Relations with Scotland and Ireland 1485–1498* (Cambridge 1932), 39–40, 48ff. Henry wrote in 1493 that at first in Ireland Warbeck claimed to be an illegitimate son of Richard III, and later claimed to be Warwick, but was at present claiming to be Edward IV's younger son, Richard duke of York – the claim on which he finally settled (Pollard, I, 93–4). For an official Tudor account of Warbeck's intrigues and invasions, André, 65ff.

114 Pollard, I, 93–5. For Henry's naval preparations, Conway, 41.

115 Vergil, *Anglica Historia*, 70ff; Pollard, I, 100–3, 109ff. FitzWalter was only executed in 1496 after plotting to escape from his prison in Guines castle (*ibid.*, 144).

116 Vergil, *Anglica Historia*, 80–3; Molinet, II, 421–2; Pollard, I, 103ff, 111–12; *Chronicles of London*, 206–7, for captured foreigners. It was reported in London that 500–600 invaders landed and that the fourteen ships which remained at sea probably carried up to 800 more. The Kentish force was 140–160 strong; it captured 169 invaders, killed 2, and others were drowned (*ibid.*, 105). Albon wrote that 140 rebels were slain or captured, de Puebla that 150 were killed and 80 captured, Molinet that 300 landed and suffered about 150 casualties (Pollard, I, 105, 107; Molinet, II, 421–2).

117 Pollard, I, 105ff. For the capture of the captains 'Jennot', 'Quentin' and 'Beld', *Memorials of King Henry the Seventh*, 147–8.

118 Vergil, *Anglica Historia*, 82–5. For Anglo-Scottish relations, Conway, *passim*; Chrimes, 86ff. See also R. L. Mackie, *King James IV of Scotland* (Edinburgh 1958), 78ff; R. Nicholson, *Scotland. The Later Middle Ages* (Edinburgh 1974), 549ff. Warbeck had been in correspondence with James in March 1492 (Conway, 39).

119 Conway, 84–6, 99; Pollard, III, 278–9. Waterford had defied the Yorkist rebels in 1487 (*ibid.*, 265–6).

120 Pollard, I, 136–7. Bothwell was also certain that Northumberland men were showing disloyal tendencies at 'march days' and secret meetings with Scots, and facilitating the escape of 'vagabonds' to join Warbeck.

121 Pollard, I, 137ff. Bothwell reports Lalain as referring to 'Richard IV' as 'Perkin' in his remarks to James, in Perkin's presence (*ibid.*, 142). Both Neville and Lalain were to serve the Yorkist pretender Edmund de la Pole (*Letters and Papers*, I, 276–8).

122 *Accounts of the Lord High Treasurer of Scotland*, I, cxxxix ff, 296ff; Mackie, 81ff. Warbeck's movements on 21 September were mysterious: he seems to have been returning to Scotland from James in England. For their quarrel, see below, p. 216.

123 Pollard, I, 143.

124 Vergil, *Anglica Historia*, 86ff. In 1497 Henry's envoy to James, Bishop Fox of Durham, was instructed to claim compensation for the destruction of castles and fortalices in the previous year's invasion, as a condition of peace (*Letters and Papers*, I, 107).

125 *Accounts of the Lord High Treasurer*, I, 297.

126 *Ibid.*, 296.

127 Nicholson, 551–2, 600ff.

128 Vergil, *Anglica Historia*, 90ff; *Tudor Royal Proclamations*, I, 39–40, no. 35; *Letters and Papers*, I, 232; Sharpe, I, 331–2; Chrimes, 90.

129 Vergil, *Anglica Historia*, 94–5; *Select Cases in the Council of Henry VII*, ed. C. G. Bayne and W. H. Dunham Jr (Selden Soc. vol. 75,

London 1958), xxix–xxx; *Letters and Papers*, I, 263ff.

130 *CPR, 1494–1509*, 117, 115.

131 Conway, 110–11; Chrimes, 90–1.

132 Pollard, I, 162–3.

133 *Ibid.*, 163ff.

134 Vergil, *Anglica Historia*, 104–5, 108–9; Pollard, I, 166–8. For the siege of Exeter, see below, p. 190.

135 Pollard, I, 167–8; Sharpe, I, 333.

136 Pollard, I, 168–9; Vergil, *Anglica Historia*, 106–7.

137 Molinet, II, 439–40; *MS Tanner 2*, in *Six Town Chronicles*, 173; Sharpe, I, 333; Vergil, *Anglica Historia*, 106ff. According to the official London version, Warbeck went from Taunton to 'Mynet' with fewer than sixty adherents. But Minehead, on the Bristol Channel, is in the opposite direction from the one Warbeck is known to have taken. He may have gone to Minehead first, and found that Henry's fleet made escape thence impossible.

138 Vergil, *Anglica Historia*, 106ff.

139 See M. Levine, *Tudor Dynastic Problems, 1460–1571* (London 1973).

Chapter 6: Military Convention and Recruitment

1   *Rot. Parl.*, V, 348.

2   *Knyghthode and Bataile*, 74.

3   Whethamstede, I, 392. Henry knighted his son, one of his opponents, after the battle (*Annales*, 776).

4   Quoted in C. T. Allmand (ed.), *Society at War* (Edinburgh 1973), 17.

5   F. H. Russell, *The Just War in the Middle Ages* (Cambridge 1975), 298; cf. *ibid.*, *passim*, and M. H. Keen, *The Laws of War in the Late Middle Ages* (London 1965), 63ff.

6   Keen, 106ff.

7   Armstrong, 36.

8   *Rot. Parl.*, V, 280–2; Armstrong.

9   See above, pp. 29–30, 34ff.

10 *Records of the Borough of Nottingham*, II, 369.

11 *English Chron.*, 81–2.

12 *Rot. Parl.*, V, 348. According to *Bale's Chron.*, 148, Henry was in the foreward at Ludford Bridge, where he would have been more vulnerable to shot.

13 See above, pp. 72, 97. The opposing sides in Yorkshire had made a brief truce in December 1460: its rupture by the Lancastrians probably prejudiced the chances of negotiation in 1461.

14 *Foedera*, II, 709–11.

15 Valera, cited in Goodman and MacKay, 92; Vergil, *English Hist.*, 225–6.

16 See above, pp. 105, 108, 115.

17 See above, pp. 57ff.

18 *HMC, Rutland MSS*, I, 3–4; cf. *Arrivall*, 17, 20.

19 See below, p. 205.

20 Richmond, 'Fauconberg's Kentish rising of May 1471', 676.

21 'Tunc rex constituit sui certaminis constabularium et principalem actorem ducem Bokyngamiae' (Armstrong, 23 and n).

22 G. D. Squibb, *The High Court of Chivalry* (Oxford 1959), 1ff; Keen, 27ff; cf. *Tudor Royal Proclamations*, I, no. 13, p. 15.

23 *Annales*, 782; Warkworth, 38–9. For the placing of prisoners in the constable's ward by King Arthur, Malory, I, 211.

24 *CPR, 1494–1509*, 34, 115. These knights were holding the offices as deputies (cf. Squibb, 228ff). For the commission, including Digby, to execute the offices on the rebel Lord Audley in 1497, *CPR, 1494–1509*, 115. At York in 1487 Sir John Turberville, knight marshal, had judged recent rebels for treason (*York Civic Records*, II, 28).

25 Squibb, 1ff.

26 *Knyghthode and Bataile*, 32–3, 44–5.

27 Pollard, I, 67–9.

28 *Tudor Royal Proclamations*, I, no. 213, pp. 14–15. For earlier proclamations on discipline in the wars, see below, p. 215.

29 Whethamstede, I, 394ff; Malory, I, 243.

30 Waurin, V, 325.

31 *Knyghthode and Bataile*, 58–9.

32 Hearne, *Collectanea*, IV, 209–10; Armstrong, 23–4; *Arrivall*, 3; *Hist. Croylandensis Continuatio*, 555. For Oxford's proposed arrangements to consult with his council and three or four Norfolk gentlemen over defence measures in 1471, *Paston Letters*, II, no. 663.

33 Waurin, V, 290–1, 293, 295–7, 299, 306, 325–6, 337.

34 See above, pp. 84–5, 87ff.

35 See above, p. 37.

36 Whethamstede, I, 338; *Knyghthode and Bataile*, 1ff.

37 Cf. *Knyghthode and Bataile*, 11, 32.

38 K. Fowler, *The Age of Plantagenet and Valois* (London 1967), 125–6; cf. Powicke, 'Lancastrian Captains', 371ff.

39 *Rot. Parl.*, V, 369; Hearne, *Collectanea*, IV, 209–10.

40 Malory, I, 232–3, 235.

41 See above, pp. 120, 75.

42 *Short English Chron.*, 75.

43 Fowler, *Age of Plantagenet and Valois*, 125–6; K. Fowler (ed.), *The Hundred Years War* (London 1971), 10; cf. Powicke, 'Lancastrian Captains', *passim*. For Harowe, below, p. 202.

44 *Annales*, 776; *Short English Chron.*, 77; Worcestre, *Itineraries*, 203.
45 *Brief Latin Chron.*, 178.
46 Vergil, *English Hist.*, 200.
47 *Coventry Leet Book*, 282–3.
48 *Records of the City of Norwich*, I, 406. For Rokewode, *Paston Letters*, I, nos 174, 201.
49 Chamberlain's Account, 1463–4, in *Records of the Borough of Nottingham*, II, 377.
50 'Gregory', 212–13.
51 Warkworth, 13–14; *Arrivall*, 3–4.
52 Vergil, *Anglica Historia*, 90ff.
53 'Gregory', 193; *English Chron.*, 64, 66; *Paston Letters*, I, p. 133n.
54 Waurin, V, 334.
55 *Bale's Chron.*, 151; *English Chron.*, 107–8. Cade had a certain 'Lovelase' in his service at Southwark in 1450 (*Paston Letters*, I, no. 99).
56 'Gregory', 214.
57 *Ibid.*, 205.
58 Waurin, V, 273, 276, 278–9, 306, 325–6; cf. *Paston Letters*, I, no. 357.
59 For some documentary illustrations, Allmand (ed.), *Society at War*, 57ff.
60 J. W. Sherborne, 'Indentured retinues and English expeditions to France, 1369–1380', *EHR*, 79 (1964); A. Goodman, 'The military subcontracts of Sir Hugh Hastings, 1380', *EHR*, 95 (1980).
61 For examples of fourteenth-century life indentures, see N. B. Lewis, 'Indentures of Retinue with John of Gaunt, duke of Lancaster' (etc.), *Camden Miscellany*, XXII (1964). For the effects of legal limitations on the grant of liveries, and a sceptical view of the importance of retaining in constituting the first duke of Buckingham's military companies, Rawcliffe, 72ff.
62 *CDS*, IV, nos 1387, 1466.
63 Allmand (ed.), *Society at War*, 74–6; *Wars of the English in France*, ed. Stevenson, II, 512–15; *English Chron.*, 85; Scofield, I, 53–4.
64 See, for example, *Foedera*, XI, 444.
65 *Rot. Parl.*, V, 348.
66 'Gregory', 226.
67 Vergil, *English Hist.*, 215–16.
68 *Paston Letters*, III, no. 874.
69 *Plumpton Correspondence*, p. 96n.
70 *Letters and Papers*, I, 112. To encourage a good response to such summonses, it was enacted in 1495 that no person attending in response to a royal summons for military service was to be liable for that cause to conviction or attaint of high treason or for any other offences (*Statutes of the Realm*, II, 568).
71 *CDS*, IV, no. 1342.

72 W. H. Dunham, Jr, *Lord Hastings' Indentured Retainers 1461–1483* (New Haven, Conn., 1955), 25.

73 See above, pp. 127, 165.

74 E.g., *CCR, 1454–61*, 408, 410, 415.

75 *Annales*, 780.

76 *Hist. Croylandensis Continuatio*, 568.

77 Lander, *Crown and Nobility*, 143 and n; *Statutes of the Realm*, II, 568 (1495 c. I).

78 For Lancastrian contracting of mercenaries in 1462, Calmette and Périnelle, 282.

79 W. Fraser, *The Douglas Book*, III (Edinburgh 1885), 92–3.

80 *English Chron.*, 79–80; 'Gregory', 204.

81 'Gregory', 212. He may have been referring to the Lancastrian magnates' servants as well as the queen's.

82 *Short English Chron.*, 78.

83 They were the queen's servant John Marfyn, Henry's purser Roger Water, the queen's yeoman Thomas Hunte, Henry's porter Robert Wattys. Also executed were Sir Thomas Fynderne, king's knight and former lieutenant of Guines (*CPR, 1452–61*, 22), and John Gosse, Somerset's carver (*Short English Chron.*, 79–80; 'Gregory', 225–6).

84 *CPR, 1452–61*, 323.

85 *Paston Letters*, I, no. 357; 'Gregory', 214; *Paston Letters*, II, no. 413.

86 *CPR, 1452–61*, 18, 335, 338; D. A. L. Morgan, 'The King's Affinity in the Polity of Yorkist England', *TRHS*, 5th ser., 23 (1973), 7–8.

87 *Paston Letters*, II, no. 463; Warkworth, 3.

88 Morgan, 7–8 and 8n; *CPR, 1467–77*, 227.

89 Morgan, 10ff.

90 *Coventry Leet Book*, 353–4. Pluralists were to send a man for each office they held.

91 *Paston Letters*, II, no. 648.

92 *Arrivall*, 7–9, 20; Warkworth, 14; Morgan, 11.

93 Morgan, 16–17; cf. below, pp. 188–9.

94 *Epístolas y otros varios tratados de Mosén Diego de Valera*, ed. J. A. de Balenchana (Madrid 1878), 91ff.

95 Vergil, *Anglica Historia*, 6–7, 10–11.

96 *Italian Relation*, 39.

97 *Statutes of the Realm*, II, 582.

98 *Ibid.*, 648–9.

99 *Arrivall*, 31–2.

100 *Plumpton Correspondence*, no. I.

101 *Stonor Letters and Papers*, I, no. 112.

102 *Paston Letters*, II, no. 653.

103 *HMC, Rutland MSS*, I, 4–5.

104 *Ibid.*, 7–8; *Household Books of John Duke of Norfolk* (etc.), 480ff.

105 *HMC, Rutland MSS*, I, 8; *Plumpton Letters*, p. 96n. Henry's summons to Vernon is dated London, 17 October. The editor thought the year was 1485, but the contents appear to refer to the Yorkshire rebellion of 1489.

106 Pollard, I, 93–5; cf. his summons to Talbot in 1497, *ibid.*, 162–3.

107 *Statutes of the Realm*, II, 426.

108 Dunham, 26ff.

109 A recent study of the first duke of Buckingham's 'affinity' has been made by Dr Rawcliffe (72ff); cf. A. J. Pollard, 'The Northern Retainers of Richard Nevill, Earl of Salisbury', *Northern Hist.*, 11 (1976), 52ff.

110 Cf. Morgan, 16 and n, 19 and n.

111 *HMC, Rutland MSS*, I, 2.

112 *Ibid.*, 3ff.

113 *Stonor Letters and Papers*, II, no. 333.

114 *Paston Letters*, III, no. 876.

115 *Ibid.*, no. 884.

116 *Ibid.*, no. 887.

117 *CPR, 1452–61*, 552–3.

118 This and the following paragraphs on commissions of array are based on M. R. Powicke, *Military Obligation in Medieval England* (Oxford 1962), *passim*, and H. J. Hewitt, *The Organization of War under Edward III, 1338–62* (Manchester 1966), 36–43.

119 Numbers were usually specified only for contingents going abroad.

120 Mounts came to be required for expeditions abroad.

121 The customary weapons were bow and arrows, sword and knife.

122 *CPR, 1452–61*, 557ff.

123 *Paston Letters*, I, no. 346. Paston added that commissions were certainly made out for various shires 'that every man be ready in his best array to come when the King send for them' – perhaps referring to the commissions of December 1459.

124 *Arrivall*, 23.

125 *Coventry Leet Book*, 341ff.

126 *Foedera*, XI, 444–5.

127 *CPR, 1452–61*, 557ff.

128 *Ibid.*, 659. 'Gregory', 211, says that March 'mustered his men without the town walls [of Hereford] in a marsh that is called Wyg mersche. And over him men saw . . . three suns shining' – perhaps the origin of the Yorkist 'sunburst' badge.

129 *Paston Letters*, II, no. 664.

130 *Ibid.*, III, no. 887. The proclamation was to say that the arrayed men were to be 'ordered according to the last commission afore this'. Frequency and continuity of summons enabled arrayers to expect that the organization would work efficiently.

131 See above, p. 42.

132 *Coventry Leet Book*, 342–3.

133 Warkworth, 53–4; cf. Edward's proclamation of 31 March, *ibid.*, 56–7.
134 *Ibid.*, 52–3.
135 See above, p. 75.
136 *Paston Letters*, III, no. 894; cf. no. 895. For confusion in 1483 caused by opponents' attempts to raise soldiers in the same region, *Plumpton Correspondence*, no. vi.
137 *Foedera*, XI, 501–2.
138 *Ibid.*, 523–4.
139 *Ibid.*, 624. The Norfolk and Suffolk array commissioned in October 1485 was to have hobelars and archers (*Paston Letters*, III, no. 887).
140 *Foedera*, XI, 680–1.
141 *Tudor Royal Proclamations*, I, no. 28, pp. 30–1.
142 *Ibid.*, no. 61, pp. 83–4.
143 *Arrivall*, 33; cf. Richmond, 'Fauconberg's Kentish rising of May 1471', 676. For the Bastard's supporters, *ibid.*, 684ff.
144 *Foedera*, XI, 523–4.
145 *Arrivall*, 8.
146 *Foedera*, XI, 706–7.
147 *Hist. Croylandensis Continuatio*, 573.
148 See pp. 145–6.
149 *Paston Letters*, II, no. 384.
150 Warkworth, 12. The Kentish and Sussex forces arrayed in 1492 for service on Henry VII's French expedition were to receive the king's wages: no such stipulation was made in the commissions to array for war with the Scots in 1497 (*Tudor Royal Proclamations*, I, pp. 30–1, 40–1). Warbeck promised recompense for arrayed service in 1497 (Pollard, I, 155).
151 Bridport Muster Roll, 1457, Dorset County Record Office, B3/FG3; *CPR, 1452–61*, 406–10.
152 *Stonor Letters and Papers*, II, no. 258; for Oxford's 1487 arrays, *Household Books of John Duke of Norfolk* (etc.), 501–3, 493ff; cf. M. J. Tucker, 'Household Accounts 1490–1491 of John de Vere, earl of Oxford', *EHR*, 75 (1960). Kingsford dated the Stonor muster as ?*c.* 1480.
153 *Coventry Leet Book*, 282–3.
154 Hudson and Tingey, I, 405–6.
155 *Records of the Borough of Nottingham*, II, 377.
156 Dominic Mancini, *The Usurpation of Richard III*, ed. C. A. J. Armstrong (Oxford 1969), 98–9, 132–3.
157 Quoted in J. Cornwall, *Revolt of the Peasantry 1549* (London 1977), 21.
158 'Gregory', 204–5, 212; *English Chron.*, 107–8.
159 *Hist. Croylandensis Continuatio*, 542.
160 *Ibid.*, 552; cf. the author of the *Arrivall*'s remarks on the poor service

which Yorkshiremen would have given if the earl of Northumberland had raised them in Edward's interest after his landing in 1471 (*Arrivall*, 6–7).

161 *Coventry Leet Book*, 308.

162 For Bridport's hire of a man to purchase gunpowder at Abbotsbury in 1465–6, Bailiffs' Account, Dorset CRO, B3/M6; for 'The harness belonging to the town' of Reading in 1488, *Reading Records*, I, 1431–1602, ed. J. M. Guilding (1892), 85. For towns' possession of guns, Turner, 84.

163 *Paston Letters*, III, no. 908.

164 *Paston Letters*, II, no. 638.

165 *Hist. Croylandensis Continuatio*, 582.

166 Cf. Commynes, *Memoirs*, ed. and trans. Jones, 81.

167 *Paston Letters*, II, no. 384.

168 'Gregory', 215.

169 Alternatively, many of the levies who had won at Wakefield may have had to be dismissed when their pay ran out, and replaced by new, perhaps less experienced and poorly financed levies.

170 *Paston Letters*, II, no. 464; cf. above, pp. 61–2.

171 *Arrivall*, 24.

172 *Ibid.*, 32.

173 Warkworth, 20.

174 *English Chron.*, 87.

175 Sir John Fortescue, *The Governance of England*, ed. C. Plummer (Oxford 1885), 137ff.

176 See J. J. Goring, 'The general proscription of 1522', *EHR*, 86 (1971), 681ff; A. C. Chibnall (ed.), *The Certificate of Musters for Buckinghamshire in 1522* (HMC 1973).

Chapter 7: Supply, Billets and Ordnance

1 Pollard, III, 44; *Italian Relation*, 23.

2 Malory, *Works*, I, 235.

3 Sir John Fortescue, *De Laudibus Legum Angliae*, trans. Grigor, 60; cf. H. J. Hewitt, *The Organization of War under Edward III, 1338–62*, 52ff; C. G. Cruickshank, *Army Royal. Henry VIII's Invasion of France 1513* (Oxford 1969), 60ff.

4 *Foedera*, XI, 449.

5 *Knyghthode and Bataile*, 41–2, 58, 85.

6 Malory, *Works*, I, 24, 228.

7 Poulson, I, 227–8.

8 *Coventry Leet Book*, 356–7.

9 *Knyghthode and Bataile*, 22–3.

10 'Gregory', 214.

11 *Arrivall*, 28. In 1484 the duke of Norfolk had made prior arrangements for the provision of horse fodder in the event of an expedition. Sir Harry Rosse and two others had undertaken 'to get my Lord's grass of his servants and tenants' (*Household Books of John Duke of Norfolk* (etc.), 492).

12 See p. 218.

13 Fortescue, *De Laudibus Legum Angliae*, trans. Grigor, 56–7.

14 See below, p. 218.

15 *Tudor Royal Proclamations*, I, no. 12, p. 13.

16 *Ibid.*, no. 13, p. 14.

17 Pollard, I, 50; *York Civic Records*, II, 25–6. Henry's 'knight herbingers' sent a copy of the royal ordinances of war to the mayor to be published through the city, prior to the royal arrival (*ibid.*, 26–7).

18 *Annales*, 775; see above, p. 43.

19 *Short English Chron.*, 76; *Brief Notes*, 155; 'Gregory', 214; *Annales*, 776–7; *York Civic Records*, I, 135.

20 *CPR, 1452–61*, 658–9.

21 *VCH Yorks., East Riding*, I, 24. For Lynn, see above, p. 44.

22 *CSP Milan*, I, p. 54, no. 71.

23 Waurin, V, 335; cf. the remarks of Bishop Beauchamp, *CSP Venice*, I, pp. 101–2, no. 371.

24 *HMC, Fifth Report*, part I, 523.

25 *Henry the Sixth. A Reprint of John Blacman's Memoir*, ed. and trans. M. R. James (Cambridge 1919), 20, 43; *Paston Letters*, II, no. 464.

26 *VCH Yorks., East Riding*, I, 25.

27 *Lincolnshire Rebellion*, 16–17; Warkworth, 54; cf. above, pp. 72–3.

28 *Lincolnshire Rebellion*, 17.

29 *Arrivall*, 31–2; see above, pp. 77, 83. The Beverley governors' account of 1460–1 contains expenses incurred as a result of the Yorkist occupation after Towton, which may have been harsh because the town had sent men to the losing side (Poulson, I, 238ff).

30 Warkworth, 6; see above, pp. 68–9.

31 *Knyghthode and Bataile*, 30.

32 *Arrivall*, 26.

33 *Tudor Royal Proclamations*, I, no. 13, p. 14; Hearne, 212.

34 Fortescue, *De Laudibus Legum Angliae*, trans. Grigor, 60.

35 Malory, *Works*, I, 172–3.

36 See above, p. 31.

37 *Arrivall*, 18, 25–6.

38 Vergil, *Anglica Historia*, 22ff.

39 *Household Books of John Duke of Norfolk* (etc.), 33, 47, 50, 67.

40 O. F. G. Hogg, *The Royal Arsenal*, I (Oxford 1963), 8ff; H. L. Blackmore, *The Armouries of the Tower of London*, I, *Ordnance* (London 1976), 1ff.

41 For fortifications, see below, pp. 181ff.

42 Hogg, 32–3.

43 Devon, 482. For the cost of transporting guns to Kenilworth the previous year, *ibid.*, 481.

44 *Short English Chron.*, 73.

45 *Wars of the English in France*, ed. Stevenson, II, pt 2, 512; Scofield, I, 50.

46 Blackmore, 3; J. R. Hooker, 'Notes on the Organization and Supply of the Tudor Military under Henry VII' *Huntington Library Quarterly*, 23 (1959–60), 26ff.

47 Blackmore, 3. Foreigners were heavily involved in the provision of firearms in England. Motte was reappointed with two subordinates by Henry VII in December 1485 (*CPR, 1485–94*, 48). In Henry's reign Nele supervised the iron foundries making royal munitions in Ashdown Forest, Sussex (Hooker, 27–8).

48 *CPR, 1485–94*, 18, 77–8.

49 *Memorials of King Henry the Seventh*, 303; 'To the City of London', in *A Choice of Scottish Verse*, ed. J. and W. MacQueen (London 1972), 33, cf. 202; *The Pylgrymage of Sir Richard Guylforde*, ed. Sir Henry Ellis (Camden Soc. 1851), 7–8.

Chapter 8: Methods of Warfare

1 For the techniques of the *chevauchée*, see Hewitt, *The Black Prince's Expedition of 1355–1357*, 46ff.

2 The terms used in the early sixteenth century were 'foreward', 'middleward' and 'rearward' (Cruickshank, *passim*). The 'battles' in which soldiers fought were not necessarily identical with those in which they had ridden: considerable regrouping often took place when an action was anticipated (Fowler, *Age of Plantagenet and Valois*, 100–1).

3 Fowler, 101, 107–8.

4 Powicke, 'Lancastrian Captains', 371.

5 Commynes, *Memoirs*, ed. and trans. Jones, 72.

6 Fowler, 59ff, 79.

7 M. Mallett, *Mercenaries and their Masters* (London 1974), 37.

8 Commynes, *Memoirs*, ed. and trans. Jones, 71; cf. 73, 76, 101, 124.

9 B. H. St J. O'Neil, *Castles and Cannon* (Oxford 1960), *passim*; Turner, 65–6.

10 *King's Works*, I, 448–9. In 1451 the south-east corner of Sandwich was fortified with the two-storey 'Bulwark', armed with guns: this may have been 'le bollewert' captured by assault by the French in 1457 (Turner, 165; Waurin, V, 385ff). For the development of gun emplacements, M. G. A. Vale, 'New Techniques and Old Ideals: The Impact of Artillery on

War and Chivalry at the End of the Hundred Years War', in *War, Literature and Politics in the Late Middle Ages*, ed. C. T. Allmand (Liverpool 1976), 61ff.

11 Cited in Bornstein, 470.

12 Fowler, 109ff; P. E. Russell, introduction to O'Neil, xiv ff; Mallett, 160ff; Hooker, 28–9; Cruickshank, 72ff; Vale, 57ff; *Knyghthode and Bataile*, 68. For *Mons Meg*, Blackmore, 108.

13 Mallett, 156ff; cf. Vale, 62ff.

14 *Paston Letters*, I, no. 67. Gairdner's tentative dating of the letter is 1449.

15 Mallett, 160–1.

16 Vale, 65ff; Basin, *Histoire des règnes de Charles VII et de Louis XI*, ed. J. Quicherat, I, 263–8, trans. by C. T. Allmand in *Society at War*, 111–13.

17 See below, p. 172.

18 Powicke, 'Lancastrian Captains', 376, 379; Fowler, 110; *CP*, II, 388; J. S. Roskell, *The Commons in the Parliament of 1422* (Manchester 1954), 153.

19 *CP*, VI, 619 and n.

20 *Ibid.*, XI, 504ff; *English Chron.*, 98.

21 *CP*, V, 281ff; *English Chron.*, 93; *CPR, 1452–61*, 243; *Wars of the English in France*, ed. Stevenson, I, 519–20.

22 *CP*, V, 284. Fauconberg was acting as lieutenant at Calais on 31 January 1461 (*CSP Milan*, I, p. 47, no. 61).

23 Other veterans who fought in the Wars of the Roses were John Bourchier, earl of Essex (d. 1483), who had been comte of Eu, William Herbert, earl of Pembroke (d. 1469), Richard Wydeville, earl Rivers (d. 1469), James Butler, earl of Wiltshire (d. 1461), Viscount Beaumont (d. 1460), who had been comte of Boulogne, Lords Audley (d. 1459), Clinton (d. 1464), de la Warr (d. 1476), Roos (d. 1461), Sudeley (d. 1473) and Wenlock (d. 1471) (*CP, passim*).

24 *Paston Letters*, I, no. 99.

25 See K. B. McFarlane, 'William Worcester, a Preliminary Survey', in *Studies presented to Sir Hilary Jenkinson*, ed. J. C. Davies (London 1957).

26 Worcestre, *Itineraries*, 204–5. Worcester also noted the French service of Welshmen who were killed at Edgcote in 1469 (*ibid.*, 338–41).

27 See above, p. 30.

28 Worcestre, *Itineraries*, 352–3; *CPR, 1452–61*, 553. For Trollope, see also pp. 52–3, 127. Another highly regarded veteran who fought in the wars was Sir Thomas Kyriel, whose experience of command in France went back at least to 1429. He was summarily executed by the queen's party after being captured at St Albans in 1461 (*English Chron.*, 108, 205; Waurin, V, 329–30).

29 See above, p. 124.

30 William Caxton, *The Book of the Fayttes of Armes and of Chyualrye*, ed. A. T. P. Byles (EETS 1937), 291.

31 'Gregory', 213–14.

32 Whethamstede, I, 162; *Cely Letters*, ed. Hanham, no. 178. Guto'r Glyn, describing Lord Herbert's invasion of Gwynedd in the 1460s, says that 'Three warbands went into Wales' (*Medieval Welsh Lyrics*, ed. and trans. Clancy (London 1965), 207).

33 Molinet, II, 332; Pollard, I, 92; Cruickshank, 29ff.

34 *Bale's Chron.*, 150–1; *Benet's Chron.*, 226, 229–30; Waurin, V, 336–7; see also above, p. 37. These complexities may be an illusion created by chroniclers' muddles.

35 *CSP Venice*, I, p. 99, no. 370.

36 Vergil, *English Hist.*, 219–20; Vergil, *Anglicae Historiae libri . . .* (1555), 561.

37 *Arrivall*, 28.

38 Vergil, *Anglica Historia*, 24–5.

39 Molinet, I, 564. According to *Bale's Chron.*, 151, the Yorkist army at Northampton was divided into four 'battles', but Whethamstede, I, 373, says it was divided into three.

40 *Knyghthode and Bataile*, 39–40.

41 See above, pp. 37, 46, 50.

42 See above, pp. 71, 83.

43 Vergil, *English Hist.*, 222ff.

44 Vergil, *Anglica Historia*, 10–11; see above, p. 97.

45 *Ibid.*, 24–5.

46 Pollard, I, 80–1; see above, p. 108.

47 See above, p. 114.

48 See above, p. 115.

49 See above, p. 82.

50 Vergil, *English Hist.*, 223; Molinet, I, 564; Pollard, I, 80–1.

51 Vergil, *English Hist.*, 145, 223.

52 See p. 24.

53 Warkworth, 6–7; see above, pp. 68–9.

54 *Arrivall*, 29.

55 Vergil, *English Hist.*, 223.

56 See above, pp. 92–3.

57 Molinet, I, 564.

58 See above, p. 165.

59 Mallett, 160–1.

60 Commynes, *Memoirs*, ed. and trans. Jones, 94ff.

61 Contamine, *Guerre, état et société à la fin du moyen âge* (Paris 1972), 299–300.

62 Commynes, *Memoirs*, ed. and trans. Jones, 65.

63 *Ibid.*, 77, 87, 101.

64 *Benet's Chron.*, 206; Whethamstede, I, 161; see above, pp. 20–1. Jack Cade's men had 'dyked and staked well about' their camp at Blackheath in 1450 ('Gregory', 190).
65 *Rot. Parl.*, V, 347; see above, pp. 22–3. At St Albans buildings and possibly parts of the town ditch provided some protection.
66 'Gregory', 204; see above, pp. 27–8.
67 'Gregory', 205; Whethamstede, I, 341–2; *Rot. Parl.*, V, 348.
68 *Knyghthode and Bataile*, 19–21, 55ff. But, being a cleric, not a soldier, he was unable to link this with advice about the deployment of guns.
69 *English Chron.*, 96–7; Waurin, V, 295, 297; Whethamstede, I, 373–4.
70 *English Chron.*, 97. Guns were fired in the brief battle, for Sir William Lucy heard them ('Gregory', 207). The Yorkists had gone to Northampton 'with great ordnance' (*Short English Chron.*, 74). For the rainy weather in the days preceding the battle, Waurin, V, 296; Whethamstede, I, 374.
71 *Short English Chron.*, 73. For Judde, see above, p. 160.
72 Scofield, I, 118–19; Whethamstede, I, 381–2; Waurin, V, 325ff.
73 Scofield, I, 262 and n.
74 'Gregory', 213–14. According to one London chronicle, there were 500 Burgundians, and 18 of them were burned and killed by their own fire (*Brief Notes*, 155). The 'wild fire' may have been naphtha, the 'Greek fire' long familiar in medieval warfare. The gunners' defences sound like a sophisticated adaptation of the *champ de guerre* principle.
75 Waurin, V, 335: 'grant plente de charriotz et charrettes chargies de vivres et artilleries'.
76 Scofield, I, 197.
77 *Paston Letters*, II, no. 464.
78 Probably in preparation for his campaign against Robin of Redesdale, on 20 June 1469 the king commissioned a group including his master of the ordnance, John Wode, to impress wheelwrights, cartwrights and other carpenters, stone-cutters, smiths, plumbers and other workmen for the works of the royal ordnance on various types of guns and other armaments (*CPR, 1467–77*, 163).
79 Warkworth, 8. On 3 March, three days before Edward set out from London, he issued an ordnance commission similar to that of June 1469 (*CPR, 1467–77*, 163).
80 Warkworth, 13. According to *Chronicles of London*, 183, Edward had 500 Englishmen and as many 'Dutchmen'. For estimates of his invasion force, see above, p. 75 and n. 30.
81 *Arrivall*, 18–19. Warkworth, 16, gives a different account of the night bombardment.
82 *Arrivall*, 24, 29. A week before the king set out from Windsor commissioners were appointed to impress workmen for the work of the royal ordnance (*CPR, 1467–77*, 259).

83 Molinet, I, 434–5; cf. above, p. 93. In his 'Yorkist' invasion of 1496, James IV brought an artillery train, but Warbeck had no siege guns with which to assault Exeter the following year (below, p. 190). Fifty gunners received wages for their service against the Cornishmen at Blackheath in 1497 (Hooker, 26n).

84 J. Smyth, *The Berkeley Manuscripts. The Lives of the Berkeleys*, ed. J. Maclean (Gloucester 1884), II, 109.

85 Allmand (ed.), *Society at War*, 66; Calmette and Périnelle, 183–4, 358–61.

86 For the royal ordnance, see above, pp. 160–1.

87 Calmette and Périnelle, 358–9.

88 Armstrong, 41.

89 Vergil, *English Hist.*, 107.

90 *Benet's Chron.*, 230; Waurin, V, 340. George Neville's account of the fight for the Aire crossing implies infantry fighting (*CSP Venice*, I, pp. 99–100, no. 370).

91 Warkworth, 16.

92 Commynes, *Memoirs*, ed. and trans. Jones, 181; cf. 195. Which nine battles was Commynes referring to? I count seven major ones in which Edward was one of the victorious commanders – Northampton, Mortimer's Cross, Ferrybridge, Towton, Losecoat Field, Barnet and Tewkesbury. He was a mere boy at St Albans in 1455.

93 Mancini, 98–101; cf. below, p. 194.

94 Poulson, I, 228; cf. above, p. 38.

95 *Knyghthode and Bataile*, 50–2, 57, 70ff.

96 'Gregory', 205.

97 *Bale's Chron.*, 149.

98 Waurin, V, 296.

99 *MS Tanner 2*, 167.

100 'Gregory', 214.

101 *Chronicles of London*, 175. For a distinction between his horsemen and footmen, *Benet's Chron.*, 229–30.

102 'Gregory', 217.

103 *Lincolnshire Rebellion*, 15, 11–12.

104 *Coventry Leet Book*, 366.

105 *Arrivall*, 27–8. After the Bastard of Fauconberg's retreat from London, Rivers led a retinue of thirty horsemen and forty footmen into Kent (Devon, I, 494).

106 *Chronicles of London*, 217; Vergil, *Anglica Historia*, 106ff.

107 *Knyghthode and Bataile*, 50–2. Cf. *ibid.*, 57–8, for the roles of horsemen in protecting those fortifying a camp, and in scouring from a camp.

108 Armstrong, 23–4.

109 'Gregory', 204–5.

110 See above, pp. 26–7.

111 See above, pp. 42–3.

112 'Gregory', 213.

113 Waurin, V, 336ff. But in the 1469 campaign Edward's intelligence network seems to have failed him badly (see above, pp. 67ff). In the 1470 campaigns it was his political rather than his military intelligence which was at fault.

114 *Arrivall*, 7–8.

115 *Ibid.*, 18.

116 *Ibid.*, 28.

117 Vergil, *English Hist.*, 216–17, 219; Hearne, *Collectanea*, IV, 210.

118 *Arrivall*, 24–5.

119 Cf. above, p. 106.

120 Vergil, *English Hist.*, 225.

121 *Arrivall*, 14.

122 Vergil, *English Hist.*, 219–20.

123 *Knyghthode and Bataile*, 70ff.

124 Waurin, V, 337–8.

125 Commynes, *Memoirs*, ed. and trans. Jones, 195; Vergil, *English Hist.*, 145–6.

126 *Arrivall*, 29–30.

127 Vergil, *English Hist.*, 224.

128 C. Ross, *The Wars of the Roses*, 108, 127.

129 *Pageant of the Birth, Life and Death of Richard Beauchamp Earl of Warwick K. G. 1389–1439*, ed. Viscount Dillon and W. H. St John Hope, plates VII and XL.

130 Malory, *Works*, I, xix ff, 19, 25ff, 35, 75–6, 235; cf. *ibid.*, 212–13, 243.

131 *Ibid.*, 238; *The Prologues and Epilogues of William Caxton*, ed. W. J. B. Crotch (EETS 1928), 82ff; cf. *The Great Tournament Roll of Westminster*, ed. S. Anglo, 19ff.

132 Scofield, I, 374–5, 414ff; Anglo (ed.), 33 and n.

133 A. Emery, 'The Development of Raglan Castle and Keeps in Late Medieval England', *Archaeological Journal*, 132 (for 1975), 185.

134 Goodman, *A History of England from Edward II to James I*, 39.

135 Turner, 13.

136 For London's defences, see p. 191. For other town defences in the fifteenth century, see Turner, *passim*, and esp. 80. In 1471 the citizens of Hull, within their sturdy walls, refused Edward admission; those of York, similarly protected, were only slightly more obliging to him (*Arrivall*, 4–5). York was to man its defences against the Scropes' assault in 1487 (see above, pp. 103–4).

137 *Arrivall*, 12–13. Turner, 118–19, for frequent repairs to Coventry's walls in the fifteenth century.

138 *King's Works*, I, 238. The Tower of London was of course well maintained (*ibid.*, 2, 728–9).

139 *Ibid.*, 238ff.

140 *Rot. Parl.*, V, 177; *English Chron.*, 67.

141 *King's Works*, II, 667; cf. above, p. 26.

142 *Ibid.*, II, 848–9.

143 *Ibid.*, I, 572, 642.

144 *Ibid.*, II, 782.

145 *Benet's Chron.*, 225; *King's Works*, II, 684–5. The author of *Knyghthode and Bataile*, 83ff, had a lot of advice for Henry VI *c.* 1460 on defending and assaulting fortifications. But he stuck to Roman methods and had nothing to say about the employment of artillery.

146 *King's Works*, I, 240.

147 Worcestre, *Itineraries*, 344–5. Alnwick even built a town wall in the fifteenth century: the first murage grant was made in 1434, and work was still incomplete in 1474 (Turner, 50).

148 Worcestre, *Itineraries*, 342–5.

149 *Ibid.*, 218–19.

150 Emery, 'The Development of Raglan Castle', 182.

151 See brief descriptions in J. Evans, *English Art 1307–1461* (Oxford 1949), 126ff.

152 Worcestre, *Itineraries*, 186–91; *Paston Letters*, II, nos 592, 641.

153 The best recent account of private castles is Emery's article, 'The Development of Raglan Castle'.

154 *CPR, 1452–61*, 527.

155 *Ibid.*, 534, 550; *Foedera*, XI, 444–6; Scofield, I, 56. For the struggle between Warwick and Somerset, based on their castles at Calais and Guines, see above, pp. 31–2.

156 *Brief Notes*, 153.

157 Waurin, V, 295.

158 *English Chron.*, 96; *Benet's Chron.*, 226–7; *Brief Latin Chron.*, 169.

159 *English Chron.*, 96. Lord Cobham and the sheriffs of London laid 'great ordnance' against the Tower on the city side; Sir John Wenlock and Harowe, mercer, 'kept on' St Katherine's side (*Short English Chron.*, 74).

160 *English Chron.*, 96, 98; Waurin, V, 302ff; *Benet's Chron.*, 226–7. *Benet's Chron.* says that the siege lasted for four weeks.

161 *Proceedings and Ordinances of the Privy Council*, VI, 302ff. Denbigh was to be delivered to 'Edward Bou . . .'., probably 'Bourchier'. Richard Grey, lord of Powis, was ordered to deliver York's castle at Montgomery to 'Wal . . . squyer', possibly Walter Devereux.

162 *Ibid.*, 304–5.

163 For York, the queen and March in this period, see above, pp. 41, 49.

164 *CPR, 1452–61*, 657. For the defence of Lynn and Castle Rising, see above, pp. 44–5.

165 *Ibid.*, 659.
166 *Brief Notes*, 155.
167 See above, pp. 48–9.
168 See above, pp. 56ff.
169 *CPR, 1461–7*, 28; cf. above, pp. 184–5.
170 *CPR, 1461–7*, 38.
171 See above, pp. 59–60. In 1461 the island of Jersey and its castle of Gorey (or Mount Orgueil) were surrendered to the French by the Lancastrian warden. They were recovered in 1468 after a long siege of the castle by a force commanded by Richard Harleston and Edmund Weston, aided by the Jerseymen (*King's Works*, II, 606; Scofield, I, 478–80).
172 *Rot. Parl.*, V, 486, 512; 'Gregory', 237; Warkworth, 3; *Chronicles of London*, 179; Scofield, I, 338–9, 458–9. The castle had been repaired in 1417–19, and its 'great bridge' had been repaired or rebuilt in 1458–9 (*King's Works*, I, 365). The castle's defenders probably used firearms (Worcestre, *Itineraries*, 204–5).
173 *Hist. Croylandensis Continuatio*, 542; J. C. Perks, *Chepstow Castle* (London 1967), 10–11.
174 *CPR, 1467–77*, 180–1; Scofield, I, 505.
175 Warkworth, 13; *Chronicles of London*, 182; Scofield, I, 540–1.
176 *Arrivall*, 8ff; Warkworth, 14–15.
177 *Arrivall*, 25–7. Considerable sums had been spent on the royal castle at Gloucester under the Lancastrians (*King's Works*, II, 656). For a plan showing the castle site and its relation to the town's fortifications, *ibid.*, 653.
178 Vergil, *English Hist.*, 154–5.
179 *CPR, 1467–77*, 293.
180 *Arrivall*, 33ff; *Brief Latin Chron.*, 184–5; Warkworth, 19–20; *Hist. Croylandensis Continuatio*, 555–6; cf. Richmond, 'Fauconberg's Kentish rising of May 1471', 677ff.
181 Warkworth, 26–7; Worcestre, *Itineraries*, 102–3; *CPR, 1467–77*, 418, 412; *CDS*, IV, no. 1412. For Fortescue, cf. Morgan, 17.
182 *CDS*, IV, no. 1413.
183 Warkworth, 27, who says that he surrendered on 15 February 1474. Worcester says that he left the Mount on 19 February (*Itineraries*, 102–3). On 20 February it was rumoured in London that Oxford had either sued for his pardon and was surrendering to the king, or that he had left the Mount well garrisoned (*Paston Letters*, III, no. 736). *Le Caricou* was at sea for six weeks after 3 February, perhaps to intercept any reinforcements for Oxford, who had not heard of his surrender.
184 G. N. Curzon, *Bodiam Castle, Sussex*, 31–3. Vergil says that, in preparation for the rising, the rebels 'held furnished fit places with force of men' (*English Hist.*, 198).
185 Owen and Blakeway, *A History of Shrewsbury*, I, 241; Rawcliffe, 34.
186 Vergil, *English Hist.*, 212–13; PRO, E.101/55/14. According to

Vergil, some Welsh castles were garrisoned against Henry's advance in 1485, but were quickly surrendered (*ibid.*, 217). In 1486 Viscount Lovell may have garrisoned Middleham castle as a centre of resistance to Henry VII (see above, p. 97).

187 See above, p. 112.

188 Vergil, *Anglica Historia*, 104–5, 108–9.

189 Raimondo de Soncino to duke of Milan, 30 September 1497, in Pollard, I, 169–70; Vergil, *Anglica Historia*, 105–6.

190 Pollard, I, 167–9.

191 Henry names as among the defenders Sir William Courtenay, Sir John Sapcotes, Sir Piers Edgecombe, Sir John Croker, Sir Walter Courtenay and Sir Humphrey Fulford.

192 Turner, 195; cf. *ibid.*, 196.

193 Pollard, I, 180–1.

194 Vergil, *Anglica Historia*, 104–5; cf. Pollard, I, 180–1 (text of *Chronicles of London*, 217); Molinet, II, 439–40. For expenditure by the city of Exeter resulting from the rebellion, including £17. 4s. 7d. spent on repairing the North Gate, Exeter City Receiver's Account Roll, 13–14 Henry VII, Devon Record Office; cf. for other repairs to the defences, *ibid.*, 14–15 Henry VII.

195 *King's Works*, II, 729.

196 *CPR, 1467–77*, 463, 470.

197 *King's Works*, I, 241, 2, 764–5.

198 Emery, 184; *CPR, 1485–94*, 64.

199 *King's Works*, II, 893–4.

200 *CPR, 1452–61*, 528. For a discussion of urban defences and the Wars of the Roses, Turner, 80.

201 *Chronicles of London*, 187–8; *Cal. of Plea and Memoranda Rolls*, 110–11 and 111n.

202 Emery, *passim*; cf. above, pp. 68–9, 186. There are no building accounts from which the Raglan works can be dated. Emery argues that, in the main, they are more likely to have been carried out by Herbert than by his father or son.

203 Emery, 180–1, 184; W. Douglas Simpson, ' "Bastard Feudalism" and the Later Castles', *Antiquaries Jnl*, 26 (1946). On 17 April 1471, just after Hastings's support of Edward's reconquest of the realm, he was licenced to crenellate houses at Ashby de la Zouch, Bagworth, Thornton and Kirby (Leics.) and at Slingesby (Yorks.) (Dunham, 23).

204 H. M. Colvin, 'Castles and government in Tudor England', *EHR*, 83 (1968).

205 See above, p. 187.

206 *Italian Relation*, 37–8.

207 C. H. Hunter Blair and H. L. Honeyman, *Norham Castle* (London 1966), 9, 12.

208 *Knyghthode and Bataile*, 22, 70ff.

209 See above, pp. 92ff.

210 See above, p. 163.

211 Commynes, *Memoirs*, ed. and trans. Jones, 226.

212 *Ibid.*, 241–2.

213 *Ibid.*, 229.

214 *Ibid.*, 252ff.

215 Molinet, I, 106.

216 A. Bernaldez, *Memorias del reinado de los Reyes Católicos*, ed. M. Gomez-Moreno and J. de M. Carriazo (Madrid 1962), 167–8; cf. E. Benito Ruano, 'La Participacion Extranjera en la Guerra de Granada', *Andalucia Medieval*, 2 (Cordoba 1978), 306–8, 318–19.

Chapter 9 : The Wars and Society

1 See above, pp. 2ff.

2 *Hist. Croylandensis Continuatio*, 529–30; translation from *Ingulph's Chron.*, trans. H. T. Riley (London 1854), 418–19.

3 Warkworth, 12. In 1463, he says, 'the people grudged sore' at the grant of a fifteenth and a half (p. 3); Edward's coinage debasement of 1464 was 'to the great harm of the common people' (p. 4); the fifteenth granted in 1469 'annoyed the people' because of their recent heavy payments (pp. 7–8). An anonymous chronicler also stresses the various exactions which Edward made in 1461–3 (*Brief Latin Chron.*, 173, 175, 177).

4 Warkworth, 21–2. For financial losses resulting from the wars, below, pp. 197, 216ff.

5 For the greater involvement of some Londoners, see p. 202.

6 *Literae Cantuarienses*, III, ed. J. B. Sheppard (Rolls ser., London 1889), no. 1079, pp. 274ff.

7 *The Travels of Leo of Rozmital*, ed. M. Letts (Cambridge 1957).

8 *Ibid.*, 45ff, 63.

9 *Italian Relation*, 28ff, 39; 'si facevano molti clientoli, e seguaci; con li quali poi infestavano la corona, et la propria patria, et in fine fra di loro medesimi, perchè in ultimo erano tutti decapitati'.

10 Fortescue, *Governance of England*, 155–6.

11 Richmond, 'The Nobility and the Wars of the Roses, 1459–61', 72–3, 78. These and subsequent figures given include attainted claimants to peerages.

12 All these figures must be regarded as approximations. Dr Richmond has listed participants in the campaigns of 1459–61 (*ibid.*, 74ff), and Professor Lander has listed participants from 1455 to 1485 (*Crown and Nobility*, Appendix A, 301–5).

13 Richmond, 'The Nobility and the Wars of the Roses, 1459–61', 83–4.

14 *Ibid.*, 84n.

15 See above, pp. 132ff.

16 See above, pp. 131ff.

17 *Annales*, 782.

18 *Brief Latin Chron.*, 176. Another source lists fifty-nine knights in his company (*Brief Notes*, 157–8).

19 See above, pp. 26–7.

20 Worcestre, *Itineraries*, 202ff, 338ff.

21 See above, pp. 97ff.

22 *Rot. Parl.*, VI, 244–9.

23 Vergil, *Anglica Historia*, 22n–23n, 106n–107n.

24 Cf. above, pp. 61–2. For arms and armour bequeathed by northern clergy in the 1470s, *Testamenta Eboracensia*, III, 202, 210, 235.

25 R. J. Knecht, 'The Episcopate and the Wars of the Roses', *Univ. of Birmingham Hist. Jnl*, 6 (1957–8), 118.

26 See above, p. 28.

27 Hearne, *Collectanea*, IV, 212; Knecht, 111ff.

28 See above, p. 196.

29 See above, p. 109. For references to the threat and use of excommunication against rebels, Goodman, 'Henry VII and Christian renewal'.

30 *Brief Latin Chron.*, 177.

31 I. D. Thornley, 'The Destruction of Sanctuary', in *Tudor Studies*, ed. R. W. Seton-Watson (London 1924), 198–200.

32 Pollard, I, 153–4.

33 *Short English Chron.*, 74.

34 *Arrivall*, 38.

35 For links between townsmen and nobles, R. B. Dobson, 'Urban Decline in late Medieval England', *TRHS*, 5th ser., 27 (1977), 14–16.

36 *Annales*, 775; 'Gregory', 211ff.

37 *Benet's Chron.*, 233.

38 Warkworth, 20; Richmond, 'Fauconberg's Kentish rising of May 1471', 684–5.

39 Robbins, 215–18. Warkworth's statement (1–2) that Edward 'for so much as he found in time of need great comfort in his commoners, he ratified and confirmed all the franchises given to cities and towns, etc. and granted to many cities and towns new franchises than was granted before' in his first parliament suggests Edward's appreciation of the urban support which he received in 1460–1.

40 See above, pp. 22–3.

41 *Records of the Borough of Nottingham*, II, 368–9. For commons' involvement in the wars, see McFarlane, 'The Wars of the Roses', 112–13.

42 *CDS*, IV, no. 1357.

43 Waurin, V, 284.

44 *Annales*, 773; *Short English Chron.*, 75.

45 *English Chron.*, 107.

46 *Annales*, 777; cf. *English Chron.*, 109. Warwick, meeting March at Burford about this time, told him that the commons were on his side ('Gregory', 215).

47 'Gregory', 221.

48 Warkworth, 7.

49 Fortescue, *Governance of England*, 137–8.

50 Ross, *Edward IV*, 126–8.

51 See above, p. 96. Allegedly, when Henry VII was in York in 1486 confronting rebellion which centred on Middleham, 'two fellows that dwelt about Middleham said [in York] that here is good gate for us to Robin of Redesdale over the walls' (*York Civic Records*, II, 5).

52 *Paston Letters*, III, no. 916.

53 Williams, 'The Rebellion of Humphrey Stafford in 1486', 188 and n. The standards which Warbeck was reputed to fly with his Cornish peasants in 1497 seem obscure in their symbolism (Pollard, I, 165).

54 For a discussion of peasants' relations with landlords in this period, and peasant revolts, see R. H. Hilton, *The English Peasantry in the Later Middle Ages* (Oxford 1975), 64ff.

55 See above, p. 67.

56 *Arrivall*, 6; Warkworth, 13–14. The invading Edward IV in these circumstances played on Yorkshiremen's respect for rightful inheritance by claiming he had only come to occupy the duchy of York, to which he was undoubted heir.

57 *Arrivall*, 23.

58 *Gloucester Annals*, 356; cf. *Brief Latin Chron.*'s verdict on Herbert (p. 183): 'a very grave oppressor and despoiler of priests and many others for many years'.

59 *Chronicles of London*, 181.

60 *The Great Chronicle of London*, ed. A. H. Thomas and I. D. Thornley (London 1938), 218.

61 For distant rebel Yorkshiremen's invocation of Becket's example, see above, pp. 107–8.

62 Griffiths, 'Local rivalries and national politics: the Percies, the Nevilles, and the Duke of Exeter, 1452–1455', 597ff.

63 *Ibid.*, 599; cf. Dobson, 'Urban Decline', 20.

64 *Arrivall*, 6–7; cf. above, p. 51.

65 *CSP Venice*, I, no. 371, p. 102.

66 *CSP Milan*, I, no. 71, pp. 55–6.

67 *English Chron.*, 97. Before the first battle of St Albans Henry VI allegedly included yeomen among those to be slain (*Paston Letters*, I, 239).

68 Worcestre, *Itineraries*, 340–1.

69 'Gregory', 216–17.

70 See below, p. 212.

71 McFarlane, *The Nobility of Later Medieval England*, 146ff.

72 *English Chron.*, 107; 'Gregory', 217; Warkworth, 7, 17; Worcestre, *Itineraries*, 340–1. For the numerous aristocratic casualties, see also McFarlane, 'The Wars of the Roses', 100.

73 Lander, *Crown and Nobility*, 129.

74 *Stonor Letters and Papers*, II, 161.

75 'Gregory', 226.

76 Commynes, *Memoirs*, ed. and trans. Jones, 180.

77 *Hist. Croylandensis Continuatio*, 568; *Ingulph's Chron.*, 492.

78 Owen and Blakeway, I, 241–2.

79 Warkworth, 16–17; *Arrivall*, 20.

80 *Paston Letters*, III, no. 821.

81 *Annales*, 776. *English Chron.*, 109, mentions the mediation only of the duchess of Buckingham.

82 *Arrivall*, 10.

83 'Gregory', 206–7; *Benet's Chron.*, 225.

84 Scofield, I, 38; cf. *ibid.*, 64.

85 'Gregory', 206.

86 *English Chron.*, 95–6; Waurin, V, 302.

87 *CPR, 1467–77*, 26. For the duchess of Somerset's plight, Scofield, I, 313.

88 Scofield, I, 518–19. The countess of Warwick took sanctuary after her husband's death in 1471 (*ibid.*, 582–3).

89 *CPR, 1485–94*, 222–3.

90 *Testamenta Vetusta*, I, 310ff; McFarlane, *The Nobility of Later Medieval England*, 29–30.

91 *The Prologues and Epilogues of William Caxton*, ed. W. J. B. Crotch (EETS 1928), 111–12. Bishop Beauchamp graphically expressed the terror that he among others felt after the Lancastrian victory at St Albans (*CSP Venice*, I, no. 371).

92 *Annales*, 771–2; *CP*, XI, 21.

93 See pp. 68–9, 75ff.

94 See above, p. 114.

95 J. Weever, *Ancient Funerall Monuments* (etc.) (London 1631), 834–5.

96 *Paston Letters*, II, no. 389.

97 *Ibid.*, III, no. 670.

98 *Arrivall*, 33.

99 Vergil, *Anglica Historia*, 82–3.

100 *Ibid.*, 94–5.

101 Malory, *Works*, III, 1229.

102 Caxton, *Prologues and Epilogues*, 108; Vergil, *Anglica Historia*, 12–13. In his epilogue to Book 2 of *The Recuyell of the Historyes of Troye*, written in 1471, Caxton had gloomily mentioned the great divisions in

England (*Prologues and Epilogues*, 6).

103 *The Berkeley Manuscripts. The Lives of the Berkeleys*, II, ed. Sir John Maclean (Gloucester 1883), 114–15.

104 Dunham, *Lord Hastings' Indentured Retainers 1461–1483*, 25.

105 Lander, *Crown and Nobility 1450–1509*, 61ff.

106 'Gregory', 190.

107 *Paston Letters*, II, no. 516.

108 Sir Henry Ellis, *Original Letters* (etc.), 2nd ser., I (London 1827), 11–13.

109 Waurin, V, 294; cf. above, p. 204 and n. 44.

110 *English Chron.*, 98.

111 Scofield, I, 136–7. His mother wrote in similar vein.

112 *Paston Letters*, I, no. 367; cf. above, pp. 44ff.

113 Whethamstede, I, 394–6.

114 *Annales*, 776. For a proclamation by Edward asserting that the Lancastrian lords had given their men licence to rob and forbidding his own men to do so, Scofield, I, 154–6.

115 Scofield, I, 537; *Tudor Royal Proclamations*, I, no. 13; Pollard, I, 50; Vergil, *Anglica Historia*, 22–3.

116 *Tudor Royal Proclamations*, I, no. 19.

117 Vergil, *Anglica Historia*, 88–9.

118 *Bridgwater Borough Accounts, 1445–1468*, p. 110, no. 815.

119 Ellis, *Original Letters*, 2nd ser., I, 139–40.

120 *English Chron.*, 82.

121 *Bale's Chron.*, 147–8.

122 *English Chron.*, 83; cf. Whethamstede, I, 344–5.

123 Waurin, I, 277.

124 *Knyghthode and Bataile*, 37; Scofield, I, 59.

125 *Annales*, 774. For Sandal, PRO, DL 29, no. 8899, m. I, cited in *The Wars of the Roses*, Catalogue of an Exhibition at the Public Record Office (1961), ed. R. L. Storey, no. 24.

126 Lander, *Conflict and Stability in Fifteenth-Century England* (3rd edn, London 1977), 85n. For alleged plundering at Totteridge (Middlesex) by the duke of Exeter's men, PRO, C I, bdle 31, no. 516, cited in Storey (ed.), *The Wars of the Roses*, no. 30.

127 *CPR, 1461–7*, 82, 87. For a theft by Welshmen (presumably Edward's soldiers) after Towton, *Testamenta Eboracensia*, III, 208–9.

128 *CDS*, IV, p. 271, no. 1333.

129 *Feodarium Prioratus Dunelmensis* (etc.) (Surtees Soc. 1871), 98–102.

130 *CPR, 1467–77*, 114.

131 *Medieval Welsh Lyrics*, ed. and trans. Clancy (London 1965), 207ff.

132 See above, p. 75.

133 Ellis, *Original Letters*, 2nd ser., I, 140–1.

134 Scofield, I, 583n; *Tewkesbury Chron.*, 376–7, in Kingsford, *English*

Historical Literature.

135 *Paston Letters*, III, no. 876.
136 *Materials*, I, 188, 201. For the sack of Tadcaster in 1487, *York Civic Records*, II, 22.
137 *CPR, 1467–77*, 208.
138 *Ibid.*, 360–1.
139 Pollard, I, 33.
140 S. Reynolds, *An Introduction to the History of English Medieval Towns* (Oxford 1977), 147.
141 For the Anglo-Burgundian war in 1471, Ross, *Edward IV*, 158–9.
142 A petition from Bristol to the earl of Warwick emphasized unemployment experienced there resulting from declining cloth manufacture, and outlined some of the burdens incurred to aid the crown – the city's waging of sixty soldiers for eleven months for the king, at a cost of £800, as well as earlier waging of men for service in the north and the cost of finding ships for operations in Wales and to convey Edward's envoys to Castile (*The Great Red Book of Bristol*, III, ed. E. W. W. Veale (Bristol Record Soc. 1951), 77–8). For Edward's impressment of Hull ships, K. J. Allison, 'Medieval Hull', *VCH Yorks., East Riding*, I, 25.
143 See above, pp. 154ff.
144 *HMC, MSS of Shrewsbury Corporation*, 29–30.
145 See above, p. 90.
146 *CPR, 1467–77*, 250.
147 Allison, 23ff; *Arrivall*, 4. In 1483 Hull sent a paid-up contingent to support Richard III against the rebels (Allison, 26).
148 *Priory of Hexham*, I, pp. cii–civ.
149 See above, pp. 196–7 and n. 3.
150 Scofield, I, 148.
151 See above, pp. 163–4.
152 'Gregory', 207; *Annales*, 773.
153 *Paston Letters*, II, no. 384.
154 *Priory of Hexham*, I, p. ci; cf. *ibid.*, pp. cxii–cxiii.
155 *Cal. of Plea and Memoranda Rolls, 1458–1482*, 57ff. For another case of the pursuit of private vengeance through opportunities provided by the dynastic conflict, PRO, C I, bdle 31, no. 485, cited in *The Wars of the Roses*, ed. Storey, no. 25.
156 *Literae Cantuarienses*, III, 276.
157 Pollard, I, 11–12.
158 *CPR, 1461–7*, 67.
159 See above, p. 184.
160 J. Blow, 'Nibley Green 1470', *English Society and Government in the Fifteenth Century*, ed. C. M. Crowder (Edinburgh 1967), 87ff.
161 Goodman, *History of England from Edward II to James I*, 258ff, 443.
162 See above, p. 165; for some examples of upward social mobility in the

Wars of the Roses, see pp. 125, 127.

163 *Annales*, 782, 791; cf. the terms of a grant to Hastings in 1467 (*CPR, 1467–77*, 26–7).

164 The garrison establishment at Calais in time of truce in the 1470s was about 780 (Lander, *Crown and Nobility*, 240n).

165 Stevenson, II, part 2, 512; *Records of the City of Norwich*, I, 406.

166 *Nottingham Borough Records*, III, 414–15; *Coventry Leet Book*, 343.

167 *Coventry Leet Book*, 355.

168 Devon, 494; *York Civic Records*, I, 118. Rivers's footmen received 8*d*. Henry VII contracted with Lord Hastings in 1492, for the French expedition, that Hastings's men-at-arms (including himself) should receive 18*d*. a day, his demi-lances 9*d*. and his archers 6*d*. (*HMC Report on the Manuscripts of R. R. Hastings*, I (1928), 306).

169 *Paston Letters*, II, no. 592.

170 Commynes, *Memoirs*, ed. and trans. Jones, 122–3, 225; *Coventry Leet Book*, 426–8.

171 *Literae Cantuarienses*, III, 282.

172 *Paston Letters*, III, nos 905, 913; Bernaldez, 167–8, 241.

173 Pollard, I, 66.

174 See above, pp. 145–6.

175 *CPR, 1467–77*, 362.

176 *Cely Letters*, ed. Hanham, no. 161. For the local purchase of 'harness' by the warden and community of Henley for the four soldiers whom they provided for the king in 1487, and the four in 1497, *Henley Borough Records . . . 1395–1543*, 94, 118–19.

177 *Cal. of Plea and Memoranda Rolls . . . 1458–1482*, 11–12. Eliot confirmed his account.

178 *CPR, 1467–77*, 25.

179 Edmund Dudley, *The Tree of Commonwealth*, ed. D. M. Brodie (Cambridge 1948).

180 Goodman, *A History of England from Edward II to James I*, 257–8.

181 See above, pp. 23, 26–7. The Marches comprised Cumberland, Westmorland and Northumberland.

182 *Short English Chron.*, 74.

183 Robbins, 213.

184 *Brief Notes*, 155.

185 *Short English Chron.*, 77.

186 *Gloucester Annals*, 356.

187 *English Chron.*, 106.

188 *Paston Letters*, I, no. 367.

189 Whethamstede, I, 171ff, 386ff.

190 See above, p. 216.

191 *Hist. Croylandensis Continuatio*, 542–3.

192 *Gloucester Annals*, 356.

Select Bibliography

Accounts of the Lord High Treasurer [of Scotland], ed. T. Dickson, I, 1473–1498 (Edinburgh 1877).

ALLISON, K. J., 'Medieval Hull', *VCH Yorks., East Riding*, I.

ALLMAND, C. T. (ed.), *Society at War* (Edinburgh 1973).

ANDRÉ, BERNARD, *De vita atque gestis Henrici septimi ... historia*, in *Memorials of King Henry the Seventh*.

ANGLO, S., *Spectacle, Pageantry and Early Tudor Policy* (Oxford 1969).

Annales [rerum anglicanum], in *Letters and Papers Illustrative of the Wars of the English in France*, II, pt 2.

ARMSTRONG, C. A. J., 'Politics and the Battle of St Albans, 1455', *BIHR*, 33 (1960).

Arrivall: Historie of the Arrivall of King Edward IV, A.D. 1471, ed. J. Bruce (Camden Soc. 1838).

Arundel MS 19, in Kingsford, *English Historical Literature*.

ASTON, M., 'Richard II and the Wars of the Roses', in *The Reign of Richard II*, ed. F. R. H. Du Boulay and C. M. Barron (London 1971).

Bale's Chronicle, in *Six Town Chronicles*.

BASIN, THOMAS, *Histoire de Louis XI*, I–II, ed. C. Samaran and M.-C. Garand (Paris 1963–6).

Benet's Chronicle: John Benet's Chronicle for the years 1400 to 1462, ed. G. L. Harriss and M. A. Harriss, in *Camden Miscellany*, vol. XXIV (London 1972).

BERNALDEZ, ANDRES, *Memorias del reinado de los Reyes Católicos*, ed. M. Gomez-Moreno and J. de M. Carriazo (Madrid 1962).

BLACKMORE, H. L., *The Armouries of the Tower of London*, I, *Ordnance* (London 1976).

BORNSTEIN, D., 'Military Manuals in Fifteenth-Century England', *Mediaeval Studies*, 37 (1975).

BRIDPORT COFFERERS' ACCOUNTS, 1469–70, 1483–4, Dorset County Record Office, B3/M6.

BRIDPORT MUSTER ROLL, 1457, Dorset County Record Office, B3/FG3.

Brief Latin Chronicle, in *Three Fifteenth-Century Chronicles.*

Brief Notes, in *Three Fifteenth-Century Chronicles.*

BURNE, A. H., *The Battlefields of England* (London 1950).

BURNE, A. H., *More Battlefields of England* (London 1952).

Calendar of Close Rolls: Henry VI, vol. VI, 1454–61; Edward IV, vols I–II, 1461–8, 1468–76; Edward IV – Edward V – Richard III, 1476–85; Henry VII, 1485–1500 (London 1949–67).

Calendar of Documents Relating to Scotland, ed. J. Bain, IV, 1357–1509 (London 1888).

Calendar of Patent Rolls, Henry VI, vol. VI, 1452–61; Edward IV, vols I–II, 1461–7, 1467–77; Edward IV – Edward V – Richard III, 1476–85; Henry VII, vols I–II, 1485–94, 1494–1509 (London 1910–16).

Calendar of Plea and Memoranda Rolls . . . of the City of London, 1458–1482, ed. P. E. Jones (Cambridge 1961).

Calendar of State Papers and Manuscripts existing in the Archives and Collections of Milan, I, 1385–1618, ed. A. B. Hinds (London 1913).

Calendar of State Papers and Manuscripts relating to English Affairs, existing in the Archives and Collections of Venice (etc.), I, 1202–1509, ed. R. Brown (London 1864).

CALMETTE, J., and PÉRINELLE, G., *Louis XI et l'Angleterre* (Paris 1930).

CAXTON, WILLIAM, *Prologues and Epilogues*, ed. W. J. B. Crotch (EETS 1928).

CAXTON, WILLIAM, *The Book of the Fayttes of Armes and of Chyualrye*, ed. A. T. P. Byles (EETS 1937).

The Cely Letters 1472–1488, ed. A. Hanham (EETS 1975).

CHARLESWORTH, D., 'The battle of Hexham, 1464', *Archaeologia Aeliana*, 4th ser., 30 (1952).

CHARLESWORTH, D., 'Northumberland in the early years of Edward IV', *Archaeologia Aeliana*, 4th ser., 31 (1953).

CHASTELLAIN, GEORGES, *Chronique*, in *Oeuvres*, IV and V, ed. K. de Lettenhove (Brussels 1864).

CHRIMES, S. B., *Henry VII* (London 1972).

Chronicles of London, ed. C. L. Kingsford (Oxford 1905).

COCKERMOUTH CASTLE MSS, Carlisle Record Office, Receivers' Account Rolls, D/Lec/28/28–9 (Neville); D/Lec/29/8 (Percy).

COMMYNES, PHILIPPE DE, *Mémoires*, ed. J. Calmette, III (Paris 1925); ed. and trans. M. Jones (London 1972); ed. and trans. S. Kinser and I. Cazeaux, II (Columbia, S. Carolina, 1973).

The Complete Peerage of England, Scotland, Ireland and the U.K., ed. G. E. Cokayne, V. Gibbs, H. A. Doubleday and others, 13 vols (London 1910–59).

Conway, A., *Henry VII's Relations with Scotland and Ireland 1485–1498* (Cambridge 1932).

Coventry Leet Book, ed. M. D. Harris, 4 pts (EETS, Original Ser., 1907–13).

DEVON: *Issues of the Exchequer*, I, ed. F. Devon (London 1837).

Dijon Relation, in Armstrong, 'Politics and the Battle of St Albans, 1455'.

DUNHAM, W. H., JR, *Lord Hastings' Indentured Retainers 1461–1483* (New Haven, Conn., 1955).

DUNLOP, A. I., *The Life and Times of James Kennedy, Bishop of St Andrews* (Edinburgh 1950).

ELLIS, SIR HENRY, *Original Letters* (etc.), 2nd ser., I (London 1827).

EMERY, A., 'The Development of Raglan Castle and Keeps in Late Medieval England', *Archaeological Jnl*, 132 (1975).

[An] English Chron[icle of the reigns of Richard II, Henry IV, Henry V and Henry VI], ed. J. S. Davies (Camden Soc. 1856).

EVANS, H. T., *Wales and the Wars of the Roses* (Cambridge 1915).

EXETER CITY RECEIVERS' ACCOUNT ROLLS, 13–14 and 14–15 Henry VII, Devon Record Office.

Fastolf Relation, in Armstrong, 'Politics and the Battle of St Albans, 1455'.

Feodarium Prioratus Dunelmensis (etc.), Surtees Soc., 58 (1871).

Foedera[, Literae . . . et Acta Publica] (etc.), I–XV (London 1704–13).

FORTESCUE, SIR JOHN, *De Laudibus Legum Angliae*, trans. F. Grigor (London 1917).

FORTESCUE, SIR JOHN, *The Governance of England*, ed. C. Plummer (Oxford 1885).

FOWLER, K., *The Age of Plantagenet and Valois* (London 1967).

FOWLER, K. (ed.), *The Hundred Years War* (London 1971).

GAIRDNER, J., 'The Battle of Bosworth', *Archaeologia*, 55 (1896).

Gloucester Annals, in Kingsford, *English Historical Literature*.

GOODMAN, A., *A History of England from Edward II to James I* (London 1977).

GOODMAN, A., 'Henry VII and Christian renewal', *Religion and Humanism. Studies in Church History*, 17, Ecclesiastical History Society (Oxford 1981).

GOODMAN, A., and MACKAY, A., 'A Castilian report on English affairs, 1486', *EHR*, 88 (1973).

'GREGORY': *The Historical Collections of a London Citizen in the Fifteenth Century*, ed. J. Gairdner (Camden Soc. 1876).

GRIFFITHS, R. A., 'Local rivalries and national politics: the Percies, the Nevilles, and the Duke of Exeter, 1452–1455', *Speculum*, 43 (1968).

GRIMBLE, I., *The Harington Family* (London 1957).

HANHAM, A., *Richard III and His Early Historians 1483–1535* (Oxford 1975).

HAWARD, W. I., 'Economic Aspects of the Wars of the Roses in East Anglia', *EHR*, 41 (1926).

HEARNE, T. (ed.), John Leland's *Collectanea*, IV (London 1770) – anonymous account of the Stoke campaign.

Henley Borough Records. Assembly Books i–iv, 1395–1543, ed. P. M. Briers (Oxford 1960).

HICKS, M. A., 'Dynastic Change and Northern Society: the Career of the Fourth Earl of Northumberland, 1470–89', *Northern Hist.*, 14 (1978).

Historiae Croylandensis Continuatio, in *Rerum Anglicarum Scriptorum Veterum*, I, ed. W. Fulman (Oxford 1684); trans. in *Ingulph's Chronicle* (etc.), by H. T. Riley (London 1854).

HOGG, O. F. G., *The Royal Arsenal*, I (Oxford 1963).

HOOKER, J. R., 'Notes on the Organization and Supply of the Tudor Military under Henry VII', *Huntington Library Quarterly*, 23 (1959–60).

Household Books of John Duke of Norfolk and Thomas Earl of Surrey 1481–1490, ed. J. Payne Collier (Roxburghe Club 1844).

Ingulph's Chronicle (etc.), trans. H. T. Riley (London 1854).

Italian Relation: A Relation, or rather a True Account, of the Island of England, ed. C. A. Sneyd (Camden Soc. 1847).

KEEN, M. H., *The Laws of War in the Late Middle Ages* (London 1965).

KINGSFORD, C. L., *English Historical Literature in the Fifteenth Century* (Oxford 1913).

King's Works: Brown, R. Allen, Colvin, H. M., and Taylor, A. J., *History of the King's Works*, 3 vols (London 1963).

KNECHT, R. J., 'The Episcopate and the Wars of the Roses', *Univ. of Birmingham Hist. Jnl*, 6 (1957).

Knyghthode and Bataile, ed. R. Dyboski and Z. M. Arend (EETS 1935).

LANDER, J. R., *The Wars of the Roses* (London 1965).

LANDER, J. R., *Crown and Nobility 1450–1509* (London 1976).

LANDER, J. R., *Conflict and Stability in Fifteenth-Century England* (3rd edn, London 1977).

Letters and Papers [illustrative of the reigns of Richard III and Henry VII], I, ed. J. Gairdner (Rolls ser. 1861).

Lincolnshire Rebellion: Chronicle of the Rebellion in Lincolnshire, 1470, ed. J. G. Nichols, in *Camden Miscellany*, 1847.

MCFARLANE, K. B., 'The Wars of the Roses', *Proc. of the British Academy*, 50 (1964).

MCFARLANE, K. B., *The Nobility of Later Medieval England* (Oxford 1973).

MCKISACK, M., *Medieval History in the Tudor Age* (Oxford 1971).

MAJOR, JOHN, *A History of Greater Britain*, trans. and ed. A. Constable (Scottish History Society, Edinburgh 1892).

MALLETT, M., *Mercenaries and their Masters. Warfare in Renaissance Italy* (London 1974).

MALORY, SIR THOMAS, *Works*, ed. E. Vinaver, 3 vols (Oxford 1967).

MANCINI, DOMINIC, *The Usurpation of Richard III*, ed. C. A. J. Armstrong (Oxford 1969).

Materials [for a History of the Reign of Henry VII], I, ed. W. Campbell (Rolls ser. 1873).

Memorials [of King Henry the Seventh], ed. J. Gairdner (Rolls ser. 1858).

MOLINET, JEAN DE, *Chronique*, ed. G. Doutrepont and O. Jodogne, I–II

(Brussels 1935).

MORGAN, D. A. L., 'The King's Affinity in the Polity of Yorkist England', *TRHS*, 5th ser., 23 (1973).

MS Tanner 2, in *Six Town Chronicles*.

O'NEIL, B. H. ST J., *Castles and Cannon* (Oxford 1960).

OWEN, H., and BLAKEWAY, J. B., *A History of Shrewsbury*, I (London 1825).

The Paston Letters 1422–1509, ed. J. Gairdner, 3 vols (Edinburgh 1910).

PIGGOT, JOHN, *Memoranda*, in Kingsford, *English Historical Literature*.

Plumpton Correspondence, ed. T. Stapleton (Camden Soc. 1839).

POLLARD, A. F., *The Reign of Henry VII from Contemporary Sources*, 3 vols (London 1913–14).

POLLARD, A. J., 'Lord FitzHugh's rising in 1470', *BIHR*, 52 (1979).

POULSON, G., *Beverlac*, I (London 1829).

POWICKE, M. R., *Military Obligation in Medieval England* (Oxford 1962).

POWICKE, M. R., 'Lancastrian Captains', in *Essays in Medieval History presented to Bertie Wilkinson*, ed. T. A. Sandquist and M. R. Powicke (Toronto 1969).

The Priory of Hexham, I (Surtees Soc. 1864).

Proceedings and Ordinances of the Privy Council of England, ed. Sir Harris Nicolas, VI (London 1837).

PUBLIC RECORD OFFICE, EXCHEQUER, VARIOUS ACCOUNTS, E. 101/55/14; ordnance received at Calais and other fortresses in France, *temp.* Edward IV–Henry VII.

RAWCLIFFE, C., *The Staffords, Earls of Stafford and Dukes of Buckingham 1394–1521* (Cambridge 1978).

Records of the Borough of Nottingham, II–III (London 1883–5).

The Records of the City of Norwich, ed. W. H. Hudson and J. C. Tingey, I (Norwich 1906).

RICHMOND, C., 'Fauconberg's Kentish rising of May 1471', *EHR*, 85 (1970).

RICHMOND, C., 'The Nobility and the Wars of the Roses, 1459–61', *Nottingham Mediaeval Studies*, 21 (1977).

ROBBINS: *Historical Poems of the XIVth and XVth Centuries*, ed. R. H. Robbins (New York 1959).

ROSS, C., *Edward IV* (London 1974).

ROSS, C., *The Wars of the Roses* (London 1976).

Rotuli Parliamentorum, ed. J. Strachey and others, 6 vols (London 1767–83).

The Royal Commission on Historical Manuscripts: Fifth Report, I, Rye, Lydd (1876); *Eleventh Report*, Appendix, part 3, Southampton and King's Lynn (1887); *Fifteenth Report*, Appendix, part 10, Shrewsbury (1899).

SCOFIELD, C. L., *The Life and Reign of Edward the Fourth*, 2 vols (London 1923).

SHARPE, R. R., *London and the Kingdom*, I (London 1894).

Short English Chronicle, in *Three Fifteenth-Century Chronicles*.

Six Town Chronicles of England, ed. R. Flenley (Oxford 1911).

The Statutes of the Realm, II (London 1816).

STONE, JOHN, *Chronicle*, ed. W. G. Searle (Cambridge 1902).

The Stonor Letters and Papers 1290–1483, ed. C. L. Kingsford, 2 vols (Camden ser. 1919).

STOREY, R. L., *The End of the House of Lancaster* (London 1966).

STOREY, R. L. (ed.), *The Wars of the Roses*. Exhibition of Records, Public Record Office, March–May, 1961 (Catalogue).

Testamenta Eboracensia, II and III (Surtees Soc. 1855–64).

THOMSON, J. A. F., ' "The Arrivall of Edward IV" – The Development of the Text', *Speculum*, 46 (1971).

THOMSON, J. A. F., 'The Courtenay Family in the Yorkist Period', *BIHR*, 45 (1972).

THOMSON, J. A. F., 'John de la Pole, Duke of Suffolk', *Speculum*, 54 (1979).

Three Fifteenth-Century Chronicles, ed. J. Gairdner (Camden Soc. 1880).

TUDOR-CRAIG, P., *Richard III* (Ipswich 1977).

Tudor Royal Proclamations, ed. P. L. Hughes and J. F. Larkin, I (New Haven, Conn., 1964).

TURNER, H. L., *Town Defences in England and Wales* (London 1971).

VALE, M. G. A., 'New Techniques and Old Ideals: The Impact of Artillery on War and Chivalry at the End of the Hundred Years War' in *War, Literature and Politics in the Late Middle Ages*, ed. C. T. Allmand (Liverpool 1976).

VERGIL, POLYDORE, *Anglicae Historiae libri viginti septem* (Basel 1555); *Three Books of Polydore Vergil's English History . . . from an early translation*, ed. Sir Henry Ellis (Camden Soc. 1844); *The Anglica Historia of Polydore Vergil A.D. 1485–1537*, trans. D. Hay (Camden ser. 1950).

WARKWORTH, JOHN, *A Chronicle of the First Thirteen Years of the Reign of King Edward the Fourth*, ed. J. O. Halliwell (Camden Soc. 1839).

Wars of The English in France: Letters and Papers Illustrative of the Wars of the English in France during the Reign of Henry VI, ed. J. Stevenson, 2 vols (Rolls ser. 1864).

WAURIN, JEHAN DE, *Recuiel des Croniques et Anchiennes Istories de la Grant Bretagne, à present nommé Engleterre*, V, ed. Sir William Hardy and E. L. C. P. Hardy (Rolls ser. 1891).

WEEVER, J., *Ancient Funerall Monuments* (etc.) (London 1631).

WHETHAMSTEDE, JOHN, *Register*, in *Registra quorundam Abbatum Monasterii S. Albani*, ed. H. T. Riley, I (Rolls ser. 1872).

White Rose: Chronicles of the White Rose of York, ed. J. A. Giles (1845).

WILLIAMS, C. H., 'The Rebellion of Humphrey Stafford in 1486', *EHR*, 43 (1928).

WORCESTRE, WILLIAM, *Itineraries*, ed. J. H. Harvey (Oxford 1969).

York Civic Records, I–II, ed. A. Raine (Yorkshire Archaeological Soc., Record Ser. 1939–41).

A Yorkist Collection, in Kingsford, *English Historical Literature*.

Yorkist Notes, in Kingsford, *English Historical Literature*.

Index

ALUMINUM DREAMS

ALUMINUM DREAMS

THE MAKING OF LIGHT MODERNITY

MIMI SHELLER

THE MIT PRESS

CAMBRIDGE, MASSACHUSETTS

LONDON, ENGLAND

MIT Press books may be purchased at special quantity discounts for business or sales promotional use. For information, please email special_sales@mitpress.mit.edu.

This book was set in Bembo and Engravers Gothic by the MIT Press. Printed and bound in the United States of America.

Library of Congress Cataloging-in-Publication Data

Sheller, Mimi.
Aluminum dreams : the making of light modernity / Mimi Sheller.
    pages   cm.
Includes bibliographical references and index.
ISBN 978-0-262-02682-6 (hardcover : alk. paper)
1. Aluminum. 2. Aluminum industry and trade—Social aspects. I. Title.
TA480.A6.S48   2014
338.4'7669722—dc23
2013021936

10   9   8   7   6   5   4   3   2   1

For Daniel Jay Schimmel

CONTENTS

ACKNOWLEDGMENTS

When my partner Dan first gave me some 1940s Alcoa Shipping Company advertisements that he found on eBay for my fortieth birthday, I wondered why an aluminum company was running passenger cruises in the Caribbean. The more I found out about the global aluminum industry, the more I wanted to know. From Jamaican bauxite mines to Iceland during summer 2007, where I heard about worldwide protests against the industry, I journeyed a long way from the Caribbean origins of this project. Through warm and cold, travels far and wide, collaborative research, gallery and museum visits, Dan has kept my interest kindled with well-timed aluminum surprises. He also played a key part in image research, photography, and magazine collection. This book is dedicated to him, because it would not exist without him.

My research was generously supported by the Faculty Research Fund at Swarthmore College during 2006–2007, which enabled me to attend the Saving Iceland "Conference against Heavy Industry" and observe part of the "Summer of Protest" there. For help during this time in Iceland I am incredibly grateful to Abby Ley for driving me to protest sites and into beautiful areas of wilderness, and to her partner Dagar for hosting me. This period also began my steadfast friendship with Esther Figueroa, a constant source of news on the Jamaican bauxite and alumina industry from the *Jamaica Gleaner* and the *Jamaica Observer,* along with her own invaluable running commentary. Thank you, Fig, for being an indefatigable supporter of this project from start to finish—I still hope we will film a documentary on it one day!

Further research was supported by a truly productive visiting fellowship at the Shelby Cullom Davis Center for Historical Studies at Princeton

University, New Jersey, during 2008–2009, and I especially want to thank Daniel Rodgers and Bhavani Raman for hosting me. Princeton's Firestone Library was a welcoming place to conduct research. Some assistance was also provided by the Center for Mobilities Research and Policy at Drexel University, which supported research into visual archives and purchase of primary sources. I want to underline that this project has neither sought nor received funding from any national funding agencies, private foundations, or corporate foundations, which has ensured the independence of my views in pursuing all avenues.

I have very much valued the opportunity to present aspects of this work at a wide range of professional conferences and public lectures since 2007, whose organizers and audiences I thank for their questions, insights, and guidance. Early research was presented at a Swarthmore College faculty seminar, where I want to thank my wonderful colleagues Robin Wagner-Pacifici, Miguel Diaz-Barriga, Sarah S. Willie-LeBreton, Farha Ghannam, Lee Smithy, Joy Charlton, Rose Maio, and the rest of the sociology and anthropology department for their warm support during my time as a visiting faculty member. In July 2008 I presented work at the Crossroads in Cultural Studies conference in Kingston, Jamaica, and later that year at Princeton's Davis Center, where I especially thank all of the brilliant members of the Cultures in Motion seminar for sharing their wisdom, and especially Jeremy Adelman, Celia Applegate, Thomas Bender, April Masten, Susan Pennybacker, Bhavani Raman, Daniel Rodgers, Bradley Simpson, and Nira Wickramasinghe, all of whom made invaluable suggestions.

In 2009 I presented aspects of the project, especially focusing on the Caribbean, at the annual meeting of the Association of American Geographers in Las Vegas; at the annual conference of the Caribbean Studies Association in Kingston, Jamaica; at the American Tropics Conference, Essex University, in Colchester, United Kingdom, where I thank Peter Hulme, Maria Cristina Fumagalli, Richard Price, and Leah Rosenberg for their interest and input; at the workshop called "Visuality/Materiality: Reviewing Theory, Method, and Practice," at the Royal Institute of British Architects, London, for which I thank Divya Tolia-Kelly and Gillian Rose for their invitation and eventual publication; and at Bucknell University, Pennsylvania, where I thank Linden Lewis for a warm welcome. In 2010 talks on the project led me to the Caribbean Studies Association Annual Conference in Barbados, where I want to thank Elizabeth DeLoughrey for organizing a wonderful panel called "Metals and Modernity," and fellow participants Candice Goucher and LeGrace Benson, who taught me much about iron. At the University of Pittsburgh in Pennsylvania, I thank Shalini Puri for the invitation to present my work, which also gave me the opportunity to make use of the Alcoa Archives at the Senator John Heinz History Center Library and Archives, where chief librarian Art Louderback was especially helpful. In 2012 I presented aspects of the book to the Department of Anthropology at Rutgers University, New Brunswick, New Jersey, where I thank David Hughes for his insights especially on smelters in Trinidad; to the West Indian Students' Association at Wesleyan University, Connecticut, with thanks to Gina A. Ulysse; and in 2013 at the Academy of Natural Sciences of Drexel University. I thank all of these organizers and audiences for their contributions.

I especially want to thank the editors and anonymous reviewers of several volumes in which aspects of this work have appeared for their thoughtful comments and careful editing. This includes chapters appearing in the following publications: "Space Age Tropics," in *Surveying the American Tropics: Literary Geographies from New York to Rio*, eds. Maria Cristina Fumagalli, Peter Hulme, Owen Robinson, and Lesley Wylie (Liverpool, UK: Liverpool University Press, 2012); "Metallic Modernities in the Space Age: Visualizing the Caribbean, Materializing the Modern," in *Visuality/Materiality: Images, Objects and Practices*, eds. Gillian Rose and Divya Tolia-Kelly (Aldershot, UK: Ashgate, 2012), 13–37; "Speed Metal, Slow Tropics, Cold War: Alcoa in the Caribbean," in *Cultures in Motion*, eds. Daniel T. Rodgers, Bhavani Raman, and Helmut Reimitz (Princeton, NJ: Princeton University Press, 2013); "Aluminology: An Archaeology of Mobile Modernity," in the *Oxford Handbook of the Archaeology of the Contemporary World*, eds. Paul Graves-Brown, R. Harrison, and A. Piccini (Oxford: Oxford University Press, 2013); and an article for a forthcoming special issue of *Theory, Culture and Society* on "Energizing Society," edited by David Tyfield and John Urry.

Along the way various other colleagues and friendly interlocutors have contributed to my understanding, sent me articles or images, or inspired and helped along my research. Special thanks to Peter Adey, Sara Ahmed, Allen Batteau, David Bissell, David Cade, David Clayton, Gene Coleman, Ian Cook, Tim Cresswell, Samarendra Das, Elizabeth DeLoughrey, Hans-Liudger Dienel, Sarah Franklin, Malene Freudendal-Pederson, Christophe Guy, David Hughes, Hana Iverson, Rivke Jaffe, Eric Jensen, Ole B. Jensen,

Meredith Kaffel, Caren Kaplan, Vincent Kaufmann, Sven Kesselring, David Lambert, Stuart Leslie, Michael McGovern, Peter Merriman, Gijs Mom, Leah Rosenberg, Charlotte Sheedy, Arthur Shostak, Skúli Sigurðsson, Divya Tolia-Kelly, Gina Athena Ulysse, John Urry, Philip Vannini, and all of my excellent colleagues at Drexel University, who have supported my work.

And of course, my family. Dad, thanks for your enthusiasm for this project—I hope you finally enjoy reading this one. Girls, thanks for putting up with me disappearing off into research or writing and talking all the time about the importance of recycling! Mom, thanks for holding the family together whenever we needed you. To the Schimmels, thanks for endless nourishment and sustenance of many kinds shared so generously with all of us.

At the MIT Press, finally, I want to thank my editor Marguerite Avery and the production team for seeing the book through the publication process, series editor Gijs Mom for bringing my project on board (and getting me involved in his journal *Transfers* and in T2M, the International Association for the History of Traffic, Transport, and Mobility), and the anonymous readers to whom I am extremely grateful for pressing me to thoroughly improve the manuscript in crucial ways. I remain responsible for any errors, mistakes, and limitations for what remains my continually evolving comprehension of a global challenge of the largest dimensions, but I hope to have at least begun to capture the global contours of the problem of technologies of lightness, speed, and modernity. My greatest dream is that this initial effort to understand aluminum will at least spark the interest of others to learn more.

If men had had to dream a metal that suited their needs best—it would have been aluminum.

—The Aluminum Association, *The Story of Aluminum*

We have often said: just like the nineteenth century was the century of iron, heavy metals, and carbon, so the twentieth century should be the century of light metals, electricity, and petroleum.

—Arnaldo Mussolini (brother of Benito Mussolini), *Alluminio*, 1932

The discovery of how to create aluminum on an industrial scale in the late nineteenth century unlocked a new material culture of mobility alongside a technological drive toward progressive acceleration in speed and lightness. The physical qualities of this light metal and its alloys contributed to the existing dream of high-speed travel and gravity-defying flight by finally making it possible. And the dreams that aluminum enabled to come true became definitive of twentieth-century modernity and its visions of the future. Aluminum became crucial to the making of modernity not simply as a new material out of which to make particular objects (especially those that we associate with streamlined modernism) but also as a means of innovating across the entire infrastructure of transport and communication (underlying many of the technologies that we associate with modernization). Over the course of around fifty years, from 1910 to the 1960s, aluminum came to play a crucial part in the transportation, electrical, construction, aeronautics, and ship-building industries, as well as in domestic design, architecture, technical equipment, and all kinds of banal aspects of everyday life (from packaging and fasteners, to antiperspirants and makeup, frying pans, and artificial Christmas trees). Once you start looking for it, it is everywhere yet often unnoticed, entering into the design and manufacture of so many artifacts that it fundamentally changed the affordances of the built environment and the motility of the human body.

This book describes how invention and innovation in the applications and meanings of aluminum, driven by military necessity and investment, transformed the twentieth century and continue to shape the world today. Items such as cans, foil, cars, houses, doors, windows, sports equipment, crutches, and walkers might all be aluminum parts of everyday modern life that pass directly through our hands. We often take less notice of the important role of aluminum in the underlying infrastructure that supports that life, such as electrical power lines, lightweight structural support systems inside vehicles and buildings, highway railings and signage, aviation and aerospace technologies, and satellite communication systems and mobile devices. The built environment that has grown up to support the contemporary world economy is a material culture based in aluminum—especially in the cars, trains, and planes that keep our economies moving; the lightweight cans and packages of aluminum-foiled foods that fill our supermarkets and feed urban populations; the high-power electricity lines that make up the long-distance power grid; the massive hydroelectric power projects that were built to support aluminum smelting; and the aluminum powders that make their way into everything from cosmetics, food, paint, and vaccines to bombs, rocket fuel, and new nanotechnologies.

This was not the first time that a new material has transformed the world. Walter Benjamin wrote eloquently about the cultural impact of cast iron, which contributed new materials and visions for the transformation of Paris in the 1820s to the 1850s into a glittering city of arcades, grand boulevards, and exciting railways. In his seminal *Arcades Project* Benjamin spins out a web of cultural connections from the cast iron structures of the gas-lit arcades, to the new department stores and the cavernous railway stations, into an entire world of capitalist spectacle and new modern attitudes. This was the beginning of a movement toward modernity, and a fascination with the speed of the galloping stagecoach, and soon the steaming locomotive thundering on its iron rails, with the instantaneity of daily newspapers and the fascination with kinetoscopes and moving pictures. Aluminum was also a material that inspired people to peer into the future and indeed to invent that future (see figure 1.1).

The electrochemical smelting of aluminum (discovered simultaneously by two twenty-three-year-old inventors, one in France and one in the

Peer into the Future . . . Alcoa Aluminum is revealed a
shining symbol of strength . . . light weight . . . enduring beauty

Even as we look, the present passes. A decade slips by and the desire for the stimulating contacts of city life has increased our urban population twice as fast as the country at large.

Crowded metropolitan space demands expansion—but how? Probably through buildings rising tier upon tier, overhead traffic lanes, roof space for aeroplane landings, aerial sidewalks, terraced parks—buildings mounting ever upward.

Peer into the future and Alcoa Aluminum is revealed. Weighing only one-third as much as metals now commonly used, Alcoa Aluminum is destined to play a prominent part in future building development.

Alcoa Aluminum resists corrosion. It need not be painted. It will not streak adjoining surfaces. It can be cast, forged, drawn, extruded,

welded and riveted. On the exteriors of buildings its beauty is already seen —its light weight and strength utilized. For the interior trim and furnishings of office buildings, stores, and residences its decorative charm is employed. Providing the architect with a metal that lends itself readily to design and fine detail, that insures permanence, that saves handling of unnecessary dead-weight, and that cuts cost of erection, Alcoa Aluminum will find ever-increasing use.

In each of our offices we have competent representatives who are familiar with the decorative and structural uses of each of the special Alcoa Aluminum alloys. The services of these representatives are available to architects. ALUMINUM COMPANY of AMERICA; 2402 Oliver Building, PITTSBURGH, PENNSYLVANIA.

ALCOA ALUMINUM

FIGURE 1.1
Alcoa Aluminum Advertisement, *Fortune Magazine*, "Peer into the Future," circa 1931.

United States, in 1886, as discussed in chapter 2), opened whole new vistas in the quest for speed and lightness. It brought the apotheosis of speed, new architectures of luminosity, and the conquest of air and outer space that nineteenth-century writers such as Jules Verne dreamed of, thrilled at, and feared.

Although iron, steel, plastics, glass, and cement all have their place in the material culture of twentieth-century modernity, aluminum demands attention not because it necessarily outpaced or outperformed these materials, nor because it is so prevalent yet so overlooked, but because it embeds crucial transnational processes right into everyday lives; and because of the conundrum it represents. It is so full of promise as a technological solution across a range of applications, yet has caused so much unacknowledged environmental and human harm. Aluminum is a material with great potential for supporting life and also inherent massive powers of destruction. Although we recognize the centrality of oil to our modern world because of the wars waged to control the oilfields, the calls for energy independence by politicians, or the consequences of global warming, we seldom notice its quiet accomplice. Those wars are waged using aluminum-skinned airplanes, aluminum armor-plated tanks, and aluminum-based explosives, including many bombs and bomb-delivery systems. Troops and military equipment are moved using aluminum vessels, cargo carriers, and long-distance aluminum logistics systems for getting the lightest-weight weaponry and material around the world as quickly as possible. Yet the same qualities that make aluminum ideal and necessary for warfare also make it ideal and necessary for new technologies of sustainability in the face of climate change: energy-efficient buildings, lighter and more fuel-efficient transportation systems, new metal matrix materials, and nanocomposite technologies.

Although steel and reinforced cement were also crucial materials for the building of modern urbanism, it was aluminum that added the leavening to make structures light enough to rise far above the ground. It was aluminum that put the portability into transport, the lift into lift off, and the oomph into the modern housewife's kitchen in the 1950s. Amid the gravity of the Cold War it was aluminum that gave us the levity of the space age and enabled the dream of landing on the moon. It was aluminum that made the bombs explode, the rockets fire, and the satellites orbit. Heavy industry became lighter, ethereal electricity flowed through expanding circuits, and aluminum put us on the path toward dreams of dematerialization of cybernetic economies running on information superhighways. The aluminum industry also inadvertently left us bound up in metallic threads that fused with our bodies, infiltrated our buildings, altered our way of life, and even made their silent way into our foods and medicines. Today aluminum is an adjuvant in vaccines, incorporated into high-tech metal matrix composites and nanomaterials, some believe leaching out of our foods and packaging and said to be accumulating in the brain tissue of Alzheimer's sufferers. All of these aspects are part of the story of aluminum, yet there is also more.

Tracing the silvery thread of aluminum across time and space draws together some of the remotest places on earth alongside some of the centers of global power, some of the richest people in the world alongside some of the poorest, and some of the most pressing environmental and political concerns we face. It is a dramatic yet little-known tale that encapsulates the making of global modernity and uneven development, the creation of multinational corporations and the displacement of native indigenous peoples around the world, the entrenchment of the United States as a world economic and military power and the current rise of China, the modernization of warfare and significance of air power, and the invention of 1950s suburbia and the pursuit of the American Dream. But it also entails many other dreams around the world, which I call *aluminum dreams*. These dreams involved hopes and idealistic projections of modernization, prosperity, and leisure-filled future utopias, as well as false hopes that led to failed technologies, pollution, social dislocation, and environmental devastation. The story of aluminum does not begin with the United States, nor does it stop there; it is a global story about nation building and the "second industrial revolution" in Europe, from World War I to World War II; about the Cold War and the Soviet-US space race; about Third World development, resource control, and struggles for national sovereignty in Africa, India, and the Caribbean; about the unleashing and reining in of transnational corporations; and about the pollution of the earth and the battle to save it.

COMPARING COMMODITY HISTORIES

Before we begin, it is instructive to compare the history of aluminum production and consumption to other materials of modernity such as steel and plastics. Thomas Misa powerfully describes the making of the modern United States as "a nation of steel" from 1865 to 1925, a history that precedes slightly but overlaps with the period covered here, roughly 1886 to the present.[1] His is an important national history and explanation of the complex forces that shape a "technological regime,"[2] forces that he argues arise not only out of scientific research, industrial innovation, or economic rationalities but also from the often contradictory social, cultural, and institutional practices that guide particular companies, government agencies, and interactions between producers and users. Misa links "the building of the world's largest steel industry" to the "emergence of the United States as a leading economic, military and political power"[3]—including the rapid expansion of railroads across the west, the rise of skyscrapers and modern cities, the making of military armor, the rationalization of factory production, and the rise of automobility—and he also shows how each of these developments was not an inevitable outcome of advances in technology, but was contingent on specific user-producer interactions that sometimes stifled innovation (and ultimately led to the collapse of the US steel industry, its factories and jobs shipped overseas). "However often technologies appear to cause changes, technical change itself is frequently the *result* of underlying changes in the availability of raw materials, in the structure of firms, and in social forms and economic conditions."[4]

Building on Misa's approach, then, we need to consider not only the discovery of aluminum smelting and the expanding uses of this new metal as an inevitable outcome of science, engineering, or even investments in research and development (which is often the assumed narrative in business histories),[5] but also the crucial role of competing capitalist firms, state interventions, and user-producer interactions in shaping markets, industrial structures, and wider social processes.[6] The rise of aluminum was neither inevitable nor steady; it faced challenges, setbacks, and at times embarrassing failures when airplanes broke apart, ships corroded, or electric wiring caught fire. Although this book takes heed of Misa's lessons about steel, it also pushes us in two other directions: first, to move beyond a national history, and second, to expand the boundaries of cultural history further into material culture. Understanding aluminum requires an almost archeological excavation of the material culture of light modernity as well as a sociological explanation of the cultural, social, political, and ecological impacts of the age of aluminum. Aluminum's meanings go beyond any single form, purpose, or nation.[7]

We are surrounded by the artifacts of the age of aluminum and by the culture that has been assembled around it. Understanding the future of technology requires a deeper understanding of its past and of the interconnections between its globally distributed actors and networks of power. I emphasize aluminum's transnational cultural history in part because of my own grounding in Caribbean studies and the history of the Atlantic World, which I first explored in my book *Consuming the Caribbean* in relation to the slave trade, the sugar trade, and the tropical fruit industry, as well as various kinds of cultural circulation of images, texts, and ideas.[8] National cultures, I suggest, are part of wider material cultures that are "cultures in motion," including empires conceived as "complex and entangled worlds, with their middle grounds, contested borders, and contact zones" and "stories of intrusion, translation, resistance, and adaptation."[9] The cultural history of aluminum production and consumption likewise embeds the history of the United States in the history of other nations and in global processes, especially the forms of colonial exploitation that had already shaped the Americas, making this "a nation among nations."[10] This is therefore a transnational story that like other recent commodity histories embeds the United States "in larger circuits of people, ideas, and resources," rather than stopping at "the water's edge," as Robert Vitalis puts it in his study of US multinationals on the Saudi Arabian oil frontier.[11]

Culture does not stop at the national border, nor does the structure of industrial firms in the aluminum industry. Perhaps because the steel industry held more of a nationally territorialized structure, with iron ore mined inside the United States, transported by rail, and turned into steel and serving consumer markets within the United States, it is easier to confine it to a national history, symbolized by the dominance of the United States Steel Corporation. Aluminum, by contrast, was from very early on a multinational enterprise, with the first North American leader, the Aluminum Corporation of America (Alcoa), becoming a dominant world producer spanning the United States and Canada, mining bauxite in Suriname and British Guiana, and soon opening refining plants, smelters, and consumer markets overseas, as well as competing (and forming cartels) with French and German firms.

Like steel, the story of aluminum also concerns battles over the legality of patents, the regulation of monopolies and cartels, and the fundamental question of the ethics of transnational corporations and the ultimate future of capitalism, which will be explored throughout this book. However, these transnational economic and business histories must be accompanied by a transnational cultural history recognizing how global markets link various parts of the world together by producing different technological cultures and different degrees of access to new technologies.

In his interesting cultural history of aluminum as an industrial material, Eric Schatzberg argues that symbolic meanings and ideologies embedded within engineering played a crucial role in shaping expectations, influencing technological innovation, and driving increased uses of aluminum even in the face of its objective shortcomings.[12] Schatzberg argues that symbolic meanings that linked aluminum with modernity drove a kind of irrational enthusiasm, even though at other times promoters of other materials (such as steel or wood) along with disappointed consumers attacked its "ersatz" qualities. Just as Misa finds the contest between the qualities of high-temperature Bessemer steel and lower-temperature open-hearth iron indeterminate, or the contest between military contracts for low-carbon steel plate versus high-carbon nickel steel armor determined by politics more than evidence, Schatzberg suggests that in their early decades of development wooden airplanes were as good a technology as aluminum airplanes in terms of price, performance, and safety; but there was a "rhetoric of enthusiasm" that linked aluminum to inevitable progress from an age of wood and handcraft toward an age of metals and scientific production—the ever deferred and always still arriving "age of aluminum."

Yet in Schatzberg's account, too, the focus on rhetorical moves and ideological conflicts interior to the United States misses out on some of the larger story of the cultural history of aluminum, ignoring some of the crucial economic factors and state interferences that are highlighted in economic or business histories. There is a remarkable parallel between the contested rhetorics surrounding aluminum (miracle metal versus flimsy substitute, in a nutshell) and those that Jeffrey Meikle has identified in his very similar national cultural history of another material, *American Plastic*.[13] Similar to aluminum, early understandings of plastic were poised between the rhetoric of scientific invention of a seemingly immortal "magic" material that would transform the world, and the more mundane positioning in which plastic is merely a cheap imitation or substitute for other materials, vulnerable to being rejected as "artificial" rather than celebrated as a product of chemistry.

However, in the cases of aluminum and plastics, I want to argue, we need to understand their entrance into the US market not simply as a matter of internal cultural contestations and rhetorical frames, but also in relation to wider cultures of technological regimes, embeddedness in institutions (including US imperialism), global struggles for economic and military predominance, and competition with other transnational actors and industries for resources, energy, and labor.

In contrast to all of the existing mainstream histories of modern materials, whether of steel, aluminum, or plastics, *Aluminum Dreams* will also explore its transnational ecological and cultural impacts alongside its domestic importance, and indeed show the connection between home and away. In this sense the story here bears some resemblance to Michael Redclift's history called *Chewing Gum: The Fortunes of Taste,* which emphasizes the geographical and cultural distance between sites of production among the Mayan *chicle* workers of Mexico's Yucatan forests and the cheerful sites of pleasurable and ephemeral consumption of chewing gum in the United States.[14] It is this distance of the tropical frontier that hides extreme disparities of power, ecological impacts, and social catastrophes, and also prevents us from learning the history of indigenous people's resistance to both transnational capitalism and to state domination by developmental states serving the interests of small elites. These are all aspects of the transnational history of bauxite mining and aluminum production, too, yet tracking this complex material also engages more than Redclift's binational approach to US-Mexican relations, for it is also about histories of world war, of North-South and East-West relations during the Cold War, and of the economic restructuring of the global economy in the late twentieth and twenty-first centuries.

Drawing on my earlier work *Consuming the Caribbean* (2003), as well as the emerging new interdisciplinary field of mobilities research,[15] this book emphasizes the simultaneous making of modern infrastructures of mobility (associated with dreams of lightness, speed, and modernity) alongside the creation of transnational regimes of immobility (associated with what I call the *dark side,* including the underdevelopment of tropical countries, the forced displacement of deeply rooted indigenous communities through imposition of hydroelectric plants and mining, and the ecological destruction and health impacts of mining and smelting). I argue that these conjoined relations between the mobilities of modernity and the "backwardness" of underdeveloped mining regions have deeply shaped the economic, ecological, and cultural relations between Global North and South.

Veins of aluminum quietly course through our culture, keeping the kinetic elite moving while sucking up eons of electrical power from not-so-modern places where people are often prevented from moving across borders or are forced out of their own lands and thrown into an unstable process of involuntary transmigration. The unheeded external effects of a material so deeply and innocently incorporated into everyday life are reminiscent of E. Melanie DuPuis's account in *Nature's Perfect Food: How Milk Became America's Drink.*[16] How does something so ordinary and seemingly harmless carry with it such a heavy ecological burden? How do state support and marketing promotions so effectively cover over the ambiguities of industrial production? And how could we possibly do without milk or aluminum, when they are so deeply embedded into the American Dream?

An overlooked cultural aspect of aluminum's metallic modernity is found in the contrast between modernity and backwardness, speed and slowness, and mobility and immobility as forms of cultural representation of the difference between the "developed" and "developing" world. I therefore pay attention not only to the internal dynamics of technological development, corporate structure, industry-state relations, and user-producer relations, but also, unlike some other national studies of single commodities, I pay far more attention to the transnational dynamics of political economy, uneven development, and ecological externalities as part of the cultural history of aluminum. The "externalities" that the industry, its engineers, and its historians have largely ignored—pollution, energy use, and health effects on workers, consumers, and those displaced by large-scale industrial development—are all crucial to understanding aluminum's ambiguous cultural history, as well as its contested future. Aluminum remains with us in the twenty-first century, for some as a renaissance material for the "green" design of a lighter, recyclable set of transition technologies that will reduce our carbon footprint and for others as a major cause of environmental devastation, warfare, and human suffering. It is a superficially lightweight topic with a surprisingly heavy history, and deserves a fuller accounting as we move into the next generation technologies of what some foresee as an inevitable postcarbon transition.[17]

A METAL FOR MOBILITY AND MODERNITY

Let us begin with an overview of aluminum's role as a metal that is crucial to mobile modernity. Above all, aluminum is a substance constitutive of modern mobility due to the crucial part it plays in the transportation, construction, and the aviation industries. It also moves our electricity, without which many other things would not be able to move. The combination of electricity and electrochemical production of metals has been called the *second industrialization,* replacing the classic canals, water, coal, iron, and steam power of the first industrial revolution. We might think of this as a shift from heavy to light modernity. Aluminum initiated this shift, and was later joined by other light substances such as plastics, fiberglass, and nylon, all spun off from the petrochemicals industry. In 2012 the main uses of aluminum globally were 24 percent in the building industry; 18 percent in cars; 13 percent in packaging; 9 percent in electrical cable, and an equal amount in miscellaneous other products; 7 percent each in mechanical equipment, appliances, and trucks; 4 percent in electrical equipment, and 2 percent in other transportation such as airplanes.[18] However, in the United States, transportation accounted for an estimated 34 percent of domestic consumption; packaging, 27 percent; building, 12 percent; electrical, 8 percent; machinery, 8 percent; consumer durables, 7 percent; and other, 4 percent.[19]

Aluminum made its way into so many places and products in part because it has special qualities as compared to other metals, both in pure form and in alloys. The weight of aluminum is about one-third of an equivalent volume of steel (with a specific gravity of 2.70 versus steel's 7.85), so engineers can use it to achieve dramatic weight reductions. This has made it especially attractive in the aviation and transport industries, as well as in lightweight packaging and fasteners. Aluminum is very malleable and versatile compared to other metals, thus, it moves around the world, changing shape as it moves, such that its myriad fluid forms change the places in which we dwell and the infrastructures that enable our movements. It can be machined, shaped, extruded, and recycled, meaning there are many different processes for working it into a desired shape. It can be turned into sheets, wire, castings, alloys, and forgings, thus creating innumerable useful products.

Aluminum also has a natural oxide layer on its surface that protects it from various types of atmospheric corrosion, aqueous corrosion, and corrosion by oil or chemicals, so it is far more durable than other metals. It will not rust like iron or turn green like copper. It can be painted, plated, or anodized to produce various surface finishes. Because it is nonferrous, it does not cause sparks and is also nonmagnetic, so it can be safely used in electronics and in the oil and gas industries. It is also incombustible, weldable, and has good electrical and thermal conductivity, making it an ideal building material that can replace copper in many applications.[20]

Aluminum was first incorporated into the rolling out of electrification projects due to the significant use of aluminum cable steel reinforced (ACSR) power lines, the creation of national energy grids, and the investment in large-scale hydroelectric power projects in many parts of the world. An advertisement by the Aluminum Company of America, appearing in *Business Week* in December 1929, declared the following:

This is the Age of Aluminum. [. . .] few people—outside of the electrical profession—realize to what extent Aluminum is acting as the vehicle for the transmission of that most intangible of all travelers—electricity. Hundreds of thousands of miles of Aluminum Cable of every conceivable size—from the great 220,000 volt high tension lines to the small telephone wire—weaves its web of civilization across the countryside [. . .] spanning deep canyons and rivers [. . .] crossing rugged mountains [. . .] bringing light and sound communication and power to remote rural districts; carrying harnessed electrical energy from the point of its generation to the point of its use.[21]

Thus it was swept up in the excitement of "electrifying America," entering into everyday life in farms, homes, and industry, and redefining US culture in myriad ways.[22]

Though electricity is often association with copper wires, these were actually more expensive and heavy than aluminum. Reynolds Metals Company in 1950 explained that "one pound of aluminum wire is equivalent electrically to two pounds of copper wire." Heavier copper transmission cables were not only expensive in themselves, but also required almost 50 percent more pylons per mile than aluminum, and aluminum pylons themselves were light and easier to erect. "ACSR permits the use of longer spans, fewer poles. On a typical line, ACSR requires only 10.8 poles per mile where the equivalent copper conductor requires 14.9 poles per mile," notes Reynolds, so that "the majority of modern high-voltage electric power lines throughout the world use it," including the "famous British 'Grid' that covers the whole of Great Britain . . . some 12,000 tons of aluminum being used in nearly 20,000 miles of overhead conductor."[23]

In the United States, Alcoa pointed out in 1969 that aluminum and electricity "grew up together," with aluminum being used in "every aspect of electric power distribution and utilization" because "pound for pound, aluminum has twice the electrical conductance of copper."[24] Starting with aluminum conductor in 1897, they then developed stranded aluminum conductor, and finally in 1909 designed ACSR "aluminum conductor, steel reinforced," the first composite kind of transmission line, which was first installed at the Southern California Edison Company in 1913. With "54 aluminum wires stranded in three layers over a seven-strand steel core," this "220,000-volt line, still in operation [in 1969], was for years the world's longest and highest-voltage line," only exceeded by later "extra-high-voltage" lines.[25] Aluminum was used not only for wire and cable but also switchyards, bus conductors of all sizes, transformers and capacitors, aluminum towers (that could be delivered fully assembled by helicopter), all-aluminum substations, distribution lines, and inside the home for lightbulb bases, electrical fittings, and appliance components, telephone lines, and eventually TV antennas, and, of course, the classic aluminum telephone booth.

Second, aluminum quickly revolutionized packaging, starting with foil cigarette wrappers and chocolate wraps, and extending into all kinds of foil, lids, linings, and above all the lightweight aluminum can, all of which enabled great weight reductions and less spoilage in the movement of foods and drink around the world, as discussed in later chapters. Most recently we have seen the rise of the Tetra Pak, which combines a thin aluminized coating with paper and plastics, making it particularly difficult to separate for recycling. Aluminum is generally considered to be nontoxic and impermeable to water and air, making it especially useful in packaging for the food industry. In terms of the wider food system, from farm to fork, the lightness of aluminum helps farmers more easily move water into their fields, feed and fence their animals, and process and store their crops. Aluminum vats serve in canteens, food-processing plants, breweries, and bottling plants, helping to industrialize modern food systems.

Aluminum foil perhaps sums up best what is appealing, beautiful, and convenient about aluminum. One side shining, the other slightly matte, it unwinds in thin precision and breaks off along the satisfying saw-toothed edge without tearing or fraying. It is part of many people's everyday home life as food cover, pan liner, cooking device, children's arts and crafts material; always useful, fun, decorative, and hard to live without.

Thanks to aluminum we have US icons such as the TV dinner in its freezer-to-oven tray with each separate food item snugly tucked in its own little geometric compartment; Jiffy Pop popcorn with its magically rising foil dome; packaged prepared foods from the supermarket ready to heat and eat in just a few minutes; and take-away containers that keep restaurant meals warm and go straight into the oven at home. Each of these reminds us that the utility of aluminum is as much about time-savings as weight-savings. It is light and fast to transport, but it also makes the chores of the kitchen lighter and faster. It was promoted as a way to free women, in particular, from some of the burdens of housework, promising a new era of easy domestic labor and instant cuisine, even though electric appliances arguably fragmented time and privatized women's work in the home.[26] But it was also part of a wider movement toward "scientific" efficiencies that would not only bring convenience into the modern home, and especially the kitchen, but also revolutionize logistics for the delivery of goods to those homes. The logistics revolution was tied to a wider transformation of US infrastructure and transportation that would also spawn "fast food," drive-through restaurants, and a throw-away culture.

Third, as I explore in more detail in chapters 4 and 5, aluminum brought new possibilities to architecture, making the process of building more mobile and the physical materiality of modern design lighter. In the case of airports, for example, aluminum expresses the essence of airspace: from the aluminum framing and cladding of modernist airport architecture to the conveyors and screening systems for moving luggage, from the check-in desks and escalators to the moving walkways and monorails for moving passengers, from the furnishings of departure lounges to the airport restaurants. It connotes the speed, ease of movement, high technology, and modernity associated with air travel (when it works smoothly, and before the era of security delays!). It also played a crucial part in the development of skyscrapers and modern suburban homes, especially in combination with other materials such as steel, plastic, and glass, not to mention in mobile homes and prefabricated homes that could be easily moved. It especially contributed to the emergence of lightweight mobile devices ("miniature mobiles") that transformed music listening, computing, and communication, from the iconic Sony Walkman in the 1970s to the equally design-savvy Apple MacBook laptops, machined out of a sharp-edged slab of aluminum. Today handheld devices such as the iPhone and iPad achieve their portability thanks to the lightness of aluminum, but also their connectivity to ubiquitous communication systems from cell phone towers to the low-earth-orbiting aluminum satellites that support their capabilities.

Fourth, at an even more human scale, this mysteriously light metal also revolutionized the capacity of the human body for prosthetic mobility in several ways, having the curious capacity to meld with our bodies to enhance their power, change their form, and allow them to move in new ways. Around the house it brought us far lighter and more portable equipment: ladders, folding chairs, window frames, screens, outdoor furniture, canoes, and small motorboats. Aluminum furniture allowed us to carry chairs easily indoors and outdoors, by the poolside or down to the beach. Aluminum ladders likewise lightened the load on trade workers, allowing people to climb higher and carry out tasks more easily—whether painting, washing windows, or screwing in lightbulbs. Other significant innovations occurred with the use of aluminum in the design of tennis rackets, bicycle frames and parts, baseball bats, crutches, walkers for the elderly, and guitars, all of which allowed the human body to be mobilized in new ways. In the realm of sports aluminum tennis rackets revolutionized the entire style of the game, bringing in an era of high-speed baseline volleys, just as aluminum baseball bats created super-human home-run hitting streaks. These changes to the sport caused controversy, but they were as irresistible as doping in making people feel stronger and faster.

A seemingly mundane technology—the walker—has allowed millions of elderly people to continue to live active lives, and aluminum crutches have gotten many people back on their feet. Aluminum has just the right combination of strength, lightness, and flex to enhance the natural capabilities of the human body to move. In the realms of aging, health, and medicine, devices made of aluminum brought new possibilities for human mobility. Otherwise incapacitated people could regain a new sense of freedom and movement, assisted by aluminum artificial limbs or prosthetic joints. Its lightness makes it perfectly suited to combination with human muscular power, and its strength and durability are up to the test of human impact, clumsiness, and wear and tear. The strength, lightness, and durability of aluminum give our vulnerable bodies access to potentials for mobility that can extend the human range of movement whether for the highest-potential sportsperson or those overcoming limited abilities to regain capacities.

On a lighter note, perhaps the best way to appreciate the significance of aluminum to our everyday lives would be to imagine a counterfactual world without it. An episode of the animated television program *The Simpsons* opens with a spoof 1950s educational documentary called *A World without Zinc,* which suggests how awful life would be without this useful element.[27] Creator Matt Groening had to defend the episode's controversial depiction of a teen suicide attempt:

"We opened the show with Bart and his class watching a scratchy black-and-white film about zinc," Groening said. "It was a send-up of those cornball education films we were forced to watch when we were growing up."

The snippet showed the teen in a dream sequence imagining a world without the element zinc. Because zinc didn't exist, the teen had no car; without a car, he lost his girlfriend. Distraught, he put a gun to his head, but when he pulled the trigger, nothing happened because there was no zinc in the firing pin.

"He wakes up thinking, 'Thank God I live in the world of zinc,'" Groening said. "If anything, it possibly cheers up suicidal teens by giving them something to laugh at."[28]

The spoof film echoes 1940s educational films such as *A Case of Spring Fever,* which hammers home the usefulness of springs by showing what happens to a man who wishes them out of existence. The makers of this film, known as Jam Handy, also made a 1956 promotional film for the Reynolds Corporation called *Aluminum on the March,* a classic of propagandistic industrial documentary that opens with a wonderful animated sequence of pieces of aluminum marching in formation, set to stirring martial music, portraying the many useful qualities of aluminum—for vehicles, for buildings, for packaging, electricity, and for myriad everyday products. It also aims to leave us with the message, "Thank God I live in the world of aluminum!" In the rest of this book I will explore our world of aluminum, and consider whether it would be possible to live without it or at least reduce our usage of it.

Why would we want to reduce our use of this miraculous metal, you might ask? In the following sections I lay out what is overlooked in almost every industrial, business, and cultural history of aluminum: its ecological and social and human rights effects on people in many "nonmodern" parts of the world, as well as on industrial workers and nearby communities in the "developed" world. While most of us buy into the aluminum dream, there are many who have experienced its darker side.

THE ECOLOGICAL IMPACTS OF ALUMINUM

One-twelfth of the earth's crust is aluminum, making it the third most common element, after oxygen and silicon; but it is extremely difficult to get it into pure form. The main source is bauxite ore, which is processed into alumina, as described further in the following and in chapter 2, in a process that separates out iron, silica, and about forty other mineral elements that are found in the ore. As a general rule, four tons of dried bauxite is required to produce two tons of alumina, which, in turn, provides one ton of primary aluminum metal. Today the world's largest producers of bauxite ore are Australia, China, Brazil, India, Guinea, and Jamaica (see table 1.1), with the largest known reserves in Guinea.

World bauxite resources are estimated to be in total fifty-five to seventy-five billion tons, distributed in Africa (32 percent), Oceania (23 percent), South America and the Caribbean (21 percent), Asia (18 percent), and elsewhere (6 percent).[29] US imports of bauxite (2007–2010), in order to feed the ten primary smelters in the country, come mainly from Jamaica (41 percent), Guinea (21 percent), Brazil (18 percent), and Guyana (8 percent).[30]

TABLE 1.1

World Bauxite Mine Production and Reserves (in thousand metric tons)

Mine production	2010	2011	Reserves
United States	NA	NA	20,000
Australia	68,400	67,000	6,200,000
Brazil	28,100	31,000	3,600,000
China	44,000	46,000	830,000
Greece	2,100	2,100	600,000
Guinea	17,400	18,000	7,400,000
Guyana	1,760	2,000	850,000
India	18,000	20,000	900,000
Jamaica	8,540	10,200	2,000,000
Kazakhstan	5,310	5,400	160,000
Russia	5,480	5,800	200,000
Sierra Leone	1,090	1,700	180,000
Suriname	4,000	5,000	580,000
Venezuela	2,500	4,500	320,000
Vietnam	80	80	2,100,000
Other countries	2,630	2,600	3,300,000
World total (rounded)	209,000	220,000	29,000,000

Source: US Geological Survey (USGS). *Mineral Commodity Summaries (MCS) 2012* (Reston, VA: USGS, Department of the Interior, 2012).

US imports of bauxite that has already been refined into alumina come mainly from Australia (38 percent), Brazil (18 percent), Suriname (17 percent), and Jamaica (16 percent).

Bauxite mining is an open pit process that leads to deforestation and leaves behind toxic "red mud" lakes that can overflow and pollute local ground water. Bauxite mining damages forests, pollutes waterways, and encroaches on agricultural land often displacing small farmers:

Strip mining and ore processing produces about two and a half tons of wet mining wastes per ton of aluminum produced. It has historically led to severe soil erosion, as millions of tons of exposed earth and crushed rock were left to wash into streams and oceans. Strip mining destroys whatever wildlife habitat has existed above the mine, and is difficult—if not impossible—to re-establish even with intentional revegetation.[31]

The production of each ton of aluminum cans, for example, requires four tons of bauxite ore to be strip-mined, crushed, washed, and refined into alumina, creating about four tons of caustic red mud residue, which can seep into surface and groundwater. All around the world, as explored in part II, bulldozers uproot ancient rainforest and the sacred mountains of indigenous tribal peoples, explosives blast away the outer crust of earth, and giant trucks move in, digging their claws deep into the exposed bauxite ore. A reddish dust fills the air, eventually settling on every leaf, roof, and lung for miles around.

The bauxite ore is then washed, strained, baked, and dried into a fine powdery dust—aluminum oxide. Alumina refining also takes place near the mining operations, with Jamaica having traditionally been one of the major suppliers to US smelters:

Dust from alumina refining and export operations has caused respiratory and aesthetic damage, and portside alumina spills have harmed coastal coral reefs. In 2000, the U.S. imported 3 million tons of bauxite and 400,000 tons of alumina from Jamaica, over 90% of which was used for primary aluminum.[32]

Poured into the deep holds of ships, the alumina crosses the world in search of cheap electricity, drawn to the raging rivers and geological forces that have been tamed to feed the smelters. Into the mile-long lines of smelter pots it pours, where a jolt of electric current awakens the secretive metal from its oxide slumber. Electrons jump to order, molten shining metal forms like lava around the cathode of a carbon crucible. The alchemical forces of the universe are unleashed, setting in motion an alluvial flow of aluminum. Out of the pots, presses, and rollers, a tidal wave of castings, forgings, and sheets of metal enter the factories of the world to be turned into finished goods such as car parts and airplane fuselages, cans and wrappers, kitchenware and foil, chairs and satellites.

Beyond mining, though, there are further ecological effects associated with aluminum production. Aluminum smelting is one of the most energy-intensive production processes on earth. Smelting uses an electrolytic process in which a high current is passed through dissolved alumina in order to split the aluminum from its chemical bond with oxygen. The electrochemical smelting of aluminum from refined bauxite ore requires between 13,500 and 17,000 kWh of electricity per ton, more energy than any other kind of metal processing. To put this in perspective, the making of one soda can is said to require the equivalent of one-quarter of the can's volume in gasoline to produce.[33] Three percent of the electricity generated worldwide goes to aluminum smelting, and in some small countries smelters consume a third or more of the national power supply.[34] Because of its high demand for electricity the process of producing aluminum produces on average thirteen tons of CO_2 emissions per ton of aluminum. The aluminum industry emits about 1 percent of global emissions of man-made greenhouse gases. Smelters are also responsible for 90 percent of all tetrafluoromethane and 65 percent of all hexafluoroethane emissions worldwide. These PFCs have global warming potentials that are 6,500 to 9,200 times higher than carbon dioxide. Other emissions and effluents include sulfur dioxide, fluoride, hydroflourocarbons, and spent pot lining.

With demand for aluminum expected to more than double between 2006 and 2025 (despite a fall in global demand during the recent global recession), this is an opportune moment to ask how sustainable the growth and intensification of bauxite mining and aluminum smelting operations around the world will be in the future.[35] By far the largest world producer (and consumer) of aluminum is China, which had capacity to produce a staggering 25 million tons in 2011, with Russia, the United States and Canada following behind with capacity of between 3 and 4.4 million metric tons each (see table 1.2). Some of the newest entrants are Bahrain, the United Arab Emirates, and Qatar, each of whom is using abundant supplies of natural gas to power new smelters. With energy usage constituting between 21 and 30 percent of the cost involved in producing aluminum, the industry has aggressively pursued low-cost energy around the world and has benefited from huge subsidies in the price it pays for electricity. During wartime, especially, aluminum production drives energy policy, for example, in World War II when Canada's "electricity generation and distribution decisions circulated around [aluminum smelter] Alcan's needs,"[36] or in the United States, as described in chapter 3, where the Grand Coulee Dam on the Columbia River powered the Bonneville Power Project, which in turn powered nearby Alcoa and Reynolds smelters, which supplied aluminum to the Boeing corporation to produce about one-third of the planes built in the United States during World War II. This is not without environmental effects; fluoride contamination from smelters on the Snake-Columbia river system in Oregon and British Columbia is linked to the collapse of the native salmon population.[37]

TABLE I.2

World Smelter Production and Capacity (in thousand metric tons)

	Production		Year-end capacity	
	2010	2012	2010	2012
United States	1,726	2,000	3,200	2,900
Australia	1,930	2,900	2,050	1,980
Bahrain	870	900	880	970
Brazil	1,540	1,450	1,700	1,700
Canada	2,960	2,700	3,020	3,020
China	16,200	19,000	23,000	25,000
Germany	394	405	620	620
Iceland	780	800	790	800
India	1,450	1,700	1,950	3,150
Mozambique	557	550	570	570
Norway	800	1,000	1,230	1,230
Qatar	190	585	585	585
Russia	3,950	4,200	4,440	4,450
South Africa	807	600	900	900
United Arab Emirates	1,400	1,850	1,800	1,850
Other countries	4,900	4,760	6,180	6,250
World total (rounded)	40,800	44,900	53,500	56,400

Source: US Geological Survey (USGS). *Mineral Commodity Summaries (MCS) 2012* (Reston, VA: USGS, Department of the Interior, 2012); US Geological Survey (USGS). *Mineral Commodity Summaries (MCS) 2013* (Reston, VA: USGS, Department of the Interior, 2013).

   The aluminum industry's needs for energy drove the damming of rivers for hydroelectric generation, especially during wartime surges in demand. The industry has turned to hydroelectric power in many places, because it is considered a clean renewable energy source, preferable to burning coal or oil, and above all offers the round-the-clock continuous current that is needed to keep the smelter pots from freezing solid. Yet in almost every case this has involved the displacement of indigenous and tribal peoples from their land and rivers, often accompanied by environmental destruction and human rights violations. From Niagara Falls and the Tennessee Valley River Authority in the early twentieth-century United States, to Oregon's Columbia River basin, Canada's Saguenay River projects and the Suriname River in South America in the mid-twentieth century, shifting in the late twentieth century to places like the Zambezi River in Mozambique, the Three Gorges Dam in China, and tributaries of the Amazon in Brazil, "histories of aluminium and dam construction go hand in glove, linked from birth."[38] In underdeveloped regions of the world the expansion of transnational aluminum corporations consumes huge amounts of electricity, straining the power generation system and depriving local populations of their own sources of energy.

There is much to learn from the history of bauxite mining and the aluminum industry about how to govern and regulate transnational corporations and promote desirable forms of technological development. As development has spread across remote aboriginal territories in Australia and untouched wilderness areas in Brazil, into tribal lands in Eastern India or politically unstable West African countries such as Guinea or Sierra Leone, it is pertinent to ask who is responsible for monitoring and regulating transnational industries. Even as global social movements unite in protest against the industry, it remains uncertain how environmental effects can be minimized and how the completion of costly cleanups can be monitored, not to mention preventing harmful developments in the first place. In many countries the industry has been able to externalize environmental costs, leaving the cleanup to future generations.

In relation to mining operations, something like the US superfund program to clean up toxic waste and heavily polluted areas left across the country by former industries could perhaps be implemented internationally to assess and address the effects of bauxite mining, alumina plants, and hydropower dams. Yet even within the United States the actual cleanup of superfund sites has been painfully slow and often simply unachievable. Countries such as Jamaica and Australia have very active programs for "restoring" bauxite mining lands, yet the infilling and grassing over of such areas never returns them to their natural state, and they often remain unsuitable for farming, whereas forested areas are turned to monoculture plantations of species such as eucalyptus, which can deal with hydrological damage. How can the industry be made to clean up its prior messes and prevent future environmental damage? Who will be able to control corporate power and rein in a global industry with little accountability to any particular legal jurisdiction?

HUMAN HEALTH AND HUMAN RIGHTS: AN ENVIRONMENTAL POISON?

In addition to the ground, water and air pollution associated with mining and smelting, there is also extensive documentation of negative health consequences for communities living near alumina refineries and aluminum smelters around the world, including increased asthma levels near bauxite mines, indications of multiple chemical sensitivity around alumina refineries, and exposure to toxic waste such as fluoride and cyanide near aluminum smelters.[39]

There are also persistent questions about its potential health effects on consumers, including possible links to Alzheimer's disease, leading some people to avoid aluminum cookware, antiperspirants, and cosmetics that contain powdered aluminum (despite claims to their complete safety from the scientific community and government safety agencies). In January 2012 a documentary called *Aluminum, Our Everyday Poison* was broadcast in France, attracting an audience of 1.4 million viewers and exploring the widespread and little known prevalence of aluminum in everyday foods, infant formula, kitchenware, foil, vaccines, and cosmetics. It reported on the growing concerns among some scientists and doctors that it is a dangerous neurotoxin, particularly due to increased exposure of infants.

At Keele University in England extensive research on human exposure to aluminum is undertaken at the Birchall Centre for Bioinorganic Chemistry of Aluminum and Silicon, led by Professor Chris Exley.[40] According to Exley,

Aluminium sulphate is added to our water to improve clarity. . . . All foods that need raising agents or additives, such as cakes and biscuits, contain aluminium. Children's sweets contain aluminium-enhanced food colouring. It is in tea, cocoa and malt drinks, in some wines and fizzy drinks and in most processed foods. It is in cosmetics, sunscreens and antiperspirants, as well as being used as a buffering agent in medications like aspirin and antacids. It is even used in vaccines. We know aluminium can be toxic, yet there is no legislation to govern how much of it is present in anything, apart from drinking water. When the amount of aluminium consumed exceeds the body's capacity to excrete it, the excess is then deposited in various tissues, including nerves, brain, bone, liver, heart, spleen and muscle [. . .] We call it the "silent visitor" because it creeps into the body and beds down in our bones and brain.[41]

Exley's research attracted increased public attention in August 2012 during the inquest into the death of Carole Cross, a fifty-eight-year-old who died from a rare and aggressive form of Alzheimer's (cerebral amyloid angiopathy) that some link to the so-called Camelford water disaster.

In 1988, in the town of Camelford where Cross lived, twenty tons of aluminum sulfate were accidentally poured into the drinking water supply and it was ingested by much of the population. Many complained of illnesses including fatigue, loss of memory, and premature aging; when Cross died an autopsy found twenty-three micrograms (mcg) of aluminum per gram of her brain, in contrast to normal levels of zero to two mcg. The coroner found a "very real possibility" that this contributed to her death, but it could not be proven as the definitive cause.[42] However, he did call for further research into the effects of aluminum on public health, an issue that is also receiving growing attention in the United States, especially in relation to its use as an adjuvant in infant and childhood vaccines.

There are, moreover, worldwide concerns about the industry's human rights effects. From the hot equatorial jungles of Suriname to the cold central highlands of Iceland, the smelting of shining aluminum from the earth's rich bauxite ores drives passionate conflicts between modern industrial "development" and alternative forms of sustainable development that are called for by environmentalists and indigenous rights movements. The building of dams and reservoirs to generate electricity has serious environmental and social impacts, especially in developing countries. As critics point out,

Dams that have been built primarily to supply the aluminum industry have flooded over 30,000 square kilometers of forested land worldwide. They have caused the relocation of over 200,000 indigenous people—from the Nile to the Caroni River in Venezuela, impinged on reindeer herds in Norway's fragile sub-Alpine plateaus, destroyed habitat and threatened biodiversity in Brazilian and Asian rainforests, enabled the spread of debilitating tropical diseases in African valleys, and submerged archaeological treasures.[43]

One example is the construction of the Afobaka dam and an artificial lake on the Suriname River in order to generate electricity for Alcoa's aluminum smelter in Paranam, Suriname, in 1966–1967. The reservoir created by the hydroelectric dam effectively blasted a hole through illegally appropriated Saamaka Maroon territory, covering over the Mamadan rapids and some forty-three villages, decimating a traditional culture that was highly place-based.[44] The Saamaka people eventually won a very important case in the Inter-American Court of Human Rights in 2007, *Saramaka People* v. *Suriname*, recognizing their collective rights to self-determination and to control development on the lands on which their ancestors had lived since the early eighteenth century,[45] as discussed further in chapter 6. The flooded lands, however, are not recoverable, the people have already suffered from the loss of their homelands, and the judgment has proved difficult to enforce. The Suriname government has continued to call for further development of the bauxite and aluminum industry, and has recently announced deals with transnational corporations (with Chinese financing) to possibly develop highways, railroads, gold mines, and new bauxite mining areas, which ignore the court ruling requiring consultation with and decision making by the Saamaka and Ndyuka Maroon communities whose lands are affected.[46]

Other specific instances of hugely damaging hydroelectric projects involving the aluminum industry, according to the International Rivers Network, include "Tucuruí, in the Brazilian Amazon, which flooded 2,860 km^2 of rainforests and displaced more than 24,000 people; the James Bay Complex in Canada, which flooded nearly 16,000 km^2 and has affected hunting grounds of the Cree and Inuit indigenous peoples; and Akosombo, in Ghana, which created the world's largest man-made lake (8,482 km^2) and displaced 84,000 people" (http://www.internationalrivers.org/dams-and-mining).

More recently, huge new hydroelectric projects such as the controversial Belo Monte Dam planned for the Xingu River, a tributary of the Amazon in Brazil, would send up to 25 percent of the energy produced to nearby smelters owned by Alcoa (which is expanding operations across Amazonia) and Norwegian state-owned Norsk-Hydro (which purchased assets from Vale do Rio Doce in 2010 including one of the world's largest bauxite mines, Paragominas; a 91 percent stake in Alunorte, the world's largest alumina refinery; and a 51 percent stake in Albras aluminum plant). The Belo Monte project will displace remote "uncontacted" indigenous tribes, damage biodiversity, and add to greenhouse gas emissions through the decomposing of flooded vegetation.[47]

The building of new aluminum smelters and the hydroelectric dams that feed them is galvanizing opposition everywhere from Trinidad and Brazil to India and Iceland. Around the world people are beginning to mobilize against the building of massive new dams that drive the power-hungry smelters, and are drawing attention to the environmental costs of bauxite mining and the effects of new smelters. A deeply committed corps of environmentalists has tirelessly attacked the global aluminum industry for a wide range of ecological and health harms attributed to its bauxite mining operations and its huge consumption of electricity for smelters. The protestors charge that the gleam of aluminum (and the gleam in the eye of capitalist profiteers) comes with a darker underside. Indigenous advocates highlight the industry's detrimental impact on native peoples around the world, peace activists berate the role of aluminum in the defense industry and note its central place in the military-industrial complex (one of the largest consumers of the metal), and environmentalists focus on the toxic waste produced by bauxite mining and the greenhouse gases emitted in the production of primary aluminum.[48] Mostly, especially when these protests occur outside the developed world, they are ignored.

The ease of high-speed travel, the convenient food packaging, the mobile communications systems, and the shining skyscrapers that serve today as the cathedrals of late modernity are grounded in the heavy (and dirty) industries of power generation, mining, refining, and smelting—and these are part of a worldwide production process controlled by a handful of huge multinational corporations with exotic acronyms: RUSAL, Alcoa, CHINALCO, Rio Tinto-Alcan, BHP Billiton, and Vedanta. These corporate powers have been accused of ignoring the rights of local people, especially disempowered indigenous peoples in the tropics; of consuming vast amounts of energy; and of exploiting the resources of poorer countries. Meanwhile, their owners accrue vast personal wealth. Across the world these global titans of industry fight for control of strategic bauxite reserves and access to hydropower, and small bands of local people and environmental activists try to stop them. Occasionally these battles garner international attention:

• In Odisha, India (formerly spelled *Orisha*) a near civil war has been raging across the heart of East India, hardly noticed by the outside world. It is in a region rich with bauxite and iron, much of it on land occupied by the *Adivasis*, or tribal peoples. The international media failed to connect the Maoist rebellion there to the encroachment of corporate interests into the lands of some of India's poorest and most disenfranchised citizens. But in April 2013 the Indian Supreme Court upheld the Dongria Kondh's right to stop Vedanta Resources from mining their sacred mountain.[49]

• In Guinea, too, there are invisible linkages among an unstable government, huge mining corporations, and people living in abject conditions right next to the largest bauxite reserves in the world. Occasionally some egregious act of violence attracts international media attention to these marginal places, yet seldom does anyone recognize how the economics of bauxite mining and aluminum production might be fundamental to producing political violence and social conditions of injustice and poverty.

• In October 2010 a catastrophe occurred in Hungary in which a massive spill of highly caustic red mud killed several people, wiped out villages and streams, and threatened the Danube River. This toxic spill brought global attention to the pollution caused by bauxite mining, an issue that has usually been ignored outside of activist social movements. It followed closely on the heels of the Deepwater Horizon oil-drilling disaster in the Gulf of Mexico, and a sensitized public was (once again) starting to look at industrial polluters with growing anger.

• In May 2011 an explosion killed three workers and injured fifteen others at a factory in Chengdu, China, that supplies Apple computers. A Hong Kong–based labor rights group had noted a problem with aluminum dust in Foxconn's Chengdu plant the previous March, saying that workers at the factory complained that "the ventilation of the department is poor. Workers polish the iPad cases to make them shiny. In the process, there is lots of aluminum dust floating in the air. Workers always breathe in aluminum dust even though they put on masks. When workers take off their cotton gloves, their hands are covered with aluminum dust."[50] Aluminum dust is an explosive when ignited.

Can societies afford the amount of energy, pollution, and government subsidies that it takes to smelt aluminum? Is a switch from coal-powered electric generation to hydroelectric or geothermal power a sustainable solution? What are the associated ecological costs and to what extent can we reduce demand for aluminum? Will moving into a postpetroleum and postcarbon economy also require that the world move into postaluminum technologies, or do we need aluminum to create the sustainable technology solutions to global warming?

This book will assist in answering such questions by providing a better understanding of the importance of this light versatile metal in shaping the modern world. Aluminum is one of the unrecognized pillars of our civilization, yet it is also the root of some of the key problems that threaten global equity and spatial justice. Until we better understand what enables our existing forms of transportation, electricity transmission, architecture, food packaging, space travel, and satellite communications, among other things, we will not be in a position to decide how best to move forward. Understanding the transnational cultural, economic, and political history of the global spread of aluminum is important because it also helps us to envision how we might advance toward reduction of its usage, increase in its recycling and reuse, and hence reduction in its profligate energy consumption and environmental pollution.[51]

OVERVIEW OF THE BOOK

This book tells the story of these times, of space machines and streamlined gadgets, mobile homes and soaring cities, and the double-edged sword of utopia and catastrophe that hastens us toward the accelerated metallic future envisioned in the twentieth century. The chapters that follow go beyond existing business histories that celebrate the age of aluminum as if it were an inevitable product of this "magic metal," but also beyond the important but one-sided environmental diatribes against heavy industry and transnational corporations, which sometimes ignore the realities of cultural dreams and desires for new technology, for modern development, and for streamlined efficient mobility. Although we might summarize much about aluminum just by looking at the numbers behind it (see box 1.1), *Aluminum Dreams* examines the technological, economic, cultural, and ecological history of aluminum, showing its full significance and repercussions for people around the world. Although each section is loosely chronologically organized, the narrative also pushes forward in each chapter to relate history to aspects of aluminum's contemporary relevance.

Part I focuses mainly on the bright side of how aluminum became a modernizing metal, transforming the speed, lightness, and mobility of the industrialized world in the Global North, and especially the United States, even as it entailed a massive military buildup with huge environmental and social consequences. Part II focuses more on the dark side of how bauxite mining and the operations of transnational corporations affect developing countries and postsocialist countries in key transition periods, bringing pollution, environmental degradation, and political turmoil around the world. Yet there are actually more nuanced shades of dark and light, past and present, in both parts of the book: just as the bright side casts a shadow of negative externalities right from the beginning of the industry, so too does the more recent dark side appear to have a silver lining in ongoing claims to

BOX 1.1
Aluminum by the Numbers

- **One-twelfth** of the earth's crust is aluminum, making it the third most common element after oxygen and silicon.
- **1** percent of global emissions of man-made greenhouse gases come from the aluminum industry.
- **3** percent of electricity generated worldwide goes to aluminum smelting; in small countries smelters consume one-third of the national power supply.
- **5** percent of the energy used in making new aluminum is needed to make the same amount in recycled materials.
- **6–8** percent fuel savings can be realized for every 10 percent weight reduction in vehicles by substituting aluminum parts for heavier materials.
- **8** mg is the amount of aluminum an average adult in the United States eats per day in his or her food.
- **18 billion** kWh of electricity were used in 1943 to produce the 920,000 tons of aluminum made in the United States that year (enough electricity to supply half the residents of the country for an entire year).
- **27** kN/m3 is the specific weight of aluminum, which is just one-third of the weight of copper or steel.
- **51 billion** aluminum cans were thrown away and not recycled in the United States in 2001, rising to an estimated **55 billion** wasted cans in 2012.
- **90** percent of all tetrafluoromethane and **65** percent of all hexafluoroethane emissions worldwide come from aluminum smelters. These PFCs have global warming potentials that are 6,500 to 9,200 times higher than carbon dioxide.
- **300** kWh of electricity are conserved for each aluminum can that is recycled, enough to run a 100-watt bulb for three hours.
- **660** degrees Celsius is the melting point of aluminum.
- **13,500** kWh of electricity are needed to produce **1** ton of aluminum. That's a lot of electricity and it has to come from somewhere.

aluminum as a recyclable "green metal" that can contribute to new sustainable technologies.

Thus brightness and darkness run as counterpoints throughout this book, mirroring various other juxtapositions: the rhetorical "hype cycles" around the promise of this "miracle metal" versus deep disappointment in it as an ersatz cheap substitution for better things;[52] the charges of antismelter activists of alleged "greenwashing" by industry brand management versus the corporate social responsibility managers who describe aluminum as a useful "energy bank" and a "green metal" that improves the efficiency of transport systems; the ethereal lightness of modernity's dreams of mobility and faster communication, on the one hand, and the heavy burdens of the weight of modernization, the gritty labors of mining, and the destructive power of weaponry, on the other. These two faces of aluminum are the two sides of this tale. Similar to many other fables of modernity the story of aluminum gropes toward moral clarity and the ethical improvement of life on earth, yet falters on the ambiguous advancements of science and technology, the ironic unintended consequences of improvement, and the limitations of human invention and ingenuity to triumph over suffering, or even to grasp its cultural causes or its ecological extent.

This book seeks to open our eyes to the metallic fabric of our modern world, and to show why some advocates today seek to slow down our hurry toward the metallic future yet others seek ever-greater streamlining, lightness, and efficiency in our sociotechnical systems through research and development of new aluminum-based technologies.

When I began researching this book the aluminum industry was in the midst of a massive global restructuring, in a flurry of mergers and acquisitions with major players in Russia, North America, Australia, Europe, Brazil, and elsewhere jostling for position. Already it had begun with Alcoa's 2000 acquisition of Reynolds Aluminum, Norsk Hydro's buyout of German VAW in 2001, and Alcan's $5 billion takeover of the French company Pechiney in 2004, soon itself to be merged into a new megacorporation, Rio Tinto Alcan. When metal prices were soaring on the commodity exchanges in 2006–2007, with projections of growing demand especially in China (where the Aluminum Corporation of China has quickly become a world leader in alumina refining), corporate giants began buying each other out while vying to control existing bauxite mines, build new capacity, and gain control over the remaining rivers and cheaper power sources across the globe.

With the bursting of the commodities bubble in 2008 some plans unraveled, production was slowed at some mines, and aluminum ingot reportedly began to pile up in China, unused, in 2012. In January 2009 the US multinational Alcoa announced a 13 percent reduction of its output, and 13,500 job cuts; but by the third quarter of 2009 it was already back in profit and its stock price started climbing again. Yet it remains a harbinger of market ups and downs, with Alcoa being the first company to announce quarterly outcomes on the stock exchange. In 2013, Rio Tinto Alcan announced it would be closing several major smelters, and the Aluminum Corporation of China announced a "temporary shutdown of 420,000 tons of production capacity, equal to 9 percent of the company's output of primary aluminum products last year."[53] It remains to be seen how the recession of 2009–2012 will affect growth projections for the industry overall.

It could be argued that the massive concentration of power in corporations such as Alcoa, RUSAL, Rio Tinto Alcan, Vedanta, or CHINALCO, who are in tight competition with each other, has to be brought under some kind of democratic jurisdiction and decision making. Otherwise, these industrial giants will continue to form cartels, benefit from government subsidies, externalize environmental and social effects, and roam the globe, devouring its limited resources without regard. And certainly the protest movements such as Saving Iceland and activist scholars such as Felix Padel and Samarendra Das are trying to do just that, in part by exposing and writing about the real effects of the industry. Padel and Das argue that truly socially responsible companies would undertake not only internalizing costs and paying taxes in full but also addressing climate change, ending deceitful public relations campaigns, ending lobbying that is against the public interest, and democratizing the workplace.[54] Here, though, I concentrate especially on the demand side, and think about their final two recommendations: reducing consumption and limiting growth. How much is our consumption of aluminum driven by the modern cultural quest for mobility, lightness, and speed, and the presumption that these qualities are always to be highly valued? By tracing aluminum's fundamental role in the rise of the military-industrial complex, its tight embedding in complex transnational processes, and its deep cultural implications, we can better address the question of how aluminum consumption might be reduced through disruptive innovation.

If spatial justice[55] concerns geographically uneven development and unequal distributions of collective goods at many different scales, ranging from the bodily to the urban to the global, then aluminum is crucially implicated in the production of spatial injustice through the location of polluting production facilities, the agglomeration of spatial control over energy production (especially the use of rivers for hydropower), and the ability to move investments across international borders seeking the lowest costs for inputs, including bauxite ore, energy, and labor.

The chapters that follow will trace the flow of aluminum around the world, like a ribbon of metal running through the fabric of modernity from one end of the world to the other. Following this thread will allow us to knit together the First World and the Third World, capitalism and communism, the North and the Tropics, battlefields and home fronts, industry and ideas, texts and images, the "modernizing" past and the "sustainable" future. It will also challenge us to confront some of the most basic questions about the future of life on earth, the amount of energy we can sustainably use, and what our lives would be like if we tried to live without certain modern conveniences predicated on aluminum's contribution to lightness, speed, and mobility.

PART I   THE BRIGHT SIDE

Electricity was a magical word then [in the 1870s], one that evoked speed, modernity, vital force, mystery, and power.

—Rebecca Solnit, *Motion Studies: Time, Space and Eadweard Muybridge*

America's "aluminum century" originated in a scientific revolution that was as important to the nation's industrial life as the American Revolution of the previous century was to its political life. That century is culminating in a period of renewal that may extend both the technology and the industry far into the next century.

—Margaret Graham and Bettye Pruitt, *R&D for Industry*

Medieval alchemists long ago pursued the secrets of metals, chemicals, and medicinal substances locked inside what they considered to be the earth's four elemental constituents: earth, air, fire, and water. Through the application of chemical solutions and heat they sought ways to transmute common metals into gold, promising kings that they might create unfathomable fortunes. But above all they sought to find the hidden "fifth element," some unknown substance that would unlock the pathway to immortality. Their schemes, which in retrospect seem like crackpot trickery, were in fact the origins of modern chemistry and medicine. The chemistry behind the discovery of aluminum stands on the shoulders of the alchemists. But the secret of unlocking pure aluminum from common oxide ores is a relatively recent discovery.

Although it is the most prevalent metallic element on earth, it took gradual developments in chemistry and understanding of the forces of electrical current at the atomic level during the course of the nineteenth century to lead to the invention of a process for freeing molecules of aluminum from common clay. And then, even with the right configuration of knowledge and practical know-how in place, it still took time and a great deal of effort for this long-awaited new element to sweep across the world.

The discovery of aluminum smelting belongs to the same period as the invention of cinema. Fast-motion photography was built on photochemistry and electric triggers, which made instantaneous photographs possible, just as chemistry and electricity would together make aluminum possible. As Rebecca Solnit has eloquently observed, railroad baron Leland Stanford supported the experimentations of photographer Eadweard Muybridge, who carried out his famous motion studies of race horses on Leland's Palo Alto estate, which later became Stanford University, the birthplace of Silicon Valley and the Internet age. The railroad and the instantaneous photograph became the progenitors of mechanized moving pictures on perforated celluloid strips.

Stanford and Muybridge also "prefigured cinema in another way; the medium at its most influential was to be the fruit of the meeting of huge monopolistic corporations and their fistfuls of dollars with dreamers and self-invented people, the marriage of business and art."[1] Just as the railroad expanded European settlement across the continent, dispossessing Native Americans and then preserving their remnant culture in the Wild West shows and the Hollywood westerns, aluminum is also a national anti-romance of the electrochemical fusion of monopolistic business and artful invention, full of visionaries, inventors, villains, and dead aboriginals.

People have had an inkling of the existence of aluminum for a long time. The ancient Egyptians and Babylonians used clay containing alum (aluminum silicates) to make pigments and medicines. It is also found in the aluminum-rich ash that Romans used to make a very long-lasting cement and the ancient Greeks and Romans "used alum to make astringent or desiccative products."[2] The existence of the metal was known to alchemists in the Middle Ages, but it was not until 1808 that the illustrious Cornish chemist Sir Humphrey Davy announced that there was a plentiful compound, alumina, which was the oxide of an undiscovered metal. Yet his efforts to isolate pure aluminum metal were fruitless. Although comprising about 8 percent of the earth's crust, aluminum is very reactive and generally comes tightly bound to other elements such as oxygen, silicon, and fluorine. "Such combinations, or compounds, of aluminum are so chemically stable that they refuse to let go of the metal without a struggle."[3] This set off a dream and a competition for fame and fortune among scientists across Europe to find a cheap way of obtaining this new element.

In 1821 the Frenchman Pierre Berthier discovered a red, firm, claylike material near the village of Les Baux-en-Provence from which aluminum oxide could be recovered, and he named this ore *bauxite*. Bauxite is plentiful throughout many parts of the world, especially in the tropics, and it serves as the basic material from which aluminum is extracted. In the 1820s several chemists obtained tiny samples of aluminum residue from processes based on a reaction between potassium solution and aluminum chloride. In 1845 the German chemist Friedrich Wöhler discovered its density and weight, demonstrating its amazing lightness for the first time. Following Robert Wilhelm von Bunsen's success in using batteries to produce very small amounts of aluminum in 1854, Antillean-born French chemist Henri Saint-Claire Deville displayed an ingot of aluminum at the Paris Exposition in 1855 under the title of "silver from clay."[4] His work caught the eye of Emperor Napoleon III, who hoped to develop lightweight helmets, armor, and artillery for his cuirassiers.

With the emperor's backing, Deville undertook experiments that improved on Wöhler's method (by replacing expensive potassium with cheaper sodium) and he invented the first way to obtain aluminum in commercial quantity, lowering its price from $90 a pound to $17 a pound by 1859, about the price of silver.[5] Yet the 1859 world production was only two tons, which a century later Alcoa could produce in about two minutes, so aluminum remained a precious metal, more expensive than gold or platinum. It was mainly artisans who worked with this unusual material, fabricating luxury products out of the new metal. In the 1850s "it adorned the banquet table in the form of finely crafted eating utensils," which delighted Napoleon III's state guests when they discovered its lightness, and it "became a fashionable substance for jewelry."[6] One of the earliest domestic objects made from aluminum was actually a baby's rattle made for the infant Prince Imperial.

Improvements in the Saint-Claire Deville chemical process gradually brought the world aluminum price down toward $8 per pound in the 1880s, but many chemists were certain that there must be a less expensive way of producing this tantalizing metal, perhaps by using an electrical current to dissolve alumina into its constituent elements. When a one-hundred-ounce pyramid of aluminum capped the Washington Monument in 1884, "the metal served as both ornament and lightning rod" at a cost of $225 (figure 2.1).[7] Above all, though, it must also have served as a beacon spurring on inventors to achieve national glory and international fame: "the cap was such a novelty that it was first exhibited in New York among the displays of fashionable jewelry in Tiffany's."[8]

Another kind of beacon was created in 1893 when a Deville-process casting was used to make the statue popularly known as *Eros* still seen today in the center of Piccadilly Circus in London. It was not simply that aluminum was immensely practical and useful that brought about its uptake; art, love, and ornament also proved as crucial as industry and technology in the desire to make use of aluminum. Thus it began as an expensive and rare material used in fine arts and handcrafted luxury goods:

Aluminum was first presented as a scientific marvel and a rare commodity, sparking the imagination of jewelry makers, silversmiths and watchmakers. From the late 1850s to the late 1870s, aluminum objects usually came in the form of small luxury or novelty items, like brooches, bracelets, medallions, candlesticks, mustard spoons and opera glasses.[9]

FIGURE 2.1
The first use of architectural aluminum in the United States: "572 feet high—setting the cap-stone on the Washington Monument" from a sketch on the spot by S. H. Nealy, Illus., in *Harper's Weekly* (December 20, 1884): 839. Courtesy of Library of Congress.

But very soon this would all change, because a race was on to see who could come up with a more economical way of mass-producing the enchantingly light metal. Electricity would provide the key for unlocking the powers of chemical energy that could release aluminum into the world, along with new capacities for speed, lightness, and imagination of the technology of the future.

SIMULTANEOUS INVENTION AND FLUIDITY OF INNOVATION

A technological revolution occurred with the invention of the electrolytic process for smelting aluminum in 1886.[10] One of the great triumphs of modern chemistry, the dramatic race to invent and secure a patent on this electrolytic process for making aluminum was achieved simultaneously by a twenty-three-year-old American, Charles Martin Hall (figure 2.2), and a twenty-three-year-old Frenchman, Paul Louis Toussaint Héroult. As historian George Smith observes, "the discovery of the modern process of smelting aluminum is one of many famous cases of simultaneous invention" in which two men working "continents apart and in complete ignorance of each other . . . devised a commercially plausible way to produce aluminum electrolytically and thereby ushered in a new era in man's use of metals."[11]

That very simultaneity should alert us to the fact that invention is not simply a matter of individual genius or luck; rather, it is a matter of convergence of information, training, purpose, perseverance, and dedication to a cause, building on existing knowledge and processes.[12] "In reality," writes Tom Geller,

both Héroult and Hall were participants in a much larger program of aluminum research that started in the 1850s and lasted until 1903, when the last major patent dispute was settled [. . .] their nearly simultaneous discovery of a process for aluminum extraction built on several decades' worth of electrochemistry and, indeed, centuries' worth of knowledge on the nature of metals.[13]

At Oberlin College, in Ohio, in 1880, the sixteen-year-old Charles Martin Hall, sixth child of a Congregational missionary, enrolled in the chemistry course of Professor Frank Fanning Jewett, who had studied with Wöhler in Germany. Professor Jewett told his students that "if anyone should invent a process by which aluminum could be produced on a commercial scale, not only would he be a great benefactor to the world but would also be able

FIGURE 2.2
Charles Martin Hall (1863–1914).

to lay up for himself a great fortune. Turning to a classmate, Charles Hall said, 'I'm going for the metal.' And he went for it."[14] Hall eventually made close to $30 million on his shares in the company he helped found, Alcoa, which was long considered the largest fortune ever made based on a single US patent.[15]

Hall's story unfolds as a classic American success story. He was interested in chemistry at a very young age, performing rudimentary experiments at home under the influence of his older sister Julia, who had also attended Oberlin College and took the same course with Professor Jewett. She may well have played an important part in encouraging and assisting his invention. Inspired by American inventors such as Alexander Graham Bell and Thomas Edison, whose telephone and lightbulb were just beginning to take off into major industrial enterprises, Hall "set up a makeshift laboratory in the woodshed adjoining the kitchen of his parents' house."[16] After their mother (also an Oberlin graduate) died in 1885, Julia took care of her siblings and clearly encouraged Charles in his pursuit of aluminum.

On graduation from Oberlin in 1886, using equipment borrowed from Professor Jewett, who had become a mentor to him, and supported by Julia, Hall devoted himself full time to experimentation with electrolytic processes to obtain aluminum from aluminum oxide. The young inventor earned money to purchase chemicals and supplies by cutting lawns, tending furnaces, and shoveling snow. Eventually, using homemade batteries and hand-fashioned apparatus, he succeeded in electrochemically dissolving alumina in a solution of synthetic cryolite (the double fluoride of sodium and aluminum) contained in a carbon crucible, obtaining his first "small globules" of the nearly pure metal in February 1886.[17] Oberlin's campus today is graced by a statue of Hall at the moment of his discovery, and his original small globules are preserved in a case and referred to in Alcoa lore as "the seeds of speed."

"This was the moment of high victory for which Hall had been striving so long," according to a commercial history of Alcoa, the company he went on to found, becoming a multimillionaire in the process. "In this successful experiment lay the seed of a great new industry. The twenty-two-year-old American boy had discovered the secret which had eluded the world's scientists for decades. Here was a low-cost method for making aluminum. How right he was is proved by the fact that his process for the electrolytic smelting of aluminum is basically the same one still used throughout the industry today."[18] Although Hall's success became "the stuff of American legend,"[19] self-congratulatory stories of the triumph of American ingenuity do not give us the full picture. Graham and Pruitt's company history instead emphasizes the challenges of starting a company, the constant need for innovation, and the difficulties in convincing others that producing and using aluminum was a good idea. This triumph over adversity and continual innovation model of business history is, though, also a kind of updated version of the plucky American capitalist narrative.

To begin with, Hall worked for a year at the leading aluminum-producing factory in the United States, the Cowles Electrical Smelting and Aluminum Company in Cleveland, trying to convince them of the commercial feasibility of his invention. But they declined to invest in his process, sticking instead to their own specialty, the electrothermal production of an aluminum-copper alloy known as aluminum bronze. Hall was also turned down by other investors in Cleveland, Boston, and New York, "all places where enterprises based on chemistry, electricity, and combinations of the two were taking shape."[20] Finally he turned to a small company in Pittsburgh, located on a two-mile-long strip along the banks of the Allegheny River, where there was a concentration of machine shops, forges, steel mills, a rolling mill, and a copper mill.

Here in the lively and inventive industrial district of the Smallman Street neighborhood Hall found a "handful of hopeful young investors well connected in steel" who formed the Pittsburgh Reduction Company (PRC) in 1888.[21] But the going was not easy at first, as Margaret Graham and Bettye Pruitt recount in their company history, *R&D for Industry: A Century of Technical Innovation at Alcoa*. Although aluminum's "weight, silvery appearance, thermal and electrical conductivity, ease of working, resistance to acid, and imperviousness to tarnish and corrosion" all made it a desirable replacement for other metals, its susceptibility to heat also made it "difficult to weld and solder, and its propensity to electrolytic (or galvanic) action made it susceptible to corrosion when in contact with other metals."[22] Thus it required special techniques, special metal-working machinery, and special training of the craft-based metal workers, all of which made existing metals industries and their workers reluctant to take it on.

It required ongoing experimentation and research by Hall and others to make aluminum smelting into a viable industry. Once they had proof of concept and a small volume business going, the PRC owners approached the famous Pittsburgh financiers Andrew W. Mellon and Richard B.

Mellon, owners of the Mellon Bank. They agreed to put up $1 million for the building of a steam-powered smelting plant in New Kensington, on the Allegheny River, sixteen miles from Pittsburgh, which opened in 1891. Even more ambitiously, in 1893 the PRC "became the first company to buy power from the new Niagara Power Company and to locate a large plant at Niagara Falls," where it later moved all of its smelting operations.[23] Thus began the search for cheap electricity, especially hydroelectric power, driving the aluminum industry around the world over the coming century in pursuit of access to powerful rivers. In the early years the PRC also had to fight another patent battle with the Cowles Company—the ones who had originally been uninterested in Hall's invention. Settlement cost them millions of dollars but finally gave them control of the Bradley patents that were used in the aluminum bronze process, plus an agreement that the Cowles Company, their only serious competitor, would withdraw from the production of pure aluminum.[24] If this reads like a national history, along the lines of Misa's *Nation of Steel*, or Meikle's *American Plastic*, it is only because we are missing half of the picture, which was taking place in Europe. The "seeds of speed" lay as much in Europe as in the United States.[25]

Meanwhile cut to France, where Paul Héroult was also born in 1863, the son of a Norman leather tanner who had once worked as a laborer at a Deville-process aluminum plant (figure 2.3). After reading Deville's famous treatise *De L'Aluminium*, the standard text on aluminum from its publication in 1859, Héroult became equally fanatical in his fascination with the light metal.[26] Enrolled at the Ecole des Mines in Paris, he studied under the famous chemist Henri le Chatelier. But he was so fixated on finding a better way to unlock aluminum from the vaults of the earth that he failed in his other courses and was expelled after a few months. Héroult himself "claimed he was ejected because he threw a wet sponge that hit the dean."[27]

The go-it-alone Héroult fortuitously inherited his father's tannery at the age of twenty-two, and somehow convinced his mother to give him fifty thousand francs for a 400-amp, 30-volt dynamo to carry out experiments with aluminum. His mother's financial support and belief in him made all the difference in getting his experiments off the ground, just as Hall's success depended on his sister's support. Using molten cryolite in an electrolytic process, just as Hall had, he filed a French patent on April 23, 1886, and a US patent on May 22, 1886, but based on a technicality of filing, Hall's slightly different US patent no. 400,766 (filed in July 1886) was given

FIGURE 2.3
Paul Louis Toussaint Héroult (1863–1914).

precedence. Eventually their two discoveries were joined in what became
known as the Hall-Héroult process, which became the industry standard for
producing aluminum electrolytically.

Héroult could not have been more different from the sober and industri-
ous Hall. Hall remained single and childless, while Héroult married twice
and had five children. Hall enjoyed reading the *Encyclopaedia Britannica* and
playing the piano in his spare time, whereas Héroult had a reputation as a
bon vivant. "He was highstrung, unruly, occasionally hard and insolent; he
did not fit the image of wise, disciplined men of science. He loved games,
the company of women, travels by land and sea; he was a free spirit in an
impetuous body." Hall dedicated himself single-mindedly to the aluminum
industry, whereas Héroult branched out into other inventions such as a helicopter prototype, an unusual boat on runners, and, most famously, the
electric arc furnace for making steel.[28] In another coincidence, both inventors died of disease in the same year, 1914.

Paul Héroult's technical knowledge and his patent and access to both bauxite and hydropower laid the groundwork for the European aluminum industry. His discoveries contributed to the French aluminum company Péchiny S.A., which became the leading supplier of aluminum to Germany and France during the buildup to World War I. Superior technical training in Europe gave them a lead over the United States, where the quality of metal lagged. The managers of Alcoa were so desperate to improve their process that when Héroult visited the United States in 1909, a manager named Fitzgerald took him out drinking and "after supplying him with about fifteen beers" plied him for technical knowledge on a specific problem of blistering in their sheet metal, but the Frenchman did not crack and "kept his secrets to himself."[29]

Nevertheless, under their extended patent protection, the PRC prospered. "By 1909, when their patent protection ran out, the PRC, renamed the Aluminum Company of America, had reduced the price of its basic product, primary aluminum ingot, by 96 percent through the exploitation of economies of scale and control of critical inputs—alumina, carbon, and electricity."[30] The foundations were now laid for a powerful monopoly that would give the company single-handed control of the North American aluminum industry for decades to come. Their main markets were in some of the burgeoning new industries of the era, including "transmission wire for electric utilities and for electric streetcars, ingot to be cast into parts for bicycles, automobiles, and trolleys, tubing for chemicals and petroleum works, and feedstock for some of the many new chemical enterprises."[31] Thus there was a synergy among all of these emerging new electrochemical industries, and aluminum rode this wave of scientific industrialization. As in the steel industry described by Thomas Misa, there was also back-and-forth interaction between producers of aluminum and eventual users of its products as they worked together to shape its end uses and form.[32]

For example, the development of one of the major markets for aluminum was power lines, which depended on extensive sharing of knowledge and experience among equipment suppliers, consultants, and "patient, flexible and knowledgeable customers" in the electrical industry, who put up with initial rollouts of cable that failed, caused massive electrical arcs, or sagged and snapped under ice and wind. Graham and Pruitt argue that it was in large part because the related electrical and electrochemical industries were also in "fluid stages" of speculative knowledge building and growth that

Alcoa could develop and take off. In this case technical innovation occurred through interactions between primary producers (Alcoa) and primary users (the electrical industry), which was also happening with the plastics industry around the same period, which Jeffrey Meikle describes as plastic itself being in a "plastic" state of flexible form.[33] From the ACSR experience Alcoa learned the need for "a systematic program of research applied to primary and metalworking processes alike."[34] Thus the craft of industrial R&D was born. This aspect of fluid interaction across industries and between primary producers and end-product manufacturers is missing in many cultural or social histories of single sectors. David Nye, for example, surprisingly, says almost nothing about the aluminum industry in his otherwise very comprehensive social history of electrification in the United States.[35] And Eric Schatzberg focuses only on the symbolic culture of science and engineering in framing aluminum's meaning, rather than on wider cultural meanings and institutional actors such as the state and the military.[36]

However, the cultural historians do remind us of the cultural struggles that take place in the adaptation of new materials such as aluminum and the importance of participants beyond the industrial research labs, who contributed the spark of imagination to product innovation and other kinds of discursive framings of new materials. Although the race for a patent inspired the first inventors, and the dream of riches inspired the first investors, the story of aluminum also involves a far wider cast of characters. Beyond the chemists, metallurgists, engineers, financiers, and business managers who made it all possible, it also took the dreamers, the artists, and the inventors who doodled, dawdled, tinkered, and drew inspiration from everything around them, lashing together ideas from one realm to another, imagining the future and bringing it into being.

The subsequent parts of this book will delve into the realms of the imagination, art, and design to show how aluminum took hold of the twentieth century, shaped the culture of modernity, and bequeathed to us a significant part of our material world. Because the Aluminum Company of America, known as Alcoa, has played such a central role in the rise of the industry, it will be a touchstone throughout the historical narrative. But it is worth noting that although Alcoa became the largest aluminum producer in the world, the company was in competition with a few others, in France and Germany in the early years, later in the Soviet Union,[37] and today a small number of very large transnational global competitors. Moreover, to truly understand the transnational character of the industry requires that we move beyond company-centered histories and national histories of progress to the sites of production where bauxite and electricity are first grasped, and which have their own cultural history wrapped up in aluminum.

Inventor, architect, and philosopher R. Buckminster Fuller offers one of the truly global histories of the temporal evolution of human and planetary history, in which he crucially links the modern era to the use of metals. Developments in mass production of steel in the mid-nineteenth century, he argues, led to an entirely new system of value that was no longer based on land ownership but on "metal buildings, metal machinery, metal tools, metal sea and land transportation systems, and, ofttimes, metal end products."[38] "Suddenly," he writes,

we had a completely new form of capitalism, which required both the large-scale financing and integration of metals, mines and mine-owners, metals refining and shaping into wholesaleable forms, all to be established around the world by the world masters of the great line of supply [e.g., maritime trade]. The world line of metals-and-alloy supply was essential in producing all the extraordinarily productive new machinery and that machinery's delivery system, as was the generation and delivery of the unprecedentedly vast amounts of inanimate energy as electricity."[39]

Fuller calls this new form of world capitalism the "*metals and mining capitalism*. Whoever owned the mines had incredible power," which when combined with control of the "line of supply," or what we would today call *logistics,* led to "the first supranational, world-around-integrated, metals cartels. They were out of reach of the laws of any one country, in a *metals cartels capitalism*"[40] Although he initially had in mind the steel cartels and the iron ore, copper, and gold mines of the world, we can extend his vision to the aluminum cartels of the early twentieth century and the ongoing importance of global "supranational" mining industries today.

UNITED STATES V. ALCOA

For most of the twentieth century Alcoa controlled the largest share of the world bauxite, alumina, and aluminum markets, raising questions about the power of big business, the legality of cartels, and the power of government to break up monopolies. Up until recently it was still possible to say that

Alcoa was the leading aluminum company in the world, and was still expanding:

Alcoa is the world's principal producer of bauxite (with mines in Australia, Guinea,
Suriname, Jamaica, Brazil, and Guyana), alumina (nearly one-quarter of global production with nine refineries in the US, Australia, Spain, Brazil, Jamaica, and
Germany), and primary aluminum (13% of world production, with 27 smelters in
the US, Canada, Australia, Brazil, Spain, Italy, and Norway), as well as fabricated
aluminum.[41]

But forces of global economic restructuring were already in play. The
breakup of the Soviet Union and subsequent privatization of its state-owned
industries in the 1990s had a large impact on mining and metals markets.
This global restructuring has now been joined by huge forces of growth in
Brazil, Russia, India, and China (BRIC), which has spurred demand for
aluminum, especially in the construction sector in China, and with it for
energy to drive the smelters. Alcoa is now rivaled by companies such as
RUSAL, CHINALCO, and Rio Tinto Alcan. BRIC production and consumption has been expanding rapidly and is driving transformations in the
global structure of aluminum markets.

Nevertheless it is still worthwhile to look back at the economic forces that
brought Alcoa into a dominant position for so much of the twentieth century. Alcoa is one of the most successful and longest-lived big businesses in
the United States. Under its protected patent for the Hall reduction process,
the Pittsburgh Reduction Company, which later became Alcoa, was able to
create one of the most vertically integrated businesses in history, which gained
near-monopoly control over the infant industry. In other words, it controlled
not only bauxite mining, alumina reduction, and aluminum smelting facilities
but also owned plants for producing sheet metal, castings, extrusions, wire,
and so on, as well as extensive metallurgical research and development wings.

Groaning under the weight of its sheer success, Alcoa also became subject to one of the most important and longest-running antitrust lawsuits in
US history during a period of active government intervention in capitalist
markets. The founding of Alcoa is associated with the famous financier Andrew Mellon, the political struggles over the antitrust Sherman Act, and the
transformation of US businesses into global corporations. Antitrust law, or
competition law, is what allows for some degree of public regulation over
private corporations. When corporations become all-powerful, it is the rule

of law that allows for government intervention to break up monopolies and allow for competition.

In the United States, the Sherman Act and the 1914 Clayton Act, building on English common law, were the main tools for prohibiting cartels, banning anticompetitive practices, and supervising mergers and acquisitions of large corporations. The famous case of *United States* v. *Alcoa* placed the aluminum industry at the center of major battles concerning price setting, cartels, monopoly, and the power of "big business" during the New Deal. It is a decision that comes back to haunt us today as US courts still struggle with antitrust issues and the problem of breaking up dominant corporations such as Microsoft and Intel, Apple and Google. US antitrust law permits a company to hold a monopoly, but it forbids a company from leveraging its dominance to restrict competition. Companies such as Microsoft in the 1990s and Intel in 2008 ran into trouble with the Federal Trade Commission for practices that are said to discourage competitors.

Alcoa's antitrust issues dated back to a 1912 consent decree that barred the company from participating in foreign cartels and from entering into restrictive contracts. Then in 1922 the Federal Trade Commission launched an eight-year investigation of Alcoa's anticompetitive practices, alleging that the company engaged in practices that hurt independent producers of cooking utensils; was monopolizing the sheet metal and sand-casting businesses, the secondary scrap market, and the ingot and raw materials markets; and that it "had violated the terms of the 1912 consent decree and had conspired over time to control the world's water power and aluminum trade."[42] In contrast to the late nineteenth-century period of "robber barons," unfettered capitalism, and US business expansion across the Western frontier and into parts of Latin America and the Caribbean, the 1920s opened a period in which the government tried to regulate big business and protect small businesses and consumers.

In 1937 the New Deal attorneys of the Department of Justice initiated an even broader federal antitrust suit, *United States* v. *Alcoa*. According to corporate historian George Smith, "Alcoa's antitrust problem was partly a matter of image":

Among all major industries where concentrated economic power existed, aluminum was most clearly a monopoly and Alcoa a monopolist. Alcoa had become the very model of industrial concentration, and its principal owners had become exemplars of the kind of corporate barony that seemed distant, powerful, and dangerous to the popular mind. [. . .] Alcoa's ties to the Mellon interests had come to appear downright nefarious.[43]

Andrew Mellon, scion of one of the richest banking families in the world, was the financier of Alcoa and was accused of being "head and front of the aluminum trust" by populists like Nebraska senator George Norris. When he served as US treasury secretary during Herbert Hoover's presidency, Mellon became known for cutting federal spending, sharply reducing corporate and personal income taxes, and opposing public works and business regulation. Populists and New Dealers ardently hated Mellon and all that he stood for. "As the nation plunged into the depths of depression [in the 1930s], A. W. Mellon became a leading scapegoat for what many saw as the failure of the American business system" and the press "turned him into a dour personification of the political and social bankruptcy of corporate capitalism."[44]

The 1937 federal anti-monopoly case against Alcoa resurrected all of the old charges of the earlier 1912 suit in regard to monopolistic horizontal control of production facilities, but also added new charges relating to the company's vertical control of bauxite, water power, alumina, virgin aluminum, and scrap markets in ways that drove competitors out of business. The case lasted for six and half months of actual trial days, 176 days longer than the previous record holder for Anglo-Saxon litigation (the 1874 case of the Tichborne claimant), and cost Alcoa more than $2 million. Alcoa won the first decision in 1942, when judge Francis G. Caffey found the defendants not guilty on every one of the more than 130 charges (reading his ruling aloud over nine days, "after sitting through twenty-six months of testimony, countless motions and procedural hagglings, and some 58,000 pages of trial record."[45]). Caffey found that Alcoa's success was due to sound business practices rather than any intent to monopolize or illegally exclude competitors. However, the case then got bogged down in various stages of appeal until 1956.

The most significant decision to ensue was the March 1945 ruling by Justice Learned Hand of the Second Circuit Court (with the stature of a Supreme Court ruling). He "savaged" Alcoa's defense according to Smith and found that the company had maintained an illegal monopoly of the ingot market.[46] Hand's decision was considered a legal landmark, but "has been deplored over the years by some scholars as deeply flawed in its economic reasoning and by some legal commentators as an unwarranted attempt by judges to transcend both the issues of the case and the intent of the law in order to make public policy, [while] others have praised the decision on precisely the same grounds."[47] It certainly opened up debate about antitrust law that remains unresolved and divisive today.

Before 1940 the US aluminum industry was synonymous with Alcoa, "the sole American producer of pig aluminum. Anyone who designed and made anything with aluminum—from architectural elements to cooking utensils—purchased their aluminum from Alcoa."[48] "The unprecedented increase in wartime demand (U.S. production of aluminum in 1938 was 143,000 short tons and in 1944, 766,000 short tons)," as discussed in chapter 3, "and Alcoa's inability to meet it, were the main factors in breaking up the company's monopoly."[49] Thanks to the wartime necessity of antitrust action, "the R.J. Reynolds Tobacco Company—long a consumer of aluminum for cigarette packaging—and the Kaiser Company—a shipbuilding and heavy construction concern—quickly established independent aluminum companies, acquired aluminum production facilities from the Surplus Property Board, and entered the market as vertically integrated primary producers of aluminum."[50] Thus, there emerged some competition among producers of aluminum goods, new pressures for research and development, and competitive marketing and advertising campaigns.

In sum, the famous US antitrust litigation against Alcoa, filed in 1937 and partially settled on appeal in 1945, placed the aluminum industry at the center of major battles concerning price setting, cartels, monopoly, and the power of politically connected financiers such as Andrew Mellon. The suit ended in a controversial decision requiring Alcoa shareholders to divest themselves of Alcan (a Canadian subsidiary) and to sell off parts of its plants and facilities to two major competitors, the Reynolds Metals Company and Kaiser Aluminum and Chemical Corporation. Assisted by the government's Defense Plant Corporation and the post–War Reconstruction Finance Corporation, this introduced much greater competition into the consumer market.[51] Yet US government activities also had crucial effects on the access of multinational corporations to "developing" countries with bauxite and hydropower resources, which helped to stifle the emergence of foreign competitors in production. Critics of the global industry argue that the amount of competition introduced was minimal, and that the friendly competitors continued to operate as an oligopoly (the boards of Alcoa and Alcan remained closely interlinked), with total control over pricing, especially in regard to the pricing of bauxite and the low levels of royalties offered to bauxite-producing countries.

As economist John Stuckey argues in his study of vertical integration of the industry, aluminum does not really function in a free market because "vertical integration and, more recently, joint ventures play a much greater role in this industry than in most others," to the extent that "there is no such thing as a free-market world price for bauxite or alumina, the industry's two upstream commodities."[52] Likewise the downstream price, we shall see, can be manipulated by investment banks like J. P. Morgan and Goldman Sachs.

ALUMINUM INDUSTRY AND GLOBAL INEQUALITY

How did Alcoa become one of the most dominant global companies of the twentieth century? First, the protection of patents in the early development of the industry led to "first-mover" advantages for the initial entrants, Alcoa in the United States, and Alusuisse (Schweizerisches Aluminum A.G.) and Péchiny Compagnie de Produits Chimique et Électrometallurgiques in Europe. Under patent protection these companies were able to build up powerful and long-lasting monopolies over the two main inputs for the making of aluminum: bauxite mines and hydropower resources. By the time the patents expired in 1909 and 1914 they had achieved such economies of scale and control over inputs that it was very difficult for others to enter the industry. With few competitors until the breakup of Alcoa after World War II, the highly vertically and horizontally integrated corporations formed cartels to maintain prices and profits under an international oligopoly. Indeed, on a continuum of raw material extractive industries, the aluminum industry falls toward the extreme end of relative scarcity, concentration of resources, technology entry barriers (protected by patents and sunk costs), and inelastic demand, encouraging a highly monopolistic or oligopolistic structure. Although these structural features do not determine outcomes, they certainly set tight conditions on the possibilities for resource-rich states to bargain with resource extractors.[53] Aluminum has been dubbed "packaged electricity" or "solidified electricity" because smelting demands so much power,[54] but it might equally be called solidified power because it tends toward such an uncompetitive industrial structure. This view offers an alternative corporate history, less about clever inventors and self-made captains of industry mobilizing the power of innovation and investment, and more about state support and locked in advantage.

Second, aluminum became so crucial to modern warfare (see chapter 3) that national governments played a major part in subsidizing and shaping the industry. During World War II, US government investment drove aluminum production to grow by more than 600 percent between 1939 and 1943, outpacing the increase in all other crucial metals.[55] During the war the United States produced 304,000 military airplanes in total, using 3.5 billion pounds of aluminum, claiming more than 85 percent of Alcoa's output. At the war's end the government had $672 million invested in fifty wholly state-owned aluminum production and fabrication plants, which were disposed of after the war through the Surplus Property Act.[56] Subsidies to favor Alcoa's competitors, stockpiling after the war, and the outbreak of the Korean War led to even greater government participation in the industry. One of those new competitors, Reynolds Metals Company, noted in a 1950 pamphlet that during the war the price of aluminum had dropped by 30 percent due to increased production, whereas for other metals it rose an average of 125 percent. One of the reasons for the low price had to do with subsidized electricity. Although the average cost to homeowners for electricity was 3.5 cents per kWh, according to Reynolds, the cost to aluminum plants was only 0.35 cents per kWh, or one-tenth.[57]

From a wartime resource of national strategic importance the aluminum industry mutated into a multifaceted industry that not only produced goods but also produced the capacity to consume more electricity, to transport more goods, and to keep the economy on the move more quickly. In other words it boosted economic capacity as it was consumed, building infrastructure as well as the goods that flowed through it, and also helping to build US global military power. As environmental historian Matthew Evenden points out, the "aluminum revolution" that increased global production by ten times in the period between World War I and World War II not only "set into motion a train of consequences for bauxite producers, shipping companies, aluminum smelters, and aircraft manufacturers" but also "triggered profound changes in the social and environmental relationships that were necessary for, and produced by, aluminum production."[58] Reaching from "bauxite mines and razed forests along the Demerara River in British Guiana," to a shipment station in Trinidad, to smelters and dammed rivers in Quebec, the wartime aluminum industry intensified global commodity chains and enabled aluminum producers in the United States and Europe to gain new kinds of territorial control and power over the resources of other parts of the world, thus locking in advantages from particularly unequal power relations. The state, and especially the military-industrial complex, played a crucial role in the development of this industry.

Canadian production was heavily reliant on bauxite mines in British Guiana, where there were further detrimental environmental and social effects, as discussed in later chapters. The United States also benefited from this supply chain, as its wartime expansion of aircraft production demanded energy and aluminum supplies from Alcan. Although Alcoa (with Alcan) is not alone in its rise to power as a user of natural resources, it offers an instructive example of the challenges local people and communities face in trying to exercise some control over the industry.

Controlling electricity production is one of the major forms of corporate national and transnational power exercised by the aluminum industry. Alcoa proudly noted in a 1969 publication that "Alcoa is one of the largest users of electricity in the nation. [. . .] During 1967, Alcoa utilized over 20 billion kilowatt hours of electricity in its domestic operations. [. . .] Alcoa's 1967 requirements, therefore, were equivalent to those of over 4,000,000 homes."[64] Its search for power took the company first to Niagara Falls in 1893, then to the construction of major hydroelectric plants in Canada and Massena, New York; then it moved into the Smoky Mountains in western North Carolina and eastern Tennessee. "It is believed that Alcoa's development of the Little Tennessee River basin [1910–25] is the earliest example of a fully planned, complete integration of hydroelectric developments on a single watershed."[65] After harnessing various other river systems, it eventually reached the point where "it is virtually impossible today for an industry to construct a hydroelectric plant for its own use. In fact, within the continental United States, almost all the economical hydro sites have been developed."[66] This drove the company, by the mid-1960s, into purchasing large coal deposits in the Ohio Valley, building coal plants in Indiana, Anglesea (Australia), and Mexico, as well as massive new hydropower developments in Norway and the fateful Brokopondo Agreement that led to the damming of the Suriname River in the 1960s (discussed in chapter 6).

Beginning in the 1960s, then, in addition to the depletion of metallurgical-grade bauxite in the United States pushing the aluminum cartels toward a transnational strategy, smelting also began to be switched to countries with low-cost energy or resources. Fuller gives an interesting account of how the metals cartels "were motivated to establish military supremacy over nonindustrialized countries in Africa, South America, and the Far East," where crucial metal ores were located.[67] He provides Ghana as a good example, being both rich in bauxite and having the Volta River:

Americans with vast capital came into Ghana, arranged to have all the inhabitants of the Volta River basin banished from that basin, then built one of the world's largest hydroelectric dams there. They used the electricity thus generated to convert the Ghanaian bauxite (which was just so much dirt to the Ghanaians) into aluminum ingots. These ingots were, and as yet are, shipped to America and Europe, where the aluminum is transformed into airplanes, cooking utensils, etc., and sold back to the Ghanaians and others around the world at such a markup in price that the Ghanaians' balance of import-export trading finds them ever deeper in debt to those countries that "developed" their natural resources. The societies in the manipulating countries call these people "the underdeveloped countries" or "the Third World."[68]

As others have called attention to, the building of the Akosombo Dam in 1965 on Ghana's Volta River powered a 174,000-ton aluminum smelter in Tema. It created a reservoir that "covered 4% of the country, inundating the homes of 80,000 people in 740 villages. The reservoir exacerbated waterborne diseases, [. . .] and has done little in the way of rural electrification or local economic development."[69] Most important, Fuller concludes, "There can be no equity until all the sovereign nations are abolished and we have but one accounting system—that of the one family of humans aboard Spaceship Earth."[70]

TRANSNATIONAL BIG BUSINESS TODAY

Between 1972 and 1982, the average cost of electricity for US industrial users rose by a factor of five, "forcing U.S. aluminum companies to close plants with high operating costs and low energy efficiencies in the early 1980s"; further energy price spikes in 2000–2001 led to "the shutdown of almost all aluminum capacity in the Pacific Northwest."[71] Today new industrial players have emerged, with growing bauxite mining in Australia, Guinea, Brazil, and China; alumina refining in Australia, China, Jamaica, Brazil, and Russia shrinking the US share; and primary aluminum smelting still led by the United States, Canada, and Russia but now joined by competitors in China, Australia, Brazil, and Norway. In considering how transnational corporations exercise territorial power it is important to understand the legal underpinnings of their market practices. Even the US federal government struggled to control big companies like Standard Oil, United States Steel, and Alcoa in the first half of the twentieth century, as the story of its antitrust battles show. Much of what was done to break up the industry in the 1940s only had a partial success, and is being undone today as a wave of mergers is again creating huge transnational, diversified corporations, unimaginable then. Whereas antitrust law may seem like obscure business and legal history, it is in fact crucial to understanding how we regulate the big multinational corporations that dominate global markets today and that consume vast quantities of natural resources and electrical power while generating vast amounts of pollution.

In the 1990s Alcoa gained further fame under the chairmanship of Paul O'Neill, who doubled its global market share and workforce. Padel and Das point out that Alcoa was the third largest contributor to the election campaign of George W. Bush, under whom Alcoa's chairman Paul O'Neill was appointed treasury secretary, "selling his Alcoa shares only after they had risen 30 percent during his first weeks in office. The cartel was thus consolidated from the apex of the US Treasury Department, just as it was when Mellon was Treasury Secretary in 1921–33."[72] Like Andrew Mellon before him, O'Neill was known for his controversial neoconservative economic views on the protection of wealth accumulation and the abolition of corporate taxation. At the same time, despite receiving several environmental awards, Alcoa received a number of fines for pollution and remained the target of numerous environmental protests around the world. The story of this company thus offers a sharply focused lens into questions of business ethics and monopoly, and competing views on global development and environmental protection. It also leads us to consider how legal instruments such as patents, corporate law, and regulatory regimes allow an industry to exercise vast influence over local trajectories of development, land use, labor relations, and environmental impact around the world.

Aluminum-producing companies today wield far more power than many of the states in which their production facilities are located, with profits larger than national gross domestic products in many states. They use their power to bargain with resource-rich nations and to threaten them with withdrawal if terms are not favorable. Through their own powers of mobility, these global giants are able to gain access to bauxite with very low royalty payments and often negotiate access to highly subsidized electricity. For example, according to a report by the International Rivers Network,

The World Commission on Dams' case study of Tucuruí Dam in Brazil found that the Albrás/Alunorte and Alumar smelters received between \$193–411 million per year in energy subsidies from a state-owned utility. The smelters recently employed the strategy of threatening to shut down and leave the country in order to obtain new, long-term contracts for subsidized electricity at far below the rates paid by other industries.[73]

When governments do try to strike tougher bargains on bauxite royalties and tax levies with the industry, as will be discussed in chapters 6 and 7, they often find themselves without an industry, because it simply moves to other countries. Countries that do welcome industrial development by the industry usually find that the expected job creation goes to low-paid foreign contract workers rather than local people, and that royalties, tax revenues, and electricity purchases are all at bargain levels that benefit the companies more than the hosts. Therefore, even with antitrust laws being applied, it is extremely difficult to control the international arena in which such corporations operate. Alongside antitrust law, most other tools for regulating multinational corporations currently depend on voluntary cooperation and have little scope for enforcement.

In 2003, for example, the EPA ordered Alcoa to pay $4 million in compensation for pollution from its Rockdale, Texas, plant, which spewed seventy-five thousand tons of pollutants into the atmosphere and was the nation's largest nonutility emitter of sulfur dioxide and nitrogen oxide. "In 1991, Alcoa agreed to pay $7.5 million in civil and criminal penalties for dumping PCBs and other pollutants, including spent pot liners, at its Massena plant," including $3.75 million in criminal penalties, which were the largest hazardous waste violation in US history.[74] And in 2004 it was ordered to pay $11.4 million for cleanup of mercury contamination, the same year it was named "one of America's most admired companies" by *Fortune* magazine and awarded for its "commitment to sustainability." Pollution is just business as usual for this industry, and these fines were considered a cost of doing business.

The appetite for applying antitrust law to rein in corporations also waxes and wanes under different administrations. Today antitrust law in the United States is in a period of flux, as the more conservative John Roberts's Supreme Court has made decisions that strike down century-old restrictions on corporate power. The court is described as "notable for overturning precedents and for victories for big businesses and antitrust defendants."[75] Jeffrey Rosen, a law professor at George Washington University, describes this as "an ideological sea change on the Supreme Court," which once viewed big business with skepticism, "ready to bend the law in favor of the environment and against the corporations.'"[76] It seems that we are seeing the dismantling of antitrust law as the court becomes more conservative and increasingly appears to uphold business interests rather than supporting consumer protection and the environment. The disclosure in July 2013 that investment bank Goldman Sachs was manipulating the price of aluminum by delaying its release from warehouses it owns in Detroit reinforces that this is a rigged market, bringing huge profits to a few at a high cost to many. The salt in the wound is that Goldman Sachs was added to the Dow Jones Industrial Average a few months later, just as Alcoa, with its faltering share price, was dropped, ending its fifty-four-year reign marking the age of aluminum.[77]

Transnational corporations today operate not only in a globalizing economy but also under a more global structure of financial governance than in the past. The International Rivers Network report on the industry points out that multilateral lending agencies such as the World Bank's International Finance Corporation or the Inter-American Development Bank have been instrumental in encouraging expansions of hydroelectric and smelter projects by furnishing credit and loan guarantees. In struggles against transnational corporations today, activists consider campaigns against the financing of aluminum complexes (especially hydroelectric projects) one of the key environmental battles globally and also one of the greatest vulnerabilities of the industry.[78]

In sum, although the industry struggled in the twentieth century to protect patents, develop markets, and overcome antitrust law, today its major battles are concerned with weathering economic volatility, fighting competitors, justifying environmental effects, and protecting corporate brand images from attacks by activists. How can an industry associated with modernization, innovation, and contributions to the mobilization of the world also be associated with the production of spatial injustice, negative development, and global inequality? That is one of the great ironies of the "light modernity" that aluminum brought to the twentieth century. To better understand these two sides of modern industry, as the following chapters will show, we need to go back to its origins, follow its industrial development across the world, and trace our everyday products back to their sources.

Aluminum has become the most important single bulk material of modern warfare. No fighting is possible, and no war can be carried to a successful conclusion today, without using and destroying vast quantities of aluminum.

—Dewey Anderson, *Aluminum for Defence and Prosperity*, 1951

War was good to Alcoa.

—George David Smith, *From Monopoly to Competition*

Aluminum has fascinated military strategists from its very earliest days. Most histories of the metal begin by noting that French emperor Napoleon III financed experiments by chemist Henri Sainte-Claire Deville in the 1850s with the hope of developing light helmets and armor for his cavalry, but it remained so expensive that all he got was a breastplate for himself.[1] However, with the establishment of the modern industry as described in chapter 2, production soared, prices plunged, and as early as 1892 the French military ordered several aluminum torpedo boats. "United States cavalrymen fighting in the Spanish-American War," notes an Alcoa popular history, "tethered their horses to aluminum picket pins, and infantry troops slept in tents pegged to aluminum stakes," while Teddy Roosevelt himself carried an aluminum canteen as he "led his troops up San Juan Hill."[2]

However, these quaint details pale in comparison to the subsequent military adoption of aluminum, which the company itself described as "massive applications of aluminum to the terrible arena of modern warfare," adding that it was its contributions to mobility and speed that made aluminum so crucial both to perpetuating war and to changing modern military strategy: "the mechanized age added speed and mobility" and "the air age revolutionized the art of war, adding speed and versatility to the techniques of attack and defense."[3]

The aluminum industry helped to modernize warfare, and warfare helped to modernize the aluminum industry. Even the official company history by George David Smith notes that "war was good to Alcoa," with World War I enabling the company to increase production by 40 percent and to export ninety million pounds of Alcoa's total primary output (152 million pounds between 1915 and 1918) to British, French, and Italian allies.[4] Smith notes that "plant facilities were hastily expanded to meet demand, and shipments of bauxite from the company's new mines in South America began in earnest." Thus the war was also key to expanding the international operations of the company. During both World Wars I and II about 90 percent of US aluminum production went into military uses, which ranged from "aircraft and automobile parts to electrical supplies and screw machine products," as well as explosives such as ammonal (ammonium nitrate and aluminum powder) and thermite used in bombs.[5] In this way "aluminum became a strategic material" and part of "the regulated command economy" of the war years.[6] After the war, aluminum production was immediately converted to civilian markets such as new visions for commercial aircraft, involving extensive advertising campaigns and promotion, such as those by the Bohn Aluminum and Brass Corporation, which are explored further in chapter 4 (see figure 3.1).

It is fair to say that the entire history of innovation and technical development in the uses of aluminum was in many respects driven by the necessities *of war,* by aluminum's terrible power *for waging war,* and by the intrigues, espionage, and industrial maneuvering for military research funding and contracts generated *by war*—leading to what Eisenhower himself in 1961 warned was a dangerous "military-industrial complex" with "unwarranted power" built in partnership with aluminum producers. Key investor in Alcoa, Andrew Mellon, "left his job as Alcoa's Chief Executive to become the US Treasury Secretary in 1921, and kept this post for eleven years, while his company expanded into Europe and Canada, buying bauxite mines as well as factories and dam sites—as one of the world's first real multinationals."[7] In other words, there were key ties between the international expansion and vertical integration of the industry, and the very heart of government. There were not only interlocking directorates across companies like Alcoa and Alcan but also linkages among the aluminum industry, the highest levels

FIGURE 3.1
Bohn Corporation advertisement: Revolutionary Rockets (circa 1943).

of government, and the government funding of warfare as described in the following.

This tells us something about the strategic importance of aluminum. Cultural historian Eric Schatzberg argues that wooden planes such as the British World War II Mosquito combat plane were just as effective as metal aircraft, and it was simply engineers who imposed the ideological frame of aluminum being a superior, more modern material.[8] By contrast, I argue that we need to understand not only the scientific discourses, but also the economic and political power structures and interlocking networks that promoted the age of aluminum. The cultural history of aluminum concerns not just national cultures, consumer preferences, or beliefs among civil engineers in the ideology of scientific modernization, but also the national *and* international social ordering of military strategies, the definition of military problems, and the social construction of technical choices by a range of interlocking governmental and nongovernmental actors involved in wartime industries. Sociotechnical change is never a simple matter of a single group of actors prevailing in imposing their ideology on others through rhetorical framing, but this does not mean that culture is not important.

One problem is that Schatzberg employs a far too instrumental view of culture. A good counterexample is John Law's account of the design, construction, and eventual cancellation of a British military aircraft known as the *TSR2,* which exemplifies the competing frames, failing materials, "obligatory points of passage" through networks, and multiplicity of actors, both human and nonhuman, that go into particular technological projects.[9] Cultural sociology includes discourses and ideologies, but we must also think beyond culture as a frame in which thought and action take place to instead describe culture as more or less durable practices and networks involving not only ideas but also materials and assemblages of people and materials, which are constantly being tried out, reconfigured, or exceeded. Culture is additionally productive of the slowly changing social orderings that produce frames, practices, networks, and assemblages in the first place.

In this chapter, therefore, I focus on some of the practices and networks within which specific forms of aluminum and technologies based on aluminum were produced, especially those pertaining to warfare; in subsequent chapters I turn to more explicit cultural practices such as industrial research and development, design, and advertising that shifted these technologies from the military to the civilian realm. This chapter traces how the international race to master aluminum technology was intimately linked with the race for military dominance in flight, transport, weaponry, logistics, and eventually in aerospace and satellite communications systems.

Beginning with the lightweighting of ancillary military equipment, I show how supplies and troops were made more easily transportable and thus quickly deployable. Next a massive research effort was put into aluminum alloys for airplanes as well as troop carriers and other ships. Applied to logistics, aluminum supported the shift toward the rapid-deployment concept, leading to lightweight aluminum alloys for armored tanks, personnel carriers, and howitzers, as well as for easily transportable bridges, pontoons, and amphibious vehicles. Aluminum was also crucial in the production of explosives and bombs of most kinds; heavily used by the US Navy and essential to the US space race, nuclear arsenal, and Cold War against the Soviet Union in the 1960s to 1970s.

Light metal continues to play a crucial role in defense. The US Army Research Lab itself points out that "aluminum alloy armor has been utilized by the US government since the outbreak of World War II, and each year, the military procures about 5,000 vehicles, which translates to more than 30 million pounds of aluminum alloys that will be procured annually."[10] It also continues to be a crucial material for military-funded research and development today, especially in regard to new nanocomposites, as discussed in chapter 9, including at the cutting-edge nanomaterials engineering research facilities of my own employer, Drexel University in Philadelphia.

Our contemporary culture of innovation and entrepreneurship remains deeply entwined with the military-industrial complex, with serious implications for our ability to address ethical issues concerning global pollution, environmental destruction, and the huge effects of aluminum production on marginalized people.

AIR POWER: FROM SCIENCE FICTION TO INDUSTRIAL ESPIONAGE

The French writer Jules Verne was one of the first to recognize aluminum's potential in his prophetic science fiction story *From the Earth to the Moon,* published in 1865. His characters turn to what was then a rare and expensive metal as the perfect material for creating a spacecraft that would be able to leave the earth: "It is easily wrought, is very widely distributed, forming the basis of most of the rocks, is three times lighter than iron, and seems to have been created for the express purpose of furnishing us with the material for our projectile."[11] He was right—the first rockets and moon landing vehicles were made from aluminum. But first came the airships and airplanes. The incredible mobility afforded by commercial aviation, which we almost take for granted today, would not be possible without this light metal. The allure of aluminum begins with the dream of flight and the conquest of space.

Some of the earliest experiments in human flight benefitted from the lightness of aluminum. The Wright brothers' airplane flown at Kitty Hawk used aluminum alloyed with copper in the engine crankcase and other parts. Aluminum castings, including the crankshaft and pistons, were crucial in the Liberty engine used in US war planes during World War I, making up as much as one-third of the engine weight.[12] In order to reduce weight, aluminum-copper alloys quickly came to be used wherever possible for aircraft engine beds, crank cases, pistons, oil pumps, and camshaft housings, and pure aluminum sheet or light alloy for gasoline tanks, fuselage, hoods, cowling, seat backs, aileron frames, navigation instruments, communication devices, and exterior reflective aluminum paint.[13] Although the Wright brothers claimed the first successful flight of a heavier-than-air, machine-powered airplane in 1903, and the story of flight is often told as a national history within institutions such as the Smithsonian Institute's National Air and Space Museum in Washington, DC, European chemists initially took the lead in the development of aluminum alloys for aerial technologies, and it was the race for military predominance that drove industrial research and development forward.

Duralumin is an extremely strong heat-treated alloy of aluminum with small percentages of copper, magnesium, and manganese, developed by German metallurgical engineer Alfred Wilm in 1909. It became the basis for the building of Zeppelin airships with aluminum structural girders during World War I, instigating a race between Britain and the United States to try to develop their own airships.[14] In the end it was the war itself that enabled Alcoa to gain access to the exact details of the Duralumin patent via "industrial espionage" according to Alcoa historian Margaret Graham. After the war US technical missions from the Bureau of Construction and Repair gained access to the German state aluminum works at Staaken, and entered plants in England and France. "The result," says Graham, "was Alcoa's 17S, an alloy almost identical in composition to Duralumin."[15]

With this "effectively stolen technology" Alcoa drove ahead in its pursuit of new strong alloys. Soon after, Alcoa's aluminum alloy known as 25S, developed in the early 1920s, "was the first strong, heat-treatable aluminum alloy that proved practical for forging, an art which made the aluminum propeller standard equipment for aircraft."[16] They finally came up with a thin sheet metal known as Alclad in 1926—with a strong alloy core and surface layers of corrosion-resistant pure aluminum integrally bonded to the core—which became indispensable in the development of military and civil aircraft.

However, Alcoa's other historian George David Smith ignores the espionage (saying simply that Wilm's patents were "appropriated by a war-time Alien Property Custodian") and emphasizes that it was not like simply getting the recipe and going into production. "Metallurgists, much like cooks who concoct recipes, could barely explain the theoretical bases for the results of many of their experiments. Wilm himself could not explain the results of his great discovery, and so his 'recipe' was hard to translate into a product."[17] Instead what happened was government-funded research, "continuing urging of the Navy, which in those days was the Government's most sophisticated consumer of technology," and the emergence of an entirely new attitude toward systematic research and innovation within the company: "The impact of the Duralumin program on Alcoa's research and development was profound."[18] And today the impact of US Department of Defense DARPA (Defense Advanced Research Projects Agency) research programs and other military research contracts continues to be profound, not only on companies but also on university research laboratories and the basic training of new materials engineers. Behind what Schatzberg perceives as the "ideology" of engineering lies a deeper social ordering of political attention, investment, and production of the means of war.

In many ways what General Dwight Eisenhower called the "military-industrial complex" was (and remains) very much a "military-aluminum complex." During World War I, US military requirements for 1917 and 1918 totaled 128,867 tons of aluminum, whereas in World War II, some 304,000 airplanes were produced by the United States alone using 1,537,590 tons of metal.[19] Western governments have therefore vociferously protected aluminum as an essential "strategic industry." States made huge investments in scientific and commercial development of their air industries,[20] as well as the aluminum industry. Padel and Das draw attention to a 1951 pamphlet written by Dewey Anderson, *Aluminum for Defense and Prosperity,* which they claim "is one of the few public documents ever released that reveal the real policies surrounding the aluminium industry, written by an insider."[21] Anderson baldly stated the facts:

Aluminum has become the most important single bulk material of modern warfare. No fighting is possible, and no war can be carried to a successful conclusion today, without using and destroying vast quantities of aluminum. [. . .] It is so critical for defense that government steps in for prolonged periods of time, determines how much aluminum there should be, expands production at government expense, and decides what part of the supply will be available for civilians. [. . .] Aluminum making is dependent on vast continuing grants of low-cost electricity.[22]

So the military need for aluminum was closely tied to the government investment in energy infrastructure such as huge hydroelectric power projects, because the large-scale harnessing of energy was crucial to the making of aluminum, and hence, readiness for war.

But aerial "readiness" was not simply about new industries and technologies; according to Peter Adey it also generated new forms of "aerial life"[23] in which activities related to aviation were promoted among the civilian population to reinforce national security. As industrialized and militarized countries competed to develop their aluminum industries the dream of aluminum's power of flight took hold. In May 1927 Charles Lindbergh made the first successful solo nonstop transatlantic flight in his single-seat, single-engine Ryan NYP, the *Spirit of St. Louis,* which had a Wright Whirlwind J-5C engine containing a substantial amount of Alcoa aluminum. His success contributed further not only to aluminum becoming firmly entrenched in the US aviation industry but also to the cultural imaginaries that equated metal-skinned planes (rather than wooden ones) with progress toward the future. The radial air-cooled Whirlwind was one of the most reliable aircraft engines of its time in the world. The Collier Trophy, the United States' most respected aviation award, was awarded in 1927 not to the pilot who had flown the Atlantic, but to Charles L. Lawrance, the designer of the engine that made it possible. The reality of aluminum-skinned airplanes hurtling across the Atlantic, flown by brave aviators, inspired a craze for aviation. Lindbergh was a national hero, and aviatrix Amelia Earhart fascinated the nation.

Aerial readiness and air-mindedness were not only a US phenomenon, so cannot be limited to a national culture. In Europe the 1930s are described as a golden age for aluminum in the domains of transportation, household products, furniture, and architecture.[24] In Italy, for example, this coincided with the rise of Mussolini's fascist government, which embraced the potentials of the light metal. In 1932 the government founded an industry review, *Alluminio,* which carried this quote on its cover: "Italy has abundant raw materials, abundant enough to forge the new productive Civilization that is already shining on the horizon: a Civilization principally based upon the ubiquity of light metals and their alloys in everything including the national defense."[25] Another industrial review described aluminum as "not only the *metal* of the Fatherland; it is also the metal of progress, the real material of unreal velocities [*la materia reale dell'irreale volocita*]."[26] The Italian Futurists especially embraced the aesthetics of mobility and dynamism and initiated an art movement that combined the worship of speed with a fascist politics of national power. Aluminum and the development of an aircraft industry were the realization of such aesthetic and political projects of modernization, and for the rest of the century to have a national airline would become the marker of a modern nation-state.

Ironically, the Soviet Union, with ample supplies of wood with which to make perfectly serviceable aircraft, was a latecomer to the race for aluminum air power, but also gained its aerial technology through industrial espionage against the United States in the 1930s. According to Mikhael Mukhin of the Russian Academy of Science, Soviet engineers knew about duralumin since the 1920s but were unable to produce it without more precise technical specifications. After failing to gain sufficient information from industrial plants in France and Britain, they sent the engineer A. V. Sibilev to the United States in 1931, where he was unsuccessful in getting any information out of Alcoa. However, he also visited US machine-building plants, where he managed to ascertain that the US duralumin industry used electric furnaces (unlike the oil-powered ones used in France) and roller mills designed for billets of 1.5 tons each. This provided enough information, combined with other know-how, to purchase appropriate-sized electric furnaces in 1932 and commission the Soviet Union's first aluminum plant in 1933, which was quickly extended into a fully vertically integrated industry in ten to fifteen years. As Mukhin argues, this act of espionage was absolutely crucial "for the victory of the Soviet Union in the Second World War. Though the USSR could not completely forgo deliveries of import aluminium, it is indubitable that the Soviet aviation industry would simply cease to exist without the advanced domestic aluminium industry."[27] This case shows us, contra Schatzberg, that the production of wooden aircraft simply could not be ramped up quickly enough for massive wartime production.

The perceived aerial superiority of aluminum over all previous metals has made possible what cultural theorist Caren Kaplan calls "the cosmic view" of militarized air power. "Mobility is at the heart of modern warfare," writes

Kaplan, and "modern war engages the theories and practices of mobility to a great extent."[28] It is lightweight aluminum-clad bombers that made such a change in military practice possible, later joined by guided missiles, satellites, and rockets, all made from the light metal. Kaplan tracks the emergence of the first phase of the weaponization of the air through Major Alexander De Seversky's famous book *Victory through Air Power* (1942), which was also made into a Walt Disney animated feature film of the same name. In the aftermath of Pearl Harbor the widely distributed book and film are said to have influenced both Winston Churchill and Franklin Delano Roosevelt and to have changed national military strategy forever. The story of flight is also the story of modern warfare and an air power that arises from dusty bauxite ores turned into shining aluminum.

In May 1940 President Roosevelt announced that the government planned to construct 50,000 airplanes over the next two years, as part of a massive war effort; this was extended to 60,000 in 1942, and an astounding 125,000 in 1943.[29] While steel production doubled, US government investment drove aluminum production to grow by more than 600 percent between 1939 and 1943, outpacing the increase in all other crucial metals.[30] "World War II demonstrated to the world the capacity and power of US industrial production and its ability to expand exponentially to meet wartime needs."[31] This was mainly driven by the frantic fabrication of warplanes, in which "[90] percent of the wings and fuselage, 60 percent of the engine, and all of the propeller was composed of aluminum," not to mention the "rivets, wires, cables, rods, radios, instrument cases, cockpit fittings, aerial cameras, and the hydraulic system that opens and closes the bomb doors and retracts the wheels of the plane."[32]

During World War II it is also notable that "the only invaders to land on the American mainland came with the purpose of 'harming as much as possible aluminum production in the United States.' In 1942, Nazi U-boats landed eight saboteurs—four in Florida and four on Long Island" whose primary mission, according to FBI investigations after their capture, "was the destruction of Alcoa plants in Alcoa, Tenn., Massena, N.Y., and East St. Louis, Ill."[33] The Nazis knew exactly where the US military strength rested.

Aluminum went on to play a crucial role in the development of new military aircraft, but its pathway was not always smooth, its failures revealing the extent it was wrapped up in government-funded projects, military contracting, and hidden subsidies. One of the more successful designs, the A-6

Intruder, designed by Lawrence Mead Jr. of Grumman Aerospace Corporation (now Northrup Grumman) and introduced in 1960, was considered "the Navy's workhorse bomber and the Marine's primary ground support aircraft in Vietnam." The bulky jet was designed around a "wing-to-wing aluminum alloy beam" that enabled it to carry up to 18,000 pounds of bombs in a vehicle weighing only 25,000 pounds, with a wingspan of about 50 feet and cruising speed up to 500 miles per hour. Grumman went on to become a member of the design team that worked on the Apollo lunar module that landed Neil Armstrong and Buzz Aldrin on the moon on July 20, 1969. The A-6 went on to serve in combat in conflicts ranging from the US invasion of Grenada to the first Persian Gulf War.[34]

The Lockheed C-5 Galaxy, introduced in 1968, is described by Alcoa as "essentially an all-aluminum aircraft," and remains among the largest military aircraft in the world (250 feet long with original maximum gross weight of 728,000 pounds), capable of carrying oversize cargos (initially up to a 100,000 pound payload) and completing long-range intercontinental strategic airlift (such as the delivery of armored vehicle launched bridges, and today the transport of up to six Apache helicopters or five Bradley Fighting Vehicles). However, the fractures in its wings and associated one billion dollar cost overrun in its design and production led to a Congressional investigation in 1968 to 1969, and ongoing problems with cracking led to the need for several expensive refits.

Such cost overruns were evidently not a reason to abandon aluminum, but instead to throw more money into research and development. As Dewey Anderson argued in 1951, "More than any other modern industry, aluminum is dependent on government policies and government action for more production and consumption,"[35] and this was why aluminum production was heavily subsidized, including a US government stockpile that was created in the run-up to the Korean War, drawing on new bauxite mines in Jamaica (see chapter 6), reaching nearly two million tons in 1963.

Aluminum also played a crucial role in advances in naval speed. Emblematic of the stunning speed potential of aluminum design was the groundbreaking ocean liner the S.S. United States, designed by Philadelphian William Francis Gibbs, which set the record for the fastest Atlantic crossing and highest average speed in 1952. To put this achievement in perspective, the first steam ships cut the Atlantic sailing time between Britain and New York from six weeks to fifteen days in 1838. As ships grew larger and faster, they competed for the Blue Riband of the Atlantic awarded to the fastest regular passenger service, which brought faster times every few years, reaching six days for the Atlantic crossing in 1900 and five days by the 1930s. In 1952, with its top speed a military secret, the *S.S. United States* easily beat the record holder, Britain's ocean liner *Queen Mary,* by sailing from Southampton to New York in three days, twelve hours, and twelve minutes.[36]

According to his recent biographer, Steven Ujifusa, Gibbs dedicated his life to designing "not just the fastest and most beautiful ship, but also the safest," and he did so by incorporating aluminum throughout the *United States.* Alcoa took pride in the ship, noting that "her 1,000 ton deckhouse was the largest single aluminum assembly in history . . . In all, more than 2,000 tons of aluminum went into the ocean giant," yet "the total decrease in displacement amounted to 8,000 tons."[37] This remarkable ship set transatlantic speed records and went on "to establish new standards in marine engineering," especially through extreme weight savings. Because it was designed to be easily converted to a troop carrier or a hospital ship, with a capacity of fifteen thousand troops, the US government underwrote $50 million of the $78 million construction cost. Indeed, the firm Gibbs & Cox was the country's leading naval-design firm, and during World War II was responsible for the design of two-thirds of all US naval ships, as well as the workhorse "liberty ships" used as cargo carriers, reminding us of the military commitment to the metals industry and research into advanced design.

Yet it was air travel that ultimately put an end to the *S.S. United States,* unable to compete for speed with the Boeing 707, which started regular transatlantic passenger service in 1958. By 1969 the fastest passenger ship in the world had to be taken out of service for lack of customers. Today it sits forlornly docked at Pier 82 on the Delaware River in Philadelphia, where preservationists are trying to save it from the scrap heap. I visited it there recently, its corroding yet graceful hull still glinting in the sunlight, a striking relic of the age of aluminum (see figure 3.2). It rests not far from the site where shipbuilders Kvaerner and FastShip Atlantic proposed in 2004 to develop superfast transatlantic container ships that would use a specially built container port designed to speed up logistical operations with roll-on–roll-off loading systems and synchronized rail and road access. Philadelphia's deputy mayor of transportation and utilities also hopes one day to connect such a port into a high-speed rail network that will stop at Philadelphia International Airport, creating an advanced logistics hub integrating sea, land,

FIGURE 3.2

S.S. United States docked on the Delaware River, Philadelphia (2012). Photo: Daniel Schimmel.

and air transport in one location. Such visions build on the trajectory of speed from road transport, to rail, to sea, to air, in which aluminum will play a crucial part.

By the 1960s this marriage of aluminum innovation with military strategy and state investment was framed in terms of the paramount need for mobility and the rise of "rapid deployment strategies" associated with fighting new kinds of warfare in the jungles of South Asia. A circa 1965 publication by the Aluminum Association, a trade association promoting uses of aluminum, takes note of the "new era of warfare in which the slow advance of great armies has been replaced by the brush fire war, and many forms that guerrilla warfare takes. For the United States, with her globe-girdling responsibilities, there's a paramount need for mobility of her fighting forces and the weapons of war, without sacrifice of her firepower or armor."[38] Aluminum was to its core associated with these strategically necessary practices of lightness, speed, and mobility. At the same time, however, it was US military power and government subsidies that enabled the rise of Alcoa as a powerful transnational corporation operating around the world. Alcoa notes how aluminum supported the "logistics revolution" of the 1960s, because containerization helped to "speed loading and unloading, cut delivery times and protect against pilferage. In some instances, these sealed, weatherproof units have served as mobile warehouses for storage of goods at various points along distribution lines," with great savings to shipping lines.[39] So in speeding up the transport of goods, aluminum helped to lay the groundwork for the beginnings of a global economy of crossborder transport, and an emerging space of flows, which supports today's militarization of logistics.[40]

BOMBS, MISSILES, AND MOON LANDINGS

Although aluminum is often described as a "speed metal" or a "metal for mobility," it would be a mistake to ignore the other side of aluminum's role in war, which is actually to produce immobility. Aluminum not only mobilizes the technologies of warfare in the form of planes, missiles, and satellites but it also immobilizes enemies in the form of arms and explosives, and stops ballistics in the form of armor. The 1901 invention of thermite unlocked the power pent up in the very atoms of the molecule:

While smelters require huge supplies of electricity in order to split aluminum from its bonding with oxygen in molecules of aluminum oxide, thermite reverses this process: a bomb is packed with iron oxide and aluminum powder. When the fuse ignites, the aluminum leaps to the high temperature of its "heat of formation"' to re-bond with oxygen, making the explosion huge. This was the basis of the first world war hand grenades, second world war incendiary bombs and napalm, and the "daisy cutters" used by American planes for "carpet bombing" from the Korean and Vietnam wars to Iraq. Aluminum is also basic to the technology of nuclear missiles.[41]

As the inventor of ammonal in 1901 explained it, "if a mixture of finely granulated aluminium is ignited by a strip of magnesium ribbon, the combustion so started attains a temperature of nearly 3,000 degrees [. . .] resulting in a violent smokeless explosion [. . .]. It has a shattering, disruptive effect, best utilized in bombs."[42] In 1950 the Reynolds Metals Company observed that "our bombs over Germany were doubled in power through the use of aluminum powder."[43] And in 1951 the company was even advertising the great utility of aluminum for its "light, strong links for the chain of command," linking the multiplication of military usage to the growth of civilian applications for aluminum (see figure 3.3).

Communications: Fire instructions received at artillery post. Weight of today's "walkie-talkie" has been brought down to 20 pounds — largely by use of aluminum.

Light, Strong Links for the Chain of Command !

Communication units ... the links of the "command chain" ... need the light weight, strength and rustproof durability of aluminum. They need aluminum for non-magnetic shielding, and for the highest electrical conductivity per pound. In shipment, many parts need the protection of aluminum foil ... as do rations and medical supplies. The military uses of aluminum multiply ... from planes and bazookas to radar towers and walkie-talkies!

And the civilian uses of aluminum multiply no less amazingly. Aluminum for *your* communications ... transmitters, antennas, receivers. And for your home-building ... windows, gutters, reflective insulation. More and more aluminum in refrigerators, washing machines, automobiles. Aluminum foil packages on your market shelves. And Reynolds Wrap, the pure aluminum foil, in your kitchen.

Military needs come first, but the goal of today's production expansion is more aluminum for civilian use, too. We face a double job: fighting shortages and inflation while we fight aggression. Reynolds is working at that double job full time, full speed.

Reynolds Metals Company, General Sales Office, Louisville 1, Kentucky.

Defense needs limit Reynolds Wrap ... Return Flight Guaranteed!

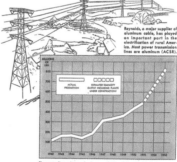

Reynolds, a major supplier of aluminum cable, has played an important part in the electrification of rural America. Most power transmission lines are aluminum (ACSR).

The expanding primary aluminum production of Reynolds Metals Company — a historic chapter in the company's 33 years of continuing growth.

REYNOLDS ALUMINUM

FIGURE 3.3
Reynolds Metals advertisement (1951)

From hand grenades to nuclear bombs, modern weaponry across the world rests on aluminum-based technology. It is worth itemizing some of these uses in order to build up a sense of how significant aluminum is to all modern technologies of warfare, and how signficant military applications are for the aluminum industry. This is what is meant by a military-industrial-aluminum complex. First, besides ammonal and thermite, aluminum is also a central ingredient of BLU-82, known as the *daisy cutter,* used for carpet bombing Vietnam and more recently in the wars in Iraq and Afghanistan. Described as "the world's largest non-nuclear weapon," it contains a slurry of ammonium nitrate, aluminum powder, and a polystyrene-based thickener, which when it explodes generates a massive pressure wave "estimated at 1,000 lbs per square inch, over an area of about 3 acres: every human being within this 'carpet' is killed."[44] In addition to bombs, Alcoa lists "a whole family of small arms [that] make use of aluminum," including the M-72 light antitank weapon, the M-16 rifle with "an aluminum housing, receiver and carrying handle," and the barrel of the M-79 grenade launcher.[45]

Second, missiles make even more significant use of the light metal, for example, the Hawk missile, which "depends largely on aluminum for its speed and maneuverability," according to Alcoa, and the Polaris missile, "one of the first potent submarine-borne deterrents, [which] requires 4000 pounds of the light metal. A few more thousand pounds of aluminum in powder form goes into the missile's propellant mix."[46] The Titan ICBM, according to the Aluminum Association, "carries aloft eight tons of aluminum in its air-frame and fuel propellant and oxidizer tanks." Russia's R-27s and India's Prithvis missile are also "made of aluminium alloys, and use aluminium in the explosive mix and as rocket fuel."[47]

Third, the Aluminum Association publicity material from the 1960s itemizes the development of new high-strength ballistic armor plate; aluminum pontoons and bridges that can be easily moved into location; and the M-102 lightweight howitzer, which could be air-dropped onto the battlefield. By 1970 the M113 armored personnel carrier introduced a new hardened aluminum armor that made it light enough for air transport as well as being moderately amphibious. Alcoa notes that "use of aluminum in this vehicle provides a number of advantages over the steel M-59 that it replaced: decreased weight, increased range and speed, fuel savings, and one diesel engine instead of two."[48] It became the most widely used armored vehicle during the Vietnam War, and a version is still made by BAE Systems.

Still widely used in the United States and other militaries around the world, the current program for developing a new Ground Combat Vehicle (GCV) infantry fighting vehicle is expected to replace existing armored personnel carriers by 2015 at the earliest.

Fourth, speed, range, and maneuverability are also capacities that aluminum lends to naval vessels. The Navy's destroyer-conversion program used "200,000 to 700,000 pounds of aluminum per ship" in order to "cut the weight of deckhouse structures by 40 to 50 percent"; whereas "great aircraft carriers, such as the atomic-powered *Enterprise,* use millions of pounds of aluminum." The Aluminum Association specifies that this vessel used 3.5 million pounds "primarily in the elevators that whisk combat aircraft quickly to her flight deck."[49] On a smaller scale, "lightning speed and easy maneuverability are designed into 50-foot, all-aluminum 'Swifty' patrol craft," says Alcoa—a ship many Americans know of today in relation to the "Swift Boat" ads that brought down John Kerry's presidential run in 2004. Alcoa also proudly notes that "firepower and speed are features of the U.S. Navy's PG (H)-1 Flagstaff, prototype hydrofoil patrol gunboat, which utilizes 43,600 pounds of Alcoa aluminum in its structural components."[50]

Another surprising use of aluminum during WWII was as a radar countermeasure in the form of "chaff." Britain's Royal Air Force first used this secret new device, code-named WINDOW, in its bombing of Hamburg in 1943. It consisted of bundles of over two thousand strips of coarse black paper with aluminum foil stuck on one side. Seven thousand bundles were dropped from a stream of 740 Lancaster and Halifax bombers and they were so highly successful in jamming Hamburg's defensive radar, that the entire warning system was blinded: Hamburg was infamously reduced to ashes, and only twelve British bombers were lost. A 1950 publication by Reynolds points out, furthermore, "that mapping jungles and other inaccessible terrain is being greatly facilitated by using aluminum foil streamers dropped from planes at key points," which would then be registered on radar equipment. "Truly, the possibilities of the magic metal, aluminum," they conclude, are just beginning to be explored. The future undoubtedly will reveal many more."[51]

Aluminum, as Jules Verne presciently foresaw, made possible the first human landing on the moon, which communicated the technological modernity of the United States, responding to the Soviet advances in this area. The USSR succeeded in launching the first man into space, the cosmonaut Yuri Gagarin, who orbited the earth on April 12, 1961, aboard the

Vostok 3KA-2. But the United States was not far behind, and prided itself on its lighter more-sophisticated rockets. NASA's famous Vehicle Assembly Building, built to house the moon-bound *Saturn V* rocket, was the world's largest building when completed in 1965, covering ten acres, enclosing 130 million cubic feet of space, and with double doors that are forty-five stories high. Its construction called for more than three million pounds of Alcoa aluminum. The *Saturn V* itself required "400,000 pounds of aluminum in its first stage [. . .] more in the form of 'Y' rings machined from 15,000-lb pieces of aluminum for the huge circles to which the skin and the end domes of the first stage" were attached, and "100,000 pounds of sheet and plate for the second stage."[52]

On July 20, 1969, the world watched Neil Armstrong and Buzz Aldrin step out of their aluminum landing craft onto the Sea of Tranquility, while the mother ship *Columbia* orbited the moon. With the achievement of low orbital and outer space technologies, aluminum truly came into its own. Aluminum has remained central to space exploration ever since its beginnings. The fuel used in the solid rocket boosters on the US space shuttles contained aluminum powder, the fuel pumps incorporated a highly cored aluminum sand casting, and the shuttles' external fuel tanks were made of an aluminum alloy. The problematic heat panels that faultily protected the exterior were made from a new kind of aluminum foam. In short, the shuttle would not exist without aluminum, which composed 90 percent of its materials.

Other crucial aerospace communication technologies also depend on aluminum. In 1962, the fifty-foot antenna of the American Telstar satellite, which used eighty thousand pounds of aluminum, beamed the first satellite television pictures back to a transmission station in Maine, ushering in the dawning of satellite telecommunications and new dreams of the gravity-defying lightness of the space age. Project Haystack, a radio telescope on a hill in Massachusetts, began operations for the Air Force in 1964 with "a fully steerable parabolic antenna 37 meters in diameter, enclosed in the world's largest space-frame radome," and was transferred to MIT in 1970. The reflector required "150,000 pounds of aluminum honeycomb sandwiched between aluminum sheets" and in all its construction required "350,000 pounds of aluminum," and was used to observe "topographical characteristics of the lunar surface [. . .] with emphasis on the proposed landing sites for the Apollo lander, and similar observations were made in support of the Viking lander on Mars."[53]

Meanwhile, far up in outer space, a ring of aluminum satellites and space debris circles the Earth like a metallic halo, though one that portends disaster due to collisions. With the shuttle returning to earth for the last time in July 2011, NASA turned to its next mission, the launch of the spacecraft *Juno* on a five-year-long journey to Jupiter. Juno is carrying "three aluminum Lego figures: of Galileo, Juno [wife of Jupiter] and Jupiter carrying his thunderbolts," further extending the reach of aluminum into interplanetary realms.[54] Few know that there is already an aluminum statuette on our moon, a three-inch figure called "Fallen Astronaut," made by Belgian artist Paul Van Hoeydonck, and placed on the Hadley-Appenine landing site (without NASA permission) by the crew of *Apollo 15* on August 1, 1971, alongside a plaque naming the eight American astronauts and six Soviet cosmonauts who had lost their lives in the space race.

The memorial reminds us of the losses that have accompanied our conquest of air and space, assisted by aluminum. Other artists are also working in outer space. At the end of 2012 artist Trevor Paglen launched his project "The Last Pictures" into geostationary orbit on a satellite called *Echostar XVI*. He "collaborated with researchers at MIT to devise an object that could theoretically withstand billions of years in space, settling on a gold-plated aluminum cannister carrying a small silicon wafer etched with the images," which include a hundred photographs representing "a sombre chronicle of modern human history," from nuclear mushroom clouds to Trotsky's brain.[55]

FUTURE MILITARY APPLICATIONS

Aluminum empowers humanity in diverse ways, but in many cases that power has been used for purposes of massive destruction, leaving behind trails of death and pollution. Speed and lightness are core elements of modern military power; as Paul Virilio puts it, "History progresses at the speed of its weapons systems."[56] Interstate competition to control energy sources, access to metals, and command of supply routes relies on having ever faster military capabilities in the form of lighter vehicles, accelerated weaponry, and the creation of smooth logistical space; this in turn depends on energy-intensive material cultures and metals-consuming infrastructures that reshape national economies and international relations. The contemporary political economy of global logistics depends on trans-territorial flows grounded in metals-mining and energy generation, often in remote parts of the world. The metals-energy complex feeds the military-industrial complex, which then controls world territory from which to extract further metals and energy.

Yet it is also understood within national military cultures that aluminum is a crucial material for protection of soldiers, and any state (or parent) sending its forces (or children) into war wants them protected to the best technological capability. Although the destructive forces unleashed by aluminum also take a more subtle form (displacement of remote populations, environmental pollution, health impacts), it is the strategic importance of aluminum as an enabler of military air power and aerospace technologies, alongside the added protection it affords to troops, that has ensured the continuing national protection of and investment in the industry, and thus ongoing research and development of new materials and applications. The aluminum-based technologies for waging aerial warfare in the twentieth century were not simply a background or underbelly of modernity, but were constitutive of fundamental power relations and representational practices that spanned art, design, technology, and shaped "the ground of everyday life."[57] Continuing research into new military applications today will also have civilian spinoffs and may potentially continue to lead to transformations of everyday life, especially in addressing the emergency situations arising from climate change, as Bucky Fuller prognosticated, such as more intense and frequent storms.

Today the US National Science Foundation supports the development of forged nanoparticle aluminum alloys for the automotive and defense industries, the market for which is expected to rise rapidly as new fuel efficiency standards are imposed in 2015. Aluminum still stands at the forefront of materials engineering research, especially new nanomaterials that will be used for military purposes. "Honeycomb nano-structures of aluminium oxide were one of the first fruits of nanotechnology," which was used to produce the fine aluminum powder solid rocket fuel used in the 1990s and used for example in the space shuttle.[58]

As already noted, the space shuttles also used aluminum-lithium alloys in their fuel tanks and aluminum spray foam in their heat shields, materials that are also finding wider applications today. The US Navy has been developing "tri-modal aluminum," which combines various ceramic and metallic materials to create a replacement for heavier steel armor on mine-resistant, ambush-protected combat vehicles and humvees, as used recently in Afghanistan.[59] Sapphire aluminum is also used as an extremely hard transparent material, replacing glass.

Companies such as Powdermet are working with "the U.S. Army and the National Science Foundation to develop micro-nanocomposite aluminum alloys that offer 30 to 50 percent higher ductility than today's state-of-the-art, high-strength aluminum alloys, such as aluminum lithium." There is also extensive research on aluminum oxynitride, commercially known as ALON, a transparent polycrystalline ceramic that is optically transparent, extremely hard (85 percent as hard as sapphire), and stable up to 1,200°C (2,190°F). Tests by the US Army Research Laboratory and the University of Dayton Research Institute in 2005 showed that it could withstand shots from a 0.50 caliber sniper's rifle with armor-piercing bullets.[60] Thus, if the costs can be brought down, it will have military applications in bulletproof and blastproof windshields for combat vehicles, possibly in infrared and radiation resistance technologies, and in body armor, being half the weight and thickness of existing body armor. Coatings of aluminum nanoparticles are also being applied to the aluminum alloys on aircraft to protect them from corrosion, and various new metal matrix composites are being developed for new applications.

Finally, we should remember that at the center of tense relations between the United States and Iran sits a shiny set of aluminum tubes, the spinning centrifuges that are used to purify uranium for Iran's nuclear reactors, and perhaps for its nuclear weapons one day. It became public knowledge in 2010 that these aluminum centrifuges were also at the forefront of secret cyberwarfare, having been the target of the Stuxnet worm that was specifically designed and launched to disrupt the operation of the centrifuges by making them spin so fast they would be broken.

As the *New York Times* first reported, and the US government eventually confirmed,

Overall, the attack destroyed nearly 1,000 of Iran's 6,000 centrifuges—fast-spinning machines that enrich uranium, an essential step toward building an atomic bomb. The National Security Agency developed the cyberweapon with [the] help of Israel.[61]

Iran was able to quickly replace the centrifuges, which were initially said to have come from "the black market" but were later linked to Pakistan's leading nuclear scientist A. Q. Khan, and continue with uranium enrichment, but it reminds us of the use of aluminum (as well as other advanced materials such as carbon fiber and maraging steels, which are used for parts inside the centrifuges) in just one more aspect of the intertwined complex of energy production, industrial manufacture, and nuclear bomb production.

Returning to some of the themes developed in chapter 2, these forms of warfare emerge in relation to metals cartel capitalism. In what Buckminster Fuller describes as "World War Gaming," states employ the most advanced, "most comprehensive and incisive, scientifically and technologically feasible capabilities to develop and mass-produce weaponry systems that will ever more swiftly devastate all enemy life-support artifacts and kill ever more enemy people at ever greater ranges in ever shorter periods of time."[62] Thus, there is a continuing investment in the technologies of lightness and speed, which Fuller referred to as "ephemeralization" and "acceleration," and in the accelerating temporalities of technological turnover and "ever-improving metal-alloy capabilities."[63]

Fuller proposes that all of these technologies that support military superiority might one day be turned to the protection and improvement of humanity by showing us how to do more with less, to conserve energy, and to use materials efficiently. There is an intriguing tension in the fact that aluminum has on the one hand so massively contributed to destructive weaponry, energy consumption, polluting industrialization, and the reign of cultures of acceleration, and on the other hand supports the very technologies and energy efficiencies that might save life on earth, being a key material for permitting energy savings because of its lightness, strength, and versatility.

In the following chapters we will consider how these temporalities of ephemeralization and acceleration of the arms race also affected the accelerating temporalities of civilian transportation and domestic life, and the associated ideologies of convenience, efficiency, and modernity that came to define the difference between the industrialized world and its counterparts in the Third World, where many of the raw materials for modernity were sourced. For Fuller the solution was not to give up on our most advanced technologies and metal alloys, but to turn them toward nonmilitary purposes.

In his World Game, which was played in the 1980s in the old gymnasium at Drexel University,[64] "the objective of the game would be to explore ways to make it possible for anybody and everybody in the human family to enjoy the total Earth without any human interfering with any other human and without any human gaining advantage at the expense of another." The World Game, Fuller proposed, would enable worldwide energy and resource accounting, instituted—crucially—in association with a "world-unifying electric power grid" (facilitated by a hemispheric connection between Russia and the USA), which he saw as the first step toward the "desovereignization" of territory. In the face of a global emergency, the world would unite to create a new energy culture based in a global power grid and a peaceful assemblage of "livingry systems."[65] The following chapters will bring us into the utopian hopes of the researchers, designers and dreamers who saw aluminum as the way towards the future.

4   SPEED METAL

For the day of lightness is here. The swan song of needless weight is being sung. Aluminum has become the *speed metal* of a new and faster age.

—ALCOA's fiftieth anniversary message, *Fortune*, 1936

Aluminum played a crucial part in creating our contemporary world both in the material sense of enabling all of the new technologies that we associate with mobile modernity and in the ideological sense of underwriting a world vision (and creative visualization) that privileges speed, lightness, and mobility.[1] The spread of an aluminum material culture from expensive military projects into everyday life occurred through a combination of new technologies, new aesthetics, and new practices of mobility.

Light metal is what set the twentieth century apart from past eras, and in many ways bequeaths to us today the distinctive look and feel of "late modern" material culture based on aeriality, speed, and lightness. In the early to mid-twentieth century the aluminum industry pioneered a modernist design aura around its products through an entire culture of cutting-edge design and advanced technological development. Stunningly eye-catching advertising campaigns promoted innovative design and helped to communicate modern style into everyday life, lending artistic and design cachet to an otherwise banal material.

Much like the promotion of Bakelite, an early kind of plastic invented by Leo Baekeland in 1907, aluminum producers had to move beyond the idea that it was an imitative substitute for other materials and toward its framing as an innovative new material associated with electricity, chemistry, and advanced metallurgy. Baekeland, argues Jeffrey Meikle, had to establish "plastic's novelty, its protean versatility, its unique ability to become whatever one wanted. Bakelite challenged inventors to discover its uses and taxed

Line cars purchased by the Port of New York Authority in 1965, and the wide use of aluminum by San Francisco's Bay Area Rapid Transit (BART) system and Chicago's Transit Authority, among others.[21]

Alcoa was also proud to note its extensive use in the building of the interstate highway system, where aluminum serves in bridges, median barriers, safe-impact sign-support systems, light poles, and so on. Thus, from a military necessity to a specialty design item, aluminum eventually became an everyday standby in the construction of twentieth-century infrastructure, where it continued to be associated with the vehicles and landscapes of speed, transit, and mobility.

Shining aerodynamic form came to influence the design of cars, buses, trains, trucks, and ships, but often the appeal was aesthetic or philosophical more than practical. R. Buckminster Fuller designed the all-aluminum Dymaxion house in the 1930s, the aluminum-bodied Dymaxion car in 1933, and eventually the geodesic dome, which achieved world fame as the centerpiece of the United States Information Agency's American National Exhibition in Moscow in 1959 (figure 4.2). The Dymaxion car was described by *Time* magazine in 1964 as "one of the most dramatic leaps forward in automotive design that have ever been made. In a pre-streamlined world, where the old-fashioned buggy's boxy look prevailed, Fuller's car was built like an airplane fuselage."[22] It was a front-wheel drive, three-wheeled vehicle in which the "steering wheel was connected to its single rear wheel, which enabled the car to run in circles around a man within a radius of a few feet or to drive straight into a parking space and swing in with only inches to spare. The body was aluminum, the chassis of chrome-molybdenum aircraft steel." Fuller's initial idea was part aircraft and part automobile, with wings that would inflate as the car lifted off the ground at higher speeds. Unfortunately, according to *Time*, one of the first prototypes was rammed by another car in Chicago that belonged to a city official, killing the driver. The offending car was quickly removed from the scene, and the Dymaxion car's reputation was tarnished. Even today it is described as a "three-wheel dream that died at take-off."[23] Fuller nevertheless became a very influential innovator in other areas involving aluminum designs for houses, bathrooms, and domes, as discussed further in chapter 5.

This vision of an aluminum-based aerodynamic modernism was further shaped by maverick inventors, designers, and dreamers. William Bushnell Stout, a pioneering aircraft designer whose 1936 aluminum-bodied Stout

FIGURE 4.2

R. Buckminster Fuller, *Time* magazine cover, by Boris Artzybasheff. Courtesy of Time/PARS International Corp.

Scarab was a minivan-like vehicle with a folding table and swivel seats (figure 4.3), had a motto: "Simplicate and add lightness."[24]

The streamline aesthetic was even more systematically advanced by designer Norman Bel Geddes, whose aluminum-bodied Motor Car Number 8 also sported a teardrop shape (figure 4.4). Bel Geddes's influential design book, *Horizons*[25] explained the principles behind aerodynamic streamlining and included his radical designs for motor cars and buses, aircraft and a floating air terminal, and houses and public buildings, all aimed at changing the future built environment to use energy and materials more efficiently. He was also the creator of the 1934 *Century of Progress* exhibition at the Chicago World's Fair, and the General Motors' *Futurama* exhibit at the 1939 New York World's Fair (with its "World of Tomorrow" theme), which brought viewers on a ride into a landscape of futuristic skyscrapers, seven-lane highways with automated driverless cars, and past a "Midwestern City of 1960" with modernist buildings, raised walkways and expressways, and surrounding natural landscapes.

The model included five hundred thousand miniature buildings, a million little trees, and paved highways over which sixteen thousand driverless cars and trucks zoomed on automated systems. His vision, which we have yet to achieve today, included a freeway with different lanes for going one hundred, seventy-five, and fifty miles per hour, which the car could be automatically set to and navigated by an electrical conductor while the driver relinquished control. Enabled in part by the fascination with light metal and electrical control systems, the idea of the driverless car remains a touchstone

FIGURE 4.3
William B. Stout's Stout Scarab (1936) from the January 1942 issue of *Popular Mechanics*.

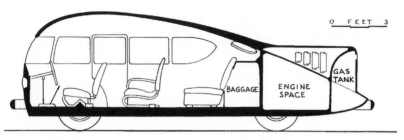

FIGURE 4.4
Norman Bel Geddes's "Motor Car Number 8" plan, from *Horizons*.

of the automobile industry and highway planning agencies today, and much of the technology is in place to make it happen.[26] We are still pursuing the aluminum dreams of the 1930s.

In the advertisements by the Bohn Corporation, we can see how lightness, strength, and speed were consciously injected into the US landscape. Bohn's early 1940s magazine ads offer a blueprint for futuristic transportation that was influential on vehicle designers. Saturated in rich colors, the images stand out from the surrounding magazine pages, catching the eye like comic book covers. Even the modern sans serif typography of the company name looks monumental, streamlined, and futuristic. In one ad, a metallic glass-fronted railcar pulls away from a city of modern skyscrapers: "Here's a railway observation car of the future, from which you may one day watch the wonders of the world of tomorrow unfold, as you spin by in this super-streamliner. And many things you see will likely be made of Bohn aluminum or magnesium. For these metals possess that matchless combination for the industrial world—strength with lightness" (see figure 4.5). Coming out of wartime shortages and intense industrial expansion for the war effort, these images hold out optimistic hope for a land of tomorrow, a future world of peace and progress.

Other futuristic designs feature a car, a trailer truck, and a boat of the future made of light alloys "designed, engineered and fabricated" by Bohn. The vehicles swoosh across the page on diagonal axes, inviting the viewer to travel into the future. They appear aerodynamic and light, making use of panoramic glass windows, and their curviness remains a feature in futuristic

FIGURE 4.5
Bohn Corporation ad: railway observation car (circa 1943).

prototypes even today. Even more fanciful departures from existing designs include oversized farm and industrial machinery that would transform not only the mobilities of people, but also of food production and freight transport, described as tomorrow's power shovel, a future cotton picker, a possible tractor of tomorrow, and a future tank truck. This series of ads suggests that Bohn design and engineering expertise might one day make possible groundbreaking conceptual designs such as future transoceanic "dream ships" that resemble the streamlined air ships and ocean liners designed by Norman Bel Geddes in the 1930s (figures 4.6, 4.7, 4.8, 4.9).[27]

Some of this Bohn series carries the signature of the well-known futurist graphic artist Arthur Radebaugh, who worked in Detroit where the company was also based. Radebaugh became especially known for his luminous

FIGURE 4.6
Bohn Corporation ad: tomorrow's power shovel (circa 1943).

FIGURE 4.7
Bohn Corporation ad: a future cotton picker (circa 1943).

airbrush illustrations of futuristic vehicles and cities, especially for *MOTOR Magazine* and the Detroit automobile industry, and he deeply influenced the streamline aesthetic and later science fiction illustrators. During World War II Radebaugh was enlisted into the Army Ordnance Department where he headed the Design and Visualization Division, working with other artists and designers (including Will Eisner, later of Disney fame) on developing

FIGURE 4.8
Bohn Corporation ad: possible tractor of tomorrow (circa 1943).

weapons of the future including armored cars, bazookas, artillery, and black light instrument panels.[28] He initially drew on Art Deco and the 1930s streamline style, which represented the aestheticization of speed and mobility: "Streamline's ideal formula is a formal compactness that lends static rigidity combined with a low weight and smooth, spherically shaped surfaces rendered in a bright, lightweight metal."[29] He was also inspired by Jules

FIGURE 4.9
Bohn Corporation ad: future tank truck (circa 1943).

Verne's science fiction, by German zeppelins, and by Norman Bel Geddes's designs. Radebaugh's designs not only invented new forms of urbanism and transport but were also widely suggestive of new modes of dwelling, working, traveling, and communicating.

Streamlined objects and futuristic ads demonstrate how aluminum's lightness, strength, and speed served as a blueprint for futuristic transportation and thereby came to influence vehicle designs that still resonate in the design of new vehicles today. From 1957 to 1962 Radebaugh worked on a syndicated comic series called "Closer Than We Think" (published nationally in newspapers with up to nineteen million readers), which depicted life in the future with all of its wondrous technologies such as mining on the moon, weather control satellites, electronic robot kitchens, and rocket mailmen. He traveled around the country in a mobile studio (a converted English Ford van) with "quasi-futuristic accessories," confirming his reputation as an "eccentric avatar of the future."[30] Radebaugh's "imagineering" depicted a futuristic world of human conveyor belts, glass-domed futuramas, elevated expressways, amphibious cars, and moveable sidewalks. His fantastical images of soaring metropolises with high-speed levitating trains, personal helicopters, zeppelin mooring masts, and so on drew heavily on the capacities of aluminum to make possible a new lightweight and malleable architecture of the future.

After the war Bohn Aluminum and Brass Corporation offered its services in design and technical advice on incorporating aluminum alloys into production processes, trying to kick-start a takeoff in new uses. A 1944 Bohn ad depicting an engine notes that new technologies would be spinoffs from military research and development:

Mechanized warfare has had a tremendous effect on the development of internal combustion engines. The lessons now being learned will appear in concrete form in the motor car engines in the after-the-war era. One thing that is definitely sure is that new engine designs will furnish greatly increased horsepower per pound of engine weight. Engines will be smaller and by the greater use of aluminum alloys will be considerably lighter.[31]

Another group of Bohn ads is signed by George W. Walker, an industrial designer who worked in Detroit where he is credited with the design of the 1949 Ford, the 1950 Lincoln, the 1951 Mercury, the 1952 Ford, and the 1955 Thunderbird. For Bohn, Walker depicts a futuristic city with a kind of levitating monorail train and multilevel expressways snaking through a forest of tall modernist buildings: "Today America's manufacturing processes are concentrated solidly on war materials for Victory. From this gigantic effort will spring many new developments of vast economic consequence to the entire universe. The City of the Future will be born—startling new architectural designs will be an everyday occurrence!"[32] (see figure 4.10).

Today America's manufacturing processes are concentrated solidly on war materials for Victory. From this gigantic effort will spring many new developments of vast economic consequence to the entire universe. The City of the Future will be born—startling new architectural designs will be an every day occurrence! New alloys—new materials—new applications—designs engineered by Bohn will be an important contributing factor in making possible a world of new products. Remember the name Bohn. Our advanced knowledge will be most helpful to many manufacturers in redesigning their products of tomorrow.

BOHN

BOHN ALUMINUM AND BRASS CORPORATION, DETROIT, MICHIGAN
GENERAL OFFICES—LAFAYETTE BUILDING
Designers and Fabricators—ALUMINUM • MAGNESIUM • BRASS • AIRCRAFT-TYPE BEARINGS

FIGURE 4.10
Bohn Corporation ad: "Forecasting by Bohn" (circa 1945).

Ironically, though, the very cars that Walker designed for the 1950s market did not convey the light, streamlined aesthetic of modernism, nor would the US city of the future have much room for trains. Instead post-WWII automobile designs were heavy and overblown, what Ford called a "living room on wheels," and US car culture would lead to massive highway construction rather than levitating trains. Aluminum struggled to enter the consumer market, appearing more in lightweight consumer goods and in hidden infrastructure than in car bodies. Yet we are still in thrall to the aerodynamic streamlined shapes of the aluminum designers and imagineers. They continue to resonate as harbingers of a technologically enhanced future, when travel will be frictionless, smooth, and fast.

During the Korean War, too, industrial designers dreamed up vehicles of the future that would be made of aluminum. In a 1951 edition of the popular magazine *Science and Mechanics,* Dean Hammond, vice president in charge of engineering at Kaiser-Frazer Corporation, describes the future: "Lightweight cars with all-aluminum bodies, which will use glass extensively to provide the motorist with more visibility [. . .] More efficient engines, weighing half as much as today's, built of aluminum, titanium and magnesium alloys, with new combustion chamber designs aimed at reducing the amount of gasoline wasted through incomplete burning."[33] Sixty years later, the automotive industry has only just started introducing such features. Yet the cover image speaks to the futuristic imaginary of aluminum that has gripped popular culture at times, influencing the depiction of future material culture in comic books and TV shows, even as disappointments in its capabilities and failures of particular technologies have burst its bubble in other periods.

Radebaugh's designs for Bohn are reminiscent of one other real vehicle of this period: the Airstream trailer. Pilot and inventor William Hawley Bowlus, who supervised the construction of Charles Lindbergh's *Spirit of Saint Louis* in 1927, designed the record-breaking Albatross sailplane in 1932. When he became interested in designing travel trailers in the early 1930s, the Bowlus travel-trailer company pioneered the use of Duraluminum in trailer design. Thus there was a direct link among an inventor who experimented in the design of airplanes, the creation of aerodynamic road vehicles, and the creators of new road vehicles (including R. Buckminster Fuller), who often turned to the airplane-building industry for the expertise in and facilities for working with aluminum materials. Travel trailers, pulled behind cars, transferred the materials, feel, and aerodynamic form of airplanes back down to ground-based transportation vehicles. When salesman Wally Byam purchased the Bowlus travel-trailer company in a bankruptcy auction in 1936, its light egg-shaped vehicles became the basis for Airstream Inc. Byam was described as "a man in motion, a mover of people and things," who led groups of Airstreams on caravan trips around the world and founded the Wally Byam Caravan Club International in 1955.[34] The doughty caravans rallied across Europe, Africa, the Middle East, Asia, and Central and South

America, going literally to all ends of the earth in a global celebration of travel, adventure, and US technology. They turned even the roughest road into a streamlined home-away-from-home while serving as global ambassadors for US modernity. The Airstream mobile home was not just a vehicle, but became a way of life (figure 4.11), a practice of mobile living and world travel, and a promotional ideology for a new light modernism.

In 1956 Wally Byam brought his caravan of Airstream travelers to Cuba, where they were escorted by a motorcade through the streets of Havana to meet with President Fulgencio Batista. "Armed soldiers lined the roofs as Batista stepped into Wally's shining zeppelin to admire an aerodynamic example of atomic-age comfort, aptly named because it rode along the highway like a stream of air."[35] Byam met Batista at the crossroads of two alternative modernities: US modernity epitomized by the gleaming Airstream travel trailer versus an alternative Caribbean modernity, here epitomized by the US-backed dictator about to be deposed by a social revolution led by Fidel Castro in 1959. The juxtaposition of the Airstream against tropical jungles and banana republics reinforced a geography of distinction that promised to bring modern technology to "developing" countries, a theme I return to in chapter 6.

FIGURE 4.11
Wally Byam, with Airstream trailer, at Airstream, Inc., California (1950s). Courtesy of Airstream, Inc.

The Airstream epitomizes the aesthetic appeal of aluminum, beckoning to us even today through its "semiotic handle,"[36] which is to say it is its look and feel that catches our attention and desire through what it signifies as much as what is does. The Airstream suggests mobility, lightness, aerodynamic speed, durability, and with these qualities implies US values such as the freedom of the road, liberation from a fixed abode, casual easy living, and maybe even the innocent optimism of modern technology. It feeds into the US national characteristic that James Jasper describes as "restlessness," arguing that "the story of America is a story about movement."[37] The airstream also has a sensually pleasing form that seems to marry what Jasper describes as a male pursuit of escape "on the road" (like Jack Kerouac's book of that title) with a somewhat more feminine pursuit of domesticity, at least in 1950s gender stereotypes. It allows for the dynamic domesticity of the mobile home, which in itself became a symbol of US road culture and US ideals.

VELOCITY, LUMINOSITY, AND ARCHITECTURE

Buildings can also express a kind of speed. Skyscrapers as we know them would not have been possible without aluminum. Architectural anodized aluminum was first used on a large scale in the spandrels of the Empire State Building, built in 1935 as the then-tallest building in the world. It was also used for the mast at the top, which was originally designed as a mooring for air ships, which were themselves braced with aluminum support structures. This architectural wonder was extolled for the speed with which it was erected, with a stream of materials being delivered with precision timing. "At one point the 'velocity' of this automatic architecture reaches 14½ stories in ten days," writes Rem Koolhaas in his homage to the building, "Empire State seemed almost to float, like an enchanted fairy tower, over New York. An edifice so lofty, so serene, so marvelously simple, so luminously beautiful, had never before been imagined."[38] Velocity and luminosity would become the hallmarks of the emerging new architecture using aluminum. In 1943 the Bohn Aluminum and Brass Corporation's promotions of futuristic designs included "factories of tomorrow [that] will utilize to full advantage the new lighting-technique—the advancements in air conditioning, ventilation and design" through the light metals aluminum and magnesium (see figure 4.12); another envisions that "a tent of aluminum is more than a possibility for the future" (see figure 4.13). By the 1920s to 1930s,

FIGURE 4.12
Bohn Corporation ad: "Factories you might see!" (1943).

aluminum did make it into many uses in farm buildings and industrial plants, as well as in experimental domestic designs as discussed in chapter 5; however, apart from some exterior features such as the spandrels of the Empire State Building, it was not until the 1950s that new processes were developed to actually make aluminum a practical material for major components of advanced urban architecture. There was more hype surrounding aluminum than actual building with it for the first half of the twentieth century, but it finally began to meet some of its promised capabilities by the 1960s.

Combined with structural steel and glass curtain walls, the light metal enabled the largest man-made structures to rise with new speed and lightness. Aluminum instigated the emergence of modernism as an architectural style not only because it allowed for the streamlining of building forms by the removal of heavy support structures and the incorporation of more glass into external walls but also because its machine-age surfaces matched the desire for a lighter, airier, modern kind of styling. Aesthetically it became the material of the moment for the new urbanism of the twentieth century, or as architect Walter Gropius called it, "the material of the future."[39]

The true demonstration of the potentials of architectural use of aluminum came in 1952 to 1953 when Alcoa completed a new company headquarters in Pittsburgh (see figure 4.14). The thirty-one-story Alcoa Building was the first multistory building to employ aluminum curtain walls. Sheathing these walls progressed at the then-remarkable speed of one floor a day. The building also demonstrated how thin self-supporting inner walls could increase usable floor space (bringing greater returns on investment). Other features included aluminum ceiling systems of radiant heat and cooling, which also added more floor space; pivoting aluminum windows that could be cleaned from inside; an all-aluminum electrical system; and aluminum plumbing on a scale never before attempted.[40]

As Stuart Leslie argues, the 1953 Alcoa Building exemplifies "'architecture parlante,' literally buildings that speak of their function and meaning." Corporations such as Alcoa "intended their signature buildings as larger than life advertisements for their signature products . . . creating a distinctly modern image" as part of an extreme corporate makeover.[41] The company proudly advertised its achievements:

Efficiency through light weight was the purpose of its builders . . . and innovation their method. Outside walls of 6 × 12 foot aluminum panels were simply hung like curtains from within—no scaffolding was required. Aluminum windows pivot on a vertical axis for safe and easy inside cleaning. A year-round aluminum radiant heating and cooling system in the ceiling is paneled with aluminum. Wiring, conduit, water tanks, ducts, elevators—are aluminum too. *Light-walled,* this building used hundreds of tons less structural steel framing than a conventional building of the same size . . . *Thin-walled,* it yields thousands of feet of extra floor space. It will require no painting—and virtually no maintenance.[42]

FIGURE 4.13
Bohn Corporation ad: "A tent of aluminum?" (1943).

The use of prefabricated aluminum panels had the potential to transform the building industry, but so too did the kinds of design and styling associated with the new metal. Architect I. M. Pei was hired to design all of Alcoa's New York corporate properties in high modernist style and he "looked forward to a day when aluminum would be permitted to do 'a total functional job in the construction of a building.'"[43]

FIGURE 4.14
Alcoa Aluminum ad, *Saturday Evening Post:* "31 Stories of Aluminum Make News"
(1953).

A 1958 article, "Alcoa's New Look for Architecture," extols the arrival
of the "youngster of the metal family" as a "primary material" for building construction. Noting that aluminum had been used for "windows and
doors, trim and ornamentation, and even electrical distribution systems," the
1953 Alcoa building was seen as "proof of its practicality" as a replacement

for conventional walls: "This achievement firmly established aluminum as a primary building material. Now the architect and builder could utilize the metal fully in curtain wall construction." And just five years later "several hundred aluminum-sheathed buildings have been completed and even more on the planning boards. From New York to Los Angeles, from Minneapolis to New Orleans," the article shows photographs of, among others, the Fairview Park Hospital in Cleveland; the Heinz Vinegar Building in Pittsburgh; the American Association for the Advancement of Science Building, in Washington, DC (with "mobile louvers" that were "timed electronically to follow the sun throughout the day"); the Civic Center in Charlotte, North Carolina, with "the largest domed roof of its kind ever constructed"; the Prudential Insurance Building in Houston; and the Pennsylvania State Office Building in Pittsburgh. Aluminum building made great strides in this period. The article even notes that a "40-man crew made history in New York by erecting the 676 aluminum panels on the 22-story office building at 460 Park Avenue in a record nine and one-half hours!" Thus aluminum is described as quick to build with, giving maximum floor space by creating especially thin walls, providing efficient insulation, and low maintenance requirements, all of which provide financial savings.

By tracing the infiltration of this metal into the material cultures of modernity we can uncover a layer of modern artifacts that expressed a certain moment in human existence, and also expressed that period's hopes for the future of humanity. But it took a great deal of advertising and promotion to bring about these kinds of associations. In 1952 Alcoa hired the advertising agency Ketchum, Macleod, and Grove, who produced a marketing campaign that they called *FORECAST*. They announced that the campaign's "principal objective is not to increase the amount of aluminum used today for specific applications, but to inspire and stimulate the mind of men."[44] They devised a multifaceted marketing campaign with weekly magazine advertisements, the publication of a periodical called *Design Forecast,* and the creation of a new kind of showroom. Most important, they commissioned twenty-two well-known designers to create products using Alcoa aluminum. The practice of forecasting and scenario building employed in this advertising campaign built on the practices of the RAND Corporation, a major player in research and development for the military-industrial complex.

Airplanes, rockets, satellites, and new architectural forms served not just as applications of aluminum but also as advertisements and exemplars of the achievements of modernity and the benefits that modernization would bring to the entire world. As the Victoria and Albert Museum's 2008 exhibition *Cold War Modern: Design 1945–1970* amply demonstrated,

Not only signs of military strength and power, but also glittering products, high-tech electronics, skyscrapers and their images were deployed by each side to demonstrate its superior command of modernity. By planting a flag on the Moon, by construct-ing the world's tallest building or quite simply by ensuring the supply of shining white refrigerators for ordinary homes, the superpowers sought to demonstrate the pre-eminence of their science, their industry, their organization and their design.[45]

When the Soviet Union launched its first *Sputnik* satellite in October 1957, the shining aluminum orb that was the first man-made object to orbit the earth captured people's imaginations around the world.

The United States and the Soviet Union entered into a "space race" as they competed to launch the first rockets, satellites, and humans into outer space. The USSR capitalized on its success by exhibiting *Sputnik* prototypes around the world. It inspired many designers to embrace sleek curvilinear shapes, fashioned out of aluminum, plastic, fiberglass, and other space-age materials. Chairs became spaceship pods, radios and televisions looked like spy equipment, and domestic objects went high-tech, with automated push-button operation echoing the technologies of the Cold War.

At the American National Exhibition held in Moscow in 1959, during the USSR's post-Stalin thaw period, US vice president Richard Nixon and Soviet premier Nikita Khrushchev held a famous discussion of the merits of US consumer culture while standing in front of a model US kitchen dis-play. Arguing over the relative achievements of their political and economic systems while contemplating the Frigidaire refrigerators, General Electric dishwashers, and automatic mixers, Nixon asked Khrushchev, "Would it not be better to compete in the relative merits of washing machines than in the strength of rockets? Is this the kind of competition you want?"[46]

During the Cold War a battle was waged not just with atomic weaponry and missiles (made of aluminum), but also with kitchenware and consumer goods (many also made of aluminum). Aluminum, in other words, was the weapon of choice whether in a war of bombing and destruction or a war of winning hearts and minds in "the kitchen wars," and it is no coincidence that we can find echoes of similar shapes and surfaces in the artifacts pro-duced in each kind of war.

Aluminum stands at every frontier where humankind has pushed the limits of our material existence to the extreme. Wherever we have challenged the constraints of gravity, of heat, of size, and of human survival in the most adverse conditions, aluminum has been there. In the midst of this space race, in 1965 Alcoa launched the "FORECAST jet," a kind of "flying showcase" that displayed the company's products and services. Described as "an aeronautical ambassador of aluminum," the DC-7CF was flown by a three-man crew and could be expanded on the ground into a "blue-vinyl-carpeted" reception area formed by "a semi-circular screen of aluminum beads," with aluminum spiral stairs rising up to an interior conference lounge furnished with woven-aluminum panels, aluminum-fabric upholstery, aluminum sand-casted lighting fixtures, and artworks in aluminum.[47] The jet "functioned both as a sign and signifier of its product as well as a metaphor for the new postwar corporation," argues Brennan; the "corporate jet—the ultimate symbol of corporate achievement—referenced the heyday of Alcoa's production of military aircraft during the war. Here the aluminum airplane—*the* war machine of World War II—transformed into a sleek communication machine in the Cold War marketplace."[48]

By 1972 "Alcoa aluminum had been used to sheath such architectural landmarks as the Vehicle Assembly Building at Cape Canaveral [1965, housing the *Saturn V* rocket that first took men to the moon], Pittsburgh's Hilton Hotel [faced in a new anodized color known as Hilton Gold], Chicago's John Hancock Center [1969, with more than 2,500,000 pounds of aluminum], and the World Trade Center in New York [1971],"[49] where it was joined by the Time-Life Building in Rockefeller Center, the Chase Manhattan Building, and structures in the Lincoln Center.[50] In other words, it was used on some of the biggest buildings in the world, built for the most powerful organizations and corporations, achieving iconic status at the heart of the global metropolis.

In chapter 9 I highlight some of the contemporary architects who are using aluminum today, for it has had a renaissance as a supposedly "green" material that can assist in energy savings and building efficiency. In some ways the early dreams of the Alcoa corporation's product research and marketing teams are finally being realized, because aluminum and its new alloys continue to be central to the architecture of the future, both on earth and in outer space. But it was in the domestic realm that it especially left its trace, and in chapter 5 we turn to the ways in which aluminum mobilized the home.

Airstreams and air power continue to serve as important "communication machines" to convey US influence globally. In a funny late-modern twist on the common appeal of the all-American Airstream trailer, Vice President Joe Biden is reported to travel in an Airstream, but this one is immobilized inside a cargo plane:

a C-17, retrofitted for vice-presidential comfort with an Airstream trailer bolted on to tracks in the center of the hold. With its porthole and shiny rivets and gleaming chrome, this strange conveyance looks like something out of Jules Verne. Captain Biden holds court in a wood-paneled galley just large enough for his half-dozen or so aides to pile into.[51]

The Airstream has finally taken to the air, streaming a new kind of global diplomacy to the world at large, with the aluminum capsule of US road culture now safely ensconced inside an aluminum capsule of US air power.

When I speak of mobile dwellings, I do not refer to camping trailers or tents, I speak of the dwellings which will stay geographically fixed for many months or years but which are readily and economically transportable and reinstallable over wide ranges of distance.

—Buckminster Fuller, *Critical Path*

In his 1934 magnum opus *Technics and Civilization,* historian and philosopher of technology Lewis Mumford argued that human history moved through phases organized around different primary materials and forms of energy consumption. In what he called the *eotechnic era,* which had prevailed for millennia, the primary materials were wood and stone, fashioned into technologies using muscle, wind, and water power. In the late eighteenth century we entered the paleotechnic era, when materials such as iron and steel came to the fore, and humanity began to draw energy from coal-powered steam engines that depended on huge extractive mining industries and industrial clock time. But the move from natural and organic materials to cold, hard metals had alienated us from the earth.

With the dawn of the twentieth century, however, he detected a move toward a neotechnic era, in which strong, lightweight alloys of aluminum along with clean, limitless hydroelectric power would restore a harmonic balance between humans and the material world.[1] For Mumford, as Jeffrey Meikle summarizes, "the dominant materials of a particular technological era exerted influence over the mood or tone of everyday life" so that today we live among materials that are "engineered, highly refined, often synthesized, doing ever more with ever less as they replaced a dark, ponderous environment with lightweight, artificially colored structures and machines."[2]

Although there still exist remnants, echoes, and revivals of the technics of previous civilizations, the predominant mood and feel of the neotechnic era is shaped by the speed and lightness of aluminum and synthetics, now joined by plastics, fiber-optic cables, silicon chips, and information superhighways. Yet Mumford's vision of a restored harmony seems a long way off. What went wrong with the neotechnic era?

When a new material like aluminum enters into a system of interrelated objects and social practices (what anthropologists describe as a *material culture*), it first appeals to the dreamers and inventors, the innovators and designers who take up this novelty to try to figure out what to do with it. "Each innovation contributes not only to instituting a particular product," argues sociologist Harvey Molotch, "but also to the regime of interrelated objects and social practices within which the product is embedded."[3]

The artifacts that make up our material culture join larger assemblages of stuff that flow over our world in waves of style, shaping the feel or atmosphere of a time and place. In this chapter I try to follow aluminum into the domestic realm where, on the one hand, inventors used it to rethink and remake homes into more mobile assemblages and, on the other hand, it became embedded into an existing matrix of interrelated objects and social practices—especially those associated with suburban life.

Sometimes the companies that make a new material also fund research, development, invention, and design to generate new uses for and applications of their product. And they use advertising to vociferously promote their products. In the post-WWII period a burgeoning middle-class consumer culture embraced the vehicles, the electric infrastructure, and the aluminum household appliances that extended the "American Dream" of suburban living to more and more people (especially white families assisted by the Federal Housing Administration and the GI Bill). Aluminum was a key part of this wider shift in US material culture, and became embedded into everyday life as infrastructure, as vehicles, and as designed objects that contributed to the aesthetics of speed and lightness.

It also played a special role in the futuristic scenarios of science fiction and creative product development that continue to influence our vision of the future today. In reading the visual images and cultural discourses surrounding the dream of aluminum on the home front we can better understand how a military industrial technology was incorporated into domestic life and interior spaces, as well as public life and public space.

In addition to aluminum's potential to accelerate transport and lighten skyscrapers, as explored in chapter 4, it was also embraced closer to home where it afforded other kinds of mobility. As early as 1909 the feminist writer Charlotte Perkins Gilman was incorporating aluminum into the future domestic technologies envisioned in her serial novel *What Diantha Did*. Gilman imagines a world in which women will be freed from domestic drudgery through the collective provisioning of ready-cooked meals delivered by a specially built futuristic vehicle. The characters marvel at a large food container purchased in Paris for use in a food-delivery service:

They lifted it in amazement—it was so light.
   "Aluminum," she said proudly. "Silver-plated—new process! And bamboo at the corners you see. All lined and interlined with asbestos, rubber fittings for silverware, plate racks, food compartments—see?"
   She pulled out drawers, opened little doors, and rapidly laid out a table service for five . . .
   "What lovely dishes," said Diantha.
   "You can't break them, I tell you," said the cheerful visitor, "and dents can be smoothed out at any tin shop."[4]

Aluminum would enable women's emancipation from the ongoing dilemma of gender inequality in the distribution of housework. A precursor to Simone de Beauvoir and Betty Friedan, Gilman recognized that women's liberation required a revolution in domestic arrangements. She gives us a glimpse of the potential for new materials to modernize not just the physical world of things but also the social world of gender relations, not just outer space but also inner space.

The new metal would indeed play a central part in the "grand domestic revolution," but as social historian Dolores Hayden shows, it was not to be the radical revolution sought by feminists and other promoters of collective housing. Instead of shared kitchens, food-delivery services, and communal nurseries, modernity would foster the individualized, privatized suburban dwelling in which wives were isolated from public life and men drove automobiles to distant workplaces. The rise of the food packaging industry as well as domestic appliances such as freezers were crucial to this process, which had deep effects on the scheduling of daily life.

Packaged foods, freezers, and later microwaves "allowed the competent housewife to order her daily routine; to cook at her convenience; to plan

THE SATURDAY EVENING POST   July 30, 1955

If it must resist rust...

This is progressive rusting—the result of oxidization of iron and steel in the presence of moisture. If not checked by painting or other costly protective measures, this rusting can completely destroy the metal.

This prevents rusting! The thin, tough film of aluminum oxide which forms naturally on aluminum protects against corrosive attack. Even if damaged, this film immediately re-forms—assuring long, trouble-free life.

THE SATURDAY EVENING POST

Money-saver! Kaiser Aluminum Roofing saves money because it won't rust, lasts for years. So light, one man can do the job. And aluminum reflects sun's rays, keeps interiors up to 15° cooler.

"Neither snow nor rain" will ever rust this rural mailbox—because it's made with Kaiser Aluminum! And this modern metal is as strong and durable as it is good looking.

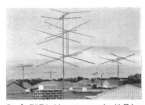

Tops for TV! Television antennas made with Kaiser Aluminum not only resist rust, they're also light, strong, easy to install. And aluminum conducts radio waves better than steel.

Long life insurance! Ever see a license plate falling apart from rust? Can't happen if the plate, frame and fasteners are made of Kaiser Aluminum! Light weight means metal goes farther, cuts costs.

Bright idea! Aluminum lighting standards and reflectors stay bright because they resist corrosion even in salt atmosphere! Reflectors greatly increase lamp brilliance due to aluminum's reflectivity.

Forget the rain! With outdoor furniture made of Kaiser Aluminum, you don't have to worry about rust. And it's light, easy to move, will keep its beauty through years of constant usage.

Beautiful protection! Chain link fences made with Kaiser Aluminum keep their good looks even when in contact with most corrosive industrial fumes. They're light, easy to install.

Handsome and rugged! Kaiser Aluminum is ideal as decorative trim for autos. Its modern beauty won't ever be defaced by rust. And its durability resists scuffing and banging.

Simple change—big benefit! A simple change to Kaiser Aluminum results in railroad and highway signs that are rustproof and strong, give years of extra service. Plus greatly increased brilliance!

think of *Kaiser Aluminum*

NEXT TIME you buy a product made of aluminum, touch your hand to its beautiful surface—and congratulate yourself.

For in aluminum you've chosen a metal that throughout its long, long life will never be marred by rust.

And think of aluminum's other advantages! It's light and strong. It conducts heat and electricity. It reflects light. It's economical. These advantages, and many others, are COMBINED in aluminum.

This *versatility* explains why aluminum is taking over in almost any field you can mention—building, transportation, appliances, packaging, electrical transmission—making better products at lower cost.

Today, more and more manufacturers think of Kaiser Aluminum —the fastest growing of the major aluminum producers—for unsurpassed customer service.

We now have the capacity to produce close to 30% of all the primary aluminum made in this country . . . and we are continuing to expand. For we believe that the future opportunities for this lightweight giant of metals are almost unlimited.

We are dedicated to the job of working with manufacturers to help realize this brighter future through aluminum. Kaiser Aluminum & Chemical Corporation, 191 Kaiser Building, Oakland 12, California.

FOR AN EXCITING PEEK INTO YOUR FUTURE WITH ALUMINUM—VISIT OUR EXHIBIT AT DISNEYLAND NEAR LOS ANGELES!

FIGURE 5.1

"If it must resist rust . . . think of Kaiser Aluminum," *Saturday Evening Post* (July 1955).

Only 2 aluminum lightweights can take on 5 heavyweights!

Emeco's amazing heat-treatment makes these aluminum chairs **tougher than steel!**

It's the perfect way to make the perfect chair:

Make it of workable aluminum, to form without distortion in the bends.

Then **heat treat** it to incredible strength, toughness, rigidity. So it can support nearly a ton — 1700 pounds — with less than ⅛-in. permanent distortion. So just **one** chair could support those wrestlers — **and a couple of their biggest friends!**

And anodize the surface into aluminum oxide, next to diamonds in hardness.

Result: the perfect chair (available in 7 models) . . . fantastically strong, corrosion-resistant, wipeable clean, light on its feet. **Far and away the lowest in cost,** when you measure service and length of life.

Send for a sample of aluminum "before" and "after". It supports our story as surely as it takes on the heavyweights.

7110-264-5339

EMECO DIVISION
Standard Furniture Company
Hanover, Pa. 17331

AVAILABLE AS GSA STOCK ITEM
FEDERAL STOCK NO. 7110-264-5339

Telephone E. F. Quinn, Government Administrator — (717) 637-5951

FIGURE 5.2
Emeco heavyweight chair ad. Courtesy of the Emeco Company.

By mid-century the hopes for a technological transformation were heavily promoted in popular magazines and advertising. Seemingly ubiquitous, aluminum underwrites the mobility and modernity of the 1950s, and locks it into material cultures in myriad forms. Alcoa Aluminum reveled in the sheer excess of aluminum applications in its advertising. A two-page Christmas spread in the *Saturday Evening Post* features, among other things, cookware, outboard motors, toys, irons, golf carts, outdoor folding chairs, cameras and tripods, snow shovels, tools, fishing tackle, vacuum bottles, a portable oven, flashlights, ladders, and grills, all made of "light, lasting, lustrous Alcoa aluminum" (figure 5.3).

An advertising series by the Kaiser Aluminum company also features many of the new products coming into general use in the mid-1950s, including roofing, rust-free mailboxes, television antennas, license plate frames and fasteners, outdoor lighting standards and reflectors, outdoor furniture, chain link fences, decorative trim on automobiles, and railroad and highway signs. Here it appears as an enabler of the modern transport system, the postal system, and other systems for the organization of space and communication. Another ad in this series emphasizes the heat conductivity and reflectivity of aluminum, featuring a barn, foil wall insulation, chicken brooders, heaters, window shades, truck bodies, shingle roofing, aluminum foil, oil storage tanks, and vacuum jugs. Another emphasizes corrosion resistance featuring a water canteen, shiny tumblers and ice buckets, irrigation pipes for crops, bridge railings, greenhouse frames, playground equipment, marquees, and storefronts. This ad notes,

When you buy a product made of aluminum, you're probably attracted by its lightness and its gleaming, almost delicate beauty. But never forget this. Aluminum also combines strength with high resistance to corrosion—thus it will last for generations. And long life is only part of the aluminum story. It reflects heat and light. It conducts electricity. It's workable and economical. In fact, aluminum combines more useful properties than any other metal. This versatility explains why aluminum is taking over in so many fields—such as building, transportation, appliances, packaging, electrical transmission—making better products at lower cost.[14]

Economy, versatility, and longevity make aluminum attractive to both producers and consumers. It flows through markets in multiplying forms, colonizing one object after another.

Sports equipment was another unexpected beneficiary of aluminum designs. By the 1970s new stronger aluminum alloys became associated with

THE SATURDAY EVENING POST

CHRISTMAS CREATIONS

OF LIGHT, LASTING, LUSTROUS

ALCOA ALUMINUM

IT'S MEALTIME MAGIC the way cookware of Alcoa Aluminum heats quickly, evenly on bottoms, sides and lids. Food-friendly aluminum cleans easily, stays attractive.

MORE POWER PER POUND from outboard motors made of Alcoa Aluminum! Aluminum outboards stay new looking with little maintenance. A perfect companion for an aluminum boat.

WHAT LITTLE GIRL wouldn't love this tea set? What little boy doesn't want a real gas engine and plane? Alcoa Aluminum makes all toys last longer, look better, more fun to play with.

COOK AT THE TABLE is the news this season with handsome electric frying pans and deep fat cookers of light, bright Alcoa Aluminum. They clean in a jiffy.

HEAT NOT WEIGHT does the ironing when electric irons are made of Alcoa Aluminum. Aluminum soleplates heat faster. Steam won't mar their bright finish. Easy to carry!

GIFTWARE of Alcoa Aluminum gaily reflects the holiday season in hammered or rich satin finish. Never cracks, peels or tarnishes. Available in rainbow colors.

EASY ROLLING golf carts of Alcoa Aluminum trail effortlessly after you. Stay smart looking in spite of weather and hard use. Stow quickly, handle easily.

STRONG, COMFORTABLE AND PRACTICAL, outdoor furniture of Alcoa Aluminum is easy to move, easy to clean. Does double duty in game room in wintertime, provides extra seating for parties.

FINE CAMERAS AND ACCESSORIES gain precision and smart looks from Alcoa Aluminum. Their lightness makes them fun to use. Their corrosion resistance makes them easy to care for.

December 3, 1955

THESE FINE STORES ARE SHOWING CHRISTMAS CREATIONS OF ALUMINUM

See "Alcoa Day on
NBC Television,"
Tuesday, December 6.

Akron, Ohio: The M. O'Neil Company	**Chicago, Ill.:** The Fair	**Knoxville, Tenn.:** Rich's, Inc.	**Providence, R.I.:** The Outlet Company
Albany, N.Y.: W. M. Whitney & Co.	**Cincinnati, Ohio:** Pickering Hardware Co.	**Los Angeles, Calif.:** The Broadway, So. Calif.	**Richmond, Va.:** Miller and Rhoads
Allentown, Pa.: Hess Brothers	**Cleveland, Ohio:** The Higbee Company	**Louisville, Ky.:** J. Bacon & Sons	**Rochester, N.Y.:** McCurdy & Company
Atlanta, Ga.: Rich's, Inc.	**Columbus, Ohio:** Moore's Stores	**Memphis, Tenn.:** Goldsmith's	**St. Louis, Mo.:** Stix, Baer, & Fuller
Baltimore, Md.: The Hecht Co.	**Dallas, Tex.:** Titche-Goettinger	**Miami, Fla.:** Burdine's	**Salem, Oreg.:** Meier and Frank Company
Birmingham, Ala.: Loveman's	**Davenport, Iowa:** M. L. Parker Company	**Milwaukee, Wis.:** Gimbels	**San Antonio, Tex.:** Joske's of Texas
Boston, Mass.: R. H. White's	**Dayton, Ohio:** The Rike Kumler Company	**Minneapolis, Minn.:** Donaldson's	**San Francisco, Calif.:** The Emporium
Bridgeport, Conn.: Howland's	**Denver, Colo.:** Denver Dry Goods Company	**Montclair, N.J.:** Hahne & Company	**Seattle, Wash.:** Ernst Hardware
Buffalo, N.Y.: Weed & Co.	**Evansville, Ind.:** The Evansville Store	**Montgomery, Ala.:** Loveman's	**South Bend, Ind.:** Wyman's
Charlotte, N.C.: Ivey's	**Fort Wayne, Ind.:** Frank's	**Newark, N.J.:** Hahne & Company	**Springfield, Mass.:** Forbes and Wallace
Chattanooga, Tenn.: Miller Brothers Co.	**Grand Rapids, Mich.:** Herpolsheimer's	**New Orleans, La.:** D. H. Holme's	**Spokane, Wash.:** The Crescent
	Hartford, Conn.: Brown Thomson, Inc.	**New York, N.Y.:** Gimbels	**Syracuse, N.Y.:** E. W. Edwards & Son
	Houston, Tex.: Braes Hardware	**Oakland, Calif.:** Capwell's	**Tampa, Fla.:** Maas Brothers
	Houston, Tex.: Joske's of Houston	**Oklahoma City, Okla.:** John A. Brown Co.	**Toledo, Ohio:** La Salle's
	Indianapolis, Ind.: The Wm. H. Block Co.	**Omaha, Nebr.:** J. L. Brandeis & Sons	**Washington, D.C.:** Woodward & Lothrop
	Jackson, Mich.: L. H. Field Company	**Peoria, Ill.:** Block and Kuhl Company	**Wichita, Kan.:** Innes
	Kansas City, Mo.: Emery, Bird, Thayer	**Philadelphia, Pa.:** Lit Brothers, All Stores	**Worcester, Mass.:** R. H. White's
		Pittsburgh, Pa.: Joseph Horne Company	**York, Pa.:** The Bon-Ton Department Store
		Pontiac, Mich.: Waite's	**Youngstown, Ohio:** The Stambaugh-Thompson Co.
		Portland, Oreg.: Meier and Frank Company	

DAD and junior, too, can clean walks in a jiffy with feather-light snow shovels of Alcoa Aluminum. Sturdy enough for wettest snows. Stay bright and clean for years.

TOOLS are really portable when made of Alcoa Aluminum. They handle easier, run cooler, require less maintenance—help any handyman do finer, faster work.

EXPERIENCED FISHERMEN praise the new, lighter, sturdier tackle made of Alcoa Aluminum. Moisture won't rust these handsome tackle boxes, rod cases, reels and nets.

EASY-TO-CARRY, easy-to-handle picnic jugs and vacuum bottles are made of Alcoa Aluminum. They keep their good looks because solid aluminum won't tarnish or peel off.

A PORTABLE OVEN for holiday meals! A coffeepot that you set and forget! Alcoa Aluminum makes roasters and coffeepots easy to handle, a pleasure to keep clean.

RELIABLE flashlights and lanterns are made of Alcoa Aluminum. Easy to handle because aluminum is light. Stay clean and bright inside and out because aluminum resists corrosion.

ALUMINUM LADDERS weigh less than ordinary ladders, are easier to move and handle. They won't rot, warp or swell. No splinters to hurt your hands.

OUTDOOR COOKING is a pleasure with a rust-resistant grill and a light portable icebox of Alcoa Aluminum. You'll enjoy them season after season because aluminum lasts.

GIVE EVERY PRESENT that extra-special sparkle with an attractive gift wrapping of aluminum foil. Easy to fold, strong and durable. Available plain and embossed in every color of the rainbow.

FIGURE 5.3

Alcoa Aluminum advertisement, *Saturday Evening Post*, "Christmas Creations of Light, Lasting, Lustrous Alcoa Aluminum" (December 3, 1955).

Called the Aluminaire, Frey's design was displayed at the Allied Arts and Building Products Exhibition in 1931 and was selected for the very first modern architectural exhibition, *The International Style: Architecture Since 1922,* held at the Museum of Modern Art in New York in 1932.[19] Kocher and Frey saw the house "as a prototype for a house of the future, able to be produced in great quantity at a low cost" and "assembled and disassembled quickly."[20] The idea was that aluminum construction techniques could lift the home off its heavy foundations, liberating modernist architecture to travel around the world. This was the beginning of a trend toward a mobilized form of dwelling, a lighter kind of living that would lead toward the US embrace of both mobile homes and prefab home building (see figure 5.4).

The exhibition of the Aluminaire was sponsored by "a group of manufacturers and industrial contractors eager to show the public their new products," with aluminum floor joists and pipe columns furnished by Alcoa.[21] It was clad with four-by-five-foot corrugated aluminum panels fastened with aluminum screws and washers. It was designed in the International Style "as an experimental house to reflect new technologies and materials and to generate new ideas,"[22] including the notion of prefabricated building. It was well received and drew interest for its other features such as built-in furniture and neon-tube lighting that changed colors. The house was purchased by Wallace K. Harrison and reassembled on his estate in Huntington, Long Island, where it eventually became the subject of a restoration project in the early 1990s.

Frey went on to become one of the key users of aluminum in a style of US domestic architecture known as Desert Modernism, which he developed after moving to Palm Springs, California, in 1934. He built the Frey House I in Palm Springs in 1940, using corrugated aluminum for the exterior walls, as in the Aluminaire, but now laid out in a low-slung building, with large horizontal windows set in aluminum frames. Even the dining table was unconventional, a shining disc hung from the ceiling with aluminum wire.

He built several other influential examples using his signature corrugated aluminum siding and ceilings, always with a light airy feel that opened the interior of the home to the expansive landscape outside. His light, open houses embodied a modernist version of the American Dream in a California landscape of hope and promise. In the 1950s he added to his repertoire futuristic aluminum turrets with porthole-shaped windows, creating a "cool" style that included vinyl fabrics, hanging staircases suspended from aluminum rods, and indoor and outdoor swimming pools.

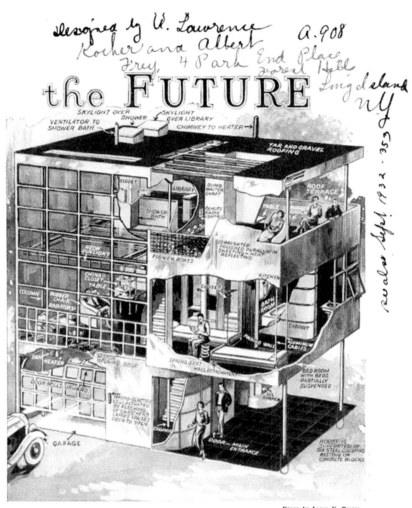

Cut-Away Representation of the Home of the Future; the House Is Constructed Entirely of Metal and Glass, with the Latest Space and Labor-Saving Features

FIGURE 5.4

"Cut-Away" drawing of Kocher and Frey's Aluminaire house from the August 1931 issue of *Popular Mechanics*.

Whereas some designers were invested in using light aluminum to revolutionize construction techniques and use industrial processes to build faster, Frey seemed to make living itself lighter, lifting the house off its foundations and dissolving its walls and conventional wooden solidity. Walter Gropius, an émigré to the United States from the German Bauhaus, was also experimenting with aluminum buildings in this period, having already experimented with copper housing and industrial processes for mass-produced building. In 1941 he was commissioned, along with Marcel Breuer, by the Federal Works Agency to design a project nicknamed Aluminum City Terrace for New Kensington, Pennsylvania, home of an Alcoa aluminum plant.[23]

Other visionaries sought to revolutionize lifestyles by making homes that could literally move. If modern cars and trains could be made into living rooms on wheels, why couldn't homes themselves become mobile? The mobile home, the trailer home, and the minivan were all ideas for streamlined living that arose out of not just the use of aluminum, but also the ideas it put into motion. Aluminum could make the home light enough to be transported, family and all, onto the smooth roadways of modernity.

William Stout designed not only the first minivan (the Stout Scarab) but also a 1936 mobile metal house that could be folded away and towed by a car. As already noted, the Airstream trailer became the most significant embodiment of an aerodynamic life on wheels—lighter, optimistic, open to the adventures of the road. In the post-WWII adjustments of the US economy and resettlement of GIs there was a craze for mobile living as young families sought out greener pastures and better jobs. But these aluminum dreams also took more conventional forms, departing from the modernist visions of European architects into something far more mundane.

Marchfield Homes brought out the Ten-Wide mobile home in 1954, and by 1968 mobile homes accounted for 25 percent of single-family homes in the United States. Many veterans, at least those who were white, also benefitted from the GI Bill mortgage support, which allowed them to move into new suburban communities linked by freeways, expressways, and parkways (all words connoting the utopian vision of privatized automobility). The epitome of this trend was the white flight into the sprawling suburbs around Los Angeles, many of which were economically based on the expanding aerospace industry.[24] Thus the very workers who were producing aluminum-clad airplanes could live in aluminum-clad suburban homes, where their wives could make use of all the new aluminum kitchenware and domestic conveniences.

LA MAISON TROPICALE

Another significant innovator in the design of aluminum homes was French designer and architect Jean Prouvé (b. 1901), who "believed in the power of design to make a better world" and whose "bold, reduced forms, inspired by the sparse aesthetic of aircraft design" played a significant role in modernizing our aesthetic expectations of domestic buildings.[25] Prouvé's father was a painter and sculptor who became a founding member of the Art Nouveau School of Nancy, where in 1931 Jean Prouvé founded his own atelier where he experimented with innovations in the use of aluminum and steel. He designed sturdy functional furniture including chairs, tables, desks, and even an elegant aluminum sideboard. Several contemporary art galleries are currently featuring revivals of his interior designs and furniture, all made from aluminum. But it is his aluminum building designs that are most striking and radical.

After World War II he worked out of a factory where he combined research, prototype development, and production. His work emphasized his "love of mobility" in several senses. He wanted to make objects that could be easily assembled and dismantled so that the objects themselves could be easily transported; he wanted to make "houses manufactured in factories like cars" so that the production process was mechanized and the product could be prefabricated and moved; and he wanted to be able to move these houses around the world. His technical solutions and pragmatic aesthetics were influential on a number of modern designers and architects, such as British architects Richard Rogers (whom Prouvé helped select to design the landmark Centre Georges Pompidou in Paris, along with Renzo Piano) and Norman Foster (who also collaborated with R. Buckminster Fuller from 1968 until Fuller's death in 1983), known for their interest in "high-tech architecture."

Extending his work on prefabricated barracks commissioned by the army and prefabricated aluminum houses for refugees after World War II, Prouvé designed a series of buildings from 1949 to 1951 including La Maison Coloniale, La Maison Metropole, and La Maison Tropicale as a lightweight, easily assembled house that could be flat-packed and shipped to French colonial Africa in cargo planes. With these three variants, "it was a system that could be adapted to vastly different climates, sites, and scales through modular expansion or pavilion-like additions."[26] The tropical design addressed the need for affordable housing and civic buildings in the colonies, and no piece was heavier than 100 kilograms to ensure that it could be carried by just two men and easily packed and air lifted. Only three were made: one was used as an office for the director of a college in Niamey, Niger; and two were sent to Brazzaville, in the Republic of Congo, where they were used by the company Aluminium Française, serving as a kind of demonstration project for the potentials of aluminum.

In 2006 one of these houses was rediscovered in Brazzaville, riddled with bullet holes, and was rescued for posterity. It was reconstructed first in New York and then in London in 2008 as an exhibit at Tate Modern to accompany a retrospective on Prouvé at the nearby Design Museum. Here I visited the house, whose clean lines and grids of small round windows still look modern, even futuristic. Practical and simplified, similar to William Stout's aircraft-inspired designs, this modern architecture also seems to "simplicate and add lightness." The house is a simple rectangle, raised off the ground and wrapped by a verandah. The verandah is shaded by adjustable louvers that prefigure the designs used on energy-conserving passive solar buildings today. The blue porthole windows make no concessions to popular taste, bathing the interior in a strangely spaceshiplike atmosphere. One can only imagine the percussive racket that would ensue when a tropical downpour pummeled the metal roof.

One of the other prototype houses now "resides on the fifth-floor terrace of the Pompidou Center in Paris."[27] Prouvé's work on mobile homes, barracks, and emergency shelters are all considered ingenious "green" designs before their time, and as "examples of a portable modular building system, they speak to a resurgent interest in prefabrication, and the engagement of architects in the design of emergency housing. Non–site specific, they are nonetheless inextricably bound up in cultural memories of colonial Africa."[28]

Prouvé was also commissioned by Aluminium Française to design an aluminum pavilion for the centenary of aluminum. For this he made a sweeping curved wave of a roof over a long open space, full of light and air. It echoes the tent of aluminum envisioned in the Bohn advertising, and extends the qualities of metallic design in directions that would be pursued by later architects. But one crucial thing about Prouvé's work is his emphasis on a new building design for the tropical colonial world. He reminds us that there were people thinking about the connections between Europe and its colonies, and about the ways in which new aluminum technologies might be applied in the tropical climate. It turns out that the modernist designers Ray and Charles Eames were also deeply interested in India, and traveled and worked there, developing a fascination with Indian material culture. So against the grain of the dominant narrative of modernity as a purely Western formation, there are hints of an interactional domain where divergent modernities met on common terrain. This kind of global outlook is even more pronounced in the work of the next inventor-designer-architect, R. Buckminster Fuller.

THE DYMAXION HOUSE

Philosopher, inventor, architect, and designer R. Buckminster Fuller is a key exemplar of the forecaster of the future who was deeply engaged with aluminum. In 1933, he designed the Dymaxion car, a three-wheeled streamlined aluminum-skinned vehicle that could carry up to ten passengers. He also designed a mobile travel trailer. But one of his most important ideas was the automated, lightweight, and mobile Dymaxion house, first designed in 1927 to be mass-produced, affordable, easily transportable inside a metal tube, and environmentally efficient. Bergdoll and Christensen of the Museum of Modern Art in New York describe it as "one of the most critical projects not only on prefabricated housing but on industry and architecture in general."[29] Fuller's work has been recently celebrated at a number of major museum exhibitions. Fuller sought to copy the automobile industry in systematizing and rationalizing the mass production of houses, and therefore "placed paramount importance on ease of shipment and assembly," as noted in the epigraph for this chapter; he was also extremely concerned with efficient use of resources, which "anticipates the sustainability movement by decades."[30] Drawing on the most advanced aluminum fabrication techniques from the aircraft industry, his aim was to make housing as light, strong, and energy efficient as possible: "Then, using the most advanced aircraft-engineering techniques and the highest-performance aluminum alloys, etc., I designed a dwell-in-able environment control . . . that in every way provided facilities and degrees of comfort equal to those of AIA's [the American Institute of Architects] optimum 1927 single-family dwelling. My aeronautical-engineering counterpart single-family dwelling weighed only three tons."[31]

Fuller designed his first prefabricated aluminum house to be suspended from a central vertical stainless-steel strut, from which wedge-shaped fans of aluminum sheet metal would hang to form the floors, ceilings, and roof. He named the house by combining the words dynamic-maximum-tension. He made only two prototypes of this early version of the Dymaxion house, which were purchased by a single investor William Graham, but the design never went into production, perhaps being too extreme for the home-buying public. After the war, in partnership with Beech Aircraft of Wichita, Kansas, which had excess aluminum assembly lines available, Fuller developed a second concept for the Dymaxion house, this time with a more rounded exterior and higher quality interior finish. Although Beech initially had plans to produce fifty to sixty thousand units a year for $6,500 each,[32] the Wichita house also ended up being made only as two prototypes, one of which was acquired by the Henry Ford Museum and reconstructed for public viewing in 2001.[33]

The round structure looks a bit like a giant Hershey's Kiss wrapped in silver foil, with a conical peak at the center (figure 5.5). The use of aluminum sheet metal for the roof, ceiling, and floor of the round design enabled the house to be naturally heated and cooled, to be storm and earthquake proof, to require little maintenance, and to offer flexibility and mobility. It also incorporated a unique revolving closet system known as the "O-volving shelf," and an aluminum prototype for a one-piece Dymaxion bathroom that used Fuller's inventions of a "fog-gun" to replace a shower or bath, and a dry toilet system that dry-packaged and removed waste for recycling, "which altogether eliminate[s] all wet plumbing and do[es] away with the need of piped-in-and-away water and water-borne wastes."[34]

Thus the house was self-sufficient and provided its own services, could be easily moved, could withstand various storm and weather conditions, and effectively anticipated adaptation to many of the emergency conditions, stressed or failing infrastructure that many cities deal with today in the face of a changing climate. The design went through several iterations, and along with Fuller's Dymaxion car, later geodesic domes, and other projects, made him one of the key futurists in the United States, gaining a national reputation that landed him on the cover of *Time* magazine in 1964, in an illustration by Boris Artzybasheff (see figure 4.2), whose work for Alcoa on the Caribbean we find in chapter 6.

The Dymaxion house seems both futuristic and primitive, like a space-age Mongolian yurt or Navajo hogan. It is certainly one of those designs that is "before its time," and Fuller believed that it would be adopted when

FIGURE 5.5
Fuller's Dymaxion house from *Fortune* magazine (April 1946).

the appropriate social conditions made it necessary. Whereas technological optimists envisioned a future made possible by the new human capabilities that might sprout from aluminum, and the new social and cultural practices it would enable, by the 1960s people were also beginning to consider the limits of our planet, and the need to conserve resources for the future of life on earth. A realization of the harmful effects of industrial pollution was also emerging, with the publication of books like Rachel Carson's *Silent Spring*. Fuller's techno-utopian vision spanned the advanced high-tech world of the military-industrial complex and the alternative countercultures of the cybernetic generation of the *Whole Earth Catalogue,* who went on to invent the Internet. Later he and his wife, Ann, would live in one of his other designs, a geodesic dome home, one of the most efficient structures ever designed in terms of materials use and energy use, as well as being easily moveable.

The geodesic dome is formed by the fourteen-sided polyhedron projected out into a spherical system of triangles to form a very strong and economical structure, for which Fuller received a patent in 1954. Fuller's geodesic domes made from aluminum or steel tubing led to new experimental building forms that were also adopted by the US military as light, strong structures that could be airlifted into place on difficult terrains. They were adopted as geodesic radomes for the Defense Early Warning system installed around the world; for the 1954 Marine Corps air-delivered geodesic domes; the

American National Exhibition pavilion in Moscow in 1959 (where Charles and Ray Eames projected their seventy-screen show "Glimpses," about a day in the life of the United States, and where Nixon and Khrushchev held their "kitchen debates" in a model ranch-style suburban home); and the US pavilion for the 1967 Montreal World's Fair. Fuller's domes represent the conundrum at the heart of aluminum dreams, for they were used not only to promote US industrial design and military readiness in the midst of the Cold War but also were embraced by the environmental and peace movements in the 1960s and 1970s, whose members also wanted to experiment with radical design and lighter living forms for transforming social relations.

In 1965 an artists' community called Drop City was built near Trinidad, Colorado, as a live-in work of "Drop Art" (inspired by the impromptu performances of John Cage, Robert Rauschenberg, and Fuller himself at Black Mountain College). The collection of aluminum-skinned domes were based on Fuller's geometric designs such as the triacontahedron and the zonohedra. Drop City was awarded Fuller's Dymaxion award for innovative and economic housing construction in 1967. Many other artists at this time were turning against the square linear forms of Modernism and the square lifestyles of the suburban United States and seeking out more organically designed forms of shelter and communal forms of living. This was the period in which the concept of inflatable buildings emerged, soft bubbles of plastic enclosure that took the concepts of lightness and mobility to an extreme. Alongside these experimentations with new materials, this was also the beginning of the ecological movement toward recycling, composting, and organic foods, the anti-war movement, the "drop out" culture and its pursuit of a slower pace of life. Fuller himself, more interested in practical advances in technology, went on to invent other living systems, including the 1952 Growth home which was based on similar principles to the Dymaxion house, but created an indoor vertically hanging growing system for food.

Most spectacularly Fuller also developed several designs for entire cities, including Old Man River City, a proposal for East St. Louis, Illinois, to inhabit a five-hundred-foot-high crater-shaped structure covered by a one-mile-diameter "geodesic-sky parasol-umbrella" made of aluminum and stainless steel trussing;[35] and in the 1960s a tetrahedronal floating city that he was commissioned to design for Tokyo Bay.[36]

Although the innovators of the 1960s initially embraced aluminum geodesic domes, cybernetics, and other futuristic schemes, this counterculture generation brought the classic age of aluminum to an end in some respects, as the movement against the Vietnam War also turned against the military-industrial complex that had supported the growth of aluminum-based technologies. But the tension between a desire for futuristic advanced technology and a desire to be earth friendly is a sociotechnical dilemma that remains at the heart of our contemporary material culture and the drive toward innovation.

It was never really resolved whether objects made from aluminum and other products of industrial processes can fit into a "green" lifestyle or should be banished altogether. Contemporary moves toward corporate responsibility and movements for ethical consumption still play on this uncertainty, but they do not address the underlying global energy and resource balance that informed Fuller's vision. He called for the worldwide complete recycling of all metal scrap, and total reduction of waste. Some of his inventions might still be the best way for an energy-scarce world to adapt to changing life conditions, and still maintain the advanced technologies that he believed were necessary to meet all human needs for shelter, comfort, mobility, self-development, and collective thriving. These are issues that I will return to in chapter 9, where I consider the possible rebirth of aluminum as a green technology.

LOSING ITS GLEAM

Unlike the experimental aluminum homes like the Aluminaire, La Maison Tropicale, and the Dymaxion house, aluminum in home design took far more banal paths in the 1960s, leading to mass-produced vernacular trailer homes, safe suburban ranchers, split levels, and pseudo-colonials for the mass market rather than to ultra-mobile space-age pods or round-sided domes. Aluminum siding became the primary external skin of suburban houses in the 1960s. Homebuilders embraced rustproof aluminum screens, along with storm doors, window frames, ductwork, gutters, and foil insulation.

The hard sell of aluminum siding is memorably captured in Barry Levinson's film *Tin Men* (starring Richard Dreyfuss and Danny DeVito) about the unethical activities of siding salesmen in the early 1960s. It shows the crackdown on these deceptive sales schemes by Baltimore's Home Improvement Commission, which investigated the industry. As it became associated with declining inner suburbs and trailer parks, and the homes themselves aged and faded, aluminum began to gain a bad reputation.

In 1965, with mounting inflation, President Lyndon Johnson decided to release aluminum from the government stockpile, driving down prices.[37] Alcoa was also involved in several urban redevelopment projects in the 1960s, and the metal became associated with cheap, low-rent housing. For those who grew up in the 1970s aluminum was already losing some of its luster on the domestic front. As philosopher Paul Ricoeur summed things up in 1961, mankind was engulfed in a consumer culture in which "one finds the same bad movie, the same slot machines, the same plastic or aluminum atrocities, the same twisting of language by propaganda, etc."[38] Whereas plastic and aluminum had once been the materials of the future, during the course of the 1960s they came to be seen as artificial, cheap, throw-away materials.

I myself grew up in an aluminum-sided suburban house in the 1970s and carried a colorful aluminum lunchbox to school, with a sandwich wrapped by my mom in handy aluminum foil. I drank from aluminum cans; traveled in cars, planes, and bikes chock-full of aluminum parts; and ate food cooked in aluminum pots and pans. Along with the suburban homes came the aluminum swimming pools and outdoor furniture, the camping equipment and golf clubs, the canoes and bicycles, the thermos and the picnic cooler—an entire American way of life. Looking at old photos of my family relaxing on those nylon-meshed aluminum folding chairs brings back chlorine-scented memories of lazy summer afternoons, playing by a poolside and piling the light chairs into forts that we covered with beach towels.

I also remember the beginning of a change in our feelings about aluminum. As the space age passed and the oil crisis set in, the chairs began to fall apart and the aluminum siding developed stains. We crushed cans under our feet to turn our sneakers into funny noisemakers and made craft projects from the pull tabs that still detached from the lid in those days. This flimsy metal began to seem worthless, and recycling campaigns seemed to increase its association with trash rather than with the chic modern design of previous decades.

A Charlie Brown Christmas, the animated TV special, premiered in 1965 featuring the newest trend in an age-old tradition: the aluminum Christmas tree. Lucy orders the hapless Charlie Brown to "get the biggest aluminum tree you can find . . . maybe painted pink" for their staging of the nativity story. Charlie Brown instead returns from the tree farm with a spindly little fir tree that caught his sympathy among the glittering metal faux-trees. Linus warns him that it "doesn't seem to fit the modern spirit," as epitomized by the silvery aluminum Christmas tree.

"The aluminum tree," according to Tom Vanderbilt (in a nostalgic essay written for an entire book on the subject), "was a shining beacon to the optimism of the space age, a monument of Pop modernism, and proof of American manufacturing prowess. Where else but in a country that had conquered a sprawling and primeval wilderness could Nature herself be improved upon?"[39] A shining emblem of the age, the reusable, economical, brightly beautiful copy of a living tree made perfect sense within this material culture.

Yet, in the end, the children embrace Charlie Brown's living tree as representing the "true meaning of Christmas." In Charles Schulz's prescient comic critique of the commercialization of Christmas, the gaudy aluminum tree stands in for all that is wrong with US culture: false, flashy, flimsy, faddish fakery. It hints at a deep-seated disquiet with the age of aluminum and all that it had wrought. It goes along with cheap siding, shoddy cookware, and a kind of lightness that had come to signify emptiness, lack of gravitas, and a never-satisfied consumer culture. With the birth of the sixties "counterculture" there was finally a backlash against aluminum-filled suburbia and a rejection of all that it stood for, including the military-industrial complex. US design preferences of the upwardly mobile middle-class for organic materials, stone-clad, or wooden-beamed houses, natural hemp, and recycled paper packages accompanied a backlash against aluminum, a retreat from futurism into a nostalgic nonurban elsewhere. However, getting rid of aluminum is not as easy as throwing out a fake Christmas tree in favor of a live one. At the retail chain Urban Outfitters for Christmas 2008 they were selling "classic" aluminum trees, which are having something of a retro comeback, with sales on eBay and articles extolling their nostalgic associations. Prefab architecture is also having a comeback, with young architects again interested in "modern prefab dwellings that combine precision and mass production in a sophisticated yet breezy and livable form," often constructed from aluminum panels.[40] It is hard to put aluminum to rest.

A wave of technological futurism is again coming into fashion, and aluminum is once again along for the ride. High-tech prefabricated construction is back on the design radar with publications such as *Dwell* magazine, which did a 2006 special issue called "Prefab Now" and a general move toward using aluminum in new "green" buildings. Perhaps the most extreme example is the Micro Compact Home by Horden Cherry Lee Architects and Haack+Höpfner Architects, which I viewed at the MOMA *Home*

Delivery exhibition in 2008 (see figure 5.6). Under the slogan "Smart living for a short stay" this seventy-six-square-foot anodized aluminum cube updates the concept of a modern "machine for living."[41]

"Taking inspiration, as so often in the history of prefabrication, from the aerospace and automobile industries, the [British and German] architects fashion a 'high performance' cocoon specifically geared toward single persons with a mobile work or leisure-oriented lifestyle."[42] Like a machine-tooled smartphone, or a spaceship, it seems to streamline life itself down to the most efficient yet well-designed elements, making "a bold statement regarding what is essential to life in the twenty-first century without sacrificing a meticulous aesthetic and brilliantly organized composition in a confident, compact package."[43] Most important, it chooses to make this bold statement in aluminum, retooling all of the associations that the industry has worked hard to achieve over the last hundred years.

We have come full circle back to some of the dilemmas that Buckminster Fuller addressed in his work. Fuller's book *Operating Manual for Spaceship Earth*[44] based on a lecture he first gave in 1967, first popularized the idea of the earth as a spaceship, and the vision of using technology to "do more with less." Indeed, even the aluminum industry took note. In 1967–1968 the Kaiser Aluminum and Chemical Corporation published two booklets, *The Dynamics of Change*[45] and *The Markets for Change,* to "examine in depth the probable technological responses that may be made in the next two decades in answer to changing attitudes about man's relationship to his global environment." In the accompanying advertising campaign they depict the globe covered with man-made objects (jet planes, ships, a rocket launch, skyscrapers, magnetic tape, geodesic radomes, and electrical equipment) with this text, drawn directly from ideas in Fuller's 1967 lecture:

What hath man wrought?

It has been suggested that the "spaceship" earth was turned over to mankind without an operation manual. Ever since—for all of his time on earth—man has been "flying blind."

His efforts affect the land, the water and the air on a global scale. The making of these marks, and the way they have been made, are extensions of human attitudes and ideas that remain largely unexamined.

The idea of "development." The idea of "progress." The concept that man "owns" the earth. Now, as the result of technological responses to these concepts becomes more and more visible, the whole relationship between man and earth is undergoing reexamination.[46]

FIGURE 5.6
Micro compact home by Horden Cherry Lee Architects and Haack+Höpfner Architects, at MOMA *Home Delivery* exhibition (2008). Photo Credit: D. Schimmel.

In a reflexive mode, Kaiser Aluminum questions development and modern progress, although the company still envisions new markets in "aluminum, chemicals, computing, specialty metals, mining and exploration, nickel, real estate, refractories, [and] international trading" as the way forward. Fuller was one of the first thinkers to argue that we as a species need to draw on energy "income"—sunlight, water power, wind power, geothermal energy—and stop drawing from our energy "savings account"—fossil fuels. He himself recognized his role as one of "prognostication," or forecasting of the future, based on the "anticipatory design science" that he had learned in the US Naval Academy. He understood the future as a transition from technologies of warfare and weaponry to technologies of life for an emerging world society that he called "completely tooled-up and organized comprehensive, anticipatory livingry systems."

In the oracular style of his 1963 book *Ideas and Integrities,* he wrote, "In a manner similar to the past evolution of weaponry systems the new, architect-designed, world-around, livingry systems will be realized in progressive, economic-industrial-plan increments predicated upon pyramidal reinvestments of the forward years' regeneratively amplifying and progressive techno-economic advantages."[47] This is the conundrum of aluminum: will it continue to be an energy-hungry technology of weaponry, polluting the world, harming health, and violating human rights, or will it become a truly global, recycled, green technology for "anticipatory livingry"? Can we reduce our use of aluminum even as we depend on it to support modern life in so many ways?

These are questions that remain unanswered fifty years later and that I explore further in part II. But before turning to the future we need to first widen our aperture beyond national cultural histories of the uses of aluminum, technological histories of innovation and design breakthroughs, or business histories of single companies. It is imperative that we understand the harms caused by the bauxite mining, alumina refining, and smelting industry around the world, if we are to take its full measure.

PART II   THE DARK SIDE

Countries in the early stages of economic development ought to derive the largest possible benefits from their natural resources. They ought not to be regarded merely as sources of cheap raw materials for metropolitan enterprises.

—Norman Washington Manley, letter to Kaiser Bauxite Co., 1956

The sea smelled of swamp; it barely rippled, had glitter rather than colour; and the heat seemed trapped below the pink haze of bauxite dust from the bauxite loading station.

—V. S. Naipaul, *Guerillas*, 1975

Although the aluminum industry took off by promoting a gleaming aero-dynamic modernism and supermobility in its primary consumer markets in the United States, it simultaneously benefited from and reproduced a very different image of an as yet unachieved modernization in the "slow" Caribbean. The heavy industry of Caribbean bauxite mines became the ground for others to reach toward the sky. There was an implicit connection between the production of the material culture and visual image of modernity in the United States in the age of aluminum and the parallel consumption of raw materials and visual images of tropical backwardness in the Caribbean.

The infrastructures of tourism and its modes of visual imagery played a crucial part in promoting this view of the Caribbean. By contrast, West Indian nationalists, internationalists, and labor movements struggled to counter these representations, to gain control over their own resources, and to participate in modernization. The desire for participation included a conflicting drive to develop their own resources, but also to possess the new technologies and goods that modernity promised to bring. US dreams of air power and space age supermodernity occurred at the very time when Caribbean states were attempting to negotiate labor rights, political rights, and national sovereignty, and to negotiate resource sovereignty with multinational aluminum corporations backed by the US government.

In W. W. Rostow's classic treatise on modernization, *The Stages of Economic Growth: A Non-Communist Manifesto*, first published in 1960, he describes economic development as a series of stages toward technological maturity that begin with a takeoff toward sustained growth. The metaphor of modernization as takeoff drew on the power of aviation, which is based on the discovery of hardened aluminum as described previously, but also references aluminum's role in the emergence of new consumer markets based on speedier transport, light packaging, and durable goods. Each society must meet certain preconditions of social structure, political system, and techniques of production in order to take off toward modernity.

Modernization was premised on motion—rural to urban, old world to new, sea power to air power—and only with mobility is takeoff achieved into a high-flying era of mass consumption of durable consumer goods and general welfare. Rostow's influential thesis was that communist societies were unable to create the preconditions for such a takeoff, but that the noncommunist "developing" societies would eventually get there and join the leaders (Europe and the United States). The very mobility offered by the aluminum industry was both a condition for producing modernity and a metaphor for modernization. Yet Rostow ignored how the takeoff to modernity was premised less on the invisible hand of the market than on the heavy hand of the state and the monopolistic control of primary commodity markets by powerful multinational corporations. To a large extent it was state intervention and business protection that enabled the industrial takeoff of the United States, including the use of patents, cartels, international trade regimes, corporate monopolies, occasional state ownership, and the benefits of military power.[1]

Aluminum has been dubbed "packaged electricity" or "solidified electricity" because smelting demands so much power, but it might equally be called "solidified power," as noted in chapter 2, because it tends toward such an uncompetitive industrial structure.[2] The industry's celebration of its own contributions to technological advancement and to modernization actually mask the behind-the-scenes work that enabled it to lock in immobilities (of technologies, capital, and people), which were often grounded in global economic inequalities that prevented development elsewhere by simply extracting raw materials without any inward investment or societal capacity building.

To tell the story of aluminum's role in modernization—and to write a transnational history of the Americas—one must recombine the North American world of mobility, speed, and flight with the heavier, slower tropical world of bauxite mining, racialized labor relations, and resource extraction. It was, ironically, precisely this juxtaposition of cultural velocities that simultaneously created a market for international tourism, the other great pillar of contemporary Caribbean economies.

Just as anthropologist Sidney Mintz argued in *Sweetness and Power*[3] that the modern Atlantic world was built on sugar consumption in the age of slavery, we could say that aluminum offers a successor to that story: a late modernity built on consumption of aluminum and all that it enabled, including speed and mobility itself. The emergence of aluminum reworks the asymmetric material relations and visual circulations between metropolitan centers of consumption and the peripheries of modernity where resource extraction and labor exploitation take place, just as effectively erasing the modernity and humanity of the laborers who produce modernity's aluminum dreams. West Indian nationalists, internationalists, and labor movements also struggled to gain control over their own resources, to participate in modernization, and to possess the new technologies and goods that modernization promised to bring. They, too, had their own aluminum dreams of Caribbean modernity.

By closely examining the aluminum industry's visual representations of its bauxite mining lands in the Caribbean alongside its US dreams of streamlined modernity, we can reconnect the valuation of modern US mobility with the fixed and immobile "premodern" ground on and against which it was produced. As Matthew Evenden argues, studying the aluminum commodity chain "helps to reveal aspects of the global environmental history of war" because "it unfolded over vast distances and imposed different environmental burdens on several locations" including companies such as Alcan, which "operated under permissive colonial conditions in British Guiana to extract wealth from tropical soils and low-waged workers."[4]

Alongside such colonial relations of extraction, the visual imaginaries and material practices of a technologically advanced mobile modernity were co-constitutive of the "backwardness" of the Caribbean. As a key location of both US bauxite mining and tourism in the twentieth century, the Caribbean became underdeveloped not merely through corporate and military power but also through the redeployment of colonial visual tropes as incitements to modern subjectivity within a modernizing material culture of consumer desire and touristic place formation. The very ideologies that promote lightness, mobility, high-tech design, and the celebration of modernity are in fact grounded in heavy industry, warfare, tropical dispossession, and economic inequalities. These dichotomies are in truth the two inseparable sides of the same coin.

The successful expansion of the market for aluminum in the 1930s to 1940s, and even more so into the 1950s, required a steady supply of high-quality bauxite. The threats posed by German U-boats to trans-Caribbean shipping during World War II prompted an interest in securing steady supplies closer to the US mainland, including Jamaica, where bauxite ore was discovered only in the 1940s. The increased demand for aluminum during World War II, the emergence of the United States as the world's largest aluminum producer, and the dangers of wartime shipping all led to the emergence of Jamaica as the primary supplier of bauxite to the US aluminum companies.[5]

The system of Allied collaboration known as "lend-lease," along with the September 1940 Destroyers for Bases Agreement, enabled the United States to provide aluminum to British wartime industries (whose European sources of bauxite and power had been seized by Germany) in exchange for air bases in British colonies, including Jamaica, Trinidad, and British Guiana.[6] The United States established a naval base in Trinidad, within which Alcan sited its bauxite transfer facility in 1942; and built the Atkinson landing strip and air base in British Guiana to protect the flow of bauxite down the Demerara River. Wartime needs forced the opening up of mineral rights in Jamaica (against landowner opposition) to Alcan, Reynolds, and Kaiser, after the breakup of Alcoa.[7]

New military bases embodied the waning of Britain's power in the region and gave the United States a valuable military foothold just as US multinationals were engaging in bargaining over access to resources, preferential tariffs, and deals for low taxation. During the war the "economies and ecologies of the Demerara [river in British Guiana] and the Saguenay [river in Quebec, Canada] were practically conjoined" as bauxite was shipped and railway freighted over four thousand kilometers across the militarized commodity chain of the British Commonwealth.[8] After the war, following negotiations with Canadian and US aluminum multinationals, Jamaica's British colonial government enacted The Minerals (Vesting) Act and The Mining

Act in 1947, which set a very low royalty payment of only one shilling per ton of bauxite mined, equivalent to about US 20 cents, and a very low level of assumed profit on which taxation would be based.

Kaiser Aluminum based its new mining operations in Jamaica and US mining companies acquired 142,000 acres of agricultural land mining leases, and Reynolds Metals gained exclusive access to 206,000 acres of Crown Land in British Guiana.[9] Reynolds Metals also expanded mining operations into Haiti in 1941, and from 1956 to 1982 exported 13.3 million tons of bauxite from Haiti to its alumina refinery in Corpus Christi, Texas. Haitian bauxite accounted for almost one-fifth of Reynolds's bauxite acquisition in that period, and Reynolds was given access to 150,000 hectares, expelling thousands of Haitian families. Haitian economist Fred Doura describes the extractive mining industry in Haiti as "a typical example of an 'enclave' industry under foreign domination where two North American transnationals exploited the minerals bauxite and copper . . . [T]he impact was practically null on the economy."[10]

Bauxite mining furthermore underpins a crucial connection between the production of the material culture and visual image of modernity in the United States and the parallel consumption of raw materials and visual images of tropical backwardness in the Caribbean. Surprisingly, the material circulation of mining and light metals is intimately linked with the visual circulation of images of the Caribbean, and the embodied practices of tourism that connect the Caribbean and the United States.

In this chapter I offer a brief overview of a striking series of luxury magazine advertisements, promoting the Caribbean tourist cruises of the Alcoa Steamship Company from 1948 to 1958, the period in which the Aluminum Company of America became the biggest producer of aluminum in the world and depended to a large extent on bauxite mined in Jamaica and Suriname, the two largest exporters of bauxite in the world. Leisure travel surprisingly came to operate as part of this circuit of commodity production, in which a West Indies lacking the luster of metallic modernity was represented as a backward region beckoning US tourists, enterprise, and adventure.

SURINAME AND THE DECIMATION OF THE SAAMAKA MAROONS

Aluminum, as already noted, is economically recoverable only in limited forms and limited locations. One of those locations is the Greater Antilles and the northern coastal jungles of South America, which share a Caribbean cultural heritage. As Alcoa's main historian points out, "In 1915, the company went to the British and Dutch Guianas to explore their rich bauxite lands, and in December 1916, Alcoa organized the Surinaamsche Bauxite Maatchappij. Thereafter, all significant additions to Alcoa's bauxite reserves would come from overseas."[11] Alcoa first mined bauxite in Suriname in 1917, and began producing alumina there in 1941. Billiton began mining there in 1942. World War II created a worldwide surge in demand for aluminum, and Suriname remained the largest producer of bauxite up until the 1960s, when it was surpassed by Jamaica. The other major producers in the Caribbean region were British Guiana, where bauxite mines fed Alcan's Canadian smelters, which also served US war production, and to a lesser extent Haiti, where Reynolds mined bauxite from the 1950s onward.

US military power was behind Alcoa's expansion into the region: "In its search for new bauxite reserves, the aircraft industry made large investments in Suriname," according to Sandew Hira. "A massive import of capital was accompanied by the stationing of a large and highly paid American army unit to protect the interests of . . . Alcoa,"[12] Military power enabled the United States to commandeer Caribbean resources, and no one consulted local people, especially indigenous people and Maroons, on the use of their lands. An Alcoa Shipping Company ad from 1948 announces the company's multiple business interests in the region:

Behind Caribbean romance lurks an export market. SURINAME—Thousands of East Indians contribute an Arabian Nights touch to this equatorial land. They also are part of a thriving Caribbean market that needs razors, sewing machines, autos, machinery and other products manufactured here in the U.S.A.[13]

The Alcoa Shipping Company not only carried bauxite out of the region at very cheap rates, but also profitably carried tourists into the exoticized lands that were simultaneously being opened up for US markets for products made from their metal. It was a win-win-win situation from their point of view.

The Caribbean could be exploited as a site for both romantic escape and business profit. Many of the customers on Alcoa's cruises were North American (and some Latin American) businessmen and their families, with an interest in the markets there; however, Alcoa's main interest in Suriname was not in export markets as much as in bauxite mining and alumina processing, and it would expand these interests in the 1950s to 1960s. In a 1955 publication on bauxite mining activities in the region, we can see the view of a Djoeka (Maroon) village from a Suralco freighter, the elevated point of view suggesting a huge ship moving through the jungle, its passengers looking down on people living with very traditional means (thatched roofs, dugout canoes, simple clothing), far removed from the purposes of this gigantic industrial conveyance (figure 6.1).

The experience is described as follows: "For the tourist, there can be few thrills equal to that of winding for 10 to 12 hours between two constantly narrowing walls of jungle greenery, broken only occasionally by primitive Djoeka villages, until the tree branches actually scrape the sides of the vessel, and then suddenly and unexpectedly bursting out upon the spectacle of a colorful and modern industrial community in the heart of the jungle."[14] This spectacle of industry against the jungle backdrop fed into the US technological sublime, and fed the desire for even grander projects of development.

"By far the largest development project ever carried out in Suriname was the construction of a hydroelectric dam and an artificial lake in order to generate electricity for an aluminum smelter" in 1966–1967.[15] Alcoa financed the Afobaka dam and the smelter at Paranam, and the Surinamese government agreed to relocate the Saamaka Maroons, whose territory was unilaterally appropriated.[16] In the 1959 Brokopondo joint venture between the

FIGURE 6.1
View of a Djoeka village from the Suralco Freighter on the Suriname River, from *Suriname Bauxite* (1955). Courtesy of the John Heinz Library and Archive, Pittsburgh, Pennsylvania.

Government of Suriname and Alcoa, the government had agreed to give Alcoa exclusive rights to "exploration for bauxite in a zone which is bounded by the Atlantic Ocean on the north, by the Fourth Parallel on the south, the Marowijne River on the east, and the Suriname River on the west." Alcoa in return agreed to build a hydroelectric plant involving several dams and a reservoir predicted to rise 50 meters over the existing river elevation. In 1969, Alcoa described its own involvement in the region in glowing terms:

Alcoa has ventured into every part of the globe, establishing complex operations where bauxite reserves and sources of hydropower occur close together. In at least one case, these overseas developments have had deep implications for the host nation, revolutionizing its economy and raising standards of living for its people. In Suriname, South America, under the terms of the Brokopondo Agreement, Alcoa constructed a dam across the Suriname River. A reservoir of about 600 square miles—one of the largest man-made lakes in the world—was created. Power from this project is used in the smelter at Paranam.[17]

Besides electricity generation and bauxite mining, the foreseen benefits of the project for Suriname included not only road construction that would make the region of the upper Suriname River more easily accessible, but also "Social Sector—Transmigration of native hinterland population [boslandbe-volking], including thereunder education, hygiene, medical attendance, intensifying agricultural and town-planning at Paranam. Recreation and Tourism—Along the edge of the lake and the nearby mountain-ranges."[18] Thus the removal of the boslandbevolking, or people of the woodland, that is, the Maroons, was actually seen as one of the benefits of the project, as was the opening up of the interior to development and the potential for tourism.

However, from the point of view of the Saamaka Maroon people who lived along the river and had treaty rights to control this territory as their own, "approximately half of traditional Saramaka territory was flooded in order to produce cheap electricity for Alcoa's new smelter near the capital. Six thousand people were forced to leave their homelands, some settling in special 'transmigration villages' to the north of the [artificial] lake, others establishing villages near its southern border."[19] The gates of the dam were first closed off in February 1964, and the flooding of the Suriname River reached its full height in July 1971, which in fact ended up eighty meters above the original level.[20] The reservoir effectively dismembered their territory, destroying significant cultural sites including covering over the rapids of Mamadan and some forty-three villages, decimating a traditional culture that was highly place-based. The transmigration villages lacked basic facilities, including electricity, even though the power lines to Alcoa's smelter ran nearby. They were also not given secure land tenure. Price goes on to describe the twenty-first century in scathing terms:

In Suriname, there are yet more blatant attempts to abrogate unilaterally the eighteenth-century Maroon treaties. The government in Paramaribo cuts up the bulk of Saramaka territory into parcels and leases them to Chinese, Indonesian, Canadian, American, and other multinational logging and mining companies. Logging roads are cut through [historic] First-Time village sites; game, birds, and fish disappear; vast expanses of red mud and white sand replace tropical forest; thousands of tons of cyanide- and mercury-laced gold-mining slag bury watercourses.[21]

In planning for Suriname's independence in 1975–1980,[22] further development plans called for "the building of a huge hydroelectric station in the west of Suriname, for an alumina and aluminium plant and for a city on the site of the present Indian village of Apoera. The plan revolved around the mining and processing of the enormous bauxite reserves in the Bakhuys mountains in the south-west of the country,"[23] considered one of the world's largest reserves. Local indigenous communities lost some of their agricultural land, protested the development, which would have flooded an area twice as large as the Brokopondo project, and "demanded legal title to an indigenous territory."[24]

Although the original plan never came to fruition, Alcoa and other companies have continued on and off negotiations with the government to revivify the "West Suriname project" for the development of a new hydroelectric dam and bauxite mining region.[25] In 1998 the US State Department called alumina exports "the backbone of Suriname's economy." "The preeminence of bauxite and Alcoa's continued presence in Suriname is a key element in the U.S.-Suriname economic relationship," according to a 1998 State Department briefing.[26]

In addition to controlling bauxite mines, Alcoa and BHP Billiton also share (55/45 percent) operations at the Suralco 1.7 million ton alumina refinery in Paranam on the Atlantic coast. Alcoa continues to expand Suralco's activities today, at the expense of Saamaka people and the ecology of the region. Since the 1990s the problems faced by these Maroon communities have continued:

These once forested communities now live in a moonscape, surrounded by blasted rock, covered in dust and debris from blasting and are subjected to high intensity lights that allow mining to take place 24 hours a day, seven days a week. Adjoema-kondre is an extreme example of the impact of Suralco's activities. It is presently surrounded by three active concessions and mining is taking place less than 200 meters from the village itself. Much of the community's agricultural and hunting lands, and in some cases houses, ha[s] been destroyed and the river that runs through the village has turned brown-orange due to run off from the mining areas. Community members also allege that their health has suffered as a consequence of environmental contamination caused by Suralco's activities.[27]

The Association of Saamaka Authorities, representing the interests of the Maroons, brought a case before the Inter-American Court of Human Rights, *Saramaka People* v. *Suriname*, "seeking collective title to the lands on which Saramakas have lived, farmed, and hunted since the eighteenth century." The Saamaka people won their case in 2007, but it remains to be seen whether the ruling against the Government of Suriname recognizing their collective land rights and right to self-determination will be enforced.[28]

In July 2010 the party of ex-dictator and convicted drug-smuggler Desi Bouterse won a parliamentary majority and chose him to be president. He quickly signed a memorandum of understanding with China to finance "a railroad and highway from Paramaribe to Manaus (Brazil), cutting right through the heart of Saamaka territory. There was no mention of the *Saramaka People* judgment nor any consultation with Saamaka representatives."[29] There are also extensive new plans for gold mining, and expansion of bauxite mining into the Nassau Mountain region. A new five-year plan approved by the national assembly includes implementation of the Tapajai project, "which would dam the Tapanahoni River, divert its waters into the Afobaka reservoir, and sink numerous Ndyuka and Saamaka villages, as well as a project to dam the Grankiiki (in Ndyuka territory) to provide electricity for the massive mining projects in Paamaka territory currently under development with Newmont Mining (gold) and Alcoa (bauxite)."[30] These plans ignore the court ruling and impose huge new ecological and social burdens on the Maroons and indigenous people, violating their human rights. The National Assembly, Price says, also "passed a law granting amnesty to Bouterse and his associates for all crimes committed 'in defense of the State' during the period of military dictatorship that began in 1980."

Today international human rights law remains one of the few tools available to protect indigenous, Maroon, and tribal peoples' collective land rights, serving as "an instrument that allow[s] their voices to be heard" in national and transnational debates,[31] despite its evident limitations. The appropriation of Saamaka Maroon lands highlights the spatial injustices of global industries both materially and through representations and global imaginaries. The Caribbean has long served as a site of tropical semimodernity, set apart from the modern West through forms of colonial exploitation and imperialist exotification of its "colorful" people, "vivid" nature, and "dream-like" landscapes.[32]

The cool space-age futurism of aluminum modernity had to be constructed via its contrast with a backward, slow world that happened to lie next door: the US fascination with the steamy jungles of the tropics, the hybrid races of the Caribbean, and the image of "the islands" as primitive, backward neighbors. This grammar of difference helped to construct what anthropologist Michel-Rolph Trouillot[33] calls "the Savage Slot," yet it depended on making *invisible* the power of US corporations to control and monopolize the mining and processing industries that make modern technology possible, and the military power that it enabled and required. It also hid the emerging modernities of the Caribbean itself, especially its political modernity, which was subsumed beneath the romantic naturalism of tourism and at best acknowledged as a potential market for US-made goods. In the following sections I examine both Alcoa's representation of the region and how it was challenged by actors within the region.

YOUR SHIP: ALCOA *CLIPPER*

The Alcoa Steamship Company played a special role in the Caribbean, not only shipping bauxite and refined alumina to the United States but also carrying cruise ship passengers, commissioning artists to depict Caribbean scenery, and even recording Caribbean music and sponsoring the Caribbean Arts Prize in the 1950s. The company operated three "modern, air-conditioned ships," each carrying sixty-five passengers, which departed every Saturday from New Orleans on a sixteen-day cruise, making stops in Jamaica, Trinidad, Venezuela, Curaçao, and the Dominican Republic.[34] These ships became not simply a conduit connecting different modernities, but were precisely one of the means by which divergent North Atlantic and Caribbean modernities were produced. David Lambert and Alan Lester argue that the "travel of ideas that allowed for the mutual constitution of colonial and metropolitan culture was intimately bound up with the movement of capital, people and texts between these sites, all dependent in the last resort on the passage of ships."[35] The mobility and increasing speed of ships as steam replaced sail in the nineteenth century reconfigured the space of the Atlantic world as "a particular zone of exchange, interchange, circulation and transmission," suggests David Armitage.[36] And as Anyaa Anim-Addo elaborates in her work on the Royal Mail Steam Packet Company in the Caribbean, "The RMSPC's ships offered an alternative modernity to the railway but also, as mobile places, provided a shifting experiential modernity at various points along the ship's routes."[37] It was precisely in riding onboard ships such as Alcoa's cruise liners, and in consuming their touristic visual grammars, that divergent mobile modernities were constituted, lived, and materialized.

The ship en route was a space of travel and mobility between allegedly separate worlds—one fast and modern, the other traditional and romantically slow—yet ironically those worlds were connected by the material potentialities of aluminum that arose directly out of the ground of the Caribbean. Alcoa's three new ships, built by the Oregon Shipbuilding Co. in 1946, were test beds for Alcoa's new magnesium-silicide Alloy 6061, thus becoming a material and symbolic realization of mobility on display:

These liners, the *S.S. Alcoa Cavalier, Clipper,* and *Corsair* used alloy 6061 for deckhouses, bridges, smokestack enclosures, lifeboats, davits, accommodation ladders, hatch covers, awnings, weather dodgers and storm railings, all connected with 6053 rivets. Other alloys, both wrought and cast, were used for doors, windows, furniture, electrical fittings, décor and for miscellaneous applications in the machinery space.[38]

The ships themselves, with their extensive aluminum fixtures and fittings, advanced technology and modernist design, were at once floating promotions for potential investors, displays of the material culture of aluminum's light modernity, and a means of consuming mobility as touristic practice. Passengers on the three ships were given pamphlets including "Let's Talk about Cruise Clothes," "Taking Pictures in the Caribbean," and "Your Ship: Alcoa *Clipper,*" which described the extensive use of the light metal in the ship, from the superstructure to the staterooms: "Almost anywhere you happen to be on Your Ship you will find some use of aluminum."[39] Thus the ships combined industrial mobilization of commodities, multisensory touristic mobilization of a mobile gaze, and subtle symbolic mobilization of the signs and icons of mobile modernity.

The same economic, political, and spatial arrangements that locked in huge market advantages for transnational mining corporations simultaneously opened up Jamaica and other Caribbean destinations for tourism mobilities. Tourism then instigated the circulation of new visual representations and material means of movement through the Caribbean. While Alcoa promoted novel products, modern skyscrapers, and metallurgical research and development in the United States, the company promoted the Caribbean as a source of bauxite, positioned it as a potential market for "superior" US products, and envisioned it as a timeless destination for tourists traveling on its modern ships to safely step back into the colorful history, exotic flora, and quaint folkways of diverse Caribbean destinations. Although these modes of both imaging and moving are not surprising (and continue in other ways today), what is striking is the degree to which the Caribbean produced here diverges from the futuristic images of supermodernity that were simultaneously being promulgated in the US consumer market for aluminum products. Appearing in the luxury publication *Holiday* magazine, the advertising images seamlessly meld together tourism, business travel, bauxite shipment, and cultural consumption, yet carefully detach these Caribbean mobilities from the light, sleek modernity being envisioned and promoted at home in the United States, in magazines such as *Fortune* and onboard the ships themselves.

The ads also strikingly ignore or erase the presence of modern technology in the Caribbean, including US military bases and the emerging infrastructure of modern ports, urban electrification, and eventually airports. As Krista Thompson has shown in her study *An Eye for the Tropics,*[40] photographic images of the Caribbean produced for tourist markets in the early twentieth century tropicalized nature by emphasizing lush and unusual plants, exoticized local people by showing them in rustic and primitive settings, and erased signs of modernity such as electric power lines or newer urban areas. It is US tourists and modern North American ships that seemed to move, and the Caribbean islands and coastal ports were pinned down like butterflies to be collected, cataloged, and made known. Here I focus on three moments of the erasure of Caribbean modernity, showing how the motions of the Alcoa ships produce the spatial disjunctures of divergent modernities through their representational practices and cultures in motion.

TOURISTS, PRIMITIVES, AND MODERN WORKERS, 1948–1952

The first series of ads, which ran from 1948 to 1949, was created and signed by the graphic artist Boris Artzybasheff. A Russian émigré to the United

States, Artzybasheff was most well-known for his cover portraits for *Time* magazine, his colorful series of Shell Oil ads, and his surreal drawings of anthropomorphic machines. For the Alcoa Steamship Company he produced an unusual series of portraits of Caribbean people. A Carib mother and child, for example, are depicted as timeless primitives, holding up fruit and peering out from dark eyes and exotically painted faces (figure 6.2), in a region described as "rich in the turbulent history of the Carib Indians, Spanish Conquistadors and bloody buccaneers."

Afro-Creole women appear in typical poses such as "dark-eyed senoritas, descended of conquistadores of old" or a stereotypical "Creole belle," wearing a madras head tie and gold jewelry (figure 6.3). Each image represents an example of racial blending or distinctiveness, portraying a male or female racialized persona in typical costume, including Carib Indians, various types of Afro-Caribbean "blends," East Indian Hindu, and Muslim (figure 6.4), and even various types of Creole "whites" of Spanish, Dutch, or Anglo-Caribbean origin. Although the images appear at first to promote cultural encounter and ethnological curiosity within touristic contact zones, such typifying images circulate within a long lineage of tropicalizing representations of Caribbean islands and people.[41]

Setting the modern US consumer-tourist apart from the ersatz primitive populations of the tropics, the text of this series emphasizes the swashbuckling colonial history of the Caribbean, which marked the region with diversity: "if you look carefully you'll see how the distinctive architecture, languages and races of this area have been blended by centuries into interesting new patterns." This kind of typifying imagery relates to earlier colonial racial typologies and Spanish *castas* paintings, which attempted to portray all of the racial "types" found through mixtures of different kinds. Each image includes a distinctive flower, colorful foliage, and often a typical bird or butterfly, suggesting a kind of natural history that conjoins island people and wildlife, naturalizing races through attachment to profusely tropical places. This is a mode of visualization that solidifies Caribbean difference as a natural distinction that sets "the blue Caribbean" apart from the mainland world inhabited by allegedly modern subjects. Above all, this "tourist gaze" produces a visual grammar of difference.[42]

Although suggestive of the complex global mobilities of people and cultures, these historically anchored images fix the Caribbean in time as a series of romantic remnants that exist for the edification and consumption of the

FIGURE 6.2

Boris Artzybasheff, Alcoa Steamship Co. ad, Carib Indian, *Holiday* (February 1948).

ALCOA *sails the* CARIBBEAN

In centuries past, "affairs of honor" between European nations were often settled in the blue Caribbean. The scars of these former quarrelsome days are now hidden by flowering frangipani trees, and lovely tropical plants. But the see-saw of races and tongues that lasted so long is reflected in the interesting people who now populate these friendly, good-neighbor lands. Plan now to visit the Caribbean—region of ageless beauty and of thriving markets—served by ships of the Alcoa fleet. Write for booklet. Alcoa Steamship Company, Inc., 17 Battery Place, New York 4, N. Y. or One Canal Street, New Orleans, 16, La.

ALCOA STEAMSHIP COMPANY, INC. • OFFICES IN: BALTIMORE, CHICAGO, MOBILE, MONTREAL, NEW ORLEANS, NEW YORK, ST. LOUIS, TORONTO

HOLIDAY/JUNE

FIGURE 6.3

Boris Artzybasheff, Alcoa Steamship Co. ad, Creole belle, *Holiday* (1948).

East meets West
on an Alcoa Caribbean Cruise

Decades ago, natives of British India were brought to Trinidad to till the fields. Today,
white minaretted mosques and colorful Hindu temples are a mark of the island. In
modern Port of Spain the mixing of East Indians, Englishmen, Negroes, Chinese and
Portuguese makes a photogenic and cosmopolitan city. On Frederick Street you'll find
fascinating shops selling the wares of the world. In addition, Trinidad offers fine sight-
seeing trips, palm-fringed beaches, handsome clubs and the amusing, racy ballads of
its famed Calypso singers. Yes, on an Alcoa cruise you can enjoy all these—plus calls
at Venezuela, Jamaica, Curacao and the Dominican Republic. Plan now to sail the
Caribbean *this Fall*, one of the best times of the year in this region of tropical beauty.

ALCOA
sails the CARIBBEAN

ASK TODAY for booklet telling about the unusually fine accommoda-
tions for fall sailings on Alcoa's three modern, *air-conditioned* ships.
All staterooms outside with private baths. *See our local travel agent* or
write: Alcoa Steamship Company, Inc., Dept. B, 17 Battery Place,
New York 4, N. Y. or Dept. B, One Canal Street, New Orleans 16, La.

ALCOA STEAMSHIP COMPANY, INC., OFFICES IN: BALTIMORE, CHICAGO, MOBILE, MONTREAL, NEW ORLEANS, NEW YORK, NORFOLK, ST. LOUIS, TORONTO

HOLIDAY/AUGUST

FIGURE 6.4

Boris Artzybasheff, Alcoa Steamship Co. ad, Trinidad Hindu, *Holiday* (1948).

modern, mobile traveler. Hindus and Muslims appear in unusual hats in front of their exotic temples, suggesting the mobility of cultures into the colonial Caribbean. A Dominican sugarcane cutter appears as noble worker in one image, with the tools of his trade in hand (figure 6.5). Yet the images simultaneously paper over the ethnic, class, and color hierarchies that fanned political unrest throughout the post-WWII Caribbean; they offer not only a visually flattened perspective but also a historically and socially flattened one.

Left-wing Guyanese labor leader Cheddi Jagan noted in 1945 that wages for workers were "only one-third to one-quarter of comparative wages in bauxite and smelting operations in the United States and Canada," and he dreamed of an independent nation with its own aluminum industry.[43] Ironically, in this very period Alcan's DEMBA mine in British Guiana (part of Alcoa when built) was using racial and ethnic divisions of labor to reinforce the occupational and political divisions between Guyanese of African and East Indian descent, and class hierarchies between black and white.[44] The DEMBA workers engaged in a sixty-four-day strike in 1947 but struggled to form an effective union in the face of company paternalism and tight discipline.

The Caribbean claims one of the most mobile working classes in the world, but it was foreign corporations that governed the patterns of labor migration—whether to work on the sugar plantations of other islands, the banana plantations of Central America, or in the building of a trans-isthmus railway and the Panama Canal. This mobile working class was at times highly politicized, cosmopolitan, and critical of the world economic system. Ideologies such as Garveyism, pan-Africanism, socialism, and communism circulated among them, and between the Caribbean and its US outposts in places such as Harlem.[45] The most organized workers in the region were the stevedores and other port workers who, along with sugar plantation workers, led major strikes including the labor rebellion of 1937–1938.[46]

Both Guyanese and Jamaicans in the labor movement struggled to shift the terms of their enrollment in the world economy and transform the ways in which their natural resources (and labor) were being mobilized for the benefit of others.[47] Only a Venezuelan worker placed in front of what is described as a "forest of picturesque oil wells," holding a sturdy wrench among some delicate pink flowers, hints at a modern industrial economy taking shape in the Caribbean, but one that is described as "*hungry* for American-made products—and all that their superiority represents." The feminization of the worker and naturalization of the industrial landscape

ON AN ALCOA CRUISE you enjoy gracious living on a modern, air-conditioned ship. Your trip is punctuated with stops at such interesting places as Dominican Republic, Jamaica, Venezuela, Trinidad, and Curacao. The Alcoa Cavalier, Alcoa Clipper and Alcoa Corsair alternate in weekly sailings from New Orleans.

Something new to see at each Alcoa port you visit

You'll find the Caribbean rich in exciting reminders of centuries long past. Take the Dominican Republic for example . . .

Discovered by Christopher Columbus—in later centuries a stopping place for treasure-laden galleons—it is rich in historical background. Part of the once regal home of Diego Columbus, built in 1510, still stands. There is also the little old Iglesia del Rosario, first church in all the Americas, and the beautiful tomb of Christopher Columbus in the spacious quiet of the old Cathedral. In the cities, modern architecture contrasts with crumbling remains of colonial Spain. In the countryside, machetes of hard-working natives harvest the fourth greatest amount of sugar in all Latin America.

Write today for booklet of all the places you visit. Alcoa Steamship Company, Inc., Dept. B, 17 Battery Place, New York 4, N. Y., or Dept. B, One Canal Street, New Orleans 16, Louisiana.

ALCOA
sails the CARIBBEAN

ALCOA STEAMSHIP COMPANY, INC. OFFICES IN: BALTIMORE, CHICAGO, MOBILE, MONTREAL, NEW ORLEANS, NEW YORK, NORFOLK, ST. LOUIS, TORONTO

HOLIDAY/APRIL

FIGURE 6.5

Boris Artzybasheff, Alcoa Steamship Co. ad, Dominican cane cutter, *Holiday* (1948).

suggest an awkward attempt to fit industrialization into older tropes of Caribbean island paradise.

The protean Caribbean appears here as a series of renaturalized yet traditional places, outside of modernity yet accessible to the mobile tourist, a "paradise for travelers, export opportunity for businessmen." Special editions of some of the images, suitable for framing, could also be ordered by mail, creating a Caribbean souvenir to take home. A second related series of ads, published in 1951–1952, depicts botanical paintings of tropical flowering trees by the respected botanical illustrators Harriet and Bernard Pertchik (figure 6.6).

These images tap into a long tradition of botanical collection and illustration of tropical plants by colonial naturalists, who collected material in the Caribbean and incorporated it into systems of plant classification and medical knowledge.[48] Natural beauty is here valued in a visual economy of touristic consumption, even though the modern light mobility of the US tourist is predicated on clearing and strip mining Caribbean forests for the precious red bauxite ore below them. Tourists themselves are depicted in the corner of each ad, frolicking on the modern space of the ship in motion.

The same corporation that transports bauxite out of the Caribbean on its freighters not only carries tourists in but also through its advertising incites the consumption of new modern products in the US consumer market, and the cruise experience itself produces the mobile modern subjects who will consume such products. This modern mobile subjectivity is explicitly contrasted against the slow, backward, romantic tropics; yet the market relations and power relations that produce these conjoined uneven modernities (including US military bases) are like photographic negative and positive, each a condition for the other.

BAUXITE, FOLK DANCE, AND VERNACULAR STYLES, 1954–1959

As Jamaica adopted universal enfranchisement in the 1940s and moved toward self-government in the 1950s, there was "an increasing sense of nationalism and concern for the protection of national resources," especially among the labor parties of the left.[49] Out of the labor movement arose a generation of nationalist leaders who pushed the British West Indies toward independence and toward democratic socialism. In October 1953 the British government, with US support, forcibly suspended the constitution of Guyana and deposed Jagan's labor-left government, elected by a majority under

PLUMIERIA RUBRA (Red Frangipani)—Second in a series of Caribbean flowering tree blossoms painted by Pertchik for Alcoa Steamship Company. A de luxe print 16" x 16" on fine paper, with wide grey mat, will be sent you for fifty cents.

Bright spot in your memory book...

A visit to the nearby Caribbean is truly a memorable adventure. The magnificence of nature displays itself in the beauty of its flowering trees, its palm-studded beaches, its majestic mountains. And when you "sail Alcoa," you travel to this tropical wonderland in comfort and relaxation. Your ship is modern and air-conditioned. Each stateroom is outside, amidships and has a private bath. For extra enjoyment you have a tiled, outdoor swimming pool, planned shipboard entertainment, exciting shore trips and the finest cuisine. Alcoa's fast freight-carrying passenger ships sail every Saturday from New Orleans for Venezuela, Trinidad, Jamaica and Curacao or the Dominican Republic. See your travel agent or write for booklet "H" describing a luxurious 16-day Alcoa cruise.

ALCOA *serves the Caribbean*

PASSENGER AND FREIGHT SERVICES

© ASCO 1951

ALCOA STEAMSHIP COMPANY, INC., 17 BATTERY PLACE, NEW YORK 4, N. Y. or ONE CANAL STREET, NEW ORLEANS 12, LA.

HOLIDAY/APRIL

FIGURE 6.6
Harriet and Bernard Pertchik, Alcoa Steamship Co. ad, botanical illustration, *Holiday* (April 1951).

universal adult suffrage, when he threatened to take back mineral resources and move the colony toward independence.[50]

Coming just as the government was in the process of passing a labor relations bill that would have protected unions and labor rights, the coup nipped in the bud Jagan's longer-term plans to create forward linkages through locally based aluminum smelters and fabrication plants using the country's significant potential for hydropower. Bolland argues that the "consequences of the suspension of Guyana's constitution and subsequent British actions were devastating for the development of politics in the colony," leading to a deep racial split within the People's Progressive Party, and long-lasting racial polarization between Afro-Guyanese and Indo-Guyanese.[51] These events make evident the external control over labor movements in the region and the degree to which they would not be allowed to assert resource sovereignty.

It is in this historical context that we can read the third Alcoa Steamship series, which ran from 1954 to 1955, a striking set of folkloric portrayals of musical performances, parades, or dances, both religious and secular, by the graphic illustrator James R. Bingham. Readers are encouraged to write in to purchase 45 rpm recordings of the music that accompanies some of the dances, including the sensationalized Banda dance of Haiti, associated with Vodou (figure 6.7), the Joropo of Venezuela, the Merengue of the Dominican Republic, and the Beguine of the French West Indies.

Other ads represent the Pajaro Guarandol "folk dance of the Venezuelan Indians," the steel pan and "stick dance" of Trinidad, the "Simadon" harvest festival of Curacao, the folk dance of the Jibaros of Puerto Rico, and the John Canoe dancers of Jamaica, whose costumes date back to the eighteenth century and possibly to West Africa (figure 6.8). This series connects touristic consumption of musical performances from across the Caribbean with an almost ethnographic project of investigation of traditional cultures and people who persist outside of modernity, a remnant of the past available for modern cruise tourists to visit, but also, as the ads note, "Uncle Sam's biggest export customer, and still growing. To appraise it for your products, write on your company letterhead for the 1955 edition of our 'Export Market Opportunities' book."

Folkloric music was played by costumed performers for the benefit of tourists. Caribbean national elites had an interest in furthering these projects of self-exotification for the tourist market, just as they had an interest in encouraging foreign investment, whether in agriculture or mining. They

FIGURE 6.7
James R. Bingham, Alcoa Steamship Co. ad, the Banda dance of Haiti, *Holiday* (August 1955).

See the exciting Caribbean the relaxing Alcoa cruise way

You'll find the Caribbean a colorful, merry-go-round of memories—from these John Canoe dancers in Jamaica to the Calypso singers of Trinidad. You'll find, also, that an Alcoa cruise is the really enjoyable way of seeing the Caribbean's wonderful sights. For 16 days your de luxe, air-conditioned Alcoa ship roams this romantic region calling at six exciting ports in Jamaica, Venezuela, Trinidad and Curacao or the Dominican Republic. Between visits you relax in luxurious comfort, enjoying the ship's outdoor pool, its superb cuisine, its many pleasant and unregimented activities. And all the way you travel in a congenial, yacht-like atmosphere, for Alcoa cruise ships carry an average of only 65 passengers. There's a sailing every Saturday from New Orleans. Or you may prefer one of Alcoa's more modest and leisurely 12-passenger freighter cruises from New York, Montreal or New Orleans. For details see your travel agent; or write for literature "H".

Sales-minded executives will find a thriving market in the friendly, nearby Caribbean. It is Uncle Sam's second best export customer, and still growing. To appraise it for your products, write on your company letterhead for the 1955 edition of our "Export Market Opportunities" book.

Bingham

ALCOA *serves the Caribbean*
WITH PASSENGER AND FREIGHT SERVICE TO 59 PORTS
ALCOA STEAMSHIP COMPANY, INC., 17 BATTERY PLACE, NEW YORK 4, N. Y. or ONE CANAL STREET, NEW ORLEANS 12, LA.
HOLIDAY/MAY

FIGURE 6.8
James R. Bingham, Alcoa Steamship Co. ad, John Canoe dance, *Holiday* (May 1955).

tried to keep their towns looking quaint and not too modern in order to encourage tourism. When modern buildings such as a new Hilton Hotel were built in the 1950s and 1960s, they became enclaves of modernity for visiting tourists from which the local populace was excluded except as service workers. Yet seldom has the direct connection between the two industries been noted: the mining of bauxite made possible the mobilities of tourism, and the touristic visualization of the Caribbean supported the materialities of dependent development that kept the Caribbean "backwards" and hence picturesque.[52] So in a sense the *absence* of aluminum architecture, vehicles, power lines, and designer objects came to define Caribbean material culture, which in contrast came to be associated with the rustic, quaint, vernacular, handmade island tradition, using natural materials and folk processes.

However, the people of the Caribbean were at the same time contesting such images, insisting on their own modernity. Independence movements in the post-WWII period began to call for self-rule, at the same time that migrants to London, New York, and other metropoles, along with the radio, carried styles of modern urban cultural consumption back to the Caribbean; and Caribbean styles of modernity were themselves carried into the metropole, so-called colonization in reverse, as Jamaican performance poet Louise Bennett called it. The potential circuits of travel of the musical recordings and dance styles hint at the powerful cultural currents emanating out of Caribbean popular cultures and circulating into US urban culture via Caribbean diasporas. Despite the appearance of frozen tradition in Bingham's portrayal of these folk dances, the vivid forms of dance and music also attest to a kind of cultural vitality that could quite literally *move* people in unexpected (and possibly dangerous) ways.[53] Writers, musicians, intellectuals, and artists grappled with the meanings of Caribbean modernity, and produced their own visualizations of the Caribbean past, present, and future.

Ironically, Alcoa incorporated these same images into their own advertising in 1958, when they started to sponsor the Caribbean Arts Prize and feature the winners in some of their campaigns (see figure 6.9). A painting by Haitian artist Castera Bazile, for example, is described as catching "much of the color and warmth of a Caribbean village on a lazy Sunday afternoon. His use of clear, bright pigments, with cool blues and greens opposing the hot colors of the middleground, give the impression of brilliant sunshine beating down through tropical foliage." The vivid action of the scene seems to contradict the idea that this is a "lazy" afternoon. The text also notes that

**CARIBBEAN ART COMPETITION
1ST GRAND PRIZE – HAITI**
In this prize-winning painting Castera Bazile, of Haiti, has caught much of the color and warmth of a Caribbean village on a lazy Sunday afternoon. His use of clear, bright pigments, with cool blues and greens opposing the hot colors of the middleground, give the impression of brilliant sunshine beating down through tropical foliage. And the geometric design of the fence and roof gable contribute a dynamic element that helps convey a feeling of movement and aliveness. The result is a painting rich in realism without being photographic.

ALCOA SAILS THE CARIBBEAN

You'll enjoy the trip of a lifetime journeying through the colorful Caribbean on a de luxe Alcoa cruise ship! She'll have air conditioning in staterooms and public rooms . . . tiled outdoor pool . . . superb cuisine . . . all staterooms outside with private baths . . . and the kind of unobtrusive personal service that Americans like. It's no wonder seasoned travelers write us "Best trip we ever took." These 16-day cruises sail every Saturday from New Orleans to six ports in Venezuela, Jamaica, Trinidad and Curacao or the Dominican Republic. Or you may prefer an Alcoa 12-passenger freighter cruise of 10 to 42 days from New York, New Orleans or Montreal. Write today to Dept. "H" for cruise booklets. Alcoa Steamship Company, Inc., 17 Battery Place, New York 4, N. Y. or One Canal Street, New Orleans 12, La.

FIGURE 6.9
Caribbean Arts Prize, painting by Castera Bazile, Alcoa sails the Caribbean advertising campaign (1958).

the image conveys "a feeling of movement and aliveness," which seems to counter Artzybasheff's frozen, still, captive figures.

In 1956 changes in the internal and external political situation led into a new conjuncture for bargaining between the Jamaican state and the transnational corporations. A major renegotiation of the terms of bauxite royalty payments and taxes was undertaken by People's National Party chief minister Norman Washington Manley (one of the founding fathers of Jamaican independence) in 1956–1957, based on the principle that "countries in the early stages of economic development ought to derive the largest possible benefits from their natural resources. They ought not to be regarded merely as sources of cheap raw materials for metropolitan enterprises."[54] The space race and the Korean War made aluminum an even more crucial "strategic material." Jamaica moved from supplying about one-quarter of all US bauxite imports in 1953 to over one-half in 1959, with 40 percent of total shipments of crude bauxite and alumina between 1956 and 1959 going into the US government stockpile.[55]

Following tough negotiations, the 1957 agreement reset the royalty paid on ore, which led to a substantial increase in revenues to the Jamaican government. Bauxite royalties contributed more than 45 percent of the country's export earnings by 1959.[56] Kaiser Aluminum, which had benefitted from the breakup of Alcoa due to the antitrust laws, expanded its operations in the country extensively. One of the few images of an industrial mine worker appears in one of their ads, showing a towering Jamaican miner against a red mining landscape, holding up a chunk of reddish bauxite ore, which matches his skin color (figure 6.10).

This image ran simultaneously with another ad depicting a white US worker, holding a shining aluminum ingot, against a blank background, with the modern end of the process literally in US hands. After independence, images of bauxite mines also appear on Jamaican postage stamps and Guyanese money, for example, showing the national importance of the industry, which in the postindependence Caribbean was still associated with modernization and development.

CARIBBEAN MODERNITY IN MOTION, 1962–1975

Ironically, in 1960 the Alcoa Steamship Company was forced to decommission its three beautiful passenger ships, the Alcoa *Corsair, Cavalier,* and *Clipper,*

FIGURE 6.10

Kaiser Aluminum, Bauxite ad with Jamaican bauxite worker (1953).

because of high costs, union struggles, and a cost-saving shift to Liberian flags of convenience.[57] A confidential internal memo at the time noted that the company would shift to chartered foreign flag freighters: "Taking advantage of the lower foreign flag operating costs, we will be able to save an estimated $2,077,000 per year immediately and $2,296,000 per year after the passenger ships are sold . . . This will eliminate jobs for American seamen and there is never a good time to do this particularly when foreign seamen will benefit."[58]

The memo goes on to note that "the passenger vessels have undoubtedly been our best form of public relations. However, the Steamship Company, by itself, can no longer justify this costly form of public relations." They would also have to cancel the cruises booked by twenty-six couples, many of whom were "customers of the Aluminum Company of America" and "prominent people." The most serious problem, however, was that the workers on the ships were primarily Trinidadian and "some smattering of Surinamers," who belonged to the Seamen and Waterfront Workers' Union in Trinidad, which at the time was trying to organize with the Seamen's International Union to strike against the cost-saving move. Alcoa executives noted that with the help of the powerful United Fruit Company they would be able to challenge the legality of such strikes, and force the workers out of their jobs before new labor contract negotiations took place.[59]

Jamaica achieved independence in 1962 when it "was the world's largest producer of bauxite" according to historical sociologists Evelyne Huber Stephens and John Stephens. "In 1965, the country supplied 28 percent of the bauxite used in the market economies of the world . . . [and] bauxite along with tourism fueled post-war Jamaican development and the two provided the country with most of her gross foreign exchange earnings."[60] Caribbean leaders also desired to escape their colonial past in order to embrace exactly the kind of modernity that US technology promised. They shared the dreams of the space age and the light modernity that aluminum could bring.

Yet the demise of the cruise ships indicates how multinational corporations were evolving into global transnational corporations. US workers would also suffer the consequences as industrial production began its shift to other parts of the world, and containerization undercut the bargaining power of port workers' unions. This was accompanied by another shift in modernization strategies, from sea power to aerial power. Ships were no longer suitable publicity machines for the company as attention shifted to the new civilian aircraft that were coming into use. If the Alcoa steamships were once "communication machines," suggesting the close relationship among material objects, semiotic meanings, advertising, and the advance of industry, by the mid-1960s they would be replaced by Alcoa's FORECAST jet, as discussed in chapter 4.

Caribbean cultures were also in motion, promulgating their own communication machines. The New World Group of economists at the University of the West Indies began to publish scathing critiques of foreign capital and the economic underdevelopment of Jamaica and began to call for the nationalization of the Jamaican bauxite industry in the early 1970s. The socialist government of newly independent Guyana nationalized the Demerara Bauxite Company in 1970 and took a 51 percent stake in Alcan's DEMBA subsidiary. In 1973 Prime Minister Michael Manley's People's National Party government "opened negotiations with the aluminum TNCs on acquisition of 51 percent equity in their bauxite mining operations, [. . .] acquisition of all the land owned by the companies in order to gain control over the bauxite reserves, and a bauxite levy tied to the price of aluminum ingot on the U.S. market."[61] In March 1974, inspired by the success of OPEC, a bauxite producer's cartel known as the International Bauxite Association was set up and was quickly able to double the price of bauxite on world markets.

However, Manley's socialist rhetoric, friendship with Fidel Castro, and support for African liberation movements such as the MPLA in Angola did not endear him to the United States or to the multinationals. In response, US aluminum companies "doubled their bauxite imports from Guinea in 1975, [and] they reduced their Jamaican imports by 30 per cent . . . Jamaica's share of the world market for bauxite plummeted."[62] The corporate powers that controlled the global aluminum industry would never allow Third World countries, especially socialist ones, to wrest control over their own resources.

The bauxite taken from the Caribbean allowed the United States to build a material culture of light aluminum, unquestionable military air power, and space-age mobility. At the same time, the terms of oligopolistic international trade and market governance that allowed this transfer of resources to take place helped to lock in place structures of global inequality that prevented Caribbean countries from exercising true sovereignty or benefiting from their own resources—for them Rostow's takeoff never came.[63] Instead, the Caribbean remained a tourist mecca, frozen in folkloric performances of the colorful past embellished with tropical foliage, for mass market tourists who now arrived on jets built with Alcoa aluminum. Most galling of all, the mined-out bauxite lands left behind deforested mountains, lakes of red mud, and environmental devastation that even government ownership could not fix, as well as populations whose health was damaged by alumina refining.

By closely examining the aluminum industry's material objects of light-weight modernity alongside its visual representations of its bauxite mining lands in the Caribbean as tourist destinations, this chapter has tried to reconnect the valuation of modern US mobility with the fixed and immobile premodern ground on and against which it was produced. The visual imaginaries and material practices of a technologically advanced mobile modernity, I argued, were co-constitutive of the "backwardness" of the Caribbean not merely through the discursive continuation of colonial visual cultures, but via a more complex redeployment of colonial visual tropes as incitements to modern subjectivity within a modernizing material culture of consumer desire and touristic place formation.

The very national ideologies that promoted lightness, mobility, and modernist design were in fact grounded in transnational heavy industry, warfare, tropical dispossession, and economic inequalities. The colonial mobilities of the Caribbean held it in a kind of slow motion, and the postcolonial struggles for democratic socialism and resource sovereignty locked the region into conflicts that were geared to spur the fast-forward motion of the United States while indefinitely delaying the Caribbean takeoff toward the promise of modernity. Today the effects of bauxite mining, alumina refining, and tourism over-development mar the Jamaican landscape, and leave behind a legacy of environmental injustice.

It seems fitting that in March 2008 the first European Space Agency Automated Transfer Vehicle, which docked successfully with the International Space Station, was launched on an aluminum Ariane 5 rocket from Kourou, French Guiana. The vehicle is appropriately named *Jules Verne*. Gazing toward the heavens, an observer of the historic launch might not have noticed the displaced Saamaka Maroons living as non-national migrants on the fringes of the neighboring French territory of Guyane, a former penal colony known for its brutal and deadly prisons, but where the capital Cayenne is now the location of the European Space Programme.[64] The modernizing society of Guyane "is trying so hard to replace its image as a penal colony with that of gleaming Ariane rockets," writes Price, but here again two modernities jarringly converge at a crossroads of sharp contrasts between the "backwards" or "slow" traditions of the Maroon past, which they refer to as "first time," and the rocket-fast, outer-space future.[65]

These Caribbean footnotes to the metropolitan world's technological achievements ought to draw our attention back down to the ground of Suriname, Guyana, and Jamaica, where an analysis of the fast *and* slow material cultures afforded by aluminum can elucidate not only the transnational cultural history of technology, design, and popular culture but also the broader currents of global political economy, mobile modernity, and its sites of contestation.

He says he's been traveling and has just come back from the Keshkal Ghats near Kanker. There are reports of bauxite deposits—3 million tonnes—that a company called Vedanta has its eye on . . . From the stray wisps of conversation and the ease with which he carries his AK-47, I can tell he's also high up and hands on PLGA [Peoples Liberation Guerrilla Army].

—Arundhati Roy, "Walking with the Comrades"

Light alloys and new products made from aluminum changed the US landscape and way of life, and spread tentacles of industrial development around the world. Yet seldom do we connect the everyday mobility capabilities of US modernity—the transport systems and airplanes crisscrossing the country, the convenient packaging and lightweight cans that transport our food and drink, the satellites and handy devices that keep us connected—with questions of development, self-determination, and environmental integrity in places like Jamaica, Suriname, Guinea, or India. Although I began research on bauxite and the aluminum industry out of an interest in Caribbean history and concerns for the future environment of the region, in the course of following aluminum I quickly realized that I would have to go beyond the Caribbean and North America to understand the activities and effects of aluminum transnational corporations. And to my great surprise (given the lack of coverage of these issues in the mainstream media), I discovered that in many of the world's main bauxite mining regions there are little-noticed conflicts, social struggles, and even wars breaking out as global corporations wrestle for control over land, resources, and energy. Even as the story of Suriname's Maroons was reaching some kind of legal resolution in the Inter-American Court of Human Rights, new human rights violations have continued to appear in association with bauxite mining and dam building for smelters in many other parts of the world today.

As noted in previous chapters, as electricity became increasingly expensive in the United States and Europe, the aluminum industry increasingly turned to the Caribbean, Africa, and Australia not only for bauxite mines and alumina refining plants, but also for the building of new smelters. In southern Africa, for example, "a single aluminum smelter near Mozambique's capital, Maputo, gobbles up four times as much power as the entire rest of Mozambique."[1] Nevertheless, a planned expansion of the Mozal smelter near Maputo rests on building the Mepanda Uncua dam on the Zambezi River, which "would flood 100 square kilometers of important pastoral land on the river's floodplain, displace an estimated 2,000 people, and further reduce valuable silt infusions into the environmentally sensitive Zambezi delta."[2] Despite opposition to the dam project by environmentalists, it is back on the table again. The Zambezi River is described as having a potential 12,000 megawatts of energy, and with Portugal having recently surrendered ownership of the Cahora Bassa dam, the energy minister of Mozambique now hopes to expand capacity by building the US$1.3 billion Mepanda Uncua dam downstream. A website promoting the project, Afrique Avenir, describes hydropower as a clean, renewable resource and laments that "less than 7% of Africa's hydropower potential is currently exploited. Hence the importance attached by most major international bodies and African states in the construction of hydroelectric dams on the continent."[3] Although new hydropower projects are described as bringing clean energy to African populations, anti–dam activists point out that much of the energy produced will instead go to aluminum smelters owned by transnational corporations, while local populations are displaced and left vulnerable to flooding.[4]

Aluminum smelting's demands for hydropower have often been met at the expense of people's health and welfare on the mining peripheries of the world. Critics continue to cite an array of ethical quagmires for the industry, which is deeply involved in building mines, smelters, dams, and other power-generating schemes around the world. One critical report entitled "Behind the Shining" describes the effects of the industry on indigenous peoples in particular:

In the eastern Indian state of Orissa, indigenous communities have been trying to stop the construction of the world's largest new bauxite mine and alumina refinery complex. [. . .]

In Brazil, the construction of the Tucurui dam displaced more than 25,000 people. More than half of the power generated by Tucurui goes to aluminum smelters in northern Brazil. The new reservoir impacted an estimated 100,000 people who drank and fished the river and farmed along the riverbed. [. . .]

In Surinam, 6,000 people were forced to move from their ancestral communities in the tropical rainforest to make way for an Alcoa/Billiton dam and smelter. A proposed new dam for a smelter in Sarawak, Malaysia, could force the resettlement of 10,000 indigenous people.[5]

In this chapter I try to track a few of these conflicts over corporate human rights violations in several of the major bauxite mining and smelting regions of the world, highlighting three of these battlefronts in Russia, India, and Guinea because these are key places on the frontier of new global developments in the industry.

The dark stories that emerge when one pursues the shining metal back to its global sites of production involve a wide range of "bad elements" not usually found in mainstream business histories or for that matter in most cultural histories of the consumption end of the industry, ranging from dictators and oligarchs, to criminal organizations and corrupt governments, to tribal resistance movements and guerrilla warfare. The international media occasionally pays attention to these forgotten places, yet seldom does anyone recognize how fundamental the economics of bauxite mining and aluminum production are to producing highly unjust and at times violent political and social conditions. Instead of the convenient packaging, gleaming skyscrapers, and futuristic transport of the aluminum dream, we see the dark side of aluminum here. The processes that produce both global and local economic inequality have left many people living in poverty and coping with the environmental and health impacts of mining bauxite and refining alumina without the benefits it allegedly brings, with many living in poverty right next to the largest bauxite reserves in the world—on their own lands.

The three countries considered in this chapter are each in the midst of different kinds of political transitions and economic restructuring. The post-Soviet transition in Russia led to a unique set of circumstances for a country that was already one of the major aluminum producers in the world, but suddenly transforming from a state-owned system to a privatized economy. The Indian transition is associated with that country's postcolonial democratization, privatization of the state sector, and recent rapid economic growth that has catapulted it to join the major industrialized nations, although still saddled with extreme poverty, inequality, and human rights challenges especially for its lowest caste peoples and listed tribal groups known as Adivasis.

In Guinea, finally, we have a postcolonial and postdictatorship state that holds 30 percent of the known bauxite reserves in the world, along with many other metals and minerals. However, it has suffered under dictatorship and unstable government, as the world's largest transnational corporations vie for control of its resources. Guinea is one of the largest producers of bauxite, yet one of the poorest countries of the world.

All three countries are affected by the huge worldwide demand for aluminum, which drove a global scramble for metals and power sources, at least until the 2012 slowdown of the Chinese economy. Chinese companies ramped up aluminum production from 3.86 million tons in the first five months of 2006 to 5.29 million tons in the first five months of 2007, to more than 13 million tons in 2010, according to the International Aluminum Institute. Other reports cite a Chinese increase in alumina production capacity from 11 percent of global capacity in 2004 to 37 percent in 2012, and an associated increase in bauxite imports from about 3 million tons in 2005 to 45 million tons in 2011.[6] These bullish analysts expect global bauxite demand to grow 6.9 percent a year, from 220 million tons in 2011 to 750 million tons in 2030. However, China does not have enough cheap power sources to apply to smelting "when its electricity systems struggle to keep up with the needs of higher-value industries, like the Chinese aerospace companies that use aluminum from Alcoa to fabricate components for Boeing 737s."[7] Chinese companies have been searching the world for access to bauxite and hydropower, leaving no stone unturned, from Australia to Guinea, and most recently instigating plans by Russian billionaire and aluminum magnate Oleg Deripaska to export electricity to China from new hydroelectric dams that RUSAL is building in the remote Siberian wilderness.

Because of this shifting terrain, the North American aluminum industry is also in flux. Between 2005 and 2006 Alcoa entered into secret talks with Canadian rival Alcan, which after fruitless negotiation resulted in Alcoa making a hostile takeover bid in early May 2007. Then, in a dramatic series of moves, the bid was rejected by Alcan in late May and finally it was British-Australian diversified mining company Rio Tinto that raised the stakes with a $38.1 billion dollar offer for Alcan in July 2007. Then Alcoa itself became a potential takeover target, with rumors emerging in June and July 2007 that the Australian mining giant BHP Billiton (with a market capitalization of $197 billion) might make a hostile bid for Alcoa. Other potential suitors include Anglo American, a South African–founded conglomerate based in London, or the Brazilian Companhia Vale do Rio Doce.[8] In another surprising turn of events in February 2008 the Aluminum Corporation of China joined with Alcoa in buying a 12 percent stake in Rio Tinto, then the world's third-largest mining company. Their "stealth move" was said to have "stunned analysts and investors," not only because it is by far China's largest foreign investment, but also because it blocked imminent efforts to buy the company (for $130 billion) by BHP Billiton, the world's largest mining company.[9] Even when BHP Billiton raised its offer to $147 billion it was still turned down by Rio Tinto, who claimed it undervalued the company. China is especially interested in gaining reserves of iron ore, used in making steel, but also in gaining control over other metals including aluminum and nickel.

All of these international industrial machinations are driving a suspenseful collision of authoritarian states, organized crime, hugely powerful corporations, and popular resistance movements. Caught in the midst of all this are some of the last remaining wilderness areas on earth, both in the tropical bauxite belt (including South America, West Africa, and Australia), and in the far reaches of the subarctic north where power is sought (including Iceland, Greenland, and Siberia).

The action begins with the period known as the "aluminum wars" in post-Soviet Russia because of the violent struggles to control the industry as it was privatized in the 1990s. Then we shift to Odisha in the 2000s, where the Indian aluminum company Vedanta has been locked in a struggle with both Maoist guerrillas fighting a civil war, and tribal peoples trying to stop the mining of their sacred mountains. Finally, in Guinea today we turn to one of the most important yet little-known industrial conflicts in the world today, as a dream of economic development through mining teeters on the brink of disaster with extremely powerful megacorporations vying for power in a country with an extremely fragile government.

RUSSIA'S "ALUMINUM WARS"

The post-Soviet economic restructuring of the Russian Federation in the 1990s created a chaotic opportunity for organized crime to take control of major sectors of the industrial economy, including mining and metals. The accumulation of capital and wealth by a few men, known as the *oligarchs,* was later converted into social capital and political influence, and it is now said that "at the beginning of the twenty-first century, Russian organized crime has established itself as a major force in the economy of the Russian Federation, blurring the lines between legal and illegal economic activities."[10]

In the 1990s former Soviet aluminum flooded onto world markets, causing prices to plummet. This contributed to the breakup of the great monopolies and oligopolies of the mid-twentieth century, and unleashed a wave of corporate restructuring and scrambling for new resources around the world. Analysts of the Russian aluminum industry (privatized along with other post-Soviet industries in 1992–1993) describe it as sharing "with that country's oil industry some of the defining features of what could be called the oligarch economy—massive profits from the export of a commodity, corporate misdeeds ranging from the dilution of minority stakeholder stakes to occasional assassinations of rivals, extreme wealth and power held by a few key entrepreneurs, and a significant place in global markets."[11]

The story of Russian corporate behemoth RUSAL is instructive. Behind it is forty-five-year-old self-made multibillionaire Oleg Deripaska, one of Russia's richest men. Deripaska emerged unscathed out of the lawless post-Soviet period known as the "aluminum wars" in part thanks to his marriage in 2001 to Polina Yumasheva, the daughter of Boris Yeltsin's chief of staff, and his close friendship with Vladimir Putin. It was President Yeltsin who oversaw the sell-off of the former Soviet Union's state-owned assets and principal industries in the 1990s, enriching a small cadre. Even now it is said that "Mr. Deripaska continues to enjoy 'protection' at the highest levels of Russian leadership."[12] For example, President Putin helped Deripaska gain a multientry visa to the United States, which had been canceled by the State Department in 2006 amid allegations of his ties to Russian organized crime.

Deripaska got his start as a young man working for Transworld Group (TWG), a metal trading company, which installed him as director of the Sayanogorsk Aluminum Works (SaAZ) at a time when TWG's opponents "claimed that it was instrumental in the criminalization of Russian industry and that its commercial operations concealed nothing more than a fraudulent exercise in asset-stripping."[13] Deripaska then "turned against his patrons" and managed to drive TWG out of SaAZ through share manipulation, assuming control over an incipient vertically integrated network of Siberian Aluminum enterprises. He then utilized bankruptcy laws to take control of Novokuznetsk Aluminum Plant (NkAZ), according to Fortescue.

In 2000, Mikhail Zhivilo, former director of NKAZ, and several other plaintiffs filed suit in the United States against Deripaska, along with more than six other major Russian businesses. Citing the United States Racketeering Influenced and Corrupt Organizations (RICO) Act, the plaintiffs accused Deripaska of "fraud, money laundering, extortion and complicity to murder" and sought damages for what he called the "illegal bankruptcy" of NkAZ. The case was dismissed, however, as not falling under US jurisdiction.[14]

The increasingly successful oligarch next consolidated his control over the industry when his main rival, Roman Abramovich, sold Deripaska a 50 percent share in RUSAL in 2003, and the balance of the company in October 2004. At this point RUSAL produced 70 to 80 percent of Russian aluminum output (2.7 million tons of primary aluminum), which was more than the entire US output of 2.5 million tons and second only to China's production.[15] In 2006 RUSAL merged with two more major players, SUAL and Glencore, capturing the remaining Russian production to become the largest alumina-aluminum multinational in the world, producing approximately 12.5 percent of global aluminum and 16 percent of global alumina through its combined assets in bauxite mining, alumina refineries, aluminum smelting, and foil production facilities.[16]

Nevertheless, there were still legal challenges to Deripaska's control of the industry. In 2008 Michael Cherney also filed a foreign lawsuit against Deripaska and RUSAL, in the United Kingdom, claiming that he deserves compensations for 20 percent stock of RUSAL that he allegedly owned. Abramovich (who became owner of Chelsea football club in England), meanwhile was the subject of a $2 billion lawsuit by Boris Berezovsky that reached the High Court in London in April 2008. Berezovsky, another one of Russia's wealthiest men, charged that Abramovich acted in concert with President Putin to use threats of state confiscation to force him to sell his interests in several companies, including RUSAL, at prices far below market value.

Berezovsky was a close associate of Aleksandr V. Litvinenko, the former KGB agent who was murdered in London in 2006 by contamination with a dose of radioactive polonium 210. Berezovsky lost the lawsuit in October 2012 and was left with huge legal fees. He was found dead in his bathroom in March 2013, with a ligature around his neck.[17] Amid this swirl of intrigue it has been rumored that a journalist working on a book about the Russian aluminum industry had to go into hiding after receiving death threats. Certainly there has not been a thorough accounting of the illegalities that accompanied the privatization and consolidation of power over Russian aluminum.

Under Deripaska's control RUSAL has generated huge private profits by exporting primary aluminum and selling off "downstream" production facilities, but still raising significant antitrust issues. Limited bauxite reserves in Russia have instigated intense pressure for the expansion of RUSAL's bauxite mining and alumina reduction operations around the world, including in Guinea, Jamaica, and Guyana. The industry is also particularly concerned with gaining control over its main cost: electricity, including both the hydroelectric plants concentrated in Siberia, currently being massively expanded by Deripaska, and Russia's coal-based generating capacity.

In 2006–2007, as already noted, the aluminum industry was in the midst of a roller-coaster global restructuring. With the price of aluminum soaring (reaching its peak at US$3,240 per metric ton in May 2006), there was a flurry of mergers and acquisitions, hostile takeover bids, and counterbids frothing up the markets. Then the global recession took hold, and the price of aluminum went nose-diving (plunging from US$3,200 per metric ton in July 2008 to US$1,476 per metric ton in December 2008).[18] The industry slammed on the brakes. Mines were shut down. Workers were laid off. Processing and fabrication companies went bankrupt. Pension funds were looted and emptied. And entire cities based on the industry, along with some of the richest men in the world, faced economic meltdown. Diversification became a crucial strategy for massive metals companies to weather price instability, so aluminum producers branched out into iron ore in some cases, or silicon and rare earth metals, or sister metals such as nickel and titanium.

In April 2008 RUSAL purchased a 25 percent stake in the Arctic mining company Norilsk Nickel, further consolidating Deripaska's control over the mining industry in Russia and raising the specter of monopoly power that rivals the scale of the former Soviet state-owned enterprises, but now under private control.[19] RUSAL borrowed $4.5 billion for the acquisition of Norilsk Nickel from a syndicate of Western investment banks including Goldman Sachs and Morgan Stanley. However, in October 2008 the company needed a $4.5 billion dollar rescue from the Russian state-owned Development Bank in order to meet these debt obligations. Deripaska's entire fortune was put in jeopardy. For the first time ever Prime Minister Vladimir Putin surprisingly scolded Deripaska, addressing him directly at a televised meeting in the small industrial town of Pikalevo, where factories have been closed and heat turned off to residential apartments: "I wanted the authors of what happened here to see it with their own eyes. Addressing these authors, I must say that you've made thousands of residents of Pikalevo hostages of your ambition, your nonprofessionalism and maybe your greed. Thousands of people. It's totally unacceptable."[20]

Deripaska also came under pressure from rival oligarch Michael Cherney, whose lawsuit against Deripaska opened in London in August 2012 and is "likely to be one of the largest ever commercial cases to be fought in a UK court." The case has offered "a rare insider's view of the chaotic and often violent consolidation of Russia's aluminum sector after the collapse of the Soviet Union." Cherney charges that Deripaska cheated him out of a 13.2 percent share of RUSAL, based on a verbal deal made in a London hotel in 2001. Deripaska charges that he was subject to a protection racket, and that his admitted $250 million payment to Cherney eleven years ago was not a business deal but an effort to end the complex protection arrangement known in Russian as "krysha" [roof].[21] As the London press follows the case, attention is focused on "one of the murkiest chapters of Russia's history when organised crime and business came together in a toxic mix. It is estimated that up to 100 people were killed and there were countless more kidnappings, beatings and general terrorism." Deripaska in his own words describes the situation as both chaotic and profitable:

You could buy a ton of aluminium for $400 and sell it for $1,200. You could make 100pc profit on trades. And if you borrowed in rubles, even though interest rates were high at 30pc, ruble depreciation was even higher. It was 1,000pc a year.

You borrowed $500,000 and six months later you [only] needed to return $100,000. People went mad with enormous fortunes that just fell on their shoulders.

You have to understand the environment. It was not just easy money. All the institutions had collapsed. The whole idea of the state, it went in a matter of weeks. No one managed the transition.[22]

Deripaska set about buying shares from employees who had been awarded them during the state privatizations but, he says, immediately "started receiving pressure from the local crime group." He describes the outbreak of the aluminum wars between organized crime and the security forces that he himself assembled from ex-KGB and Red Army veterans. "In 1993 and

1994 more than 34 people in Krasnoyarsk were shot dead because of this struggle for control"; after numerous threats and assassinations he recounts, "this was how finally I decided it was better to pay [gangs] for the moment to stay alive and for my people to stay alive . . . We had strong security and then when [Vladimir] Putin came there was a lot of optimism and strong state service, around 2000 to 2002. We managed then to quit the relationship [with organized crime]."

This period of the aluminum wars in Russia flooded the market with cheap aluminum, and destablized the international oligopolies that controlled pricing. It also led to a new political role for the aluminum oligarchs. Deripaska's political connections have generated extensive political controversy, not only in Russia but also across the world. In January 2008 the *Washington Post* reported on an unseemly meeting of Republican presidential candidate John McCain with Deripaska via a meeting set up by his political advisor, lobbyist Rick Davis.[23] McCain has been a critic of the Russian oligarchs, yet like Andrew Mellon in his day, the financiers of the twenty-first-century aluminum industry have deep pockets and long arms of political influence. In October 2008 another story broke in the British press concerning Deripaska's meetings with Peter Mandelson when he was European Trade Commissioner and approved decisions that exempted RUSAL from a 14.9 percent import tariff on aluminum foil in 2006, as well as approving RUSAL's acquisitions of Glencore and Sual and a reduction of customs duty on raw aluminum in 2007.

The merger with Glencore brought the Windalco and Alpart bauxite mines in Jamaica under RUSAL's control in a period of crisis in the mining industry, when aluminum prices were rapidly falling. This means Jamaica's economic future is now wrapped up with the decisions made by this extremely powerful transnational company owned by a Russian oligarch. With the Jamaican government facing a budget crisis and weak economic growth, including falls of 60 percent in bauxite and alumina production because of the global economic crisis, in 2010 it had to accept a $1.27 billion IMF loan with the usual conditions of public sector shrinkage and imposed rules for "efficiency" and "fiscal responsibility."[24] Thus the government greeted with relief the announcement in October 2012 that RUSAL would invest US$100 million in the Ewarton alumina-producing plant in Saint Catherine, Jamaica, saving the six hundred jobs there. However, the cost of this investment was that the government had to waive the bauxite levy on the plant for one year, which is valued at US$7 million and will involve the building of a coal-fired thirty-megawatt electric generation station. The bauxite levy waiver is described as a "sweetener" by Jamaica's energy minister Phillip Paulwell, and the overall deal as a "win-win" situation, but Jamaican environmental activists argue that it is a capitulation of the Jamaican government, which is in an extremely weak bargaining position.[25]

The current global consolidation of the mining and smelting industries, whether in Russia, North America, or elsewhere, raises pressing questions about monopoly power, global financing, environmental protection, and the failure of government regulation. Will RUSAL's investments lead to renewed pressure to open up further bauxite mines in Jamaica's protected Cockpit Country and Maroon territories? Will coal-fired power plants add to air pollution in Jamaica? Will there be further "sweeteners" needed to keep RUSAL's investment in Jamaica, thus undermining the hard-won bauxite levy? When corporations become so powerful, what government is able to stand up to them? And if governments cannot regulate them, what chance do people have to control the industrial behemoths in their own backyards and communities?

It is worth remembering one other little-known catastrophe associated with the Russian aluminum industry. In August 2009 there was a massive failure of Russia's largest hydroelectric dam, the Sayano-Shushenskaya dam in Siberia, which resulted in at least seventeen people dead and fifty-eight missing. The dam accounted for 15 percent of Russia's hydroelectric power and 2 percent of its overall power, of which about 70 percent was dedicated to the use of RUSAL. The accident took 6,000 megawatts offline, and was estimated at the time to cost $1.25 billion to repair.[26]

VEDANTA AND THE SACRED MOUNTAIN

In Odisha, India, formerly known as Orisha, there is another kind of aluminum struggle taking place. India's largest mining conglomerate, Vedanta Resources, Plc., is trying to displace forest-dwelling tribal peoples, the Dongria Kondh ("one of the few peoples in India still classified as a Primitive Tribe"[27]), from their sacred mountains in the Niyamgiri range in order to gain the 72 million tons of bauxite ore estimated to lie beneath its forests.

Extensive detailed research on the activities of Vedanta and the resistance movements against it has been published in a seven-hundred-page exposé

by Felix Padel and Samarendra Das, very active participants in campaigns to
stop bauxite mining and aluminum smelters. Although not wanting to cover
the same ground, it is worthwhile here to summarize some of their findings
because the book has been published by Orient Black Swan Press in New
Delhi and may not be widely known in the United States. They suggest that
"Vedanta's rise is one of the most rapid of any mining company, ever. Its
lofty aims of benefits for people in Odisha contrast sharply . . . with ground
realities of obliterating landscapes, pollution, corruption and death. The stories of this company are both unique and symptomatic of what is happening
in many parts of the earth."[28]

The Indian government has development plans that encompass a vast expansion in the scale of mining of bauxite, iron ore, coal, and chromite, plus
the building of aluminum refineries and smelters, steel plants, and coal-fired
power stations and hydro-electric dams to power them. These growth plans,
along with privatization, unleashed new forces in the economy. Similar to
Deripaska in Russia, Anil Argarwal, the owner of Vedanta Resources, Plc.,
also began from humble roots as a scrap metal trader in Patna and then
Mumbai to become one of the wealthiest men in the world, with homes in
London's Mayfair section, in Russia, and a seafront villa in Mumbai. Also
like Deripaska, Argarwal benefited from the privatization of India's mining
industry in the 1970s, and is seen by many as exercising undue influence
over local politics. Alongside his mining and smelting interests, Argarwal
has grandiose plans to create Vedanta University as the first interdisciplinary university of humanities, science, engineering, and medicine in India.
It is planned to encompass a huge campus built in the pattern of a Hindu
mandala, with one hundred thousand students supported by new college
towns and sports facilities built in the surrounding area. He models his civic
contribution after Leland Stanford's founding of Stanford University in Palo
Alto, California, which was built on his fortune made in building the trans-
continental railways, and Andrew Carnegie, who built Carnegie-Mellon
University in Pittsburgh, Pennsylvania, the capital of the US steel industry.
Yet in Odisha, with its rich water and mineral resources, protection of the
environment and of tribal peoples easily fall by the wayside just as they did
in the days of Stanford and Carnegie in the late nineteenth-century United
States, another place and time driven by so-called robber barons and their
visions of modernization and development.

With an aluminum refinery and a new smelter built in 2004–2006 in Lanjigarh, Vedanta obtained a mining lease for Niyam Dongar, "one of Odisha's best forested mountains, possessing the most extensive and wildest forest in the entire range" with wildlife including "elephants, tigers, leopards, bears, king cobras, pythons and monitor lizards."[29] The forest has been preserved because the Dongria people who live there, for whom it is a sacred location, have a taboo on cutting trees on the summit. Padel and Das also suggest that they live in harmony with nature, with a kind of natural wealth that modern societies should learn from rather than destroy in the name of development.

Nearby in Kashipur another bauxite mining and alumina complex is being built in "a strange and hauntingly beautiful region, ringed by several of the greatest bauxite Mailes; a high-altitude plain of rolling hills, largely deforested. Yet the soil is fertile from its high alumina content."[30] The alumina producers interested in the area have changed hands several times, from Norsk and Indal in the 1990s to Alcan and Hindalco most recently. In both regions a struggle has been taking place in which the local Adivasis, or tribal peoples, have tried to block development and hold onto their land, only to be arrested, attacked by company "goons," tear-gassed, and even shot by police.

Environmental and indigenous rights activists have been waging a major campaign to protect the rest of Odisha before it is too late and suffers the fate of mining lands elsewhere, where the "legacy landscape" of bauxite mining is described as "lunar: pocked, mineralized surfaces, devoid of topsoil, flora or fauna. Such landscapes take years (even with active rehabilitation programs [. . .]) before they can be colonized by plants and animals."[31] Thousands of Adivasis have blocked mining roads and smashed machinery, saying, "We won't give up Niyamgiri for any price," "We are the children of Niyamgiri," "Niyamgiri is our soul." Their supporters have taken protests to the company gates, to corporate annual general meetings, to government offices, and to overseas embassies in places like London.

Many villages in Odisha were also flooded out by the building of the Indravati complex of seven dams and a reservoir in the 1980s to 1990s, with World Bank funding, for the main purpose "almost certainly to supply electricity and water to proposed aluminium plants, though the rapid siltation occurring at this reservoir means the hydropower is much less than planned. None of the remote villages in the reservoir's vicinity have received the electricity they were promised."[32] Hundreds of workers died in the building of tunnels for the river diversion, and forty thousand people were displaced, receiving little or no compensation. Soil erosion has been a serious problem in the area, agricultural land was destroyed, lower portions of rivers have dried up, and people resorted to cutting forests for firewood as one of the only ways to survive.

The connection between megadams and aluminum smelting is fundamental, with hydro-projects giving an "essential stimulus to the aluminium industry . . . while the aluminium companies help finance the dams."[33]

Few people understand aluminium's true form or see its industry as a whole. Hidden from general awareness are its close link with big dams, complex forms of exploitation in the industry's financial structure, and a destructive impact on indigenous society that amounts to a form of genocide. At the other end of the production line, aluminium's highest-price forms consist of complex alloys essential to various "aerospace" and "defence" applications. The metal's high "strategic importance" is due to its status as a key material supplying the arms industry. In these four dimensions—environmental, economic, social and material—it has some very destructive effects on human life.[34]

These destructive effects have been especially pernicious for indigenous communities living in remote areas and lacking in political clout. "In Guyana, Suriname, Jamaica, Brazil, Australia, New Zealand, Guinea, Ghana, Sierra Leone, and other countries, these effects on indigenous peoples and nature have generally intensified," argue Padel and Das, "often accompanied by a high degree of foreign financial and political control."

International NGOs such as Action Aid, Concern, Oxfam, and Greenpeace have all campaigned on this issue. For example, Survival International, an organization that protects threatened indigenous groups around the world, filed a successful charge against Vedanta in a UK-based complaint under the Organisation of Economic Co-operation and Development Guidelines for Multinational Enterprises, which upheld their complaint that Vedanta failed to consult the affected communities and violated the rights and freedoms of the Dongria Kondh people. They produced a short film called *Mine: Story of a Sacred Mountain,* narrated by Joanna Lumley; protests were held on numerous occasions in Lanjigarh, and in front of the company headquarters in London; and Vedanta was blocked from receiving the "Golden Peacock Award" for corporate environmental governance from the World Environment Foundation following a petition campaign against the nomination in 2008.

The campaign has garnered further international publicity through the writings of Arundhati Roy, and publications by activist-scholars such as Padel and Das.[35] They argue that in some ways the NGOs have been compromised in their actions, depoliticizing the movement by collaborating with corporate responsibility managers. Ultimately, though, there was a glimmer of justice in April 2013: "In a landmark ruling, the Indian Supreme Court . . . rejected an appeal by Vedanta Resources to mine the Niyamgiri hills. In a complex judgement, the court decreed that those most affected by the proposed mine should have a decisive say in whether it goes ahead."[36]

Against the glossy images of aluminum as a "green metal" and the corporate responsibility managers who burnish the industry's image, we have to consider the actual economic and political structure of the industry. The industry is putting the very foundations of Indian democracy in jeopardy, according to the writer and political activist Arundhati Roy, because it corrupts the government and overturns the rule of law. Roy writes,

On the outskirts of Raipur, a massive billboard advertises Vedanta (the company our Home Minister once worked with) Cancer hospital. In Orissa, where it is mining bauxite, Vedanta is financing a University. In these creeping, innocuous ways mining corporations enter our imaginations: the Gentle Giants who Really Care. It's called CSR, Corporate Social Responsibility. [. . .] This CSR masks the outrageous economics that underpins the mining sector in India. [. . .] We're talking about daylight robbery to the tune of billions of dollars. Enough to buy elections, governments, judges, newspapers, TV channels, NGOs and aid agencies. What's the occasional cancer hospital here or there? [. . .] I'm twisted enough to suspect that if there's a cancer hospital, there must be a flat-topped bauxite mountain somewhere.[37]

In the writings of Padel, Das, and Roy we see an effort to shift the cultural framing of the aluminum industry by revealing its dark underside. Bauxite, similar to other natural resources, seems to come with a curse in which the means of progress are also the seeds of destruction. In turning this ore into gleaming aluminum, the culture of modernity generates both our best dreams of science, technology, and a better future, and our worst nightmares of ecological despoliation, cultural destruction, and perpetual strife.

Padel and Das suggest that in its natural state bauxite actually plays a key part in preserving the fertility of the earth by enabling the soil to bond with water and retain moisture. "In its earth-bound state, alumina binds minerals together, collects nutrients, and feeds these into the roots of plants."[38]

In contrast, when stripped out of the mountains it decreases soil fertility, destroys water resources, and in addition to its direct human effects also produces weapons of destruction. India's aluminum industry, similar to those elsewhere around the world as described in chapter 3, feeds into its weapons systems, including the nuclear-capable Agni, Prithvi, and Akaash missiles, as well as its satellites and its emerging space program. Thus they argue that aluminum production "has some extremely destructive effects—environmental, economic, social and military—on human life itself."[39]

"Mining and metal consumption," moreover, "have not yet assumed the key place they deserve in climate change debates. In fact, one result of the new environmental awareness is that richer nations are outsourcing their most polluting industries to India and other Third World countries, where the environment is lower on the political agenda, and legislation to protect it is enforced weakly, if at all."[40] Following our products and conveniences back to their source is one way to begin to create greater environmental awareness and a public debate about such outsourcing.

BAUXITE AND POVERTY IN GUINEA

Guinea, the largest bauxite producer in the world today, remains one of the poorest countries in Africa, in many ways exemplifying the problems of transnational capitalism. Bauxite was first discovered here in 1954, and Africa's first alumina reduction plant was developed near Fria by the French company Pechiny; but when the country rejected in a referendum General de Gaulle's proposal of being part of the French community, France abruptly withdrew, leaving the country independent in 1958 under president Ahmed Sékou Touré (1922–1984). Guinea was described as "a country of immense promise after independence in 1958, with gold, diamonds, verdant banana fields, seemingly limitless aluminum ore and gushing rivers ideal for hydropower. It was considered one of the gems in the French colonial crown."[41] The government of President Ahmed Sékou Touré pursued socialist policies, joined the Non-Aligned Movement, and had close ties with Eastern Bloc countries. After his death Guinea was then under the long dictatorship of General Lansana Conté, who took power in 1984.

The town of Fria was built around the Kimbo-Fria alumina refinery under paternalistic company policies in which housing was built according to worker's rank, along with schools, stadiums, swimming pools, and youth centers. It later became the Aluminum Company of Guinea, which after 1997 was owned by the Government of Guinea and the Reynolds Metals Company. Although the Institute for the History of Aluminum has produced a very positive history of the Fria complex, which was essentially a company town and even today remains dependent on the alumina refinery for water, electricity, and jobs, others offer a far more critical analysis of how Guinea was incorporated into international exploitation of its resources and conditions of economic dependency.[42] Although some might blame Guinea's poverty on its corruption and mismanagement, it might also be worthwhile to consider the role of the bauxite industry, and of transnational corporations more generally, in perpetuating global inequalities from which they draw advantages. The industry does not have a good record in Africa.

Joint ventures in bauxite mining and alumina refining are crucial to Guinea's economy, having long provided about 80 percent of Guinea's foreign exchange earnings. Guinean bauxite is of the highest grade, rich in alumina, and mainly obtained from three open pit mines of Sangaredi, Kindia, and Fria in the Boke Bauxite Belt. Rio Tinto Alcan notes in its own press releases that it "has had a presence in Guinea since 1921 and bauxite began to be shipped to Rio Tinto Alcan's alumina facility in Canada in the 1950s." In partnership with the Compagnie des Bauxite de Guinée it now owns the world's third-largest bauxite mine there, which produces about twelve million tons annually.[43]

In the 1990s, under International Monetary Fund and World Bank structural adjustment agreements, the government began to reduce the state sector through extensive privatization and a 1998 investment code that opened up the country to foreign investment and allowed for repatriation of profits. The exchange rate was allowed to float, leading to a huge depreciation in the value of the currency after 2004, and price controls were removed from basic consumer goods such as gasoline, leading to a 30 percent inflation rate in 2005. These adjustments were complicated by the existence of black markets for fuel on the borders with Mali and Sierra Leone, which did not have state subsidies, as well as black markets for currency that existed outside of the official exchange rate. The overall economic effects on the population were negative. There has been little investment in infrastructure, and much of the population faces shortages of water and electricity. In line with neoliberal polices elsewhere in the world, structural adjustment has increased hardships and led to political unrest.

The new mining code "mandates for the nationalisation of a 15 per cent stake in mining projects, with the government to also hold an option to buy up to another 20 per cent. Royalties have been increased, while custom duties have jumped from 5.6 per cent to 10 per cent." Based on calculations offered by Aleksey Gordymov, the director of commercial markets for RUSAL, the new code would lead Guinea's royalties on bauxite to rise to $US14.45 a ton, up from $US1 to $US3 a ton, leaving only a 6 percent profit margin for the transnational corporations, and 36 percent for the government of Guinea.

The mining industry giants were not happy. An article in the business section of the *Australian* reporting on these developments, describes this as "pain," "woe," and a warning to the iron ore sector.[49] Other world mining market analysts condemned the move as making bauxite mining in Guinea "unworkable":

Up until this year, Guinea's well-established bauxite industry had been on to a good thing, pumping out bauxite and alumina for the European market and planning major expansions.

That picture has since changed dramatically. An overhaul of the Guinea mining code carried out with the input of legendary fund manager Mr George Soros has left the country's bauxite industry contemplating a future of razor thin margins. The expansions that were being considered now look increasingly unlikely and some appear to have been pulled altogether.[50]

Just as mining companies had fled Jamaica in the 1970s (instigating the original expansion into Guinea) due to their government's efforts to gain greater sovereignty over their own resources, now the mining companies are threatening to abandon Guinea. The only thing keeping them there, according to the *Australian*, is worries that China will develop the resources and steal their Asian markets.

In April 2011, Rio Tinto, the second-largest mining conglomerate in the world, paid the government of Guinea a "so-called settlement agreement" of $700 million, to allow it access to the Simandou iron ore field, which would also allow it to go ahead with the $US1.35 billion sale of a 44.65 percent stake to Aluminum Corp. of China Ltd., the state-owned Chinese aluminum and metals group. Whereas the Chinese interests in iron ore are crucial here, these complex business deals are entangled with the aluminum industry, too. As the *Australian* article notes,

According to those watching the situation closely, this leaves [mining companies] Rio [Tinto] and Vale playing a game where they develop the projects at the slowest pace acceptable to the Guinea government, but not a day faster.

The Guinea government wants to see its resources exploited as quickly as possible, but under a taxation regime that provides maximum benefit to its people.

Unfortunately, with investment in the bauxite industry drying up, it may have gone too far with one of its core resources. Rio and Vale will be hoping the government doesn't make the same mistake with iron ore.[51]

With threats of the withdrawal of investment so blatantly circulating, it remains doubtful whether the people of Guinea will ever see any benefits from these deals, and whether its mineral riches will help strengthen democracy and the dream of development. In December 2011 Rio Tinto Alcan dispatched its chief executive, Tom Albanese, to Guinea on his third trip of the year, in something of a public relations tour. He met with government officials, elders of the Beyla tribe who live adjacent to the Simandou iron ore mining project (expected to open in 2015), and "stakeholders" including ministers, NGO representatives, ministers, and members of the diplomatic corps. He iterated the company's commitment to working "hand-in-hand with contributions to the social and economic development of the country. During this visit we have underscored our commitment to working with our partners and communities to bring mutual benefits."[52]

With the election of Conde in 2010, and despite criticism from human rights groups and the United Nations for continued violent government crackdowns against opponents, in October 2011 the United States returned Guinea to "most-favored nation" trading status, opening the way for increased investment and indicating an improvement in the human rights situation and moves toward rule of law. Crowning this transition, in September 2012 it was announced that "Guinea secured $2.1 billion in debt relief from the World Bank and the IMF Heavily Indebted Poor Countries (HIPC) initiative, paving the way for accelerated development of the minerals-rich West African state, officials said."[53] According to Reuters,

Guinea's Finance Minister Kerfalla Yansané said the debt relief, which clears two-thirds of the country's total foreign debt, will allow the country to invest in infrastructure, water, electricity, and food security. [. . .] "Guinea needs to follow a more democratic path, in consultations, in collaboration, so that we can have a sustainable development and growth that can be shared by all including the poor," he said.[54]

Meanwhile, the country has also contracted former British prime minister Tony Blair as an advisor, through his charity the African Governance Initiative (AGI), which aims both to instill good governance and to attract foreign investment. One West African diplomatic source told the *Sunday Telegraph*: "AGI's dealings are part business and part charity. While some people in his organisation are pushing the shepherding bit of his operation, others are doing business on the mineral resources side of things."[55]

Those granting favored-nation status and debt relief transparently link it to the development of mining in Guinea, while papering over ongoing human rights issues, electoral manipulation, and a poverty rate that remains over 50 percent of the population. In September 2012, on the third anniversary of the stadium massacre, Human Rights Watch took note that no one had yet been charged with the crimes or prosecuted, and called for a government investigation to take place.[56] Meanwhile the CIF was reported to be moving on the Simandou project in May 2012, cutting secret deals to provide rail infrastructure in exchange for commodities, promising "to turn Guinea into a natural resources powerhouse."[57] In July 2012 it was reported that the world's largest mining company BHP Billiton had pulled out of its iron ore project in Guinea, while "a source at Vale said [in September that] the company was putting its planned Simandou development down its list of priorities."[58] Presumably they did not like the terms the government was trying to impose.

As in other aluminum dreams around the world, it seems likely that transnational mining industries operating in a weak state will squeeze out maximum profits, while potentially leaving a wide swathe of pollution, violence, and injustice that are then blamed on local misgovernance. Articles on Guinea in the international press tend to sensationalize the violence without linking it in any way to structural problems within the global metals and mining economy. The latest reports indicate that since calling an election for June 30, 2013, opposition groups protesting the Conde government have been met with violent repression: up to fifty people have been killed and more than 350 wounded, with conflicts said to be degenerating into ethnic conflict between Malinke and Peul tribes.[59] Who is monitoring the effects of mining in Guinea? Does the government have the power to negotiate with incredibly powerful corporations? And do the people of Guinea have control over the deals cut by its government, especially when there is so little transparency? Who ultimately will benefit from Guinea's rich natural resources?

THE EXTRACTIVE INDUSTRIES TRANSPARENCY INITIATIVE

The Extractive Industries Transparency Initiative (EITI) has developed a set of rules for membership and principles that it is calling on all mining countries to sign on to and implement.[60] Guinea has been in the process of joining the EITI, and submitted its final validation report in August 2012. If these principles were to be implemented it would be of great benefit to the people of Guinea:

The EITI Principles

1. We share a belief that the prudent use of natural resource wealth should be an important engine for sustainable economic growth that contributes to sustainable development and poverty reduction, but if not managed properly, can create negative economic and social impacts.

2. We affirm that management of natural resource wealth for the benefit of a country's citizens is in the domain of sovereign governments to be exercised in the interests of their national development.

3. We recognise that the benefits of resource extraction occur as revenue streams over many years and can be highly price dependent.

4. We recognise that a public understanding of government revenues and expenditure over time could help public debate and inform choice of appropriate and realistic options for sustainable development.

5. We underline the importance of transparency by governments and companies in the extractive industries and the need to enhance public financial management and accountability.

6. We recognise that achievement of greater transparency must be set in the context of respect for contracts and laws.

7. We recognise the enhanced environment for domestic and foreign direct investment that financial transparency may bring.

8. We believe in the principle and practice of accountability by government to all citizens for the stewardship of revenue streams and public expenditure.

9. We are committed to encouraging high standards of transparency and accountability in public life, government operations and in business.

10. We believe that a broadly consistent and workable approach to the disclosure of payments and revenues is required, which is simple to undertake and to use.

11. We believe that payments' disclosure in a given country should involve all extractive industry companies operating in that country.

12. In seeking solutions, we believe that all stakeholders have important and relevant contributions to make—including governments and their agencies, extractive industry companies, service companies, multilateral organisations, financial organisations, investors and non-governmental organisations.

These are the kinds of steps in the right direction that will begin to establish some international oversight of the mining industry. Following these principles would help countries like Guinea to bolster efforts to negotiate transparent and effective contracts with transnational mining corporations, to monitor how much income is paid to the government and where it goes, and to ensure that profits are invested in programs that benefit the entire population in countries from which basic resources are extracted.

Nevertheless, improvements in the financial transparency of the extraction end of the industry are only one part of the solution. As John Maxwell, one of the great gadflies of the mining sector in Jamaica points out, Jamaica's Mining Act "requires mining companies to compensate Jamaica for every hectare of land mined but not restored," which requires rehabilitating the land and returning it to the government. Yet in 2009 there were

at least 2,669 hectares on which the companies owe us US$66,725,000 in one-time compensation, at the rate of $25,000 per hectare. In addition, the companies owe the people of Jamaica an additional US$2,500 per hectare for every year the land is not rehabilitated. According to my calculations, which are probably an underestimate, the companies owe us another US$150 to 350 million. We are talking real money here, our money—between US$200 million and US$400 million. When is the Government going to collect this debt?[61]

Yet, as noted previously, the Jamaican government was instead forced into waiving the bauxite levy to tempt RUSAL back to the country. At the same time in Haiti the new government of Prime Minister Laurent Lamothe has already promised to make the country more "business-friendly," in part by removing crucial clauses from the existing mining conventions. Article 26.5 put a cap on the expenses a company could claim at 60 percent of revenues, and article 26.4 ensured that profits were split 50–50 between the mining company and the government. These were taken out by a minister who is now a paid consultant to a major gold mining company, Newmont Venture; a geologist who was then head of the Bureau of Mines and Energy who objected to the violation of the law was removed from his position. What concerns observers "is the likely incapacity of Haiti's 'weak state' to control the mining companies and the potential environmental damage."[62] This is the global economics of mining and metals, pitting one country against another in a race to the bottom.

In chapter 8 I turn to Iceland in order to examine a wider set of issues concerning the worldwide expansion of aluminum smelting, and the question of what kind of energy sources can power its growth. Here we are not dealing with a developing country or an unstable government subject to easy corruption or a weak negotiating position, but a highly developed Western European setting, where grave environmental (and economic) issues are nonetheless at stake.

In chapter 9 a glimmer of light reappears, with the renaissance of aluminum in new materials, technologies, and design trends, along with a renewed discourse of innovation and technological fixes to the challenges of sustainability. Once again we will see how cultural processes and cultural framing are as significant as global economic development processes in driving the market for aluminum.

In the final chapter, we also turn attention back to the consumption end of the process and the role of aluminum users in all of this, alongside possible improvements in the production process itself and the life-cycle issues of the recycling of primary aluminum. Stepping back from the oligarchs, dictators, and activists, we will return to the realm of the everyday and domestic uses of aluminum that make "modern" lives possible.

The environmentalists were trying to save Iceland.
The industrialists were trying to save Iceland. Everyone was trying to save Iceland.
"A mental civil war," somebody called it.
A war of dreams.

—Marguerite Del Giudice, *National Geographic*

"We do not want your filthy lucre here."

—Yvonne Ashby, quoted by Attilah Springer of the Trinidad Rights Group at the Saving Iceland conference

From an Iceland Express flight, my first view of the "land of fire and ice" is a black crust of lava rock set off against sparkling blue sea and surprisingly lush green pasture. The bright white glint of glaciers stretches across the land like a crumpled sheet of foil. Sitting on the volcanic mid-Atlantic ridge, scoured by powerful glacial rivers, the earth's energy churns Iceland into "one of the most concentrated sources of geothermal and hydroelectric energy on Earth—clean, renewable, green energies that the world increasingly hungers for."[1] Or so some would claim. But others see it differently.

A new geothermal power plant steams ominously on the outskirts of Reykjavik—promising a new era of cleaner, greener development. As we approach the capital the road skirts past the Alcan aluminum smelter, sitting innocently enough by the shoreline. Well before the economic collapse of this small northern island-nation's banking system and currency in 2008, a global network of activists was protesting the arrival of heavy industry in the pristine wilderness of Iceland's remote subarctic highlands. I devote a chapter to this particular case because it exemplifies the struggle between claims of "green" production technologies (the cleanest in the industry) and economic development in remote areas versus global social movements against heavy industry and the ecological costs of aluminum smelting.

I first traveled here in July 2007 to witness the International Summer of Dissent led by the Saving Iceland movement, a loosely organized international group of young, fiercely dedicated environmental activists who are trying to stop the aluminum industry around the world. Although smelting aluminum with coal-fired power stations is clearly a major contributor to greenhouse gases and air pollution, these movements against worldwide heavy industry claim that geothermal and hydroelectric energy may not be so clean or renewable, and the motives behind the industrial development of Iceland may not be so noble. At issue in Iceland is whether human societies ought to harness remote wild rivers as an energy source for heavy industrial development or protect them as some of the last rare and beautiful natural places untouched by human industry.

When the activists chained themselves to machinery, blocked the entrance to smelters, and disrupted the offices of multinational corporate business, few knew that the Icelandic banking system was teetering on the brink of disaster. One year later Iceland was beset by a complete collapse of its currency and a precipitously plummeting economy, which some analysts have linked to the building of Europe's largest hydropower dam, Kárahnjúkar, along with the runaway free market neoliberalism of a group referred to as the *New Vikings*. The question now is, Will the protestors prevail or will aluminum rise like a shining phoenix out of the sulfurous ashes of Iceland's battered economy?

Iceland was "a highly coveted strategic location during World War II" and "was zipped into the center of geopolitics during this global conflagration when technological systems and industrial power linked the United States and its allies in Europe."[2] Icelandic historian Skúli Sigurðsson argues that "fundamental changes in the relationship between science, technology and the military wrought by World War II and the Cold War and a strategic location boosted Iceland into a high technological orbit" involving extensive electrification. These developments were linked to the country joining NATO in 1949, the return of US forces to the country in 1951 during the Korean War, a symbolic position culminating in the famous meeting of US president Ronald Reagan and Soviet leader Mikhail Gorbachev in Reykjavik in October 1986, which was meant to halt the nuclear arms race.[3]

Thus Iceland became a key site of advanced technological infrastructure (the US-NATO base at Keflavik, electrification, nuclear submarines, radar stations, an undersea sound surveillance system, hydroelectric projects, and advanced geothermal power plants) despite its remote location, inhospitable weather, and highly paid workforce. This special technoscientific positioning continued at the opening of the twenty-first century, generating a deep ambivalence in the country about the symbolic nature of progress and its ecological costs.[4]

In 2004 Alcoa broke ground on one of the world's largest aluminum smelters, just outside of the tiny former fishing village of Reydarfjördur (pop. 650) in the remote East Fjords region. Traditionally one of the poorest parts of the country, the region stood to gain from a Goldrush-style economic boom. Built by Bechtel for $US1.25 billion dollars, it is a colossal industrial plant plunked down in a region with a total population of only 5,522 people, in a country of only 300,000 people spread over 39,800 square miles, with most concentrated in the capital Reykjavik. According to Sigurður Arnalds, the spokesman for the Icelandic national power company Landsvirkjun, the government's grand idea was to "export electrical power on ships in the form of aluminum."[5]

The best way to export electricity in a country with comparative advantages in its production is to package it in the form of a very energy-intensive product: aluminum. Iceland's center-right government spent twelve years in power trying to encourage foreign investment by tempting electricity-starved aluminum producers with the promise of dedicated, cheap, "clean" (noncoal) energy production. For an industry that requires massive amounts of energy, Iceland is a perfect location not only because of its accommodating politics and friendly green image but also because of the fact that the Kyoto Protocol granted it the right to increase its greenhouse emissions by 10 percent above 1990 levels, the biggest increase granted to any country in the world. De Muth argues that in effect, "Alcoa is buying Iceland's license to pollute, as well as cheap electricity"[6]

The Kyoto Protocol also gave power-intensive industries that made use of renewable energy sources such as hydro- and geothermal power the right to emit an extra 1.6 million metric tons of carbon dioxide a year until 2012.[7] And beyond that, in Iceland, "the ministry of environment also gave Alcoa a license to emit 12kg of sulphur dioxide (SO_2) per tonne of aluminium produced—12 times the level the World Bank expects from modern smelters. SO_2 and fluoride, the most dangerous pollutants in terms of public health and land damage, will be pumped directly into the air via giant chimneys."[8]

In its defense, Alcoa points to its record of having cleaned up smelting. The company claims that its state-of-the-art smelter is based on far cleaner technology than in the past, and will produce only 1.8 metric tons of carbon dioxide for every ton of aluminum produced, as compared to the 13 metric tons produced per ton of aluminum by coal-fired smelters such as those in China. "The emissions from this facility will be less than for any other facility of this size elsewhere in the world," said company spokesman Kevin Lowery.[9]

To power the enormous smelter at Reydarfjördur, Landsvirkjun undertook the $US3 billion-dollar construction of a massive hydroelectric power plant at Kárahnjúkar, a remote upland region where two of the country's most powerful and awesome rivers flow north from Europe's largest glacier, Vatnajökull. The highly controversial Kárahnjúkar Hydropower Project has involved the rerouting of a glacial river through forty-five miles (seventy-three kilometers) of tunnels and a series of nine dams, the largest of which has already flooded a dramatic canyon and pristine highland wilderness area with what will eventually be a twenty-two-square-mile (fifty-seven-square kilometer) reservoir (see figure 8.1). Although largely uninhabitable by humans, the flooded region is the home of wild reindeer, nesting pink-footed geese, gyrfalcons, snowy owls, and ptarmigan. A further thirty-two miles of overland transmission lines have been built to carry electricity to the mile-long Alcoa smelter, built on the edge of a quiet and undeveloped fjord. Parts of the dramatic engineering can be seen on a documentary on the *Discovery Channel,* proudly narrated as an exciting conquest of technology over natural obstacles. With a 650-foot high dam (the largest in Europe), the power plant can generate 4,600 gigawatt hours of electricity annually, equivalent to half of what the entire nation was using, but all dedicated to the Alcoa smelter.

Opponents claimed that the flooding of a protected area at the foot of the glacier set a dangerous precedent for the sacrifice of other supposedly protected areas for the sake of industrial development. It was predicted that it would contribute to dust storms and likely lead to silting up of Iceland's longest lake, Lagarfljot, which indeed has sadly come to pass. The project's own environmental impact statement ascertained that the multiple dams, tunnels, and roads would disrupt nesting areas, reindeer migrations, river sediments, and atmospheric dust. Many are also concerned that the project lies in a geologically active area where earthquakes and volcanic activity, as well as glacial surges, are likely to occur.[10] Large-scale heavy industry is certainly detrimental to tourism, which has grown rapidly in recent years.

FIGURE 8.1
Construction of Kárahnjúkar dam, Iceland, from the film *Dreamland* (dir. Þorfinnur Guðnason and Andri Snær Magnason). Courtesy of Ground Control Productions (2009).

Unspoiled nature and untouched wilderness areas are a large part of Iceland's appeal, and the country is heavily marketed as an eco-friendly "green" destination for adventure tourism.

Nevertheless, the Icelandic government plans numerous other developments of hydroelectric dams and smelters throughout the country. Rural areas struggling with the imposition of fishing quotas and loss of jobs have faced an exodus of young people in recent years. Cheap hydro- and geothermal power are some of Iceland's main economic assets. Power plants and aluminum smelter projects have been proposed at Helguvik and Straumsvik, just outside of Reykjavik, and at Husavik in the north. In 2007 pending proposals called for four new dams, as many as eight new geothermal and hydroelectric power plants, two new smelters (one owned by Alcoa), and the expansion of capacity at Alcan's existing smelter. "If all are built, foreign companies would have the capacity to produce as much as 1.6 million tons of aluminum in Iceland a year."[11] Much of that aluminum would head for the United States, to be turned into automobiles, airplanes, weapons, and all the conveniences of modern life.

Supporters of industrialization in Iceland include the government, the foreign companies involved, and some of the rural population who have benefited from new sports halls, swimming facilities, condominiums, and amenities such as shops and movie theaters. Alcoa, of course, also defends the project. Del Giudice notes that the company's local representative Tómas Már Sigurðsson,

a native Icelander with a degree in environmental engineering who considers himself an environmentalist, was upbeat and idealistic. Alcoa's mission, he said, was to be a good neighbor in the community—while creating the most efficient, safe, and eco-friendly smelter on the planet, by recycling materials and using state-of-the-art technologies to minimize waste and control the sulfur dioxide fumes that are a by-product of smelting.[12]

Other regions slated for development have been promised new infrastructure such as roads, bridges, as well as jobs. However, although the Kárahnjúkar Hydropower Project was promoted as bringing jobs to the region, up to 80 percent of the workforce were foreign contract laborers, mainly from Eastern Europe. The extreme weather conditions at the remote work site were extremely challenging, with multiple delays in the underground tunneling. It is also reported that four workers died in building the dam, ten suffered irrecoverable injuries, and more than one-hundred others had long-term disabilities, some of the highest rates of workplace injury in Iceland.[13]

Public opinion polls conducted by the Institute of Social Sciences at the University of Iceland and Gallup in 2002 found that of all the respondents 54.3 percent were in favor of the project, 30.2 percent opposed, 12.3 percent were undecided, and 3 percent refused to answer.[14] Although the majority of the opponents live in the capital, one local farmer, Gudmundur Beck, has publicly spoken in opposition to the smelter. A soft-spoken, passionately serious man with tussled graying hair, he points out at the Saving Iceland conference in July 2007 that many people lost their homes, their farmland, and their fjords to create electricity that would not even be for Icelanders but for a transnational corporation whose aluminum is used to produce weapons. Some people in the East Fjords were against the smelter and dams, he argued, but they did not know how to unify, and the government suppressed their voices and covered up opposition to the project. Opponents of the project included some of the more urban population in Reykjavik, opposition political parties, environmental groups, as well as international activists such as the Saving

Iceland coalition, the World Wildlife Fund, Friends of the Earth, and so on. Many accuse the government of corruption and the corporations of lies and deceit in getting the project through environmental assessments. "In August 2001, Iceland's National Planning Agency (NPA) rejected the Kárahnjúkar project on the grounds of 'substantial, irreversible negative environmental impact' [. . . Yet] four months later, that decision was overturned by minister for the environment Siv Fridleifsdottir, in a move that prompted a series of lawsuits and raised concern about the nature of democracy in Iceland."[15]

In 2003 these political concerns contributed to large demonstrations of up to ten thousand people in Reykjavik against the project and public statements against the dam by some of Iceland's leading cultural figures, such as the singer Björk who played a protest concert. The country's most famous television personality Ómar Ragnarsson launched a boat into the flooding reservoir to collect samples and film the land that was being lost. And Icelandic writer Andri Snaer Magnasun published *Dreamland: Self-Help for a Frightened Nation* an indictment of the government's industrialization plans that became a local best-seller and bolstered the conservation movement.[16] It was also made into a stunning documentary film about "the dark side of green energy." His idea of Iceland as a dreamland points toward the dreams (and the delusions) behind the aluminum industry, not only here but around the world.

Do smelters bring real prosperity, or is the gleam of aluminum as much of a false promise as the financial wheeling and dealing of the New Vikings who brought Iceland's economy to ruin? Controversy continues to swirl around the government's behind-the-scenes decision-making process, the role of aluminum companies in masking the real environmental damage they cause, and the failure of democratic channels of opposition. This "democracy deficit" has led some protestors to turn to direct action—nonviolent action to disrupt business as usual and radically draw attention to saving the Icelandic wilderness. And in doing so they have also reached out to antismelter activists around the world, contributing to a global protest movement that stretches from India and South Africa to Jamaica, Trinidad, and Brazil.

THE ACTIVISTS SAVING ICELAND

With their lanky, thin frames draped in baggy black and khaki clothing, skin tattooed, some with long hair in dreadlocks, the antismelter activists look primed to take on the aluminum-military-industrial complex (figure 8.2).

They are ready to put their young bodies on the line for the cause. Mistrustful of the manipulations of mainstream, democratic, party politics, they tend toward a philosophical anarchism and a do-it-yourself ethos. Their heroes and heroines are the anti-road protestors of Twyford Down and Newbury in Britain and the Earth First!ers who stop dams and logging by breaking machinery, spiking trees, or locking themselves together to block sites.

They also have great respect for the people of the Global South who have stood up against the mega-projects of multinational corporations, often making greater sacrifices of life and health than many in the developed world. Their attitude is not so much the naive idealism of earlier generations, but rather a kind of gritty determination to fight a last-ditch battle in the final hours of the world war against heavy industry.

The organization Saving Iceland has been at the forefront of efforts to publicize what is going on in Iceland, to try to stop it from going forward, and to build international networks that can work together as a counterforce against heavy industrial development in many parts of the world. At the conference "Saving Iceland: Global Perspectives on Heavy Industry and

FIGURE 8.2
Photo of Saving Iceland activists, Summer of Protest (2007), including Reverend Billy of the Church of Stop Shopping, bottom left.

Large Dams," I met invited speakers including writer Andri Snaer Magnasun, filmmaker and environmentalist Omar Ragnarssen, Trinidadian journalist and activist Attilah Springer, East Fjords farmer Gudmundur Beck,
South African activist Lerato Maria Maregele, and Brazilian activist in the
Movement of Dam-Affected People Cirineu da Rocha (see figure 8.3).

The conference was organized to kick off the 2007 "Summer of Protest,"
which followed previous actions in 2005 and 2006 to try to stop the Kárahnjúkar Hydropower Project. Direct actions have included protest camps, local
actions to invade corporate offices and hang protest banners, "rave against
the machine" street parades, and human blockades of the roads leading to
smelters. Many of the actions have a carnivalesque element, with costumes,
parodies, and music, but the intent is always very serious. The conference
is moderated, for example, by a surreal character from New York known
as Reverend Billy, whose Church of Stop Shopping embraces evangelical
fervor to defend small places, local economies, real neighborhoods, and the
"commons" from corporate power and consumerism. Although slightly out
of place in Iceland, Reverend Billy's experience with retail intervention

FIGURE 8.3
Photo of Attilah Springer, Lerato Maria Maregele, and Abby Ley at Saving Iceland
conference (summer 2007).

workshops, anticonsumption revival services, and parades and other public actions comes in very handy.[17] They charge the industry not only with environmental devastation and pollution but also damaging human health and undermining democratic process (see figure 8.4).

The challenge for direct action groups such as Saving Iceland is how they can gather public support and galvanize local people to take action to protect their own lands. Iceland does not have a tradition of political protest or radical movements. In some ways the radical tactics of direct action seem a far cry from the everyday people of Iceland and their forms of politics, discussion, and decision making. There is a risk that the activists may alienate the very people whom they wish to draw into mass public action against the corporations. Icelanders describe the rift between the two sides in the debate as a civil war, and the suspicious perception of the activists as outside agitators, or young unwashed anarchists, may be counterproductive to the cause.

The secretive nature of the planning of the protest actions, understandably done to protect the participants from arrest, makes it difficult to open

FIGURE 8.4
Saving Iceland protest banner: "Stop Ecocide for Aluminium" making use of aluminum sign post.

democratic dialogues with local people. In making my way to the conference I myself had to trust in a website instructing participants to go to a coffee shop in Reykjavik, where they could find out the location and possibly arrange transportation to get there (bringing their own camping gear). Later, when the protest camp moved to an even more secretive location, I had to call various cell phone numbers until I was finally given instructions to a rural road where we were told to look for "a blanket wrapped around a stick," indicating the turn off onto a farm track leading to the hidden campsite. Later protest events that summer alienated some locals, because the protesters locked the doors to a major shopping mall in one instance and blocked the main road leading to the hospital in another instance.

Even at the anti-industry protest camps, there are ironies left by our aluminum-based material culture. The conference is held in a hotel clad with aluminum panels and window frames. The communal vegan meals are prepared in convenient lightweight aluminum cookware. Many of us sleep in tents held up by folding aluminum poles and tent pegs. We document the event with cameras mounted on aluminum tripods. Our very mobility to get here, whether by airplane, automobile, or bicycle, is enabled by the very metal that is detested and protested.

How easy will it be to wean ourselves off of the versatile miracle metal that props up our modern lives? Perhaps we need to acknowledge our own dependence on aluminum before we try to convince others to reject it. How do we know that protest in one place is not simply going to shift the industry to poorer disempowered regions of the world (such as Guinea), even more desperate than Iceland for development? And what if the industry itself claims to be promoting recycling, renewable energy, and sustainable practices?

Even more difficult for Iceland, in the first quarter of 2008 the country plunged into an economic crisis, with high inflation and the global credit crunch leading to a sharp devaluation of the currency, the krona, which lost 22 percent of its value between January and April 2008. With its banking sector on the ropes, 15.5 percent interest rates, and its credit rating cut by Standard & Poor's, Iceland's recent years of rapid growth and investment became a bubble that suddenly burst. Was the rapid expansion of the aluminum industry in any way responsible for the national bankruptcy? The huge current account deficit that underlies the credit worries was created in part due to the government borrowing capital to finance the building of the hydropower project, plus the massive import of materials to build the Alcoa smelter. Economists suggested that the Icelandic government's borrowing to finance industrial development would lead to a significant increase in the current account deficit, whereas the injection of borrowed capital would overheat the economy and cause increased inflation. This contributed directly to the banking crisis when European banks called in their debts from IceSave, triggering the currency collapse. Most outside analysts blamed the banking crisis on currency speculation and possible manipulation by foreign hedge funds, yet they failed to report on the role of the aluminum industry in weakening government finances in the first place.[18]

It remains to be seen whether the new heavy industrial economy in Iceland will rebound and what its ultimate impact will be both in economic terms and in environmental and social terms. Meanwhile, the corporations have turned their attention to Greenland, an even more remote and untouched wilderness, where potential development beckons. Alcoa entered into a memorandum of understanding with the Greenland self government to conduct a feasibility study for constructing an aluminum smelter with a 340,000 metric-ton-per-year capacity in West Greenland (located on the northwestern tip of Maniitsoq Island on the southwest side of Greenland), along with a hydroelectric power station affecting two separate locations, related infrastructure, and a port. An environmental impact assessment was conducted throughout 2009, and was presented at public meetings in 2010. With the antismelter group Against Aluminum Smelter in Greenland campaigning against it, Alcoa hired a public relations director to manage positive publicity for their Greenland Development project.[19] Anthropologist Mark Nuttall suggests that

the proposed smelter is a prime example of the global restructuring process the aluminium industry has been undergoing. Production has moved away from its traditional industrial heartlands of Western nations, such as the United States, to parts of the world where cheap energy and cheap labour can be accessed readily, and to places where environmental impact assessment and regulation procedures can be moved through swiftly. For Alcoa and other international multinationals, Greenland is a remote extractive periphery where the regulatory process and less than stringent legal requirements for environmental hearings make it an attractive place to invest.[20]

The Alcoa smelter is anticipated to bring in two thousand foreign workers, and create only six hundred permanent jobs of which only about three hundred will go to local people; and it is anticipated to emit 4,600 tons of sulfur dioxide and 450,000 tons of carbon dioxide.

Saving Iceland's analysis of the Icelandic situation points out that before their economy collapsed there had been early predictions that government costs for the development of large-scale industrial projects such as this one in Iceland would be an economic drain rather than a benefit to the country, in part due to indirect effects on demand, inflation, interest rates, and the exchange rate. Moreover, the companies were able to negotiate very low electricity prices, tied to the price of aluminum; thus, they were protected when prices fell and the government had to absorb the costs at taxpayer's expense.

Some economists believe this contributed to the weakening of Iceland's banking sector in 2008:

In the run up to Iceland's dramatic financial crash in 2008 the OECD concluded their country report by warning Iceland that "large-scale public investments are inherently risky" and strongly advised them not to approve further aluminium developments until it was clear whether they would get a long term profit from existing ones: *"No major investments in energy-intensive projects, including those already in the planning phase, should proceed without prior evaluation within a transparent and comprehensive cost-benefit framework (including environmental impacts and inter-generational effects)."*[21]

Thus the antismelter movement aims to take on the industry in regard to both its environmental claims to sustainability and its economic claims to producing jobs and benefiting the economies where they are located. Such movements are starting to link up around the world, sharing resources and information.

GLOBAL PROTEST NETWORKS: "THIS SMELTER TING IS ALL 'O US BIZNESS"

With dreadlocks running down her back and a winning smile, journalist and activist Attilah Springer (see figure 8.3) is a striking spokesperson for the Rights Action Group, working to stop the building of aluminum smelters in Trinidad. Far away from Iceland, Trinidad is another key location on the frontlines of the battle between heavy industrial development and local rights. Speaking at the Saving Iceland conference in July 2007, she opens her talk with the story of the small settlement of Union Village, which one morning in 2005 awoke to the rumbling sound of heavy machinery. Bulldozers had begun leveling their local forest, tearing up their productive mango hills, encroaching from every direction unannounced.

As the ravenous machines indiscriminately uprooted everything in their path, animals from the surrounding forest, seldom seen within the village, started running through yards and streets—fleeing some unseen danger behind the trees. It was the time of year when all of the forest animals were carrying young and just one band of monkeys was left in the middle of the forest, clinging to their trees with babies and pregnant bellies. The workers, uncertain what to do, stopped their machines, climbed out and started viciously clubbing the defenseless animals to death. The terrified monkeys fled helter-skelter into people's yards and houses, trying to find shelter anywhere they could. As the chaotic stomach-churning scene unfolded the people of Union Village were in shock, even grown men had tears in their eyes. Attilah's voice broke as the gruesome tale unfolded, and her audience too had tears in their eyes.

Eight hundred acres were cleared near Union Village, without warning or consent of the inhabitants, as part of the government's "Vision 2020" plan for Trinidad and Tobago to reach developed status by 2020. The plan calls for the building of three aluminum smelters in southwestern Trinidad, as well as other gas-based and chemical industries. Alcoa was contracted to build one of the smelters and the other was to be built via a joint venture of Alutrint (a partnership between national government and a Venezuelan company, Sural). Two of the planned smelters were within ten miles of each other, one within three miles of a major town (Pt. Fortin) and the other within six miles. About twenty-five thousand people live within a ten-mile radius of these smelters. All this on an 1,864-square-mile Caribbean Island with one of the highest population densities on the planet of 550 people per square mile. Lush with rainforests and spectacular bird watching, according to tourist brochures, it is also one of the few Caribbean islands with extensive natural resources including oil, natural gas, and pitch.

When Alcoa came into Chatham, ten miles south of Union Village, to hold a "public consultation" about their plans to build a smelter there, the people were prepared to stop it in its tracks. Despite the company's "it's a done deal" attitude, seventy-one-year-old Yvonne Ashby told the company representatives, "we do not want your filthy lucre here." She had been a district nurse in Carronage, a nearby bauxite trans-shipment point, and she knew how the clouds of white dust would settle over people's homes causing outbreaks of respiratory ailments. Local people also feared that the smelter was to be sited on the old Bucongo slave burial ground, where their

ancestral spirits dwelled. The next time the company men came back to the
area they brought armed guards.

But the people of Chatham had made their will felt, initiating the first
big environmental struggle in Trinidad and Tobago since independence in
1966. At Carnival that year there were five bands with antismelter calyp-
sos, such as "Helter-Smelter"; children put on school plays about industrial
pollution with names such as "Smelly"; and on Good Friday, Labor Day,
and Environment Day people paraded effigies of Alcoa and protested their
smelter-building plans. In his Christmas Day message of 2006, the prime
minister under growing pressure finally announced that the plans for the
Alcoa smelter at Cap-de-ville–Chatham were no longer going ahead.

The Trinidad and Tobago government is still pressing ahead anyway
with accelerated plans to develop a new industrial estate on the offshore site
known as Otaheite Bank to include ethylene, polyethylene, propylene, and
polypropylene plants. The prime minister Patrick Manning even bragged at
a 2007 meeting of the African Union in Addis Ababa, Ethoiopia, that "by
2012, we should be among the top three per capita users of electricity in
the world."[22] With the Alcoa smelter suspended, there were still plans to go
ahead with the second smelter in the La Brea and Union Village area.

The Alutrint smelter, financed by the Chinese government, was planned
to have a fifty-seven-hectare buffer zone of trees, shrubs, and grasses to protect surrounding populations. The community of La Brea learned from the
activists in Chatham Village about some of the negative effects of the development, and shared lessons on nonviolent resistance. Following community
opposition to the smelter, in May 2009 a high court judge revoked the certificate of environmental clearance that had been provided to Alutrint, and
the joint partner, Sural, dissolved their partnership.[23]

For Springer, the antismelter movement in Chatham was an example to
the country of how people can stop powerful corporations in their path—
"we don't always have to give way"—and an inspiration to people around
the world facing similar development debacles. Springer's words served as
a warning to the people of Iceland and an incentive to keep up the fight
against Alcoa, and the movement in Chatham provided an inspiration to
the nearby community of La Brea. Thus the antismelter movement is both
local and global, encompassing environmental justice issues in a broad understanding of spatial justice and how uneven development moves around
the world, drawing places into relations based on inequity.

Yet, as chapter 9 will explore, the production and use of aluminum is not so easily displaced. We all depend on it in many ways, and it is even having a renaissance within green design. The contradictions embedded in the history of aluminum continue to shape its future. Will it bring human destruction of the earth, or is it the route toward salvation in next generation sustainable technologies? How do alternative cultural framings influence the future of large-scale technologies, infrastructure decisions, and economic development? And what is the ongoing role of military investments and state-driven interests in determining where we invest our research and development dollars and minds?

the improvement of the brand image of the industry by continuing to emphasize its innovation and "contributions to modern lifestyles," especially
predicting aluminum's increasing use in lightweight vehicles (if it meets the
challenges of other upcoming lightweight materials such as carbon fiber).

The new US federal corporate average fuel economy (CAFE) standards
will require automakers to meet a fleet average of 54.5 miles per gallon by
2025. Today the automotive industry continues to move toward the replacement of steel with lighter aluminum parts. In 2002, David Schlendorf
of Alcoa Automotive Structures proclaimed that "the aluminum-structured
car will progressively displace the steel car over the next 20 years" because
it delivers weight reductions along with safety improvements, high performance, good handling, better fuel economy, production efficiencies, and
cost savings.[11] The Audi A8, the world's first car built on an entirely aluminum platform, debuted in Europe in 1994 and North America in 1997 using
multiple aluminum parts produced by Alcoa at its manufacturing facility in
Soest, Germany. The new aluminum alloy forming the inner structure of
the A8 contributes to "enhanced performance, quicker handling and better
fuel consumption" in a car described as "graceful" and "athletic." BMW has
introduced a new gasoline direct-injection twin-turbo V-8 engine made of
all aluminum and novel design principles, based on the metal's durability at
high temperatures.[12] The new Jaguar F-series sports car, first shown at the
Paris Auto Show in September 2012 and discussed further in the following,
incorporates all-new aluminum alloys that are said to add lightness without
compromising strength. Although battling against new high-strength steels
and comparatively expensive carbon fiber composites, Alcoa vigorously pro-
motes use of aluminum in the auto industry. Randall Scheps, their director of ground transportation, "points to cars like the 2013 Range Rover,
whose all-aluminum body is up to 39 percent lighter than older models"
and the "new Cadillac ATS uses many aluminum components, including
the engine, hood and wheels," because of aluminum's weight advantages
over steel, absorption of energy during a crash, and advantages in corrosion,
handling, and braking.[13] Certainly these developments help to reposition
aluminum as a material that is found in the most advanced luxury goods, but
does it really contribute to sustainability and corporate responsibility?

Although European car manufacturers especially are making strides in
the reduction of production waste and reuse of automotive aluminum, most
of the growth in primary production in the BRIC countries is going into

image in response to the "oil shock" of 1973–1974—a steep rise in world oil prices (due to OPEC's control of supply) that contributed to "stagflation" in the United States. As energy prices rose, recycling was not only politically attractive to manufacturers but was also embraced by the industry because it lowered the costs of production by requiring so much less electricity.

During the oil crisis Alcoa's advertising campaigns began to emphasize the energy savings afforded by lighter cars and trucks: "American cars must become smaller and lighter and less expensive to operate. Part of their diet to lose weight will be strong, lightweight aluminum alloys." They then describe how a car put on "an aluminum diet" could be reduced from 3,600 pounds to about 3,150. And "after the car has served us and gone on to scrap, we could use it. Aluminum brings about $200 a ton as scrap, so it's worth recycling." The company even touted its conservation efforts in a brochure called "Energy, Aluminum and the Automobile."[20] This was the same period in which idealistic designers like Bucky Fuller were experimenting with aluminum, seeing its potential as a "mine above ground" that could be endlessly recycled and reused.[21] Fuller developed some of the first life-cycle analyses of aluminum recycled across decades, but his 1981 vision of existing metals being able to meet all future needs through recycling within a generation depended on stopping the potential for huge population growth and reducing energy use and greenhouse gas emissions. He would probably find the current state of the world population, resource usage, and already-occurring climate change irredeemable.

Used beverage containers were a prime vehicle for promoting recycling efforts because of their high visibility and presence in daily life. Alcoa advertising in 1975 took pride in the expansion of recycling. "Collections for recycling are expanding at an amazing rate all over the country," it noted, "from 100 million cans in 1970 to over 2¼ *billion* in 1974." Recyclers had gathered in 85 million pounds of used aluminum cans in 1974, and since 1970 "over 30 million dollars have been paid to the collecting public, and over 6 billion aluminum cans have been collected."[22] Other ads in the mid-1970s, under the slogan "Aluminum: Pass it on," pointed out that "when you recycle aluminum, you save energy. It takes only 5 percent of the energy it takes to make it the first time. Once it's made, it can be recycled repeatedly, at a tremendous saving in energy." In addition to promoting the recycling of cans, the industry also tried to meet conservation targets by making cans thinner and thinner, using less aluminum to produce each can.

"In the 1970s the aluminum in beverage cans was nearly as thick as aluminum gutters, .015 inches. Lightweighting progress leveled-off in the early 80s, then resumed in 1984 due in part to computer modeling," finally reaching less than 0.012 inches in 1992 according to researchers at Alcoa laboratories.[23] As production processes improved, "over the course of a single decade the weight of aluminum cans in the United States was reduced by 40%."[24]

Although this was a positive development in terms of energy savings, "the reduced weight of individual cans has made it increasingly difficult for low-income individuals to collect cans for supplemental income. Whereas in 1987 it took about 27 cans to make a pound (worth 50 cents), it took 33 cans to make a pound (also worth 50 cents)—in 1998."[25] With a five-cent or ten-cent refundable deposit on cans, collecting discarded cans for recycling became a source of income for many people in US cities, especially the homeless, and across the world; but without their unpaid labor to collect the cans, fewer were recycled. Other changes in the economics of recycling contributed to reduced throughput and the closing down of many buy-back centers in the 1990s, because running costs exceeded revenues. In fact the industry's calculations of recycling rates are based on total processing of "used beverage containers" (UBCs), which includes cans imported into the United States from other countries. Rates of recycling within the United States are actually lower than claimed, and have been shrinking rather than growing. The Container Recycling Institute published an important report by Jennifer Gitlitz entitled *Trashed Cans,* which details the huge costs in energy consumption and other environmental impacts of our low recycling rates, which have actually declined since their peak in the 1980s.[26] Gitlitz argues that industry statistics on the success of recycling programs mask the fact that in the United States we are *failing* to recycle on a huge scale, with our recycling rate dropping from about 65 percent in 1992 to only 45 percent in 2004, according to the Container Recycling Institute.

We cannot afford to remain ignorant about the environmental and social impacts of our carefree and careless use of aluminum. As Gitlitz argues,

In the year 2001, 50.7 billion cans were *not recycled* in the United States: just over half of the 100 billion cans sold that year—and 50% more than were wasted in 1990. [. . .] Had the 50.7 billion cans wasted in 2001 been recycled, they could have saved the energy equivalent of 16 million barrels of crude oil—enough energy to generate electricity for 2.7 million U.S. homes for a year, or enough to supply over a million cars with gasoline for a year. [. . .] Since the first Earth Day in 1970,

Americans have thrown away 910 billion cans worth over $25 billion in current dollars.[. . .] We have also wasted a tremendous amount of energy making new cans from raw ore to replace those that were not recycled. The energy required to replace three decades of wasted cans—16 million tons of aluminum—is equivalent to about 342 million barrels of crude oil.[27]

If we take wastage of UBCs alone, the Container Recycling Institute calculates a needless expenditure of 4.09 metric tons of carbon equivalent (MTCE) per ton of waste (i.e., the difference in GHG emissions between making one ton of containers from 100 percent virgin materials versus 100 percent recycled materials), which can be compared to the average US car, which emits 1.3 MTCE/year. Recovery of postconsumer scrap aluminum is also weak. We continue to produce and consume ever more primary aluminum and to recycle smaller percentages. Higher rates of recycling would have a large impact: "Were we to achieve a national aluminum can recycling rate of 90 percent—a rate which has already been surpassed in Michigan—we could save an additional 610,000 tons of aluminum: an amount equivalent to the annual production of at least three major Pacific Northwest smelters."[28]

Like other areas of the aluminum dream, convenient, lighter packaging also had unintended consequences. More efficiency in packaging does not necessarily reduce the amount that is used, transported, and disposed of, but may simply encourage more usage. Convenience packaging was also linked to the rise of sprawling exurbia and its automobile-based culture, with the aluminum foil–wrapped McDonald's burger (ordered at a drive-through window and easily eaten in the car) perhaps epitomizing an era of US car culture, strip malls, and suburban sprawl. As Annie Leonard argues in her book and anti-overconsumption project *The Story of Stuff,*

In the United States we consume about 100 billion cans per year, or 340 per person: almost one a day. That's ten times more than the average European . . . People like cans because they're light, they don't break, they chill quickly, and they have a reputation for being widely recycled. If the real story were more widely known, people might stop using aluminum cans so carelessly.[29]

She, too, cites the research by the Container Recycling Institute showing that recycling rates in the United States have been declining for decades, and links this to a culture of mobility. "We're recycling about 45 percent of cans today, down from 54.5 percent in 2000 and the peak rate of 75 percent in 1992. In part this is because Americans are spending ever more time commuting and consuming beverages on the go, while there are few recycling bins in places away from home."[30] Because of these low recycling rates "more than a trillion aluminum cans have been trashed in landfills since 1972, when records started being kept. If those cans were dug up, they'd be worth about $21 billion in today's scrap prices."[31]

Life Cycle Studies of aluminum cans by World Watch suggest that the eight hundred thousand tons of cans that went straight into US landfills in a single year, if recycled, would have saved sixteen billion kWh of energy, or enough to power more than two million European homes for a year.[32] The OECD study of sustainable materials management using a life-cycle approach also concludes that "the substitution of secondary for primary aluminum product can significantly reduce greenhouse gas emissions," from about 11 metric tons of CO_2 equivalent in the European Union countries annually, for example, to only 0.88 and 0.96 Mt of CO_2 equivalent for secondary remelting and refining.

Yet focusing only on consumer choices and failure to recycle cans misses some of the bigger picture, even though it may be a good educational tool. First, it reinforces a national narrative, in which aluminum appears to occur within a single nation-state, in competition with others, rather than showing its wider transnational connections to mining, energy export, and far-flung smelting, with all of their associated environmental pollution and human rights issues. Second, it ignores the role of the military-industrial complex which, as noted in chapter 3, drives investment in primary smelting as a national security strategy. Third, aluminum is far more deeply embedded in our culture than the simple use and trashing of cans, given its connections to dreams of modernization, convenience, and material culture, as argued in chapter 5. The ongoing struggles over its cultural framing and meaning, its infrastructural importance, and its necessity for crucial technologies all influence social behavior, markets, state-led research, and the availability of aluminum.

In sharp contrast to environmentalist's depiction of the harm caused by the aluminum industry, many industrial economists have long argued that aluminum is a green metal because the use of lighter-weight transportation, packaging, and building materials improves efficiency in the use of oil and reduces greenhouse gas emissions across the economy. At an international symposium of the major European aluminum producers and government

or the US space shuttles, all of which the Russian company RUSAL notes on its website are made from aluminum, linking itself to a globalized world of high-tech industry. Today aluminum also continues to hold an important place in the high-end design world, the visual arts, and fashion. It has made an appearance in numerous recent art exhibitions, design shows, and new products.

Designers and product developers have especially turned to recycled aluminum as a green material. The Emeco chair company, for example, has continued its collaborations with famous designers, making chairs designed by Phillippe Stark, Frank Gehry, and BMW Design Group.[45] Gehry designed the Superlight chair in 2004, which can be lifted with one hand, and has more recently designed a one-off Tuyomyo nine-foot-long aluminum bench, which debuted at the Milan Furniture Fair. The company today publicizes not only its designers but also its green credentials because its chairs are made with 80 percent recycled aluminum, half of which is post-consumer recycled cans and half of which is recycled industrial waste. They also try to use renewable energy sources, and emphasize the lifelong guarantee on their products, showing how a company can value and add value to the special qualities of aluminum. Use of their furniture can even help building projects get LEED certification. In a playful advertising campaign for their Navy chair ("Standard U.S. Navy issue since 1944"), the brushed aluminum version is photographed with chunky Petty Officer FTG3 in the buff and a svelte "Parisienne socialite" posing in the nude. In fact their retro designs are so popular now that there has been a problem with unauthorized reproduction, including a "Naval chair" by Restoration Hardware that so closely resembled the Emeco Navy chair that it is currently the subject of a lawsuit and withdrawal of the imposter chair from the market.[46] Whereas Emeco actually uses recycled aluminum, other designer products often simply make claims to the "recyclability" of aluminum.

Mobile computing and phone companies are also enamored with aluminum. Apple Computer in particular features recycled aluminum in some of its new products such as the MacBook Air and the iPhone. The laptop computer is just the latest incarnation of a culture of lightness, mobility, agility, and "instantaneous" communication, wrapped in a seamless aluminum skin as the most appropriate expression of those values. Consumers tap into the aesthetic history of our entire technoculture when they tap at the anodized aluminum keyboard of the Apple iMac or admire its recycled aluminum frame with its "all-in-one design" made from a single sheet of aluminum, reminding us of the streamline aesthetic. Apple uses "friction-stir welding," which it describes as "commonly used on airplane wings, rocket booster tanks, and other parts that simply can't fail. This process uses a combination of intense friction-generated heat and pressure to intermix the molecules of the two aluminum surfaces—creating a seamless, precise, and superstrong join."[47]

The ultra-slimmed-down Apple MacBook Air is especially touted as featuring a "feather-light aluminum design":

It's a stunningly beautiful aluminum slab, three-quarters of an inch thick. Its edges are beveled to look even thinner. [. . .] This laptop's cool aluminum skin and smooth edges make it ridiculously satisfying to hold, carry, open and close. You can't take your eyes or your hands off it.[48]

How sleek, how slender, how slick our technology seems and makes us feel as we touch its shimmering surfaces. These light luminous packages of computing power put the benefits of modernity in our hands and open new kinds of windows on the world. They transport knowledge-economy workers effortlessly onto the World Wide Web even as they ride the train to work or sip lattes at Starbucks, the new roadside service stations of the information age. But even as I rest my arms on the coldly seductive brushed aluminum of my MacBook Pro, its sharp chiseled edge bites into my wrists, troubling me that there must be some sharper truths upholding the easy lightness of this wondrous technology. Concerns percolate to the surface as stories of labor struggles at the Foxconn factories producing Apple products in China keep resurfacing, and there seems to be little follow-up by companies producing e-waste on whether, where, and how their products are recycled.

Design and advertising are very powerful tools for corporate branding, and for masking the complex realities of heavy industry behind the attractive facades of desirable commodities and enticing images of a simplified life of lightweight conveniences. Beyond advertising, brand imaging also extends to associating the company logo with the arts and culture, whether through amassing corporate art collections or sponsoring the latest cultural events and arts institutions. As has already been discussed, Alcoa engaged a number of prominent artists in its advertising campaigns in the 1940s to 1950s, and sponsored the Caribbean Arts Prize in the late 1950s. Alcan also built up an extensive art collection over the years, based around the

Airstream Clipper, it is wrapped in riveted aluminum sheet, shining like a silver bullet. Built to commemorate Airstream's seventy-fifth anniversary, this nostalgic style of riveted aluminum can also be seen in an entire recent furniture collection from the company Restoration Hardware.

Noted Japanese designer Naoto Fukasawa also works with aluminum and is known for designing objects that seem so simple and obvious that "it makes them feel light and almost effortless."[62] He created a series of nine chairs for the 2007 Vitra Edition program of limited-edition objects by cutting-edge architects and designers, each one in a material that people commonly perch on. The "Chair" series included a boxy aluminum-clad chair that looks amusingly like the aluminum suitcases that people perch on at an airport.[63] It is suggestive of the qualities of light travel and being on the move that are the essence of aluminum. Even when we are stopped, stilled, and delayed, the aluminum chair represents a metaphor for movement, promising we will soon be on our way. It matches the aesthetics of the airport, and makes our waiting seem less heavy in these inescapable places of stillness on the way to mobility.[64]

The rows of chairs at an airport gate are flexible and moveable, adding to the dynamic flow of airport space, keeping our bodies on the move even as we wait to fly. As airfields were gradually transformed into more permanent airport architectures, the buildings themselves were imagined and designed to embody lightness and flexibility. As Peter Adey points out,

> The first airport designs were premised upon fluidity, with many research papers in engineering and architectural journals celebrating themes of flexibility. The airport designs of the 1930s embodied the progress of modernity, as speed and plasticism materialized, not only in style and symbolism such as art deco architecture, but also in the workings of the terminal structure.[65]

Most important, of course, were the airplane hangars, giant sheds clad in aluminum. Airports of today are also constantly flexing, growing, adding new terminals, and restructuring their internal spaces, passageways, and corridors such that "the airport forms a nexus of movement."[66] And supporting all of that flexibility there is in many cases an underlying architecture of light aluminum panels, ductwork, wiring, seating areas, doorways, curtain walls, and ceilings.

One of the new twists in contemporary design is the use of repurposed aluminum, in keeping with the industry's new green image. Boris Bally's

Transit Chairs, shown in the *Aluminum by Design* exhibition, are made from aluminum signs salvaged from scrap yards. To directly salvage a metal—without even melting it down and refabricating it—indicates a reuse of the energy stored in it, and a recapture of its potential to become other things. In the exhibit *Second Lives: Remixing the Ordinary* at the Museum of Arts and Design in New York City other objects made of repurposed aluminum were on display. The beautifully shimmering tapestry made by El Anatsui out of cut and bent pieces of aluminum cans turned consumer waste into a subtly textured and colored fabric. At its best such works of repurposing re-cast banal domestic goods into more ephemeral objects that nevertheless call into question our consumption of aluminum and failures to recycle much of it. But how do you change a whole economy, an entire material culture, and the way of life that it supports? What part did designers play in the advent of the age of aluminum, and what role might designers play in the process of changing our use of aluminum in the future?

Molotch suggests that making change in the stuff of life "means dealing not with one element alone but with all the others—material, emotional, and political—with which it has come to be bound"; from an "aesthetics of movement" to significant rites of passage, a "whole economy, in sector after sector, results from iterative buildups that increasingly merge as a single global system of sentiments, institutions, and physical material."[67] Alumi-num, too, is caught up in an iterative buildup of sentiments, institutions, and physical material that support each other and make it difficult to undo any single element.

You could say that not only is aluminum tightly bonded with other ele-ments at the atomic and molecular level but also with our material cul-ture and way of life, from our homes to our national security. Our use of aluminum, moreover, is tightly bound up with feelings about modernity, ideologies of lightness, speed, development, progress, and new technology. It underwrites our fantasies of the future and of what the present could be.

Today the corporate support of culture raises questions not only about the role of art institutions in creating value that supports potentially unethi-cal forms of capitalist excess but also the role of democratically elected gov-ernments in selling off public space and institutions to the same corporations, along with the natural resources they already monopolize. Ironically, since the merger of Alcan with the even larger company Rio Tinto, to become Rio Tinto Alcan, the company has become even more deeply involved in support for the arts. They have funded a major landmark building in Montreal in a public-private partnership with contributions of $1.5 million from Canadian Heritage and $1,476,584 from Canada Economic Development:

> The Blumenthal building, a Montréal architectural gem, has been renovated to serve as the year-round home of the *Maison du Festival Rio Tinto Alcan*. This permanent infrastructure gives Montréal a new tourist attraction on which to further build its international reach, while showcasing the history and evolution of jazz music in Montréal and Canada. The uniqueness of this new facility and its strategic location in the heart of the city's entertainment district promise to make the *Maison du Festival Rio Tinto Alcan* a major magnet for music industry artists, media, contractors and creators.[68]

By building up their brand images and so-called corporate citizenship, remote corporations operating in distant locations scattered around the world become the friendly face of regional arts and local cultural festivals, sponsors of academic conferences, and contributors to urban renewal via the "creative economy." Aluminum companies appear to be extremely media-savvy directors of public relations, deflecting much criticism, managing corporate relations with small communities via public meetings and information-packed websites, and producing myriad corporate responsibility initiatives. The real challenge for repurposing aluminum is not simply to use it in different ways, but to find ways of engaging with transnational corporations through means that promote transparency, democratization, environmental justice, and spatial justice. A true aluminum renaissance would connect the dots between the local and the global in ways that allow all of us to understand the global impacts of aluminum production, the harm caused by its wasteful consumption, and the role corporations and states play in avoiding its actual costs.

We can juxtapose the word "slow" with many of the basic terms that define our modern lives. Slow economy, slow technology, slow science, slow food, slow design, slow bodies, slow love . . . This kind of wordplay may hold the potential to liberate our imaginations. It directs our attention toward alternatives at odds with the dominant common sense of modern society—toward alternative economics, alternative technologies, alternative sciences, alternative diets, alternative aesthetics—even alternative forms of love.

—Shin'ichi Tsuji (Oiwa Keibo), *Slow Is Beautiful*

In this book I set out to trace the global economic and cultural history of aluminum in order to better understand how we might do without it, or how we might better manage our relation to technology, to global ecologies, and to others. In doing so I came to realize that aluminum was not only a crucial material in making the modern world but also that it underwrites an entire set of attitudes toward the desirability of mobility, lightness, and speed, and everything they bring us (as well as an opposite image, of some places as slower, backward, outside of modernity, or places that simply failed at modernization). Our use of aluminum is related to its combination with plastics, glass, steel, and other materials; to the everyday activities we undertake with such things; to its embedding in everyday infrastructures such as buildings, electric grids, and communication systems; and the routines of convenience and time-savings that we associate with its use. We might follow Elizabeth Shove in thinking about this as a kind of "path dependency" that "refer[s] to the interrelatedness of artifacts with other artifacts, infrastructure and routine."[1] What routines would need to change if we were to reduce our use of aluminum artifacts and infrastructure? Could we still have a modern world without aluminum? Are there alternative technologies and sciences emerging that could liberate us from our dependence on this ener-gy-hungry light metal? Or should we consider slowing down, loving alu-minum less, as a way to change the aesthetics and ethics of modern design?

One approach to green transitions premised on reducing energy con-sumption presumes that if we simply have the facts at hand, and could com-municate them more effectively to consumers, then people would begin to make the right choices. However, as Simon Guy and Elizabeth Shove point out in their sociological study of energy efficiency in buildings, it seldom works that way. Knowledge does not bring clarity of action. If this were the case, then our aim would simply be to reveal the "reality" behind our mate-rial world, and overcome the barriers of human ignorance that prevent ev-eryday energy conservation. Instead "it is the sheer familiarity of energy use, and its deep embeddedness in taken for granted patterns of everyday life" that make it so hard for us "to 'see' the energy embodied in an aluminum window frame" for example.[2] They argue that rather than simply trying to promote the visibility of facts and change people through enlightenment (i.e., as Al Gore did with his lectures and film *Inconvenient Truth* or as Annie Leonard does with *The Story of Stuff*), we need to do far greater "justice to the social ordering of choices, problems and practices."

Substituting aluminum for energy in their argument, we could ask, "What services, activities and lifestyles does [aluminum] consumption make possible?" Asking this "might lead us to think about how expectations of comfort evolve and the extent to which they are, for example, the cause or the consequence of the rapid spread of air conditioning [or other aluminum-based conveniences] around the world."[3] Studies of large-scale sociotechni-cal transitions demonstrate that such patterns do change over time, slowly, and will change in the future, through some interaction between changes at the micro-level of people's everyday practices and new niche innovations, at the meso-level of governing regimes and institutional practices, or at the macro-level of broad changes in the landscape (e.g., energy availability, re-source depletion, climate change).[4] But such transition theories often over-look the cultural aspects of how things get locked in, and how they change.

For example, one way to think about aluminum concerns the ways in which it shapes infrastructures and remakes the "spatial fix" that locks in certain kinds of mobilities and immobilities. Aluminum can ultimately be thought of not just as a metal for a consumer end product that one can choose to use or not, recycle or not, but as a complex network of actors and connections between them, involving, as I have tried to show throughout this book

• The mobilization of resources, corporate networks, market economies, and state power around the world
• The mobilization of technical instruments such as patents, electrolytic conversion processes, and technologies of power generation, mining, smelting, transport, and fabrication
• The mobilization of consumers, the products they use, and the circulating representations of such products in advertising and marketing
• The actual material flux and "agency" of the multiplicitous forms that aluminum takes: bauxite ore, alumina, molten aluminum, forgings, castings, extruded shapes and sheets of metal, and a multitude of finished products, waste products, and recycled aluminum that flow around the world

So changing aluminum (and energy) consumption requires some recombination of all of these elements, not just telling consumers to recycle their cans. Aluminum shapes infrastructures and remakes "spatio-temporal fixes"[5] that stabilize certain kinds of spatial patterns and their associated mobilities (of electricity, of communication, of transportation) and immobilities (of pylons, of highway systems, of infrastructure), and also stabilize certain kinds of political and economic structures such as so-called developed versus developing countries.

My argument is not only that we can analyze aluminum as a metal for mobility (though this is an important part of what I hope this book will achieve), whose rapid, reliable, reasonably priced transport and communications systems became the sine qua non of our modern way of life, keeping the wheels turning and the global village talking, texting, and twittering. I also want to emphasize how aluminum's potential mobilities also became a metaphor for the very making of modernity, as well as an embodiment and display of modernity based on speed, lightness, and movement of all kinds, as I argued in part I. At the same time, as explored in part II, it is not enough to describe the bright gleam of mobile modernity within everyday life without also tracking its mobilities back to the sources of production, which cast a dark shadow over modernity. The making of aluminum's mobile modernity crucially depended on both the extraction of raw materials from less-developed places on the global periphery, and the representation of those places as backward, slow, and outside of modernity. These spatial relations then served to perpetuate uneven distribution of the benefits and costs of new technologies. The mobilities and flows of commodities, transport, and communication that aluminum afforded were dependent on various kinds of immobilities and spatial fixes, generating not only pollution and environmental degradation but also spatial injustice and political conflict across many parts of the world.

Shove's analysis of the temporalities of comfort, cleanliness, and convenience suggests one of the ways in which we might interpret the distinction between the speedy modernity of the aluminum age and the associated construction of the "slowness" of tropical underdeveloped places where bauxite is mined. As she argues, "it is important to understand the personal and collective scheduling of practice in order to understand the transformation of convention."[6] Most important,

the diffusion and appropriation of things like freezers, washing machines and answerphones [and we could add cars, airplanes, and laptop computers] paradoxically increases the problems of scheduling and co-ordination and inspires the search for new, yet more convenient arrangements. In addition, and just as relevant for the present argument, reliance on convenient solutions has the cumulative effect of redefining what people take for granted.[7]

The taken-for-granted availability of aluminum and of the variety of things and services that it affords us has been built up over time through many cumulative efforts to make life easier—to lighten loads, to speed delivery, to modernize our homes and built environment. People around the world have been inadvertently drawn into the sociotemporal dynamics of the speed metal, as well as into its sociotechnical network. If the appropriation of objects and their integration into practice matters, Shove concludes, then "there might be political, social and technological scope for intervention with respect to the temporal organization of society."[8]

In this concluding chapter I want to think about the temporalities of aluminum and its particular pace of life in relation to questions of how we might slow down, in a positive way. A number of social movements have emerged that call for "slow food," "slow technology," "slow cities," and so on. Yet slowing down, downshifting, or embracing simplicity, as many environmental movements have advocated, cannot be imposed on people or even be made an individual voluntary choice unless we also address the wider configuration of the capitalist system and its temporalities,[9] or more specifically the military-industrial system described in previous chapters.

Changes in such everyday spatio-temporalities need to be thought about in relation to more macro-level "spatio-temporal fixes" that shape the relations within and between cities, nations, and regions. This story of aluminum and its global entanglements offers an alternative way of thinking about spatial relations between different parts of the world, and the question of what some, following Edward Soja, call spatial justice.[10] As noted at the outset, spatial justice concerns geographically uneven development and unequal distributions of collective goods at many different scales ranging from the bodily to the urban to the global. Aluminum is caught up in all of these scales, and in producing uneven benefits and burdens across them.

The material infrastructures and the discursive formations of metallic modernity described in this book are crucially implicated in the production of spatial injustice through the location of polluting production facilities, the agglomeration of spatial control over energy production (especially the use of rivers for hydropower), and the ability to move investments across international borders seeking the lowest costs for inputs, energy, and labor. Military power, state subsidies, and unregulated transnational corporations all drive the structure of the aluminum industry, and in doing so shape uneven development across the world. In seeking spatial justice (as well as reduced energy consumption and pollution) we need not simply to advocate speed limits or call for simpler ways of life but also to build civil society's powers to exercise greater democratic control over corporations in order to restrain their ability to produce space and roam the globe, taking resources at will (or in collusion with state actors). In addressing our own investment in the lightness and speed of modernity, and trying to reduce our dependence on aluminum, we also need to find ways of being responsible to the impact of our government and state-supported industries on others and on the planet. To do so requires not simply "seeing" the problems with aluminum, although this is a necessary first step, but also thinking about how to intervene in the social ordering of choices, problems, and practices, as Shove suggests. This intervention will pivot on how we turn the current attention being given to cultures of slowness into actionable transformations in sociotechnical regimes.

The emergence of aluminum-based practices of mobility, alongside modern ideologies and representations of that mobility, pivoted on the co-production of other regions of the world as backward, slow, and relatively immobile —bauxite-bearing regions that would be mined by multinational corporations for the benefit of those who could make use of the "magical metal," as well as "energy islands" that could export power in the form of aluminum ingot. Such relative mobilizations and demobilizations are constitutive of the connections and disconnections between North America and the Caribbean, and between the Global North and Global South (and other peripheries such as the sub-arctic), with patents, tariffs, tax regimes, and military power locking in the spatial formations and spatiotemporal fixes that allow disjunctive modernities to exist side by side. To "fix" the problem in the social ordering of aluminum consumption, then, also demands that we grapple with some of the problems in the social ordering of global inequalities, the power of transnational corporations and the military-industrial complex, and the uneven temporalities of places perceived as "advanced" versus "backward," modern versus traditional, urban versus rural, metropolitan versus peripheral. This is an even bigger problem than most approaches to sociotechnical change would have us believe.

The apparently airy lightness of aluminum and its associated imaginaries of metallic modernity speeding toward the future were wrenched out of the heavy tropical earth of specific places subjected to modern forms of domination and associated pollution. Toxic red mud from bauxite mining, water and air pollution from alumina refining, excessive energy use for aluminum smelting, and negative health effects on workers and nearby populations are as much a product of the age of aluminum as are elegant MacBook Air notebook computers with their "featherlight aluminum design" and promise of mobile connectivity at our fingertips. Advertising and alluring objects continue to enroll us in the fantasy of mobile modernity, and tourist mobilities hide the global rifts on which easy circulation is premised. As Jussi Parikka argues, we need a media archeology that gets at the slower temporalities of geological formation. The field of "media archaeology" calls for

a more geologically oriented notion of depth of media that is interested in truly deep times—of thousands, millions, billions of years and in depth of the earth; a media excavation into the mineral and raw material basis of technological development, through which to present some media historical arguments as to how one might adopt a material perspective in terms of ecological temporality.[11]

If "the materiality of information technology starts from the soil, and underground"—in metals such as cobalt and gallium, tantalum and germanium, and, I would add, bauxite and aluminum—we find ourselves in a "double bind that relates media technologies to ecological issues; on the one hand, acting as raw material for the actual hardware, from cables to cell phones; on the other hand, as an important epistemological framework."[12] In particular, we can unearth not only the metallic basis of contemporary material cultures of transport and communication, in their widest senses but also their epistemological basis in the valuation of lightness, speed, and mobility.

In contrast to the aluminum dreams of the past in both the "developed" industrial world and in the "developing" world of resource extraction, both the Global North and the Global South need to wake up from the aluminum dream and work together to produce more just spatial and temporal relations with each other. For, as we have seen, these two worlds of the modern and the underdeveloped are not really separate; they have interdeveloped together, and the extraction of metals and minerals is one of the key processes that makes them each what they are, and ultimately connects them together.

Awakening from the aluminum dream, we will realize that fast, modern, "developed" places are contingent on slow, backward, "developing" places. Not only is speed relative but the conditions, resources, technologies, and labor that enable some to take flight, to lighten their burden, to launch rockets and satellites, are also precisely the same ones that leave other places and people burdened with pollution, excluded from modern infrastructures, and imagined as outside of modernity or forever catching up, forever trying to take off. This is not simply a European or North American problem either; the same goes for the operations of Chinese corporations in Africa, of Russian corporations in Siberia, or of Brazilian corporations in Amazonia, where pressures for economic development have been at the expense of wilderness areas and indigenous peoples. We as a species ultimately need to be aware of our own limits, the limits of the earth, and the limits on speed that will be necessary to live on this earth in the future.

WAKING UP FROM THE ALUMINUM DREAM

How can individuals and societies around the world break the social orderings of choices, problems, and practices that continue to reinforce their unbridled use of aluminum? One approach taken by the industrial producers themselves is to reduce energy consumption and pollution in the primary production of aluminum, basically creating a technical fix that will allow business as usual to continue further into the future. A recent comparative analysis of steel and aluminum production processes by Julian Allwood and Jonathan Cullen shows that about one-third of the cost of producing aluminum is solely to purchase energy, which ought to drive the industry to work as efficiently as possible given existing technology, and also to seek out the cheapest possible sources of electricity. Nevertheless, 40 percent of the liquid metal formed during the electrolysis, melting, and casting-rolling process never reaches finished products but is scrapped in production.[13] So improvements in the industrial production process itself are offered as one way to improve efficiencies in production by decreasing wastage. This would of course be in the interest of the industry and its profitability, so it would seem that they are already working on such technical solutions.

A second approach is to increase recycling and promote more thoughtful use of such a special and costly material. Yet demand for aluminum is expected to double in the next forty years, at the same time that there is pressure to halve energy emissions. Allwood and Cullen argue this is unachievable. Beyond greater efficiencies, they also suggest the need to use less aluminum by design, to reduce demand (in part by reusing old metal and reducing yield loss in production), and to design longer life goods as other ways to reduce our use of aluminum. They suggest a number of improvements in the design and production process that could yield improvements and optimize the amount of metal that is used for particular production processes of metal forming. The assumption here is that we will still continue to need aluminum for its many versatile affordances but that we will use it more carefully. Is this enough?

On the first point—energy consumption—the industry claims to be cleaning up its act, going on a strict diet of low-emissions energy. Although Alcoa trumpets its use of renewable energy, however, critics such as Saving Iceland note that hydropower is not necessarily a clean and green energy source because of the harmful environmental and social impacts of large dams across the world. Aluminum companies have also turned to other low-carbon energy sources. Alcoa in particular is involved in the development of geothermal power in Iceland. The company announced in August 2007 that it was supporting the Iceland Deep Drilling Project, a research consortium composed of three leading Icelandic power companies and Alcoa.[14] Bernt Reitan, Alcoa executive vice president, said, "Geothermal energy is exactly what the world needs to tap into almost limitless, clean, natural energy and to substantially reduce greenhouse emissions."[15]

Corporate leaders show an understanding of their industry as one that is reducing greenhouse gases, contrary to most ecological arguments. Making aluminum production more energy efficient is certainly one starting point, yet with regard to the switch to geothermal energy in Iceland (or Greenland, which is considered another crucial site of development), we have already seen some of the controversies over the development of heavy industry in wilderness areas. Other kinds of changes will be needed beyond such technological fixes, which are also going to maintain existing social practices of open-pit bauxite mining, energy-intensive aluminum consumption, externalized environmental costs, and uneven development.

Although ecologists focus on the greenhouse gases emitted in the production of primary aluminum, industry insiders focus on the reductions in emissions enabled by the metal's overall contribution toward lighter, more energy-efficient transport and the movement toward greater rates of recycling. But we have to ask whether there would be an overall reduction in the volume of transport if we didn't have aluminum in the first place. Isn't the current magnitude of global mobility in part an outcome of the age of aluminum and its ideologies of speed and lightness? Wouldn't a reduction in greenhouse gas emissions actually require that humanity reduce the overall amount of travel, freight movement, and energy consumption? And what can we learn from the history of aluminum about how to govern and regulate transnational corporations and promote alternative social orderings of technology?

Despite its rising cost prior to the recession, demand for aluminum (along with other metals) continued to grow. China, especially, has been ramping up aluminum production and with it the production of massive amounts of greenhouse gases. China's CO_2 emissions "are most likely to continue growing substantially for years to come," according to one *New York Times* article, because "China is heavily dependent on coal and has seen its most rapid growth in some of the world's most heavily polluting industrial sectors: cement, aluminum and plate glass."[16] When it comes to China, it's OK for the US media to refer to aluminum as a heavily polluting industrial sector. You will not often find such forthright statements about "our" industry, which hides behind the green veil of hydropower and geothermal energy, recycling, and upcycling. The aluminum industry has worked hard to become associated with building the infrastructure of new eco-friendly technologies such as wind-turbines, solar-powered buildings, and prefabricated architecture, often touted in trendy magazines such as *Dwell*.

The aluminum industry's claims to environmental sustainability appear to be going down well among designers and architects, as noted in chapter 9. Nevertheless, resistance by local communities, activists, and transnational social movements continues to challenge the aluminum industry to live up to higher standards. The governments that support it as a desirable form of economic development have to answer for its environmental, social, and health impacts. How many of us actually realize the extent of aluminum's use in our everyday lives? If we were really to stop the expansion of aluminum smelting (without simply pushing it to even more poorly regulated and politically oppressed places), what impact would it have on everyday life?

To cut down on our use of aluminum might require more than a diet to reduce our consumption of light metal; it conceivably will require an entire change of lifestyle and of spatial practices, including a new material culture and more radical reenvisioning of the built environment. Developing such future scenarios will be crucial to reformulating notions of sustainability in ways that might realize a revolutionary transformation in everyday practices and material cultures as extreme as the aluminum revolution that created twentieth-century light modernity.

SLOW GOING: EMERGENCE BY EMERGENCY

In his vision of "emergence by emergency," Buckminster Fuller explains how some of his anticipatory technologies will one day be taken up and widely adopted, once humanity faces an emergency in which they become necessities. Climate change and the imperative to reduce greenhouse gases may be precisely such an emergency. But it was Fuller's realization that we would still need advanced technologies, including many that he himself based on aluminum, to survive future emergencies. His solution to this conundrum was a second realization: that so much metal has already been unearthed and processed that "humanity need do very little further mining," with a few rare exceptions.

He argues that the "metals already scrapped from obsolete machinery and structures, which recirculate on a sum-total-of-all-metals-average every twenty-two years, are now able to do so much more work with ever less weight per each given function with each recirculation as to make the present scrap resources of almost all metals adequate to take care of all humanity's forward needs."[17] In other words, he envisioned a closed-loop system in which we keep recycling scrap metal and putting it to ever lighter, stronger applications, accomplishing more per each unit of weight of material involved with each recirculation. This was precisely what he aimed to achieve with his geodesic domes, demonstrating how "to do more with less." Ironically, though, it was the military strategists who first adopted his geodesic domes and radomes, seeing their potential to lighten military logistics and communications systems.

To reduce our use of aluminum might require twenty-first-century societies to question our very attitudes toward mobility, lightness, and speed, attitudes that are deeply embedded in all kinds of everyday objects and ways of doing things, but also in our national security systems and state infrastructures. The post-aluminum age, whether by choice or of necessity, may be a time when we take more care with how we produce the materials we require, put more effort into recycling energy-costly metals, and value aluminum for the special qualities it affords us.

It is not simply that we need to reject speed or ban aluminum altogether, an impossible cultural project given its prevalence in the production of ever more efficient technologies at reduced weight. However, we do need to think about the global spatial relations between differential speeds (uneven mobilities) and how "modernization" enables some places to gain military and economic advantages to the detriment of others (uneven geographies).

Seeking spatial justice and mobility justice will require some degree of transparency about industrial processes and democratization of transnational decision making about the siting of production processes and the globalization of commodity chains. This requires a public discussion about how we value speed and lightness, what choices we might have, and what we are willing to sacrifice in order to reduce the harmful impacts of mining and smelting. And this will vary in different local contexts and situations, and for different individuals.

Fuller's own suggestion for addressing this world democracy deficit was the creation of what he called the *World Game,* a system for participatory open data sharing and global governance (which would be far more possible with today's computer technologies than those under which he began to imagine it). This would enable worldwide energy and resource accounting, instituted in association with a "world-unifying electric power" grid, which he saw as the first step toward the "desovereignization" of territory.[18]

However, the world does not seem ready for such a radical vision of desovereignty yet. The current forms of emergency instead continue to lead to continuing weapons proliferation of interstate warfare, as well as infrawarfare against hidden networks such as terrorists and cyberwarfare against the modern infrastructures that support life. Until the emergence of one-world Spaceship Earth as envisioned by Fuller, it seems that our next best option is to slow down our use of primary metals and reconsider the kinds of cultural values that modernity is based on.

Jeffrey T. Schnapp framed the exhibition *Speed Limits,* which I viewed at the Canadian Centre of Architecture in October 2009, in terms of the relation between speed and slowness. The exhibition suggests the importance of speed in shaping twentieth-century cultures of modernity, from transport and architecture to the efficient kitchen and the physically trained body; but it also shows the longing for slowness, escape, and nostalgia for the past as a concurrent facet of modern culture. Arguably the desire to be ever faster is no longer the key characteristic of late modern culture. It is only at the dawn of the twenty-first century, as things begin to slow down, that we can look back and appreciate the power of mobility, lightness, and speed as organizing motifs of the twentieth century. And we can begin to look forward not just to a slower future, but to a cultural system not organized around the master trope of speed and perpetual rapid growth.

Physical lightness and the ever-greater capacity for movement and speed were the defining qualities of twentieth-century transport and material culture more generally. This is what sets it apart from the heavy iron and coal technologies of the nineteenth century and also from the new era we are moving into. The space race—the zenith of speed, lightness, and gravity-defying aeronautics—seems almost antiquated, with NASA finally retiring its aging space shuttle fleet and manned space flights now outsourced to the aging Russian Baikonur Cosmodrome.

Back on earth, the *Concorde,* that great symbol of high-speed luxury travel (and huge fuel consumption), was also wheeled into a retirement home. Drivers are going slower to conserve gasoline. The merits of walking and bicycling, and livable cities with "complete streets" policies are being touted. What are the implications of these transformation for the once "slow" parts of the world, that is, parts of the Caribbean or Africa or the Amazon that have been constructed as "backward" and outside of modernity? Can we rethink the very processes of global modernization by decoupling development from the notion of takeoff?

Airports and air travel remain a major conduit and switch node of the global economy, moving all the parts that keep it running smoothly. Although engaging the designs of major architects to create airport-cities as attractions in themselves, airports are nevertheless also points of friction and contestation. Travel is increasingly slowed by security risks and by the labyrinthine systems for passenger surveillance and baggage checks. Yes, people still travel, but air travel has lost some of its romance as no frills service and budget airlines ply the skies. Although a small kinetic elite may be speeded along by premium access and iris-scanning identity checks, the majority of air travelers face longer lines, slower travel, and more time waiting at airports for the foreseeable future. And in economic terms, many smaller regional airports are closing, and some passengers must choose indirect flights with one or more transfers, because direct flights have become increasingly expensive. Others have curtailed air travel altogether, either foregoing trips or going by train or bus. Even long-haul flights are being cut back, as airlines review their fuel efficiency and wait for more efficient fleets (built with carbon composites) to come online.

Today informational speed has become more significant than physical speed in many ways, the unencumbered flow of bits and bytes more important than aerodynamics and acceleration. Technologists are always pursuing the newest device, the faster connection, the latest network, 4G, 5G, LTE. Streaming of information has overtaken streamlining of objects in our cultural imagination. As we move toward more portable devices and nanotechnology, scaling things down has become more important than lightness per se, and this increasingly involves nanotechnologies and new nanomaterials (some of which include aluminum).

Yet the promise of high-speed "instantaneous" communication nevertheless remains tethered to underground media archaeologies, that is, mining and e-waste and their associated pollution and heavy metals that once again affect the underdeveloped world most.[19] Moreover, access to communications technology is uneven and always under threat, with the call for "net neutrality" seeking to prevent the fragmentation of the Internet into high-speed business channels and low-speed slow lanes for the electronically disenfranchised. Geographers talk of the "splintering of urbanism"[20] as software is used to sort the "kinetic elite" into a "fast lane" while the rest languish.

Others would promote a transition into an era of slow food, slow design, and slow travel, seeking out refuge from these dangerous times, ecological solace for the planet, and more time to appreciate the basics of life. As the "Slow Food Manifesto" first put it when published in 1989:

> Our century, which began and has developed under the insignia of industrial civilization, first invented the machine and then took it as its life model.
>
> We are enslaved by speed and have all succumbed to the same insidious virus: Fast Life, which disrupts our habits, pervades the privacy of our homes and forces us to eat Fast Foods. [. . .]
>
> In the name of productivity, Fast Life has changed our way of being and threatens our environment and our landscape. So Slow Food is the only truly progressive answer.[21]

The proliferation of canned goods and fast foods was dependent, of course, on aluminum—from the industrial farming equipment and transport systems that move food from farm to market, to the packaging in which our lightweight beverages, TV dinners, drive-in burgers, Tetra Paks, and take-away meals often come wrapped. If one takes the time to buy organic, locally grown food, it comes without packaging, naked and unprocessed; it seems to call for glass or ceramic cookware, or better yet can be eaten raw, not cooked in some Teflon-coated aluminum pan.

Japanese writer Shin'ichi Tsuji also reembraces "culture as slowness," proclaiming that "slow is beautiful." He contrasts the pace of industrial time to the biological temporalities of living organisms; trees are unable to shift in response to climate change, plants are unable to absorb the carbon dioxide spewed out by industry. "Modern society, with its emphasis on getting 'more, faster,'" he argues, "has also given rise to grotesque disparities between North and South, developed and developing countries. Isn't it time for those who speak of justice, fairness, equality, and democracy, to start seriously considering ways to live with 'less, more slowly?'"[22]

Slowness, then, is not just a negative opposition to the fast life but is the positive promotion of a form of global justice and ecological balance. Is slow the future, and if so, what will sustainable development look like?

REENCHANTMENT

Fleet-footed Mercury, the messenger of the gods, Italo Calvino reminds us, is locked in brotherhood with Vulcan, "a god who does not roam the heavens but lurks at the bottom of craters, shut up in his smithy, where he tirelessly forges objects . . . To Mercury's aerial flight, Vulcan replies with his limping gait and the rhythmic beat of his hammer."[23] The ancients understood that the swift-footed messenger depends on the maker of weaponry. Lightness and weightiness, beautiful arts and destructive weaponry, flight through the air and descent into the dark depths of the earth, are all part of aluminum's meaning and impact.

Those without the material culture of aluminum seem to exist in a more primitive era of heavy technologies and grinding immobility. They seem weighted down like cave men wielding stone tools, armor-suited knights heaving ponderous swords, or old "iron horses" fired by hand-shoveled coal and tied to iron rails. In our light vehicles we have broken free of friction and gravity. Living in a sci-fi fantasy we imagine ourselves floating free above the earth, traveling to Mars, dwelling on the moon, communicating with the universe.

Through stories of invention and discovery, entrepreneurship and imagination, *Aluminum Dreams* has uncovered our profound attachment to this elemental metal of modernity. But if we are attached to this metal and the prosthetic powers it affords our flesh-and-bone bodies, it is time that we gave its production more thought and its recycling more care. Above all, we must become reenchanted with the magic of aluminum's contribution to our capacity for lightness, speed, mobility, and flight, but also wary of its destructive capacities as a weapon and as matrix for uneven global development and environmental destruction.

If we once again experienced the fantastic wonder of the airplane, the bullet train, and the humble can; the kinesthetic joy of moving with the lightweight bicycle, the tennis racket, or the walker; and the marvel of electricity flowing across our world on aluminum cables and into the aluminum appliances in our homes and personal devices we carry with us, perhaps we would stop treating these inventions of the aluminum dream as routine expectations. We might stop treating aluminum as a cheap throw-away material if we recognized not only the costliness of its production but also the great value of the many things it provides for us.

At the same time, it would benefit developing countries not to depend on bauxite or hydropower as the sole route toward economic takeoff. Over-reliance on a single resource (and the oligopolistic multinational companies that often control the market) leads not only to environmental overexploitation but also often produces political corruption and economic instability.

The larger question, though, is how the global community can exercise control over transnational corporations in an era of privatization, denational-ization, and globalization. The old antitrust laws used the power of national state jurisdiction to rein in the power of multinational corporations, but they seem far less effective today, when global institutions such as the World Trade Organization or the International Monetary Fund seem to promote the opening up of markets and the hollowing out of national jurisdictions over territory. The old vision of national resource sovereignty seems rather antiquated in this context.

We need to not only slow down the speed at which we travel but also the speed at which capital flows around the world, unsettling the earth along with the communities who dwell on it. The massive concentration of power in corporations such as RUSAL, Rio Tinto Alcan, Vedanta, or CHINALCO (as well as investment banks like J. P. Morgan and Goldman Sachs) has to be brought under some kind of democratic jurisdiction and decision making, otherwise these industrial giants will continue to roll unimpeded over the planet, devouring its limited resources without regard. The aluminum dream so easily turns into an aluminum nightmare for those who dwell near the mines or who find their rivers dammed and valleys flooded for hydroelectric power. And the governments who cut deals with these industries are often selling their sovereignty to the highest bidder, at great cost to democratic accountability and the rights of citizens. We are allowing giant mining cor-porations and energy companies to destroy the last remaining natural areas in remote parts of the world such as the highlands of Iceland, the Cock-pit Country of Jamaica, remote parts of Brazilian Amazonia, the outback of Australia, the sacred mountains of Odisha, and the interior of Guinea, while using vast amounts of energy to make a metal that allows economies to grow and to modernize, thus demanding even more energy and more resources. A technological fix cannot solve these structural problems of spatial injustice.

Actions are being taken by environmental activists, by local communities and citizens, by governments and by consumers around the world to stand up to unbridled corporate power and to state injustice. The situation is by no means hopeless. But the vast majority of us, when we pick up an alumi-num can, get into an aluminum-laced vehicle, or cradle an aluminum laptop computer, we have limited awareness of the magnitude of the industrial expansion happening in very remote places, of the scale of growth in the industry, or of the massive size of the facilities and corporations that brought these products to us.

We take for granted the conveniences of modern life, comparing our lightness, speed, and mobility against those who lack them, and coveting those things that will bring us more. Similar to the consumers of sugar in the age of slavery, we are largely unaware of our role in the age of aluminum, of our global connectivity, and of our ethical implication in extremely harmful processes of production. The more of us who wake up from the aluminum dream, the more power we will have to reshape markets, influence government decision making, and force corporations to accountability. Only our own reenchantment with our one-and-only world and all of the material capacities it brings to us will enable us to save this world from our own destructive capacities.

As I write the final words of this book Hurricane Sandy has pummeled the East Coast of the United States, where I live, reminding us of what we already know: climate change is on us; storm intensities are increasing; sea levels are rising; storm surges are growing; low lying lands are at ever-increasing risk. A tree has fallen on the roof of my house. Power was out for four days. Roadways were blocked. But I still feel lucky not to be in worse-hit places, such as lower Manhattan, Staten Island, or Long Beach Island, New Jersey, where we have built on barrier islands and marshlands soon to be reclaimed by the sea. And I am not in Haiti where the storm wiped out agricultural crops, roads, and bridges.

I think of Bucky Fuller's lessons, that we only change our ways when crisis is on us, "emergence through emergency." He designed technologies and ways of living in advance of the crisis, knowing it would come, and optimistically hoping that humanity would adopt his designs when the time was right. Yet he thought this would have to happen within a generation, otherwise it might be too late for humanity. Perhaps we are living in the times of too late.

But I like to think that if we slow down the rate of resource consumption and the ever-faster acceleration of modernity, if we value metals like aluminum and reuse them more carefully, if we use less energy and take more care in resource extraction, maybe our children and grandchildren will still have a chance to live more lightly on this, our earth.

NOTES

I INTRODUCTION

1. Thomas J. Misa, *A Nation of Steel: The Making of Modern America 1865–1925* (Baltimore: Johns Hopkins University Press, 1995).

2. Ibid., 482.

3. Ibid, 273.

4. Ibid, xvii.

5. In the United States, classic business histories of the aluminum industry include those sponsored by Alcoa: George David Smith, *From Monopoly to Competition: The Transformation of Alcoa, 1888–1986* (Cambridge, UK: Cambridge University Press, 1988); and Margaret G. W. Graham and Bettye H. Pruitt, *R&D for Industry: A Century of Technical Innovation at Alcoa* (Cambridge, MA: MIT Press, 1990). These are joined by a wide range of industry pamphlets, films, and advertising that also emphasize invention and innovation.

6. This approach to the mutual interaction between social and technological change is influenced by science and technology studies including those by W. E. Bijker, T. P. Hughes, and T. J. Pinch, eds., *The Social Construction of Technological Systems: New Directions in the Sociology and History of Technology* (Cambridge, MA: MIT Press, 1987); W. E. Bijker and J. Law, eds., *Shaping Technology / Building Society: Studies in Sociotechnical Change* (Cambridge, MA: MIT Press, 1994); and Lucy Suchman, *Human–Machine Reconfigurations: Plans and Situated Actions* (Cambridge, UK: Cambridge University Press, 2007).

7. A transnational approach is taken by some economists who take the worldwide vertically integrated aluminum industry as unit of analysis, for example, John A. Stuckey, *Vertical Integration and Joint Ventures in the Aluminum Industry* (Cambridge, MA: Harvard University Press, 1983). A more political world economy approach is developed by Bradford Barham, Stephen Bunker, and Denis O'Hearn, *States, Firms, and Raw Materials: The World Economy and Ecology of Aluminum* (Madison: The

University of Wisconsin Press, 1994), building on earlier political economies of bauxite mining such as Norman Girvan, *Foreign Capital and Economic Underdevelopment in Jamaica* (Mona: University of the West Indies, Institute of Social and Economic Research, 1971).

8. Mimi Sheller, *Consuming the Caribbean: From Arawaks to Zombies* (London: Routledge, 2003).

9. Daniel Rodgers, Bhavani Raman, and Helmut Reimitz, eds., *Cultures in Motion* (Princeton, NJ: Princeton University Press, 2013).

10. Thomas Bender, *A Nation among Nations: America's Place in World History* (New York: Hill and Wang, 2006).

11. Robert Vitalis, *America's Kingdom: Mythmaking on the Saudi Oil Frontier* (Stanford, CA: Stanford University Press, 2007). Thanks to Bradley Simpson for this source and to all of the participants in the Cultures in Motion group at the Shelby Cullom Davis Center for Historical Studies at Princeton University, who contributed to my thinking on these issues.

12. Eric Schatzberg, "Ideology and Technical Choice: The Decline of the Wooden Airplane in the United States, 1920–1945," *Technology and Culture* 35, no. 1 (January 1994): 34–69; Eric Schatzberg, "Symbolic Culture and Technological Change: The Cultural History of Aluminum as an Industrial Material," *Enterprise & Society 4,* no. 2 (June 2003): 226–271.

13. Jeffrey L. Meikle, *American Plastic: A Cultural History* (New Brunswick: Rutgers University Press, 1997).

14. Michael Redclift, *Chewing Gum: The Fortunes of Taste* (New York: Routledge, 2004).

15. Sheller, *Consuming the Carribbean.* For an introduction to the interdisciplinary field of mobilities research see M. Sheller and J. Urry, "The New Mobilities Paradigm," *Environment and Planning A: Materialities and Mobilities* 38 (2006): 207–226; K. Hannam, M. Sheller, and J. Urry, "Mobilities, Immobilities and Moorings," Editorial introduction to *Mobilities* 1, no. 1 (March 2006): 1–22; Tim Cresswell, "Mobilities I: Catching up," *Progress in Human Geography* 35, no. 4 (2010): 550–558; Tim Cresswell, "Mobilities II: Still," *Progress in Human Geography* 36, no. 5 (2012): 645–653.

16. E. Melanie Dupuis, *Nature's Perfect Food: How Milk Became America's Drink* (New York: New York University Press, 2002).

17. On postcarbon transitions see John Urry, *Societies beyond Oil: Oil Dregs and Social Futures* (London: Zed Books, 2013); David Tyfield and John Urry, eds., "Energizing Societies," Special Issue of *Theory, Culture and Society* (forthcoming).

18. Julian M. Allwood, and Jonathan M. Cullen, *Sustainable Materials: With Both Eyes Open* (Cambridge, UK: UIT, 2012).

19. US Geological Survey (USGS), *Mineral Commodity Summaries (MCS) 2012* (Reston, VA: USGS, Department of the Interior, 2012), 16. Available online at http://minerals.usgs.gov/minerals/pubs/mcs.

20. Hugues Wilquin, *Aluminium Architecture: Construction and Details* (Basel: Birkhäuser, 2001), 10, 12–13.

21. "Aluminum Company of America," *Business Week* (December 25, 1929); "Records of Alcoa, 1857–1992" (Pittsburgh: Heinz History Center, n.d.), MSO 282.

22. David Nye, *Electrifying America: Social Meanings of a New Technology* (Cambridge, MA: MIT Press, 1992).

23. Reynolds Metals Company, *The A-B-C's of Aluminum* (Louisville, KY: Author, 1950), 26.

24. *Aluminum by Alcoa* (Pittsburgh: Aluminum Corporation of America, 1969), 70.

25. Ibid., 71.

26. Nye, *Electrifying America,* chapter 6.

27. Season Three, Episode No. 51, "Bart the Lover." First aired February 13, 1992. Thanks to Eric Jensen for bringing this to my attention.

28. "Cartoonist Groening Defends 'Simpsons' Suicide Scene," *San Francisco Chronicle* (February 15, 1992).

29. USGS, *Mineral Commodity Summaries (MCS) 2012,* 27.

30. Ibid.

31. Jennifer Gitlitz, *Trashed Cans: The Global Environmental Impacts of Aluminum Can Wasting in America* (Arlington, VA: Container Recycling Institute, June 2002), 17.

32. Ibid.

33. Annie Leonard, *The Story of Stuff: The Impact of Overconsumption on the Planet, Our Communities, and Our Health—And How We Can Make It Better* (New York: Free Press, 2010), 65.

34. This can be compared, for example, to the data storage industry; data server centers in the United States consume approximately 76 billion kWh per year, or roughly 2 percent of all electricity consumed in the country (James Glanz, "Power, Pollution and the Internet," *New York Times* [September 23, 2012]: A1). But in smaller countries, such as New Zealand, for example, the Tiwai Point smelter is the largest electricity consumer in the country, and uses approximately one-third of the total energy consumed in the South Island and 15 percent of the total energy nationwide.

35. Projections of demand are based on W. D. Menzie, J. J. Barry, D. I. Bleiwas, E. L. Bray, T. G. Goonan, and G. Matos, "The Global Flow of Aluminum from 2006 through 2025," US Geological Survey, Open-File Report 2010-1256 (Reston, VA: USGS, 2010); see also Jennifer Gitlitz, *The Relationship between Primary Aluminium Production and the Damming of World Rivers,* Working Paper 2 (Berkeley, CA: International Rivers Network, 1993); Felix Padel and Samarendra Das, *Out of This Earth: East India Adivasis and the Aluminium Cartel* (Delhi: Orient Blackswan, 2010).

36. Matthew Evenden, "Aluminum, Commodity Chains, and the Environmental History of the Second World War," *Environmental History* 16, no. 1 (January 2011): 85.

37. Evenden, "Aluminum, Commodity Chains, and the Environmental History of the Second World War." For developments in the Pacific Northwest see http://www.nwcouncil.org/history/aluminum.

38. Padel and Das, *Out of This Earth,* p. 72; see also Gitlitz, *The Relationship between Primary Aluminium Production and the Damming of World River.*

39. Glenn Switkes, *Foiling the Aluminum Industry: A Toolkit for Communities, Activists, Consumers and Workers* (Berkeley, CA: International Rivers Network, 2005).

40. See http://www.keele.ac.uk/aluminium/mediaandpresentations on Exley's research center as well as information on the French television broadcast *Aluminium, Notre Poison Quotidien,* shown on France 5 on January 22, 2012 (download available).

41. Liz Bestic "Is Aluminum Really a Silent Killer?" *Telegraph* (March 4, 2012). Available online at http://www.telegraph.co.uk/health/9119528/Is-aluminium-really-a-silent-killer.html.

42. Available online at http://www.bbc.co.uk/news/uk-england-cornwall-17367243.

43. Jennifer Gitlitz, *Trashed Cans,* 24.

44. Richard Price, *First-Time: The Historical Vision of an Afro-American People* (Baltimore: Johns Hopkins University Press, 1983); Richard Price, *Travels with Tooy: History, Memory, and the African American Imagination* (Chicago: University of Chicago Press, 2008).

45. Richard Price, *Rainforest Warriors: Human Rights on Trial* (Philadelphia: University of Pennsylvania Press, 2011).

46. I thank Richard Price for sharing with me the Postface to the French edition of *Rainforest Warriors* (2012), which updates the situation, and in which he writes "it is difficult not to feel discouraged by what has happened in the interim [since the original publication of his book]. Suriname continues to proceed largely as if the judgment in *Saramaka People* v. *Suriname* never happened. And despite the patient

and persistent efforts of the Saamaka people and their legal representatives to get Suriname to implement the judgment, very little further action has been taken." Note that the former spelling of *Saramaka* has been changed more recently to *Saamaka*.

47. International Rivers, "Belo Monte: Massive Dam Project Strikes at the Heart of the Amazon"(March 2010), http://internationalrivers.org.

48. For an overview, see Padel and Das, *Out of This Earth.*

49. Ibid. And see http://www.survivalinternational.org/news/9155.

50. Available online at http://sacom.hk/archives/844.

51. For a related argument on the importance of cultural processes as well as the structure of firms and state regimes in leading toward a postautomobile transition, see Mimi Sheller, "The Emergence of New Cultures of Mobility: Stability, Openings, and Prospects," in Geoff Dudley, Frank Geels, and René Kemp, eds., *Automobility in Transition? A Socio-technical Analysis of Sustainable Transport,* 180–202 (London: Routledge, 2011).

52. Eric Schatzberg, "Symbolic Culture and Technological Change: The Cultural History of Aluminum as an Industrial Material," *Enterprise & Society* 4, no. 2 (June 2003): 226–271.

53. See reports at http://www.nytimes.com/2013/06/08/business/global/austra lian-gold-miner-takes-big-hit-as-price-slides.html?emc=tnt&tntemail0=y&_r=1& and http://www.mineweb.com/mineweb/content/en/mineweb-fast-news?oid=17 6988&sn=Detail.

54. Padel and Das, *Out of This Earth,* 546.

55. Edward W. Soja, *Seeking Spatial Justice* (Minneapolis: University of Minnesota Press, 2010).

2 INVENTORS, INVESTORS, AND INDUSTRY

1. Rebecca Solnit, *River of Shadows: Eadweard Muybridge and the Technological Wild West* (New York: Penguin, 2003), 219.

2. Hugues Wilquin, *Aluminium Architecture: Construction and Details* (Basel: Birkhäuser, 2001), 24. On Roman cement in comparison to modern Portland cement, see http://www.theatlanticcities.com/technology/2013/06/could-2000-year-old-rec ipe-cement-be-superior-our-own/5800.

3. Aluminum Company of America, *Aluminum by Alcoa: The Story of a Light Metal* (Pittsburgh: Aluminum Company of America, 1954), 5–6. [Form AD 429 A1154.125]

4. Wilquin, *Aluminium Architecture,* 204.

5. Aluminum Company of America, *Aluminum by Alcoa,* 4–5; Tom Geller, "Aluminum: Common Metal, Uncommon Past," *Chemical Heritage* (Winter 2007/2008): 34.

6. George David Smith, *From Monopoly to Competition: The Transformation of Alcoa, 1888–1986* (Cambridge, UK: Cambridge University Press, 1988), 2.

7. Ibid., 7.

8. The Aluminum Association. *Uses of Aluminum* (New York: The Aluminum Association, circa 1965), 5.

9. Sarah Nichols, "Aluminum by Design: Jewelry to Jets," *Aluminum by Design* (Pittsburgh: Carnegie Museum of Art, 2000b).

10. This section draws on several company histories as well as popular pamphlets produced by Alcoa. For celebratory insider's accounts of Alcoa see the history written by the company's director of public relations, Charles C. Carr, *Alcoa: An American Enterprise* (New York: Rinehart and Co., 1952); and Junius Edwards, *The Immortal Woodshed: The Story of the Inventor Who Brought Aluminum to America* (New York: Dodd, Mead & Co., 1955). A more objective company history is George David Smith, *From Monopoly to Competition.*

11. Smith, *From Monopoly to Competition,* 8–9.

12. Just a few years later, in the 1890s, there was the comparable parallel invention of motion pictures by Thomas Edison in the United States, Auguste and Louis Lumiere in France, and Max Skladanowsky in Germany.

13. Geller, "Aluminum: Common Metal, Uncommon Past," 33.

14. Smith, *From Monopoly to Competition,* 10.

15. Margaret G. W. Graham and Bettye H. Pruitt, *R&D for Industry: A Century of Technical Innovation at Alcoa* (Cambridge, MA: MIT Press, 1990), 36.

16. Ibid., 12.

17. Smith, *From Monopoly to Competition,* 14–15.

18. Aluminum Company of America, *Aluminum by Alcoa,* 7.

19. Graham and Pruitt, *R&D for Industry,* 36.

20. Ibid., 29.

21. Ibid., 30.

22. Ibid., 33.

23. Ibid., 45–46.

24. Ibid., 40.

25. On Europe's aluminum industry, which I cannot fully address here, see Florence Hachez-Leroy, *L'aluminium Français; L'invention d'un Marché, 1911–1983* (Paris: CNRS Editions, avec le Concours de l'Institut pour l'Histoire de l'Aluminium,1999); Ivan Grinberg and Florence Hachez-Leroy, eds., *Industrialisation et sociétés en Europe occidentale de la fin du XIXe siècle a nos jours: L'age de l'aluminium* (Paris: Armand Colin, 1997); and Luitgard Marschall, *Aluminium: Metall der Moderne* (München: Oekom Verlag, 2008).

26. Henri Sainte-Claire Deville, *De l'aluminium, ses propriétés, sa fabrication et ses applications* (Paris, 1859).

27. Geller, "Aluminum: Common Metal, Uncommon Past," 35–36.

28. Ibid., 36.

29. Graham and Pruitt, *R&D for Industry*, 109–110.

30. Ibid., 32.

31. Ibid.

32. Thomas J. Misa, *A Nation of Steel: The Making of Modern America 1865–1925* (Baltimore: Johns Hopkins University Press, 1995).

33. Jeffrey L. Meikle, *American Plastic: A Cultural History* (New Brunswick, NJ: Rutgers University Press, 1997).

34. Ibid., 96.

35. David Nye, *Electrifying America: Social Meanings of a New Technology* (Cambridge, MA: MIT Press, 1992).

36. Eric Schatzberg, "Ideology and Technical Choice: The Decline of the Wooden Airplane in the United States, 1920–1945," *Technology and Culture* 35, no. 1 (January 1994): 34–69; Eric Schatzberg, "Symbolic Culture and Technological Change: The Cultural History of Aluminum as an Industrial Material." *Enterprise & Society* 4, no. 2 (June 2003): 226–271.

37. The Soviet Union was late to gain smelting technology, as discussed further in the next chapter. See Mikhail Mukhin, "Aluminium for Red Airforce: Foreign Technology in the Making of Soviet Aluminium Industry, 1928 to 1941." Paper presented at *Les Techniques et la Globalisation: Échange, Réseaux et Espionnage Industriel au XXe Siècle* [Technology and Globalization: Exchange, Development and Industrial Espionage in the 20th Century], March 29–31, 2012, EHSS—Université de Paris VII. Thanks to Allen Batteau for providing this paper to me.

38. R. Buckminster Fuller, *Critical Path* (New York: St. Martin's Griffin, 1981), 98.

39. Ibid., 98–99.

40. Ibid., 99. Emphasis in original.

41. Glenn Switkes, *Foiling the Aluminum Industry: A Toolkit for Communities, Activists, Consumers and Workers* (Berkeley, CA: International Rivers Network, 2005), 38.

42. Smith, *From Monopoly to Competition,* 194.

43. Ibid., 196.

44. Ibid., 198.

45. Ibid., 201.

46. Ibid., 209–210.

47. Ibid., 210.

48. Dennis P. Doordan, "Promoting Aluminum: Designers and the American Aluminum Industry," *Design Issues* 9, no. 2 (Autumn 1993): 45.

49. Sarah Nichols, *Aluminum by Design* (Pittsburgh: Carnegie Museum of Art, 2000a), 44.

50. Doordan, "Promoting Aluminum," 46.

51. Detailed histories of the government's involvement with the industry are provided in Carr, *Alcoa,* and Smith, *From Monopoly to Competition.*

52. John A. Stuckey, *Vertical Integration and Joint Ventures in the Aluminum Industry* (Cambridge, MA: Harvard University Press, 1983), 2, 5.

53. Bradford Barham, Stephen Bunker, and Dennis O'Hearn "Raw Material Industries in Resource-Rich Regions," in *States, Firms, and Raw Materials: The World Economy and Ecology of Aluminum,* ed. Bradford Barham, Stephen Bunker, and Dennis O'Hearn (Madison: The University of Wisconsin Press, 1994), 29. This profile, they argue, leads to a market structure with a few large corporations, consumer-state involvement to secure stable supplies, producer-state involvement seeking "rents," and in which strategic behavior and bargaining are central to the market structure. See also Evelyne Huber Stephens, "Minerals Strategies and Development: International Political Economy, State, Class, and the Role of the Bauxite/Aluminum and Copper Industries in Jamaica and Peru," *Studies in Comparative International Development* 22, no. 3 (1987): 60–97.

54. On average 13,500 kWh of electricity are needed to produce one ton of aluminum, although the figure was higher in the first half of the twentieth century; eighteen billion kWh of electricity were used in 1943 to produce the 920,000 tons of aluminum made in the United States that year (enough to supply half the residents of the country for an entire year); today approximately 3 percent of electricity generated worldwide goes to aluminum smelting; in several less-developed countries aluminum smelters consume up to one-third or more of the national power supply.

55. Doordan, "Promoting Aluminum," 46.

56. Carr, *Alcoa,* 257, 263–264.

57. Reynolds Metals Company. *The ABC's of Aluminum: From Raw Material to Application* (Louisville, KY: Reynolds Metals Company, 1950), 28–29.

58. Matthew Evenden, "Aluminum, Commodity Chains, and the Environmental History of the Second World War," *Environmental History* 16, no. 1 (January 2011): 70.

59. Aluminum Company of America, *Aluminum by Alcoa: The Story of a Light Metal* (Pittsburgh: Aluminum Company of America, 1954), 27–29.

60. Ibid., 19–20.

61. Paragraph based on ibid., 20–21.

62. Evenden, "Aluminum, Commodity Chains, and the Environmental History of the Second World War," 72.

63. Jennifer Gitlitz, *Trashed Cans: The Global Environmental Impacts of Aluminum Can Wasting in America* (Arlington, VA: Container Recycling Institute, June 2002), 25.

64. Aluminum Company of America, *Aluminum by Alcoa,* 18.

65. Ibid.

66. Ibid., 20.

67. Fuller, *Critical Path,* 201.

68. Ibid., 202.

69. Gitlitz, *Trashed Cans,* 24.

70. Fuller, *Critical Path,* 202.

71. The Aluminum Association. *Aluminum Industry Vision: Sustainable Solutions* (Washington, DC: The Aluminum Association, November 2001), 7.

72. Felix Padel and Samarendra Das, *Out of This Earth: East India Adivasis and the Aluminium Cartel* (Delhi: Orient Blackswan, 2010).

73. Switkes, *Foiling the Aluminum Industry,* 21.

74. Ibid., 40.

75. Stephen Labaton, "Supreme Court Lifts Ban on Minimum Retail Pricing," *New York Times* (June 29, 2007): C1.

76. Jeffrey Rosen, "Supreme Court Inc.," *New York Times Magazine* (March 16, 2008): 40.

77. David Kocieniewski, "The House Edge: A Shuffle of Aluminum, but to Banks, Pure Gold," *New York Times* (July 21, 2013): A1.

78. Switkes, *Foiling the Aluminum Industry*, 23.

3   METAL OF WAR, FOR WAR, AND BY WAR

1. George David Smith, *From Monopoly to Competition: The Transformation of Alcoa, 1888–1986* (Cambridge, UK: Cambridge University Press, 1988).

2. Aluminum Company of America, *Aluminum by Alcoa* (Pittsburgh: Aluminum Company of America, 1969), 78. [Form 01–12292]

3. Ibid.

4. Smith, *From Monopoly to Competition*.

5. Ibid., 128.

6. Ibid., 127.

7. Felix Padel and Samarendra Das, *Out of This Earth: East India Adivasis and the Aluminium Cartel* (Delhi: Orient Blackswan, 2010), 271.

8. Eric Schatzberg, "Ideology and Technical Choice: The Decline of the Wooden Airplane in the United States, 1920–1945," *Technology and Culture* 35, no. 1 (January 1994): 34–69; Eric Schatzberg, "Symbolic Culture and Technological Change: The Cultural History of Aluminum as an Industrial Material," *Enterprise & Society* 4, no. 2 (June 2003): 226–271.

9. Although I do not fully employ the methodologies of John Law's *Aircraft Stories: Decentering the Object in Technoscience* (Durham, NC: Duke University Press, 2002), with its emphasis on oscillation, interference, fractional coherence, and rhizomatic networks, I take inspiration from his view of the contested military roles and political attributes of objects as part of the effort to make them cohere—that is, to become aluminum airplanes, rather than wooden ones.

10. *Five ARL Scientists Receive DoD Standardization Award*. United States Army Research Lab (March 8, 2012). Available from http://www.arl.army.mil/www/default.cfm?page=905.

11. Jules Verne, *From the Earth to the Moon* [De la Terre à la Lune] (Paris: Pierre-Jules Hetzel, 1865), cited in The Aluminum Association, *Uses of Aluminum* (New York: The Aluminum Association, circa 1965), 31.

12. Margaret G. W. Graham and Bettye H. Pruitt, *R&D for Industry: A Century of Technical Innovation at Alcoa* (Cambridge, MA: MIT Press, 1990), 119.

13. Charles C. Carr, *Alcoa: An American Enterprise* (New York: Rinehart & Co., 1952), 160; Smith, *From Monopoly to Competition,* 128.

14. Margaret Graham notes that "because it had no copper, Germany relied more heavily on aluminum than any of the other belligerents" in World War I. They were also leaders in chemistry and metallurgical research, including Count Ferdinand von Zeppelin who "developed new structural concepts for the rigid airship that involved girders made of aluminum parts stamped out from sheet metal and assembled." Margaret Graham, "R&D and Competition in England and the United States: The Case of the Aluminum Dirigible," *Business History Review* 62, no. 2 (Summer 1988): 265.

15. Ibid., 274.

16. Carr, *Alcoa,* 140.

17. Smith, *From Monopoly to Competition,* 130.

18. Ibid., 131.

19. Carlton E. Davis, *Jamaica in the World Aluminium Industry, 1838–1973* (Vol. I) (Kingston: Jamaica Bauxite Institute, 1989), 49–50.

20. Mark Whitehead, *State, Science, and the Skies: Governmentalities of the British Atmosphere* (Oxford: Wiley-Blackwell, 2009).

21. Padel and Das, *Out of This Earth,* 274–275.

22. Dewey Anderson cited by Padel and Das, *Out of This Earth,* 276–277.

23. Peter Adey, *Aerial Life: Spaces, Mobilities, Affect* (Oxford: Wiley-Blackwell, 2010).

24. Jeffrey T. Schnapp, "The Romance of Caffeine and Aluminum," *Critical Inquiry* 28, no. 1 (Autumn 2001): 244–269.

25. Ibid., 255–256, note 17.

26. Ibid., 256, note 18.

27. Mikhail Mukhin, "Aluminium for Red Airforce: Foreign Technology in the Making of Soviet Aluminium Industry, 1928 to 1941," paper presented at *Les Techniques and la Globalisation: Échange, Réseaux et Espionnage Industriel au XXe Siècle* [Technology and Globalization: Exchange, Development and Industrial Espionage in the 20th Century], March 29–31, 2012, EHSS—Université de Paris VII, 5.

28. Caren Kaplan, "Mobility and War: The Cosmic View of US 'Air Power,'" *Environment and Planning A* 38, no. 2 (February 2006): 395.

29. Annmarie Brennan, "Forecast," in *Cold War Hothouses: Inventing Postwar Culture, from Cockpit to Playboy,* ed. Beatriz Colomina, Annmarie Brennan, and Jeannie Kim (New York: Princeton Architectural Press, 2004).

30. Dennis P. Doordan, "Promoting Aluminum: Designers and the American Aluminum Industry," *Design Issues* 9, no. 2 (Autumn 1993): 44–50.

31. Brennan, "Forecast," 60.

32. Ibid.

33. Aluminum Company of America, *Aluminum by Alcoa*, 78.

34. Dennis Hevesi, "Lawrence Mead Jr., Aerospace Engineer, Dies at 94," *New York Times* (August 30, 2012). Available online at http://www.nytimes.com/2012/08/31/business/lawrence-mead-jr-aerospace-engineer-who-helped-design-a-6-bomber-dies-at-94.html?emc=tnt&tntemail0=y.

35. Cited in Padel and Das, *Out of This Earth*, 277.

36. Steven Ujifusa, *A Man and His Ship: America's Greatest Naval Architect and His Quest to Build the S.S. United States* (New York: Simon & Schuster, 2012).

37. Aluminum Company of America, *Aluminum by Alcoa*, 63.

38. The Aluminum Association, *Uses of Aluminum*, 27.

39. Aluminum Company of America, *Aluminum by Alcoa*, 60.

40. Deborah Cowen, *Rough Trade* (Minneapolis: University of Minnesota Press, 2014).

41. Padel and Das, *Out of This Earth*, 15.

42. H. Goldschmidt cited in Padel and Das, *Out of This Earth*, 270.

43. Reynolds Metals Company, *The ABC's of Aluminum: From Raw Material to Application* (Louisville, KY: Reynolds Metals Company, 1950), 68.

44. Padel and Das, *Out of This Earth*, 278.

45. Aluminum Company of America, *Aluminum by Alcoa*, 81.

46. Ibid., 83.

47. Padel and Das, *Out of This Earth*, 280.

48. Aluminum Company of America, *Aluminum by Alcoa*, 81.

49. The Aluminum Association, *Uses of Aluminum*, 29.

50. Ibid., 81–82.

51. Reynolds Metals Company, *The ABC's of Aluminum*, 69.

52. The Aluminum Association, *Uses of Aluminum*, 31.

53. Ibid., 30; see also http://www.haystack.mit.edu/hay/history.html.

54. Kenneth Chang, "For NASA, Return Trip to Jupiter in Search of Clues to Solar System's Origins," *New York Times* (August 5, 2011) A12.

55. Jonah Weiner, "Prying Eyes: Trevor Paglen Makes Art out of Government Secrets," *New Yorker* (October 22, 2012): 60–61.

56. Paul Virilio, *Speed and Politics*. Trans. Semiotext(e) and Mark Polizzotti. (Los Angeles: Semiotext(e), 2006 [1977]), 90.

57. Caren Kaplan, "The Balloon Prospect: Aerostatic Observation and the Emergence of Militarized Aeromobility," in *From Above: War, Violence, and Verticality*, ed. Peter Adey, Mark Whitehead, and Alison J. Williams (London: Hurst, 2013).

58. Padel and Das, *Out of This Earth*, 280.

59. Grace V. Jean, "Researchers See Aluminum as Alternative to Steel Armor," *National Defense* (October 2008). Available online at http://www.nationaldefen semagazine.org/archive/2008/October/Pages/Researchers%20See%20 Aluminum%20As%20Alternative%20to%20Steel%20Armor.aspx.

60. Andrew Nusca, "Powdermet Pursues Nanoparticle-infused Aluminum Alloys for Auto Industry, Military," *SmartPlanet* (May 21, 2012). Available online at http:// www.smartplanet.com/blog/smart-takes/powdermet-pursues-nanoparticle-infused-aluminum-alloys-for-auto-industry-military/26629. LiveScience, "Military: New Aluminum Windows Stop .50-Caliber Bullet" (October 18, 2005). Available online at http://www.livescience.com/420-military-aluminum-windows-stop-50 -caliber-bullet.html.

61. David E. Sanger, "Obama Order Sped up Wave of Cyberattacks against Iran," *New York Times* (June 1, 2012). Available online at http://www.nytimes. com/2012/06/01/world/middleeast/obama-ordered-wave-of-cyberattacks-against-iran.html?pagewanted=1&_r=2; Ellen Nakashima and Joby Warrick, "Stuxnet Was Work of U.S. and Israeli Experts, Officials Say," *Washington Post* (June 1, 2012). Available online at http://www.washingtonpost.com/world/national-secu rity/stuxnet-was-work-of-us-and-israeli-experts-officials-say/2012/06/01/gJQAl nEy6U_story.html. And see David Sanger, *Confront and Conceal: Obama's Secret Wars and Surprising Use of American Power* (New York: Random House, 2012), although cyber-security experts have challenged the technical details of his account (see, e.g., John Leyden, "Prof Casts Doubt on Stuxnet's Accidental 'Great Escape' Theory: How DID the Super-Weapon Flee Iran's Nuke Plant?" *Register* (September 13, 2012). Available online at http://www.theregister.co.uk/2012/09/13/stuxnet/).

62. R. Buckminster Fuller, *Critical Path* (New York: St. Martin's Griffin, 1981) 203.

63. Ibid., 216.

64. As a World Fellow in Residence at University of Pennsylvania, Fuller had offices in the University City Science Center, in a building designed by Robert Venturi,

renovated and reopened in 2012 as the URBN Center of Drexel University's West-phal College of Media Arts and Design.

65. Fuller, *Critical Path*, 69, 202.

4   SPEED METAL

1. Tim Cresswell, *On the Move: Mobility in the Modern Western World* (New York: Routledge, 2006), describes mobility as consisting of physical movement, meanings and representations of movement, and embodied practices; all three dimensions are involved in my understanding of aluminum.

2. Jeffrey L. Meikle, *American Plastic: A Cultural History* (New Brunswick, NJ: Rutgers University Press, 1997), 30.

3. Ibid., 33.

4. Ibid., 55.

5. Ibid., 51.

6. Meikle, *American Plastic*.

7. Florence Hachez-Leroy, *L'aluminium Français: L'invention d'un Marché, 1911–1983* (Paris: CNRS Editions, avec l'Institut pout l'Histoire de l'Aluminium, 1999).

8. Dennis P. Doordan, "Promoting Aluminum: Designers and the American Alumi-num Industry," *Design Issues* 9, no. 2 (Autumn 1993): 49.

9. Ibid.

10. Henry Dreyfuss cited in Doordan, "Promoting Aluminum," 48.

11. Meikle, *American Plastic,* 116.

12. Ibid., 115–116.

13. Harvey Molotch, *Where Stuff Comes From: How Toasters, Toilets, Cars, Computers, and Many Other Things Come to Be as They Are* (New York: Routledge, 2005), 62.

14. Ibid. 87.

15. The Aluminum Association, *Uses of Aluminum,* 9.

16. David Nye, *American Technological Sublime* (Cambridge: MIT Press, 1994).

17. F. T. Marinetti, *Futurist Manifesto* (1909), *Three Intellectuals in Politics*, trans. James Joll (New York: Pantheon Books, 1960), 181.

18. Alcoa's fiftieth anniversary message, printed in *Fortune* magazine in May 1936.

19. Alcoa Aluminum ad from the *Saturday Evening Post*, October 11, 1930, 106.

20. Aluminum Company of America, *Aluminum by Alcoa* (Pittsburgh: Aluminum Company of America, 1969), 58. [Form 01-12292]

21. Ibid, 60–62.

22. Douglas Auchincloss, "The Dymaxion American," *Time* 83, no. 2 (January 10, 1964): 49. The article was written with research by Miriam Rumwell in Chicago and Nancy Gay Farber in New York. A famous portrait of Fuller is on the cover, by artist Boris Artzybasheff, who also is discussed in chapter 6 in relation to his imagery of the Caribbean for Alcoa.

23. Phil Patton, "A 3-Wheel Dream That Died at Takeoff," *New York Times* (June 15, 2008), accessed at http://www.nytimes.com/2008/06/15/automobiles/collectibles/15BUCKY.html?_r=0. The only existing Dymaxion car was featured in an exhibition on Fuller's designs at the Whitney Museum of American Art, New York, in June–July 2008.

24. Phil Patton, "A Visionary's Minivan Arrived Decades Too Soon," *New York Times*, Automotive Section (January 6, 2008): 6.

25. Norman Bel Geddes, *Horizons* (Boston: Little, Brown, 1932).

26. Jeremy Packer, "Automobility and the Driving Force of Warfare: From Public Safety to National Security," in *The Ethics of Mobility*, ed. T. Sager and S. Bergmann (Farnham and Burlington: Ashgate, 2008), 39–64.

27. Bel Geddes, *Horizons*.

28. Available online at Matt Novak's blog, http://www.paleofuture.com.

29. Bryan Burkhart and David Hunt, *Airstream: The History of the Land Yacht* (San Francisco: Chronicle Books, 2000), 53.

30. Available online at Matt Novak's blog, http://www.paleofuture.com.

31. "Tomorrow's Engine?" Bohn Aluminum and Brass Corporation ad, *Time* magazine [date unknown, page unknown].

32. "Forecasting by Bohn," Bohn Aluminum and Brass Corporation ad, *Fortune* magazine [date unknown], 45.

33. Dean A. Hammond, "Kaiser-Frazer Plans Aluminum-Glass Car," *Science and Mechanics* (October 1951): 65.

34. Burkhart and Hunt, *Airstream,* 39–40.

35. Ibid., 19.

36. Molotch, *Where Stuff Comes From,* 82.

37. James M. Jasper, *Restless Nation: Starting Over in America* (Chicago: University of Chicago Press, 2000), xii.

38. Rem Koolhaas, *Delirious New York: A Retroactive Manifesto for Manhattan* (New York: Monacelli Press, 1994), 141, 143.

39. Hugues Wilquin, *Aluminium Architecture: Construction and Details* (Basel: Birkhäuser, 2001), 26.

40. "31 Stories of Aluminum Make News," Alcoa Aluminum ad, *Saturday Evening Post* (April 4, 1953), 101.

41. Thanks to Stuart Leslie for sharing his work with me. Stuart W. Leslie, "The Strategy of Structure: Architectural and Managerial Style at Alcoa and Owens-Corning," *Enterprise & Society* 12, no. 4 (2011): 863–902.

42. "31 Stories of Aluminum Make News," 101.

43. Aluminum Company of America, *Aluminum by Alcoa,* 49.

44. Annmarie Brennan, "Forecast," in *Cold War Hothouses: Inventing Postwar Culture, from Cockpit to Playboy,* ed. Beatriz Colomina, Annmarie Brennan, and Jeannie Kim (New York: Princeton Architectural Press, 2004), 71–72.

45. David Crowley and Jane Pavitt, eds., *Cold War Modern: Design 1945–1970* (London: V&A Publishing, 2008), 13.

46. Ibid., 12.

47. Brennan, "Forecast," 86–87.

48. Ibid., 88–89.

49. George David Smith, *From Monopoly to Competition: The Transformation of Alcoa, 1888–1986* (Cambridge, UK: Cambridge University Press, 1988), 338.

50. Aluminum Company of America, *Aluminum by Alcoa,* 50.

51. James Traub, "After Cheney," *New York Times Magazine* (November 24, 2009).

5 MOBILE HOMES

1. Lewis Mumford, *Technics and Civilization* (New York: Harcourt, Brace, 1934).

2. Jeffrey L. Meikle, "Materials," in *Speed Limits,* ed. Jeffrey T. Schnapp (Montreal: Canadian Centre for Architecture, 2009), 60.

3. Harvey Molotch, *Where Stuff Comes From: How Toasters, Toilets, Cars, Computers, and Many Other Things Come to Be as They Are* (New York: Routledge, 2005), 233.

4. Dolores Hayden, *The Grand Domestic Revolution: A History of Feminist Designs for American Homes, Neighborhoods, and Cities* (Cambridge, MA: MIT Press, 1981), 220–221.

5. Elizabeth Shove and Dale Southerton, "Defrosting the Freezer: From Novelty to Convenience," *Material Culture* 5, no. 3 (2000): 308.

6. Elizabeth Shove, *Comfort, Cleanliness and Convenience: The Social Organization of Normality* (New York: Berg, 2003), 178.

7. Jeffrey L. Meikle, *American Plastic: A Cultural History* (New Brunswick, NJ: Rutgers University Press, 1997).

8. Sarah Nichols, *Aluminum by Design* (Pittsburgh, PA: Carnegie Museum of Art, 2000).

9. Jeffrey T. Schnapp, "The Romance of Caffeine and Aluminum," *Critical Inquiry* 28, no. 1 (Autumn 2001): 245.

10. Ibid., 245.

11. Nichols, *Aluminum by Design*; and see Maureen Byko, "Aluminum Exhibits Its Versatility in Art, Life," *JOM* 52, no. 11 (2000): 9–12. Available online at http://www.tms.org/pubs/journals/JOM/0011/Byko-0011.html.

12. See http://www.emeco.net/material/recycled-aluminum.

13. Pat Kirkham, *Charles and Ray Eames: Designers of the Twentieth Century* (Cambridge, MA: MIT Press, 1998), 249.

14. Kaiser Aluminum ad, *Saturday Evening Post* (December 10, 1955), 87.

15. Jessica McCahon, "Alcoa Aluminum Bat History," *Livestrong.com* (May 26, 2011). Available online at http://www.livestrong.com/article/377484-alcoa-aluminum-bat-history.

16. Timothy Onkst, "Comparison of Wooden Bats & Aluminum Bats," *Livestrong.com* (June 14, 2011). Available online at http://www.livestrong.com/article/356634-how-have-aluminum-baseball-bats-changed-college-baseball/#ixzz29erLPNet.

17. Pat Borzi, "Making Metal Bats Play Like Wood," *New York Times* (June 18, 2011). Available online at http://www.nytimes.com/2011/06/19/sports/baseball/metal-bats-that-play-like-wood-alter-college-baseball.html?.

18. R. Buckminster Fuller, *Critical Path* (New York: St. Martin's Press, 1981), 283.

19. H. Ward Jandl, "With Heritage So Shiny: America's First All-Aluminum House," *Association for Preservation Technology (APT) Bulletin* 23, no. 2 (1991): 38.

20. Ibid., 39.

21. Ibid.

22. Ibid., 43.

23. Barry Bergdoll and Peter Christensen, *Home Delivery: Fabricating the Modern Dwelling* (New York: The Museum of Modern Art, 2008), 20–21.

24. Edward W. Soja, *Seeking Spatial Justice* (Minneapolis: University of Minnesota Press, 2010), 129–133.

25. *Jean Prouvé: The Poetics of the Technical Object,* Design Museum, London, February–April 2008, exhibition pamphlet.

26. Bergdoll and Christensen, *Home Delivery,* 22.

27. Ibid., 108.

28. Robert Rubin in ibid., 113.

29. Bergdoll and Christensen, *Home Delivery*, 58.

30. Ibid.

31. Fuller, *Critical Path,* 148.

32. Bergdoll and Christensen, *Home Delivery,* 90.

33. Available online at http://www.hfmgv.org/museum/dymaxion.aspx.

34. Fuller, *Critical Path*, 149.

35. Ibid., 315–323.

36. Ibid., 333.

37. Annmarie Brennan, "Forecast," in *Cold War Hothouses: Inventing Postwar Culture, from Cockpit to Playboy,* ed. Beatriz Colomina, Annmarie Brennan, and Jeannie Kim (New York: Princeton Architectural Press, 2004), 85.

38. Paul Ricoeur, "Universal Civilization and National Cultures" (1961), *History and Truth,* trans. Chas. A. Kelbley (Evanston, IL: Northwestern University Press, 1965), 276.

39. See Tom Vanderbilt, "Trees for an Age of Glitter," in J. Shimon and J. Lindemann, *Season's Gleamings: The Art of the Aluminum Christmas Tree* (New York: Melcher Media, 2004), 71.

40. *Dwell* magazine, special issue "Prefab Now: High Style, Flexible Design" 7 (November 2006): 165.

41. Bergdoll and Christensen, *Home Delivery,* 190.

42. Ibid.

43. Ibid., 193.

44. R. Buckminster Fuller, *Operating Manual for Spaceship Earth* (Southern Illinois University Press, 1969).

45. Don Fabun, *The Dynamics of Change* (Englewood Cliffs, NJ: Kaiser Aluminum with Prentice Hall, 1967).

46. Kaiser advertising copy citing Fuller, *Operating Manual for Spaceship Earth.*

47. Fuller quoted in Jeffrey T. Schnapp, *Speed Limits,* 283.

6   ALCOA CRUISING THE CARIBBEAN

1. I thank the Shelby Cullom Davis Center for Historical Studies at Princeton University for supporting my research as a Davis Fellow in 2008–2009, and the participants in the "Cultures and Institutions in Motion" seminar, especially Jeremy Adelman, for bringing Rostow to my attention.

2. Bradford Barham, Stephen Bunker, and Dennis O'Hearn, "Raw Material Industries in Resource-Rich Regions," in *States, Firms, and Raw Materials: The World Economy and Ecology of Aluminum* (Madison: The University of Wisconsin Press, 1994).

3. Sidney Mintz, *Sweetness and Power: The Place of Sugar in Modern History* (New York: Penguin, 1986).

4. Matthew Evenden, "Aluminum, Commodity Chains, and the Environmental History of the Second World War," *Environmental History* 16, no. 1 (January 2011): 73.

5. Carlton E. Davis, *Jamaica in the World Aluminium Industry, 1838–1973* (Vol. I) (Kingston: Jamaica Bauxite Institute, 1989), 135.

6. Ibid.; O. Nigel Bolland, *The Politics of Labour in the British Caribbean* (Kingston: Ian Randle; London: James Currey, 2001), 443.

7. Evenden, "Aluminum, Commodity Chains, and the Environmental History of the Second World War," 81, 85.

8. Ibid., 80.

9. Gerald Horne, *Cold War in a Hot Zone: The United States Confronts Labor and Independence Struggles in the British West Indies* (Philadelphia: Temple University Press, 2007), 160.

10. Fred Doura, *Économie d'Haïti—Dépendence, crise et développement* (Vol. 1) (Montréal: Les Editions DAMI, 2001), quote as cited at http://canadahaitiaction.ca/

content/gold-rush-haiti-who-will-get-rich. See also Alex Dupuy, *Haiti in the World Economy—Class, Race and Underdevelopment* (Boston: Westview Press, 1989).

11. George David Smith, *From Monopoly to Competition: The Transformation of Alcoa, 1888–1986* (Cambridge, UK: Cambridge University Press, 1988), 98.

12. Sandew Hira, "Class Formation and Class Struggle in Suriname: The Background and Development of the Coup d'Etat," in *Crisis in the Caribbean,* ed. Fitzroy Ambursley and Robin Cohen, 166–190 (New York: Monthly Review Press, 1983), 166.

13. Alcoa Steamship ad, *Holiday* Magazine, circa 1948, n.p.

14. *Surinaams Bauxiet/Suriname Bauxite: A Story of Cooperation in the Development of a Resource* (Paramaribo, Suriname: Suriname Bauxite Co., 1955), 112. [In Dutch and English, published on the occasion of the first ever visit to Suriname by a sovereign of the Kingdom of the Netherlands, Her Majesty Queen Juliana.]

15. Ellen-Rose Kambel, "Land, Development, and Indigenous Rights in Suriname: The Role of International Human Rights Law," in *Caribbean Land and Development Revisited,* ed. Jean Besson and Janet Momsen (New York: Palgrave Macmillan, 2007), 72.

16. Richard Price, *First-Time: The Historical Vision of an Afro-American People* (Baltimore: Johns Hopkins University Press, 1983); Richard Price, *Travels with Tooy: History, Memory, and the African American Imagination* (Chicago: University of Chicago Press, 2008), 174, 398; Richard Price, *Rainforest Warriors: Human Rights on Trial* (Philadelphia: University of Pennsylvania Press, 2011).

17. Aluminum Company of America, *Aluminum by Alcoa* (Pittsburgh: Aluminum Company of America, 1969), 21. [Form 01–12292]

18. Alcoa Archives, MSS 282, Subseries 6: Suriname Bauxite Company, Suriname, 1929–1973, Box 18, Booklet: "BROKOPONDO joint venture SURINAME-SURALCO," stamped October 1, 1959, pp. 39, 41. [Contract in Dutch and English]

19. Price, *First-Time,* frontmatter.

20. Alcoa Archives, MSS 282, Box 17, Folder 5, Fact Sheet: "Suriname Aluminum Company."

21. Price, *Travels with Tooy,* 175.

22. Dutch Guiana became the independent Republic of Suriname in 1975, but about 40 percent of the population chose to emigrate to the Netherlands prior to independence. "Within five years, the political system had totally collapsed, and the country was under martial law between 1980 and 1988," and continued to be ruled by army commander Lt. Col. Desire Bouterse, who was eventually elected president in 2010.

23. Hira, "Class Formation and Class Struggle in Suriname," 186.

24. Kambel, "Land, Development, and Indigenous Rights in Suriname," 72.

25. "Maroon Community Petitions Suriname Government about the Operations of a US-owned Bauxite Mining Company," *Forest Peoples Programme* (September 17, 1998).

26. Bureau of Inter-American Affairs, "Background Notes: Suriname," US Department of State (March 1998), cited in "Behind the Shining: Aluminium's Dark Side" (2001).

27. Ibid.

28. Price, *Rainforest Warriors.*

29. Many thanks to Richard Price for advice on some details in this section, and especially for sharing with me the Postface to the French edition of *Rainforest Warriors* (2012), which updates the situation.

30. Ibid.

31. Kambel, "Land, Development, and Indigenous Rights in Suriname," 71.

32. Mimi Sheller, *Consuming the Caribbean: From Arawaks to Zombies* (London: Routledge, 2003); Krista Thompson, *An Eye for the Tropics* (Durham, NC: Duke University Press, 2006).

33. Michel-Rolph Trouillot, *Global Transformations: Anthropology and the Modern World* (New York: Palgrave Macmillan, 2003).

34. The company also ran several freighters out of New York, Montreal, and New Orleans, each of which carried twelve passengers and made longer, slower trips, delivering bauxite and alumina for Reynolds, Kaiser, and Alcoa.

35. David Lambert and Alan Lester, "Introduction: Imperial Spaces, Imperial Subjects," in *Colonial Lives across the British Empire: Imperial Careering in the Long Nineteenth Century,* ed. David Lambert and Alan Lester (Cambridge, UK: Cambridge University Press, 2006), 10.

36. David Armitage, "Three Concepts of Atlantic History," in *The British Atlantic World, 1500–1800,* ed. David Armitage and Michael J. Braddick (Basingstoke, UK: Palgrave Macmillan, 2002), 16.

37. Anyaa Anim-Addo, *Place and Mobilities in the Maritime World: The Royal Mail Steam Packet Company in the Caribbean, c. 1838 to 1914,* PhD thesis (London: Department of Human Geography, Royal Holloway, University of London, 2011), 137.

38. Heinz History Center Library and Archives [HHC], MSS 282, Box 11, Folder 7, David Macintyre, "Some Practical Aspects of Aluminum in Shipbuilding," 4.

58. HHC, MSS 282, Box 11, Internal Correspondence, September 22, 1960, F. A. Billhardt, Alcoa Steamship Company, Inc., New York Office to Mr. L. Litchfield Jr., Pittsburgh Office, Re: Economic Study of Passenger Ships, Alcoa Steamship Company, Inc.

59. HHC, MSS 282, Box 11, Internal Correspondence, January 22, 1960, F. A. Billhardt, Alcoa Steamship Company, Inc., New York Office, to Mr. F. L. Magee, Aluminum Company of America, Pittsburgh Office, Re: PAN-ORE Fleet.

60. Stephens and Stephens, *Democratic Socialism in Jamaica,* 26.

61. Stephens, "Minerals Strategies and Development."

62. Clive Y. Thomas, *Dependence and Transformation: The Economics of the Transition to Socialism* (New York: Monthly Review Press, 1974), 83.

63. For an argument against the Caribbean's capacity to "reach out beyond the extractive stage of production," see Sterling Brubaker, *Trends in the World Aluminum Industry* (Baltimore: Johns Hopkins University Press, 1967), a publication sponsored by the Ford Foundation-funded nonprofit Resources for the Future, Inc.

64. Peter Redfield, *Space in the Tropics: From Convicts to Rockets in French Guiana* (Berkeley: University of California Press, 2000).

65. Price, *Travels with Tooy,* 194.

7 DARK DREAMS

1. Michael Wines, "Toiling in the Dark: Africa's Power Crisis," *New York Times* (July 29, 2007): 10.

2. Jennifer Gitlitz, *Trashed Cans: The Global Environmental Impacts of Aluminum Can Wasting in America* (Arlington, VA: Container Recycling Institute, June 2002), 26.

3. Staff writer, "Africa has an exceptional hydroelectric potential," Inamibia.co.na, June 29, 2011. Available online at http://www.inamibia.co.na/news/africa/item/9658-africa-has-an-exceptional-hydroelectric-potential.html.

4. Danielle Knight, "Enviros Blame Aluminum Industry for Dam Boom," *Monitor* (February 25, 2002). Available online at http://www.albionmonitor.com/0202a/copyright/aluminum.html.

5. "Behind the Shining: Aluminium's Dark Side," authored by the grass-roots movement in Kashipur; An IPS/SEEN/TNI report (2001). No longer available at http://www.saanet.org/kashipur/docs/seenalum.htm.

6. Martin Creamer, "South Africans Spearheading New Guinea Bauxite Thrust," *Mining Weekly* (April 17, 2012). Available online at http://www.miningweekly.com/article/south-africans-spearheading-new-guinea-bauxite-thrust-2012-04-17.

7. Ian Austen, "Aluminum: Quarry for Mining Companies," *New York Times,* Business Section (July 25, 2007): C3.

8. Ibid.

9. David Barboza and Julia Werdigier, "Alcoa and Chinese Rival Buy 12% Stake in Rio Tinto," *New York Times,* Business Section (February 2, 2008).

10. Kelsey Willingham, "Corruption, Capitalists, and the Crime-State Nexus: Criminal Infiltration of the Russian Economy and Implications for the Future," *New Voices in Public Policy* IV (Spring 2010): 2.

11. Stephen Fortescue, "The Russian Aluminum Industry in Transition," *Eurasian Geography and Economics* 47, no. 1 (2006): 76.

12. Ethan Burger and Rosalia Gitau. "The Russian Anti-Corruption Campaign: Public Relations, Politics or Substantive Change?" Georgetown University Law Center, discussion paper (2010): 30. Available online at http://scholarship.law. georgetown.edu/fwps_papers/126.

13. Fortescue, "The Russian Aluminum Industry in Transition," 77.

14. Ibid., 12; Lyuba Pronina, "U.S. Rejects $3Bln Suit against RusAl," *Moscow Times* (2003).

15. Fortescue, "The Russian Aluminum Industry in Transition," 77, note 2.

16. According to a RUSAL press release of February 14, 2007, when the merger was approved by the Federal Antimonopoly Service of Russia, the unified company included RUSAL's Bratsk, Krasnoyarsk, Novokuznetsk, Sayanogorsk Aluminum Smelters, Achinsk Alumina Plant, Nikolaev and Boksitogorsk Alumina Refineries, Friguia Alumina Plant (Guinea), Compagnie des Bauxites de Kindia (Guinea), Bauxite Company of Guyana, a stake in the Queensland Alumina Refinery (Australia), Eurallumina (Italy), as well as ARMENAL, SAYANAL, and a cathode plant in China. SUAL Group contributed Irkutsk, Urals, Kandalaksha, Bogoslovsk, Nadvoitsy, Volgograd, and Volkhov Aluminum Smelters, Zaporozhye Aluminum Combine, Pikalevo Alumina Refinery, SUBR, Urals Foil, as well as Silicon, SUAL-Silicon-Ural, and SUAL-PM. Glencore contributed the alumina refineries Aughinish in Ireland, Windalco and Alpart in Jamaica, and Eurallumina in Italy, along with Kubikenborg Aluminum Smelter in Sweden.

17. John F. Burns, "Russian Feud Goes to Court in London," *New York Times* (April 18, 2008). Available online at http://www.nytimes.com/2008/04/19/world/europe/19britain.html?ref=world. John F. Burns and Ravi Somaiya, "Russian Tycoon Loses Multi-billion Dollar Case Over Oil Fortune to Kremlin Favorite," *New York Times* (August 31, 2012). Available online at http://www.nytimes.com/2012/09/01/world/europe/russian-tycoon-loses-5-8-billion-case-against-ex-partner. html?pagewanted=all. Sarah Lyall, "For a Homesick Russian Tycoon, Instant of Ruin

Came in Court," *New York Times* (March 24, 2013). Available online at http://www.nytimes.com/2013/03/25/world/europe/for-homesick-russian-tycoon-instant-of-ruin-came-in-court.html?ref=europe.

18. Prices are from Felix Padel and Samarendra Das, *Out of This Earth: East Indian Adavasis and the Aluminium Cartel* (Delhi: Orient Black Swan, 2010), Appendix V. World Metal Prices, 686–687; they also have been checked against prices listed on the London Metals Exchange. For recent prices, which averaged US$1,900 per metric tonne in the third quarter of 2012, falling to US$1,800 per metric tonne in the first quarter of 2013, see http://www.infomine.com/investment/metal-prices/aluminum/all. Low global demand and oversupply in China are predicted to continue downward pressure on prices.

19. Andrew Kramer, "Russian Aluminum Tycoon Buys 25% of Nickel Giant," *New York Times*, Business Section (April 25, 2008). Available online at http://www.nytimes.com/2008/04/25/business/worldbusiness/25nickel.html.

20. Ellen Barry, "Putin Plays Sheriff for Cowboy Capitalists," *New York Times* (June 4, 2009). Available online at http://www.nytimes.com/2009/06/05/world/europe/05russia.html.

21. Clara Ferreira-Marques, "Metals Magnates Trade Blows as London Case Opens," *Reuters* (July 9, 2012).

22. This and the following Deripaska quotes are drawn from Kamal Ahmed, "Oleg Deripaska: Why I Paid Crime Gangs for Protection," *Telegraph* (April 21, 2012). Available online at http://www.telegraph.co.uk/finance/newsbysector/industry/mining/9218657/Oleg-Deripaska-Why-I-paid-crime-gangs-for-protection.html.

23. Jeffrey Birnbaum and John Solomon, "Aide Helped Controversial Russian Meet McCain," *Washington Post* (January 25, 2008): A01.

24. "IMF Approves $1.27 Billion Loan for Jamaica," *IMF Survey Magazine* (February 4, 2010). Available online at http://www.imf.org/external/pubs/ft/survey/so/2010/new020410a.htm.

25. Edmond Campbell, "Bauxite Jobs Saved: UC RUSAL to Fire up Ewarton with Coal Plant," *Jamaica Gleaner* (October 3, 2012). Available online at http://jamaica-gleaner.com/gleaner/20121003/lead/lead1.html; Ingrid Brown, "Gov't Gives up US$7 Million in Bauxite Levy," *Jamaica Observer* (October 4, 2012). Available online at http://www.jamaicaobserver.com/news/Gov-t-gives-up-US-7-million-in-baux-ite-levy_12674924. Many thanks to Esther Figueroa for forwarding me bauxite news from the Jamaican press over several years.

26. Andrew E. Kramer, "Catastrophe with Soviet Roots," *New York Times* (August 21, 2009): B1, B4.

27. Padel and Das, *Out of This Earth*, 140.

28. Ibid., 159.

29. Ibid., 140.

30. Ibid., 103.

31. Quote describing South American mining areas, from Matthew Evenden, "Aluminum, Commodity Chains, and the Environmental History of the Second World War," *Environmental History* 16 (January 2011): 83.

32. Padel and Das, *Out of This Earth*, 96.

33. Ibid, 39.

34. Felix Padel and Samarendra Das, "Double Death: Aluminium's Links with Genocide," *Voice of the Wilderness*, pamphlet published by Saving Iceland (July 2007): 10. Available online at http://www.savingiceland.org/2007/08/double-death.

35. Padel and Das, *Out of This Earth*. See also reports on the issue such as those by Saving Iceland, available online at http://www.savingiceland.org/2010/07/out-of-this-earth-east-india-adivasis-and-the-aluminium-cartel-2.

36. Survival International, "Ban Upheld: Avatar Tribe 'to Decide' Future of Vedanta Mine" (April 18, 2013). Available at http://www.survivalinternational.org/new/9155.

37. Arundhati Roy, "Walking with the Comrades," *Outlook India* (March 21 2010). Available online at http://www.outlookindia.com/article.aspx?264738.

38. Padel and Das, *Out of This Earth*, 29–30.

39. Ibid., 5.

40. Ibid., xvii.

41. Jeffrey Gettleman, "Military Coup Succeeds Easily in Guinea," *New York Times* (December 26, 2008): A14.

42. For a glowing history of the company town see Jacques Larrue, *Fria en Guinée: premiere usine d'alumine en terre d'Afrique* (Paris: Editions Karthala, Publié avec le Concours de l'Institut pour l'Histoire de l'Aluminium, 1997). For a far more negative assessment of the impact of aluminum corporations on Guinea's development see Bonnie K. Campbell, *Les enjeux de la Bauxite: Le Guinée face aux multinationales d'aluminium* (Montréal: Les Presses de l'Université de Montréal, 1983). Thanks to Michael McGovern at Yale University for some pointers on recent events in Guinea (Personal communication, July 11, 2011).

43. "Rio Tinto Top Executives Visit Guinea and Emphasise Commitment to Project Development and Local Communities," *Rio Tinto* (December 9, 2011). Available

online at http://www.riotintosimandou.com/ENG/media/media_releases_1030
.asp.

44. Saliou Samb, "Guinea Secures $2.1 Billion Debt Relief from IMF, World Bank,"
Reuters (September 26, 2012). Available online at http://www.trust.org/alertnet/
news/guinea-secures-21-billion-debt-relief-from-imf-world-bank.

45. Jon Lee Anderson, "Downfall: The End of West African Dictatorship," Letter
from Guinea, *New Yorker* (April 12, 2012): 26–33.

46. Human Rights Watch, *Guinea: Stadium Massacre Victims Await Justice* (September
29, 2012). Available online at http://www.hrw.org/news/2012/09/29/guinea
-stadium-massacre-victims-await-justice.

47. "Guinea Town Paralysed as Pay Strike Shuts Aluminium Plant," *Radio Netherlands
Worldwide* (August 26, 2012). Available online at http://www.rnw.nl/africa/bulletin/
guinea-town-paralysed-pay-strike-shuts-aluminium-plant.

48. B. Biswas, "Bauxite Mining in West Africa," *Alcircle* (September 11, 2012). Available online at http://blog.alcircle.com/?p=118; "Alufer Plans $400 Million Guinea
Bauxite Mine," *Reuters* (July 9, 2012). Available online at http://www.reuters.com/
article/investingNews/idAFJOE86806F20120709.

49. Paragraph based on Paul Garvey, "Guinea Bauxite Woes a Warning for Ore
Miners," *Australian* (December 12, 2011). Available online at http://www.theaustra
lian.com.au/business/opinion/guinea-bauxite-woes-a-warning-for-ore-miners/
story-e6frg9if-1226219374257.

50. "Change in Taxes to Make Guinea Bauxite Unworkable," *Worldal* (December
13, 2011). Available online at http://www.worldal.com/news/others/2011-12-
13/132375656437696.shtml.

51. Garvey, "Guinea Bauxite Woes a Warning for Ore Miners."

52. "Rio Tinto Top Executives Visit Guinea and Emphasise Commitment to Project
Development and Local Communities."

53. Ibid.

54. Ibid.

55. Robert Mendick, "Tony Blair Extends His African Empire into Mineral-Rich
Guinea," *Sunday Telegraph* (March 11, 2012). Available online at http://www.tele
graph.co.uk/news/politics/tony-blair/9136126/Tony-Blair-expands-his-African-
empire-into-mineral-rich-Guinea.html.

56. Human Rights Watch, *Guinea*.

57. "Chinese Tycoons Plan to Take Guinea Mine Simandou from Rio," *Australian*
(May 7, 2012). Available online at http://www.theaustralian.com.au/business/min

ing-energy/chinese-tycoons-plan-to-take-guinea-mine-simandou-from-rio-tinto/
story-e6frg9df-1226348137452.

58. Samb, "Guinea Secures $2.1 Billion Debt Relief from IMF, World Bank."

59. Saliou Samb, "Guinea says death toll from protest rises to 12," Reuters, May 27,
2013. Available at http://www.reuters.com/article/2013/05/29/us-guinea-protests-
idUSBRE94S0NN20130529.

60. *EITI Rules*, 2011 Edition, including the Validation Guide (Oslo, Norway: EITI
International Secretariat, November 2011).

61. John Maxwell, "Bauxite Owes Jamaica Millions," *Jamaica Observer* (August 9,
2009). Thanks as always to Esther Figueroa for updates.

62. Haiti Grassroots Watch, *Goldrush in Haiti! Who Will Get Rich?* Canada Haiti
Action Network (May 30, 2012). Available online at http://canadahaitiaction.ca/
content/gold-rush-haiti-who-will-get-rich.

8 FROZEN ELECTRICITY

1. Marguerite Del Giudice, "Power Struggle: The People of Iceland Awaken to a
Stark Choice: Exploit a Wealth of Clean Energy or Keep Their Land Pristine,"
National Geographic (March 2008). Available online at http://ngm.nationalgeo
graphic.com/2008/03/iceland/del-giudice-text.

2. Skúli Sigurðsson, "The Dome of the World: Iceland, Doomsday Technologies, and
the Cold War," in *Aspects of Arctic and Sub-Arctic History, Proceedings of the International
Congress on the History of the Arctic and Sub-Arctic Regions* (June 18–21, 1998) (Reykjavik: University of Iceland Press, 2000), 476.

3. Marguerite Del Giudice, "Power Struggle."

4. Many thanks to Skúli Sigurðsson for sending me some of his work on electrification in Iceland, which builds on Thomas P. Hughes's *Networks of Power: Electrification in Western Society, 1880–1930* (Baltimore: Johns Hopkins University Press, 1983),
but develops an argument about large-scale technological systems in the unique
geopolitical and cultural context of Iceland. His book *Ísland Rafvoett (Iceland Electri-
fied)* is published by the University of Iceland Press.

5. Del Giudice, "Power Struggle."

6. Susan De Muth, "Power Driven," *Guardian Weekend* (November 20, 2003). Available online at http://www.guardian.co.uk/weekend/story/0,3605,1094541,00
.html.

7. Sarah Lyall, "Smokestacks in a White Wilderness Divide Iceland in a Development Debate," *New York Times* (February 4, 2007): 16.

8. De Muth, "Power Driven."

9. Lyall, "Smokestacks in a White Wilderness Divide Iceland in a Development Debate," 16.

10. De Muth, "Power Driven." On current environmental effects of the project, see Saving Iceland, "The Biological Death of River Lagarfljót—Yet Another Revelation of the Kárahnjúkar Disaster," April 25, 2013. Available at http://www.savingiceland. org/2013/04/the-biological-death-of-river-lagarfljot-yet-another-revelation-of-the-karahnjukar-disaster.

11. Lyall, "Smokestacks in a White Wilderness Divide Iceland in a Development Debate," 16.

12. Del Giudice, "Power Struggle."

13. Saving Iceland, "Unusually High rate of Work Related Accidents in Kárahnjúkar", August 13, 2010. Available at http://www.savingiceland.org/2010/08/unusually-high-rate-of-work-related-accidents-in-karahnjukar.

14. The sample consisted of six hundred people. The question asked was, Are you in favor of or opposed to the Kárahnjúkar hydro station and the building of an aluminum plant in Reydarfjordur? "Attitudes Toward an Aluminium Plant in Reydarfjördur and the Kárahnjúkar Hydroelectric Project," available online at http://www.docstoc.com/docs/26476337/Toward-an-Aluminium-Plant-in-Reydarfjördur-and-the-Kárahnjúkar.

15. De Muth, "Power Driven."

16. Andri Snaer Magnason, *Dreamland: A Self-Help Book for a Frightened Nation*, 2nd ed., trans. Nicholas Jones (London: Citizen Press, 2008). The book is available via Amazon in the UK only. Information on the book and film are available at http://www.andrimagnason.com/books/dreamland.

17. See http://www.savingiceland.org and http://www.revbilly.com/index.php.

18. Mark Landler, "Iceland, a Tiny Dynamo, Loses Steam," *New York Times* (April 18, 2008). Available online at *www.nytimes.com/2008/04/18/business/worldbusiness/18iceland.html?*.

19. On Alcoa's plans in Greenland see http://www.alcoa.com/greenland/en/home .asp. A presentation on the Environmental Impact Assessment is available at http://www.alcoa.com/.../ERM_Baseline_Presentation_January_2010_(en).pdf. On opposition to the project see Miriam Rose, "Alcoa in Greenland: Empty Promises?" *Saving Iceland* (April 4, 2011). Available online at http://www.savingiceland.org /2011/04/alcoa-in-greenland-empty-promises.

20. Mark Nuttall, "Self-Rule in Greenland: Towards the World's First Independent Inuit State?" *Indigenous Affairs,* nos. 3–4 (2008): 68.

21. Rose, "Alcoa in Greenland." *Economic Survey of Iceland,* Policy Brief (February 2008). Paris: Organisation for Economic Co-operation and Development (OECD).

22. Sean Douglas, "2 Smelters by 2012," *Trinidad and Tobago Newsday*, January 30, 2007. Available online at www.newsday.co.tt/news/0,51538.html.

23. Trinidadian environmentalist Wayne Kublalsingh led protests against Alutrint. See, e.g., Wayne Kublalsingh, "Alutrint AD: Freedom of disinformation," *Trinidad Guardian Commentary*, October 20, 2009. Available at http://www.greentnt.org/content/alutrint-ad-freedom-disinformation. For views in favor of the smelter project see Keith Subero, "The Alutrint Whirlwind," *Trinidad Express*, January 9, 2011. Available at http://www.trinidadexpress.com/commentaries/The_Alutrint_whirlwind-113179659.html.

9   ALUMINUM RENAISSANCE

1. Available online at http://www.alumifuelpowercorp.com. For the sake of full disclosure, this company has ties to Drexel University, my employer, through the Nanotechnology and Materials Consortium, but I have no direct relationship with them.

2. John J. Geoghegan, "Designers Set Sail, Turning to Wind to Help Power Cargo Ships," *New York Times* (August 27, 2002). Available online at http://www.nytimes.com/2012/08/28/science/earth/cargo-ship-designers-turn-to-wind-to-cut-cost-and-emissions.html?.

3. Joseph M. Cychosz and Jerry M. Woodall, "Aluminum-Rich Bulk Alloys: An Energy Storage Material for Splitting Water to Make Hydrogen Gas on Demand," *NanoHUB* (June 30, 2010). Available online at http://nanohub.org/topics/SplittingWaterUsingAluminum.

4. Chuck Squatriglia, "Metal 'Foam' Could Mean Lighter Ships," *Wired.com* (January 4, 2011). Available online at http://www.wired.com/autopia/2011/01/metal-foam-could-mean-lighter-ships. Aluminum-titanium hydride powder was developed at Fraunhofer Institute for Machine Tools and Forming Technology in Chemnitz, Germany.

5. "Aluminum Statistics, 1900–2010," *United States Geological Survey* (September, 2011). Available at http://minerals.usgs.gov/ds/2005/140/#aluminum.

6. OECD Global Forum on Environment, *Sustainable Material Management, Case Study 2: Aluminum* (October 25–27, 2010) (Mechelen, Belgium: OECD Environment Directorate, 2010), 5.

7. "The IAI [International Aluminium Institute] and its member companies have adopted through the Alumina for Future Generations program a number of performance targets related to the release of certain production wastes. Among these goals

is the reduction of PFC emissions by 2020 to 50% of 2006 levels. This corresponds to a level of emissions of .5 t of CO_2 equivalent per ton of aluminum. The IAI has adopted a goal of achieving a 33% reduction from the 1990 level of 2.4 kg of fluorine per ton of aluminum produced by 2010. IAI also adopted a goal to reduce the amount of electrical energy used in aluminum smelting by 10% to 14.5 mega watt hours from 1990 levels by 2010. Finally, IAI adopted a goal of reducing energy use per ton of alumina refined by 10% from 2006 levels to 14.4 Giga joules per ton of aluminum by 2020" (Ibid, 36; and see International Aluminum Institute, "Aluminum for Future Generations—2009 update" [2009]. Available online at http://www.world-aluminium.org/cache/fl000336.pdf).

8. "Classic New York Skyscraper Clad in Alcoa Architectural Building Material," *BusinessWire* (August 10, 2010). Available online at http://alcoa-news.newslib.com/story/6659-3250560.

9. The Aluminum Association, *Aluminum Industry Vision: Sustainable Solutions* (Washington, DC: The Aluminum Association, November 2001), 1. See also The Aluminum Association, *Aluminum: The Element of Sustainability*, A North American Aluminum Industry Sustainability Report, September 2011. Available at http://aluminum.org/Content/.../Aluminum_The_Element_of_Sustainability.pdf.

10. Ibid., 2, emphasis added.

11. Available online at http://www.alcoa.com/global/en/news/info_page/news room.asp.

12. Tim Moran, "BMW Rethinks the V-8 Engine," *New York Times* (January 20, 2008). Available online at http://www.nytimes.com/2008/01/20/automobiles/autoshow/20V8.html.

13. Jim Motavelli, "For Lightweight Cars, a Materials Race," *New York Times* (October 11, 2012). Available online at http://www.nytimes.com/2012/10/12/automobiles/for-lightweight-cars-a-race-among-steel-aluminum-and-carbon-fiber.html.

14. OECD Global Forum on Environment, *Sustainable Material Management, Case Study 2*, 39.

15. Ibid., 61.

16. George David Smith, *From Monopoly to Competition: The Transformation of Alcoa, 1888–198*. (Cambridge, UK: Cambridge University Press, 1988), 339–340.

17. Ibid., 341.

18. Ibid., 348.

19. Ibid., 349.

20. Alcoa advertising campaign, 1975, "The Reasons for Using Aluminum Are Found in Aluminum Itself."

21. R. Buckminster Fuller, *Critical Path* (New York: St. Martin's Press, 1981).

22. Alcoa advertising campaign, 1975, "Aluminum. Recycled Cans Are Winning the West."

23. A. B. Trageser and R. E. Dick, "Aluminum Can Design Using Finite Element Methods," presented at the Society of Manufacturing Engineering Can Manufacturing Technology Symposium, September 14–16, 1988, Schaumburg, IL. Available online at http://www.psc.edu/science/ALCOA/ALCOA.html.

24. Harvey Molotch, *Where Stuff Comes From: How Toasters, Toilets, Cars, Computers, and Many Other Things Come to Be as They Are* (New York: Routledge, 2005), 241.

25. Jennifer Gitlitz, *Trashed Cans: The Global Environmental Impacts of Aluminum Can Wasting in America* (Arlington, VA: Container Recycling Institute, June 2002), 31.

26. Ibid., whole book.

27. Ibid., 9, 13.

28. Ibid., 25.

29. Annie Leonard, *The Story of Stuff: The Impact of Overconsumption on the Planet, Our Communities, and Our Health—And How We Can Make It Better* (New York: Free Press, 2010), 64.

30. Ibid., 67.

31. Ibid.; see also Elizabeth Royte, *Garbageland: On the Secret Trail of Trash* (New York: Little, Brown, 2005), 155.

32. Leonard, *The Story of Stuff,* 67.

33. D. N. Ernst, "The Importance of Aluminium for the Automotive Industry." *Aluminium + Automobil.* Lectures held on an international symposium organized by the Aluminum-Zantrale, Düsseldorf, 1980, 2/1 (Düsseldorf: Aluminium-Verlag GmbH, May 1981).

34. Ibid.

35. M. Wintenberger, "Aluminium in the Motor Car, the Energy Balance." *Aluminium + Automobil.* Lectures held on an international symposium organized by the Aluminum-Zantrale, Düsseldorf, 1980, 3/2 (Düsseldorf: Aluminium-Verlag GmbH, May 1981).

36. "Jaguar F-Type Unveiled at the Paris Auto Show 2012," *Paddock Talk* (September 27, 2012). Available online at http://paddocktalk.com/news/html/story-205897.html.

37. Available online at http://www.alcoa.com/global/en/news/news_detail.asp?pa geID=20080122006127en&newsYear=2008.

38. "3-Month Price of Aluminum up after 2-Day Decline on Daily Index," *MetalMiner* (August 21, 2012). Available at http://agmetalminer.com/2012/08/21/month-price-aluminum-after-two-day-decline and see http://agmetalminer.com/2013/08/16.

39. Ann Farmer, "Recycling Metal: Loud, Dirty and Suddenly Lucrative," *New York Times*, Metro Section (June 27 2008): B7.

40. See photographs by Pieter Hugo, "A Global Graveyard for Dead Computers in Ghana," *New York Times Magazine* (2010). Available online at http://www.nytimes.com/slideshow/2010/08/04/magazine/20100815-dump.html.

41. Sunil Heart, "Major Threats from E-Waste: Current Generation and Impacts," *Chemistry Views Magazine* (April 5, 2011), doi: 10.1002/chemv.201000065. Available at http://www.chemistryviews.org/details/ezine/1037973/Major_Threats_From_E -Waste_Current_Generation_And_Impacts.html.

42. Alcoa Business Wire, "Alcoa Helps the Airbus A380 Make Its First Flight" (April 27, 2005). Available online at http://www.alcoa.com/fastening_systems/aerospace/en/news/releases/A380_takes_off.asp.

43. Nicola Clark, "High Stakes for Airbus in Getting New Jet to Market," *New York Times* (October 21, 2012). Available online at http://www.nytimes.com/2012/10/22/business/global/high-stakes-for-airbus-in-getting-new-jet-to-market.html?.

44. K. Lu, "The Future of Metals," *Science* 328, no. 5976 (April 2010): 319. doi: 10.1126/science.1185866.

45. Eames Demetrios, grandson of Charles Eames, made a series of films on how Emeco designs are crafted, including *Citizen Starck,* which shows the creation of Starck's "Icon" version of the Emeco's famous aluminum chair for the US Navy. Available online at http://vimeo.com/10212235.

46. Julie Lasky, "Once Again, Seeing Double," *New York Times* (October 10, 2012). Available online at http://www.nytimes.com/2012/10/11/garden/copying-classic-designs-is-the-focus-of-a-lawsuit-against-restoration-hardware.html?

47. Apple, "We've gone to extraordinary lengths. And widths." Available online at http://www.apple.com/imac/design.

48. David Pogue, "Gizmos, Gadgets and Steve Jobs, Too," *New York Times* (January 17, 2008). Available online at http://www.nytimes.com/2008/01/17/technology/personaltech/17pogue.html?.

49. "Joann Meade, "Forging the Corporate Identity with Art: Four Montreal Corporations, Alcan Aluminum Ltd., Martineau Walker, Banque Nationale du Canada,

Loro-Quebec, with a Focus on Alcan," PhD Thesis, McGill University, Montreal (November 2000).

50. Ali Kriscenski, "Nokia 'Re-made' Concept Phone Made from Recycled Materials," February 18, 2008. Available online at http://inhabitat.com/nokia-remade-concept-phone-made-from-recycled-materials.

51. Available online at http://www.kithaus.com.

52. Arthur Lubow, "Face Value," *New York Times Magazine* (June 8, 2008): 52.

53. Ibid., 50.

54. Nicolai Ouroussoff, "New Look for the New Museum," *New York Times*, Weekend Arts Section (November 30, 2007): E46.

55. Lubow, "Face Value," 52.

56. Keller Easterling, "New Monuments," *Artforum International* (Summer 2008): 149; Paolo Soleri, *Arcology: The City in the Image of Man* (Cambridge, MA: MIT Press, 1969).

57. Ibid, 150.

58. Meade, "Forging the Corporate Identity with Art."

59. Text available at http://dome.mit.edu/handle/1721.3/3249 and http://dome.mit.edu/handle/1721.3/3250.

60. Yves-Alain Bois, "The Antidote, (on Hans Haacke)", October Magazine, Winter 1986, pp. 129-144; Fredric Jameson, "Hans Haacke and the Cultural Logic of Postmodernism," *Hans Haacke: Unfinished Business,* ed., Brian Wallis (New York: the New Museum of Contemporary Art, and Cambridge, MA: MIT Press, 1986); both cited in Ntongela Masilela, "The Unfinishable Business of South Africa in the Work of Hans Haacke." Available online at http://pzacad.pitzer.edu/NAM/general/essays/haacke.htm.

61. Roberta Smith, "How Art Is Framed; Exhibition Floor Plans as a Conceptual Medium," *New York Times*, Arts Section (March 8, 2008). Available online at http://www.nytimes.com/2008/03/08/arts/design/08ashe.html.

62. Alice Rawsthorn, "Designing the Inevitable," *New York Times*, T Magazine (March 16, 2008): 126.

63. Pilar Viladas, "In Situ," *New York Times Magazine* (July 1, 2007). Available online at http://www.nytimes.com/2007/07/01/magazine/01stylechair-t.html?.

64. Gillian Fuller and Ross Harley, *Aviopolis: A Book About Airports* (London: Black Dog Publishing Ltd., 2005).

65. Peter Adey, *Aerial Life: Spaces, Mobilities, Affect* (Oxford: Wiley-Blackwell, 2010), 196.

66. Ibid.

67. Molotch, *Where Stuff Comes From,* 232.

68. Canada Economic Development for Quebec Regions, "Government of Canada supports Maison du Festival Rio Tinto Alcan" (June 29, 2009). Available online at http://www.dec-ced.gc.ca/eng/media-room/news-releases/2009/06/2017.html.

10   CONCLUSION

1. Arie Rip and René Kemp, "Technological Change," in *Human Choice and Climate Change,* vol. II, *Resources and Technology,* ed. S. Rayner and E. L. Malone (Columbus, OH: Battelle Press, 1998), 354; Elizabeth Shove, *Comfort, Cleanliness and Convenience: The Social Organization of Normality* (New York: Berg, 2003), 12.

2. Simon Guy and Elizabeth Shove, *A Sociology of Energy, Buildings and the Environment: Constructing Knowledge, Designing Practice* (London: Routledge, 2000), 5.

3. Ibid., 139.

4. Shove, *Comfort, Cleanliness and Convenience*; Geoff Dudley, Frank Geels, and René Kemp, eds., *Automobility in Transition? A Socio-technical Analysis of Sustainable Transport* (London: Routledge, 2011).

5. Bob Jessop, "Spatial Fixes, Temporal Fixes and Spatio-Temporal Fixes," in *David Harvey: A Critical Reader,* ed. Noel Castree and Derek Gregory (New York: Blackwell, 2006), pp. 142–166.

6. Shove, *Comfort, Cleanliness and Convenience,* 170.

7. Ibid.

8. Ibid., 185.

9. Ibid., 172.

10. Edward W. Soja, *Seeking Spatial Justice* (Minneapolis: University of Minnesota Press, 2010).

11. Jussi Parikka, "A Call for an Alternative Deep Time of the Media," *Machinology* (September 28, 2012). Available online at http://jussiparikka.net/2012/09/28/a-call-for-an-alternative-deep-time-of-the-media. And see Jussi Parikka, *What Is Media Archaeology?* (London: Polity, 2012).

12. Ibid.

13. Julian M. Allwood and Jonathan M. Cullen, *Sustainable Materials: With Both Eyes Open* (Cambridge, UK: UIT, 2012).

14. Hitaveita Sudurnesja Ltd., Landsvirkjun, and Orkuveita Reykjavikur, together with Orkustofnun (National Energy Authority). On progress of the Iceland Deep Drilling Project, see http://iddp.is/about.

15. Mark Gongloff, "Alcoa Can't Wait . . . to Get Geothermal," *Wall Street Journal* (September 11, 2007). Available at http://blogs.wsj.com/environmentalcapital/2007/09/11/alcoa-cant-waitto-get-geothermal.

16. Elisabeth Rosenthal, "China Increases Lead as Biggest Carbon Dioxide Emitter," *New York Times* (June 14, 2008).

17. R. Buckminster Fuller, *Critical Path* (New York: St. Martin's Press, 1981), 208.

18. Ibid., 202.

19. Parikka, *What Is Media Archaeology?*

20. Stephen Graham and Simon Marvin, *Splintering Urbanism: Networked Infrastructure, Technological Mobilities and the Urban Condition* (London: Routledge, 2001).

21. Folco Portinari, "Slow Food Manifesto" (November 9, 1989). Available at http://slowfoodaustralia.com.au/history/slow-food-manifesto.

22. Shin'ichi Tsuji (Oiwa Keibo), *Slow Is Beautiful: Culture and Slowness* (Tokyo: Heibonsha, 2001) cited in Jeffrey T. Schnapp, ed., *Speed Limits* (Montreal: Canadian Centre for Architecture, 2009), 304.

23. Italo Calvino, "Quickness," *Six Memos for the Next Millennium* (Cambridge, MA: Harvard University Press, 1988).

BIBLIOGRAPHY

ARCHIVES

Alcoa Archives, Senator John Heinz History Center Library and Archives, Pittsburgh.

PRIMARY SOURCES

The Aluminum Association. *The Story of Aluminum*. New York: The Aluminum Association, circa 1965. [Form 01–11952]

The Aluminum Association. *Uses of Aluminum*. New York: The Aluminum Association, circa 1965.

The Aluminum Association. *Aluminum Industry Vision: Sustainable Solutions*. Washington, DC: The Aluminum Association, November 2001.

The Aluminum Association. *Aluminum: The Element of Sustainability*, A North American Aluminum Industry Sustainability Report, September 2011.

Aluminum Company of America. *A Brief Story of Aluminum and Alcoa*. Pittsburgh: Aluminum Company of America, n.d. [Form 01–11889]

Aluminum Company of America. *Aluminum by Alcoa: The Story of a Light Metal*. Pittsburgh: Aluminum Company of America, 1954. [Form AD 429 A1154.125]

Aluminum Company of America. *Aluminum by Alcoa*. Pittsburgh: Aluminum Company of America, 1969. [Form 01–12292]

Anonymous. "Alcoa's New Look for Architecture" (1958).

Auchincloss, Douglas. "The Dymaxion American." *Time* 83, no. 2 (January 10, 1964): 46–51. [with cover image by Boris Artzybasheff]

"Behind the Shining: Aluminium's Dark Side," Authored by the grass-roots movement in Kashipur; An IPS/SEEN/TNI report (2001).

Bel Geddes, Norman. *Horizons.* Boston: Little, Brown, 1932.

Deville, Henri Sainte-Claire. *De l'aluminium, ses propriétés, sa fabrication et ses applications.* Paris, Mallet-Bachelier, 1859.

Ernst, D. N. "The Importance of Aluminium for the Automotive Industry." *Aluminium + Automobil.* Lectures held on an international symposium organized by the Aluminum-Zantrale, Düsseldorf, 1980, 2/1–2/4. Düsseldorf: Aluminium-Verlag GmbH, May 1981.

Extractive Industries Transparency Initiative (EITI). *EITI Rules* (including the Validation Guide). Oslo, Norway: EITI International Secretariat, November 2011.

Fabun, Don. *The Dynamics of Change.* Englewood Cliffs, NJ: Kaiser Aluminum with Prentice Hall, 1967.

Fahnestock, Samuel, ed. *Design Forecast 1 & 2.* Pittsburgh: Alcoa, 1959.

Fanning, Leonard M. *Charles Martin Hall: Father of the Aluminum Industry.* Fathers of Industries Series. New York: Mercer Publishing Company, 1956.

Fortune Magazine, 1950–1958 (personal collection).

Hammond, Dean A. "Kaiser-Frazer Plans Aluminum-Glass Car." *Science and Mechanics* (October 1951): 65–69.

Holiday Magazine, 1946–1965 (personal collection).

International Aluminium Institute, *Aluminium for Future Generations.* London: International Aluminium Institute, 2009. Available online at http://www.world-alumin ium.org/media/filer_public/2013/01/15/none_28.

Menzie, W. D., J. J. Barry, D. I. Bleiwas, E. L. Bray, T. G. Goonan, and G. Matos, G. "The Global Flow of Aluminum from 2006 through 2025," US Geological Survey, Open-File Report 2010-1256. Reston, VA: USGS, 2010.

OECD Global Forum on Environment, *Sustainable Material Management, Case Study 2: Aluminium,* October 25–27, 2010, Mechelen, Belgium.

Plunkert, Patricia. *Aluminum Recycling in the United States in 2000.* U.S. Geological Survey Circular 1196-W, Flow Cycles for Recycling Metal Commodities in the United States. Washington, DC: US Department of the Interior, 2000. Available online at http://pubs.usgs.gov/circ/c1196w/c1196w.pdf.

Reynolds Metals Company, *Aluminum on the March* (DVD, Jam Handy, 1956). Available at Prelinger Archives, http://archive.org/details/Aluminum1956.

Reynolds Metals Company. *The ABC's of Aluminum: From Raw Material to Application.* Louisville, KY: Reynolds Metals Company, 1950.

US Geological Survey (USGS). *Mineral Commodity Summaries (MCS) 2012.* Reston, VA: USGS, Department of the Interior, 2012.

Verne, Jules. *De la terre à la lune* [From the Earth to the Moon]. Paris: Pierre-Jules Hetzel, 1865.

Wintenberger, M. "Aluminium in the Motor Car, the Energy Balance." *Aluminium + Automobil.* Lectures held on an international symposium organized by the Aluminum-Zantrale, Düsseldorf, 1980, 3/1–3/5. Düsseldorf: Aluminium-Verlag GmbH, May 1981.

SECONDARY SOURCES

Adey, Peter. *Aerial Life: Spaces, Mobilities, Affect.* Oxford: Wiley-Blackwell, 2010.

Allwood, Julian M., and Jonathan M. Cullen. *Sustainable Materials: With Both Eyes Open.* Cambridge, UK: UIT, 2012.

Anderson, Jon Lee. "Downfall: The End of West African Dictatorship," Letter from Guinea. *New Yorker* (April 12, 2012): 26–33.

Anim-Addo, Anyaa. *Place and Mobilities in the Maritime World: The Royal Mail Steam Packet Company in the Caribbean, c. 1838 to 1914.* PhD thesis. London: Department of Human Geography, Royal Holloway, University of London, 2011.

Antonellie, Paola. "Aluminum and the New Materialism." In *Aluminum by Design*, ed. S. Nichols, 166–189. Pittsburgh: Carnegie Museum of Art, 2000.

Appadurai, Arjun. *Modernity at Large: Cultural Dimensions of Globalization.* Minneapolis: University of Minnesota Press, 1996.

Armitage, David. "Three Concepts of Atlantic History." In *The British Atlantic World, 1500–1800*, ed. David Armitage and Michael J. Braddick, 11–27. Basingstoke, UK: Palgrave Macmillan, 2002.

Arnold, David. *The Tropics and the Traveling Gaze: India, Landscape and Science, 1800–1856.* Seattle: University of Washington Press, 2006.

Austen, Ian. "Aluminum: Quarry for Mining Companies." *New York Times*, Business Section (July 25, 2007): C3.

Barham, Bradford, Stephen Bunker, and Denis O'Hearn. *States, Firms, and Raw Materials: The World Economy and Ecology of Aluminum.* Madison: The University of Wisconsin Press, 1994.

Bender, Thomas. *A Nation among Nations: America's Place in World History.* New York: Hill and Wang, 2006.

Benjamin, Walter. *The Arcades Project.* Ed R. Tiedemann. Trans. H. Eiland and K. McLaughlin. Cambridge, MA: Belknap Press of Harvard University Press, 2002.

Bergdoll, Barry. "Home Delivery: Vicissitudes of a Modernist Dream from Taylorized Serial Production to Digital Customization." In *Home Delivery: Fabricating the Modern*

Dwelling, ed. Barry Bergdoll and Peter Christensen, 12–26. New York: The Museum of Modern Art, 2008.

Bergdoll, Barry, and Peter Christensen. *Home Delivery: Fabricating the Modern Dwelling.* New York: The Museum of Modern Art, 2008.

Bijker, W. E., T. P. Hughes, and T. J. Pinch, eds. *The Social Construction of Technological Systems: New Directions in the Sociology and History of Technology.* Cambridge, MA: MIT Press, 1987.

Bijker, W. E., and John Law, eds. *Shaping Technology/Building Society: Studies in Sociotechnical Change.* Cambridge, MA: MIT Press, 1994.

Blainey, Geoffrey. *White Gold: The Story of Alcoa in Australia.* St. Leonards, New South Wales: Allen and Unwin, 1997.

Bois, Yves-Alain. "The Antidote (on Hans Haacke)," *October* (Winter 1986), 129–144.

Bolland, O. Nigel. *The Politics of Labour in the British Caribbean.* Kingston: Ian Randle; London: James Currey, 2001.

Borzi, Pat. "Making Metal Bats Play Like Wood," *New York Times*, June 18, 2011.

Brennan, Annmarie. "Forecast." In *Cold War Hothouses: Inventing Postwar Culture, from Cockpit to Playboy*, ed. Beatriz Colomina, Annmarie Brennan, and Jeannie Kim. New York: Princeton Architectural Press, 2004.

Bunker, Stephen, and Paul Ciccantell. "The Evolution of the World Aluminum Industry." In *States, Firms, and Raw Materials: The World Economy and Ecology of Aluminum*, ed. Bradford Barham, Stephen Bunker, and Denis O'Hearn, 39–68. Madison: The University of Wisconsin Press, 1994.

Burger, Ethan, and Rosalia Gitau. "The Russian Anti-Corruption Campaign: Public Relations, Politics or Substantive Change?" Georgetown University Law Center, discussion paper (2010). Available online at http://scholarship.law.georgetown.edu/fwps_papers/126.

Burkhart, Bryan, and David Hunt. *Airstream: The History of the Land Yacht.* San Francisco: Chronicle Books, 2000.

Byko, Maureen. "Aluminum Exhibits Its Versatility in Art, Life," *JOM* 52, no. 11 (2000): 9–12.

Calvino, Italo. *Six Memos for the Next Millennium.* New York: Vintage, 1993.

Campbell, Bonnie K. *Les enjeux de la bauxite: Le Guinée face aux multinationales d'aluminium.* Montréal: Les Presses de l'Université de Montréal, 1983.

Carr, Charles C. *Alcoa: An American Enterprise.* New York: Rinehart & Co., 1952.

Chang, Kenneth. "For NASA, Return Trip to Jupiter in Search of Clues to Solar System's Origins," *New York Times* (August 5, 2011), A12.

Cook, Ian. "Follow the Thing: Papaya." *Antipode* 36, no. 4 (2004): 642–664.

Cowen, Deborah. *Rough Trade.* Minneapolis: University of Minnesota Press, 2014.

Cresswell, Tim. *On the Move: Mobility in the Modern Western World.* London: Routledge, 2006.

Cresswell, Tim. "Mobilities I: Catching Up." *Progress in Human Geography* 35, no. 4 (2010): 550–558.

Cresswell, Tim. "Mobilities II: Still." *Progress in Human Geography* 36, no. 5 (2012): 645–653.

Crowley, David, and Jane Pavitt, eds., *Cold War Modern: Design 1945–1970.* London: V&A Publishing, 2008.

Dathan, Patricia W. *Bauxite, Sugar and Mud: Memories of Living in Colonial Guyana, 1928–1944.* Ste. Anne-de-Bellevue, Quebec: Shoreline, 2006.

Davis, Carlton E. *Jamaica in the World Aluminium Industry, 1838–1973* (Vol. I). Kingston: Jamaica Bauxite Institute, 1989.

Del Giudice, Marguerite. "Power Struggle: The People of Iceland Awaken to a Stark Choice: Exploit a Wealth of Clean Energy or Keep Their Land Pristine." *National Geographic* (March 2008). Available online at http://ngm.nationalgeographic.com/2008/03/iceland/del-giudice-text/.

De Muth, Susan. "Power Driven." *Guardian Weekend* (November 20, 2003). Available online at http://www.guardian.co.uk/weekend/story/0,3605,1094541,00.html.

Doordan, Dennis P. "Promoting Aluminum: Designers and the American Aluminum Industry." *Design Issues* 9, no. 2 (Autumn 1993): 44–50.

Doordan, Dennis P. "From Precious to Pervasive: Aluminum and Architecture." In *Aluminum by Design,* ed. S. Nichols, 84–111. Pittsburgh: Carnegie Museum of Art, 2000.

Doura, Fred. *Économie d'Haïti—Dépendence, Crise et Développement* (Vol. 1). Montréal: Les Editions DAMI, 2001.

Dudley, Geoff, Frank Geels, and René Kemp, eds. *Automobility in Transition? A Sociotechnical Analysis of Sustainable Transport.* London: Routledge, 2011.

Dupuis, E. Melanie. *Nature's Perfect Food: How Milk Became America's Drink.* New York: New York University Press, 2002.

Dupuy, Alex. *Haiti in the World Economy—Class, Race and Underdevelopment.* Boston: Westview Press, 1989.

Easterling, Keller. "New Monuments." *ArtForum International* (Summer 2008): 149–150.

Evenden, Matthew. "Mobilizing Rivers: Hydro-Electricity, the State and World War II in Canada." *Annals of the Association of American Geographers* 99 (December 2009): 940–947.

Evenden, Matthew. "Aluminum, Commodity Chains, and the Environmental History of the Second World War." *Environmental History* 16, no. 1 (January 2011): 69–93.

Evenett, Simon J., Alexander Lehmann, and Benn Steil, eds. *Antitrust Goes Global: What Future for Transatlantic Cooperation?* Washington, DC: The Brookings Institution; London: Royal Institute of International Affairs, 2000.

Farmer, Ann. "Recycling Metal: Loud, Dirty and Suddenly Lucrative," *New York Times* (June 27, 2008), B7.

Feltham, Cliff. "Mining Rich Seam of Merger Mania." *The Independent* (July 13, 2007). Available at http://www.independent.co.uk/news/analysis_and_features/article2765588.ece.

Fortescue, Stephen. "The Russian Aluminum Industry in Transition." *Eurasian Geography and Economics* 47, no. 1 (2006): 76–94.

Friedel, Robert. "A New Metal! Aluminum in its 19th-Century Context." In *Aluminum by Design*, ed. S. Nichols, 58–83. Pittsburgh: Carnegie Museum of Art, 2000.

Fuller, Gillian, and Ross Harley. *Aviopolis: A Book about Airports.* London: Black Dog Publishing Ltd., 2005.

Fuller, R. Buckminster. *Operating Manual for Spaceship Earth.* Carbondale: Southern Illinois University Press, 1969.

Fuller, R. Buckminster. *Critical Path.* New York: St. Martin's Griffin, 1981.

Garn, Andrew, ed. *Exit to Tomorrow: World's Fair Architecture, Design, Fashion, 1933–2005.* New York: Universe Publishing, 2007.

Geller, Tom. "Aluminum: Common Metal, Uncommon Past." *Chemical Heritage* (Winter 2007/2008): 32–36.

Gettleman, Jeffrey. "Military Coup Succeeds Easily in Guinea." *New York Times* (December 26, 2008), A14.

Girvan, Norman. *Foreign Capital and Economic Underdevelopment in Jamaica.* Mona: University of the West Indies, Institute of Social and Economic Research, 1971.

Girvan, Norman. *Corporate Imperialism: Conflict and Expropriation.* New York: Monthly Review Press, 1976.

Gitlitz, Jennifer. *The Relationship between Primary Aluminum Production and the Damming of World Rivers,* Working Paper 2. Berkeley, CA: International Rivers Network, 1993.

Gitlitz, Jennifer. *Trashed Cans: The Global Environmental Impacts of Aluminum Can Wasting in America.* Arlington, VA: Container Recycling Institute, June 2002.

Glanz, James. "Power, Pollution and the Internet." *New York Times* (September 23, 2012): A1, A20–A21.

Graham, Margaret. "R&D and Competition in England and the United States: The Case of the Aluminum Dirigible." *Business History Review* 62, no. 2 (Summer 1988): 261–285.

Graham, Margaret G. W., and Bettye H. Pruitt. *R&D for Industry: A Century of Technical Innovation at Alcoa.* Cambridge, MA: MIT Press, 1990.

Graham, Stephen, and Simon Marvin. *Splintering Urbanism: Networked Infrastructure, Technological Mobilities and the Urban Condition.* London: Routledge, 2001.

Grinberg, Ivan, and Florence Hachez-Leroy, eds. *Industrialisation et sociétés en Europe occidentale de la fin du XIXe siècle à nos jours: L'âge de l'aluminium.* Paris: Armand Colin, 1997.

Grove, Richard. *Green Imperialism: Colonial Expansion, Tropical Island Edens and the Origins of Environmentalism, 1600–1860.* Cambridge, MA: Cambridge University Press, 1995.

Guy, Simon, and Elizabeth Shove. *A Sociology of Energy, Buildings and the Environment: Constructing Knowledge, Designing Practice.* London: Routledge, 2000.

Hachez-Leroy, Florence. *L'aluminium Français: L'invention d'un Marché 1911–1983.* Paris: CNRS Editions, avec le Concours de l'Institut pour l'Histoire de l'Aluminium, 1999.

Halpern, Sue. "Eight Days, No Nights." *Condé Nast Traveler* (July 2007): 78–128.

Hannam, Kevin, Mimi Sheller, and John Urry. "Mobilities, Immobilities and Moorings." Editorial Introduction, *Mobilities* 1, no. 1 (March 2006): 1–22.

Hayden, Dolores. *The Grand Domestic Revolution: A History of Feminist Designs for American Homes, Neighborhoods, and Cities.* Cambridge, MA: MIT Press, 1981.

Hays, K. Michael, and Dana Miller, eds. *Buckminster Fuller: Starting with the Universe.* New York: Whitney Museum of American Art in association with Yale University Press, New Haven, CT, 2008.

Heart, Sunil. "Major Threats from E-Waste: Current Generation and Impacts," *Chemistry Views Magazine*, April 5, 2011. doi: 10.1002/chemv.201000065.

Hira, Sandew. "Class Formation and Class Struggle in Suriname: The Background and Development of the Coup d'Etat." In *Crisis in the Caribbean*, ed. Fitzroy Ambursley and Robin Cohen, 166–190. New York: Monthly Review Press, 1983.

Holloway, Steven K. *The Aluminium Multinationals and the Bauxite Cartel*. Houndmills, UK: Macmillan, 1988.

Horne, Gerald. *Cold War in a Hot Zone: The United States Confronts Labor and Independence Struggles in the British West Indies*. Philadelphia: Temple University Press, 2007.

Hughes, Thomas P. *Networks of Power: Electrification in Western Society, 1880–1930*. Baltimore: Johns Hopkins University Press, 1983.

International Rivers Network. *Belo Monte; Massive Dam Project Strikes at the Heart of the Amazon*. Berkeley, CA: International Rivers Network, March 2010.

Isenstadt, Sandy. "Visions of Plenty: Refrigerators in America around 1950." *Journal of Design History* 11, no. 4 (1998): 311–321.

Jameson, Frederic. "Hans Haacke and the Cultural Logic of Postmodernism." In *Hans Haacke: Unfinished Business*, ed. Brian Wallis. New York: The New Museum of Contemporary Art, and Cambridge, MA: MIT Press, 1986.

Jandl, H. Ward. "With Heritage So Shiny: America's First All-Aluminum House." *Association for Preservation Technology (APT) Bulletin* 23, no. 2 (1991): 38–43.

Jasper, James M. *Restless Nation: Starting Over in America*. Chicago: University of Chicago Press, 2000.

Jessop, Bob. "Spatial Fixes, Temporal Fixes, and Spatio-Temporal Fixes." In *David Harvey: A Critical Reader*, ed. Noel Castree and Derek Gregory., 142–166. New York: Blackwell, 2006.

Kambel, Ellen-Rose. "Land, Development, and Indigenous Rights in Suriname: The Role of International Human Rights Law." In *Caribbean Land and Development Revisited*, ed. Jean Besson and Janet Momsen, 69–80. New York: Palgrave Macmillan, 2007.

Kaplan, Caren. "Mobility and War: The Cosmic View of US 'Air Power.'" *Environment and Planning A* 38, no. 2 (February 2006): 395–407.

Kaplan, Caren. "The Balloon Prospect: Aerostatic Observation and the Emergence of Militarized Aeromobility." In *From Above: War, Violence and Verticality*, ed. Peter Adey, Mark Whitehead, and Alison J. Williams. London: Hurst, 2013.

Kirkham, Pat. *Charles and Ray Eames: Designers of the Twentieth Century*. Cambridge, MA: MIT Press, 1998.

Koolhaas, Rem. *Delirious New York: A Retroactive Manifesto for Manhattan*. New York: Monacelli Press, 1994.

Krater, Jaap, and Miriam Rose. "Development of Iceland's Geothermal Energy Potential for Aluminium Production—A Critical Analysis." In *Sparking a World-wide Energy Revolution: Social Struggles in the Transition to a Post-Petrol World*, ed. K. Abrahamsky, 319–333. Edinburgh: AK Press, 2010.

Labaton, Stephen. "Supreme Court Lifts Ban on Minimum Retail Pricing." *New York Times* (June 29, 2007): C1.

Lambert, David and Alan Lester. "Introduction: Imperial Spaces, Imperial Subjects." In *Colonial Lives across the British Empire: Imperial Careering in the Long Nineteenth Century*, ed. David Lambert and Alan Lester, 1–31. Cambridge, UK: Cambridge University Press, 2006.

Larrue, Jacques. *Fria en Guinée: Première usine d'alumine en terre d'Afrique*. Paris: Editions Karthala, 1997.

Lash, Scott, and John Urry. *Economies of Signs and Space*. London: Sage Publishing, 1994.

Law, John. *Aircraft Stories: Decentering the Object in Technoscience*. Durham, NC: Duke University Press, 2002.

Leonard, Annie. *The Story of Stuff: The Impact of Overconsumption on the Planet, Our Communities, and Our Health—And How We Can Make It Better*. New York: Free Press, 2010.

Leslie, Stuart W. "The Strategy of Structure: Architectural and Managerial Style at Alcoa and Owens-Corning," *Enterprise & Society* 12, no. 4 (2011): 863–902.

Litvak, Isaiah A., and Christopher J. Maule. "Nationalisation in the Caribbean Bauxite Industry." *International Affairs* 51, no. 1 (January, 1975): 43–59.

Litvak, Isaiah A., and Christopher J. Maule. "The International Bauxite Agreement: A Commodity Cartel in Action." *International Affairs* 56, no. 2 (Spring 1980): 296–314.

Lu, K. "The Future of Metals." *Science* 328 (April 2010): 319–320.

Lubow, Arthur. "Face Value." *New York Times Magazine* (June 8, 2008).

Lyall, Sarah. "Smokestacks in a White Wilderness Divide Iceland in a Development Debate." *New York Times* (February 4, 2007). Avaiable at http://www.nytimes.com/2007/02/04/world/europe//04iht-web.0204iceland.4460265.html.

Magnason, Andri Snaer. *Dreamland: A Self-Help Book for a Frightened Nation*. (2nd ed.). Trans. Nicholas Jones. London: Citizen Press, 2008.

Marinetti, F. T. *Futurist Manifesto* [1909]. In *Three Intellectuals in Politics*, ed. James Joll. New York: Pantheon Books, 1960.

Marschall, Luitgard. *Aluminium: Metall der Moderne*. München: Oekom Verlag, 2008.

Massey Doreen. "Power-Geometry and a Progressive Sense of Place." In *Mapping the Futures: Local Cultures, Global Change*, ed. J. Bird, B. Curtis., T. Putnam, G. Robertson, and L. Tickner. London: Routledge, 1993.

Mathur, Saloni. "Charles and Ray Eames in India." *Art Journal* 70, no. 1 (Spring 2011): 35–53.

Meikle, Jeffrey L. *American Plastic: A Cultural History*. New Brunswick, NJ: Rutgers University Press, 1997.

Meikle, Jeffrey L. "Materials." In *Speed Limits,* ed. Jeffrey T. Schnapp. Montreal: Canadian Centre for Architecture, 2009.

Miller, David P. "Joseph Banks, Empire, and 'Centers of Calculation' in Late Hanoverian London." In *Visions of Empire: Voyages, Botany, and Representations of Nature*, 21–37. Cambridge, UK: Cambridge University Press, 1996.

Mintz, Sidney. *Sweetness and Power: The Place of Sugar in Modern History*. New York: Penguin, 1986.

Misa, Thomas J. *A Nation of Steel: The Making of Modern America 1865–1925*. Baltimore: Johns Hopkins University Press, 1995.

Mitchell, W. J. T. *Landscape and Power.* (2nd ed.) Chicago: University of Chicago Press, 2002.

Molotch, Harvey. *Where Stuff Comes From: How Toasters, Toilets, Cars, Computers, and Many Other Things Come to Be as They Are.* New York: Routledge, 2005.

Mukhin, Mikhail. "Aluminium for Red Airforce: Foreign Technology in the Making of Soviet Aluminum Industry, 1928 to 1941." Paper presented at *Les techniques et la globalisation: échange, Réseaux et espionnage industriel au XXe siècle* [Technology and Globalization: Exchange, Development and Industrial Espionage in the 20th Century], March 29–31, 2012, EHSS—Université de Paris VII.

Naipaul, V. S. *Guerrillas.* New York: Vintage, 1990 [1975].

Mumford, Lewis. *Technics and Civilization.* New York: Harcourt, Brace, 1934.

Neptune, Harvey. *Caliban and the Yankees: Trinidad and the United States Occupation.* Chapel Hill: University of North Carolina Press, 2007.

Nichols, Sarah. *Aluminum by Design*. Pittsburgh: Carnegie Museum of Art, 2000a.

Nichols, Sarah. "Aluminum by Design: Jewelry to Jets." In *Aluminum by Design,* 12–57. Pittsburgh: Carnegie Museum of Art, 2000b.

Nuttall, Mark, "Self-Rule in Greenland: Towards the World's First Independence Inuit State?" *Indigenous Affairs*, 3–4 (2008): 68–70.

Nye, David. *Electrifying America: Social Meanings of a New Technology.* Cambridge, MA: MIT Press, 1992.

Nye, David. *American Technological Sublime.* Cambridge: MIT Press, 1994.

Ouroussoff, Nicolai. "New Look for the New Museum." *New York Times,* Weekend Arts Section (November 30, 2007): E46.

Packer, Jeremy. "Automobility and the Driving Force of Warfare: From Public Safety to National Security." In *The Ethics of Mobility,* ed. T. Sager and S. Bergmann, 39–64. Farnham: Ashgate, 2008.

Padel, Felix, and Samarendra Das. *Agya, What Do You Mean by Development?* 2007a. Available online at http://www.savingiceland.org/2007/08/agya-what-do-you -mean-by-development.

Padel, Felix, and Samarendra Das. "Double Death: Aluminum's Link with Genocide." In *Voice of the Wilderness.* Published by Saving Iceland (July 2007b): 10–17. Available online at http://www.savingiceland.org/2007/08/double-death.

Padel, Felix, and Samarendra Das. *Out of This Earth: East India Adivasis and the Aluminium Cartel.* Delhi: Orient Blackswan, 2010.

Parikka, Jussi. *What Is Media Archaeology?* London: Polity, 2012.

Patton, Phil. "A Visionary's Minivan Arrived Decades Too Soon." *New York Times,* Automotive Section (January 6, 2008): 6.

Patton, Phil. "A 3-Wheel Dream That Died at Takeoff." *New York Times* (June 15, 2008).

Petroski, Henry. *Invention by Design: How Engineers Get from Thought to Thing.* Cambridge, MA: Harvard University Press, 1996.

Post, Ken. *Arise ye Starvelings: The Jamaican Labour Rebellion of 1938 and Its Aftermath.* The Hague: Martinus Nijhoff, 1978.

Price, Richard. *First-Time: The Historical Vision of an Afro-American People.* Baltimore: Johns Hopkins University Press, 1983.

Price, Richard. *Travels with Tooy: History, Memory, and the African American Imagination.* Chicago: University of Chicago Press, 2008.

Price, Richard. *Rainforest Warriors: Human Rights on Trial.* Philadelphia: University of Pennsylvania Press, 2011.

Quamina, Odida T. *Mineworkers of Guyana: The Making of a Working Class.* London: Zed Books, 1987.

Redclift, Michael. *Chewing Gum: The Fortunes of Taste.* New York: Routledge, 2004.

Redfield, Peter. *Space in the Tropics: From Convicts to Rockets in French Guiana.* Berkeley: University of California Press, 2000.

Rip, Arie, and René Kemp, "Technological Change." In *Human Choice and Climate Change.* Vol. II, *Resources and Technology*, ed. S. Rayner and E. L. Malone. Columbus, OH: Battelle Press, 1998.

Robinson, Cedric J. *Black Marxism: The Making of the Black Radical Tradition.* Raleigh: University of North Carolina Press, 2000.

Rodgers, Daniel, Bhavani Raman, and Helmut Reimitz, eds. *Cultures in Motion.* Princeton, NJ: Princeton University Press, 2013.

Rodney, Walter. *A History of the Guyanese Working People, 1881–1905.* Baltimore: The Johns Hopkins University Press, 1981.

Rosen, Jeffrey. "Supreme Court Inc." *New York Times Magazine* (March 16, 2008): 40.

Rosenthal, Elisabeth. "China Increases Lead as Biggest Carbon Dioxide Emitter." *New York Times* (June 14, 2008).

Rostow, W. W. *The Stages of Economic Growth: A Non-communist Manifesto.* (3rd ed.) Cambridge, UK: Cambridge University Press, 1990 [1960].

Royte, Elizabeth. *Garbageland: On the Secret Trail of Trash.* New York: Little, Brown, 2005.

Sanger, David. *Confront and Conceal: Obama's Secret Wars and Surprising Use of American Power.* New York: Random House, 2012.

Schatzberg, Eric. "Ideology and Technical Choice: The Decline of the Wooden Airplane in the United States, 1920–1945." *Technology and Culture* 35, no. 1 (January 1994): 34–69.

Schatzberg, Eric. "Symbolic Culture and Technological Change: The Cultural History of Aluminum as an Industrial Material." *Enterprise & Society* 4, no. 2 (June 2003): 226–271.

Schivelbusch, Wolfgang. *The Railroad Journey: The Industrialization of Time and Space in the Nineteenth Century.* Berkeley: University of California Press, 1986.

Schlendorf, David. "Alcoa and the Aluminum Auto." Reprint from *Ingénieurs de l'automobile* (September 1998). Available online at http://www.alcoa.com/global/en/news/whats_new/2002/audi.asp.

Schnapp, Jeffrey T. "The Romance of Caffeine and Aluminum." *Critical Inquiry* 28, no. 1 (Autumn 2001): 244–269.

Schnapp, Jeffrey T., ed. *Speed Limits.* Montreal: Canadian Centre for Architecture, 2009.

Sheller, Mimi. *Consuming the Caribbean: From Arawaks to Zombies.* London: Routledge, 2003.

Sheller, Mimi. "The Emergence of New Cultures of Mobility: Stability, Openings, and Prospects." In *Automobility in Transition? A Socio-technical Analysis of Sustainable Transport,* ed. Geoff Dudley, Frank Geels, and René Kemp, 180–202. London: Routledge, 2011.

Sheller, Mimi. "Metallic Modernities in the Space Age: Visualizing the Caribbean, Materializing the Modern." In *Visuality/Materiality,* ed. Gillian Rose and Divya Tolia-Kelly. Aldershot, UK: Ashgate, 2012.

Sheller, Mimi. "Space Age Tropics." In *Surveying the American Tropics: Literary Geographies from New York to Rio,* ed. Maria Cristina Fumagalli, Peter Hulme, Owen Robinson, and Lesley Wylie. Liverpool: Liverpool University Press, 2013a.

Sheller, Mimi. "Speed Metal, Slow Tropics, Cold, War." In *Cultures in Motion,* ed. Daniel Rodgers, Bhavani Raman, and Helmut Reimitz. Princeton, NJ: Princeton University Press, 2013b.

Sheller, Mimi, and John Urry, eds. "Materialities and Mobilities." Special Issue of *Environment and Planning D,* Vol. 38 (2006a).

Sheller, Mimi, and John Urry. "The New Mobilities Paradigm." *Environment and Planning A, Materialities and Mobilities* 38 (2006b): 207–226.

Shimon, John, and Julie Lindemann. *Season's Gleamings: The Art of the Aluminum Christmas Tree.* New York: Melcher Media, 2004.

Shove, Elizabeth. *Comfort, Cleanliness and Convenience: The Social Organization of Normality.* New York: Berg, 2003.

Shove, Elizabeth, and Dale Southerton. "Defrosting the Freezer: From Novelty to Convenience." *Material Culture* 5, no. 3 (2000): 301–319.

Sigurðsson, Skúli. "The Dome of the World: Iceland, Doomsday Technologies, and the Cold War." In *Aspects of Arctic and Sub-Arctic History, Proceedings of the International Congress on the History of the Arctic and Sub-Arctic Regions,* Reykjavik, June 18–21, 1998, 475–485. Reykjavik: University of Iceland Press, 2000.

Slater, Candace. "Amazonia as Edenic Narrative." In *Uncommon Ground: Rethinking the Human Place in Nature,* ed. William Cronon. New York: W. W. Norton, 1996.

Smith, George David. *From Monopoly to Competition: The Transformation of Alcoa, 1888–1986.* Cambridge, UK: Cambridge University Press, 1988.

Smith, Roberta. "How Art Is Framed; Exhibition Floor Plans as a Conceptual Medium." *New York Times* (March 8, 2008).

Soja, Edward W. *Seeking Spatial Justice*. Minneapolis: University of Minnesota Press, 2010.

Soleri, Paolo. *Arcology: The City in the Image of Man*. Cambridge, MA: MIT Press, 1969.

Solnit, Rebecca. *River of Shadows: Eadweard Muybridge and the Technological Wild West*. New York: Penguin, 2003.

Sparke, Penny. "Cookware to Cocktail Shakers: The Domestication of Aluminum in the United States, 1900–1939." In *Aluminum by Design*, ed. S. Nichols, 112–139. Pittsburgh: Carnegie Museum of Art, 2000.

Stephens, Evelyne Huber. "Minerals Strategies and Development: International Political Economy, State, Class, and the Role of Bauxite/Aluminum and Copper Industries in Jamaica and Peru." In *Studies in Comparative International Development* 22, no. 3 (1987): 60–97.

Stephens, Evelyne Huber, and John D. Stephens. "Bauxite and Democratic Socialism in Jamaica." In *States versus Markets in the World System*, ed. Peter Evans, Dietrich Rueschemeyer, and Evelyne Huber Stephens. Beverly Hills: Sage Publications, 1985.

Stephens, Evelyne Huber, and John D. Stephens. *Democratic Socialism in Jamaica: The Political Movement and Social Transformation in Dependent Capitalism*. Princeton, NJ: Princeton University Press; London: Macmillan, 1986.

Stuckey, John A. *Vertical Integration and Joint Ventures in the Aluminum Industry*. Cambridge, MA: Harvard University Press, 1983.

Suchman, Lucy. *Human-Machine Reconfigurations: Plans and Situated Actions*. Cambridge, UK: Cambridge University Press, 2007.

Switkes, Glenn. *Foiling the Aluminum Industry: A Toolkit for Communities, Activists, Consumers and Workers*. Berkeley, CA: International Rivers Network, 2005.

Thomas, Clive Y. *Dependence and Transformation: The Economics of the Transition to Socialism*. New York: Monthly Review Press, 1974.

Thompson, Krista. *An Eye for the Tropics*. Durham, NC: Duke University Press, 2006.

Traub, James. "After Cheney." *New York Times Magazine* (November 24, 2009).

Trouillot, Michel-Rolph. *Global Transformations: Anthropology and the Modern World*. New York: Palgrave Macmillan, 2003.

Tsuji, Shin'ichi (Oiwa Keibo). *Slow Is Beautiful: Culture and Slowness*. Tokyo: Heibonsha, 2001.

Ujifusa, Steven. *A Man and His Ship: America's Greatest Naval Architect and His Quest to Build the S.S. United States*. New York: Simon & Schuster, 2012.

Urry, John. *The Tourist Gaze.* (2nd ed.) London: Sage, 2002.

Urry, John. *Societies beyond Oil: Oil Dregs and Social Futures.* London: Zed Books, 2013.

Virilio, Paul. *Speed and Politics.* Trans. Semiotext(e) and Mark Polizzotti. Los Angeles: Semiotext(e), 2006 [1977].

Vitalis, Robert. *America's Kingdom: Mythmaking on the Saudi Oil Frontier.* Stanford, CA: Stanford University Press, 2007.

Vogel, Craig. "Aluminum: A Competitive Material of Choice in the Design of New Products, 1950 to the Present." In *Aluminum by Design*, ed. S. Nichols, 140–165. Pittsburgh: Carnegie Museum of Art, 2000.

Weiner, Jonah. "Prying Eyes: Trevor Paglen Makes Art out of Government Secrets." *New Yorker* (October 22, 2012): 54–61.

Weinman, Edward. "Boom Towns." *Iceland Review* 44, no. 3, (2006): 50–57.

Whitehead, Mark. *State, Science and the Skies: Governmentalities of the British Atmosphere.* Oxford: Wiley-Blackwell, 2009.

Williams, Brackette. *Stains on My Name, War in My Veins: Guyana and the Politics of Cultural Struggle.* Durham, NC: Duke University Press, 1991.

Willingham, Kelsey. "Corruption, Capitalists, and the Crime-State Nexus: Criminal Infiltration of the Russian Economy and Implications for the Future." *New Voices in Public Policy* IV (Spring 2010).

Wilquin, Hugues. *Aluminium Architecture: Construction and Details.* Basel: Birkhäuser, 2001.

Wines, Michael. "Toiling in the Dark: Africa's Power Crisis." *New York Times* (July 29, 2007).

Young, B. S. "Jamaica's Bauxite and Alumina Industries." *Annals of the Association of American Geographers* 55, no. 3 (September 1965): 449–464.

INDEX

Note: Page numbers in italics refer to figures.

Bureau of Mines and Energy, 202
Burj Dubai, 240
Business Week, 11–12
Byam, Wally, 103–104

Cadillac ATS, 225
Cadmium, 234
Caffeine, 119, 122
Caffey, Francis G., 50
Cage, John, 138
Cahora Bassa dam, 180
Calvino, Italo, 260–261
Camara, Moussa Tiégboro, 196
Camelford water disaster, 23
Canada, 7
    Alcan and, 19, 25, 29–30, 48, 51, 55–
        56, 62, 149–150, 152, 164, 176, 182,
        191, 195–197, 199, 205, 209, 237,
        241–242, 245–246, 262
    alumina and, 195
    British Columbia and, 19, 55
    consumptions rates of, 225
    hydroelectric plants and, 56
    industrial issues and, 48, 55–57
    James Bay Complex and, 24, 55
    Mellon and, 62
    modernity and, 7, 19–20, 24
    Montreal Opera and, 241–242
    National Gallery of, 241
    Quebec and, 53, 55, 150, 300n68
    Saguenay River and, 21, 150
    smelting and, 55, 57, 164
    tourism and, 246
Canada Economic Development, 246
Canadian Heritage, 246
Cancer, 193
Cans, 28, 260
    brewers and, 227
    consumption rates of, 230
    high art and, 245
    Life Cycle Studies and, 231
    lightweight, 2, 179, 229–230
    modern home and, 118, 140

as noisemakers, 140
production of, 18
pull-top, 227
recycling and, 28, 221, 227–231, 233,
    236, 249
rigid container sheet (RCS) and, 227
steel, 227
upcycling and, 238
Carbon dioxide, 19, 28, 207–208, 216,
    231, 255, 260, 295n7
Carbon footprint, 10
Caribbean. *See also* Specific country
    advertising and, 151–173, *173,* 176
    Alcoa and, 136, 147, 150–177
    alumina and, 151–152, 155, 157, 173,
        177, 180
    architecture and, 160, 171
    Artzybasheff and, 159–160, *161–163,*
        166, 171
    Atkinson landing strip and, 150
    backwardness and, 147, 149, 151, 177,
        286n63
    bauxite and, 147, 149–159, 164–177,
        179–180
    consumption and, 6, 9, 147–151, 159–
        160, 166, 168, 171
    cruise ships and, 151–173, *173,* 175
    electricity and, 147–148, 153–159,
        180
    exports and, 166, 168
    folk dances and, 168, 171
    indigenous peoples and, 152, 155–156,
        192
    material culture and, 171, 176–178
    military and, 152, 159, 166, 176
    Minerals (Vesting) Act and, 150
    mining and, 147, 149–158, 166, 168,
        171–173, 176–177, 179–180
    mobility and, 147–150, 158, 164–166,
        176–177
    modernity and, 147–178
    Royal Mail Steam Packet Company
        and, 158